A Historical Guide to the U.S. Government

A Historical Guide
to the
U.S. Government

Editor in Chief

George Thomas Kurian

Consulting Editors

Joseph P. Harahan

Morton Keller

Donald F. Kettl

Graham T. T. Molitor

OXFORD UNIVERSITY PRESS

New York   1998   Oxford

OXFORD UNIVERSITY PRESS

Oxford   New York

Athens   Auckland   Bangkok   Bogotá   Bombay
Buenos Aires   Calcutta   Cape Town   Dar es Salaam
Delhi   Florence   Hong Kong   Istanbul   Karachi
Kuala Lumpur   Madras   Madrid   Melbourne
Mexico City   Nairobi   Paris   Singapore
Taipei   Tokyo   Toronto   Warsaw

and associated companies in
Berlin   Ibadan

Library of Congress Cataloging-in-Publication Data
A historical guide to the U.S. government / editor in chief
George T. Kurian, consulting editors Joseph P. Harahan . . . [et al.].
p.   cm.
Includes bibliographical references and index.
ISBN 0-19-510230-4
1. United States—Politics and government—Encyclopedias.
2. Administrative agencies—United States—Encyclopedias.
3. Executive departments—United States—Encyclopedias.
I. Kurian, George Thomas.   II. Harahan, Joseph P.
JK9.H57   1998
352.3'0973—dc21   97-47442

Printing (last digit): 9 8 7 6 5 4 3 2 1

Printed in the United States of America
on acid free paper

Contents

Preface

The U.S. federal government is one of the largest public institutions in the world. It is enormous in every sense of the term. It employs almost three million civilians, and its annual budget as well as its public debt are the largest in the world. It is also one of the largest owners of real estate in the United States. Size apart, it is acknowledged to be one of the most efficient governments in the world, with a civil service that is among the least elitist and authoritarian. Contrary to public perception, the United States is also one of the least governed nations in the world, with more sectors in the hands of private enterprise than is the case in most developed countries. For example, most governments own railways, airlines, mines, heavy industries, banking, broadcasting, and other public utilities and services that are outside U.S. government control or ownership.

In popular speech, the term *government* is used in two ways. First, it refers to the three branches of the federal government exercising together their constitutionally mandated powers. Second, and in a more restricted sense, it refers to the executive branch of the government, headed by the president and consisting of a myriad of agencies, departments, bureaus, and their branches. In this sense, the government is also referred to as the *executive* or the *administration*. *A Historical Guide to the U.S. Government* deals with this second definition. It therefore excludes both the judiciary and the U.S. Congress from consideration. However, because the boundaries of these three branches of government are sometimes vague and permeable, certain agencies lying within these other two branches of government are dealt with herein.

A Historical Guide to the U.S. Government presents a composite profile of the U.S. government through a history of the various departments and agencies that constitute it. Theories of public administration abound, but they do not explain why the parts work so well together (or not) unless one looks closely at the ways in which these parts have evolved during the course of the last two centuries and the political, economic, and social influences that have shaped them. A history of U.S. government is part of the history of the American people, and thus this book illustrates the social, cultural, intellectual, and economic ideas and movements that have energized the course of U.S. history. The growth of American government hews closely to the great historical cycles, with wars and depressions fueling growth and peace and prosperity restraining it. This book also explains why the U.S. government is not so monolithic and unitary as it often appears to be. Peter the Great once remarked, "Not I, but ten thousand clerks rule Russia." This is equally true of the United States. Although each administration carries an overall presidential character, the average citizen generally comes into contact only with lower-level officials in departments, agencies, and their branches. These points of contact determine how well a government performs and how well it discharges its duties as a servant and not a master.

Historical Overview

Americans have always been ambivalent about the type of government they want. They want strong government but at the same time fear big government. The fear of big government goes back to colonial times. The Declaration of Independence complains that King George III had "erected a multitude of new offices and sent . . . swarms of officers to harass our people and eat out their substance." Americans want (and have always wanted) a government that is frugal but generous in providing public services, efficient without being authoritarian, strong without curtailing civil liberties, responsive and accountable without being subject to the shifting tides of public opinion, honest and incorruptible without being rigid and unadaptive. Obviously, America has not achieved an ideal government at any time in its history, but the history of U.S. public administration as been a ceaseless quest in that direction.

The huge increase in size of the American government is a twentieth-century phenomenon. The American Revolution had little or no effect on the way the new republic was governed. The British already had an efficient—perhaps too efficient—governmental system in the American colonies, and since it seemed to work well, there was little motivation to change it. "Reinventors" of U.S. government forget the fact that it was never invented in the first place; it was just copied. The founding fathers were comfortable with grand concepts and ideas but had little patience for details. The principal functions of the new government were to maintain a standing army, to collect revenues, and to run the post office. Between 1776 and 1880 the development of public administration was uneven, except for the steady, if unimpressive, growth in the number of public employees. This period was marked by historic events in many other areas: the territorial expansion of the nation, the opening of the West, the Civil War and the settlement of the slavery question, the establishment of political parties, the Morrill Act, and many others. But there was no consistent effort to improve the quality of administration or to define executive functions.

The word *administration* does not appear in any of the early documents of the republic. Article II of the Constitution opens with the sentence, "The executive Power shall be vested in a President of the United States of America." But the terms *executive* and *power* are only partially defined elsewhere. The Constitution leaves the whole field untouched; there are references to organization or procedures, regulations or rulemaking, planning or civil service. The silence did not, however, arise because of neglect or oversight; the Founders were well aware of the importance of good government as a bulwark of the liberties guaranteed by the Constitution. On the closing day of the Constitutional Convention, Benjamin Franklin said, "There is no form of government but what may be a blessing to the people, if well administered. . . . I hope, therefore, for our own sakes, as part of the people, and for the sake of posterity, that we shall act heartily and unanimously in recommending this Constitution . . . and turn our future thoughts and endeavors to the means of having it well administered." A few months later Alexander Hamilton, in *The Federalist*, no. 68, asserted that the "true test of a good government is its aptitude and tendency to produce a good administration." Both men were, however, echoing the poet Alexander Pope's famous couplet, "For forms of government let fools contest; / Whate'er is best administered is best."

The founding fathers were generally in favor of less rather than more government. They had a well-grounded fear that a strong administration would be tempted to deprive people of their hard-won liberties. The Constitution and related documents had more to say on what could not be done than on what could be done, and during the first fifty years of the republic a bureaucracy existed only in a very rudimentary form. George Washington had only four assistants, or clerks, yet he found time not only to run the affairs of state but to attend to his personal estate as well. The number of federal civilian employees had reached only 6,914 by 1821, and the number had grown to only 36,672 by the time of Abraham Lincoln's administration.

None of the departments or agencies of the federal government is specified in the Constitution. Beginning in 1789, the first two departments created were the Department of Foreign Affairs (later the Department of State) and the Department of War (now the Department of Defense). In setting them up, Congress enjoined them to conduct their affairs "in such manner as the President of the United States shall from time to time order or instruct." This established the executive branch as a presidential domain. The Treasury Department was the next to be established, but Congress retained substantial control over the financial affairs of the republic. Another act established the Office of the Attorney General. As a part-time legal adviser to the government, the attorney general had no staff at all and was placed on retainer. It was not until 1870 that the Department of Justice was established with the attorney general at its head. It was required that the heads of these early departments be appointed by the president, with the advice and consent of the Senate, but it took many debates before the president's authority to fire them was firmly established.

For the next hundred years, little change was made in the mechanisms of government. The next executive department, the Department of the Interior, was not created until 1845. Only one other department was established in the nineteenth century, that of Agriculture in 1889. Much of the work of the executive branch was carried out by offices, such as that of the Census, and by offices, such as that of Education, some of which prefigured later departments. Admittedly, the nation had some great administrators and bureaucrats, some of whom looked upon their duties as a sacred calling. The relative slowness in the evolution of governmental structures and forms was attributable to many factors peculiar to American history: the open frontier, the strength of private enterprise, the prevailing laissez-faire philosophy, the fear of big government, and the principle of dual federalism, according to which the federal government was expected to keep out of areas specifically assigned to states and localities. Under the doctrine of the Separation of Powers, Congress and the White House were constantly bickering over their respective jurisdictions, and for most of the nineteenth century Congress dominated, thus inhibiting the growth and development of a unified and responsive executive. Yet another factor that prevented growth of federal power was the influence of the spoils system and the infiltration of political parties in government. Federal jobs were seen as the loaves and fishes of office, and the job turnover of public servants was extremely high after every election.

Beginning in the last decades of the nineteenth century, the United States underwent what is generally called the Management Movement. This arose not only from a growing backlash against political corruption but also from a growing professionalism among public servants. Ironically, the calls for reform and scientific management arose from the local levels and were later adopted at the state and federal levels. The catchwords were efficiency and honesty. Schools for public service were established in numerous cities. The Management Movement matured during the first two decades of the twentieth century and came to full flowering in the New Deal of Franklin Delano Roosevelt.

The Management Movement had three goals. The first was to develop an honest civil service and to reform government personnel selection and procedures. Its second goal was to integrate related activities in departments and bureaus, to establish channels of authority and responsibility, and to modernize and rationalize agency procedures. The third goal was to better plan and control budgets within the executive branch.

The origins of civil service reform began under Ulysses S. Grant. In 1871 Congress passed a rider to an appropriation bill consisting of one sentence:

> That the President of the United States be, and he is hereby, authorized to prescribe such rules and regulations for the admission of persons into the civil service of the United States as will best promote the efficiency thereof, and ascertain the fitness of each candidate in respect to age, health, character, knowledge, and ability for the branch of service which he seeks to enter; and for this purpose the President is authorized to employ suitable persons to conduct said inquiries, to prescribe their duties, and to establish regulations for the conduct of persons who may receive appointments in the civil service.

Under the terms of this act, a body that later became the Civil Service Commission was set up. Although the commission went out of existence in 1875, it led to the Civil Service (Pendleton) Act of 1883. It was based on a lengthy report by Dorman B. Eaton, who had studied the British experience and made recommendations for the U.S. system.

In 1887 Congress took the first step toward creating a regulatory commission— a step that would profoundly affect the character of government operations. Both population and territory were expanding, and the American economy was moving into new sectors, such as railroads, that were unheard of before the Civil War. Congress created the Interstate Commerce Commission as a first attempt by the federal government to create a bureaucratic agency with functions that transcended those specified in the Constitution.

By the time of Grover Cleveland's first administration (1885–1889), it was obvious that the federal executive was hopelessly obsolescent. Its machinery was inefficient, its sources of revenue were shrinking, its bureaucrats were blatantly corrupt, and it was increasingly unfit to cope with the problems related to post–Civil War peace and prosperity. However, a series of piecemeal, half-hearted reforms made any real solution even more difficult. Between 1887 and 1912, both Congress and presidents sponsored a number of reform committees and proposals. These included the Cockrell Committee of 1887–1889, the Dockery-Cockrell Committee of 1893–1895, Theodore Roosevelt's Commission on Department Methods, better known as the Keep Commission, of 1905–1909, and the Commission on Economy and Efficiency during William Howard Taft's administration (1909–1913).

Although Franklin Delano Roosevelt's New Deal is considered the watershed in U.S. administrative history, it was preceded by significant reforms in the 1920s. The Budget and Accounting Act of 1921 established the Bureau of the Budget in the Department of the Treasury. Later, in 1939, it was transferred to the Executive Office of the President and in 1970 became the Office of Management and Budget. The Budget and Accounting Act has been described as "the greatest landmark of our administrative history except for the Constitution itself." Meanwhile, the civil service became more professional with the passage of the Classification Act of 1923. This act authorized what is now called the Civil Service Commission and introduced the concept of equal pay for equal work for all federal employees. Position classification became a key element for measuring and evaluating work force performance and helped increase efficiency.

FDR may be described as the true architect of modern American government. Within the course of only a few years the New Deal revolutionized the systemic bases of governance and shifted the foci of power to a host of new governmental agencies and departments. He also introduced the era of proactive government by redefining administrative functions and inaugurated the era of big government that was to last nearly half a century. The New Deal adopted, invented, and extended a variety of administrative devices to meet new challenges in society and the economy. It also meant government involvement in a number of areas that had been closed to government for the first 150 years of U.S. history: farm subsidies, welfare, regulation of financial markets, Social Security, unemployment compensation, and government participation in labor-management disputes. FDR's initiatives on the reorganization of government were inspired by the Brownlow Committee Report, which made the president manager of the executive branch. The Brownlow Committee Report was followed by the Reorganization Plan No. 1 of 1939 and Executive Order 8248 of 1939, both of which are considered among the most significant documents of public administration. In 1940 the Hatch Acts prohibited public employees from participating in overt political activities.

New Deal thinking dominated American government for nearly a third of a century after World War II. Even the Republican opposition accepted the fundamental premise that more government was necessary to cure certain social and economic ills. By 1980 the number of government departments had risen to fourteen and the number of federal agencies to several hundred. It was a period marked by few innovations. The most notable of the efforts at reorganization during the period was the first Hoover Commission, which has been described as the most ambitious and comprehensive study of administrative operations in American history. It represented the culmination of the Management Movement.

By 1980, when Ronald Reagan was elected to his first term, the New Deal tide had begun to ebb, and opponents of big government were able to gain positions of authority within the federal government itself. The downsizing of American government began on a variety of fronts. States rights were restored in many areas, and more power was increasingly devolved to the states. Under the rubric of fiscal conservatism and better management methods, public services were curtailed and in some cases abandoned altogether. Under the banner of deregulation and privatization, controls on the conduct of business were eased or eradicated.

The historian Theodore Mommsen said "Every revolution is followed by a restoration." The Roosevelt revolution was followed by the Reagan restoration. The top-heavy growth of the federal government finally yielded to the pruning knives of the neoconservatives and supply-siders. Even the Clinton administration, although Democratic in name, joined the movement toward leaner government. The scaffolding of the New Deal survived, but the philosophical bases of government had shifted. *A Historical Guide to the U.S. Government* traces the trajectory of federal departments, agencies, and bureaus, their growth, evolution, and sometimes demise, through more than two centuries of "the experiment entrusted to the hands of the American people."

How To Use This Book

A Historical Guide to the U.S. Government is arranged by entry term alphabetically, letter by letter rather than word by word. Three varieties of cross-referencing are employed, the most general being blind entries, which appear within the alphabetical range of headwords as synonyms, related subjects, inverted terms, and acronyms of the actual entry term under which the topic is discussed. Within the text of an article, cross-references alert readers to subjects that are treated as separate entries elsewhere in the volume. Finally, cross-references may be found at the end of many entries, directing the reader to related or expanded discussions in other entries.

Following most entries readers will find selected bibliographies of works that will be helpful if they wish to learn more about the subject of the entry. The name of the author (or authors) of each article follows the bibliographies. To find all the articles written by a single author, the reader can consult the Directory of Contributors.

At the end of the volume, readers will find an appendix consisting of many of the more important documents of public administration. For example, the texts of the actual acts that established the first five executive departments of the federal government, the departments of Foreign Affairs (now State), War (now Defense), the Treasury, Justice, and the Office of the Attorney General, may be found on pp. 627–629. The appendix also contains the texts of a number of presidential executive orders that have been instrumental in reorganizing and reforming the executive branch over the years, all arranged chronologically by year of passage or issuance. The index following the appendix will help readers locate information on topics, concepts, and individuals not covered by separate entries.

Acknowledgments

Oxford University Press is the home of many of the finest reference books in the world. During the gestation of this project I understood why. I was privileged to work with a fine editorial team—a group of people who were very supportive of and receptive to good ideas and who shared generously with me their vast expertise in every field. Claude Conyers, vice president and editorial director of the Scholarly and Professional Reference Department, is a veteran reference editor who is also mentor to an entire generation of editors. Chris Collins, with whom I worked closely, is a keen and perceptive intellect, at home in many subject areas. He made significant contributions to the shaping of the project. Stephen Chasteen, the project editor who was in charge of the day-to-day shepherding of the work through production, was a model of unobtrusive efficiency and sharp editorial skills. Also closely involved with the project were Jeffrey Edelstein, managing editor of the department, and Karen Casey, vice president and marketing director.

A Historical Guide to the U.S. Government had a distinguished board of editors. Graham T. T. Molitor, the chair of the editorial board of *The Encyclopedia of the Future*, is a personal friend and colleague who was unstinting in support and advice. He brought a rich and varied experience within both government and the private sector to the project. Joseph P. Harahan was president of the Society of

Federal Historians when the project began and was instrumental in obtaining the participation of a number of its members in the project. Morton Keller is an outstanding authority on the history of the federal government. Donald F. Kettl, director of both the Robert M. La Follette Institute of Public Affairs at the University of Wisconsin–Madison and the Brookings Center for Public Management, was a pillar of strength to whom I could always turn in time of need. I am grateful to all of them. Above all, I must thank Annie, my beloved wife and faithful companion, for her unfailing support and encouragement.

—George Thomas Kurian
Yorktown Heights, New York
December 1997

Directory of Contributors

Herbert E. Alexander
Director, Citizens' Research Foundation, University of Southern California
ELECTION COMMISSION, FEDERAL

Deane J. Allen
Historian, Defense Intelligence Agency
DEFENSE INTELLIGENCE AGENCY

Nancy V. Baker
Associate Professor, Department of Government, New Mexico State University
JUSTICE, DEPARTMENT OF

Edward Berkowitz
Professor, Department of History, George Washington University
HEALTH AND HUMAN SERVICES, DEPARTMENT OF; HEALTH CARE FINANCING ADMINISTRATION; SOCIAL SECURITY ADMINISTRATION

Douglas E. Bowers
Section Head, Economic Research Service, Department of Agriculture
AGRICULTURE, DEPARTMENT OF

William T. Bowers
Department of the Army, retired
ARMY, DEPARTMENT OF THE

Alan C. Brennglass
Formerly, Professor, John Jay College of Criminal Justice, City University of New York
INTERNATIONAL DEVELOPMENT COOPERATION AGENCY

William Bushong
Office of the Architect of the Capitol
ARCHITECT OF THE CAPITOL, OFFICE OF THE

Mark Byrnes
Assistant Professor, Department of Political Science, Middle Tennessee State University
FEDERAL BUREAU OF INVESTIGATION; NATIONAL AERONAUTICS AND SPACE ADMINISTRATION

Frederick S. Calhoun
U.S. Marshals Service
MARSHALS SERVICE

George C. Challou
National Archives
NATIONAL ARCHIVES

Jeanne Nienaber Clarke
Associate Professor, Department of Political Science, University of Arizona
FISH AND WILDLIFE SERVICE; LAND MANAGEMENT, BUREAU OF

Jeffrey E. Cohen
Associate Professor, Department of Political Science, University of Kansas
COMMERCE, DEPARTMENT OF

Katherine A. Collado
Center for Legislative Archives, National Archives
PEACE CORPS

Shelley L. Davis
Formerly, Internal Revenue Service
INTERNAL REVENUE SERVICE

Martha Derthick
Professor, Department of Government, University of Virginia
STATES AND THE FEDERAL GOVERNMENT

I. M. Destler
Institute for International Economics
TRADE REPRESENTATIVE, OFFICE OF THE U.S.

Veronica D. DiConti
Freelance Writer
EDUCATION, DEPARTMENT OF, FEDERAL COMMUNICATIONS COMMISSION; FEDERAL TRADE COMMISSION; GOVERNMENT ETHICS, OFFICE OF; HOUSING FINANCE BOARD, FEDERAL; NATIONAL CAPITAL PLANNING COMMISSION; PRISONS, FEDERAL BUREAU OF; RESOLUTION TRUST CORPORATION; SMALL BUSINESS ADMINISTRATION; SPECIAL COUNSEL, OFFICE OF

Melvin Dubnick
Independent Scholar
ARMY CORPS OF ENGINEERS; CUSTOMS SERVICE; FOREST SERVICE

Robert F. Durant
Research Professor, Schaeffer Center for Public Policy,
University of Baltimore
INTERIOR, DEPARTMENT OF THE

Daniel J. Fiorino
Office of Policy Development, Environmental Protection
Agency
ENVIRONMENTAL PROTECTION AGENCY

Patrick Fisher
Assistant Professor, Department of Political Science,
Slippery Rock University of Pennsylvania
BUDGET PROCESS

Ben A. Franklin
Journalist
VETERANS AFFAIRS, DEPARTMENT OF

Abby L. Gilbert
Historical Association, Department of the Treasury
FINANCIAL MANAGEMENT SERVICE; MINT, U.S.;
TREASURY, DEPARTMENT OF THE

Joel K. Goldstein
Professor, School of Law, St. Louis University
PRESIDENTIAL SUCCESSION AND DISABILITY; SUPREME
COURT DECISIONS ON THE PRESIDENCY; TWENTY-SECOND
AMENDMENT; VICE PRESIDENCY

Hugh Davis Graham
Professor, Department of History, Vanderbilt University
CIVIL RIGHTS COMMISSION; EQUAL EMPLOYMENT
OPPORTUNITY COMMISSION

R. Dale Grinder
Historian, U.S. Department of Transportation
TRANSPORTATION, DEPARTMENT OF

Elizabeth M. Gunn
Formerly, Senior Analyst, Office of Technology
Assessment
TECHNOLOGY ASSESSMENT, OFFICE OF

Wendy L. Hansen
Associate Professor, Department of Political Science,
University of New Mexico
INTERNATIONAL TRADE ADMINISTRATION;
INTERNATIONAL TRADE COMMISSION

Joseph P. Harahan
Senior Historian, On-Site Inspection Agency, U.S.
Department of Defense
HISTORY AND HISTORIANS IN THE FEDERAL
GOVERNMENT; ON-SITE INSPECTION AGENCY

Victoria A. Harden
Historian and Director, De Witt Stetten, Jr., Museum of
Medical Research, National Institutes of Health,
Bethesda, Md.
NATIONAL INSTITUTES OF HEALTH

Magaera Ausman Harris
Historian, Corporate Information Service, U.S. Postal
Service
POSTAL SERVICE

J. Douglas Helms
Senior Historian, Natural Resources Conservation
Service, U.S. Department of Agriculture
NATURAL RESOURCES CONSERVATION SERVICE

Pamela Henson
Director, Institutional History Division, Smithsonian
Institution
SMITHSONIAN INSTITUTION

Vicki Hermann
Librarian, Bureau of Alcohol, Tobacco and Firearms
ALCOHOL, TOBACCO AND FIREARMS, BUREAU OF

Gwen-Torges Hoffman
Independent Scholar
INDIAN AFFAIRS, BUREAU OF

Tom Hoffman
Independent Scholar
INDIAN AFFAIRS, BUREAU OF

Jack M. Holl
Professor, Department of History, Kansas State
University
ENERGY, DEPARTMENT OF

David Honness
Freelance Writer
MARITIME ADMINISTRATION; MARITIME COMMISSION,
FEDERAL

Ari Hoogenboom
Professor, Department of History, Brooklyn College,
City University of New York
INTERSTATE COMMERCE COMMISSION

Karen Hult
Professor, Department of Political Science, Virginia
Polytechnic Institute and State University
ADVISING THE PRESIDENT

Patricia W. Ingraham
Professor, Department of Public Administration,
Syracuse University
CIVIL SERVICE

Robert E. Johnson
U.S. Coast Guard, retired
COAST GUARD; LIFE-SAVING SERVICE; LIGHTHOUSE
SERVICE; REVENUE-CUTTER SERVICE

John Kamensky
National Performance Review
NATIONAL PERFORMANCE REVIEW

Don E. Kash
Hazel Chair of Public Policy, Institute of Public Policy, George Mason University
TECHNOLOGY ASSESSMENT, OFFICE OF

W. D. Kay
Associate Professor, Department of Political Science, Northeastern University
SCIENCE AND TECHNOLOGY POLICY, OFFICE OF

Morton Keller
Spector Professor of History, Department of History, Brandeis University
POLITICAL PARTIES AND THE FEDERAL GOVERNMENT

Donald F. Kettl
Director, Robert M. La Follette Institute of Public Affairs, University of Wisconsin–Madison
REFORM OF THE FEDERAL GOVERNMENT

Anne M. Khademian
Assistant Professor, Department of Political Science, University of Wisconsin–Madison
FEDERAL DEPOSIT INSURANCE CORPORATION; SECURITIES AND EXCHANGE COMMISSION

Nick A. Komons
Historian, Federal Aviation Administration, retired
FEDERAL AVIATION ADMINISTRATION

John J. Kornacki
Historical Office, U.S. House of Representatives
HOUSE OF REPRESENTATIVES

Tom Lansford
Graduate Program in International Studies, Old Dominion University
DRUG ENFORCEMENT ADMINISTRATION; NATIONAL SECURITY COUNCIL

Barry Mackintosh
National Park Service
NATIONAL PARK SERVICE

Judson MacLaury
Historian, U.S. Department of Labor
LABOR, DEPARTMENT OF

Gerald A. Mann
Bureau of the Census, retired
CENSUS, BUREAU OF THE

Martin J. Manning
Archivist, U.S. Information Agency
UNITED STATES INFORMATION AGENCY

Janet M. Martin
Associate Professor, Department of Government, Bowdoin College
WOMEN AND THE EXECUTIVE BRANCH

George T. Mazuzan
Historian, National Science Foundation
NATIONAL SCIENCE FOUNDATION

Jerry Mechling
Professor, John F. Kennedy Insitute of Government, Harvard University
ELECTRONIC GOVERNMENT

Graham T.T. Molitor
President, Public Policy Forecasting, Inc., and Vice President and Legal Counsel, World Future Society
ADVISORY AGENCIES

Kathryn E. Newcomer
Professor and Chair, Department of Public Administration, George Washington University
ACCOUNTABILITY IN THE FEDERAL GOVERNMENT

David C. Nice
Professor, Department of Political Science, Washington State University
AMTRAK; BUDGET PROCESS; CITIES, LOCALITIES, AND THE FEDERAL GOVERNMENT

David M. O'Brien
Professor, Department of Political Science, University of Virginia
JUDICIAL BRANCH

Kay Oliver
Chief Historian, Central Intelligence Agency
CENTRAL INTELLIGENCE AGENCY

Armando Palacios-Sommer
Graduate Program, Robert M. La Follette Institute of Public Affairs, University of Wisconsin–Madison
PUBLIC DEBT, BUREAU OF THE

John Parascandola
Professor, History of Medicine Division, Uniformed Services University of the Health Sciences
PUBLIC HEALTH SERVICE

William D. Pederson
Professor, Department of Social Sciences, Louisiana State University in Shreveport
BROWNLOW COMMITTEE

James P. Pfiffner
Professor, Institute of Public Affairs and International Development, George Mason University
CABINET; CHIEF OF STAFF TO THE PRESIDENT; PERSONNEL MANAGEMENT, OFFICE OF; PRESIDENT, EXECUTIVE OFFICE OF THE; PRESIDENTIAL PERSONNEL, OFFICE OF; WHITE HOUSE OFFICE

Roger A. Pielke, Jr.
National Center for Atmospheric Research
ATMOSPHERIC RESEARCH, NATIONAL CENTER FOR; GLOBAL CHANGE RESEARCH PROGRAM

Richard M. Pious
Professor, Department of Political Science, Barnard College
ECONOMIC ADVISERS, COUNCIL OF; EXECUTIVE POWER; MANAGEMENT AND BUDGET, OFFICE OF; PRESIDENT AS CHIEF EXECUTIVE

Walter S. Poole
Joint History Office, The Pentagon
JOINT CHIEFS OF STAFF

Christine Smith Ritter
Doctoral Program in Public Administration, George Washington University
ACCOUNTABILITY IN THE FEDERAL GOVERNMENT

Mike Roberts
History Division, U.S. Navy
NAVY, DEPARTMENT OF THE

Nadia Rubaii-Barrett
Director, Master of Public Administration Program, New Mexico State University
CONSUMER PRODUCT SAFETY COMMISSION; OCCUPATIONAL SAFETY AND HEALTH ADMINISTRATION

Mike Sampson
Archivist, U.S. Secret Service
SECRET SERVICE

Jeffrey D. Schultz
Professor, Department of Political Science, Colorado College
GENERAL SERVICES ADMINISTRATION; TENNESSEE VALLEY AUTHORITY; TRAVEL AND TOURISM ADMINISTRATION

Pamela Scott
Independent Scholar
ARCHITECTURE OF THE FEDERAL GOVERNMENT

Edwin H. Simmons
Director, Marine Corps History Museum
MARINE CORPS

William Z. Slany
Historian, Department of State
STATE, DEPARTMENT OF

Marian L. Smith
Historian, Immigration and Naturalization Service
IMMIGRATION AND NATURALIZATION SERVICE

Robert J. Spitzer
Professor, Department of Political Science, State University of New York College at Cortland
ENVIRONMENTAL QUALITY, COUNCIL ON

Jesse Stiller
Office of the Comptroller of the Currency
COMPTROLLER OF THE CURRENCY, OFFICE OF THE; ENGRAVING AND PRINTING, BUREAU OF; THRIFT SUPERVISION, OFFICE OF

Brit Allen Storey
Senior Historian, Bureau of Reclamation
RECLAMATION, BUREAU OF

John P. Swann
Historian, Food and Drug Administration
FOOD AND DRUG ADMINISTRATION

Donald G. Tannenbaum
Professor, Department of Political Science, Gettysburg College
SENATE CONFIRMATION OF PRESIDENTIAL APPOINTEES

Roger R. Trask
Department of Defense, retired
DEFENSE, DEPARTMENT OF; GENERAL ACCOUNTING OFFICE

J. Samuel Walker
Historian, Nuclear Regulatory Commission
NUCLEAR REGULATORY COMMISSION

Paul F. Walker
Defense Consultant; former Senior Adviser to House Armed Services Committee
ARMS CONTROL AND DISARMAMENT AGENCY

George M. Watson, Jr.
Department of History, U.S. Air Force
AIR FORCE, DEPARTMENT OF THE

Wendy Wolff
Historical Editor, U.S. Senate
SENATE

Robert Wood
Senior Fellow, John W. McCormack Institute of Public Affairs, University of Massachusetts Boston
HOUSING AND URBAN DEVELOPMENT, DEPARTMENT OF

Margaret J. Wyszomirski
Director, Arts Management Program, Case Western Reserve University
NATIONAL ENDOWMENTS FOR THE ARTS AND HUMANITIES

A Historical Guide to the U.S. Government

A

Accountability in the Federal Government

The U.S. government operates with the "consent of the governed," and the governed hold their representatives accountable through periodic elections. However, elections do not hold career public administrators accountable for their behavior. Instead, the U.S. Congress has instituted accountability mechanisms inside the federal bureaucracy. These oversight offices are called upon by Congress to obtain information about program implementation. These oversight agents are used to ensure that public servants ethically provide quality public services within the confines of the U.S. Constitution and pertinent statutes.

Over the years, the U.S. Congress and president have developed multiple oversight mechanisms and agents to hold the federal bureaucracy accountable as program size, complexity, and responsibilities have grown. The strategies used by both the president and Congress to exert oversight have also evolved over time.

Congress has traditionally approached accountability through requesting information about specific programs or incidents. Frederick Mosher identifies three requisites of accountability: information about decisions and actions, outside receivers of information, and the recourse to sanction or praise. In order to control decisions and actions, the outside receivers carefully monitor activity, ensuring quality public services through strict compliance with legislated procedures. In general, such systematic receipt of information and such careful attention have not been the case for the U.S. Congress, and the sanctions have typically been negative, not positive. In fact, the approach to accountability taken throughout most of the U.S. federal experience has been backward-looking. Oversight agents judge the efficacy of past activity and punish for improper actions. In the federal government the strategy has been to enforce financial compliance accountability, through audits of financial records, and program compliance accountability, through evaluations of program implementation to ensure legislative intent. However, initiatives have recently been undertaken by both the executive and legislative branches to promote oversight through assessing programmatic results. Paul Light has recently distinguished these different approaches toward accountability and labeled the traditional approach compliance accountability, as opposed to a forward-looking approach that looks for evidence of performance. This essay traces the evolution of the U.S. federal government's oversight mechanisms and strategies.

Until the beginning of the twentieth century, the federal government remained fairly small, providing basic services such as defense and mail delivery. Through this period, the appropriations process and personnel action provided sufficient oversight. At the turn of the century, the good government reform movement advocated a greater concentration of power in the executive branch to combat the entrenchment of machine politics and the improper use of tax revenues at the local level. Reformers specifically advocated the use of a comprehensive budget proposal by the executive that would outline each fiscal year's expenditures, an idea that gained popularity at the federal level.

The reform movement reached fruition in the 1921 Budget and Accounting Act, creating an executive budget. [*See* Appendix: Budget and Accounting Act (1921).] To balance the concentration of executive power in an executive budget, Congress created an independent General Accounting Office (GAO) to "investigate, at the seat of government or elsewhere, all matters relating to the receipt, disbursement, and application of public funds . . ." (P.L. 67-13, 42 Stat. 20). In creating the GAO, Congress sought to institutionalize its ability to control public expenditures. Congress created the GAO to exercise financial compliance accountability, but the word *application* later enabled the GAO to broaden the scope of its activities to include nonfinancial matters.

Up until World War II, the GAO ensured that executive expenditures complied with legislated appropriation by reviewing every agency's expenditure vouchers for compliance with the law. The GAO became the government's accounting firm. Eventually, expansive growth in government programs during the New Deal and World War II made it impossible for the GAO to review every agency voucher. Instead, the GAO moved to install accounting responsibilities in each agency and concurrently redefined its financial accountability role toward oversight of accounting systems, providing standards and technical assistance. The "comprehensive" audit of accounting systems replaced voucher checking as the primary form of financial compliance accountability. The Budget and Accounting Act of 1950 (P.L. 101-576, 104 Stat. 2855) formalized this development.

The GAO began to broaden the scope of compliance activities beyond financial matters when it began auditing the government corporations created during the Great Depression. The GAO not only audited these corporations but assessed their effectiveness in carrying out their designated purposes. Eventually, the GAO boasted a sizable Office of Investigations and began to use the comprehensive audit selectively, identifying trouble spots for special attention. Culminating in the Truth in Negotiations Act, the heightened focus on contract auditing led to more rigorous procurement procedures to ensure that private compliance with the intent of appropriated public expenditures was respected.

In the late 1960s, the GAO officially broadened the concept of financial accountability to include program accountability, using program evaluations to assess President Johnson's social programs. Senator Prouty initiated the first serious round of GAO program evaluations with an amendment to the Economic Opportunity Act of 1967 requesting a complete evaluation of Johnson's poverty programs. The 1970 Legislative Reorganization Act further empowered GAO program evaluation by granting the ability to conduct cost-benefit analysis of programs (P.L. 91-510, 84 Stat. 1140), and the Congressional Budget and Impoundment Control Act of 1974 enabled the GAO to establish a separate Office of Program Review and Evaluation. The GAO's ability to control executive implementation now included reviewing both financial and program compliance with legislation.

During the 1960s and 1970s, both Congress and the president began to place greater responsibility for monitoring program compliance in the agencies. Congress initiated agency evaluation with a provision in the 1965 Elementary and Secondary Education Act requiring the administering agency to report on its implementation of Title I. For the first time, program administrators were required to devote time and resources to evaluating their efforts. Johnson's Program-Planning-Budgeting-System required agencies to identify performance objectives when compiling their budget, and in 1979 the Office of Management and Budget released circular A-117, which officially endorsed program evaluation and urged agencies to evaluate the effectiveness of their programs.

In the late 1970s, the combined effects of Watergate and tightening government revenues heightened the desire to control executive program implementation, resulting in searches for executive waste, fraud, and abuse. Although the GAO continued to respond to congressional requests for information about financial and program compliance, larger, more complex executive agencies and public programs prevented the GAO from constant monitoring. The increased number of congressional requests for evaluations spread the GAO's resources thinly over the entire executive branch.

To supplement the oversight information provided them by the GAO, Congress established inspectors generals in executive agencies, beginning slowly with one statutory inspector general in 1976 and quickly creating the bulk of the positions under the Inspectors General Act of 1978 (P.L. 95-452, 92 Stat. 1109) and the 1988 amendments to the act. The intent of the 1978 act was to establish a consolidated oversight office within each federal agency that would report directly to Congress and would be vigilant against fraud and abuse in executive agency spending. Reports by inspectors general of extensive savings from identifying fraudulent agency expenditures and program mismanagement fell on receptive congressional ears.

The intensity of congressional oversight over public managers increased further during the 1980s. Declining federal resources, a growing federal deficit, and the political orientation of the Reagan White House to identify waste, fraud, and abuse translated into punitive reactions for noncompliance. Congress and the executive reduced the size of agency program evaluation and budgeting staffs, forcing rapid-feedback, management-oriented reviews. Congress requested even more program evaluations and policy analyses from the GAO, and also increased the staff and scope of Inspector General Offices. Some of the increased efforts to ensure accountability resulted in high-profile investigations, such as uncovering significant expenditure fraud at the Department of Housing and Urban Development.

During the 1990s a growing concern with assessing the quality of program performance led to an increased emphasis on ensuring accountability through measuring performance. The move to assessing performance reflected several changes in the economic and political environment. A weak economy and increasing taxes pushed frustrated taxpayers to demand visible results. The growing federal deficit ignited calls to redesign public service delivery. The growing prominence of contracting for services to contain costs increased the need for visible results. Peters and Waterman's seminal book *In Search of Excellence* renewed an interest in customer service and client satisfaction. Finally, the availability of powerful technology eased the burden of collecting data on program outcomes. All of these developments supported both executive and legislative demands that agencies support

budgetary requests with hard evidence, that is, by providing program costs and results. The move to holding public administrators accountable for their programmatic performance has manifested itself in three recent pieces of legislation and the Clinton administration's National Performance Review.

The Chief Financial Officers Act of 1990 (CFOA; P.L. 101-576, 104 Stat. 2838) and the Government Management and Reform Act of 1994 (GMRA; P.L. 103-356, 108 Stat. 34) emphasized both measuring performance and improving management systems to enhance accountability. The CFOA legislated the first link between setting performance goals and costs. In conjunction with the Office of Management and Budget's Bulletin 94-01, the CFOA calls for agencies to show how program outcomes supported agency missions. The CFOA also requires agencies to report the final costs of each program. The CFOA requires after-the-fact accounting of financial expenditures through audited annual financial statements to obtain the true cost of federal programs. Although annual audits continue to emphasize compliance with accounting standards, financial statements also provide a final cost for any given program. Further, the CFOA requires agencies to report their expenditures under accrual based accounting. Accrual accounting, which considers future project costs and counts costs when goods are received and not when bills are due, had been legislated for all agencies in the 1960s but had never been fully implemented. Linking true program costs with measures of program performance provides improved performance information. The GMRA extended audited financial statements to almost all government agencies and requires a government-wide annual financial statement by March 1998.

The CFOA and the GMRA were designed to improve systems to support oversight by redesigning human resource and financial management systems. The acts strengthened the executive branch's management functions, creating new management and financial management roles within the Office of Management and Budget. They also authorized the appointment of a chief financial officer in each agency who is responsible for all budgeting, accounting, and other financial management activity. The GMRA streamlined personnel leave and pay policies and made both congressional and management reporting requirements more flexible.

Although the CFOA requires each federal agency to provide "systematic measurement of performance," the government moved to institute performance measurement in its own right with the Government Performance and Results Act of 1993 (GPRA; P.L. 103-62, 107 Stat. 285). Under the GPRA, agencies must develop three important pieces of a performance measurement system: strategic plans, annual performance plans, and annual performance reports. In line with performance measurement, agencies must compile a long-term plan to fulfill the agency's mission; a short-term performance plan for each program with identified performance measures and goals for those measures; and after-the-fact reporting of program results. The GPRA's commitment to holding public managers accountable for performance even offers agencies the possibility to waive administrative procedures if they inhibit goal achievement. Agency-initiated plans and performance goals, as well as internal tracking of performance by program evaluation and accounting resources, ensure greater agency involvement. The collaboration of both agency personnel and accountability mechanisms represents a forceful move away from traditional control strategies.

The Clinton administration has taken initiatives to promote holding public managers accountable for programmatic performance. The Clinton White House initiated a national review of all federal government operating procedures and concluded that much government ineffectiveness and inefficiency results from too much emphasis on procedures and too little emphasis on outcomes. The National Performance Review made specific recommendations to streamline various government procedures that will enhance management's ability to provide quality public services. Although many reforms have not been implemented, this Clinton initiative stresses the need to obtain performance data as one means of holding public managers accountable.

Today the U.S. federal government still wishes to control government activities, retaining an emphasis on compliance in some areas—continued GAO program evaluation and Ig audits by inspectors general, for example. However, both the president and Congress have taken several steps to promote proactive incentives to enhance government performance and demonstrate programmatic accountability. This move reflects a general belief that holding people or organizations accountable for results, rather than simply compliance with procedures, will improve the quality of public services. This trend also emphasizes that each agency's internal accounting and program evaluation resources will play a greater role in identifying goals and providing supporting information.

Those who disagree with the current emphasis on performance accountability often support alternative approaches to improving government performance. For example, Ronald Moe disputes the effectiveness of waiving management rules to achieve desired outcomes. Moe believes greater adherence to legal management practices will improve the quality of public services. He also promotes building government management capabilities. Coming from a quite different perspective, Michael Harmon calls for a complete redefinition of the traditional public administrator role to enhance individuals' personal responsibility for public service delivery. Harmon would improve the ethical delivery of quality public services by including public servants in the process of defining program activity, simultaneously instilling in each participant a personal responsibility for providing quality public services.

Ensuring accountability will challenge future administrations and congresses as government programs grow more intricate. Exerting oversight after the fact and punishing public managers for wrongdoing is not sufficient, as most critics have recognized. Ultimately, promoting performance will require creative incentives for public administrators, as well as positive collaborative relationships between those conducting oversight and those being overseen.

[See also General Accounting Office; Management and Budget, Office of; and National Performance Review.]

BIBLIOGRAPHY

Gore, Al. *From Red Tape to Results: Creating a Government That Works Better and Costs Less; Report of the National Performance Review.* New York, 1993.

Harmon, Michael M. *Responsibility at Paradox: A Critique of Rational Discourse on Government.* Thousand Oaks, Calif., 1995.

Light, Paul C. *Inspectors General and the Search for Accountability.* Washington, D.C., 1993.

Moe, Ronald C. "Traditional Organizational Principles and the Managerial Presidency: From Phoenix to Ashes." *Public Administration Review* 50, no. 2 (1990): 129–140.

Moe, Ronald C. "The 'Reinventing Government' Exercise: Misinterpreting the Problem, Misjudging the Consequences." *Public Administration Review* 54, no. 2 (1994): 111–122.

Mosher, Frederick C. *The GAO: The Quest for Accountability in American Government.* Boulder, Colo., 1979.

Newcomer, Kathryn E. "Recent Trends in the Evaluation of Public Policies and Programs in the U.S. Federal Government." *Chinese Journal of Administration* 54 (1993): 71–86.

Newcomer, Kathryn E. "Evaluating Public Programs." In *Handbook of Public Administration,* edited by James Perry. San Francisco, 1996.

Trask, Roger R. *GAO History, 1921–1991.* GAO-OP-3-HP. Washington, D.C., 1991.

Wholey, Joseph S., and Kathryn E. Newcomer, eds. *Improving Government Performance.* San Francisco, 1989.

—KATHRYN E. NEWCOMER and
CHRISTINE SMITH RITTER

Act to Regulate Commerce.

See Appendix: Basic Documents of Public Administration.

Administrative Procedure Act.

See Appendix: Basic Documents of Public Administration.

Advising the President

ESSAY Presidential advising is a multifaceted task, performed by myriad individuals in and out of government. Presidents sometimes seek out advice; other times, they confront virtual overload. Here, *advising* refers to providing input into or offering support for presidential decision-making; its actual influence on presidential decisions becomes a separate question.

The more cognitive dimensions of advising include "providing information, defining problems, structuring choices, generating alternatives, and communicating viewpoints" (Hult, p. 112). Meanwhile, advising also may provide presidents with socioemotional support, reinforcing presidential values or reassuring them that their decisions are appropriate.

TRENDS IN PRESIDENTIAL ADVISING

The twentieth century has witnessed a "swelling of the presidency" (Cronin). As aides and specialized staff units have proliferated, the number of channels through which advice can reach presidents has multiplied, in turn reducing the centrality of any single source of counsel and heightening competition among advisers. Contemporary presidents confront increasingly complex policy problems and a fragmenting political system, with exploding numbers of interest groups, frequently divided government, more independent members of Congress, and a road to the White House that runs through the primary states rather than party bosses' smoke-filled rooms. As presidents relentlessly seek information and counsel relevant to their own political and policy objectives, they have centralized advising in and around the White House and turned more frequently to personal staffers for advice ("politicization"). The focus of advising also may be shifting toward an emphasis on public relations.

Cabinet

The cabinet has been perhaps the biggest loser. To be sure, the Framers never intended the cabinet to be a collective body (instead envisioning the U.S. Senate as a sort of privy council for the president), and few presidents have used the cabinet as an advisory forum. Even the more specialized cabinet councils of Presidents Ronald Reagan and George Bush handled mostly second-tier issues, typically under the guidance of a senior White House staffer. Still, presidents since George Washington have sought the advice of individual cabinet members, especially those in the "inner" cabinet, who head the State, Defense, Treasury, and Justice departments. Richard Nixon, however, dramatically undermined this practice, beginning his second term with an explicit charge that cabinet secretaries be managers and leave advising to the (presumably more loyal) White House staff.

More than one president's suspicion and distrust were involved in this further weakening of the cabinet. Through the 1960s and 1970s, as presidents' dependence on political parties plummeted, they brought tasks formerly performed by the parties into the White House, relying on aides to maintain links with interest groups and the public and to plot reelection bids. These changes eroded the independent political bases of individual cabinet members, making them less attractive and necessary as political or policy advisers.

Executive Office

More appealing to presidents have been the growing number of specialized aides in the increasingly complex Executive Office of the President (EOP). Throughout the twentieth century, presidents have turned to their staffs for advice. Only after the EOP was created in 1939, however, did presidential aides begin to offer substantive policy (as opposed to political strategic) advice. [*See* Appendix: Reorganization Plan No. 1, (1939).] Since then, staffers' involvement in advising has grown.

The centralization and politicization of the EOP began in earnest under Dwight Eisenhower, who appointed the first noncareer official to head the Bureau of the Budget and created the posts of national security assistant and economic policy adviser in the White House Office. Propelled by a fragmenting political system and the systematic strategies of Presidents Nixon and Reagan, these trends accelerated. As a result, "the White House Office has gradually eclipsed the EOP [of which it is a part] as the core advisory resource" (Campbell, p. 188), and political appointees throughout the Executive Office have constrained the access of career officials to the president.

Not surprisingly, the exact nature of advisory arrangements within the EOP varies with the type of policy. In *economic* policy, for example, the Council of Economic Advisers (CEA) formally was the primary source of advice from its creation by the Employment Act of 1946 until 1993, when President Bill Clinton established the National Economic Council. Yet the CEA has had diminishing influence on presidents since Lyndon Johnson, facing mounting competition from other economic advising units within the EOP and throughout the executive branch. That the boundaries between "domestic" and "international" economic issues and among "economic," "domestic," and "national security" policies continue to blur further complicates the generation of coherent advice.

While most presidents have been content to rely on experts outside of the White House itself for substantive economic policy input, domestic and national security policy have been pulled closer to the presidential orbit. In *domestic* policy, presidents have experimented with a variety of arrangements, but since Herbert Hoover White House aides have focused on specific issues. In July 1970 Nixon added a unit in the EOP for domestic policy (to house staff for a new Domestic Council), a practice followed by all his successors. Yet, as with economic policy, fragmentation of advice and fuzzy jurisdictional boundaries persist. The influence of the EOP unit has varied considerably with the standing in the White House of the president's assistant for domestic policy.

In contrast, in the *national security* arena, arrangements in the EOP have been more stable and less fragmented. When Congress established the National Security Council (NSC) in 1947, many hoped it would inject a wider range of input from cabinet members into foreign policy decision-making and discourage the dominance of a Franklin Roosevelt. Instead, the White House–based national security assistant and the NSC staff have only added to centralization. Despite the decreased visibility of the national security assistant following the Nixon-Kissinger era and renewed efforts to rein in the NSC staff in the wake of the Iran-*contra* revelations, the assistant and NSC staff continue to be key foreign policy advisers.

Vice Presidents

Vice presidents, too, have grown in significance as presidential advisers. Indeed, the enhanced access to the president and policy involvement of Nelson Rockefeller and Walter Mondale signaled the emergence of a "new vice presidency." Since then, external expectations and precedent likely have made the vice president's participation as an adviser part of the job description. Still, their advisory tasks (and influence) typically vary with vice presidents' political skills, staff resources, and compatibility with the president. Presidents with little Washington experience have tended to depend more on vice presidents' strategic advice than have "insider" presidents.

Presidential Advisory Committees

Although presidents have turned to advisory committees throughout U.S. history, their use accelerated as the tasks performed by and expected of the federal government multiplied. Sometimes the creation and operation of these advisory mechanisms have triggered controversy (e.g., the Clinton Task Force on Health Care Reform). Most often, though, presidents use such committees less to provide advice than to build support for administration proposals or to indicate concern about particular problems.

Presidential Kin

Presidents also have been looking more frequently to family members for information, counsel, and moral support. Barbara Kellerman traces this shift to 1960 and the frenetic campaign activities of the extended family of John F. Kennedy.

At the same time, involvement of presidential kin in political and policy advising has sparked controversy. Although Eisenhower's dependence on his brother Milton as an informal adviser drew little negative reaction, Kennedy's appointment of his brother Robert as attorney general was the target of considerable criticism. The most hostility, however, has been directed at presidential spouses. Abigail Adams, Edith Galt Wilson, and Eleanor Roosevelt, of course, generated withering disapproval. Yet a shift toward "more activist First Ladies" has intensified since the 1970s, producing more heated debate. Of greatest concern to some are presidential spouses like Rosalynn Carter and Hillary Rodham Clinton, who appear to be actively engaged in policy advising. Doubtlessly, much of this resistance is to strong, independent women. "But among serious students of government . . . [Rodham Clinton's] ascendancy as a formal policy adviser raises questions about the institution of the presidency and the proper relationship between advisees and advisers" (Rockman, p. 335).

Public Relations

Presidents must focus on more than the details of substantive policy. They have drawn advising closer to the White House, worked to politicize the EOP, and relied more on kin in order to increase the likelihood that the advice they receive will be refracted through the prism of presidential political interests. These tendencies are reinforced by changes in the electoral system that give first-term presidents more incentives to hire campaign workers as White House staffers and to view governing primarily in electoral terms. More generally, advances in communications and closer direct ties between presidents and publics make governing ever more like campaigning. In such a setting, advice on public relations strategies may receive more attention than substantive policy input, and media advisers like Gerald Rafshoon (in the Carter administration) and Michael Deaver (under Reagan) have become White House fixtures.

CONTINUITIES IN PRESIDENTIAL ADVISING

Still, one ought not overstate the changes in presidential advising. Most presidents, for example, routinely turn to a few trusted individuals for counsel and emotional support. These frequently have been members of the White House staff, like Lawrence Richey in the Hoover administration and Louis Howe under FDR. Other times, close advisers have no official position (e.g., Colonel Edward House for Woodrow Wilson), and become part of presidents' "kitchen cabinets."

Two more general factors also affect advising.

First, over the course of a term in office, as relationships grow more predictable, presidents tend to rely less on formal arrangements. Moreover, as an administration's agenda becomes fixed and constraints multiply, presidents often see less need for hearing competing points of view, and the advisory circle shrinks. Second, in situations of political or policy "crisis" (e.g., the 1929 stock market crash, the Watergate scandal) or when secrecy is deemed to be critical (as is often true when national security issues are involved), presidents may be more apt to turn away from established procedures and rely instead on more *ad hoc* advising networks. At these times, too, the number of advisers and the range of advice proffered may contract dramatically.

PROSPECTS FOR CHANGE

Few disagree that arrangements for presidential advising have grown more complex, more centralized, and more politicized. More unsettled are the desirability of these developments and the possibility for change.

Critics contend that, as presidents increasingly rely on White House aides, they may receive less diverse advice and be buffered from the counsel of executive branch officials with substantive expertise and experience. Furthermore, expansion of the EOP has complicated presidential ability to shape and monitor how advice reaches them, while increasing the likelihood that aides may overlook, screen out, or distort information and analysis or even act independently (as happened, for example, during Iran-contra).

Such concerns have generated numerous prescriptions for reining in presidential staff and increasing the amount of "objective, expert" advice that presidents receive. Frequently suggested are White House "custodians" of the advisory process to ensure that diverse information and arguments reach the president and that weaker positions and advocates receive fair hearings.

Others, however, question these proposals. Some maintain that advising arrangements both should and inevitably do reflect presidential preferences. Individual presidents, for example, participate more or less actively in the advising process, differ in their tolerance for conflict among advisers, and vary in their receptivity to advice. At least as important, centralization and politicization serve presidents' demands for advice that is relevant to and consistent with their political and policy objectives. This drive for "responsive competence" can be expected to lead presidents to ignore prescriptions that stress gathering more "neutral" advice from sources outside the White House.

A transforming U.S. political system, thorny policy problems, and the institutional legacies of past administrations all shape presidential advisory arrangements. At the same time, much about advising presidents remains irreducibly personalized. Prescriptions that neglect individual presidents' preferences, policy objectives, and political interests likely are doomed to fail.

[*See also* Cabinet; Economic Advisers, Council of; National Security Council; President, Executive Office of the; Vice Presidency; *and* White House Office.]

BIBLIOGRAPHY

Burke, John P. *The Institutional Presidency.* Baltimore, 1992.

Bybee, Jay S. "Advising the President: Separation of Powers and the Federal Advisory Committee Act." *Yale Law Journal* 104 (1994): 51–128.

Campbell, Colin, S.J. "The White House and Cabinet under the 'Let's Deal' Presidency." In *The Bush Presidency: First Appraisals,* edited by Colin Campbell, S.J., and Bert A. Rockman. Chatham, N.J., 1991.

Caroli, Betty Boyd. *First Ladies.* New York, 1987.

Cohen, Jeffrey E. *The Politics of the U.S. Cabinet: Representation in the Executive Branch, 1789–1984.* Pittsburgh, 1988.

Cronin, Thomas E. *The State of the Presidency.* Boston, 1975.

Destler, I. M. "National Security Advice to Presidents: Some Lessons From Thirty Years." *World Politics* 29 (1977): 143–176.

George, Alexander L. *Presidential Decision-Making in Foreign Policy.* Boulder, Colo., 1980.

Hart, John. *The Presidential Branch: From Washington to Clinton.* 2d ed. Chatham, N.J., 1995.

Hess, Stephen. *Organizing the Presidency.* 2d ed. Washington, D.C., 1988.

Hult, Karen M. "Advising the President." In *Researching the Presidency: Vital Questions, New Approaches,* edited by George C. Edwards III, John H. Kessel, and Bert A. Rockman. Pittsburgh, 1993.

Janis, Irving L. *Victims of Groupthink.* Boston, 1972.

Johnson, Richard Tanner. *Managing the White House: An Intimate Study of the Presidency.* New York, 1974.

Kellerman, Barbara. *All the President's Kin.* New York, 1981.

Light, Paul C. *Vice Presidential Power.* Baltimore, 1984.

Meltsner, Arnold J. *Rules for Rulers: The Politics of Advice.* Philadelphia, 1990.

Moe, Terry M. "The Politicized Presidency." In *The New Direction in American Politics,* edited by John E. Chubb and Paul E. Peterson. Washington, D.C., 1985.

Pika, Joseph A. "The Vice Presidency: New Opportunities, Old Constraints." In *The Presidency and the Political System,* 4th ed., edited by Michael Nelson. Washington, D.C., 1995.

Rockman, Bert A. "Leadership Style and the Clinton Presidency." In *The Clinton Presidency: First Appraisals,* edited by Colin Campbell and Bert A. Rockman, Chatham, N. J., 1996.

Walcott, Charles E., and Karen M. Hult. *Governing the White House: From Hoover Through LBJ.* Lawrence, Kans., 1995.

Williams, Walter. *Mismanaging America: The Rise of the Anti-Analytic Presidency.* Lawrence, Kans., 1990.

—KAREN HULT

Advisory Agencies

ESSAY Advisory committees provide basic findings and rationale that play important roles in developing public policy, establishing priorities, and shaping agendas for new policies and programs. Advisory commissions may be described as *ad hoc* institutions formally and officially established to make recommendations and consult with host government agencies on prescribed topics. Advisory committees span the institutional spectrum, including committees, boards, commissions, councils, conferences, panels, task forces, and similar groups. Subcommittees and subgroups also are included but may not be held to statutory obligations imposed on parent groups.

Federal advisory committee roles in fashioning public policies are too numerous to fully portray in this brief description. The purpose here is to highlight the history, general characteristics, statistical profile, organizational and operational requirements, objectives and attributes (both good and bad), and rules governing creation and use.

HISTORY OF FEDERAL ADVISORY UNITS

Governing authorities have relied on advisory assistance throughout history. Among the very first known was the senate of Rome, composed of one hundred elders (*patres*) whose responsibilities were advisory in nature. Dating back to 750 B.C., this advisory council was intended perhaps more as a check on powers and prerogatives of an elected (not hereditary) king. Sound counsel provided by outside unbiased experts always has been a hallmark of responsible government.

Advisory assistance institutionalized at the federal level has contributed to public policy decision-making throughout U.S. history. President George Washington appointed a commission to help resolve the 1794 Whisky Rebellion that arose over opposition to a 1791 liquor tax. President Van Buren (1837–1841) established an advisory commission to study European postal systems. (The new American government had much to learn from the long experience amassed in other countries. France had established the first post office in 1461, nearly three centuries before the founding of the U.S. post office in 1727.) The Aldrich Commission led to the establishment of the Federal Reserve System in 1907. An outgrowth of President Taft's Commission on Economy and Efficiency was the Budget and Accounting Act (1921), which required the president to submit an annual budget to Congress and established the Bureau of the Budget and the General Accounting Office. [*See* Appendix: Report of the (Taft) Commission on Economy and Efficiency (1912).]

Maintaining that President Theodore Roosevelt relied excessively upon advisory groups, Congress attached a rider to the Sundry Civil Act in 1909 that denied commission funding unless authorized by law. President Hoover convened sixty-two advisory agencies during his initial sixteen months in office; most notable were the Commission on Law Observance and Enforcement (Wickersham Commission) and the President's Research Committee on Social Trends, Inc. (1929–1932). President Franklin Roosevelt appointed over one hundred commissions during his first two terms in office; the Brownlow Committee on Administrative Management (1936–1939), for example, led to the Reorganization Act of 1939 creating a wide-ranging and more powerful Executive Office. [*See* Brownlow Committee *and* Appendix: Reorganization Act of 1939.]

Advisory committees played key roles in fostering and developing new enterprise. The National Advisory Committee for Aeronautics (NACA), established by Congress during 1915 (U.S.C. title 50, sec. 151), laid milestones that led to U.S. predominance in aviation. The NACA operated aeronautical laboratories from coast to coast that contributed to aircraft and engine design as well as piloting and navigational techniques, thus benefiting military, commercial, and private aviation. Appointed by the president, the committee consisted of two members each from the aviation sections of the War and Navy departments, one each from the Smithsonian Institution, the Weather Bureau, and the National Bureau of Standards, and eight other experts in the field of aeronautics. Commencing with a modest appropriation of $5,000 in 1915, funding soared and peaked during 1945 at $45 million. Contributions proved vital to Allied air victories during World War II.

Advisory groups proliferated thanks to the drastic increase in federal intervention during World War II. National calamity prompted the creation of other advisory agencies, including the Kerner Commission on Civil Disorders (1967–1968) in the aftermath of the disastrous Newark and Detroit inner-city riots during 1968, and the Warren Commission on the Assassination of President Kennedy (1963–1964).

Advisory agencies take many different forms. National conferences have proved successful in generating interest and mobilizing support. A White House Conference on Children and Youth led in 1912 to the establishment of the United States Children's Bureau and the enactment of child labor laws. President Eisenhower convened sixteen such conferences during his term of office, including an important White House Conference on Aging. Pre-inaugural task forces and transition teams also have become an advisory mainstay in reorienting incoming administration focus.

From time to time, advisory committees are chartered to come up with sweeping visionary perspectives. Stepping back and looking ahead to the longer range is an ideal assignment for advisory groups. Reconnoitering the national landscape and recommending panoramic strategies for optimizing national interests has become common over the years: perhaps the most notable effort to establish a sweeping national vision of the future was the President's Research Committee on Social Trends, Inc., established in September 1929 by President Hoover. Its massive two-volume report of 11 October 1932 was financed by the Rockefeller Foundation. The President's Commission on National Goals, an eleven-member panel established by President Eisenhower to study the entire range of contemporary problems submitted its visionary report on 16 November 1960. This presidentially appointed commission was unique in that it was supported by private funds (from eight private foundations), administered by the American Assembly of Columbia University, and commercially published by Prentice-Hall, Inc. Although clearly in the nature of an advisory committee, its status was separate and distinct from laws regulating government units.

A Panel on Social Indicators was established pursuant to President Johnson's request to develop indicators for monitoring the social landscape that would be analogous to the economic indicators promulgated by the Bureau of Labor Statistics and the Council of Economic Advisers. Modeled after President Hoover's Research Committee on Social Trends, the panel summarized its findings in *Toward a Social Report,* submitted to President Johnson on 11 January 1969, the last day of his term in office. Several months later, President Nixon announced on 13 July 1969 the formation of a National Goals Research Staff within the White House to "illumine the possible range of national goals for 1976—our 200th anniversary." Although many outsiders were involved in this project, it more or less operated as a staff unit within the White House rather than, strictly speaking, an advisory committee. Following up on the Panel on Social Indicators recommendations, and spurred by the British example (*Social Trends,* published 1970 and thereafter), the White House Office of Management and Budget (OMB) under President

Nixon also published several editions (1974, 1977, and 1981) of *Social Indicators,* each one supported by advisory committees.

Vice President Rockefeller, who in the late 1960s organized and chaired a forty-two-member Commission of Critical Choices for Americans, switched to an *ex officio* status on the commission after assuming federal office. The commission's six panels churned out an entire shelf of books dealing with priority issues that helped to fashion decisions made during the Ford-Rockefeller tenure. The commission was financed through the Third Century Corporation, a nonprofit unit financed by the Rockefellers and other financial scions. Nelson Rockefeller had initiated a similar searching scrutiny of national issues during the late 1950s, and a compendium of the reports, *Prospect for America: The Rockefeller Panel Reports,* was published in 1961. (Numerous other similar public and private efforts could be cited.) Finally, the President's Commission for a National Agenda for the Eighties (1978–1980), a forty-five-member commission established by President Carter, issued a series of pamphlets reporting on a broad issue spectrum.

Concern over collusion and the antitrust implications of recourse to business advisers during the post–World War II economic boom prompted the Justice Department to issue advisory committee guidelines in 1950 that were reaffirmed by Bureau of the Budget directive in 1959 and reiterated by President Kennedy in 1962 (Executive Order 11007). Lacking the force of law, these guidelines were largely ignored. During the early 1970s, legislative attention focused on duplication, waste, cost, minor impact on public policy, and undue influence. Hearings eventually resulted in enactment of the Federal Advisory Committee Act, or FACA (P.L. 92-463, effective 5 January 1973), which provided a sense of order and new levels of responsible conduct.

Every administration is hallmarked by important advisory commission findings and recommendations. The Presidential Commission on Health Needs of the Nation (1951–1952) provided impetus for enactment of the first national health insurance laws. The President's Commission on the Assasination of President John F. Kennedy (1963–1964), commonly referred to as the Warren Commission, probed the culprits and reasons behind this tragic event. During the Johnson administration, the Commission on Technology, Automation and Economic Progress (1964–1966) delved into the wrenching dislocating effects of advancing technologies, and the Kerner Commission on Civil Disorders (1968) gave rise to a new round of civil rights protections.

Congress sometimes collaborates with the executive branch to thrash out the issues, as was the case with the Hoover Commission on Organization of the Executive Branch of the Government (1947–1949 and 1953–1955). [*See* Appendix: Concluding Report of the Commission on Organization of the Executive Branch of Government (First Hoover Commission) (1949).] Occasionally, the collaboration is overtly with private groups: the Joint Commission on Mental Illness and Health (created by the Mental Health Study Act of 1955) was spearheaded by the American Psychiatric Association and the American Medical Association, was administered by the National Institute of Mental Health, and received about ten percent of its funding from private groups.

Congress, of course, has its own retinue of what might be considered advisory groups. Standing committees and their subcommittees regularly call upon outside opinion in considering public policy, and a host of other special units often function in a manner similar to advisory agencies: the Kefauver Special Committee to Investigate Organized Crime in Interstate Commerce; the infamous McCarthy Subcommittee on Investigations; and a plethora of investigative committees in recent years, one of them actually bringing about resignation of an incumbent president.

Politicians frequently cave in to special-interest pleaders. To stiffen resolve and ease political pressures, advisory commissions sometimes are organized to provide a first line of defense against political compromise. The Defense Base Closure and Realignment Commission short-circuited political pressures that previously prevented Congress from closing unneeded facilities. Excess base capacity at the Cold War's end had to be reduced, but local communities and the congressional members representing them consistently frustrated these efforts. As structured, advisory recommendations were allowed to be voted up or down, thereby barring pork-barrel efforts to save favored local installations. Either house of Congress was empowered to reject final recommendations, but only *in toto;* only the president was empowered to send the commission's recommendations back for further consideration. This approach proved successful. Commission recommendations succeeded in closing 243 domestic military bases. Cost saving calculations vary, but congressional estimates placed them in excess of $49 billion over twenty years—meaningful savings compared with the $13 million the commission cost taxpayers.

Divided government may encourage separate branches to put forward their own empaneled experts to speak out on the issues in a manner calculated to advance their specific views and pet projects. Rivalries between different branches of government controlled by opposing political parties exacerbate such situations. Confronted by gridlock brought on by the House's being controlled by one political party and the Senate by another, President Hoover, to curry favor for his programs, resorted to the appointment of sixty commissions, boards, and similar bodies during a sixteen-month period. Carried to an extreme, advisory committees can be arrayed as a "shadow" government to offset and upstage an opposing political party. Vice President Gore's 1994 memorandum to all executive departments and agencies declared that "the Administration will not support legislative language that establishes new advisory committees [and advocates] reduc[ing] the number of advisory committees required by statute." The ostensible purpose was to resist any further addition of mandated or authorized statutory advisory agencies by a Congress dominated by the opposing political party. Politically, the underlying thrust may have been to discourage formation of legislative-sponsored advisory groups for partisan purposes.

Not infrequently, advisory groups may be used to advance political purposes. Presidential election campaigns often rely on advisory commissions to come up with expert recommendations on nettlesome issues that candidates can seize upon to bolster their positions. The President's Council on Sustainable Development, appointed in 1993, issued a 1996 report whose recommendations were widely acknowledged as the blueprint for a strong pro-environmental stance by the Clinton-Gore ticket in the 1996 elections. The Republican-controlled Congress empaneled a fourteen-member Kemp Commission whose 1996 report laid out a basis for tax reductions, revisions, and reforms at odds with the policies of the incumbent Democratic administration. In short, staking out pivotal issues for forthcoming elections may be the purpose behind certain mission-oriented advisory units. On other hand, apolitical purposes may provide the motivation. The very purpose of constituting an advisory agency may be to transcend politics and provide an unbiased assessment of controversial issues without regard to their influence upon upcoming elections.

GENERAL CHARACTERISTICS OF ADVISORY AGENCIES

Federal advisory committees—about one thousand of which have been active during any recent year—provide valuable outside opinion and input concerning government policies and programs of all kinds. Currents of popular opinion influence the subjects addressed and the number and nature of advisory groups. Over one hundred new committees are established every year. Nearly the same number go out of business, having concluded their work or outlived their purposes.

Advisory committees are established: pursuant to presidential authority, usually by executive order; by statutory mandates; pursuant to statutory authorizations (permitted but not compelled to be established); or by inherent (implied) regulatory authority. Most committees are mere continuations of previously established units. Among advisory agencies active during fiscal year 1994, thirty-six percent (429) were required by statute; thirty-four percent (423) were authorized by statute; twenty-eight percent (316) were organized pursuant to agency authority; and only two percent (27) were established by presidential directive.

Federal advisory committees sponsored by fifty-one federal departments and agencies numbered 1,195 throughout fiscal year 1994, involved 30,446 members, and required 1,174 federal staff support years. Issued reports numbered 1,245, based on 4,109 meetings (1,826 open, 1,502 totally closed, and 781 partially closed). On average each committee met 3.4 times during the year, about the same as in previous years. Annual cost totaled $133.4 million. [*See* Appendix 1: Federal Advisory Agencies, Tables 2, 3, and 4.]

Advisory groups come and go—1,088 units were in existence at the end of fiscal year 1993; during fiscal year 1994 another 107 units were established and 188 were terminated, leaving 1,007 units at the end of fiscal year 1994. Elimination of eighty-one groups amounted to a decline of about seven percent.

Five government hosts accounted for nearly two-thirds (62%) of all members serving on the advisory committees in existence during fiscal year 1994 (19,013 of the 30,446)—8,085 of them in the Department of Health and Human Services; 6,181 in the National Science Foundation; 1,779 in the Department of the Interior; 1,602 in the Department of State; and 1,366 in the Environmental Protection Agency. The Department of Health and Human Services usually has the most advisory agencies, primarily because of the numerous advisory committees established by the National Institutes of Health.

Advisory Agencies Reporting Directly to the President

Advisory committees that report directly to the president generally reflect priority issues, especially controversial ones. Reporting directly to the president each year are about fifty such agencies, typically confined to high-priority matters; other *ad hoc* groups typically number about fifty in a given year. Independent and (supposedly) impartial appraisal and recommendations can help to advance the president's agenda.

Health care reform involved the most important advisory committee effort in recent years. The President's Task Force on National Health Care Reform engaged at least three-hundred federal officials and fourty "special government employees" (i.e., persons "employed to perform, with or without compensation, for a period not to exceed 130 days during any period of 365 consecutive days, temporary duties either on a full-time or intermittent basis"). The task force was chaired by the First Lady, Hillary Rodham Clinton, characterized by the court as a *de facto* federal employee; this determination placed the group outside the pale of the FACA because it was composed of full-time federal employees. Working groups that included outsiders, however, were subject to the law.

Reflecting the political salience of issues important to the times, advisory committees established during 1995 addressed entitlement reform, personal motor vehicle greenhouse gas reductions, and human radiation experiments. During the preceding year other high-priority task forces addressed trade policy and negotiations, unemployment compensation, the "glass ceiling," aging, HIV/AIDS, educational goals, acid precipitation assessment, telecommunications, critical technologies, and defense base closure and realignment.

Are Advisory Committees Increasing or Decreasing?

Given free rein, advisory committees very likely would proliferate enormously. Excessive use of such committees could be self-defeating, cheapen their value, and frustrate the purpose for which they are established. Laws and presidential directives constantly are interjected to keep the number of such groups within bounds, thereby augmenting, not diminishing, their import.

President Carter directed a "zero-based review of all advisory committees" (memorandum, 15 February 1977) that eliminated 284 committees. The number dropped from 1,159 in 1976 to 875 in 1977, and hit a low of 816 in 1978. The number of new units established per year plunged to a mere twenty-one units in 1977, and funding costs plummeted to only $10.5 million from $60 million in the previous year.

Campaigning for the presidency in 1991–1992, Bill Clinton urged "reinventing" government and paring back bureaucracy, specifically including advisory agencies. Following the election, President Clinton touted "as one of my first acts as President" Executive Order No. 12838 (effective 10 February 1993), which directed "terminat[ing] not less than one-third of the advisory committees. . . ." As reported above, however, there was an overall decline of only seven percent as of the beginning of fiscal year 1994. Indeed, instead of decreasing, spending for federal advisory committees is escalating. Fiscal year 1994's $133 million was projected to jump to $161 million, a twenty-one percent increase. The plain facts reveal, by almost any objective measure, that advisory committee presence is increasing. Washington, however, has its own statistical ways, and legerdemain can alter perceptions. President Clinton declared in his fiscal year 1994 report to Congress: ". . . we have reduced the overall number of *discretionary committees* [emphasis added] by 335 to achieve a net total of 466 chartered groups by the end of fiscal year 1994. This reflects a net reduction of 42 percent over the 801 discretionary committees in existence at the beginning of my Administration—substantially exceeding the one-third target. . . ." This contrived count conveniently eliminated all statutory advisory agencies—an artful tabulation, to say the least.

Politicians like to appear to be both for and against things at the same time. Forwarding the *23d Annual Report of the President on Federal Advisory Committees,* President Clinton not only boasted of "substantially exceeding the one-third target," but, in an artful display of the political straddle, went on to urge "more thoroughly involv[ing] the Nation's citizens in the development of Federal decisions" and to extol "citizen involvement as an essential . . . strategic resource that must be maximized." Reconciling cutting citizen involvement simultaneously with increasing their involvement is not easily accomplished.

OBJECTIVES AND ATTRIBUTES OF ADVISORY COMMITTEES

- Fulfilling Informed Deliberation. Sound democratic decision-making is enhanced by well-informed choice. The very essence of democracy entails government rule by the people. To the extent that the number of citizens involved in public policy making can be enlarged and enhanced, the cause of democracy is advanced. Information comes from many sources. Advisory agencies provide additional means for registering citizen opinion in decision-making. Advisory groups simply provide another way for the voice of the people to be heard.

- Advancing Fundamental Freedoms. Advisory groups buttress constitutional provisions that foster freedom of speech, of the press, of assembly, and of petition. Advisory groups reinforce deliberation, a fundamental prerequisite of democracy.

- Augmenting Representative Democracy. Representative democracies delegate decision-making to duly elected or otherwise duly constituted surrogates. The ideal of direct democracy—individuals participating directly in the shaping of policy—is advanced by citizen participation in advisory groups. Extending outreach moves the nation a step further toward enlarging democratic deliberation.

- Supplementing Insider Elitism. Reaching out beyond an "inner circle" of advisers provides government with fresh insight. These forums provide a convenient and efficient process for utilizing intelligent people that transcends established government circles. Nonfederal perspectives play an important role in achieving balanced consideration of policy options. Enlarging participation diminishes (at least to some degree) the elitism implicit in small circles of insiders making all the decisions.

- Acquiring Independent Judgment. Tapping independent counsel to secure fresh insight and analysis is a basic reason for constituting advisory groups. Objectivity and impartiality are ideal hallmarks of advisory committee deliberations and recommendations.

- Obtaining "Balanced" Consideration. Balanced composition of advisory committee memberships contributes to more broadly representative consensus. Decisions are best made by involving qualified citizens of diverse backgrounds, interests, and viewpoints. The give-and-take of advisory group deliberations provides a means to reach consensus. Balanced consultation enlarges the area of agreement and narrows areas of disagreement, thereby encouraging convergence.

- Achieving Broad Consensus. To work well, democracy must rest on expert judgment moderated by broad-based public consensus. Assembling a large and representative group of experts in advisory forums is conducive to melding a spectrum of opinion. Recommendations that reflect diverse expertise may carry enough weight and merit that opposition is mollified. Expert opinion of prestigious persons may be too powerful and persuasive to prompt serious opposition.

- Tapping Expertise. Properly constituted advisory committees ideally bring together the nation's very best experts. Tapping collective judgment of the country's best minds helps to generate the best answers to pressing national problems. Quality, not quantity, is what matters.

- Obtaining Expert Counsel in a World of Growing Complexity. The awesome breadth of complex issues prompts marshaling the best thinkers to deal with them. The urgency is compounded by the accelerating pace of change that necessitates in-depth and informed review by the best and smartest. The more expertise that can be brought to bear, the better.

- Obtaining an Expert "Stamp of Approval." Drawing upon advisory committee expertise provides an "intellectual jury" on the issues and a means for "clearing" policies with experts and interested parties. Proposals that are not quite ready for widespread popular acceptance may be made more palatable by having a group of highly respected experts give it their "stamp of approval." Such groups often lend respectability to controversial concepts.

- Obtaining Expert Advice at Low Cost. *Ad hoc* advisory committees provide a means to gather expert advice quickly and in a cost-effective manner. Expertise is expensive and always in short supply, so that there is a recurring need to tap talent outside of government circles. The need for high-priced talent grows apace but increasingly is beyond the financial means of government to maintain in-house and full-time. Unable to afford retaining all the experts that may be needed—either directly as employees or as consultants—government turns to outsiders willing to volunteer their time and talent. Remuneration of advisers is minimal, consisting of a modest *per diem,* travel costs, and other direct expenses. Federal staff support accounted for forty-six percent or $61 million, of the $133.4 million attributed to these undertakings during fiscal year 1994. Operating costs were projected to increase to $161 million in 1995.

- "Stacking" Membership to Bias Findings. Advisory agency membership may be biased to favor the political leanings of the originators. Despite bipartisan declarations and intentions, handpicking members inclined to support the host's viewpoint is possible. The "loyal opposition" may be co-opted. True political balance in membership of advisory agencies is rarely achieved.

- Advancing Consultation and Consensus. Fashioning of consensus is facilitated when persons having contrasting views and representing competing interests come together in neutral forums and work toward resolving differences amicably.

- Avoiding Unproductive Haggling. Perhaps an overlooked advantage of advisory groups is that bringing discordant interests together in amicable settings can shift responsibility for time-consuming debate and deliberation to a collateral group, thereby freeing organizers to concentrate on more pressing matters.

- Minimizing Political Demagoguery. If constituted on a bipartisan basis, advisory committees provide an opportunity to resolve political differences under conditions that minimize opportunities for "grandstanding" and that require a certain level of statesmanship. The higher plane of involvement may temper political issues that immobilize government decision-making.

- "Rising above" Politics. Rational decision-making is enhanced by deferring policy development to carefully selected experts who are "above" politics and self-seeking. Politically uncharged conditions hold out the promise for amicable resolution of differences.

- Building Program Support. Advisory agencies often are established expressly to help build public support for controversial programs. Indeed, such groups may serve as a "soapbox" for generating and securing approval of recommendations to follow a particular course of action. The advisory process by its very nature is a means to attract and channel public attention.

- Mobilizing Support for Pet Objectives. Prominent, prestigious, and vocal expert advisers can play instrumental roles in mobilizing popular support for controversial issues. Bringing in the "big guns" on key issues is a newsworthy event in its own right, and the views of such renowned authorities regarding policy may be played up in the media. Their endorsement of recommended change carries weight with decision makers and the public.

- Gathering and Assessing Facts. Advisory committees make an important contribution to government as fact finders and triers of facts. Laying a solid foundation for fully informed decision-making is a laborious process. Weighing claims and counterclaims, winnowing the chaff from the wheat, to arrive at a comprehensive and objective statement of problems to be addressed is a task made all the more difficult by the vested interests, sensationalized coverage, and blatant propaganda that becloud many issues.

- Putting Impractical Ideas to Rest. Advisory committees occasionally may be relied upon to lay to rest "harebrained schemes" championed by powerful groups. The opinions of impartial experts may succeed in dampening enthusiasm for impractical proposals without offending affected parties.

- Demonstrating a Sense of "Doing Something." The mere act of appointing an advisory group sends out a dramatic signal that problems are receiving immediate attention. It creates a sense that issues are being confronted and that a particular urgency is involved.

- Diverting/Attracting Media Attention. Time-consuming deliberations can wear down the opposition, defuse tension, and lull the public into forgetfulness. Protracted undertakings keep interested parties busily immersed in serious fact-finding. Prolonged familiarity may dissipate interest, instill boredom, and divert attention to other issues. Obversely, well-orchestrated media promotion can help to focus public attention and create a sense of urgency concerning the issues at stake. It all comes down to a matter of emphasis and how the game is played.

- Deferring Responsibility to Others. Advisory groups may be established for the purpose of relieving pressure on accountable parties. Transferring decision-making responsibility to third parties tends to deflect attention from originating parties.

- Buffering Sponsors from Direct Responsibility. Advisory groups may be constituted to buffer proper authorities from the dissatisfaction or outrage associated with controversial matters. Environmentalists and timber interests recently clashed over logging and its effect on the fate of the spotted owl, a matter that eventually was shunted off to a Federal Ecosystem Management Advisory Team for further study.

- Abdicating Responsibility. Advisory groups regularly are attacked for usurping administrative responsibilities vested in the host government unit. Why establish and maintain an elaborate civil service, it is argued, if you are only going to call in outsiders to second-guess its judgment? Elected officials, meanwhile, complain that advisory committees are not answerable to the electorate. A fundamental distinction is that advice is *not* policy-making, and inputs are merely an adjunct for government policy-makers to take into account as they choose.

- Opening the Way for Undue Influence. By providing insider access to government policymakers and an official forum for airing views, it has been argued, advisory groups pave the way for government officials to become instruments of outside influence and parties to the advancement of special interests. The National Industrial Pollution Control Council, established during the Nixon administration, was among the business-dominated groups assailed for undue influence. The fine line between soliciting objective views and succumbing to special-interest pleaders warrants vigilance. Although advisory groups are not free of bias; their advice probably is more impartial than that obtained from other professionals in the course of government decision-making.

- Affording More Time for Careful Deliberation. Sometimes pressure to reach a decision immediately—when more time for careful deliberation is needed—can be reduced by establishing an advisory group. Interposing such a group into the decision-making process buys time for collateral deliberation and provides additional breathing space for less pressured deliberation. Studies, and the time required to conduct them, provide a convenient pretext for not taking immediate action.

- "Buying Time" to Obstruct Decision-Making. Advisory groups may be established as buffers against coming to grips with problems or being forced to premature commitment, or in the hope that policies or programs will be obstructed and eventually killed altogether. Thanks both to the time delays inherent in the process itself and to the difficulties in reaching consensus concerning controversial topics, such undertakings simply require considerable amounts of time to wend their way to conclusion. Obversely, advisory committees can be managed in a manner that trumpets a sense of urgency. Properly orchestrated, deliberations and findings of advisory committees can be manipulated to speed up decision-making.

- Obtaining Objective Perspectives. Activist demands, especially when played up by sympathetic mass media, can be difficult to fend off. Objective appraisal by prestigious advisory groups may offset or overcome these pressures.

- Waylaying Activists. Tactically, "diversionary" efforts such as time-consuming advisory committee deliberations sidetrack activists, capture and contain them, and divert them from pressuring change. The additional time afforded helps to defer and to stave off crises of the moment. Outreach through advisory groups provides a way of channeling and institutionalizing special-interest response. "Throwing a sop" to interested parties may help to placate them. Establishing a blue-ribbon advisory group to assess the situation simply may be enough to satisfy them. In a Machiavellian vein, President Hoover once asserted that the "greatest silencer . . . for foolishness is to associate him [the crusader] on a research committee with a few citizens who have a passion for truth. . . ."

- Securing Unrestrained Response. Operating in an advisory committee environment, bureaucrats may have less fear of retribution and feel freer to assert themselves. Uninhibited insight and freedom from institutional constraints can provide a rationale for resorting to outside advisory committees. Bureaucrats who fear that they will lose their jobs for speaking their mind act with restraint. Internal decision-making can become "hidebound," and expected answers inhibit decision-making.

- Resolving Inter-Agency Differences. Bureaucratic infighting may be a major argument for establishing an advisory committee. Petty jealousies and turf fights between branches and units of government may obstruct and stymie meaningful response. In a neutral forum, these obstacles can be overcome.

- Breaking away from Stale Bureaucracy Viewpoints. Sometimes thinking within a government agency may become so insular, so detached from reality, so blinded by dogma that outside views are essential. Fresh insights of independent outsiders can alter entrenched mind-sets.

- Reversing Established Policies without Embarrassment. In the event of a failure of governmental machinery, advisory groups may be instituted with a view to easing away from or rescinding unwise decisions while shielding those responsible from humiliation or embarrassment. Advisory committees have been hailed in such instances as "the last refuge of administrative incompetence."

- Whitewashing Issues. Decisions rendered by advisory committees may be belittled or dismissed as "whitewash." The real purpose in such circumstances is not so much to illumine the issues or find the best answers, but rather merely to put a good face on things.

- Honoring the Deserving. Advisory group membership is considered an honor and bestows recognition and prestige on participants. The invitation to participate attests to the wisdom, competence, and expertise of the distinguished few who serve.

- Fulfilling Civic Responsibilities. Civic duty— a citizen's contribution to governing—is among the highest obligations of citizenship. For most citizens, civic duty is limited to periodic exercise of their franchise. Participation in groups constituted to provide advice on contemporary problems involves an elevated form of civic duty. Advisory groups involve part-time obligations that enable public service participation without requiring giving up private obligations.

- Shaping Policy Outcome. Finally, there is a widely held notion that government advisory reports are never read or used, amount to a waste of time and money, wind up as little more than ponderous paperweights, and that recommendations are ignored and considered unimportant to public policy decision-making. Yet the fact remains that blue-ribbon panels of the country's best generate sound ideas that sooner or later wend their way into public policy.

Advisory recommendations do not automatically become law. Seldom do they move with the speed of summer lightning. Full appreciation of their importance and impact requires viewing them over the long term. Although it may take ten to twenty years or longer, a surprisingly large number of these recommendations do become law. Well over fifty percent of the numerous recommendations developed by the two Hoover commissions on organization of the executive branch of government were implemented. Follow-up by the Citizens Committee for the Hoover Report, a privately financed lobbying group, contributed to implementation. But even without follow-up by lobbying groups established to oversee implementation, advisory recommendations make a vital contribution to American public policy.

RULES GOVERNING ADVISORY AGENCIES

Establishing, reestablishing, or renewing advisory committees entails compliance with basic statutory requirements. Public disclosure and reporting requirements imposed by law provide notification and access to the creation, activities, and reports of federal advisory committees. Balance between secrecy and candor, between formal and informal deliberations, between limited and protracted debate is scrupulously sought.

Duly constituted advisory committees are composed of 1) a group of persons 2) established pursuant to statute or "utilized" by a government agency 3) for the purpose of giving advice, individually or as a group. Courts favor facilitating interchange of views between private groups and the public sector over hobbling inputs with burdensome openness and public participation as stipulated by the FACA. Whether outside groups are deemed to be "established" or "utilized" generally turns on whether the group has been constituted as an official institution. Private groups include those that were formed privately, lack official connections or government auspices, are not under government control, receive no federal funding, or offer incidental inputs. The more routine and regular, the more formal and structured, the less unstructured and random are the meetings, and the more reliant the host becomes upon any *ad hoc* inputs, the less likely will be a finding of informal give-and-take. Even though this input may occur on a regular or preferred basis, it is unlikely to be considered "utilized" by government recipients. Private groups have a right to convey their views to government (i.e., a right to petition government, a right to "lobby").

Protecting Informal Consultation

Questions may arise involving government outsiders frequently, periodically, or regularly meeting with government officials to discuss issues. At what point and under what conditions do such meetings constitute an "advisory committee" subject to FACA controls? Every consultation does not involve formal advisory relationships. One-time meetings between a government official and two or more outsiders does not constitute an advisory committee. Infrequent and informal information exchanges were not intended to be covered by the FACA. Strictures such as these would frustrate the very essence of democratic exchanges between citizens and their government. Only when the trappings become more formal and regular and take on an institutional character does the question become more difficult to classify.

Chartering Advisory Committees

Charters are filed with the General Services Administration (GSA) including justification as to why it is essential to conduct agency business; how the committee is in the public interest; why functions cannot be performed by the agency, other existing advisory committees, or other means (such as public hearings); and how membership "balance" has been achieved. Chartering

requires routine disclosures including committee name, objectives, duration, organization/person to whom responsible, supporting organization, description of duties, operating costs, number and frequency of meetings, termination date (if less than two years), and filing date. Charters also must be furnished to the Library of Congress and to standing committees of Congress with jurisdiction over the sponsoring agency. All duly constituted units are required to file annual reports with the GSA summarizing activities.

The GSA must respond to charter filings within fifteen days of submission. The GSA review requires concurrence or nonconcurrence. Filing and review procedures are more in the nature of a *pro forma* consultation that does not include the power to veto or "kill" the establishment of an advisory unit.

Failure to comply with filing requirements can be fatal. Errors open up the opportunity for litigation challenging the status of the group, including the possibility of enjoining illegally constituted groups from rendering advice, or its use for any purpose.

GSA Committee Management Secretariat

Administrative and oversight responsibilities were transferred from the OMB to the Administrator of the GSA, effective 20 November 1977 (Executive Order 12024). The Committee Management Secretariat was constituted at the GSA to manage these functions. Participating departments and agencies are directed to establish committee management officers to centralize and coordinate advisory committee activities within individual units. Individuals representing their parent organizations formed a Federal Advisory Committee Management Association in 1980. An Interagency Committee on Federal Advisory Committee Management, a liaison organization with responsibility for developing improvements to pertinent acts and regulations, also has been established.

Meeting Notice

Advance public notice of meetings is mandatory. Ample notice helps to assure that government decisions are made in the open and that interested parties have an opportunity to submit their views. *Federal Register* notice must be made at least fifteen days beforehand and specify committee name, time and date (must be reasonable), place (must be reasonably accessible), purpose, agenda summary, and whether the session is open or closed. Previous OMB overseers also encouraged more broad-scale notice by way of press releases and mailed notices to persons and groups known to be interested in the subject matter. Advances in electronic communications have prompted recommendations to substitute outmoded *Federal Register* "constructive" notice with more easily accessed electronic media notification—e-mail, electronic bulletin boards, World Wide Web sites, and homepages.

Conduct of Meetings

Meetings must be open to the public. Accommodations must be appropriate to the occasion, and meeting room size must be sufficiently large to accommodate members of the public likely to attend. In addition, provision must be made for interested parties to participate and voice their opinions or file written statements.

Closed Meetings

Closed meetings may be required for national security reasons and for peer review of grant proposals (to encourage candid commentary without fear of libel, slander, or invasion of privacy). Open or partially open meetings totaled 2,603 in fiscal year 1994, amounting to 63% of the total. Closed meetings are mostly confined to four host units: the Department of Defense, the Department of Health and Human Services, the National Endowment for the Arts, and the National Science Foundation. These four hosts accounted for seventy-nine percent of all closed meetings. The National Science Foundation conducted 481 closed advisory committee meetings during fiscal year 1993, 404 of them totally closed (the largest number by any federal agency).

Meeting Records

Reports and other relevant documents must be filed with the GSA Secretariat and the Library of Congress. Most documents maintained are available to the public for inspection, copying, and use. Minutes of meetings must be detailed and fairly represent what transpired. Materially unrepresentative renditions are not acceptable. To help assure compliance, chairmen are required to certify the minutes.

Balanced Membership

Committee composition is governed by laws requiring "balanced" membership. This requires evenhanded representation of stakeholders, points of view, disciplines, geography, sex, race, age, personal characteristics, practical wisdom, and so forth.

Statutory provisions sometimes specify members or groups from which members must be drawn. The council of the American Historical Association, by statute, is accorded authority to appoint two members to the National Historical Publications Commission. The American Marketing Association, American Statistical Association, and American Economic Association each are entitled to appoint one member to Bureau of Census advisory committees.

Some organizations are so prominent and politically influential that their views and/or approval of proposed members for advisory committees usually are sought. It is unlikely, for instance, that the White House would not consult union representatives in clearing appointments to committees of direct interest to organized labor.

Formation of advisory groups is subject to challenge. Big business often is charged with exclusively dominating these groups. So-called "stacking" is a perpetual complaint leveled against advisory groups of almost any sort. Despite statutory efforts to balance representation, advisory committees tend to reflect the political bias of the appointing agency. When power shifts to an opposing political party, there usually is a concerted effort to purge previously established advisory groups. "Wiping the slate clean" reconstitutes self-serving support to bolster voter mandates.

Peer reviews, a form of advisory committee, often are challenged for bias in that advisers are drawn mostly from the small number of institutions receiving the bulk of funding. The National Institutes of Health, the National Science Foundation, the Environmental Protection Agency, and the National Endowments for the Arts and Humanities rely heavily upon peer review, generally treating them as advisory agencies.

Statutory Controls

Regulation of advisory agencies is controlled by a bevy of laws and further circumscribed by judicial interpretation. The FACA, the primary directive, is only one among a number of statutes intended to promote open government and safeguard the public interest.

- The FACA (P.L. 92-463, effective 5 January 1973) confers the power to establish new committees subject to compliance with basic administrative specifications, regulations, and guidelines. Private consultations with government officials that fall outside the FACA's scope may be available to interested parties pursuant to provisions of the Freedom of Information Act.

- Sunset provisions, written into the FACA, stipulate a two-year (renewable) limit to the life of such committees. Statutory specification of duration overrides this limit. The president or other host agencies can continue advisory agencies by two-year increments. The number of extensions is not expressly limited.

- The Government in the Sunshine Act (P.L. 94-409, effective 12 March 1977) mandates open meetings except when such participation would impair national security, invade privacy, compromise confidentiality and privileged information, or otherwise vitiate the general welfare. Meetings must be reasonably accessible in terms of location, time, and convenience. [See Appendix: Government in the Sunshine Act.]

- The Freedom of Information Act (P.L. 89-554), along with FACA provisions, requires that most records (reports, transcripts, minutes, appendixes, working papers, drafts, studies, agendas, and other documents) be available for inspection and copying at a single location. Most often, the offices of the advisory committee itself or the agency to

which the committee reports are utilized. [See Appendix: Freedom of Information Act.]

- The Unfunded Mandates Reform Act of 1995 exempts meetings and communications between federal officials and state and local elected officials and their agents pursuant to joint implementation of federal programs. This recent provision is intended to facilitate essential communications between government officials at all levels.

- The Ethics in Government Act of 1978 and the Ethics Reform Act of 1989 (P.L. 101-194) impose standards of ethical conduct on advisory committee participants.

- Conflicts of interest provisions impose further limitations that keep conflicting interests and other biases in check.

- Executive privilege, inherent in governmental powers, also can be invoked. Cloaking proceedings in secrecy may be invoked when national security, military affairs, or diplomatic relations are at issue, or when the executive and legislative branches are controlled by opposing political parties and hope to maintain control and direction of activities.

Avoiding Restrictions on Acquiring Advice

Impairing the executive branch's ability to solicit or receive advice from outside groups cannot be unduly restrictive. Congress cannot unreasonably interfere with the president's ability to carry out the duties of his office. Among the criteria of reasonableness in seeking advice, balancing input by competing interests is considered essential to fair play.

Constitutional provisions purposely establish separate but equal branches of government. Subdividing government into three separate but equal branches—legislative, executive, and judicial—diffuses power. This separation of powers was intended to avoid concentration of power and prevent the undue influence of any one branch over another. As structured, each branch is intended to serve as a check or balance upon the powers of the others. Tripartite division of authority limits the ability of any one branch to impose its dictates on another.

ROYAL COMMISSIONS

Royal commissions deserve a few words in closing. Blue-ribbon advisory agencies in other nations are equally well—perhaps even better—suited to the task of resolving nettlesome problems and establishing a base of impartial expertise upon which sound decisions can be made. No nation has a monopoly on ideas, but a few nations consistently produce superior results. Most notable is the work done by royal commissions in Great Britain and Sweden. British Royal Commission reports enjoy a long and well-earned tradition of being regarded as the best and most carefully researched of any such documents. The tradition of relying on such agencies dates back to the early 1800s. Supreme Court Justice Felix Frankfurter fittingly asserted: "The history of British democracy might in considerable measure be written in terms of the history of successive Royal Commissions."

Swedish Royal Commission reports tend to be a useful barometer in determining where U.S. public policy is headed. Generally speaking, the goals set forth in these Swedish reports are adopted within the next five to twenty years by the United States as well. Swedish Royal Commissions address public policy issues by bringing together a cross-section of representative interests to sort out problems deliberately, impartially, and rationally. Swedish commissions are structured to be devoid of demagogic upstaging and crass emotionalism. A "remiss" or review procedure provides for full and fair commentary by interested parties before final determination of recommendations.

BIBLIOGRAPHY

Annual Report of the President on Federal Advisory Committees. Washington, D.C., 1972–present.

Berg, Richard K. "Conflict of Interest Requirements for Members of Federal Advisory Committees." *Federal Bar News and Journal* 37 (1990).

Bybee, Jay S. "Advising the President: Separation of Powers and the Federal Advisory Committee Act." *Yale Law Journal* 104 (1994): 51–128.

Cardozo, Michael H. "The Federal Advisory Committee Act in Operation." *Administrative Law Review* 33 (1981).

Cardozo, Michael H. "Implementation of the Federal Advisory Committee Act: An Overview." *Federal Bar Journal* 38 (1989).

Cronin, Thomas E., and Sanford D. Greenberg. *The Presidential Advisory System.* New York, 1969.

Cronin, Thomas E., and Norman C. Thomas. "Federal Advisory Processes: Advice and Discontent." *Science,* February 26, 1971.

Hanser, Charles J. *Guide to Decision: The Royal Commission.* Totowa, N.J., 1965.

Marblestone, A. "The Coverage of the Federal Advisory Committee Act." *Federal Bar Journal* 35 (1976).

Markham, J. "The Federal Advisory Committee Act." *Pittsburgh Law Review* 35 (1974): XXX–XXX.

Nuszkiewicz, Michelle. "Twenty Years of the Federal Advisory Committee Act: It's Time for Some Changes." *Southern California Law Review* 65 (1992).

Perritt, Henry H., Jr., and James A. Wilkinson. "Open Advisory Committees and the Political Process: The Federal Advisory Committee Act after Two Years." *Georgetown Law Journal* 63 (1975).

Popper, Frank. *The President's Commissions.* New York, 1970.

Tuerkeimer, Barbara W. "Veto by Neglect: The Federal Advisory Committee Act." *American University Law Review* 25 (1975).

Wegman, Richard A. *The Utilization and Management of Federal Advisory Committees.* Dayton, 1983.

—GRAHAM T. T. MOLITOR

Aging, Administration on.

See Health and Human Services, Department of.

Agricultural Marketing Service

The largest regulatory body within the Department of Agriculture, the Agricultural Marketing Service (AMS) is headed by an administrator and includes units covering cotton, dairy products, fruits and vegetables, livestock and seed, poultry, tobacco, and scientific support. The AMS issues marketing orders to manage the flow of agricultural commodities to the marketplace. It also regulates such activities as fair trading, truth in labeling, and nondiscriminatory practices. Among the acts that it administers are the Perishable Agricultural Commodities Act, the Federal Seed Act, the Plant Variety Protection Act, the Agricultural Fair Practices Act, and the Export Fruit Act. Its Market News Service provides current information to producers to promote orderly marketing and distribution. The Transportation and Marketing Division assists farmers in transporting their products to the appropriate markets, and it also oversees the National Organic Standards Board. The AMS tests and classifies farm products and seeds, develops standards, and offers grading services to buyers and sellers. It is the agency responsible for purchasing food for distribution through programs of the Food and Nutrition Service, such as the school lunch program, nutrition programs for the elderly, and supplemental food program for women, infants, and children. [*See* Food and Nutrition Service.] In addition, the AMS oversees the quality of food purchased by government agencies and issues specifications for federal food purchases. In its procurement programs the AMS applies federal laws giving preferences to minority- and women-owned businesses. The AMS conducts research and promotion programs designed to improve the quality of agricultural commodities and develop new markets. The service also administers the Egg Products Inspection Act, providing continuous inspection of all egg-producing facilities. Under the Agricultural Marketing Act of 1937, the AMS issues marketing orders to help stabilize markets for certain farm products. These orders help to forestall gluts as well as shortages, keep high-quality produce on the markets, standardize packing of containers, and establish reserves of storable commodities. The Science Division provides centralized scientific support through laboratory analyses. The Science Division also issues certificates of protection for new varieties of sexually reproduced plants and collects and analyzes data on pesticide residue levels in agricultural commodities. —GEORGE THOMAS KURIAN

Agricultural Service, Foreign.

See Foreign Agricultural Service.

Agricultural Stabilization and Conservation Service

Established in 1961 as an agency within the Department of Agriculture, the Agricultural Stabili-

zation and Conservation Service (ASCS) administers programs that assure an adequate and reliable supply of food, feed, and natural fibers for domestic and foreign markets at fair prices. The agency also administers land-use programs that protect, expand, and conserve farmlands, wetlands, and forests. Under the Department of Agriculture Reorganization Act of 1994, the farm programs of the ASCS will be consolidated under a new agency, the Agriculture Service Agency.

The principal ASCS program is commodity stabilization, which applies to wheat, corn, cotton, soybeans, peanuts, rice, tobacco, milk, wool, mohair, barley, oats, sugar beets, sugarcane, sorghum, rye, and honey. Commodity loans are the basic means of price support, but the ASCS also resorts to quotas, allotments, direct payments, and purchases. Loans are arranged and financed through the Commodity Credit Corporation, a $30 billion corporation wholly owned by the federal government. Deficiency payments are made to agricultural producers to assure them a return at least equal to a specified target price established by the Secretary of Agriculture. There are statutory ceilings on such deficiency and diversion payments. The ASCS establishes acreage allotments for certain crops to ensure that supply will equal demand. Crop land set-aside and acreage reduction programs operate similarly, as do marketing quotas. The ASCS may also purchase certain products in bulk when the supply threatens to glut the market. Other ASCS programs include: the Warehouse Licensing Program; the Agricultural Conservation Program, funding environmental protection practices on farms; the Dairy Indemnity Payment Program in the event of the contamination of milk by chemical or toxic residues; emergency programs to help farmers struck by natural disasters; the Forestry Incentives Program to subsidize tree planting; the Grain Reserve Program; the Water Bank Program to preserve and protect wetlands adjacent to farmlands; the Wool and Mohair Incentive Program; and the Agricultural Resource Conservation Program, an omnibus program fostering adoption of conservation strategies by farmers.

—GEORGE THOMAS KURIAN

Agriculture, Department of

The establishment of the United States Department of Agriculture (USDA) in 1862 was the culmination of a long movement to bring government assistance to what was then the nation's largest occupation. At the time of the Revolution, farmers made up some ninety percent of the labor force. The more advanced farmers of the day had a strong interest in improving agricultural practices, and most citizens of the new republic believed that a healthy agriculture, with independent, landowning farmers, was vital to the nation's character. The first two American agricultural societies, in Philadelphia and Charleston, were founded in 1785 to promote agricultural experimentation and to exchange information and ideas. Members included such forward-looking farmers as George Washington and Thomas Jefferson. When President Washington prepared to leave office in 1796, he recommended that Congress create a board of agriculture charged with collecting and distributing information about agriculture and offering prizes to "assist a spirit of discovery and improvement."

Washington's proposal was not acted on, but in the first decades of the nineteenth century a number of local agricultural societies were formed to promote better farm practices through fairs and other means. Renewed attempts to establish a national board of agriculture after the War of 1812 failed on the grounds that such a board might be a greater extension of government power than the Constitution permitted. Congress and many state legislatures, however, set up committees on agriculture to handle agricultural issues. Moreover, federal land laws made it increasingly easy for farmers to buy public land in small quantities and at low prices.

The earliest explicit federal assistance to agriculture came through the efforts of the first commissioner of the Patent Office, Henry Ellsworth, who took office in 1836. Impressed by patents for new farm machinery, Ellsworth made his office the unofficial center for agricultural information in Washington. He coordinated the collection and distribution of new plants and seeds, many gathered overseas. In 1839 Congress granted Ellsworth a small fund to collect agricultural statistics and for other agricultural purposes. By 1842 Ellsworth's annual Patent Office reports were being filled with agricultural statistics, reports on crops, and advice. These became very popular for congressmen to send to constituents and continued most years through the 1850s. From time to time Congress made a modest appropriation for agricultural research. In 1856 it set aside six acres near downtown Washington to be used as an experimental garden.

Despite growing interest in new federal efforts to stimulate agricultural innovation, the establishment of a separate department to handle agriculture had to await the Civil War, when Southern fears of too strong a central government could be overridden. The United States Agricultural Society did much to keep the issue before the public in the 1850s. In 1862 Republicans in Congress pushed through three significant laws relating to agriculture—the Morrill Act, setting up a system of land-grant colleges in each state to teach agriculture, among other things; the Homestead Act, which granted bona fide settlers 160 free acres of public land; and the act, signed 15 May 1862, creating the USDA. President Lincoln later referred to the new department as the "people's department" because farming, with half the labor force in 1860, was still the most common occupation. It was the first federal department devoted to the interests of a particular economic group. Lincoln appointed a progressive dairy farmer, Isaac Newton of Pennsylvania, as the department's first commissioner.

The new department had just a handful of employees but began with a broad mandate. According to the act, the Department of Agriculture was "to acquire and to diffuse among the people of the United States useful information on subjects connected with agriculture in the most general and comprehensive sense of that word . . . ." It was also to "procure, propagate, and distribute" new seeds and plants. Its first task was to expand the work already begun in the Patent Office. Horticulturalists, entomologists, chemists, and other scientists were hired to study plants, insects, and soils. Regular statistical series on crop conditions, prices, and production of crops and livestock began to be published between 1863 and 1867. The department's annual reports were the chief source of information on agricultural developments in the United States.

USDA research grew in the 1870s and 1880s with the hiring of a number of new scientists. In 1884 the department established the Bureau of Animal Industry, the first of several important scientific bureaus. Research received a substantial boost from the Hatch Experiment Station Act, passed in 1887. This act initiated a unique government relationship—a cooperative federal-state program of research into all aspects of agriculture. With federal assistance, experiment stations were set up at each land-grant college. The state stations could do research on problems of special interest to their areas while the whole effort was coordinated by a federal Office of Experiment Stations (1888). With the Hatch Experiment Station Act, the United States was moving in the direction that would make it the world's most important center for agricultural research. In 1889 the department's growing stature was recognized when it became a cabinet-level department; six years later it adopted an official seal. Norman J. Colman, a well-known farm editor and the last commissioner, became the first secretary of agriculture. With the appointment of Iowa state experiment station director James Wilson as secretary in 1897, the department began a period of rapid growth, especially in research. Wilson remained in office through the end of the Taft administration (1913), making him the longest-serving secretary.

In the late nineteenth century, attitudes toward government and its functions changed from a belief in strictly limited government to a more positive conviction that government should intervene actively in the economy and society to protect the public welfare. It was during these years that the Department of Agriculture began to expand its mission into several lines of work beyond research and the dissemination of information. First was the protection of public health from food-borne diseases. Complementing its research on animal diseases, the Meat Inspection Act of 1890 charged the department with inspecting exported pork, bacon, and

live animals. Imported animals were to be quarantined upon arrival. These provisions were soon extended to cover live animals whose meat would be sold in interstate commerce. Meat inspection was strengthened in 1906 and the Pure Food and Drugs Act of that year required the department to examine foods for adulteration.

In 1891 Congress authorized setting aside public lands as forest reserves for recreational purposes and to protect the timber supply. The USDA's Division of Forestry had been studying forest management and had, in 1898, been placed under conservationist Gifford Pinchot. In 1905 the division became the Forest Service and the U.S. forest reserves were transferred to it. In time, the Forest Service grew to be the largest agency in the department. In 1893 the USDA began to study the construction of roads, owing to the poor state of country roads. The advent of rural free delivery in 1896 and the automobile led to greatly expanded research on road building. The USDA became the center of federal road building. Another function acquired by the USDA was the Weather Bureau, which became a part of the department in 1890. Also in the 1890s, the department began to promote the export of American agricultural products abroad and to do research on the nutritional properties of food. In 1894 its annual report became the *U.S. Department of Agriculture Yearbook,* filled with statistics and information from USDA research projects. By 1900 the department had grown to 3,100 employees overseeing a $4 million budget. In 1912, near the end of Wilson's tenure, it had nearly 14,000 employees and a budget of $21 million.

The department's duties continued to grow in the first two decades of the twentieth century. Research by the USDA and experiment stations had been very fruitful, but the department had experienced difficulty getting the results of that research into the hands of ordinary farmers. In 1914 the Smith-Lever Act formally established a cooperative extension service to bring the best agricultural techniques directly to farmers. The extension service went beyond the USDA–experiment station model to bring local communities as well as land-grant universities into the planning and funding of extension work. By the

THE DEPARTMENT OF AGRICULTURE HEADQUARTERS IN WASHINGTON, D.C. *Completed in 1936, the Department of Agriculture occupies the only building on the Mall that does not participate in the Mall's public life.*

end of World War I extension agents were at work in most rural counties visiting farmers, giving lectures, and passing out literature on the whole range of agricultural problems, including cultural practices, variety selection, conservation, and farm management. Farm women also received assistance from a growing body of home economists, who taught food preservation, nutrition, and homemaking skills.

Farmers began receiving assistance in other ways, too, during these years. In 1914 the Cotton Futures Act gave the USDA its first responsibility for regulating the marketing of a farm product. A group of 1916 acts marked the department's formal entry into the regulation of grades, in-

cluding standards for grain quality, fruit containers, and agricultural warehouses. The 1916 Federal Farm Loan Act instructed the department to set up land banks to provide farmers inexpensive credit when purchasing land. These would be joined by intermediate credit banks in 1923.

During World War I the department's authority expanded substantially to meet the war emergency. While the USDA did its best to encourage farmers to produce more food, a separate agency, the United States Food Administration (1917), headed by Herbert Hoover, controlled the distribution of food. The two agencies cooperated closely. By setting the prices at which the government would buy food, the Food Administration was able to help the USDA in its task of stimulating greater production. Farm prices rose, as did the price of agricultural land. Fragile lands in the Great Plains were plowed up to plant wheat for the war effort.

Following the war, government controls were dropped. When continuing high production and contracting demand led to a collapse in farm prices in 1920, farmers began to demand a more permanent form of government intervention in the marketplace. Proposals for government purchases of surpluses failed to become law but foreshadowed Hoover and Roosevelt administration farm policies. In other areas, the department's role widened during the 1920s. Regulation was extended to meat packers through the Packers and Stockyards Act of 1921 and to grain futures trading the same year. Economic and statistical work expanded with the creation of the Bureau of Agricultural Economics in 1922. The Capper-Volstead Act of 1922 exempted farmer cooperatives from antitrust legislation, giving a boost to cooperative marketing associations. By 1926 the Bureau of Agricultural Economics' Division of Cooperative Marketing was fostering farmer cooperatives through research and education. Forestry work was also enlarged during the 1920s, both in the national forests and in programs to assist farmers who desired to grow timber or plant windbreaks. The department's road work grew to the point where most of the USDA's budget went to road programs. As the federal highway system spread across the nation, the Bureau of Public Roads not only funded major construction projects but conducted extensive research on road building.

The Great Depression, which began in 1929, ushered in the greatest era of USDA expansion. It was during the Depression, especially the New Deal, that the modern Department of Agriculture took form. The Hoover administration overcame its reluctance to enlarge government responsibilities and took several steps to counteract the Depression. The Agricultural Marketing Act of 1929 created the Federal Farm Board with a revolving fund of $500 million to enable farmer cooperatives to stabilize prices by buying surplus commodities and taking them off the market. The magnitude of the price decline after 1929 made

this a futile effort. In the early 1930s the department provided jobs and relief through stepped-up road and forestry work and disaster loans for feed and seed to farmers suffering from floods or drought. In 1932 the department made disaster loans to over a half-million families who had trouble obtaining commercial credit.

The administration of Franklin D. Roosevelt, which took office in March 1933, had a much more activist attitude toward government. Roosevelt appointed Iowa farm journalist and hybrid corn breeder Henry A. Wallace as secretary of agriculture. Wallace moved boldly on several fronts to confront the farm crisis, provide relief, and make permanent improvements in farm practices and rural life that would put farmers in a better economic position and narrow the differences between rural and urban standards of living. Under Wallace, the USDA became one of the principal centers of innovative New Deal policies.

The farm problem came first. Since World War I, farmers had been able to produce substantially more than they could find markets for without depressing prices. Wallace and economists like M. L. Wilson, who had worked for the Federal Farm Board, believed that only by controlling production could the supply of farm products be brought into line with demand. The Agricultural Adjustment Act (AAA), passed 12 May 1933, gave the secretary a number of options for reducing production and boosting prices. The object was to bring the purchasing power of farm products back to the level farmers had enjoyed during the prosperous 1909–1914 period. The secretary could enter into voluntary agreements with farmers to cut the production of major crops and livestock, make commodity loans, and limit marketing through marketing agreements. Establishment of the Commodity Credit Corporation later in 1933 permitted the use of nonrecourse loans on farm commodities, which set a floor under farm prices. These loans, in conjunction with acreage controls, became the most important farm policy strategy. Although intended to meet the emergency of 1933, the AAA also aimed to find solutions to long-term agricultural problems. It contained most of the tools found in subsequent farm programs. It also became an example of the democratic administration of federal programs through the state and local committees of producers. These committees, elected by farmers or appointed by extension agents, gave farmers a chance to participate in the programs that soon became a significant part of their economic well-being. Thus farm programs joined experiment stations and the extension service as examples of the USDA's federalist approach to many administrative problems.

The Agricultural Adjustment Act of 1938 expanded mandatory programs that had been tried earlier for cotton and tobacco to include wheat, corn, and rice. The 1938 AAA provided that when projected surpluses of one of those commodities reached a certain point, voluntary programs would be supplanted by controls mandatory on all producers of the commodity, if two-thirds of those producers approved in a referendum. This second AAA became part of what is still today the permanent legal basis for farm programs. The two Agricultural Adjustment Acts of the 1930s helped raise farm income and stabilize prices. Since farm families still made up a majority of the rural population, providing aid to farmers also helped stimulate the economies of hard-pressed rural areas.

Later in the 1930s soil conservation became an important part of farm programs. Dust storms on the Great Plains (culminating in the Dust Bowl of 1934) and flooding in the eastern half of the country dramatically revealed the lack of conservation practices on many American farms. In 1933 a Soil Erosion Service was set up in the Interior Department; transferred to the USDA in 1935 and renamed the Soil Conservation Service (SCS), it carried out research and funded demonstration projects to show farmers and other private landowners how terracing, contour plowing, windbreaks, and similar techniques could prevent erosion by wind and water. After joining the USDA, the SCS began to form soil conservation districts throughout the country so that farmers would participate in carrying out conservation measures in their areas. These legal entities had the same democratic aims as the farmer committees administering the Agricultural Adjustment Acts. The use of soil conservation techniques was tied to farm program benefits by pas-

sage of the Soil Conservation and Domestic Allotment Act of 1936.

The department also began several other programs during the 1930s to assist farmers and achieve related social objectives. A 1935 law gave the USDA the authority to subsidize exports to meet foreign competition and to impose import quotas when imports threatened to interfere with price support programs. Research was augmented, especially research on industrial uses for agricultural products as a means of absorbing surpluses. Acts in 1935 and 1938 created a series of regional laboratories to work on problems associated with particular areas and industrial utilization. The department's loan offerings were extended significantly, with much emphasis being put on poorer farmers and tenant farmers. The Resettlement Administration, formed in 1935, joined the department in 1937 and shortly thereafter was renamed the Farm Security Administration. This agency provided both short-term relief for impoverished farm families through rehabilitation loans and longer-term solutions through tenant purchase loans and through purchases of submarginal lands unsuited for cultivation and resettlement of the farm families on them to more productive lands. One of the most ambitious projects of this type was the establishment of greenbelt communities—planned suburbs for moderate-income families that combined the virtues of urban and rural living. These resettlement activities raised the controversial specter of federal land-use planning and were dropped after several years. A more lasting legacy was left by the corps of talented Farm Security Administration photographers who documented rural America during the Depression. Credit programs for commercial farmers were consolidated in the Farm Credit Administration, established in 1933 as an independent agency and transferred to the USDA in 1939. This agency focused on emergency loans to stave off mortgage foreclosures and also provided intermediate credit to farmers.

The 1938 AAA included a pilot crop insurance program as an additional safeguard in years when natural disaster or other causes prevented farmers from harvesting their normal crops. The USDA also began a number of food programs in the 1930s with the dual purpose of providing food relief and disposing of surplus farm production. In addition to distributing surplus commodities to meet emergency situations, the USDA began an experimental food stamp program in 1939 in which people on public assistance purchased stamps entitling them to receive certain surplus foods free. Also in the 1930s a school lunch program began as a means of improving children's diets by distributing surplus food to schools. In 1939 the USDA's Federal Surplus Commodities Corporation enlarged the program so it could reach several million children. A subsidized school milk program began in 1940.

The New Deal also made a concerted effort to improve the quality of rural life, which had lagged far behind urban areas in many modern conveniences. The Bureau of Public Roads put more emphasis in the 1930s on local farm-to-market roads. This permitted the widespread use of road work for relief purposes while also extending transportation improvements far beyond the main highways. The most significant change to rural life, however, came through the work of the Rural Electrification Administration (REA). Private electric utility companies had been reluctant to extend service to rural areas because of their lower population density. When the REA began in 1935 as a separate agency, only about a tenth of U.S. farms had electricity. Many other nonfarm rural residents were in the same predicament. The REA made loans principally to rural electric cooperatives of local users that built transmission lines in the countryside and purchased or generated power. By the time it joined the USDA in 1939 the number of farms with power had doubled. Power on the farm meant electric lights, refrigeration, electric water pumps for indoor plumbing, and a host of other improvements affecting farming and everyday life.

By 1940 the Department of Agriculture had grown to about 100,000 employees, four times the number a decade earlier and close to its present size. The great majority of these employees were based in local field offices or national forests, administering price support, credit, and conservation programs, and doing forestry work. The addition of new action agencies to what had been largely a group of research bureaus created a complex and overlapping bureaucratic structure

that became increasingly difficult to coordinate. In the late 1930s department administrators devoted much time to improving coordination. The Mount Weather Agreement of 1938, for example, clarified the relationship between the USDA, the land-grant colleges, and the extension service in the planning of action programs, which remained at the federal level, and land use planning, where states and local committees would have the main say. In 1938 the Bureau of Agricultural Economics became the center of the department's program planning, an arrangement that proved short-lived. The USDA's growth came despite the transfer of some functions out of the department as they grew away from their initial close association with agriculture. In 1939 the Bureau of Public Roads joined the Commerce Department, followed by the Weather Bureau in 1940. Also in 1940 the Food and Drug Administration left to join the Federal Security Agency.

America's entry into World War II in 1941 brought about a sharp reversal of the agricultural situation. Instead of surpluses, it soon became apparent that wartime demands at home and abroad would require all-out production. In December 1942 President Roosevelt added substantial responsibilities to the USDA's list of duties, including estimating total domestic, military, and foreign food needs; gearing production to meet those needs; and allocating food in the most efficient manner among competing priorities. To do these things, the department folded most of its action programs into a powerful new food agency, which became known as the War Food Administration in 1943. The USDA also had authority to ration foods, which it delegated to the Office of Price Administration, a separate agency that also regulated prices. Meat, sugar, fats and oils, processed fruits and vegetables, and coffee were among the foods in short supply that were rationed. To encourage production, the USDA lifted acreage controls and raised price supports. The department's Victory Garden program likewise encouraged people to contribute to food production by growing some of their own food. The War Food Administration worked to make sure farmers received sufficient fertilizer, machinery, fuel, and labor to keep output rising.

To counteract caps on food prices, the USDA paid subsidies to farmers for a number of commodities. Wartime prosperity helped end the agricultural depression, raising farm income, reducing the need for relief, and allowing even many poorer beneficiaries of USDA loan programs to reduce their debts.

The War Food Administration ended on 30 June 1945, and the agencies in it returned to their separate identities. Shortly thereafter, production, marketing, and crop insurance functions were combined in one large unit, the Production and Marketing Administration. The immediate postwar period was a rocky one, as demand for food exports to relieve the devastated countries of Europe kept supplies tight in the United States and prices high. Millions of bushels of grain were shipped to Europe, and additional aid was sent under the Marshall Plan starting in 1948. Some price controls had to be maintained until 1947–1948. High wartime price supports remained on basic commodities. The Korean War created new demands for food and fiber. Yet the possibility of surpluses kept the USDA interested in promoting exports beyond relief shipments. The Office of Foreign Agricultural Relations assisted in negotiating the General Agreement on Tariffs and Trade (GATT, 1947), to encourage freer trade, and the International Wheat Agreement (1949), which sought to stabilize the international wheat trade.

Meanwhile, the department's agricultural research and extension efforts were showing dramatic successes. Farmers took advantage of better incomes to buy improved seed varieties and more machinery, to use more chemical fertilizers and pesticides than ever before, and to practice better farm management, all of which had been advocated and in many cases developed by the USDA. Productivity began to soar as the yields for most crops and livestock went through their most dramatic rise in history. The result was a technological revolution that brought many changes to agriculture, including larger and more specialized farms, greater reliance on credit, and more scientific training for farmers. The once-common general farm, with its varied mix of crops and livestock, nearly disappeared among full-time farmers. The Research and Mar-

keting Act of 1946 tried to extend the USDA's successes in production research into the field of marketing by greatly expanding research in that field in order to lower industry and consumer costs. The department also continued efforts to improve rural life. In 1949, for example, the Rural Electrification Administration received authority to make loans for rural telephone lines, an area where service badly trailed that offered to urban consumers. The Farmers Home Administration, which replaced the Farm Security Administration in 1946, continued that agency's focus on small farms and also made a number of loans to veterans in the postwar years.

President Eisenhower's secretary of agriculture, Ezra Taft Benson, accepted the basic range of programs established during and after the New Deal but wished to put more emphasis on market forces and private enterprise. Benson carried out a major reorganization of the department in 1953 with the goal of simplifying administration and making agencies more responsive to the secretary's office. A number of functions were consolidated in new agencies, and economic research was divided among action agencies.

In the 1950s the Department of Agriculture faced the challenge of dealing with the consequences of the technological revolution it had helped create. Surplus production returned following the end of the Korean War in 1953. Secretary Benson wished to end high price supports. Congress, however, would only agree to make supports more flexible. Public Law 480 (1954) extended the government's ability to dispose of surpluses abroad through sales for foreign currency, relief donations, and barter for commodities needed in the United States. Farm exports reached record levels in the 1950s. The Soil Bank program began in 1956 to take land out of production. The long-term conservation reserve part of the program aimed to divert land to conserving uses for up to ten years. A special Great Plains program also began in 1956, following a drought, with the goal of converting farms in dry land areas from cultivated crops to grasslands. Despite these efforts, production outstripped both foreign and domestic demand, lowering farm prices and leaving the department to store huge surpluses by the late 1950s, especially grain.

By the mid-1950s another result of the technological revolution was becoming evident. As farms grew larger and machines supplanted human and animal labor, the farm population began its sharpest and most sustained decline ever. From over six million farms in 1940, the number of farms had slipped below four million by 1960. The decline affected the entire country, but especially the South, where thousands of tenants moved off the land. Many families leaving agricultural also left rural life, moving to cities to look for work. Since people living on farms still accounted for nearly half the rural population in 1950, this loss dealt a sharp blow to many rural communities. In 1954 the Benson administration began a pilot rural development program to provide training and encourage nonfarm jobs so that people leaving their farms would be able to find opportunities in rural communities.

Orville Freeman, secretary during the Kennedy and Johnson administrations (1961–1969), brought a significant change in the department's direction. Freeman saw opportunity in the mounting farm surpluses. While U.S. farmers were producing more than commercial markets could absorb, many Americans as well as people overseas still suffered from malnutrition. Freeman believed that American abundance could be put to use to feed the poor. Any surpluses remaining could be controlled by mandatory production controls. Congress spurned mandatory controls but revised price support programs to lower support levels while giving farmers income supports and making some payments in surplus commodities. These steps, along with export programs, greatly reduced government stocks by the end of the decade. Symbolically, President Kennedy's first executive order on assuming office was to expand the domestic distribution of surplus food. A pilot food stamp program soon followed, and in 1964 the Food Stamp Act became a major contributor to President Johnson's War on Poverty. The Child Nutrition Act of 1966 expanded the school lunch program and began a breakfast program. Use of Public Law 480 also continued as a means of promoting friendly relations with less developed countries while using

up surplus stocks of agricultural commodities. In addition, the USDA did more to promote commercial sales abroad.

In other ways, too, the Freeman administration sought to broaden the department's role. The rural development program was intensified and funding increased substantially. The environment became a serious issue as the effects of pesticides on wildlife and human health were increasingly publicized. The USDA withdrew some pesticides from the market and searched for safer pesticides and alternative ways of handling insect and disease problems. Environmental concerns were also a factor in the passage of the Wilderness Act in 1964, the highway beautification movement, and the greater attention paid to recreational uses of farm and forest land. Freeman also made it clear that the department would pay more attention to consumers. This could be seen in new meat and poultry inspection acts in 1967 and 1968 and in a 1965 reorganization that refashioned the chief marketing agency as the Consumer and Marketing Service. Within the department Freeman gave the first serious attention to protecting the civil rights of minority employees, though he had greater success in Washington than in the field offices. All these efforts could be considered part of President Johnson's Great Society. However, funding for some of them, such as the poverty programs and rural development, had to be scaled back because of the Vietnam War.

The advent of the Nixon and Ford administrations brought a renewed interest in market orientation in farm programs and, in general, enhancing the role of the private sector. Farm bills in 1970 and 1973 gave farmers more flexibility and placed limits on income supports when market conditions were good. Farm prices were, indeed, very good for most of the 1970s thanks to a boom in export sales that was touched off by large purchases from the Soviet Union. The cost of farm support programs fell to a postwar low. While the focus in the secretary's office shifted back to farmers, the department's nonfarm work remained important. Funds for food stamps and other food programs grew strongly, becoming more than half the department's budget. Rural development laws were consolidated in the Rural

Development Act of 1972, and the program was given a more local and private character by the administration. Environmental protection was also stepped up as scientists learned more about the harmful effects of pesticides.

The Carter administration worked to reemphasize the importance of consumers, food programs, rural development, and the environment to the USDA's mission. Consumer interests were highlighted by the appointment of a new assistant secretary for Food and Consumer Services, who stressed better nutrition, inspection, and labeling of foods. In agriculture, the department studied the changing structure of agriculture and explored ways to improve conditions for small farmers, who were finding it increasingly hard to compete in a market dominated by large commercial farmers. The administration sought to redirect research more toward small farms. It reorganized research and extension to strengthen coordination from Washington but ran into opposition from the state experiment stations. After grain prices dropped back from their mid-decade highs, farmers in a new group, the American Agriculture Movement, brought their tractors to Washington in 1978–1979 to demand higher supports. Some supports were raised and acreage reduction reinstituted for several crops. But farmers reacted with dismay when President Carter declared a partial suspension of exports to the Soviet Union in early 1980 for its invasion of Afghanistan.

The Reagan administration brought important new farm legislation during a difficult period for American farmers. The administration's most pervasive theme was cutting the federal budget deficit, though it had little success doing this for farm programs. Reagan ended the Soviet embargo and sought to repeal most price support and adjustment legislation to reduce federal outlays so that farmers would depend on the market to set prices and guide planting decisions. The rigid supports of the 1981 Agriculture and Food Act, however, proved very costly. Exports peaked in 1981, then fell and left the government with record surplus stocks. A financial crisis affected many farmers in the mid-1980s, leading to a restructuring of farm credit programs. The Food Security Act of 1985 reapplied many of the solu-

tions of the 1950s and 1960s to farm surpluses. It lowered price support loans to near world levels but retained income supports, began a new long-term conservation reserve program similar to the Soil Bank, and aggressively promoted farm exports.

Budget containment was more successful in other areas during the Reagan years. Eligibility for food stamps was tightened and school lunch and breakfast subsidies trimmed. These programs remained expensive, but the administration succeeded in moderating budget increases. The administration worked to reduce federal involvement in rural development, but the slowdown in the rural economy in the 1980s—a sharp contrast to the booming 1970s—made major budget cuts impossible. Efforts were also made to render meat and poultry inspection more efficient while reducing regulation. The Animal and Plant Health Inspection Service (APHIS) aimed to save money through more user fees and cooperative partnerships with the private sector and other levels of government. Still, it was able to expand overseas projects designed to stop plant and animal diseases before they reached this country and in the late 1980s stepped up its efforts to license the products of biotechnology. Administrative reforms sought to improve efficiency throughout the department by better cost management and more effective use of computer technology. The Reagan administration could not escape the environmental conflicts that were increasingly affecting USDA programs. Fresh outcries over pesticide use led the APHIS to explore new biological controls against insects. Animal rights advocates questioned the department's research procedures. Finally, millions of acres were added to Forest Service wilderness areas, but controversy over the habitat of the endangered spotted owl raised new questions about logging on federal lands.

The Bush administration continued the major themes of the Reagan era. Early in the administration, trade development took center stage. The United States had proposed sweeping reforms of the General Agreement on Tariffs and Trade in 1988 to reduce international trade barriers and farm subsidies. A free trade agreement with Canada in 1988 pointed to the direction in which the United States wished to go. The department used export subsidies to counter subsidies coming from other countries. Trade subsidies helped agricultural exports recover most of their lost ground. New farm legislation in 1990 gave farmers more planting flexibility while cutting program costs.

By the early 1990s the department was coming under increasing criticism for inefficiency and an organizational structure that had not kept pace with changing priorities. A particular point of contention was the presence of farm agency field offices in counties that now had few farmers to serve. Prodded by Congress, the department studied ways to streamline its organization.

The department continued work on restructuring government under the Clinton administration. In 1994 the USDA went through a major reorganization in which the number of agencies was reduced from forty-three to twenty-nine and many field offices were consolidated or closed. For the first time, most of the programs serving farmers directly were put in a single unit, the Farm Service Agency. Congress proposed a number of other budget reforms in 1995 that would have affected the USDA, including converting food programs to block grants to the states, but opposition by the Clinton administration prevented many of these changes from becoming law. The Federal Agriculture Improvement and Reform Act of 1996, however, made the most thorough overhaul of farm programs since the 1930s, removing planting restrictions and leaving income support payments as the major federal subsidy. The department's food safety inspection system also came under scrutiny owing to several outbreaks of food-borne illness. In foreign trade, a new GATT agreement was signed in 1993 that further liberalized agricultural trade, although it failed to end domestic subsidies as in the original U.S. proposal. The North American Free Trade Agreement lowered trade barriers between the United States, Canada, and Mexico effective 1 January 1994.

In 1996 the Department of Agriculture had some ninety-eight thousand employees divided into nine broad program and administrative areas headed by an under secretary or assistant

secretary. Its budget of about $65 billion went mainly for food programs. Since its founding in 1862, the department had grown into a wide-ranging institution with research, education, and action programs dealing with agriculture, foreign and domestic agricultural trade, food assistance, forests, the environment, and consumer protection. It remained one of the largest federal departments, ranking fifth among civilian agencies.

[*See also* Animal and Plant Health Inspection Service *and* Forest Service.]

BIBLIOGRAPHY

Baker, Gladys L. *Century of Service: The First 100 Years of the United States Department of Agriculture.* Washington, D.C., 1963.
Gaus, John M. *Public Administration and the United States Department of Agriculture.* Chicago, 1940.
Rasmussen, Wayne D., and Gladys L. Baker. *The Department of Agriculture.* New York, 1972.

—DOUGLAS E. BOWERS

Air Force, Department of the

In compliance with the passage of the National Security Act on 26 July 1947, the Department of the Air Force was established on 18 September of that year; W. Stuart Symington became the first secretary of the Air Force and Carl A. Spaatz the first Air Force chief of staff. As founded, the civilian side was to have precedence over the military, but Symington, who had previously served as the assistant secretary of war for air, saw the military as being better equipped to evaluate the vicissitudes of war and to train and ready a force for conflict. The newly created Department of the Air Force authorized the Office of the Secretary of the Air Force, an under secretary, and two assistant secretaries. Both the secretary of the Air Force and the chief of staff attained coequal status with their counterparts within the Army and Navy.

This new status was not achieved without struggle. Rather, it was a culmination of years of effort by many advocates of air power and proponents of an independent air component. Army aviation activities had included Signal Corps balloon observations during both the Civil and the Spanish-American wars, the foundation of the Aeronautical Division of the Signal Corps in 1907, the award to the Wright Brothers of the first airplane contract in 1909, the establishment of the Aviation Section, Signal Corps, in 1914, and the valiant efforts of the First Aero Squadron during the punitive expedition against Pancho Villa in Mexico in 1916 and 1917. Yet on the eve of U.S. entry into World War I, the Army's air arm found itself ill-equipped and -prepared— fifty-six pilots and fewer than 250 aircraft, most of which were obsolete; altogether the nation's aircraft manufacturers had produced but a thousand planes. The U.S. response to France's request for forty-five hundred aircraft and fifty thousand men was enthusiastic but naive, for even with congressional approval of Secretary of War Newton D. Baker's request of $640 million for aviation, the Signal Corps had failed by the spring of 1918 to achieve its goals. A reorganization was deemed essential, and on 20 May of that year President Woodrow Wilson ordered the War Department to establish an Air Service. This entity was to consist of two agencies, one under a civilian to deal with the manufacturers, the other under a military officer for training and organizing units. This setup was further streamlined in August 1918 when President Wilson charged John D. Ryan, as aviation "czar," to fix the problem.

The most significant American contribution to the air war effort was the Liberty engine, not its aircraft, for nearly all of the 740 American airplanes at the French front at war's end had been built in Europe. The American Air Service did enjoy some success in its brief wartime stint. With Major General Mason M. Patrick organizing the Air Service efforts and Brigadier General William Mitchell in charge of air combat, the air arm found immediate work flying reconnaissance missions that in many instances proved invaluable in locating enemy troop formations and operations for American ground forces. In air-to-air encounters the American pilots made a good showing, listing seventy-one American aces (five

or more kills), with Captain Eddie Rickenbacker leading the way with twenty-six victories. During seven months of combat, American air forces launched some 150 bombing missions and claimed 756 enemy aircraft and 76 balloons while losing 289 aircraft, 48 balloons, and 237 crewmen.

Few could ignore the important role that air power had played during World War I. Its achievements fueled a two-decades-long movement among air proponents to establish an independent air force. Supporters of the concept pointed to the experience of Great Britain, which in 1918 had combined its Army and Navy aviation elements into the Royal Air Force (RAF) under an Air Ministry. But the U.S. Army's leaders viewed the airplane primarily as a support weapon for the infantry and relegated the Air Service a status similar to that of the field artillery or the engineers, limiting it to procuring aircraft and training flying units. In addition, between 1920 and 1926, attempts to legislate needed changes in the nation's air defense were blocked by jurisdictional conflict between the Air Service on the one hand and the War Department and the Navy on the other. The Air Service at the time was dominated by a small group of men like Brigadier General William Mitchell who were dedicated to and bound together by their passion for and practical knowledge of military aviation. Holding firmly that the Air Corps should support the advancement of aeronautical science, they doubted that it could do so under the direction of those whose views on aviation diverged from their own. During this period a series of boards and commissions studied and restudied the air organization issue, leading eventually to the passage of the Army Air Corps Act of 1926. While the act did not grant independence or autonomy, it did establish the Army Air Corps, granting it more personnel, aircraft, and, in effect, more prestige than its predecessor, the Air Service, had enjoyed. The act also called for the inclusion of Air Corps representation on the Army General Staff and reestablished a second assistant secretary of war—the assistant secretary of war for air. F. Trubee Davison was the first to hold this position, where he remained until 1932.

Despite opposition to a separate service and a lack of funding that was felt by all the services, the Air Corps managed significant achievements during the interwar period. Record-breaking flights for speed, distance, and endurance were accomplished by civilian and military flyers alike; meanwhile, an Air Corps doctrine of precision bombing of industrial targets by heavily armed long-range bombers began to emerge. A major reorganization in March 1935 led to the creation of the General Headquarters Air Force— or GHQ, as it was usually referred to—which allowed the Air Corps to achieve unified command over its combat units. This command, headed by Brigadier General Frank Andrews, a bomber enthusiast and advocate of an independent air force, succeeded in removing combat air units from the control of local commanders by obtaining jurisdiction over all questions relating to the organization of units, maintenance of aircraft, and operation of technical equipment, maneuvers, and training. Benjamin D. Foulois, chief of the Air Corps, retained responsibility for supply and procurement and for developing all doctrine affecting the employment of air elements.

Despite efforts by the Army General Staff to obtain larger appropriations for the Army air arm during the mid-1930s, the aircraft inventory of the Air Corps fell in 1936, and only a few of the new four-engined B-17s specifically designed for strategic bombing were authorized for purchase. As late as 1938 only thirteen B-17s were in the inventory.

With the advent of World War II, the fortunes of air power and its advocates rose as accounts from Europe in 1939 and 1940 showed clearly that the airplane now played a dominant role in war. On 20 June 1941 a further reorganization occurred when Major General Henry H. Arnold, chief of the Air Corps, took the title of chief of the Army Air Forces and assumed command of the Air Force Combat Command, as the GHQ had been renamed. Less than a year later, in March 1942, Arnold became the commanding general, Army Air Forces (AAF), which now made him coequal with the commanders of Army Ground Forces and Services of Supply. He now reported directly to General George C. Marshall, chief of staff of the Army, and the pair agreed

that while the AAF would have full autonomy within the War Department, any move toward an independent Air Force would be postponed until the end of the war.

In the meantime the civilian side of the Air Corps boosted its cause with the April 1941 appointment of Robert A. Lovett to the Office of the Assistant Secretary of War for Air, which had remained vacant since Davison's departure in 1932. Lovett was an investment banker who had served in the Naval Air Service during World War I and had retained a keen interest in aviation throughout the interwar years. Although not actually granted statutory power to direct procurement, Lovett was encouraged by Secretary of War Henry L. Stimson to promote aircraft production. While advising Stimson, Lovett worked closely with military leaders and was free to offer opinions on a variety of questions outside the formal chain of command.

From April 1940 until the end of World War II, Lovett was vitally concerned that nothing threaten industry's adherence to realistic aircraft production schedules. He attempted to settle labor disputes and sometimes intervened when the Office of Production Management and, subsequently, the War Production Board were at odds with AAF contractors, subcontractors, and suppliers. During the war Lovett acted as a sounding board for industry's complaints and requests. Stimson had a clearer conception of Lovett's role and told him, "Whatever authority the secretary of war has, you have."

Lovett and Arnold formed a superb partnership in fashioning the AAF as the world's most powerful air force. Indeed, from 20,000 men and 2,400 aircraft in 1939, by war's end there were 2.4 million personnel in the AAF while American industry produced almost 160,000 aircraft for the forces. Some of the outstanding wartime performers were the B-17 Flying Fortress and the B-29 Superfortress, the bomber workhorses of the European and the Pacific theaters, respectively; two fighters, the P-47 and the P-51; and the stalwart transport the C-47 Skytrain. The tremendous increase in size necessitated a reorganization that replaced Air Force Combat Command with four air forces in the continental United States. This force was subsequently complemented with twelve additional overseas air forces.

While tactical air units supported Operation Torch (the November 1942 invasion of North Africa), the Eighth Air Force supported the RAF as the focal point of a strategic bombing offensive against Germany. Mission after mission pounded a myriad of targets in Germany, although often enduring heavy losses. Beginning in early 1944 the P-51, equipped with drop tanks, allowed full-mission bomber escort and proved the decisive factor in gaining Allied air superiority. Coordinated attacks by the Eighth Air Force and Fifteenth Air Force stationed in Italy specifically against German petroleum industry targets along with tactical air support of the ground armies continuously frustrated enemy maneuvers. Indeed, with the Allied landings in Normandy on 6 June 1944, Allied control of the air had been attained. By war's end the AAF's strategic bombing effort had dropped 1.36 million tons of bombs on Germany at a cost of 67,646 personnel and 8,325 bombers.

In the Pacific General Douglas MacArthur chose a strategy of amphibious assaults on selected islands; as these fell into American hands, he built airfields on them to station his air forces, thereby moving his bombers ever nearer to the Japanese homeland. In addition, the AAF supported Admiral Chester Nimitz's aircraft carriers in their island-hopping efforts in the central Pacific, and it did the same for Allied forces in Burma and China. From Washington, General Arnold directed the Twentieth Air Force in its B-29 bombing of the Japanese home islands. Notwithstanding the fact that many firebombed Japanese cities were so devastated that Arnold believed that a ground invasion might already have been rendered unnecessary, atomic bombs would be dropped on Hiroshima and Nagasaki before the Japanese emperor finally ordered a surrender. In any event, it was abundantly clear that air power would play a significant role in future wars.

After the war, the AAF and the newly appointed assistant secretary of war for air, Stuart Symington, worked toward the independence the war had delayed. As the Air Force demobi-

lized, Symington sought to instill cost-control measures such as establishing an Office of the Comptroller to satisfy an austerity-minded Congress and the public. He believed the AAF "had an unusual opportunity to look toward efficiency, no past heritages, no barnacled procedures to first overcome." He and General Carl Spaatz, the new AAF chief of staff, worked toward a goal of seventy combat groups with 400,000 men and eight thousand planes.

In addition, the postwar era witnessed the creation of three major combat commands in the United States: the Strategic Air Command (SAC), the Tactical Air Command (TAC), and the Air Defense Command. The Strategic Air Command, under its commanding general, Curtis E. LeMay (1948–1957), became the dominant Air Force command. Even though the Military Air Transport Service played the key role in airlifting supplies during the Berlin airlift and tactical air forces were built up during the Korean conflict, SAC reigned supreme. Although Symington left office in April 1950 disappointed at not being able to attain a seventy-group Air Force, the Korean war provided a spurt in funding for an ample buildup in air forces, new weapon systems, and personnel so that Air Force leaders like Secretary Harold E. Talbott (1953–1955) could concentrate on more mundane issues such as military housing.

During the 1950s three pieces of legislation curtailed the authority of the secretary of the Air Force as well as of the department that the National Security Act of 1947 had established. The 1949 amendments gave more power to the secretary of defense by granting him an under secretary of defense and three assistant secretaries. The secretary of the Air Force and the other service secretaries lost their seats on the National Security Council, where they had been coequal with the secretary of defense. [See National Security Council.] The 1953 Reorganization Act further restrained the power of the service secretaries by adding six more assistant secretaries to the Department of Defense. Finally, the 1958 Reorganization Act took the service secretaries out of the direct chain of operational (combat) command, which now went from the president to the secretary of defense to the unified and specified commands, leaving the service secretaries with responsibility for operational support activities such as training and logistics. It was Secretary of Defense Robert S. McNamara, appointed by President John F. Kennedy, who took full advantage of the powers imbedded in this legislation.

That same decade witnessed the beginnings of missile technology under the inspired guidance of Trevor Gardner, an assistant secretary of the Air Force for research and development, and Major Bernard A. Schriever, who founded the Space and Ballistic Missiles Organization and would later become the first commander of Air Force Systems Command. Under Schriever the Air Force developed the Atlas, Titan, and Minuteman intercontinental ballistic missiles (ICBMs) and established the basis for the Air Force space program. Spurred on by the shock of Sputnik and fears espoused by "missile gap" theorists, SAC in 1959 began the process of complementing its bomber fleet with land-based missiles so that by the end of the 1960s over a thousand intercontinental missiles were in place while bomber numbers had dwindled. So the Air Force possessed two key elements of the ever-important "triad" of strategic weaponry—bombers and land-based missiles—while the Navy retained the third element—submarine-launched missiles. During the early 1960s TAC benefited from the Kennedy-McNamara emphasis on conventional forces that could respond to several protracted conflicts under the still-necessary nuclear umbrella.

U.S. strategy in Vietnam was to hold off North Vietnam until South Vietnam became a viable nation able to defend itself. To this end, between 1965 and 1974 the United States dropped three times the number of bombs that it did during World War II. To avoid expanding the war into an all-out nuclear conflict with the Soviet Union and China, the United States specified that Laos and Cambodia would remain off-limits for bombing attacks during most of the war, as would targets close to the Chinese border.

During the Rolling Thunder campaign against North Vietnam (March 1965–October 1968) the Air Force faced the strongest air defense system ever constructed. This effort was hampered by restrictive rules of engagement, such as a ten-mile limit around Hanoi, where North Vietnamese Migs were based. Rolling Thunder, which caused $300 million in damages to the North Vietnamese economy at the expense of over a $1 billion in U.S. aircraft, failed in its aim to thwart Communist efforts in the south.

Supplying and transporting troops was a major Air Force war mission as C-47 Skytrains, C-119 Boxcars, C-123 Providers, and C-130 Hercules maneuvered vast supplies about the jungle terrain while C-141 and C-5 Galaxies, assisted by commercial airlines, moved troops and supplies from the United States to Vietnam. SAC B-52 bombers and tactical forces assisted the U.S. and South Vietnamese armies in South Vietnam and struck at North Vietnamese army supply lines along the Ho Chi Minh trail and in southern Laos, where the air strikes supported counterinsurgency efforts of the Laotian government. In addition, operations were carried out over Cambodia to support the war in South Vietnam.

The Air Force performances at Khe Sanh and during the Tet Offensive of 1968 and the Easter Offensive in the spring of 1972 proved notable but could not alone bring the enemy to its knees. Anxious to settle the conflict, President Nixon, in pursuit of his "Vietnamization" policy, ordered a massive bombing campaign (Linebacker I, May–October 1972) against targets in North Vietnam and the mining of Haiphong and other ports. As Communist negotiators employed delaying tactics at the Paris peace talks, President Nixon ordered Linebacker II, an eleven-day bombing effort that began on 18 December. It brought the North to the negotiating table where a treaty was signed the following April. Two years later a North Vietnamese offensive sealed their victory.

Following the war, the Air Force once again had to adjust to stringent budgets and at the same time build up its strategic forces and maintain a readiness in Europe, a theater that had been neglected during the conflict in Southeast Asia. The early 1970s witnessed the development of smaller, lighter warheads that could be installed on ICBMs and submarine-launched missiles and that were complemented by the introduction of multiple independently targeted reentry vehicles.

After taking office in January 1981, President Ronald Reagan announced an extensive effort to modernize the Air Force's strategic forces. The B-1B program, canceled in 1977, was revitalized, and the bomber reached initial operational capability in September 1986. The Air Force modified its B-52H and G models to carry air-launched cruise missiles, and it modernized its intercontinental ballistic missile force by deploying Peacekeeper (formerly M-X) missiles in Minuteman silos. The F-15 and the F-16 fighters of the 1970s were complemented by two stealth aircraft that flew for the first time during the decade, the F-117A flying in June 1981 and the B-2A in 1989.

The Reagan administration also devoted considerable attention to space. Air Force Space Command was activated on 1 September 1982, and the following March Reagan introduced the Strategic Defense Initiative (SDI), a wide-ranging effort to investigate technologies that could contribute to a ballistic missile defense. (The Air Force would transfer its SDI efforts to the Strategic Defense Initiative Organization in 1994.) During the early to mid-1980s, Air Force budgets enjoyed five years of unprecedented double-digit percentages of real growth, affording Air Force Secretary Vern Orr (1981–1985) the luxury of concentrating on issues such as housing and the advancement of women.

When Iraq invaded Kuwait in August 1990, President George Bush mobilized an international coalition and ordered U.S. military units to carry out Operation Desert Shield, an enormous deployment of forces to defend Saudi Arabia. Within six weeks, Air Force cargo aircraft brought more tonnage to Southwest Asia than they had carried during the entire fifteen-month-long Berlin Airlift. The Desert Shield transporters eventually moved 500,000 passengers and nearly 3.7 million tons of dry cargo—roughly the equivalent of all the citizens of Denver, Colorado, with all their possessions—a third of the way around the world in about seven months.

Saddam Hussein continued his brutal occupation of Kuwait for five and a half months, defying a series of United Nations resolutions and a naval embargo. After exhausting every effort to reach a diplomatic settlement of the crisis, on 17 January 1991 (16 January EST) the United States and its allies began Desert Storm, a military operation to liberate Kuwait. The Gulf War which followed was remarkable for its brevity, relatively low Allied casualties, and decisive result. The Air Force component of United States Central Command, United States Central Air Forces (CENTAF), provided the centerpiece of the victory. The war lasted only forty-three days, thirty-nine of them devoted to a stunningly successful coalition air campaign against targets throughout Iraq and the Kuwaiti theater of operations (southern Iraq and Kuwait). CENTAF aircraft destroyed Iraq's air defenses and leveled many of its nuclear, biological, and chemical warfare facilities. The coalition air attacks against the Iraqi forces occupying Kuwait, particularly the armor and equipment of the elite Republican Guard divisions, made possible the rapid success of the ground campaign that followed. The Allies drove the Iraqis from Kuwait within a hundred hours.

With the Cold War's end, the Air Force entered another era of austerity: fiscal year 1992 and fiscal year 1994 budgets showed, respectively, −10.0 and −8.5 percent real growth. Faced with the reality of a reduced force structure as well as the need to address a blurring of the distinction between strategic and tactical missions that had been evident during the Gulf War, the Air Force began to reorganize several of its major commands. On 1 June 1992 the Air Force activated Air Combat Command, which combined all the assets of TAC with most of those of SAC and a small portion of those of Military Airlift Command (MAC). On the same day, Air Mobility Command, which blended most of MAC's force structure with a few key SAC resources, came into existence. Finally, Air Force Materiel Command, combining the resources of Air Force Systems Command and Air Force Logistics Command, was activated a month later. Part and parcel of the realities of downsizing and retrenchment that the Air Force faced in the mid-1990s was the focus on streamlining mission requirements under the objective "Global Reach, Global Power," whereby the Air Force posited itself as the service of the future and the guarantor of world stability while steadfastly adhering to its goals of retaining air and space superiority.

[*See also* Defense, Department of, *and* Joint Chiefs of Staff.]

BIBLIOGRAPHY

Craven, Wesley F., and James L. Cate, eds. *The Army Air Forces in World War II.* Washington D.C., 1983.

Davis, Richard G. *Carl A. Spaatz and the Air Force in Europe.* Washington, D.C., 1993.

Futrell, Robert F. *The United States Air Force in Southeast Asia: The Advisory Years to 1965.* Washington, D.C., 1981.

Futrell, Robert Frank. *The United States Air Force In Korea, 1950–1953.* Washington, D.C., 1983.

Futrell, Robert Frank. *Ideas, Concepts, Doctrine: Basic Thinking in the United States Air Force, 1907–1984.* Maxwell Air Force Base, Ala., 1989.

Gropman, Alan L. *The Air Force Integrates, 1945–1964.* Washington, D.C., 1978.

Hallion, Richard P. *Storm over Iraq: Air Power and the Gulf War.* Washington, D.C., 1992.

Keaney, Thomas A., and Eliot A. Cohen. *Gulf War Air Power Survey Summary Report.* Washington, D.C., 1993.

Mark, Eduard. *Aerial Interdiction: Air Power and the Land Battle in Three American Wars.* Washington, D.C., 1994.

Maurer, Maurer. *Aviation in the U.S. Army, 1919–1939.* Washington, D.C., 1987.

Maurer, Maurer, ed. *The U.S. Air Service in World War I.* Washington, D.C., 1978.

Moody, Walton S. *Building a Strategic Air Force, 1945–1953.* Washington, D.C., 1995.

Nalty, Bernard, John F. Shiner, and George Watson. *With Courage: The U.S. Army Air Forces in World War II.* Washington, D.C., 1994.

Neufeld, Jacob. *The Development of Ballistic Missiles in the United States Air Force, 1945–1960.* Washington, D.C., 1990.

Schaffel, Kenneth. *The Emerging Shield: The Air Force and the Evolution of Continental Air Defense, 1945–1960.* Washington, D.C., 1991.

Schlight, John. *The United States Air Force in Southeast Asia: The War in South Vietnam.* Washington, D.C., 1988.

Shiner, John F. *Foulois and the U.S. Army Air Corps, 1931–1935.* Washington D.C., 1983.

Van Staaveren, Jacob. *The United States Air Force in Southeast Asia: Interdiction in Southern Laos, 1960–1968.* Washington, D.C., 1993.

Watson, George M., Jr. *The Office of the Secretary of the Air Force, 1947–1965.* Washington, D.C., 1993.

Wolk, Herman S. *Planning and Organizing the Postwar Air Force.* Washington, D.C., 1984.

—GEORGE M. WATSON, JR.

Alcohol, Tobacco and Firearms, Bureau of

The U.S. Bureau of Alcohol, Tobacco and Firearms (ATF) is a tax-collecting, enforcement, and regulatory arm of the U.S. Department of the Treasury. In common with all other members of the executive branch, ATF's responsibility is established by congressional action. ATF cannot enact a law, nor can it amend the law. Charged as it is with fiscal oversight of some of the most controversial topics in Western civilization, ATF strives to maintain professional neutrality while giving a 35-to-1 return on every dollar it spends. ATF has the best cost-to-collection ratio in the federal family.

ATF is the youngest tax-collecting Treasury agency, separated from the Internal Revenue Service by Treasury Department Order No. 120-1 (former No. 221), effective 1 July 1972. Notwithstanding, ATF traces its roots across two hundred years of American history.

In 1789 under the new Constitution, the first Congress imposed a tax on imported spirits to offset a portion of the Revolutionary War debt assumed from the states. Administration of duties fell to the Department of the Treasury, whose secretary, Alexander Hamilton, had suggested them. Congressional lawmakers were favorably impressed by the results. The imports tax was augmented by one on domestic production in 1791. Taxpayers had grumbled over import duties. Some of them greeted the domestic levy—as they do today—with political resistance, escalating in that early case to the short-lived Whisky Rebellion of 1794. Both revenue sources survived rebellion—as they do today. Although these particular taxes were eventually abolished, similar devices for revenue came and went as needed until 1862. By an act of 1 July 1862, Congress created an Office of Internal Revenue within the Treasury Department, charging the commissioner with collection, among others, of taxes on distilled spirits and tobacco products that continue, with amendments, today. Because taxation so often does evoke resistance, including criminal evasion, during 1863 Congress authorized the hiring by Internal Revenue of "three detectives to aid in the prevention, detection and punishment of tax evaders." Tax collecting and enforcement were now under one roof. Before decade's end, the Office of Internal Revenue had its own counsel, another component descending in unbroken line to ATF today.

In 1875 federal investigators broke up the "Whisky Ring," an association of grain dealers, politicians, and revenue agents that had defrauded the government of millions of dollars in distilled spirits taxes. Responding to the scandal, Congress undertook the first Civil Service reform acts, acknowledging formally that effectiveness of law depends on the quality of its administrators.

The commissioner's annual report for 1877 refers to his office as the Bureau of Internal Revenue, a title that it retained for the next seventy-five years. In 1886, a single employee from the Department of Agriculture came to the Bureau of Internal Revenue under authority of the Oleomargarine Act to establish a Revenue Laboratory. The first samples received in the laboratory that 29 December were of butter suspected of adulteration with oleomargarine. In its second century, ATF's laboratory staff includes—but is not limited to—chemists, document analysts, latent print specialists, and firearms and toolmark examiners, supported by its own highly sophisticated facilities at Rockville, Maryland, Atlanta, Georgia, and Walnut Creek, California. That first chemist would recognize some aspects of laboratory service today (analysis of alcohol and tobacco products, for instance) although tools such as chromatography and electrophoresis might seem magic. There was nothing in 1886 to foreshadow the laboratory's sought-after forensic skills in arson, explosives, and criminal-evidence examination, a resource now available to law enforcement personnel worldwide.

Ratification of the Eighteenth Amendment to the Constitution in 1919, in combination with the Volstead Prohibition Enforcement Act of that year, brought to prominence those officers—"revenoors"—charged with investigating criminal violations of the Internal Revenue law, including illicit manufacture of liquors, who coalesced by 1920 into the Prohibition Unit. Evolution of this unit reflects the difficulty of enforcing a nationwide ban on "manufacture, sale or transportation of intoxicating liquors for beverage purposes." Internal Revenue's orientation has been toward collection throughout its history. Enforcement efforts, albeit necessary, never came easily. On April Fool's Day, 1927, Treasury elevated the Prohibition Unit to bureau status within the department. Congress was impatient with the results. On 1 July 1930 Congress created certain confusion for later historians by transferring "the penal provisions of the national prohibition act" from Treasury's Bureau of Prohibition (which then ceased to exist) to the Department of Justice's new Bureau of Prohibition—with an important exception: tax-related and regulatory activities, "the permissive provisions," remained at Treasury, under a new Bureau of Industrial Alcohol. The most illustrious enforcer during that tumultuous era was Eliot Ness, the "T-man" who toppled Chicago's organized-crime king Al Capone on tax-evasion charges.

The Twenty-first Amendment to the Constitution, repealing Prohibition, achieved ratification with unanticipated speed by 5 December 1993, catching Congress in recess. As an interim measure to manage a burgeoning legitimate alcohol industry, by executive order under the National Industrial Recovery Act, President Franklin Roosevelt established the Federal Alcohol Control Administration (FACA). The FACA, in cooperation with the Departments of Agriculture and Treasury, endeavored to guide wineries and distilleries under a system based on brewers' voluntary codes of fair competition. The FACA was relieved of its burden—and effectively vanished from history—after just twenty months, when President Roosevelt in August 1935 signed the Federal Alcohol Administration (FAA) Act. The new FAA received a firm departmental assignment: Treasury once more found itself regulating the alcohol industry.

Although Prohibition was officially over, the era's side effects continued for decades to mold the shape of ATF. On 10 March 1934 Justice's Prohibition enforcement duties folded into the infant Alcohol Tax Unit (ATU), Bureau of Internal Revenue, Department of the Treasury. At the same time, the FAA, functioning independently within Treasury, was carrying forward its mandate to collect data, establish license and permit requirements, and define the regulations that ensure an open, fair marketplace for the alcohol industry and the consumer. In 1940 the FAA as an administration merged with the ATU. The FAA Act continues today as one foundation of ATF's enabling legislation.

National dismay over the weaponry wielded so conspicuously by organized crime during Prohibition led to passage in 1934 of the National Firearms Act, followed in four years by the Federal Firearms Act. The newly regulated articles might be firearms, but taxes were involved as ever. The Miscellaneous Tax Unit, Bureau of Internal Revenue, collected the fees. In 1942 enforcement duties for the "Firearms Program" fell to the ATU, which was accustomed to managing controversial industries. In a major Internal Revenue reorganization of 1952, the nearly-century-old Miscellaneous Tax Unit was dismantled. Its firearms and tobacco tax responsibilities went to the ATU. The Bureau of Internal Revenue became the Internal Revenue Service (IRS) we know today. Acknowledging a portion of ATU's new burden, the IRS renamed it the Alcohol and Tobacco Tax Division. This incarnation lasted until 1968 passage of the Gun Control Act, which gave to the laboratory, among other things, responsibility for explosives. The division title shifted to Alcohol, Tobacco and Firearms (ATF) Division. Title XI of the Organized Crime Control Act in 1970 (Title XI) formalized ATF Division explosives expertise. In the same year, moved by a growing perception that the IRS's revenue-collecting bias did not reflect ATF Division's enforcement skills, overtures began toward ATF independence.

Treasury Department Order No. 120-1 (originally No. 221), effective 1 July 1972, transferred to ATF from the IRS those functions, powers, and duties related to alcohol, tobacco, firearms, and explosives. (During the mid-1970s at Treasury's direction ATF briefly assumed responsibility for wagering laws; that task returned to the IRS in less than three years.) Throughout the 1970s, based on determination that accelerants used in arson, when explosions might occur, meet Title

XI's definition of explosives, ATF began demonstrating in court its ability to prove arson. In the Anti-Arson Act of 1982, Congress amended Title XI to make it clear that arson is a federal crime, giving ATF responsibility for investigating commercial arson nationwide.

ATF continues a mutually beneficial interface with its legitimate industries, while refining unique enforcement skills. With developments such as the state-of-the-art Integrated Ballistic Identification System (a computerized matching program for weapons and the ammunition fired from them), accelerant- and explosives/weapons-detection canines, and the Gang Resistance Education and Training (GREAT) program (which gives children the tools to resist membership in violent gangs), ATF leads and supports law enforcement internationally.

In its first quarter-century ATF has had only four directors: Rex Davis, G. R. Dickerson, Stephen Higgins, and John Magaw. The director is appointed by the secretary of the Treasury, and reports to the under secretary (enforcement). ATF headquarters are in Washington, D.C., although most personnel and many ATF operations are decentralized throughout the country, with a few stations overseas. ATF agents, inspectors, and support staff are involved in investigating some of the most violent crimes in society, in regulating some of the most important and sensitive industries in America, and in collecting over $13 billion in annual revenue. ATF is a young federal agency, yet it is heir to the whole experience and proud tradition of "these United States."

BIBLIOGRAPHY

Annual Report of the Commissioner of Industrial Alcohol. Washington, D.C., 1931–1933.
Annual Report of the Commissioner of Internal Revenue. Washington, D.C., 1863–present.
Annual Report of the Commissioner of Prohibition. Washington, D.C., 1927–1930.
ATF Facts—History. Washington D.C., n.d.
A Report on the Bureau of Alcohol, Tobacco and Firearms: Its History, Progress and Programs. Washington, D.C., 1995.
United States Government Manual, 1994/1995. Washington, D.C., 1994. See pp. 496–498.

—VICKI HERRMANN

American Folklife Center.

See Library of Congress.

American Workplace, Office of the

Established in 1993, the Office of the American Workplace (OAW) works with business, labor, and government to promote the adoption of high-performance work practices and coopera- tive labor-management relations as a means of achieving higher productivity. The OAW consists of three offices: the Office of Work Technology Policy, which identifies and promotes the use of high-performance work technologies; the Office of Labor-Management Programs, which fosters labor-management partnership; and the Office of Labor-Management Standards (OLMS), which monitors the financial integrity and democratic practices of labor unions. The OLMS administers the Labor-Management Reporting and Disclo- sure Act of 1959, which protects the rights of union members vis-à-vis their own officers as well as management.

—GEORGE THOMAS KURIAN

Amtrak

During the 1920s a long-term decline in Ameri- can passenger train service began. The decline continued, with a major interruption during World War II, through the 1960s. The number of passenger trains fell, and the total mileage of routes served by passenger trains shrank. Passen- ger volume also declined, and the nation's rail- roads reported large financial losses arising from passenger operations. As a number of railroads in the northeastern United States faced bankruptcy and as railroad executives became increasingly unwilling to bear the financial losses resulting from passenger services, the nation faced the possibility of having no intercity passenger train service at all as the 1960s drew to a close.

The possible disappearance of passenger trains alarmed a number of observers. Some were con- cerned by the environmental problems caused by exclusive reliance on highway and air trans-

portation. Some were concerned by the serious congestion problems facing a number of major airports and highways. Other observers noted that millions of Americans do not have access to a car and that millions of Americans can- not travel by air. Several proposals to preserve passenger rail service were considered; the na- tional government ultimately created a semipub- lic corporation, originally named Railpax and later named Amtrak, to provide passenger train service.

Amtrak began operations with little opportu- nity for advance planning and amid conflicting expectations. Much of its equipment, obtained from the private railroads, was old and in poor condition. Track conditions, especially in the northeastern states, were not conducive to high- speed operations, and many train stations showed signs of neglect. In addition, most of the actual work of providing the services was in the hands of employees of private railroad compa- nies; Amtrak did not own passenger train sta- tions, terminals, or maintenance facilities. Providing high-quality service was, therefore, initially quite difficult.

One priority for improving service was mod- ernizing the equipment fleet, particularly loco- motives and passenger cars. Because private rail- roads had largely stopped investing in new passenger rolling stock prior to Amtrak's cre- ation, no state-of-the-art equipment was avail- able in the United States. Amtrak management began by retiring the worst equipment, rebuild- ing cars that were structually sound, and by de- veloping designs for a new generation of passen- ger cars. New locomotives, largely adapted from existing freight locomotives, were purchased but were not particularly successful. A second gener- ation of locomotives developed specifically for passenger use proved more successful, and a third generation began to enter service in the mid-1990s. Budgetary problems since the early 1980s have, however, led to a gradual aging of the locomotive fleet, with old locomotives re- maining in service beyond their optimal op- erating life.

New passenger car designs were also devel- oped, although the first new cars were not deliv- ered until 1975, four years after Amtrak first be- gan operations. Two different fleets of new cars were developed: Amfleet cars for the eastern United States, where tunnel and bridge clearances are lower, and Superliner cars for the western United States. By the mid-1990s, a new type of long-distance car for eastern routes was being tested and will, budget considerations permitting, eventually replace the bulk of the existing car fleet in the east.

Amtrak management also worked to gain more control over the personnel who provided services to the traveling public and to modernize work rules in order to increase employee productivity. Amtrak created the first nationwide, automated reservation system for passenger rail service in American history. Immediately prior to Amtrak's creation, the United States had thirteen separate passenger train reservation systems, none of which was automated.

Amtrak has experimented with a number of techniques to attract customers, from discount fares and new equipment to on-board movies and other service amenities. The results have been striking: the number of passenger miles generated by passenger trains fell almost every year from 1945 through 1971, the year of Amtrak's creation. By contrast, from 1972 through 1993, passenger miles rose in roughly three out of every four years, from 3.0 billion passenger miles in 1972 to 6.2 billion in 1993.

Amtrak's financial situation has been a matter of continuing concern. From the beginning its costs have exceeded passenger revenues, a common phenomenon for passenger trains in many countries. One major reason for that tendency is heavy government subsidies for other transportation modes. However, Amtrak's financial performance has improved substantially over the years. In 1971, Amtrak's revenues (excluding subsidies) covered barely half of its costs; by 1993, revenues covered eighty percent of costs. Some of that improvement appears to be due to increased passenger volume, for passenger rail service is more economical with high traffic volume. Routes that attract relatively few passengers have been trimmed in order to reduce costs. Amtrak's management has also explored other sources of revenue, including mail and express services, and has negotiated new labor agreements to increase productivity. At the same time, federal funding has been tight and some-

what erratic; in 1986, federal funding for new equipment amounted to only $2 million, about the price of two passenger cars. Low and erratic funding levels have hampered efforts to develop and maintain a consistent program of equipment modernization.

Amtrak has worked with state governments to provide services beyond what the national government has been willing to support. Since Amtrak's creation, a number of states have experimented with state-subsidized Amtrak service, although not all of those services have survived for extended periods. States that continue supporting Amtrak service over the long term tend to have relatively large populations, which make passenger rail service more economical, and to have a moderate-to-liberal political climate. However, as of 1996, some of the states that previously terminated their support for Amtrak service were moving to resume support. Amtrak has also become heavily involved in operating local commuter rail services; in 1994, commuter services generated over $271 million in revenues for Amtrak.

BIBLIOGRAPHY

Annual Report. National Railroad Passenger Corporation.
Bradley, Rodger. *Amtrak.* Poole, U.K., 1985.
Hilton, George. *Amtrak.* Washington, D.C., 1980.
Nice, David. "Program Survival and Termination: State Subsidies of Amtrak." *Transportation Quarterly* 42(1988):571–585.
Nice, David. "Financial Performance of the Amtrak System." *Public Administration Review* 51(1991): 138–144.
Nice, David. "Passenger Train Ridership in the Amtrak System." *Transportation Quarterly* 45(1991):121–132.
Wilner, Frank. *The Amtrak Story.* Omaha, 1994.
Zimmerman, Karl. *Amtrak at Milepost 10.* Park Forest, Ill., 1981.
—DAVID C. NICE

Animal and Plant Health Inspection Service

Created in 1972 as an agency within the Department of Agriculture, the Animal and Plant Health Inspection Service (APHIS) is responsible for programs to eradicate diseases and pests affecting animals and plants, for conduct of animal and plant health and quarantine programs, and for the control of predatory animals. Through inspection of all shipments and arrivals at major air, sea, border, and offshore points of entry, APHIS screens out undesirable and diseased animals and plants. APHIS is empowered to refuse entry after inspection or to require that plants and animals be quarantined or treated prior to entry. APHIS inspectors also work in several foreign countries, where they examine and certify shipments of agricultural products to the United States. Domestic plants and animals for export are certified to be pest and disease free before they are shipped abroad.

Within the United States, APHIS concentrates on control and eradication of pests and diseases. It surveys pest activity, population, and spread in various areas, and when evidence of such activity reaches dangerous levels, an emergency is declared and an areawide quarantine may be invoked. Generally, control efforts take the form of chemical sprays, introduction of a pest's natural enemy into an affected area, and sterilization of the male pests to reduce their breeding. In addition to its quarantine stations at air and sea terminals, APHIS licenses private bird quarantine stations and certifies and inspects processing plants that handle animal products. The service also administers regulations that require humane handling of dogs, horses, cats, primates, and zoo animals during transportation or public display. It regulates the manufacture of biological products used in the treatment of animals. In 1986, the Animal Damage Control Program was transferred to APHIS from the U.S. Fish and Wildlife Service. This program, based on the Animal Damage Control Act of 1931, protects livestock and crops as well as forests and rangelands from marauding animals and birds. In addition the program helps protect human health and safety through the control of animal-borne diseases and hazards to aircraft caused by birds.

—GEORGE THOMAS KURIAN

Architect of the Capitol, Office of the

One of the oldest and most influential agencies in federal service, the Office of Architect of the

Capitol today is responsible for the design, construction, repairs, and general housekeeping of the 271-acre United States Capitol complex, which includes the Capitol building and grounds, the Library of Congress, the House and Senate office buildings, the Supreme Court, the Judiciary Office Building, the Botanic Garden, and the Capitol Power Plant. The agency's history has been deeply influenced by the contributions of nine designers and builders of the Capitol complex. This group includes the famous architects William Thornton, Benjamin Henry Latrobe, Charles Bulfinch, and Thomas U. Walter, as well as their administrative successors Edward Clark, Elliott Woods, David Lynn, J. George Stewart, and George M. White.

The origins of the Office of the Architect derive from President George Washington's appointment of three commissioners to carry out the provisions of the Residence Act of 1790. This important legislation established the new capital along the Potomac River and charged the first presidential commission in American history with providing for the accommodation of Congress, the president, and the public offices of the United States.

The commissioners held the first design competition for the Capitol in 1792 and, with President Washington's and Secretary of State Thomas Jefferson's approval, selected Dr. William Thornton's design for the Capitol. In 1794 President Washington appointed Thornton (1759–1828) a commissioner, and he used his official position to protect his winning design. Professionally trained architects Stephen Hallet, George Hadfield, and James Hoban superintended the Capitol's construction generally according to Thornton's plan, completing the Senate (north) wing in 1800. As the building's initial designer and an active commission member directing the erection of the President's House and the Capitol, Thornton has been recognized by historians as the first Architect of the Capitol.

Soon after establishment of the national government in Washington in 1800, Congress abolished the three-member board of commissioners and placed the Capitol's construction and maintenance under the control of a single official called the superintendent (1802–1817) and later the commissioner of public buildings

(1817–1867). These presidentially appointed officials managed the public works in Washington, D.C., including the Capitol and the White House. Under their charge, master architects such as Latrobe and Bulfinch provided design services and superintended construction while holding such titles as "surveyor of public buildings" and "Architect of the Capitol."

In 1803 President Thomas Jefferson offered the talented English architect Benjamin Henry Latrobe (1764–1820) the position of surveyor of public buildings. During the first phase of his association with the Capitol's design and construction (1803–1811), Latrobe politely acknowledged Superintendent Thomas Munroe's administrative authority. However, his now-famous architectural collaboration with Jefferson resolved all design issues.

By 1811 the impending conflict with Great Britain cut off appropriations for the Capitol's construction, and Latrobe moved to Pittsburgh to pursue business ventures there. The burning of the Capitol by the British during the War of 1812 left the building a charred ruin and led to Latrobe's being recalled to rebuild the structure in 1815. Latrobe restored the Capitol, nearly completing the Senate and House wings of the old Capitol before his resignation in 1817. Charles Bulfinch (1763–1844), considered America's first native-born professional architect, succeeded Latrobe and designed the Capitol's western portico, the old Library of Congress, the original dome, and the landscaping of the grounds. Having held a position in Boston similar to that of commissioner of public buildings, he did not bridle at having to defer to officials involved in public building projects. His experience greatly simplified matters of construction after several decades of conflict and delay. He remained at the job for nearly twelve years, completing the Capitol in 1829.

No further construction was necessary until 1851, when Congress, citing the need for more space thanks to the influx of senators and representatives from the states that had joined the Union since 1830, appropriated $100,000 for an extension and authorized President Millard Fillmore to select an architect. In so doing Congress bypassed the commissioner of public buildings and modified the previous system of oversight concerning the design and construction of the Capitol. President Fillmore appointed Thomas U. Walter (1804–1887) of Philadelphia, a fellow Whig and the leading professional architect of his day, to design and superintend the erection of the Senate and House extensions and, later, the Capitol dome (1851–1865). However, following a controversy concerning the extension's materials and building contracts, Congress transferred administration of the Capitol Extension to the War Department. Appointed as the new superintendent by Secretary Jefferson Davis, Captain Montgomery C. Meigs (1817–1892) of the Army Corps of Engineers took charge of administrative details and the engineering problems. Walter retained control of the design work.

After a feud between Meigs and Walter concerning the architect's professional rights caused several serious construction delays, Congress transferred project oversight to the Department of the Interior in 1862. Secretary Orville Browning again assigned Walter control of the building's design and construction. This arrangement continued until Walter's retirement in 1865 as the building neared completion. Edward Clark, Walter's apprentice and draftsman, succeeded his mentor as the architect of the Capitol Extension.

Clark (1822–1902) initially shared responsibilities for oversight of the Capitol with Commissioner of Public Buildings Benjamin B. French, but in 1867 Congress abolished the office of commissioner, assigning its duties at the Capitol to the architect of the Capitol Extension. Since then the architect of the Capitol has maintained responsibility for the Capitol's design, construction, management, repair, and housekeeping services.

Scrupulously honest and nonpartisan in his service to Congress, Clark solidified the status of the Office of the Architect as a permanent agency. In 1876 Congress reaffirmed the Architect's responsibility for the repair and maintenance of the Capitol building and grounds, dropping "Extension" from the title and stipulating that the incumbent occupy an office in the building (19 Stat. 417).

Recognizing his limitations as a designer, Clark routinely brought in outside experts to install modern amenities at the Capitol. During his tenure he directed installation of the first elevator in the Capitol in 1874, introduced modern plumbing and drainage in 1893, and wired the entire building with electricity in 1897. However, his greatest legacy was the execution of Frederick Law Olmsted's landscape plan for the Capitol grounds (1874–1892), defined by the broad eastern plaza, west terraces, and the romantic naturalistic landscape treatment of the Capitol grounds that we know today.

When Clark became incapacitated by illness in 1898, Congress appointed his chief assistant, Elliott Woods (1865–1923), as acting Architect of the Capitol. After Clark's death in 1902, the American Institute of Architects opposed Woods's promotion on the grounds that he was not a trained professional architect. Eventually Congress and President Theodore Roosevelt, who supported the architectural profession's position, struck a compromise that resulted in a change of the agency head's title to "superintendent of the Capitol building and grounds" without altering the salary or responsibilities.

Woods proved to be an excellent appointment, directing more than $25 million of building projects including the construction of the first congressional office annexes—the Cannon House Office Building (1908) and the Russell Senate Office Building (1909)—and the House and Senate subways. By the end of his career, Woods had earned the respect of the architectural profession and accepted an honorary membership in the American Institute of Architects. In 1921 Congress reinstated the title of the agency as the Office of the Architect of the Capitol with widespread professional approval.

David Lynn, Woods's "right-hand man," assumed control of the agency's operations after Woods's death in 1923. He had risen through the ranks, advancing from laborer to superintendent before finally gaining an executive position as a Capitol engineer in 1910. He also became Woods's chief assistant. News stories announcing his appointment by President Calvin Coolidge in 1923 noted he was a natural successor and that his specialized experience paralleled Woods's own tutelage under Clark.

From a dozen permanent employees during Clark's administration, the agency's personnel expanded to more than nine hundred near the end of Lynn's term in the 1940s, largely reflecting the explosion of custodial and managerial tasks associated with the growth of the Capitol complex. The Longworth House Office Building (1925), the Supreme Court Building (1935), and the John Adams Building of the Library of Congress (1939) were all completed during Lynn's tenure.

With Lynn's retirement at the advanced age of eighty-one, President Dwight D. Eisenhower appointed sixty-four-year-old J. George Stewart (1890–1970) as Architect on 1 October 1954, ending the practice of promoting the "right-hand man" from within the ranks of the office. Stewart had powerful connections as the friend of House Speaker Sam Rayburn and House Minority Leader Joseph Martin.

Compared to Woods and Lynn, Stewart's professional qualifications as a registered civil engineer, practical experience as a landscape contractor (1919–1942), and political knowledge as a former Republican congressman from Delaware (1935–1937) and clerk of the Senate Committee on the District of Columbia (1947–1951) seemed an ideal preparation for the new head of the Office of the Architect. Ironically, Stewart received more criticism for his lack of professional qualifications than either of his predecessors. Stewart was the straw man for a torrent of critical remarks leveled at the design and construction costs of the Dirksen Senate Office Building (1947), the East Front extension (1958), and the Rayburn House Office Building (1965). These controversial building projects provided Congress with the facilities needed to respond to the dramatic growth of the national government and congressional staff after World War II. The work force of the office almost doubled to approximately 2,000 employees during the expansion of the Capitol complex between 1955 and 1971. About 70 professionals formed the Architect's core administrative staff, with most of the work force composed of custodial and maintenance workers employed for the upkeep of the buildings and grounds.

After the design controversies of Stewart's tenure, George M. White's appointment in 1971 was widely praised as a welcome change. His credentials as a professional architect and administrator were beyond reproach. A *New York Times* editorial lauded White's appointment as Architect in 1971 as a "stunning and welcome departure from recent practice in which professionalism has been eliminated in favor of party service."

White has had a distinguished career at the Capitol, including noteworthy restorations of the old Senate and old Supreme Court chambers, the National Statuary Hall, and the canopy of the Capitol Rotunda. The Ohio native also administered the design and construction of a series of important new structures including the Hart Senate Office Building, the James Madison Building for the Library of Congress, and the Thurgood Marshall Judiciary Office Building. Of all the architectural projects, nothing epitomizes White's professional approach to the job better than the development of a *Master Plan for the United States Capitol* (1981). Although Congress has not adopted the scheme, this comprehensive study created a flexible, rational plan for the Capitol complex that projects the needed expansion of Congress well into the twenty-first century.

Although White received his share of critical press about a proposed West Front extension and the Hart Senate Office Building cost overruns in the 1980s, he has rehabilitated the image of the office, which today is generally considered an apolitical and highly professional agency. White's career achievements as Architect of the Capitol culminated in 1992 when the American Institute of Architects bestowed on him the Thomas Jefferson Award for Public Architecture, created to honor individuals who have made long-term contributions to the field. He retired from federal service in 1995. Congress enacted legislation in 1989 to ensure that a successor will have a ten-year term limit and will be selected by the president from a list of candidates submitted by the House and confirmed by the Senate.

At the end of the twentieth century, the Architect of the Capitol remains unrecognized as an important federal official. Over time, magazine and newspaper profiles have proclaimed the architect of the Capitol to be the "emperor" or "king" of Capitol Hill. But the office has no arbitrary or independent power. Congress has the express legal authority to appropriate funds for the Capitol, and since the early Republic the custodians of the Capitol, whether architects, superintendents, or commissioners, have been accountable to the president and Congress as the ultimate arbiters and shapers of one of our nation's most revered buildings.

[*See also* Architecture of the Federal Government.]

BIBLIOGRAPHY

Allen, William C. *The United States Capitol: A Brief Architectural History.* Washington, D.C., 1991.
Allen, William C. *The Dome of the United States Capitol: An Architectural History.* Washington, D.C., 1992.
Allen, William C. *"In the Greatest Solemn Dignity": The Capitol's Four Cornerstones.* Washington, D.C., 1995.
Architect of the Capitol. *Art in the United States Capitol.* Washington, D.C., 1978.
Bushong, William, et. al. *Uncle Sam's Architects: Builders of the United States Capitol.* Washington, D.C., 1994.
Documentary History of the Construction and Development of the United States Capitol Building and Grounds. Washington, D.C., 1904.
Fairman, Charles E. *Art and Artists of the Capitol of the United States of America.* Washington, D.C., 1927.
Frary, Ihna T. *They Built the Capitol.* New York, 1940.
Kerwood, John R. *The United States Capitol: An Annotated Bibliography.* Norman, Okla., 1973.
Scott, Pamela. *Temple of Liberty: Building the Capitol for the New Nation.* New York, 1995.

—WILLIAM B. BUSHONG

Architectural and Transportation Barriers Compliance Board

Commonly known as the Access Board, the Architectural and Transportation Barriers Compliance Board (ATBCB), was established under Section 502 of the Rehabilitation Act of 1973 to enforce the provisions of the Architectural Barriers Act of 1968. Under this act all facilities owned, rented, or funded in any part by the federal government must be accessible to and usable by persons with disabilities. Since the enactment of the Americans with Disabilities Act of 1990 (ADA), the ATBCB is charged with the responsibility for developing ADA accessibility guidelines for places of public accomodation, public housing, schools, parks, commercial facilities, state and local government facilities, and transportation vehicles. These standards are codified in the Uniform Federal Accessibility Standards.

The board is an independent federal agency with 25 members, of whom 13 are members of the public (the majority of whom are required to be people with disabilities) appointed by the president and the remaining 12 represent the major executive departments of the federal government. The ATBCB may conduct investigations, hold public hearings, and issue orders. Its orders are final and binding on all federal agencies. In some cases, it may initiate legal proceedings before an administrative law judge.

—GEORGE THOMAS KURIAN

Architecture of the Federal Government

ESSAY The authority for federal buildings is found in Section 8, Article 17, of the Constitution: "To exercise exclusive legislation in all cases whatsoever, over such district (not exceeding ten miles square) as may, by cession of particular States, and the acceptance of Congress, become the seat of government of the United States, and to exercise like authority over all places purchased by the consent of the legislature of the State in which the same shall be, for the erection of forts, magazines, arsenals, dockyards, and other needful buildings." The 1790 Residence Act located the federal district on the banks of the Potomac River and charged President George Washington with having the federal city ready for the government's occupancy by December 1800. The executive branch historically has overseen most federal architectural matters; presidents frequently played decisive roles in the choice of architects or designs for the major public buildings and monuments. The government's vast array of civil buildings has been and continues to be designed by staff architects or obtained by public competition or appointment.

The first building designed specifically for national purposes was Federal Hall, a renovation of New York's City Hall, where the Stamp Act Congress had met briefly in 1765. The project was undertaken in 1788, soon after the Constitution was ratified by New York's Common Council. In hopes of convincing Congress to remain permanently in New York, they chose Pierre Charles L'Enfant to create an elegant and impressive building to express and promote the new union of the states. L'Enfant, an engineer who came to America in 1777 with French troops to fight in the Revolution, consciously designed Federal Hall to be different from all existing Colonial statehouses. He chose, perhaps in consultation with George Washington, the modern neoclassical style of architecture with an expansive white marble, porticoed facade overlooking Wall Street. This new facade gave the impression of solidity and permanence in stark contrast to adjacent step-gabled red brick rowhouses, the remnants of New York's Dutch past.

L'Enfant invented new American symbols and adapted traditional or recent American ones to express Federal Hall's purpose as the seat of the national government. These included elements borrowed from the flag chosen in 1777—thirteen stars in the entablature—and the Great Seal of the United States adopted in 1782—a heraldic eagle in the pediment and arrows and olive branches in relief-carved panels on the third story. Individual decorative schemes for the Senate and House chambers combined European and American motifs to stress literally the states united under one government. On 30 April 1789, Washington was inaugurated the first president on Federal Hall's second-story balcony, which was connected to the Senate chamber. Congress remained there for only a year, but such significant legislation as the Bill of Rights was enacted in Federal Hall.

Washington and Secretary of State Thomas Jefferson actively influenced design decisions in the new federal city, named in honor of Washington in September 1791. Earlier in the year Washington had appointed L'Enfant to design the city and all of its public buildings; Jefferson conducted the public competitions to choose plans for the President's House and Capitol after L'Enfant's dismissal a year later. The extraordinary size of L'Enfant's city—6,100 acres—and its unique blend of baroque and Picturesque traditions was in itself an emblem of the geography and the history of the founding of the country. Fifteen boulevards (Vermont and Kentucky were about to become states) traversed the city, connecting a variety of public squares. These named avenues were clustered in the northern, central, and southern parts of the city according to where the states fell geographically in the country. The three longest boulevards traversing the entire city—Massachusetts, Pennsylvania, and Virginia—were named for the three largest states. They were also the states with the most important Revolutionary War activity, both civil and military. Pennsylvania Avenue seems to have been given pride of place, bisecting the city because of its central location in the country with six states above it and six below it. In addition, such pivotal events as the signing of the Declaration of Independence, the Constitutional Conventions, and the encampment at Valley Forge took place in Pennsylvania.

The President's House, called the White House as early as 1803 because its porous brown sandstone exterior was painted to act as a vapor barrier, has been redecorated, renovated, and enlarged numerous times during the last two centuries. Yet its basic architectural character, an American adaptation of English neo-Palladian Renaissance and neo-Roman traditions, remains the same. The White House's design was won in competition by the Irish-born and -trained architect James Hoban (c.1762–1831), who used Leinster House (1745–1851) in Dublin as his model. Unlike its European antecedents, the two stories of the White House's main block were raised only slightly above ground to enhance its relationship with its beautiful site. Two imposing projecting porticoes were added in the 1820s following drawings commissioned by Jefferson during his presidency (1801–1811). The rectangular one at the north entrance was a porte cochere while the semicircular portico on the south served partially as a sun screen shading the central public rooms. Aesthetically, both porticoes added a dimension of grandeur that Hoban's initial building lacked. Although the White House's function was to look like, as well as be, the grandest house in America, it was built following a familiar domestic formula and presented no great design or construction difficulties.

The Capitol, however, had to express symbolically the new form of government. It was the first complex building project undertaken by the government and is still evolving, with new offices added behind the renovated west terrace in the early 1990s and a future underground visitor's center planned for the next decade. None of the designs submitted to the 1792 Capitol competition was entirely satisfactory; after a year a composite plan that combined William Thornton's (1759–1828) elegant exterior pattern with Stephen Hallet's (1755–1825) internal arrangement began to be constructed. The major feature of Thornton's design was a central rotunda and low dome patterned on the Roman Pantheon (probably influenced by Jefferson's stated preferences); Hallet's House chamber was shaped like a Roman hippodrome with its seating pattern similar to that adopted in 1789 by the French National Assembly. Contrary to European precedents for neoclassical buildings, Jefferson suggested that the floors of both two-story chambers be at ground level. Only the north wing was completed by 1800; it was occupied by the Senate, House of Representatives, Supreme Court, and the Library of Congress.

In 1803 President Jefferson hired Benjamin Henry Latrobe (1764–1820) to complete the Capitol. Over the next decade both the Capitol's interiors and exterior were slowly altered. Jefferson collaborated in the design of a new eastern portico that incorporated a grand staircase leading to the rotunda, the "Hall of the People." He suggested skylights for the House of Representatives ceiling to make it, in his view, "the most beautiful room in the world." Following Latrobe's suggestion both the House and Senate chambers were raised to the second level; the Supreme Court was placed beneath the Senate, as its tenancy in the Capitol was thought to be temporary. Latrobe designed three American columns for the Capitol's north wing, all based on native species: corn, tobacco, and the magnolia tree. He devised a complex interweaving of subsidiary spaces to increase visually the size of a relatively small building. Much of his and Jefferson's attempts to aggrandize the Capitol and have it express the unique experience of being American was destroyed in August 1814, when the Capitol was burned by British troops toward the end of the War of 1812. Latrobe returned in 1815 to rebuild the interiors of the burnt-out shell; he redesigned the House chamber (currently Statuary Hall) to be semicircular and proposed a projecting west wing overlooking the Mall to house the Library of Congress and much-needed congressional committee rooms and offices. When Latrobe resigned in 1818, construction of the Capitol's central section—the rotunda and dome—had not yet begun.

The Boston-born and -educated architect Charles Bulfinch (1763–1844) completed the Capitol between 1818 and 1829. He carried out Latrobe's general schemes for the west wing and east portico, making only decorative changes, but redesigned the rotunda in a structurally and aesthetically more conservative manner. Figural and decorative sculptural panels and eight history paintings ornamented Bulfinch's rotunda; their overall theme was manifest destiny, the belief that Euro-American civilization should and would dominate the continent. Against Bulfinch's wishes and better judgment, a high dome with a profile based on a stilted arch was chosen by President James Monroe and Secretary of State John Quincy Adams to insure the Capitol's visibility from any point in the city.

California was a state by the time the Capitol was extended in the 1850s, and eclectic Victorian styles of architecture had replaced neoclassicism as the canon of good taste. The Philadelphia architect Thomas U. Walter (1804–1887) designed semidetached lateral wings and a tall colonnaded dome in the Renaissance Revival style, transforming the Capitol from a sedate building to an exuberant, highly articulated one. Montgomery C. Meigs (1817–1892) of the Army Corps of Engineers worked with Walter on the design and rapid construction of the cast-iron dome, this material chosen because the rotunda could not support the greater weight of a masonry dome.

Meigs was in charge of the painters and sculptors who decorated the Capitol Extension; collectively, American heroes and events were cast as traditional European allergorical figures. In the canopy painting suspended between the double domes, "The Apotheosis of George Washington," the first president is raised to the status of a god.

He is attended by allegorical groups that celebrate America's nineteenth-century achievements: Neptune, the sea god, lays the transatlantic cable, while Ceres, the goddess of agriculture, drives the team of horses that pulls a McCormick reaper. In 1863 Thomas Crawford's statue of "Freedom" was placed atop the dome and his pedimental group of sculpture entitled "The Progress of Civilization" was installed above the Senate wing's portico. The Capitol's final major iconographic sculpture was Paul Barlett's pedimental group for the House wing. Completed in 1916, "The Apothesis of Democracy" has as its dual themes the life and labors of contemporary Americans.

Between the time the original Capitol was finished and the Capitol Extension begun, executive department office buildings were needed to replace those destroyed by fire. Originally four brick Anglo-Palladian buildings designed by George Hadfield (1763–1826) flanked the White House, those housing the Treasury and State Departments on the east, and the War and Navy Departments on the west. On 4 July 1836 President Andrew Jackson appointed Robert Mills (1781–1855) to design and supervise construction of the new fireproof Treasury Building and carry out the plan by Ithiel Town (1784–1844) and William P. Elliot (1807–1854) for the Patent Office (now the National Portrait Gallery). Both are landmark Greek Revival structures, still imposing in appearance because Mills built them to respond to the scale of L'Enfant's city. Mills's General Post Office (1839–1841) completed a triad of new federal office buildings. For them he used the three major ancient orders of architecture—the Doric Patent Office, Ionic Treasury, and Corinthian Post Office—and based each on a different building type: temple, stoa, and palazzo, respectively.

Like his mentors Jefferson and Latrobe, Mills believed that public architecture was the highest calling and that federal buildings should convey some fundamental American concept. In displaying this architectural diversity he may have intended both to express the pluralism of American society and to provide exemplars of historical architecture for the edification of his countrymen. His design for the Washington

Monument, chosen in 1845, was sponsored by private individuals, although it was eventually completed in 1884 at government expense by the Army Corps of Engineers.

Private beneficence historically has founded many of the country's national museums. No one knows why British scientist James Smithson bequeathed to the U.S. government his fortune to found in Washington an institution for the "increase and diffusion of knowledge among men." The government officials who conducted the 1846 competition deliberately sought a medieval revival design because they believed it would be less expensive and more flexible than Mills's classical office buildings. In 1849 Congressman Robert Dale Owen of Indiana wrote *Hints on Public Architecture,* proposing that James Renwick's winning design for the Smithsonian Institution be a model for future public buildings. His arguments had little effect on the immediate development of federal architecture.

During the early 1830s Mills was hired to design four customs houses for New England towns. They were built with exterior granite walls and brick-vaulted interiors: sober, dignified, and quite small in scale, but monumental in appearance. The government's great customs houses of the period were in the largest ports. The perceived need that the government be housed in buildings that expressed power and permanence, as well as dignity, was met in different ways by these massive buildings. The loss of records when the Treasury Building was destroyed by fire in 1833 was so serious that Congress mandated that federal buildings be built of stone.

Ithiel Town and Alexander Jackson Davis (1803–1892) articulated the flanks of the marble New York Custom House (1833–1842; now Federal Hall National Memorial because it occupies the site of Federal Hall) with a deep "pilustrade," rectilinear buttresses in place of a colonnade. The architects claimed this as their own enhancement to the classical temple form and terminated the gable end with a full Greek Doric portico, topping the whole with a Roman dome (hidden under the roof when finally constructed). Ammi B. Young's (1798–1874) granite Boston Custom House (1837–1847) was daring

in both its design and construction. Located on an open site, the rectangular building fused a peripheral Greek Doric temple with the Roman Pantheon. Giant porticoes, each composed of six monolithic, 32-foot-high columns, equal the dome's diameter and span nearly half the width of the north and south facades. The east and west wing walls were remarkably transparent, with engaged columns connected to narrow wall segments that acted together as buttresses to open the intervening walls to large expanses of windows. Alexander T. Wood (d. 1854) designed the New Orleans Custom House (1848–1881) as a stark, sober, almost forbidding structure. The largest of the great Greek Revival federal buildings, Wood's design depended on flat expanses of gray granite punctured by unframed windows organized in an unusual vertical rhythm, as well as uncommon Egyptian-inspired lotus capitals, for its imposing, even aggressive, architectural character.

These diverse stone buildings had counterparts in many other cities, including Savannah, Georgia (John S. Norris, architect; 1848–1853), and Charleston, South Carolina (Edward B. White and Ammi B. Young, architects; 1850–1879), in places and at a time when large-scale commercial and local civic structures were competing for the supremacy of the skyline. The government's willingness to fund "636 3/4 days of work hammering and carving four large Granite Bannister Posts for principal stairways" of the Boston Custom House reflected the importance of their functions. Custom duties were the government's major source of revenue; these customs houses embodied the government's vital participation in the health of the local economy and consequently the strength of the nation as a whole. Their designs were chosen in competition, with the best local architects willing to submit plans because they expected to be employed for several years superintending their construction.

The design and construction history of each of these customs houses was tumultuous. In 1852 the Office of the Supervising Architecture was established in the Treasury Department in recognition that the government should control the building of courthouses, customs houses, post offices, mints, marine hospitals, and assay offices needed across the rapidly expanding country. Apparently because the Boston Custom House was an aesthetic and functional success and had been built more expeditiously than other contemporary federal buildings, Ammi Young was appointed the first supervising architect. Alexander T. Bowman (1803–1865) of the Army Corps of Engineers was placed in charge of the Construction Division. Together they designed a series of prototypical designs for federal buildings that were lithographed so that multiple copies could be sent to contractors and local superintendents. Between 1850 and 1858, eighty-eight Young-Bowman buildings were spread from Portsmouth, New Hampshire, to Galena, Illinois. Each was a unique design but recognizable as part of a larger whole, the consistent, coherent, well-built federal building. Many were built of granite quarried on Dix Island, Maine; they conveyed solidity, security, and permanence without ostentation. Often the only emblematic decoration that identified them as federal buildings was the Great Seal eagle above the door and the American flag flying from the roof.

Over the next century the position of the supervising architect of the Treasury was held by fifteen individuals. Few were leaders in the profession nationally as Latrobe, Mills, and Young had been. The *Official Register of the United States* for 1859 lists 2 clerks and 4 draftsmen working in the Office of the Supervising Architect; 20 years later there were 4 clerks, 2 civil engineers, 38 draftsmen (6 of whom were women), 21 computers (estimators of the amount and cost of materials), 35 architects in the field superintending construction, and a variety of other specialists including two photographers. By 1899 there were 7 division chiefs, 2 designers, 34 draftsmen, 22 on-site superintending architects, and dozens of clerks, tracers, computers, and office workers. By 1907 there were drastic cutbacks to the Washington office staff. In the twentieth century, as America's influence became international, other federal agencies took on the responsibility of providing for their own architectural needs.

The most notable among the supervising architects were Alfred Bult Mullett (1834–1890),

William Appleton Potter (1842–1909), and James Knox Taylor (1857–1929). Mullett was the product of the apprenticeship system, entering the Cincinnati office of Isaiah Rogers in 1856 after less than two years at the Ohio Farmers' College, where he studied mathematics and mechanical drawing. Mullett followed Rogers to Washington when the latter was appointed supervising architect in 1863. Three years later Mullett forced out his mentor, and over the next eight years he resolutely changed the image of government buildings from the staid Renaissance-inspired Italianate classicism fostered by his two predecessors to the avant-garde French Second Empire style. Recent immigrants and American architects who studied at the Ecole des Beaux-Arts in Paris popularized this French revival, one of several Victorian architectural vocabularies popular after the Civil War. A few famous baroque monuments featuring mansard roofs, broken masses, and layered wall surfaces provided Mullett with a staid architectural paradigm that was more conservative than the lighter, sculpturally ornate models emulated by most of his contemporaries.

Thus Mullett's thirty-six massive government buildings erected in major cities as widely separated as Boston and San Francisco were notable for their heaviness and solidity and immediately identifiable as federal buildings. Criticized by the private architectural profession when they were built, and excoriated during the early twentieth century as exemplifying the nadir of Victorian bad taste, most were destroyed. Their solidity of construction, however, was never questioned; a wrecking ball was broken when the New York Courthouse and Post Office was being dismantled in 1939. Those few that have survived, including those in St. Paul, Minnesota, and St. Louis, Missouri, are now highly regarded local landmarks. Mullett did not slavishly copy prototypes but redefined them within the context of contemporary American public needs, functions, and aspirations.

Mullett's successor, W. A. Potter, was appointed in response to complaints from the profession that America's largest architectural office was covering the continent with repetitive, inferiorly designed federal buildings. Only thirty-three years old when he was appointed in 1875,

Potter was educated in chemistry at Union College before being apprenticed to his half-brother. Edward Tuckerman Potter was one of America's leading practitioners of the High Victorian Gothic style of architecture. John Ruskin's thinking is reflected in the fine craftsmanship, varied materials and textures, as well as the flexible planning of W. A. Potter's government buildings; a notable surviving example is his Evansville, Indiana, Custom House and Post Office.

So many federal buildings were designed between 1852 and 1878 that several were unfinished when each successive architect was appointed. Because their ideologies differed so greatly, Mullett altered Young's and Rogers's designs for those buildings still under construction, and Potter changed Mullett's. The resulting hybrids added to America's increasingly eclectic mix of historical architecture and contributed to the erosion of the notion of stereotypical government buildings. In concert with prevailing theories, eclectic late Victorian federal buildings were intended to avoid monotony, be expandable and flexible, and reflect architecturally the great strides made by nineteenth-century civilization. Most of the government architects of this period are little known today: James G. Hill (1839/1841–1913) served for eight years, but Mifflin E. Bell (1846–1904), James G. Windrim (1840–1919), Willoughby J. Edbrooke (1843–1896), Jeremiah O'Rourke (1833–1915), and William Martin Aiken (1855–1908) had tenures lasting from two to four years. Their federal buildings were by no means neither insignificant nor poorly designed, and they continued to have a positive impact in their communities. They were, however, both derivative and *retardataire*. Edbrooke's massive rock-faced limestone federal buildings, including the Old Post Office (1892–1899) on Pennsylvania Avenue in Washington, were ungainly renditions of Henry Hobson Richardson's famous Allegheny County Courthouse (1883–1888) in Pittsburgh, Pennsylvania.

The monopoly the supervising architect's office had over the design of government buildings began to be challenged by private architects in the late 1860s. Because of a controversy surrounding an aborted competition sanctioned by Congress in 1869 for the New York Courthouse

and Post Office and recurring scandals about faulty construction of government buildings, the American Institute of Architects (AIA) led a movement to open the design of government buildings to private architects. In 1893 former Supervising Architect Windrim helped the AIA draft the Tarnsey Act, legislation that called for open competitions for public buildings with the winner having ultimate responsibility for the proper construction of the design. The greatest of the thirty-one buildings done under the Tarnsey Act between 1897 and 1912 was Cass Gilbert's New York Custom House (1899–1907), now considered an examplar of Beaux-Arts classicism. By 1900 American architects routinely went to Paris to finish their educations. Skilled emigrant craftsmen, the availability of fine materials, the country's increased wealth, and firsthand knowledge of monumental European architecture all contributed to sophisticated interpretations of classical traditions.

James Knox Taylor, supervising architect from 1898 to 1912 and the first incumbent chosen by a civil service examination, was educated at what is now the Massachusetts Institute of Technology and for eight years was Gilbert's partner in St. Paul, Minnesota. Recognizing the enormous scope of work undertaken by the office, Taylor favored designs by private architects for large federal buildings in major cities. His staff of talented young draftsmen was responsible for dozens of small- and medium-sized post offices, compact, beautifully proportioned Beaux-Arts-inspired structures. Although Taylor approached each building as an individual problem and varied their exterior and interior details, most reflected his interest in Italian and French Renaissance pavilions. In Taylor's post offices the ideal of identifiable civic architecture was resurrected. After his resignation, the Public Buildings Act of 1913 enforced a policy of standardization, primarily to contain costs.

While government buildings were built in hundreds of towns and cities during the last half of the nineteenth century, the greatest concentration was erected in Washington. Between 1855 and 1869 wings were added to the Treasury Building to form a square figure eight following a suggestion by Thomas U. Walter. This shape maximized the ground area while allowing for light and air courts on the interior of an apparently solid structure. This form was common for Washington office buildings until the advent of modern climate control. The three architects who carried out the Treasury Building's extensions conformed generally to Walter's scheme of central and corner porticoes. Each, however, left his distinctive stamp on the interiors, where cast iron was used extensively for both structure and decoration. There, Native American symbols were revived, including a new American capital and gas lighting fixtures depicting Native Americans, buffalo, and rattlesnakes.

Mullett's State, War and Navy Building (1871–1888; now the Old Executive Office Building) displaces the same ground area as the Treasury Building. It is considered his masterpiece and one of the nation's outstanding French Second Empire buildings. Little about its exterior proclaims that it is a government building; three libraries designed specifically to serve the original departments, however, represented allegorically their functions. The State, War and Navy Building was widely criticized for its lavishness: why should government employees be accommodated in a palace?

Army engineer Montgomery Meigs designed a less expensive solution for a large government office building with his design for the Pension Building (1882–1887). He had two other major interests, devising a natural air conditioning system and glorifying the victorious Union Army, of which he had been quartermaster general during the Civil War. A huge rectangular courtyard served as a chimney to draw air introduced via outside vents through offices located around the building's twelve-hundred-foot perimeter. Meigs combined several Italian Renaissance models to create the Pension Building's historicizing form. His principal source for the exterior was the Roman Palazzo Farnese (1515–1534), to which he added a sculptural frieze that depicted the victorious Union Army returning home. The sole purpose of the Pension Building was to dispense government benefits to disabled Union veterans and their widows and orphans.

When John Smithmeyer (1832–1908) and Paul Pelz (1841–1918) won the competition in 1873 for the Library of Congress, they could not have anticipated that they would endure fifteen years of site and design changes only to be replaced by the twenty-three-year old son of the Army engineer in charge of construction. From the 1870s to the 1890s, Lieutenant Colonel Thomas Lincoln Casey (1831–1896) completed construction of the Washington Monument, the State, War and Navy Building, and the Library of Congress. The ever-present rivalry between architects and engineers on government building projects was particularly intense in Washington during the last half of the century. For the Library of Congress, Smithmeyer and Pelz responded directly to the call for a functional plan centered on an octagonal reading room. Books were to be organized according to the new Library of Congress classification system that divided knowledge into eight categories. The decorative scheme proposed by the architects revolved around two parallel themes, allegories of "Wisdom" and American cultural and scientific achievements with Benjamin Franklin taking pride of place. The architectural prototype finally settled on was the recent Paris Opera House (1861–1875), itself a compendium of French contributions to the performing arts.

The full realization—and expansion—of L'Enfant's 1791 plan for Washington was a twentieth-century phenomenon. The Senate Park Commission Plan of 1901–1902, chaired by Senator James McMillan (1838–1902) of Michigan, more than doubled the size of the Mall, transforming it from a naturalistic public garden designed by Andrew Jackson Downing (1815–1852) in 1851 to a monumental landscape park. A team of planners, architects, and landscape architects led by the Chicago-based architect Daniel Burnham (1846–1912) conceived and carried out Washington's new monumental core. Dominant and subordinate vistas connected the Capitol and White House to new memorial structures: Henry Bacon's Lincoln Memorial (1912–1922) is two and a quarter miles west of the Capitol and John Russell Pope's Jefferson Memorial (1939–1943) terminates the axis south of the White House. Considered two of America's greatest Beaux-Arts commemorative structures, the first was executed at the height of the movement, the second near its end. Both exploit their landscape settings, their architectural forms and details, large-scale statues, and the written word to explicate their meaning. The Lincoln Memorial went far beyond simply honoring the sixteenth president. The thirty-six exterior columns represent the states at the outbreak of the Civil War; forty-eight eagles and state seals that decorate the attic story stand for the states when the memorial was begun. The Roman Pantheon was chosen as the prototype for the memorial to Jefferson because he preferred it as the model for the U.S. Capitol. The Pantheon's basic function as the temple to all the gods may have influenced Jefferson's thinking when he sought an appropriate historical prototype for the temple dedicated to all the people.

The Federal Triangle (seven new executive department office buildings bounded by Pennsylvania and Constitution avenues and Sixth and Fifteenth streets, designed by several architects and erected between 1928 and 1938), Carrère and Hastings's Senate and House office buildings (1905–1908), and Hornblower and Marshall's Natural History Museum (1901–1911) were among several additional buildings mandated by the comprehensive 1902 plan. Burnham wanted to replace the red brick and sandstone Victorian buildings on the Mall with white marble ones, unified by color, a common cornice line, and a classical architectural heritage. The Beaux-Arts-inspired buildings erected on the Mall as a result of the Senate Park Commission were both publicly and privately sponsored. Museums donated by Charles L. Freer and Andrew Mellon (the National Gallery of Art) continued the tradition initiated by James Smithson. The Agriculture Department Building (Rankin, Kellogg, and Crane; 1903–1930) is now the Mall's sole remaining federal building that is neither museum nor monument. It, and the Smithsonian's Natural History Museum, were completed before the Mall was realigned to bring the Washington Monument to the center of its east-west axis, a major component of the Senate Park Commission Plan. Each was angled twenty-five feet to respond to this future condition. We now recognize that the immense scale and the iconographically potent and controlled organization of Washington's monu-

mental core reflects President Theodore Roosevelt's imperialistic aspirations.

The sheer number of twentieth-century federal buildings is staggering. Federal courthouses (and jails) are not confined to large cities, but were and are being built in county seats, of which there are more than thirty-one hundred. Many of America's 128,000-plus "named places" have more than one post office. Hundreds of thousands of public housing units, many designed by the country's brightest and most socially conscious architects, have been sponsored by numerous government agencies since the Federal Housing Adminstration was founded in 1934. The Army's Construction Division, under the Quartermaster Corps until 1941, when it was merged with the Corps of Engineers, was responsible for providing posts (miniature towns, in effect), veterans' hospitals, supply depots, cemeteries, chapels, and even monuments. The architects of many military structures responded to regional traditions, demonstrated by Spanish Revival buildings at Fort Wingate, New Mexico (1906). To insure against monotony, private architectural firms as prestigious as Cass Gilbert and McKim, Mead and White were hired to design buildings as diverse as Gilbert's Army Supply Base in Brooklyn, New York, and the Army War College (1903) at Fort McNair in Washington, one of many federal projects undertaken by McKim, Mead and White, the largest firm of the period. The American eagle and flag were ever-present icons, guardians as well as virtual address labels.

When the stock market collapsed in 1929, the federal government created jobs for thousands of Americans on federal works projects. New Deal architectural projects numbering in the several hundreds, principally for post offices and federal courthouses (but also for building typologies as diverse as national park facilities and airports), brought together architects and artists whose collaborative efforts created a distinctively American body of work. Murals recounting local and national historical events enlivened the interiors of buildings that combined classicism and modernism, the result often ponderous but always substantial. Government architects in the 1930s sought out their own history, honoring Robert

Mills as their professional ancestor by erecting a monument above his unmarked grave in Washington's Congressional Cemetery. From 1930 until 1946, the Association of Federal Architects, founded in 1927, published a journal, *The Federal Architect,* to defend the range and quality of their restrained classicizing works.

One example of the interaction of government agencies commissioning and making federal buildings is the Wright Brothers Memorial in Kitty Hawk, North Carolina. Two commissions were appointed; the second, the Kill Devil Hills Memorial Association, was successful in obtaining congressional sponsorship from Representative Lindsay Warren of Beaufort County, North Carolina. The War Department held the national design competition in 1927–1928; the Commission of Fine Arts, quartermaster general of the U.S. Army, and the secretaries of war and navy approved the premiated design by Robert Perry Rodgers (1895–1934) and Alfred Easton Poor (1893–1991). Construction of the memorial was overseen by the Army's Construction Division; in 1950, its stewardship was transferred to the National Park Service, part of the Department of the Interior. The Wright Brothers Memorial is a simple instance of the complex network of local constituents, congressional interests, and federal oversight necessary to build and maintain nearly every twentieth-century federal building project.

In 1910 Congress created the Commission of Fine Arts to regulate the development of Washington's public areas including buildings, artwork, and landscapes. The commission has a permanent staff and revolving members composed of architects, sculptors, artists, and historians who have successfully moderated Washington's development in the spirit of unity and continuity mandated by the 1902 plan. The Senate Park Commission and its monuments, as well as the finest of Washington's high visibility twentieth-century federal buildings—Bertram Grovesnor Goodhue's National Academy of Sciences (1924), Paul Cret's Federal Reserve Board Building (1937), Cass Gilbert's Supreme Court (1929–1935)—were commissioned from architects in private practice. The Office of the Supervising Architect and its successor, the Public Buildings Service (established in 1939), designed dozens of office buildings, many of them of a mundane character, to serve the government's basic needs. The difference in quality was sometimes a function of budget rather than talent.

Several excellent architects were repeatedly awarded government commissions. Generally their tastes were conservative, their business abilities finely honed, and their civic services extensive. Many served terms on the Commission of Fine Arts, arbitrating the designs of their colleagues. Cass Gilbert (1859–1934) was an arch-conservative politically (he corresponded with Mussolini) as well as architecturally. He based the dome of his Minnesota State Capitol (1896–1903) on that of the U.S. Capitol, the New York Custom House (his first important government commission) on the Paris Opera House, and the central "temple of justice" of the Supreme Court on the Parisian Madeleine Church. Although Gilbert manipulated each of his models to create something unique, he felt that the authority of history should resonate throughout important public buildings. All were exemplars of the French Beaux-Arts system; in 1901 Gilbert equated this hierarchical design method with good government: "Order and system, a high state of organization, are elemental conditions of government."

John Russell Pope (1874–1937), the designer of seventeen Washington buildings, belonged to the second generation of Beaux-Arts-educated architects. His aesthetic allegiance, however, was not primarily French, but rather the quiet repose of earlier classical traditions, including ancient Roman and Renaissance models. Pope combined a sense of grandiosity with refinement, paring down the classical language to essential geometries at the same time that he created monumental designs. He initially planned the Jefferson Memorial (1939–1943) to be one and a half times the size of the Lincoln Memorial. Small sculptural elements, such as eagles, were eschewed by Pope in favor of large allegorical sculptural works. Both entrances to his National Archives Building (1931–1935) are flanked by heroic figural groups representing abstractions: *Heritage, Guardianship, Future,* and *Past.* The pedimental groups relate to the building's function, both actual and abstract; that facing the Mall is entitled *Recorder of the Archives,* and *Destiny* overlooks Pennsylvania Avenue. Most Beaux-Arts-inspired federal buildings conveyed their specific purpose through some iconographical program, sculpted or painted.

Paul Cret (1876–1945), born and educated in Lyons, France, emigrated to the United States in 1903 to teach the Beaux-Arts system of design at the University of Pennsylvania. Cret led the profession out of the impasse of Beaux-Arts classicism versus European modernism, the former focused on formal, hierarchical, and rational planning, and the latter on ahistorical, pure geometric form, to create a hybrid called modern classicism, or stripped classicism, by the 1930s. In association with Albert Kelsey (1870–1950), Cret won in 1907 the competition for the Washington headquarters for the International Bureau of American Republics (subsequently the Pan American Union; now the Organization of American States) sponsored by the American government.

Cret's greatest work of architecture for the government was the Federal Reserve Board Building (1935–1937) on Constitution Avenue in Washington. Cret distinguished between the board's functional and metaphorical purposes, creating a central "temple" flanked by lower office wings, the whole an elegant and reserved fusion of modernist and traditional forms. Its quality was achieved through finely tuned proportional relationships and beautifully crafted materials; its national function announced by the ubiquitous eagles, but also by its stateliness. Cret began and ended his career with federal commissions, his last work being the U.S. Naval Hospital (1945) in Beaufort, South Carolina. Whatever their functional purposes, Cret brought to his buildings an integrity of purpose that transcends any stylistic considerations. His Central Heating Plant (1931) in Washington was as admired as his Federal Reserve Board Building (1932) in Philadelphia. The final issue of *The Federal Architect* was dedicated to Cret.

During the same period that these stellar American architects were designing showcase federal buildings, the Office of the Supervising Architect (after 1939 the Public Buildings Service) continued to turn out a great number of substantial, competently designed and well constructed federal buildings. They were primarily post offices that often replaced structures designed by their predecessors. Most Americans visit some national site, perhaps make a pilgrimage to Washington, and are awed by the great federal monuments, designed, in part, specifically to evoke such a response. Daily exposure to more mundane buildings erected at contained costs to serve everyday needs may also be an important architectural encounter. Government architects consciously strove to design buildings reflective of national ideals, but under considerable financial, political, and aesthetically conservative constraints. In 1937 Eliel Saarinen, the father of Eero and the Finnish-American architect-educator who founded Michigan's Cranbrook Academy, exhorted members of the Association of Federal Architects to remember that "architecture is not the expression of a person, or a year, but of a civilization."

America's presence abroad has three major architectural expressions: diplomatic enclaves, commemorative cemeteries and related monuments, and military installations. Until the Foreign Service Building Commission was established by Congress in 1926 to oversee a coherent program for the design of embassies and legations, the State Department either purchased or rented necessary buildings. However, embassies were the official residences of ambassadors, and the prestige of the United States depended on their architectural character. Initially many were designed by architects appointed by the Foreign Service Building Office as neo-Renaissance palaces similar to contemporary country estates or city mansions erected by wealthy Americans in many parts of the United States. Delano and Aldrich's American Embassy in Paris (1928–1932) was an appropriate example of this Beaux-Arts-inspired approach, both because of the embassy's historic location and the educational background of its architects, who had studied in Paris. The desire for an image that distinctively evoked "America" led Congressman Stephen G. Porter of the House Committee on Foreign Affairs to suggest that the White House be used as a model. White House replicas, or near-replicas, include

Jay Morgan's American Consulate (1932) in Yokohama, Japan, the American Legation (1938) in Monrovia, Liberia, designed by the Office of the Supervising Architect, the American Legation (1938) in Baghdad, Iraq, and the American Embassy in Chungking, China, the latter two by unknown architects.

In its first two decades of operation, the Foreign Service Building Office executed two-hundred projects in seventy-two countries. In 1954 an architectural advisory panel of private architects signaled a change. Stodgy, pedestrian buildings were no longer acceptable avatars to represent America around the world. Eero Saarinen (1910–1961), one of America's great twentieth-century architects, designed the chancelleries for Oslo, Norway (1955–1960), and London (1956–1959), the latter criticized by a British architectural journal for its aggressive monumentality. Ambassador Ellsworth Bunker, noting the resemblance between Edward Durrell Stone's (1902–1978) New Delhi Embassy (1962) and some of Stone's commercial buildings, feared that the modernist vocabulary would deprive government buildings of their important national and international symbolic meaning. The variety of architectural vocabularies exhibited in the several embassies built in the 1950s were attempts to respond to local climatic and historical conditions within the tenets of modernism. Currently the State Department's Foreign Buildings Operations objectives are to build embassies that "demonstrate respect for the architectural customs and traditions of the host country," according to Kevin Spence, who has overseen three-hundred projects designed by a number of American firms.

The American Battle Monuments Commission, created by Congress in 1923, erected eight military cemeteries and chapels and nineteen monuments on the European battlefields where the American Expeditionary Forces fought between 1917 and 1919. From Cret's Aisne-Marne Monument (1926–1930), a modern interpretation of a Greek theater set atop a hill overlooking the town of Chateau-Thierry, France, to Arthur Loomis Harmon's (1878–1958) modest truncated obelisk (1927–1932) at Cantigny, France, stylized Great Seal eagles identified these classicizing

monuments as American. To avoid any confusion with European imperial eagles, the stars and stripes of the American flag also were often part of the sculptural program.

Fourteen cemeteries and monuments on foreign soil were erected after the Second World War. Although some government architects by the 1950s were excited by the new expressive possibilities of modernism, many Washington officials, including congressmen appropriating the funds, viewed modern architecture as un-American. Consequently, the American monuments at the Normandy and Nettuno military cemeteries, for example, carried on the New Deal traditions of modern classicism. Sculptural programs integral to the World War II monuments also were allied to America's sculptural and mural traditions of the 1930s and 1940s. Dean Cornwall's panels decorating the sides of the Ardennes Military Cemetery monument are naturalistic depictions of American military forces and their equipment, ranging from battleships to tanks, in action. The underlying messages were America's technological supremacy and its position of power on the international scene.

In 1962 a presidential committee recommended that the government abandon its official architectural style, a rather heavy-handed interpretation of stripped classicism. Few federal buildings of the mid-century era are much more than pedestrian in quality, even those designed by such renowned architects as Marcel Breuer (1902–1981), whose headquarters of the Departments of Housing and Urban Development (1963–1968) and Health, Education, and Welfare (1976) in Washington emulated Le Corbusier's ideal of a universally applicable reinforced-concrete architecture. By mid-century, complex "federal centers" that housed a wide variety of government offices were erected in medium-sized and large cities. The most architecturally distinguished of these was built in Chicago in 1973. It was designed by Ludwig Mies van der Rohe (1886–1969), the German-born and -trained architect who brought Bauhaus modernism directly to America. The Chicago Federal Center's function cannot be distinguished from that of similar International Style office buildings, as, for example, Mies's Seagram Building (1958) in New

York. It and other federal buildings erected since 1963 are often identifiable in cityscapes by large pieces of public sculpture on entrance plazas. In 1963 the General Services Administration initiated its Art-in-Architecture program, setting aside one percent of total building costs for artworks to be displayed in public areas. Works of modern architecture considered great on a world scale that were sponsored by the federal government include Eero Saarinen's Gateway Arch (1963–1965) in St. Louis, Missouri, and his Dulles Airport (1958–1962) in Chantilly, Virginia. Both have survived into the era of postmodernism with their reputations intact because they are exciting, innovative architectural solutions that engage the mind and emotions while carrying out their functional purposes.

At the end of the twentieth century, the United States government is the largest patron of architecture in the history of the world. Largely through the efforts of Senator Daniel P. Moynihan, there has been a renaissance in federal design during the last quarter of the century. The realization that great civilizations historically produced great architecture has been a powerful stimulus to architects, who once again consider public commissions prestigious. Architectural analogies, once commonplace, that equated abstract qualities and durability of buildings with the vitality and validity of political and civic values have been revived during the postmodern period. In 1994, following the success of a pilot program begun in 1985, the General Services Administration (the umbrella agency of the Public Buildings Service) initiated a "Design Excellence" program aimed at once again involving the country's best architects in federal buildings. During the first decade of the twenty-first century, 156 new federal courthouses will be built from Albuquerque, New Mexico, to White Plains, New York, their architects chosen through a variety of innovative competitive processes. The Boston Federal Courthouse (1994–), designed by Henry N. Cobb of Pei Cobb Freed and Partners, is a vivid and thoughtful response to its city; contextually responsible attitudes and excellent architecture unite the varied courthouse designs already commissioned from America's best designers. New government office and research

campuses like the Environmental Protection Agency Research and Administration Building in Research Triangle Park, North Carolina, by Hellmuth Obata Kassabaum, also have put a premium on high-quality design.

Enlightened political leadership is fundamental to the production of quality civic architecture. In his effort to realize the construction of the Supreme Court, William Howard Taft queried: "If General Washington, at a time when his country was a little hemmed-in nation, boasting but a single seaboard, with a population of only five million, and with credit so bad that lot sales, lotteries, and borrowing upon the personal security of individuals had to be resorted to in order to finance the new capital, could look to the future and understand that it was his duty to build for the centuries to come and for a great nation, how much more should we do now?" For more than two centuries thoughtful architects of America's great and small national buildings have recognized their responsibility, and their power, to instill pride in and love of country in its citizens through their buildings.

[See also Architect of the Capitol, Office of the.]

BIBLIOGRAPHY

Brown, J. Carter, ed. *Federal Buildings in Context: The Role of Design Review.* Washington, D.C., 1995.

Caemmerer, H. Paul. *Washington. The National Capital.* Washington, D.C., 1932.

Craig, Lois, and the staff of the Federal Architecture Project. *The Federal Presence.* Cambridge, Mass., c. 1978.

"Federal Architecture: A New Era." *Architecture* 85 (1996).

Fryd, Vivien Green. *Art and Empire. The Politics of Ethnicity in the U.S. Capitol, 1815–1860.* New Haven, Conn., 1992.

Grossman, Elizabeth G. "Architecture for a Public Client: The Monuments and Chapels of the American Battle Monuments Commission." *Journal of the Society of Architectural Historians* 43 (1984): 119–143.

Guerney, George. *Sculpture and the Federal Triangle.* Washington, D.C., 1985.

Irish, Sharon. "Beaux-Arts Teamwork in an American Architectural Office: Cass Gilbert's Entry to the New York Custom House Competition." *New Mexico Studies in the Fine Arts* 7 (1982): 10–13.

Kohler, Sue A. *The Commission of Fine Arts. A Brief History, 1910–1990.* Washington, D.C., 1990.

Lee, Antoinette J. *Architects to the Nation: History of the*

Supervising Architect of the U.S. Treasury Department. Forthcoming.

Loeffler, Jane C. "The Architecture of Diplomacy: Heyday of the United States Embassy Building Program, 1954–1960." *Journal of the Society of Architectural Historians* 49 (1990): 251–278.

Longstreth, Richard, ed. *The Mall in Washington, 1791–1991.* Washington, D.C., 1991.

Lowry, Bates, ed. *The Architecture of Washington, D.C.* 2 vols. Washington, D.C., 1976–1979.

National Capital Planning Commission. *Worthy of the Nation.* Washington, D.C., 1977.

Reiff, Daniel D. *Washington Architecture, 1791–1861.* Washington, D.C., 1971.

Reps, John W. *Monumental Washington.* Princeton, N.J., 1967.

Reps, John W. *Washington on View: The Nation's Capital since 1790.* Chapel Hill, N.C., 1991.

Robin, Ron. *Enclaves of America: The Rhetoric of American Political Architecture Abroad.* Princeton, N.J., 1992.

Rouse, John E., Jr. *Urban Housing: Public and Private.* Detroit, 1989.

Scott, Pamela. *Temple of Liberty: Building the Capitol for a New Nation.* New York, 1995.

Scott, Pamela, and Antoinette J. Lee. *Buildings of the District of Columbia.* New York, 1993.

Seale, William. *The President's House.* 2 vols. Washington, D.C., 1986.

Short, C. W., and R. Stanley Brown. *Public Buildings: Architecture under the Public Works Administration, 1933–39.* Reprint. New York, 1986.

Thayer, R. H. *History, Organization and Functions of the Office of the Supervising Architect of the Treasury Department.* Washington, D.C., 1886.

—PAMELA SCOTT

Arms Control and Disarmament Agency

John F. Kennedy, while campaigning for the White House in 1960, observed that ". . . no problem is more vital or more urgent in the struggle for peace than the problem of effective arms control. Yet, in the past eight years, this problem has been virtually ignored, we have had no real disarmament policy. And we have completely failed to provide the effort and the leadership which the pursuit of disarmament demands." (Milwaukee, Wise, 23 October 1960). Eleven months later his new Democratic administration created the world's first independent, cabinet-level organization for arms control—the U.S. Arms Control and Disarmament Agency (ACDA).

This new agency, a direct result of Kennedy's political campaign promises, was established, however, only after a long and contentious process of public and congressional debate in the middle of the Cold War, shortly after the so-called "bomber gap" and "missile gap," and just preceding the Cuban missile crisis and Bay of Pigs incident.

After World War II, responsibility for arms control activity within the United States rested within the Department of State in the Office of United Nations Affairs, later to be called the Bureau of International Organization Affairs. The staff was small, often necessitating that studies and work be contracted among various other executive departments and nongovernmental organizations.

In 1955 President Dwight D. Eisenhower appointed Harold E. Stassen to be his special assistant for disarmament, with cabinet rank, and a White House staff to assist him. Two years later the Stassen unit was transferred to the Department of State and subsequently disbanded less than a year later in February 1958. Next, the position of special assistant to the secretary of state for atomic energy and disarmament was created, taking over the disarmament functions of the Bureau of International Organization Affairs. This remained the central focus for disarmament planning until 1960.

In September 1960, with several congressional bills pending to establish a disarmament agency, Eisenhower founded the U.S. Disarmament Administration with a staff of fifty-four within the Department of State. In addition, he established a special assistant to the president for scientific affairs, the President's Science Advisory Committee, and a Committee of Principals (consisting of cabinet officials in military, intelligence, and foreign affairs) to handle arms control matters.

President Kennedy first introduced his idea for an "Arms Control Research Institute" during his 1960 campaign in a Durham, New Hampshire, speech: "Here is a gap equally as serious as the missile gap [also a central theme of Kennedy's presidential campaign]—the gap between America's incredible inventiveness for destruction and our inadequate inventiveness for peace. We prepare for the battlefield, but not for the bargaining table" (*Disarmament Document Series,* 1 December 1960). He committed himself in his 1961 inaugural address to a policy of arms control and disarmament and six months later introduced to Congress a draft bill to establish a "U.S. Disarmament Agency for World Peace and Security" (*Congressional Record—House,* 29 June 1961). In September he addressed the United Nations, presenting a six-point "new Disarmament Program," and announced the creation of "a new now-statutory agency fully endorsed by the Congress to find an approach to disarmament" (*Disarmament Document Series,* 26 September 1961). On 26 September 1961, President Kennedy signed the bill mandating the new agency.

The Arms Control and Disarmament Act was widely supported by a broad coalition of Republicans and Democrats in Congress, partly owing to its active sponsorship by Kennedy's disarmament adviser, John J. McCloy, a highly respected Republican, and by several high-ranking military officers. However, the act and the agency were strongly opposed by a vocal minority who viewed the effort as a "sign of weakness, another sign of our willingness to surrender." It was feared by some that the agency could possibly "provoke war" and would therefore be dangerous during a time of mounting international tensions—the Berlin Wall was constructed in August 1961 and nuclear test ban talks had just broken down in Geneva. Other critics alleged that such an organization would "cause great confusion and misunderstanding among the peoples of the earth," would be a "masterpiece of bad timing," and would be a sign of "appeasement and weakness" on the part of the United States (Congressman John R. Pillion, R-N.Y., and Senators Richard B. Russell, D-Ga., Barry Goldwater, R-Ariz., and Karl E. Mundt, R-S.D.).

The act was passed in the end by a large majority on both sides of Capitol Hill but was avidly supported by very few and was amended several times to change its title, require high-level security clearances for employees, establish an outside advisory committee, limit its director's autonomy, and restrict its treaty-negotiating authority. Most telling in this early history of the agency was the lengthy debate over whether both terms, "arms control" and "disarmament," should be in its title and in what order. Senator Hubert Humphrey, an avid supporter, finally resolved the debate by arguing that the "baby should be named after both grandparents."

The broad purpose of the ACDA was set forth in the act's preamble: " . . . to provide impetus toward this goal by creating a new agency of peace to deal with the problem of reduction and control of armaments looking toward ultimate world disarmament" (Sec. 2, U.S.C. 2551; *Congressional Record—House,* 23 September 1961). The ACDA's more specific responsibilities were also laid out in the act in four parts:

- to conduct research for arms control and disarmament policy formulation

- to prepare for and manage U.S. participation in international negotiations

- to disseminate and coordinate public information

- to manage the verification of arms control and disarmament agreements.

For the past thirty-five years the ACDA has sought to fulfill these four major functions with mixed success. Expectations for the new agency were understandably high in 1961. The United States and the Soviet Union were on the brink of armed confrontation over Berlin, and strategic nuclear arsenals were undergoing a historic expansion to include intercontinental and submarine-launched ballistic missiles. Proponents hoped that the ACDA could help effect successful limits to the nuclear and conventional arms races and, in particular, help to carry forth a ban on nuclear testing. Critics were concerned, as noted earlier, that such a new agency would only confuse enemies and allies and possibly undermine a strong American foreign and military policy.

In spite of such mixed expectations, the ACDA became quickly involved in a number of relevant national security issues: strategic nuclear weapons, nuclear testing, nuclear proliferation, chemical and biological warfare, conventional arms sales, defense budgets, and many related topics. The Soviets and Americans had traded nuclear arms control proposals, primarily in speeches before the United Nations, throughout the 1950s; these included President Dwight Eisenhower's 1953 "Atoms for Peace" speech, the Soviet's 1955 resolutions for a ban on atomic and hydrogen weapons, and the U.S. suggestion in 1957, in response to Soviet intercontinental ballistic missile and Sputnik launches, to limit nuclear delivery systems.

By 1962 the ACDA began providing research and support for three major international arms control fora: in the United Nations under Ambassador Adlai Stevenson, in Geneva on nuclear test bans led by Ambassador Arthur Dean, and at the reconvened Eighteen-Nation Disarmament Committee (ENDC) in Geneva led by Ambassador Charles C. Stelle. Two of the ACDA's early studies were on "the general problem of verifying compliance" and on "measures dealing with levels of strategic weapons systems" (*Documents on Disarmament, 1962*).

One year later two major arms control agreements, in which the ACDA took active part, were signed by the United States and the Soviet Union: 1) the Hot-Line Agreement, upgrading communications between Washington and Moscow, largely a result of the Surprise-Attack Conference which had been unofficially recessed since the late 1950s; and 2) the Limited Test Ban Treaty, prohibiting nuclear testing in the atmosphere, underwater, and in outer space. These first two Cold War arms control agreements were impressive accomplishments for the new agency and encouraged follow-on efforts, especially concerning nuclear weapons. Defense Secretary Robert S. McNamara, among others, publicly expressed skepticism over the burgeoning nuclear arms race; he commented before the Senate Foreign Relations Committee that "I cannot allege that the vast increase in our nuclear forces, accompanied as it was by large increases in Soviet nuclear stockpiles, has produced a comparable enhancement in our security." Indeed, a Pentagon study at the time advocated bilateral and equal ceilings of five-hundred on strategic nuclear delivery vehicles, far below the Soviet and American strategic arsenals, which would each eventually surpass fourteen thousand warheads and bombs.

The ACDA's first opportunity for direct participation, rather than backstopping the State Department, in arms control came in 1964 when it

drafted President Lyndon B. Johnson's speech, one of his first as president, before the ENDC talks in Geneva. Written primarily by ACDA deputy director Adrian Fisher, the speech focused on a "freeze" of nuclear weapons. Ten days later ACDA director William Foster fully delineated the freeze proposal in Geneva (which ironically failed in 1964 but took public hold in the United States two decades later).

Since its early years, the ACDA has played at times a central role, at other times a support role, in several dozen formal and hundreds of informal arms control and disarmament talks, both bilateral and multilateral. ACDA directors Gerard Smith and Paul Warnke, rather than State Department ambassadors, led the two sets of Strategic Arms Limitation Talks (SALT) for over a decade (1969–1979). The agency has also played a key role in the follow-on Strategic Arms Reduction Talks (START), initiated in 1985, which have produced two treaties; in current Comprehensive Test Ban talks, likely to culminate in a 1996 treaty; in twelve years of talks that produced the 1993 Chemical Weapons Convention, signed by over 150 nations; and in the ongoing Standing Consultative Commission and the Joint Compliance and Inspection Commission (JCIC) established by SALT and START agreements.

The ACDA, with an initial staff of 126, was small when first founded in 1961 and has remained so over its thirty-five-year history. Its budget averaged under $10 million annually for the first decade and is now under $50 million; its staff has seldom surpassed 250 employees, although its responsibilities for ongoing arms control negotiations have grown steadily since the 1960s. About twenty-five percent of its staff has annually come on loan from the State and Defense Departments, partly in recognition of the fact that it must coordinate its work closely as an independent agency with both cabinet-level departments.

The agency produces a number of annual studies and reports; for example, its *World Military Expenditures and Arms Trade* report is widely read and used by foreign affairs specialists. This study is a combination of two prior annual reports—*World Military Expenditures* and *World Arms Trade*. Earlier reports, such as its *Arms Control and Disarmament: A Quarterly Bibliography* and the annual *Documents on Disarmament* have been widely used by scholars. Much of its work also involves classified background and planning memoranda for ongoing negotiations and verification efforts.

The ACDA is also very active in advocating for ratification of arms control agreements before the U.S. Senate. The current ACDA director, John Holum, along with other colleagues, has testified most recently on behalf of ratification of the START II agreement and the Chemical Weapons Convention. Such public advocacy, however much of the original intent of the ACDA's creators, brings the agency directly into the political crossfire on Capitol Hill.

Foreign, defense, and arms control policies have always been controversial—for both international and domestic reasons—in American politics. The ACDA therefore finds its annual funding at times threatened by opponents. In 1974, for example, congressional hearings addressed the ACDA's role in foreign affairs. In 1995 the new chairman of the Senate Foreign Relations Committee, Senator Jesse Helms, demanded that the administration dismantle the agency along with the U.S. Information Agency and the Agency for International Development. The political compromise was to agree to a sizable reduction in annual appropriations for foreign affairs agencies, including the State Department, which may force at least one of the agencies to close its doors during the 1990s.

With the support of the White House and National Security Council, historically shown to be critical to the ACDA's effectiveness, the agency continues to be very active in ongoing bilateral and multilateral arms control talks and programs. ACDA ambassador Stephen Ledogar, for example, represents the United States in Geneva negotiations on a nuclear test ban; ACDA ambassador Stanley Riveles leads Russian-American discussions on clarifying theater missile defense under the SALT I Anti-Ballistic Missile Treaty; and ACDA ambassador Steven Steiner heads the United States JCIC delegation in ongoing talks.

A number of other countries have since followed the American lead in creating an independent agency or specially dedicated department for arms control and disarmament issues. Although politically controversial, reflecting the nature of its role as an advocate and leader of arms control and disarmament, the ACDA remains in the eyes of many observers not only an effective policy player but also an important symbol of a historic American bipartisan commitment to more peaceful world politics.

BIBLIOGRAPHY

Clarke, Duncan L. "The Arms Control and Disarmament Agency: Effective?" *Foreign Service Journal* (December 1975): 12–14, 28–30.

Drew, Elizabeth. "An Argument Over Survival." *New Yorker,* 4 April 1977, 99–117.

Holum, John D. "The Administration's Arms Control Agenda: Gaining Ground Under Fire." *Arms Control Today* 26, no. 2 (March 1996): 3–6.

Humphrey, Hubert H. "Government Organization for Arms Control." In *Arms Control, Disarmament, and National Security,* edited by Donald G. Brennan, pp. 391–403. New York, 1961.

Isaacs, John. "Cold Warriors Target Arms Control." *Arms Control Today* 25, no. 7 (September 1995): 3–7.

Keeny, Spurgeon M., et al. "U.S. Arms Control Policy: Progress and Prospects." *Arms Control Today* 26, no. 2 (March 1996): 7–13.

Newhouse, John. *Cold Dawn: The Story of SALT.* New York, 1973.

Smith, Gerard C. *SALT: The First Strategic Arms Negotiation.* New York, 1978.

U.S. Arms Control and Disarmament Agency. *Annual Report of the U.S. Arms Control and Disarmament Agency.* Washington, D.C., annually.

U.S. Arms Control and Disarmament Agency. *Documents on Disarmament.* Washington, D.C., annually.

U.S. Arms Control and Disarmament Agency. *World Military Expenditures and Arms Transfer, 1993–1994.* Washington, D.C., 1995.

—PAUL F. WALKER

Army, Department of the

Much of the Department of the Army's history has been influenced by traditions and beliefs extending back to Britain and the American colonies. Distrust of a standing army and concern for strong civilian control over the military helped to shape its organization and its role in society. The early history of the department is largely a story of the struggle between the need for an effective army in the field and a dislike for centralized authority in the department headquarters. As the United States assumed a larger role in the world, the Department of the Army evolved to meet increasingly larger and more complex challenges.

Early in the American Revolution, on 14 June 1775, which is considered the traditional birthdate of the United States Army, the Second Continental Congress voted to raise its own troops. On the following day Congress appointed George Washington as commander in chief of the Colonial forces. Washington soon built strong bonds of trust with Congress by consistently deferring to civilian legislative authority. Within a short time, Congress realized that it must assume greater responsibility for organizing, administering, and supplying its military forces. Consequently, on 12 June 1776 Congress created a Board of War and Ordnance, the lineal ancestor of the Department of the Army. This body struggled to deal with the details of mobilizing and maintaining an army. Although the composition of the board changed over the next few years, its performance remained generally unsatisfactory both because of a lack of authority to obtain needed resources and because of the inadequacies of its members. On 7 February 1781 Congress created a War Department headed by a secretary at war and a small staff. Benjamin Lincoln was appointed the first secretary. The result was improved administrative efficiency, although the war ended before the full effects could be seen.

When the Constitutional Convention assembled in 1787, the nature of the national military establishment was one of the primary issues debated. The Constitution provided a system of checks and balances by stating that Congress would have the power to raise armies and make rules to govern and regulate them. The president would have executive power as the commander in chief of the army. On 7 August 1789 Congress created the War Department headed by a secretary of war. Henry Knox, the first secretary, who had handled military affairs under the previous government, merely continued with his duties, although now he was responsible to the president instead of Congress.

During the period 1789–1812, the Army averaged less than ten thousand men, requiring little in the way of centralized management. As the nation prepared for war in 1812, Congress moved to increase the size of the Army and improve its supply system. However, Congress specifically rejected a request to increase the size of the War Department's staff, which when war came proved to be too small to cope with a rapid mobilization. Moreover, the secretary of war, William Eustis, was a poor administrator, lacking the skills or strong character needed to deal with the situation. Supply conditions rapidly deteriorated, and orders to commanders in the field were incomplete, confusing, and poorly crafted, often resulting in defeat. Eustis was replaced as secretary by John Armstrong, who immediately instituted needed reforms such as expanding the War Department staff to include professional military officers with technical expertise in supply, personnel, and ordnance. Despite these changes, the overall efforts of the department were inadequate to the demands of war.

Following the War of 1812, Secretary of War John C. Calhoun effected additional changes to improve the War Department. He expanded, formalized, and made permanent the staff offices established by Secretary Armstrong. Calhoun's so-called bureau system provided management of the administrative and logistical needs of the Army into the mid-twentieth century. To fill the void of professional military expertise in Washington so noticeable in the War of 1812, Calhoun selected the senior general of the Army, Jacob Brown, and brought him to the capital to fill a position that eventually became known as the commanding general of the Army.

Although efficient management of the Army was undoubtedly enhanced, Calhoun's reforms introduced issues with which the War Department struggled for many years. In order to provide coherent and coordinated management for the Army in the field, the individual bureaus needed a strong, knowledgeable guiding hand. However, the commanding general was not to control the staff bureaus, and in fact it was unclear what his duties were or what relationship he had with the secretary of war. Capable secretaries of war were required in order to manage the bureaus and provide appropriate control and direction for the commanding general. Unfortunately, the War Department had held a low priority in previous presidential administrations, and talented secretaries seemed to be the exception, not the rule.

The value and the flaws of Calhoun's reforms were evident in the Mexican War. Although few preparations had been made for war, the bureaus performed reasonably well in mobilizing an army, moving it to Mexico, and keeping it supplied. The commanding general, Major General Winfield Scott, provided sound military advice to President James K. Polk and Secretary of War William L. Marcy. However, the overall direction of the war effort was fragmented within the War Department. Marcy was a weak administrator and was unable to control the bureau chiefs or to coordinate their activities. Polk distrusted Scott because of suspected political ambitions and frequently quarreled with him. Since there was no office responsible for mobilization and strategic planning, Scott performed these duties single-handedly. Polk took an active role by assuming many of Marcy's responsibilities, including bringing the bureau chiefs under more effective control, selecting field commanders, and preparing their orders based on options and recommendations provided by Scott. However, when Scott departed Washington to lead an army against Mexico City, the secretary of war and the president were left without professional military counsel. Fortunately, the war was brought to a speedy conclusion. Polk had exercised strong civilian control over the military during the war, and thus he established a precedent which would be followed by future presidents.

The situation in the War Department at the beginning of the Civil War was somewhat similar to that in the Mexican War. The bureaus remained strong and were staffed by men with extensive experience but resistant to change or attempts to control or coordinate their activities. The secretary of war, Simon Cameron, had been appointed to his position as a result of a campaign promise and not because of expertise or strength of character. General Scott attempted to perform the planning and coordinating role he had in the Mexican War. The problems, however, were of a much greater magnitude, and he was too old and infirm to provide the vigorous direction that was needed. President Abraham Lincoln lacked military expertise but believed strongly in fulfilling his responsibilities as a wartime commander in chief.

Because of initial Union setbacks and the demonstrated incapacity of Cameron to deal with the situation, Lincoln selected Edwin M. Stanton to be the new secretary of war in early 1862. Stanton was businesslike, energetic, and ruthless in bringing the staff bureaus under control. Supply operations and personnel mobilization were soon functioning efficiently, but the matter of overall strategic direction for the war remained unsettled. Both Lincoln and Stanton recognized that they did not have the military knowledge or experience needed to control military operations for all of the Union armies. For the next two years, they searched for a capable commanding general and a workable arrangement between the roles of the president as commander in chief, the secretary of war as the president's executive agent in controlling the Army, and the professional military expertise provided by the commanding general. Only with the emergence of Major General Ulysses S. Grant was an effective command arrangement put in place. Grant provided coherent and decisive strategic control for all of the Union field armies; an office in the War Department translated his directives into specific orders and provided the status of ongoing operations in the different theaters of war upon which he based his decisions. Stanton ensured that the armies were administratively and logistically supported, and Lincoln oversaw the entire effort. Despite its success, the temporary command arrangement, dependent as it was on personality and without basis in law, disappeared at the end of the war.

Although there were attempts following the Civil War to find a solution to the command problem, there was no permanent resolution. Moreover, the situation with the bureaus continued unchanged. Consequently, at the outbreak of the Spanish-American War, the War Department was unprepared to wage a war overseas, even against a weak opponent. Supply and transportation difficulties quickly emerged, as did the familiar problem of overall direction of the war effort. There was friction and bickering between the commanding general, Nelson A. Miles, and the secretary of war, Russell A. Alger, a weak administrator who was incapable of bringing order or guidance to the War Department bureaucracy.

The obvious inability of the War Department to operate effectively provided impetus for reform following the Spanish-American War. Elihu Root, who served as secretary of war from 1899 to 1904, quickly identified the need to end the uncertain division of authority between the secretary of war and the commanding general and to bring the bureau chiefs under tighter control. Root proposed abolishing the office of commanding general and creating a new position, chief of staff of the Army, who would advise the secretary of war as well as control the actions of the bureaus. Root also urged the creation of a general staff to prepare plans and coordinate their execution. Although Congress eventually passed the necessary legislation, Root's reforms merely provided a foundation for a more effective organization. The bureaus maintained their former roles almost unchanged because of army tradition and inertia, congressional restrictions on the activities of the general staff, and a general lack of interest in further change by most of the succeeding secretaries of war. Uncertain of their proper functions and lacking strong direction from the president or secretary of war, the chiefs of staff and the general staff failed to achieve the positions Root had envisioned for them.

On the eve of the United States' entry into World War I, the bureau chiefs retained their independence from effective control by either the secretary of war or the chief of staff. Indeed, the National Defense Act of 1916 had specified that each of the bureaus was a statutory agency that could not be abolished or changed without congressional approval. Each bureau had its own budget and answered directly to Congress. The role of the chief of staff in this situation was uncertain. The general staff was an ineffective planning agency, consisting of only nineteen officers. Overall, the War Department was unprepared to deal with the massive challenge of mobilizing and supporting a large army overseas.

On 12 May 1917, soon after war was declared, Congress passed an act that increased the size of the general staff and provided that the chief of staff would have rank and precedence over all other officers in the Army, thus giving him control over the bureau chiefs. Initially Secretary of War Newton D. Baker did not make use of this authority and continued to deal directly with each of the bureaus. The chief of staff was limited to overseeing the general staff, which continued to have only a planning role. The lack of effective control over the War Department bureaus, particularly those dealing with supply, produced chaos. Within four months of the beginning of the war, there were over 150 purchasing organizations, each competing with one another for scarce supplies and with no overall control over priorities for procurement or transportation. By the winter of 1917–1918 an economic and logistical disaster was imminent. In these circumstances, Secretary Baker brought in General Peyton C. March to be the new chief of staff in March 1918. March immediately acted to establish firm control over the bureau chiefs. Thanks to his use of the general staff to control specific functions such as training and manpower mobilization, improvements in efficiency were soon apparent. In April 1918 March established the Purchase, Storage, and Traffic Division of the general staff to consolidate control of the supply function. Thus the general staff was transformed from a planning body into a directing staff to coordinate and oversee all activities.

Following World War I, Congress moved to reestablish the prewar situation in the War Department. The technical bureaus regained their independence subject to congressional supervision while the general staff became merely another bureau responsible for planning. Although theoretically the chief of staff still was charged with controlling the bureaus, his power was limited since the bureau chiefs had direct access to and received their budgets from Congress.

At the beginning of World War II Congress passed emergency legislation authorizing federal agencies to reorganize. The chief of staff, General George C. Marshall, faced circumstances far different from earlier experience. Military operations would be conducted on multiple fronts around the world, requiring close coordination among the Army and Navy and with allied military forces. Moreover, President Franklin D. Roosevelt was an active commander in chief and was not inclined to delegate broad authority to the secretary of war or commanders in the field over matters of strategy or national policy. It was obvious to Marshall that a reorganization of the War Department was required to handle effectively the multiple facets of global war.

Using the emergency legislation, in early 1942 Marshall reorganized the War Department staff by creating three field commands to deal with supply and services, training, and the Army Air Forces. Most of the bureaus were placed under the supply and services command. Most offices of the general staff were reduced in size and limited solely to planning and coordinating and were supervised by a deputy chief of staff. Thus Marshall was freed from administrative detail so that he could devote most of his time to advising the president and dealing with the larger questions of strategy, determination of priorities, and direction of worldwide operations of the armies in the field. To assist him in this effort, a new general staff office was created, the Operations Division, which functioned as the command headquarters for the field armies. The secretary of war, Henry L. Stimson, strongly supported Marshall while concentrating his own efforts on issues of manpower, scientific development, and civil affairs and dealing with the numerous civilian agencies concerned with the war on the home front.

Marshall's War Department reorganization effectively dealt with most of the vast and complex aspects of World War II. However, at the end of the war, most of the organization was dismantled. The Operations Division was dissolved and the supply and service field command was disbanded, thus allowing the bureaus to regain their prewar status. For the next few years, the War Department went through numerous internal changes in seeking to regain the effectiveness of Marshall's wartime organization.

In response to the increased global responsibilities of the United States as well as the growing cost and complexity of military operations, the National Defense Act of 1947 created a National Military Establishment, soon to become the Department of Defense, under a secretary of defense to provide general direction for the military services. The Joint Chiefs of Staff, consisting of the military heads of the individual services and a small professional military staff, would support the secretary of defense. As a result of the act, the War Department's name was changed to the Department of the Army, and the Army Air Forces became a separate Department of the Air Force.

Over the years the authority of the secretary of defense increased, producing a fundamental change in the role and functions of the Department of the Army. In 1949 the Department of the Army was changed from a separate executive department to a military department under the Department of Defense. At the same time, the authority of the secretary of defense was increased to enable him to more effectively coordinate such areas as financial management and research and development among the services. Also in 1949, a chairman was provided for the Joint Chiefs of Staff.

During the Korean War, the Joint Chiefs of Staff controlled military operations in the field, dispatching their directives through their executive agent, the chief of staff of the Army. A change in 1958 further refined the command relationship for field operations by directing that the secretary of defense, acting for the president and assisted by the Joint Chiefs of Staff, would control operations in the field without going through one of the military departments. As a result, the Department of the Army was restricted to providing administrative and logistical support for forces assigned to field commands controlled by the Department of Defense. During the Vietnam War, the forces in the field were under the firm authority of the secretary of defense, with the Army performing a support role. The Office of the Joint Chiefs of Staff was further strengthened by the Goldwater-Nichols Defense Reorganization Act of 1986, which made the chairman of the Joint Chiefs of Staff the primary military adviser to the president, eliminating the need to consult the other service chiefs or forward their dissenting views in giving advice to the president.

Along with substantial changes in the relationship between the Department of the Army, the Department of Defense, and military forces in the field, there were also major modifications in the internal administration of the Department of the Army. The increased importance of research and development, financial management, and common supply and services led to development of Department of Defense programs requiring conformity by the Department of the Army. The trend further accelerated with the changes directed by Secretary of Defense Robert S. McNamara. As a result, in 1962 two new field commands were created to supervise Army supply activities and to determine the organization and doctrine associated with new weapons and equipment. Recently this trend has continued with the Department of the Army constantly refining its organization to better support its forces in the field and the mission of the Department of Defense.

[*See also* Defense, Department of; Joint Chiefs of Staff; *and* Appendix: An Act to Establish . . . the Department of War.]

BIBLIOGRAPHY

Hewes, James E., Jr. *From Root to McNamara: Army Organization and Administration, 1900–1963.* Washington, D.C., 1975.
Millett, Allan R., and Peter Maslowski. *For the Common Defense: A Military History of the United States of America.* New York, 1984.
Shubert, Frank N., and Theresa L. Kraus, eds. *The Whirlwind War: The United States Army in Operations* Desert Shield *and* Desert Storm. Washington, D.C., 1995.
U.S. Army Center of Military History. *American Military History.* Washington, D.C., 1989.
Weigley, Russell F. *History of the United States Army.* New York, 1967.

—WILLIAM T. BOWERS

Army Corps of Engineers

The U.S. Army Corps of Engineers Civil Works Directorate (hereafter, the Corps) is a unique and somewhat odd entity among federal government agencies. Although located in the military complex, it has played a significant role in the design, construction, and maintenance of civilian public infrastructure. In a governmental system that re-

wards incrementalism and short-term responsiveness, the Corps's primary mission and professional norms demand rationality and long-term commitments. And in an agency populated by professionals who regard politics as unprofessional, success has historically depended on the cultivation of political connections and the honing of political skills.

The uniqueness and methods of the Corps make greater sense in historical perspective. To better understand the agency, two closely related factors must be highlighted: the military roots of the engineering profession and the importance of the role of French military advisers in establishing the Army Corps of Engineers.

The modern professional of civil engineering was born and nurtured in the military. The very term *engineers* comes from the French term applied to combat technicians who designed and maintained the "engines" of siege—whether defensive fortifications to withstand attack or the roads and various implements of war that sustained an offensive campaign. It is not surprising that the "science" of engineering would be nurtured in a country like France, where fortifications and sieges formed the stage upon which wars were fought. As the historian Todd Shallat notes, this stands in sharp contrast to modern British military history, where sieges were relatively rare after the consolidation of royal control and the high seas formed the principal stage for action. It was in France that the science and profession of engineering would be cultivated.

French soil also proved to be fertile ground for the adaptation of military engineering to civil works. From at least the seventeenth century onward, France was focused on the challenges to both political centralization and economic expansion posed by its interior landscape. Britain, in contrast, faced the challenge of the open seas. Thus, while England became the center for technical advances in marine instrumentation, mapping, and naval architecture, France nurtured the civilian capacities of its military engineer corps and its capacity to plan and build roads, canals, and other projects that became part of its vast public infrastructure. Among the British, those who would perform the tasks of "engineers" emerged from the ranks of craftsmen—carpenters, masons, millwrights—who developed and honed their skills on the job, learning from trial and error as they went from project to project. Their approach would be neither scientific nor professional, but pragmatic and infused with the craftsman's pride of problem solving.

The story of the birth of the Corps is rooted in the distinction between those contrasting traditions represented by France and Britain. The military knowledge and skills of the rebelling colonists were steeped in the British tradition for obvious reasons. This posed a problem for General George Washington almost from the outset. Facing the challenge of defending Boston against a superior British force in 1776, Washington had to rely on a congressionally appointed artillery officer, sixty-five-year-old Colonel Richard Gridley, to help establish fortifications to meet the challenge. While Gridley served as the army's first engineer, it was Lieutenant Colonel Rufus Putnam, a millwright by trade, who eventually assumed the role of chief military engineer for the U.S. forces as the war moved to New York. Putnam had established his credentials with Washington by constructing a defensive position at Boston's Dorchester Heights that led the British to change their minds about launching an attack on that position. Putnam later acknowledged that he owed his success at that site to a passage in an English translation of a French military field manual that he had found among Washington's possessions.

That episode, along with the international reputation already established by the French engineers, led the Continental Congress to request that its key ally, Louis XVI, consider sending engineers among the group of officers France had promised to provide in support of the revolutionary effort. Sixteen French engineer officers would serve between 1777 and 1781, most of them trained at Mézières, the school for military engineers. The influence of these officers on both the American war effort and the military's view of the engineering corps would prove significant. Especially important was the role played by Louis Lebébue Duportail, who became the engineering commander of Washington's forces in 1777. Much credit is given to Duportail for the

eventual success of the revolutionary forces, especially in designing the siege of Cornwallis at Yorktown that ended the war. Duportail left the United States in 1783, and would play an equally impressive role in the French military during its period of revolutionary turmoil. The American revolutionary army's engineer corps disbanded in 1784, when most of the French officers returned to Europe. Nevertheless, Duportail's influence (and that of other French officers) continued, and their reports on the needs of the new U.S. military proved critical in eventually convincing Washington and the U.S. Congress to establish a military component that included engineers—the Corps of Artillerists and Engineers, which was formally commissioned in 1794.

In 1802 President Jefferson created a distinct Army Corps of Engineers and offered the chief engineer's position (as well as the rank of colonel) to a civilian and fellow savant of the period, Jonathan Williams. Included in William's charge was the task of establishing a military school of engineering (after the French model) at West Point. For Jefferson and others this was the first step in the creation of a national university that would serve the civilian as well as military interests of the new nation.

Such desires notwithstanding, there followed an era reflecting a return to the less professionalized British view of civil engineering. Carpenters, masons, and other practical craftsmen became the builders of canals and other engineering projects as local and private endeavors filled the void left by the lack of a national civil works agenda. Some French engineers (including Duportail) returned to the United States in the face of revolutionary terror in France, but many joined the thriving private sector endeavors focused on the relatively simple job of building more canals. The only major public project of note, the design and construction of the new federal city on the Potomac River, was placed in the hands of a French engineer, Pierre Charles L'Enfant, who had served under Duportail during the American Revolution.

With one major exception, however, most of this was accomplished without the involvement of the few military engineering officers in the Corps of Artillerists and Engineers. The immediate reason for the establishment of that Corps in 1794 was the need for the newly established national government to deal with reinforcing coastal fortifications in light of perceived threats from Britain. With such military activities to occupy them, the small cadre of engineers in the Corps did not get involved in civilian undertakings, even after the enhancement of their status in 1802. If anything, the military's view of the major civilian projects of the day was critical, reflecting the attitudes of the French-trained engineers who dominated the Corps and the curriculum at West Point. They regarded the unscientific and unplanned nature of most canal and road building as a tragedy in the making. Such attitudes did not facilitate cooperation between the Corps and other entities when the opportunities arose, nor was it helpful that Americans were becoming increasingly tired of what they regarded as French cultural snobbishness. The first decades of the nineteenth century, in short, were not conducive to an extension of the Corps's functions into the civilian arena.

The major exception was in the federal city itself. While the city had been designed and its public buildings constructed without significant assistance from military engineers, the vulnerability of the capital in the War of 1812 and the lack of any decent public infrastructure (e.g., roadways and drainage) led President Madison to ask for their involvement. With headquarters in Brooklyn, New York, the Corps at first limited its work in the District of Columbia to enhancing the fortifications in and around the city. Ordered by President Monroe to move its offices to Washington in 1817, the chief engineer, Colonel Joseph G. Swift, soon had the Corps involved in a number of civic improvement projects to make the federal city more livable and commercially viable. Civilian endeavors among the Corps's builders, however, were limited primarily to the District of Columbia.

The other major point of involvement for the Corps of Engineers during this period resulted from the role that several of its officers played on the U.S. Board of Engineers for Internal Improvement. Established in 1824 at the urging of President John Quincy Adams (a strong advocate of the national government's positive role in eco-

nomic and scientific matters), the board provided a base for influencing some of the major projects being developed at the time. While anti-Corps sentiment prevented the Corps from directly undertaking many civil works projects on its own, many Corps personnel were sent to "study" or assist those who were in charge.

During this period, historically relevant events were unfolding for another group of military engineers, that is, the topographical engineers, or "topogs." Topographers and surveyors had occupied a distinct section of Washington's revolutionary army, although they often worked closely with Duportail's construction engineers. Disbanded after the war, the topogs sometimes found positions with boundary commissions, lighthouse districts, and other government entities. A "Topographical Section" reemerged in the War Department in 1813, with the role of assisting the military in its growing role of exploring and opening the West. Section members were soon assigned to Army units, and the Washington office of the section received separate bureau status in 1816 and was given the task of collecting and storing maps and reports generated by topogs and others in the field. In 1818, the six-member bureau was placed in the War Department's Engineer Department.

Passage of the General Survey Act of 1824 generated increased demand for the services of topogs and an opportunity for the bureau to expand. The head of the bureau at the time, Major Isaac Roberdeau, adapted the agency to the changes, but it was his successor (in 1829), Colonel John J. Abert, who took the bureau on a more active course. By 1831 he had obtained departmental status for the topogs under the secretary of war's office, and in 1838 the unit became the Corps of Topographical Engineers. With thirty-six officers, most of them graduates of West Point and thus steeped in the scientific view of engineering, the new Topographical Corps now had independence from the priorities of the fortification-minded Corps of Engineers to pursue its role of meeting growing civilian demands for more explorations and surveys of the trans-Mississippi West.

For the next twenty-three years, the Topographical Corps would launch numerous expeditions that not only fed the growing American thirst for knowledge of the West but also served the political agendas of individual members of a Congress who sponsored and supported these efforts on an *ad hoc* basis. Until the 1850s there was no national policy on western exploration, and thus Abert and his topogs honed the political skills needed to sustain the agency. When a national policy did develop in the 1850s, however, Abert's political nemesis, then–Secretary of War Jefferson Davis, created a separate office to oversee the new policy.

The Civil War radically altered War Department priorities and led to the merger of the Topographical Corps into the Corps of Engineers. During the postwar period, demand for topog services had been significantly changed. The settlement of the West was now progressing, and from the perspective of the War Department the civilian needs were more for military protection than for exploration and surveying. In addition, many West Point graduates and Corps veterans returned to civilian life and helped establish a nonmilitary cadre of professional engineers through curricula at Yale, Harvard, Rensselaer, and Dartmouth. The Corps of Engineers itself took advantage of these developments, for when it mounted major surveying expeditions after the Civil War it did so by funding civilian-led parties. Civilian agencies emerged as major competitors for the Corps's topogs, particularly in the Department of the Interior. Political battles among the agencies and various scandals ultimately led Congress to establish the U.S. Geological Survey in 1879. [*See* Geological Survey.] Thus the Corps had once again had its civilian role reduced. Nevertheless, the legacy of the topogs would be an established tradition of Corps involvement in civilian projects on a national scale.

For the Army Corps of Engineers in general, the post–Civil War period proved to be both the best and worst of times. The devastation resulting from the war brought demands for civil works to repair all forms of public infrastructure. In 1866 the Corps had a budget of $3.4 million and an agenda of forty-nine projects and twenty-six surveys; by 1882 there were 371 projects and 135 surveys to conduct, and a budget of

$19.5 million. New levees, dredging, rebuilding bridges and rail lines, removing sunken vessels, and many other jobs were the obvious tasks at hand, but there was also considerable pressure for new projects to take advantage of the economic boom times. The Corps thus found its services in demand. The problem was that it was not authorized to increase its officer corps to a number sufficient to deal with the expanded demand. In fact, in 1872 the Corps actually had only ninety-seven officer engineers (not many of senior rank or with sufficient experience), a dozen fewer than it was authorized to have. The agency found itself relying on a growing cadre of civilian "assistants" (110 in 1872), many of them young and inexperienced. Stretched thin in the higher ranks, senior Corps officers were overseeing as many as twenty or more projects at any point in time. The inevitable result was that the Corps suffered from both poor management and a poor reputation.

The problems of the Corps during these boom years were compounding quickly. In 1866 it lost its control over West Point amid charges that the academy's graduates were of low quality and in light of growing intraservice rivalry. The wastefulness and mismanagement of Corps operations were the subject of many articles in the professional and popular political press of the time, and a growing list of fiascoes was being used by the agency's enemies to challenge its effort to develop a more comprehensive civil works program.

General Andrew A. Humphreys, a major theoretician in the field of hydraulics and the chief engineer of the Corps from 1866 to 1879, proved himself politically ineffective in dealing with key issues. Just as he lost the battle to maintain the primacy of the topogs in performing surveying functions for the nation, he and the Corps were made to look inept and foolish by entrepreneurial civilian engineers who opened up the lower Mississippi to navigation by implementing approaches that the agency (relying on Humphreys's theoretical writings) vehemently opposed. By the time Humphreys left, the Corps had reached a low point politically and a critical juncture in its historical development. The final blow to Humphreys and the Corps came a few days before the chief engineer's decision to retire in the form of congressional action to establish the Mississippi River Commission. The Corps would have three of the seven positions on the commission, including that of president. The leaders of the Corps argued that it alone was capable of making decisions about the river basin's flow, but to no avail. In fact, similar constraints were placed on its jurisdiction over other river basins where it had enjoyed growing discretion.

That particular juncture in 1879 was key to the future of the Corps, for in hindsight it is conceivable that agency leaders could have abandoned the Corps's role in civil works and focused its attention exclusively on its still-substantial military functions. But there were at least two major factors at work countering such a choice. First, despite well-publicized problems in the field and significant political defeats, the Corps remained engaged in many public works projects throughout the country. Second, and perhaps of greatest importance, the devoted professionals who comprised the agency's leadership were incapable of making such a choice. The legacy of both their professional roots and long-standing institutional commitments would have made a retreat from civil works extremely difficult. And yet the Corps of Engineers had to face the reality of an American political scene that was filled with powerful competitors and was inherently suspicious of the kinds of massive government planning efforts so central to the Corp's self-assumed mission.

During the 1880s, the Corps survived several congressional attempts to create a federal civilian public works agency that would take over its civil projects entirely. To placate some of the agency's critics, the civil works directorate was organized and five regional divisions were established in 1888 to make the Corps more responsive to local demands. The regions, in turn, would contain district offices at key localities. This organizational move would prove both permanent and critical for the future operations of the Corps. Officers and civilian staff would find that service to—and support from—local interests in their regions was a key ingredient to long-term success and stability for the agency. The decentralization

of the Corps may have saved it politically, but it also changed its culture fundamentally. The professionalism of its past now mixed with a commitment to being responsive to powerful interests within regional and district boundaries.

For the most part, the history of the Corps since the 1880s is a history of the individual regional and district divisions of the agency. A series of rivers and harbors acts in the 1890s and afterwards authorized specific projects that focused on navigation improvements and other tasks that favored commercial development in each locale. In the larger river basins where the Corps operated under the authority of commissions such as those set up in 1879, the agency's representatives were able to establish the Corps's primacy by working more closely with local interests.

In all these locales, the Corps's civil works management structure created a unique situation where political responsiveness was nurtured and constantly reinforced. Regional and district offices were formally headed by military officers who rotated through their assignments on a regular basis, at first serving in a district (initially as a deputy engineer, and eventually as a district engineer), then in a region, then at headquarters, and in other components of the Army as well. Trained in engineering (typically at West Point), they carried with them the professionalism and national perspective of the Corps. At the same time, their stints in district offices as young officers gave them greater appreciation of the need to be responsive to local interests.

At the same time, each office was staffed by a cadre of permanently assigned civilian engineers whose focus was primarily on local projects and needs. The military officers relied on these civilians to do the actual work assigned to the Civil Works Directorate in each locale, and their relationship with the top civilian manager (usually called the chief of the engineering division) was critical to the agency's success. The resulting dynamic has become the norm in the management of the Corps.

The general mission of the Corps has been dynamic as well, responding to changing conditions in the agency's environment. As a consequence of its work on navigation, the Corps naturally found itself involved in flood control as a secondary task. In 1917, after several disasters, the Corps was formally authorized by Congress to undertake flood control as a major component of its mission in the Mississippi and Sacramento river basins. Outside those areas, however, the Corps's work on flood control was strictly on an *ad hoc* basis, and generally the directorate did not seek that as a primary mission among its civil works. During the Great Depression, however, the pressure for creating more jobs through public works led the Corps to undertake flood control projects that it might have passed up earlier. Finally, in 1936, Congress passed a Flood Control Act that made such projects a "proper activity" of the federal government and gave the Corps authority for implementing that national responsibility.

Just as flood control emerged from the Corps's work on navigation, so two additional Corps missions emerged from its flood control efforts. The 1936 act contained provisions that made the damming of rivers the method of choice for flood control projects, and with dams came the opportunity to generate hydroelectric power. Thus, it was not surprising that amendments were made to the Flood Control Act in 1938 that extended the authority of the Corps by permitting it also to engage in the generation and sale of power at those dam sites. A related development was the growing role of the Corps in providing water for irrigation to farmers near the dam sites, thus enhancing the Corps' mission even further.

The regional offices reacted to these developments with lists of potential projects, and soon the construction and maintenance of three-hundred reservoirs were among the Corps's responsibilities. As the reservoirs came on line, still another function was added: the management of recreation and other public facilities created as a result of the construction of dams and reservoir lakes.

Thus, as the Corps entered into the business of damming rivers, it soon found itself in competition with a number of other federal agencies, from agencies dealing with soil conservation to those charged with managing national parks. But its greatest nemesis was the Department of the Interior's Bureau of Reclamation, which had been providing water and power to the arid western United States for decades. The two agencies worked around each other for years, but in the 1940s both found themselves making plans for similar projects in the high Sierra and in the Midwest. Representatives of the two agencies finally met and drew up an agreement that effectively divvied up responsibilities for water projects and allowed each to work without threat of constant political competition from the other. Although disagreement arose from time to time, both the Corps and the Bureau of Reclamation continued to flourish through the 1950s and 1960s. [*See* Reclamation, Bureau of.]

The organization of the Corps became even more decentralized as its fortunes improved after World War II. The original five regional divisions of the Civil Works Directorate expanded to eleven. In addition, thirty-seven district offices were opened in locales from New York to Honolulu and from Walla Walla to Jacksonville. By the mid-1970s the agency employed nearly thirty-five thousand workers in the civil works area alone, and an additional three hundred military officers were assigned to key positions at headquarters and top positions in the division and district locations. Its $2.5 billion budget at the time was to pay for nearly three hundred projects actively under way, with an equal number in "active backlog" status and six hundred more projects on the drawing boards. Large as those numbers were, they reflected a relative decrease in Corps expansion.

Twenty years later (fiscal year 1996), the budget had increased to $3.2 billion and the civilian work force had declined slightly (to just under thirty thousand—a figure reached in the middle 1980s), while the number of military officers assigned was reduced to 213. Although the backlog of projects had decreased, the number of active projects had gone up to 352. There were now many more completed projects to manage (e.g., 383 major lakes and reservoirs, 75 hydroelectric generation facilities, 463 recreation areas containing over 4,300 sites, etc.), but fewer "start-up" projects each year to deal with. Regulatory activities, environmental protection, and emergency response operations have been playing a greater role for the Corps.

Despite the relative stability achieved by the Corps in recent years, it remains one of the more controversial agencies in the federal government. Environmentalists have raised questions about the wisdom of the Corps's projects and methods, and critics inside and outside government protest the continuation of pork barrel politics and inefficient operations. While flooding and similar emergencies keep the engineers busy, current trends portend a shift toward a service agency that devotes more work hours to operating facilities instead of constructing them.

The history of the Army Corps of Engineers Civil Works Directorate is a case study in the complexities that characterized the emergence of an administrative state within a democratic context. In its current form, the Corps bears the formal and organizational scars that emerged from attempts to bring a rational, highly professional commitment to public good (at least as defined by the pre-1879 Corps leadership) into sync with the highly individualistic American political culture. Ironically, another Frenchman, Alexis de Tocqueville, foresaw the troubles facing any grand agenda for a national public works program in a democracy when he observed that "useful undertakings requiring continuous care and rigorous exactitude for success are often abandoned in the end, for . . . the people proceed by sudden impulse and momentary exertions." What the Corps has achieved through organizational decentralization and the honing of political skills can be regarded as a necessary adaptation to the realities of applying rationality in a democratic arena.

BIBLIOGRAPHY

Cowdrey, Albert E. *A City for the Nation: The Army Engineers and the Building of Washington, D.C., 1790–1967.* Washington, D.C., 1978.
Maass, Arthur. *Muddy Waters: The Army Engineers and the Nation's Waters.* Cambridge, Mass., 1951.
Mazmanian, Daniel, and Jeanne Nienaber. *Can Organizations Change? Environmental Protection, Citizen Participation, and the Corps of Engineers.* Washington, D.C., 1979.
McPhee, John. "Atchafalaya." In *The Control of Nature.* New York, 1989.
Reisner, Marc. *Cadillac Desert: The American West and Its Disappearing Water.* Rev. ed. New York, 1993.
Reuss, Martin. "Andrew A. Humphreys and the Development of Hydraulic Engineering: Politics and Technology in the Army Corps of Engineers, 1850–1950." *Technology and Culture* 26, no. 1 (January 1985).
Schubert, Frank N. *Vanguard of Expansion: Army Engineers in the Trans-Mississippi, 1819–1878.* Washington, D.C., n.d.
Shallat, Todd. *Structures in the Stream: Water, Science, and the Rise of the U.S. Army Corps of Engineers.* Austin, 1994.
—MELVIN DUBNICK

Atmospheric Research, National Center for

Located in Boulder, Colorado, the U.S. National Center for Atmospheric Research (NCAR, pronounced "en-car") is a federal government–sponsored laboratory that conducts scientific and technological research. The center was established under the guidance of Walter Orr Roberts in 1960 under the auspices of the National Science Foundation to complement and enhance university-based research in the atmospheric sciences and was originally named the National Institute for Atmospheric Research (NIAR, or *rain* spelled backwards). Since that time, NCAR has focused its efforts on addressing fundamental research in the atmospheric sciences and providing major computing, observational, and instrument facilities to the university community. In meeting these objectives NCAR seeks to contribute to a better understanding of climate and weather at local, regional, and global scales.

NCAR conducts and oversees research in the atmospheric sciences in a wide range of areas including large-scale atmospheric and ocean dynamics, atmospheric chemistry, solar physics, local- and regional-scale weather, and relationships between society and the atmosphere. The wide range of research seeks to address (in the words of the center's 1980 annual report) "questions that are important for science, for the nation, and for humanity; and on the production of knowledge that can lead to more informed policy and action concerning the atmosphere as an environment and a resource."

Some of the issues that NCAR research seeks to address include: global climate change and variability, aviation safety, prediction of severe storms, global impacts of the El Niño phenomenon, and societal vulnerability to weather and climate. NCAR also offers a number of facilities to the broader atmospheric science research community, including a state-of-the-art supercomputing center and data archives that are accessible to scientists around the world and an aviation facility that houses a research aviation fleet.

NCAR is managed for the National Science Foundation by a not-for-profit consortium of more than sixty universities called the University Corporation for Atmospheric Research. The consortium manages, in addition to NCAR, projects in the atmospheric sciences sponsored by the Departments of Commerce, Energy, Defense, the Environmental Protection Agency, the Federal Aviation Administration, and several private sources. For 1996 NCAR had an estimated budget of $97 million. Approximately $62 million of this total is funded by the U.S. National Science Foundation, with about sixty percent going to support facilities and forty percent supporting research. Extensive information about NCAR and its programs of research can be found on the World Wide Web at http://www.ucar.edu.

[See also National Science Foundation.]

BIBLIOGRAPHY

National Center for Atmospheric Research. *Annual Report, Fiscal Year 1980.* Boulder, Colo., 1981.
National Center for Atmospheric Research. *Strategic Plan, Fiscal Year 1991—Fiscal Year 1996* Boulder, Colo., 1990.
University Corporation for Atmospheric Research. *Preliminary Plans for a National Institute for Atmospheric Research.* Washington, D.C., 1959.

—ROGER A. PIELKE, JR.

B

Brownlow Committee

The Committee on Administrative Management—popularly known as the Brownlow Committee—was appointed by President Franklin D. Roosevelt to recommend the administrative infrastructure necessary for the chief executive to efficiently manage the modern welfare state that resulted from implementation of New Deal measures. Within the context of the spread of European fascism abroad and the development at home of modern social science—especially public administration—the president's committee represented the spirited response of a gifted political leader who was willing to consult academia to refute fascist claims that democracy was inadequate to meet the demands of the twentieth century. The committee's report was an imaginative elaboration on America's most original political office, the presidency. The committee used as its foundation political theory propounded by Alexander Hamilton in *The Federalist,* no. 70: "Energy in the Executive is a leading character in the definition of good government." From that theoretical basis, the committee determined that the proper response to the fascist allegations against democracy lay in strengthening the American presidency by bestowing upon the chief executive managerial power commensurate with presidential responsibility. The challenge for the Brownlow Committee was to strengthen the role of the chief executive within the democratic system of checks and balances prescribed by the Constitution. Initial attempts to implement the committee's recommendations failed in Congress; however, many of the legislative concerns were addressed subsequently in the Reorganization Act of 1939. More significantly, the Brownlow Committee's report clearly delineates the beginning of the modern presidency and a shift in power from the legislative to the executive branch of government. It serves also to mark the coming of age of public administration, an acknowledged contributor to effective government in a democratic society.

THE PROBLEM

In the two decades following the Civil War, Congress launched several initiatives to investigate governmental efficiency. Every president since Theodore Roosevelt had called for governmental reorganization. These efforts, however, brought little action. Congress tended to tinker too much with the details; cabinet secretaries jealously guarded against encroachment on their prerogatives. Conservatives fixated on reorganization efforts solely for economic reasons. Franklin Roosevelt had firsthand experience of the problems of modern administration both as an administrator, having served as secretary of the Navy under President Woodrow Wilson, and as an elected executive, having served as governor of New York. During his second term as governor, he enlisted the services of the newly created Institute of Public Administration to examine the issue of reorganization of local government and in February 1932 requested that the New York legislature appoint a committee of experts to make the revisions. Unlike the conservatives who sought change for economic reasons, Roosevelt believed the primary purpose of governmental reorganization was to improve management.

Ever the politician, Franklin Roosevelt as president dealt with issues of immediate concern to the public. While the New Deal was launched during his first term, he undertook little action after the passage of the Economy Act of 1933, which was designed to reorganize the federal government. By the end of this first term, however, he realized that the greatly expanded role of the federal government demanded greater presidential administrative latitude to assure its success.

THE RESPONSE

Creation of the Committee on Administrative Management is attributed to Harold Ickes, President Franklin Roosevelt, and Charles E. Merriam (1874–1953), the originator of the idea. Merriam soon recruited Louis Brownlow (1879–1963), and Luther H. Gulick III (1892–1993), who later was named by the president to the Committee on Administrative Management.

Besides being the originator of the idea that led to the Brownlow Committee, Charles Merriam is recognized as the father of the behavioral movement in political science and for his pioneering roles in the Social Science Research Council (1923), the American Political Science Association (1924), and the Public Administration Clearing House (1930). He exemplified the academic specialist in the emerging role of governmental consultant.

Born and reared in Iowa, Merriam received his LL.D. from Columbia University in 1900. He spent most of his professional career at the University of Chicago. Yet his interests extended beyond political theory into the realm of practical politics. He served as a Chicago alderman for six years and ran unsuccessfully for mayor in 1911. His commitment to the Progressive party led Robert La Follette to dub him "the Woodrow Wilson of the West." Herbert Hoover appointed him to the President's Research Committee on Social Trends in 1929.

Because of his service on the Social Science Research Council and the fact that he was a former progressive Republican, he was appointed by Harold Ickes to what eventually became known as the National Resource Planning Board, which attempted to utilize social science research in the development of public policy. Both Roosevelt and Ickes always referred to Merriam as "Uncle Charley," indicative of their reliance on him for advice.

In October 1935, in response to President Roosevelt's request and after the Public Works Administration approved $35,000 for the National Planning Board, Merriam prepared a memorandum on the need for a "plan for a plan," which ultimately resulted in the creation of the Brownlow Committee. The president needed authority commensurate with his responsibility in order to coordinate and manage the plethora of new governmental units created to implement New Deal legislation. Roosevelt wanted to integrate the new emergency agencies into the regular departments of the federal government. Merriam assigned the task for developing such a plan to the Public Administration Committee of the Social Science Research Council, chaired by his friend Louis Brownlow.

Like Merriam, Brownlow was a midwesterner. Born in Missouri, he shared with Franklin Roosevelt an interest in both journalism and the Democratic party. Brownlow was a prominent journalist for fifteen years before he was appointed by President Wilson as a commissioner of the District of Columbia (1915–1920). He subsequently served as a city manager in Petersburg, Virginia, and Knoxville, Tennessee. Backed by Rockefeller funding, he and Merriam cofounded the Public Administration Clearing House in Chicago to assist administrative organizations and provide for exchange of research findings among them. He served as its director for fifteen years (1930–1945). Brownlow declined an offer from the Roosevelt administration to serve as assistant secretary of commerce, but he served as an unofficial adviser to Harold Ickes and Harry Hopkins.

In February 1936, in response to Merriam's request, Brownlow drafted "Rough Notes on Kind of Study Needed," a précis limited to one page since Brownlow knew that Roosevelt, like Wilson, thought presidential memos should be restricted to a single page. The theme of the Brownlow memo carried over into the final thrust of the eventual report of the Brownlow Committee. Ever sensitive to congressional politics, Roosevelt made it clear that he did not want the Social Science Research Council involved in the study because it was supported by a Rockefeller Foundation grant. Brownlow met with Roosevelt in early March 1936 and agreed to chair the president's committee.

After careful review of several names suggested, Gulick eventually was named as the final person appointed to the Brownlow Committee. Educated in the Midwest, Gulick became a student of the Progressive historian Charles A. Beard at Columbia University. He succeeded Beard as the director of the Training School for Public Service of the New York Bureau of Municipal Research. After working with the Council of National Defense and the War Department during World War I, Gulick returned to Columbia University, where he received his doctorate in 1920; he then established the Institute of Public Administration, serving as its president for more than forty years. As a Republican he had helped to organize the Massachusetts budget system during Calvin Coolidge's governorship. He later deserted the Republican party. His works on public budgeting, personnel management, and governmental reorganization gained national exposure following his appointment by the Social Science Research Council to direct the Commission of Inquiry on Public Service Personnel (1933–1935).

Maneuvering to stay ahead of Congress, President Roosevelt on 22 March 1936 announced the formation of the committee, which would focus on improving the managerial role of the president rather than on governmental reorganization. Congress by that time already had established two separate committees to study reorganization, as the issue was traditionally viewed as a congressional initiative. Harry F. Byrd had appointed a Senate committee on the reorganization of the executive agencies. Brownlow and Gulick were among those Byrd asked to serve on the advisory committee; Brownlow was asked to serve as chairman. Roosevelt wanted Brownlow to chair his committee as well as the Senate and House committees. Both Brownlow and Gulick, who earlier had worked with Byrd when the latter was governor of Virginia, urged the senator to use the Brookings Institution to study the problems of reorganization, duplication, and overlapping of federal agencies.

Initially, Roosevelt supported Brownlow's chairmanship of the House advisory committee on reorganization, and over Brownlow's objection had offered for Brownlow to work in cooperation with the House committee. Brownlow had known Speaker of the House Joseph W. Byrns for

thirty-five years, but Byrns was unable to persuade Representative James P. Buchanan to appoint an advisory committee in cooperation with Brownlow. Buchanan, chairman of the House Appropriations Committee, was a conservative Democrat from Texas and preferred to abolish aspects of the federal government's New Deal.

The president's committee had a nine-month deadline to research and prepare its findings. To assist the three-man committee, Brownlow recruited Dr. Joseph P. Harris as the research director supervising a staff of twenty-five experts, more than half of whom held doctorates and more than two-thirds of whom held academic positions. Many of the staff later became well-known political scientists—for example, Robert E. Cushman (1889–1969), Merle Fainsod (1907–1972), Arthur N. Holcombe (1884–1977), and Arthur W. Macmahon (1890–1980). The committee established its offices in the Commercial National Bank Building, at Fourteenth and G streets, Washington, D.C., the same building that housed the National Emergency Council.

In June 1936 Congress passed legislation appropriating $100,000 for the president's committee. Representative Buchanan, House Appropriations Committee chairman, mandated that the funds be divided as follows: the Brookings Institution staff, which was working for the U.S. Senate, received $30,000; the House Committee, $20,000; the Brownlow Committee, $50,000.

THE REPORT

The completed report was timed for issuance after the November 1936 elections, so that its results would be presented to the winning presidential candidate. Strict secrecy was maintained by the committee and its large staff during research and preparation of the final report. Unlike the Senate (Brookings Institution) and House committee staffs, which used questionnaires, the Brownlow Committee staff relied primarily on interviews. By early November 1936, Brownlow had outlined the draft report, and by mid-November he and Gulick had presented it personally to President Roosevelt. Roosevelt liked the findings and requested a draft report by 17 December 1936.

The report proposed strengthening the American presidency in five ways:

- enlarging the president's staff
- expanding the merit system
- improving fiscal management
- creating a permanent planning agency
- adding two additional cabinet posts and placing every executive agency, including the regulatory commissions, under the major cabinet departments.

Overall, the theme of the report was to give the president managerial power commensurate with his role as the chief executive of the largest bureaucracy in the world.

The report developed the modern concept of the White House staff. Finding that the "the President needs help" because of the major expansion of presidential duties associated with the proliferation of governmental programs that grew out of the Great Depression, it called for six executive assistants charged with acting as additional pairs of hands to assist the president, not as assistant presidents or cabinet secretaries, but merely as executive assistants. Franklin Roosevelt pointedly rejected the post–World War I British model with a secretariat under a single person. He refused to limit himself to one person as his source of information. The president intended to serve as his own chief of staff. Brownlow had traveled to Europe in the summer of 1936 to interview Tom Jones, deputy to Sir Maurice Hankey, head of the British cabinet secretariat and a former secretary to three British prime ministers. Jones advised Brownlow that the staff pattern should fit the American presidential model rather than the British parliamentary system. His model administrator should have characteristics of Sir Maurice, an individual with competence, energy, and "a passion for anonymity." The latter was incorporated into the report and became perhaps its best-known phrase. Though the media caricatured these assistants as "passionate anonyms," the Brownlow Committee's first recommendation was the heart of the report. Not only should presidents be of good character, but first-rate citizens devoted to the democratic ideal should be entrusted to assist the president with his expanding responsibilities. Now was the time for the public administrator to come to the aid of his and her country against the threat of a totalitarian political system. Not surprisingly, Brownlow himself was the American prototype of such an individual. Neither an academician nor a politician, his life personified the evolving role of the public administrator in democratic government. The call for six additional assistants to the president would, over time, be transformed into the White House Office, signifying the institutionalization of the modern presidency.

In tandem with the first recommendation, the second dealt with the role of the Civil Service Commission and the issue of the merit system. The Civil Service Commission during Franklin Roosevelt's first term was inadequate to perform its assigned task. It was not selecting model candidates for governmental positions to be filled. The committee traced most of the problems to the boards and commissions that oversaw the selection process at the state and local levels. Gulick believed a competent personnel director was needed to assure that the civil service system functioned as intended.

The third recommendation dealt with the president's exercising fiscal management within the executive branch. The comptroller general, established in 1921 with a fifteen-year term appointment, was appointed to serve as the fiscal agent of the Congress, to prescribe the rules and regulations governing executive branch expenditures, and to audit governmental business. The committee recommended separating the control and audit functions of the comptroller general's office. Government fiscal policy needed to reflect modern accounting practices by relinquishing control of expenditures to the executive and providing Congress with a post-audit. The comptroller general in office had been assuming public policy power to frustrate implementation of New Deal legislation, giving added impetus to the committee recommendation. Eventually this recommendation led to creation of the Office of Management and Budget during the Nixon administration. [*See* Management and Budget, Office of; *and* Appendix: Budget and Accounting Act (1921).]

The fourth recommendation called for the creation of a National Resource Planning Board to use social science methodology to collect data. Long-range government planning had a crucial role to play in avoiding repetition of crises such as the Great Depression. This recommendation clearly reflected the values of the political scientists on both the committee and its staff.

The final recommendation dealt with expanding and reorganizing the administration to bring executive agencies and regulatory commissions under the jurisdiction of the major cabinet departments. Abraham Lincoln had supervised eleven executive agencies; the number in 1936 stood at sixty-three. Roosevelt did not have time to give attention to every department, agency, and commission. The committee feared that the overload on the president would ultimately undermine the office. Reflecting Roosevelt's view, the report labeled the independent commissions as a "headless fourth branch of government" lacking proper executive oversight and direction. The report also called for two new cabinet departments (Public Works and Welfare) and for extending presidential authority to transfer agencies. The Department of the Interior would be changed to the Department of Conservation. In short, the report called for a powerful presidency with qualified personnel, a planning staff, and fiscal power requisite to implementing and managing public policies.

THE REACTION

Brownlow took the page proofs of the report to Franklin Roosevelt on 1 January 1937. On 8 January, Roosevelt informed the cabinet about the report and briefed congressional leaders. In response to the president's request, Brownlow had already drafted a bill and recruited Gulick to draft the presidential message to accompany it. On 11 January, the president held a news conference about the report, which he transmitted to Congress the next day.

The Congress created a Joint Committee on Government Reorganization to consider the message and the report. Hearings began in mid-February 1937. Initial reaction to the report seemed favorable, helped in no small measure by the overwhelming Democratic majorities in each chamber of Congress. However, Roosevelt made

the fatal mistake, just as he did with the Supreme Court packing plan introduced that same February, of not consulting any members of Congress in advance for their suggestions, and of insisting on total secrecy while the Brownlow Committee prepared its findings. After the president announced the Supreme Court packing plan, attention was diverted to that issue, causing Congress to stall on implementation of the Brownlow Committee's report. Roosevelt turned responsibility for the Brownlow legislation over to his son, James, while he concentrated on the Supreme Court battle. On 31 May 1937, Brownlow had a heart attack, removing him from the legislative battle. Opponents now termed the Brownlow bill a call for executive dictatorship. The reorganization bill was finally defeated by a narrow margin in April 1938.

Thus a combination of factors caused defeat of the Brownlow recommendations in the short term; as in his battle with the Supreme Court, however, Roosevelt eventually got what he sought. The Reorganization Act of 1939 and subsequent reorganization legislation passed in future administrations enacted most of the bold vision that the Brownlow report outlined for the American presidency. Unfortunately, most of the original recommendations of the report have been completely distorted. For example, what was recommended to be a small increase in staff has mushroomed into a six-hundred-employee White House Office, and presidential assistants are noted for anything but their anonymity. Violating the spirit of the Brownlow Report, these excesses have created an environment that permitted Watergate and the Iran-*contra* affair. Yet the fact remains that the recommendations of the Brownlow Committee have been the most important contributions to the philosophy of a strong and responsible presidency since publication of the *Federalist Papers,* the benchmark of creative American political theory.

[*See also* White House Office *and* Appendix: Reorganization Act of 1939.]

BIBLIOGRAPHY

Brownlow, Louis. *A Passion for Anonymity: The Autobiography of Louis Brownlow.* Chicago, 1958.
Hart, John. *The Presidential Branch.* Elmsford, N.Y., 1987.

Karl, Barry D. *Executive Reorganization and Reform in the New Deal.* Cambridge, Mass., 1963.

Pederson, William D., and Stephen N. Williams. "The President and the White House Staff." In *Dimensions of the Modern Presidency,* edited by Edward N. Kearney, pp. 139–156. Saint Louis, 1982.

Pfiffner, James P., ed. *The Managerial Presidency.* Belmont, Calif., 1991.

Polenberg, Richard. *Reorganizing Roosevelt's Government: The Controversy over Executive Reorganization, 1936–1939.* Cambridge, Mass., 1966.

Report of the President's Committee on Administrative Management. Washington, D.C., 1937.

—WILLIAM D. PEDERSON

Budget Process

ESSAY At first the federal budget process was a relatively simple system that did not directly affect many people's lives. Political pressures on the system were initially modest, for the national government played a small role in domestic policy making, and the United States played a comparatively small role in the international arena as well. Budgetary decisions, as a result, were initially quite simple.

In the beginning, when federal agencies needed money, they submitted requests to the Treasury Department, which compiled the requests and submitted them to Congress. Agencies and Congress freely exchanged information regarding agency needs, and the president was usually not involved in budgeting decisions—although there were significant exceptions.

Within Congress, a division of labor gradually emerged. One facet of budgetary decisions involved authorizing agencies to exist and to operate programs. This facet did not usually provide funding for operations but did sometimes place limits on spending for particular programs. A second facet involved appropriating money for agencies and programs that had been authorized, and a third facet involved raising revenues to fund programs. As the congressional committee system developed, one set of committees began to handle authorization decisions; a single committee in each house of Congress handled both the appropriations decisions and revenue decisions. Congress also experimented with a single appropriations bill funding all programs but

changed to using several appropriations bills by the 1820s and 1830s.

As the federal government and federal budget grew, the workload produced by the appropriations and revenue bills also grew. At the same time, some members of Congress felt resentful of the power wielded by the single committee in each house that handled both appropriations and revenue bills. People who were concerned by the rising cost of government began to believe that separating the revenue and appropriations decisions might produce closer scrutiny of government spending. As a result, Congress created the appropriations committees in the 1860s. That decision helped to spread the workload more evenly, gave more members a chance to participate in important decisions, and weakened the linkage of revenue decisions and spending decisions, at least as far as the committee system was concerned.

The appropriations committees tried to limit spending on many programs, an effort that angered many members of the authorization committees. Their power to authorize programs would mean little if the programs were denied adequate funding. In a series of decisions in the 1870s and 1880s, Congress gave responsibility for some appropriations bills to authorization committees, which proved to be more generous in funding their own programs. The appropriations committees, faced with extinction if that process continued, became less restrictive in funding programs. The result was a seemingly haphazard system, with some appropriations bills being handled by the appropriations committees and other appropriations bills being handled by the authorization committees.

By the early years of the twentieth century, pressures to change the budget process were building again. The growth of federal spending, frequent budget deficits, and the prolonged battle over the federal income tax led to complaints that the budget process was no longer adequate. Reformers believed that involving the president in the budget process would help overcome congressional parochialism, improve coordination of various budget-related decisions, offset the power of interest groups and party bosses, and, consequently, curb wasteful spending.

The proposal to give the president a major

role in budgeting troubled many members of Congress, who regarded presidential involvement as a threat to Congress's power of the purse. The pressures for reform were quite powerful, however, and the result was the Budget and Accounting Act of 1921. The law required the president to submit a budget proposal to Congress each year. It also created the Bureau of the Budget, initially housed in the Treasury Department, to assist the president in formulating the budget proposal. Agencies were required to submit their budget requests to the Bureau of the Budget, which attempted to bring those requests into line with the president's budget priorities. [*See* Appendix: Budget and Accounting Act (1921).] In a series of decisions from 1919 through 1921, Congress also returned control of most appropriations bills to the appropriations committees; members hoped that change would strengthen fiscal discipline and coordination.

The president's role in the budgetary process was (and is) vulnerable to being undercut by agencies going directly to Congress. In the 1920s the Bureau of the Budget tried to cope with that threat by instituting *central clearance,* which required agency proposals and agency testimony with budgetary implications to be reviewed by the Bureau of the Budget. Only proposals consistent with the president's budgetary policies could be presented to Congress. Agency testimony would be accompanied by a statement from the Bureau of the Budget regarding whether the agency's position was consistent with the president's budgetary policies. Official agency communications with Congress, then, became subject to review and regulation to reduce the risk that agencies would try to seek funding beyond what the president had approved. Unofficial communications are much more difficult to control.

The system established in 1921, with comparatively minor modifications, lasted for more than fifty years. Presidents, along with the Bureau of the Budget (renamed the Office of Management and Budget in 1970) and other advisers, tried to monitor the performance of the economy and focus on large-scale budgetary issues, such as total revenues and expenditures. Beginning in the 1930s and 1940s, presidents also began to emphasize using the budget to help manage the economy, though controversies abounded regarding how that could best be done.

From 1921 through 1973, Congress generally dealt with the budget as a considerable number of decisions that were only somewhat related to one another. The president's budget proposal was normally divided into several separate bills. Total spending levels emerged from a series of decisions about spending for various programs rather than from an explicit congressional decision about the ideal level of total spending.

Frictions between the authorization committees and the appropriations committees, along with broader concerns about safeguarding the flow of funding to some programs, led members of the authorization committees to draft legislation to limit the control of the appropriations committees. A number of methods to achieve that goal were devised, including laws that gave eligible program beneficiaries a legal right to benefits, laws permitting agencies to borrow money that the federal government would later be obligated to repay, and laws enabling agencies to sign contracts that the federal government would later be required to finance. The result was a gradual rise in so-called *uncontrollable spending*—spending that could not be controlled within the budget process (but that could be controlled by changing the authorization legislation).

Another important development in the budget process in the decades following the 1930s was the increasingly direct impact of federal spending on many people's lives. With the growth of Social Security, Medicare, Medicaid, financial aid to college students, and many other programs, including subsidies to businesses, the number and range of people affected by federal budget decisions dramatically expanded. As a result, the political pressures on the White House and Congress at budget time could escalate dramatically when programs were threatened with spending cuts.

The relatively slow economic growth of the 1970s added more pressure to budget decisions. When the economy grows rapidly, revenues rise rapidly as well; finding additional revenues to fund higher program costs is fairly easy. With slower economic growth comes slower revenue growth, which makes accommodating higher program costs more difficult.

Frictions between the White House and Congress during the Nixon presidency placed further strain on the budget process. Members of Congress came to doubt the accuracy of budgetary information provided by the White House, and the Nixon administration criticized Congress's failure to pay adequate attention to the overall size of the budget and budgetary priorities. Conflicts also erupted over President Nixon's use of *impoundment,* the withholding of funds from certain programs even though Congress had appropriated the money. Although a number of presidents had occasionally impounded funds over the years, President Nixon impounded on a much larger scale and largely withheld funds from programs he disliked. Many members of Congress feared that widespread use of impoundments would greatly weaken congressional influence over the budget. The combined result of all these problems was pressure to reform the budget process again.

Congress responded to those pressures by enacting the Budget and Impoundment Control Act of 1974. Before the act, Congress had no formal means to make integrated decisions on overall levels of taxing and spending. The 1974 Budget Act appeared to be a radical departure from traditional congressional practices because Congress would now make program decisions within a context of fiscal policy guidelines.

The 1974 Budget Act reflected the political conflicts of the time. Members of Congress wished to strengthen its position vis-à-vis the president. Mistrust of the White House led to the act's creation of the Congressional Budget Office, which was to serve as Congress's independent budget analysis office. The act established House and Senate budget committees to focus attention on overall budgetary totals and the allocation of funds among various functional areas of governmental activity. The law also established a new budgetary timetable. After the president submitted budget recommendations to Congress in January, Congress (working through the House and Senate budget committees) would adopt a bud-

get resolution that established the overall blueprint for the budget. The beginning of the fiscal year was moved from 1 July to 1 October in order to give Congress more time to complete work on the budget.

The 1974 Budget Act mandates that following passage of the concurrent budget resolution in the spring, subcommittees of the appropriations committees consider specific spending bills, and the revenue committees consider revenue bills. Those actions are to remain within the guidelines established by the concurrent budget resolution. The budget committees serve as watchdogs, making certain that legislation is consistent with the resolution. Enforcing budget resolutions has often proved difficult, however.

The 1974 Budget Act has disappointed many analysts. In fact, some critics believe that some provisions of the act have made budgeting even more difficult. By expanding Congress's flexibility in making spending decisions, the law may have encouraged higher spending. The law protects entitlement programs and may encourage greater program advocacy by many congressional committees. In addition, some members tend to treat the budget resolutions as the minimum spending levels to be built upon rather than as limitations that must not be exceeded.

The Budget Act of 1974 provided Congress with the means to deal with broad budget policy issues and therefore had the potential for altering the balance of influence between Congress and the White House. Not all supporters of the new law, however, agreed on the need to control congressional spending. Furthermore, the act enlarged the potential range of conflict within Congress because it expanded the scope of participation in budgetary decisions and compelled Congress to make more explicit and integrated budget choices than before. Before the act, the various parts of the budget could be dealt with separately. The provisions of the Budget Act changed the process so that very few financial decisions could be made by just one set of committees. The decisions of the revenue and appropriations committees needed to be coordinated in the development of congressional budget policy.

Owing to disagreements over budget priorities, Congress has often been unable to pass spending bills by the beginning of the fiscal year. As a result, Congress has often funded agencies by continuing resolutions, which provide budget authority for agencies when the regular appropriations bill has not been enacted on schedule. The growing flexibility regarding what is allowed in continuing resolutions and supplemental appropriations bills (which are usually used when a budget needs modification during the fiscal year) means that important budgetary decisions are now being made in them. By relying heavily on continuing resolutions and supplemental appropriations bills, the budget process has become even more difficult to coordinate. As a result, congressional efforts to balance the budget face the constant problem of additional spending demands even after the new fiscal year has begun.

The postwar transformation of federal budgeting from a control-oriented process to one oriented toward spending growth has upset the relationship between available resources and demands on the budget. Claims on the budget became stronger when budgeting was an expansionary process, fueled by a rapidly growing economy, and it has not been easy for Congress to reverse course as the climate has become more constrained. Budgeting for growth (for example, the 1950s and 1960s) differs from budgeting when resources are growing slowly or even declining. When resources are expanding rapidly, pleasing large numbers of claimants is relatively easy; tax rates do not need to be raised to accommodate rising demands.

Coping with slow economic growth is made more difficult because only approximately twenty-five percent of the budget is "controllable" through the budget process, and much of that twenty-five percent is politically difficult to alter as well. Some seventy-seven percent of uncontrollable expenditures are devoted to entitlement programs. Once a program benefit is given the status of an entitlement in law, a recipient who meets the criteria has a right to the benefits. Entitlement programs range from very large and costly ones, such as Social Security and Medicare, to quite small ones, such as an indemnity program for dairy farmers whose milk is contaminated by chemicals. When the number of program beneficiaries rises, especially if program benefits are also indexed to automatically rise with inflation, entitlements can cause substantial increases in budget costs. Congress and the president may act to change the authorization legislation that sets benefit levels and eligibility requirements, and that has been done at times, but it is politically difficult to curtail benefits or eligibility for benefits for large entitlement programs.

One feature of the 1974 Budget Act might have helped control entitlement spending: the reconciliation process. Reconciliation was adopted to ensure consistency among the various congressional decisions affecting the budget. If spending or revenue decisions deviated from the original budget resolution, or if conditions changed substantially as work on the budget progressed, a reconciliation bill could direct various congressional committees to revise their previous actions. Spending and/or revenue levels might be adjusted, and the budget resolution might be modified if needed. The budget committees were initially reluctant to use the reconciliation process because it might anger members of the powerful appropriations and revenue committees. Reconciliation was used with significant results in 1981, the first year of Ronald Reagan's presidency, but many members were concerned by the bypassing of the traditional budget processes.

Reconciliation aroused conflict by changing the scope of involvement in budgetary decision making and possibly changing the balance of political power. Members of the budget committees and party leaders might use reconciliation to influence other congressional committees involved in the budgetary process. The result could be a more centralized system of budgetary decision making. Reconciliation has not been very successful in helping Congress to produce greater consistency between substantive legislation and budgeting or in closing the gap between revenues and expenditures.

Frictions between the White House and Congress have contributed to budgetary conflicts since the 1960s. Each side wants to please its supporters and wants to appear successful to the other side. Each side blames the other for any serious problems with the budget. That has been particularly common during divided party control, as has been common since 1968. The result has been frequent conflict.

Chronic deficit spending is widely regarded as the most conspicuous problem of the federal budget. Although the national government has run deficits every year since 1969, deficits reached unprecedented levels (for peacetime) beginning in the Reagan administration. The administration's fiscal policy helped to dramatically increase the size of the deficit when actual revenues failed to match administration projections. Congress and the White House have struggled with the deficit since then; the deficit peaked in 1992 at $290 billion.

The substantial pain involved in eliminating huge budget deficits, either by large tax increases or large program cuts (or a combination of both), has made Congress and the White House reluctant to tackle the deficit directly. In 1985, Congress enacted the Gramm-Rudman-Hollings Emergency Deficit Control Act, which established a set of deficit reduction targets. If the targets were not met, an automatic mechanism would cut spending until each deficit target was met. However, the law's effectiveness was undercut by a combination of loopholes and "blue smoke and mirrors"—budgetary actions that complied with the letter of the law but did not change the budget fundamentally. The deficit targets were amended to provide more time to reach a balanced budget, and then Gramm-Rudman-Hollings was repealed in 1990 amid continuing deficits.

The persistent deficits and conflict between the White House and Congress led to enactment of the Budget Enforcement Act of 1990. This law included a package of revenue increases and spending cuts and established some new budgetary rules to encourage more centralized control over the budget. Some accounting functions were transferred from the Congressional Budget Office to the White House's Office of Management and Budget, and new spending limits were adopted, although those limits can be exceeded in emergencies.

Americans tend to criticize government spending in the abstract but to welcome it for specific programs that benefit them. They also grumble about taxes, which actually take a smaller percentage of incomes in the United States than in most other industrialized democracies. The result is chronic deficits. Most officials want to reduce the deficit but fear the political consequences of tax increases and program cuts. With high expectations for public services, the indexing of a number of program benefits, and relatively sluggish economic growth since 1970, Congress and the president have struggled with the conflicting pressures bearing on the budget. During 1995 and 1996, a number of deficit-reduction proposals were discussed; virtually all of them recommended postponing painful actions until several years into the future.

[See also Management and Budget, Office of.]

BIBLIOGRAPHY

Fisher, Louis. *Presidental Spending Power.* Princeton, N.J., 1975.
Fisher, Louis. "Ten Years after the Budget Act: Still Searching for Controls." *Public Budgeting* 5(1985):3–28.
Ippolito, Dennis. *Congressional Spending.* Ithaca, N.Y., 1981.
LeLoup, Lance. *Budgetary Politics.* 2d ed. Brunswick, Ohio, 1980.
Neustadt, Richard. "Presidency and Legislation: The Growth of Central Clearance." *American Political Science Review* 48(1954):641–671.
Rubin, Irene. *The Politics of Public Budgeting.* 2d ed. Chatham, N.J., 1993.
Schick, Allen. *Congress and Money.* Washington, D.C., 1980.
Schick, Allen. *Reconciliation and the Congressional Budget Process.* Washington, D.C., 1981.
Schick, Allen. "The Evolution of Congressional Budgeting." In *Crisis in the Budgetary Process,* edited by Allen Schick, pp. 3–54. Washington, D.C., 1986.
Schick, Allen. *The Capacity to Budget.* Washington, D.C., 1990.
Thurber, James, and Samantha Durst. "The 1990 Budget Enforcement Act: The Decline of Congressional Accountability." In *Congress Reconsidered,* 5th ed., edited by Lawrence Dodd and Bruce Oppenheimer, pp. 375–397. Washington, D.C., 1993.
Wildavsky, Aaron. *The New Politics of the Budgetary Process.* 2d ed. New York, 1992.

—PATRICK FISHER and
DAVID C. NICE

Bureau of _____.
See under latter part of name.

C

Cabinet

The term *cabinet* is not mentioned in the Constitution, probably because the Framers explicitly rejected limiting the chief executive with any advisory body that would imply collective responsibility for the executive branch. The Constitution does, however, provide that the president "may require the Opinion, in writing, of the principal officer in each of the executive Departments." In George Washington's administration the executive departments were the Departments of State, War, and Treasury. Washington consulted with his cabinet secretaries regularly along with his attorney general (the Justice Department was not created until 1870). By 1794 the term *cabinet* was commonly used to denote the cabinet secretaries as chief advisers to the president.

As the country grew and presidents needed to please different factions in their political coalitions, cabinet members often were chosen in order to build political support rather than solely because of loyalty to the president and his policies. Since some of these appointees were not well known to the presidents who selected them, presidents occasionally sought policy advice from their closest political supporters and confidants. Thus arose the "Kitchen Cabinet" in Andrew Jackson's administration, close policy and political advisers who had no formal role in the government but who were trusted by the president. During the nineteenth century most presidents used their cabinets for policy advice. Jackson preferred to consult his Kitchen Cabinet and did not meet with his official cabinet for his first two years in office. James Polk, in contrast, convened his department heads 350 times in his single term. Throughout the rest of the nineteenth and the early twentieth centuries presidents tended to use their cabinets as their primary advisory mechanisms.

The cabinet in the United States must be distinguished from the cabinet in a parliamentary system, where cabinet members are also members of parliament. Political parties choose ministers from among the leadership of the controlling party in parliament. They retain their full voting membership in the legislature at the same time that they are cabinet ministers in charge of the executive departments (ministries). They are thus dependent on their party in the legislature, where party loyalty is expected, and the prime minister is the first among equals. In the United States, however, cabinet secretaries are wholly dependent on the president for their appointment, and the Constitution forbids membership in both branches at the same time. Cabinet secretaries serve at the pleasure of the president, who can dismiss them at any time. The U. S. cabinet as such has no formal power, and its influence comes from the president's willingness to listen to its advice. Individual departmental secretaries, however, do have the legal authority to manage their departments as long as they are in office.

SELECTING CABINET MEMBERS

Since the official duty of a cabinet officer is to act as the president's agent in running the major departments, presidents must select people who agree with their philosophy of governance and who have managerial ability. But the professional qualifications of managerial ability and policy expertise are not the only criteria that presidents use in selecting their cabinet officers. From the time of Washington, presidents have used cabinet appointments for partisan and geographic balance, and contemporary presidents have added several other balancing factors.

A new president of one wing of the political party might choose a representative of the opposite wing (or occasionally of the other political party) to attempt to unify the nation after a divisive election. Just as Washington balanced his cabinet geographically, modern presidents strive to ensure that their cabinets do not represent only one region of the country. Modern presidents also use their cabinets to demonstrate that their administrations will be broadly representative of the whole country. Thus presidents often take into account factors such as religion, sex, and ethnicity to demonstrate inclusiveness or diversity. So cabinet officers are chosen not only for their loyalty to the president, but also for other reasons that may cut against that loyalty.

Although all departmental secretaries are members of the cabinet, presidents can also elevate other government officials to cabinet rank. In this way presidents have symbolized their priorities or demonstrated their personal regard for members of their administration. Since Eisenhower began the practice, presidents have granted cabinet rank to officials such as the U.S. representative to the United Nations, the U.S. trade representative, the director of the Office of Management and Budget, and the director of the Central Intelligence Agency.

THE ROLE OF CABINET OFFICERS

Cabinet officers are obliged not only to serve the president but also to fulfill their legal duties as department heads. They are responsible for managing the large, complex programs and agencies within their departments. Cabinet secretaries must answer to Congress as well as the president for the conduct of their official duties, and control of their programs often lies with congressional decisions on the scope of the programs they run as well as their funding. Cabinet secretaries must also be sensitive to the interest groups that form the constituencies of their departments, groups that often differ with the president over the direction of policy.

This combination of factors—responsiveness to Congress, concern with their policy constituencies, sensitivity to career bureaucrats—causes cabinet secretaries to be perceived as advocates for their departments. They are legitimately ambivalent because they have official duties to Congress and their departments as well as to the president who appointed them. Charles G. Dawes, the first director of the Bureau of the Budget, reflected this reality when he said, "Cabinet secretaries are vice presidents in charge of spending, and as such are the natural enemies of the president."

The tendency toward departmental advocacy can be explained in part by the background of departmental secretaries, for they have often spent most of their careers becoming experts in the policy area they are now administering. But lack of absolute loyalty to the president by departmental secretaries is inherent in the American political system, both because of the reasons for their recruitment and because they are legally bound to carry out the law and may be called before Congress to account for their actions and justify their budgets. In providing effective leadership for their departments, secretaries must be seen to stick up for the career civil servants who implement the laws and presidential priorities. Ironically, cabinet secretaries can sometimes be of more long-term use to the president by paying close attention to the needs of their own departments and their constituencies.

COLLECTIVE DELIBERATION AND THE DECLINE OF THE CABINET

In addition to consulting members of their cabinets individually for advice, presidents have met with their cabinets collectively to deliberate major issues in their administrations. The advantages of such collective deliberation are that the give-and-take of talented and intelligent people can improve a president's perspective on the issues, and presidents have often proclaimed the value of the collective advice of their cabinets. But despite presidents occasionally polling their cabinets, the authority of the U.S. cabinet—in contrast to the collective policy-making authority of the British cabinet—is strictly limited to advising the president. As President Lincoln said when his cabinet unanimously recommended delaying the release of the Emancipation Proclamation, "Seven nays, one aye. The ayes have it."

There are practical limits to the utility of the cabinet as a deliberative advisory body to the president. Members of the cabinet often have conflicting interests and are thus rivals for resources and jurisdictional turf. In seeking advantage, individual cabinet members are likely to want to petition the president individually rather than laying their own priorities open to criticism at the cabinet table. FDR's secretary of commerce, Jesse H. Jones, expressed it this way: "My principal reason for not having a great deal to say at cabinet meetings was that there was no one at the table who could be of help to me except the president, and when I needed to consult him, I did not choose a cabinet meeting to do so."

Since 1960 the cabinet has lost significance as adviser to the president and as developer of administration policy. The reasons for the decline include an expanded White House staff capacity, the crosscutting nature of many policy issues, and the tendency of cabinet secretaries to be advocates for their own departments. In 1939 the Executive Office of the President was established as the institutional base for the White House staff. Since then the size and capacity of the White House staff has grown considerably, with a major spurt in growth during the 1970s. With a White House Office of four hundred within an Executive Office of the President of two thousand, much of the work of policy development and advice to the president has been internalized in the presidency at the expense of the cabinet.

This has been particularly evident in national security policy making. From the 1970s through the 1990s the National Security Council and its staff have overshadowed the Departments of State and Defense in formulating national security policy. The domestic policy staff in the White House is more important than any of the domestic cabinet departments on most domestic policy issues. The Office of the U.S. Trade Representative in the Executive Office of the President now dominates trade policy, and the Office of Presidential Personnel in the White House, rather than the departmental secretary, dominates political appointments in the departments. Thus many functions that used to be performed in cabinet departments are now handled by the president's staff.

This arrangement is preferable from the presidential perspective because most issues that reach the Oval Office cut across cabinet jurisdictions. Consequently, presidents seek to view their options from a standpoint other than that of a potentially prejudiced and self-interested cabinet secretary. Members of the White House staff as well tend to see recommendations from cabinet members as self-serving or representing the perspectives of Congress, interest groups, or the bureaucracy rather than the best interest of the president. Only advisers close to the president are thought to have the breadth of perspective to make the crosscutting policy decisions that are necessary at the top of the federal government. In advising the president, White House staffers have the advantage of proximity and the ability to focus solely on the president's current concerns; they do not have the far-reaching legal and managerial duties of cabinet secretaries. Thus presidents tend to rely on their own staffers rather than their cabinets for advice.

The perspective of cabinet secretaries, however, is different. They often feel that they are forced into the role of advocacy because they so seldom get to see the president. The natural friction between cabinet secretaries and White House staffers is exacerbated by differences in age and stature, with young White House aides often having the clout to be able to tell senior administration officials what to do.

At times presidential reliance on White House staffers has resulted in ineffectiveness or scandal. Because of this, presidential candidates in the 1970s and 1980s often promised "cabinet government" if they were elected. Cabinet government—in the American sense, that is, with the separation of powers, not a parliamentary system—was practiced most effectively in the modern era by Dwight Eisenhower. Eisenhower delegated a certain amount of leeway in policy development to his cabinet secretaries, and he used his cabinet as a deliberative body to advise him on the major issues of his administration. He expected that members of his cabinet would not confine their advice to their own policy areas but would speak out on the broad issues facing his administration.

The seriousness with which Eisenhower took cabinet deliberations was demonstrated by his establishment of a cabinet secretariat to prepare agendas for cabinet meetings and make sure that all background papers were in the hands of secretaries well before cabinet meetings. Members of the secretariat also made a record of each meeting and followed up on presidential decisions to ensure cabinet compliance. The secretary to the cabinet is still important in coordinating the actions of the presidency and the cabinet.

While Presidents Kennedy and Johnson rejected placing such heavy reliance on their cabinets, Presidents Nixon, Ford, Carter, and Reagan each promised that the cabinet would play an important role in their administrations. They intended to delegate authority to their cabinet secretaries and seek their collective advice, but each soon became disillusioned and centralized control in his White House staff. The problem was that the cabinet secretaries would often pursue priorities at odds with White House policies.

President Reagan, while promising to involve his cabinet, ended up with a White House staff–dominated administration. Reagan did, however, institute "cabinet councils" as subgroups of the cabinet and White House staffers who would meet to develop policy. The cabinet council system was a useful mechanism, thought it met with mixed success. President Bush used his cabinet effectively because he knew most of his secretaries personally, though he made no attempt to return to cabinet government. President Clinton met with his cabinet only seven times in his first year in office and continued to use the White House staff as the primary formulator of his administration's policies, most notably his 1993 health care reform task force.

Over two centuries of American history the cabinet has been an enduring structure that presidents have used in a variety of ways. Despite the trend in the latter twentieth century of presidents depending on their White House staffs at the expense of the cabinet, presidents still call on cabinet secretaries for advice and depend upon them for leadership of the executive branch. Whether or not future presidents decide to use their cabinets for collective deliberation, the president's cabinet will continue to play an important role in the U.S. presidency.

[*See also* Advising the President.]

BIBLIOGRAPHY

Cohen, Jeffrey. *The Politics of the U.S. Cabinet.* Pittsburgh, 1988.
Fenno, Richard F. *The President's Cabinet.* New York, 1959.
Hess, Stephen. *Organizing the Presidency.* Washington, D.C., 1988.
Patterson, Bradley. *The President's Cabinet.* Washington, D.C., 1976.
Pfiffner, James P. *The Modern Presidency.* New York, 1994.
Pfiffner, James P. *The Strategic Presidency.* 2d ed. Lawrence, Kans., 1996.
Porter, Roger B. *Presidential Decision Making.* Cambridge, U.K., 1980.
Seidman, Harold, and Robert Gilmour. *Politics, Position, and Power.* New York, 1986.
Warshaw, Shirley Anne. *Powersharing: White House–Cabinet Relations in the Modern Presidency.* Albany, 1996.
—JAMES P. PFIFFNER

Census, Bureau of the

The principal function carried out by the Bureau of the Census is specifically described in the U.S. Constitution (Art. I, Sec. 2): "Representatives and direct taxes shall be apportioned among the several States which may be included in this Union, according to their respective numbers. . . . The actual enumeration shall be made within three years after the first meeting of the Congress of the United States, and within every subsequent term of ten years, in such manner as they shall by law direct." This requirement has been expanded and codified over the years (mostly in Title 13, U.S. Code) to include censuses and surveys of nearly all economic and demographic aspects of American society.

During the early years of the nation, the decennial censuses were conducted under the direction of the secretary of state, and later of a superintendent appointed by Congress or by the Secretary of the Interior. It was not until 1902 that a permanent Bureau of the Census was established, and the superintendent at that time was named its first director.

THE CENSUS OF 1790: THE FIRST ENUMERATION

The first census act was signed by President George Washington on 1 March 1790, providing for a period of enumeration of nine months, from 2 August 1790 through April 1791. The 1790 census was conducted under the direction of Secretary of State Thomas Jefferson, who delegated the actual work to the seventeen U.S. Marshals, who hired six hundred assistants called "enumerators." The enumerators were paid less than one cent per person counted and were required to provide their own paper on which to record their counts. The first census presented several difficulties: boundaries were uncertain, roads and bridges were scarce, and travel was mostly by horseback. A trip between New York and Boston took six days.

While the Constitution required only a head count, James Madison and others in Congress argued for collection of additional information as an aid to legislation. They were outvoted, and the first census asked only five questions, mainly classifying people as free or slave, and by race and sex. "Free white males" were counted as "16 years and upward" or "under 16 years" to provide information for military conscription.

The 1790 census cost $44,377.29 and counted 3,929,214 people, including 558,000 "heads of households" and 694,000 slaves. The only names entered were, by law, those of the heads of households—master, mistress, steward, overseer, or other principal person. The final report was a single volume of fifty-eight pages.

THE CENSUSES OF 1800–1830: A VIGOROUS NATION HANDICAPPED BY A PRIMITIVE CENSUS

The census of 1800 was conducted in essentially the same way as the first census. However, in 1810 the international situation that would lead to the War of 1812 persuaded Congress to add inquiries concerning manufacturing establishments and manufactures. This first attempt at an industrial census failed because businessmen were not yet major users of census data, and they were reluctant to report facts that might interest their competitors. Further, the U.S. marshals had little enthusiasm for collecting business statistics, and their reports were of poor quality, with some reporting crops and livestock as manufactures and other variations. Collection of manufacturing data was dropped entirely in 1830, and the census retreated to essentially the same population questions used forty years earlier. Also in 1830, uniform census schedules were supplied by the census office for the first time.

THE CENSUSES OF 1840–1870: THE CENSUS CATCHES UP WITH THE NATION

As Madison had anticipated, Congress found it impossible to legislate without facts. By 1840 the census comprised six schedules with 142 items relating to population, health, mortality, literacy, pauperism, occupation, income, wealth, agriculture, manufactures, mining, fishing, commerce, banking, insurance, transportation, schools, libraries, crime, taxes, and religion. New states pressed for data for legislation and tax structures, and experts in economics, education, and social sciences found ever-broader uses for census data.

While few quarreled with the need for more data, nearly everyone complained about slow publication of results and rampant errors. The American Statistical Association decried the "extraordinary contradictions and improbabilities" in some census tabulations, and census officials themselves testified to serious weaknesses in the data. Nonetheless, Congress called it "the most complete census any nation has ever had."

In 1849, responsibility for the census was moved from the State Department to the Department of the Interior. For the census of 1850, census takers began writing down the names of all people counted, not only heads of households, and classified them by age, sex, race, and place of birth. Thus, the individual became the unit of enumeration rather than the family.

Other notable events of this period included the first enumeration of American Indians as a separate group and the collection of data on Chinese immigrants in the census of 1860. In the census of 1870, women were included in the labor force count, freed blacks were identified by name, and data were collected on Japanese immigrants. Results of the 1870 census were presented in map charts, and the first *Statistical Atlas of the United States* was published. In 1878 the first *Statistical Abstract* was published.

THE CENSUS OF 1880: THE CENTENNIAL CENSUS

In its first century, the American nation increased tenfold in population, extended its boundaries to the Pacific Ocean, and moved from a simple agrarian society to a complex industrial one. Slavery had been abolished and the Union preserved.

The census of 1870 had suffered from many of the same weaknesses as previous ones, and subsequently Congress ordered a committee headed by General James A. Garfield to find ways to improve enumeration procedures. The resulting legislation: 1) replaced the overloaded U.S. marshals with civilian supervisors, who were required to take a confidentiality pledge; 2) liberalized staffing and pay; and 3) instituted quality checks. For the first time, women were used as enumerators.

"Special agents"—professionally qualified people—were hired to collect and tabulate the economic and social statistics. Under the supervision of Henry Gannett, nearly two-thousand enumeration districts were organized and assigned, which greatly simplified and clarified the enumerators' work. As a result of all these innovations, the coverage, accuracy, and speed of the 1880 census were sharply improved.

A movement for a special centennial census in 1875 failed to gain wide support, but the census of 1880 was befitting a centennial: 13,010 items of data were collected, and the mass of completed schedules weighed well over one-hundred tons. The final report comprised twenty-two volumes. Although legislative changes had improved the efficiency of the census, the lack of a continuing organization still handicapped advance planning, and slow processing of data caused some reports to reach the public as late as 1887.

THE CENSUSES OF 1890 AND 1900: BREAKTHROUGH—MECHANICAL DATA PROCESSING

Although a mechanical tallying machine (the Seaton device) was introduced in 1872, the census of 1890 saw the first systematic use of mechanical tabulation equipment, along with punch cards. This equipment and system were invented by Dr. Herman Hollerith, a former census employee. Greatly improved by 1900, these devices brought under control the enormous costs of massive data processing and made it possible to publish census reports within a reasonable time span.

ESTABLISHMENT OF A PERMANENT CENSUS ORGANIZATION

From the middle to the end of the nineteenth century, the idea of a permanent census office was expressed repeatedly, and by the 1890s this movement had gained widespread support. The recommendations of the Garfield committee and the efforts of census pioneers such as General Francis A. Walker and Colonel Charles W. Seaton lent weight to the movement. Leading figures in the American Economic Association and the American Statistical Association, as well as commercial interests represented by the National Board of Trade, petitioned Congress for a permanent and independent census office. At about the same time, Carroll D. Wright, commissioner of labor, prepared a draft bill describing the basic model of a permanent office.

Legislation moved slowly through Congress in 1898, and final legislation was enacted in 1899 establishing a temporary census office in the Interior Department. In 1899, William R. Merriman was confirmed by the Senate as director and Frederick H. Wines as deputy director. In 1901, within three months of his succeeding to the presidency after the death of McKinley, Theodore Roosevelt recommended to Congress that the census office be made permanent. A bill for this purpose was soon taken up, and in March 1902 it was enacted, leaving the new Census Office under the Department of the Interior.

Finally, on 14 February 1903, President Roosevelt signed into law a bill creating a new Department of Commerce and Labor and transferring the Census Office from Interior to that department. This could be considered the birth of the modern Census Bureau, from which point grew the great statistical organization now known as the "Factfinder for the Nation."

In the new organization, professional staff members corresponding to earlier "special agents" assumed responsibility for specific programs. A census geographer was appointed to tackle the long-standing problem of overlapping jurisdictions, and a small research staff began collecting information on census methodologies all over the world. With a permanent Census Bureau staff, planning for the next census could be started while the last reports from the previous census were being issued; and there was the beginning of an "institutional memory" of successes and mistakes that, over time, would contribute to increasingly accurate and timely collection, processing, and publication of census data.

THE FIRST THREE DECADES OF THE CENSUS BUREAU

The Permanent Census Act of 1902 not only established a permanent Bureau of the Census, it also called for a number of censuses and surveys to be conducted between decennial censuses. Among these intercensal activities were an annual compilation of vital statistics, a mid-decade census of manufacturers, and collections of data on crime, social conditions, religious bodies, and public finance. Thus the foundation was laid for the broad program of statistical tasks now performed by the Census Bureau.

From 1902 until 1929 there were no significant changes in census legislation, but a number of interesting events occurred during that period. In 1903 the bureau began its "age-search" operation, through which citizens could confirm their date and place of birth from census records, in the absence of official local records. In 1906 the first report on current industrial statistics (*Facts on File*) was published. In 1910 the first census tracts were delineated. In 1913, when the Department of Commerce and Labor was split, the Bureau of the Census was placed organizationally in the Department of Commerce, but its statistical programs remained essentially the same. In 1917 the bureau conducted several surveys of war industries, and in 1919 it conducted the first biennial census of manufacturers. Disaster struck in 1921, when a fire destroyed most of the records from the 1890 census.

LEGISLATIVE CHANGES

Beginning with the Census Act of 1929, which provided for the census of 1930, a number of

laws were enacted over the next twenty years that led the way toward stronger programs for collecting current statistical data and expanded the scope of the censuses. The act of 1929, in contrast to previous census acts, did not specify which questions were to be included but left the choice to the director of the Census, subject to the approval of the secretary of commerce. This act also specified that a decennial census of distribution (retail and wholesale trade) be taken, the first significant addition to the collection of economic statistics since the mining and agriculture censuses were first taken in 1840. The 1929 act also provided for a census of construction and for automatic reappointment of congressional districts based on decennial census results.

In 1939 legislation was enacted to require a census of housing, which has been conducted in conjunction with the decennial census of population ever since. In 1948 Public Law 671 was enacted. This law changed the frequency of the census of manufactures from every two years to every five years, and the frequency of the censuses of business and mineral industries from every ten years to every five. The law also called for a census of transportation to be taken every five years. All four censuses were to be conducted for years ending in 3 and 8 (changed in the late 1960s to years ending in 2 and 7). In 1933 the first census of selected service industries was conducted.

INTRODUCTION AND REFINEMENT OF SAMPLING TECHNIQUES

During the 1930s, a group of mathematical statisticians and other survey methodologists at the Census Bureau, under the direction of Morris H. Hansen, began carrying out research and developing scientific statistical methods for conducting sample surveys and censuses. Their work included the development of sampling theory, the establishment of formal quality control methods for surveys, and the derivation of theory and models for analyzing nonsampling errors. Both the statistical methods they developed and the form of research staff they organized had a profound effect on survey methods and statistical agencies worldwide. Hansen and his close friend and associate William N. Hurwitz were widely recognized for their seminal contributions to sampling theory. Their work, more than any other factor, elevated the U.S. Bureau of the Census to its current preeminence in the field of statistics.

THE WAR YEARS AND THE BIRTH OF THE ELECTRONIC COMPUTER

The 1940 decennial census marked several milestones for the Census Bureau. It was the first decennial census to use scientific sampling techniques. It also included the first census of housing and showed data for city blocks in major urban areas. Also in 1940, the Census Bureau began providing technical assistance in survey and census methods to countries overseas, which was to provide the basis for an ongoing and expanding program of international training and research through the 1990s.

In 1941 the Census Bureau began issuing data on foreign trade, and during the war years it conducted numerous special surveys to collect data for the war effort. In 1942 the bureau was given responsibility for the *Monthly Report on the Labor Force* (later to become the current population survey) and moved from downtown Washington, D.C., to its current location in suburban Suitland, Maryland.

By the 1940s it had become apparent that the increased number of censuses and surveys and the growing complexity of data tabulations required were overwhelming the capabilities of the bureau's electromechanical punch card equipment. Some of the Census Bureau staff were familiar with the uses of electronic computers to perform scientific calculations, including military applications, and so, in 1946, the Census Bureau asked the National Bureau of Standards to investigate the feasibility of using electronic computers to process statistical data.

In 1950, the Universal Analytical Computer, model I (Univac I), was put into full operation in Philadelphia, and it was used to perform some of the data processing for the 1950 decennial census over the next three years. Large staffs of clerical operators were used to read questionnaire responses and key them into card-punch machines; the punched cards provided the input to the computer. (Parts of Univac I are now on display at the Smithsonian Institution.) During this time a much faster device was under development to capture information from census questionnaires and feed it into the computer—this device was designated Film Optical Sensing Device for Input to Computers (FOSDIC). The FOSDIC equipment photographed questionnaire pages onto negative microfilm; the negatives showed clear dots where circles had been filled in on the forms, and these dots were "read" in the same manner as the holes in punch cards.

FULL AUTOMATION FOR DATA ANALYSIS AND PUBLICATION

Throughout the 1950s rapid improvements were being made to all aspects of electronic data processing. The Univac computer was made faster and more powerful, new programming languages and techniques allowed more sophisticated tabulations and quality checks, and high-speed line printers were developed. Some of the field forms for the 1960 decennial census were FOSDIC-readable, although the questionnaires were not FOSDIC forms. As a result of all these developments, there was a quantum increase in the speed with which the Census Bureau could tabulate and publish the enormous amounts of data gathered in the 1960 decennial census. It was the first census to be tabulated completely electronically.

In preparation for that census, the Census Bureau in 1958 opened its first field facilities: one in Pittsburg, Kansas, and the other in Jeffersonville, Indiana. The Jeffersonville facility was used to assemble and mail out questionnaire packages, record the receipt of returned questionnaires, and perform the FOSDIC scanning of the questionnaires. The Pittsburg office took over the age-search function. (This office was closed in July 1991 because the number of age-search queries had dwindled greatly as a result of the establishment of vital records in nearly all parts of the country by the turn of the century and the deaths of most people born in the 1800s. Age-search service is now available through the Jeffersonville facility.) The Jeffersonville facility continues in use for the many monthly, quarterly, and annual surveys conducted by the Census Bureau, as well as the economic and agriculture censuses conducted every five years.

The 1960 decennial census was the first in

which some people were asked to enumerate themselves by filling in a questionnaire, rather than being visited by an enumerator who marked down their responses. The use of the mail for sending and returning questionnaires was tested in this census.

For the 1980 decennial census, the Census Bureau opened two field offices, in addition to Jeffersonville, in Laguna Niguel, California, and New Orleans, Louisiana, to process questionnaires returned from their regions. These temporary facilities were closed in 1982 after the processing was completed. Six temporary field processing offices were established for the 1990 decennial census, with facilities located in Albany, New York; Austin, Texas; Baltimore, Maryland; Jacksonville, Florida; Kansas City, Missouri; and San Diego, California.

REFINING AND EXTENDING THE METHODS AND MEANS

During the 1960s, 1970s, and 1980s the Census Bureau continued its development of new methods of gathering and publishing statistical data, as well as adding new censuses and surveys to provide the information demanded by government and private interests. The Census Bureau conducted the first census of transportation in 1963, the first annual revenue-sharing survey in 1971, and the first Annual (now American) Housing Survey in 1973. Numerous other economic and demographic surveys are conducted on monthly, quarterly, and annual bases, and data are collected and reported monthly on exports and imports. In addition, the Census Bureau conducts a set of economic and agriculture censuses every five years, for years ending in 2 and 7; these include a Census of Agriculture, Census of Construction Industries, Census of Manufacturing, Census of Mineral Industries, and Censuses of Retail and Wholesale Trades and Service Industries.

In 1967–1968 the Geographic Base File/Dual Independent Map Encoding (GBF/DIME) system was developed for computerizing census geography, and in 1970 the first computerized address coding guide was developed. In the late 1980s these systems were supplanted by the far more sophisticated Topologically Integrated Geographic Encoding and Reference (TIGER) system; consequently, data collected in the 1990 decennial census were automatically assigned to the correct geographical areas, and tabulations based on geographic locations were produced quickly and accurately. The TIGER system was also used to produce most of the maps used by enumerators. For the 1990 decennial census, the entire country, including rural areas, was divided into city blocks or their equivalents, and statistics were tabulated and published at that level. For the 2000 census, the Census Bureau is working with the U.S. Postal Service to produce a master address file, containing every address in the United States, which will be integrated with TIGER to increase the speed and accuracy by which economic and demographic data are linked with the correct geographic areas.

For the 1970 decennial census, the mailout/mailback procedure was expanded to cover more than eighty percent of the nation's inhabitants. In 1971 the Census Bureau began its Federal-State Cooperative Program for Population Estimates, and in 1972 it obtained funding to develop a Standard Statistical Establishment List (SSEL). The SSEL streamlines the process of obtaining and tabulating statistics on the enormous variety of businesses in the country. In 1975 a program developed by the Census Bureau permitted computer generation of multicolor map charts to display statistical data by states and by countries; this program was first used to produce the *Urban Atlas* publication series. In 1983 the Census Bureau was given responsibility for the Survey of Income and Program Participation (SIPP), which gathers data on income, labor force participation, and eligibility and participation in such government programs as food stamps.

During this same thirty-year period, the Census Bureau's computer equipment—which by the early 1960s had become indispensable to large-scale data processing—was continually modernized and updated. Giant mainframe Univac computers operating with vacuum tubes were made faster and more reliable, then were supplemented by smaller and vastly more powerful IBM and DEC computers using first transistors and then integrated circuits; magnetic tape handlers were supplanted by high-density, rapid-access magnetic disk drives; and punch-card and magnetic tape inputs gave way to programs and data entered directly from personal computers operated by statisticians and analysts.

In September 1995 the Census Bureau broke ground for a new computer facility in Bowie, Maryland. In a cooperative working arrangement with the University of Maryland, the university will pursue research in supercomputing technologies, and the Census Bureau will perform research in record linking and file matching of very large data sets and in advanced image processing and optical character recognition techniques. Completion of the facility is scheduled for March 1997, in time to handle the processing needs of the 2000 decennial census.

The FOSDIC system was further refined for the 1990 decennial census and renamed Film Automated Camera Technology for 1990 (FACT-90). For the 2000 census, this technology will be replaced by digital image capture and optical character recognition techniques, which will greatly increase the speed of data input from questionnaires.

Although the amount of statistical data being gathered and tabulated continues to grow, in the late 1980s and early 1990s the volume of printed reports began declining for the first time, owing to demands from users for data in computer-readable forms. Consequently, the Census Bureau's outputs were increasingly provided on magnetic tapes, computer diskettes, and compact discs (CD-ROMs). Most recently, the Census Bureau has established a "home page" on the World Wide Web area of the Internet, where computer users can review data from current reports. (The Uniform Resource Locator—the Internet address—for the Census Bureau's home page is http://www.census.gov.)

PLANNING FOR THE FUTURE

On 28 February 1996, the bureau released *The Plan for Census 2000,* which describes the key goals and strategies, major features, and estimated costs involved in planning and conducting the next decennial census. The announced goals of this far-reaching plan are to: 1) make it easier for everyone to be counted; 2) provide a complete census of the nation's population and housing; 3) reduce the differentials in the completeness of counts among various components of the population; and 4) reduce costs, compared with those of the 1990 census, on a real, per-unit basis.

Along with improving many aspects of the census process, such as "building partnerships" with state, local, and tribal governments, community groups, and the U.S. Postal Service, the Census Bureau expects to make some significant changes:

- Use of private-sector "partners" to manage telecommunications, processing activities, and training of temporary field staff

- Development of a comprehensive master address file in cooperation with the U.S. Postal Service

- "User-friendly" reporting forms to be available in stores, malls, schools, civic and community centers, and other locations where large numbers of people often go, in addition to the regular mailing to all households

- Toll-free telephone numbers for people to call in their responses to the reporting form, in place of filling in and mailing the form

- Direct digital "capture" of completed forms, eliminating the previously used step of photographing forms onto microfilm (FOSDIC and FACT-90) and speeding up processing

- Use of a sample for field interviews of nonrespondents after responses have been received from ninety percent of all addresses

- A "second census" of 750,000 addresses nationwide to assure the integrity of the apportionment process and the completeness of Census 2000

The Census Bureau believes that the innovations described above, along with improvements in all other parts of the census process, will produce a "one-number" census that will provide a complete picture of the nation's population and housing and that will eliminate the differentials in completeness of coverage that have existed among groups in all earlier censuses.

Of course, many of the innovations developed

for use in the 2000 census will be applied to the other censuses and surveys conducted by the Census Bureau. Other initiatives also are under way, such as working with Canada and Mexico to develop a modern system of industrial classification to replace the sixty-year-old Standard Industrial Classification (SIC) system.

ORGANIZATIONAL STRUCTURE

The Bureau of the Census is part of the Department of Commerce. Its current organizational structure comprises three major areas:

- The Office of the Director, which is responsible for determining policies and directing the programs of the bureau. It includes the deputy director as well as the assistant director for communications, to whom report the Congressional Affairs Office, the Public Information Office, and the Stakeholder Relations Office.

- The Office of the Principal Associate Director and Chief Financial Officer, which is responsible for the overall management activities of the bureau. Reporting to this office are the Equal Employment Opportunity Office, the Commerce Administrative Management Systems Implementation Office, the Associate Director for Planning and Organization Development, the Office of the Associate Director for Administration, the Office of the Comptroller, and the Office of the Associate Director for Information Technology.

- The Office of the Principal Associate Director for Programs, which is responsible for the overall management of field operations, demographic and economic programs, the decennial census, and statistical design, methodology, and standards. Reporting to this office are the Customer and Product Development Office, the Office of the Associate Director for Field Operations, the Office of the Associate Director for Demographic Programs, the Office of the Associate Director for Economic Programs, the Office of the Associate Director for the Decennial Census, and the Office of the Associate Director for

Statistical Design, Methodology, and Standards.

In addition to these functions, which are housed at headquarters in Suitland, Maryland, the Census Bureau maintains twelve regional offices around the country. These offices provide vital assistance to local organizations in finding and using census data and to the Census Bureau itself by coordinating the work force of field representatives who conduct sample surveys. The regional offices also oversee data collection efforts for each decennial census; for example, for the 1990 decennial census the regional offices hired, supervised, and paid over 250,000 temporary workers. It was unclear whether the Census Bureau would be allowed by Congress to use sampling methodologies recommended by the National Academy of Sciences as the twenty-second decennial census of 2000 approached.

BIBLIOGRAPHY

Anderson, Margo J. *The American Census: A Social History.* New Haven, Conn., 1988.
Duncan, Joseph W., and William C. Shelton. *Revolution in United States Government Statistics, 1926–1976.* Washington, D.C., 1978.
Eckler, A. Ross. *The Bureau of the Census.* New York, 1972.
Halacy, Dan. *Census: 190 Years of Counting America.* New York, 1980.
U.S. Bureau of the Census. *Counting for Representation: The Census and the Constitution.* Washington, D.C., 1987.
U.S. Bureau of the Census. "History and Organization." *Factfinder for the Nation,* CFF no. 4, rev. Washington, D.C., May 1988.
U.S. Bureau of the Census. *Census and You,* Bicentennial Issue, vol. 25, no. 8. Washington, D.C., August 1990.
U.S. Bureau of the Census. "Historical Notes." Appendix B, *1987 Census of Agriculture.* Washington, D.C., 1992.
U.S. Bureau of the Census. *History of the 1987 Economic Censuses.* Washington, D.C., 1992.
U.S. Department of Commerce. *Department Organization Order No. 35-2B.* Washington, D.C., Nov. 2, 1995.
—GERALD A. MANN

Centers for Disease Control and Prevention.

See Public Health Service.

Central Intelligence Agency

The public view of the Central Intelligence Agency (CIA) and the role it plays in shaping American foreign policy is often greatly distorted. Television, the movies, novels, and newspapers and magazines all portray a selective, often twisted and misunderstood image of the agency. For many, the fictional James Bond, high-tech espionage gadgets, secret operations, and Tom Clancy accounts characterize the CIA. This view is unfortunate. While it is true that the CIA is charged with the conduct of covert action operations, it is primarily responsible for the collection and analysis of quality national intelligence and its presentation to U.S. policymakers—the president, the National Security Council, the Department of State, and the Department of Defense. In recent years the Congress and many other departments and agencies have also become major users of the intelligence the CIA provides. In addition, the CIA has major counterintelligence responsibilities.

CREATION OF THE CIA

Until the creation of the CIA in 1947, the United States had never had a peacetime civilian organization devoted solely to intelligence. The Japanese surprise attack on Pearl Harbor in 1941 and the emergence of the Soviet Union as a major security threat to the United States following the war convinced most Americans of a need for a peacetime central intelligence service.

The concept of a peacetime civilian intelligence agency had its origins in World War II with the Office of Strategic Services (OSS). The wartime OSS provided the organizational precedent for the CIA. Its major components included a Research and Analysis Branch, which provided economic, social, and political assessments; a Secret Intelligence Branch, which engaged in clandestine collection; a Special Operations Branch, which conducted sabotage and worked with resistance forces; a Counterespionage Branch, which sought to protect U.S. intelligence opera-

tions from enemy penetration; a Morale Operations Branch, which was responsible for cover or "black" propaganda; an Operational Group unit, which conducted guerrilla operations in enemy territory; and a Maritime Unit, which carried out maritime sabotage.

In November 1944 General William J. Donovan, drawing on his experiences during World War II as head of the OSS, outlined for President Franklin D. Roosevelt a similar structure for a postwar centralized civilian intelligence organization that would report directly to the president. This proposal received little support from the rest of the intelligence community—the Department of State, the military services, and the Federal Bureau of Investigation (FBI). President Harry S. Truman abolished the OSS at the end of the war, dismissing Donovan's plan.

In January 1946 Truman created the Central Intelligence Group (CIG) to coordinate the work of the existing intelligence departments. The CIG, the CIA's immediate predecessor, was conceived and established as a strictly coordinating body to minimize duplicative efforts of the military services and the Department of State in intelligence. The CIG's anomalous structure and initially limited mission reflected the opposition of the other intelligence agencies to a truly centralized intelligence service. It was a creature of the other departments, which were determined to retain for themselves an independent intelligence capability and a direct advisory role to the president on intelligence matters. Rear Admiral Sidney W. Souers, the first director of central intelligence (DCI), chose not to challenge the independent positions or power of the departmental intelligence services. The departments retained autonomy over their respective intelligence services, and the CIG budget and staff were drawn from these separate agencies, primarily the Department of State, the War Department, and the Navy. The CIG was a feeble organization at its beginning.

The appointment of Lieutenant General Hoyt Vandenberg as DCI in June 1946 accelerated the CIG's emergence as an independent intelligence producer. Under Vandenberg the CIG began to move beyond a strict coordinating role to acquiring a clandestine collection capability of its own. Souers had already arranged for the CIG to gain the remnants of the OSS's foreign collection and counterintelligence functions, which had been transferred to the War Department. Vandenberg absorbed the Strategic Services Unit from the War Department, using its personnel to create an Office of Special Operations for espionage and counterespionage. He also arranged for the transfer of the FBI's foreign intelligence responsibilities in Latin America to the CIG.

The Central Intelligence Agency emerged from the reform efforts of the National Security Act of 1947. The act attempted to unify military command by creating an Office of the Secretary of Defense. Added to the act, however, was an independent U.S. Air Force and a new Central Intelligence Agency. The new CIA was originally established to rectify some of the weaknesses of the CIG by giving central intelligence statutory authority and an independent budget. Under the act, the CIA's mission was very loosely defined. The agency was made responsible for coordinating, evaluating, and disseminating intelligence affecting national security. By reviewing and analyzing the data collected by itself and the other departments, the CIA was to provide senior policymakers with high-quality, objective intelligence. The new agency was to be civilian in character, under the control of the new National Security Council (NSC). Its role in domestic affairs was to be extremely limited because of congressional fears of creating a police state or a Gestapo. There was no mention in the legislation of authority to perform covert operations, although the act did contain a provision that directed the CIA to "perform such other functions and duties related to intelligence affecting the national security as the National Security Council may from time to time direct." This catchall clause was purposely included in the act to provide for unforeseen contingencies.

Despite its rather modest beginnings, the CIA was soon in the forefront of the superpower struggle between the United States and the Soviet Union and the U.S. battle against international communism. The agency would be shaped and formed by the Cold War as it evolved into a major tool for U.S. policymakers in the foreign and military policy process.

Within two years of its creation (by September 1949), the CIA assumed functions very different from its original principal mission. With the departments resisting providing their intelligence data to the new agency, thus preventing if from fulfilling its designated role as the producer of "coordinated intelligence," the CIA added its own collection and production aspects to U.S. intelligence. It became a competing producer of current intelligence. The military intelligence services and the Department of State continued to jealously guard their intelligence data. The military particularly resented having to provide a civilian agency with military intelligence data. It argued that civilians could not understand, let alone analyze, military intelligence data. The U.S. military also refused to provide the new agency with information on the capabilities and intentions of U.S. armed forces for comparative purposes. The Army, Navy, and Air Force all had independent clandestine collection operations. The result was often an excessive duplication and competition for the same agents and assets. The agency soon changed from its original purpose of producing coordinated national intelligence estimates to becoming a producer of current intelligence in its own right.

THE MODERN CIA

The modern CIA emerged from the Korean War and the subsequent reforms instituted by DCI General Walter Beddell Smith. Soon after becoming director, Smith organized a Directorate for Plans to coordinate and oversee all clandestine activities. (Under DCI James Schlesinger in 1973 this became the modern Directorate for Operations.) Smith also grouped analytical functions under the Directorate for Intelligence (DI) and created a Directorate for Administration. This basic organizational structure still exists today. (The Directorate for Science and Technology was created in 1962.) Smith failed, however, to resolve some of the fundamental jurisdictional conflicts among the intelligence players. By 1953 the agency had achieved the basic structure and scale it retained for the next forty years.

COVERT ACTION

No activity of the CIA has engendered more controversy than its responsibilities in the covert action arena. Even today, the CIA is identified more in terms of its covert action capabilities than anything else. As used by CIA officials, covert action is "any clandestine operation or activity designed to influence foreign governments, organizations, persons, or events in support of US foreign policy." CIA covert operation programs have generally been designed to accomplish one of the following objectives: 1) subversion of Communist regimes or movements (Cuba, Guatemala, Iran, Nicaragua, Afghanistan); 2) support to a friendly government (Laos, Chile); or 3) unconventional support to a larger war effort (Korea, Vietnam, Laos).

In December 1947 the NSC provided the CIA with authority to conduct psychological warfare in its directive NSC/4A. The acquisition of this mission had a profound impact on the development and direction of the agency. The precedent for covert action, of course, came from OSS activities during the Second World War. By late 1947 U.S. officials had become preoccupied with the Soviet threat. The perception of the Soviet Union as a global threat demanded new modes of conduct in U.S. foreign policy. When Secretary of State George Marshall refused to have the Department of State assume operational responsibility for covert action, the NSC adopted NSC/4A, giving the mission to the CIA. Following the Soviet refusal to withdraw its forces from Iran in 1946, a civil war in Greece in 1947, Communist power grabs in Poland, Hungary, and Romania, a Communist coup in Czechoslovakia, and Communist-led strikes in France and Italy, in June 1948 the NSC adopted NSC 10/2, which authorized a dramatic increase in the range of CIA covert operations directed against the Soviet Union and created the Office of Policy Coordination (OPC) as a quasi-autonomous office to run them.

Policymakers believed at the time that covert political action would serve strictly as a support function for U.S. foreign and military policy. The Departments of State and Defense and the military services would define the scope of covert activities in specific terms. A CIA component, the OPC, headed by Frank Wisner, emerged to coordinate this effort. Although it was a CIA component, the DCI had little authority in determining OPC activities. Policy guidance came from State and Defense. Only when DCI Smith took over the OPC in October 1950 did the CIA gain firm control over covert operations.

The outbreak of the Korean War in the summer of 1950 also had a major impact on covert operations as the OPC became the major organization conducting covert activities against North Korea and China. The budget and scope of its activities soared. In 1949, for example, the OPC's total personnel strength was 302; in 1952 it was 2,812, plus 3,142 overseas contract personnel. In 1949 the OPC's budget was $4.7 million; in 1952, $82 million.

On 21 October 1951 NSC 10/5 replaced NSC 10/2 as the governing directive for covert action. It provided a broad justification for large-scale covert activity by the OPC. In August 1952 DCI Smith integrated the OPC with the Office of Special Operations in the Directorate for Plans (DDP).

By the end of the Korean War the CIA was an important independent government agency commanding personnel and budget far exceeding anything originally imagined. During the 1950s and 1960s the agency emerged as an integral part of high-level U.S. policy making. Rather than simply functioning in a strict support role to the State and Defense Departments, the CIA became a major player in covert operations.

The Eisenhower administration regarded the CIA as a major weapon to be used against the spread of communism, and covert operations became a vital tool in the pursuit of U.S. foreign policy objectives. The CIA and covert operations during this period were regarded by U.S. policymakers as "operational successes" following the overthrow of Premier Mohammed Mossadegh in Iran in 1953 and the coup against President Jacobo Arbenz Guzmán of Guatemala in 1954. The report of General James Doolittle in 1954 on U.S. intelligence set the tone for CIA activities for the next twenty years. The report saw the Soviet Union as the "implacable enemy" and urged the United States to "subvert, sabotage, and destroy our enemies by more clever, more sophisticated, and more effective methods than those used against us." During this period the Clandestine Services of the DDP occupied a pre-eminent position within the CIA. They commanded the major portion of agency resources. By 1953 the DDP commanded the major share of the agency's budget, personnel, and resources—sixty percent of agency personnel and seventy-four percent of its budget. Between 1953 and 1961 clandestine collection and covert operations absorbed an average of fifty percent of the agency's total annual budget.

Until 1955 no formal approval mechanism existed outside the agency for such covert action projects. In March and December 1955 the NSC issued NSC 5412/1 and NSC 5412/2, which outlined control procedures for review and approval of covert action projects, and established the 5412 Committee or "Special Group" to oversee covert actions. In 1958 the NSC officially assigned the CIA the primary responsibility for all clandestine activities abroad.

During the 1960s the CIA's covert operational capability continued to dominate agency activities. It was used by various presidents in paramilitary activities in support of counterinsurgency and military programs in Cuba, Laos, Vietnam, and Cambodia. Under the direction of the Kennedy administration, for example, the CIA initiated paramilitary programs in Cuba, Laos, and Vietnam. After the Bay of Pigs fiasco, the agency assisted in Operation Mongoose against Fidel Castro's Cuba. (It consisted of collection, paramilitary, sabotage, and political propaganda activities aimed at destabilizing the Castro regime.) There were also full-scale paramilitary assistance programs in Laos and Vietnam. By the early 1970s, although the number of operations radically declined, covert action operations had become a regularized, ongoing element in the conduct of U.S. foreign policy. For nearly four decades U.S. policymakers considered covert action vital in the struggle against international communism.

During the 1970s, however, there was a general decline in covert action. Détente rather than confrontation characterized U.S. foreign policy. Events abroad in the late 1970s, however, shifted the Carter administration's priorities, and CIA covert operations once again came to the forefront. The Soviet invasion of Afghanistan and the war there prompted the Carter administration to mount a major covert operation to supply arms to the Afghan Mujahideen resistance fighters. Following the triumph of the Sandinistas in Nicaragua, the Carter administration initiated another covert action program to promote democracy in Nicaragua. It was DCI William Casey and the Reagan administration, however, who greatly expanded these operations. Casey, the first DCI to be given cabinet rank, shared President Reagan's conviction that the Soviet Union needed to be confronted and checked throughout the world. They were determined to use the CIA to defeat perceived Soviet inroads in Afghanistan and Central America. Reagan's Executive Order 12333 gave the CIA the exclusive right to conduct covert action operations, or "special activities." The CIA's efforts to aid the Afghan Mujahideen, unlike the help given the anti-Sandinista *contras,* was supported by Congress and the American public. Despite these major operations, covert action continued to decline.

ANALYSIS

Although CIA covert action activities garner most of the attention of the media and the American public, the main purpose of the CIA is to provide the president, his chief advisers, and Congress with information about events abroad. Within the CIA the Directorate for Intelligence is the core element in the production of finished national intelligence. The DDI produces daily, weekly, and monthly publications aimed at U.S. decision makers. These publications are usually far more detailed, wide-ranging, and up-to-date than any other intelligence source.

DCI Smith established the Office of National Estimates within the DDI in 1950. Its task was the production of coordinated "national estimates" incorporating the views of the entire U.S. intelligence community. (The intelligence community includes the CIA, the Defense Intelligence Agency, the National Security Council, the

Federal Bureau of Investigation, and the intelligence components of the departments of State, Treasury, Energy, and the four military services.) Smith called on Harvard historian William Langer, who had directed the Research and Analysis Branch of the OSS, to organize the effort. In 1951 Smith also created an Office of Current Intelligence to handle increasing demands for current intelligence. It produced various publications from all kinds of intelligence sources with a view toward providing advanced warnings of impending crises. In addition, Smith announced a new Office of Research and Reports to produce economic intelligence research focused on the Soviet Union and its satellite areas. The size and structure of the DDI remained constant during the 1950s.

Soon the overriding aim of U.S. intelligence became the assessment of the Soviet Union and its nuclear arsenal and delivery systems. A 1951 State-CIA agreement gave the CIA exclusive responsibility for economic research and analysis relating to the Soviet Union and its satellites. At the insistence of the U.S. military, the agency was officially excluded from doing any military analysis on the Soviet Union. Nevertheless, the agency challenged some of the basic military judgments concerning the Soviet Union's long-range bomber capabilities and missile technology. Gradually, the agency assumed ascendancy over the U.S. military in strategic analysis. Nevertheless, until the mid-1950s the production of intelligence on military matters remained primarily the responsibility of the Department of Defense. The "bomber gap" and "missile gap" controversies opened the door for increasing the CIA's role in foreign military research. This role has continued to expand ever since.

During the 1960s the agency further expanded its finished intelligence production in strategic and economic analysis. The growing importance of the strategic arms race between the United States and the Soviet Union helped drive this expansion. The agency's discovery of Soviet missiles in Cuba in 1962 was also crucial. In the mid-1960s, in an exchange of letters, Deputy Secretary of Defense Cyrus Vance recognized that the CIA had primary responsibility for intelligence on the cost and resource impact of for-

eign military and space programs. In addition, during the bombing campaign against North Vietnam the CIA provided regular bomb damage assessments and information on the flow of men and supplies from the North into the South. CIA analysis, in general, painted a rather pessimistic view of the escalating ground and air war in Vietnam.

It was not until the mid-1960s that the agency focused a major effort on economic analysis. In the earlier years the agency had concentrated its economic research largely on the Communist states. The emergence of an independent Africa, however, promoted a growth in non-Communist economic intelligence and inquiries into trading partnerships and trade rivals.

DCI William Colby in 1973 reorganized the Office of National Estimates and established a group of specialists in functional and geographical areas to coordinate U.S. intelligence estimates. These became known as national intelligence officers (NIOs), and they are still the major coordinating mechanism for producing estimates. Today this information is still presented to U.S. policymakers in the form of national intelligence estimates (NIEs). All of the intelligence agencies contribute, and the CIA coordinates the effort. The estimates cover a range of issues from strategic weapons to food distribution efforts, to weather and climate forecasts, to political conditions, to energy resources and international finances, to terrorist and drug activities.

DDI analysts usually provide the bulk of the staff work for the NIEs which are prepared under the auspices of the NIOs. The DDI also produces daily intelligence publications such as the *President's Daily Brief*, designed "to alert the foreign affairs community to significant developments abroad and to analyze specific problems as broadly-based trends in the international arena."

Under William Casey, the DDI was reorganized into geographically oriented units to focus on the Soviet Union, Europe, the Middle East, South Asia, East Asia, Africa, and Latin America. William Gates, who served as DCI in 1991–1992, was the first intelligence analyst to rise to director. The directorship hitherto had been dominated by military men and OSS veterans. Gates nevertheless faced charges of politicizing the intelligence process and the intelligence estimates. Today the CIA devotes most of its analytical resources to evaluating information relating to the capabilities and intentions of adversaries or potential adversaries and to forecasting political, economic, and military developments that might affect U.S. security interests.

COLLECTION

Despite intensive espionage activities on the part of the CIA and other parts of the U.S. intelligence community, U.S. intelligence on the Soviet Union was meager during the late 1940s and early 1950s. DCI Smith warned, for example, in 1952 that the U.S. intelligence system was incapable of providing strategic intelligence on the Soviets or advanced warning of any sudden attack on the United States by the Soviet Union. This led to a major technological effort on the part of the agency and the U.S. intelligence community to improve espionage and collection capabilities.

The development of sophisticated overhead reconnaissance systems in the 1950s and 1960s revolutionized U.S. intelligence collection capabilities and the CIA. In July 1955, only eighteen months after first covertly contracting with the Lockheed Corporation, the agency produced the U-2 strategic reconnaissance aircraft. It enabled the United States to monitor Soviet bomber and missile capabilities and development. The further advancement of manned reconnaissance with the OXCART (Blackbird or SR-71) and the dramatic successes of the CORONA satellite systems further expanded the CIA's capabilities to collect raw intelligence data.

On 4 October 1957 the Soviet Union rocked U.S. policymakers by orbiting Sputnik I, the first artificial earth satellite. The shock was compounded by the paucity of information within the U.S. intelligence community on Soviet missile development. Many claimed that the Soviet Union now had a large lead over the United States in the development of long-range missiles—hence the emergence of the "missile gap" arguments. To counter the perceived threat, the Eisenhower administration ordered the CIA, with the assistance of the Air Force, to speed up not only its manned reconnaissance program

but to produce a reconnaissance satellite as well. The satellite program became Project CORONA, which proved to be the pioneering program for NASA's efforts in manned space flight. After numerous failures, on 10 August 1960 the CORONA team successfully launched and recovered its first payload from space. On 19 August, as U-2 pilot Francis Gary Powers went on trial in Moscow for spying after his U-2 spy plane was shot down over the Soviet Union, the CIA successfully launched and recovered a photoreconnaissance satellite that had overflown Soviet territory. The recovered CORONA capsule produced more photographic intelligence of the Soviet Union and Communist China than was gathered during the entire U-2 program.

The development of overhead reconnaissance systems created a major need for photographic interpretation. In 1961 President Eisenhower established the National Photographic Interpretation Center (NPIC), staffed by CIA and military personnel. The NPIC grew out of two earlier CIA organizations, the Photographic Intelligence Division, established in 1953, and the Photographic Intelligence Center, created in 1958. The NPIC became the principal mechanism for the exploitation of imagery-derived intelligence, playing a major role in the detection and analysis of Soviet missiles in Cuba during the Cuban missile crisis of 1962. In 1973 it became part of the Directorate for Science and Technology (DS&T), where it remains. This move helped consolidate in one directorate the agency's technical collection and processing functions. By the 1980s, the NPIC had become an important item in the DS&T budget, and its analytical attention focused on terrorism, the war between Iran and Iraq, Central America, and the Soviet Union.

The development in technical collection programs, including overhead reconnaissance, highlighted the need within the agency for centralizing collection and analysis of scientific intelligence. In 1961 scientific and technical intelligence operations were scattered among the other directorates. DCI John McCone created the Directorate for Research (DDR) in 1962 in an attempt to solve the problem. After severe infighting, in 1963 McCone created the DS&T to replace the DDR. It was established with the assumption that it would rely on outside expertise in the scientific and industrial communities in the private sector. This pattern persists today.

The DS&T consists of several offices, including the NPIC and the Foreign Broadcast Information Service (FBIS). The mission of the FBIS is to provide information from foreign news media. This involves the systematic monitoring of radio, television, and press agency transmissions; scrutiny of foreign newspapers, periodicals, and commercial data bases; and the acquisition of maps and other publicly available media. The FBIS is rather unique in that most of its products are unclassified and are disseminated to a broad range of consumers inside and outside the U.S. government.

The FBIS was originally established to monitor Axis propaganda broadcasts. It was first called the Foreign Broadcast Monitoring Service and existed within the Federal Communications Commission. With the United States' entry into World War II, the monitoring service expanded and was renamed the Foreign Broadcast Intelligence Service. In 1946 it became part of the new Central Intelligence Group and was renamed the Foreign Broadcast Information Service. When the CIA was formed in 1947, the FBIS became a founding component.

COUNTERINTELLIGENCE

Counterintelligence (CI) is often the overlooked aspect of the CIA's intelligence effort. Counterintelligence is a special form of intelligence activity, separate and distinct from other intelligence disciplines. Its purpose is to discover hostile foreign intelligence operations aimed at the United States and destroy their effectiveness; to guard against espionage, spying, and sabotage directed against the United States; and to protect the U.S. government against infiltration by foreign agents. Offensively, it attempts to control and manipulate adversary intelligence operations.

The concept of an ever-present security threat was one of the fundamental premises on which the CIA operated from its very beginning. The new CIA drew on the CI assets and concepts inherited from the OSS and its work against Axis intelligence organizations. The small CI unit, working closely with the Office of Security,

sought not only to safeguard intelligence information and screen prospective employees to ensure that CIA officers were not working for a hostile power, but to protect CIA intelligence collectors and covert action programs from penetration.

While the CIA was able to protect itself from penetrations at home, most CIA operations inside the Soviet bloc came to be compromised in the late 1940s and early 1950s. Aware of the Soviet penetration of the OSS during World War II, the CIA, working with military intelligence, the National Security Council, and the FBI, helped uncover several Soviet spy rings operating in Great Britain and the United States during this period. Operations to counter efforts of the Soviet intelligence and CI services became a major feature of agency CI operations for the next twenty years. In December 1954 DCI Allen Dulles created a separate CI Staff in the Directorate for Plans, responsible for monitoring the agency's entire CI effort. James Jesus Angleton, a veteran officer of the Counterespionage Branch of the OSS, headed the new staff. Angleton regarded CI as the "queen of the intelligence chessboard," believing that CI should not only protect its service from penetration but actively manipulate adversary services. Under Angleton, the CI Staff became responsible for double agents, provocateurs, deception, and operational interrogations. Angleton was also the DCI's personal adviser on all CI matters. In addition, he came to control the CIA's counterterrorism activities and all agency liaison with the FBI.

The combined efforts of the CI Staff and the Office of Security yielded mixed results in the 1950s and 1960s. There were few actual penetrations of the CIA's professional staff during this period, although some people were unjustly fired or made to resign when they fell under suspicion. There were also spectacular successes, most notably the recruitment of Soviet major Vladimir Popov and Soviet colonel Oleg Penkovsky and the arrest and conviction of Soviet spy Rudolph Abel. (Abel was later exchanged for U-2 pilot Francis Gary Powers in February 1962. Popov and Penkovsky were arrested by the Soviets and executed for their espionage activities.) Despite such successes, many in the agency did not welcome the CI Staff on their turf. They resented the skepticism of the CI officers and resisted attempts to divert energy and resources to CI. Counterintelligence became a world unto itself by the 1960s.

During the 1960s CI work increasingly focused on defectors from the Soviet Union and Soviet deception. Convinced that the CIA could have escaped neither the sort of penetration that had been proved in other Western intelligence organizations nor Soviet disinformation efforts, Angleton unleashed an extended search for a Soviet-controlled "mole" in the top echelons of the CIA. Angleton believed there was a Moscow-directed conspiracy to subvert the CIA by controlling key CIA officials. Accusations and counter-accusations about the reliability of Soviet defectors Anatoli Golytsin and Yuri Nosenko flew about the agency for years. CIA morale sagged.

DCI William Colby, convinced that Angleton and his work had become counterproductive, fired Angleton in December 1974. Colby diffused the CI work among the various divisions and reorganized the CI Staff. This brought charges from Angleton and others that Colby had destroyed the effectiveness of the agency's CI efforts.

In fact, there was some truth to the charges. David H. Barnett, a career CIA officer, was arrested in 1980, tried, and convicted of spying for the Soviet Union since 1976. In January 1977 Christopher Boyce and Andrew Lee ("the Falcon and the Snowman") were arrested for passing secret satellite information to the Soviets. In 1978 William Kampiles, another former CIA officer, was arrested for selling the Soviets a copy of the manual for the KH-11 photoreconnaissance satellite system.

The revolution in technical collection capabilities was not protected. The CI Staff was not involved in any of the original overhead reconnaissance planning. The Office of Security did provide some degree of security to private-sector contractors such as Lockheed and TRW, which were producing many of the new systems, but the revolutionary collection technologies were soon compromised by the likes of Kampiles, Boyce, and Lee.

The year 1985, "The Year of the Spy," once again thrust the agency's CI effort into the public spotlight. In one year at least six different espionage cases exploded in the press—the John Walker and Jerry Whitworth spy ring, which compromised high-level U.S. Navy cryptographic systems to the Soviets; the defection of former CIA case officer Edward Lee Howard, who gave the Soviets sensitive information on CIA operations in Moscow; the arrest and conviction of Ronald Pelton, a former communications specialist with the National Security Council, who sold the Soviets highly classified intelligence information; the charging of Jonathan Jay Pollard, a Navy intelligence specialist, who provided the Israelis with classified documents; the arrest of Larry Wu-tai Chin, a CIA translator and foreign media analyst, for his work on behalf of the Chinese government; and the conviction of Sharon Scranage, a low-level CIA employee posted to Ghana, for passing classified information to Ghanaian intelligence officials. The public disclosures of these spy cases, plus the defection and re-defection of Soviet intelligence officer Vitaly Yurchenko, the revelation of KGB penetration of the new U.S. embassy building in Moscow, and the news that a Cuban double-agent and deception operation had stymied U.S. efforts to infiltrate Cuban intelligence raised public and congressional concern about security in the U.S. intelligence community during the 1980s.

Unknown to the media or the public was the fact that in the same year the CIA lost almost all of its agents in the Soviet Union. Vital technical operations against Soviet communications were also compromised and lost. Something had gone terribly wrong. Perhaps there really was a Soviet agent inside the CIA who was betraying the agency's operations to the KGB.

Most high-level agency officials placed the blame on known defector Edward Lee Howard and took little action. Only a small special task force within the CIA was assigned to the problem in 1986. The arrest and disclosure of the espionage activities of CIA officer Aldrich H. Ames in February 1994 once again raised the prospect of serious CI and security problems within the agency. Ames had successfully avoided detection since 1985 and had succeeded in depriving the United States of valuable intelligence by destroying CIA sources within the Soviet Union. It was a CI nightmare from which the agency is still recovering.

CONGRESSIONAL OVERSIGHT AND CIA ACCOUNTABILITY

The Truman administration conceived and organized the CIA as an agent of the executive branch. Drawing on the OSS experiences during World War II, the Truman administration drew up plans for a peacetime civilian intelligence agency without much input from Congress. Even the congressional debates over its creation did not much change its projected structure or character. From its origin in 1947 the agency's only formal relationship to Congress was through the appropriations process. The concept of congressional oversight in the sense of scrutinizing and being fully informed of agency activities did not exist in the 1950s and 1960s. Congress, in general, accepted the CIA mission and projected an unquestioning and uncritical attitude toward the agency. Any oversight was informal in nature and generally sympathetic. No formalized covert action reporting requirements existed between the CIA and Congress until the mid-1970s.

The congressional structure set up to deal with agency activities was *ad hoc* and informal. A few key congressional leaders and committee chairmen provided what passed for oversight. They did not challenge either the executive branch in its direction of U.S. foreign policy or the actions of the agency in support of those policies. In fact, they carefully guarded their jurisdiction over CIA affairs and their own access to intelligence information from their fellow congressmen. For their part, CIA officials readily adapted to this loose informal system of oversight and worked to cultivate the friendship and support of the key congressional leaders. What emerged during the 1950s and early 1960s was a special relationship between these congressional figures and the agency. Congress under the guidance of Richard Russell, Carl Hayden, Carl Vinson, and Clarence Cannon did not carefully scrutinize agency operations and provided a liberal budget approval process for agency financial matters.

This general consensus began to break down during the Vietnam War as Congress took a more assertive role in U.S. foreign policy decisions. As part of this new role, the CIA came in for closer congressional and public scrutiny. Press and congressional investigations and allegations of CIA involvement in the 1973 overthrow and death of Chilean president Salvador Allende moved Congress in late 1974 to enact the Hughes-Ryan amendment to the annual Foreign Assistance Act. The Hughes-Ryan amendment formalized the reporting requirements on covert action, specifying that the president himself had to inform the Congress of any covert operation and had to certify that the activity was essential to U.S. security.

The Watergate scandal and journalist Seymour Hersh's December 1974 charge that the agency was involved in massive domestic spying activities drove Congress to demand broader review of CIA operations. President Gerald Ford attempted to preempt a major legislative inquiry into the CIA by creating a commission, headed by Vice President Nelson Rockefeller, to look into Hersh's charges. Despite the executive branch investigation, both houses of Congress moved in early 1975 to establish special investigative committees to determine whether the CIA and the intelligence community had been involved in improper or illegal activities. On 21 January 1975 the Senate established its own investigation into illegal and improper or unethical activities engaged in by the agency and other parts of the intelligence community, the Senate Select Committee to Study Governmental Operations with Respect to Intelligence Activities (the Church Committee). The House voted to create a House Select Intelligence Committee (the Nedzi/Pike Committee) on 19 February 1975. For the first time since its founding, the agency faced hostile congressional committees determined to expose CIA and intelligence community abuses and promote major changes in oversight procedures.

The committees' review revealed extensive CIA involvement in domestic intelligence activities (Operation MHCHAOS), illegal mail openings, drug testing on unsuspecting U.S. citizens (MKULTRA), and assassination attempts against several foreign leaders. Specifically, however, the congressional committees found that the CIA was not "out of control" or "a rogue elephant." According to the committees, on the whole the CIA had acted on higher authority and was responsible to internal and external review and executive branch authorization and requirements.

The most important and lasting effect of the Church and Pike committees' investigations was the creation of the permanent Senate Select Committee on Intelligence and the House Permanent Select Committee on Intelligence to oversee the CIA and the intelligence community. The new intelligence oversight committees moved away from the confrontational, adversarial model of the Church and Pike committees to become strong supporters of the agency and the intelligence community. Congress also became a major consumer of CIA intelligence products at this time.

The years of the Reagan administration and DCI William Casey produced a complex relationship between the Congress, its intelligence oversight committees, and the CIA. Despite bickering over a host of issues and major conflicts over the CIA covert action operations in Angola and Nicaragua, what emerged in the 1980s was overwhelming congressional support for the agency and its budgets. There was a basic consensus between the Reagan administration and the Congress on maintaining, strengthening, and expanding U.S. intelligence operations and capabilities. Even the Iran-*contra* scandal, although it tarnished the agency's image, did not break this essentially cooperative partnership arrangement. The congressional oversight committees remained advocates, apologists, protectors, and defenders of the agency. Congress now has access to intelligence information essentially equal to that of the executive branch. The CIA is in a remarkable position, poised nearly equidistant between the executive and legislative branches.

THE FUTURE OF THE CIA

Although the Japanese attack on Pearl Harbor supplied the initiative for the establishment of a civilian central intelligence agency to guard against similar surprise attacks in the future, the new CIA quickly became a creature of the Cold War and the confrontation between the Soviet Union and the United States. Despite the breakup of the Soviet Union and the end of the Cold War, the role of the CIA in providing objective intelligence to U.S. policymakers remains crucial for America's security. The CIA remains the principal conduit of intelligence to the president and U.S. policymakers. The DCI serves both as director of the CIA and as head of the U.S. intelligence community. The DCI also continues to serve as the president's chief intelligence officer.

The chief priority of the CIA will remain its traditional one of monitoring threats to the security of the United States. The CIA continues to serve as the eyes and ears of the United States government regarding national security matters. It must continue to assist U.S. policy makers in understanding and dealing with an often dangerous and unpredictable world.

[*See also* Defense Intelligence Agency; Federal Bureau of Investigation; *and* National Security Council.]

BIBLIOGRAPHY

Andrew, Christopher. *For the President's Eyes Only: Secret Intelligence and the American Presidency from Washington to Bush.* New York, 1995.

Beschloss, Michael R. *Mayday: Eisenhower, Khrushchev and the U-2 Affair.* New York, 1986.

Breckinridge, Scott. *The CIA and the United States Intelligence System.* Boulder, Colo., 1986.

Brugioni, Dino A. *Eyeball to Eyeball: The Inside Story of the Cuban Missile Crisis.* New York, 1990.

Burrows, William. *Deep Black: Space Espionage and National Security.* New York, 1986.

Colby, William E., and Peter Forbath. *Honorable Men: My Life in the CIA.* New York, 1978.

Darling, Arthur B. *The Central Intelligence Agency: An Instrument of Policy, to 1950.* University Park, Pa., 1990.

Draper, Theodore. *A Very Thin Line.* New York, 1991.

Epstein, Edward Jay. *Deception: The Invisible War between the KGB and the CIA.* New York, 1989.

Grose, Peter. *Gentleman Spy: The Life of Allen Dulles.* New York, 1994.

Hersh, Burton. *The Old Boys: The American Elite and the Origins of the CIA.* New York, 1992.

Jeffreys-Jones, Rhodri. *The CIA and American Democracy.* New Haven, Conn., 1989.

Koch, Scott A., ed. *Selected Estimates on the Soviet Union, 1950–1959.* Washington, D.C., 1993.

Laqueur, Walter. *A World of Secrets: The Uses and Limits of Intelligence.* New York, 1985.

Leary, William M., ed. *The Central Intelligence Agency.* University, Ala., 1984.

Mangold, Tom. *Cold Warrior: James Jesus Angleton: The CIA Master Spy Hunter.* New York, 1991.

Martin, David. *Wilderness of Mirrors.* New York, 1980.

McAuliffe, Mary S., ed. *CIA Documents on the Cuban Missile Crisis, 1962.* Washington, D.C., 1992.

Miller, Nathan. *Spying for America: The Hidden History of U.S. Intelligence.* New York, 1989.

Montague, Ludwell L. *General Walter Bedell Smith as Director of Central Intelligence, October 1950–February 1953.* University Park, Pa., 1992.

O'Toole, G. J. A. *The Encyclopedia of American Intelligence and Espionage: From the Revolutionary War to the Present.* New York, 1988.

Persico, Joseph. *Casey: The Lives and Secrets of William J. Casey from the OSS to the CIA.* New York, 1990.

Phillips, David Atlee. *The Night Watch: 25 Years of Peculiar Service.* New York, 1977.

Powers, Thomas. *The Man Who Kept the Secrets: Richard Helms and the CIA.* New York, 1979.

Ranelagh, John. *The Agency: The Rise and Decline of the CIA.* New York, 1987.

Ruffner, Kevin C., ed., *CORONA: America's First Satellite Program.* Washington, D.C., 1995.

Schecter, Jerrold L., and Peter S. Deriabin. *The Spy Who Saved the World.* New York, 1992.

Smith, R. Jack. *The Unknown CIA: My Three Decades with the Agency.* Washington, D.C., 1989.

Steury, Donald P., ed. *Sherman Kent and the Board of National Estimates: Collected Essays.* Washington, D.C., 1994.

Steury, Donald P., ed. *Estimates on Soviet Military Power, 1954 to 1984: A Selection.* Washington, D.C., 1994.

Thomas, Evan. *The Very Best Men: Four Who Dared: The Early Years of the CIA.* New York, 1995.

Troy, Thomas F. *Donovan and the CIA: A History of the Establishment of the Central Intelligence Agency.* Frederick, Md., 1981.

Turner, Stansfield. *Secrecy and Democracy: The CIA in Transition.* New York, 1985.

Turner, Stansfield. *Terrorism and Democracy.* Boston, 1991.

Warner, Michael S., ed. *The CIA under Harry Truman.* Washington, D.C., 1994.

Wise, David. *Molehunt.* New York, 1992.

Wise, David. *Nightmover: How Aldrich Ames Sold the CIA to the KGB for $4.6 Million.* New York, 1995.

Woodward, Bob. *Veil: The Secret Wars of the CIA, 1981–1987.* New York, 1987.
—KAY OLIVER

Chief Executive.

See Executive Power *and* President as Chief Executive.

Chief of Staff to the President

The office of chief of staff to the president was established as the post–World War II White House became more institutionalized. Up to the 1970s presidents could choose to organize the White House on a collegial basis or in a more hierarchical manner by using a chief of staff. Since the 1970s, however, each president has sooner or later designated a chief of staff, and some scholars argue that it is now a virtual necessity for managing the White House.

Dwight Eisenhower was the first president to use a chief of staff to manage the White House; he chose Sherman Adams, who acted in the president's stead much of the time. Adams had full range of the domestic side of the government and coordinated White House operations authoritatively. Adams's official title was "assistant to the president" because Eisenhower did not want to create an appearance of military organization in the presidency. Nevertheless, his function was to be similar to the military chiefs of staff with whom Eisenhower had worked during his years in the Army. When Adams was forced to resign because of appearing to help a business friend with government regulations, Wilton Persons became Eisenhower's chief of staff.

John Kennedy and Lyndon Johnson, both with legislative rather than executive careers, chose to organize their presidencies along collegial rather than hierarchical lines. Each had several aides reporting directly to him in what has been called a "spokes-of-the-wheel" model of White House organization. During the 1960s the White House staff was small enough to allow this type of traditional approach to White House management to work effectively.

When Richard Nixon was elected, he returned to the more hierarchical approach of his White House years as vice president and designated H. R. ("Bob") Haldeman to be his chief of staff. During the Nixon presidency the White House staff grew considerably in size, and Haldeman ruled it with an iron hand. He advised Nixon on the full range of presidential issues and ensured that all presentations to the president were fully "staffed out" and ready for presidential consideration. When Haldeman was forced to resign during the

Watergate scandal, Alexander Haig took over as Nixon's chief of staff.

When Gerald Ford assumed the presidency he decided not to have a chief of staff because he felt that the tightly closed Nixon hierarchy contributed to the Watergate problems. He thus began his presidency with nine people reporting directly to him, but soon became overwhelmed with coordinating the large White House staff that had grown under the Nixon administration. He then asked Donald Rumsfeld to be his "staff coordinator"—in reality, his chief of staff. When Rumsfeld was appointed secretary of defense, his deputy, Richard Cheney, became Ford's chief of staff.

Jimmy Carter also began his presidency without a chief of staff for the same reason that Ford did: he wanted to distinguish his administration sharply from that of Nixon and to steer clear of any suggestion of Watergate. But Carter also had nine people reporting directly to him and in 1979 finally admitted that he could not run the White House without a chief of staff. Hamilton Jordan first held the position; upon taking over the Carter reelection campaign, he was replaced by Jack Watson.

The lessons of the Ford and Carter experiences were not lost on Ronald Reagan, and when he was elected in 1980 he designated James Baker as his chief of staff. Baker did not have as complete control of the White House as had his predecessors Sherman Adams and H. R. Haldeman, but he held the official title, occupied the traditional corner office, controlled White House personnel and office space, and coordinated the administration's policy agenda. Access to President Reagan, however, was shared with Edwin Meese and Michael Deaver, who played important roles during Reagan's first term in office. After the 1984 election Baker traded positions with Secretary of the Treasury Donald Regan, who, in contrast to Baker, took a very controlling approach to his job, jealously guarding access to Reagan and dominating the White House staff. Regan was forced out after the Iran-*contra* scandal, and former Senator Howard Baker (and later Kenneth Duberstein) took over Reagan's White House.

Governor John Sununu of New Hampshire had played a crucial role in George Bush's victory in the 1988 state Republican primary, and upon gaining the presidency, Bush asked Sununu to be his chief of staff. Sununu was very intelligent but a domineering personality, and unlike previous chiefs of staff had strong policy preferences. Thus, in addition to his chief of staff duties, Sununu served as liaison to the right wing of the Republican party and the protector of conservative values in the Bush White House. Sununu took a particularly controlling approach to the White House staff and antagonized many colleagues as well as members of Congress. He was forced to resign after it was disclosed that he had abused his perks as chief of staff and taken a number of trips, many of which did not seem to be related to his official duties. He was succeeded by Samuel Skinner; less than a year later Skinner was replaced by James A. Baker who resigned as secretary of state to become Bush's chief of staff in the summer of 1992.

Bill Clinton was the first Democratic president to begin his term with a chief of staff, naming Thomas ("Mack") McLarty, a childhood friend, to the post. Unlike other chiefs of staff, McLarty spent a good portion of his time as a high-level emissary from Clinton to Capitol Hill and the business community and only about one-third of his time managing the White House as a traditional chief of staff. After Clinton's tumultuous first year of mixed policy success, McLarty was replaced in mid-1994 by Leon Panetta, who had previously been chair of the House Appropriations Committee and director of the Office of Management and Budget in the Clinton White House.

Several lessons can be drawn from the experience of these presidents. The first is that in the contemporary White House, a chief of staff is a virtual necessity. No president since Lyndon Johnson has run the White House successfully without one, and no one since Jimmy Carter has tried. On the other hand, a too domineering approach to the job can easily result in trouble. There have been four domineering chiefs of staff (Adams for Eisenhower, Haldeman for Nixon, Regan For Reagan, and Sununu for Bush). Each of these men alienated members of Congress, alienated members of his own administration, had reputations for a lack of common civility, and had hostile relations with the press. And each of them was forced to resign in disgrace after various degrees of scandal.

The job can be done well, however, and in that case the chief of staff performs a number of essential services for the president. The chief of staff must enforce staff discipline by organizing information flow to the president and ensuring that all issue analyses are ripe for presidential involvement. The chief must orchestrate administration policy development by coordinating policy input from cabinet departments and agencies and ensuring that all appropriate officials have had a chance to comment on administration initiatives. Access to the president must be regulated so as to ensure that differing perspectives are brought to bear on administration policies and that limited presidential time is protected. All of this must be done with the chief of staff acting as a neutral broker. That is, his actions must be, and be perceived to be, neutral among different perspectives and members of the administration. Each significant presidential adviser and member of the administration must have confidence that his or her advice is getting through to the president without distortion. If this is not done, back channels of communication to the president will be created, and organizational discipline will be undermined.

Chiefs of staff also serve their presidents by acting as high-level negotiators in crisis situations or by negotiating among members of the cabinet who are in disagreement. No one else besides the president has the clout to assuage the large egos in the cabinet or enforce the president's wishes on reluctant members of the administration. The chief enforces presidential directives and often delivers the bad news if a White House staffer must be fired. He or she also protects the president by taking the blame for incidents that might be embarrassing to the president. The chief of staff is the person who has a close-enough relationship with the president and a broad-enough perspective to make sure that the politics of the president and the policies of the administration mesh as smoothly as possible.

The bottom line is that somebody short of the president must be in charge of the White House. The president's job is too overwhelming to include managerial duties and overseeing the White House staff. The chief of staff should be as informed as the president on all of the dimensions of presidential policy making. But delegated power must be monitored; the president must make sure that the White House is being managed to his specifications and that the chief of staff does not abuse the great amount of authority that is delegated to him.

BIBLIOGRAPHY

Buchanan, Bruce. "Constrained Diversity: The Organizational Demands of the Presidency." In *The Managerial Presidency*, edited by James P. Pfiffner. Pacific Grove, Calif., 1991.

Hess, Stephen. *Organizing the White House.* 2d ed. Washington, D.C., 1988.

Johnson, Richard Tanner. *Managing the White House.* New York, 1974.

Kernell, Samuel, and Samuel Popkin. *Chief of Staff: Twenty-Five Years of Managing the Presidency.* Berkeley, Calif., 1986.

Neustadt, Richard. *Presidential Power and the Modern Presidents.* New York, 1990.

Neustadt, Richard. "Does the White House Need a Strong Chief of Staff?" In *The Managerial Presidency*, edited by James P. Pfiffner. Pacific Grove, Calif., 1991.

Patterson, Bradley. *Ring of Power.* New York, 1988.

Pfiffner, James P. "The President's Chief of Staff: Lessons Learned." *Presidential Studies Quarterly* 23 (Winter 1993): 77–102.

Pfiffner, James P. *The Strategic Presidency: Hitting the Ground Running*, 2d ed. Lawrence, Kans., 1996.

—James P. Pfiffner

Children and Families, Administration for.

See Health and Human Services, Department of.

CIA.

See Central Intelligence Agency.

Cities, Localities, and the Federal Government

ESSAY Relationships between the federal government and the many local governments in the United States have taken a variety of forms over the years. Over the long term, and with many deviations, the relationships have become more numerous and more complex. Some of the relationships have also been frequently controversial.

The growth and increasing complexity of federal-local relations are due to many factors. The growth of America's urban population meant that people were increasingly affected by one another's actions, which led to increasing calls for governmental intervention to deal with problems ranging from poverty to crime and pollution. Those pressures were magnified by the Great Depression, which simultaneously added to the burdens facing local governments and reduced their ability to raise funds on their own. State governments were also in financial difficulty and unable to provide adequate assistance to their localities. Many local governments turned to the federal government for help, and the result was a fairly durable set of bonds between the two levels.

The mobilization of local political influence further encouraged the development of federal-local ties. That mobilization took many forms, from the growing voting power of urban areas and the power of some local party organizations (such as New York City and Chicago in the early 1900s) to the formation of associations of local officials, such as the U.S. Conference of Mayors, organized in part to lobby the federal government. Private groups concerned about specific local problems worked with agency specialists, such as educators or police officers, to press for federal assistance.

Strains and conflicts between states and localities also encouraged localities to seek help from the federal government. When state officials have been unwilling or unable to respond to local needs, local officials have sometimes found the federal government to be more helpful. That has not always been the case, but it has been true often enough to encourage local officials to take their concerns to Washington, D.C., from time to time. The emergence of direct national-local relations has sometimes encouraged state officials to be more attentive to local concerns in order to prevent the development of even more national-local ties.

Changing beliefs about the federal system also helped to produce more contact between the national government and local governments. Beginning in the 1930s, public officials and scholars came to think about federalism in a new way, with a greater emphasis on sharing of powers and responsibilities and less emphasis on separating different levels from one another. In the 1950s and 1960s, greater acceptance of local governments as full partners in the federal system encouraged development of even more national-local contact. Federal judges came to be more accepting of federal laws applying to local governments and to be more willing to hear lawsuits against local governments.

National-local relations also became more important and complex with the development of the national grant system. The U.S. Constitution gives the national government broader powers in raising and spending money than in passing ordinary laws, and those financial powers provided an important foundation for cooperation between the national government and localities. Direct grants from the national government to localities grew from only $10 million in 1932 to $22 billion in 1981, then declined to approximately $15 billion by 1992. In addition, a substantial share of the much larger amount of federal grant money given to state governments ultimately trickles down to local government coffers.

National-local relations take a great many forms. Some arise from national programs that do not officially involve local governments but that may significantly affect cities and other local governments. A decision to open or close a major federal facility, such as a military base, may greatly affect the economy of a community. Federal transportation and tax policies have also influenced local economies, in part by affecting where businesses locate and where families decide to move. Social programs have helped reduce the local burden of caring for the elderly, poor, and sick.

Federal-local relations also take the form of joint involvement in many programs. From law enforcement, environmental protection, and public health to transportation, education, and even foreign trade, federal and local (and state) officials find themselves trying to deal with common problems. Virtually all major public policies today involve activities by all three levels of government. Federal and local officials provide one another with advice and technical assistance on many subjects; as the technological complexity of many programs and policies has increased over the years, officials at one level of government often need ideas and guidance from officials at another level.

Federal-local relations emerge in their most dramatic form during emergencies. When a hurricane, earthquake, or major flood strikes, the combined resources of national, state, and local governments will be needed in order to repair the damage and help the victims. After the emergency is over, the experience of cooperation to solve a pressing problem may help to encourage future cooperation on less dramatic matters.

Relationships between the national government and local governments are very complex, in part because of the large number of local governments in the United States (more than eighty thousand). In addition, the powers and responsibilities of local governments vary considerably from state to state and within individual states as well. A task that is assigned to city governments in one state may be assigned to county governments in another state and to special district governments in a third. Large cities within a state may have powers and responsibilities that are not given to small cities in the same state. Many national-local programs include various private-sector organizations as well as local governments; nonprofit organizations, both public and private, are eligible to participate in nearly half of all federal grant programs, for example. The task of keeping track of all of the many participants is extremely difficult.

Federal and local officials sometimes have very different priorities and sometimes face very different political climates; both conditions add further complexity to national-local relations. An interest group that is very powerful in some communities may be relatively weak nationwide. A program may affect some communities much more than others and, therefore, produce different reactions in different communities. Complications also arise from legislation that is vague and, therefore, does not give clear guidance to national or local administrators regarding how the program should operate. In that situation, of-

ficials in different settings may interpret the law in very different ways. Taken together, the various sources of complexity in federal-local programs have sometimes created serious problems for those programs.

Longer-term assessments of national-local programs present a somewhat more encouraging picture, however. Many of those programs apparently go through an initial phase in which many problems surface. Developing a smooth working relationship among a number of different agencies and organizations may take several years. Program goals may be initially unclear, and some procedures may be ineffective. Some personnel in key roles may need to be replaced or need additional experience before they can perform adequately. Improvements are not automatic, but with sustained effort program performance gradually improves in many cases as goals are clarified, working relationships improve, and procedures are fine-tuned.

One strategy that has sometimes been used to improve the administration of national-local programs is to include program clienteles, the people served by the program, in program administration. Those efforts have not always officially included local governments in the process, but the efforts have significantly affected national-local relations. One attempt to involve program clienteles occurred in the 1960s during the War on Poverty. The Community Action Programs, which tried to combat poverty, were to be carried out with substantial participation by poor people in the areas being served. Reformers hoped that residents of poor neighborhoods would provide valuable information on the specific problems of their individual neighborhoods and add their own efforts to the battle against poverty. Controversies erupted in many communities, in part over who would control the programs and in part owing to established agencies' resentment of the new programs being run by other people. Local officials in some areas were publicly criticized by the new antipoverty activists. In the wrangling that followed, many of the Community Action Agencies were closed down; others came under the control of local governments. The poor lost influence over program operations.

Federal programs regulating grazing on public lands have also tried to involve clienteles in program administration. Although those efforts have also produced controversy, the results have been notably different. When the federal government began those regulations in the 1930s, local associations of ranchers were involved in deciding which ranchers would receive grazing permits, and their involvement often had considerable influence. Since then, the associations of ranchers have sometimes mobilized to fight proposed policy changes, such as higher grazing fees and environmental regulations. These controversies have not, however, led to efforts to exclude ranchers from program operations.

The development of direct relationships between the national government and local governments has been a controversial one in many respects. Officials at different levels of government have somewhat different perspectives, and there are also differing views among officials in the same level of government. With significant exceptions, national officials are primarily interested in individual policies rather than broad issues of federalism or intergovernmental relations. One sign of that emphasis is the fact that the vast majority of federal grants to states and localities is in the form of grants for narrowly defined purposes; those grants distributed about eighty-nine percent of all federal aid funds in 1995. Although federal officials sometimes talk about broad issues of federalism, that discussion is frequently a somewhat roundabout way of trying to advance specific policy goals. That is, officials often try to move program decisions to arenas where they believe that their policy views are most likely to receive a friendly response.

National officials' concern for individual programs encourages the use of numerous mechanisms for affecting how local officials manage those programs. Local officials may have to submit detailed plans for review by federal officials before taking action and may have to submit reports from time to time regarding program operations. Federal officials may inspect local operations and sometimes investigate local actions that appear inconsistent with federal policies. Some federal programs include numerous guide-lines regarding the procedures localities must use in order to participate in the program. Federal courts also review local actions from time to time. The vast bulk of all this activity is focused on individual programs and agencies.

Federal officials are particularly concerned about monitoring local programs when the federal government is paying a large percentage of program costs. Federal officials sometimes worry that local officials may be tempted to use federal funds for unauthorized activities, a worry that is sometimes justified.

Federal officials are also concerned by the difficulty of coordinating federal-local programs. Part of the difficulty stems from inconsistencies among federal programs. Interest group pressures, the power of congressional committees, and agency parochialism, among other forces, sometimes produce national policies that contradict one another. Coordination problems also arise at the local level in two respects. First, the actions of various actors (national, state, local, and private) working in the same program area need to be coordinated. Second, activities involving different programs sometimes must be drawn together. If they are not, different programs may interfere with one another's operations. For example, resources expended to revitalize a neighborhood may be wasted when the neighborhood is then destroyed to make way for a new freeway or shopping mall.

Coordination in the field is difficult for many reasons. The large number of local governments, variations in their powers, and overlapping jurisdictions of cities, counties, and other local governments all create coordination problems. In addition, local officials do not always want to coordinate their actions with one another, and the same can be said for state, private, and even federal actors. A variety of reforms to improve coordination in the field have produced disappointing results, a pattern that reflects the strength of forces resisting coordination.

National officials seeking to influence local program operations and improve coordination in the field face an awkward dilemma. Overly rigid national controls may prevent necessary adaptation of programs to local conditions and may antagonize local officials, sometimes to the point of creating political problems for national officials. Moreover, local officials may decide not to participate in federal grant programs if federal controls are unduly burdensome, particularly for grant programs involving relatively small amounts of money. Conversely, too little federal oversight may lead to a neglect of federal priorities and diversion of funds to inappropriate uses. Striking the right balance between too much and too little federal control is far from easy.

Local perspectives on national-local relations present a somewhat different pattern. Local officials generally appreciate receiving financial help from the federal government, and many local officials at least occasionally appreciate being able to deal with Washington, D.C., directly. That has been particularly the case for local officials from large cities, which have sometimes had difficulty in dealing with their respective state governments.

Many local officials criticize federal policies that are too rigid and federal monitoring that is too intrusive. The volume of paperwork needed to participate in a number of federal-local programs has been reduced in recent years, but local officials still find the burden excessive at times. The federal government's recurrent difficulty in passing its budget on time creates additional difficulty for local officials. They may have to adopt their own budgets before funding decisions for federal grants are completed. If the federal funding is less generous than expected, local budgets may have to be cut. The declining purchasing power of direct national-local grants since the 1970s has also generated numerous complaints.

Local officials with broad responsibilities, officials such as mayors and city managers, also express concern over the federal government's emphasis on individual programs. When a federal grant must be spent for a narrowly defined purpose or returned to the federal government, the grant may enhance the autonomy of local bureaucracies at the expense of elected officials. When many of the interactions between the federal government and local governments involve agency specialists at each level, generalists such as mayors may find themselves on the sidelines.

Local officials, too, face a dilemma. They value federal assistance but also want local autonomy. Federal officials rarely want to give localities large sums of money without some say in how the money is used. Local autonomy also can carry political risks; more than one local official has occasionally used federal regulations or guidelines to provide political cover for a controversial action.

State officials frequently have mixed feelings regarding national-local programs. Some state officials, particularly the more conservative ones, oppose national-local programs as excessive federal intrusion in domestic policy making. State officials also worry that direct national-local ties threaten state control over local governments. This concern sometimes seems excessive in view of the broad array of powers that states have over local governments. However, many state programs are jointly administered by states and their localities; state officials sometimes fear that national influence may jeopardize state policies being implemented at the local level.

State officials also recognize that national-local programs satisfy demands that might otherwise gravitate to state capitals. Even when state officials complain loudly about federal intrusiveness, many of those same officials appreciate federal assistance for vital programs.

Republican and Democratic party perspectives on national-local relations at the national and state levels have been noticeably different since the 1930s. Generally speaking, Democrats have been more supportive of federal aid to urban areas and of an active federal role in dealing with local governments overall. Republicans have generally preferred a more limited federal role, with more discretion being left to the states, and have preferred channeling federal aid through state governments rather than dealing with local governments directly. Those general tendencies, however, are sometimes overriden by specific policy concerns.

The conflicting perspectives regarding national-local relations, coordination problems, and other considerations have periodically led to calls to reduce the amount of direct contact between the national government and local (and state) governments and reduce the national government's role in domestic policy making generally. Those efforts include the first and second Hoover Commissions in the 1940s and 1950s, the Joint Federal-State Action Committee of the late 1950s, and the New Federalism of the Reagan administration.

A recent effort to reduce direct national-local contacts occurred during the 1995–1996 congressional term. The results of that effort are yet to be fully assessed, but some familiar patterns seem to be emerging. All efforts to reduce national-local contacts produce complaints from people who are concerned that the reduction will harm programs that they support. In addition, local officials are fearful that the loss of federal aid will add to local financial difficulties that are already considerable in many localities. Some local officials also fear that reduced access to the federal government will leave localities at the mercy of state governments. If the past is any guide, efforts to reduce direct national-local contacts are likely to face considerable difficulty, particularly in the long run. President Reagan was able to reduce local governments' access to the White House during his presidency, for example, but Presidents Bush and Clinton made local officials much more welcome again. The American political system has many access points; keeping out active, persistent people is very difficult for any length of time.

BIBLIOGRAPHY

Characteristics of Federal Grant-in-Aid Programs to State and Local Governments: Grants Funded, Fiscal Year 1995. Washington, D.C., 1995.

Graves, W. Brooke. *American Intergovernmental Relations.* New York, 1964.

Grodzins, Morton. *The American System.* New Brunswick, N.J., 1984.

Martin, Roscoe. *The Cities and the Federal System.* New York, 1965.

McConnell, Grant. *Private Power and American Democracy.* New York, 1966.

Moynihan, Daniel. *Maximum Feasible Misunderstanding.* New york, 1970.

Murphy, Jerome. "The Education Bureaucracies Implement Novel Policy: The Politics of Title I of ESEA, 1965–72." In *Policy and Politics in America,* edited by Allan Sindler, pp. 160–199. Boston, 1973.

Nice, David, and Patricia Fredericksen. *The Politics of Intergovernmental Relations.* 2d ed. Chicago, 1995.

Peterson, Paul, Barry Rabe, and Kenneth Wong. *When Federalism Works.* Washington, D.C., 1986.

Pressman, Jeffrey, and Aaron Wildavsky. *Implementation,* 2d ed. Berkeley, 1979.

Schattschneider, E.E. *The Semisovereign People.* New York, 1960.

Significant Features of Fiscal Federalism. Washington, D.C., 1991, 1994.

Wright, Deil. *Understanding Intergovernmental Relations.* 3d ed. Pacific Grove, Calif., 1988.

—DAVID C. NICE

Civil Rights Commission

The U.S. Commission on Civil Rights is an independent advisory agency created when Congress passed the Civil Rights Act of 1957. The commission was initially established on a temporary basis to provide a bipartisan fact-finding forum to study problems of voting discrimination against African American citizens in the South. Congress directed the commission to:

- Investigate complaints of voting discrimination

- Study and collect information concerning the denial of equal protection of the laws on account of race, color, religion, and national origin

- Assess the effectiveness of federal laws and policies against discrimination

- Serve as a national clearinghouse for civil rights information

- Advise the president and Congress.

The commission lacks enforcement authority but is empowered to hold hearings, subpoena witnesses, publish reports, issue findings, and submit recommendations.

Between 1957 and 1968 the commission won wide respect for reports documenting racial discrimination in the South and for recommendations that helped shape the Civil Rights Act of 1964, the Voting Rights Act of 1965, and the Open Housing Act of 1968. Although an agency with a small staff and budget, the commission from the beginning maintained a prominent public profile, holding hearings and issuing influential reports on voting discrimination, school desegregation, fair housing, equal employment opportunity, and the administration of justice.

In the 1970s the policy agenda of the commission expanded and shifted to reflect the addition by Congress, the federal courts, and regulatory agencies of new protections and remedies. In addition to race, religion, and national origin the commission monitored discrimination by sex, age, and disability. In addition to nondiscrimination policies, the commission supported controversial affirmative action remedies, including school busing for racial balance, minority hiring preferences, "comparable worth" standards to reduce gender differences in pay, the Equal Rights Amendment, and "race norming" in employment test scores. By the late 1970s the commission was attacked by conservatives and Republicans as a "captured" agency serving the interests of liberal advocacy groups, especially African American, feminist, Hispanic, and Native American organizations.

Following the election of 1980 the Reagan administration attempted to replace sitting commissioners with appointees critical of "reverse discrimination." The result was a political battle during 1981–1982 that split the agency and damaged its credibility and effectiveness. In 1983 Congress compromised with the president, expanding the number of commissioners from six presidential appointees to eight, four of them appointed by the president and four by Congress. As civil rights policy has grown more complex in the 1980s and 1990s, constituency groups benefiting from enforcement policies have grown in number and competition for enforcement attention among protected groups has increased. As a consequence, the ideological clarity of civil rights disputes has become blurred and controversy over the Civil Rights Commission has declined.

BIBLIOGRAPHY

Ball, Howard. "United States Commission on Civil Rights." In *Government Agencies,* edited by Donald R. Whitnah, pp. 130–133. Westport, Conn., 1983.
Dulles, Foster Rhea. *The Civil Rights Commission, 1957–1965.* East Lansing, Mich., 1968.
Lawson, Stephen F. *Black Ballots: Voting Rights in the South, 1944–1969.* New York, 1976.
—HUGH DAVIS GRAHAM

Civil Service

The three fundamental purposes of civil service systems are to recruit qualified personnel, to compensate and develop members of the public's work force, and to provide a basic framework of guidelines and procedures for how the work force should be organized. Every modern nation assumes or legislates that the members of the civil service system should also be responsive to the wishes and demands of elected officials. These are straightforward responsibilities. They do not, however, reflect the real complexity of the civil service in modern nations. They most certainly do not reflect the complexity of the United States's federal civil service system.

To fully understand the reality of the federal system, it is necessary to know the evolution of the jobs and tasks performed by the civil service. Of equal significance, it is essential to understand the close, but always uncomfortable, relationship between the civil service—or merit—system and the political system that provides both its environment and its leadership.

THE ORIGINS OF THE MERIT SYSTEM

It has frequently been argued that one of the enduring problems of the federal civil service is the failure of the Constitution to provide for its role in government. Quite clearly, the Founding Fathers visualized a more limited role for a professional service than that which has emerged after two hundred years. At the same time, they consciously divided responsibility for overseeing whatever that role might be. The president, as director of the executive branch, would have direct responsibility for the administration of government. The Congress, as holder of the purse strings, would also have responsibility, however: that of oversight and budgetary control. The arrangement was never the most comfortable of fits. Alexander Hamilton's view that the quality of government would be judged by its administration implied a strong executive to ensure that quality. Madison's commitment to divided power ensured tension and conflict as the federal bureaucracy grew in size and responsibility.

The early growth in the bureaucracy was also accompanied by changes in its demographic and educational composition. Early members of the public service corps were persons like the Founding Fathers themselves: wealthy, well-educated, white male landowners. As politics became more diverse, and as mass politics became a defining characteristic of the United States, the public service changed as well. Patronage—the awarding of a public job for partisan service or affiliation—created a civil service that looked much more like the society at large than did the earlier elite groups. Gender and racial discrimination continued to cause the group to be almost totally white and male, however.

Andrew Jackson is the president most often charged with patronage excesses. In fact, however, he only continued the practices of his predecessors with a bit more enthusiasm and with a different group of partisan appointees. Further, the practice of patronage continued to grow in size and scope after the Jackson presidency. During the Civil War, a common joke attributed the Union loss at Bull Run to the announcement of a federal job opportunity in New York; essentially the entire Union force, said the joke, left the battlefield to apply for the job.

The continued growth of patronage had two major effects on the federal service: it caused large numbers of employees to leave with every presidential election, and over time, it devalued the quality and the purpose of the service. If a job could be bought—with party service, favors, or cash—it would not be held in high esteem. Over time, recognition of the debilitating effect of patronage and public displeasure with its abuses led to the formation of good government leagues in several of the states. The assassination of President Garfield by a deranged office seeker in 1881, combined with upcoming congressional elections in which reform would be a major issue, provided dramatic impetus for reform legislation. The Pendleton Act, the first major legislation to address the federal civil service, was passed in 1883.

The Pendleton Act created what is now referred to as the merit system. Initially, the provisions of the act covered only ten percent of the federal work force. The legislation mandated that, for the covered positions, admission to the federal service would be only through neutral competitive examinations. While the Pendleton Act was clearly modeled on the British civil service, it had been molded to reflect strongly held American values, the most notable being the emphasis on common sense and "common" knowledge rather than on the educational requirements found in European systems. The act also created a bipartisan Civil Service Commission, whose purpose was to oversee the operation of the merit system, and also to advise the president on the remaining components of patronage, which were very substantial.

In very important ways, the Pendleton Act institutionalized the tensions between politics and merit in the American federal service. The ability of the president and the Congress to influence placement in the merit system itself was seriously constrained. Since the act covered only ten percent of the work force, however, ample opportunity for patronage continued to exist. In addition, the president would, as the Constitution provided, appoint the top decision-makers in each executive department—the policymakers. As early as 1887, Woodrow Wilson's description of the different roles that politics and the merit system would play in government—what has been termed the "politics/administration dichotomy"—made clear the continuing issues related to politics and merit.

THE GROWTH OF MERIT

Growth of the merit system occurred incrementally and in a disjointed way. By 1900 about forty percent of the federal service was "classified," or covered under the terms of the Pendleton Act. Much of the growth occurred when entire agencies were converted or "blanketed in" to the merit system at the end of presidential terms. The effect of this, of course, was to convert former political appointees to merit employees. Growth of the federal civil service continued in an essentially incremental way until the New Deal; the programs associated with New Deal policies increased the growth of the federal service dramatically. At the same time, President Franklin Roosevelt's distaste for the "neutral competence" of the merit system led him to create many new agencies outside of Civil Service Commission jurisdiction.

The strong emphases of the early development of the merit system were on neutrality and efficiency. The competitive and objective entrance examination was intended to ensure neutral application of skills and expertise. In keeping with the scientific management administrative theories of the time, standardization of practices and procedures across government was intended to produce the most efficient means of achieving government objectives. The civil service was organized to achieve both of these objectives; classification and compensation were tightly linked. The Classification Act of 1923 classified and graded the nearly one million federal employees by duties and responsibilities. In the application of one of its most significant components, the arranging of jobs within the organization in ascending order of responsibility and authority, the Classification Act created rigid, hierarchical federal organizations. Skills and positions were very narrowly defined and boundaries between jobs were strict.

The 1923 act also created compensation schedules for 1) the Professional and Scientific service; 2) the Subprofessional service; 3) the Clerical, Administrative and Fiscal service; 4) the Custodial service; and 5) the Clerical-Mechanical service. These broad categories are generally descriptive of the nature of federal jobs at the time. The act provided that no salary increase could occur in the system without ". . . attainment and maintenance of appropriate efficiency ratings" (Ingraham, p. 39).

Despite early and intense criticism of both classification and compensation schemes, reforms were slow in coming. The Classification Act was not reformed until 1949, following the report of the first Hoover Commission. Federal employment had exploded in the years from 1938 to 1945, growing from about 800,000 to almost four million. The Hoover Commission's motto—"Better Government for a Better Price!"—reflected the desire to focus once again on economy and efficiency in the operation of the civil service. As had the Brownlow Committee a decade earlier, the Hoover Commission argued that the *management* of the civil service needed to be emphasized and that reformed structures would facilitate improved management. [*See* Brownlow Committee *and* Appendix: Concluding Report of the Commission on Organization of the Executive Branch of Government (First Hoover Commission) (1949).]

UNDERSTANDING THE COMPLEXITY

In fact, however, by the end of World War II, the formal classification and compensation structures of the federal civil service did not even begin to describe its real operation and full complexity. Veterans' preference, excepted hiring authorities, and special hiring authorities had become significant components of federal recruiting, hiring, and promotion policies and practices. Later, unions and collective bargaining added participation and complexity to the process.

Veterans' preference had been a part of public personnel practice since before the Civil War; provisions for Civil War veterans were part of the Pendleton Act's provisions. Essentially, veterans' preference provides that all veterans have additional points added to their competitive examination scores; disabled veterans receive more points than those veterans who are not disabled. Particularly in the two decades after World War II, the impact of these preferential points was notable on the demographic composition of the federal work force as large numbers of veterans entered the public service and spent most of their careers there.

Excepted and special hiring authorities are also important. Two excepted authorities, called Schedule A authority and Schedule B authority, were created shortly after the passage of the Pendleton Act. Schedule A permits the hiring, without additional testing, of persons whose professions conduct nationally accepted examinations. Examples of persons hired under this authority are lawyers and accountants. Schedule B authority permits specialized hiring for occupations whose national labor pool is too small to warrant a national examination effort. In the 1980s, after the centralized Professional and Administrative Career Examination was abolished because of its discriminatory impact, Schedule B became the only hiring authority available to those federal agencies who needed to hire persons who did not qualify under Schedule A authority. (A new central examination, the Administrative Careers with America examination, was introduced in 1990.)

Schedule C, the third major excepted authority, was created in the Eisenhower administration to permit hiring of partisan associates into policy-sensitive positions. To that time, the president's appointment authority in policy positions had been limited to those appointments that needed Senate confirmation. These were at the highest levels of the executive departments and agencies, and included the departmental secretaries, under secretaries, and assistant secretaries. Schedule C permitted the hiring of both lower-level and support positions for these appointments. The president also has the power to appoint ten percent of the members of the Senior Executive Service (created in 1978), ambassadors, members of standing commissions, and a limited number of other appointees; the total number of appointments available to the president government-wide is now about three thousand.

Special hiring authorities allow the hiring, without examination or with more limited examining, of special groups. One example of a special hiring authority is that for Outstanding Scholars: any recent college graduate with a GPA of at least 3.5 can be hired directly and without examination. Temporary and part-time hiring is also common in the civil service.

Compensation, as noted earlier, is linked to grade and level of responsibility. Although the standardized system has operated from the foundation of "equal pay for equal work," blue collar rates have been linked to local labor market wages for many years. For most other civil servants, until 1962 Congress had to pass legislation specifically intended to increase pay; the very highest members of the career service continue to have their pay level capped at the level of congressional salaries. To increase the salaries of members of the Senior Executive Service, therefore, it is necessary for Congress to increase its own pay as well.

Federal Pay Acts in 1962 and 1970 gave the president a major voice in the pay-setting process for white collar employees and included the principle of comparability with private sector pay scales. Federal labor unions are also involved in the annual review of federal salaries. It has been the historic pattern that, except for cost-of-living adjustments, long periods of time elapse between federal pay increases. The National Commission on the Public Service (1989) estimated that federal pay—particularly executive-level pay—lagged behind private sector counterparts by as much as two-thirds at the end of the 1980s. This problem was addressed by the Bush administration, which successfully argued for a substantial salary increase for members of the Senior Executive Service and for the passage of the Federal Employee Pay Comparability Act of 1990. That legislation allowed white collar wages to be linked to regional rates in most large metropolitan areas of the United States. In addition, performance-related pay incentives were introduced for the Senior Executive Service in 1978 and for mid-level managers in 1981. The mid-level program was discontinued in 1993, but many agencies continue to operate some kind of performance pay system for upper-level managers.

The final complexity that is important is the creation of entire personnel systems outside of the core civil service. The Foreign Service has always had its own system; the Postal Service has its own system as well. The General Accounting Office, an agency of Congress, also has an independent personnel system. The splintering occurred in pay systems as well as personnel. Over thirty different pay systems currently operate in the federal service. Decentralization and delegation of authority, which has often proceeded without clear central guidelines or monitoring, have served to increase ambiguity in the areas of personnel and pay.

REFORMING THE CIVIL SERVICE SYSTEM

Not surprisingly, this complexity and confusion led to efforts at reform. In fact, efforts at reform are nearly as old as the merit system itself. In the United States there has been a major commission on reform on the average of every seven years since 1900. Two of the most recent efforts are notable: Jimmy Carter's Civil Service Reform Act of

1978 and the Clinton administration's efforts to "reinvent" government.

The Carter reform was the first effort to comprehensively reform the civil service since the passage of the Pendleton Act. It was a major focus of the Carter presidency. While the act contained many provisions, three are of enduring significance: the Civil Service Commission was abolished, the Senior Executive Service was created, and performance-based pay was formally introduced for managers and senior executives at Grade 13 and above. The Senior Executive Service and performance-based pay have already been mentioned; their intent was to break traditional civil service patterns in promotion and mobility and to create a more flexible, performance-oriented set of government managers. The Senior Executive Service was modeled on the British higher civil service; the concept of pay for performance was borrowed from the private sector. The Senior Executive Service was composed of the former members of the top rungs of the career service: grades 16–18. Performance pay applied to both the Senior Executive Service and lower-level managers. Neither of these reforms has accomplished all of its goals; as noted earlier, mandatory mid-level performance pay was discontinued by Congress in 1993.

The Civil Service Commission was replaced by the Office of Personnel Management and the Merit Systems Protection Board; the intent was to clearly separate the function of oversight of merit from other central personnel functions. The director of the Office of Personnel Management became a presidential appointee, while the Merit Systems Protection Board was governed by a bipartisan board. The Civil Service Reform Act also created the Federal Labor Relations Authority, an appellate body for collective bargaining processes and grievances. With the passage of the act, collective bargaining rights were codified for the first time in the federal government. [See Personnel Management, Office of.]

Despite some successes, the concomitant failures of the Civil Service Reform Act are made clear by the efforts at reform which followed it. The Reagan election shortly after its passage clearly changed the political and governmental environment in which the act was implemented; other components of the act required more fundamental changes than the law proposed to be effective. Pay for performance is the leading example.

The most recent effort at reform is the Reinventing Government initiative of the Clinton administration. This is a controversial set of reforms that are premised on the foundation of entrepreneurial government; the intent is to increase the authority and discretion of federal agencies and managers and to emphasize customer (i.e., citizen) service and satisfaction. The activity produced no major legislation in human resource management but did abandon the massive Federal Personnel Manual. Spearheaded by Vice President Al Gore, Reinventing Government remained a major initiative of the Clinton administration throughout its term, but again, it produced mixed results in attempting to solve the thorny problems of the federal civil service. That remains a political, as well as a personnel, issue. [See National Performance Review.]

There is no question, however, that reforms will continue. Both the structure and the operation of the civil service are likely to change as the emphasis turns away from traditional bureaucracy and rigid standardization to flexibility, increased discretion, the separation of policy from operations and service delivery, and smaller decentralized agencies. How the civil service will be employed, rewarded, and held accountable in such circumstances will be key questions for future civil service reforms.

[See also Appendix: Civil Service (Pendleton) Act (1883) and Classification Act (1923).]

BIBLIOGRAPHY

Carroll, James D. "The Rhetoric of Reform and Political Reality in the National Performance Review." *Public Administration Review* 55 (May–June 1995): 302–310.

Gulick, Luther, and Lyndall Urwick, eds. *Papers on the Science of Administration.* New York, 1937.

Ingraham, Patricia Wallace. *The Foundation of Merit: Public Service in American Democracy.* Baltimore, 1995.

Ingraham, Patricia W., and David Rosenbloom. "The New Personnel and the New Public Service." *Public Administration Review* 49 (March–April 1989): 116–125.

Ingraham, Patricia W., and David Rosenbloom. *The Promise and Paradox of Civil Service Reform.* Pittsburgh, 1992.

Kettl, Donald F. *Reinventing Government? Appraising the National Performance Review.* Washington, D.C., 1994.

Mosher, Frederick C. *Democracy and the Public Service.* New York, 1968.

National Commission on the Public Service. *Leadership for America: Rebuilding the Public Service.* Lexington, Mass., 1989.

National Performance Review. *Reinventing Government: Creating a Government That Works Better and Costs Less.* Washington, D.C., 1993.

Osborne, David. "Resurrecting Government." *Washington Post Magazine,* 8 January 1995, 13–17, 28–32.

Rohr, John. *To Run a Constitution.* Lawrence, Kans., 1986.

Rosenbloom, David. *Public Administration and the Law.* New York, 1983.

Rossiter, Clinton, ed. *The Federalist Papers.* New York, 1961.

Skrowonek, Stephen. *Building a New American State: Expansion of National Administrative Capacities.* New York, 1982.

Van Riper, Paul. *History of the United States Civil Service.* Evanston, Ill., 1958.

Wilson, Woodrow. "The Study of Administration." *Political Science Quarterly* 2 (June 1887): 200–213.

—Patricia W. Ingraham

Classification Act.

See Appendix: Basic Documents of Public Administration.

Coast Guard

The U.S. Coast Guard was formed on 28 January 1915, when President Woodrow Wilson signed legislation merging the Revenue-Cutter Service and the Life-Saving Service. The act specified that the Coast Guard should be a military service, although more than half of its personnel, some twenty-three hundred men of the former Life-Saving Service, had been civilians, most of whom continued to serve for only ten months each year. In fact, the two services had been merged at the top only, the lifesaving branch of the Coast Guard retaining its separate identity under the chief of operations, who had his desk in the commandant's office at headquarters in Wash-

ington, D.C. The Coast Guard continued to be under the Treasury Department; in time of war or when the president might direct, it would be transferred to the Navy Department.

The new service was responsible for all of the duties previously assigned its predecessors, most notably the protection of life and property at sea, which included the International Ice Patrol, created as a result of the *Titanic* disaster, and enforcement of the nation's maritime laws. Licensing merchant marine lifeboatmen was added a short time later, leading to a growing involvement in matters pertaining to the merchant marine.

On 6 April 1917 the Coast Guard was transferred to the Navy Department when the United States declared war on the German Empire. Six of the largest cutters went to the war zone to escort slow convoys between the United Kingdom and Gibraltar, while the remainder served on escort and patrol duties in American waters and trained naval personnel. One of the former, the *Tampa,* was torpedoed and sunk with all hands in September 1918, the U.S. Navy's greatest combat loss during World War I. Meanwhile, surfmen at the lifesaving stations were kept on duty throughout the year as coast watchers; henceforth they would serve full time.

At the war's end, a large majority of the Coast Guard's officers wished that their service be retained by the Navy, believing it would fare better under the larger sea service. Captain-commandant Ellsworth P. Bertholf and a few of his subordinates at Coast Guard headquarters disagreed, pointing out that the peacetime duties of the two services were fundamentally different and that the Coast Guard could not long survive as a separate organization under the Navy Department. The latter group carried the day; President Wilson returned the Coast Guard to Treasury Department control by executive order on 28 August 1919.

The immediate postwar period was difficult, primarily because of personnel shortages—until 1924, the service had fewer than four thousand officers and men, little more than three-fifths of its authorized strength. That year, however, saw the beginning of the Coast Guard's involvement in Prohibition enforcement; within a short time, the service's personnel more than doubled, enabling numerous additional vessels, including twenty-five of the Navy's older destroyers, to be manned. Although many of these ships, including the destroyers, were employed principally against rumrunners, the Coast Guard's other duties were not neglected, and the commandant, Rear Admiral Frederick C. Billard, insisted that the saving of life must remain the primary concern of all units.

Prohibition brought about the true birth of Coast Guard aviation. A number of officers had received flight training at the Navy's Pensacola aviation training station during World War I, but the postwar personnel shortage caused these men to be ordered to other duties. In 1926 five aircraft were purchased for reconnaissance purposes, and thereafter aviation continued to be an increasingly important part of the service; by 1934 it had forty aircraft flying from six air stations.

The Coast Guard Academy, which provided many of the service's officers, underwent a considerable improvement during this period. Its course of instruction was increased from two years to four in 1930, and two years later the school was moved from its inadequate campus at an abandoned Army post in New London, Connecticut, to its present location on the bank of the Thames River in the same city. In 1940 the Coast Guard Academy was formally accredited as a degree-granting institution.

Repeal of the Eighteenth Amendment in 1933 found the Coast Guard at a strength of more than twelve thousand officers and men, a number soon cut to ten thousand. Many of the vessels acquired for Prohibition enforcement were disposed of, including the destroyers, but some fifty seagoing cutters built during the 1920s were retained. Seven larger and faster cutters, each carrying a seaplane—the famous Treasury class—were commissioned in 1936–1937. New lifeboats were designed and built as well, and some lifesaving stations were rebuilt.

Rear Admiral Russell R. Waesche, who became commandant in 1936, completed the merger of the service's cutter and lifesaving branches; at the same time he undertook the politically sensitive task of closing lifesaving stations that had

been made redundant by the disappearance of sailing vessels (which had been relatively susceptible to shipwreck) and by the use of more modern and mobile equipment. Waesche also supervised the Coast Guard's most dramatic expansion, beginning late in 1936, when President Franklin D. Roosevelt directed the service to assume responsibility for icebreaking in domestic waters. Little more than a year later, administration of the new Maritime Service and the training of merchant seamen thereunder devolved on the Coast Guard.

The rapid spread of recreational boating during the 1930s taxed the regulating ability of the Coast Guard, especially because much of this activity occurred on inland waterways and lakes, while lifesaving stations were located on the nation's seacoasts and the Great Lakes. Regulation of the small-craft sailors by the more experienced among their number under Coast Guard supervision was the solution; Congress passed legislation creating the Coast Guard Reserve in June 1939, and enrollment of personnel began that autumn. Applicants had to prove their knowledge of navigation laws, rules of the road, aids to navigation, and boat handling, and their craft were inspected to assure the proper condition and equipment. Within a year the Coast Guard Reserve numbered twenty-six hundred men and twenty-three hundred boats. These part-time Coast Guardsmen, who served without compensation, assisted the service in performing search-and-rescue missions, inspecting small boats, instructing recreational boaters, and patrolling regattas. This proved to be a very popular solution to a potentially perplexing problem; small-craft sailors doubtless found regulation by their fellows less onerous than would have been the case had members of the regular Coast Guard assumed the responsibility, and service in the Reserve continued to attract large numbers.

On 1 July 1939 Congress enacted legislation in accordance with President Roosevelt's Reorganization Plan No. 2, under which the Bureau of Lighthouses was transferred from the Department of Commerce to the Treasury Department for consolidation with the Coast Guard. Thus, a military service numbering some ten thousand officers and men incorporated a civilian organization numbering more than five thousand full- and part-time employees who were responsible for manning or maintaining about thirty thousand aids to navigation, ranging from lighthouses and lightships to buoys and daymarks. Relatively few of the former Lighthouse Service personnel accepted induction into the Coast Guard, preferring to continue as civilians until they reached retirement age, but within a few years most had been replaced by Coast Guardsmen. Former Lighthouse Service and Coast Guard districts were consolidated, and the boundaries of the new districts were aligned more closely with those of naval districts to facilitate transfer of the Coast Guard in the event that the United States became actively involved in the war that began in Europe in September 1939.

The beginning of this conflict resulted in further expansion of Coast Guard duties; as in World War I, senior officers were appointed captains of the port in major seaports with responsibility for enforcing neutrality legislation and supervising the handling of hazardous cargoes. Within a short time a number of the larger cutters joined naval vessels in patrolling the two-hundred-mile neutrality zone off the Atlantic coast, and under the guise of the International Ice Patrol, German activity in Greenland was effectively countered by Coast Guard ships. The beginning of transoceanic air service led to the assignment of six Treasury-class cutters to ocean station duty in the Atlantic Ocean in 1940; Weather Bureau aerographers aboard them provided meteorological information, and aircraft encountering trouble might seek to alight in the vicinity of a cutter. These ships were required for escort duty in the autumn of 1941; former cargo vessels of World War I construction took their places, and when these became unserviceable, a variety of other Coast Guard–manned craft served on "weather patrol" through the remainder of the war.

Ten 250-foot cutters were transferred to Britain's Royal Navy for escort duty by Lend-Lease in the spring of 1941, whereupon their crews manned four Navy transports. Surfmen from lifeboat stations were assigned to teach naval personnel the difficult art of landing small craft through the surf and to man landing craft em-barked in the Navy's amphibious vessels. Most of the cutters were placed under naval control during the summer, and the Coast Guard itself was transferred to the Navy Department by executive order on 1 November 1941, by which time its personnel numbered more than twenty thousand; a full-time Reserve had been established by Congress nine months earlier, the erstwhile Reserve having become the Coast Guard Auxiliary. Members of the latter called to active duty for prolonged periods were dubbed the Temporary Reserve.

The Coast Guard expanded rapidly during World War II, reaching a peak strength of more than 171,000 by mid-1945. Its Women's Reserve numbered some ten thousand, and the Temporary Reserve ultimately had more than fifty thousand. The Temporary Reserve included defense factory police, harbor pilots, a variety of civil servants, and merchant marine inspectors from the former Bureau of Marine Inspection and Navigation, most of whose duties associated with merchant marine licensing and inspection were assumed by the Coast Guard in 1942; meanwhile, the new War Shipping Administration took over the merchant marine training responsibilities heretofore borne by the Bureau of Marine Inspection. During the war, Coast Guard personnel manned 351 naval vessels, most of which were engaged in amphibious warfare or escort duties, and 288 Army service craft. The service's own fleet was expanded by the acquisition of a number of private vessels and the construction of thirty-nine seagoing buoy tenders and five large icebreakers, three of which were transferred to the Soviet Union by Lend-Lease. Thirteen 255-foot cutters were completed too late for war service.

Primary responsibility for development of the electronic navigational system called LORAN (LOng RAnge Navigation) and naval use of the helicopter went to the Coast Guard, which would be associated with both long after the war. Construction of LORAN stations on coastlines of the nation and its possessions was well advanced by the war's end, and thereafter the series of stations reached global dimensions. All were manned by service personnel. The helicopter's antisubmarine role was emphasized at first, but

Coast Guard aviators involved in the program realized that its rescue capabilities would be more important for their service, especially in peacetime.

The Coast Guard was returned to the Treasury Department on 1 January 1946, by which time demobilization was proceeding rapidly, although some Coast Guardsmen continued to serve on board naval vessels for a few months thereafter. Planning for the postwar period, which had begun in 1943, anticipated that some thirty-five thousand officers and men would be necessary to perform the Coast Guard's duties, including LORAN and ocean stations and those formerly assigned to the Bureau of Marine Inspection and Navigation. By mid-1947, the service had little more than half that number, resulting in the curtailment of a number of activities, while members of the Auxiliary volunteered to assist with others.

The wartime expansion of Coast Guard responsibilities, several of which had been added without legislative authority, led Congress to order a thorough investigation of the service and its operations by a private management consulting firm, Ebasco Services, Inc., of New York, in 1947–1948. While recommending some changes, including a clear mandate of the service's mission, the investigators found that generally the Coast Guard's activities were in the public interest and were being performed efficiently. Passage of the necessary legislation followed in 1948.

The personnel shortage had forced the cessation of most of the ocean station activity by cutters, but in 1948 this was reestablished by international agreement, with the Coast Guard manning four stations in the Atlantic Ocean and two in the Pacific. This required more large cutters, so fifteen of the Navy's small seaplane tenders were transferred to the smaller service and refurbished for ocean station duty. Manning them was easier because selective service had been reinstated in 1948, and former Coast Guard and Navy petty officers were permitted to reenlist with their earlier rates.

Meanwhile, the development of electronic aids to navigation continued, with LORAN-C supplementing the older type. In 1956, the service was charged with coordinating search-and-rescue operations in the nation's maritime region under the National Search and Rescue Plan, and in 1958 AMVER, a system whereby merchant vessels reported regularly their positions, courses, and speeds to the Coast Guard for storage in a computer memory bank, was begun. Those closest to a vessel in distress could be diverted to assist, and in the event of a medical emergency, the ship could be directed to the nearest vessel with a doctor aboard. This voluntary program was immensely successful; begun in the North Atlantic, it was soon extended to other ocean areas.

By 1960 a number of the prewar cutters required replacement, so planning of new vessels began. All were to be capable of operating helicopters, which required ships of at least two hundred feet in length. A newly designed forty-four-foot lifeboat would later be described as "probably the finest rescue boat in the world"; more than one hundred such boats would serve for the next thirty years. In 1965 the Navy transferred its five icebreakers to the Coast Guard, which assumed responsibility for supporting the nation's programs in the Arctic and Antarctic regions.

Unlike the Korean War, to which the Coast Guard's sole contribution had been increased port security and ocean station activity, that in Vietnam brought much greater involvement: twenty-six eighty-two-foot patrol boats joined the inshore patrol force in Operation Market Time, supported by a number of the larger cutters; explosive-handling details were invaluable in supervising the offloading of large quantities of munitions; additional LORAN-C stations were established; buoy tenders serviced other aids to navigation; and a merchant marine detail dealt with disciplinary and other problems in merchant ships. The patrol boats were turned over to South Vietnam in 1970, as were four larger cutters, and the last Coast Guardsmen left Vietnam early in 1973.

Continuation of the Coast Guard's more traditional duties during the Vietnam conflict required a further expansion of personnel, to more than thirty-five thousand officers and men by 1966. The service itself was transferred from the Treasury Department to the Department of

Transportation when the latter was formed in 1967. Its missions remained many—indeed, they increased during the following decades, although the advent of jet aircraft and meteorological buoys led to the curtailment of the ocean stations, from which the last cutter was withdrawn in 1977. The larger cutters henceforth patrolled the two-hundred-mile economic resources zone and increasingly participated in efforts to regulate emigration from West Indian islands. The importation of illegal drugs from Latin America proved to be a greater challenge than Prohibition enforcement had been a half-century earlier, while tanker disasters led to environmental protection activities demanding a much greater share of the service's resources.

Although the Coast Guard's experience with integration during World War II had compared quite favorably with the other services, its relatively few blacks were all enlisted men thereafter until the early 1960s, when President John F. Kennedy ordered that blacks be admitted to the Academy. Women joined the Coast Guard's officer and enlisted ranks in 1973, and in 1977 they began to be assigned to regular billets in cutters, with all restrictions on their duties being removed a year later. A Coast Guard lieutenant (junior grade) became the first woman to command a U.S. warship in 1979, and the service has since striven to encourage women and minorities alike.

Electronic harbor traffic control experiments in the 1960s were unsuccessful; in 1972, a Vessel Traffic System, with two radar sets for marine traffic surveillance and control, began operation in San Francisco. Similar systems soon followed in the nation's major seaports, made the more necessary because of the tanker traffic necessitated by the country's growing dependence on imported petroleum. These have generally been very successful, notwithstanding the *Exxon Valdez* grounding that resulted in a major oil spill in Alaska's Prince William Sound in 1989.

Efforts to privatize a number of the Coast Guard's missions during the 1980s were less successful. A proposal that it be made a civilian service was abandoned when the National Security Council argued the importance of the Coast Guard's military role in defense plans. Budgetary limitations continued to plague the service— "doing more with less" had long since become a Coast Guard tradition. A number of its ships of World War II construction served more than fifty years; some will probably continue into the twenty-first century. Icebreakers are not among them; the last of these was decommissioned in 1989, leaving only two ships built during the 1970s in the nation's polar icebreaker fleet (although another is under construction, as are thirty seagoing and coastal buoy tenders). Minimum manning has been one of the responses to budgetary constraints; thus, new 225-foot buoy tenders will require twenty percent fewer personnel than the considerably smaller vessels they are to replace, although this may inhibit their usefulness for other than their designed missions. A new patrol boat to replace the long-lived eighty-two-footers is under design, and production of a number of forty-seven-foot lifeboats to replace the aging forty-four-footers has begun.

In the mid-1990s the Coast Guard's multimission role continued, albeit with fewer resources. By 1998 it was to have cut some four thousand people from its roster to save $400 million. To make this reduction without affecting the service's mission capabilities is the latest of the challenges the Coast Guard has faced during the past eighty years.

[*See also* Life-Saving Service; Lighthouse Service; *and* Revenue Cutter Service.]

BIBLIOGRAPHY

Bell, Kensil. *"Always Ready": The Story of the United States Coast Guard.* New York, 1943.

Bragaw, Louis K. *Managing a Federal Agency: The Hidden Stimulus.* Baltimore, 1980.

Canney, Donald L. *U.S. Coast Guard and Revenue Cutters, 1790–1935.* Annapolis, 1995.

Capron, Walter C. *The U.S. Coast Guard.* New York, 1965.

Johnson, Robert E. *Guardians of the Sea: History of the United States Coast Guard, 1915 to the Present.* Annapolis, 1987.

Kaplan, H. R., and James F. Hunt. *This Is the Coast Guard.* Cambridge, Md., 1972.

MacGregor, Morris J. *Integration of the Armed Forces, 1940–1965.* Washington, D.C., 1980.

Nalty, Bernard C. *Strength for the Fight: A History of Black Americans in the Military.* New York, 1986.

Nalty, Bernard C., Dennis L. Noble, and Truman R. Strobridge, eds. *Wrecks, Rescues, and Investigations:*

Selected Documents of the U.S. Coast Guard and Its Predecessors. Wilmington, Del., 1978.

Piercy, Arthur. *A History of Coast Guard Aviation.* Annapolis, 1989.

Scheina, Robert L. *U.S. Coast Guard Cutters and Craft of World War II.* Annapolis, 1982.

Scheina, Robert L. *U.S. Coast Guard Cutters and Craft, 1946–1990.* Annapolis, 1990.

Smith, Darrell H., and Fred W. Powell. *The Coast Guard: Its History, Activities, and Organization.* Washington, D.C., 1929.

Thomas, Charles W. *Ice Is Where You Find It.* New York, 1951.

Townsend, Linda, and Dupree Davenport. *The History of Blacks in the Coast Guard from 1790.* Washington, D.C., 1977.

Tulich, Eugene N. *The United States Coast Guard in Southeast Asia during the Vietnam Conflict.* Washington, D.C., 1975.

Waters, John M., Jr. *Rescue at Sea.* Rev. ed. Annapolis, 1989.

Willoughby, Malcolm F. *The U.S. Coast Guard in World War II.* Annapolis, 1957.

—ROBERT E. JOHNSON

Commerce, Department of

The United States has long had policies to promote business, but it was not until the early part of the twentieth century that a cabinet-level department was created expressly with the task of promoting business interests. Thus, the Commerce and Labor Department was created in 1903.

The Commerce and Labor Department was not the first department created to represent the interests of an important segment of the economy. Given the importance of commerce historically, this may appear odd.

Agriculture interests were represented before business's with the creation of the Agriculture Department in 1889. At this time agriculture was the primary occupation of the American work force and was among the largest sectors of the economy. Yet also at this time agriculture as the core of the U.S. economy was declining, with manufacturing and industry supplanting agriculture's primacy. In part, the Agriculture Department was created to deal with these and other pressures that the new industrial sector was placing on agriculture. For instance, farmers were feeling intense financial pressure from railroads and banks. Farm groups organized and successfully pressed their case for supportive policies, which included not only the Agriculture Department, but regulatory agencies, such as the Interstate Commerce Commission, which was to regulate the railroads.

Following agriculture's lead, manufacturing and big business also sought governmental representation. Several factors were involved in business's move toward government. Among these were the implementation of business regulations in the late 1800s and the suspicious attitude of the public toward big business and the monopolies and trusts of the era. Also, the Panic of 1893, which deeply depressed the economy, motivated the manufacturing sector to seek favorable governmental policies. The stirring of the nascent labor movement created yet another incentive for manufacturing to try to influence government policy against unions.

As a result of these forces, the business sector organized and pressed its case for representation in the cabinet and government. The business community was not without opponents to the idea of a Commerce Department. Some opposed the idea of expanding the government, and labor advocates, who sought labor representation, fought business representation without labor representation. Still, sentiment favored creating a Commerce Department, with support coming from the Theodore Roosevelt administration as well. Roosevelt's support, however, rested less with the aid that the new department would provide business than with the placement of a regulatory agency, the Bureau of Corporations, in the new department. Finally, a compromise in Congress was hammered out and the Department of Commerce and Labor was created, providing both sectors with cabinet representation.

FINDING A MISSION FOR THE NEW DEPARTMENT

The Commerce and Labor Department was given a wide but not very specific mission. Its organic mandate stated that "it shall be the province and duty of said Department to foster, promote, and develop the foreign and domestic commerce, the mining, manufacturing, shipping, and fishing interests, the labor interests, and the transportation facilities of the United States" (32 Stat. L. 825).

The department was composed of other agencies that were transferred to it as well as new units. This amalgam of functions and units led to competing views of the department's mission. For instance, it was responsible to further both the interests of business and labor, which at the time were quite antagonistic toward each other. It was to both regulate and promote business, while also trying to find foreign markets for U.S. goods, a task that it shared with the State Department, leading to much bureaucratic rivalry between the two departments.

Building the department mostly from units transferred to it did not help, as they tended to be either statistical collection agencies or performed very narrow service functions. Thus, from the Treasury Department came the Lighthouse Board, Lighthouse Establishment, Steamboat Inspection Service, Bureau of Navigation, United States Shipping Commission, National Bureau of Standards, Coast and Geodetic Survey, Commissioner and Bureau of Immigration, and Bureau of Statistics. From the Interior Department came the Census Office, Bureau of Labor, Fish Commission, and Office of the Commissioner of Fish and Fisheries. And from the State Department came the Bureau of Foreign Commerce.

Aside from the Secretary's Office, two new bureaus were created, the Bureau of Manufacturers and the Bureau of Corporations. Tension existed between these two bureaus, the first being primarily responsible for promotion, the latter for regulation. Moreover, the Bureau of Corporations was not able to develop its regulatory functions, feeling pressures from the promotional side of the department. A series of "gentleman's agreements" evolved in which big business granted government access to information and the Bureau of Corporations approved most mergers.

Arising from these internal pressures, as well as external demands and the general aimlessness of the department, several organizational reforms were implemented in the dozen or so years after creating the department. The most famous

was the separation of labor from commerce, with the creation of a new cabinet Department of Labor in 1913. This reorganization came about as the Wilson administration sought to repay labor for its help in the 1912 elections. Not only was a Democrat elected president for the first time in over two decades, but Democrats captured both houses of Congress, another rare event during this political era. Union leaders were placed in key Labor Department posts, including the former union activist W. B. Wilson as the first secretary, and the son of Samuel Gompers, the famous union leader, was named to a departmental high post.

Another important reorganization merged the Bureaus of Manufactures and Statistics in 1912, creating a more competent statistical collection agency. Also important was the transfer of the Bureau of Corporations to the Federal Trade Commission in 1914. No longer would the Commerce Department be split between promotion and regulation of the business sector. The department that resulted from these reorganizations focused on promoting business, not regulating it, and was more bureaucratically competent.

EARLY DEPARTMENT POLICIES AND EFFORTS

The Department of Commerce and Labor was created with the mission to help business, especially in finding foreign markets for goods. Early on the department focused on aiding big business, but big business was less in need of government assistance than small business. Small business, however, rarely sought foreign markets, except when the U.S. economy turned down. To build a small-business constituency, the early secretaries of the department sought to organize the business community.

Secretary Oscar Strauss, who served during Theodore Roosevelt's second term and whose family owned Macy's, the giant department store, initiated an early effort to organize the business community. From his urging, the National Council of Commerce (NCC) was created, comprising local business and national associations. The NCC ran into early troubles. First came the perennial split between big and small business. More importantly, Strauss wanted the NCC to support a policy of trade reciprocity with

THE DEPARTMENT OF COMMERCE HEADQUARTERS IN WASHINGTON, D.C. *Located on the Federal Triangle, The Commerce Department Building, when it was completed in 1932, was the largest government building in the country, with thirty-seven acres of floor space and eight miles of corridors.*

other nations, although prevailing business sentiment was staunchly protective. Consequently, the NCC fell apart.

Strauss's successor, Charles Nagel, who served under Taft, had more success, shifting policies further in the direction of helping small business. Nagel's small business bias was consistent with the orientation of the Taft administration, which had a reputation for taking stronger antitrust actions than Theodore Roosevelt's administration. Under Nagel's tenure, the Chambers of Commerce were created.

During these formative years the department developed services for the business community. These included the collection and publication of

data on trade and foreign markets. Also, the department established a corps of representatives, who would be based in foreign nations. This corps would build contacts and learn about markets in these nations. Still, the Commerce Department generated little in the way of foreign markets for U.S. products. What success the United States had in exporting came mainly from the efforts of big business.

William Redfield, Woodrow Wilson's secretary, embarked on a new policy course and also attempted to make the department the center of foreign trade marketing and policy in the United States. Redfield and Wilson, unlike Nagel and Taft, were not antagonistic to big business, and

Redfield refocused the department on this sector of the economy. He also won a bureaucratic dispute with the State Department by gaining access to State Department materials relevant to foreign trade, with Congress backing this plan. Redfield also engaged in a public education campaign to sell the value of foreign trade, arguing that the increasing productivity and expansion of the U.S. economy required foreign markets. As a part of this campaign, Redfield opened Commerce Department offices in many cities. He hoped this would increase business access to the Commerce Department.

In a major legislative action, Redfield and big business convinced Congress to ease antitrust restrictions on business combinations that engaged in foreign commerce. They argued that the relaxation was necessary to compete with other nations, especially Britain, Germany, and Japan, which successfully exploited business combinations in pursuit of foreign markets. Redfield was a strong-enough leader to convince President Wilson to support the changes, though Wilson was a strong believer in antitrust.

By the First World War, Commerce had emerged as the paramount agency with regard to foreign trade. This position, however, began to unravel with the World War. New agencies were given important economic powers under wartime authority, and Commerce lost its lead role. Thus, before U.S. entry into the war, the Bureau of War Risk Insurance was created to insure shipping companies, which were threatened by Europe's hostilities. That agency was located in the Treasury Department, under the direction of Robert McAdoo, a close adviser to Wilson. The U.S. Shipping Board was also created, with powers to regulate the shipping industry, including rates, service, and routes as well as to construct and purchase ships for the U.S. merchant marine. Lastly, once the U.S. entered the war, another body was created, the War Trade Board (WTB), which was primarily responsible for conducting trade efforts during the war. Rather than trying to expand trade, the WTB was more concerned with winning the war and restricted businesses from trading when it felt such action was necessary for the war effort.

The domestic economy was heavily controlled and regulated during the war, with the railroads nationalized. The most important economic agency during the war was the War Industries Board, which helped foster cooperative relations between business and government, while also possessing some regulatory powers. The Commerce Department also played but a small part in that domestic economic policy effort. All of these wartime efforts pushed Commerce from its lead position and limited Commerce's ability to open new markets or to influence the domestic economy.

After the war, Commerce found itself in a further-weakened state. The State Department, not Commerce, was given the task after the war of dismantling the WTB. Secretary Redfield tried to reassert Commerce's position and primacy after the war, but those efforts failed. There was strong business sector demand for some sort of coordination of government effort, but government was more intent on dismantling the war agencies that provided wartime coordination. Congress failed to appropriate funds to revive the Commerce Department's prewar trade expansion and coordination efforts, and the little coordination that existed was given to the State Department's Economic Liaison Council, which worked, not at the secretarial level, but at middle levels of the bureaucracy among the several departments with a trade mission.

Perhaps most critical, Wilson and Congress were more concerned with peace efforts in Europe, pushing Redfield's efforts far from the top of the nation's agenda. In defeat, Redfield left the administration in 1919. It was not until Herbert Hoover became secretary in 1921 that the Commerce Department emerged from its postwar doldrums.

THE HOOVER ERA

Herbert Hoover was the longest-serving secretary of commerce, serving for seven years (1921–1928). The reputation that he built in the postwar reconstruction of Europe catapulted him in the public's mind. His service at Commerce reinforced and enhanced that public esteem, positioning him for the Republican nomination in 1928, and then the presidency itself.

Prior to the First World War, Commerce was

out of step with the prevailing political policies toward business. Commerce was fundamentally a promotional agency, though most business policy was regulatory. Experience during the First World War with the WTB and the War Industries Board, along with the exhaustion of the regulatory movement, created an atmosphere more conducive to Commerce's prime mission of helping business.

Sensing this mood, Hoover accepted the commerce secretary post, declining to head the Interior Department. In a three-pronged move, Hoover revitalized the Commerce Department, among the few government agencies to grow during the 1920s. By the time he became president, the Commerce Department was constructing the then-largest government office building.

First, Hoover reorganized the department along functional lines. He created the Commodity Divisions of the Bureau of Foreign and Domestic Commerce. Seventeen divisions were established around important sectors and industries of the economy. These divisions would send information and statistics on each industry, through their trade associations, to operating businesses. This, Hoover hoped, would cut down on overly aggressive competition and allow some coordination and rationalization within each competitive market. To seal ties to the sectors, Hoover sought people from the industry itself for posts within each division.

To further promote cooperation between business and government and to rationalize competition, Hoover created the Division of Simplified Practice in the Bureau of Standards. Here Hoover sought to reduce economic waste by developing standards for manufacturing processes and products. This division proved very popular with business.

Lastly, Hoover increased the public presence of the department. Public relations became a high priority for Hoover. Top journalists were hired and publicity about the agency was channeled through the specialized business press. Appointments were widely publicized. A vigorous leader and agency were presented to the public, with both Hoover and Commerce developing such a reputation. The 1920s represented the heyday of the Department of Commerce, yet its "golden age" would be short-lived.

THE GREAT DEPRESSION AND BEYOND

The Department of Commerce was pushed into the background during the Depression after Franklin Roosevelt assumed office. The department was too closely associated with Hoover for political comfort, as Hoover was blamed for the Depression. Also, the New Deal was a time of experimentation, often without much of a theoretical guide. What was felt, however, was that the old ways of doing things had not worked, and Commerce was associated with the old way of doing things. Other agencies and ideas moved to the forefront, ahead of Commerce.

Commerce suffered severe budgetary cutbacks under FDR. Twenty-one of the fifty-three local offices of the Bureau of Foreign and Domestic Commerce were closed, and some New Dealers suggested closing the entire department. One such piece of legislation was actually introduced. The department was an easy political target and scapegoat.

During the 1930s a pattern of shuffling agencies to and from Commerce began that has continued well into this day. Often new governmental responsibilities were initially housed at Commerce, only later to be moved to other agencies once they grew too big or too important to be located there. Thus, aviation was moved to the Civil Aeronautics Authority in 1938 but came back to Commerce in 1940 when the Civil Aeronautics Board (CAB) was created, an independent agency retaining regulatory powers and responsibilities.

Two venerable Commerce agencies, the Lighthouse Bureau and Fisheries Bureau, were transferred to the Coast Guard and Department of the Interior, respectively. And the important Bureau of Foreign and Domestic Commerce was transferred to the State Department. The Weather Bureau was moved into Commerce in 1940 and, with the Bureau of Standards, became the core of the scientific agencies established in Commerce. After the war, the National Technical Information Service was established.

Also after the war, the Bureau of Public Roads and the Maritime Administration were located in

Commerce. Along with the Aviation Authority, Commerce became the principal transportation agency for government until the establishment of the Department of Transportation in 1966. As the economy modernized and as government became increasingly involved in the economy during the postwar years, new bureaucracies were created to serve these interests, often becoming bureaucratic rivals to Commerce.

In the postwar era Commerce again seemed to be lost, as it was in the pre-Hoover era. Turnover among secretaries was high, though many highly respected individuals served there, including Henry A. Wallace (1945–1946), W. Averill Harriman (1946–1948), Peter G. Peterson (1972–1973), and Elliot L. Richardson (1976–1977).

THE MODERN COMMERCE DEPARTMENT: CURRENT POLICIES AND PROGRAMS

The Commerce Department today is divided into four basic functions: trade, economics, economic development, and science. Each function includes several agencies and bureaus.

Trade

The lead trade agency in commerce is the International Trade Administration (ITA). The Commerce Department has often competed with the State Department for primary control over trade development. Trade functions in Commerce suffered a blow when foreign offices were closed owing to budgetary cutbacks in the 1930s and in 1953, when the Bureau of Foreign and Domestic Commerce was abolished. Two new offices were created in its place, the Bureau of Foreign Commerce and the Business and Defense Services Administration. While trade expansion retained a major role in Commerce in the post–World War II years, export licensing became a new, critical function.

Export licensing importance rose as foreign trade became an instrument of foreign policy. Policy leaders feared that other nations might use imported U.S. goods for military purposes. Thus, control over exports became a top U.S. priority, with half of all U.S. exports requiring licenses by 1948.

Another problem, the growing trade deficit, began to force a realignment in the Commerce Department in the 1960s. At Lyndon Johnson's request, Commerce developed a plan to deal with the growing trade deficit. This culminated in 1968 in the creation of the Office of Foreign Direct Investment. The aim of the office was to stem the outflow of U.S. capital. While the program met with some success, the trade imbalance remained.

The trade deficit soared in the late 1970s, stimulating another realignment of trade offices and functions. In 1980 the ITA was created. Commercial attachés, who had once been located in Commerce but were transferred to the State Department, were returned to Commerce in 1978. And supervision of the Trigger Price Mechanism, which focused on unfair trade practices of U.S. trading partners, was relocated from Treasury to Commerce. Thus, the trade imbalance led to a centralization of some trade policies in Commerce. Still, some trade offices, like that of the U.S. Trade Representative, are not housed in Commerce.

The current ITA is divided into four major components. The Division of Trade Development promotes U.S. exports and provides advice to business on trade matters. The U.S. Foreign and Commercial Service has offices throughout the nation and the world and provides liaison between the U.S. business community and potential markets. International Economic Policy parallels the work of Trade Development but is organized geographically into national desks, like the State Department's organization. Trade Development is organized around industrial sectors. Lastly, Trade Administration oversees export licensing and foreign unfair trade practices. Two minor trade offices also exist, the Bureau of Export Administration (BEA) and the U.S. Travel and Tourism Administration (USTTA). The BEA, created in 1987, oversees exports of commodities and technologies that might harm U.S. national security. The USTTA, formally created in 1981, is the successor to the U.S. Travel Service. It oversees foreign travel to the United States, promoting travel and aiding foreign travelers and tourists in the United States. (The USTTA was discontinued in 1996.)

Economics

The economics component of the Commerce Department helps develop U.S. economic policy and collects data on economic performance and trends. The umbrella economics agency for Commerce is the Office of Economic Affairs. The office coordinates the analyses and information collected by its two premier units, the Bureau of Economic Analysis and the Census Bureau.

The Bureau of Economic Analysis uses a wide variety of data and reports to track the economy. It publishes the important *Survey of Current Business,* a distillation and analysis of its data collection. It estimates national income, annually and quarterly, as well as estimates U.S. direct foreign investment, business plans, and foreign ownership of U.S. business.

The Bureau of the Census is among the most venerable of government agencies. It is mentioned in the U.S. Constitution, making it unique among federal bureaucracies. Until 1880 the ten-year census counts were conducted by U.S. marshals. In 1880 civilian census officials replaced the marshals, and in 1902 the Census Bureau became a permanent agency and its data collection responsibilities expanded. The next year the bureau was moved into the Department of Commerce and Labor, its permanent home. Over time the bureau gained responsibility for issuing the annual statistical abstract of the United States, the monthly labor report (now called the Current Population Survey). It is now the largest statistical collection agency in the world.

There are also several minor offices in the Office of Economic Affairs. The Office of Productivity, Technology, and Innovation seeks to boost economic productivity and promote private sector use of federal research and development funding. The National Technical Information Service produces reports on scientific, technical, and engineering information and analysis, disseminating these reports to business. Most costs of the National Technical Information Service are recovered through sale of these reports and associated services.

Economic Development

Another important Commerce Department function concerns economic development, especially with regard to economically distressed areas and minority business development. The constituency of this Commerce function differs from the business establishment that has served histori-

cally as Commerce's prime constituency. Three agencies spearhead Commerce's economic development programs, the Economic Development Administration (EDA), the Minority Business Development Agency, and the Office of Business Liaison.

The EDA, created in 1965, was mandated to deal with economic development in multistate and regional groupings. Its responsibilities have expanded to include programs to help displaced workers, especially in high unemployment areas. Aid to areas adversely affected by natural disasters also became an EDA charge.

The Office of Minority Business Enterprise was created in 1969 by Richard Nixon through an executive order. In 1979, the agency was renamed the Minority Business Development Agency. It is mandated to coordinate federal minority programs, to promote growth of the minority business sector, and to provide information and assistance to minority-owned businesses.

The Office of Business Liaison, which began in 1971 as the Ombudsman for Business program, was reorganized under its present name in 1979. It functions as a clearinghouse for people conducting business overseas or with the federal government. The office offers information, responds to inquiries, serves as a place where people can file complaints, and proposes remedies for problems that businesses may have in dealings with the federal government.

Science

Science activity, especially as it affects business, has become one of the largest Commerce functions in terms of budget authority and expenditure. The combination of these activities and the economic data collection of Commerce makes Commerce one of the most important scientific and technological agencies of the federal government. Commerce houses four major science/technology agencies: the National Oceanic and Atmospheric Administration, the National Bureau of Standards (NBS), the Patent and Trademark Office, and the National Telecommunications and Information Administration.

The National Oceanic and Atmospheric Administration, whose mission is to gather knowledge of the natural environment, especially as it pertains to weather, is Commerce's largest agency. Though formally established in 1970, its constituent parts have much older roots. The National Ocean Service, which began in 1807 as the Coast Survey and later became the Coast and Geodetic Survey, was the nation's first scientific agency. Originally charged to chart the nation's coast, its duties expanded to air charting as the airline industry was established.

A second unit, the National Weather Service, also has roots in the early 1800s and was previously called the Weather Bureau. The service collects data on weather, predicts weather (a service begun in the 1870s), and in coordination with the National Aeronautics and Space Administration, operates weather satellites.

The NBS, an outgrowth of the Office of Weights and Measures of the Treasury Department, was created in 1901. It was charged with the custody, comparison, and creation of standards. The NBS conducts tests of standards and, to further develop its capabilities, houses a basic science program that ranges over the fields of physical, engineering, and, now, computer sciences.

THE SECRETARIES

In the eighty-three years that the Department of Commerce has existed, there have been thirty-one secretaries, plus four others who headed the combined Commerce and Labor Department. The average length of service of a Commerce Department secretary is a little over two and a half years, about average for all cabinet departments. Two women have headed the department, Juanita Kreps, under President Jimmy Carter, and Barbara Hackman Franklin, under George Bush. And there has been only one black secretary, Ronald Brown, Bill Clinton's appointee. All of the other secretaries have been middle-aged white males, as is the general case for all cabinet secretaries.

Generally, Commerce Department secretaries come from the president's party, as has been the case for about three-quarters of these appointees, and the overwhelming percentage, over eighty percent, have some type of business background or experience. Still, nearly half had some type of government office holding experience before

their secretarial appointment, and many had other political experiences and duties as well. Most Commerce secretaries, however, are employed in the private sector immediately before their appointment. Thus, it is quite common for Commerce secretaries to move in and out of government and the private sector.

This career pattern suggests that Commerce secretaries are not professional politicians but rather tend to be business people who do some limited service in government. In this sense, they truly are representatives of the business community in government, but then many other cabinet secretaries have a similar business background, so the Commerce Department cannot lay exclusive claim to representing business in the cabinet.

Moreover, the Commerce secretaries bring to government more than mere business experience by possessing some earlier government and/or political experience. Nor do they lack party ties, with so many having the same party affiliation as the president who appointed them. One sees in these secretaries the convergence and intermixing of the private, public, and partisan sectors in their backgrounds, experiences, and careers, and in this sense they resemble all other cabinet secretaries.

THE ATTACK ON THE COMMERCE DEPARTMENT

In the 1994 midterm congressional elections Republicans took majorities in both houses for the first time in forty years. The victorious Republicans brought with them an agenda to reduce the size of government and to dismantle many venerable agencies, functions, and programs. The Commerce Department was one object of this agenda.

In the summer of 1995, bills in both houses were entered to eliminate the Commerce Department, one of the few cabinet departments to be so radically threatened. The proposed legislation would eliminate all programs and functions of Commerce. Some would be privatized or paid for by user fees, while some would be transferred to other departments.

Critics of the Commerce Department charged that the department was a complex maze of programs and functions, many not exclusive to Commerce but shared with other agencies. A report by the General Accounting Office counted the Commerce Department as sharing its programs with seventy-one other federal agencies and estimated that sixty percent of its budget was not central to its mission. Included in this budget tally were the National Oceanic and Atmospheric Administration and the other scientific units of Commerce.

Programs slated for outright elimination included the Minority Business Development Agency, the U.S. Travel and Tourism Administration, and the Office of the Secretary. Many transfers were also proposed. These included moving the National Institute of Standards and Technology to the National Science Foundation; the Patent and Trademark Office to the Justice Department, where it would be heavily supported through user fees; the Economic and Statistics Administration and Bureau of the Census to the Justice Department; the Bureau of Economic Analysis to the Federal Reserve System; and the Export and Trade Administration to the Office of the U.S. Trade Representative.

Other units would be privatized. This was the fate proposed for the National Technical Information Service and much of the National Oceanic and Atmospheric Administration. The Congressional Budget Office estimated that over $7 billion would be saved by these changes over a five-year period.

The legislative move to realign the department's functions got caught in the 1995 budget impasse. The Clinton administration balked at such massive changes for Commerce. Secretary Ron Brown fought actively to save Commerce, arguing that the Commerce Department helped the business community, especially in trade matters, and that eliminating the department would mean that business would have no voice in the administration. Republican critics were skeptical of Brown's assertions, stating that the entire cabinet represented business.

Surprisingly, most of the big-business community was silent on the proposed changes. Still, polls of corporate chief executive officers found large majorities supporting the cutbacks in Commerce, perhaps an indication that they felt that a fiscally sounder federal government was worth the cost of eliminating a department that served them.

The small-business community was not so silent, however, and lobbied Congress to save the U.S. Foreign Commercial Service, which proponents originally slated to abolish. Small business argued that it relied heavily on information from the service about export possibilities. Congressional sponsors of the legislation relented to small-business lobbying by modifying the proposal. The service would be moved to a new Department of Trade, along with the U.S. Trade Representative.

The fate of the Commerce Department is as yet unresolved, being caught in the budget talks. In the face of intense debate between the president and the Republican Congress over Medicare, welfare reform, and taxes, the projected savings from dismantling Commerce appear quite small. Moreover, the debate over the fate of Commerce has gotten lost as the president and Congress focused on these other matters.

[See also Census, Bureau of the; Economic Development Administration; Export Administration, Bureau of; International Trade Administration; Oceanic and Atmospheric Administration, National; Patent and Trademark Office; Standards and Technology, National Institute of; Technical Information Service, National; Trade Representative, Office of the U.S.; and Travel and Tourism Administration.]

BIBLIOGRAPHY

Arnold, Peri E. "The 'Great Engineer' as Administrator: Herbert Hoover and Modern Bureaucracy." Review of Politics 42, no. 3 (1980): 329–348.

Becker, William H. The Dynamics of Business Government Relations: Industry and Exports, 1893–1921. Chicago; 1982.

Blackford, Mansel G., and K. Austin Kerr. Business Enterprise in American History. 3d ed. Boston; 1994.

Bowers, Helen. From Lighthouses to Laserbeams: A History of the U.S. Department of Commerce, 1913–1988. Washington, D.C., 1988.

Cohen, Jeffrey E. The Politics of the U.S. Cabinet: Representation in the Executive Branch, 1789–1984. Pittsburgh, 1988.

—JEFFREY E. COHEN

Commodity Credit Corporation

A wholly owned federal corporation within the Department of Agriculture, the Commodity Credit Corporation (CCC) was created in 1933 as part of the New Deal and incorporated in 1948 under the Commodity Credit Corporation Charter Act. The CCC administers federal programs designed to stabilize the supply and price of farm products and facilitate their distribution. The corporation is governed by an eight-member board appointed by the president and confirmed by the Senate. The secretary of agriculture serves as chairman of the board; the vice president, secretary, and general counsel are also senior officials of the Department of Agriculture.

The CCC has the authority to borrow up to $30 billion from the U.S. Treasury as well as private lending agencies. The CCC also has the authority to license and inspect warehouses that store insured commodities. Commodities purchased by the CCC under commodity stabilization programs are sold in domestic or foreign markets or donated to domestic and foreign agencies. Under the 1985 Food Security Act farmers receive dollar-denominated commodity certificates for their federal crop subsidies. Commodity certificates are also used for payments in acreage reduction and land diversion programs, disaster assistance programs, and related programs.

—GEORGE THOMAS KURIAN

Commodity Futures Trading Commission

Established in 1975 as an independent agency to administer the Commodity Exchange Act of 1936, the Commodity Futures Trading Commission (CFTC) was originally authorized for a term of four years but has since had its life extended by two- and four-year terms. The purpose of the CFTC is to regulate the futures market, ensure its integrity and efficiency, and protect participants from fraud, deceit, and other abuses. In seeking a more efficient operation, the commission promotes mechanisms for offsetting price risks as well as more equitable distribution and marketing.

The commission is composed of five members appointed by the president and confirmed by the Senate, each member serving a five-year term on a staggered basis. No more than three members of the commission may belong to the same party. In addition to annual congressional appropriations, the CFTC receives fees for services, such as approval of contracts and registration of leverage commodities. The commission oversees futures and options trading on nine exchanges and trading in certain off-exchange trade options. It monitors the trading in over one hundred actively traded futures contracts, including physical products such as lumber, metals, precious metals, petroleum products, coffee, frozen concentrated orange juice, livestock, grains, and pork bellies and intangibles such as Treasury bonds, Eurodollars, exempted securities (other than municipal securities), and currencies. Under the 1982 authorizing legislation the CFTC shares some of its regulatory responsibilities with the industry's self-regulatory group, the National Futures Association (NFA). The CFTC has since delegated to the NFA the authority to register brokers, audit records and bank accounts, and enforce compliance with CFTC rules.

The commission has three operating divisions: the Division of Enforcement, the Division of Economic Analysis, and the Division of Trading and Markets. In broad terms, these three divisions are charged with five duties:

- Regulation of exchanges and maintenance of orderly markets

- Approval of futures and options contracts traded on each exchange and the setting of ceilings on the number of contracts a single speculator may trade or hold

- Registration of traders, in which group are counted commodity brokers, commodity pool operators, trading advisers, and floor brokers

- Protection of customers and adjudication and settlement of customer complaints

- Monitoring of information contained in market letters, reports, and statistics.

Where the commission finds wrongdoing, it has the power to enforce law through administrative proceedings or by filing cases in the federal district court.
—GEORGE THOMAS KURIAN

Comptroller of the Currency, Office of the

Created as a bureau of the Treasury Department by the National Currency Act of 25 February 1863, the Office of the Comptroller of the Currency (OCC) was charged with the responsibility of organizing and administering a system of nationally chartered banks and a uniform national currency. In June 1864 the legislation underwent substantial amendment and became known as the National Bank Act. It remains the basic statute governing the national banking system today.

The president appoints the comptroller to a five-year term, subject to Senate confirmation. The 1863 legislation contained an unprecedented provision requiring the Senate's consent before the comptroller, an executive branch official, could be removed from office. Constitutional concerns led lawmakers to drop the consent provision from the National Bank Act in favor of a requirement that the president "communicate" to the Senate his reasons for a comptroller's removal.

The National Currency and National Bank Acts were not the federal government's first foray into banking. In 1781 the Continental Congress granted a charter (a license to operate) to the Bank of North America, which served as the government's depository and fiscal agent during the last years of the Revolutionary War. After independence, at the urging of Secretary of the Treasury Alexander Hamilton, Congress chartered the Bank of the United States in 1791. A joint public-private venture, the bank collected and disbursed government revenues, financed government debt, issued paper money redeemable at par (face value), and generally served as a stabilizing force over the fast-growing U.S. economy and banks chartered by the states. The bank's power inevitably attracted enemies, who defeated attempts to renew its charter after the twenty-year limit specified in the 1791 legislation ran out. The financial difficulties encountered by the government in prosecuting the War of 1812 became a strong argument for chartering the Second Bank of the United States in 1816. It, too, became a victim of its own success, as President Andrew Jackson turned it into a symbol of monopoly and privilege and vetoed a rechartering bill in 1832.

The period between 1833 and 1860 is sometimes called the era of free banking in the United States. This meant, generally, that prospective bankers could organize under general laws of incorporation of the respective states instead of requiring a special legislative enactment. In practice, it meant a large increase in the number of banks operating throughout the country. By 1860 there were more than fifteen hundred banks taking deposits and issuing notes supposedly redeemable in coin. Most met their obligations. A notorious minority, however, either fled or failed, leaving behind a trail of worthless notes and diminished confidence in the banking system. With as many as ten thousand different notes in circulation, counterfeiting was a serious problem, especially in interstate commerce.

It was largely to remedy this situation that the National Currency Act was passed. To qualify for a charter, organizers had to raise capital (a minimum of $50,000 to $100,000, depending on the population of the bank's place of business) and purchase at least $30,000 worth of U.S. government bonds. The bonds were kept on deposit as security with the Treasury Department; in return, the bank received ninety percent of their face value in national bank notes, which they placed into circulation by lending them to borrowers. It was the OCC's responsibility to arrange for printing the notes (a job first assigned to private printers, then entrusted to the Bureau of Engraving and Printing), registering them, and getting them into the hands of the bank. [See Engraving and Printing, Bureau of.] The notes bore the name of the issuing bank and the signatures of its president and cashier; otherwise, each denomination of national currency was identical, which simplified their circulation throughout the country.

The National Currency Act obviously stimulated sales of U.S. government securities, and some scholars have contended that this was the primary, or even the exclusive, purpose of its passage. By the end of 1861, Treasury reserves had shrunk to $2 million; the government was paying twelve percent per annum on short-term debt; some military contractors had stopped deliveries on credit. The government's fiscal plight forced some lawmakers to vote in favor of the bill despite their misgivings about various aspects of it, especially its impact on existing state banks. It should be remembered, however, that the founders of the national banking system were disciples of Hamilton, who recognized the importance of a reliable money supply and stable banks in promoting the nation's economic development. The Hamiltonian vision also inspired such vital Civil War legislation as the Homestead Act of 1862 and the Pacific Railway Acts of 1862 and 1864.

Among the distinguished state bankers who had come to Washington to work against the National Currency Act was Hugh McCulloch, president of the Bank of Indiana. Having failed to block passage of the bill, McCulloch was persuaded by Secretary of the Treasury Salmon P. Chase to assume the leadership of the system he had opposed. McCulloch became the first comptroller of the currency on 9 May 1863.

The national bank legislation made provision for two routes to a national bank charter: new organization and conversion of existing state-chartered banks. McCulloch emphasized the second approach, which he believed would bring more experienced bankers and fewer novices into the national system and lead eventually to unified banking under federal control. Nevertheless, most state bankers saw limited benefits and many drawbacks to conversion. They were reluctant to exchange old and valued corporate names for the sterile title of "national bank" preceded by an ordinal number. They were wary of the more rigorous banking standards imposed by federal law and OCC regulations. The National Bank Act forbade loans secured by real property and in other ways limited bankers' flexibility. It required them to furnish quarterly reports of condition and to submit to regular examinations

by the comptroller's agents, which some regarded as an unwarranted intrusion. With conversions lagging, Congress in March 1865 imposed a ten percent tax on the note issues of state-chartered banks. This induced hundreds of state banks into the national fold. By 1870 there were five times as many national as state banks, holding resources almost eight times greater.

This advantage proved temporary. In its early years the national banking system was national in name only. In 1869 there were 829 national banks in the four most populous eastern states— as opposed to twenty-six in eight southern states combined. This imbalance not only angered non-easterners and cost the national system important political support, it also contributed to a resurgence of state banking. State authorities imposed lower minimum capital requirements or eliminated them altogether; they conducted perfunctory examinations or none at all; they removed lending limits and other restrictions upon what bankers could legally do. For the first of many times in its history, the OCC had to confront the dilemma central to its mission: how to make a safe and sound banking system also a competitive one. Beginning in the 1870s comptrollers generally argued that national banks needed greater operational freedom in order to compete successfully with other financial providers. Through a combination of congressional action and favorable regulatory rulings by the OCC itself, national banks have been able to achieve a rough parity with state-chartered institutions, if not in the number of offices than in the share of the nation's total banking assets.

By the turn of the century, the supervision of national banks had eclipsed the currency function in the OCC's mission. By then eighty percent of the nation's business was being conducted by check. Bankers found that they could employ their capital more profitably by lending it to business than to the government, and so most held no more government bonds (and, therefore, no more national currency) than the law required. National bank notes declined still further after 1913 with the introduction of Federal Reserve notes, which were obligations of the government instead of the individual banks. Beginning in 1935 national bank notes were withdrawn from circulation, as the bonds backing them were retired. Today, contrary to its name, the OCC has no direct responsibility for the nation's money supply.

By law, the comptroller was a member of the Federal Reserve Board (an arrangement ended in 1935), and all national banks became members of the Federal Reserve system; for state-chartered banks, membership was (and is) optional. Member banks obtained access to the Fed's check-clearing services and to the "discount window," where they could convert certain assets into emergency cash; national banks acquired new powers that helped them to expand their activities at home and abroad.

The Federal Reserve Board acquired the authority to examine all member banks. Eager to attract new members and to avoid driving off existing ones (national banks could convert to state nonmember status) by imposing new regulatory burdens, the Board opted to rely upon examination reports prepared by the OCC and state examiners instead of requiring their own. A similar policy was adopted for similar reasons by the Federal Deposit Insurance Corporation (FDIC), which was established in 1933 to restore public confidence in the banking system after its virtual collapse during the Great Depression. Not until well after World War II did the FDIC and Federal Reserve assume primary responsibility for examining the banks under their jurisdiction.

From 1930, just after the stock market crashed, until March 1933, when newly elected President Franklin D. Roosevelt declared a bank holiday, almost fifty-eight hundred banks (886 national banks) failed. After the holiday the OCC reorganized and licensed banks to reopen and liquidated the assets of those that never would, ensuring that depositors realized the maximum recovery of their funds. After 1933 the FDIC automatically became the receiver and liquidator of national banks declared insolvent by the OCC.

The Banking Acts of 1933 and 1935 embodied a particular set of assumptions about the banking catastrophe of 1930–1933. First, there was a widespread belief that the country had "too many banks and too few bankers." Although the numbers had been in slow decline since 1921, when a remarkable 8,150 national banks and 20,600 state banks were in operation, it was in-

disputably true that many of those still in business in 1930 were so badly capitalized and managed that their failure was almost a certainty when the economy sank. From this Congress concluded that federal regulators should strictly limit the number of new charters. Indeed, between 1935 and 1960, a period of rapid population growth and resettlement, especially in the West, new national charters averaged fewer than twenty per year, less than the number of banks lost to merger and liquidation. A related assumption behind the New Deal banking acts was that competition in banking was not in the public interest. Thus, the 1933 legislation prohibited the payment of interest on checking accounts and required regulators to establish uniform interest-rate ceilings on savings accounts. Third, there was a general sense, supported by anecdote but not by empirical evidence then or since, that many bank failures were traceable to speculative ventures unrelated to the basic business of banking. Thus, the laws enacted during the 1930s forced bankers to divest securities affiliates and to confine themselves to deposit-taking and commercial loan-making functions, and gave the OCC and other regulators new powers to police the industry.

Under this rigorous regulation, banking stabilized. Bank failures became a rarity. By 1961, however, when James J. Saxon became the twenty-first comptroller of the currency, bankers were losing shares of the financial services market to credit unions, finance companies, savings and loan institutions, and the commercial paper market. Saxon, a central figure in the history of American banking, undertook to reverse this trend with a succession of regulatory rulings that permitted national banks to offer new products and services. He also approved large increases in the number of new banks and branch offices. Saxon's crusade to restore competition within the banking industry encountered opposition from state banking interests, nonbank financial providers, other regulators, and Congress, which accused him of bypassing its authority. Comptrollers since Saxon have continued the effort to reduce Depression-era restrictions on bank activity.

[See also Federal Deposit Insurance Corporation and Federal Reserve System.]

BIBLIOGRAPHY

Davis, Andrew M. *The Origin of the National Banking System*. Publications of the National Monetary Commission, vol. 5. Washington, D.C., 1910.

Dewey, Davis R. *The Second Bank of the United States*. Publications of the National Monetary Commission, vol. 4. Washington, D.C., 1910.

Hammond, Bray. *Banks and Politics in America from the Revolution to the Civil War*. Princeton, N.J., 1957.

Hammond, Bray. *Sovereignty and an Empty Purse: Banks and Politics in the Civil War*. Princeton, N.J., 1970.

Holdsworth, John T. *The First Bank of the United States*. Publications of the National Monetary Commission, vol. 4. Washington, D.C., 1910.

Kane, Thomas P. *The Romance and Tragedy of Banking* (1922). New York, 1980.

Kinley, David. *The Independent Treasury of the United States and Its Relation to the Banks of the Country*. Publications of the National Monetary Commission, vol. 7. Washington, D.C., 1910.

Klebaner, Benjamin J. *American Commercial Banking: A History*. Boston, 1990.

Robertson, Ross M., and Jesse H. Stiller. *The Comptroller and Bank Supervision*. Washington, D.C., 1995.

White, Eugene N. *The Comptroller and the Transformation of American Banking, 1960–1990*. Washington, D.C., 1992.

—JESSE STILLER

Congress.

See House of Representative *and* Senate.

Congressional Research Service.

See Library of Congress.

Consumer Product Safety Commission

Established during the social regulation regime of the late 1960s and the 1970s, the Consumer Product Safety Commission (CPSC), like many of its contemporaries, was given a broad scope of authority to regulate in the interest of human health and safety. Specifically, the CPSC was created to regulate the risks of accident and disease associated with products purchased and used by consumers.

Prior to the creation of the CPSC, relatively few products were regulated for safety reasons. Individuals injured by the vast majority of consumer products had only one recourse: to file a lawsuit after damages had occurred. In 1968, in response to concerns raised by consumer groups based on their testing of consumer products and anecdotal evidence indicating safety hazards, President Lyndon Johnson appointed a National Commission on Product Safety. This commission investigated the nature and extent of the consumer product safety problem. In a June 1970 report the commission documented over 20 million incidents of persons injured by consumer products, 110,000 individuals permanently disabled, and 30,000 who were killed. The annual cost in dollars of these product-related accidents was estimated to approach $5.5 billion.

Immediately following the issuance of the commission's report, both chambers of Congress introduced bills to create a Consumer Product Safety Commission; however, no action was taken on these bills in 1970. In 1971 President Richard Nixon attempted to avert strong consumer product legislation and preempt the creation of a new regulatory agency by instead advocating educational programs in the Department of Health, Education, and Welfare. Congress ignored the president's proposals and focused on what type of agency to create to address the issue of consumer product safety. The Nixon administration and business leaders favored regulation by existing departments in the executive branch. Senator Warren Magnuson and consumer groups favored a new independent commission. Senator Magnuson's bill would have given this new agency not only responsibility for consumer products, but also would have transferred regulation of food, drugs, cosmetics, and meats to this new agency. The compromise version that was passed created a new agency but left the regulation of food, drugs, cosmetics, and meats to their original agencies. The bill passed quickly in 1971, as there was not yet an organized opposition to consumer protection.

The Consumer Product Safety Act of 1972 (P.L. 92-573) charged the CPSC with protecting consumers from "unreasonable risk of injury from hazardous products." The act reflected a change in the approach to regulating hazardous products. Earlier efforts at regulating fabrics, refrigerators, and other products were directed at specific hazards. The 1972 act took a broad approach against hazardous products and vested authority to remove or reduce such hazards in a single agency. The CPSC was also given responsibility for implementing provisions of the Refrigerator Safety Act of 1956, the Federal Hazardous Substances Act of 1960, the Flammable Fabrics Act of 1953, and the Poison Prevention Packaging Act of 1970.

Almost all consumer products are within the jurisdiction of the CPSC. The only items that are exempt from CPSC regulation are those assigned to other agencies (e.g., automobiles, food, drugs, cosmetics, medical devices, aviation and boating equipment, pesticides, alcohol, tobacco, and firearms). This leaves to the CPSC responsibility for consumer products ranging from the obvious to the obscure, including everything from lawn mowers, children's toys, and swimming pool slides to matchbook covers and architectural glass. Despite its broad scope—it covers over ten thousand consumer products not regulated by other agencies—the agency is somewhat hampered by the statutory requirement to balance the risks and benefits in setting standards, by procedural requirements imposed by Congress, and by periods of low levels of public and political support.

Unlike most social regulatory agencies, which are housed within a cabinet department in the executive branch, the CPSC is structured as an independent regulatory commission. Five commissioners, each appointed by the president and subject to Senate confirmation, govern the activities of the agency. One member of the commission is appointed as chair. Commissioners are appointed for seven-year staggered terms and can only be removed for cause.

The independent regulatory commission form is generally seen as most appropriate for single-industry economic regulation, but the CPSC is an exception to that rule. The decision regarding the organizational structure was based largely on political considerations. Congressional advocates of an agency to regulate consumer products

sought to avoid the experiences of excessive control exercised by President Nixon and industry groups over the Food and Drug Administration. The CPSC was designed to be as independent as possible. Under the original statutory authority, the chair could not be removed by the president except for cause. This was in direct contrast to other agencies in which the commissioners are protected from removal, but the president is free to designate who will serve as chair and the chair serves at the pleasure of the president.

The CPSC is intended to serve several public functions. The agency protects the public against unreasonable risks of injury from consumer products, assists consumers in evaluating the comparative safety of consumer products, develops uniform safety standards for consumer products, minimizes conflicting state and local regulations, and promotes research and investigation into the causes and prevention of product-related deaths, illnesses, and injuries.

In an effort to accomplish its mandate, the CPSC engages in several regulatory activities. The agency requires manufacturers to report defects in products that could create substantial hazards and requires, where appropriate, corrective action with respect to specific substantially hazardous consumer products already in commerce. Agency officials conduct research and collect information on consumer product–related injuries and maintain a comprehensive Injury Information Clearinghouse. Wherever possible, the agency encourages and assists in the development of voluntary standards related to the safety of consumer products. If voluntary standards are not developed, the agency has the legislative authority to impose mandatory product standards, ban products, or order recalls of products already on the market. The CPSC has used all three powers at different times: for example, standards were applied to insure the safety of lawn mowers, urea formaldehyde foam insulation was banned (although this action later reversed by a court ruling), and asbestos hair dryers were recalled. Regulations promulgated by the CPSC are located in Title 16 of the Code of Federal Regulations, Parts 1000 to End.

Because CPSC regulations affect a multitude of manufacturing industries in the economy, the industry coalitions vary from issue to issue. The Business Roundtable has been active at a general level in opposing excessive CPSC regulation. Supporting CPSC activism are a number of consumer groups, such as the Consumers Union, the Public Interest Research Group, and the Consumer Federation of America.

The CPSC was widely criticized in the 1970s as ineffective or a failure. The agency issued few rules in its early years, and those rules that were issued caused quite a stir. A major controversy developed and the agency received extensive media coverage regarding how it had handled the matter of the safety of children's cotton sleepwear. The CPSC initially issued standards in 1972 requiring manufacturers to treat all children's sleepwear with a flame-retardant chemical called Tris. Tris was later discovered to be a carcinogenic, and the CPSC subsequently banned its use in 1977, forcing a recall of a product that the agency had forced into production. In 1978, a court ruled that the agency could not ban the export of Tris-coated sleepwear. Contributing to the questions about the agency's regulatory prowess were observations regarding consumer behavior. In keeping with CPSC guidelines for reducing flammability, children's sleepwear is made of polyester, but children's playwear is still made of cotton. Many parents simply buy playwear for their children to sleep in, thereby negating the effectiveness of the agency's regulations.

Another major scandal surrounding the CPSC developed at approximately the same time. In 1973, based on a report that suggested a possible link between a spray adhesive commonly used by hobbyists and an increased risk of birth defects, the CPSC not only issued a ban on the sale of the product but also issued a warning to those who had been exposed to the product to consider delaying pregnancy as a safety precaution. After some women aborted their pregnancies in response to the CPSC warning, the link was found to be untenable.

In direct contrast to the horror stories of agency foibles, the CPSC has also had some significant regulatory successes. The CPSC is responsible for childproof caps on containers of medicines and poisons. In an effort to accommodate manufacturers of such containers, the agency used performance standards rather than design standards in specifying the regulatory requirements. The CPSC also played a lead role in reducing the risk of strangulation of babies in their cribs by regulating the size of spaces between crib slats. CPSC regulations have also minimized choking hazards and sharp edges on children's toys, reduced dangerous kickbacks on chainsaws, and recalled deadly electrified lamp housings. The CPSC is also responsible for requiring that refrigerator doors be openable from inside, thereby reducing the risk of a trapped child's being suffocated.

The original procedures used by the CPSC were unique. The agency applied a process called the offer system, in which it advertised the area of rule making and accepted proposals (from offerors) to write the rule. The offerors chosen were required to solicit participation from consumers, small-business owners, and retailers in the process. The finished rule was then submitted to the CPSC, which could either accept or reject it. The intent of Congress in establishing this process was to maximize participation of interested parties in the rule-making process. The cumbersome offeror process was, in part, to blame for the agency's slow response to safety issues.

The agency was initially staffed by young consumer advocates who were hostile to industry and had a tendency to try to overregulate. As a consequence, the CPSC frequently spread itself too thin and tried to regulate too many products. The lack of effective regulation, in turn, resulted in declining congressional and consumer support for the agency, while industry opposition flourished.

President Jimmy Carter considered abolishing the CPSC in 1977. Instead of elimination, subsequent congressional authorization for the CPSC made the chair of the commission serve at the pleasure of the president. Congress also modified the offeror process and has encouraged the commission to rely more heavily on voluntary standards. These changes in the congressional authorizations were accompanied by an implicit threat that the agency might be abolished if it did not alter its ways. Between 1978 and 1981, the CPSC issued seventy-five standards, only five of which were mandatory; the remaining seventy were developed voluntarily by the industries in question.

In 1981 President Ronald Reagan and Office of Management and Budget Director David Stockman pushed to abolish the CPSC, but even regulatory opponents cited the CPSC as an agency that attempted to balance costs and benefits. Congressional reauthorizations in 1981 placed additional restrictions on the CPSC. Congress abolished the offeror process, subjected CPSC rules to one-house legislative veto (a provision that was later ruled unconstitutional), limited the agency to performance standards regulations, and altered the rule-making procedures. Under the revised statutory guidelines, the CPSC was only allowed to issue mandatory standards if voluntary standards were unlikely to reduce risk or would not result in compliance. The CPSC must also demonstrate that mandatory rules have benefits that exceed costs and are the least burdensome manner of reducing the risk of injury.

Several presidents have tried to reduce the problems associated with overlapping jurisdiction or conflicting regulations among regulatory agencies. Beginning in the Carter administration and continuing through the "regulatory relief" plans of President Ronald Reagan and President Bill Clinton's National Performance Review, efforts have been under way to increase the levels of communication and coordination among the CPSC and other regulatory agencies. In response to its past experiences and the criticisms that have been directed at the agency, the CPSC has begun to set priorities for which products to address based on the severity of the risks involved, the size of the population exposed, the characteristics of the exposed population, and the circumstances of the exposure.

BIBLIOGRAPHY

Eisner, Marc Allen. *Regulatory Politics in Transition.* Baltimore, 1993.
Greer, Douglas F. *Business, Government and Society.* New York, 1983.
Lammers, Nancy, ed. *Congressional Quarterly's Federal Regulatory Directory, 1983–4.* Washington, D.C., 1983.
Lave, Lester B. *The Strategy of Social Regulation: Decision Frameworks for Policy.* Washington, D.C., 1981.
Litan, Robert E., and William D. Nordhaus. *Reforming Federal Regulation.* New Haven, Conn., 1983.
Meier, Kenneth J. *Regulation: Politics, Bureaucracy, and Economics.* New York, 1985.
Pittle, R. David. "The Consumer Product Safety Commission." In *Protecting the Consumer Interest,* edited by Robert N. Katz. Cambridge, Mass., 1976.
Reagan, Michael D. *Regulation: The Politics of Policy.* Boston, 1987.

—NADIA RUBAII-BARRETT

Copyright Service.
See Library of Congress.

Credit Union Administration, National

An independent agency established by a 1970 amendment to the Federal Credit Union Act of 1934, the National Credit Union Administration (NCUA) is governed by a three-member board appointed by the president and confirmed by the Senate. Members serve six-year terms.

The credit union movement dates from 1909, when the first credit union was started in Massachusetts under a state law. State credit unions operate under state charters and federal credit unions under NCUA charter. As of 1996, the NCUA supervised and insured 7,152 federal credit unions and insured 4,240 state-chartered credit unions. Assets at federally insured institutions, which served 67 million members, totalled $307 billion. In addition to its chartering authority, the NCUA has the right to examine the accounts of federally chartered credit unions; regulate the operations of the Central Liquidity Facility, the central bank for the system; and administer the National Credit Union Share Insurance Fund, authorized in 1970 as the credit union counterpart of the Federal Deposit Insurance Corporation. The NCUA formulates standards and requirements for insured credit unions.

—GEORGE THOMAS KURIAN

Crop Insurance Corporation, Federal

The government-owned and -operated Federal Crop Insurance Corporation (FCIC) was created in 1938. Under the Department of Agriculture Reorganization Act of 1994, the FCIC will be eventually merged with the proposed Agriculture Service Agency. The FCIC offers all-risk crop insurance to cover unavoidable losses owing to insects, adverse weather, floods, plant disease, fire, and earthquake. The coverage extends to more than fifty agricultural commodities. The federal government subsidizes thirty percent of the premiums through the sixty-five percent coverage level. The corporation's administrative costs and agent commissions are paid by congressional appropriations.

—GEORGE THOMAS KURIAN

Customs Service

 As a function of government, the work of customs services spans the history of the American experience from colonial times to the present. Historically, it can claim status as the first national government program with a local presence, and in several areas (e.g., public health, immigration, consumer protection) it was the administrative forerunner of other major federal agencies. Furthermore, its shifting roles and operations reflected the changes that took place as America evolved from a colonial settlement to a world power. Administratively, it often found itself at the center of criticism and the object of the latest push for reform and reorganization. In many respects, the administrative history of the American customs services is a history of American public administration.

THE COLONIAL EXPERIENCE

Customs took two forms during the colonial period. First, it existed as a fundamental part of British colonial policy; second, it played a central role in financing the operations of colonial government.

As British policy, the beginning of customs services in America was a product of the mercantilist mentality that fostered colonial settlement. The collection of customs duties was established as policy for the Colony of Virginia by the British Privy Council in 1621. Seeking the greater advantage for "his Majesties subjectes," the council ordered that "henceforth all Tobacco and other commodities whatsoever" should not be exported "into any forraine partes until the same have been first landed here and his Majesties Customes paid therefore." Collection and enforcement in the colonies was under the jurisdiction of the colonial governors, who, until the 1670s, received an annual salary for their work overseeing the collection of these earliest duties.

The Navigation Acts of 1660, 1663, and 1673 enhanced mercantilist efforts to restrict the commerce of the colonies to England's benefit through the application of customs regulations and duties. The act of 1660 limited all trade to English shipping and specified certain key commodities—for example, tobacco, sugar, cotton—that could only be shipped to England or its colonies. The 1663 act required that all shipments to the colonies must be transited through England, and the 1673 law added a "Plantation Duty" to be paid on each measure of enumerated commodities such as tobacco.

Poor enforcement of these various acts and general suspicion of the colonial governor's collection efforts led Whitehall to appoint the first royal customs officer for the colonies in 1671. Posted to Virginia (the center of the tobacco trade, which provided the greatest source of revenue for many years), the first royal agent was paid an annual salary. Under the 1673 act, however, the appointment of customs officers was once again left to colonial governors and the compensation shifted to a percentage of collections.

The decision to rely on the governors was facilitated by the fact that customs policies and collection machinery were also in place for raising revenues to support the operations of colonial governments. Although there was a wide variation among the colonial policies, they typically included the collection of four types of duties: tonnage duties on shipping in and out of colonial ports; export taxes on tobacco; import duties on slaves; and duties on wines and liquors as well as other enumerated items.

Tonnage duties were imposed on all shipping, although they were usually designed to give some advantage to local shippers through specific exemptions. Tobacco export duties were especially important for Maryland and Virginia, but almost every colony grew some of this exportable commodity, which proved to be a central source of revenue for many governments. Imposed in addition to the British plantation duties, these colony-specific duties had a relatively minor impact on the overall price of the exported crops. Import duties on slaves were a key revenue generator for some states (e.g., South Carolina), and by the 1700s were used as a means for controlling the influx of slaves across colonial borders as well as from abroad. Import duties on enumerated items beyond the tobacco and general tonnage levies also varied from colony to colony. Some states imposed high duties on specific items such as wines and liquors, while others (e.g., Rhode Island, New Jersey) did not seem to have any levy on specific goods.

The wide use and application of British and colonial duties did not necessarily translate into the effective enforcement of these various policies. There was constant evasion of customs duties. One indicator is the mismatch uncovered between figures related to imports and revenue collections. For several years before the American Revolution, for example, the ports of New York processed goods valued at £500,000 annually. Yet despite a duty of five percent during that period, records show that not much more than one-fifth of the expected amount (£5,000) was ever collected in any of those years. In part these figures reflected an inefficient, if not blatantly corrupted, administration. It was well known that customs agents found it easier and more profitable to turn a blind eye toward smuggling.

The problems of customs administration in the American colonies were so commonplace that until the 1760s there was a pervasive sense of frustration and resignation among those in Whitehall that little could be done to correct the situation. There is evidence, in fact, that those overseeing colonial administration until the 1760s regarded tolerance of smuggling and other forms of customs avoidance as the price to be paid for peace and economic profitability in the American colonies. The case of the Molasses Act of 1733 is illustrative. Passed at the insistence of politically significant British sugar planters in the West Indies, the act imposed a duty intended to dampen the growing illegal sugar trade between New England rum merchants and French West Indies planters. While passage of the act appeased the British West Indies' landowners, extremely lax enforcement of the duty was accepted as a means for satisfying the New Englanders. Rough estimates are that the 1733 act generated £2,000 annually at a yearly administrative cost of £7,000! In the meantime, the French sugar remained a primary ingredient in New England rum.

Locally, there were additional pressures against stringent enforcement practices of the British duties. A sufficient number of violent incidents against customs agents who attempted to stringently apply the law seemed to promote a reluctance to push enforcement too hard. "To be a customs official in the colonies," notes Theodore Draper, "was not a peaceful occupation."

The years 1763 through 1767 proved to be a watershed for both general customs administration and the future of the American colonies. Histories of the American Revolution often point to the proliferation of British acts from 1763 forward as the sparks that eventually resulted in the Revolution. More important, perhaps, was the fact that 1763 also marks the year that British colonial administrators became serious about enforcement of their customs laws. As part of an effort to stabilize England's financial condition and economize in its administration, Chancellor of the Exchequer George Grenville instituted a variety of reforms in colonial administration. British naval officers were given commissions as customs officials, and the prosecution of smuggling came under the jurisdiction of officials perceived as outside agents. In 1764 adjudication of customs violations was shifted to the Admiralty Courts in London and Halifax, where violators were less likely to escape adverse judgment. Hostile reaction to these and other measures in the colonies eventually led Britain to pass the Townshend Acts in 1767, which, among other things, moved the central administrative body for colonial customs—the American Board of Customs Commissioners—from London to Boston. With these enhancements in the administration of customs laws and the mercantilist system, the British assured the growth of revolutionary sentiment. The history of specific events leading to the Revolution is filled with episodes related to the efforts to effectively enforce British customs laws—from mob actions caused by the British seizure of John Hancock's vessel *Liberty* in 1768 to the Boston Tea Party in 1773.

IMPLEMENTING THE CONSTITUTION: THE ESTABLISHMENT OF A NATIONAL CUSTOMS SERVICE

Given the key role that the administration of duties played in stirring colonial resentment and eventual upheaval, it is not surprising that there was considerable reluctance to give the new national government (organized under the Articles of Confederation) the power to impose duties. Proposals to that effect emerged from the Continental Congress as the newly formed government faced financial crises in 1781 and 1783, but there was never sufficient support from the states to carry the day. Even those proposals that gained serious consideration included provisions that would rely on state and local officials for collection and thus avoid the issue of creating a national customs service.

The new Constitution of 1787 was clear in its provisions giving Congress the power to "levy and collect taxes, duties, imposts and excises" as well as to "regulate commerce with foreign nations, and among the several states" (Art. I, Sec. 8). Also included was an express prohibition on the states' ability to levy duties on imports, exports, or shipping tonnage without the express consent of Congress. As for restriction on Congress, it could not impose export duties and was forbidden to show any preference among the states or their ports in the design and implementation of customs policies.

The importance of these provisions for the newly constituted government is indicated by the high priority given by the first Congress to establish tariffs for raising revenues. Only the constitutionally mandated task of establishing subordinate courts took precedence. Legislation creating the administrative machinery for collecting customs duties emerged from Congress a month later, at the end of July 1789. The legislation created fifty-nine customs districts in the eleven states that had ratified the Constitution to that date, with the majority of districts being distributed to Massachusetts (20), Virginia (12), and Maryland (9). These districts were to be manned by collectors, surveyors, and naval officers.

Collectors were essentially the district managers, having overall charge of the office operations as well as responsibility for receiving information on all shipments and calculating and collecting the appropriate duties. The surveyors were the field managers of the group, overseeing the inspection and processing (e.g., weighing and measuring) of relevant shipments. The job of the naval officers was to receive copies of all relevant paperwork and inspection reports and to countersign all permits and other clearances issued by the collector. (In 1922, the naval officer's title was changed to comptroller of customs.) Appointment of these officials was made by the president with the advice and consent of the Senate, and there was no formal term of office designated. It was not until 1820 that Congress passed legislation limiting these appointments (and those of other federal officials) to four-year terms. Compensation was based on specified fees set by law, with the collector also receiving a commission on monies paid to the U.S. Treasury. The costs for operating each district were to be paid by the collector who, in turn, would share some of those costs with the naval officers.

ANTEBELLUM CUSTOMS: BEYOND REVENUE RAISING

It is difficult to understate the importance of the customs offices during the first decades of the new government. Between 1789 and 1800, for example, eighty-eight percent of all revenues raised by the national government were derived from customs service activities. In addition, customs officials were the most visible of national officials at the local level. With the exception of judicial officials, customs personnel were often the only local representatives of the national government throughout the states. Taking advantage of their placement and high reputation (many collectors were local heroes from the Revolution), Congress assigned them additional functions to perform on behalf of the central government. For example, almost immediately collectors were assigned duties as superintendents for federal lighthouses within their districts and as pension agents who distributed benefits to eligible veterans. Secretary of the Treasury Hamilton also assigned them the task of gathering information on the local economy to be used in his Report on Manufactures.

Over time, even more functions were given to the customs officials. They were drawn into the implementation of foreign policy: in light of attacks on U.S. ships by both sides in the war between England and France declared in 1793, Congress and the president had the customs officials enforce intermittently imposed embargoes on American shipping to the belligerents. They were also involved in the first efforts at health care policy when, in 1798, customs collectors were authorized to assess set fees from shippers that were used to pay for the relief of sick and disabled seamen. In larger ports these funds were used to pay for the creation of the Marine Hospital Service (forerunner of the Public Health Service), and the collectors often became *de facto* directors of the hospitals and other facilities established under that service. Complementing these tasks was the collectors' role as federal enforcers of state health laws and local quarantines.

Customs officials even acted as the nation's first immigration officials. In 1803 Congress required that the customs districts maintain a list of crew members aboard ships bound for foreign ports and collect a bond that would assure the return of each listed seaman. By 1820 customs collectors were required to obtain a list of all passengers aboard ships arriving in U.S. ports, and to determine that there were sufficient provisions to handle the number of passengers on departing ships. Most of these immigration func-

tions amounted to little more than collecting statistics, but the information provided could be used by litigants to take judicial action against a vessel's owner.

The tasks of customs personnel became more regulatory in nature during the pre–Civil War period. Congress passed specific regulations regarding the conditions of passenger vessels in the late 1840s and gave enforcement powers to the customs offices. In 1848 Congress gave them jurisdiction over the importation of drugs, medicines, and chemical preparations, allowing for the appointment of special examiners at major ports who would determine if the relevant goods met standards established by the leading pharmacopoeias of the day. Inferior or adulterated goods falling below those standards would not be permitted in the country. Two years later the customs service was formally empowered to establish and maintain a national system of recording deeds and titles for marine property, and in 1852 they were given a central role in the regulation and inspection of domestic steamboat commerce.

Little is known about the details of how customs officials carried out their multiple and diverse functions during this period. We do know that the lines of accountability were changed in the 1790s when the secretary of the Treasury directed the comptroller of the Treasury to assume oversight of the function. This arrangement was modified in 1849, when Congress authorized creation of a commissioner of customs to conduct the supervision of customs. In both instances, however, the supervisory power was limited to overseeing the collection and receipt of customs duties. Their supervisory jurisdictions did not relate to the growing number of other tasks undertaken by the proliferating district and subdistrict offices.

If legislative action is any indication, then a central administrative concern during this period was the problem of appraising the value of assessed shipments. Initially the customs officials relied on the value of goods stated on the invoice and supported by the sworn statement of the shippers; formal appraisal was undertaken only for damaged or uninvoiced goods. Reacting to an obvious pattern of undervaluation, appraisers were appointed to work at some of the major ports to help provide a solution to this problem. Disagreements were to be settled through a variety of reappraisal systems that permitted the shipper to bring in outside experts to help establish the correct value of a shipment.

As for the day-to-day operations of a customs house during this period, the only major documentation remaining is the introductory chapter ("The Custom-House") to Nathaniel Hawthorne's *Scarlet Letter.* A reflection on his three years as the surveyor at the Salem, Massachusetts, customs house in the late 1840s, it is as much a commentary on the impact of the patronage system as it is a vehicle for explaining the discovery of the scarlet "A" that is central to the classic novel that followed. Hawthorne pictures the workers of the customs house as "ancient sea-captains . . . who, after being tost on every sea, and standing up sturdily against life's tempestuous blast, had finally drifted into this quiet nook; where, with little to disturb them, except the periodical terrors of a Presidential election, they one and all acquired a new lease of existence." His description of their work is hardly flattering, giving the impression that they went through the formalities of office but essentially were ineffective in accomplishing their jobs.

IN THE ERA OF REFORM: CUSTOMS AT THE CENTER OF SCANDAL

Given the significance of customs houses in the overall scheme of the national government's administrative infrastructure during the last half of the nineteenth century, it is not surprising their operation was the focal point of efforts to reform government. Immediately after the Civil War, the editors of *The Nation,* an influential weekly, began to publish articles on the corruption and inefficiency of the New York Custom House. The scandals publicized by them and *Harper's Weekly* became a *cause célèbre* among reformers and eventually proved important in the adoption of the Pendleton Act in 1883. [*See* Civil Service.]

Ironically, civil service reform came very slowly to the customs service itself. As the focal point of controversy, many positions in the New York district customs house were brought under

civil service by the 1890s. As a member of the civil service commission, the young Theodore Roosevelt gave a great deal of attention to spreading the Pendleton Act's coverage to Philadelphia and other ports. Overall, however, the effort was incremental rather than comprehensive.

More characteristic of the period from the 1850s to the turn of the century were shifts in the organization and operations of the customs service. A Division of Customs was created in the Treasury Department as part of a more general reorganization of that unit. Not much is known about the duties of that unit, although it is assumed that the head of the division played a greater role in supervising the districts than did the Commissioner of Customs Office that preceded it. A major problem facing the division administrators was the number of different acts of Congress they were to oversee. All told, there were more than 263 relevant tariff acts being enforced by the service by the turn of the century. A revision of federal statutes in 1873 helped make sense of the disarray, but the problem remained a major one for those charged with enforcement.

Another major administrative change during this period involved how the customs system was funded. Legislation passed in 1849 required all receipts to be turned in to the Treasury Department, which would in turn allocate appropriated funds to each district to cover expenses. Under this system, receipts for storage, cartage, and other local functions would be retained at the local level to deal with those specific costs. The amount that the Treasury Department was permitted to spend on customs operations was a gross amount set by Congress from time to time. In 1849 that sum was set at $1.56 million; in 1858 it was raised to $3.6 million; $4.2 million in 1866; and $5.5 million in 1871. It wasn't until 1913 that Congress began making annual appropriations to fund the customs service.

The appraisal issue continued to be a sensitive one and was addressed more systematically in 1890 with the appointment of a Board of General Appraisers. Comprising nine members appointed for life, the board was one of the first examples of federal administrative law courts. If either a collector or importer questioned an appraisal done at the local level, the dispute could be brought to one of the board members. If not satisfied with the resulting decision, either party could have the dispute heard before a group of three board members. From this point, appeals could be taken to the U.S. Circuit Court of Appeals, and ultimately to the Supreme Court. Because of the burden this process created in the federal circuit courts, as well as the resulting inconsistency emerging from the decisions of different circuits, the Congress established a special Court of Customs Appeals in 1909, which was given exclusive jurisdiction over appeals from the Board of General Appraisers.

CUSTOMS IN THE TWENTIETH CENTURY

Organizationally, the customs service was ripe for reform as it entered the twentieth century. During the 1800s, and building on the original fifty-nine districts, Congress had created a structural puzzle that made no operational sense and proved very costly. By 1912 there were 126 districts and 38 independent ports. Some covered vast territories; the New Orleans district, for example, stretched from the Gulf of Mexico to La Crosse, Wisconsin. Expenses for running fifty of the districts exceeded the receipts they generated, including nine districts that generated no receipts at all. Politically, however, customs houses and the patronage they provided proved difficult to change. Calls by the Treasury Department for authorization to reorganize the districts fell on deaf congressional ears. Finally, in 1912, in the face of critical studies and negative press coverage, Congress authorized the president to submit a reorganization plan for the customs service. As a result, a plan was implemented that reduced the number of districts to forty-nine. That effort also included the abolishment of all fee-based compensation, and all customs personnel were placed on salaries.

The next flurry of administrative change took place in the early 1920s. The position of naval officer was changed to "comptroller of customs," and their jurisdiction was extended to cover all districts rather than just the one to which they were assigned. A Special Agency Service that acted as an investigatory unit was established separate from the Division of Customs, and various administrative codes and procedures were re-written and consolidated into a single code. In addition, several information-gathering functions were transferred from the Customs Service to the newly formed Department of Commerce. Personnel policies within the Division of Customs were also changed at this time, with formalized duties being given to the director and his assistants and, over an extended period, many more of the lower-level employees of all the districts being placed under the classified civil service.

This period of administrative change occurred in the context of equally significant additions to the agency's missions. Especially noteworthy was its role in the enforcement of two major pieces of "social" legislation that were seemingly extraneous to the service's fundamental revenue collection roles. With passage of the Chinese Exclusion Act in 1882, customs officials had become deeply involved in the nation's efforts to "stem the yellow tide." Until their major immigration obligations were taken over by other agencies in 1910, customs officials had the task of keeping out all Chinese male laborers and prostitutes while certifying reentry for those who were American residents returning from trips home. In the process, the service established incarceration camps where hundreds were detained in facilities that were notably less than safe and sanitary. At the same time, the service did gain a reputation for honoring the civil rights of those who fell under the exclusion law.

The other major social policy that customs had to deal with during this period was Prohibition. The customs service had always played a role in the regulation and taxation of alcohol, and liquor smuggling was a major issue plaguing the agency throughout its history. But Prohibition demanded a greatly expanded role, and the efforts to control alcohol smuggling took an ever-greater toll on the customs service's resources throughout the 1920s.

The story of the customs service since the 1930s has been one of mission expansion, adaptation, and modernization. The growth of air transport for both goods and passengers has become a major feature of contemporary customs work. Customs has also taken on major roles in the nation's fight against child pornography and the war on drugs. During both world wars and the Cold War, the service played central roles in the regulation of trade and related intelligence operations. In the 1970s a corps of "sky marshals" was created to deal with aircraft hijackings. In each instance, new divisions were created within the agency to meet the diverse needs of each new challenge.

Organizationally, the service became increasingly rationalized, professionalized, and automated over the past seven decades. By 1965 presidential appointment was limited to the very top officials in the customs service, and the traditional office titles of collector, surveyor, and appraiser were abolished. Consolidation of districts began in the late 1960s, and regional offices were developed to facilitate unity of command at appropriate operational levels. Additional reorganizations during the 1970s and 1980s led to the centralization of key financial, personnel, and logistical functions. As it entered the 1990s, the customs service included a headquarters unit, seven regional offices, forty-two districts, 301 ports of entry, and over a hundred residential and special agents with distinct operational duties. Data processing and automated systems became a major focus of the service starting in the late 1960s, and by 1985 the agency had developed a mainframe-based Automated Commercial System (ACS) that enhanced its enforcement capabilities in a variety of areas.

THE FUTURE: REENGINEERING THE U.S. CUSTOMS SERVICE

In what might be the most significant administrative changes in the long history of the U.S. Customs Service, the agency adopted a major reorganization plan in 1993 that is unlike any changes previously undertaken. Behind these plans are provisions of the North American Free Trade Agreement Implementation Act of 1993 that specifically called for the modernization of the service. Termed the "Mod Act" by agency insiders, those provisions effectively lifted many of the arbitrary organizational constraints that had held back agency changes for decades. In response, the customs service developed a plan that called for the structural and operational transformation of the agency.

By fiscal year 1996 all districts were abolished and replaced by a multilevel structure emphasizing process and function rather than hierarchical reporting relationships. At the "field operations level," most of the ports and residential agent offices were retained and given more autonomy to deal with local needs and requirements. At the "field management level," district and regional offices were replaced with twenty Customs Management Centers that were to provide administrative support for, and facilitate coordination and cooperation among, the operational units under their jurisdiction. In addition, five Strategic Trade Centers were created to deal with special areas of concern such as antidumping and intellectual property rights issues. A headquarters level was retained in order to assure national consistency of customs policies and to provide the necessary management coordination through offices dealing with finances, human resources, and information/technical services.

The explicit objective of these and related operational changes was to convert the customs service into a more mission-driven agency that stressed customer needs and partnerships while reducing and minimizing management overhead. If successfully implemented, these changes will create an agency that is culturally, as well as structurally, different from the customs service of the past. And it is that point that makes these efforts to "reengineer" the service so different from past efforts. The customs service of the past was structurally and procedurally the product of responses to external constraints and immediate needs. Reorganizations and procedural reforms were reactive, typically dealing with the need to bring the service in line with changed environments and to address issues raised by negative press coverage. The reform agenda of the 1990s, in contrast, is based on an explicit desire to create a customs service capable of adapting quickly to changes in its constantly changing environment, especially when it comes to the needs of service "customers" such as importers, shippers, and passenger airlines. Internally, the changes emphasize streamlining, structural flattening, teamwork, and enhanced responsibility at the field operations level. Whether the U.S. Customs Service is transformed by these changes or not, its contribution to the development of America's federal administrative infrastructure should not be overlooked.

BIBLIOGRAPHY

Colonial Dames of America, National Society of the. *Three Centuries of Custom Houses.* Washington, D.C., 1972.

Draper, Theodore. *A Struggle for Power: The American Revolution.* New York, 1996.

Maier, Pauline. *From Resistance to Revolution: Colonial Radicals and the Development of American Opposition to Britain, 1765–1776.* New York, 1972.

Miller, John C. *Origins of the American Revolution.* Boston, 1943.

Prince, Carl E., and Mollie Keller. *The U.S. Customs Service: A Bicentennial History.* Washington, D.C., 1989.

Schmeckebier, Laurence F. *The Customs Service: Its History, Activities and Organization.* Baltimore, 1924.

U.S. Customs Service. *People, Processes, Partnerships: A Report on the Customs Service for the 21st Century.* Washington, D.C., 1994.

—MELVIN DUBNICK

D

DEA.
See Drug Enforcement Administration.

Defense, Department of

 The National Security Act (26 July 1947) created the National Military Establishment (NME), which became the Department of Defense in 1949. Although there had been interest in unification of the military services earlier in the twentieth century, two events in the 1940s—World War II and the emergence of the Cold War—provided the impetus for action. World War II demonstrated the need for improved teamwork and coordination of activities among the services and between the United States and its allies. The dangers of the post–World War II ideological, political, military, and economic competition between the United States and the Soviet Union—the Cold War—became obvious by 1947.

Before World War II ended, Congress began considering the concept of unification. The Army, which favored it, first put forward a proposal in the spring of 1944, and the Joint Chiefs of Staff (JCS) later presented a similar plan. Another Army plan in late 1945 envisioned a Department of the Armed Forces headed by a secretary, with a chief of staff of the armed forces heading Army, Navy, and Air components. While the Army and the Army Air Corps favored this plan, the Navy objected to the proposed single integrated command plan, arguing that it would sacrifice the balancing of separate military elements and the principle of civilian control. More specifically the Navy worried about losing its autonomy and some of its components—naval avi-

ation and the Marine Corps. A 1945 Navy plan, which rejected service unification, included three "coordinate" War, Navy, and Air Departments and retention by the Navy of its air arm.

In December 1945 President Harry S. Truman proposed creation of a unified Department of National Defense, with coordinated land, naval, and air forces. Among other things, Truman stressed the need for integrated strategic plans, a unified military program and budget, civilian control of the military, and coordination between the military and the rest of the government. At Truman's request, Secretary of War Robert P. Patterson and Secretary of the Navy James V. Forrestal, who had led the Navy's opposition to unification, agreed on a plan and the matter came before Congress. The result was the National Security Act of 1947.

Title II of the National Security Act created the NME, including a secretary of defense and Army, Navy, and Air Force *executive* departments under individual secretaries. The secretary of defense was to have three special assistants and other civilian and military staff, creating a group that eventually became the Office of the Secretary of Defense. The secretary of defense received the power to "establish general direction, authority, and control" over the NME. The service secretaries had substantial independent authority, retaining "all powers and duties relating to . . . [their] departments not specifically conferred upon" the secretary of defense. Title II also placed within the NME the War Council, the JCS—making the World War II organization a statutory body—the Munitions Board, and the Research and Development Board. The National Security Act did not bring unification of the armed forces, but rather a loose confederation of three coordinate departments and other agencies, boards, and offices.

Title I of the National Security Act established

several other components of the new national security system—the National Security Council (NSC), the Central Intelligence Agency, and the National Security Resources Board. Forming these agencies as well as the NME was, according to the law's declaration of policy, "to provide for the establishment of integrated policies and procedures for the departments, agencies, and functions of the Government relating to the national security. . . ."

James V. Forrestal, the first secretary of defense (1947–1949), faced several serious challenges during his first year—a crisis in Czechoslovakia, the Berlin Blockade, and the first Arab-Israeli War. The passage of the Marshall Plan and creation of the North Atlantic Treaty Organization (NATO) also occurred during Forrestal's term, reflecting the adoption by 1947 of a key principle of postwar defense policy, containment. Containment rejected concessions to the Soviet Union, sanctioned negotiations with that nation to achieve U.S. objectives and win support from allies, and emphasized provision of economic and military aid to allies. The United States also relied on its monopoly (until 1949) on atomic weapons, and then began development of the hydrogen bomb as a new deterrent.

Forrestal also had to contend with disputes among the services over roles and missions; the Navy pushed for aircraft carriers as a key element of the defense system, while the Air Force preferred strategic bombers. Forrestal also differed over the NME's budget with President Truman, who wanted to keep defense spending at modest levels.

In 1949 Forrestal proposed amendments to the National Security Act; based on his experience, he concluded that the NME's organization, and the secretary of defense's powers, needed to be strengthened. With support from Truman, Congress approved changes in the act in August 1949. The NME became the Department of Defense (DOD); the secretary of defense gained "direction, authority, and control" (rather than general direction) over the Army, Navy, and Air Force, all of which became *military* (rather than executive) departments without cabinet status. Forrestal himself, who had begun the process of reducing the military services' autonomy and centralizing authority in the secretary of defense,

resigned in March 1949 and died tragically two months later.

In response to Truman's request for a review of national security policy in the aftermath of the detonation by the Soviet Union of an atomic device in 1949, NSC-68, a comprehensive plan for the national security of the United States, was completed in April 1950. The report emphasized the aggressiveness and growing military capabilities of the Soviet Union and recommended that the United States expand both its inventory of atomic weapons and the conventional forces of itself and its allies. Implementation of NSC-68 would require increases in several areas—military spending, foreign economic and military assistance, and intelligence and covert operations. When North Korea attacked South Korea in June 1950, the Truman administration began to implement NSC-68, increasing the defense budget for fiscal year 1951 from the planned $13.5 billion to $48.2 billion. Secretary of Defense Louis A. Johnson (1949–1950), who earlier supported the president's limited defense budget, recommended large increases after the Korean conflict started. Johnson took some of the blame for U.S. military unpreparedness and military reverses early in the war. He resigned at Truman's request in September 1950.

Truman then appointed General George C. Marshall as secretary of defense (1950–1951) to direct the military effort in Korea and the long-term expansion of the armed forces. Under Marshall the defense budget climbed and the size of the armed forces doubled. After the late 1950 intervention of Communist China into the Korean struggle, the Truman administration adopted a limited war approach, which General Douglas MacArthur, the United Nations supreme commander in Korea, publicly challenged. Marshall supported Truman's decision to remove him. The core objectives of Truman's defense policy in 1951 were to negotiate an end to the Korean conflict and build up the defensive power of the United States and its allies against international communism. Secretary of Defense Robert A. Lovett (1951–1953) ably led the DOD in working toward these objectives.

Charles E. Wilson (1953–1957), Neil H. McElroy (1957–1959), and Thomas S. Gates, Jr. (1959–1961), headed the Defense Department under

THE PENTAGON. *Home to the Department of Defense, the Pentagon, located in Arlington, Virginia, opened in January 1943 and remains one of the largest office buildings in the world, with 23,000 employees, 17.5 miles of corridors, and 100,000 miles of telephone cable.*

President Dwight D. Eisenhower, who in effect served as his own secretary of defense. Under Wilson, a 1953 DOD reorganization eliminated some agencies, including the Munitions Board and the Research and Development Board, and created six new assistant secretary of defense positions with functions prescribed by the secretary of defense. The plan also increased the power of the JCS chairman, making him (rather than the joint chiefs collectively) responsible for management of the Joint Staff, while retaining the prerogative of the full JCS to give major assignments to the staff. Wilson generally pushed decentralization of authority in the DOD and assigned more responsibility and importance to the ser-

vice secretaries. This decentralization, Wilson thought, would "make possible the effective exercise of civilian authority throughout the defense establishment."

Eisenhower's defense policy, termed the "New Look," assumed that any major war would become nuclear and placed heavy reliance on nuclear weapons delivered by strategic air forces. The new approach also espoused conventional forces cuts, expanded continental defense, and fostered reserve forces modernization. Controlling the size of the defense budget was central to Eisenhower's plan. The New Look provoked much controversy, both inside and outside of the DOD. To many critics, the policy ruled out limited, non-nuclear war, and ensured that a conflict between major powers would be a nuclear conflagration. The Army, which stood to lose many personnel, questioned the New Look's reliance on "massive retaliation" and criticized the replacement of balanced forces (land, sea, and air) with strategic air power.

The launching by the Soviet Union of the first satellite (Sputnik) in October 1957 shocked the Defense Department and caused Secretary McElroy to order accelerated development and production of intermediate range ballistic missiles and their deployment in England and Europe to counter the Soviet Union's placement on its own soil of intercontinental range ballistic missiles (ICBMs) aimed at the United States. The United States at the same time began development of the Minuteman ICBM, to be deployed in hardened underground silos in U.S. locations. By 1960 an alleged "missile gap," related to U.S.-Soviet competition in missile development, became a domestic political issue, based on charges that the Soviet Union was ahead of the United States in missile development. During the 1960 presidential campaign, the Democrats blamed the Eisenhower administration for the missile gap, but after he became president in 1961, John F. Kennedy learned that the charge was not valid.

During the same period, under Secretaries McElroy and Gates, the DOD underwent another wave of reorganization. In 1958 McElroy created the Advanced Research Projects Agency to work on satellite and antimissile projects. The Defense Reorganization Act (1958) put the JCS in the military chain of command in place of the service secretaries, further strengthened the role of the JCS chairman, and gave the secretary of defense power to transfer, reassign, abolish, and consolidate functions. Later, based on this power, successive secretaries of defense established numerous unified defense agencies; by 1995 there were sixteen such organizations.

The 1958 act also created the position of director of defense research and engineering, reflecting the accelerating efforts in the missile, aircraft, and nuclear submarine fields. Gates instituted regular meetings between the JCS and the secretary of defense to facilitate discussion and agreement on important issues. He also set up the Joint Strategic Target Planning Staff, under the Strategic Air Command, to control strategic weapons targeting, which had become an issue between the Air Force and the Navy. By this time the U.S. strategic triad—land-based ICBMs, submarine-launched ballistic missiles (SLBMs), and manned bombers—was fully operational.

Robert S. McNamara, the president of Ford Motor Company, became secretary of defense in 1961 and served for seven years. Under President Kennedy's direction, McNamara developed a policy of "flexible response," which meant discarding massive retaliation and giving the United States a choice of responses to threats and aggressive acts, options, as Kennedy put it, between "inglorious retreat or unlimited retaliation." Resisting communist wars of national liberation was one goal of the new strategy. This required increases in conventional strength and training for counterinsurgency operations. During McNamara's term, the U.S. armed forces increased from about 2.4 million (1961) to more than 3.5 million (1968).

McNamara paid much attention to nuclear strategy. He first espoused a "no-cities" approach—abstention from bombing urban areas in response to a surprise nuclear attack—with the hope that the Soviet Union would not attack cities. Because critics argued that promise of limited use of nuclear weapons would increase the risk of nuclear war, McNamara deemphasized the no-cities approach. He then adopted a policy of "assured destruction," again a deterrent policy, which meant maintaining the capability to inflict massive damage on an enemy, even after a surprise first strike. To implement this strategy, McNamara emphasized weapon and delivery systems modernization, including the Minuteman, the Polaris SLBM, and the Titan II missile. He questioned the future strategic value of the manned bomber, leading him to cancel development of the B-70 aircraft. He opposed developing an antiballistic missile system because of its high cost and the likelihood that the Soviet Union would be able to counterbalance it.

McNamara was an active manager who pushed centralization of authority in the Office of the Secretary of Defense. He recruited a civilian group, the so-called "Whiz Kids," who used systems analysis as an approach to decision making. Using this approach, McNamara canceled weapon programs such as the Skybolt missile, but promoted the controversial TFX (F-111) aircraft, to be used by both the Air Force and the Navy. Relationships between McNamara and the military services deteriorated, in part because McNamara relied so heavily on civilian advisers and made decisions opposed by the services.

McNamara played a major role in directing U.S. forces in a series of crises during his term—the disastrous Bay of Pigs invasion of Cuba (1961), the Cuban missile crisis (1962), the conflict in the Dominican Republic (1965), and most obviously, the Vietnam War. McNamara and Presidents Kennedy and Lyndon B. Johnson (1963–1969) believed that U.S. involvement in Vietnam was an example of flexible response, requiring the calibration of means to needs. As a result the nature and incidence of U.S. participation in the Vietnam conflict escalated; by 1968 the United States had nearly 550,000 troops in Vietnam, casualties were very high, victory was fleeting, and a strong antiwar movement had developed at home. McNamara publicly supported President Johnson's policies in Vietnam, including large troop increases and the bombing of North Vietnam, but privately he became increasingly skeptical of the effectiveness of these policies. He was disturbed by the antiwar movement's criticism of the Pentagon, the divisiveness in American society, and the carnage in Vietnam. He resigned as secretary of defense in February 1968. In recently published memoirs (1995), McNamara admitted that he and other national security officials in the 1960s made errors of judgment in determining the U.S. course in Vietnam.

McNamara's successor, Clark M. Clifford (1968–1969), eventually adopted McNamara's departing position on Vietnam: stopping both troop increases and the bombing of North Vietnam, negotiating with the enemy, and gradually disengaging from the war. The new president in 1969, Richard M. Nixon, chose Representative Melvin R. Laird as secretary of defense. Laird's "Vietnamization" posited gradual shifting of the fighting burden to South Vietnam. He withdrew U.S. troops, cutting the total to less than seventy thousand by the spring of 1972. Continuing negotiations led to a settlement with North Vietnam in January 1973; U.S. prisoners held by North Vietnam would be released and U.S. fighting forces would withdraw. Laird then discontinued the controversial military draft and began the shift to an all-volunteer force.

Nixon's administration adopted a policy of "strategic sufficiency," hoping that the Soviet Union and the United States would practice mutual restraint rather than trying to surpass each other in the development and stockpiling of nuclear weapons. Under this policy the United States required nuclear capacity sufficient to deter nuclear attacks by making it clear that a potential enemy would suffer an unacceptable level of retaliatory damage after an attack on the United States. The Nixon Doctrine, aimed at shifting a larger share of the defense burden to U.S. allies, was related to strategic sufficiency.

Secretary of Defense James R. Schlesinger (1973–1975) adopted a partial counterforce strategic policy, with emphasis on attacking military targets and avoiding attacks on population centers. As the first secretary of defense in the post-Vietnam era, Schlesinger's goals for the DOD included restoring military morale and prestige, increasing the defense budget, stressing research and development, and modernizing strategic doctrine and programs. His plan included building up both U.S. and allied conventional forces in NATO. Schlesinger's rather insistent arguments for larger defense budgets irritated both Congress and President Gerald R. Ford (1974–1977), Nixon's successor, and eventually contributed to his dismissal late in 1975. Ford supported Secretary of Defense Donald Rumsfeld's (1975–1977) efforts to move ahead with new weapon systems—the B-1 bomber, the Trident nuclear submarine, and the MX ICBM. Although Congress agreed to modest defense budget increases, the fiscal year 1977 budget in constant dollars was only slightly more than the 1956 level.

In 1976 the Democrats argued for substantial cuts in defense spending, and with Jimmy Carter's election to the presidency in that year, the new administration initially went in that direction, with the budget decreasing slightly in constant dollars in fiscal years 1978 and 1979. Secretary of Defense Harold Brown (1977–1981), consistent with Carter's pledge to control the defense budget, pressured the major allies of the United States—the members of NATO and other nations such as Japan and South Korea—to assume larger shares of the defense burden. But several crises in 1979—the fall of the shah of Iran, the taking of U.S. hostages in Iran by the new regime, and the Soviet invasion of Afghanistan—forced Carter and Brown, faced with Republican criticism, to begin a defense buildup. There were significant increases in the defense budget during Carter's last two years in office.

Brown adopted a program of "essential equivalence" in the nuclear balance with the Soviet Union to make it clear that the U.S. nuclear capacity was neither in appearance or fact inferior to that of the Soviets. He pushed an upgrading of the strategic triad by supporting development of the MX ICBM, the Trident submarine, and stealth technology (to provide aircraft with low radar profiles). Brown's and Carter's "countervailing strategy" sought to make it clear to the Soviet leadership that the U.S. response to any intermediate level of aggression would be to use selective nuclear attacks to destroy at unacceptable levels the Soviet political and military control, nuclear and conventional forces, and industrial capacity. At the same time Brown pushed arms control, including the Strategic Arms Limitation Talks (SALT) II treaty (1979).

President Ronald Reagan (1981–1989) argued that the strategic capabilities of the United States had declined in comparison to the Soviet Union's, and he committed himself to a large defense buildup. His five-point approach, announced in 1981, included improvement of communications, command, and control systems; strategic bomber modernization; deployment of a new SLBM; enhancement of the survivability and accuracy of the new ICBMs; and improvement in strategic defenses. In practical terms, the program envisioned producing one hundred B-1b bombers and one hundred MX ICBMs, developing a stealth bomber and the Trident II SLBM, improving air surveillance systems, and creating an antisatellite system. In 1983 Reagan proposed an expensive space-based antimissile system, familiarly known as "Star Wars," and Congress appropriated funds to begin its long-range development. Reagan's first secretary of defense, Caspar W. Weinberger (1981–

1987), aggressively promoted the president's efforts to build up the nation's defenses against the Soviet Union, which Reagan described as the "evil empire." He succeeded initially in getting large increases in the defense budget. In current dollars, the budget increased during Reagan's term, from fiscal year 1981 to fiscal year 1989, from about $176 billion to more than $291 billion, but after 1985 there was negative real growth in the budget. As time passed, especially after 1985, Congress appropriated less than Weinberger requested and became increasingly unwilling to approve large increases. Nevertheless, the Defense Department had significantly more money during the 1980s than it had had in the previous decade.

Reagan was more willing than his immediate predecessors to commit U.S. military forces to overseas action. He sent troops in 1982–1983 to enforce a cease-fire in a civil war in Lebanon and in 1983 to expel a Marxist dictatorship from the Caribbean island of Grenada. In 1986, in order to stop alleged Libyan terrorism, Reagan dispatched U.S. fighter planes to bomb Libyan installations. Even though he promoted the military expansion of the United States, Reagan began strategic arms limitation talks with the Soviet Union in the mid-1980s. He signed an Intermediate Nuclear Forces Treaty with Soviet premier Mikhail Gorbachev in 1987 and then undertook negotiations to limit longer-range weapons; this effort resulted in a treaty after Reagan left office.

In 1986 Congress passed a very important law, the Goldwater-Nichols Department of Defense Reorganization Act (P.L. 99–433, 1 October 1986). Sentiment in Congress that defense organization was faulty, not agreement on the need within the DOD, led to passage of this law. Congress wanted to strengthen civilian authority in the DOD, improve the substance of military advice to civilian leaders, including the president, give the unified commanders more stature and authority, and improve the management and output of the Joint Staff of the JCS. The act increased the responsibilities of the JCS chairman, designating him as the principal military adviser to the secretary of defense, the president, and the NSC. The chairman could attend meetings of the NSC. He was to assist the president in strategic direction of the armed forces and preparation of strategic and other plans, and advise the secretary of defense on military requirements, programs, and budgets, including budget proposals for each unified and specified combatant command. He was to have full authority over a strengthened Joint Staff.

The Goldwater-Nichols Act also created the position of vice chairman of the JCS; this officer was to direct the JCS in the absence of the chairman as well as perform other duties as directed by the chairman. He was to come from a service other than the chairman; in rank he was second to the chairman and above all other officers of the military services. The act prescribed the chain of command and increased the authority and responsibility of the unified commanders to direct subordinate commands, employ forces within commands, and assign command functions. Also, the law strengthened the service secretaries by authorizing them to make organizational changes to transfer activities and personnel from military headquarters staffs to their own staffs. The law in general clarified command lines and individual service responsibilities by transferring some authority from the military services' uniformed heads to the department secretaries, the JCS chairman, and the combatant commanders. The effects of the law were particularly apparent during the Gulf War (1991), when General Colin L. Powell served as chairman of the JCS.

The realignment of the unified commands was an especially important result of Goldwater-Nichols. By the mid-1990s, nine unified commands existed, five geographic and four functional. The geographic commands were the European Command, the Pacific Command, the Atlantic Command, the Southern Command (Caribbean and Latin America), and the Central Command (Southwest Asia). The functional commands were the Space Command, the Special Operations Command, the Transportation Command, and the Strategic Command. The services tended to resist the movement toward jointness represented by the unified commands, which they considered rivals in the military establishment. General Powell, who strongly favored jointness, was a strong force in achieving changes in the unified command plan during his term as JCS chairman.

By the time Frank C. Carlucci succeeded Weinberger as secretary of defense in November 1987, the Reagan defense buildup had slowed significantly. Carlucci, who served earlier (1981–1983) as deputy secretary of defense, managed the DOD well and improved the department's congressional relations, which had deteriorated somewhat during the Weinberger years. Carlucci was less strident than Weinberger in arguing for the defense budget and demonstrated willingness to adapt defense policy to the changing international situation.

Richard B. Cheney, a prominent member of the House of Representatives, replaced Carlucci after George Bush became president in 1989. Cheney faced two major challenges during his term—directing the changes that were necessary in the defense establishment following the breakup of the Soviet empire and the accompanying diminishment of the nuclear threat, and directing Operations Desert Shield and Desert Storm after Iraq invaded Kuwait in August 1990. General Powell, the JCS chairman during Cheney's term, collaborated with him to deal with these challenges, aided significantly by the enhanced powers he had as a result of the Goldwater-Nichols Act.

The collapse of the Soviet satellite system in Eastern Europe, symbolized by the destruction of the Berlin Wall in 1989, had begun after Mikhail Gorbachev came into power in the Soviet Union in 1985. He pushed arms control agreements with the United States and reform within the Soviet Union; he was unwilling, unlike his predecessors, to use military force to keep the restive satellite states in line. By 1991, the Eastern European nations had all broken away, and the Soviet Union itself fell apart, leaving Russia as the largest of the former Soviet republics along with more than a dozen others operating independently. In effect the Cold War was over; the challenge for President Bush and Secretary Cheney was to adapt defense policy to this momentous change.

Pressure from Congress and the public to decrease the defense budget led to significant cuts. The fiscal year 1991 budget had been more than $310 billion; the following year it was $25 billion less, and in fiscal year 1993, Bush's last year in office, it was down to less than $270 billion. In terms of real growth, the DOD budget declined more than eighteen percent for fiscal years 1992 and 1993. This forced significant downsizing of defense personnel, both military and civilian, as well as cuts in money available for new weapons systems, training, and maintenance of defense facilities worldwide. Cheney presided over the closing or downsizing of hundreds of military bases and installations, according to recommendations of a base closure commission. Given the pressure to cut the level of deficit spending that the United States had been experiencing since 1970 and the diminishment of the military threat to the United States, the Defense Department had to accommodate itself to reduced forces and budgets.

Iraq's invasion of Kuwait in August 1990, and the concurrent threats to U.S. allies in Southwest Asia, including Saudi Arabia and its oil supplies, proved that local or regional conflict was still a reality. President Bush quickly made the decision that Iraqi president Saddam Hussein's takeover in Kuwait could not be allowed to stand, and the United States began to move troops and equipment to the Persian Gulf area. In the Pentagon Cheney and Powell directed the military buildup, which reached over 500,000 U.S. forces by January 1991. With the sanction of the United Nations, a fighting coalition led by the United States attacked Iraq's forces in mid-January 1991, with the objective of driving them out of Kuwait. The Gulf War began with an extensive bombing campaign and ended with a four-day ground campaign in late February 1991. These efforts drove Iraqi forces out of Kuwait and ended the conflict with an armistice. Saddam Hussein remained in power, but Iraq, which suffered much loss of life and physical destruction during the war, remained under an economic embargo. President Bush's decision, with the support of Cheney, Powell, and other national security leaders, to end the military campaign without removing Saddam Hussein, was widely debated in the aftermath of the war.

During Desert Shield/Desert Storm, the Defense Department demonstrated well its ability to handle the logistical problems accompanying the crisis, including the task of moving a half million troops and accompanying military equipment to the Persian Gulf area in a short

time. The military phases of Desert Storm, both in the air and on land, accomplished their objectives quickly, with minimal casualties on the UN coalition side. Secretary Cheney and General Powell worked together very successfully in managing the military effort from Washington, while relying heavily on the field commander, General H. Norman Schwarzkopf. The expanded powers given the JCS chairman in the Goldwater-Nichols Act proved very important in enabling Powell to play a critical role in collaboration with Cheney during the Gulf War.

Although the Gulf War proved the continuing need for the United States to maintain substantial military forces to handle local or regional conflicts, the general downsizing of the defense establishment continued after 1991. President Bill Clinton, elected in 1992, faced persistent pressure to control the budget deficit, and he believed that further reduction of the armed forces and defense expenditures were possible. His secretaries of defense, Les Aspin (1993–1994) and William J. Perry (1994–1996), and William S. Cohen (1997–) worked to implement these policies. There were further cuts in DOD's military and civilian personnel, and the budget continued to decline under Clinton—from about $251 billion in fiscal year 1994 to a projected $244 billion for fiscal year 1997. Funds for procurement—the purchase of new weapons and equipment—were especially tight, raising the question about the dangers of not replacing aging ships, aircraft, and other equipment. At the same time there were pressures to continue spending on weapon systems that the Pentagon did not want, for example, the B-2 bomber. In 1996 Clinton decided not to build more B-2s in addition to the twenty already ordered, even though seven previous secretaries of defense, both Democratic and Republican, argued that the nation's future security depended in part on continuing production of the aircraft.

Amidst the downsizing, the DOD found it necessary, in implementing decisions at the presidential level during the Clinton administration, to send U.S. forces on a variety of missions, to places such as Somalia, Haiti, and Bosnia. Clinton in effect added such peacekeeping and humanitarian efforts to the mandate of the armed forces, believing that such missions would diminish the chance of more major conflicts affecting or involving the United States. Secretary Perry traveled widely around the world in peacekeeping efforts and visits to U.S. allies. In his first two years as secretary of defense, Perry traveled to almost sixty countries, many more than any of his eighteen predecessors.

Almost immediately after its creation in 1947, the DOD became one of the largest and most important cabinet-level departments. Its role, and that of its leader, the secretary of defense, has been critical in maintaining the nation's security, and from time to time—in Korea, Vietnam, the Persian Gulf, and other places—it has been necessary to fight to protect the national interest. Although its mission changed and continues to change in the aftermath of the Cold War, it is clear that the DOD will remain preeminent, because maintaining national security will continue to be a central challenge to the government of the United States.

[*See also* Air Force, Department of the; Army, Department of the; Central Intelligence Agency; Defense Intelligence Agency; Joint Chiefs of Staff; Marine Corps; National Security Council; *and* Navy, Department of the.]

BIBLIOGRAPHY

Art, Robert J., Vincent Davis, and Samuel P. Huntington, eds. *Reorganizing America's Defense: Leadership in Peace and War.* Washington, D.C., 1985.
Barrett, Archie D. *Reappraising Defense Organization.* Washington, D.C., 1983.
Brown, Harold. *Thinking About National Security: Defense and Foreign Policy in a Dangerous World.* Boulder, Colo., 1983.
Caraley, Demetrios. *The Politics of Military Unification: A Study of Conflict and the Policy Process.* New York, 1966.
Cole, Alice C., et al., eds. *The Department of Defense: Documents on Establishment and Organization, 1944–1978.* Washington, D.C., 1978.
Condit, Doris M. *History of the Office of the Secretary of Defense.* Vol. 2, *The Test of War, 1950–1953.* Washington, D.C., 1988.
Enthoven, Alain C., and K. Wayne Smith. *How Much is Enough? Shaping the Defense Program, 1961–1969.* New York, 1971.
Freedman, Lawrence. *The Evolution of Nuclear Strategy.* New York, 1981.
Gaddis, John Lewis. *Strategies of Containment: A Critical Appraisal of Postwar American National Security Policy.* New York, 1982.
Geelhoed, E. Bruce. *Charles E. Wilson and Controversy at the Pentagon, 1953 to 1957.* Detroit, 1979.
Hoopes, Townsend, and Douglas Brinkley. *Driven Patriot: The Life and Times of James Forrestal.* New York, 1992.
Korb, Lawrence J. *The Joint Chiefs of Staff: The First Twenty-Five Years.* Bloomington, Ind., 1976.
Leffler, Melvyn P. *A Preponderance of Power: National Security, the Truman Administration, and the Cold War.* Stanford, Calif., 1992.
McNamara, Robert S. *The Essence of Security: Reflections in Office.* New York, 1968.
McNamara, Robert S., with Brian VanDeMark. *In Retrospect: The Tragedy and Lessons of Vietnam.* New York, 1995.
Powell, Colin L., with Joseph E. Persico. *My American Journey.* New York, 1995.
Rearden, Steven L. *History of the Office of the Secretary of Defense.* Vol. 1, *The Formative Years, 1947–1950.* Washington, D.C., 1984.
Shapley, Deborah. *Promise and Power: The Life and Times of Robert McNamara.* Boston, 1993.
Trask, Roger R. *The Secretaries of Defense: A Brief History, 1947–1985.* Washington, D.C., 1985.
Weinberger, Caspar W. *Fighting for Peace: Seven Critical Years in the Pentagon.* New York, 1990.

—ROGER R. TRASK

Defense Intelligence Agency

 The purpose of the Defense Intelligence Agency (DIA)—the nation's primary collector and producer of foreign military intelligence—is to reduce uncertainty for decision-makers and war-fighters by providing knowledge of the military capabilities and intentions of other nations during peace as well as war. The formation of national security policy and the conduct of foreign affairs hinges on accurate and timely intelligence—intelligence that can be used at the highest levels as well as by forces in the field.

The military intelligence legacy in the United States began with procedures and operations established by George Washington during the Revolutionary War. Formal intelligence organizations did not exist, however, until the Navy and Army formed the Office of Naval Intelligence in 1882 and the Military Intelligence Division in

1885, respectively. Because they were considered the domain of the military, and therefore, unimportant when there was no war to fight, the United States had to reestablish its intelligence functions, networks, and procedures with each war. Thus, the buildup of intelligence during wartime and the dissolving of intelligence elements during peacetime continued as a major theme until World War II.

Pearl Harbor brought major change to the intelligence discipline in this country. The need for permanent organizations became obvious, and improving the way in which intelligence was conducted, a necessity. Thus, World War II ushered in a new era of American intelligence. Whereas Pearl Harbor had represented the consequences of intelligence failure, conversely the fruits of successful intelligence were evidenced in June 1944 as the Allies stormed the beaches at Normandy.

The distinction between tactical and strategic intelligence emerged during World War II. Heretofore intelligence had supported a small battlefront and had been utilized by only the field commander; now the focus was widened to take in the big picture. Planners, strategists, politicians, and commanders in centralized headquarters required information in order to run the war. Strategists needed aerial photography to plan and assess bombing operations throughout Europe and the Pacific. An elaborate spy system in all theaters was required to gather and channel information. The development of technology for indications and warning purposes became critical, and so did new means of communication and of securing that communication.

Thus, the concept of American intelligence expanded. Tactical intelligence needs were not ignored, but instead were included as one aspect of the broader field of intelligence information. Intelligence had become vital to national security. Former president Herbert Hoover later termed it the nation's "first line of defense." The needs of fighting a war had brought major changes to the concept of intelligence, and in a few areas, to its practice.

Following the war, the military departments separately collected, produced, and disseminated intelligence for their individual use. However, this system proved to be redundant, costly, and ineffective, as each service produced estimates that lacked dependability and national focus. The search for a better means of organizing the nation's military intelligence activities led to the establishment of the DIA, which became operational on 1 October 1961, within the Department of Defense (DOD). "The principal objectives in establishing a Defense Intelligence Agency," said Defense Secretary Robert S. McNamara, "are to obtain unity of effort among all components of the DOD in developing military intelligence and a strengthening of the overall capacity of the DOD for the collection, production, and dissemination of intelligence information. Although perhaps of lesser priority, but certainly not of lesser importance, are the objectives of obtaining a more efficient allocation of scarce intelligence resources, more effective management of all DOD intelligence activities, and the elimination of all duplicating facilities, organizations, and tasks."

Thus, the agency—heir to the military intelligence legacy—fulfilled the critically important need for a central producer and manager for intelligence in the DOD. Its advent represented the culmination of an ongoing centralization process that was heralded as the most significant organizational development in military intelligence since World War II. The drawdown from Korea, tight defense budgets, the need for reliable intelligence, and shifting national security priorities forced centralization in military intelligence. The DOD sought to build weapon systems that included intelligence technologies that carried expensive price tags. The centralization of intelligence and the sharing of the cost of these new technologies across several service budgets clearly was advantageous.

Statutory authority for establishing the DIA stemmed from the National Security Act of 1947 and the Defense Reorganization Act of 1958. These acts empowered the secretary of defense to run the affairs of the DOD and all its organizations and agencies as the secretary deemed appropriate. Subsequent legislation clarified and expanded this authority.

The DIA directly supported the secretary of defense, the Joint Chiefs of Staff (JCS), other policymakers, and the war-fighting intelligence needs of the military forces. The agency's mission included the continuous task of collecting, processing, evaluating, analyzing, integrating, producing, and disseminating military intelligence for the DOD. Air Force Lieutenant General Joseph F. Carroll was named the DIA's first director.

Many intelligence activities that had been the province of the services were added in the early 1960s. Among these were the Defense Intelligence School in 1962 and the JCS's intelligence School in 1962 and the JCS's intelligence duties in 1963. The agency became fully operational in 1964, and it assumed responsibility for the Defense Attaché System in 1965.

The DIA received its first major test in 1962 with the detection of Soviet missiles in Cuba. Subsequently, the U.S. military's involvement in Vietnam launched a major production effort that lasted into the 1970s. Concurrently, the continuing Soviet military threat and numerous conflicts on nearly every continent occupied the DIA's analytical efforts in a decade that had begun with Cold War tension at the breaking point over the crisis in Berlin.

During the 1970s the agency became the chief authority for vital foreign military inputs to national-level intelligence products. The DIA's emphasis on foreign military technology translated to a superior capacity to provide crucial intelligence support to crisis situations involving the Soviet Union's military buildup, strategic arms control, space issues, and conflicts in Asia, the Mideast, Africa, and Latin America. Intelligence requirements soared to an all-time high, while sweeping decrements following Vietnam reduced personnel strength by nearly thirty-five percent. As a result, the DIA explored cooperative ways to produce key intelligence with service-level producers. Collaborative efforts centered on data-base production and maintenance, which were essential to supporting the battlefield commander.

The DIA focused heavily on the intelligence needs of field commanders during the 1980s. Recognizing the critical value of intelligence as a force multiplier during crises, the agency bolstered its support to war-fighting commanders

and expanded its capabilities to meet major wartime intelligence requirements.

The Goldwater-Nichols Department of Defense Reorganization Act of 1986 further codified the DIA's role in support to war-fighters by designating the DIA as a combat support agency. Among the many efforts springing from this act was the development of joint doctrine regarding intelligence support to joint worldwide operations. Subsequent defense authorization acts served to further unify military intelligence within the DIA and have supported the director of the DIA's role as leader of the military intelligence community.

The DIA's contributions to the national security issues of the 1980s and beyond—particularly terrorism, arms control, support for war-fighting elements, counternarcotics, and regional conflict—reflected its motto, "Committed to Excellence in Defense of the Nation." The annual publication of *Soviet Military Power* from 1981 until 1990 received wide acclaim. The long-awaited opening of the Defense Intelligence Analysis Center at Bolling Air Force Base, Washington, D.C., in 1984 consolidated agency locations from eleven to four and brought the advantages of collocated functions. In 1986 the agency received from the secretary of defense a Joint Meritorious Unit Award for its timely and effective intelligence support during the TWA and *Achille Lauro* hijackings and the Philippine crisis. The DIA received a second Joint Meritorious Unit Award in 1991 for its Gulf War activities.

Support to Operations Desert Shield and Desert Storm included around-the-clock intelligence monitoring by two thousand DIA employees, the deployment to the theater of nearly one hundred personnel, and daily tailored intelligence products for coalition forces. As a result, the defense intelligence community contributed to lowering U.S. casualties and to the decisive victory. General Norman Schwarzkopf said, "Tactically, no commander in the history of warfare had a more comprehensive infusion of intelligence or better picture of the enemy he faced. . . . The challenge was considerable and the Intelligence Community met it head on."

The 1991 collapse of the Soviet Union toppled the bipolar world and ended the Cold War. With the Soviet Union and its client states no longer the predominant focus of the defense intelligence community, the resulting new era of regional challenges and dramatic reductions in resources brought the most fundamental reexamination of U.S. national security policy since the 1940s.

The climate of systemic change caused a vastly increased level of military intelligence support as the agency organized for the next century. When U.S. forces were called to new challenges, including peacekeeping, counternarcotics, and counterproliferation operations, the objective of the agency remained the production of integrated all-source assessments based on the inputs from independent intelligence disciplines such as human sources, signals intelligence, and imagery. The DIA fused these and all other sources into a unified analysis in support of national security needs.

Throughout the 1990s, the DIA continued its uniquely tailored support to the war-fighter while adjusting its mission and organization to better support new national security initiatives. In 1994 the DIA received from the secretary of defense an unprecedented third Joint Meritorious Unit Award for its intelligence support to U.S. forces in Somalia, the former Yugoslavia, and Haiti. Furthermore, the defense intelligence community achieved an unprecedented integration of effort among the DIA, the military services, and the combatant commands by focusing on the missions of military intelligence and working within the common functional areas of collection, production, and infrastructure.

BIBLIOGRAPHY

Allen, Deane J. *History of the Defense Intelligence Agency.* Washington, D.C., 1985.
DIA, Moving toward the 21st Century: A Statement of Philosophy and a Guide for Action. Washington, D.C., 1995.
—DEANE J. ALLEN

Democratic Party.

See Political Parties and the Federal Government.

Department of _____.

See under latter part of name.

Disease Control and Prevention, Centers for.

See Public Health Service.

Drug Enforcement Administration

The creation of the U.S. Drug Enforcement Administration (DEA) in July 1973 answered a perceived need to coordinate and combine the numerous federal agencies and task forces involved in the effort to curtail the manufacture or importation, sale, and use of illegal drugs in the United States. The administration of President Richard M. Nixon pushed for the establishment of the DEA in an effort to end replication of function among federal agencies such as the Bureau of Narcotics and Dangerous Drugs (BNDD) and the narcotics division of the Federal Bureau of Investigation (FBI), and to curb a significant rise in illegal drug use in the United States. Although the U.S. Customs Service has remained the primary federal agency in the interdiction of illegal drugs at the border, the DEA has emerged as the main element in overseas interdiction and in the investigation of major drug cartels both within the United States and abroad.

On 1 July 1972 Nixon announced that he was going to merge the BNDD, the Office of National Narcotics Intelligence, and the Office for Drug Abuse Law Enforcement into a new agency, the DEA, under the auspices of the Justice Department. The DEA also assumed the law enforcement functions of the Law Enforcement Assistance Administration and the White House Office of Science and Technology. Agents in the drug enforcement divisions of agencies such as Customs, the Internal Revenue Service (IRS), the Central Intelligence Agency (CIA), and the FBI were transferred to the new organization. The DEA began with some four thousand agents and was fashioned to resemble the structure of the FBI. John R. Bartels was appointed the first director of the agency.

The new agency had the same powers as the FBI, including the ability to seek wiretaps and "no-knock" warrants. Furthermore, it had liaisons with both the IRS and the CIA and had access to the resources of these agencies. The DEA was also authorized to send agents abroad and establish field offices in foreign countries. With these powers and assets, the DEA began systematic investigations of the international drug trade. These investigations produced the first detailed analyses of the sources, routes, and actors involved in the international drug trade.

The DEA adopted a multipronged approach to eliminating the sale and importation of illegal drugs. By coordinating efforts with foreign governments, the DEA attempted to stop the flow of drugs at their source. In exchange for cooperation in eradication efforts, foreign nations were given American aid. For instance, from 1973 to 1977, Turkey received $35 million in exchange for collaboration with the DEA in destroying opium fields while Mexico received $50 million for destroying marijuana fields.

The DEA also sought to establish in-depth coordination among federal, state, and local agencies involved in the fight against illegal drugs. This usually took the form of joint task forces between state and local police and federal agencies such as the FBI or the IRS. This increased the range of offenses available to prosecutors to charge drug traffickers with—including tax evasion and smuggling. In addition, beginning in 1977, the DEA has used the National Guard in the identification and eradication of drug fields in the United States. The success of this effort resulted in the establishment of the DEA's Domestic Cannabis Eradication/Suppression Program (DCESP) in 1979, which provides training and resources to state and local governments and coordinates activities between these local bureaus and federal agencies such as the National Park Service and the Fish and Wildlife Service, among others. Between 1982 and 1990 the DCESP destroyed more than 664 million marijuana plants. In 1974 the DEA also established the El Paso Intelligence Center (EPIC) in an effort to coordinate intelligence about illegal drugs. EPIC gathers information from state and local law enforcement as well as information from federal agencies such as the CIA and the Department of Defense. EPIC offers eleven federal agencies and the police departments in all fifty states the ability to exchange information on drug trafficking. EPIC is also central in the DEA's efforts to assist the Customs Service and the Coast Guard in stopping drugs at the American border.

Despite the resources and powers of the DEA, the agency initially failed to fulfill expectations and was often the subject of considerable controversy. The agency failed to stem the tide of illegal drugs into the United States and was often accused of inflating drug seizure statistics in an effort to magnify its successes. Its first director, Bartels, resigned under pressure in May of 1975 amid charges that he covered up misconduct by subordinates. His temporary replacement, Henry Dogin, resigned six months later and was replaced by Peter Bensinger, who became the first DEA administrator to serve a full term with the administration. DEA successes in capturing shipments of narcotics or destroying poppy fields in Turkey or Southeast Asia were overshadowed as international traffickers were able to establish alternate routes to transport heroin and as drug cartels in Central and South America were able to ship ever-increasing quantities of cocaine into the United States.

Nonetheless, throughout the 1970s, the DEA was able to build significant ties with the drug enforcement agencies of other nations and thus take concrete steps toward international cooperation in combating the trade in illegal drugs. The DEA instituted a mobile training school that traveled to foreign countries and provided one-to four-week education programs for foreign police officers. The DEA also established the Advanced International Drug Enforcement Training School in Washington, D.C., to offer in-depth training for foreign officials. Furthermore, the DEA became the central agency for coordinating drug interdiction operations with other nations and international organizations such as the International Criminal Police Organization (Interpol).

In 1982 the administration of Ronald Reagan formally proclaimed a "war on drugs" in response to increased drug use and increased importation of cocaine. In light of manpower shortages and a perceived lack of effectiveness, the FBI was given concurrent jurisdiction with the DEA over the enforcement of drug laws. This vastly increased the number of personnel involved in the fight against illegal drugs but also made antidrug coordination efforts more complicated. The Reagan administration further expanded the war on drugs through the Department of Defense Authorization Act of 1982, which permitted military equipment and personnel, such as Navy E2C "Hawkeye" aircraft and both land and satellite radar, to be used to monitor against drug shipments (although the military was forbidden to make arrests). There was also a marked increase in the budget of the DEA, which doubled between 1981 and 1986 and then doubled again between 1986 and 1992.

In an effort to capitalize on these developments, the DEA established the South Florida Task Force in the same year. This multiagency task force was made up of agents from the DEA, FBI, Customs Service, IRS, and state and local law enforcement as well as Coast Guard and military personnel, and proved to be highly successful. By 1990 forty-six percent of all the cocaine seized in the United States was confiscated in Miami. Because of the increased interdiction efforts, there was a shift in cocaine trafficking routes away from south Florida and to Texas and California. The success of the South Florida Task Force led to the establishment of other large task forces, including Operation Alliance, which focused on interdiction along the Texas-Mexico border.

At the same time that it was increasing its interdiction efforts through combined task forces with other agencies, the DEA also began a major endeavor to reduce domestic demand for drugs. The central component of this strategy was the DEA's Drug Reduction Program (DRP), established in 1987. The DRP is made up of a number of programs that range from demand reduction training for local law enforcement officers to programs designed to reach minority and high-risk youths.

The DEA also began the "targeting kingpin organizations" (TKO) program. According to the strategy here, the purpose of drug investigations would be broadened to include not only the prosecution of drug "kingpins" but the weakening of the organization's entire infrastructure as well. The TKO strategy involves the destruction of an organization's means of production or supply, its transport network, its finances—including money-laundering methods—by means of multiple investigations and by exploiting a cartel's communications network through wiretaps and electronic surveillance. The TKO initiative has proved to be so successful that the DEA launched collaborative TKO operations with foreign governments. In 1992 one such operation, "Green Ice," brought together drug enforcement officials from the United States, Canada, the Cayman Islands, Colombia, Italy, Spain, and the United Kingdom, and resulted in 167 arrests and the seizure of $54 million in assets.

Through the development of new strategies and increased cooperation with other federal agencies and state and local law enforcement, the DEA has attempted to adapt to the changing nature of the drug trade. Although not completely successful in winning the war against illegal drugs, the DEA has nonetheless been a significant factor in the overall decline in drug use in the United States through its mission as the primary federal agency in the interdiction and investigation of illegal drugs and as the main coordinating body for collaborative operations with foreign law enforcement bodies.

BIBLIOGRAPHY

Bugliosi, Vincent T. *Drugs in America: The Case for Victory.* New York, 1991.
Drug Abuse Council. *Facts About "Drug Abuse."* New York, 1980.
Tonry, Michael, and James Q. Wilson, eds. *Drugs and Crime.* Chicago, 1990.
U.S. Congress. *Drugs in the Cities: The Federal Response.* Washington, D.C., 1992.
U.S. Justice Department. *Justice Expenditure and Employment in the U.S., 1971–1981.* Washington, D.C., 1984.
U.S. Justice Department. *Multijurisdictional Drug Control Task Forces, 1988–1990: Critical Components of State Drug Control Strategies.* Washington, D.C., 1992.
U.S. Justice Department. *Drugs and Crime Facts, 1992.* Washington, D.C., 1993.
U.S. Justice Department. *Drugs, Crime, and the Justice System.* Washington, D.C., 1993.

—TOM LANSFORD

E

Economic Advisers, Council of

The responsibilities of the Council of Economic Advisers (CEA), a unit of the Executive Office of the President established by the Employment Act of 1946, are spelled out in Reorganization Plan No. 9 of 1953. The three council members are appointed by the president with the advice and consent of the Senate. One of them is designated by the president as chair; often it is someone who has already served on the council or who has been on its staff. The members of the council are assisted by a staff of approximately thirty professionals, the majority of whom are economists and all of whom are appointed by the chair. Members of the council and the professional staff enter and leave with each new administration, so there is no institutional memory in the organization.

The CEA provides the president with economic data and with advice on policies involving growth, price stability, employment, sectoral performance, international competitiveness, and international trade. It advises about decisions involving international monetary coordination, particularly in currency crises involving the United States or its major trading partners. It provides microeconomic perspectives on issues ranging from deregulation of telecommunications to immigration policies. It prepares *The Annual Economic Report of the President,* which is transmitted to Congress annually each January along with a presidential message on the economy. The annual report involves analyses and policy recommendations, but it is not an action-forcing document and does not have the immediate impact of the presidential budget requests on the congressional work load. The CEA members and staff play a major role in planning new domestic programs. Its members chaired or participated in task forces that created much of John Kennedy's New Frontier and Lyndon Johnson's Great Society programs. In the presidencies from Ford through Clinton, members served on task forces dealing with deregulation of industry, energy policy, and international economic negotiations.

The chair of the CEA serves as one of the president's principal advisers, sitting in cabinet meetings and at the daily sessions of the White House senior staff. The chair is one of the members of the "triad" (the other two members being the director of the Office of Management and Budget (OMB) and the secretary of the Treasury) who have met regularly since 1962 to discuss fiscal and budget issues in the administration. The chair also serves in the "quadriad" (the triad plus the chair of the Federal Reserve Board) in talks designed to coordinate, as much as possible, the administration's fiscal policy with the Federal Reserve Board's monetary policy. The chair also serves on, or consults with, economic coordinating councils established by the president, such as the Economic Policy Board (Ford), the Economic Policy Group (Carter), the Cabinet Council on Economic Affairs (Reagan), the Economic Policy Council (Bush), and the National Economic Council (Clinton).

Members of the CEA play several roles. Some are professional economists who provide expert advice, others are public spokespersons or policy advocates. Edwin Nourse, the first chair of the CEA, observed in a letter to President Harry Truman, "There is no occasion for the Council to become involved in any way in the advocacy of particular measures or in the rival beliefs and struggles of the different economic and political interest groups." Nourse was reluctant to testify before congressional committees on behalf of Truman's program. He not only advised Truman but also tried to educate him with a crash course in academic economics, and Truman resented it.

Nourse was soon gone, as Truman replaced him with liberal lawyer Leon Keyserling, a passionate advocate of the president's liberal programs.

Congress almost abolished the agency in 1952 as a reaction to Keyserling's advocacy role. President Dwight Eisenhower's first chairman, Arthur Burns, managed to restore congressional confidence in the council. He was a strong advocate of policy within the CEA but did not go public with his policy recommendations. Burns also showed that an adviser with tact can educate a president on technical economic issues, as he did in weekly sessions with Eisenhower. John Kennedy appointed a professional economist, Walter Heller, but Heller also was an architect of administration programs (such as the War on Poverty) and an effective public advocate for his programs. Heller would also act as a "point man" who would argue positions that the president was not ready to publicly embrace. He engaged in a bitter conflict with Secretary of Labor Willard Wirtz over antipoverty policies in the Johnson administration, with Wirtz calling for a massive jobs program and Heller backing task forces proposing a program of "community action," a battle that Heller eventually won.

Most presidents want advisers with political savvy who can help advance the presidential program rather than academic experts who become embroiled in public disputes with cabinet secretaries or members of Congress. President Johnson's CEA chair Gardner Ackley observed that "if his economic advisor refrains from advice on the gut questions of policy, the president should and will get another one." Most CEA chairs become policy advocates before Congress and testify before the House and Senate Budget Committees and the Joint Economic Committee. Some chairs work on the inside as problem-solvers, studying particular parts of the economy, such as Laura D'Andrea Tyson, President Clinton's appointee, whose area of economic expertise involved analysis of domestic economic sectors and how they might become more productive in the world economy.

Occasionally, the CEA takes an operational role, as it did in overseeing wage-price guidelines during the Kennedy and Johnson administrations, and in issuing "inflation alerts" to the public during the early years of the Nixon administration to focus attention on areas of the economy in which prices were rapidly increasing. The CEA, according to former Secretary of Labor George Shultz, also serves as a voice of economic rationality in an administration, making it a counterweight to the influence of constituency-oriented departments dealing with economic affairs such as Labor, Commerce, Agriculture, Transportation, and Energy.

Presidents are selective in the economic advice they take. They usually support CEA requests for tax cuts, as did Eisenhower in 1954, Kennedy in 1963, Ford in 1975, and Reagan in 1981. When the CEA proposes higher taxes, presidents usually balk, as Johnson did in 1966 and Reagan did in 1983 and 1985 (though President Clinton accepted CEA recommendations for a tax hike in 1993). The CEA is likely to square off against the Treasury in forecasting the impact of high deficits: the Treasury almost always argues that deficits will "crowd out" private investment and result in a rise in interest rates that make Treasury refinancing of debt more difficult, while the CEA often has taken a stimulative approach. The president can rarely obtain a consensus from his advisers. The CEA concentrates on moderating the business cycle and on tradeoffs involving price stability, growth, and unemployment, while other economic agencies have different responsibilities, particularly the Treasury, which must manage the national debt. The CEA may call for lower interest rates as a way of stimulating the economy, while the Federal Reserve Board may keep rates higher than the administration wishes, in order to protect the value of the dollar in international markets or to "lean against the wind" of a stimulative fiscal policy. The CEA may take the lead in "jawboning" the Fed to take an accomodationist position.

The CEA helps make fiscal policy through its forecasts of future economic performance and projected revenues. These estimates are used to prepare the president's budgets and tax proposals. The CEA often projects lower revenues than the Treasury Department and higher spending levels than the OMB, which sometimes leads to conflicts within the presidential advisory system. The CEA has formal input into fiscal year budget planning just prior to the OMB's first call to the departments for preliminary budget estimates, and it continues its input in November and December prior to submission of the president's budget to Congress. It plays a major role in defending the president's economic forecasts each spring when Congress takes up the budget resolution, and again in September when Congress considers the budget reconciliation bill.

The CEA has reflected the policy orientations of the administration, and its economic theories are usually reflective of administration priorities. Truman's CEA was heavily influenced by Keynesian economic theory (which had never gained a real foothold under President Franklin Roosevelt), and it emphasized deficit spending to ensure that the postwar economy would not revert into a depression. The Truman administration believed that it was the role of government to "prime the pump" and ensure sufficient demand. As pent-up wartime demand for goods was adequate to prevent depression or recession, the CEA eventually found itself more concerned with moderating inflation than in stimulating demand. Eisenhower's CEA reflected the administration's concern over price stability, although Eisenhower did not necessarily believe that budgets should be balanced each year: instead, he adopted the principle that the budget should be balanced "over the cycle," so that in recessionary periods some deficits would be permitted, while in expansionary periods the spending should be more restrictive. Kennedy, concerned about paying for a military expansion and intent upon demonstrating that the U.S. economy could outgrow that of its Cold War rival, the Soviet Union, called for a "propulsive" economy in which growth was paramount. Lyndon Johnson, beset with inflation caused by the Vietnam War, became a "natural monetarist" and looked to the Federal Reserve Board to restrain inflation with higher interest rates rather than to the CEA to propose lower spending—something he ruled out while creating his domestic Great Society programs. Richard Nixon seemed torn between a desire for high growth (based in part on his 1960 defeat, which he blamed on a recession) and his fear of inflation. Nixon embraced the concept of a "full employment balanced budget": his CEA calculated the amount of revenues that would be obtained if the economy were at full employ-

ment; this figure would then be the maximum permitted for expenditures. Although the budget would not be in balance under this approach, it provided a rule that would limit the overall deficit. The Reagan administration, intent on carrying into effect a tax cut for individuals and business and reductions in domestic social spending, embraced the principles of the supply-side economists, who argued that increasing incentives for producers, by way of corporate, capital gains, and income tax cuts, would stimulate the economy more than would increasing government expenditures (demand-side policies).

During the Reagan, Bush, and Clinton presidencies, the CEA could no longer use macroeconomic policy to stimulate the economy. Tax cuts proposed by the supply-siders did not result in the huge economic boom they had forecast for the early 1980s. The inflexible deficit targets under the Gramm-Rudman-Hollings Act of 1986 were designed to reduce deficits to zero within a five-year period, ending attempts by the CEA to propose stimulative deficits as a policy tool. In 1990 a budget summit between President Bush's budget advisers and congressional leaders resulted in an agreement to scrap budget deficit targets but to institute expenditure caps instead. The caps also inhibited the CEA from recommending stimulative spending. As of 1995 the Republican-dominated Congress and President Clinton had reached agreement that the budget should be in balance by 2002, a principle that would eliminate the possibility that the CEA could use macroeconomic policy to influence the course of the economy.

Presidents Bush and Clinton created interagency groups to provide a broad range of economic advice, with the CEA participating in each. Bush created the Economic Policy Council, an interagency group, but it did not provide him with memoranda setting forth his options, and he found the advice of key aides confusing and sometimes indecipherable. In 1991 Bush named Clayton Yeutter, former secretary of agriculture and GOP national chairman, to be his coordinator, but Treasury Secretary Nicholas Brady insisted on chairing all economic policy groups under the council, again splitting authority. Within this advisory structure, Brady had bitter conflicts with CEA chairman Michael Boskin, claiming the CEA had become irrelevant to policy-making.

In 1993 President Clinton created the National Economic Council (NEC), modeled in part after the National Security Council, to formulate policy options, in effect relegating the CEA to a secondary role of providing technical analyses and forecasts. The CEA chairs who served in Clinton's first term nevertheless continued to play an important role in deliberations on the NEC and to act as highly visible spokespersons and defenders of administration policy. Clinton's promotion of Laura D'Andrea Tyson from the CEA to chair the NEC seemed to indicate a new path to influence, with the CEA serving as a second-tier position while the chairmanship of the NEC would be the top tier.

With the increase in "intermestic" policies (part international and part domestic) that cut across national boundaries, such as pollution, labor standards, and telecommunications policies, no single advisory body can provide the president with all the relevant information and analysis, so the CEA increasingly has had to share its advisory function with the departments and *ad hoc* task forces. In light of the difficulties within the economics discipline of developing effective data and theories—especially predictive theories—presidents seem to have put a premium on advisers (and advisory agencies) that can deal with microeconomic and sectoral issues, can offer viable policy options, and are capable of mounting a spirited defense of presidential economic performance.

[*See also* Advising the President; Federal Reserve System; Management and Budget, Office of; Treasury, Department of the; *and* Appendix: Employment Act of 1946.]

BIBLIOGRAPHY

Flash, Edward S. *Economic Advice and Presidential Leadership*. New York, 1965.
Frendreis, John P., and Raymond Tatalovich. *The Modern Presidency and Economic Policy*. Itasca, Ill., 1994.
Hargrove, Erwin C., and Samuel A. Morley, eds. *The President and the Council of Economic Advisers*. Boulder, Colo., 1984.
Heller, Walter. *New Dimensions of Political Economy*. New York, 1967.
Norton, Hugh S. *The Employment Act and the Council of Economic Advisers, 1946–1976*. Columbia, S.C., 1977.
Nourse, Edwin G. *Economics in the Public Service*. New York, 1953.
Rowen, Hobart. *Self-Inflicted Wounds: From LBJ's Guns and Butter to Reagan's Voodoo Economics*. New York, 1994.
Shultz, George. *Economic Policy beyond the Headlines*. New York, 1977.
Stein, Herbert. *Presidential Economics*. New York, 1984.
Weir, Margaret. *Politics and Jobs: The Boundaries of Employment Policy in the United States*. Princeton, N.J., 1992.
—RICHARD M. PIOUS

Economic Development Administration

An agency within the Department of Commerce created by the Public Works and Economic Development Act of 1965, the Economic Development Administration (EDA) administers programs providing assistance to states, counties, cities, and communities suffering from substantial and persistent unemployment or from sudden and severe economic deterioration. Its programs include financial assistance and planning grants, technical assistance, public works, research grants, economic adjustment assistance, and trade adjustment assistance. The EDA has six regional directors responsible for coordinating Overall Economic Development Programs in consultation with local communities. The EDA provides assistance to state and local governments as well as businesses.

—GEORGE THOMAS KURIAN

Education, Department of

The Department of Education Reorganization Act, approved by Congress in May 1980, established the thirteenth cabinet-level agency, the U.S. Department of Education. The department's express mission is to strengthen the federal commitment to education. Through several approaches, such as assuring equal access to educational opportunity for every individual, for example, the government fortifies its commitment to education. Improvements in the quality and usefulness of education also come from federally supported research, evaluation, and the sharing of information. Finally, through various programs, the department supplements and complements the efforts of the states, the local school systems, the private sector, nonprofit educational research institutions, community-based organizations, parents, and students to improve the quality of education.

THE HISTORY OF THE DEPARTMENT OF EDUCATION

Before there was a cabinet-level Department of Education, there was no federal agency specifically concerned with education. To some degree, however, Congress addressed educational issues. As early as 1867, for example, Congress created a non-cabinet-level Department of Education. Its purpose was to improve American education by providing educational information to the state and local authorities to help them establish efficient school systems. The department, headed by a commissioner, had a staff of three persons. Even in an age of small government and meager budgets, the Department of Education was a minuscule operation.

Despite the agency's small size and limited authority, the first U.S. commissioner of education, Henry Barnard, believed that the agency could bring about a vast improvement in American education through the dissemination of information. To help accomplish this mission, Barnard brought part of his extensive book collection to Washington.

Barnard also firmly believed that the production of scholarly reports on educational history and the condition of education in foreign countries was essential for understanding the contemporary condition of American education. Many members of Congress, however, did not appreciate this academic approach and soon began to attack the department as a waste of money. The annual appropriations act approved by Congress in July 1868 reduced funding for the education agency and stated that after June 1869 it would lose its independent status and become the Office of Education within the Department of the Interior. In 1870 Congress renamed it the Bureau of Education and in the process lowered the agency's status.

The name Office of Education, however, would return in 1929, but the education division would remain in the Department of the Interior for another ten years. In 1939 the Office of Education, removed from the Department of the Interior, became part of a newly created Federal Security Agency. Through the war years the Office of Education retained its autonomy. In 1953 the Federal Security Agency was legislatively upgraded into the Department of Health, Education, and Welfare (HEW).

The Health, Education, and Welfare Department made educational policy. During the 1960s in particular, the history of federal education policy was limited almost exclusively to federal grant programs and the enforcement of civil rights laws—access to aid to help give disadvantaged elementary and secondary students equal footing in education.

In 1969 Richard M. Nixon began his first term in office, and the new president expressed interest in establishing an educational research office separate from HEW's Office of Education. A separate office would enhance the quality of government-sponsored education research. Nixon's focus on a research office separate from the existing Education Department, to serve the needs of the president and the public, perhaps detracted from the possibility of elevating Education to cabinent level. Instead, at the behest of the administration, Congress created the National Institute of Education. Independent of the Office of Education, it, along with the Office of Education, formed part of HEW's Education Division.

The Office of Education finally reached cabinet-level status when members of the Ninety-sixth Congress returned to Washington in 1979 and in September of that year gave the bill creating a separate Department of Education final approval. A cabinet-level department, supporters argued, would lay the foundation for a significant new federal involvement in the lives of parents, their children, and the schools. A cabinet-level department would also improve the coordination of federal education programs. This in turn would result in greater accountability of federal education programs to the president, the Congress, and the public.

The new Education Department was a scaled-down version of the original proposal sent by President Jimmy Carter to Congress in 1978. Although the legislation perished in the Ninety-fifth Congress, Carter's second proposal faced little controversy, mainly because it excluded controversial items such as the transfer of the child nutrition program from the Department of Agriculture to the Education Department and other reorganization proposals that aroused strong congressional opposition.

PRESIDENTIAL POLICY-MAKING AND THE DEPARTMENT OF EDUCATION

When the Department of Education achieved cabinet-level status, the new department combined nearly 150 existing federal education programs into a single organization in the hope of being more responsive to the needs of educators and students by providing coherent policy and better service for those dependent on it. But from its inception, presidential hopefuls and presidents have effectively pressed their own political agendas on the secretary of education and the department. In many cases, politics rather than questions of educational substance dominated the department's policy efforts.

For example, presidents, both Democratic and Republican, have used the Department of Education as a means of fulfilling campaign promises founded on notions of congenial management strategies. Nowhere is this more evident than during President Jimmy Carter's 1976 presidential campaign. The connection became evident the day following congressional approval of the Department of Education, when the National Education Association (NEA) endorsed Carter for his second presidential run. The NEA was also the leading force behind Carter's first Oval Office bid in 1976, placing the financial and political resources of the 1.8-million-member organization behind his candidacy in return for his support of an elevated status for education in the United States.

On the campaign trail Carter was able to take his promise of a federal patron for education to the NEA and effectively use it as part of his public management pledge to the people. In general, during the 1976 campaign Carter campaigned on the need for reorganization in the federal government. Calling the new department one of his "highest legislative priorities," President Carter described the Department of Education as a "significant milestone" in his effort to make the federal government more effective. In the area of education, Carter told voters of the need to improve administration with a cabinet-level advocate who had direct access to the president.

Serious objections arose with respect to Carter's proposal for a new Department of Education in the cabinet. Opposition to the Education Department's creation stemmed mainly from the traditional notion that states and their localities should have the authority to control their own school systems. Conservative opponents argued that educational priorities would be incorrectly set at the federal level. The view of conservatives was not unpopular. In fact, local control and financing of public schools are a tradition that sets the United States apart from most other Western democracies, which have national curricula and national student examinations. Americans, mistrustful of big government, have long delegated responsibility for education to the states, which in turn have farmed out this responsibility to local school districts, which now number roughly fifteen thousand. Therefore, opponents concentrated on two key questions about the new department: Would it expand the federal education bureaucracy and would it undermine school independence?

An answer to the two questions came easily. At a 1979 Governmental Affairs Subcommittee meeting, Office of Management and Budget Director James T. McIntyre gave administration testimony that an autonomous education bureaucracy would eliminate the top layer of administrative offices that were then reporting to the HEW secretary. In the process, local school district independence would increase. By consolidating functions of the assistant secretary for education and the commissioner of education, McIntyre argued, the new department would cut time for issuance of regulations in half and actually reduce the federal bureaucracy by five hundred positions. In fact, by 1981, the reorganization eliminated 570 positions.

One of the original fears expressed by opponents was that the NEA would dominate the new department. But Carter allayed his opponents' fears when he selected the first cabinet secretary, who had few connections to the education community, particularly the teachers' unions, and acknowledged that she had never managed a bureaucracy. Carter appointed Shirley M. Hufstedler of the U.S. Ninth Circuit Court of Appeals. The California jurist, a Johnson appointee, had received high praise for her work on the bench since 1969. When announcing her nomination, Carter called Judge Hufstedler "one of the best minds in the country." Support for Hufstedler was widespread, coming from an overwhelming majority of congressional committee members, including chairman Senator Samuel I. Hayakawa of the Senate Labor and Human Relations Committee. During the judge's nomination hearing, the chairman called her a "skilled and brilliant generalist" who would take a fresh and innovative look at education. But Hufstedler's tenure at the Department of Education was short-lived largely because the voters did not return Carter to office for a second term.

Following Carter's defeat at the polls on election day 1980, his successor, President Ronald Reagan, began his first term in office by condemning the Department of Education as a symbol of intrusion into matters that should be left to state and local control. Reagan founded his philosophy of governance upon the ideal of limited central government and, what is most important, some return to state-centered federalism.

Ironically, to preside over the demolition of the Department of Education, Reagan selected Terrance Bell, a man who promoted the department's creation when he was U.S. commissioner of education in the Ford administration. Bell began his education career as a high school science teacher in Idaho in 1946, then served in Utah as a school superintendent and state chief of both elementary and secondary education. His tenure in Washington from 1974 to 1976 covered a period of attempted cuts in education spending by the Ford administration. Yet Bell nonetheless retained the support of the education community.

Following the president's inauguration in January, surprisingly, Bell argued that a "separate department was no longer necessary" and was able to affirm his interest in strengthening both local and state responsibility for education. In his meetings with the president before accepting the post, Bell reached an agreement with Reagan whereby consideration would be given to establishing an independent agency of lesser status than a cabinet department, but education would not be placed back into HEW.

Despite all the rhetoric and talk about abolishing the agency, the hallmark of the Reagan administration's education policy-making did not come until April 1983, with the release of *A Nation at Risk,* which warned of "a rising tide of mediocrity" sweeping across the nation's schools. The report, which revealed that low student achievement levels were threatening the nation's international competitiveness, aroused public concern. Commissioned by the Department of Education, *A Nation at Risk* identified deficiencies plaguing the system. In its recommendations the commission emphasized the place of technology, scientific research, and mathematics in the workplace, commerce, and manufacturing. Reagan, however, used the report to reiterate his opposition to the "federal intrusion into education" and pledged to continue to work for programs that would decrease the federal role, such as the passage of tuition tax credits, vouchers, and educational savings accounts.

Reagan continued his educational agenda into his second term in office and began his next administration by replacing Bell, a man with a low-key approach to pushing the administration's agenda, with a new education secretary, William J. Bennett. Bennett came to the secretary's post with high abilities as an educator and as an administrator. Before his appointment to the National Endowment for the Humanities in 1981, Bennett served as president and director of the National Humanities Center, a think tank at Research Triangle Park, near Durham, North Carolina. In addition to being a Doctor of Philosophy and a lawyer, Bennett taught at the University of Southern Mississippi, the University of Texas, Harvard, the University of Wisconsin, and Boston University.

Despite Bennett's qualifications as an educator, the Senate Labor and Human Resources Committee unanimously recommended confirmation of Bennett only after President Reagan assured skeptical committee members in a letter that he had shelved past proposals to abolish the Department of Education. In his message to Orrin G. Hatch (R-Utah), the committee's chair, Reagan said he still believed that a cabinet-level department was not needed to administer federal education aid effectively. But he also acknowledged that his proposal to replace the Education Department with a stripped down Education Foundation had "very little support in Congress."

In line with the president's philosophy, Bennett charged into office and issued a series of pronouncements about the poor status of American education. In particular the new education secretary advocated the need for tuition tax credits and government-sponsored vouchers for parents who sent their children to private schools as a way to remedy the problems plaguing the public schools in particular. For the most part, however, members of Congress did not perceive the secretary's support of the Reagan tuition tax credit and voucher programs as a way to strengthen public education. Many congressmen and congresswomen opposed vouchers on the grounds that the plans undermined the public education system. In fact, even with the efforts of the new education secretary, both proposals failed to win support from Congress because of fears that such a system would undermine the public school system by directing money to private schools. Vouchers were considered a radical form of "parent choice" because the concept would allow students to bypass the public system of education completely—at government expense.

Despite the opposition to voucher programs during both terms of the Reagan administration, President George Bush, Reagan's vice president and successor in the White House, proposed using vouchers as a solution to many of the problems in education. Like the two presidents before him, Bush utilized the Department of Education to press his overall strategy for government reorganization in general. In particular, Bush's support of vouchers conformed to his approach to the problems presented to government.

For example, to address domestic problems during his administration, Bush outlined a "New Paradigm" in 1990. The paradigm, or model, emphasized decentralized decision-making, individual empowerment, market forces, personal choice, and pragmatism. Bush's "New Paradigm" had its philosophical roots in the long-held Republican belief about the primacy of the individual, distrust of big governmental institutions, and fear of centralized public authority.

Bush's approach to education particularly fit this model. His second education secretary, former Tennessee governor Lamar Alexander, introduced several new education initiatives during the Bush administration. (Secretary Alexander replaced Lauro F. Cavazos, who fell into disfavor with President Bush.) While most of them focused on accountability and efficiency, the hallmark of the Bush educational program was the use of vouchers. Like many conservatives, the president envisioned education as a free market, with families choosing public, private, or parochial schools—all paid for with public money in the form of vouchers. To show federal support for this strategy, the United States Department of Education opened the Center for Choice in December 1990 to provide information and guidance to teachers, administrators, and parents who wanted to explore the Choice approach to educational reform.

Bush, however, only served one term as president. Defeated in 1992 by Democrat William Clinton, his plans for education, particularly a voucher program, never made their way successfully through Congress.

Education, however, was also high on President Clinton's agenda for the United States. Clinton's rise to national prominence was due, in part, to his education reform record in Arkansas. As governor, Clinton's push for educational change began in 1983 with a legislative program that established standards for teachers and students, mandated smaller classes, and included the nation's first eighth grade test that students had to pass before beginning high school. Clinton's educational reform effort culminated in 1989, when at his urging the overwhelmingly Democratic Arkansas General Assembly enacted a choice plan that would allow students to choose to attend virtually any public school in the state.

With the passage of the Arkansas Open Enrollment Plan, Clinton became part of a nationwide restructuring movement and enacted a reform that would gain him popularity with both conservative and moderate Republican voters. At the same time, however, Clinton was able to retain the political support of the traditional Democratic liberal constituency. For example, because Clinton's choice proposals as governor of Arkansas and as a presidential candidate in 1992 included only public schools, he received the endorsement of the country's two major teachers' unions, the NEA and the American Federation of Teachers. In agreement with the president's agenda for education and the Department of Education, both unions, which collectively represent over two million teachers, gave their resources and attention to the Clinton campaign during the presidential election.

THE DEPARTMENT TODAY

Despite two decades of presidential influence in the nation's educational agenda, the secretary of education is responsible for the overall direction, supervision, and coordination of the department's activities. In fact, from time to time the education secretary has put forth his or her own agenda for the schools. For example, in 1993 Clinton's education secretary, Richard Riley, identified critical issues that, he stated, would need the nation's attention. These issues included improved safety and discipline, challenging academic standards for every student, and a greater connection between school and work.

Additionally, the "Family Involvement Partnership for Learning" promotes Secretary Riley's belief in the family's importance in children's learning. The partnership is not a federal program, but a long-term partnership with states, communities, and more than 130 national organizations that represent parents, schools, employers, and religious organizations.

To meet the objectives of the president and the secretary, the Department of Education, headquartered in Washington, D.C., runs its operations with a central staff of approximately thirty-six hundred. Ten regional offices, each headed by a regional representative, house an additional thirteen hundred employees. These representatives serve as liaisons to state, local, and private education organizations.

The representatives also serve as advocates at the local level for the administration's policies. The regional staff involves itself primarily in representing the department's goals and views within the region, particularly in the areas of student financial assistance, civil rights enforcement, and vocational rehabilitation. Within the department there are six operational units running specific programs: the Office of Bilingual Education and Minority Languages Affairs; the Office for Civil Rights; the Office of Educational Research and Improvement; the Office of Elementary and Secondary Education; the Office of Postsecondary Education; and finally, the Office of Special Educational and Rehabilitation Services.

DEPARTMENT OF EDUCATION RESOURCES

The Department of Education shares the latest research findings and information on education with parents, teachers, school board members, policymakers, and the public. The department has several resources available to the general public. For example, the Department of Education funds ten regional educational laboratories that develop materials and provide assistance to states and local educators based on the most recent knowledge about improving teaching and learning. The Eisenhower National Clearinghouse for Mathematics and Science Education (ENC) provides an illustration of one such facility. Located at Ohio State University, the ENC, established in 1992, is the national repository for kindergartern through twelfth grade mathematics and science instructional materials. The depository also provides an on-line search resource for descriptions of those materials.

Additionally, the Department of Education supports research on effective educational practices for all students and monitors the performance of the American education system through the collection of statistics and evaluation of data. For example, the department supports long-term research and development through its national institutes and their university-based education research centers.

Another important resource found at the Department of Education is the Educational Resources Information Center, or ERIC. Since 1966 ERIC has distributed information on subjects ranging from elementary and early childhood education, to education for disabled and gifted children, to rural and urban education. ERIC is the world's largest data base on education and is available through libraries. More than 500,000 people use the ERIC data base each year.

Additional resources include the department's National Center for Education Statistics, which annually publishes the primary reference volume on education in the nation, *The Digest of Education Statistics*. The *Digest* is a comprehensive review of education statistics on elementary, secondary, postsecondary, and adult education. A second publication by the center is the *Condition of Education*, an annual report that includes information on enrollment rates, dropout rates, trends in academic achievement, and education spending. The department also funds the National Assessment of Educational Progress (NAEP), which serves as the "the nation's report card." The NAEP is the only nationally representative assessment of U.S. students' achievement. The NAEP is also the primary source of data on educational achievement in the core academic subjects. In 1990 the NAEP began collecting and publishing state-level data. Data at this level allow the states to track how their students are performing, both over time and relative to other states.

Finally, in March 1994, Congress authorized the establishment of the National Library of Education (NLE), thereby making the Department of Education Research Library a national library. The mission of the NLE is to ensure the improvement of educational achievement at all levels by becoming a principal center for the collection, preservation, and use of research and other information relating to education. The library, already the largest federally funded library in the world solely devoted to education, is the government's center for information and referral on education. The NLE houses more than 200,000 publications and about 750 periodical subscriptions in addition to studies and reports. The library also houses ERIC microfiche and CD-ROM data bases and more than 450,000 microforms. Special collections include rare books published before 1800, mostly in education; historical books from 1800 to 1964; early American textbooks from 1775 to 1990; modern American textbooks, 1900–1959; U.S. Department of Education reports, archived speeches, correspondence, and policy papers; and children's classics. The resources of the library are open to the general public.

ELEMENTARY AND SECONDARY SCHOOL PROGRAMS

The department delivers almost $13 billion to states and school districts for elementary and secondary education, primarily through formula-based grant programs. The grants, designed to support improvements in basic and academic skills, school safety, parent involvement, and teacher quality, also help the states and school districts meet the special needs of schools and students. Several programs respond to the new emphasis and help young people and adults develop the knowledge and skills they need for careers that often demand ever-higher levels of education and training. The 1994 School-to-Work Opportunities Act, administered jointly by the Department of Education and the Department of Labor, provides seed money to every state and to interested communities to develop and launch comprehensive school-to-work systems. These systems combine school-based and work-based learning with activities designed to prepare students for a first job. The school-to-work program expires in 1999. Six programs, however, account for about ninety-five percent of the department's funding to elementary and secondary education: The Goals 2000: Educate America Act; Title I of the Elementary and Secondary Education Act (ESEA); the Dwight D. Eisenhower Professional Development Program; the Safe and Drug-Free Schools and Communities Program; Impact Aid; and Part B of the Individuals with Disabilities Act.

The first program, Goals 2000, became a reality following a historic governors' meeting in Charlottesville, Virginia, in 1989, when the governors of the fifty states adopted national education goals for the education of all U.S. students. The Goals 2000: Educate America Act is the department's education program that seeks to help parents, teachers, and community leaders to improve their schools by raising academic standards; addressing safety, discipline, and basic skills; attracting and training better teachers; and strengthening parent involvement.

The Improving America's Schools Act, passed by Congress in 1994, reauthorized the ESEA, which at $10 billion is the federal government's largest investment in elementary and secondary education. The ESEA addresses four key priorities:

- Ensuring access to quality education for the most disadvantaged students so they can learn the basics and improve achievement geared to challenging academic standards

- Achieving safe, disciplined, and drug-free schools

- Ensuring that today's and tomorrow's teachers have the training and skills necessary so that all children meet challenging academic standards

- Assisting states by alleviating burdens caused by federal activities, such as federally owned land that provides no tax revenues.

The Title I program, established in 1965, directs about $7 billion to helping disadvantaged children in about half of all the schools in the country. Most of the funds go to high-poverty schools where students score at much lower levels than their peers in low-poverty schools on achievement tests—levels that contribute greatly to high dropout rates, illiteracy, and poor employment prospects. High-poverty schools use Title I funds to help close the gap. As reauthorized in 1994, Title I emphasizes high academic standards and accelerated learning in the core academic subjects rather than the low expectations often found in remedial instruction. High-

poverty schools are encouraged to develop schoolwide programs aimed at raising the basic and academic performance of all students, not just those eligible for Title I.

The Dwight D. Eisenhower Professional Development Program supports locally guided teacher training in the core academic subjects. The program distributes funds to states and school districts to help ensure that teachers are prepared to teach higher academic standards.

The third major priority in the ESEA, the Safe and Drug-Free Schools and Communities Program, responds to the continuing crisis of violence and drugs in our schools by supporting comprehensive school- and community-based drug abuse and violence prevention programs. The Impact Aid Program is the major program assisting states and local communities affected by federal activities, such as the presence of a military base or federal ownership of a significant percentage of local property. In these districts the federal presence reduces the local property tax base that ordinarily serves as a major source of school funding. Impact Aid replaces this lost revenue.

Finally, the department also helps states and school districts to meet their responsibility to provide a free appropriate public education for physically challenged children. Two landmark federal court decisions in the early 1970s established the constitutional right of children with disabilities to equal educational opportunity. In 1975 a federal law, now known as the Individuals with Disabilities Education Act, provided a framework for appropriately serving these children as well as federal financial assistance to help pay for their education. In 1994 the department allocated nearly $3 billion through three state formula grant programs intended to help states meet the developmental and educational needs of more than five million children with disabilities from birth through age twenty-one.

HIGHER EDUCATION

Although the Department of Education devotes a good deal of time and resources to elementary and secondary education, approximately forty-five percent of its budget goes to postsecondary education. Most of these funds, however, go to student financial aid. In the United States there has been a long history of federal financial assistance at the postsecondary level. In fact, the history of federal financial assistance to college students goes back to the GI Bill of 1944, which served to elevate millions of American servicemen and their families into the middle class through the opportunities presented by obtaining a college degree.

By the 1990s the federal government funded about seventy-five percent of all student financial aid in the nation. Much of the funding comes from loan programs operating through the Department of Education. The department operates two major student loan programs for which almost all students are eligible. The first is the William D. Ford Direct Loan Program, which lends funds directly from the federal government to postsecondary students and provides a wide variety of repayment options, including income-contigent repayment. The second major student loan program is the Federal Family Education Loan Program, which since 1965 has provided loan subsidies and guarantees against default on loans made to students by private lenders.

The loan programs, however, are plagued by problems such as high default rates and inadequate loan collections. To combat these problems, Congress and the Department of Education are actively trying to reduce the default rate. Their actions to reduce defaults include management reforms and refusing loans to students who attend postsecondary institutions with high default rates.

The federal Pell Grant program makes grants averaging over $1,500 to nearly four million postsecondary students annually. Most Pell recipients are from families earning less than $20,000 a year.

There are also funds available for vocational training and for individuals with disabilities. The Perkins Act vocational education state grants help pay for vocational training programs at both the secondary and postsecondary levels. Another significant federal support to assist states in preparing individuals for employment is that of vocational rehabilitation. The department provides vocational rehabilitation state grants that assist one million adults with disabilities, most of them severe, in achieving employment and independent living.

Finally, in addition to these programs that seek to prepare students and individuals with disabilities for changing employment opportunities, the department supports literacy and basic skills training through a combination of state formulas and competitive grant programs. The Adult Education Act state grant program helps approximately four million educationally disadvantaged adults achieve literacy, certification of high school equivalency, and English language proficiency. The Even Start Program delivers formula grants to states for the support of intergenerational literacy projects combining early childhood literacy with adult reading programs.

BIBLIOGRAPHY

Bell, Terrel H. *The Thirteenth Man.* New York, 1988.
Burt, Richard, Adam, Clymer, Leonard Silk, and Hedrick Smith. *Reagan, the Man, the President.* New York, 1980.
Carter, Jimmy. *Keeping Faith.* New York, 1983.
"Education Department Passes House." *Congressional Quarterly Almanac.* Washington, D.C., 1979.
"Education Department Wins Final Approval." *Congressional Quarterly Almanac.* Washington, D.C., 1979.
"From the Professional Stream." *Public Administration Review* 37 (1979): 4.
Leuchtenburg, William E. *In the Shadow of F.D.R.: From Harry Truman to Ronald Reagan.* New York, 1985.
Nathan, Richard P. "The Reagan Presidency in Domestic Affairs." In *The Reagan Presidency: An Early Assessment,* edited by Fred I. Greenstein. Baltimore, 1983.
"Major Congressional Action." *Congressional Quarterly Almanac.* Washington, D.C., 1982. 502.
Miles, Rufus E. "A Cabinet Department of Education: An Unwise Campaign Promise or a Sound Idea?" *Public Administration Review* 37 (1979): 79–86.
Seidman, Harold and Robert Gilmour, *Politics, Position and Power: From the Positive to the Regulatory State.* New York, 1986.
"Senate Confirms Bennett as Education Secretary." *Congressional Quarterly Almanac.* Washington, D.C., 1985.
Sundquist, James L. "Jimmy Carter as Public Administrator: An Appraisal at Mid-Term." *Public Administration Review* 37 (1979): 36–51.
U.S. Department of Education Documents. U.S. Department of Education, Washington, D.C., 1996.
U.S. Senate, Ninety-Sixth Congress. *Hearing before the Committee on Labor and Human Resources, First Ses-*

sion, on Shirley M. Hufstedler, of California, to Be Secretary of Education, November 27, 1979. Washington, D.C., 1980.

U.S. Senate, Ninety-Sixth Congress. *Hearing before the Committee on Labor and Human Resources, First Session, on Dr. Terrel H. Bell, of Utah, to Be Secretary of Education, January 15, 1981.* Washington, D.C., 1981.

U.S. Senate, Ninety-Sixth Congress. *Hearing before the Committee on Labor and Human Resources, First Session, on William J. Bennett, of North Carolina, to Be Secretary of Education, January 28, 1985.* Washington, D.C., 1985.

"Weekly Reports." *Congressional Quarterly Weekly Report,* 6 October 1979, 5.

—Veronica D. DiConti

Election Commission, Federal

The establishment of the Federal Election Commission (FEC) under the 1974 amendments to the Federal Election Campaign Act (FECA) came as part of the sweeping post-Watergate reform of political finance law. An independent and bipartisan regulatory agency, the main functions of the FEC include administering and enforcing federal campaign finance laws, administering the presidential public financing program, serving as a repository for public disclosure documents concerning federal elections, and serving as the Clearinghouse on Election Administration for the compilation of information and review of procedures with respect to the administration of elections.

Since its creation, criticism of the FEC has been continual; from the start members of Congress as well as the agency's commissioners and staff have been uncertain or contradictory about what the commission's mandate should be. The FEC remains controversial owing to the lack of political consensus over its appropriate role in overseeing federal campaigns and elections. Some observers believe the FEC should be a tough watchdog while others fear excessive use of its powers, sitting astride the electoral process with potential to intervene in ongoing campaigns for federal office, and possibly inhibiting free speech and rights of association guaranteed by the First Amendment to the U.S. Constitution. While the commission is an agency that actively investigates campaign spending irregularities upon complaint or on its own initiative, hands down punishment for violations, and generally seeks to assure compliance with the law, the extent and lightness or severity of its enforcement actions remains controversial. Some observers would be content if the agency acted primarily as a repository of public disclosure documents containing political and campaign fund data.

Formally organized in April 1975, the FEC was created to centralize the administrative and enforcement functions that had been divided among the General Accounting Office, the secretary of the Senate, and the clerk of the House of Representatives in the original 1971 FECA legislation. Initially, responsibility for compliance with the new law was shared by the clerk of the House, the secretary of the Senate, and the comptroller general of the General Accounting Office, with the Justice Department responsible for prosecution. But following the abuses of campaign finance laws during the 1972 presidential election, this method proved ineffective, which led to the creation of the FEC. Under the 1974 FECA amendments, two commissioners each were appointed by the president, the president *pro tempore* of the Senate, and the Speaker of the House. But the Supreme Court found this method to be unconstitutional in its 1976 ruling in *Buckley v. Valeo* as violating the constitutional theory of separation of powers. The ruling prohibited the FEC from enforcing campaign finance laws and certifying public matching fund payments to candidates for a limited time during the 1976 presidential campaigns.

Congress then enacted the 1976 FECA amendments to conform the laws to the *Buckley* decision; this allowed the FEC to reassume its executive powers. In accord with the 1976 amendments, the FEC was composed of eight members: the secretary of the Senate and the clerk of the House, or their designees, who served *ex officio* and without the right to vote; and six voting members appointed by the president and confirmed by the Senate. The terms of the appointments are staggered and are for six years each. No more than three of the voting appointees may be affiliated with the same political party. The commission elects from among its members a chair and a vice-chair—each of a different political party—and the chair serves a term of only one year to prevent a particular party or interest from dominating agency decisions and actions. Following a case decided by the U.S. Supreme Court in 1994, the FEC no longer has *ex officio* members from Congress. In *FEC v. NRA Political Victory Fund,* the Court ruled that Congress had acted unconstitutionally under the separation of powers doctrine when it appointed two of its own members to the commission.

The commission is charged with administering the FECA, disbursing public funds to presidential candidates, enforcing the expenditure and contribution limits, and providing comprehensive disclosure of political receipts and expenditures. The FECA vests the FEC with its authority and designates its responsibilities regarding federal election practices. Although the FEC has jurisdiction over civil enforcement of federal political finance laws, it does not have formal authority to act as a court of law. Like other independent regulatory agencies, it cannot compel a party to agree to a conciliation agreement, to admit a violation, or to pay a fine. The commission can levy a fine upon a party voluntarily participating in conciliation, and it can pursue litigation in the courts.

A major goal of the FEC has been to induce voluntary compliance. The commission has issued numerous booklets, manuals, and guides to ease the burden of compliance. It also has established a toll-free "hot line" to answer questions, and it holds seminars throughout the country to educate candidates and committee staffs about their responsibilities under the law. Before the establishment of the FEC, the Department of Justice had sole authority in cases of campaign finance law violation. From 1975 to 1979, the FEC and the Justice Department divided jurisdiction by mutual agreement. All "serious and substantial" violations of the act were the responsibility of the Justice Department, and the commission handled less serious violations. The 1979 amendments, however, gave the commission "exclusive

jurisdiction" over all civil matters relating to the act. Although the FEC can initiate civil actions to enforce the FECA, or can refer litigation to the Justice Department, the act specifically calls for encouragement of voluntary compliance. The commission is mandated to make every endeavor to correct or prevent violations by informal methods of conference, conciliation, and persuasion and to enter into conciliation agreements with the parties involved whenever possible. The commission follows the policy that civil enforcement action is to be used only when absolutely necessary.

Complaints regarding federal elections must be approved by a majority of the six-member FEC; only later can redress and nonvoluntary enforcement be sought through litigation or through referral to the attorney general. An enforcement proceeding can be initiated either as a result of a complaint filed with the commission, usually by an opposing candidate or political party, or from information generated from within the FEC itself. Then, the FEC's Office of General Counsel analyzes the complaint and determines whether there is "reason to believe" a violation has either occurred or is about to occur. An investigation is then initiated by the commission if four of the six commissioners agree that a violation has occurred. The fact that the FEC membership is divided equally between the two major parties sometimes has made a majority of four difficult to obtain because it requires some element of bipartisanship. Nonetheless, any decisions reached by the commission, including deadlocks, are subject to judicial review by the United States District Court for the District of Columbia, and can be appealed.

The enforcement process as outlined under the FECA has been criticized both for its lack of due process for those investigated and for its inability to deter effectively violations of campaign finance laws. Respondents are not allowed to address the commission in person, nor are they allowed to view all of the evidence gathered during the investigation. The FECA also does not always deter participants in the electoral process from violating current laws, since deadlocked decisions made along party lines are possible, thus reducing the chance for an investigation of some possible violations. Even when violations are pursued by the commission, penalties usually come long after the election is over. This leads to another major criticism of the FEC: that it exercises its enforcement powers too selectively, resulting in unjustified costs and burdens on campaigns that must now employ lawyers and accountants to ensure compliance. The agency has had to spend considerable time and resources defending itself, often at the expense of administration and enforcement of the law. The FEC's budget, determined by Congress, has grown but generally has not kept up with inflation over the years.

In addition to the FEC's statutory responsibility to provide information and studies on voter participation and to commission objective studies of various aspects of registration, elections, and election law through its Clearinghouse on Election Administration, the commission also has been given duties by new laws: to monitor the work of the states under the National Voter Registration Act of 1993, and to assist in polling place accessibility under the Americans with Disabilities Act of 1990.

Defenders of the commission contend that many criticisms are unfair because the agency is required to follow the law enacted by Congress and is too often blamed for merely implementing the law. The most approved and respected functions of the FEC are its disclosure activities—including the easy availability of information through its automated facilities in a ground-floor office—and the compilations of political fund data through its computer services. Overall, problems with the FEC spring less from the agency's shortcomings than from Congress's reluctance to create a truly independent commission.

BIBLIOGRAPHY

Alexander, Herbert E., and Anthony Corrado. *Financing the 1992 Election.* Armonk, N.Y., 1995.

Hedlund, Elizabeth, and Lisa Rosenberg. *Plugging in the Public: A Model for Campaign Finance Disclosure.* Washington, D.C., 1996.

Jackson, Brooks. *Broken Promise: Why the Federal Election Commission Failed.* New York, 1990.

Sorauf, Frank J. *Money in American Elections.* Glenview, Ill., 1988.

—HERBERT E. ALEXANDER

Electronic Government

ESSAY Human activities are carried out within an evolving division of labor and are controlled by a combination of physical, biological, and social forces. In hunter-gatherer societies work was physically difficult but relatively unspecialized, concentrated in interactions within the family or tribe. Over time, both work and social groupings have grown more complex, creating the need for complex institutions of governance. Societal structures have adapted to the growing complexity: as the development of agriculture encouraged more stable yet diversified population concentrations, so mass-production technologies encouraged the growth of nation-states.

During the last half of the twentieth century, the development of digital computing and telecommunications technologies—often referred to as the "Information Revolution"—is stimulating what many consider to be yet another fundamental restructuring of society. As the Information Revolution continues, what concepts or theories are guiding efforts by government in the United States to become highly computerized, or "electronic"? What is the status of such efforts so far? What are their prospects for the future? To understand the evolution and impacts of electronic government, it is important to set the context by briefly examining the roles and performance of government.

GOVERNMENT ROLES AND PERFORMANCE

While the units of American government are numerous and complexly interrelated, they collectively address three primary concerns:

Governance—Issues Related to Establishing Societal Values and Resolving Conflicts

Under the American Constitution, the people give authority to the government to protect and enhance social welfare and to resolve conflicts that cannot be voluntarily resolved. Governmental authority is exercised by legislatures and executive agencies (through laws and regulations, respectively) and the judicial system (through the application of constitutional principles or particular laws). The government defines community values (for example, setting standards for drinking water) and then resolves conflicts to protect those values (enforcing drinking water standards).

While conflicts tend to increase as society becomes more heterogeneous, conflict and heterogeneity also lead to social learning. Thus, the optimal level of social conflict is not zero, but rather enough to balance near-term welfare (tranquility) against longer-term welfare (change). A society that is too single-minded can be as vulnerable as one paralyzed by internal conflicts.

Spillovers—Issues Related to Correcting Market Imperfections

Within the American system individuals have great freedom to conduct their affairs and trade with others so long as they do not harm uninvolved third parties. The belief is that free markets maximize general welfare, largely by encouraging efficiency and innovation. Progress flows through the creative destruction wrought by highly motivated entrepreneurs, as it did when Bill Gates and many others fostered the microcomputer revolution and destroyed large parts of the mainframe and minicomputer industries.

Transactions between individuals, however, may "spill over" and require governmental regulation to protect the larger society. Thus we have speed limits to protect against undue traffic risks, environmental regulations to protect against pollution, and tax laws to protect against "free riders" who could otherwise benefit without paying for public services such as national defense and local policing, thus either reducing the level of those services or imposing additional financial burdens on others.

Equity—Issues Related to Equality and Fairness

Equity issues are a particularly problematic "spillover," given that free trade often leads to unequal and unfair distributions of wealth and opportunities. To some, equity is primarily an efficiency concern, as too great a disparity in economic rewards leads to conflicts that pull down total production; to most, however, equity is primarily a moral concern, with fairness preferred

even if it leads to less total production. Whether justified by efficiency or mortality, equity provides the guiding rationale for much of taxation and other governmental policy. In general, government attempts to improve equity by protecting those who are unable to protect themselves.

Several trends are particularly relevant from these and other points and are essentially pessimistic:

- As a portion of the economy, government has grown larger during periods of war, with strong growth continuing following World War II. While the government sector has recently retrenched, and while it is smaller than in most European societies, government expenditures still account for approximately one-third of all spending.

- The economy overall continues to grow more productive, but at a substantially lower rate than during the decades immediately following World War II, and at a lower rate than in other countries, especially the countries of East Asia.

- Productivity in the governmental sector is difficult to measure but is estimated as lower than in the economy overall; government is widely seen as rigid and inefficient, even by those working in the government.

- As growth in *per capita* income has leveled off, the gap between rich and poor—which had been narrowing in the first two-thirds of the twentieth century—has again grown wider. Over the past decade, those in lower and middle income groups have experienced a reduction in real income.

- As the private economy has become more "problematic" (failing to keep up with high post–World War II expectations), so too have traditionally public sector concerns: crime has risen dramatically, schools seem unable to educate children effectively, environmental degradation has become a major issue, and society has grown less community-oriented and cohesive.

- These and other trends have left the American public uncharacteristically pessimistic about the future, with a growing distrust of government. While more than seventy-six percent of Americans felt that government could be trusted to do the right thing "most of the time" in 1964, less than twenty-two percent hold that level of trust at the end of the century.

American government thus plays an important role in society, but its performance is increasingly called into question. As arbiter of conflicts, government finds the level of conflict growing rapidly; as regulator of market spillovers, government finds itself charged with inefficiency and ineffectiveness; and as promoter of equity, government finds itself relatively impotent against forces that push in the opposite direction.

These challenges are serious. In this context, with the government under significant stress, what effects will "electronic government" have?

ELECTRONIC GOVERNMENT IN THEORY

The costs of production in advanced economies are made up largely of the costs of managing information. Fortunately, computers can often manage information more efficiently than could earlier manual methods. This is the central reality that is driving the movement toward electronic government.

Rapid Growth in Productivity Thanks to Information Technologies

A computer processor can recognize an incoming pattern of "on" and "off" lines (the IF conditions) and switch them into an outgoing pattern (the THEN conditions) as instructed by the software under which the processor is operating. This ability to execute instructions, draw conclusions, and/or take action based on pattern recognition makes computers useful, since much human work involves recognizing a pattern of inputs and then taking an action that adds value as the next step in the production process. The execution of IF → THEN instructions can result in calculating checks for a payroll, plotting numbers as a graph, or enumerating the diseases that may cause a specified set of symptoms.

The productivity of computer processing—as measured by the number of instructions executed per dollar expended—continues to grow much more rapidly than the productivity of manual processing. Over the years, fabrication techniques have allowed computer switches to become smaller. This allows signals to travel shorter distances and use less material and electricity. Processing productivity has doubled about every two years over the past thirty years. Such growth is expected by most forecasters to continue for the next decade or more. For any given calculation, computers are more than 32,000 times more productive in 1996 than they were in 1966.

The networks that carry computer signals from one location to another are also growing more cost-effective. This is due to many factors, including the transmission efficiency of optical fiber and the economies of scope and scale that become available as networks grow larger.

Applications of Information Technologies

The productivity of information technologies (ITs) would not be very important if only a small fraction of the nation's workload were affected. But this is not the case.

The quantity of "knowledge work" in comparison to agricultural, industrial, and service work has increased dramatically over the course of the nineteenth and twentieth centuries. By definition, knowledge work processes symbols (numbers, letters, sounds, and pictures) rather than substances (agricultural or industrial materials). Such work is performed by accountants, teachers, architects, clerical workers, and, in general, by "white collar" rather than "blue collar" workers. Many government workers are classified as knowledge workers.

Knowledge work, as the most costly component of work in advanced economies, provides an attractive target for computerization. Computers reduce the cost of knowledge work by allowing workers to handle tasks that otherwise would require support from other workers. For example, a worker with ready access to computers and approximately organized information can often answer a client's question without the delays and expense required if the question had to be referred to someone else. In this way the computer cuts cost by eliminating "handoffs" as work moves from one specialized worker to another.

Computer networks also make work more efficient by permitting handoffs to take place over the network. This reduces the need for travel and face-to-face meetings. While meetings will obviously remain desirable in work and other settings, the barriers of time and space can often be dramatically reduced when "meetings" take place over computer networks. Work can be "re-engineered," eliminating many handoffs and allowing others to take place asynchronously and remotely, at substantial savings.

For instance, some insurance companies have recently reformed their process for determining an applicant's eligibility. In one well-publicized case, an insurance company employed nineteen separate specialists to examine applications. Applicants waited an average of twenty-two days before receiving the decision on whether they were eligible. During that time the application was actually worked on for less than an hour. Most of the twenty-two days was spent waiting for the internal mail system to carry the application from one worker's out-box to another's in-box.

In this case, the company reorganized the work to take advantage of networked computers. By putting the rules that guided eligibility into computerized form, the company found that a single caseworker could manage much more of the process than had been assumed under the earlier division of labor. In the new process caseworkers determined some twenty percent of the eligibility decisions without needing to consult with other workers; for these cases they were able to provide answers to applicants within an hour.

Even for the other eighty percent of the cases, the improvements were dramatic. Applications are now immediately scanned into the network, making the data available to several workers at once, rather than one at a time. Messages between the caseworker and those providing specialized assistance take place over the network. Work continues with fewer stops for meetings and telephone calls. Fewer interruptions lead to higher productivity.

By radically redesigning the work flow to re-duce and streamline handoffs, the company reduced the time required to determine eligibility from twenty-two days to a maximum of two days. Further, the redesigned work flow cut costs by nearly fifty percent. Used in this way, the benefits from computer applications are now often quantum leaps rather than incremental steps—fifty-percent reductions in cost and ninety-percent reductions in delivery time, while holding constant or improving the other dimensions of service quality.

It is important to recognize that radical goals for computer-assisted productivity improvement are often risky to pursue. To reduce risk, the vast majority of computerization since the mid-1950s has focused on simple automation, or the imitation and reinforcement of preexisting work flows. Applications have been targeted at work that was highly structured (easy to program) and highly repetitive (large returns, once the "setup" costs were absorbed).

Instead of merely imitating and reinforcing existing methods, however, new IT applications often seek to reorganize work tasks and relationships in fundamental ways. Many workers find such change threatening. They often oppose it—perhaps because of a fear of change itself, fear of technology, fear of not being able to grasp the new skills required, or fear of becoming superfluous. In many cases, these fears have been fully justified.

The technical problems of computerization, while vexing, can usually be fixed. The problems that cause a project to fail are more often political, involving changes in power and social relationships. This seems even more true in government than in the private sector.

Information Technologies and Government

The rising use of ITs holds significant implications for the organization of government work and also for governance itself.

The organization of government work. Government, like other institutions, must coordinate the activities of its individual workers. As other institutions are being pushed to coordinate work more efficiently, so too is government.

While efficiency is less a life-or-death matter for government than for corporations, both sectors are seeking to improve it by developing networked modes of organization, with empowered teams of frontline workers, fewer middle management layers, and remotely executed handoffs from one worker to the next and even directly to customers or citizens.

Government is going electronic in two ways, one incremental and the other more radical. The incremental approach concentrates on developing network-delivered services to improve service accessibility and apparent (or "virtual") integration. The network allows a single phone call or computer connection to reach many governmental programs. Citizens appreciate not having to travel to a number of separate offices.

The more radical—and highly publicized—approach calls for "reinvented" or "reengineered" government. Instead of merely putting existing services "on the Internet," the reengineering approach eliminates or radically restructures many of the jobs involved. This offers greater returns but at a greater risk of failure and a greater concern about who bears the costs of transition. Deciding whether to proceed incrementally or radically—that is, on the best balance of return and risk—is ultimately an ethical and political choice.

Governance itself. Governance involves shaping community values and resolving conflicts. As it becomes electronic, government may find that access to more detailed and analyzable information makes it easier to measure the effects of various activities. In this sense, government as regulator may find better approaches for establishing standards and resolving conflicts.

In other ways, however, the Information Age may make governance more difficult. In earlier eras geography shaped community values. Further, within small and well-defined communities, everyone knew everyone else and it was not easy to escape responsibility for transgressions. This gave people strong motivations to conform. More recently, given the anonymity of large metropolitan areas and global electronic markets, geography is losing power as a shaper and enforcer of values. This may make it harder to create strong communities and—ultimately—to govern. The tools and concepts of governance are under challenge. We have much to learn about how to shape values and resolve conflicts in the dispersed and temporary "communities" emerging on computer networks.

One way or another, we are creating "electronic" government. In theory, this could improve governmental efficiency while simultaneously making it both easier and harder to govern. That's the theory. But what seems to be happening at the level of pragmatic reality?

ELECTRONIC GOVERNMENT: PRACTICE SO FAR

People in government are relying more heavily on computers and telecommunications. This increased usage is reflected in money spent, applications developed, approaches to organization and control, and a variety of policy concerns and perspectives.

Increased Spending on Computers and Telecommunications

In the early years, government was the most important supporter of computer research and development, focusing on applications to improve military capacity. Since the 1970s, however, it is generally acknowledged that governmental computing has failed to keep up with computing in the private sector.

Nevertheless, the growth of government spending on computing and telecommunications has been impressive. Expenditures by U.S. governments for computer hardware, software, and services were roughly $65 billion in 1995, or about $3,365 for every governmental worker. Since the late 1980s, as spending on other government programs has been cut back or grown only slowly, spending on computing has risen in inflation-adjusted dollars, on a per-worker basis, and as a portion of total spending. While about half of all governmental IT spending is federal, with about half of that defense-related, the most rapid recent growth is in nondefense and nonfederal governmental sectors. Note that these data include the relatively "hard" spending reported through the procurement process but do not include spending for many of the indirect costs of training, operations, and maintenance.

Studies suggest that such indirect costs account for about eighty-five percent of total costs, raising our cost estimate to perhaps $360 billion per year, or about $18,516 per worker. As measured by cost, electronic government is a sizable phenomenon.

While governmental IT spending is large, it is smaller than comparable spending in the private sector. Over the past decade large corporations have placed about half of their new capital investments into computing and telecommunications. While the records are not kept in a way that would make the comparison easy or reliable, this is probably significantly greater than the investment rate in government. Further, government spends only 0.5 percent of its total revenue on telecommunications, compared to an industry average of 1.9 percent. Governmental spending on IT has room yet to grow.

Applications: From Mainframe, to Micro, to Network-based Customer Service and "Virtual" Organizations

As IT spending has grown, applications have evolved through several primary eras.

The mainframe and micro eras. Early computing was expensive and technically complicated. In World War II, applications focused on scientific and computationally intensive tasks such as calculating artillery trajectories and breaking encryption codes. By the middle 1950s, however, costs had come down enough to handle clerical tasks such as the "big four" accounting applications: payroll, accounts payable, accounts receivable, and general ledger. The data for these applications were stored on reels of tape in sequences designed to make the processing as efficient as possible. When the payroll application ran, it would read the entire payroll tape to make all the modifications required in one pass. This was called sequential batch processing.

Over time, cheaper disk-based storage devices became available, enabling data to be accessed in nonsequential or "random" order. More complex computers were developed to handle more than one application and more than one operator at the same time. This led to "random, on-line" processing for tasks such as making airline reser-

vations or for dispatching police, fire, and other emergency-response vehicles. On-line applications grew dramatically during the 1970s, as did the use of cheaper and smaller "mini" computers.

During the 1970s and 1980s, specialized data base management systems (DBMSs) were developed to manage data independently of the individual applications that used the data; thus, for example, a name and address record could be modified once in the DBMS and subsequently used by the payroll, accounts payable, or jury notification applications. The earlier approach would have required a separate file for each application, so the same name and address would have had to be changed in many places. DBMS software also made it easier to produce reports that analyzed data in ways that had not been anticipated when the original applications were being programmed.

As computing technology continued to change, it was ultimately possible to put an entire processor on a single chip (a microprocessor). This enabled the creation of personal computers—PCs—that were small and cheap enough to be purchased and controlled by individuals. PCs sparked an incredible growth in computing during the 1980s and early 1990s, once PC-based spreadsheets and word processing software were developed.

PCs, in government and elsewhere, enticed many people to expand the depth and variety of their computing. As users became more involved, they sought and gained more control over computing. As software markets grew, applications were increasingly bought "off the shelf" rather than built by internal programmers. Whereas early applications had focused on recording and looking up individual transactions (time sheets and payroll checks), the new applications used spreadsheets and other software to analyze previously captured data (using payroll data to look for trends and causes of overtime spending).

The networking era. During the 1980s computing growth concentrated on stand-alone personal computing, where individual users controlled their own machines and the machines were not connected to networks. However, as users saw the advantages of linking to each other and to outside sources of data, they sought to connect their stand-alone computers into networks. Small networks were built so that users in a given office or series of offices could share printing or electronic mail. Larger and more elaborate networks—and interconnections among networks—were also built. Networking's growth was aided by *de facto* open standards developed by defense research and turned later into more general application as "the Internet." The Internet has become the centerpiece of the "networking era." It has grown at roughly ten percent per month over the past seven years. In 1996 some eight percent of American adults were using the heavily graphical portion of the Internet known as the World Wide Web.

The growth of networking infrastructure has encouraged initiatives in both the private and public sectors to improve customer service and develop "virtual" organizations (sets of activities integrated as tightly as if coordinated within a single organization, but coordinated instead by cooperation among multiple organizations).

Networks improve customer service by offering access many hours of the day from many locations. Back when the Social Security Administration (SSA) was supported only by manual record keeping, citizens had to go to a local office, stand in line for approximately forty-five minutes before staff were available, then request what they wanted (for example, to learn the balance in their account or to track down a missing check). Instead of immediately receiving the service they requested, they were told to come back in about ten days, since the records could not be searched quickly enough for faster service.

With computers, however, the SSA has developed what has grown to be the world's largest toll-free telephone number, and citizens can now ask many questions via telephone. Supported by the phone network and a large data communications network, SSA staff receiving such calls can be located anywhere in the country. They often look up the information they need in real time, completing many transactions while the citizen is still on the line. The use of networks by the SSA has turned transactions that once required

multiple trips—to hard-to-find government offices open only during "normal" office hours—into simple phone calls from almost anywhere at almost any time.

Another example of improved service is "voice mail for the homeless" in Seattle. In this project the city made voice mailboxes available to homeless people to help them in searching for jobs. As job applicants, the homeless had no way to receive messages from potential employers. The voice mail service corrects this problem. The homeless find jobs more quickly and efficiently, thus reducing the costs of unemployment insurance and other services.

The U.S. Business Advisor is an example of a "virtual" one-stop service on the Internet. Through a single computer address (a home page on the Internet's World Wide Web) businesses can access some sixty government programs that either regulate them or offer financial or other assistance. The system both disseminates information and allows transactions to be completed directly over the network. To access these services before the Internet version was established, the businesses had to call, visit, or write to many separate offices.

The service offered by the U.S. Business Advisor is considered a "one-stop" service because it can be accessed through one computer session. But the staff of the various programs that share the network have not had to co-locate or cross-train—at least not yet—to engage in very much of the politically difficult work of standardizing forms and eliminating redundancies. Virtual one-stop is a way to get a large portion of the benefits of service integration for a small portion of the costs. Note also that the Business Advisor has turned many transactions into "self-service" operations; this reduces cost as it also expands access.

Organization and Management: The Expanding Influence of General Managers

In computing's early years the problems of implementation were predominantly technical and managers had to rely on programmers. Most applications were concerned with routinized record keeping and were located within the financial functions of the organization. Such applications were of little interest to operating managers or senior general managers. As a result, computing staff typically reported to the financial and administrative officers of the agency, and to middle rather than top management.

Over time, however, the nature of computing and telecommunications has shifted. Budgets are getting bigger. Training and staff support require more resources. Agency operations have become much more dependent upon computing and telecommunications infrastructure. More software is purchased from outside markets. End-users are no longer passive recipients of systems developed by others, but active designers of their own systems. The difficult problems of computing have become organizational rather than technical.

In response to the new problems, general managers and political managers are getting more directly involved in the management and oversight of computing. Many organizations are creating the position of chief information officer (CIO). The CIO, like the chief financial officer, is the senior official in charge of a major category of organizational resources. The role of the CIO is to integrate IT into the organization and, most significantly, to serve on the senior management team so that IT developments and issues can be clearly understood and acted upon. In the mid 1990s, CIO positions were being created in a large number of American federal, state, and local agencies.

Unintended Consequences and Policy Issues

The movement toward electronic government has consequences for more than just the accessibility and efficiency of government services. Three additional concerns relate to privacy, equity, and the nature of governance.

Privacy—What should be done to protect it in a world of easily shared information? By sharing information widely, ignorance and redundant data collection can be reduced. But sharing also implies that information given to one organization for one purpose can be used by other organizations for other purposes, thus reducing privacy. Anyone with the right computer access and a social security number can learn an incredible amount, including names and ad-

dresses, family members, neighbors, cars driven, mortgage amounts, approximate incomes, personal interests, etc.

To some extent one's desire for privacy is a desire to be left alone. But it is also a desire to prevent others, especially a "Big Brother" government, from gaining and abusing power. Should the U.S. Department of Education, which has difficulty collecting from people who default on department-backed student loans, be allowed to match a list of defaulters with a list of their own employees? (Most people answer "yes" to this question, although the union representing the workers was strongly opposed.) Should they be allowed to search Internal Revenue Service records to find ways for those in default on their loans to repay? (Most people answer "no" to this, which, in any case, is forbidden by law.)

A privacy principle that is gaining support is to forbid reusing information about an individual for purposes other than that for which it was originally gathered, unless consent is gained from the individual. An exception is to waive permission from the individual when the purpose is to enforce laws, and to require instead permission through some due process, such as that that requires the police to go to the courts before conducting a wiretap.

So far, the views of the public are mixed and unstable on privacy issues. The public opposes the "Clipper Chip," a device proposed by the government to preserve the ability of law enforcement officials to "wiretap" within digital networks. On the other hand, the public supports the extensive use of hand scanners and other technology-based surveillance such as was used to protect against terrorism at the 1996 Olympics in Atlanta.

Equity—What should government do to promote it? Many people are concerned that the combination of IT and global competition is unnecessarily disruptive and may even lead to a permanent class of "have-nots." To counteract Information Age inequality, some argue that government should assume a more active role in fostering open standards and subsidizing computer-based services. Typical proposals call for free access to electronic government through libraries, schools, and hospitals. Others argue that recent indicators of rising inequality are both misleading and not likely to endure. Those in opposition to governmental intervention to promote equity argue that the best hope for broad and equal access is low unit costs, and that costs are cut most reliably by the innovation spawned by competitive markets. Still others argue that the real problem is simply globalization, and that government should create barriers to protect American workers from unfair competition.

So far, the debates about equity have not become very loud, and the government's role in IT-related equity issues has been limited. Compared to the governments in Japan or Europe, the U.S. government relies more on private markets and less on government for the creation of information infrastructure.

Governance—How should government respond to the diminishing importance of geographical boundaries and physical property? As economic and social interactions flow freely through digital networks, geography becomes less a factor in shaping communities. Satellite-based television makes it difficult for any nation to resist external cultural influences, and free-flowing capital markets make it futile to establish a fixed currency exchange rate.

In the United States such developments are raising fundamental issues about governance in the Information Age, but the issues have not yet entered the political arena in a serious way. It is feared that copyright and patent laws are no longer adequate for resolving disputes about software and other intellectual property that can be digitally manipulated. It is also feared that the Internet and other networks may reduce social cohesion and weaken traditional communities. So far, however, little progress has been made in crafting broadly supported proposals for new laws or governmental structures.

The Status of Electronic Government So Far

Most of the work on electronic government has been done to make traditional services more efficient and accessible. To a lesser degree, work is also proceeding on privacy, equity, and governance in general. Progress so far can be characterized as noticeable, but a long way yet from revolutionary. But what are the prospects for the future?

ELECTRONIC GOVERNMENT: FUTURE PROSPECTS

In many ways, electronic government is just gaining momentum. Many applications are still reinforcing old missions and operating procedures. Innovative applications are often too new to form the basis for confident predictions about the future. Nevertheless, although with some hesitation and uncertainty, we can make the following predictions about future impacts on technology, efficiency, equity, and governance.

Impacts on Technology: Computing Becomes Ubiquitous

Technology trends are likely to continue, with the productivity of processors doubling every eighteen months to two years through at least the first decade of the twenty-first century. Much of this expanding productivity will be used for "friendlier" interfaces and portability. Voice recognition systems—which today must be "trained" to understand a handful of particular individuals and a limited vocabulary (as for verbal data entry of medical records by nurses)—should, in the near future, be able to understand a large number of speakers and a large vocabulary. This would allow visually and physically impaired users to interact comfortably with systems. Good voice recognition would also make it easier for the general public to speak and listen directly to government systems ("When will Hurricane Bob hit Boston? What steps should I take to protect my home and family?").

Computer networks will become dramatically more pervasive, with both fixed and mobile networks and with increasingly open interoperability among different protocols. The "telephone" system will carry full-motion video, the "cable TV" network will offer phone and data services, and people hiking in remote areas will carry small and inexpensive devices that serve as pagers, telephones, global positioning indicators, and personal computers.

Such technological capacities are, in fact, already available. The difference will be their penetration into more locations, with more devices and more applications. While computing today is something that people do primarily at the office, it is rapidly becoming "ubiquitous"—available always and everywhere, and used for personal and social as well as work-related activities.

Impacts on Efficiency: Significant Improvement via Growth in Networked Delivery and Production

So far, networked delivery of government services has been limited to adventuresome experiments. Soon, however, the idea of getting anything, at any time, from any place over the network will become a common and reasonable expectation. As this happens, citizens will no longer need to travel to government buildings, as the government will increasingly come to its citizens, much as police and fire officials do today. Consequently, face-to-face interactions will be much less necessary; citizens will interact with government perhaps via a self-service interface, or perhaps via a video conference, but without the disruptions of physical travel.

Network-delivered services will be more highly customized than is possible with the rudimentary record keeping of today. At present it is all too possible for doctors to prescribe medications that interact badly with other medications the patient is taking. In some jurisdictions, however, bad interactions are becoming greatly reduced as systems become more universally interconnected and aware of patients' medical histories.

Advances in computer-assisted service distribution are already well under way. Their expansion over the next decade is a virtual certainty. Advances in networked methods of service production will continue. This will result in lower overhead and more efficient services. These reforms will not occur as quickly or extensively in the public sector as in globally competitive markets, since the equity concerns of downsizing are of greater concern in government. Nevertheless, self-service, remote service, and outsourcing will all continue to expand, and will result, ultimately, in lower unit costs for government services.

Impacts on Equity and Governance: Uncertain, but Likely to Be Large

As the Information Age continues, issues of equity and governance are likely to become extremely important. The transition period will be disruptive, as jobs and careers change and people are forced to cope with an uncertain future. While Americans have characteristically been an optimistic people, optimism has eroded considerably in the late twentieth century. Especially in the middle classes, Americans worry that their children will not find jobs and will not be as successful as they themselves have been.

Added to the economic worries are concerns about society. In a recent study by Canadian officials of the impacts of the Information Age, the dominant prediction was that society was headed for rapid economic growth accompanied by social fragmentation and conflict. In this scenario, the well-educated rich would continue to retreat behind private walls, to seek protection by private guards, to send their children to private schools, and to entertain themselves in private health clubs and resorts. Outside the private walls, the scenario predicted a public world destabilized by gang warfare and an inability to develop and protect cohesive community values.

It is highly debatable whether such a negative future will ever develop. The growth in the gap between rich and poor may or may not continue. It is probable that concerns about equity and community will claim more attention and work, much as they did earlier in the twentieth century. People will be concerned about developing strong communities at the local level along with strong economies at the regional level. They will also focus on regulating economic and other behavior when the "system" is essentially global. Political attention will swell and flood to local and global issues, and erode away from national and state issues.

Taking the long view, it seems clear that productive technologies have always led, eventually, to improved living conditions. On average, people are richer, healthier, and happier today than before the invention of agriculture or industrial mass production. So too, the Information Age will likely lead, eventually, to a substantially improved future. But, as many are now noticing, the problems to be resolved in getting from here to there will also be substantial. As in the ancient saying, we are cursed to live in "interesting" times.

As the Information Age deepens, governments are making themselves increasingly electronic. They are using networks as distribution channels, so citizens can access services over the telephone, television, fax machine, and computer. They are creating "one-stop" services, sometimes merely by allowing agencies to share the same networks, and sometimes by using networks to redesign production and delivery in more fundamental ways.

While expenditures for computing each year amount to some $3,365 per government worker, there is room remaining for further growth. The effects on work of eliminating handoffs or allowing them to be made over networks are just beginning. Even more important, the potential impacts of electronic government on equity and governance are only just beginning to be understood.

BIBLIOGRAPHY

Barzelay, Michael. *Breaking through Bureaucracy: A New Vision for Managing in Government*. Berkeley, Calif., 1992.

Beninger, James R. *The Control Revolution*. Cambridge, Mass., 1986.

Branscomb, Anne Wells. *Who Owns Information?* New York, 1994.

Connors, Michael. *The Race to the Intelligent State: Towards the Global Information Economy of 2005*. Oxford, U.K., 1993.

Davenport, Thomas H. *Process Innovation: Reengineering Work through Information Technology*. Boston, Mass., 1993.

Hammer, Michael, and James Champy. *Reengineering the Corporation*. New York, 1993.

Hiltz, Starr Roxanne, and Murray Turoff. *The Network Nation*. Cambridge, Mass., 1993.

Leebaert, Derek. *Technology 2001: The Future of Computing and Communications*. Cambridge, Mass., 1991.

Magna Carta for the Knowledge Age: Cyberspace and the American Dream. Progress & Freedom Foundation, 1994.

National Performance Review. *Reengineering through Information Technology*. Washington, D.C., 1993.

Osborne, David, and Ted Gaebler. *Reinventing Government: How the Entrepreneurial Spirit Is Transforming the Public Sector*. Reading, Mass., 1992.

Pool, Ithiel de Sola. *Technologies without Boundaries: On Telecommunications in a Global Age*. Cambridge, Mass., 1990.

Sproul, Lee, and Sara Kiesler. *Connections: New Ways of Working in the Networked Organization*. Cambridge, Mass., 1991.

Toffler, Alvin, and Heidi Toffler. *Creating a New Civilization: The Politics of the Third Wave*. Atlanta, Ga., 1994.

—JERRY MECHLING

Employment Act of 1946.

See Appendix: Basic Documents of Public Administration.

Employment and Training Administration

An agency within the Department of Labor, the Employment and Training Administration (ETA) funds and regulates training and employment programs administered by state and local agencies and also oversees employment service and unemployment insurance programs. The ETA also establishes standards for apprenticeship programs. The ETA's employment and training programs are authorized by the Job Training Partnership Act of 1982. Some of these programs are targeted to seniors, Native Americans, migrants, and persons with disabilities. The ETA administers the United States Employment Service (USES), which matches vacancies with qualified applicants. In most urban areas, the USES has daily updated computerized job banks. The USES certifies hard-to-employ workers, whose employers receive tax breaks under the Targeted Jobs Tax Credit. Under the NAFTA Transitional Adjustment Assistance program, workers displaced as a result of the implementation of NAFTA provisions or the shift of production facilities from the United States to Mexico or Canada receive employment counseling, job training, job placement, and relocation allowances. The ETA's other major responsibility is monitoring unemployment insurance programs to ensure compliance with federal laws and regulations.

—GEORGE THOMAS KURIAN

Employment Standards Administration

The responsibilities of the Employment Standards Administration (ESA), a regulatory agency within the Labor Department, are carried out by three main offices: the Office of Federal Contract Compliance Programs, the Office of Workers'

Compensation Programs, and the Wage and Hour Division. The ESA has the authority to correct a wide range of unfair employment practices and working conditions.

The Office of Federal Contract Compliance Programs administers Executive Order 11246, which prohibits discrimination by federal contractors and subcontractors against employees on the basis of race, color, religion, national origin, and sex. It promotes affirmative action. The office also administers programs under section 503 of the Rehabilitation Act of 1973 requiring contractors and subcontractors to hire and promote Vietnam veterans as well as qualified persons with disabilities. The Office of Worker's Compensation Programs administers claims under three major disability programs. The Wage and Hour Division administers the Fair Labor Standards Act governing minimum wages, child labor, and the keeping of proper records.

—GEORGE THOMAS KURIAN

Energy, Department of

Established as the twelfth cabinet-level department on 1 October 1977, the United States Department of Energy represented the centerpiece of President Jimmy Carter's national energy policy. In response to the global energy crisis, the Carter administration created the new department out of several predecessor agencies to coordinate national energy policy and to manage federal energy programs, including production, distribution, research, development, regulation, pricing, and conservation. Energy issues had been muted during the presidential campaign of 1976, but Carter had promised dramatic innovation in federal energy policy. Immediately following his inauguration, Carter asked James R. Schlesinger, assistant to the president, to work directly with Congress to ease the energy shortage. Establishing his headquarters in the Old Executive Office Building, Schlesinger assembled an experienced team of energy experts to forge Carter's energy

strategy. Schlesinger himself, former chairman of the Atomic Energy Commission, secretary of defense, and director of the Central Intelligence Agency, was quickly recognized as Carter's "energy czar." By 2 February, Carter declared a national energy emergency. That evening, in his televised "fireside chat" with the American people, the president solicited sacrifice, conservation, and patience while the new administration fashioned its energy policy. Reminiscent of Franklin Roosevelt's New Deal during the Great Depression, Carter and his energy advisers worked feverishly during the administration's first one hundred days to develop a comprehensive national energy plan.

Although Carter's rhetoric advocated the first "comprehensive" national energy policy, the federal government had been involved directly and indirectly in energy matters for years. But Carter was correct that government energy policy had rarely been centrally coordinated from Washington. During decades of cheap and abundant energy before the 1973 energy crisis, the government's role in managing domestic energy resources was not only greatly limited, but the government's few activities were also dispersed among several agencies. Although the government established naval oil reserves and sponsored a variety of research programs, for the most part Americans believed that private industry should establish energy production, distribution, and marketing policies except where "natural monopolies" in interstate transmission of electricity and gas precluded competitive pricing. On occasion when national emergencies or the public interest required national action, the federal government funded large energy research and development enterprises, especially expensive hydroelectric and nuclear reactor projects. But even when the government's initiatives were extensive, such as in establishing the Tennessee Valley Authority or promoting hydroelectric development of the Columbia River valley, federal energy management was restricted both by region and technology.

Until the 1970s the federal government had not played a vigorous role in managing America's energy resources. In the interests of national security, the government had collected energy

OAK RIDGE NATIONAL LAB. *Founded in 1942 as part of the Manhattan Project to develop an atomic bomb, the U.S. Department of Energy's Oak Ridge National Lab, near Knoxville, Tennessee, is shown here in 1950. The lab now conducts basic and applied research to advance the nation's energy resources, environmental quality, and scientific knowledge.*

data. But even during World Wars I and II, when the federal government imposed strict controls over energy production and distribution, including rationing, Americans regarded government regulations as temporary emergency measures. More typically, peacetime energy programs that arose out of the New Deal, such as dam building, power marketing, and rural electrification, sought to promote growth in energy industries to ensure consumers plentiful and inexpensive energy. Energy supply rather than energy pricing dominated government attention.

Thus, from the 1920s to the 1970s, while energy programs were dispersed throughout the vast federal bureaucracy, the federal government served as a relatively benign overseer of energy management as a whole. In fact, government officials generally focused on fuels, technologies, or resources rather than on "energy." Each fuel or technology, with its special characteristics or problems, developed its own constituency of producers, consumers, and government stewards. In the interest of national security, for example, the Departments of State and Defense sought to secure reliable sources of both foreign and domestic oil. In some agencies, however, fuel and related technologies were handled almost independently of one another, as in the Office of Oil and Gas and the Office of Coal Research within the Department of the Interior. The Bureau of Mines' relationship to the highly decentralized and labor-intensive coal industry contrasted sharply with the Atomic Energy Commission's monopoly of nuclear technology prior to 1954. The Federal Power Commission sought to assure "fair prices" in interstate transmission of oil and gas, while the Federal Trade Commission encouraged competition among energy technologies. Energy research, largely sponsored by the Department of the Interior and, after 1946, by the Atomic Energy Commission, was conducted at diverse national laboratories, research stations, and development centers scattered around the country.

Frequently, America's energy policy became intertwined with other federal policies and programs. During the New Deal, the Roosevelt administration constructed "multipurpose" dams that not only generated electricity but also promoted conservation, reclamation, and recreation. For example, Bonneville Dam, built by the Army Corps of Engineers east of Portland, Oregon, embodied federal energy policy. As a New Deal public works project, Bonneville Dam was built both to provide immediate stimulation of the economy of the Pacific Northwest and to provide the region with inexpensive electrical energy in the long run. But depression economics and energy supply were not the only considerations behind the government project. Bonneville also contributed to national security by providing reliable power to the aluminum, aircraft, and other defense industries located in the Pacific Northwest. The Columbia River project was also important for flood control, irrigation, and navigation. Large concrete dams, of course, significantly altered the environment, particularly by blocking upstream migration of spawning fish and flooding ancient fishing sites. At Bonneville, the Corps of Engineers built ingenious fish ladders and channels to assist migratory fish around the seventy-foot-high dam. While the success of these various stratagems has been questioned, federal energy policy, as expressed in the construction of Bonneville Dam, was regionally and technologically focused, promoted plentiful cheap energy and national secu-

rity, and evidenced awareness of Bonneville's impact on the river's ecology.

In summary, before the energy crisis of 1973, the federal government moved cautiously in energy policy, acting more as a broker among diversified interests than as a master planner. Controversy surrounding the Tennessee Valley Authority and seemingly endless debates between public and private power interests precluded aggressive national planning. Even when energy allocation became a national issue during World War II, the government limited action to immediate problems at hand, leaving the task of long-range postwar planning to private industry or state, local, and regional authorities. Mostly, when energy resources seemed limitless, the American people did not expect the federal government to make hard decisions about America's energy future.

CONSUMPTION AND SKEPTICISM

Unfortunately, hard decisions were in the offing. By the 1960s, conflicts between energy and environmental systems forecast difficult and bitter choices that lay ahead. In addition, the nation experienced some sharp, if minor, energy shortages in the great blackout of 1965 and the subsequent "brownout" of 1971. Richard M. Nixon, perhaps the first modern president to realize that America was heading for an energy crisis, warned Congress that the United States could not take its energy supplies for granted. Since 1967, Nixon cautioned, the United States' consumption of energy had outpaced its production of goods and services. To help private enterprise secure new sources of abundant energy, Nixon proposed establishing a Department of Natural Resources that would unify all federal energy development programs in one agency. In response to Nixon's energy message, Congress authorized the Atomic Energy Commission to pursue research and development projects related to superconducting power transmissions, energy storage, solar energy, geothermal resources, and coal gasification. These programs implemented the commission's large commitment to the development of nuclear power reactors also encouraged by Nixon's and preceding administrations.

Nixon's prophetic energy plans gained little

support because the American public did not believe that annoying energy shortages were more than temporary or regional. As late as 1971, few Americans worried about an impending "energy crisis" as long as there was abundant cheap gasoline for their cars, electricity and fuel for their homes, and power for their industries and businesses.

The 1973 energy crisis reinforced Nixon's determination to develop a comprehensive national energy policy as well as to concentrate the government's energy programs into one agency. Although largely unappreciated, ironically, Carter's energy initiatives were anticipated by the Nixon administration. In April 1973, six months before war again broke out in the Middle East, Nixon predicted that the United States would soon face energy shortages and increased prices. As in 1971, again he warned that the United States' energy "challenge" would become a *bona fide* crisis if American consuming habits did not change rapidly. Foreseeing only deepening energy problems, Nixon amended his earlier proposal for a cabinet department—now requesting Congress to create a Department of Energy and National Resources with responsibility for energy policy and management as well as research and development. In the meantime, Nixon formally organized a team of energy advisers in the White House to coordinate energy policy and analysis among federal offices and agencies.

Again, Nixon's energy proposals stalled in Congress, but he did not give up hope for an energy department. At the urging of Roy L. Ash, director of the Office of Management and Budget, Nixon established an Energy Policy Office to recommend and coordinate the president's energy policies. If he could not persuade the Democratic Congress to create a Department of Energy, as a compromise Nixon suggested creating an Energy Research and Development Administration responsible for central management of the government's energy research programs and promotion of industrial initiatives to foster new energy technologies. The new energy administration would combine the energy research programs of the Atomic Energy Commission and the Department of the Interior, while continuing the former's licensing and regulatory responsibil-

ities in a five-member Nuclear Energy Commission.

Thus, before the Yom Kippur War of October 1973, the principal outline of Nixon's energy policy was already in place waiting for congressional action. The war, of course, greatly exacerbated American energy problems. The consequences of the Israeli victory quickly spread to North America when the Organization of Petroleum Exporting Countries (OPEC) placed an Arab oil embargo on crude shipped to the United States. By November oil reserves were critically low, creating America's most severe petroleum shortages since World War II. Long gas lines that snaked through virtually every city, coast to coast, underscored that the nation was in serious trouble. No longer merely a regional nuisance, the 1973 energy crisis spread nationwide and threatened virtually every sector of the economy.

On 3 November 1973, in a special message on the energy emergency, Nixon asked Americans to lower thermostats, drive slower, and eliminate unnecessary lighting. Evoking the Manhattan Project, which had built the atomic bomb, and the Apollo Project, which had landed two Americans on the moon, Nixon reassured citizens that American science and technology would soon free the United States from dependence on foreign oil. Proclaiming "Project Independence," Nixon pledged increased funding for energy research and development. Optimistically, the president believed that the United States could achieve energy self-sufficiency by 1980. Across the nation, Americans hunkered down to a gloomy holiday season, during which communities reduced outdoor lighting and devised various schemes for allocating scarce supplies of gasoline and heating oil. Gas lines became more irksome than crowded shopping malls. With stunning swiftness, a half-century of energy affluence ended.

For the first time since World War II, Nixon moved to establish federal energy pricing and production controls. Asking William Simon, former deputy secretary of the Treasury, to head the Federal Energy Office, Nixon assigned the Federal Energy Office the task of establishing a comprehensive allocation program including gasoline, aviation fuel, propane, butane, residual fuel oil, crude oil and refinery yield, lubricants, petrochemical feedstocks, and middle distillates. In addition, Simon accepted responsibility for gathering energy data, coordinating the administration's energy policy, and implementing Project Independence. To assist the White House, Simon recruited staff from the energy office of the Treasury Department and transferred key personnel from four offices in the Interior Department: Petroleum Allocation, Energy Conservation, Energy Data and Analysis, and Oil and Gas. He also received assistance from the Oil Import Administration in the Interior Department, the energy division of the Cost of Living Council, and Internal Revenue Service personnel who enforced allocation and pricing regulations.

The American public remained skeptical about the real causes behind the energy shortages. Few Americans accepted responsibility for the crisis. A Gallup public opinion poll published in January 1974 indicated that most Americans believed that the energy emergency was artificial, and surprisingly, only seven percent blamed the Arab nations for the long gas lines. Americans held the oil companies and the federal government equally responsible (twenty-five percent and twenty-three percent, respectively) for the shortages that drove up energy prices. Indeed, distrust of Nixon was such that nineteen percent held the president or his administration responsible for the energy price inflation. Only nineteen percent of the public thought American consumers were at fault. Almost no one believed that depletion of national or worldwide petroleum reserves had contributed to the winter's energy crisis. Thus, as the Federal Energy Office implemented its emergency plans, the Nixon administration encountered a skeptical public that felt that the government itself was a major cause of the energy problem. In March 1974 Congress granted Nixon a small victory by authorizing creation of the Federal Energy Administration as a temporary agency to manage petroleum allocation and pricing, the strategic oil reserve, energy information and analysis, energy conservation, and efficient use of energy resources.

The Watergate crisis of 1974 soon overshadowed Nixon's federal energy policy, programs, and reorganization. The consolidation of federal energy programs into a single cabinet-level Department of Energy would not be accomplished until long after Nixon's resignation as president. In the political battles that followed, Nixon's contributions to federal energy policy and programs were either forgotten or ignored. When, during the 1976 presidential campaign, Jimmy Carter promised to be the first president to propose a "comprehensive" federal energy policy, even the Republicans failed to remind voters that Nixon had taken the first steps toward such a goal as early as 1971 and had fully committed his administration to the development of a comprehensive federal policy following the energy crisis of 1973.

Nixon's energy policies had gained sufficient momentum, however, for Congress to pass the Energy Reorganization Act of 1974, which President Ford signed on 11 October. The act abolished the Atomic Energy Commission, created a Nuclear Regulatory Commission to license and regulate private nuclear facilities, and established the Energy Research and Development Administration to centralize federal research programs. The legislation also authorized the Energy Resources Council, including the heads of the Federal Energy Administration and the Energy Research and Development Administration, which was given a mandate to develop a unified federal energy policy and program.

During the Ford administration, the Energy Research and Development Administration under the leadership of Robert C. Seamans, Jr., became the government's principal energy agency. Seamans's agency inherited by far the largest portion of the Atomic Energy Commission's budget and personnel. In addition, the Energy Research and Development Administration incorporated all of the commission's national laboratories, the research and development functions of Interior's Office of Coal Research, and the Bureau of Mines' research centers. The National Science Foundation relinquished its solar and geothermal research activities, and the Environmental Protection Agency transferred its programs relating to innovative automotive systems. Seamans organized his agency along the lines of traditional fuels and technologies—fossil, nuclear, solar, geothermal, and advanced energy systems. He also created units to focus on conservation, the environment, and safety. Inheriting a tradition of civil control of nuclear weapons, the Energy Research and Development Administration also retained the Atomic Energy Commission's military application program, which managed research, development, and testing of nuclear weapons.

Despite the easing of the energy crisis in the summer of 1975, U.S. dependence on foreign imports increased, while supplies of natural gas remained alarmingly low. Seeking alternatives to energy dependency, Ford asked Congress to establish an Energy Independence Authority to assist in the construction of nuclear power plants, coal-fired power plants, oil refineries, synthetic fuel plants, and other energy production facilities. Concurrently, the president sought deregulation of natural gas, opening of the naval petroleum reserves, and increased funding for nuclear power development. None of Ford's initiatives significantly inspired the American voter, however. As the United States entered its bicentennial year, the American public continued to believe that there was no real energy crisis; that energy shortages were temporary; and that the problems had been created by Arab oil producers, the major oil companies, the federal government, or all three.

Although no one was able to exploit the energy issue in the 1976 presidential election, both candidates knew that energy issues would be a major concern of the next administration. In his final energy message to Congress, Ford offered a mixed warning. While he worried about the expanded federal role in energy, Ford also cautioned that delay in solving the nation's energy problems could exact a high price. Free of requirements to oversimplify issues for the voters, Ford stressed the complexity and difficulty of the choices that had to be made. The most challenging problems were reconciling politically popular low consumer prices with adequate and secure energy supplies, and balancing environmental objectives with energy production and use. Ford predicted that Americans might have to adjust to limited economic growth as well as be willing to take greater environmental risks with energy technologies.

BIRTH OF THE DEPARTMENT OF ENERGY

The winter of 1976–1977 turned bitterly cold. While the thermometer plunged to record lows, electric utilities responded to record demands. Natural gas supplies in New England fell worrisomely low. In several states, industries and businesses closed or curtailed working hours, affecting over 200,000 workers. Thousands of schoolchildren received extended or unscheduled winter vacations. The nation shivered, perhaps as much from this new energy uncertainty as from the weather. Reminiscent of the Great Depression days when a worried nation waited for a new administration to take office, the inauguration of Jimmy Carter promised vigorous action on energy legislation by a Democratic White House and Congress.

Within ninety days of Carter's inauguration, Schlesinger developed the administration's basic energy reorganization plans and energy policy strategies. Carter, who had meticulously edited Schlesinger's drafts, presented his energy reorganization legislation to Congress on 1 March 1977. Thereafter, in April, Carter sent his National Energy Plan to Capitol Hill. In a somber tone that would come to characterize much of his presidency, Carter predicted that the continuing energy crisis would not only challenge American character but would also test the ability of the president and Congress to govern. Indeed, with the exception of preventing war, Carter believed that the energy emergency was the nation's foremost priority. Borrowing from the philosopher William James, Carter characterized America's testing as the "moral equivalent to war." Carter's rhetoric was significant because only during actual wartime had the president asked for such comprehensive authority to manage the nation's energy resources.

Carter's National Energy Plan consisted of approximately one hundred proposals ranging from administrative changes to new laws and regulations. The president placed heavy emphasis on "soft" alternatives: encouraging conservation, reducing consumption, and fostering environmentally benign energy technologies. Little in Carter's plan was new, but in contrast to Nixon and Ford, who had promoted increased domestic energy production to make up energy shortages, Carter encouraged belt-tightening and conservation to ease energy deficits. Carter also abandoned the illusion of achieving energy "independence," but he believed the United States could lessen dependency on foreign resources by slowing growth in energy demand, reducing gasoline consumption, increasing coal production, and installing insulation and solar energy in millions of homes and business. To implement his national energy policy, Carter asked Congress for speedy establishment of the Department of Energy. "Continued fragmentation of government authority and responsibility of our energy program for this nation," he warned, "is both dangerous and unnecessary." The day after Carter signed legislation creating the Department of Energy (P.L. 95–91), he named Schlesinger as the first secretary of energy. The new department was activated on 1 October 1977 with about twenty thousand employees and an annual budget of $10.4 billion.

While Carter wanted to promote energy efficiency and conservation, to achieve a centralized government energy manager he created a large, sprawling bureaucracy. The Department of Energy not only combined the responsibilities and programs of the Energy Research and Development Administration with those of the Federal Energy Administration; the new cabinet agency also assumed functions from the Departments of the Interior, Defense (Navy), Commerce, and Housing and Urban Development, as well as from the Interstate Commerce Commission. Additional transfers included the Alaska, Bonneville, Southeastern, and Southwestern power marketing administrations from Interior and the Navy oil and oil shale reserves from the Department of Defense. To preserve the independent regulatory authority of the Federal Power Commission, the Federal Energy Regulatory Commission was established as an independent agency within the Department of Energy. The commission inherited most of the authority of the Federal Power Commission, including licens-

ing and regulation of hydroelectric power projects, the regulation of electric utilities, the transmission and sale of electric power, the transportation and sale of natural gas, and the interstate operation of natural gas and oil pipelines.

Regulatory programs not included in the Federal Energy Regulatory Commission were placed under the Economic Regulatory Administration, one of the two administrations created in the department. The Economic Regulatory Administration assumed the oil pricing, allocation, and import programs that had been administered by the Federal Energy Administration. Most of these programs had been established during the 1973–1974 oil embargo under the Emergency Petroleum Act and extended through subsequent legislation. Other regulatory programs included emergency and contingency planning, controls over importing and exporting natural gas, supervision of utilities and industry converting from oil and gas to coal, establishment of priorities for natural gas curtailment, and coordination of regional power systems.

The department's second administration, the Energy Information Administration, consolidated the government's many and diverse energy data systems. By centralizing the most important data-gathering activities, the Energy Information Administration would provide comprehensive data and timely analysis for the president, the department, Congress, and the public. In addition to predicting long-term energy trends, the administration was expected to develop systems for estimating national fuel reserves and reporting the financial status of energy-producing companies.

Finally, the Department of Energy inherited about forty regional and field offices, research centers, university programs, and laboratories from the predecessor agencies. These varied from the ten regional regulatory offices of the Federal Energy Administration to the Bureau of Mines research laboratories at Bartlesville, Oklahoma, Morgantown, West Virginia, Pittsburgh, Pennsylvania, and Laramie, Wyoming; the Atomic Energy Commission's national laboratories at Argonne, Illinois, Berkeley, California, Brookhaven, New York, Los Alamos, New Mexico, Livermore,

California, and Oak Ridge, Tennessee; and the new Solar Energy Research Institute established by the Energy Research and Development Administration. Also included were the Atomic Energy Commission's operations offices, production facilities, and weapons laboratories. The Department of Energy thus kept intact the network of national laboratories that the scientific community regarded as an irreplaceable national resource.

In his first State of the Union message in January 1978, Carter reviewed progress on his energy program but reminded Congress that, aside from creating the Department of Energy, much legislation crucial to implementing his National Energy Plan had yet to be enacted into law. The heart of Carter's energy plan consisted of five major acts: The National Energy Conservation Policy Act, the Powerplants and Industrial Fuel Use Act, the Public Utilities Regulatory Policy Act, the Energy Tax Act, and the Natural Gas Policy Act. By November Congress enacted the president's energy legislation minus proposed tax measures whose aim had been to reduce oil imports. Nevertheless, Energy Secretary Schlesinger hailed the National Energy Act as a historic watershed. "The era of cheap and abundant energy is recognized to be over," he proclaimed, ". . . for the first time energy conservation is recognized as an indispensable ingredient in national energy policy."

Although Carter was elated to achieve most of his national energy plan, the unlucky president suffered cruel shocks to his energy policies in 1979. Unfortunately, conflict in the Middle East, which would ultimately prove disastrous to Carter's presidency, renewed uncertainty about oil supplies. With increasing trouble in Iran, including cessation of oil exports and the flight of the shah on 16 January, Schlesinger warned Congress that the Iranian crisis might lead to greater oil shortages than those created by the Arab oil embargo of 1973–1974. Then in the early morning of 28 March, just as the oil situation seemingly eased with the resumption of limited Iranian exports, Americans learned of the frightening accident at the nuclear power plant at Three Mile Island, Pennsylvania. For almost two weeks the nation watched with both fascina-

tion and apprehension as scientists, engineers, and technicians worked to shut the plant down. Following its emergency plans, the Department of Energy dispatched more than two hundred people to Three Mile Island to assist in containing the crisis. President Carter and his wife, Rosalynn, also personally inspected the control room of the stricken reactor.

Shortly after his return from Three Mile Island, Carter addressed the nation for a second time about the energy crisis. Again using the rhetoric of war and national sacrifice, Carter rallied Americans to join the battle for energy security. The economic welfare of the nation had become "dangerously dependent on a thin line of oil tankers stretching half-way around the Earth." Ominously, Carter also impugned the oil companies, whom he accused of enjoying excess profits from energy shortages. Moving from his urgent and moralistic rhetoric, Carter characteristically offered a highly detailed and complex analysis of world energy economics. There was no simple answer, but his major prescription was clear—the United States had to find more effective ways to curtail oil consumption, perhaps through easing price controls while imposing a windfall profits tax to reduce the profits of the oil companies.

Despite Carter's plea for aggressive conservation, during the spring and early summer of 1979 gasoline shortages again plagued American motorists. In late June, OPEC raised the price of crude oil by fifteen percent. Although he had predicted trouble, the severity of the gasoline shortage, measured by ever-lengthening lines of automobiles, surprised even the president. Carter called his energy advisers together in a "domestic summit conference" at Camp David to prepare yet another energy message for the American public. Distressingly for the White House, a Gallup poll indicated that Americans still did not believe the energy crisis was "real." On the eve of the president's energy speech, George Gallup reported that Americans were "misinformed, bewildered, and cynical about the management of the Nation's energy supplies." Forty-two percent of Americans now blamed the oil companies for the gasoline crisis, while twenty-three percent (the same as in 1974) blamed the federal government. More familiar with, if not more enlightened about, the Middle East, Americans now held OPEC and the Arab countries (thirteen percent) more responsible for energy shortfalls than the consumption habits of the American people themselves (eleven percent). No doubt Carter found small comfort in the fact that only eleven percent thought the president was responsible, as compared to the nineteen percent of Americans who believed Nixon responsible for the energy crisis in 1974. Most discouragingly, the vast majority of Americans continued to believe that the energy "crisis" was artificially and deliberately contrived by actions of the oil companies, the government, and oil-producing nations.

In his 15 July energy address, Carter soberly and insistently returned to themes that he had expounded previously. Could he convert profligate Americans to energy austerity with his post–Independence Day jeremiad? The president believed that the United States stood at a major crossroads but had lost its self-confidence. If the nation walked uncertainly down the "path that leads to fragmentation and self-interest," America would jeopardize its social and political fabric. Instead, Carter hoped Americans would strike out boldly on the "path of common purpose and restoration of American values." As he had predicted two years before, the energy crisis tested the soul of the nation. Prophetically, Carter offered to lead Americans to a more secure energy future through an Energy Security Corporation to produce oil substitutes, an Energy Mobilization Board empowered to expedite the construction of non-nuclear energy facilities, and a ceiling on oil imports not to exceed 1977 levels.

Perhaps Americans heard the president's exhortations; perhaps cold, hard economics intervened. In any event, by the end of the summer the energy crisis had largely passed. Gasoline lines vanished as Americans adjusted to the higher prices that accompanied lower supplies. Much to the surprise of some observers, American drivers actually began to abandon their gas-guzzling sedans and station wagons in favor of more fuel-efficient compact cars. With gasoline again available at the nation's service stations,

energy faded as an immediate political issue. Between 1979 and 1980, U.S. energy consumption declined four percent, while oil consumption declined even more significantly, by over eight percent. Even more dramatically, oil imports had fallen twenty percent.

Neither federal energy policy nor the Department of Energy became a major political issue during the 1980 presidential campaign. For the most part, both candidates were satisfied to let energy issues remain in the background. Carter, of course, highlighted the success of his energy policies, adding that the "battle to secure America's energy future has been fully and finally joined." On the other hand, Ronald Reagan criticized the vast bureaucracy created to manage energy affairs, and promised to abolish the Department of Energy because he believed the "free market" would do a better job than the government in regulating energy production and consumption. But energy issues, while related, were not central to Reagan's presidential agenda, which focused sharply on the economy, national defense, and the need to balance the budget and reduce federal spending and employment.

Reagan's national energy plan, "Securing America's Energy Future," broke sharply with that of the previous Democratic administration. Rather than promoting conservation and alternative energy systems, the Reagan administration encouraged increased production of conventional fuels, especially oil and gas. Confident that free enterprise would solve long-range energy problems, the Reagan administration sought to reduce federal energy spending, taxes, and regulation. "All Americans are involved in making energy policy," wrote Reagan's energy advisers. "When individual choices are made with a maximum of personal understanding and a minimum of governmental restraints, the result is the most appropriate energy policy." Reagan did not exactly promote a dog-eat-dog, laissez-faire energy policy, but he believed that the promotion and funding of energy technologies should be left to private industry and that the government should refrain from subsidizing or intervening to maintain artificially low energy prices. He realized that high energy prices had a major impact on the poor, but he did not believe that social policy should be confused with sound energy policy. Specifically, Reagan was confident that his economic policies, which dealt with the burdens of inflation and unemployment, would provide greatest relief to the disadvantaged. Nevertheless, the Reagan administration also pledged continued assistance to the neediest households through block grants of aid to be administered by state and local governments.

Although he could not eliminate the Department of Energy, Reagan sought to return the federal government to its historically limited role in national energy management. Established in 1977 by President Jimmy Carter as a political symbol indicating the federal government would accept a large responsibility for solving the nation's energy crisis, five years later, under the Reagan administration, the Department of Energy had become an equally potent symbol of the ineffectiveness of "big government" in dealing with national problems.

[*See also* Army Corps of Engineers; Energy Regulatory Commission, Federal; Nuclear Regulatory Commission; *and* Tennessee Valley Authority.]

BIBLIOGRAPHY

Byset, Clark. "The Department of Energy Organization Act: Structure and Procedure." *Administrative Law Review* 30 (Spring 1978): 193–236.

Cantelon, Philip L., and Robert C. Williams. *Crisis Contained: The Department of Energy at Three Mile Island.* Carbondale, Ill., 1982.

Daniels, George H., and Mark H. Rose, eds. *Energy and Transport: Historical Perspectives on Policy Issues.* Beverly Hills, Calif., 1982.

Fehner, Terrence R., and Jack M. Holl. *Department of Energy, 1977–1994: A Summary History.* Washington, D.C., 1994.

Goodwin, Craufurd, ed. *Energy Policy in Perspective: Today's Problems, Yesterday's Solutions.* Washington, D.C., 1980.

Holl, Jack M., ed. *Institutional Origins of the Department of Energy.* Washington, D.C., 1982.

Ray, Dixy Lee. *The Nation's Energy Future.* Washington, D.C., 1973.

U.S. Department of Energy. *Securing America's Energy Future: The National Energy Policy Plan.* Washington, D.C., 1981.

U.S. Senate Committee on Energy and Natural Resources. *Executive Energy Documents.* Washington, D.C., 1978.

—Jack M. Holl

Energy Regulatory Commission, Federal

Created by the Department of Energy Organization Act of 1977, The Federal Energy Regulatory Commission (FERC) replaced the Federal Power Commission (FPC), which had been established in 1920. An independent agency, the FERC is within but separate from the Department of Energy. Subsequently, the FERC assumed the oil pipeline valuation and rate regulation functions from the Interstate Commerce Commission.

The FPC was a three-member (later five-member) body created by the Federal Water Power Act of 1920 to coordinate the construction of hydroelectric projects on federal lands and waterways. Before the 1920 act, each private hydroelectric project on federal lands and waterways required a special act of Congress. During the FDR administration, the FPC's regulatory scope increased after the Federal Power Act was passed in 1935 to replace the Federal Water Power Act. The FPC assumed responsibility for regulating the wholesale rates and transactions of electric utilities. The Natural Gas Act of 1938 extended FPC powers to the wholesaling and transportation of natural gas by pipeline companies engaged in interstate commerce. In 1942 the certification of facilities for transporting natural gas was added to its purview. Until 1978 the FPC had control only over natural gas in interstate commerce; the Natural Gas Policy Act of that year extended its powers to intrastate natural gas prices and sales. Beginning in 1985 the act also established a schedule for phased deregulation of natural gas even though natural gas drilled before 1977 remained under control. This tiered pricing system was intended to encourage the discovery of new gas supplies. Under Reagan, wellhead prices of new natural gas were decontrolled in 1985. About half of the nation's gas supplies were then free of federal controls. In 1984 the FERC issued Order 436 changing its regulations governing the transportation of natural gas by pipelines and broadening access to pipelines by shippers and consumers. The FERC also made it easier for pipelines to serve new markets if they were willing to accept total risk. The FERC followed with Order 451 (vacated by the U.S. Fifth Circuit Court of Appeals in 1989 but upheld by the Supreme Court in 1991) establishing a new pricing structure for old gas that collapsed the previous vintage, or classification, system into a single higher ceiling price. Order 636 mandated the complete separation of pipeline services, or unbundling, and allowed pipelines to sell gas at unregulated prices. In 1989 Congress lifted all price controls on natural gas.

Meanwhile, the natural gas marketplace had become increasingly deregulated. However, high transportation costs neutralized much of the savings to consumers. In 1991 the FERC proposed a new rule, officially known as Docket No. RM91–11, with several provisions relating to pipeline transportation. Under these provisions, pipelines could continue to market gas to customers by setting up discrete marketing affiliates, but had to unbundle their services, making it possible for their customers to buy only the services they needed; pipelines had to set separate prices for each of the services they offered. The rule was incorporated into Rule 636, later expanded into 636A and 636B. The Energy Policy Act of 1992 loosened existing restrictions on Canadian natural gas and also directed the FERC to streamline consideration of rate changes. After deregulation became complete, the FERC focused on two issues left over from Rule 636. During 1993 and 1994 there was an FERC-led push to develop working groups on computerization. These groups later coalesced into the Gas Industry Standards Board. The second issue related to a reform of the gathering systems, or methods by which interstate pipelines collect and retrieve natural gas from the suppliers. Since interstate pipelines are not necessarily located near gas wells or gas fields, they are dependent on unregulated gathering systems that collect the gas, take it to a processing plant, separate natural gas from other petroleum liquids, and then transport the gas to the appropriate pipeline. In May 1994 the FERC announced eight decisions on gathering systems, forming the broad lines of an emerging policy.

Although natural gas dominated FERC activity in the Reagan era, changes in the electricity industry were also far reaching. In 1989 the FERC set up a task force to reevaluate its electricity transmission regulations. In 1992 Congress passed a new bill amending the 1935 Public Utility Holding Company Act. Under this act the FERC was authorized to order a utility to transmit power from wholesale electrical generators if it were deemed to be in the public interest. Prior to 1992 it was not possible for an electric utility to purchase electricity from any other provider than the one that served the grid in its area. Now, wholesale customers were able to shop around for electricity anywhere in the country. The legislation also restricted self-dealing whereby utilities bought power from wholly or partly owned affiliates at inflated rates. According to Chairwoman Elizabeth Moler, the FERC is committed to developing competitive open transmission access. Five elements of this new vision are new compatibility of transmission services, lighter regulatory control, recovery of stranded costs or costs that a utility incurs when a customer stops buying power and simply pays for transmission services to reach a different supplier, greater flexibility in transmission pricing, and formation of regional transmission groups.

The FERC is composed of five members appointed by the president and confirmed by the Senate. Since 1990 terms of office have been set at five years. The FERC has jurisdiction over natural gas, oil, and electricity. In the field of natural gas, the FERC regulates transmission in interstate commerce, construction and operation of interstate pipelines, and construction and operation of pipeline facilities. In the field of oil, it regulates the rates and practices of oil pipeline companies engaged in interstate commerce. In the field of electricity, it regulates the transmission and wholesaling of electricity, conditions, rates, and charges among electric utilities, environmental compliance by nonfederal hydroelectric projects, and the sale of securities by electric utilities. The commission may initiate formal rule making on its own and also review certain rules proposed by the Department of Energy. An administrative judge presides over commission hearings on proposed rules. Company requests for rate increases, adjustments, and curtailments of service follow a similar procedure. The FERC has the authority to enforce compliance. Most enforcement is through administrative or judicial action.

The commission issues different types of licenses and certificates. Licenses are issued for construction of nonfederal hydroelectric projects and gas plants, and certificates for construction of gas pipelines and facilities.

In addition to administrative divisions, the FERC has three separate regulatory offices: the Office of Electric Power Regulation, the Office of Hydropower Licensing, and the Office of Pipeline and Producer Regulation. There are five regional offices, in Atlanta, Chicago, New York, Portland, and San Francisco. The FERC publishes *The Chronicle,* a monthly newsletter, in addition to staff reports.

BIBLIOGRAPHY

The Federal Energy Regulatory Commission: Its Organization and Operations. Washington, D.C., 1996.

—GEORGE THOMAS KURIAN

Engraving and Printing, Bureau of

The facility that would come to be known as the Bureau of Engraving and Printing (BEP) originated in the act of 17 July 1861 authorizing the United States to issue up to $250 million in paper money. The act further required that this currency carry the original signatures of designated Treasury Department officials. Thus, after the plates were engraved and the notes printed by private suppliers—the American Bank Note Company and the National Bank Note Company, both located in New York—they were shipped to Washington, D.C., where a cohort of clerks hired for the purpose at $1,200 per year hand-signed each and every one. The notes, printed in sheets of four, were then handed off to another battalion of clerks armed with shears, who separated and trimmed them.

This tedious process offended an engineer in Treasury's bureau of construction, who persuaded Secretary Salmon P. Chase to obtain modification of the legislation of 17 July, allowing facsimile signatures in lieu of the real thing. This efficiency-minded public servant was Spencer M. Clark, and he was not content with the comparatively small savings that followed immediately from the switch to machine-produced signatures and machine-cut and -trimmed sheets. It was evidently his intention from the outset to centralize the whole production process, including the engraving and printing, in the government itself. Having been won over to the first part of Clark's scheme, Secretary Chase now embraced the rest, overcoming considerable opposition to win the legislation, approved on 11 July 1862, authorizing the Treasury to undertake the production of the nation's paper money. By the end of 1864, the fledging BEP employed over five hundred workers and two hundred pieces of heavy equipment—presses, ink mills, numbering machines, and so forth—in the manufacture of government securities and currency of various kinds.

The new bureau faced early threats from its business and bureaucratic competitors as well as from private citizens opposed to paper money whatever the source. The New York bank note companies probably were most directly threatened, and they fought hard to discredit the BEP and regain their control over the government's engraving and printing business. Allegations of waste and fraud and worse led to a formal congressional investigation in 1864. The most sensational charge centered on the bureau's women clerks. Women were then uncommon in the government workplace, but the wartime manpower shortage, coupled with the BEP's rapid expansion, left the bureau without other options. Washington society was scandalized, and this sense of offended morality was exploited by the bureau's enemies, who drew lurid pictures of promiscuity and incompetence in BEP operations. In the end, Clark and the bureau were cleared of all charges, although proposals to dismantle it recurred through the 1870s.

The infant BEP's uncertain status within the Treasury Department increased its vulnerability to external enemies. At the beginning, without a statutory designation, it was known by a variety

THE BUREAU OF ENGRAVING AND PRINTING IN WASHINGTON, D.C. *The bureau prints all the currency and postage stamps used in the United States, plus a large range of other official cerificates and documents.*

of titles: the "small note bureau," the "small note department," the "note bureau," and the "national note bureau." This last appellation seemed to associate it with the Currency Bureau, today known as the Office of the Comptroller of the Currency, which had been founded in February 1863 to organize and administer a system of federally chartered banks and a uniform national currency. The *Official Register of the United States* for 1863 listed the printing bureau as the "First Division of the National Currency Bureau," and Clark soon after started referring to himself as the "division chief," but the relationship was disavowed by the first comptroller, Hugh McCulloch, who opposed the printing of national bank notes by the government. As secretary of the Treasury from 1865 to 1869, McCulloch was even better positioned to influence policy, and so it was not until 1877 that the BEP became the

exclusive printer of national currency. Eventually it acquired distinct legal status from Congress, with appropriations earmarked specifically for it instead of for Treasury generally, and a statutory mandate spelling out the duties of the BEP director and his relationship to the secretary.

BEP's new status was recognized with a permanent home. Clark, that apostle of efficiency, was almost as horrified by the conditions under which his bureau initially had to operate as he was with the system he meant it to supplant. The BEP and its heavy machinery had been relegated to the attic and basement of the Treasury Department, with a dumbwaiter connecting the two locations. Clark complained about the clumsiness of this arrangement as well as the security problems it presented. At a time when the doors of government offices—even the White House—were wide open to all, he worried about Treasury

Department visitors helping themselves to a "souvenir" or two from the carts of finished money that moved about the bustling floors—a problem that actually came to pass occasionally. The BEP's answer was a secure building to call its own. A site was chosen at Fourteenth and B streets, S.W., and on 1 July 1880 the new fire-proof red-brick building opened for operation. As the BEP's business increased, it outgrew even these accomodations, and since 1914 it has occupied its present site just south of the original one.

The year 1880 was a significant one in the BEP's history for yet another reason, and that was the transfer to it of printing responsibilities for all U.S. government securities. In 1894 it gained the exclusive rights to print the nation's postage stamps as well. These were hardheaded business decisions by Congress and the Post Office rather than cases of bureaucratic favoritism, for in each instance the bureau was obliged to prove—and to continue to prove—that it could produce these fiscal documents at lower cost than the private sector.

Its ability to meet that test was partly the result of its ability to take advantage of various economies of scale. From the very beginning, the need to compete with the private printers kept the bureau on the cutting edge of printing technology, and many improvements in the design of the presses and related machinery were devised in-house by BEP personnel. Clark himself was a skilled engineer responsible for important developments in the science of dry printing, which, when it was later perfected, obviated the necessity of repeatedly wetting the paper, with all the attendant shrinkage and mess. Less than a year after a U.S. patent was granted to James Milligan of Brooklyn, N.Y., for a steam-powered plate printing machine, his machine was undergoing trials at the BEP, which in 1878 adopted the Milligan device (and the inventor himself, for he later joined the BEP staff). It was not long before the Milligan presses were cast aside in favor of more advanced models. Rapid advances also arrived in stamp production and the development of improved papers and inks. So impressive was the bureau's record of sponsoring technological progress in its area of competence that, for a time, it became a primary target of orga-

nized labor for its alleged contribution to the reduction of skilled labor in the printing trades. Not until 1938 did a formal office of research and development come into being at the BEP, solidifying a long-standing worldwide reputation in those areas.

The bureau may not have been on the front lines during World Wars I and II, but those two national emergencies tested its resourcefulness and ability to improvise. During World War I, especially, the BEP's supplies of ink, paper, labor, and space shrunk even as demand for its products rocketed. In 1914 the bureau learned the risks of dependence upon a single supplier of any basic commodity when shipments of German dyestuffs were imperiled by a British blockade; only by a special (and precarious) arrangement with the British government was the stock of ink maintained. Meanwhile the BEP was hastening to develop domestic alternatives, which served it well when the United States went to war with Germany again in 1941.

The demands on the bureau's resources during World War I stemmed primarily from the Liberty Bond program. Between 1917 and 1919, it printed, numbered, and controlled more than 100 million bonds. It required twenty-four-hour shifts, more than one thousand new employees, and the phasing out of the last of the hand-presses in favor of power machinery to get the job done.

The turmoil of the war years, bad as it was, in some ways was not as traumatic as the upheaval of the period between the wars. The bureau was rocked by scandal. It began with a number of employees who were let go when the bureau's work load dropped off after 1921. Some of them charged that the bureau's senior management had defrauded the government in connection with the Liberty Bond program and that, furthermore, their own release from employment was retribution for having sounded the alarm about the alleged transgressions. Hearings and investigations led to the removal from office of twenty-nine ranking bureau employees—all but two of whom were subsequently exonerated when the original charges were discovered to have been based on a misunderstanding. Still, the affair shook the bureau to its core and occasioned an unprecedented turnover at the position of director.

It did not take a return to war for the BEP to return to a state of full mobilization, for the Great Depression and the government programs adopted to alleviate it during the 1930s seriously taxed its capacities. First, there was the contraction, prompted by the contracting economy, which led to employee furloughs and a general slowdown in demand for the bureau's products. Then came the New Deal, with immediate stimulative effects on the money supply. The emergency banking legislation of 9 March 1933 authorized a new issue of Federal Reserve notes to restore liquidity to the economy, and once again the BEP moved into high gear. Millions of government checks to the millions of new recipients of government transfer payments, millions of U.S. savings bonds (an entirely new product), and millions of newly designed silver certificates, gold certificates, and Federal Reserve notes streamed from the bureau's presses. Thus, when World War II arrived, the BEP was well prepared for its stresses and easily managed the switch in production from savings bonds to war bonds, from circulating currency to special issues for use by the military in liberated territories, and from regular stamps to military postage.

In the years since World War II, the bureau has faced a variety of technological challenges. Most recently, its ingenuity and the security of the American money supply have been tested by increasingly resourceful counterfeiters armed with high-resolution color copiers. In 1996, after many piecemeal changes and years of research and development in cooperation with the U.S. Secret Service, the Federal Reserve system, and other government agencies, the BEP began production of new $100 bills embodying the latest anti-counterfeiting advances. It amounted to the most comprehensive overhaul of the basic currency design in four generations. Today, the BEP operates with a work force of some three thousand and maintains production facilities in Washington, D.C., and Forth Worth, Texas.

BIBLIOGRAPHY

Hessler, Gene. *The Comprehensive Catalog of U.S. Paper Money.* Port Clinton, Ohio, 1995.

Schmeckebier, Laurence F. *The Bureau of Engraving and Printing: Its History, Activities, and Organization.* Baltimore, 1929.

U.S. Treasury Department. *History of the Bureau of Engraving and Printing, 1862–1962.* Washington, D.C., 1964.

—JESSE STILLER

Environmental Protection Agency

 During the 1960s and early 1970s, people in the United States and other nations became more aware of the harmful effects of industrial development on the quality of the environment. After two decades of steady economic growth since the end of World War II, citizens in the United States, Europe, Japan, and elsewhere began to call for government intervention to reduce levels of air and water pollution and to remedy the effects of past industrial pollution.

In the early 1970s many nations created government agencies or ministries to respond to these growing environmental concerns. The United Nations Conference on the Human Environment, held in Stockholm in 1972, drew attention internationally to environmental issues. As part of this trend, the United States Environmental Protection Agency (EPA) was created in December 1970. Since then, the EPA has come to be recognized as one of the leading environmental agencies in the world. Other nations turn to it for scientific expertise. Experts often use environmental and health standards that the EPA has issued as a reference point. And yet, the EPA's policies are controversial because of their substantial effects on the economy as well as their ecological and health implications. This article examines the EPA's origins, the institutional setting in which it operates, its organization, history, and changing role.

ORIGINS AND INSTITUTIONAL SETTING

The EPA was not created through an organic law, as environmental agencies in many countries were, but as part of a reorganization of the executive branch authorized by President Richard Nixon in December 1970. This reorganization combined health and regulatory responsibilities from across the federal government into one agency. The EPA was patched together from the Department of Health, Education, and Welfare (air quality, solid waste, and drinking water); the Department of the Interior (water quality, pesticides research); the Department of Agriculture (pesticides regulation); and other agencies, such as the Food and Drug Administration and the Atomic Energy Commission. Because the EPA and its many legal authorities were pieced together from several sources, it is not as fully integrated as environmental agencies in other nations. As a result, the EPA is "not a single organism with a single will but a series of different organisms with different wills" (Marcus, p. 201).

This aspect of the EPA's creation was reinforced by the several different laws that establish its authority. Rather than pass one environmental law, Congress passed several laws, each responding to a different kind of problem. The EPA was granted regulatory authority over sources of air pollution in 1970, surface water pollution in 1972, drinking water quality in 1974, the generation and disposal of hazardous wastes in 1976, the manufacture and marketing of chemicals in 1976, and cleanup of abandoned waste sites in 1980. Separate legal authorities exist for such varied issues as protection of estuaries and coastal areas, removal of asbestos from schools, handling and disposal of medical wastes, lead abatement and control, and many others.

This fragmentation in its legal authorities affects the EPA and the operation of its programs. Each law specifies different goals, requires different approaches to balancing risks and benefits, and relies on different implementation strategies. Both the EPA and most state-level environmental agencies are organized along programmatic (air, water, waste, and chemicals) lines. As a result, many critics argue, U.S. environmental programs are not well integrated.

American federalism is an important influence on the EPA and U.S. environmental programs. Although many pollution standards are set nationally, much of the authority for implementing them is assigned to state governments. In air, water, and waste pollution control programs, the EPA sets national ambient or technical standards that states are charged with implementing and enforcing. For example, in the control of common air pollutants, such as nitrogen oxide, Congress directed the EPA to establish National Ambient Air Quality Standards that set air quality goals, but gave the states responsibility for developing State Implementation Plans for achieving those standards. Federal and state authorities work in a close and often complex partnership. A trend in recent years has been to shift more authority to states to allow for more state and local discretion over problems that are geographically limited.

The EPA functions within the particular institutional setting of the U.S. policy system. The constitutional principle of separation of powers divides power among legislative, executive, and judicial branches of government. Although the EPA's authority is established by the Congress, through the enactment of such laws as the Clean Air Act, it is part of the executive branch of government and is accountable to the president as well. Regularly in recent years, the White House and Congress have come into direct conflict in their oversight of the EPA. The federal courts also review the EPA's decisions on a regular basis, and they have authority to reverse or remand decisions when they are inconsistent with the authorizing law or are not grounded adequately in the available evidence. Interest groups that represent a range of views on environmental matters—from regulated companies, to trade associations, to nonprofit environmental and citizens' groups—participate actively in legislative, executive, and judicial arenas to influence policy.

THE EPA'S ORGANIZATION AND RESPONSIBILITIES

When the EPA was established in 1970, many people argued that it should function as part of a larger Department of Natural Resources that would also include the current Department of the Interior. To the advocates of an aggressive national pollution control agency, however, this meant that environmental issues and concerns would be subordinated to the goals of resource development and exploitation, which characterize much of the Interior Department's agenda today. Instead, the EPA was established as a separate organization within the executive branch, and thus is formally accountable to the president, but not as part of a cabinet-level department. Like cabinet-level secretaries, the administrator of the EPA is appointed by the president and confirmed by the U.S. Senate for the position. Although the administrator is not formally a member of the president's cabinet, recent presidents (George Bush and Bill Clinton) have invited administrators to cabinet meetings and accorded them cabinet status, as a measure of commitment to environmental protection programs. [See Cabinet.]

The formal organization of the EPA reflects many basic features of the federal government in the United States. One such feature is a distinction between the top layer of political appointees and the much larger number of career officials who staff federal agencies. In addition to the administrator, a deputy administrator and ten assistant administrators are formally responsible for setting the policy direction of the agency. They are publicly accountable for the EPA's decisions. Like the administrator, all of these officials are appointed by the president and confirmed by the Senate. They serve at the pleasure of the president, and they almost always are replaced during a change in presidential administrations. Regional administrators, responsible for policy and implementation in ten geographic areas of the United States, are also appointed by the president.

Although political appointees are allowed a limited number of staff positions that may be filled outside the civil service, the rest of the EPA is staffed by career officials. As part of the federal civil service, career staff are protected from changes in political administrations and may spend their entire career with the EPA or other federal agencies. The EPA's career staff in 1995 numbered some eighteen thousand. It is a highly professional group; two-thirds have college degrees, and one-third have graduate degrees. The largest single discipline represented is engineering, followed by law and business; health, agricultural, and biological sciences; physical

and environmental sciences; and the social sciences. Agency staffing declined from about 13,000, at the start of Ronald Reagan's administration, to about 11,000 in 1983, then rose to its peak of about 18,000 in 1995. It has declined since then, to some 17,000 in 1996, owing to debate over its policies and spending limits imposed by the budget deficit.

Assistant administrators lead each of the main operating units of the EPA. Responsibility for main pollution control programs (such as air, water, and waste) lies with assistant administrators for Air and Radiation; Water; Solid Waste and Emergency Response; and Prevention, Pesticides, and Toxic Substances. Other assistant administrators lead offices with functional rather than program responsibilities. These are the Offices of Policy, Planning, and Evaluation; Research and Development; Enforcement and Compliance Assurance; International Activities; Administration and Resources Management; and General Counsel. There are ten regional offices.

Presidents Bush and Clinton both proposed elevating the EPA to the status of a cabinet-level agency as a sign of the importance of environmental issues to the nation. Although a law creating a cabinet-level Department of Environmental Protection was passed by the Senate in 1993, it failed in the House of Representatives, owing to disagreement on peripheral issues regarding EPA decision-making. When the Republican party gained control of both houses of the U.S. Congress in 1995, the proposal for elevating the EPA to cabinet status was lost in the broader debate over the EPA's budget and policies. The EPA remains a separate agency with nondepartmental status, a situation that is more important at a symbolic than at a practical level.

By 1995 the EPA's annual budget was nearly $7 billion. In current dollars, this was slightly above its funding for 1981; so in real terms, the EPA lost ground, despite the apparent expansion in its resources. Less than half of this total is available to the EPA for its operating budget. The remainder is used for hazardous waste cleanup, construction of water treatment facilities, and grants to state environmental programs. After the Republican victories in the 1994 congressional elections, however, and given the continuing effort to reduce the U.S. budget deficit, spending for the EPA will be under close scrutiny in the coming years.

Unlike environmental agencies in many other countries, the EPA does not hold authority over the use and preservation of natural resources. Most of those programs are assigned to the Department of the Interior. Nor is it responsible for national energy policy, which is assigned to the Department of Energy. The EPA's authority is focused on the control, prevention, and cleanup of pollution and scientific, planning, and other activities associated with it. Many issues with environmental effects—natural resources, energy, transportation, agriculture—lie outside its direct control.

THE EPA'S TURBULENT HISTORY

Environmental protection inevitably involves a clash of many important social values. It pits the advocates of economic growth against the defenders of environmental preservation; those who want to use natural resources against those who want to conserve them; those who believe the market should operate free of restraint and those want government intervention to protect the interests of society as a whole. The EPA has been at the center of such conflicts.

Under its first administrator, William Ruckelshaus, the EPA set out to define an aggressive enforcement profile. Highly visible problems of industrial air and water pollution had created a public demand for action. The new agency moved quickly to take advantage of this public support by issuing rules for controlling pollution and enforcing them as visibly as possible. This invited criticism from many people, who argued that environmental regulation would cost jobs, slow economic growth, and add to inflation. Yet the EPA was able to maintain the necessary level of political support to build credibility as an institution to expand pollution control programs.

The 1970s were a period of expanding legal authority for the EPA. Congress passed new laws regulating hazardous and solid wastes and reauthorized earlier laws on air and water pollution. In the late 1970s the energy crisis, high inflation rates, and a troubled economy brought environ-

mental policies under close scrutiny. More and more, from the mid-1970s on, the EPA was required to analyze and justify the economic effects of its regulations. To maintain the EPA's political support, Administrator Douglas Costle (1977–1981) began to cast the agency more as a health than an environmental agency, especially in its efforts to identify and reduce risks from cancer. It was not until the late 1980s that ecological issues again began to compete with health issues (principally cancer) on the EPA's agenda.

More than a decade of steady growth in EPA resources and legal authority ended abruptly in 1981, when President Ronald Reagan took office. An advocate of reduced government interference in economic activity, Reagan set out to reverse the growth in environmental regulation. Reagan's appointee as EPA administrator, Anne Gorsuch, set out to reduce the EPA's legal authority, cut its budget, pare back its regulations, and delegate more authority to state and local governments. Although the Reagan administration was responding to some genuine political and economic concerns, its effort to dismantle the nation's environmental programs encountered intense opposition. Public support for environmental protection remained high, and Congress did not accede to proposals to reduce the EPA's authority.

Unable to achieve its legislative goals, the administration instead pursued a budgetary and administrative strategy for change. The new political leadership at the EPA tried to insulate itself from career staff, weakened the agency's enforcement capabilities, cut research budgets, and catered to industry influences, often in violation of administrative procedures. Public opposition to the administration's environmental policies, combined with conflict with Congress, led by March 1983 to the resignation of nearly all of the EPA's political leadership. The administration's strategy to roll back national environmental protection programs had failed.

To repair the damage done by the failed leadership at the EPA, President Reagan asked William Ruckelshaus to return as the head of the EPA in the spring of 1983. Ruckelshaus rebuilt the agency and its credibility by restoring the budget, improving morale, rebuilding enforcement programs, and mending relations with Congress. Despite lukewarm White House support, Ruckelshaus and his successor, Lee Thomas, were able to restore the EPA's credibility and capacities. In Congress, however, distrust of the administration led to passage of more stringent and prescriptive laws that covered waste management, waste cleanup, drinking water, and surface water quality issues.

When he took office in 1989, President George Bush adopted a more environmentally friendly posture than his predecessor. He named William Reilly, leader of an international environmental organization, as the EPA administrator. For a time Reilly enjoyed a close relationship with the White House. The administration supported the EPA's programs and worked with the Democratic Congress to enact a major reauthorization of the Clean Air Act in 1990. Reilly stressed the importance of international environmental issues and the EPA's role in working with other countries on such problems as global climate change, deforestation, and transboundary pollution. As the 1992 election approached, however, the Bush administration decided to stress economic over environmental concerns. By the time of the United Nations Conference on the Environment and Development, held in Rio de Janeiro in June 1992, the administration had beat a tactical retreat on environmental issues. It was criticized for abdicating the U.S. (and the EPA's) role as international leader.

Another phase in the EPA's history began with President Bill Clinton's appointment of Carol Browner as administrator in 1993. The new administration pledged to maintain environmental programs as well as to improve them in a broad effort to "reinvent government." But many of the administration's initiatives were derailed by the Republican party's victories in the 1994 congressional elections. With a majority in the House and the Senate, the Republicans challenged many environmental regulatory programs and led efforts to reduce the EPA's authority and budget. As of mid-1996, those efforts had enjoyed very limited success, because the American public again (as in the early 1980s) showed strong support for environmental values. However, the Republican proposals set off a debate about the EPA's role and its programs.

THE EPA'S ROLE AND THE FUTURE OF U.S. ENVIRONMENTAL POLICY

In the United States, more than in other countries, policymakers have relied on a strategy of direct regulation to achieve their goals. The EPA issues regulations that define standards for industry, usually based on a judgment about the available technologies, requires reports and conducts inspections to ensure compliance, and takes enforcement action against pollution sources that fail to meet the standards. Often the laws and the regulations that implement them are detailed and prescriptive; they give industry little discretion for deciding how to achieve environmental goals most effectively. Relations between the EPA and industry have often been adversarial.

The EPA reflects this orientation toward direct regulation. Its primary task over the first twenty-five years of its existence was to issue and enforce pollution standards. Often these standards were based, as required, on judgments about the "best available technology" that would control pollutants in different industry categories.

Even within the EPA, debate has been growing about what its role should be. Should it continue mainly as a national regulator, with standard setting and enforcement its most visible activities? Or should it move toward a new conception that recognizes the limits of a purely regulatory approach? This conception pictures the EPA less as a regulator and more as a source of education, technical advice, technological innovation, and international leadership. Instead of deciding what new technology requirements to place on industry, the EPA would act more as a leader in a national debate about environmental problems and priorities. Rather than focus on pollution control, the EPA would work with industry and other interest groups to devise and promote better methods of preventing pollution at the source.

This debate took on a new dimension when

the Republicans took control of the U.S. Senate and House of Representatives in 1995. Congressional critics of environmental regulation argued that it was too costly, too inflexible, and often addressed problems that posed too small levels of environmental and health risk. The House passed and the Senate considered a bill that would have required extensive cost-benefit analyses and risk assessments for major regulations. Critics of federal regulation argued for delegations of authority to state and local levels of government and for a streamlining of reporting, permitting, and compliance programs. Congress voted for severe reductions in the EPA's budget, in part as disapproval of the costs and complexity of environmental programs. President Clinton accepted a need for change. In March 1995 he announced initiatives for "Streamlining Environmental Regulation."

By the late 1990s, the EPA and environmental policy in the United States were at a crossroads. Supporters could document clear evidence of progress on many environmental indicators. The levels of many pervasive air pollutants had declined. Major water bodies were far cleaner than they had been in the 1960s. International cooperation was supporting progress on global issues. Public opinion polls demonstrated strong levels of support for environmental protection. And yet the role of government in American society and the economy was the subject of debate. Although the public supported the goals of the nation's environmental programs, many people questioned the means by which those goals were being achieved. Many observers recommended efforts to better integrate the EPA's internal programs (regarding air, water, waste, and chemicals use) as well as to integrate with environmentally related programs at other agencies (such as energy, resources, transportation, and others). Even defenders of environmental programs called for changes to make them more flexible, performance-based, and effective. Accomplishing these changes while maintaining the needed levels of environmental protection will present the EPA with major challenges in the coming decades.

[See also Agriculture, Department of; Environmental Quality, Council on; Health and Human Services, Department of; Interior, Department of the; and Science and Technology Policy, Office of.]

BIBLIOGRAPHY

Davies, J. Clarence, III, and Barbara S. Davies. *The Politics of Pollution*. 2d ed. Indianapolis, 1975.
Fiorino, Daniel J. *Making Environmental Policy*. Los Angeles, 1995.
Fiorino, Daniel J. "Toward a New System of Environmental Regulation: The Case for an Industry Sector Approach." *Environmental Law* 26 (1996): 101–132.
Kraft, Michael E. *Environmental Policy and Politics: Toward the Twenty-First Century*. New York, 1996.
Landy, Marc K., Marc J. Roberts, and Stephen R. Thomas. *The Environmental Protection Agency: Asking the Wrong Questions*. New York, 1990.
Lester, James P., ed. *Environmental Politics and Policy: Theories and Evidence*. 2d ed. Durham, N.C., 1995.
Marcus, Alfred A. *Promise and Performance: Choosing and Implementing an Environmental Policy*. Westport, Conn., 1980.
Melnick, R. Shep. *Regulation and the Courts: The Case of the Clean Air Act*. Washington, D.C., 1983.
National Academy of Public Administration. *Setting Priorities, Getting Results: A New Direction for EPA*. Washington, D.C., 1995.
Portney, Paul R., ed. *Public Policies for Environmental Protection*. Washington, D.C., 1990.
Ringquist, Evan J. *Environmental Protection at the State Level: Politics and Progress in Controlling Pollution*. Armonk, N.Y., 1993.
Vig, Norman J., and Michael E. Kraft, eds. *Environmental Policy in the 1990s*. 2d ed. Washington, D.C., 1994.

—DANIEL J. FIORINO

Environmental Quality, Council on

Created by an act of Congress as part of the National Environmental Policy Act of 1969 (P.L. 91–190; 83 Stat. 852), the Council on Environmental Quality (CEQ) was established to formulate and recommend national policies aimed at improving the quality of the environment by issuing studies and reports for Congress and the president. The CEQ's responsibilities are divided into three categories for budget purposes: development and analysis of environmental policy; coordination of environmental programs among other agencies; and the gathering and assessment of environment-related information. As a part of the Executive Office of the President (EOP), the CEQ does not have cabinet status; the chair of the council does, however, interact at the cabinet level and also serves in the cabinet's Council on Natural Resources and Environment. [*See* Cabinet.]

The council consists of a three-member board appointed by the president, one of whom is designated by the president to serve as chair. All three are subject to advice and consent of the Senate. The council is supported in its work by the Office of Environmental Quality (OEQ), which contains the staff support that carries out the work of the council. The OEQ is directed by the chair of the CEQ. For most of its existence, the CEQ has played a less significant role in shaping environmental policy than other environment-related agencies, in part because of its very broad responsibilities.

The CEQ was the brainchild of Senator Henry M. Jackson (D-Wash.), who had previously proposed the idea in 1967. President Richard Nixon argued against creation of such a special board and instead created a cabinet-level Environmental Quality Council by executive order on 29 May 1969, in part to stave off Jackson's proposal. Jackson argued that Nixon's interagency council would be less effective and that a special office was needed to coordinate the twenty-seven executive and independent agencies in the government involved with environmental matters. When the Environmental Policy Act was presented to Nixon, it included creation of the CEQ. Nixon signed the bill on 1 January 1970 despite his misgivings about placing such an office within the EOP. On 25 March 1970 Congress passed the Environmental Quality Improvement Act (P.L. 91–224; 84 Stat. 112), which included a provision to create and staff the OEQ to support the CEQ's activities. The council delivered its first report to Congress in August 1970. Nixon's first nominee to head the CEQ was Under Secretary of the Interior Russell E. Train. The other two board members included an environmental reporter for the *Christian Science Monitor,* Robert Cahn, and Gordon MacDonald, vice chancellor of the University of California at Santa Barbara.

Despite Nixon's initial opposition to the office, the CEQ had a staff of sixty by the end of his administration.

Throughout the 1970s the CEQ was a relatively active force in advancing a wide variety of environment-related issues, although its emphasis shifted according to the policy preferences of the president. The Nixon administration lost some of its enthusiasm for environmental concerns as it shifted toward a more strongly pro-industry stand, a trend accelerated by the energy crisis of the early 1970s. This pattern continued during the administration of Gerald Ford.

The CEQ acquired a more aggressive voice and enhanced influence during the administration of Jimmy Carter. It researched and issued reports on subjects as diverse as water quality and farm land loss. Two weeks after Carter signed a bill extending the deadline for some cities to meet federal water pollution standards in 1980, for example, the CEQ issued a report citing evidence linking water additives with cancer rates. Land use planning received a boost from CEQ research on the sacrifice of the nation's available farmland to shopping centers, public works projects, and other nonfarming activities.

In 1981 and 1982 Congress acceded to budget requests of the administration of Ronald Reagan to dramatically cut the budget and staff of the CEQ. As part of the Reagan administration's move to reduce environmental regulations, the CEQ budget was cut by seventy-two percent, its staff was reduced from forty-nine to fifteen members, and its influence within the Executive Office was dramatically diminished. (In fact, the CEQ suffered a sort of banishment when it was relocated to offices at some remove from those of the rest of the EOP.) CEQ reporting activities were also cut back, and the agency focused its attention on the economic costs and effectiveness of existing environmental efforts. By the time Reagan left office, the CEQ staff had been reduced to nine. This diminished policy role for the CEQ continued throughout the Bush administration. Nevertheless, Bush expanded the staff to thirty during his term.

Bill Clinton entered office similarly skeptical about the role of the CEQ, but for somewhat different reasons. Clinton was far more sympathetic to environmental concerns than his predecessors. In the early days of his presidency, for example, he proposed elevating the Environmental Protection Agency (EPA) to cabinet status. His desire to shrink government and minimize duplication prompted him to propose the abolition of the CEQ and its replacement by a smaller statistics bureau that would gather and coordinate the distribution of environment-related data among agencies like the EPA and the Interior Department. In addition, Clinton created a White House Office of Environmental Policy (OEP) to coordinate the diverse environment-related actions of other government agencies.

Congress and environmental interests opposed Clinton's proposal to abolish the CEQ, however, and because the agency was created by statute, only Congress could authorize its abolition. In the fall of 1993, Clinton reversed his stand and merged the OEP with the CEQ. Even so, in 1994, the CEQ was the smallest of the eleven divisions making up the EOP. Its budget was $375,000, and no staff lines were initially allocated for the agency because of Clinton's plan to abolish the agency. Congress approved a small appropriation to keep the office going for the year, which allowed the CEQ to hire up to seven people. In 1995, the office's appropriation was $1 million.

[*See also* Environmental Protection Agency *and* President, Executive Office of the.]

BIBLIOGRAPHY

Fitzsimmons, Allan. "Environmental Quality as a Theme in Federal Legislation." *Geographical Review* 70 (July 1980): 314–327.
Goodwin, Craufurd D., ed. *Energy Policy in Perspective.* Washington, D.C., 1981.
Hart, John. *The Presidential Branch from Washington to Clinton.* Chatham, N.J., 1995.
Pfiffner, James P. *The Strategic Presidency.* Pacific Grove, Calif., 1988.
Relyea, Harold, ed. *The Executive Office of the President.* Westport, Conn., 1996.

—ROBERT J. SPITZER

EPA.
See Environmental Protection Agency.

Equal Employment Opportunity Commission

 Established in 1965, the Equal Employment Opportunity Commission (EEOC) is an independent federal agency that works to combat employment discrimination. Originally proposed by President Truman in 1948 as the Federal Employment Practices Commission but blocked by southern opposition in Congress, the commission was authorized by Title VII of the Civil Rights Act of 1964 under a compromise limiting its power to investigation and conciliation. In 1972 Congress extended the EEOC's jurisdiction to state and local governments and empowered it to bring discrimination suits in federal court against private and public employers.

The agency is composed of five commissioners and a general counsel, appointed by the president and confirmed by the Senate to fixed terms. It enforces laws prohibiting employment discrimination on the basis of 1) race, color, national origin, religion, or sex, and 2) pregnancy, childbirth, and related medical conditions, as well as laws 3) protecting men and women against pay discrimination based on sex, 4) protecting workers aged forty and older from age discrimination in employment, and 5) prohibiting job discrimination against disabled individuals. Additionally, the EEOC coordinates federal enforcement of equal employment opportunity and protects the employment rights of federal employees.

During the 1970s the EEOC fell chronically behind in processing individual complaints and was criticized in General Accounting Office studies for poor management. [*See* General Accounting Office.] Yet the agency developed a strong enforcement program by 1) issuing guidelines, rules, and regulations, 2) suing employers in federal court, and 3) bringing commissioner charges against employers based on "systemic" patterns of underrepresentation of minorities and women. Federal court decisions, most notably *Griggs v. Duke Power Co.* (1971), upheld EEOC guidelines on employment testing and proportional representation in the work force. Enforcement doctrine relied on the "adverse (or disparate) impact" standard, which presumed a norm of proportional representation in the work force for minorities and women, absent discrimination. Employers carried the burden of proof to justify hiring standards or job requirements producing underrepresentation. By adopting EEOC-approved affirmative action plans, employers won protection from "reverse discrimination" lawsuits filed by white males.

As a consequence of these developments, conservatives during the 1970s accused the EEOC of requiring hiring quotas, thereby practicing the very discrimination the agency was established to prevent. During the Reagan presidency the EEOC under chairman Clarence Thomas (1982–1990) shifted enforcement from negotiating large-scale affirmative-action agreements with major employers, a practice developed by EEOC chair Eleanor Holmes Norton during the Carter administration, to seeking full remedies for individuals in cases of proven discrimination. The Supreme Court in 1989 limited the agency's enforcement powers, but most of these were restored by Congress in the Civil Rights Act of 1991. In 1990 President Bush signed the Americans with Disabilities Act, bringing an additional forty-three million citizens under EEOC protection and swamping the agency's complaint-processing machinery. By the 1990s the EEOC was no longer at the center of controversy, but the agency struggled under accumulating demands from competing constituencies in an era of divided government, partisan conflict, and legal uncertainty.

BIBLIOGRAPHY

Blumrosen, Alfred W. *Modern Law: The Law Transmission System and Equal Employment Opportunity.* Madison, Wis., 1993.
"Equal Employment Opportunity Commission." In *Federal Regulatory Directory,* 7th ed., pp. 113–139. Washington, D.C., 1994.
Graham, Hugh Davis. *The Civil Rights Era: Origins and Development of National Policy, 1960–1972.* New York, 1990.
—Hugh Davis Graham

Executive Orders.

For the texts of Executive Orders 8242, 12044, 12291, 12498, and 12866, see Appendix: Basic Documents of Public Administration.

Executive Power

ESSAY   Article II of the Constitution assigns presidents the "Executive Power" of the United States, allows them to appoint, by and with the advice and consent of the Senate, the "officers of the United States," permits them to request reports in writing from the heads of departments, and requires them to "take care that the laws be faithfully executed." But the Constitution of 1787, although it anticipated that presidents would provide political direction to officials, did not provide presidents with much in the way of specific administrative powers over the departments of government. It specified no removal power, budget authority, or management functions for presidents, and provided them with no administrative staff. Moreover, it did not refer at any point to a presidential cabinet, nor to an "executive branch."

The framers of the Constitution intended the president to superintend the departments and prevent wrongdoing within them, rather than to function as a chief executive directly supervising their activities. Acting on this understanding, the Treasury Department and Post Office were initially organized by Congress without direct presidential controls. As Attorney General William Wirt understood it in 1823, "The constitution assigns to Congress the power of designating the duties of particular officers; the President only is required to take care that they execute them faithfully."

Congress, not the president, was granted most of the specified powers over the departments by the Framers. In Article I it was given the power to create departments, organize and reorganize them, provide all legal authority for their operations, provide all their funds, and conduct investigations to oversee their operations. The Senate was given the power to consent to presidential nominations and could remove officials from office through the impeachment power. At times in American history, most notably in the Whig presidencies and the period of "congressional government" after the Civil War until the end of the nineteenth century, Congress relied on these constitutional powers to dominate the departments. Daniel Webster, speaking for the Whigs in the aftermath of Jackson's assertions of supervisory powers over the departments, argued that the executive power was not an independent grant of power. In the aftermath of the Civil War, Woodrow Wilson could write a treatise on American government entitled *Congressional Government,* in which he could claim that congressional committee leaders held department secretaries in their "leading strings." As late as 1926 Supreme Court Justice Oliver Wendell Holmes could write in a dissenting opinion in *Myers v. U.S.* that "the duty of the President to see that the laws be executed is a duty that does not go beyond the laws or require him to achieve more than Congress sees fit to leave within his power." Yet the Constitution is sufficiently ambiguous about the "Executive Power of the President" to allow for interpretations that make the president a chief executive—interpretations that have been dominant throughout the twentieth century.

The Framers who attended the Constitutional Convention were suspicious of a strong presidency, but they were also unhappy with the existing administrative apparatus of national government. The Articles of Confederation had provided for a weak Congress and no executive. Almost as an afterthought the Articles provided for a "Committee of States" to sit only when Congress was in recess. The committee was to "execute in the recess of Congress, such of the powers of Congress as the United States, in Congress assembled, shall by the consent of nine states, from time to time, think expedient to vest them with." Government operations were left to *ad hoc* or standing committees of Congress, supplemented by boards operating under their direction. The Marine Committee dealt with the navy, the Board of War and Ordnance with the army; the Committee of Secret Correspondence handled diplomacy. Congress initially began with a superintendent of finance, but replaced Robert Morris near the end of the revolution with a Treasury Board. By 1781 these arrangements had proven unsatisfactory, and Congress created several departments, including Foreign Affairs, War, Marine, and Treasury. But no executive council or president gave direction to the departments, and results remained chaotic. Congress insisted that the secretaries report to it and take its directions. The departments were weak appendages of the legislature, and not an executive branch. They remained inefficient, vacillated in making policy during the war, and were administered corruptly thereafter. General Washington, his aide-de-camp Alexander Hamilton, and others assigned by Congress to support the Continental armies all called for a stronger administrative state as a result of their experiences during the Revolution.

Many delegates at the Constitutional Convention of 1787 wanted to provide the presidency with specific but limited executive powers granted directly by the Constitution. The Committee on Detail, chaired by James Wilson, reported a draft of the Constitution that provided several enumerated powers: The president was to appoint officers otherwise not provided for, take care that the laws be faithfully executed, command the armed forces, and command the militia when called into federal service. These provisions were authored by James Wilson and based in part on a draft written by Charles Pinckney, which in turn had been inspired by the executive powers granted to the governor in the New York State constitution. The "take care" clause received little discussion at the convention and was lifted from provisions of state constitutions, based on the separation of power doctrine. The delegates may have intended it to be read in conjunction with Article I, section eight, paragraph 18, which states that Congress has the power "to make all Laws which shall be necessary and proper for carrying into Execution the foregoing [seventeen enumerated] Powers, and all other Powers vested by this Constitution in the Government of the United States, or in any Department or Office thereof." In this clause Congress was granted the power to legislate on (i.e., to regulate) the executive and administrative powers of the president. Congress, under this provision, would have the power to determine the organization and many of the duties of the presidential staff (organized much later into the White House Office and the Executive Office of the President). [*See* President, Executive Office of the *and* White House Office.]

The Committee on Postponed Matters added the presidential power to appoint, by and with the advice and consent of the Senate, ambassadors and justices of the Supreme Court, and provided that the president "may require the opinion in writing of the principal officers in each of the executive departments, upon any subject relating to the duties of their respective offices." No longer would department heads report only to Congress, the practice under the Articles of Confederation. Some Framers seemed to conceive of the Senate as the functional equivalent of a council of state that would share the power of appointment and supervision of administration, much as Councils of Appointment had done in several state legislatures. Others viewed the requirement for Senate consent as an important check and balance against unbridled presidential patronage that might otherwise corrupt the administration. As Alexander Hamilton explained in *The Federalist,* "a man who had himself the sole disposition of offices, would be governed much more by his private inclinations and interests, than when he was bound to submit the propriety of his choice to the discussion and determination of a different and independent body." Near the end of the convention the delegates struck out a provision that would have given Congress the power to appoint the head of the Treasury; instead, they made the Treasury subject to the same appointment process as the other departments. The delegates also defeated a plan submitted by Gouverneur Morris and Charles Pinckney that would have put in the Constitution a detailed plan for the departments and that would have granted the president sole appointing and removal power over the departmental secretaries. The convention also rejected a plan by Morris and Pinckney, and another proposed by James Madison, that would have formally established a council of state: the Morris-Pinckney plan would have created a council out of the department secretaries, along with the

Chief Justice of the United States; Madison's council would have involved the geographical representation of the Northern, Middle Atlantic, and Southern states. Thus the convention delegates simultaneously beat back proposals to remove key departments from presidential supervision, as well as proposals to require the presidency to function in a collegial body.

James Madison told the convention that the presidency must be granted sufficient power to check and balance Congress, but he called on the convention "to fix the extent of the Executive authority" which "should be confined and defined." Not all delegates agreed, especially not those who wanted a strong executive functioning within a stronger national government. After all, if they had wanted to continue with administrative powers diffused and checked, they could simply have continued with the existing boards and commissions under the Articles of Confederation. The delegates who intended to create a presidency that could wield executive power over the departments included George Washington, Alexander Hamilton, and Gouverneur Morris. They wanted more general terms and ambiguous language that presidents could interpret broadly. The Committee on Detail provided that the "Executive Power of the United States shall be vested in a single person," without specifying the limits of such a power. Gouverneur Morris, chairman of the Committee on Style, later revised this provision into the opening words of Article II: "The Executive Power shall be vested in a President of the United States of America." This was a general term, sufficiently ambiguous so that no one could say precisely what it meant. It was possible that the words referred to more than the specific powers that followed, and might confer a set of otherwise unspecified executive powers: the power to give orders to department secretaries, and the power to remove officials who did not follow presidential policies. When Morris and his allies used the term *executive power* they were seeking deliberately to build into the Constitution an open-ended clause that might later expand the powers of the presidency. As a result of their efforts, the limits to presidential power were not fixed in the Constitution.

The lack of fixed limits on the executive was

a major cause of the criticism mounted by the Anti-Federalists against the new Constitution. Some, such as George Mason, argued that the president and the Senate would combine in a "cabal" that would "destroy all balances" and would corrupt the government, centralize power, and destroy the liberties of individuals and the powers of the states. Mason and others claimed that the lack of one or more executive councils, especially a Council of Revision (to share in the veto power) or a Council on Appointments, would leave the president with too much executive discretion. Federalist defenders compared the president's executive powers to those of the New York and Massachusetts governors, prompting New York's governor George Clinton, an opponent of the Constitution, to warn that "if the President is possessed of ambition, he has the power and time sufficient to ruin the country. This government is no more like a true picture of your own," Clinton warned New Yorkers, "than an Angel of Darkness resembles an Angel of Light." In the Albany Manifesto, New York Anti-Federalists proposed a Council on Appointments and removal of presidential control over the armed forces. Eventually, it was for Alexander Hamilton, speaking to the New York constitutional convention, to make the plea for a strong executive: "When you have divided and nicely balanced the departments of government," he told the delegates, "when you have strongly connected the virtue of the rulers with their interest, when, in short, you have rendered your system as perfect as human forms can be, you must place confidence, you must give power." Hamilton was later, in *The Federalist,* to argue that the administrative powers of the presidency resembled those of the New York governor, and he took pains to play down ambiguities in the document; this discussion must be understood as tactical propaganda to win ratification, rather than a good faith effort to describe the limits on the president's executive powers.

Presidents since Andrew Jackson have fused the "Executive Power," their oath of office, and their duty to take care that the laws be faithfully executed into a "resulting power" that they use to claim that department secretaries are their subordinates. Franklin Pierce's attorney general Caleb Cushing argued, "I think here the general rule to be . . . that the Head of Department is subject to the direction of the President. I hold that no Head of Department can lawfully perform an official act against the will of the President." Franklin Roosevelt argued that "the Presidency was established as a single strong Chief Executive Office in which was vested the entire executive power of the National Government." President Harry Truman observed that "it is not the business of Congress to run the agencies of government for the President." Modern presidents in the twentieth century have obtained from Congress vast powers over the departments: broad delegations of routine and emergency powers, upheld by the Supreme Court in a series of cases starting with *United States v. Grimaud* in 1911 and the various cases upholding New Deal programs in the 1930s, followed by the Presidential Subdelegation Act passed in 1950 permitting presidents to determine the duties of officials based on the broad statutes. Congress has provided presidents with preliminary budgeting and impounding authority, reorganization authority, and the power to recommend pay and benefits for the bureaucracy—all subject to final congressional approval.

Presidents direct officials by issuing executive orders, although no such power of direction was granted in the literal Constitution. The first such order, promulgated by George Washington on 8 June 1789, instructed the heads of departments to make a "clear account" of matters in their departments. Since then executive orders have been used to regulate the civil service, to determine holidays for federal workers, to recognize federal employee unions, to fire employees in illegal strikes, to institute security programs, to classify government documents, to organize federal disaster assistance efforts, to organize the intelligence agencies at the beginning of every president's term in office, to stabilize internal White House organization, and even to create government agencies: President Franklin Roosevelt used executive orders to create New Deal and wartime agencies without going through Congress, until in 1994 Congress prohibited funding of such agencies. President John Kennedy established the Peace Corps in 1961 by executive order. In 1968 Congress passed a law prohibiting creation of presidential commissions, councils, or study groups that were not authorized by Congress.

The reach of the president's executive power is not specified, but it does run up against constitutional and legal limits. Constitutional law, beginning with *Marbury v. Madison* in 1803, distinguishes between "executive" and "ministerial" powers. The former are confided to the president and involve political direction. The latter involve duties and procedures that can be specified so that they may be performed without discretion. The president, through the executive power, exercises the former power, but Congress by statute can control the departments through the latter. But often the presidential claim of executive authority will clash with the congressional power to establish ministerial responsibilities.

Provided that it is based either on his constitutional powers or laws passed by Congress, an executive order has the force of law and will be enforced by the courts. But an order that conflicts with existing law will not be judicially enforced: when President Richard Nixon tried to dismantle several agencies by executive order his actions were blocked by federal courts, since Congress had not abolished them. Similarly, when President Nixon ordered the impoundment of funds appropriated by Congress, federal courts in more than fifty cases required officials in the departments to expend the funds. An executive order may be superseded by new legislation. When President Bill Clinton proposed to end discrimination against homosexuals in the military by issuing an executive order, opponents in Congress threatened to overturn the action by new legislation. An executive order that is unconstitutional, such as President Truman's seizure of steel mills during the Korean War, can be nullified by the Supreme Court or lower federal courts.

When an executive order or other command issued by the president conflicts with a law passed by Congress, officials are duty bound to execute the laws, and if they do not, the federal courts will require them to do so. In 1838, for example, the Supreme Court in *Kendall v. U.S.* required Postmaster General Amos Kendall to carry out the terms of a law passed by Congress and pay private postal carriers an amount determined by the solicitor of the Treasury, in spite of an order that had been issued by President Andrew Jackson not to pay these postal carriers anything. The rules and regulations promulgated by the bureaucracy itself have the force of law, and will be upheld by the courts even if the president or his subordinates have issued orders that conflict with them. In 1974, for example, in *Nader v. Bork,* the federal courts ruled that the firing of special prosecutor Archibald Cox during the Watergate crisis by acting Attorney General Robert Bork was illegal, because the firing violated regulations about the independence of the prosecutor that had been promulgated by his predecessor, Attorney General Elliot Richardson. Officials who are appointed by the president do not take an oath to obey him, but rather take an oath to obey the Constitution and the laws of the land. This oath is no formality: officials have multiple responsibilities, and enforcing presidential priorities does not take precedence over enforcing the law.

Although presidents now function as chief executives, much of the original constitutional legacy still remains in place. Political scientists have developed a theory of the "administrative state," which follows the observation of James Madison in *The Federalist,* no. 51, that the Constitution is based on the principle of *partial* rather than *complete* separation of powers. According to this principle, Congress does not possess all legislative powers, the president does not possess all executive powers, and the federal courts do not possess all judicial powers. Partial separation was instituted by the Framers in 1787 to prevent Congress from utilizing its legislative powers to unbalance the entire system and establish a legislative tyranny. In the twentieth century, its effect has been to limit the power of the "chief executive" by providing for three separate lines of control over governmental agencies: the departments and agencies actually function as a separate administrative establishment—a "fourth branch" of government—that is supervised concurrently by the Congress, the federal courts, and the presidency.

[*See also* House of Representatives; Judicial Branch; President as Chief Executive; Presidential Succession and Disability; Senate; Supreme Court Decisions on the Presidency; Twenty-Second Amendment; Vice Presidency; *and* Women and the Executive Branch.]

BIBLIOGRAPHY

Bessette, Joseph, and Jeffrey Tulis, eds. *The Presidency in the Constitutional Order.* Baton Rouge, 1981.

Corwin, Edward S. "The President as Administrative Chief." In *Presidential Power and the Constitution: Essays by Edward S. Corwin,* edited by Richard Loss. Ithaca, N.Y., 1976.

Cronin, Thomas E. "The President's Executive Power." In *Inventing the American Presidency,* edited by Thomas E. Cronin. Lawrence, Kans., 1989.

Fisher, Louis. "The Efficiency Side of Separation of Powers." *Journal of American Studies* 5, no. 2 (August 1971): 113–131.

Guggenheimer, Jay Caesar. "The Development of the Executive Departments, 1775–1789." In *Essays in the Constitutional History of the United States,* edited by J. Franklin Jameson. Boston, 1889.

Kenyon, Cecilia. *The Antifederalists.* Boston, 1985.

Phelps, Glenn A. *George Washington and American Constitutionalism.* Lawrence, Kans., 1993.

Robinson, Donald. "Gouverneur Morris and the Design of the American Presidency." *Presidential Studies Quarterly* 17, no. 2 (Spring 1987): 319–328.

Sanders, Jennings B. *Evolution of the Executive Departments of the Continental Congress, 1774–1789.* Chapel Hill, N.C., 1935.

Thach, Charles. *The Creation of the Presidency, 1775–1789.* Baltimore, 1922.

—RICHARD M. PIOUS

Export Administration, Bureau of

 Established in 1987, the Bureau of Export Administration (BXA) works to stem the proliferation of weapons of mass destruction by controlling exports and reexports of dual-use commodities and technical data from the United States. Dual-use commodities are those for a primarily civilian market but with a potential for use in military technology. These export controls are designed to undergird national security concerns and to combat terrorism. The BXA also functions as the watchdog under the Nuclear Nonproliferation Act of 1978, with its safeguards against the manufacture and sale of chemical and biological weapons.

—GEORGE THOMAS KURIAN

F

FAA.
See Federal Aviation Administration.

Farm Credit Administration

An independent agency established under the Farm Credit Act of 1971, the Farm Credit Administration (FCA) it is responsible for regulating the activity of the Farm Credit System, a nationwide system of borrower-owned financial institutions organized as cooperatives. The FCA is governed by a three-member board appointed by the president and confirmed by the Senate. Members serve six-year terms but are not eligible for reappointment.

The Farm Credit System is chartered by Congress to lend money to two types of banks: farm credit banks and banks for cooperatives. In 1995 a new type of bank, the agricultural credit bank, was authorized to make loans to agricultural producers and utility cooperatives. The farm credit banks were created through the 1988 merger of federal land banks and federal intermediate credit banks in eleven Federal Credit System districts. The number of lending associations within the Federal Credit System dropped from 800 in 1984 to 238 in 1994 because of the merger of some federal land bank associations and production credit associations into agricultural credit associations. A fourth type of bank, the federal land credit association, has the authority to provide long-term real estate loans. The farm credit banks also provide short- and intermediate-term loan funds for the purchase of fertilizers, seeds, and chemicals. The Central Bank for Cooperatives and ten of the twelve district banks for cooperatives merged into a National Bank for Cooperatives in 1989. In addition to participating

banks within the Federal Credit System, the FCA monitors the financial activities of the Federal Farm Credit Banks Funding Corporation (through which the Farm Credit System raises its loan funds on the New York bond market), Farm Credit System Financial Assistance Corporation, Farm Credit Leasing Services Corporation, Farm Credit System Insurance Corporation, and the Federal Agricultural Mortgage Corporation (Farmer Mac).

—George Thomas Kurian

Farmers Home Administration

Responsibility for the nation's rural housing needs belongs to the Farmers Home Administration (FmHA), a credit agency within the Department of Agriculture. Under the Department of Agriculture Reorganization Act of 1994, the FmHA will be absorbed by a new agency, the Farm Service Agency (FSA). The mission of the FSA will be to stabilize farm income, provide credit to new or disadvantaged farmers and ranchers, and help farm operations recover from the effects of disasters. The FSA will incorporate programs from several agencies.

The FmHA is headed by an administrator appointed by the president and confirmed by the Senate. The agency operates forty-seven state offices, 265 district offices, and nearly seventeen hundred county offices. Its principal task is to regulate the terms of the loans, grants, and agreements and to draw up and enforce guidelines. In addition to making direct loans to farmers without other sources of credit, the FmHA guarantees loans through private commercial lenders. The loans are made available under two sets of programs: the farmer programs offer loans for operating expenses, farm land purchases, disaster emergencies, soil and water resource improvements, and Indian tribal land acquisitions; the rural housing programs provide loans for low-income and moderate-income housing, rural rental housing, farm labor housing, and land development. The Farm Credit Reform Act of 1992 authorizes the FmHA to receive money from the Treasury for making these loans.

BIBLIOGRAPHY

Farmers Home Administration. *Brief History of the Farmers Home Administration.* Washington, D.C., 1995.

—GEORGE THOMAS KURIAN

FBI.

See Federal Bureau of Investigation.

FCC.

See Federal Communications Commission.

FDA.

See Food and Drug Administration.

FDIC.

See Federal Deposit Insurance Corporation.

Federal Aviation Administration

Since its establishment by the Federal Aviation Act of 1958 (49 U.S.C. 106), the Federal Aviation Administration (FAA) has been entrusted with the dual mission of fostering air commerce and promoting aviation safety. It carries out that mission by promulgating and enforcing air safety rules, certificating airmen and aircraft, designating and establishing airways, administering a grants-in-aid-to-airports program, and maintaining and managing a common system of air navigation and air traffic control for military and civil aircraft.

The FAA has had its present name and occupied its present place in the federal executive branch since 1 April 1967, the day it was folded into the newly created U.S. Department of Transportation. It has existed in some recognizably similar form, however, since 1926, the year the federal government resolved to play an active role in civil aviation's development.

That aviation became a reliable and efficient means of moving people and goods was not entirely owing to the airplane. The invention of this machine was only the first step in aviation's development. The essential second step came with the realization that the airplane was a highly dependent machine and if it was ever to become a viable tool in commerce it needed the support of an elaborate ground organization.

The early fliers navigated by visual reference to known landmarks. Instead of electronic aids, they relied on their own sensory aids, the feel and sound of the wind and the sight of the ground. As the U.S. Air Mail Service learned soon after its establishment in 1918, this method of navigation has its limitations. The service could fly only during daylight. Pilots could not fly by visual landmarks if they could not see those landmarks. Accordingly, the U.S. Air Mail Service recognized early in its operations the need for ground-based airways equipped with rotating light beacons, emergency landing fields, and radio stations. By the mid-1920s the Post Office was flying the mail on a fixed schedule over a lighted airway that stretched between New York and San Francisco. In doing this the Post Office demonstrated to the business community the practicability of air transport. But prospective investors in air transportation realized that if they were to profit from the Post Office's trailblazing efforts, government must play a direct role in the development of the infant industry. Government had done no less for other transportation modes. It dredged harbors, built highways and canals, and subsidized the westward expansion of railways with munificent land grants. If government developed highways and seaways, why should it not develop airways?

Airway development was not all that the aviation community wanted of the federal government. In 1924 the U.S. Air Mail Service experienced one fatal accident for every 463,000 miles flown; in contrast, commercial fliers suffered a fatal accident every 13,500 miles. A U.S. Senate committee, in examining these figures, noted that the Post Office used only pilots and planes approved by federal authority. "The inference is obvious," the committee noted in its report. Others made the same inference and began lobbying for federal regulation of flying activities. Most important among those joining the chorus was the aviation community itself. "It is interesting to note," Secretary of Commerce Herbert Hoover wrote to an influential congressman, "that [aviation] is the only industry that favors having itself regulated by government."

The aviation industry got its wish when Congress enacted the Air Commerce Act of 1926, thus linking civil aviation activities to federal policy. The act charged the secretary of commerce with establishing and operating airways and air navigation aids, controlling air traffic, licensing pilots, certificating aircraft for airworthiness, and investigating accidents.

To carry out these responsibilities, the act created the position of assitant secretary of commerce for aeronautics. Hoover selected William P. MacCracken, Jr., a Chicago lawyer and World War I pilot who had lobbied for passage of the Air Commerce Act, to fill this post. To perform the functions contemplated by the act, Hoover organized a small unit of bureau rank, the Aeronautics Branch, and placed it under MacCracken.

The Aeronautics Branch continued, indeed, improved upon, the airway development pioneered by the Air Mail Service. The lighted airway had made night flying possible. But the technique of flying a lighted airway is similar to following a picket fence, except that you can see the beacon at night. But you cannot see the beacon if the weather is overcast. To solve this problem, the Department of Commerce turned to radio, specifically to the four-course radio range. The facility beamed two distinct Morse Code signals—an "a" and an "n"—that could be picked up by an aircraft equipped with a radio receiver. In the center of the radio beam, or at the point where both signals could be heard with equal intensity, the signals meshed like the teeth of a gear, and all that could be heard was a long dash. The pilot flew along this center of equal intensity. It was with this device—and with such air transports

as the Boeing 247 and the Douglas DC-2—that modern air transportation came into its own.

When MacCracken turned to aviation safety, he set the federal government on a regulatory course that, in many ways, is still followed today. For example, he insisted on and encouraged the participation of the aviation industry in the regulatory process. Accordingly, the rules promulgated by the Aeronautics Branch, the Air Commerce Regulations, had been hammered out by industry and government representatives at a series of conferences. Today the FAA uses other forums more extensively to exchange ideas with industry. Conferences, however, still play a role in the making of rules.

In addition to establishing standards for the licensing of pilots, mechanics, and other airmen and setting forth air traffic rules, the Air Commerce Regulations provided for the certification of aircraft. MacCracken and Aeronautics Branch personnel recognized at the outset that aircraft certification must begin at the manufacturing plant. If it did not, branch personnel would be forced to pick apart every aircraft sold into interstate commerce. The Aeronautics Branch hit upon a clever solution: a single certificate to cover all aircraft of identical design and construction. When federal inspectors found that a new aircraft type conformed with federal airworthiness standards, they issued the aircraft's manufacturer a certificate that authorized the company to produce aircraft of "an exact similarity of type, structure, materials, assembly and workmanship" to the test model. Type certification proved such an efficient procedure that it soon expanded into other areas—first to propellers and then to engines and other components. Today the approved type certificate is at the core of FAA procedures for the certification of aeronautical products.

The Aeronautics Branch did not long survive the Democratic landslide of 1933. It was reorganized—actually given greater structural integrity—and, on 7 July 1934, renamed the Bureau of Air Commerce.

Franklin Roosevelt came into office prepared to pump some life into an economy battered by the worst economic depression ever experienced by the American people. There was one area of the economy, however, that did not need priming: the air transport industry. Buoyed by mail subsidies and the construction of three transcontinental airways, air carriers were doing a thriving business. Indeed, business was so good that it strained the capacity of the airway system. It also raised the specter of impending midair disasters. The problem lay in the fact that no one controlled the flow of en route traffic. Aircraft arrived randomly at terminal areas, where they were forced to compete with each other for a portion of the congested airspace.

In cooperation with an airline consortium, the bureau got into the business of en route traffic control. By 6 July 1935 it was operating air route traffic control centers at Newark, Chicago, and Cleveland. By the end of the decade, the embryonic control system had sprouted an additional nine centers. The federal government had thus assumed the responsibility of controlling the flow of en route traffic.

The rapid growth of the air transport industry during the 1930s had other consequences. The old-line mail contractors that came into existence during the Coolidge and Hoover administrations were being confronted for the first time by serious competition on their passenger routes. And that competition had a sharp edge—the Douglas DC-3, the first airliner that could turn a profit just by hauling passengers. Suddenly airmail contractors began calling with one voice for the federal government to regulate airline economics.

There was also a call from other quarters for other reforms. The Air Commerce Act was flawed. It charged the secretary of commerce with investigating aviation accidents and determining their probable cause. There was a clear conflict of interest when the same entity was responsible for maintaining safety on the airways and for determining the probable cause of accidents on those airways.

In 1935 a U.S. senator from New Mexico, Bronson M. Cutting, was killed in an air transport accident near Kansas City. Though unsupported by the evidence, FDR's critics in the Congress charged that the accident was caused by malfunctioning ground-based navigational aids. The affair brought into question the effectiveness of the Bureau of Air Commerce as the safety regulator of the nation's airways.

The concerns over safety combined with the economic concerns of the airline industry led to the enactment of the Civil Aeronautics Act of 1938, which took the federal civil aviation responsibilities out of the Department of Commerce and entrusted them to a new organization, the Civil Aeronautics Authority, an independent agency composed of a five-man board responsible for safety and economic rule making, a three-man board responsible for investigating accidents and determining probable cause, and an administrator responsible for air traffic control, the establishment and maintenance of airways, safety-rule enforcement, and fostering air commerce.

The authority stayed in business two years. Franklin Roosevelt did not like the authority's complex organization and, on 30 June 1940 he exercised executive powers newly granted him by the Congress to split the authority into two organizations, the Civil Aeronautics Board (CAB) and the Civil Aeronautics Administration (CAA). Roosevelt lodged in the CAB the quasi-judicial and quasi-legislative powers of the five-man and three-man boards. The executive functions of the administrator went to the CAA, which was placed in the Department of Commerce.

The CAA controlled the U.S. airways during the next eighteen years—years that saw U.S. entry into World War II, the start of the Cold War, the sudden eruption of the Korean conflict, the expansion of aviation on a global scale, and the introduction of jet transports into the civil air carrier fleet. All these events had an effect on the CAA.

Even before the Japanese attacked Pearl Harbor, the CAA's responsibilities in air traffic control expanded impressively. In 1940, at the urging of the War Department, Congress empowered the CAA to operate towers at airports that the military services certified as essential to the national defense. At war's end the agency was operating more than one hundred towers. Neither the CAA nor its successor agencies ever relinquished this responsibility.

It was also during World War II that the federal civil aviation agency became involved in airport development. In 1940, largely in response to the military buildup, Congress charged the CAA with the development of defense landing areas. During the war years the CAA built 535 such projects. Then, in 1946, this time largely out of civil concerns, Congress passed the Federal Airport Act, which authorized the CAA to award grants-in-aid to municipalities for airport development. Federal allotments were to be matched by local funds.

The immediate postwar period saw major technological innovations make their appearance on the civil airways, of which radar was the most important. Radar transformed air traffic control from an uncertain art to a reliable technique rooted in technology. The first-generation air traffic control system was a manual system that relied on the ability of controllers to visualize in their minds the movement of aircraft in three-dimensional space. With radar controllers could actually track the traffic they controlled on an electronic screen. When long-range radar was combined with an airborne transponder and a ground interrogator, the result was spectacular. Controllers could safely reduce the minimum horizontal distance between aircraft flying the same route at the same altitude by a factor of six. Hence, radar could have a potentially dramatic effect on system capacity.

Though the technology existed to modernize and increase the capacity of the air navigation and air traffic control system, scant progress was made. One impediment was that authority in airway matters was divided between competing civilian and military interests; when these interests failed to agree on the precise aids to install, the result was stalemate. Another impediment was a lack of funds—a lack that became more pronounced with the outbreak of the Korean War and was not addressed by the Eisenhower administration at war's end.

A wake-up call came on 30 June 1956, when a TWA Super Constellation and a United DC-7 collided over the Grand Canyon, killing 128 people. The airliners were flying under visual flight rules because the air traffic system did not possess the physical resources to require every scheduled airliner to fly under instrument flight rules in controlled airspace. The solution seemed obvious: require instrument flight over certain portions of the airspace irrespective of weather conditions. That meant deploying long-range radar on a massive scale and bolstering the ranks of an overworked air traffic controller work force.

Two years and two major midair collision later Congress dismantled the CAA and replaced it with a more broadly empowered independent agency, the Federal Aviation Agency. The FAA was given not only all the functions of the CAA, but also the safety-rule-making functions of the CAB. At the same time the new legislation removed one of the major roadblocks to airway modernization by vesting in the new organization the sole responsibility for developing and operating "a common system of air traffic control and air navigation for both military and civil aircraft."

Elwood R. Quesada was the first administrator of the FAA. In the two short years that he was at the FAA's helm he devoted most of his energies to safety regulation and enforcement. The air disasters of the 1950s had engendered a widespread feeling among the public that the CAA was soft and feckless and that a perilous laxness permeated its regulatory practices. Quesada plunged headlong into tightening up rules, prosecuting violators, and applying a dash of discipline to flying activities. The crackdown went a long way in reassuring the public that safety on the airways was being enforced.

Eisenhower left the business of developing a modern airway system to John Kennedy, whose administration produced early in his tenure a long-range plan that called for the massive use of computers in a semiautomated system that could relay real-time information to controllers by electronically tagging radar targets with luminous letters and numerals that indicated the target aircraft's identity and altitude. With this system the computer performed tedious chores that were previously performed by the controller. And the computer performed them faster and more accurately.

By the time the Kennedy administration came to an abrupt end, the FAA was poised to field-test two automated systems, one for terminal traffic, the other for en route traffic. Little progress was made from that point till the end of the decade. Airway modernization was not on Lyndon Johnson's agenda. The Texan's budget priorities ran from the Great Society to Vietnam.

Johnson could claim credit for one transportation accomplishment, the establishment of the Department of Transportation, which brought together the half-dozen or so transportation agencies scattered throughout the executive branch. That meant a change of name for the FAA, from "agency" to "administration," and the loss of direct access to the White House, which made the organization's funding problems more difficult to resolve.

The modernization program languished until 1970, when Richard Nixon signed the Airport and Airways Development and Revenue Acts of 1970 into law. That legislation created an Airport-Airways Trust Fund fed by user-tax revenues used exclusively for airport and airway development. By the mid-1970s the airway system envisioned by Kennedy was finally in place.

The painful period of economic austerity was not without lasting consequences. In the five years that Lyndon Johnson resided in the White House, air traffic increased by more than 50 percent while the air traffic controller work force increased by a mere 8.5 percent. That made the 1960s a nightmare for controllers.

Out of that nightmare emerged the Professional Air Traffic Controllers Organization (PATCO), a militant labor union founded in January 1968 with assistance from criminal attorney F. Lee Bailey. PATCO overplayed its hand by staging three illegal job actions during the first two years of its existence. In 1970 it jettisoned its militant leaders, including Bailey, and replaced them with a more moderate group, which remained in control of the union over the next ten years. The union grew in power, wealth, and influence during the 1970s. Moreover, with the semiautomated system in place, working conditions improved considerably. Nevertheless, in January 1980 a more aggressive faction took control of the union and, in August 1981, in an attempt to achieve for controllers economic parity with airline pilots, staged a disastrous strike that led to Ronald Reagan's firing nearly 12,300 strikers and to PATCO's demise.

The PATCO strike had not caught the FAA by surprise. Indeed, when the Reagan administra-

tion took office it found that a strike contingency plan had already been developed at the FAA by the departing Carter administration. The plan worked, with the agency severely restricting aviation traffic while rebuilding its controller work force.

By 1996 the FAA had 17,200 controllers out of a total permanent work force of 47,900. In 1995 these controllers handled 33,600 aircraft at 21 air route traffic control centers and logged 52,400 aircraft operations at 476 air traffic control towers. They performed these function at a cost of $12.2 billion, or 24 percent of the FAA fiscal year 1995 budget of $9 billion.

BIBLIOGRAPHY

Briddon, Arnold E., Ellmore A. Champie, and Peter A. Marraine. *FAA Historical Fact Book: A Chronology, 1926–1971.* Washington, D.C., 1974.
Brooks, Peter W. *The Modern Airliner: Its Origins and Development.* London, 1961.
Kent, Richard J., Jr. *Safe, Separated, and Soaring: A History of Federal Civil Aviation Policy, 1961–1972.* Washington, D.C., 1980.
Komons, Nick A. *The Cutting Air Crash: A Case Study in Early Federal Civil Aviation Policy.* Washington, D.C., 1973.
Komons, Nick A. *Bonfires to Beacons: Federal Civil Aviation Policy under the Air Commerce Act, 1926–1938.* Reprint, Washington, D.C., 1989.
Komons, Nick A. "William P. MacCracken, Jr." In *Aviation's Golden Age: Portraits from the 1920s and 1930s,* edited by William M. Leary. Iowa City, Iowa, 1989.
Komons, Nick A. "Professional Air Traffic Controllers Organization." In *Encyclopedia of American Business History and Biography: The Airline Industry,* edited by William M. Leary. New York, 1992.
Leary, William M. *Aerial Pioneers: The U.S. Air Mail Service, 1918–1927.* Washington, D.C., 1985.
Preston, Edmund. *Troubled Passage: The Federal Aviation Administration during the Nixon-Ford Term, 1973–1977.* Washington, D.C., 1987.
Rochester, Stuart I. *Takeoff at Mid-Century: Federal Civil Aviation Policy in the Eisenhower Years, 1953–1961.* Washington, D.C., 1976.
Thomas, David D. "ATC In Transition, 1956–1963." *Journal of Air Traffic Control* (October–December 1985).
U.S. Department of Transportation, Federal Aviation Administration. *Annual Report '94.* Washington, D.C., 1995.
U.S. Department of Transportation, Federal Aviation Administration. *Administrator's Fact Book.* Pamphlet. Washington, D.C., 1996.
Wilson, John R. M. *Turbulence Aloft: The Civil Aeronau-*

tics Administration amid Wars and Rumors of Wars, 1938–1953. Washington, D.C., 1979.

—NICK A. KOMONS

Federal Bureau of Investigation

As the main investigative branch of the Department of Justice, the Federal Bureau of Investigation (FBI) handles all violations of federal law except those explicitly assigned to other federal agencies. The FBI's mission has enabled it to capture the public's attention and imagination in a way few other government agencies have, and the agency has acquired a near mythic quality. Yet some of the FBI's activities, particularly in the realm of domestic intelligence, have sparked considerable protest.

THE CREATION OF THE FBI

In the nation's first century, state and local governments did most of the law enforcement owing to the limited role of the federal government and the traditional American ambivalence toward centralized power. With the growth in the size and scope of the federal government came the need for more federal investigations, however, so Congress authorized an investigative agency to be part of the Department of Justice it created in 1870.

For several decades the new Justice Department followed the federal government's practice of hiring private detectives (usually from the Pinkerton Agency) or relying on agents from other departments (especially the Treasury Department's Secret Service) when investigations were required. But in 1893 Congress prohibited the Justice Department from hiring private detectives and in 1908 banned the department from using Secret Service agents (after two members of Congress were convicted of land fraud based on evidence collected by Secret Service agents working for the Justice Department).

President Theodore Roosevelt denounced the prohibitions and directed Attorney General Charles J. Bonaparte to develop an investigative agency within the Justice Department. In July 1908 Bonaparte created an investigative force, soon named the Bureau of Investigation, and staffed it with about thirty-five special agents. After a series of name changes, the agency officially became known as the FBI in 1935.

EARLY YEARS

Because of the relatively small number of federal criminal laws at the time, the agency had limited jurisdiction in its early years, focusing mainly on bankruptcy frauds, antitrust matters, and neutrality violations. The bureau's jurisdiction expanded as Congress designated more federal crimes in laws such as the Mann Act of 1910, which made it a crime to transport women across state lines for purposes of prostitution, and the Dyer Act of 1919, which prohibited transporting stolen vehicles across state lines. The agency also grew as it began conducting "intelligence" investigations (that is, efforts to collect noncriminal information about certain persons or organizations).

During World War I the agency received responsibility for sedition, espionage, sabotage, and draft violations. Thus empowered, the bureau shifted its focus from investigating crimes to investigating potential subversives. Both during the war and in the unsettled period after the war, the agency conducted a series of raids against supposed radicals, arrested many of them without warrants, and violated other civil liberties.

These events prompted a public and congressional backlash against the bureau and the entire Justice Department. In 1924 newly appointed Attorney General Harlan Fiske Stone named J. Edgar Hoover, a young lawyer serving as the bureau's assistant director, as head of the organization. Stone ordered the bureau to stop investigating political radicals and directed Hoover to reform and professionalize the organization.

J. EDGAR HOOVER

John Edgar Hoover exercised enormous influence over the FBI, serving as director for nearly fifty years. A native of Washington, D.C., Hoover joined the Department of Justice in 1917 and moved to its Bureau of Investigation two years later. There he formed his lifelong conviction that Communists and other subversives posed grave danger to America. Hoover also quickly proved to be a master politician, building an impressive power base for himself and the bureau.

Throughout his career, Hoover—convinced that popular support for the agency was vital—carefully cultivated the FBI's public image. Through newsreels, movies, comic books, radio shows, and television programs, Hoover sent the message that criminals could not escape the effective and incorruptible agents of the FBI. He produced crime statistics to support his claims.

Hoover worked hard to maintain good relations with Congress and with each of the eight presidents under whom he served as director. Yet his considerable political power also sprang from his infamous private files. Over the decades the bureau collected sensitive information on thousands of prominent Americans, including politicians and government officials. Hoover's control of that information, kept in closely guarded files in his office, gave him and the bureau political insulation and helped ensure his continued tenure as FBI director.

From the 1930s until his death, Hoover's closest friend and constant companion was FBI associate director Clyde Tolson. The relationship sparked speculation that the never-married Hoover may have been a homosexual, but no evidence proving that claim has appeared.

THE GANGSTER ERA

After his appointment Hoover moved quickly to remake the FBI. He insisted that hirings and promotions be based on qualifications and merit rather than political connections, and the bureau began recruiting college graduates with training in the law or accounting. He intensified the training program for agents and enforced high standards for their personal behavior and grooming. He sought to remove the bureau from partisan politics and successfully argued that the bureau should report only to the attorney general and no other executive branch official.

Hoover also enhanced the bureau's crime-fighting technology. In 1924 he established the FBI's Identification Division as a national clearinghouse for fingerprint files, and in 1932 he set up the bureau's famous crime laboratory. By sharing these resources with state and local law enforcement agencies, and by creating the National Academy to train local officers, the FBI took a major role in national law enforcement.

Prohibition helped spawn the "gangsterism" of the 1920s and early 1930s. Robbers, kidnappers, and other criminals could often elude local authorities by crossing state lines, so in 1934 Congress granted the FBI greatly increased jurisdiction and power, including authority over kidnapping, bank robbery, and interstate fugitives. FBI agents, nicknamed "G-men" (for "government men"), were also empowered to make arrests and carry firearms.

The FBI vigorously used its new authority and grabbed national attention in the mid-1930s by pursuing a series of notorious yet somehow glamorized criminals. FBI agents ultimately arrested George ("Machine Gun") Kelly and killed in shootouts Charles ("Pretty Boy") Floyd, Arizona ("Ma") Barker and her son Fred, George ("Baby Face") Nelson, and—most famously—John Dillinger. Hoover's aggressive public relations campaign highlighted the bureau's attack on crime. The gangster era waned, but not before Hoover and his "G-men" had become popular heroes.

WORLD WAR II AND THE COLD WAR

As war again loomed in Europe, the FBI renewed its involvement with domestic intelligence. At the direction of President Franklin D. Roosevelt, in 1936 the agency began secretly collecting information on Americans who belonged to potentially subversive groups such as Communist or fascist organizations. Three years later Roosevelt gave the FBI overall responsibility for all investigations of espionage, sabotage, and neutrality violations. The Smith Act of 1940, which made it illegal to advocate the forceful overthrow of the government, provided additional statutory authority for the FBI's work in domestic intelligence. The bureau began keeping records of suspected subversives.

The FBI's law enforcement functions generated more publicity, but its restored role in domestic intelligence also led to higher funding and enhanced power. The agency also used the sensitive information it gathered through domestic intelligence to solidify its political position.

The bureau employed a variety of techniques—including wiretapping, opening mail, warrantless searches, physical surveillance, and covert break-ins (so-called "black bag jobs")—in its domestic investigations during and after World War II. Some of these tactics had presidential approval (often through secret directives), but others were of questionable legality. Yet the agency conducted no wholesale roundup of aliens or supposed radicals as it had in World War I.

The FBI conducted several high-profile operations during the war. In 1941 the bureau arrested members of a German spy ring which had been transmitting U.S. military secrets to Germany. A year later the FBI captured eight German saboteurs who had been put ashore in New York and Florida with plans to carry out a bombing campaign.

America's fixation on communism and the accompanying obsession with national security kept the FBI busy in the years after World War II. In fact, the bureau helped fuel the anti-Communist hysteria by feeding information to Senator Joseph McCarthy and other conservative politicians. Hoover and the FBI warned of the Communist threat and praised the bureau's response to it in numerous speeches, magazine articles, movies, and books—including Hoover's own chronicle of the bureau's struggle with the "Red menace" in *Masters of Deceit* (1958).

In an effort to prevent Communists or their sympathizers from gaining influence in the federal government, the bureau began doing background checks on applicants for sensitive federal jobs in addition to investigating government employees who were deemed possible security risks. The FBI also worked to discredit Communists and their sympathizers.

In retrospect, many of the perceived threats investigated by the FBI during the Cold War were imaginary. Yet the agency did crack some major espionage cases during the period. The FBI discovered that Klaus Fuchs, a British scientist working on the U.S. atomic program in the 1940s, had passed atomic secrets to the Soviets. The bureau also played a pivotal role in the famous case of

Ethel and Julius Rosenberg, who were convicted of transferring secrets of the American atomic program to the Soviets. In 1957 the bureau apprehended Soviet spy Rudolph Abel.

ORGANIZED CRIME AND CIVIL RIGHTS

Senate hearings in the 1950s highlighted the existence of organized crime in America. Hoover saw little incentive for the FBI to get involved in the area, but in the early 1960s Attorney General Robert Kennedy demanded action. Congress gave the bureau jurisdiction over organized crime and the associated gambling and racketeering activities in a series of laws—most notably the Racketeer Influenced and Corrupt Organizations Act of 1970 (RICO). Since then bureau investigations have resulted in convictions of dozens of mob figures from around the country, including John Gotti in 1992.

The 1960s also brought the growth of the civil rights movement. Hoover had little sympathy for African Americans and viewed the leaders of the civil rights movement as subversives. Hoover especially hated Martin Luther King, Jr., whom he considered immoral and a Communist dupe. Hoover subjected King to long-term surveillance and electronic eavesdropping and sought to destroy King's reputation by releasing some of the unflattering information he acquired.

Many civil rights protesters suffered abuse at the hands of local law enforcement in the South. Because of Hoover's views on the subject and the bureau's desire to maintain good relations with the local law enforcement agencies, the FBI did not intervene on behalf of the protesters in the early years of the movement. But that stance changed when three civil rights workers disappeared in Mississippi in 1964. The FBI investigated vigorously and eventually arrested six people for the abduction and murder of those workers. Presidential encouragement and a changing political environment prompted the FBI to take a more active role in civil rights.

SCANDALS

From 1956 to 1971, the FBI engaged in a variety of operations known as "counterintelligence programs," or COINTELPROs, against organizations it deemed subversive. Targeted organizations included the Communist Party of the U.S.A., the Socialist Workers Party, black nationalist groups, "New Left" groups, and the Ku Klux Klan. COINTELPROs were designed to disrupt the organizations and neutralize their political effectiveness. The FBI conducted break-ins to acquire membership lists and other information, monitored and recorded telephone conversations, intercepted mail, planted informers in organizations, and leaked sensitive information to the press. Many of the FBI's COINTELPRO tactics were illegal.

The FBI also investigated and kept files on individuals—and not just persons associated with subversive groups. Political figures such as Adlai Stevenson and Eleanor Roosevelt, authors such as Ernest Hemingway and John Cheever, actors such as Charlie Chaplin and Jane Fonda, and various reporters all were subjects of FBI probes.

Hoover died in May 1972. President Richard Nixon named his friend L. Patrick Gray acting director and nominated him for the permanent job. Gray's chances for Senate confirmation evaporated, however, when it became known that he had destroyed documents as part of the Watergate cover-up. With the Nixon administration in shambles over Watergate, lawyer William Ruckelshaus served a brief stint as acting FBI director in 1973.

In addition to dramatic leadership changes, the early 1970s also brought intense congressional and public scrutiny of the FBI. The press began publishing stories about the bureau's COINTELPROs and other activities, based on data acquired under the Freedom of Information Act and on files stolen from an FBI office and given to the media. [See Appendix: Freedom of Information Act.] The revelation that the FBI had engaged in massive and often illegal operations against American citizens sparked a storm of public protest (and prompted Hoover to end COINTELPROs in 1971). The controversy severely tainted the FBI's public image.

The bureau's image suffered even more damage when it was discovered that Hoover, at the request of Nixon, had tapped the telephones of reporters and White House employees who were suspected of leaking sensitive information to the press in protest over the Vietnam War. Because of the scandals, both Congress and the Justice Department increased their oversight of the bu-

reau and issued new guidelines for its behavior, including restrictions on domestic intelligence.

THE FBI SINCE HOOVER

In 1973 Clarence M. Kelley, a former FBI agent and Kansas City chief of police, became the FBI's second permanent director. Kelley led the bureau through the very difficult period of fierce criticism and ensuing reform in the 1970s.

In 1978 President Jimmy Carter selected federal appellate judge William Webster to be FBI director. Webster earned the reputation as a hard-working, demanding, and by-the-book boss. Yet he also was seen as innovative and fair, and he opened FBI employment to women and minorities, whom Hoover had kept out. Webster also ended the bureau's tendency to concentrate on solving relatively easy cases to generate good statistics—a favorite tactic of Hoover's—and authorized long-term investigations into difficult areas such as organized crime, drug trafficking, public corruption, and white collar crime.

Webster presided over some controversial operations. In a sting operation known as "Abscam," the FBI videotaped members of Congress accepting bribes from agents posed as Arab businessmen seeking to buy influence. The investigation led to the convictions of one senator and six representatives but also received criticism as entrapment. From 1983 to 1985, in an operation reminiscent of a COINTELPRO, the FBI investigated the Committee in Solidarity with the People of El Salvador (CISPES), a peaceful group that protested President Ronald Reagan's policy on Central America.

The bureau had mixed success in uncovering foreign spies during Webster's tenure. The bureau let CIA traitor Edward Howard escape to the Soviet Union in 1985, but eventually captured spies John Walker in 1985, Ronald Pelton in 1986, and Aldrich Ames in 1994. The FBI was highly embarrassed when it caught one of its own agents, Richard Miller, passing secret information to the Soviets during the 1980s.

In 1987 Webster left the FBI to become the director of the Central Intelligence Agency. President Reagan chose William Sessions, a federal judge in Texas who had worked in the Nixon Justice Department, to replace Webster as FBI director. Sessions was an outsider whose detached leadership style alienated FBI careerists. Critics wondered whether the soft-spoken Sessions had the management skills needed to run the bureau. In addition, some charged that the director's wife, Alice Sessions, interfered in bureau matters.

In late 1992 Sessions came under fire for abusing the perks of his job. Morale at the bureau plummeted under the discredited director, but Sessions refused to heed calls to resign. In July 1993 President Clinton fired Sessions and selected Louis J. Freeh to succeed him. Freeh, who had served as an FBI agent, prosecutor, and federal judge, was a popular choice with the bureau and the public. He quickly moved five hundred agents from desk jobs in FBI headquarters to working cases.

Controversy continued to swirl around the FBI, however, as the bureau received harsh criticism for its role in two dramatic cases. In 1992 an FBI sniper killed the wife of white separatist Randy Weaver during a siege at his cabin at Ruby Ridge, Idaho. The following year the FBI helped mount the assault on the Branch Davidian cult compound at Waco, Texas, which resulted in the death of eighty cult members.

Other cases brought better results. The agency apprehended suspects in both the 1993 bombing of the World Trade Center in New York City and the 1995 bombing of the Murrah Federal Building in Oklahoma City. In 1996 FBI agents apprehended suspected "Unabomber" Ted Kaczynski at his cabin in Montana.

THE FBI TODAY

The FBI's headquarters is housed in the J. Edgar Hoover Building in Washington, D.C. (The guided tour of FBI Headquarters, taken by almost 500,000 people a year, is one of the most popular attractions in Washington.) The FBI director is appointed by the president, subject to Senate confirmation, to a ten-year term. The director runs the bureau with the assistance of a deputy director and nine assistant directors.

The bureau maintains fifty-six field offices in major cities, each overseen by a special agent in charge. The FBI also has about four-hundred satellite offices, called resident agencies, four specialized field installations, and twenty-two liaison posts in other countries. The FBI currently employs about ten-thousand special agents and over thirteen-thousand support personnel. Training takes place at the FBI Academy in Quantico, Virginia. The bureau's total annual funding is approximately $2.2 billion.

Today the FBI has jurisdiction in over two hundred categories of federal crimes. The FBI currently divides its investigations into seven categories: applicant matters, civil rights, counterterrorism, foreign counterintelligence, organized crime/drugs, violent crimes and major offenders, and white collar crime. The bureau also administers several criminal justice information services—including the National Crime Information Center (NCIC), which contains records on crimes and criminals, fingerprint records, and crime statistics—that are used by local, state, federal, and international law enforcement agencies.

[See also Central Intelligence Agency and Secret Service.]

BIBLIOGRAPHY

Jeffreys, Diarmuid. The Bureau: Inside the Modern FBI. Boston, 1995.
Kessler, Ronald. The FBI: Inside the World's Most Powerful Law Enforcement Agency. New York, 1994.
Morgan, Richard E. "Federal Bureau of Investigation: History." In Encyclopedia of Crime and Justice, edited by Sanford H. Kadish. New York, 1983.
Poveda, Tony G. Lawlessness and Reform: The FBI in Transition. Pacific Grove, Calif., 1990.
Powers, Richard Gid. G-Men: Hoover's FBI in American Popular Culture. Carbondale, Ill., 1983.
Rosenfeld, Susan. "J. Edgar Hoover." In Dictionary of American Biography, suppl. 9. New York, 1994.
Theoharis, Athan. The FBI: An Annotated Bibliography and Research Guide. New York, 1994.
Theoharis, Athan. J. Edgar Hoover, Sex, and Crime: An Historical Antidote. Chicago, 1995.
Theoharis, Athan G., and John Stuart Cox. The Boss: J. Edgar Hoover and the Great American Inquisition. Philadelphia, 1988.
Ungar, Sanford J. FBI. Boston, 1975.
U.S. Federal Bureau of Investigation. FBI: Facts and History. Washington, D.C., 1990.
U.S. Federal Bureau of Investigation. FBI Fact Sheet. FBI Home Page, World Wide Web, 1996.

—MARK BYRNES

Federal Bureau of Prisons.

See Prisons, Federal Bureau of.

Federal Communications Commission

 An independent federal regulatory agency responsible directly to Congress, the Federal Communications Commission (FCC) is charged with regulating interstate and international communication by radio, television, wire, satellite, and cable. Its jurisdiction covers the fifty states, the District of Columbia, and the U.S. possessions of Guam, the Virgin Islands, and Puerto Rico. All FCC rules and regulations have the force of law unless challenged in court.

THE BEGINNING OF BROADCAST REGULATIONS

The notion of regulating the nation's airwaves got its impetus from a well-known tragedy: the sinking of the luxury cruise ship *Titanic*. Investigation into the disaster revealed that the Marconi station in Newfoundland received the *Titanic*'s distress signal. As news broke, however, amateur radio operators filled the air with questions, rumors, and most of all, interference. Consequently, the Marconi Company complained that its operation encountered interference by "outside unrecognized stations."

The sinking of the *Titanic* was not the first incident in which amateur radio operators hindered important operations at sea. These "outside unrecognized" stations had already fallen into disfavor with the United States Navy. Despite the existence of the Wireless Ship Act of 1910 (the first radio law adopted by Congress), according to which radio was to be limited to use only as a lifesaving device at sea, amateur radio operators continued to use the airwaves for other, less desirable, purposes. For example, more than one naval ship had received false sailing orders by radio, and simultaneous radio transmissions had drowned out numerous military messages.

Following the *Titanic* incident, Congress enacted a new law, the Radio Act of 1912, which would clear the airwaves for distress. But the Radio Act of 1912 also established several key legal and regulatory principles that continue to underlie broadcast regulation almost a century later. First, the federal government would control broadcasting. No one could broadcast without a license from the secretary of commerce and labor. Second, the spectrum would be allocated between uses and users. Congress recognized some communications as more important than others, and the government would determine which was which. For example, distress calls took precedence. The military was second in the spectrum ranking. The "commercial" category was next and was for uses such as over-the-air or "wireless" usage with a direct charge. The amateur category was last. The amateur category covered communications put out for anyone to receive; amateurs could listen anywhere along the spectrum, but could transmit only on the short waves. This is the use that would eventually evolve into broadcasting as it is known today.

BROADCASTING EMERGES

Under the direction of Herbert Hoover, then commerce secretary and later the thirty-first president of the United States, the Commerce Department allocated a single wavelength for broadcasting. When it became obvious that one would not be enough, another was added, mainly for weather forecasts and crop reports. Despite the new band, privately operated radio stations interfered with each other's programming. The Commerce Department, however, regulated by the Radio Act of 1912, could do little to solve the problem and continued to issue transmitter licenses.

By the end of 1925, with 578 stations broadcasting, the band was full again. Furthermore, as the industry matured, stations began to broadcast for longer hours with increased power, which again led to widespread interference. Hoover first addressed the problem by urging stations to work out time-sharing agreements or to agree to have one station buy the other's license. But the industry, growing at all levels, could not agree on how to operate, and cooperation remained an elusive goal. Finally, in desperation, radio station managers formed the National Association of Broadcasters in 1922 and called for an expanded governmental role. To accomplish this task, industry leaders encouraged the government to call a series of radio conferences to try to deal with the mounting problems.

They were unsuccessful in conferences one, two, and three, which managed to flesh out problems but not solve them. However, they did manage to reach some agreement by the end of the fourth, which Hoover convened in 1925. The four hundred delegates voted to limit the number of stations, even if it meant driving some off the air. From that conference, the basis of the Radio Act of 1927 emerged.

The Radio Act of 1927 replaced the statute enacted after the *Titanic* disaster, and a newly created commercial radio broadcasting industry emerged. The Radio Act of 1927 had three key aspects. The first was the declaration that there could be no private ownership in the entire spectrum. Although the 1912 act had required a license to use the air, it had been silent on the issue of ownership of the airwaves. The 1927 act was not. Second, the act, in a related decision, mandated that users of the spectrum would operate and receive a license under the public interest standard. Finally, the act put the Federal Radio Commission (FRC) into place.

The FRC was to allocate frequencies according to the "public interest, convenience or necessity," a phrase that originated with an amendment to the Interstate Commerce Act. Yet radio programming is not comparable with the services of a railroad company. Unlike the railroads that the Interstate Commerce Act regulated, the FRC could not regulate individual programs: conceivably, such regulation could amount to nothing more than censorship. Nor could the commission set the rates charged for airtime. The FRC's limited programming authority resulted at least in part from the fear of a federal radio "censor." The creation of an independent radio commission, rather than an augmented authority within the Commerce Department, would limit governmental interference in expression.

Therefore, what the public interest meant was left to the FRC to decide. Another task facing the commission was deciding how many stations to allow on the air, their location, and under what conditions they would operate. This task grew more complex by a 1928 amendment to the Radio Act that mandated an equalization of sta-

tions among five geographical zones. The act sought to replace stations in the more populous East with newcomers in the South and West. License renewal, occurring at an interval of every three years, would continue to be the province of the FRC.

Although the commission had formidable responsibilities, Congress never gave the FRC long-term authority, preferring to renew its life from year to year. The agency had to share its authority with the more established Commerce Department and Interstate Commerce Commission, although several proposals surfaced to consolidate federal regulation of broadcasting into one agency.

In 1933, however, newly elected President Franklin D. Roosevelt argued that rapid growth in all areas of the communications field necessitated better coordination of those regulatory functions. In an apparent wish to consolidate communications regulatory bodies, President Roosevelt recommended to Congress that government oversight of telephone and telegraph, heretofore the charge of the Interstate Commerce Commission, be combined with that of radio, and that all be placed under the authority of a seven-member commission appointed by the president for staggered seven-year terms and called the FCC.

Despite its new status, and except for a clause regarding powers to limit the height of radio towers, the new commission would essentially assume the FRC's limited prerogatives. Not surprisingly, the communications industries offered little, if any, opposition to the conglomeration. Both houses passed the measure in 1934 by voice vote after limited debate, and the Communications Act of 1934 took effect on 1 July of that year. The new law incorporated most of the provisions of the 1927 act and established the FCC.

The new federal agency would regulate interstate and foreign communication for the United States and its territories. The commission's charge was to provide for the orderly development and operation of broadcasting services while at the same time having an efficient nationwide and worldwide telegraph and telephone service at reasonable charges. Additionally, the commission would promote the safety of life and property through the use of wire and radio communication and employ communications facilities for strengthening the national defense.

Since its inception, however, the commission has been a source of controversy. Broadcasters have been some of its harshest critics. In general, they accuse the agency of moving too slowly to regulate or shape an industry wherein technological advances at every level all too often render existing regulations obsolete.

For example, nothing more exasperated the independent agency's critics in the postwar decade than the FCC's awarding of the new and limited number of television licenses. Soon after the beginning of regular telecasts in 1948, the value of a TV station in a major market jumped. Despite high start-up costs incurred from new equipment and programming, TV stations commanded increasingly impressive revenues from the sale of time to advertisers. In turn, the commissioners found themselves overwhelmed with applications for more television channels. But despite the rush for stations, the FCC failed to abide by a consistent procedure in awarding new licenses. Instead, applicants competed against one another by stressing various strengths, any one of which might be the basis for a grant.

By the late 1950s, the FCC came under closer scrutiny. The possibilities of improprieties became public in 1957 when two magazine stories asserted that the commission had granted licenses in Boston, Miami, and St. Louis for political reasons. Following these accusations, the commission emerged from a Congressional Oversight Committee hearing in 1958 with a thoroughly tainted record. There were charges of political influence stemming mainly from the fact that the FCC's four-to-three Republican majority favored Republican applicants. This charge, however, remained difficult to prove. Other charges of improprieties forced one commissioner to resign in disgrace and face prosecution. Publicly reprimanded by House members for his *ex parte* social contacts, the FCC chairman and nearly all commissioners received gifts, free meals, and loans from license applicants and their lobbyists.

From the proceedings, ostensibly for the guarantee of fair treatment, Senator Ernest E. McFarland of Arizona offered a series of amendments to the 1934 Communications Act. The "McFarland amendments," enacted in 1952, created a bureaucratic layer immune from commission control—the review staff, set up to present cases before the hearing examiners. At the same time, the commission must now conduct hearings upon the insistence of any party actually seeking a licence. Additionally, the full commission and not a single commissioner have to meet to handle a petitioned hearing. Finally, the amendments restricted the FCC's power in reviewing the transfer or sale of a licence.

THE COMMISSIONERS

Today, five commissioners run the agency; all are presidential appointees with approval by the Senate. No commissioner can have any financial interest in any of the businesses that the FCC regulates. The normal appointment is for five years, except for someone appointed to fill out an unexpired term. The president appoints one of the commissioners as chairman. The chairman serves at the pleasure of the president.

The chairman presides over all commission meetings, coordinates and organizes the work of the commission, and represents the agency in legislative matters and in relations with other government departments and agencies. If the chairman is absent or the office is vacant, the commission designates one of its commissioners to act temporarily as chairman.

The commissioners hold regular open and closed agenda meetings and special meetings. They also may act between meetings by "circulation," a procedure whereby a document circulates to each commissioner individually for consideration and official action. The committee as a whole makes policy decisions.

The chairman also delegates management and administrative responsibility to the managing director. Within the FCC there are several bureaus with separate and distinct responsibilities. For example, the Wireless Telecommunications Bureau (WTB) handles all FCC domestic wireless telecommunications programs and policies, except those involving satellite communications. Wireless communications services include cellular telephone, paging, personal communications service, public safety, and other commercial and private radio services. The WTB regulates wireless telecommunications providers and licenses.

The Mass Media Bureau (MMB) regulates television and radio stations in the United States. The bureau issues broadcast licenses specifying the community of license as well as the channel and operating power of the station. The conditions of the license ensure that the broadcast will be picked up without interference. If problems arise, the bureau investigates and resolves the problems. The MMB can fine a station or revoke its license if it finds that a broadcaster is violating FCC rules.

The Cable Services Bureau provides a single point of contact for cable-related issues before the commission. The bureau carries out the Cable Television Consumer Protection and Competition Act of 1992.

The International Bureau is the central clearinghouse for the commission's international policies and activities. The International Bureau develops, recommends, and administers policies, standards, procedures, and programs for the regulation of international telecommunications facilities and services and the licensing of satellite facilities under its jurisdiction. The bureau advises and recommends to the commission, or acts for the commission under delegated authority, in the development and administration of international telecommunications policies and programs. The International Bureau assumes the principal representational role for commission activities in international organizations through its three divisions, Planning and Negotiations, Satellite and Radiocommunication, and Telecommunications.

The Complaints and Information Bureau (CIB) is the commission's primary point of contact with the public. Through its field office personnel, it carries out the enforcement, public service, and engineering programs of the agency. The Compliance Program ensures observation of U.S. radio laws and FCC rules. The CIB resolves interference problems, monitors the radio spectrum to make sure that channels remain usable and free from interference, certifies radio-equipped ships to sail, and assists rescue agencies. The bureau pursues administrative and criminal sanctions against parties that violate the laws and rules. The CIB also distributes forms for franchises and complaints.

Within the agency, the Common Carrier Bureau regulates interstate wireline "common carrier" services such as telephone and telegraph companies. The bureau's Enforcement Division monitors and investigates complaints about common carriers. Other divisions within the Common Carrier Bureau help enforce FCC regulations.

For example, the Accounting and Audits Division is the bureau's primary contact point for state regulators and the National Association of Regulatory Utility Commissioners with respect to the jurisdictional separations of costs, including Federal-State Joint Boards established pursuant to Section 410 of the Communications Act. The division is responsible for developing and administering universal service policies and programs, including the Universal Service Fund and the Lifeline and Link Up America programs. The Accounting and Audits Division is also responsible for developing and administering the cost accounting, auditing, and reporting requirements of the commission necessary to effectively carry out the rate regulation requirements of the Communications Act. The division conducts regular audits of local telephone companies (principally the regional Bell Operating Companies and GTE) to assure compliance with the commission's cost accounting regulatory safeguards. The division also receives and reviews information submitted under the Automated Reporting Management Information (ARMIS) program and conducts specialized cost and financial analysis of telephone company cost showings, to support work of other divisions.

Another division, Network Services, oversees network reliability, telecommunications relay services, and wireline hearing aid compatibility. Issues handled by the Network Services Division include, but are not limited to, network services and reliability issues, including the work of the

Network Reliability Council and efforts to prevent network outages. The division also handles numbering issues, which include the use of toll-free numbers, the introduction of new area codes, the designation of a new North American Numbering Plan administrator, caller ID, and other network functionality issues. The division has overseen the creation of a conservation plan designed to ensure a smooth transition for 800 to 888 toll-free numbers, successfully concluded a Negotiated Rulemaking on Hearing Aid Compatibility issues, and developed fair rules for the introduction of nationwide caller ID services.

The Enforcement Division handles all consumer protection issues and complaints, as well as mergers and acquisitions. The division is also responsible for developing and setting up the bureau's consumer protection programs, as well as conducting the bureau's investigations into possible violations of the Communications Act. The Informal Complaints and Public Inquiries Branch also prepares responses to most written congressional inquiries related to common carrier matters—about 150 each month.

The Formal Complaints and Investigations Branch answers requests for information pursuant to the Freedom of Information Act. [See Appendix: Freedom of Information Act.] The branch also responds to complaints sent to the commission. The number of written complaints received by the branch has increased seventy-eight percent from 1994 to 1995, and the branch receives twenty thousand written complaints and handles about twenty-five thousand telephone calls annually from consumers.

A REGULATORY AGENCY WITH LIMITED AUTHORITY

The scope of authority of FCC is limited. For example, there are rules to ensure that candidates for public office are able to have access to the air for their paid political advertisements. In an effort to meet its charge that the communications facilities in the United States operate in the "public interest," the FCC can affect content without controlling it. The FCC has the ability to enforce restrictions on television and radio broadcasters by means of congressional mandates such as the fairness doctrine (now rescinded); the equal time

rule; Section 415; the indecency clause; regulations regarding cross-ownership of media properties, concentration of ownership of properties, and quantity and type of ownership of communications facilities; and much more.

The FCC has jurisdiction only over interstate telecommunications, for it is the state public utilities commissions that set rates for local service. Additionally, FCC rules generally do not govern the selection of programming that is broadcast. The main exceptions are that broadcasters may not broadcast obscene programming; they may broadcast indecent programming only when there is a strong probability that no children are in the audience; and they must limit the number of commercials aired during programming aimed at children.

BIBLIOGRAPHY

Baughman, James L. *Television's Guardians: The FCC and the Politics of Programming, 1958–1967.* Knoxville, Tenn., 1985.
Breyer, Stephen. *Regulation and Its Reform.* Cambridge, Mass., 1982.
Federal Communications Commission Authorization Act of 1983: Report Together with Additional and Dissenting Views. United States Congress, House Committee on Energy and Commerce. Washington, D.C., 1983.
Federal Communications Commission Authorization Act of 1991: Report to Accompany H.R. 1674 (Including Cost Estimates of the Congressional Budget Office). United States Congress, House Committee on Energy and Commerce. Washington, D.C., 1991.
Federal Communications Commission: Strategic Focus Needed to Improve Information Resources Management: Report to the Chairman, Subcommittee on Government Information, Justice, and Agriculture. Committee on Government Operations, House of Representatives. United States General Accounting Office. Washington, D.C., 1990.
Flannery, Gerald V. *Commissioners of the FCC, 1927–1994.* Lanham, Md., 1995.
Franklin, Grace A., and R. B. Ripley. *Congress, the Bureaucracy, and Public Policy.* Chicago, 1987.
Havick, John J. *Communications Policy and the Political Process.* Westport, Conn., 1983.
Hilliard, Robert L. *The Federal Communications Commission: A Primer.* Boston, 1991.
Krasnow, Erwin G., L. D. Longley, and T. A. Herbert. *The Politics of Broadcast Regulation.* New York, 1982.
Krattenmaker, Thomas G., and L. A. Powe, Jr. *Regulating Broadcast Programming.* Cambridge, Mass., 1994.
Rourke, Francis E. *Bureaucracy, Politics, and Public Policy.* Boston, 1984.

—VERONICA D. DICONTI

Federal Crop Insurance Corporation.

See Crop Insurance Corporation, Federal.

Federal Deposit Insurance Corporation

Since its establishment in 1933 the Federal Deposit Insurance Corporation (FDIC) has provided insurance for depositors in commercial banks in the event of a bank failure. Today depositors are insured for their savings up to $100,000. Banks pay an assessment fee to the bank insurance fund for every $100 they hold in deposits. The FDIC manages the fund, making disbursements to pay off depositors in failed banks, to facilitate the purchase and assumption of a failed bank's deposits by another healthy bank, and to provide capital to a bank in order to prevent failure. Liquidation of a failed bank's assets is also an FDIC responsibility, with the sale revenue going to the bank insurance fund. FDIC operating expenses are covered by the fund, including its responsibilities for supervising state banks that do not belong to the Federal Reserve system, litigation, and the training of FDIC personnel. The FDIC also maintains and manages the Savings Association Insurance Fund and administers the Federal Savings and Loan Insurance Corporation Resolution Fund. At the end of 1996, the FDIC's Bank Insurance Fund balance was $26.9 billion.

Between 1929 and March of 1933 more than nine thousand commercial banks failed or suspended operations. The stock market crash in October of 1929 and the public's loss of confidence in the banking system fueled the failures. During the early 1900s the banking industry grew dramatically, reaching a high point of approximately twenty thousand state-chartered banks and eight thousand nationally chartered banks in the 1920s. In a more competitive environment, banks turned to the growing stock market as an option and often used depositors' funds to underwrite new issues of securities or to purchase securities in secondary trading. The market crash meant the crash of bank assets as well.

Banks also suffered from a loss of depositor confidence that took hold in one state or in one bank and spread to others. Rumors that a bank was unable to meet depositors' demands prompted a panic and a run on the bank. The problem was compounded in 1933 as revelations of the outrageous banking practices by the nation's largest and most prestigious banks were pronounced almost daily by the investigative staff of the Senate Banking and Currency Committee.

On 7 March 1933 President Franklin Roosevelt declared a national bank holiday in an effort to restore confidence in the nation's banking system. Banking activities were immediately suspended by emergency legislation that specified the procedures for reopening banks for business. More important, Senator Carter Glass (D-Va.) and Representative Henry B. Steagall (D-Ariz.) sponsored the Banking Act of 1933 to provide depositor insurance as a means to restore the public's confidence in the banking system and prevent runs on banks. (Also included was the provision known as the Glass-Steagall Act that prohibited banks from engaging in investment banking activities such as the underwriting of securities.) The FDIC was established to administer a temporary insurance fund for national and state-chartered banks and was made permanent in 1935.

The FDIC is a government corporation. Its five-member board of directors consists of a chairman, a vice chairman, a director, and two *ex officio* members, the comptroller of the currency and the director of the Office of Thrift Supervision (OTS). (The Office of the Comptroller of the Currency and the OTS are bureaus in the Treasury Department responsible for chartering and supervising national banks and thrifts, respectively.) The vice chairman and director of the OTS were added to the FDIC's board in 1989, when the Financial Institutions Reform, Recovery and Enforcement Act was passed, giving the FDIC responsibility for managing the Savings Association Insurance Fund for thrifts. All board members are appointed by the president and confirmed by the Senate.

Between 1943 and 1981 the FDIC collected more revenue from the insurance premiums charged to banks than it needed to pay off depositors in failed institutions. On average, only five banks failed each year. In 1983, however, insurance losses began to exceed assessment revenue as the number of bank failures escalated to forty-three for the year. In 1987 the number of annual bank failures escalated to more than two hundred. By 1990, more than one thousand banks failed, and in 1991 the FDIC projected a negative net worth of $7 billion dollars for the fund. More than $25 billion was spent to resolve failed institutions and protect depositors.

Congress responded to the banking crisis with the FDIC Improvement Act of 1991 (FDICIA). The primary role of the legislation was to provide the bank insurance fund with authority to borrow up to $70 billion from the Treasury Department to deal with problem banks that were projected to fail. In order to protect the bank insurance fund in the future from expensive bank failures, the FDICIA requires the FDIC (and other federal banking supervisors) to close banks in the least costly manner and to automatically close banks with capital less than two percent of assets.

The legislation was controversial. While supporters viewed it as a means to protect runs on the bank insurance fund in the future by making banking more safe and sound, critics viewed it as an excessive regulatory measure that will burden the banking industry, rather than make it stronger.

By 1993 the banking industry recorded a record year in profits, and the bank insurance fund rebounded with a balance of $13 billion. The FDIC has since paid back with interest its borrowings from the Treasury to resolve bank failures. As the banking industry continues to change and grow owing to mergers of banks and the development of new banking products, the FDIC's role as manager of the bank insurance fund will change as well.

[*See also* Comptroller of the Currency, Office of the; Federal Reserve System; Resolution Trust Corporation; *and* Thrift Supervision, Office of.]

BIBLIOGRAPHY

Federal Deposit Insurance Corporation, *The First Fifty Years: A History of the FDIC, 1933–1983.* Washing-ton, D.C., 1984.

Golembe, Carter. "The Deposit Insurance Legislation of 1933." *Political Science Quarterly* 76 (June 1960): 181–200.

Kaufman, George G, and Robert E. Litan, eds. *Assessing Bank Reform: FDICIA One Year Later.* Washington, D.C., 1993.

Kennedy, Susan Estabrook. *The Banking Crisis of 1933.* Lexington, Ky., 1973.

Konstas, Panos. "The Bank Insurance Fund: Trends, Initiatives, and the Road Ahead." *FDIC Banking Review* 5 (Fall–Winter, 1992): 15–23.

Ritchie, Donald A. "The Pecora Wall Street Expose; 1934." In *Congress Investigates: A Documented History, 1792–1974,* vol. 4, edited by Arthur Schlesinger, Jr., and Roger Brums, pp. 2555–2731. New York, 1975.

Robertson, Ross M. *The Comptroller and Bank Supervision: A Historical Appraisal.* Washington, D.C., 1968.

Simmons, Craig A., and Stephen C. Swain. "Girding for Competition: Instead of Trying to Define the Future, the New Banking Act Helps Prepare for It." *GAO Journal* 15 (Spring–Summer 1992): 3–9.

—ANNE M. KHADEMIAN

Federal Election Commission.
See Election Commission, Federal.

Federal Energy Regulatory Commission.
See Energy Regulatory Commission, Federal.

Federal Grain Inspection Service.
See Grain Inspection Service, Federal.

Federal Highway Administration.
See Highway Administration, Federal.

Federal Housing Finance Board.
See Housing Finance Board, Federal.

Federal Maritime Commission.
See Maritime Commission, Federal.

Federal Railroad Administration.
See Railroad Administration, Federal.

Federal Register

The origin of the *Federal Register,* the official newspaper of the federal government, can be traced to a curious bureucratic mix-up. In 1933 Franklin D. Roosevelt issued a series of six executive orders on petroleum quotas. A seventh executive order revoked the first, but the revocation was not recorded. When a refining company sued the government over the first order, the Supreme Court discovered the mistake, and Chief Justice Charles Evans Hughes took the government to task for not publishing the revocation. In response, Congress passed the Federal Register Act, mandating a daily publication documenting presidential proclamations, executive orders, and agency regulations. The act also established that government regulations have no legal force until published. Supplemental legislation called for codifying the rules in the *Code of Federal Regulations* (CFR). The system of codifying regulations parallels that of legislation. Laws enacted by Congress are compiled annually in *Statutes at Large* and codified in the *U.S. Code* by subject titles. Rules and regulations are published daily in the *Federal Register* and then codified by subject title in the *CFR.*

The *Federal Register* includes announcements of proposed federal regulations being drafted for the purpose of soliciting public comments. The "Proposed Rules" section announces early or final drafts of rules with deadlines for public comments. In each issue of the *Federal Register,* documents are arranged under five heads: "Presidential Documents," "Rules and Regulations," "Proposed Rules," "Notices," and "Sunshine Meetings." Agencies are required to publish rules in the *Federal Register* thirty days before they are to take effect.

The "Notices" section includes documents other than rules and proposed rules, such as notices of hearings and investigations, committee meetings, agency decisions and rulings, delegations of authority, filing of petitions and applications, issuance or revocation of licenses, announcements of advisory committee meetings, notice of filings of environmental impact statements, and grant application deadlines. Sun-

shine Act meetings are published in accordance with the provisions of the Sunshine Act. [*See* Appendix: Government in the Sunshine Act.] Several kinds of finding aids are published each day, including contents arranged by agency and type of document, selected subjects affected by rules and proposed rules, and a list of *CFR* parts affected.

The *CFR* is divided into fifty titles according to broad subject areas affected by regulatory action. Within each title, consisting of one or more volumes, subjects are further broken down into chapters numbered in Roman numerals, and chapters are further subdivided into parts numbered in Arabic. A section is a unit consisting of a short, simple presentation of one proposition The *CFR Index and Finding Aids* is revised annually and appears as a separate volume. The *CFR* also publishes every month a cumulative list of changes in the regulations since they were published in the latest annual code. There is no single annual issue of the cumulative lists; rather, four of the monthly issues include cumulative lists for certain titles. —GEORGE THOMAS KURIAN

Federal Reserve System

Created by act of Congress in 1913, the Federal Reserve System (commonly known as the Fed) is the central bank of the United States, charged with making and administering the nation's credit and monetary policy. It also supervises and regulates bank holding companies, state-chartered banks that are members of the system, overseas activities of U.S. banks, and U.S.-based operations of foreign banks.

The Federal Reserve System was the third such bank chartered in the United States. The first Bank of the United States, chartered in 1791 for twenty years, did not survive the expiry of its lease in 1811. A Second Bank was chartered in 1816 but ran afoul of the Democratic administration of Andrew Jackson, who made its demise one of his primary goals and refused to renew its charter in 1836. For the next twenty-five years, the banking system consisted of a chaotic network of unregulated state-chartered banks plagued by insufficient capital, risky loans, and floating currency values. Neither the bank notes nor deposits were guaranteed by the state. The first attempt to remedy the situation came, ironically, in the midst of the Civil War. In 1863 the Congress passed the National Bank Act establishing federally chartered banks and the Office of the Comptroller of the Currency to control them. [See Comptroller of the Currency, Office of the.] One goal of this measure was war-related: to stabilize money in the Union and, correspondingly, to devalue that in the Confederacy.

By 1913 the growing economy called for an overhaul of the entire monetary system that would allow money to be transferred from one financial institution to another anywhere in the nation. Legislators were also concerned with the need to avoid financial panics and to even out fluctuations in the money supply by creating a central authority to make loans to banks through a discount window. The act establishing the system stated its purpose as follows: "To provide for the establishment of Federal Reserve banks, to furnish an elastic currency, to afford a means of rediscounting commercial paper [and] to establish a more effective supervision of banking in the United States."

During the 1920s the Fed discovered new tools to influence money creation and supply. One was the sale and purchase of U.S. Treasury securities. By buying securities from a bank, the Fed increased the bank's reserves and enabled it to make more loans at a lower interest rate; conversely, by selling securities, the bank's reserves fell, and credit shrank, pushing up interest rates. Early use of this tool tended to be uncoordinated and to depress the market. It was only in 1922 that the Fed established the Open Market Investment Committee to fine-tune the control mechanisms. The banking acts of the Roosevelt era increased the power and autonomy of the Fed by removing the secretary of the Treasury and the comptroller from its board of governors. The acts also stripped the regional Fed banks of their power to sell and buy securities and invested that power solely in the Federal Open Market Committee (FOMC)—successor to the Open Market Investment Committee—which operated through the Federal Reserve Bank of New York.

At the outset membership in the Fed was mandatory for all national banks and voluntary for state-chartered banks. Member banks were required to keep interest-free reserves at the Fed in return for certain Fed services. As the interest rates rose in the 1970s, the cost of keeping interest-free reserves at the Fed outweighed the advantages to member banks, and many of them consequently withdrew and converted to state-chartered banks. To counteract the erosion of membership, the Monetary Control Act of 1980 required all depository institutions, regardless of their membership status, to keep reserves at the Fed. The Fed was also required to charge fees for its check-clearing and other services and offer them to nonmember banks.

FUNCTIONS AND OBJECTIVES OF THE FED

The preeminent function of the Fed is the conduct of monetary policy. In its broadest sense, monetary policy refers to the management of financial conditions through a set of policy directives aimed at controlling the flow of money by setting interest rates and other variables. The Fed is recognized as the guardian of monetary policy, and its function is clearly stated in Section A of the Federal Reserve Act as amended by the Full Employment and Balanced Growth (Humphrey-Hawkins) Act of 1978: "To maintain the long-run growth of the monetary and credit aggregates commensurate with the economy's long-run potential to increase production, so as to promote effectively the goals of maximum employment, stable prices, and moderate long-term interest rates." Long-term monetary policy is set by the Board of Governors and the short-term policy is implemented by the FOMC, which is composed of members of the Board of Governors as well as five presidents chosen from the twelve Federal Reserve Banks. The FOMC meets every five to eight weeks, and its instructions are carried out by the "Operations Desk," or simply "the Desk," located in the Federal Reserve Bank in New York.

Obviously, the broad goals of monetary policy are the same as the overall national economic policy, and therefore it should work in tandem with the latter as well as with the administration's fiscal policy (budgets) rather than at cross-purposes with them. Sometimes, the goals of monetary policy are contradictory: it is not always possible to achieve strong growth, price stability (low inflation), and high employment at the same time or by the same means. The vagaries of a global interdependent economy can also influence domestic economy in ways that are difficult to measure, let alone predict.

The Fed chairman testifies twice yearly to the House and Senate Banking Committees, explaining the Fed's monetary policy, and sometimes he appears at other congressional committees as well. These testimonies are among the most closely watched in the banking world, and the chairman's usually laconic statements are analyzed endlessly to find some clues as to the Fed's intentions.

A closely related goal is the stability and liquidity of the banking industry and other financial markets. At the time the Fed was created, commercial banks were the dominant financial institutions. Before 1980 only commercial banks were members of the system, with regular access to the discount window. The Monetary Control Act of 1980 extended this privilege to all institutions receiving deposits subject to the Reserve requirements, including savings banks, savings and loan associations, credit unions, and U.S. branches and agencies of foreign banks. However, the Fed's responsibility to maintain the liquidity of the financial system is a responsibility to the system rather than to individual institutions. The purpose is to prevent liquidity problems at a single institution or a small group of institutions from spreading and disrupting the system as a whole. Also, the Fed strongly encourages institutions to seek funds from other sources before coming to the window. Indeed, the Fed is referred to as the lender of last resort. In addition to the discount window, the Securities and Exchange Act of 1934 requires the Fed to regulate extensions of credit by securities brokers, banks, and other lenders for the purpose of buying or carrying specified securities. [See Securities and Exchange Commission.]

The third function of the Fed is to supervise and regulate commercial banks and to ensure the safety and soundness of the banking system and the efficiency of its operations. It shares these responsibilities with other federal and state financial regulatory agencies. The terms *regulation* and *supervision* are often used loosely as synonyms but in fact refer to two distinct duties. Regulations are systemic rules anchored in federal statutes and laws. Supervision, on the other hand, refers to oversight—mostly through on-site inspections—of domestic banks, branches of foreign banks, and branches of U.S. banks abroad. The landmark Depository Institutions Deregulation and Monetary Control Act of 1980 expanded the Fed's regulatory authority in some areas, but reduced it in others. Deregulation, coupled with the economic turbulence of the 1980s, has seriously challenged the Fed's supervisory resources.

The fourth function of the Fed is to protect the consumer and communities from the depredations of the unregulated sectors of the economy. The Fed has been given the responsibility to write regulations implementing laws governing consumer credit and community reinvestment and development. Among the most important statutes covering consumer financial transactions are the Truth in Lending Act, the Fair Credit Billing Act, the Equal Credit Opportunity Act, the Fair Credit Reporting Act, the Consumer Leasing Act, the Real Estate Settlement Procedures Act, and the Electronic Fund Transfer Act. The Fed is advised by a Consumer Advisory Council in carrying out its consumer-related regulatory responsibilities. The principal statutes governing community reinvestment and development are the Home Mortgage Disclosure Act and the Community Reinvestment Act.

Although the Fed is independent of the U.S. Treasury in a legal sense and under the terms of the "Accord of 1951," the two work as closely as possible to harmonize their operations. The Fed is the "fiscal agent" of the Treasury and essentially its banker. The Fed also carries out on behalf of the Treasury routine operations related to issuing, servicing, and redeeming Treasury securities. The Treasury's disbursements and receipts affect the volume of reserves available to the banking system. The Treasury informs the Fed early each business day of its projected expenditures and receipts to enable the latter to take off-setting actions.

In addition to fiscal services to the Treasury, the Fed offers a number of services to depository institutions. These services, actually provided by the twelve Federal Reserve Banks, are related to the payments mechanism. Among these services are 1) the distribution of coin and currency in response to needs, and 2) the clearing and settlement of checks, including wire transfers of funds through FedWire and automated clearinghouses.

The Fed's international responsibilities are as broad as its domestic ones. It is constantly in consultation with the central banks of most industrial nations. It charters and regulates international banking subsidiaries called Edge Corporations (after Senator Walter Edge). The Foreign Bank Supervision Enhancement Act of 1991 expanded the Fed's jurisdiction over U.S. activities of foreign banks, and it has the right to suspend operations of foreign banks, as it did in the case of Daiwa Bank in 1995. The Federal Reserve Bank of New York also performs some fiscal agent functions for foreign central banks.

STRUCTURE OF THE FEDERAL RESERVE SYSTEM

The institutional position of the Fed within the overall structure of the federal government is distinctive and unusual. These characteristics reflect the troubled history of central banking in the United States in earlier times and the political compromises and trade-offs that marked the passage of the Federal Reserve Act in 1913. Both the private and the public sectors participated in the two central banks that were established in the nineteenth century. The conflict between the powerful private banking interests of the Northeast and southern political populists led to the creation of a hybrid structure that is both public and private.

The Board of Governors is the central governing body. It is an agency of the federal government consisting of seven members appointed by the president of the United States with the advice and consent of the Senate. The full term of a member of the board is fourteen years, with one member's term expiring every even-numbered year. A member who has served a full term may not be reappointed. The president appoints one of the members as chairman and another as vice

chairman for four-year terms, again with the advice and consent of the Senate. Members of the board constitute a majority of the voting members of the FOMC. The board also reviews and approves all discount rate actions taken by the Federal Reserve Banks, and it has the authority to alter the reserve requirements of depository institutions within limits specified by law. The board exercises general supervisory authority over the activities of Federal Reserve Banks. It appoints one member of the board of directors of each bank, and it must approve the appointment of each bank's president and first vice president. The board is directly responsible to Congress but funds its expenditures through assessments on the Federal Reserve Banks rather than through congressional appropriations. In addition to its annual report, it publishes the *Federal Reserve Bulletin* and other publications.

The FOMC directs the Fed's domestic open market operations and also oversees the system's activities in foreign exchange markets. The chairman of the Board of Governors is traditionally chairman of the committee. In addition to the seven members of the Board of Governors, the FOMC includes five of the Reserve Bank presidents as voting members. The president of the Federal Reserve Bank of New York is a permanent voting member and also the vice chairman of the committee, and the four remaining voting memberships rotate among the other eleven Reserve Bank governors. There are twelve Federal Reserve Banks whose head offices are located in the following cities: Boston, New York, Philadelphia, Cleveland, Richmond, Atlanta, Chicago, Saint Louis, Minneapolis, Kansas City, Dallas, and San Francisco. There are branches of these banks in twenty-five other cities.

The corporate structure of the Reserve Banks is similar to that of private commercial banks. Each bank has a board of directors that elects the bank's officers. The banks also issue capital stock. Although the banks are designed to promote public interest and are not profit-driven, they earn substantial profits through their routine operations. Each of the Reserve Bank board of directors has nine members, divided into three categories of three members each: Category A directors are commercial bankers; Category B members are drawn from the public and elected by member banks within the district; Category C directors are drawn from the public but appointed by the Board of Governors. One of the Category C directors is named as chairman and another as vice chairman. Several informal arrangements exist to facilitate communication among Reserve Banks. The Conference of Chairmen of Federal Reserve Banks meets twice a year in Washington, D.C., and a Conference of Presidents of Reserve Banks meets several times each year at one of the banks. There is also a Conference of First Vice Presidents.

A number of advisory councils and committees exist in the system. The Federal Advisory Council has twelve members, one elected annually by each of the twelve Reserve Bank boards. These are typically prominent commercial bankers. The council meets at least four times a year with the Board of Governors. Other advisory groups include the Consumer Advisory Council, made up of thirty members, and the Thrift Institutions Advisory Council.

The Fed is often described erroneously as "independent." The framers of the Federal Reserve Act did seek to insulate the Fed from routine political pressures in order to avoid the abuse of monetary policy for partisan benefit. It has greater freedom in practice than comparable government entities since its actions do not have to be ratified by the president, its expenses are funded from its own earnings and not through congressional appropriations, and its members have unusually lengthy terms in office. However, the Fed is not independent in a legal, constitutional, or historical sense. It is not a separate branch of government protected by the Constitution like the judiciary. It is a creature of Congress, created by an act of Congress, and it can be altered or abolished at will by the Congress. Although the Fed is not accountable for its decisions in the usual sense, it cannot, without a high degree of political risk, embrace economic policies that are at variance with those of the administration. If its policies cause an economic downturn or fail to stimulate a recovery, it will, like any other department or agency, face considerable criticism from the public, and especially from the business community. The accountability element in the Fed's relationship with the executive and the legislature is dramatized by the

appearances of the chairman or members of the board before Congress, a ritual that is closely watched by the media. The Fed's positions and decisions are sometimes controversial, and congressional hearings can be contentious, albeit that the chairman's delphic statements may baffle his interlocutors.

Even the Fed's influence over the nation's monetary and fiscal conditions is somewhat exaggerated. Its influence is inherently indirect. The Reserve System has direct administrative control over only one interest rate, the discount rate, and it has no direct control over the other aggregations of currency, bank deposits and other liquid assets that constitute the national money supply. What the Fed can influence directly is the volume and growth of reserves held by private commercial banks and other depository institutions through regulating the balances held by them at Federal Reserve Banks. A restrictive approach to the provisions of reserves by the Fed puts an upward pressure on the short-term interest rate charged in the so-called federal funds market. This, in turn, causes other interest rates to rise, which acts to reduce the supply and demand for money and credit and hence their growth. The Fed's influence on the economy also is not scientifically quantifiable. A cause-and-effect relationship is assumed to exist between the Fed's actions and the state of the economy, but this is based on debatable premises. Even if the Fed is able to influence monetary and financial conditions, it may not achieve what are known in economic jargon as "goal variables," such as price stability, full employment, and economic growth. Although conventional economic wisdom is that the rate of growth of money supply influences the rate of inflation, the relationship is not precise enough to be manipulated through the tools wielded by the Fed.

The Fed did not have a clear long-term strategy for monetary policy before the 1970s. However, the growing influence of monetarist doctrine among economists as well as legislators led to the passage in 1975 of House Concurrent Resolution 133, requiring the Fed to manage the longer-term growth of monetary and credit aggregates and keep that growth consistent with the nation's broad economic goals. In 1978 the Full Employment and Balanced Growth (Humphrey-Hawkins) Act made the resolution into law. In accordance with this act the Fed has established targets for growth of various monetary and credit aggregates. At its meeting in February of each year, the FOMC sets target ranges for three monetary aggregates, M1, M2, and M3, and a monitoring range for one credit aggregate, domestic nonfinancial debt outstanding, for the period running from the fourth quarter of the preceding year to the fourth quarter of the current year. The base for each target range is the actual level of the relevant aggregate in the fourth quarter of the preceding year. These targets are normally set as growth rates, and the widths of the ranges have generally been three or four percentage points, sometimes wider. The committee may make several changes in specific targets in its July meeting, changing both the percentage growth rates and the base period.

The Fed uses three principal instruments in the conduct of day-to-day monetary policy: 1) open market operations, 2) the discount rate, and 3) reserve requirements. Of these the most important are open market operations, which are simply purchases and sales of securities in the open and bond markets. The purpose of these purchases and sales is to affect the aggregate reserve position of depository institutions. The vast majority of the operations are carried out using Treasury securities. Factors other than open market operations continuously influence the aggregate reserve position of the depository institutions. These include an increase in the public demand for currency, as happens before Christmas, large payments by the federal government for the purchase of goods and services, and a large influx of money into the Treasury, as on 15 April. The Fed carries out the majority of its operations with forty so-called primary securities dealers, about a third of which are departments of large money center banks, and the remainder securities brokerage houses. The Fed makes most of its transactions using an auction-like procedure. The Fed can also affect reserves through financial dealings with foreign central banks.

The second instrument of monetary policy is the discount rate, that is, the interest rate charged for withdrawals from the Fed's discount window by depository institutions making short-term adjustments. Although most loans were dis-

counted formerly, such loans are now generally advances secured by acceptable collateral. Each of the twelve Federal Reserve Banks has a discount window, and the boards of directors of the respective banks set the rates subject to the approval of the Fed Board of Governors. These rates are uniform across the country except for brief transitional differences when the rates are being readjusted. The Fed uses the discount rate to reinforce its efforts to manage reserves through open market operations.

The third instrument of monetary policy is the reserve requirement. Under current law all depository institutions must hold required reserves against their net transaction accounts, nonpersonal time deposits, and Eurocurrency liabilities. The Board of Governors sets the requirements within specific ranges for each category of reservable liabilities.

The process by which the Fed arrives at its decisions begins with the meeting of the FOMC. The FOMC holds eight regular meetings each year, attended by voting members as well as nonvoting presidents of the regional banks and senior advisers. Prior to the meeting all members receive the Green Book and the Blue Book and other documents. The Green Book contains comprehensive macroeconomic and financial projections for upcoming quarters. The Blue Book summarizes recent financial and monetary data and includes a set of two or three alternative directives or operating instructions to the manager of domestic operations. The Blue Book may also present alternative sets of ranges for monetary aggregates together with projections of important economic variables, such as growth of real gross national product. At the end of the meeting the FOMC considers and votes on a written short-term directive to the manager of the Desk to guide open market operations until the next meeting. Each directive is about six paragraphs long. The first few paragraphs provide background financial and economic information; a later paragraph states long-term target ranges for the monetary and credit aggregates and any special circumstances relevant to these ranges; the last and key paragraph contains the detailed short-run operational instructions to the manager. It is this paragraph that financial market watchers analyze closely to find some clue as to the Fed's intentions. The other policy-making process relates to the setting of the discount rate every fourteen days. Once approved by the Board of Governors, discount rate changes are announced late in the afternoon, after financial markets have closed, to minimize disruption.

On occasion the Fed also carries out certain foreign currency operations that directly affect exchange rates. These operations are conducted by the manager for foreign operations at the Federal Reserve Bank of New York according to a Foreign Currency Directive established by the FOMC. The Fed's foreign currency operations have been greatly facilitated in recent years by the so-called Swap network of reciprocal currency exchange arrangements under which the Fed can acquire foreign currencies from its counterparts abroad to support the dollar in foreign exchange markets.

[*See also* Treasury, Department of the.]

BIBLIOGRAPHY

Broaddus, Alfred. *A Primer on the Fed*. Richmond, 1988.
Greider, William. *Secrets of the Temple: How the Federal Reserve Runs the Country*. New York, 1989.
Jones, David M. *Politics of Money*. New York, 1991.
Kettl, Donald. *Leadership at the Fed*. New Haven, Conn., 1986.
Woolley, John T. *Monetary Politics: The Federal Reserve and the Politics of Monetary Policy*. New York, 1984.

—GEORGE THOMAS KURIAN

Federal Trade Commission

 The objective of the Federal Trade Commission (FTC) is to ensure that the nation's markets function competitively and are free of undue restrictions. The commission works to eliminate unfair or deceptive practices by enforcing a variety of federal antitrust and consumer protection laws. For example, the Federal Trade Commission Act prohibits exclusionary practices such as price fixing, tie-in selling of two separate commodities, reciprocity, price discrimination, and vertical mergers. Such practices may be either signs of vigorous competition or monopolistic tactics. It has been the commission's responsibility to develop "special competence" to distinguish between the two tactics because they have the potential to exclude competitors from certain outlets in the marketplace and affect consumer choices.

THE BEGINNING OF ANTITRUST LEGISLATION

The commission's antitrust enforcement authority comes from two sources: the Federal Trade Commission Act and the Clayton Act, both passed by Congress in 1914. Protective government regulation, however, did not begin with the passage of the 1914 legislation. Congress enacted the Clayton Act to further strengthen antitrust legislation passed in 1890 under the Sherman Antitrust Act. The Sherman Antitrust Act sought to regulate trusts created to achieve monopolies in the provision of various goods. But this antitrust legislation was weak in that it only referred to present conspiracies. The Clayton Act, on the other hand, would deal futuristically with conduct whose effect might be to lessen competition substantially.

Although the FTC opened its doors in March 1915, the agency's history actually began in 1903, when Congress created a Bureau of Corporations within the newly created Department of Commerce and Labor. The bureau's function was to investigate possible abuses by industrial corporations engaged in interstate commerce and to make public reports on the findings of its investigations. Many of these reports raised the issue of unfair competition. By 1912 a movement began in Congress when Senator Newlands originated a bill to create an Interstate Trade Commission. The new agency that Newlands proposed was necessary largely because the bureau could not rectify the conditions it disclosed.

Newlands's bill, however, languished in Congress for two years until President Woodrow Wilson adopted the idea as part of his program for the federal government. (It was renamed the FTC before the passage of the final bill, to avoid confusion with the Interstate Commerce Commission.) Wilson did not view the agency as a dangerous experiment in government regulation as some in Congress and those in the business community had argued, but rather as a safe and sensible agency created to define unfair methods of competition. Such a commission would serve to provide "information and publicity, as a clearing house for the facts by which both the public mind and managers of great business undertakings should be guided." The new trade commission would work to prevent monopoly in its incipiency through the use of cease-and-desist orders. The government's top prosecuting agency, the Department of Justice, would deal with any individual or company found to be engaged in such unfair practices.

The cease-and-desist order, however, proved an ineffectual weapon against outright violations of the Sherman Antitrust Act. Conduct illegal under the Sherman Antitrust Act also violates section five of the Federal Trade Commission Act. Therefore, in 1938, Congress strengthened the law by making failure to obey a commission order punishable by a civil penalty of up to $5,000 for each violation. This would apply to all commission orders, even those against enterprises as small as candy lotteries.

PRESIDENTIAL AUTHORITY AND THE COMMISSION

Upon taking office in 1933, Democratic president Franklin D. Roosevelt, frustrated by holdover Republican members of independent regulatory commissions, tried to assert control by notifying a Republican member of the FTC, former Representative William E. Humphrey (R-Wash.), that his services were no longer desired. The commissioner responded to the president's order with a lawsuit in order to keep his job. The Supreme Court decided the case in Humphrey's favor after his death in the 1934 decision *Rathbun* (Humphrey's Executor) *v. United States*. The Court reasoned that commission members who adjudicate cases, and who thus wield quasi-judicial power, should be free from fear of the reprisal of removal if their decisions displease the president.

Thus the Court established that the commission was to be relatively free from the most potent presidential influence of all—removal. The president's authority over the independent commissions would remain confined to his power to appoint their members, who would then be beyond the reach of his dismissal power in most circumstances. Although presidential authority

in the appointment process may be limited, there is some congressional oversight. For example, Congress monitors the FTC and controls its budget.

Today the FTC, headquartered in Washington, D.C., has four commissioners and a chairperson. The chairperson is a presidential appointment that requires the advice and consent of the Senate. In addition to the Washington office, there are ten regional offices located in Atlanta, Chicago, Dallas, Los Angeles, San Francisco, Boston, Cleveland, Denver, New York, and Seattle. FTC regional offices frequently sponsor conferences for small businesses, local authorities, and consumer groups on concerns in the marketplace for the commission. Additionally, the regional offices conduct investigations and litigation, provide advice to state and local officials on the competitive implications of proposed actions, recommend cases, provide local outreach services to consumers and business persons, and coordinate activities with local, state, and regional authorities.

VIOLATIONS OF ANTITRUST LAWS

To detect violations of antitrust laws in the United States, there are two agencies, the Department of Justice's Antitrust Division and the FTC. But how do the two agencies "detect" antitrust violations? Detection relies almost entirely on complaints that, for the most part, come from business people, but also from consumers and others who feel they have been injured by firms. The FTC may begin an investigation in several different ways. Letters from businesses, congressional inquiries, or articles on consumer or economic subjects may trigger an action by the FTC. However, letters from consumers are often the first indication of a problem in the marketplace and may provide the initial evidence to begin an investigation. Although the agency cannot act to resolve individual problems, it can act when it sees a pattern of possible law violations. When an investigation does occur, it may be either public or nonpublic. Generally, FTC investigations are nonpublic in order to protect both the investigation and the company. If the FTC believes a violation of the law occurred, it may attempt to obtain voluntary compliance by entering into a consent order with the company. Consent orders settle many matters. A consent order occurs when the commission and the respondent agree to the entry of an order and upon its terms. Under this procedure, conducted by both field offices and central bureaus, formal proceedings terminate with the entry of an agreed-upon order, subject to the approval of the commission. A company that signs a consent order does not necessarily admit to violating the law, but it must agree to stop the disputed practices outlined in an accompanying complaint.

The FTC may issue an administrative complaint if the two parties fail to reach a consent agreement. After issuing an administrative complaint, a formal proceeding similar to a court trial begins before an administrative law judge with evidence submitted, testimony heard, and witnesses examined and cross-examined. If a law violation is found, the commission will issue a cease-and-desist order or other appropriate relief. Plaintiffs have the right of appeal before the full commission following initial decisions by administrative judges.

If relief cannot be found, plaintiffs have the right to appeal to the United States Supreme Court after final decisions are issued by the commission. If the Supreme Court upholds the commission's position, the FTC, in certain circumstances, may then seek consumer redress in court. If the company ever violates the order, the commission may also seek civil penalties or an injunction. In some circumstances, the FTC can go directly to court to obtain an injunction, civil penalties, or consumer redress. This usually happens in cases of ongoing consumer fraud. By going directly to court, the FTC can stop the fraud before it affects a large number of consumers.

In addition to the litigious path of consent orders, the commission can also issue a trade regulation rule. When issued, these rules have the force of law. If the FTC staff finds evidence of unfair or deceptive practices in an entire industry, it can recommend that the commission begin a rule-making proceeding. Throughout the rule-making proceeding, the public may attend hearings and file written comments. The commission considers these comments along with the entire rule-making record—the hearing testimony, the staff reports, and the presiding officer's report—before making a final decision on the proposed rule. Although it has the force of law, an FTC rule can undergo the appellate process in any of the U.S. Courts of Appeal.

ENFORCEMENT OF ANTITRUST LAWS

The FTC's Bureau of Competition and the Antitrust Division of the Department of Justice enforce violations of antitrust laws. The Bureau of Competition is responsible for the development of cases from the initial investigatory phase (usually assigned to a field office) for the trial before an administrative law judge and for the appeal, held before the full commission.

The bureau's attorneys carry out the commission's enforcement directives in federal court and before administrative law judges. The bureau also promotes competition by participating in an advocacy program through which the commission's three operating bureaus file briefs with the courts and present comments to other government agencies.

The Department of Justice, on the other hand, focuses to a large extent on those activities that warrant criminal penalties. Before beginning an investigation, the FTC and the Justice Department agree which agency will conduct the government's antitrust review.

CONSUMER PROTECTION

Although the FTC protects the competition when it focuses on preventing unfair business practices, it also protects the consumer. In general, the commission's efforts are directed toward stopping actions that threaten consumers' opportunities to exercise an informed choice. The FTC has developed expertise in those segments of the economy in which consumers make a substantial portion of their expenditure, such as health care, other professional services, food, and energy. In fact, the FTC has attacked the practices of large firms since its inception. It has entered orders, for example, against the Aluminum Company of America, General Motors, and the Ford Motor Company. Additionally, the commission successfully sought to impose a trade regulation rule on cigarette manufacturers requiring health warnings well before the wave of adverse criticism that appeared in the early 1960s following the surgeon general's report.

The commission also scrutinizes advertising. Viewing advertising as a major means of competition, the FTC used its original mandate to prevent unfair methods of competition by bringing cases against firms that engaged in deceptive advertising aimed at specific rivals and competing products. Beginning in 1971 the commission developed several new remedies and a new technique to elicit information and deter extravagant advertising claims. The new remedies included orders of corrective or retroactive advertising and orders of restitution or repayment; the new technique is to treat a claim that an advertiser does not substantiate as an unfair act, thus apparently shifting the burden of proof. Such consent orders have usually required that a business devote a given percentage of advertising time to the corrective advertisement. Some orders, on the other hand, have required respondents to advertise corrections, as in the case of alleged false claims by trade associations.

To accomplish its objectives for the consumer, the FTC utilizes a second internal bureau, the Bureau of Consumer Protection. The bureau enforces a variety of consumer protection laws enacted by Congress, as well as trade regulation rules issued by the commission. The bureau seeks to protect consumers against unfair, deceptive, or fraudulent practices through individual company and industrywide investigations, administrative and federal court litigation, rule-making proceedings, and consumer and business education. In addition, the bureau contributes to the commission's ongoing efforts to inform Congress and other government entities of the impact that proposed actions could have on consumers. The Bureau of Consumer Protection has five divisions, each with its own area of expertise: The Division of Advertising Practices protects consumers from deceptive and unsubstantiated advertising, and the Division of Credit Practices enforces many of the nation's consumer credit statutes, including (but not limited to) the Equal Credit Opportunity Act, the Fair Credit Reporting Act, and the Truth in Lending Act. The third division, called the Division of Enforce-

ment, monitors compliance with cease-and-desist orders issued by the commission and enforces a number of laws and trade regulation rules, including the Mail or Telephone Merchandise Rule, the Care Labeling Rule, and the Negative Option Rule. All these rules require proper disclosure by makers of products regarding purchases.

The Division of Marketing Practices also engages in enforcement activities; however, it concentrates on various marketing and warranty practices, such as fraudulent telemarketing schemes, 900-number telephone programs, and the Magnuson-Moss Act, which requires that warranty information be available before a purchase is made. Additionally, the division enforces the Franchise and Business Opportunities Rule, which requires certain business disclosures before selling a franchise, and the Funeral Rule, which requires funeral directors to disclose price and other information about funeral goods and services. Finally, the Division of Service Industry Practices addresses a variety of consumer frauds and market failures that impose substantial costs on consumers. Specific enforcement activities focus on consumer fraud owing to deceptive advertising or marketing, and anticompetitive and deceptive practices in the writing and implementation of industry standards and certification programs. Finally, the division also enforces the court orders it obtains through the prosecution of contempt actions, and it frequently assists other law enforcement authorities in the prosecution of law violations.

The third and final bureau, the Bureau of Economics, provides analysis and support to antitrust and consumer protection casework and rule-making. It also analyzes the impact of government economic regulation on competition and consumers and when requested provides Congress and the executive branch with economic analyses of various aspects of the American industrial economy. All three bureaus participate in an advocacy program wherein they present comments to other agencies concerning the effect of regulation on competition and consumers. The advocacy program has recently taken up such topics as the effects of significant

U.S. import restraints on manufacturing, food labeling regulations, and certificate-of-need regulation in the health care field.

In addition to the three bureaus, the federal agency comprises seven offices. The Office of Congressional Relations works closely with members of Congress and their staffs and provides information to the commissioners and the FTC staff regarding Capitol Hill issues, policies, and pending legislation. It also coordinates the preparation of both congressional testimony and responses to congressional inquiries concerning FTC policies and programs.

For example, in the 1960s the agency began to focus on corporate mergers. In 1962 the FTC instituted an advisory program for the business community designed to provide legal opinion as to whether prospective courses of conduct were likely to violate a law administered by the commission. The agency required that the FTC receive notification in advance of certain types of mergers. By 1965 the commission had issued policy statements on particular industries, the purpose of which was to establish guidelines on various types of questionable mergers.

The Office of Public Affairs provides information to the public through the media. It issues news releases on all significant commission actions, responds to inquiries, and arranges media interviews for FTC officials. The Office of General Counsel is the FTC's chief legal adviser. The office's major functions are representing the commission in court and providing legal counsel to the commission, operating bureaus, and other offices.

The Office of the Secretary is the commission's "court clerk," responsible for implementing the commission's voting procedures, creating official records, and coordinating the preparation of responses to congressional constituent inquiries. The Office of the Executive Director is the FTC's chief operating manager, responsible for such administrative matters as budget, personnel, policy planning, and information management. The office also handles all initial requests for information under the Freedom of Information Act. [See Appendix: Freedom of Information Act.] Although enforcement activities are cleared through appropriate bureaus, the commission's regional offices operate under the general agreement of the executive director.

The Office of the Inspector General acts as the "agency cop" and is responsible for the detection and prevention of waste, fraud, and abuse in the agency programs. The inspector general conducts audits and investigates allegations of wrongdoing within the agency.

The Office of Consumer and Competition Advocacy oversees the advocacy program. The program shares its consumer and competition expertise as requested by other government and self-regulatory entities concerning the possible effects of their proposed actions on consumers and competition. It coordinates the efforts of the bureaus and regional offices in preparing testimony, comments, and amicus curiae ("friend of the court") briefs for presentation to federal, state, local, and self-regulatory agencies, legislative bodies, and courts. At the request of lawmakers or agency officials, the division provides comments to assist legislatures' consideration of pending bills or to assist agency rule-making proceedings.

Finally, the commission undertakes economic analysis to support its law enforcement efforts and to contribute to the policy deliberations of Congress, the executive branch, and independent agencies. In addition to carrying out its statutory enforcement responsibilities, the commission advances the policies underlying congressional mandates through cost-effective nonenforcement activities such as consumer education. The commission also provides assistance to state and local governments when requested.

[See also Food and Drug Administration.]

BIBLIOGRAPHY

Bork, Robert H. *The Antitrust Paradox: A Policy at War with Itself.* New York, 1978.

Breyer, Stephen. *Regulation and Its Reform.* Cambridge, Mass., 1982.

Bring, Danny A. "Origins of the Federal Trade Commission Act: A Public Choice Approach." Ph.D. diss., George Mason University, 1993.

Federal Trade Commission Documents. Washington, D.C., 1996.

Franklin, Grace A., and R. B. Ripley. *Congress, the Bureaucracy, and Public Policy.* Chicago, 1987.

Friedman, Barry D. *Regulation in the Reagan-Bush Era: The Eruption of Presidential Influence.* Pittsburgh, 1995.

Grieson, Ronald E., ed. *Antitrust and Regulation.* Lexington, Mass., 1986.

Harris, Richard A., and S. M. Milkis. *The Politics of Regulatory Change: A Tale of Two Agencies.* New York, 1989.

Miller, James Clifford. *The Economist as Reformer: Revamping the FTC.* Washington, D.C., 1988.

Phillips, Almarin. *Perspectives on Antitrust Policy.* Princeton, N.J., 1965.

Rourke, Francis E. *Bureaucracy, Politics, and Public Policy.* Boston, 1984.

Stone, Alan. *Economic Regulation and the Public Interest: The Federal Trade Commission in Theory and Practice.* Ithaca, N.Y., 1977.

—Veronica D. DiConti

Federal Transit Administration.

See Transit Administration, Federal.

Financial Management Service

 One of the oldest and most basic functions of the Department of the Treasury—receipt, custody, and disbursement of public monies, maintenance of government accounts, and preparation of monthly reports on the status of government finances—is the responsibility of the Financial Management Service (FMS). These functions were originally performed by the treasurer and the register of the Treasury. By an act of 2 September 1789 the treasurer was charged with receiving, keeping, and disbursing public money; the register was responsible for keeping the accounts of these receipts and expenditures (1 Stat. 66, 67). (In the late nineteenth century the register was a prominent African American, Blanche K. Bruce. The Register's Office was abolished in 1956.)

In 1920 the Office of the Commissioner of Accounts and Deposits was established by Treasury Secretary Carter Glass. By Executive Order 6166 of 10 June 1933, President Franklin Roosevelt centralized disbursing under the Treasury Department, closing twenty-two hundred disbursing offices belonging to dozens of government agencies. The new Division of Disbursement, created in December 1933, was placed under the Bureau of Accounts.

In 1940 the Fiscal Service was created by President Roosevelt's Reorganization Plan No. 3 (54 Stat. 1231), which consolidated under a fiscal assistant secretary the related functions of the Bureau of Accounts, the Bureau of the Public Debt (into which the Register's Office was incorporated), and the Office of the Treasurer of the United States. In February 1974 the Bureau of Government Financial Operations was created, incorporating both the Bureau of Accounts and the treasurer's functions. The secretary renamed the Bureau the Financial Management Service in October 1984. With the name change, the service was given broader responsibilities, including the lead role in improving cash management systems government-wide.

The FMS is responsible for the world's largest disbursal and collection system, accounting in each case for over $1.2 trillion. Each year the FMS makes over 840 million nondefense payments, forty-nine percent electronically and the remainder as Treasury checks. It maintains a network of more than fifteen thousand financial institutions to collect revenues on behalf of federal agencies. The FMS also oversees the federal government's central accounting and reporting system and keeps track of its monetary assets and liabilities. It helps federal agencies to develop uniform accounting and reporting practices. It manages over one hundred separate federal accounts and provides a wide array of financial services to government trust funds, including those of the Social Security Administration and the Federal Highway Administration. In addition, the agency gathers and publishes the Treasury's financial information, including the *Daily Treasury Statement, Monthly Treasury Statement, Treasury Bulletin,* the annual *Consolidated Financial Statement,* and the *U.S. Government Annual Report.* Three-quarters of the agency's staff of twenty-two hundred is stationed in Washington, D.C., and the rest work in one of the six regional centers located in Austin, Birmingham, Chicago, Kansas City, Philadelphia, and San Francisco.

—ABBY L. GILBERT

Fish and Wildlife Service

 The precursor of the U.S. Fish and Wildlife Service was created in 1871, when legislators of the Reconstruction Era voiced concern over the possible "diminution in the number of food fishes of the coasts and lakes of the United States." To study the issue and to regulate the fishing industry, Congress passed a resolution creating the position of commissioner of fish and fisheries within the Treasury Department. That office soon expanded to become the U.S. Fish Commission, and in 1903, with the conservation-minded Theodore Roosevelt in the White House, Congress transferred the commission's functions to a new agency, the Bureau of Fisheries, in the Department of Commerce and Labor. The bureau's primary functions were to preserve the nation's fishery resources while also promoting the domestic industry, particularly the large salmon industry of Alaska and the Pacific Northwest.

In 1924 Congress passed the White Act, giving the Bureau of Fisheries stronger regulatory authority. In 1940, as a result of President Franklin Roosevelt's reorganization of the executive branch, the Bureau of Fisheries was transferred from the Commerce Department to the Department of the Interior, as was the Agriculture Department's Bureau of Biological Survey. These two agencies were combined under Interior Secretary Harold Ickes to become the Fish and Wildlife Service. As a result of the merger, the new service became a more diversified organization whose mission was not limited solely to policing the fishing industry; it also had responsibility for protecting and managing the nation's wildlife refuges and fish hatcheries. These authorities were codified in the 1900 Lacey Act, the 1918 Migratory Bird Treaty Act with Canada, and the "Duck Stamp" and Fish and Wildlife Coordination Acts of 1934.

The union of commercial and preservation missions within a single agency proved to be unstable. Spokesmen for the fishing industry felt that their interests were being ignored, so a 1956 congressional statute created two separate agencies within the Interior Department, a Bureau of Commercial Fisheries and a Bureau of Sports Fisheries. In 1970 the Bureau of Commercial Fisheries was transferred back from whence it came, to the Commerce Department, while the Bureau of Sports Fisheries was renamed, again, the Fish and Wildlife Service. The present agency is thus descended from what one scholar referred to as a "roving parentage."

The Fish and Wildlife Service today has primary responsibility for managing a national wildlife refuge system composed of nearly five hundred separate units. The system encompasses ninety-one million acres, with approximately eighty-five percent of the total acreage found in three large Alaskan refuges: the Arctic, Yukon Flats, and Yukon Delta. Most of the lands in the refuge system are managed to accommodate a variety of wildlife-oriented public recreational activities, including fishing, hunting, birdwatching, and hiking. In addition, the agency manages about seventy national fish hatcheries where basic and applied research is conducted. The service also acts as a coordinator, or liaison, with other federal agencies and with state and local governments on fish and wildlife issues. Since the 1970 reorganization the agency describes its general mission as one of conserving, protecting, and enhancing fish, wildlife, and their habitats for the continuing benefit of the American people.

The director of the Fish and Wildlife Service is nominated by the president and confirmed by the Senate. As compared with other federal resource-managing agencies, the service is small: its annual operating budget through the 1990s has been in the $700-million range and its permanent work force numbers seventy-four hundred. Agency officials observe that a chronic problem for the Fish and Wildlife Service has been an imbalance between its congressionally mandated responsibilities and the resources it is given to carry them out.

The agency's work force and budget were reduced in 1993 when Secretary Bruce Babbitt reorganized the Interior Department and created, by secretarial order, the National Biological Service. Although some personnel from other agencies within the department were transferred to the new agency, the majority came from the Fish and Wildlife Service. Significant opposition to the National Biological Service has surfaced in Congress, however; thus it appears doubtful that the new agency will survive for very long.

As its chaotic organizational history implies, the Fish and Wildlife Service frequently has been at the center of controversy regarding resource use and protection. With the passage of the National Environmental Policy Act of 1969, the Federal Water Pollution Control Act amendments of 1972, and the Endangered Species Act of 1973, the service's role in environmental protection increased greatly. Under these statutes the agency became responsible for reviewing federal environmental impact statements, for assisting in the preservation of wetlands, and for listing endangered and threatened species of flora and fauna in the United States.

One of the earliest controversies over endangered species occurred in the 1970s in the case of the Tennessee Valley Authority's construction of the Tellico Dam and its potential impact upon the snail darter. The highly publicized case, which pitted environmentalists against public power developers, ultimately was heard by the Supreme Court. While the Court, citing the Endangered Species Act, found in favor of preserving the habitat of the fish, Congress subsequently passed an amendment exempting the snail darter and therefore allowing the construction of the Tellico Dam. A more recent controversy involving the Fish and Wildlife Service's listing of endangered species concerns the spotted owl and its habitat in the forests of the Pacific Northwest. A resolution of this case to the satisfaction of the timber industry, the rural communities that are dependent on logging for their survival, and the environmentalists has yet to be found.

Because so much local controversy has been generated by these national environmental protection statutes, both the 104th Congress and the Clinton administration are working with the Fish and Wildlife Service and other federal resource agencies on streamlining the regulatory process. Whatever reforms emerge from the "reinventing government" effort will be codified in the legislation to reauthorize the Clean Water and Endangered Species Acts. These statutes are likely to create a new role for the Fish and Wildlife Service with respect to habitat protection on private property, but they also will likely continue the agency's authority to manage the nation's ninety-one million acres of wildlife refuges and its fish hatcheries.

BIBLIOGRAPHY

Clarke, Jeanne Nienaber, and Daniel McCool. *Staking Out the Terrain: Power and Performance in Natural Resource Agencies.* 2d ed. Albany, 1996.
Cooley, Richard A. *Politics and Conservation: The Decline and Fall of the Alaskan Salmon.* New York, 1963.
Simon, Benjamin, Craig Leff, and Harvey Doerksen. "Allocating Scarce Resources for Endangered Species Recovery" *Journal of Policy Analysis and Management* 14 (Summer 1995): 415–32.
Yaffe, Steven Lewis. *The Wisdom of the Spotted Owl.* Washington, D.C., 1994.

—JEANNE NIENABER CLARKE

Food and Drug Administration

The jurisdiction of the U.S. Food and Drug Administration (FDA)—a scientific, regulatory, and public health agency that oversees items accounting for twenty-five cents of every dollar spent by consumers—encompasses most food products (other than meat and poultry), human and animal drugs, therapeutic agents of biological origin, medical devices, radiation-emitting products for consumer, medical, and occupational use, cosmetics, and animal feed. The agency grew from a single chemist in the U.S. Department of Agriculture in 1862 to a staff of approximately ninety-three hundred employees and a budget of $856 million in 1994, comprising chemists, pharmacologists, physicians, microbiologists, veterinarians, pharmacists, lawyers, and others. About one-third of the agency's employees are stationed outside the Washington, D.C., area, staffing field offices and laboratories in six regional offices, twenty-one district offices, and 130 resident posts. The FDA monitors the manufacture, import, transport, storage, and sale of about $1 trillion worth of products annually at a cost to taxpayers of about $3 per person. Investigators and inspectors visit more than fifteen thousand facilities a year, collecting approximately eighty thousand samples for examination. Beginning as the Division of Chemistry and then (after July 1901) the Bureau of Chemistry, the modern era of the FDA dates to 1906 with the passage of the Pure Food and Drugs Act; this added regulatory functions to the agency's scientific mission.

The Bureau of Chemistry's name changed to the Food, Drug, and Insecticide Administration in July 1927, when the nonregulatory research functions of the bureau were transferred elsewhere in the department. In July 1930 the name was shortened to the present version. The FDA remained under the Department of Agriculture until June 1940, when the agency was moved to the new Federal Security Agency. In April 1953 the agency again was transferred, to the Department of Health, Education, and Welfare (HEW). Fifteen years later the FDA became part of the Public Health Service within HEW, and in May 1980 the education function was removed from HEW to create the Department of Health and Human Services, the FDA's current home. To understand the development of this agency is to understand the laws it regulates, how the FDA has administered these laws, how the courts have interpreted the legislation, and how major events have driven all three.

ORIGINS

States exercised the principal control over domestically produced and distributed foods and drugs in the nineteenth century, control that was markedly inconsistent from state to state. Federal authority was limited mostly to imported foods and drugs. Adulteration and misbranding of foods and drugs had long been a fixture in the American cultural landscape, though the egregiousness of the problems seemed to have increased by the late nineteenth century (or at least they became more identifiable). By this time science had advanced significantly in its ability to detect this sort of fraud. Also, legitimate manufacturers were becoming more concerned that their trade would be undermined by purveyors of deceitful goods. Quinine-containing cinchona bark powder could be made less therapeutically effective—and much more profitable—by cutting it with just about anything, alum and clay masked poor wheat flour and thus netted a heftier return for the unethical company, and sufferers of any number of serious or self-limited diseases were relieved only of their finances by vendors of worthless nostrums. Even the so-called ethical drug firms were guilty of this practice.

The Division of Chemistry began investigating the adulteration of agricultural commodities as early as 1867. When Harvey Washington Wiley arrived as chief chemist in 1883, the government's handling of the adulteration and misbranding of food and drugs took a decidedly different course, which eventually helped spur public indignation at the problem. Wiley expanded the division's research in this area, exemplified by *Foods and Food Adulterants*, a ten-part study published from 1887 to 1902. He demonstrated his concern about chemical preservatives as adulterants in the highly publicized "poison squad" experiments, in which able-bodied volunteers consumed varying amounts of questionable food additives to determine their impact on health. And Wiley unified a variety of groups behind a federal law to prohibit the adulteration and misbranding of food and drugs, including state chemists and food and drug inspectors, the General Federation of Women's Clubs, and national associations of physicians and pharmacists.

While Wiley was stumping for a law, muckraking journalists such as Samuel Hopkins Adams exposed in vivid detail the hazards of the marketplace. In fact, the nauseating condition of the meat-packing industry that Upton Sinclair captured in *The Jungle* was the final precipitating force behind both a meat inspection law and a comprehensive food and drug law. Since 1879 nearly one hundred bills had been introduced in Congress to regulate food and drugs; on 30 June 1906 President Roosevelt signed the Pure Food and Drugs Act, known simply as the Wiley Act, a pillar of the Progressive Era.

This Act, which the Bureau of Chemistry was charged to administer, prohibited the interstate transport of unlawful food and drugs under penalty of seizure of the questionable products and/or prosecution of the responsible parties. The basis of the law rested on the regulation of product labeling rather than pre-market approval. Drugs, defined in accordance with the standards of strength, quality, and purity in the *United States Pharmacopoeia* and the *National Formulary,* could not be sold in any other condition unless the specific variations from the applicable standards were plainly stated on the label. Foods were not defined according to analogous standards, but the law prohibited the addition of any ingredients that would substitute for the food, conceal damage, pose a health hazard, or constitute a filthy or decomposed substance. Interpretations of the food provisions in the law led to many, sometimes protracted, court battles. If the manufacturer opted to list the weight or measure of a food, this had to be done accurately. Also, the food or drug label could not be false or misleading in any particular, and the presence and amount of eleven dangerous ingredients, including alcohol, heroin, and cocaine, had to be listed.

The bureau's regulatory emphasis under Wiley centered on foods, which he believed posed a greater public health problem than adulterated or misbranded drugs. Wiley generally held a dim view of chemical additives to foods, championing an approach that considered most to be unnecessary adulterants. On this he clashed often with Secretary of Agriculture James Wilson, and on occasion President Roosevelt himself had to decide government policy on food regulation. Wiley's personal administrative authority under the act was diluted early on when Wilson created

a Board of Food and Drug Inspection in 1907 to establish agency policy in enforcing the law. Similarly, the creation of the Referee Board of Consulting Scientific Experts in the following year to advise the department on safety issues associated with food additives undercut Wiley's scientific authority. The bureau had been developing informal standards for many foods in collaboration with outside experts since 1903, an activity that continued throughout the period. However, courts differed on the role these informal standards could play in cases. Separate laws established standards for some specific foods, such as apples and butter, as well as for canned foods.

After Wiley's resignation in 1912, the bureau devoted more effort to drug regulation, with some emphasis on the so-called patent medicines. While the law was much clearer about drug standards than standards for foods, misbranding was the source of considerable controversy in the regulation of drugs. A year earlier the Supreme Court ruled that the law did not—contrary to the government's interpretation—apply to false therapeutic claims. An amendment in the year of Wiley's resignation attempted to correct the language of the law but put the bureau in the difficult position of attempting to prove in court that manufacturers of drugs labeled with false therapeutic claims intended to defraud consumers. The bureau lost several cases against egregious products, but seizures of misbranded and adulterated drugs nevertheless increased in the 1920s and 1930s.

With the election of Franklin Roosevelt and the death in 1930 of the embodiment of the 1906 act—Wiley—the FDA now had a receptive ear to petition for needed changes in the law: legally mandated quality and identity standards for foods, prohibition of false therapeutic claims for drugs, coverage of cosmetics and medical devices, clarification of the FDA's right to conduct factory inspections, and control of product advertising, among other items. A new generation of muckraking journalists and consumer protection organizations aided in pushing a reluctant Congress to sponsor a bill to replace the old law. The FDA itself exemplified the state of affairs in the marketplace by assembling a collection of products that illustrated shortcomings in the

1906 law. It included Banbar, a worthless "cure" for diabetes that the old law protected; Lash-Lure, an eyelash dye that blinded many women; numerous examples of foods deceptively packaged or labeled; Radithor, a radium-containing tonic that sentenced users to a slow and painful death; and the Wilhide Exhaler, which falsely promised to cure tuberculosis and other pulmonary diseases. A reporter dubbed this exhibit "the American Chamber of Horrors," a title not far from the truth since all the products exhibited were legal under the existing law.

Languishing in Congress for five years, the bill that would replace the 1906 law was ultimately enhanced and passed in the wake of a therapeutic disaster in 1937. A Tennessee drug company marketed a form of the new sulfa wonder drug that would appeal to pediatric patients, Elixir Sulfanilamide. However, the solvent in this untested product was a highly toxic chemical analogue of antifreeze; over one hundred people died, most of whom were children. The public outcry not only reshaped the drug provisions of the new law to prevent such an event from happening again, it propelled the bill itself through Congress. FDR signed the Food, Drug, and Cosmetic Act on 25 June 1938.

THE MODERN FDA

The new law brought cosmetics and medical devices under control, and it required that drugs be labeled with adequate directions for safe use. Moreover, it mandated pre-market approval of all new drugs, such that a manufacturer would have to prove to the FDA that a drug were safe before it could be sold. It irrefutably prohibited false therapeutic claims for drugs, although a separate law granted the Federal Trade Commission jurisdiction over drug advertising. The act also corrected abuses in food packaging and quality, and it mandated legally enforceable food standards. Tolerances for certain poisonous substances were addressed. The law formally authorized factory inspections, and it added injunctions to the enforcement tools at the agency's disposal.

Enforcement of the new law came swiftly. Within two months of the passage of the act, the FDA began to identify drugs such as the sulfas

that simply could not be labeled for safe use directly by the patient—they would require a prescription from a physician. The ensuing debate by the FDA, industry, and health practitioners over what constituted a prescription and an over-the-counter drug was resolved in the Durham-Humphrey Amendment of 1951. From the 1940s to the 1960s, the abuse of amphetamines and barbiturates required more regulatory effort by the FDA than all other drug problems combined. Furthermore, the new law ushered in a flood of new drug applications, over six thousand in the first nine years, and thirteen thousand by 1962.

A new drug law in that year, the Kefauver-Harris Amendments, derived in large part from hearings held by Senator Estes Kefauver. As with the 1938 act, a therapeutic disaster compelled passage of the new law; in this case the disaster was narrowly averted. Thalidomide, a sedative that was never approved in this country, produced thousands of grossly deformed newborns outside the United States. The new law mandated efficacy as well as safety before a drug could be marketed, required the FDA to assess the efficacy of all drugs introduced since 1938, instituted stricter agency control over drug trials (including a requirement that patients involved must give their informed consent), transferred from the Federal Trade Commission to the FDA regulation of prescription drug advertising, established good manufacturing practices by the drug industry, and granted the FDA greater powers to access company production and control records to verify those practices. Three years later Congress gave the FDA enhanced control over amphetamines, barbiturates, hallucinogens, and other drugs of considerable abuse potential in the Drug Abuse Control Amendments of 1965, a function that was consolidated within the predecessor of the Drug Enforcement Administration in 1968.

The first food standards to be issued under the 1938 act were for canned tomato products; by the 1960s about half of the food supply was subject to a standard. As food technology changed and the number of possible ingredients—including fortifying nutrients—grew, the agency developed recipe standards for foods, lists of ingredients that could lawfully be included in a product. A product that varied from the recipe would have to be labeled an imitation. Following hearings in the early 1950s under Representative James Delaney, a series of laws addressing pesticide residues (1954), food additives (1958), and color additives (1960) gave the FDA much tighter control over the growing list of chemicals entering the food supply, putting the onus on manufacturers to establish their safety. While tolerances could be established for many chemicals, a provision of the 1958 law, the Delaney Clause, banned any carcinogenic additive.

The FDA pursued numerous cases of food misbranding in the 1950s and 1960s, most deriving from false nutritional claims and unscientific enrichment, with mixed success in the courts. In 1973, following hearings the agency convened to address the vitamin fortification of foods and the claims made for dietary supplements, the FDA issued regulations for special dietary foods, including vitamins and minerals. The public response to these regulations helped lead Congress in 1976 to prohibit the FDA from controlling the potency of dietary supplements, although the agency maintained authority to regulate enriched foods.

Cosmetics and medical devices, which the Post Office Department and the Federal Trade Commission had overseen to a limited extent before 1938, came under FDA authority as well after 1938. While pre-market approval did not apply to devices, in every other sense the new law equated them to drugs for regulatory purposes. As the FDA had to deal with both increasing medical device quackery and a proliferation of medical technology in the post–World War II years, Congress considered a comparable device law when it passed the 1962 drug amendments. The legistlation having failed to develop, the secretary of HEW commissioned the Study Group on Medical Devices, which recommended in 1970 that medical devices be classified according to their comparative risk and regulated accordingly. The 1976 Medical Device Amendments, coming on the heels of a therapeutic disaster in which thousands of women were injured by the Dalkon Shield intrauterine device, provided for three classes of medical devices, each requiring a different level of regulatory scrutiny—up to pre-market approval.

The 1938 act required colors to be certified as harmless and suitable by the FDA for their use in cosmetics. The 1960 color amendments strengthened the safety requirement for color additives, necessitating additional testing for many existing cosmetics to meet the new safety standard. The FDA attempted to interpret the new law as applying to every ingredient of color-imparting products, such as lipstick and rouge, but the courts rebuffed this proposal.

Another agency responsibility, veterinary medicine, had been stipulated since the 1906 act; foods included animal feed, and drugs included veterinary pharmaceuticals. Likewise, animal drugs were included in the provisions for new drugs under the 1938 law and the 1962 drug amendments. However, the Food Additives Amendment of 1958 had an impact too, since drugs used in animal feed were also considered additives—and thus subject to the provisions of the food additive petition process. The Delaney Clause prohibiting carcinogenic food additives was modified by the DES proviso in 1962, named for diethylstilbestrol, a hormone used against miscarriages in humans and to promote growth in food-producing animals. The proviso permitted the use of possible carcinogens in such animals as long as residues of the product did not remain in edible tissues. The Animal Drug Amendments of 1968 combined veterinary drugs and additives into a unified approval process under the authority of the Bureau of Animal Drugs in the FDA.

In the late 1960s and 1970s the FDA lost some of its responsibilities but acquired many more. Shortly after the FDA became a part of the Public Health Service, HEW transferred several functions administered by other agencies of the Public Health Service to the FDA, including regulation of food on planes and other interstate travel carriers, control over unnecessary radiation from consumer and professional electronic products, and pre-market licensing authority for therapeutic agents of biological origins. The latter originated under the predecessor of the National Institutes of Health in the Biologics Control Act of 1902, which followed the deaths of over a dozen children from a tetanus-tainted batch of diphtheria antitoxin in St. Louis, and nine pediatric fatalities from similar circumstances in Camden, New Jersey. Congress authorized the FDA to regulate consumer products such as potential poisons, hazardous toys, and flammable fabrics in a number of laws dating back to 1927, but this function was transferred to the Consumer Product Safety Commission in 1973. [*See* Consumer Product Safety Commission.]

Changes in the work of the FDA have come rapidly in the past twenty years, shaped at least in part by political pressure, consumer activism, and industry involvement. Patient advocacy groups influenced a law to stimulate industry interest in developing so-called orphan drugs for rare diseases, and they played a role in the agency's development of accelerated techniques for drug approval, beginning with drugs for AIDS. Congress passed a law that simultaneously extended patent terms to account for time consumed by the drug approval process and facilitated the approval of generic human and animal drugs to offer a lower-cost alternative to brand-name pharmaceuticals. Recently Congress instituted procedures for industry to reimburse the FDA for review of drugs and biologics to speed the agency's evaluations.

Other laws have mandated reporting of adverse reactions to medical devices, post-market monitoring of implants and other devices that pose a serious health risk, recall authority for the FDA over medical devices, and certification and annual inspection of mammography facilities. Among food regulatory issues in the past two decades, Congress issued a singular prohibition against the FDA's banning saccharin under the Delaney Clause on the grounds that the sweetener had been shown to cause cancer in laboratory animals; instead, saccharin would have to carry a label warning. In 1990 Congress passed the Nutrition Labeling and Education Act, which completely reformulated the way food products convey basic nutritional information. Four years later, after intense lobbying by the dietary supplement industry, Congress permitted supplements to carry substantiated statements about the role of such products in health, provided they issued a disclaimer that the FDA had not

evaluated the statements. Moreover, the FDA rather than industry had the burden of proving that a dietary supplement was misbranded or adulterated.

Recent interest in reinventing government and regulatory reform has very much included the work of the FDA, with the greatest interest focusing on the agency's time spent in evaluating therapeutic and other products. These are by no means original developments, at least as far as the FDA is concerned. Numerous congressional investigations, external and internal committee reports, independent fact-finding missions, and other venues of inquiry have studied the agency's mission and needs through much of this century, precisely what one would expect for one of the oldest consumer regulatory agencies in the government, with such a broad responsibility for the public health, sometimes covering issues that have polarized large segments of American society. Such issues included sodium benzoate, sulfur dioxide, and other food preservatives during the Wiley era; Banbar in the 1930s; aminotriazole-tainted cranberries in the 1950s; vitamins in the 1970s; and breast implants in the 1990s. But these and other high visibility cases were just a small fraction of the work the agency has done, arcane to most of the public, but nevertheless a key ingredient in twentieth-century U.S. history.

[*See also* Federal Trade Commission.]

BIBLIOGRAPHY

American Institute of the History of Pharmacy. *The Early Years of Federal Food and Drug Control.* Madison, Wis., 1982.
Anderson, Oscar E., Jr. *The Health of a Nation: Harvey W. Wiley and the Fight for Pure Food.* Chicago, 1958.
Blake, John B., ed. *Safeguarding the Public: Historical Aspects of Medicinal Drug Control.* Baltimore, 1970.
Dowling, Harry F. *Medicines for Man: The Development, Regulation, and Use of Prescription Drugs.* New York, 1970.
Foote, Susan Bartlett. *Managing the Medical Arms Race: Public Policy and Medical Device Innovation.* Berkeley, Calif., 1992.
Hutt, Peter Barton. "Investigations and Reports Respecting FDA Regulation of New Drugs." *Clinical Pharmacology and Therapeutics* 33 (1983): 537–548, 674–687.
Hutt, Peter Barton. "A History of Government Regulation of Adulteration and Misbranding of Medical

Devices." *Food Drug Cosmetic Law Journal* 44 (1989): 99–117.

Hutt, Peter Barton, and Peter Barton Hutt II. "A History of Government Regulation of Adulteration and Misbranding of Food." *Food Drug Cosmetic Law Journal* 39 (1984): 2–73.

Janssen, Wallace. "Outline of the History of U.S. Drug Regulation and Labeling." *Food Drug Cosmetic Law Journal* 36 (1981): 420–441.

Levenstein, Harvey W. *Revolution at the Table: The Transformation of the American Diet.* New York, 1988.

McFadyen, Richard E. "Thalidomide in America: A Brush with Tragedy." *Clio Medica* 11, no. 2 (1976): 79–93.

Marcus, Alan I. *Cancer from Beef: DES, Federal Food Regulation, and Consumer Confidence.* Baltimore, 1994.

Marks, Harry M. *The Progress of Experiment: Science and Therapeutic Reform the United States, 1900–1990.* Cambridge, U.K., 1997.

Okun, Mitchell. *Fair Play in the Marketplace: The First Battle for Pure Food and Drugs.* De Kalb, Ill., 1986.

Soave, Orland. "History of Veterinary Medicine in the Food and Drug Administration." *Journal of the American Veterinary Medical Association* 199 (1991): 38–42.

Taylor, Michael R. "History of Cosmetic Color Additive Regulation: Creative Maneuvering by FDA Bodes Well for the Future." *Food Drug Cosmetic Law Journal* 37 (1982): 152–162.

White, Suzanne. "The Chemogastric Revolution and the Regulation of Food Chemicals." In *Chemical Sciences in the Modern World,* edited by Seymour H. Mauskopf. Philadelphia, 1993.

Whorton, James. *Before Silent Spring: Pesticides and Public Health in Pre-DDT America.* Princeton, N.J., 1974.

Young, James Harvey. *The Medical Messiahs: A Social History of Health Quackery in Twentieth-Century America.* Princeton, N.J., 1967.

Young, James Harvey. "Sulfanilamide and Diethylene Glycol." In *Chemistry and Modern Society: Historical Essays in Honor of Aaron J. Ihde,* edited by John Parascandola and James C. Whorton. Washington, D.C., 1983.

Young, James Harvey. *Pure Food: Securing the Federal Food and Drugs Act of 1906.* Princeton, N.J., 1989.

Young, James Harvey. "Federal Drug and Narcotic Legislation." *Pharmacy in History* 37 (1995): 59–67.

—JOHN P. SWANN

Food and Nutrition Service

Responsibility for a number of the nation's nutrition programs belongs to the Food and Nutrition Service (FNS), an agency of the Department of Agriculture. These include the food stamp program, the national school lunch program, the food donation program, the special supplemental food program for women, infants, and children, the nutrition program and supplemental food program for the elderly, commodity distribution to charitable institutions, and the emergency food assistance program. The FNS programs also supply milk to schoolchildren and food for day-care centers, special children's summer programs, school lunch programs, and programs for American Indians and Pacific Islanders. The FNS also sets eligibility requirements for the food stamp program, approves applications from food retailers participating in the food stamp program, establishes procedures for states, sets standards for school lunch programs, and regulates the nutritional value and composition of breakfasts and lunches served in schools. The Agricultural Marketing Service is the purchasing agent for the FNS.

[*See also* Agricultural Marketing Service.]

—GEORGE THOMAS KURIAN

Food Safety and Inspection Service

Headed by an administrator who is appointed by the secretary of agriculture, the Food Safety and Inspection Service (FSIS) is an agency within the Department of Agriculture that regulates the meat and poultry industries and inspects all meat and poultry plants that ship the products in interstate and foreign commerce. It approves the facilities, equipment, and procedures of slaughtering and processing plants and sets standards for and oversees the labeling of all food products containing more than three percent fresh meat and two percent cooked poultry meat. The Inspections Division operates a network of five regional offices, twenty-six area offices, and 185 inspection circuits. More than eight thousand inspectors monitor over eight thousand meat and poultry slaughtering and processing plants. The inspection extends to the slaughter of animals to ensure that the techniques used comply with the Humane Methods of Slaughter Act. On request the agency inspectors also certify products not subject to mandatory inspection, such as venison, buffalo, and meat and poultry products intended for use as pet food. The FSIS Meatborne Hazards Control Center deals with contamination problems arising from microbiological hazards. Under the Talmadge-Aiken Act, state employees are allowed to carry out inspections of federally inspected plants. The FSIS certifies foreign plants and assures the safety and labeling accuracy of meat and poultry exported to the United States. The FSIS evaluates and sets standards for food ingredients and additives used in the preparation and packaging of meat and poultry products. Under the Nutrition Labeling and Education Act, the FSIS ensures that mandatory labels used on meat and poultry products are consistent with labels used by the Food and Drug Administration on food products.

—GEORGE THOMAS KURIAN

Foreign Agricultural Service

Established in 1953 as a promotion and information agency within the Department of Agriculture, the Foreign Agricultural Service (FAS) on the one hand gathers information about crops, production, and supply and demand abroad and distributes the data to U.S. producers and exporters, and on the other, provides information about U.S. products and supplies to foreign importers and cooperates with U.S. exporters in their efforts to establish and expand foreign markets. The FAS is headed by an administrator who is appointed by the secretary of agriculture. Its regulatory powers are limited to imports, particularly the administration of quotas imposed by the president when imports of certain items reach a level that threatens the price stability of U.S. farm products. The primary segment of FAS responsibilities is information. The FAS publishes annually more than 140 commodity reports that present data on production, consumption, and trade flows for over one hundred crop and livestock commodities. These reports analyze trading conditions and suggest market opportunities for U.S. exports. The second element is promotion of agricultural products through exhibits at

trade shows, advertisements in the media, and diplomatic liaison. The FAS operates AgExport Services to provide U.S. firms with the names of foreign importers. Through its Office of International Cooperation and Development the FAS promotes U.S. agriculture's global competitiveness, coordinates the Department of Agriculture's international training and technical assistance programs, and serves as the department's liaison with international food and agriculture organizations as well as the General Agreement on Tariffs and Trade. The FAS oversees the agricultural provisions of trade agreements and negotiations between the United States and other countries. In addition, the FAS is responsible for all of the Department of Agriculture's export credit and market development programs and administers the Commodity Credit Corporation's Export Credit Sales Guarantee Program. It also coordinates government-to-government sales of agricultural commodities on long-term credit and the donation of farm products to relieve hunger under Public Law 480, the Food for Peace Program. —GEORGE THOMAS KURIAN

Foreign Service.

See State, Department of.

Forest Service

As with many older agencies of the U.S. federal government, the functions of the U.S. Forest Service can be traced back to colonial roots. In this case, the needs of the British navy for timber resulted in policies reserving the harvesting of certain hardwood trees for that purpose. In Britain by the end of the seventeenth century the same concerns had led to the development of forest management programs based on the new science of siviculture. But while government policies related to the active husbandry of forests spread throughout Europe during the 1700s, there was little perceived need for similar policies in the American colonies given the seemingly unlimited supply of timber.

After the American Revolution the concern for reserving certain types of tree harvesting for government purposes was replaced by a broader concern for acquiring and disposing of public lands, many of them forests. States relinquished claims on lands west to the Mississippi River to the national government, and these were eventually placed under the jurisdiction of the General Land Office. The Louisiana Purchase of 1803 and purchase of Florida from Spain in 1819 added to the burden of the Land Office, as did the annexation of Texas in 1845 and the large tracts of land gained from the Mexican War and through the Gadsden Purchase in 1853. Millions of additional acres were added in 1867, when Secretary of State William H. Seward arranged for the purchase of Alaska from Russia. Thus, by the late 1800s the national government had considerable land holdings, many dense with trees. The objective of the Land Office, however, was disposing of—not managing—those lands.

A perceived need for U.S. government to engage in forest management first emerged during the Civil War. The stimulant for this interest was the 1863 publication of a book by George Perkins Marsh on *Man and Nature*. Arguing that man damages himself by damaging nature, Marsh's work proved popular and converged with both a growing fascination with nature (already in evidence in the antebellum North) and the intellectual revolution sparked by publication of Darwin's *Origin of Species* in the late 1850s. Among those most profoundly influenced was a New England physician, Franklin B. Hough, who lobbied Congress to deal with what he contended was a coming timber famine.

Congress's willingness to take action came slowly, aided by events as well as the growing popularity of Marsh's ideas. A key event was an 1871 forest fire in Wisconsin that took fifteen hundred lives and burned over a million acres of woods. The call for a forest management policy gained further ground two years later when Hough's paper "On the Duty of Government in the Protection of Forests" was enthusiastically received by members of the influential American

Association for the Advancement of Science. Congress responded with the Timber Culture Act of 1873, which encouraged tree planting by settlers in the Great Plains states. Although of little real significance, the act set the stage for further government action. In 1875 the lobbying effort was strengthened with the formation of the American Forestry Association, and soon forestry curricula began to appear at agricultural colleges.

In 1876 legislation to establish forest reserves adjacent to navigable rivers was seriously considered by Congress. Although the bill ultimately failed to pass, the fact that it was on the congressional agenda reflected the growing acceptance of the idea that the nation's forests needed greater government attention.

What did pass in 1876 was a bill calling for the appointment of a "special agent" in the Department of Agriculture to study how best to preserve and renew America's forest resources. Hough was named that special agent, and in 1878 he delivered a report that documented the need for forest protection policies and programs. By 1881 Hough was able to convince Congress to establish a Division of Forestry within the Agriculture Department with a budget of $2,000, and he was appointed the nation's first chief forester with the mandate to conduct further studies. What he was not given was authority over any of the forest land held by the federal government. That remained under the Land Office.

Hough served as chief forester until 1883, when he was replaced by a patronage appointee who did little to build on the foundation Hough had set. From 1886 to 1898, however, Bernhard Eduard Fernow, the former head of the American Forestry Association and a professional forester (trained in his native Germany, where forestry had developed into a major science), took over at the division (which consisted of two foresters during much of this period). Fernow established the agency's reputation as a primary leader in the effort to expand the government's role in forest preservation and management.

As did Hough, Fernow actively lobbied Congress to create forest reserves, and in 1891 it did so with passage of the Forest Reserve Act. Within a year fifteen reserves covering thirteen million acres had been set aside; by 1897 that figure had risen to forty million acres. There was, however, no provision in the 1891 act for the administration of those new reserves. Jurisdiction remained with the Department of the Interior's General Land Office, which had no experience at managing forests and complained bitterly that it had neither the funds nor expertise to do the job. As it did with the national park lands set aside by Congress in earlier legislation (Yellowstone in 1872, Mackinac Island in 1875, and Yosemite, Sequoia, and General Grant parks in 1890)—the Land Office appointed a corps of agents to administer the reserves. In 1897 a Division of Forestry was established within the Land Office, employing over four hundred such agents. Few, if any, of those agents were trained in forestry, and critics of that office constantly pointed to frequent abuses of the forest reserves under Land Office administration, despite the fact that Congress had attempted to address administrative issues in the Forest Management Act of 1897. That act, however, did more harm than good, for its provisions were so phrased as to promote the exploitation of the reserves by private interests.

Among those who worked in the Interior Department during this period was Gifford Pinchot, a charismatic reformer who left that post when he was named to succeed Fernow as chief forester in the Department of Agriculture division in 1898. Openly critical of the Land Office's administration of the forest reserves, he popularized the idea of conservation and, with an initial core group of eleven employees, began to build what would become the modern Forest Service. With no lands of its own to manage, Pinchot's division offered free assistance to private landowners who sought advice on the "scientific" management of their forest holdings. Working with Fernow (who had moved on to teach at Cornell) and others, Pinchot and the division helped to develop forestry schools at Cornell, Vanderbilt, and Yale. With the help of his close friend and supporter Theodore Roosevelt, Pinchot was able to withstand the attack of opponents who believed the division under his leadership had exceeded its legislative authority. When Roosevelt became president, Pinchot's influence was even greater. Finally, faced with popular pressure stirred by Pinchot and Roosevelt as well as stories of widespread scandal and incompetence in the Land Office's Division of Forestry, Congress passed the Transfer Act of 1905, which shifted jurisdiction over all U.S. forest reserves to Pinchot's agency, now recast as the U.S. Forest Service.

Among other accomplishments, and despite strong opposition from several quarters, Pinchot added to and strengthened regulations governing the use of the reserves and was able to get Roosevelt to set aside an additional 132 million acres before the latter left office in 1909. He enhanced the research function of the service and established the first forest experimental stations and cooperative labs with major universities.

Pinchot's confrontational style would not fare as well under President Taft, who dismissed him in 1910 after a bitter and very public dispute. His successor, Henry Graves, spent much time and energy fending off attempts to return jurisdiction over forest reserves to the Interior Department. Beyond the threat of reversing the Transfer Act, the greatest challenge came from the creation of the National Park Service in the Interior Department in 1916. From the outset the Park Service attempted to transfer large portions of the forest reserves to its jurisdiction. [See National Park Service.]

Despite these challenges, the Forest Service was organizationally and politically stronger by the time Graves left his position in 1920. The agency had gained new authority (under the Weeks Act of 1911), allowing it to purchase private lands to help protect watersheds in the East where there had been few or no public landholdings. Until so authorized under Weeks, the agency was limited to acquiring parcels of the public domain as forest reserve land, and all of that from public holdings in the western United States. The Weeks Act also facilitated a greater role for states (through interstate compacts and matching fund grants) in forest management, thus putting the service at the forefront of intergovernmental relations. In 1915 Graves oversaw the establishment of a separate Research Branch, whose activities soon became a high priority in the service. In his final years as head of the service, Graves also led an effort to enhance the regulatory role of the agency, especially in regard to timber cutting practices on private lands. In short, the active management of America's forests, stressed with political vigor by Pinchot, was the focus of his successor as well.

The agency's regulatory regime changed in 1920 with the appointment of William B. Greeley as chief forester. Greeley's more benign view of the service's relationship with timber and community interests was reflected in the Clarke-McNary Act of 1924, which promoted cooperation with local officials and the private sector. The 1924 act, for example, extended the acquisition powers of the service to cover the purchase or subsidization of privately held land as a means for enhancing timber production. Thus, large timber firms found a friend in the agency, which would acquire underutilized land and make its growth available for harvest. The McSweeney-McNary Act of 1928 reflected congressional support for a greatly expanded experimental and research function that stressed increasing the economic value of public and private forests.

The pendulum swung back toward regulatory tasks under the leadership of Robert Y. Stuart (1928–1933) and Ferdinand A. Silcox (1933–1939). However, while stressing forest management through regulation and public ownership, neither abandoned the idea of cooperation with state and private owners.

Politically, the greatest external threat to the service during the pre–World War II era remained the Interior Department, whose powerful secretary under Franklin Roosevelt, Harold Ickes, coveted the agency and its holdings. Bolstered by the Brownlow Committee's 1938 recommendation that the Forest Service be integrated within similar Interior functions, Ickes obtained the backing of FDR for such a move. But the political atmosphere in Washington was not conducive to such a change, and Roosevelt's support proved lukewarm. In addition, Gifford Pinchot—now a prominent Republican, having served as governor of Pennsylvania—led the strong opposition to the shift. The service survived the period intact.

Internally, during the 1930s the agency was driven by a policy of "intensive management" of all timberlands. The agency's approach was supported by a 1933 congressional study (the Copeland Report) and FDR's enthusiasm for Forest Service projects that fit into the New Deal mold. Of special note was the popular Civilian Conservation Corps (CCC), which operated for the most part in Forest Service areas. Nevertheless, the policies and programs of the service were controversial in many quarters—so much so that Earle H. Clapp, who served as acting chief forester from 1939 through 1943, could not get Senate confirmation because of opposition to his support of strong regulatory and public ownership policies.

During World War II the Forest Service oversaw the Timber Production War Project, which sought to maximize needed wood production with minimal waste. After the war the pent-up and growing demand for lumber politically outweighed the service's assessment that demand was outpacing supply and that a crisis loomed in the future. The best that could be accomplished under Chief Forester Lyle Watts (1943–1952) was passage of the Cooperative Forest Management Act of 1950, which called for increasing forest management assistance for private landowners and timber firms.

By the time Richard McArdle became chief in 1952, the major problem facing the service was the multiple and sometimes conflicting demands being made on the agency. In addition to the traditional stress on conservation and management for improved timber production, the postwar period had witnessed a push for more recreational use, wilderness preservation, and wildlife protection programs related to the forests. Beyond internal responses to these pressures, McArdle pushed for passage of the Multiple-Use Sustained-Yield Act of 1960, which gave the service flexible authority to decide on the "most judicious use of the land" for some or all of several purposes. No longer would priority be placed on timber. There was now a greater degree of discretion given to the Forest Service and its professionals.

Within the Forest Service the push and pull of multiple use demands was aggravated by the diversity of local demands made on the agency. At this time Herbert Kaufman published a classic study of the internal operations of the Forest Service, showing how the agency contended with the tensions created by these conflicting forces. His work not only highlighted agency policies and practices, but also the high degree of professionalism among the Forest Rangers who were dealing with the contradictions on the line. What emerged from Kaufman's study was a picture of a mature agency that relied on professional consensus to help keep itself together and on track.

Challenges to that professional consensus began to emerge from outside the agency in the mid-1960s. A stronger form of preservationism was developing among conservation and environmental groups, and concern for the environment was becoming politically popular. Legislation such as the Wilderness Act of 1964, the Rare and Endangered Species Act of 1966, the National Wild and Scenic Rivers Act of 1968, and the National Environmental Policy Act of 1970 each had a significant and growing impact on Forest Service operations and policies. Chief Edward Cliff (1962–1972) found himself heading an agency that had less and less ability to use the discretion it had fought so hard to get throughout the 1950s. While many in the agency sought to develop more cooperative programs, the mandates from Congress increasingly forced them to engage in regulation.

Eventually the shift in attitudes toward the environment was felt among the ranks of the Forest Service professionals. Ecological studies supported by a variety of government funding agencies soon gained favor among researchers in the service, and the results were a fundamental challenge to the assumptions underlying agency policies and programs. Past debates within the agency had focused on variations of two approaches to forest management—cooperation with or regulation of private sector timber interests. Behind both approaches was a consensus assumption that it was government's role to actively engage in the management of the forests to insure their growth and sustainability. The ecological perspective, however, raised questions about the wisdom of such managerial intervention in natural habitats.

In its most extreme form—often called "deep ecology"—the ecological approach advanced a view that government's role is to protect the nation's forests, and especially "old growth" woods, from any human actions that might interfere in the "natural" workings of the habitat. This included retreating from the forest management practices that had characterized the service's functions from the outset. Based on a "biocentric" philosophy, the deep ecology movement argued for a change in Forest Service policies that would necessarily place the agency in direct opposition to timber interests. Just such situations developed in the northwestern and southwestern regions of the United States during the 1980s and 1990s. Armed with legislation and court decisions, environmental activists were able to halt or shift Forest Service policies on millions of acres of both public and adjoining private land.

The agency leadership has bent in response to such pressure, but it has not radically altered its fundamental mission or commitments. Before 1994, the Forest Service's mission statement made no reference to ecology, although an "ecological approach" to the management of national forests and grasslands under its jurisdiction was mentioned in 1993 as part of the agency's "guiding principles." The emphasis was on achieving "quality land management under the sustainable multiple-use management concept to meet the diverse needs of the people." In 1994, however, the top echelon of the Forest Service were using different "buzzwords" in their mission statements: the primary task for the agency, stated Chief Jack Ward Thomas, was "ecosystems management," defined as "an approach to the management of natural resources that strives to maintain or restore the sustainability of ecosystems and to provide present and future generations a continuous flow of multiple benefits in a manner harmonious with ecosystem sustainability." Compared to the agency's mission statement of just a year earlier, the change seemed significant—at least on the surface.

But while some of the key words had changed in 1994, the same could not be said of the underlying mission. The commitment to multiple-use land management was adjusted to the broader concept of ecosystems sustainability. What this meant, however, was little different from the general approach of the service in the past. As articulated in the new language of ecosystems management, the objectives of the service were to "enhance protection of ecosystems," "restore deteriorated ecosystems," and "provide a variety of benefits within the capabilities of ecosystems." In historical perspective, the break with the past was minimal.

This is not to imply that nothing changed as a result of this reworking of the service's mission. Operationally, the service undertook an extensive review of relevant legislation to consider proposed changes to better fit the new political reality. There was also greater emphasis placed on cooperation with other agencies to deal with the more encompassing ecosystems approach. Personnel training also became an issue as Forest Rangers and others in the agency had to shift from work skills that stressed land management to the new demands of protecting and restoring ecosystems. The shift toward ecological approaches has been most noticeable to timber interests and landowners, who have been extremely critical of the Forest Service's policies in recent years. In the Northwest, issues related to Forest Service policies are placed high on the region's political agenda. In the Southwest, county governments passed ordinances that attempted to nullify service jurisdiction at the local level. Successfully challenged in federal court as unconstitutional, those laws reflected a growing hostility against the Forest Service and other land management agencies that has led to the possibility of violent confrontations between rangers and local property owners.

Despite all these changes and challenges, the structure of the Forest Service remains as it has for decades. Ten regions reporting to a national headquarters deal with the more than 180 million acres of land under the service's jurisdiction.

With the increased attention to mapping and reframing their task environment, research and experimental stations play an even more critical role in the organization. With its designation as a lead agency under the "reinventing government" initiatives of the Clinton administration, the service has also enhanced its intergovernmental programs and efforts to develop "partnerships" with both local communities and the private sector.

In many respects, the challenges facing the Forest Service of the 1990s are quite different from those it has faced in the past. What the agency has operating in its favor is its proven historical capacity to deal with such challenges in a manner that maintains its founding core values.

[See also Interior, Department of the.]

BIBLIOGRAPHY

Chase, Alston. In a Dark Wood: The Fight over Forests and the Rising Tyranny of Ecology. Boston, 1995.

Clawson, Marion. The Federal Lands Revisited. Baltimore, 1983.

Frome, Michael. The Forest Service. 2d ed. Boulder, Colo., 1984.

Kaufman, Herbert. The Forest Ranger: A Study in Administrative Behavior. Baltimore, 1967.

Langston, Nancy. Forest Dream, Forest Nightmares: The Paradox of Old Growth in the Inland West. Seattle, 1995.

Robinson, Glen O. The Forest Service: A Study in Public Land Management. Baltimore, 1975.

—MELVIN DUBNICK

Freedom of Information Act.

See Appendix: Basic Documents of Public Administration.

G

General Accounting Office

The Budget and Accounting Act of 1921 created the United States General Accounting Office (GAO). Described as "independent of the executive departments," the GAO was to "investigate, at the seat of the government or elsewhere, all matters relating to the receipt, disbursement, and application of public funds" and to "make such investigations and reports as shall be ordered by either House of the Congress or by any committee of either House having jurisdiction over revenue, appropriations, or expenditures." The GAO also received authority to settle and adjust all claims by or against the government, to report to Congress on illegal expenditures and contracts, and to prescribe the forms, systems, and procedures for accounting in executive agencies.

The head of the GAO, the comptroller general of the United States, was to be appointed by the president for a single fifteen-year term. In creating a long-term position, Congress intended to safeguard the comptroller general's prerogatives and insulate him from politics. During the GAO's first seventy-five years (1921–1996), six persons served as comptroller general. All except one served at least ten years, and three had full fifteen-year terms. The long tenure of the comptrollers general has had a profound impact on the course of the GAO's history; the men who have filled the office have had time to shape the GAO according to their conceptions of how it ought to operate.

John Raymond McCarl, the first comptroller general, entered office on 1 July 1921. A lawyer and former Republican party official, McCarl worked hard to develop the GAO's independence as the "watchdog" of the nation's money. McCarl insisted that his decisions, based on the Budget and Accounting Act, could not be challenged, even by the attorney general.

McCarl's decisions, sometimes appearing harsh and heartless, contributed to outside efforts to change or abolish the GAO in the 1920s and 1930s. For example, McCarl stopped General Douglas MacArthur, Army chief of staff, from buying Purple Heart decorations from surplus clothing funds, and he denied reimbursements to General John J. Pershing and Major George C. Marshall for costs of Pullman accommodations when they accompanied the body of President Warren G. Harding on a funeral train from San Francisco to Washington in 1923.

Much of the GAO's work during McCarl's term was the checking of vouchers, which were documents providing support for government receipts and expenditures. The GAO also issued reports on substantive issues. In the 1930s it audited the New Deal relief and recovery efforts and, as a result, expanded operations in the field outside of Washington.

President Franklin D. Roosevelt delayed three years after McCarl retired in 1936 before selecting Fred H. Brown, a former Democratic senator from New Hampshire, as comptroller general. Brown served from April 1939 to June 1940, when he resigned because of ill health. Roosevelt then chose Lindsay C. Warren, a prominent Democratic representative from North Carolina; he entered office on 1 November 1940.

During Warren's term, the GAO's workload expanded greatly, at first owing to World War II, which brought a tremendous increase in audit activity, especially on war contracts and government transportation costs. Between 1940 and 1945, the GAO's staff grew from five thousand to fifteen thousand, and its annual budget increased from $10.5 million to $38.4 million. At the end of the war the GAO faced a backlog of thirty-five million unaudited vouchers and a large accumulation of transportation and war contract payments.

In 1945 the Government Corporation Control Act assigned to the GAO a major new duty—annual audits, including reviews of financial management and internal controls, of government corporations (more than one hundred existed in 1945). To do this work, the GAO recruited certified public accountants and other college-trained accountants. In 1949 Warren and his counterparts in the Treasury Department and the Bureau of the Budget (BOB) began a Joint Accounting Improvement Program designed to modernize and improve federal financial management.

Also in 1949, Warren instituted the "comprehensive audit" to determine whether an agency carried out its activities consistent with congressional authorization, properly accounted for revenue, adequately controlled and used its assets, and provided reports fully disclosing the nature and scope of its activities. The GAO conducted comprehensive audits at agency operations sites rather than examining their records at GAO headquarters in Washington.

In the Budget and Accounting Procedures Act (1950) Congress gave legislative recognition to the Joint Accounting Improvement Program and the comprehensive audit. The law stated that financial reporting and accounting systems were executive branch responsibilities and that the comptroller general should prescribe accounting principles and standards and cooperate with agencies in developing systems. The law was consistent with Warren's effort to transform the GAO into a vital force in federal financial management.

The number of reports the GAO produced increased during the Warren period and covered issues of substance, such as a proposed inter-American military cooperation program; foreign military and economic aid programs; Puerto Rico; slums in Washington, D.C.; local public health services; and the status and problems of American Indians. To facilitate reporting work, Warren in 1952 created a formal regional offices

system and a European Branch in Paris. When he retired in March 1954, Warren calculated that between 1941 and 1954 the GAO had collected $915 million due the government, twice the cost of running the GAO during that period.

Warren's successor, Joseph Campbell, a certified public accountant and former member of the Atomic Energy Commission, continued the effort to modernize the GAO. Less interested in federal financial management than Warren, Campbell let the Joint Accounting Improvement Program, renamed the Joint Financial Management Improvement Program (JFMIP), languish. He focused on improving and increasing the number of GAO reports. He brought in many new professional staff each year—mainly accountants—and trained them extensively. He concentrated report preparation in two major units, the Defense and Civil Accounting and Auditing Divisions. Campbell emphasized the work of the regional offices and established a second overseas branch in Tokyo in 1956.

During Campbell's term the GAO paid more attention in audits to program objectives and accomplishments. Reports during these years covered such civil agencies as the Corps of Engineers, the Bureau of Indian Affairs, the Department of Agriculture, the Census Bureau, the Panama Canal Company, and the Tennessee Valley Authority. Reports on international activities also increased.

Campbell's greatest interest was in defense contract audits. These audit reports, with strident titles, bluntly criticized contractor and Department of Defense (DOD) practices, named persons allegedly involved in fraud and malpractice, and referred such cases to the Department of Justice. Complaints by the DOD and defense contractors about these approaches led to hearings in 1965 conducted by Representative Chet Holifield, chair of the Military Operations Subcommittee, House Committee on Government Operations. The hearings resulted in a detailed analysis of the GAO's defense contract auditing and recommendations for improvement.

Holifield's subcommittee issued a report in March 1966 summarizing the major issues raised in the hearings. By this time the GAO already had taken steps to tone down its defense contract reports. The GAO agreed to delete from its reports referral of alleged illegal activity to the Department of Justice and the names of officials recommended for disciplinary action, to limit recommendations for voluntary contractor refunds, and to take other steps to defuse the controversy. In fact, the GAO had pulled back somewhat from its emphasis on defense contract reporting. Campbell elected to retire on medical disability just as the Holifield hearings ended in July 1965.

Elmer B. Staats, deputy director of the BOB, became comptroller general in March 1966. Staats was more dedicated than Campbell to improving federal financial management, leading to the strengthening of the JFMIP. At the request of Congress, the GAO, BOB, and DOD undertook a study that led to the establishment in 1970 of the Cost Accounting Standards Board, charged with developing and promulgating standards to achieve uniformity and consistency in cost accounting principles for defense contracts over $100,000. The GAO also led in developing uniform audit standards for application to federal, state, and local governments, resulting in the 1972 publication of *Standards for Audit of Government Organizations, Programs, Activities, and Functions,* familiarly known as the Yellow Book. Eventually the federal government required use of the standards in audits of state and local governments receiving federal financial assistance.

In 1967 Congress directed the GAO to evaluate the poverty programs carried out by the federal Office of Economic Opportunity and by local agencies. A team of about 250 GAO auditors spread over the nation, studying programs such as the Job Corps, Head Start, VISTA, and the Rural Loan Program.

This assignment was a great challenge to the GAO. With the aid of consultants, it had to develop methods to evaluate social programs and indicators of progress. In its report (March 1969) the GAO identified as a major problem the coordination of programs authorized by the Economic Opportunity Act (1964) and those administered by other agencies. The GAO concluded that there had been progress but much remained to be done. For example, Head Start had provided benefits for children, but parent participa-

tion, a primary program objective, had been insufficient. The Community Action Program had administrative deficiencies, and the program had achieved less than could be expected given the amount of money spent.

The poverty programs work, the most extensive job the GAO had done in response to a statutory requirement, demonstrated its ability to do program evaluation. In the Legislative Reorganization Act (1970) Congress endorsed program evaluation work, which became the central focus of the GAO's report efforts thereafter.

To equip the GAO to do program evaluations, Staats emphasized staff recruitment and training. The GAO began to recruit from a variety of disciplines rather than basically from accounting—such as systems analysis, computer technology, economics, the social sciences, and engineering. The GAO's recruitment program also worked to attract women and members of minority groups. Earlier the GAO's professional staff had been essentially composed of white males.

In the mid-1970s the GAO developed "issue areas," such as environmental protection, health, energy, income security, economic and military assistance, and tax policy. The GAO's divisional structure evolved to reflect the emphasis on program evaluation and the emergence of new issues—the Energy and Metals Division and the Program Analysis Division were prime examples.

The subjects of reports in the 1970s reflected the GAO's changing emphasis. A congressionally mandated GAO Office of Federal Elections (1972–1974) issued regulations on spending limits for candidates for federal office and audited the 1972 presidential and vice presidential campaigns. Its most important report (August 1972) was an audit of President Richard M. Nixon's finance committee, including funds spent to support the Watergate burglary. In the 1970s the GAO began to audit the Internal Revenue Service and international organizations supported by the United States, including the United Nations, the World Bank, and the International Monetary Fund. Other representative reports concerned the New York City fiscal crisis, the illegal drug trade, the Panama Canal treaties, the MX missile, and the farm credit system.

The GAO changed extensively during the

Staats period, reflecting the shift to program evaluation, the emergence of new foreign and domestic problems, and Congress's increasing assertiveness in its relations with the executive branch. The proportion of the GAO's work in response to direct congressional requests increased from about ten percent to forty percent during Staat's term. The GAO estimated financial benefits derived from its work between 1966 and 1980 at $19.4 billion.

Staats's term ended in March 1981. In October 1981 Charles A. Bowsher, a partner in the accounting firm of Arthur Andersen and Co. and a former assistant secretary of the Navy for financial management (1967–1971), became comptroller general. Bowsher was very interested in improving the GAO's products. For years the timeliness issue—preparing reports in time for effective use by Congress and executive agencies—had persisted. Bowsher fostered improvement of staff quality and skills through extensive training programs, a team approach to job execution, a job planning system, quality assurance mechanisms, more attention to human resources issues, and improved design of an expanded product line. He strengthened the regional and overseas offices and took steps to integrate their work with that of the divisions in Washington. In addition to the traditional blue cover reports, the GAO developed letter reports, fact sheets, and briefing reports. Congressional testimony by Bowsher and other GAO officials increased significantly.

Bowsher emphasized the GAO's financial management work. In 1985 he proposed an overhaul of the federal financial management system—strengthened accounting, auditing, and reporting; improved planning and programming; a streamlined budget process; and systematic measurement of performance. The Federal Managers' Financial Integrity Act (1982) authorized the GAO to establish internal controls standards and required executive agencies to report annually on compliance with these standards. The GAO played a major role in development of the Chief Financial Officers Act (1990), which placed a chief financial officer in the Office of Management and Budget and chief financial officers in executive departments and major agencies.

Bowsher also strongly supported the JFMIP and was a very active leader in the International Organization of Supreme Audit Institutions.

From the beginning of his term, Bowsher called attention to federal budget problems and the accumulating deficits. The Balanced Budget and Emergency Deficit Control Act (1985) required the comptroller general, after an independent analysis, to inform the president and Congress how much a projected deficit within a fiscal year would surpass established ceilings, and to determine the amount of any required spending reduction. Eventually the Supreme Court ruled (*Bowsher v. Synar,* 1986) that this procedure was unconstitutional, a violation of the principle of separation of powers because the law gave executive decision-making authority to the comptroller general.

During Bowsher's term the GAO issued reports on highly important issues; they put the GAO into the forefront of thinking and action on these issues. Examples were reports on the Bigeye bomb, the Lavi aircraft, the B-1B bomber, the nuclear weapons complex, the Persian Gulf War, the liquid metal fast breeder reactor, the savings and loan bailout, problems in the Department of Housing and Urban Development, the Social Security Trust Fund, and the 1987 stock market crash. The GAO's reports and testimony contributed significantly to congressional legislation or other action on these issues, stimulated national debate, and in many cases led to substantial savings on federal programs.

The GAO's activities during the Bowsher period did not take place without controversy. Sometimes it appeared that the GAO took a policy stand in its reports, causing critics to argue that its role was to present the facts and leave policy determinations to Congress and the White House. On occasion, congressional committees or individual members disagreed with the GAO's facts or conclusions. By 1993 these problems had resulted in threats to cut the GAO's budget, then over $440 million. This situation, combined with continued federal budget problems and the downsizing efforts of the Clinton administration beginning in 1993, resulted in significant cuts in the GAO's budget for fiscal years 1996 and 1997, initiated by Congress itself, totaling about twenty-five percent. This forced the GAO to streamline its organization—abolishing one division, several regional offices, and the two overseas branches—and to reduce its staff from about fifty-one hundred in 1993 to thirty-four hundred in 1996.

Between 1921 and 1996 the GAO's staff evolved from voucher checkers to highly trained professionals, reflecting the ethnic and gender variety of the nation as a whole and doing a wide variety of work on major issues. By the 1990s the GAO did more than eighty percent of its work at the request of Congress. The GAO's history is the history of an organization that has changed to meet the changing needs of the nation and Congress. This evolution is likely to continue as the GAO faces the challenges of the twenty-first century.

[*See also* Management and Budget, Office of; *and* Appendix: Budget and Accounting Act (1921) *and* Government Corporation Control Act (1945).]

BIBLIOGRAPHY

Brown, Richard E. *The GAO: Untapped Source of Congressional Power.* Knoxville, Tenn., 1970.
Havens, Harry S. *The Evolution of the General Accounting Office: From Voucher Audits to Program Evaluations.* Washington, D.C., 1990.
Kloman, Erasmus H., ed. *Cases in Accountability: The Work of the GAO.* Boulder, Colo., 1979.
Mansfield, Harvey C., Sr. *The Comptroller General: A Study in the Law and Practice of Financial Administration.* New Haven, Conn., 1939.
Mosher, Frederick C. *The GAO: The Quest for Accountability in American Government.* Boulder, Colo., 1979.
Mosher, Frederick C. *A Tale of Two Agencies: A Comparative Analysis of the General Accounting Office and the Office of Management and Budget.* Baton Rouge, 1984.
Pois, Joseph. *Watchdog on the Potomac: A Study of the Comptroller General of the United States.* Washington, D.C., 1979.
Sperry, Roger L., Timothy D. Desmond, Kathi F. McGraw, and Barbara Schmitt. *GAO, 1966–1981: An Administrative History.* Washington, D.C., 1981.
Trask, Roger R. *GAO History, 1921–1991.* Washington, D.C., 1991.
Trask, Roger R. *Defender of the Public Interest: The General Accounting Office, 1921–1966.* Washington, D.C., 1996.
Walker, Wallace E. *Changing Organizational Culture: Strategy, Structure, and Professionalism in the U.S. General Accounting Office.* Knoxville, Tenn., 1986.
Willoughby, William F. *The Legal Status and Functions of the General Accounting Office of the National Government.* Baltimore, 1927.

—ROGER R. TRASK

General Services Administration

 An independent central management agency charged with managing government procurement, property, and telecommunications, the General Services Administration (GSA) was created in 1949 out of the recommendations of the first Hoover Commission, which derived its authority from the Federal Property and Administrative Service Act. The agency currently has about 19,500 employees. While the agency's budget is only $210 million a year, it has influence over nearly $45 billion in government purchases.

Headquartered in Washington, D.C., the GSA maintains eleven regional offices that are responsible for carrying out the policies set by the central office. The agency is headed by a director who is appointed by the president with approval and consent of the Senate. As an executive officer, the director serves at the pleasure of the president. The agency has three principal offices: the Federal Supply Service (FSS), the Public Buildings Service (PBS), and the Office of Information Technology Service (ITS). In addition, the GSA is responsible for the government's telecommunication systems.

The FSS is charged with purchasing and distributing goods and services for governmental use. The FSS handles goods from advanced scientific equipment to general office supplies. It provides services to facilitate the movement of goods and maintenance and repair of equipment. The Interagency Fleet Management System (IFMS) manages eleven repair centers across the country and oversees a motor pool of 145,000 vehicles. The FSS is also responsible for developing regulations and procedures governing management and oversight of all federal government motor vehicles except those exempted by law. These functions include developing government-wide fleet management policy, administering government-wide credit card programs, establishing safety programs and initiatives, reviewing and determining the impact of proposed legislation, and complying with energy conservation mandates and fuel economy standards. In addition, the FSS runs the federal government's extensive travel programs.

The PBS was reorganized in 1995 in order to streamline operations and to become more competitive with the private sector. The PBS functions as a builder, developer, lessor, and manager of federally owned and leased properties. The office provides a full range of real estate services including brokerage, property management, repairs, security services, and property disposal. The PBS has developed specific offices to carry out its assigned functions. Through the property disposal unit, the PBS may distribute resources among federal agencies, sell surpluses, or donate them to state and local governments. In association with the Federal Emergency Management Agency, the office also maintains emergency stockpiles of strategic and critical materials.

The ITS coordinates products and services including telecommunications, data processing, office automation, and information management. It accomplishes these goals through two principal divisions. First, the Office of Information Security provides secure information for government organizations conducting classified, sensitive, diplomatic, or military missions worldwide. Second, the Office of Information Technology Integration plans, manages, and operates government-wide information technology programs including software, hardware, systems integration, information technology facilities, office systems, and planning services.

The GSA also operates the Federal Telecommunications System, the largest private telephone system in the world. The agency is developing its plans for intercity communication to replace its Federal Telecommunications System 2000, whose contracts expire in 1998.

The GSA has come under increasing fire in the 1990s. Critics argued that the agency's monopolistic approach to acquisitions was neither cost effective nor efficient. In addition, many critics of the agency, citing the fact that the GSA has had seventeen directors in twenty-three years, claim that it is a bastion of political spoils—a good agency in which to place generous political donors. Others have argued that the agency is wasteful of taxpayers' money. Even the inspector general, an employee of the GSA, has concerns over the management of funds. In a 1995 report, the inspector general stated that the agency was torn between the prudent spending of taxpayers' money and the demands of its customers (other federal agencies). The report cited two specific extravagances that the agency approved because of pressure from other federal employees. In response to ongoing requests from federal judges, the agency approved the installation of expensive carpeting in New York City's Foley Square court complex, and in Chicago the agency approved the Environmental Protection Agency's request for mesquite flooring.

The GSA began a reorganization in 1995 that was the result of the White House's attempt to "reinvent government." Vice President Albert Gore's National Performance Review of the agency found that the dual roles of service provider and regulator have led to conflicts with the agency's clients. Therefore, the National Performance Review recommended that the GSA shed its enforcement role, that each federal agency be responsible for its own procurement, and that the GSA act as a consultant to other agencies. However, critics argue that if the roles of provider and enforcer are removed, then the agency should be dismantled altogether, as the private sector would better serve client agencies as consultants.

The agency is currently in a state of transition. In response to the National Performance Review and congressional attempts to downsize government bureaucracy, the GSA's future roles are in doubt. If calls to privatize many of the agency's functions are heeded or if the movement toward decentralized procurement and management is continued, the GSA could be a structure without a function. One indication of the decline of the agency has been the bilateral support for cutting its budget. President Bill Clinton included the GSA in a package of over $19 billion in spending cuts he proposed to Congress. The Republican-controlled Congress has been even more aggressive in wanting to cut the agency's budget and influence. In the end, the agency will likely continue to lose funds and authority, especially if the era of big government comes to an end.

[*See also* National Performance Review.]

BIBLIOGRAPHY

Office of the Vice President. *Creating a Government That Works Better and Costs Less: General Services Administration.* Washington, D.C., 1993.

—JEFFREY D. SCHULTZ

Geological Survey

 The United States Geological Survey (USGS) was established within the Department of the Interior by an act of 3 March 1879 that called for "the classification of the public lands and examination of the geological structure, mineral resources and products of the national domain." Authorization was expanded in 1962 to include activities outside the United States. The agency consists of the headquarters at Reston, Virginia, regional centers in Denver and Menlo Park, California, four mapping centers, water resources offices in fifty states, and eight Earth Science Information Centers. In addition to its geological surveys and investigations, the USGS identifies potential natural hazards and monitors water quality and use. One of its major services is the publication of authoritative geologic, topographic, and mineral resource maps and data bases.

BIBLIOGRAPHY

U. S. Geological Survey. *U.S. Geological Survey Yearbook.* Denver, 1996.

—GEORGE THOMAS KURIAN

Global Change Research Program

Around the world in the 1980s, global environmental change emerged as a matter of concern at the highest political levels. At the top of the global change agenda has been concern about a possible human-induced climate change—more popularly known as "global warming." Since 1990 the primary response to this concern in the United States has been the Global Change Research Program (GCRP). The program's congressional mandate is to provide "usable information" to policymakers who seek to develop and implement policies in response to global change. In spite of continuing and sometimes acrimonious scientific and political debate over the nature, causes, and potential impacts of global warming, through 1996 the program largely enjoyed sustained bipartisan support to become one of the largest and most ambitious programs of scientific research ever conducted by the government of the United States.

Through 1996 the program received more than $10 billion in congressional appropriations. For 1996 the program requested funding of $2.16 billion. The program consists of joint efforts by twelve federal government agencies, including the Departments of Agriculture, Commerce, Defense, Energy, the Interior, and Transportation as well as the National Science Foundation and the National Aeronautics and Space Administration (NASA). Within the agencies more than thirty government bureaus receive funding under the program for global change research. The program's scientific research agenda is broad; in 1996 it identified as its focus four major scientific challenges:

- Seasonal to interannual climate fluctuations, including research on the periodic phenomenon of El Niño

- Climate change over the next few decades

- Stratospheric ozone depletion and increased ultraviolet radiation

- Changes in land cover and in ecosystems.

Program officials expect that meeting these four challenges will support the program's more general mission to provide "short- and long-term benefits to the nation."

The largest single component of the GCRP is the Mission to Planet Earth, which accounts for approximately sixty percent of the total program budget. A NASA project, the Mission to Planet

Earth consists of a number of satellites designed to observe the Earth from space in order to document processes of global change. By far the most visible single project within the Mission to Planet Earth is the Earth Observing System (EOS), which accounts for more than seventy percent of the NASA global change budget. Initially established in 1983 as part of the NASA Space Station program, the EOS became part of the GCRP in the early 1990s and has since become a competitor with the NASA Space Station program for the agency's increasingly limited funds.

The congressional mandate of the GCRP is found in Public Law 101-606, which was passed with little debate by Congress and signed by President George Bush in 1990 (15 U.S.C. 2921). The law finds that human activities "are contributing to processes of global change that may significantly alter the Earth habitat within a few generations." In addition to concern about global warming, the law expresses the concern of policymakers about aspects of global environmental change other than global warming such as stratospheric ozone depletion owing to the release of human-produced chlorofluorocarbons into the atmosphere and the loss of biodiversity associated with the loss of natural habitats. Concern about issues related to global change led Congress and the president to create the program to "provide usable information on which to base policy decisions relating to global change" (P.L. 101-606). Acting on their mandate to answer the decision-making needs of policymakers, program officials stated that it "is a critical investment for the future of this nation, its economy, and the health and safety of its citizens."

The program was developed from an interagency process of budgetary coordination among agencies that sponsored a significant amount of global change research. The coordination process was begun in 1987 in the White House by William Graham, science adviser to President Ronald Reagan. Graham turned to the ten-year-old Federal Coordinating Council on Science, Engineering and Technology (FCCSET, pronounced "fix-it")—which until then had gone largely unused—to invigorate the interagency coordination process. The process of budgetary coordination for global change was first used in the executive branch simply to identify already-budgeted federal government–sponsored research related to global change. The interagency process was given high marks by many observers for its ability to bring different agencies together to focus on the goal of budgetary coordination.

As the issue of global warming gained more visibility in the late 1980s, demands for government action increased. One consequence was that when the agencies expressed interest in using the budget coordination process to build the framework of a research process, some in Congress saw it as an opportunity to request from the scientific and agency communities information that would be usable in policy development. Meanwhile, in the eyes of the Bush administration (led on the climate issue by Chief of Staff John Sununu), the proposed program would demonstrate to the U.S. public and the world that action was being taken on global warming yet would entail no specific policy choices other than funding research. The objectives of these various interests were realized by the establishment of the GCRP. Implementation of this massive effort is overseen by a subcommittee of the White House Committee on Environment and Natural Resources (CENR), itself one of nine committees that constitute the president's National Science and Technology Council. (The National Science and Technology Council was established by President Bill Clinton in 1993 to replace the FCCSET.) The Subcommittee on Global Change Research under the CENR is responsible for day-to-day implementation of the program and established in July 1993 the Office of the GCRP to facilitate coordination of the program.

In 1993 Congress expressed concern that the program was not meeting its mandate—that is, that it was not producing "usable information." At the request of several congressional committees, an assessment of the program was conducted by the Congressional Office of Technology Assessment. Its 1993 report found that "although the results of the program, as currently structured, will provide valuable information for predicting climate change, they will not necessarily contribute to the information needed by public and private decisionmakers to respond to global change." As a consequence of such criticism, program administrators began to change the focus of the program. In 1994 Robert Watson, chair of the CENR, stated in congressional testimony that "the administration recognized the scope of the existing program was too narrow to provide effective comprehensive assessments of global change; thus the needs of the policymakers was [sic] not being met." One step that administrators of the program have taken to improve its performance has been the development of an assessment function to "help policy makers develop options for responding to global change."

Through early 1996 the GCRP continued to receive high marks for its coordination of agency budgets. It has garnered less favorable reviews regarding its coordination of the different agencies and disciplines that fall under its purview. Despite these difficulties, the program has been praised by the scientific community for its contributions to a fundamental understanding of the global earth system. Whether scientific support will continue to translate into large budgets in an era of tight limits on the overall federal budget is an open question.

[See also National Aeronautics and Space Administration; National Science Foundation; and Science and Technology Policy, Office of.]

BIBLIOGRAPHY

Brunner, R. "Policy and Global Change Research: A Modest Proposal." *Climatic Change* 32(1996): 121–147.
Committee on Earth and Environmental Sciences. Federal Coordinating Council for Science, Engineering, and Technology. *Our Changing Planet: An Investment in Science for the Nation's Future.* Washington, D.C., 1990–1993.
Committee on Environment and Natural Resources. National Science and Technology Council. *Our Changing Planet: An Investment in Science for the Nation's Future.* Washington, D.C., 1994–1996.
Edwards, P. "Global Comprehensive Models in Politics and Policymaking." *Climatic Change* 32(1996): 149–161.
Lambright, W. H. "Administrative Entrepreneurship and Space Technology: The Ups and Downs of 'Mission to Planet Earth.'" *Public Administration Review* 54(1994): 97–104.
Monastersky, R. "The $1.5 Billion Question: Can the U.S. Global Change Research Program Deliver on its Promises?" *Science News* 144(1993): 158–159.
National Research Council. *A Review of the U.S. Global Change Research Program and NASA's Mission to Planet Earth/Earth Observing System.* Washington, D.C., 1995.
Office of Technology Assessment. *Preparing for an Uncertain Climate.* 2 Vols. OTA-O-568. Washington, D.C., 1993.
Pielke, R. A., Jr. "Usable Information for Policy: An Appraisal of the U.S. Global Change Research Program." *Policy Sciences* 28(1995): 39–77.
Taubes, G. "Earth Scientists Look NASA's Gift Horse in the Mouth." *Science* 259(1993): 912–914.
Wakefield, J. "Geophysical Science in the 1996 Budget." *EOS: Transactions of the American Geophysical Union* 76(1995): 77–78.
                                                    —ROGER A. PIELKE, JR.

Government Corporations Control Act.

See Appendix: Basic Documents of Public Administration.

Government Ethics, Office of

In response to the ethical and legal transgressions uncovered in the 1970s during the Watergate scandals of the Nixon administration, Congress created the Ethics in Government Act of 1978. The act in turn established the U.S. Office of Government Ethics (OGE), a division of the Office of Personnel Management. By October 1989 the OGE became a separate agency. The agency, lawmakers argued, would ensure a higher standard of conduct for elected officials while at the same time restoring public faith in government.

Although the OGE is a separate agency, each federal agency has primary responsibility for the administration of the "Ethics in Government" program. To ensure compliance with the act, agencies designate an ethics official responsible for coordinating, managing, and enforcing the agency's program. In addition to providing ethics counseling, ethics officials must report any information relating to a violation of the criminal code, Title 18 of the United States Code. Attorney-client privilege, however, does not protect disclosures made by an employee to an ethics official.

While the federal agencies are involved in the administration of the program, the OGE, as a regulatory authority, develops, recommends, and reviews executive branch–wide regulations. The agency director, appointed by the president to a five-year term with the advice and consent of the Senate, is responsible for the enforcement of executive branch policies related to standards of ethical conduct. Within the OGE four departments report to the director: the Office of General Counsel and Legal Policy, the Office of Education, the Office of Program Assistance and Review, and the Office of Administration.

Two basic sources permit the OGE and its staff to pursue allegations of an ethics violation. These are the Criminal Conflict of Interest Statutes (chapter 11 of Title 18, United States Code) and the Administrative Standards of Ethical Conduct Regulation (5 Code of Federal Regulations Part 2635). The conflict of interest statutes prohibit a federal employee from engaging in activities that would place the employee's own interest above the government's interest. For example, a federal employee may not represent the interests of private parties in matters in which the United States has an interest. At the same time the standards of conduct regulation establishes principles of ethical conduct for employees. For instance, the regulation covers such topics as gifts from outside sources, gifts between employees, outside activities, and seeking other employment.

The agency also reviews executive branch public financial disclosure reports of certain White House officials and presidential appointees to determine if any entries on the forms may give rise to violations of applicable laws and to recommend any appropriate corrective action. Additionally, the OGE oversees the creation and operation of blind trusts and issues certificates of divestiture for those who must sell assets to avoid conflicts.

Finally, the OGE monitors agency ethics programs, reviews agency compliance, and refers possible violations of conflict of interest laws to the Department of Justice. The OGE also has authority to order any corrective action or, in unusual circumstances, recommend individual disciplinary action.

BIBLIOGRAPHY

A Brief Wrap on Ethics. Washington, D.C., 1995.
Lardner, George Jr. "The Assault on Watergate Reforms; Overreaction to 'Watergate Overreaction.'" *Washington Post,* 5 July 1981, Cl.
May, Clifford D. "Washington Talk: Office of Government Ethics." *Washington Post,* 18 August 1987, B6.
Pound, Edward T. "Prosecutor Law Not So Special Now." *Washington Post,* 20 December 1981, D4.
Second Biennial Report to Congress. Washington, D.C., 1992.
Standards of Ethical Conduct for Employees of the Executive Branch: Final Regulation Issued by the U.S. Office of Government Ethics. Washington, D.C., 1992.
Take the High Road. Washington, D.C., 1993.

—VERONICA D. DICONTI

Government Information

ESSAY Thomas Jefferson defined information as the currency of democracy. The United States is an open and information-rich society, and one of the most fertile sources of information is the executive branch of government. The term *government information* includes and subsumes government publications (publicly available, free or priced) and government documents (with restricted access). Both publications and documents suggest print-only formats, but, in fact, government information is becoming increasingly electronic, available on film and in audio, video, CD-ROM, and on-line formats. The United States is the only major industrialized nation without a formal government information policy. Rather, it operates under an informal national information policy, emanating from laws and regulatory decisions and based on budgetary priorities, buraucratic decisions, and congressional oversight. The seed laws governing this informal information structure date from 1895, with the Printing Act, and continued with the Depository Library Act, the Freedom of Information Act, the Copyright Act, and the Paperwork Reduction Act. Like many other types of government activity, information creation is decentralized. Each of the fifty-eight hundred agencies and units of the federal government has the right—and often the duty—to provide appropriate information to the public and other agencies, but there is little or no interagency coordination. However, production and dissemination are monitored by two bodies, the Joint Congressional Committee on Printing and the Office of Management and Budget, authorized by the Paperwork Reduction Act of 1980 to oversee the entire life cycle of government information. The two major dissemination agencies are the Government Printing Office and National Technical Information Service.

Arnold Hirshon defines four types of presidential papers: public/published, executively controlled, official, and personal. The first category includes materials issued by the White House, such as proclamations, executive orders, and presidential messages, speeches, and statements. The second category consists of privileged documents shielded from disclosure because they are classified as top secret, national security directives, and policy-generating documents such as official memos, drafts, notes, and tapes. Raymond Greselbracht identifies four eras in the history of presidential papers. When Washington left office, he took, in the absence of any archive in the Capitol, all his papers with him to Mount Vernon. This practice was followed by most presidents who followed him until the end of the nineteenth century. The second era began at the turn of the century, when the Library of Congress began collecting presidential papers in its Manuscript Division, even though it had no legal powers to do so. The third era began with Franklin D. Roosevelt, who erected the first presidential library on his own land in 1939. Truman followed this model, and the Presidential Libraries Act of 1955 formally authorized the creation of presidential libraries to be maintained with the help of tax dollars. The fourth era began when Congress seized the Nixon papers in the aftermath of Watergate and passed two laws, the first giving the government control over them and the second designating all future presidential papers as national property. The Presidential Records Act of 1978 has governed all presidential papers after Carter's.

The president communicates with the Congress and the American public through various means: proclamations, executive orders, and messages. George Washington's first executive order asked his cabinet for a clear account of the government, and his first proclamation, also in 1789, declared Thanksgiving Day as the third Thursday in November. Executive orders were not numbered or issued uniformly until 1907 and not published until the *Federal Register* was created in 1936. Since 1936 every executive order has been published in the *Federal Register* and later codified in Title 3 of the *Code of Federal Regulations*. When issued with legal authority, both executive orders and proclamations have the same effect as laws. The president's oral and written communications to Congress and the public are called presidential messages and include speeches, radio addresses, press conferences, and press releases. Bills introduced in Congress with presidential endorsement may be accompanied by presidential messages. All public documents emanating from the White House, including transcripts of news conferences, messages to Congress, and speeches, are included in the *Weekly Compilation of Presidential Documents*. The *Public Papers of the Presidents* was initiated in 1957 as a documentary record of each presidential administration with both subject and name indexes.

[*See also* Federal Register; Government Printing Office; Library of Congress; National Archives; Technical Information Service, National; *and* Appendix: Freedom of Information Act *and* Paperwork Reduction Act.]

BIBLIOGRAPHY

Hernon, Peter, and Charles R. McClure. *Federal Information Policies: Conflicts and Issues.* Norwood, N.J., 1987.
Hernon, Peter, and Charles R. McClure. *Public Access to Government Information: Issues, Trends and Strategies.* Norwood, N.J., 1988.
McClure, Charles, Peter Hernon, and Harold C. Relyea. *United States Government Information Policies: Views and Perspectives.* Norwood, N.J., 1989.

—GEORGE THOMAS KURIAN

Government in the Sunshine Act.

See Appendix: Basic Documents of Public Administration.

Government Printing Office

 Title 44 of the U.S. Code designates the Government Printing Office (GPO) as the federal government's printer and binder. The GPO, which is overseen by the Congressional Joint Committee on Printing, is headed by the public printer, who is nominated by the president and confirmed by the Senate. Under him is the superintendent of documents (SuDocs), who oversees depository libraries, sale of documents, and the compilation of the *Monthly Catalog*. About three-quarters of GPO printing is done on contract by commercial printers, and the balance is done at GPO regional printing offices. Because of the presence of the International Typographical Union, GPO printing costs are generally higher than those of commercial printers.

The GPO opened for business in 1861 on the day Lincoln was inaugurated. Until the middle of the nineteenth century there was no official printer, and printing was done by a motley crew of private presses and newspaper publishers, called "publick printers." Public printing was a chaotic profession dominated by lazy, inaccurate, and messy workers who were regularly fired from jobs, who tried to win contracts through bribery, while overcharging the government, and who occasionally lost manuscripts. Congressional investigations having failed to solve the problem, by 1833 the Senate was discussing a government printing office; opponents of this proposal, inspired by public printers, turned violent, and there was a celebrated duel in the chamber between an advocate and an opponent. Finally, in 1860, the measure to set up a government printing office passed Congress. Lincoln's Emancipation Proclamation was among the first documents to be typeset. In 1895 sale and distri-

bution were added to the responsibilities of the GPO.

The GPO is the largest publisher in the nation, but no one actually counts the number of publications that it issues. As early as 1938 it was estimated that it required 1,750 railroad cars to store all the government publications. The GPO itself claims that the official paper trail could circle the earth fifteen times each year, or, to put it differently, it produces eight pounds of documents for every man, woman, and child in the United States. However, the GPO is not a true publisher but a printer. It neither initiates publication nor controls editorial content. Editorial responsibility belongs to the issuing agency. Also, the GPO does not handle all government printing. Some agencies are granted waivers to do their own printing and distribution. Further, the rise of desktop publishing and privatization of some major GPO series have threatened GPO's near-monopoly.

Although it is historically a print publisher, the GPO has been swept into the electronic publishing revolution since the late 1980s. Many of its publications are now in CD-ROM format only, and other titles are on magnetic tapes and computer disks. GPO's first CD-ROM was the *Toxic Release Inventory* in 1990, followed by the *Congressional Record* in 1991. The ability of CD-ROM to store massive amounts of archival data makes it ideal for the GPO. For example, the paper-based *Congressional Record* was over fifty thousand typeset pages, weighing 225 pounds and requiring seven feet of shelf space. By contrast, its CD-ROM version consists of two disks weighing 2.4 pounds. (Besides its utility as a storage device, CD-ROM is relatively cheap, making it an affordable medium in budgetary hard times. The Commerce Department's *National Trade Data Bank* stores 100,000 separate documents issuing from fifteen agencies at a cost of about $50 per month; the cost of publishing each document in print would be $9,000 per month. The Department of Commerce publishes more than half of all federally produced CD-ROMs. Within the department, the largest CD-ROM producers are the National Oceanic and Atmospheric Administration and the Bureau of the Census. The latter publishes the decennial censuses, the eco-

THE GOVERNMENT PRINTING OFFICE IN WASHINGTON, D.C. *Since 1860 the GPO has printed, bound, and distributed the publications of Congress as well as those of the executive departments and the offices of the federal government. Distribution of the documents is increasingly being accomplished via electronic media.*

nomic censuses, *County and City Data Book,* and *County Business Patterns* on dBase-compatible CD-ROMs.)

The process of redefining the GPO began in 1993 with the Government Printing Office Electronic Information Access Enhancement Act. The act directs the GPO to create and maintain a directory of federal electronic documents and to provide on-line access to the *Congressional Record* and the *Federal Register.* While this act was designed to strengthen the GPO, the opposite was the intention of the Government Information Dissemination and Printing Improvement Act of 1993. This bill decentralizes government pub-

lishing and turns over much agency printing to the private sector. The act also ends the free distribution of electronic documents to depository libraries.

BIBLIOGRAPHY

Government Printing Office. *GPO/2001.* Washington, D.C., 1991.
Kling, Robert E., Jr. *The Government Printing Office.* New York, 1970.
Schmeckebier, Laurence F. *The Government Printing Office: Its History, Activities, and Organization.* Washington, D.C., 1925.

—GEORGE THOMAS KURIAN

Grain Inspection Service, Federal

A unit of the Department of Agriculture, the Federal Grain Inspection Service (FGIS) administers the Grain Standards Act of 1976 and the Grain Standards Act Amendment of 1990. It is headed by an administrator who is appointed by the president and confirmed by the Senate. The service establishes or revises federal standards for grain and performs inspections to enforce compliance. It also regulates the weighing of grain before export.

The FGIS is divided into four major divisions: 1) Compliance is concerned with evaluations and inspections; 2) Field Management oversees field offices and establishes industry-wide standards for grain, rice, and other commodities; 3) Quality Assurance and Research Development recommends specifications and approves grain inspection instrumentation; and 4) Resources Management is concerned with training, budget, information, health, and safety. The FGIS also inspects, or authorizes the inspection of by state or certified private firms, nearly all grain exported from the United States. Disputes resulting from these inspections may be appealed ultimately to the FGIS Board of Appeals and Review. All individuals and companies engaged in large-scale grain export must register with the FGIS and supply ownership and management information. Registered exporters are granted an annually renewable certificate. —GEORGE THOMAS KURIAN

H

Hatch Act.

See Appendix: Basic Documents of Public Administration.

Health and Human Services, Department of

Although the Department of Health and Human Services (HHS) officially came into existence on 4 May 1980, its true origins date from the establishment of the Federal Security Agency (FSA) on 1 July 1939. The FSA, a product of President Franklin Roosevelt's desire to reorganize the government, united the social welfare agencies of the second New Deal, notably the Works Progress Administration (WPA) and the Social Security Board, and the other federal agencies concerned with health, education, and welfare.

The federal government's involvement in social welfare policy stretched back to the earliest days of the nation. In 1798, for example, the federal government established a hospital for merchant seamen and initiated what became the Public Health Service (PHS) in the Department of the Treasury. For the most part, however, the programs of the FSA started in this century. In the Progressive Era, Congress approved the Food and Drug Act (1906) and created the Food and Drug Administration. During the New Deal, Congress passed the Social Security Act (1935) and started the modern welfare, Social Security, and unemployment compensation programs. It housed these programs in the Social Security Board, an independent agency.

THE FEDERAL SECURITY AGENCY

After President Roosevelt won a landslide victory in 1936, he turned his attention to reorganizing the government. He established the President's Committee on Administrative Management to guide the effort. The committee's 1937 report recommended that the president be allowed to submit reorganization plans to Congress. These plans would automatically be approved, unless they were specifically rejected within sixty days. The committee's report precipitated a major battle between Roosevelt and Congress that lasted until 1939. In the intervening period, the president asked the members of the Committee on Administrative Management for specific reorganization plans. Among the plans that the committee devised was one to create a Department of Social Welfare. The law as passed did not give the president the power to establish cabinet-level departments. Hence, the suggestion for a Department of Social Welfare emerged instead as a proposal for a sub-cabinet FSA, headed by an administrator. On 25 April 1939 the president sent Congress a reorganization plan that included the FSA.

Headed by an administrator and an assistant administrator, the FSA included the Social Security Board, the National Youth Administration, and the Civilian Conservation Corps from the WPA, the Office of Education from the Department of the Interior, the United States Employment Service from the Department of Labor, and the PHS and the American Printing House for the Blind from the Department of the Treasury. Through these executive transfers the president hoped to unite all of the disparate federal agencies "concerned with the promotion of social and economic security, educational opportunity, and the health of the citizens of the nation." The president also sought to reduce expenditures, increase efficiency, and eliminate duplication of effort.

Under the terms of the reorganization legislation, the president's proposals became law by the end of June 1939. Congressional Republicans objected to the consolidation of emergency New Deal welfare programs in the new agency. "The only economy in these proposals is the practical assurance that we shall continue to be asked to spend from two to three billion dollars a year on these wasteful agencies," a conservative New York congressman noted. Still, conservatives lacked the necessary votes to block the reorganization plan.

When the FSA began operations on 1 July 1939, attention shifted to the appointment of the first administrator. Washington rumors centered on Arthur Altmeyer, the chairman of the Social Security Board, Josephine Roche, a former assistant secretary of the Treasury in charge of the PHS, and Clarence Dykstra, president of the University of Wisconsin, as possible candidates. The president confounded expectations and named Paul McNutt, a former governor of Indiana, to the job on 10 July. McNutt, who had been dean of the law school at the University of Indiana, hoped to run for president in 1940. By appointing McNutt to the FSA, the president subordinated McNutt's political ambitions to his own. He also established the precedent that the FSA would be headed by a political executive rather than an expert in the field of social welfare.

When the FSA started, the job programs of the WPA remained large. Popular and media attention focused on them rather than on the Social Security program or on the federal government's health activities. In 1939, for example, the Civilian Conservation Corps ran fifteen hundred camps and had 272,000 enrollees. The programs of the National Youth Administration reached 264,460 young people who had left school and more than half a million students in high school and college. The FSA itself started with twenty-one thousand employees and an annual budget of about $800 million.

The beginning of the FSA coincided with the start of the national defense program. Instead of concentrating on such measures as the estab-lishment of national health insurance, the new agency instead focused on defense-related activities. Enrollees in the Civilian Conservation Corps, for example, turned away from conservation measures, such as planting trees, to such practical skills as truck maintenance.

On 11 April 1940 the president submitted his fourth reorganization plan and enlarged the scope of the FSA. When this plan became effective on 30 July 1940, the Food and Drug Administration moved to the agency from the Department of Agriculture, and several federally aided hospitals and charitable institutions, including St. Elizabeths and Freedmen's Hospitals and the Columbia Institution for the Deaf (later Gallaudet), were transferred from the Department of the Interior.

Paul McNutt served as the head of the FSA through the war years, although his time was largely taken up by special wartime duties. During his tenure the agency utilized an assistant administrator, four assistants to the administrator, and seven counsels (lawyers) as its lead officials.

In 1945 McNutt resigned and Watson B. Miller, his assistant administrator, assumed the job. Miller, born in 1878, had fought in World War I and later become the American Legion's national rehabilitation director. His rehabilitation experience appeared appropriate to address the problems of postwar adjustment that the country faced between 1945 and 1947, Miller's years of service as federal security administrator.

The agency continued to grow in these years. President Truman's second reorganization plan of 1946 abolished the Social Security Board and transferred its powers and duties to the federal security administrator. Instead of being governed by a three-person board, the Social Security program would function within a Social Security Administration (SSA), headed by a commissioner. The former chairman of the Social Security Board became the commissioner of Social Security. As part of the same reorganization, the Children's Bureau moved from the Department of Labor to the SSA, and the National Office of Vital Statistics transferred from the Department of Commerce to the FSA.

Even in this period of growth, the FSA failed to realize its major legislative goals. When Oscar

Ewing took over as FSA administrator in 1947, he made the passage of President Truman's health program an agency priority. Although pieces of this program, such as the Hill-Burton hospital construction program and the National Institute of Mental Health, received congressional approval and augmented the responsibilities of the PHS, the expansion of the Social Security program to cover health and disability insurance never came close to passage. At the same time, the FSA engaged in a debilitating competition with the Department of Labor for control of the United States Employment Service and the unemployment compensation program. Between 1945 and 1949 the United States Employment Service moved to the Department of Labor, back to the FSA, and then back to the Department of Labor. In 1949 the unemployment compensation program joined the employment service in the Department of Labor.

Oscar Ewing, like his two predecessors, came from Indiana. A Harvard-educated lawyer and former head of the Democratic National Committee, he campaigned between 1947 and 1953 to transform the FSA into a cabinet-level department. "I hate to have one tied behind when trying to make progress," he complained. Ewing believed that as the head of an agency he could not command the same attention from the media that he could as a member of the cabinet.

On 20 June 1949 President Truman signed the Reorganization Act of 1949 and submitted a plan to Congress to establish a Department of Welfare. The department would have contained the same programs and agencies as the FSA. In particular, it would have included the SSA (with the Children's Bureau and the Bureau of Public Assistance that ran the welfare programs), the PHS, the Office of Special Services (with the Food and Drug Administration and the Office of Vocational Rehabilitation), the Office of Education, and the federally aided corporations, such as Howard University. The Civilian Conservation Corps and the National Youth Administration no longer existed, having been eliminated by a conservative Congress in 1942. Congress failed to acquiesce in the creation of the new department; opponents of national health insurance and of Oscar Ewing blocked its passage.

During the 1940s the interests of the FSA began to shift from the relief programs of the New Deal toward the problems of postwar adjustment. Ewing's 1949 report no longer mentioned work relief programs. Instead, he stressed the "appalling crisis in education" as manifested in "overcrowded classrooms and lack of teachers." Instead of dispensing relief to the nation's unemployed, the agency should strengthen "the foundation on which the individual can proceed confidently to build his own life."

THE DEPARTMENT OF HEALTH, EDUCATION, AND WELFARE

President Dwight Eisenhower did not approve of such Fair Deal programs as national health insurance, but he did lend his approval to the elevation of the FSA to cabinet status in 1953. When Eisenhower and the Republicans took over, the FSA had thirty-eight thousand employees and disbursed $1.8 billion worth of aid, nearly double the amount distributed in 1941. These figures did not include the money in the Social Security trust fund. In 1951 this fund collected $3.8 billion and paid out about $2 billion in old-age and survivors' benefits. The growth of the agency in the 1940s and early 1950s was exemplified by the PHS, which had 6,200 employees in 1939 and 15,170 in 1953. The growth resulted from such new federal endeavors as providing funds for hospital construction and supplying the bulk of the nation's support for medical research through the National Institutes of Health (NIH). Eisenhower believed that an agency so intertwined with so many areas of American life deserved cabinet status.

For the Republicans, the creation of a new cabinet-level social welfare agency served not only the cause of efficiency but also practical political ends. Creating a new department enabled the Republicans to appoint a secretary in charge of administering programs inherited from the New Deal. In addition, the Republicans wrote the legislation in a way that allowed them to remove the head of the SSA from civil service protection and make him a presidential appointee. Similarly, the reorganization provided a means to convert the position of head of the Bureau of Public Assistance into a presidential appointment. Despite incumbent Jane Hoey's plea that "poverty wasn't political," she lost her job as bureau chief. Such moves satisfied the desires of Republican congressmen to sweep away the remnants of the New Deal. "I'd leave the charwomen and the janitors," said Representative Clare Hoffman (R-Mich.).

Despite these political maneuvers, the Eisenhower administration advisers left the basic structure of the FSA in place in creating the Department of Health, Education, and Welfare (HEW). The plan for the new department, submitted by President Eisenhower on 12 March 1953 and signed into law on 11 April 1953, called for a secretary, under secretary, two assistant secretaries with unspecified duties, and a special assistant to the secretary for health and medical affairs. The President assured the American Medical Association that the special assistant would come from outside the government.

When Eisenhower appointed Oveta Culp Hobby, the former commander of the Women's Air Corps and the publisher of the *Houston Post,* as federal security administrator, he made it clear that Mrs. Hobby would also become the first HEW secretary. The name for the new department reflected in part the desires of Senator Robert Taft (R-Ohio), who preferred that it not be called the Department of Welfare. The senator believed that the Department of Human Resources sounded too totalitarian. Hence, the administration settled on what Rufus Miles, the department's unofficial biographer, describes as the long but inoffensive title of HEW. On 28 May 1953 the president appointed Nelson Rockefeller, the future governor of New York, as the first under secretary of HEW. Other appointments, such as that of John Tramburg, the director of Wisconsin's public welfare department, as commissioner for social security lagged into the fall.

The team of Hobby and Rockefeller, with the strong assistance of Assistant Secretary Roswell Perkins, a lawyer and close Rockefeller associate, launched HEW. At first Mrs. Hobby expressed some reticence about putting forward a social welfare program for the administration. Among her first actions was the appointment of a former agent of the Federal Bureau of Investigation to oversee the loyalty of HEW officials. By the fall of 1953, however, she began in earnest to prepare a complete legislative program for HEW. Her health insurance proposals, complicated plans to reinsure the beneficiaries of private insurance, failed to make congressional headway. Her disability proposals, including expansions of the vocational rehabilitation, Social Security, and hospital construction programs, received congressional approval in 1954. The design and execution of this program demonstrated the secretary's ability to coordinate policy proposals from three different branches of the agency—the Office of Vocational Rehabilitation, the SSA, and the PHS.

When the Democrats regained control of Congress in 1955, Eisenhower's HEW secretaries found it harder to advance their legislative agendas. These secretaries included Marion Folsom, who served three years beginning in August 1955, and Arthur Flemming, who completed the remainder of Eisenhower's term. Mrs. Hobby attracted considerable controversy over her handling of the distribution of Dr. Jonas Salk's polio vaccine, which became available in the spring of 1955. The adverse publicity hastened her departure in favor of Folsom, a former treasurer of the Eastman Kodak Company and an expert on private and public pension plans. Folsom devoted much of his attention to the nation's response to the Sputnik challenge in September 1957. To many the fact that Russia successfully orbited a satellite around the earth implied a failure in the American education system. Working closely with Assistant Secretary Elliot Richardson, Folsom devised what became the National Defense Education Act of 1958. Arthur Flemming, the former president of Ohio Wesleyan University and civil service commissioner, concentrated on regulatory matters, such as a 1959 controversy over the safety of the cranberry crop and a 1960 showdown with the governor of Louisiana over the state's proposal to cut children living in unsuitable homes from the welfare rolls.

John F. Kennedy named Abraham Ribicoff, midway through his second term as governor of Connecticut, as his secretary of HEW. Kennedy's plans for the New Frontier relied heavily on HEW's administrative capacity. In particular, he hoped to pass a health insurance program for the elderly (Medicare), to establish a program of federal aid to elementary and secondary education, to raise Social Security benefits, and to reform the welfare system. The demands of the job proved difficult for Ribicoff. When he left office in July 1962 to run for the Senate, he complained that the department was so large and so diverse as to be unmanageable. After becoming a senator in 1962, Ribicoff consistently supported legislation to dismantle the department.

The managerial difficulties that faced Ribicoff and Anthony Celebrezze, the former mayor of Cleveland, who served from the summer of 1962 to the summer of 1965, stemmed from the fact that, even as the department's budget and responsibilities grew, its organizational structure remained the same. That meant that Ribicoff governed HEW with the assistance of an under secretary and two assistant secretaries, one of whom concentrated on legislation and the other on finance. The Office of the Secretary served as little more than a holding company, a mere $7.5 million entity in a $3.8 billion agency (not including Social Security) that was barely able to manage large organizations such as the NIH. The years of a Democratic Congress and a Republican president between 1955 and 1961 had encouraged the heads of the NIH to establish independent relationships with powerful congressmen such as Representative John Fogarty (D-R.I.) and Senator Lister Hill (D-Ala.). Wilbur Cohen, the assistant secretary for legislation between 1961 and 1965, noted that "Senator Hill and Mr. Fogarty gave the definite impression that they were running the health aspects of the department and not Kennedy and Ribicoff."

Ribicoff's frustrations were heightened by the fact that Kennedy's major legislative proposals failed to pass during his presidency. Congress did approve a 1962 welfare reform proposal that strengthened the rehabilitative aspects of public assistance. Passage of these amendments encouraged Anthony Celebrezze to create the Welfare Administration in 1963. The Welfare Administration merged the Bureau of Family Services (formerly the Bureau of Public Assistance) and the Children's Bureau of the SSA with smaller offices concerned with social services, such as the Office of Juvenile Delinquency. In addition, Ribicoff elevated the Office of Vocational Rehabilitation to the Vocational Rehabilitation Administration, headed by Mary Switzer, a seasoned veteran who had worked in the department ever since the FSA's creation in 1939.

President Lyndon Johnson turned Kennedy's legislative proposals into laws. During fiscal 1965 and the first months of fiscal 1966, Congress passed thirty-five major acts relating to HEW. The three most important were the Civil Rights Act of 1964, which made it illegal for recipients of federal funds to discriminate on the basis of race, the Social Security Act amendments of 1965, which created Medicare, and the Elementary and Secondary Education Act of 1965, which provided federal funds to virtually every school district in the nation.

Just as Medicare, the last of the three major acts, became law, a new leadership team arrived at HEW. John Gardner, the former head of the Carnegie Corporation and one of the nation's leading authorities on education, became secretary on 18 August 1965. A few weeks earlier, Wilbur Cohen, who had worked for the Social Security program from 1935 to 1953 and enjoyed a reputation as one of the nation's foremost experts on social welfare policy, was promoted to under secretary. With these appointments, the department came the closest it ever would to professional, rather than political, management.

Gardner changed the bureaucratic structure that had persisted, largely unaltered, since 1953. As HEW secretary until 1 March 1968, when Cohen succeeded him, Gardner greatly expanded the Office of the Secretary. In 1966 the department added new assistant secretaries for health and scientific affairs, education, program coordination (later planning and evaluation), individual and family services, and administration. In addition, a new Administration on Aging administered the programs created by the Older Americans Act of 1965; new agencies, such as the Water Control Administration, oversaw environmental programs; and new special assistants, such as ones for public affairs and for civil rights, attended to the special concerns of the secretary.

In addition to expanding the Office of the Secretary and accomodating new legislation, Gardner reorganized the department's welfare programs. In the summer of 1967, he established the Social and Rehabilitation Service, headed by Mary Switzer, and placed public assistance (welfare payments), the Administration on Aging, Medicaid (medical care for welfare beneficiaries and the medically indigent), and the vocational rehabilitation program within it. The new organization lessened the number of independent agencies within the department.

These measures were John Gardner's way of bringing coherence to what the *New York Times* described as the department's "vast array of operating agencies" which produced "loosely organized" and "chaotic" results. Wilbur Cohen, who served for the remainder of Johnson's presidency, tried to finish what Gardner started by issuing a reorganization order in March 1968 that revamped the PHS. Secretary Cohen transferred all functions of the PHS and the Food and Drug Administration to the supervision of the assistant secretary for health and scientific affairs. He placed the National Library of Medicine and the Bureau of Health Manpower Education within the NIH, and he consolidated all other functions of the PHS into a new entity called the Health Services and Mental Health Administration.

Uniquely among those appointed secretary of HEW, Cohen relished his time on the job. In a valedictory essay he wrote that the secretary held a "demanding, versatile, important, exciting and intensely human job" and that his had been "a rich and gratifying stewardship." Cohen rejected the notion that HEW be broken up into separate departments concerned with health, education, and welfare. Instead, he proposed there be an under secretary for each of these areas and an under secretary for management. Cohen's proposal echoed one made earlier by John Gardner that HEW follow the model of the Department of Defense, in which secretaries for the various services reported to a secretary of defense.

The return of a Republican president in 1969 meant the appointment of Robert Finch as the seventh HEW secretary. Finch, who had known President Nixon since 1947 and managed his 1960 presidential campaign, came to HEW after serving as lieutenant governor of California. He said he accepted the job because HEW was "where the action is," and he wanted to prove that the department could be managed. A liberal

Republican, Finch hoped to achieve substantive reform, such as establishing a floor under federal welfare payments that would eliminate disparities among the states. As matters turned out, Finch, far from overseeing welfare reform, became the first of Nixon's cabinet officers to leave. The pressure on him became so intense that he developed health problems that forced a brief hospitalization and extended rest. Elliot Richardson, the former assistant secretary of HEW, lieutenant governor of Massachusetts, and under secretary of state, replaced him on 24 June 1970.

The sixties had permanently altered HEW. In 1960 total expenditures amounted to $15 billion, and in 1970 they were nearly $54 billion. When Elliot Richardson took over, the department employed 110,000 people, compared with 62,000 people in 1960. The department ran at least three hundred separate programs and participated in a plethora of social activities that were products of the social legislation of the sixties, such as HEW's mandates to withhold federal funds from segregated schools and finance medical services for the poor. In addition, the department's core programs continued to grow. To cite just one example, NIH appropriations of $430 million in 1960 had more than tripled by 1970.

With the creation of the Environmental Protection Agency in June 1970, President Nixon transferred responsibility for environmental policy from HEW to the new agency. Although he proposed that HEW be made part of a superdepartment of Human Resources that would include many of HEW's and the Department of Labor's programs, he moved to stem the growth of HEW's programs. Early in his second term, he appointed Caspar Weinberger, a former director of the Bureau of the Budget and a self-described "fiscal puritan," as secretary of HEW. Liberals objected to the appointment. Senator Harold Hughes (D-Iowa) called Weinberger "a hatchet man."

Weinberger discovered, as had his predecessors, that much of HEW's budget fell into the "noncontrollable" category. Programs such as Old-Age Insurance and Aid to Families with Dependent Children functioned as open-ended entitlements whose level of expenditures depended on the number of people eligible, not on some predetermined budgetary allocation.

As HEW secretary, Weinberger spent much of his time attempting to reorganize HEW to make it more efficient. He created the new position of assistant secretary for human development and placed such agencies as the Administration on Aging and the President's Council on Mental Retardation under it. He also rearranged the health programs into six large blocks: the NIH, the FDA, the Centers for Disease Control, the Health Resources Administration, the Health Services Administration, and the Alcohol, Drug Abuse, and Mental Health Administration.

When President Ford appointed David Mathews as secretary of HEW in August 1975, Mathews, the president of the University of Alabama, said, "I hope everybody fully realizes what a hard and often thankless task this post has become." In 1975 HEW spent one-third of all federal dollars but still faced enormous budgetary constraints. Rising welfare rolls and rising costs for Social Security gave the secretary little or no discretionary power over the budget. In addition to the frustrations of financial management, the HEW secretary faced growing dilemmas in the area of school desegregation, such as whether to condone the practice of forced busing.

Like his immediate predecessors, President Carter hoped to gain control over the $146 billion budget for HEW. He appointed Joseph Califano, a lawyer and former staff member in the Johnson White House, as secretary. Califano, who enjoyed more visibility than any HEW secretary since John Gardner, said he wanted to make HEW "a symbol of the manageability—not the unmanageability—of the government" and immediately announced a reorganization of the department that he promised would save the government $2 billion by 1981. Califano created the Health Care Financing Administration (HCFA), uniting Medicare, previously run by the SSA, and Medicaid, previously run by the Social and Rehabilitation Service. Califano also put Aid to Families with Dependent Children in the SSA, where it joined the Supplemental Security Income Program, an amalgamation of welfare programs serving the aged, blind, and disabled. In the same reorganization, Califano abolished the Social and Rehabilitation Service and created a new assistant secretary for human development to run the vocational rehabilitation program. He appointed an inspector general to root out fraud and abuse in the department, thus, it was hoped, holding down expenditures.

Despite this concern for the department's bureaucratic ranks, Califano ran the department from the top down. He wanted regional directors of HEW, who previously had enjoyed a great deal of autonomy, to report more directly to the secretary. He relied on personal assistants, many of whom were lawyers, to decide important questions, such as whether to sign regulations making educational facilities accessible to the handicapped. Furthermore, he made himself the center of attention in the battle against smoking, which he called "slow motion suicide."

Califano was the first HEW secretary to occupy what Congress designated in October 1977 as the Hubert Humphrey Building. Located on Independence Avenue, near the House offices, the modern and utilitarian building contained flexible interior space that could be altered as the structure of HEW changed. Across the street were two older office buildings, one named for Mary Switzer and the other for Wilbur Cohen (in 1988). Beyond these core buildings, the department fanned out across the Washington area and the nation. The NIH occupied a large campus in Bethesda; the SSA had its own large complex just outside of Baltimore, not to mention over one thousand field offices from coast to coast.

By making himself so visible and by refusing to hire people referred from the White House for many political appointments, Califano came under attack from the White House staff. In the summer of 1979, President Carter announced a major reshuffling of his cabinet, fired Califano, and replaced him with Patricia Roberts Harris. Harris, who had graduated first in her class at George Washington University and served President Carter as secretary of housing and urban development, was considered to be more of a team player than Califano. "You'll never see her fooling around with cigarettes," one HEW staffer noted.

TOWARD THE DEPARTMENT OF HEALTH AND HUMAN SERVICES

Being a team player meant endorsing the creation of a separate Department of Education. In his campaign and later in his 1978 State of the

Union address, President Carter committed himself to this goal. The pressure to create this department came from the National Education Association, which had 1.8 million members and had endorsed Carter in the 1976 election. Califano tried to dissuade Carter from separating education from HEW, arguing that the action would increase interest group pressure on the president and pointing to the fact that none of the groups that had studied governmental reorganization in the Johnson and Nixon administrations had recommended a Department of Education. Califano lost the argument within the Carter administration. "I don't know anything about the merits, but I know the politics and politically the NEA is important to us and it's important for the President to keep his word," said Hamilton Jordan of Carter's staff. Vice President Walter Mondale and Senator Ribicoff also strongly favored the department's creation. President Carter signed the Department of Education Organization Act into law in 1979.

It fell to Secretary Roberts to preside over the dismantling of HEW. On 4 May 1980 the Department of Education began with 17,000 employees and a $14 billion budget. The new Department of Health and Human Services (HHS) started with 140,000 employees and a budget of $226 billion. In addition to transferring its Education Division, HEW also lost the vocational rehabilitation program. Otherwise, the structure of HHS in 1980 was the same as that of HEW in 1979. The four major operating agencies of HHS consisted of the Office of Human Development Services, the PHS, the HCFA, and the SSA. Only the department's name, flag, and seal changed.

The Reagan and Bush eras were marked by a continuation of trends begun in the Carter era. Richard Schweiker, a former senator from Pennsylvania with a special interest in health care, concentrated on Social Security financing reform and changes in reimbursing hospitals in the Medicare program. Margaret Heckler, a former congresswoman from Massachusetts, who took over on 9 March 1983, implemented the reforms initiated by Schweiker and coped with a political crisis caused by the administration's removal of nearly half a million people from the disability rolls. Otis Bowen, the former governor of Indiana and physician known as Doc, served from late

1985 until the end of the Reagan administration and made the passage of catastrophic health insurance for Medicare beneficiaries his priority. Although he convinced Congress to pass the program, Congress later rescinded it. Louis Sullivan, a medical doctor and dean of the Morehouse Medical School, kept a low profile as George Bush's secretary of HHS and the only black in the cabinet. Perhaps as a result, he lasted for Bush's entire term, setting a record for longevity.

The only major organizational change in the Reagan and Bush years occurred in 1986, with the establishment of the Family Support Administration. This new agency effectively undid one of Califano's reforms by moving the Aid to Families with Dependent Children program out of the SSA and placing it with child support enforcement.

During the Clinton administration the department once again lost an important component. On 31 March 1995 the SSA became an independent agency. Senator Daniel Patrick Moynihan (D-N.Y.) was a leading supporter of the Social Security Independence and Program Improvements Act of 1994, signed into law on 15 August. At the White House signing ceremony the president used one of the pens with which Roosevelt had signed the 1935 Social Security Act.

The departure of the SSA left the PHS, with such major subdivisions as the NIH, the FDA, and the Centers for Disease Control and Prevention, as the largest operating division in the department. The three other components of the department included the HCFA, the Administration on Aging, and the Administration for Children and Families (which had been established in 1991 as a successor to the Family Support Administration).

Donna Shalala, the former president of the University of Wisconsin, presided over a department that at the end of 1995 ran 250 programs, employed 60,000 people, and maintained a budget of $332 billion. Although Franklin Roosevelt's desire to unite all the federal agencies "concerned with the promotion of social and economic security, educational opportunity, and the health of the citizens of the nation" had not been realized, HHS was the largest department of the federal government.

[*See also* Food and Drug Administration; Health Care Financing Administration; National Institutes of Health; Public Health Service; *and* Social Security Administration.]

BIBLIOGRAPHY

Altmeyer, Arthur J. *The Formative Years of Social Security.* Madison, Wis., 1966.

Berkowitz, Edward. *America's Welfare State: From Roosevelt to Reagan.* Baltimore, 1991.

Berkowitz, Edward. *Mr. Social Security: The Life of Wilbur J. Cohen.* Lawrence, Kans., 1995.

Califano, Joseph. *Governing America: An Insider's Report from the White House and the Cabinet.* New York, 1981.

Derthick, Martha. *Policymaking for Social Security.* Washington, D.C., 1979.

Derthick, Martha. *Agency under Stress.* Washington, D.C., 1991.

Miles, Rufus. *The Department of Health, Education, and Welfare.* New York, 1974.

Strickland, Stephen P. *Politics, Science and Dread Disease: A Short History of United States Medical Research Policy.* Cambridge, Mass., 1972.

Sundquist, James L. *Politics and Policy: The Eisenhower, Kennedy and Johnson Years.* Washington, D.C., 1968.

Witte, Edwin E. *The Development of the Social Security Act.* Madison, Wis., 1963. —EDWARD BERKOWITZ

Health Care Financing Administration

When Lyndon Johnson signed the Social Security Act amendments of 1965 into law on 30 July he set in motion the events that led to the founding of the Health Care Financing Administration (HCFA) in 1977. The 1965 law started three important programs in the field of health care finance. Medicare Part A helped to pay the hospital bills of elderly Social Security beneficiaries. Supplementary Health Insurance, or Medicare Part B, enabled these individuals to pay many of their doctor bills. Medicaid reimbursed the states for some of the expenses involved in providing medical care for individuals on welfare.

MEDICARE AND MEDICAID

The push to pass Medicare preoccupied the Social Security Administration (SSA) between 1961 and 1965. During these years the leaders of the pro-Medicare forces, such as Robert Ball of the SSA, made many concessions in order to gain congressional acceptance of the bill. At the core of the Medicare concept was the notion that hospital insurance would be financed through social insurance. That meant that people would pay for this insurance through payroll taxes assessed on them and their employers. Upon retirement they would become eligible for hospital insurance. Social Security leaders and their allies never questioned the fact that it would be the existing hospitals that would provide the necessary care. No thought was given to the establishment of federal or state hospitals. The Medicare proponents also agreed to allow private and quasi-private institutions, such as the regional Blue Cross organizations, to do the actual processing of hospital bills. No hospital had to deal directly with the SSA. Instead the hospital could send its bills to the local intermediary, usually the local Blue Cross organization.

Supplementary Health Insurance relied on a complex combination of general revenues and beneficiary contributions for its financing. Unlike hospital insurance, it was a voluntary program. Those who elected to participate usually paid their portion of the costs through a deduction in their Social Security paychecks, as well as through such standard insurance devices as co pays and deductibles. As with hospital insurance, private insurance carriers, acting under contract to the federal government, processed the actual bills.

To administer both parts of Medicare, the SSA established a major new operating division. Arthur Hess, a veteran Social Security bureaucrat who had helped to put disability insurance into operation in the period between 1954 and 1958, received the assignment of implementing Medicare through the Bureau of Health Insurance. Hess skillfully conducted negotiations with doctors, hospitals, and health insurers. On 1 July 1966 Wilbur Cohen, the under secretary of health, education, and welfare, wrote a note to Vice President Hubert Humphrey: "We put Medicare into operation at 12:01 this morning. It is a great day."

Medicaid, the third of the 1965 programs, had a different pedigree. Its creators worked for the Welfare Administration, which, beginning in

1960, administered a program that made grants to some of the states to defray some of the expenses of paying for the medical care of the elderly who could not otherwise afford it. Medicaid represented an expansion of this program. Instead of applying only to the elderly, Medicaid would apply to all categories of welfare recipients. Administration of the federal end of Medicaid was the responsibility of the Welfare Administration in the Department of Health, Education, and Welfare (HEW). In 1967 the Social and Rehabilitation Service (SRS), headed by respected bureaucrat Mary Switzer, became the successor agency to the Welfare Administration. Within this agency the Medical Services Administration supervised the federal part of Medicaid.

In 1965 the chief issues in health insurance centered on access. After the passage of Medicare and Medicaid, the issues shifted to cost. Since both Medicare and Medicaid became very expensive very quickly, policymakers turned their attention to containing the costs of the programs. In 1967, for example, Medicare Part A cost $3.4 billion, and in 1968, $4.3 billion. Despite sporadic efforts on the part of the Johnson and Nixon administrations to pass forms of national health insurance, Congress showed greater interest in legislation designed to reduce Medicare and Medicaid costs. Even as Congress expanded Medicare to include those on Social Security Disability Insurance in 1972, for example, it also mandated the use of "professional services review organizations" to monitor hospital admissions.

STARTING THE HCFA

In 1976 HEW Secretary David Mathews created a task force to examine the internal organization of the department. This group, led by Assistant Secretary John Young, issued its report on 15 December 1976. Although the report made no specific recommendations, it included the creation of an independent health care financing component as one of the options worthy of study. This component would unite Medicare and Medicaid as part of an "overriding need for consistency in a wide range of policy and operating decisions."

Eight days after the appearance of this report, President-elect Jimmy Carter named Joseph Ca-

lifano as his choice for secretary of HEW. As one of his first actions in January, Califano put together a working team of career bureaucrats to explore ways of reorganizing the department. Califano gave this team the explicit advice that he wanted Medicare and Medicaid together. He later explained that his motivation in undertaking the reorganization was his desire "to prove that Great Society programs could be managed." Because Califano wanted no interference from Congress or private interest groups, he made sure that the group worked in total secrecy. Among those who participated in this exercise were Don Wortman, who had headed the SRS, and Bruce Cardwell, the commissioner of social security. Califano, Under Secretary Hale Champion, and counsel Dick Beatty met with the team numerous times to review its recommendations.

On 2 March 1977 Califano briefed the president on his reorganization plans. In keeping with the tight security surrounding the project, Califano had the necessary documents and charts printed in a basement of the Pentagon. According to his later recollections, the president was ecstatic about the reorganization, and Vice President Mondale, who had recommended Califano to Carter, shared the president's feelings. Carter gave Califano permission to make a public announcement of the reorganization.

Califano unveiled his reorganization plans on 8 March 1977 at a press conference at which he said that he was initiating "the most far-reaching reorganization in the Department's 24-year history." An urgent need existed to place "HEW's disparate health care financing mechanisms, especially Medicare and Medicaid, under a single-minded, cost-conscious administrator." Because President Carter, the Congress, and the nation's governors recognized that need, Califano ordered the creation of the HCFA.

In essence, the HCFA consisted of the Bureau of Health Insurance from the SSA, the Medical Services Administration from the SRS, and the Bureau of Quality Assurance from the Health Services Administration of the Public Health Service (PHS). Califano promised that the HCFA would provide "basic quality control" and tackle "the problems of fraud and abuse." Along with "the introduction of basic managerial techniques," these initiatives would mean the savings of "literally hundreds of millions of dollars." Califano asserted that the Carter administration did not undertake this reform merely because of a "managerial fascination with box-shifting and line-drawing on an organizational chart" but rather because of a commitment to make government "credible because it is humane *and* efficient."

Within a matter of weeks, Califano recruited Robert Derzon, the director of the medical center at the University of California at San Francisco and an experienced hospital administrator, to serve as the first head of the HCFA. Since Califano believed that over-hospitalization was the reason for health care cost inflation, he wanted an expert on hospitals to be the HCFA administrator.

In the period between March and June, Derzon worked on the establishment of the HCFA. He later noted that he was "at some disadvantage" in the process because of his lack of experience with federal civil service rules. He worried that the SSA, the SRS, and the PHS withheld their best employees from the HCFA. It also became apparent that the directors of the agencies combined in the HCFA would fight hard to maintain the independence of their respective operations. Thomas Tierney of the Bureau of Health Insurance had little desire to merge his operations with those of M. Keith Weikel of the Medical Services Administration. Along with Dr. Michael Goran of the Bureau of Quality Assurance, these federal administrators resisted organizing along functional lines. As the HCFA went into operation, Medicare, Medicaid, and the process of certifying and setting standards for health care providers such as hospitals all remained separate operations.

Derzon soon earned Califano's displeasure, and on 22 September 1978 he resigned as HCFA administrator. In November, Leonard Schaeffer, the assistant secretary for management and budget at HEW and previously budget director for the state of Illinois and vice president of Citibank, took over the job. Schaeffer received instructions to merge the Medicare and Medicaid programs and to run the agency along more functional lines.

After visiting the many offices in which HCFA employees worked, Schaeffer decided that he needed to consolidate HCFA operations in Woodlawn, outside of Baltimore. That meant that former SRS employees who worked in downtown Washington and former Bureau of Quality Assurance employees who worked in Rockville, Maryland, would have to join the Medicare employees already at Woodlawn and relocate to suburban Baltimore. At the same time, Schaeffer reorganized the agency into five operating bureaus. In particular, a single Bureau of Program Operations would consolidate all contracting and state operations in the Medicare and Medicaid programs. A single Bureau of Program Policy would bring together all policy activities in Medicare, Medicaid, and the Office of Reimbursement Policies. Schaeffer announced this reorganization on 29 March 1979.

For the rest of his tenure, which lasted until June 1980, Schaeffer struggled to implement the changes that he had set in motion. Howard Newman, an experienced health care administrator who had run the Medicaid program between 1970 and 1974, succeeded Schaeffer and served for the rest of the Carter administration. In 1980 the HCFA had about five thousand permanent employees but relied upon eighty thousand nonfederal employees who worked under contract to the federal government in the Medicare program or who worked for the state Medicaid programs. The HCFA, which spent about $50 billion a year, utilized congressional appropriations of approximately $21 billion. The rest of the money came from the Medicare trust funds and from the states. Considered in terms of the money expended, rather than appropriated, the HCFA ranked as the third most expensive item in the federal budget, after Social Security and defense.

DIAGNOSIS RELATED GROUPS AND OTHER REAGAN INITIATIVES

Ronald Reagan chose Richard Schweiker, the former Pennsylvania senator, to head the renamed Department of Health and Human Services (HHS). (HEW had been dismantled during the late stages of the Carter administration.) Schweiker, in turn, named Carolyne Davis, a trained nurse and the associate vice president for academic affairs at the University of Michigan, as his HCFA administrator. Davis, who served until 1985, enjoyed the longest tenure of any HCFA administrator. During her administration she worked on cost containment measures in both Medicaid and Medicare. As Davis noted in congressional testimony in April 1981, Medicaid's growth had averaged more than fifteen percent over the past five years. The administration hoped to put a cap on Medicaid expenditures. Instead it settled for a scheme to reduce federal contribution rates by 4.5 percent by 1985. Davis and the administration also worked to substitute competition for what they regarded as heavy-handed regulation. Hence, she proposed phasing out federal support for the professional standards review organizations that had been created in 1972. Congress showed little interest in this initiative.

Davis worked hardest on designing and implementing a major change in hospital reimbursement procedures under Medicare. The HCFA funded much of the research that went into the development of "diagnosis related groups" (DRGs). The concept of DRGs represented a scheme for shifting to prospective, rather than cost-based retrospective, reimbursement under Medicare. In the old system hospitals received money according to the costs they accrued. In 1982 this system came under heavy attack in Congress. Under the Tax Equity and Fiscal Responsibility Act of that year, Congress tried to limit reimbursements and asked HHS to come up with a system, in Schweiker's words, "to eliminate perverse incentives and thereby to reverse the inflationary spiral in hospitals." In a report that reached Congress at the end of the year, HHS and the HCFA seized on the concept of DRGs that had been developed some ten years earlier at Yale.

According to this system, reimbursement would be linked to the diagnosis of people discharged from the hospital. Each discharge was classified by the diagnosis for a specific disease, the age of the patient, whether there had been surgery, and the physical status of the patient at discharge. That classification allowed the patient to be put into one of 467 DRGs. Although there were many exceptions, such as for teaching hos-

pitals, and variations were permitted by region of the country, the hospital received only the amount of money allowed for that particular DRG. An efficient hospital might make money. An inefficient hospital might lose money. In this way the administration hoped to give hospitals an incentive to reduce Medicare costs, rather than allowing them simply to pass along their increasing costs to the program.

The new prospective payment system became law as part of the Social Security financing reforms of 1983. Secretary Schweiker, in one of his last actions as secretary, made the decision to link Medicare and Social Security reform. He realized that no congressman could vote against the bill to save Social Security from bankruptcy. Hence, he secured the passage of DRGs by attaching them to "must" legislation. As a further means of winning the support of hospitals for the new proposal, payments under the system were calculated so as to be "budget neutral" through fiscal 1985. That meant that the hospitals did not lose any money under the new arrangement.

It took three years to phase in the new system. Even though this period coincided with the arrival of a new secretary of HHS, Boston-area congresswoman Margaret Heckler, Carolyne Davis decided that she needed to stay at the HCFA through the implementation period. By the end of September 1984, a total of 5,405 hospitals, or eighty-one percent of all Medicare-participating hospitals, were operating under the prospective payment system.

In May 1986 William Roper, an Alabama physician with a strong background in public health, became the new HCFA administrator. He expressed his priority as moving the Medicare and Medicaid programs toward greater reliance on private health plans. He was successful in promulgating regulations to allow Medicare beneficiaries to enroll in private health plans. In this way Medicare and its beneficiaries might take advantage of the savings involved in managed care. Roper also authorized that money be given to William Hsiao, a Harvard health economist, to perfect the system known as the "resource based relative value scale." This scale became the basis for changes in physician reimbursement in the Medicare program at the end of the decade.

In the Roper era the agency accounted for 10.3 percent of the federal budget. In fiscal 1988 the agency spent $179.4 billion, including $85.5 on Medicaid and $29 billion on the federal portion of Medicaid. Research and other administrative costs accounted for the rest. The central staff of the agency consisted of 4,046 people.

George Bush chose Gail Wilensky, the director of the Center for Health Affairs at Project Hope, to head the HCFA. She created a new administrative structure that featured four associate administrators for communications, management, operations, and program development. She also established a Medicaid Bureau that marked, in part, a return to the agency's structure in the days before Leonard Schaeffer.

THE HCFA IN THE CLINTON ERA

Bruce Vladeck, President Clinton's appointee as HCFA administrator, took office on 26 May 1993. Vladeck had been the president of the United Hospital Fund of New York City since 1983. Before that he had worked as a vice president of the Robert Wood Johnson Foundation, New Jersey's assistant commissioner for health planning and resources, and as a professor of public health and political science at Columbia.

Vladeck issued a statement in which he proclaimed that the HCFA was the largest health insurer in the country. In fiscal year 1993 over sixty-nine million beneficiaries received health care services through the Medicare and Medicaid programs. Outlays approached $222 billion, which equaled fourteen percent of the total federal budget. Considered as part of the health care system, Medicare and Medicaid represented thirty-four cents of every dollar spent on health care in the United States and accounted for forty-four cents of every dollar received by U.S. hospitals.

In addition to running the basic programs, the HCFA monitored the quality of care in Medicare through "peer review organizations" and worked with the states to survey some sixty thousand health care providers who participated in Medicare and Medicaid. The agency adminis-

tered the Clinical Laboratories Improvement Act and in this manner attempted to assure that the operation of some 152,000 laboratories met quality standards. Nor did these various forms of quality assurance exhaust the agency's responsibilities. The HCFA ran an extensive research program that, among other things, tested alternative delivery and payment schedules and maintained the largest collection of health care data in the world. The agency also assisted the states in the regulation of Medigap insurance. Because Medicare beneficiaries had to pay for many expenses out of pocket, an industry had developed to insure the beneficiaries against these costs. As a private form of health insurance, these Medigap policies were regulated by the states but with the HCFA's help and supervision.

In order to carry out these various responsibilities, the agency's staff in Vladeck's era numbered some 4,100. The bulk of these employees worked in Baltimore and Washington, but 1,500 were assigned to the agency's ten regional offices. In addition, the agency conducted its operations through eighty-one claims processing centers that employed 28,500 people, through fifty-three peer review organizations with 3,200 workers, and through 40,000 employees of state Medicaid agencies.

Vladeck concentrated his energy on two main projects. In February 1994, as a result of his urging, the agency issued a strategic plan. "We assure health care security for beneficiaries," the statement said, and "HCFA is dedicated to serving its customers." Vladeck hoped that the agency would expand its customers by means of President Clinton's health security bill, the second of Vladeck's major projects. This bill failed to pass in the period between 1992 and 1997.

In the summer of 1995, despite the disappointment over President Clinton's health plan, the agency celebrated an important occasion. In an era of government austerity, the agency opened an impressive new national headquarters in Woodlawn, Maryland. The new building featured some 668,000 square feet of usable space, including a large freestanding auditorium and a fitness center with direct access to the 57.4-acre site's walking and jogging trails. In the past the

HCFA's central staff had worked in numerous buildings near the SSA headquarters in Woodlawn. With the opening of the new building, all HCFA central staff employees were located in one office complex. In that regard the objectives of Joseph Califano's 1977 reorganization had been met.

BIBLIOGRAPHY

Baltis, Alan. "The Reorganization of DHEW: What Happened, Why, and So What?" *Journal of Health and Human Resources Administration* 1 (1979): 504–525.

Berkowitz, Edward. *Mr. Social Security: The Life of Wilbur J. Cohen.* Lawrence, Kans., 1995.

Califano, Joseph. *Governing America: An Insider's Report from the White House and the Cabinet.* New York; 1981.

David, Sherri I. *With Dignity.* Westport, Conn., 1965.

Kingson, Eric, and Edward Berkowitz. *Social Security and Medicare: A Policy Primer.* Westport, Conn., 1993.

Miles, Rufus. *The Department of Health, Education, and Welfare.* New York; 1974.

—EDWARD BERKOWITZ

Highway Administration, Federal

An agency within the Department of Transportation, the Federal Highway Administration (FHWA) sets safety standards for the design, construction, and maintenance of the nation's highways and for motor carriers using these highways. The FHWA is headed by an administrator appointed by the president and confirmed by the Senate. The agency administers the federal highway aid program, which distributes federal funds to the states to construct and improve the national highway grid. Engineering technology is the principal tool used by the agency to review and modify highway design so as to reduce traffic fatalities and accidents and increase the efficiency of traffic flows. The FHWA also regulates commercial motor carriers by setting safe operating standards. It has the right to inspect trucks on the road. In addition, it regulates the movement of dangerous cargo on highways and administers programs to reduce motor carrier noise. The FHWA administers the National Highway Institute and the highway beautification program and undertakes construction of certain types of roads on Indian reservations and in national parks and forests.

—GEORGE THOMAS KURIAN

Highway Traffic Safety Administration, National

An agency within the Department of Transportation that administers federal programs designed to increase motor vehicle safety, the National Highway Traffic Safety Administration (NHTSA) issues standards for vehicle and road safety, fuel economy, and damage liability. Headed by an administrator appointed by the president and confirmed by the Senate, the NHTSA is responsible for such areas as: development of mandatory minimum safety standards for vehicles and vehicle equipment such as lights, tires, and child restraints; establishment of average fuel economy standards for all vehicles; administration of maximum speed limits on highways; administration of anti–drunk driving programs; and administration of vehicle recalls and enforcement of laws against odometer tampering. Many auto safety features now common in most vehicles, such as air bags, automatic safety belts, high mounted stop lamps, safety windshields, dual brake systems, and steering columns able to absorb impacts, owe their development to the agency.

Charged with the authority to collect information on vehicular safety and to enforce compliance, the agency operates a toll-free auto safety hotline through which consumers provide it with most of its information on vehicle defects. If a pattern of complaints points to a potential safety defect, investigations may be conducted, public hearings held, and the manufacturer ordered to recall the vehicle or product. Driver and pedestrian safety programs are supervised through grants to states, including programs to combat drunk driving as well as others dealing with emergency medical services, police traffic services, and traffic records. A nationwide file of drivers with suspensions for drunk driving is maintained in the National Driver Register. In addition, the NHTSA may fine manufacturers who fail to comply with fuel economy standards

and offer credit to manufacturers who exceed them.
—GEORGE THOMAS KURIAN

History and Historians in the Federal Government

ESSAY In the late eighteenth century the United States established its federal system of government and elected its first national leaders at the high tide of the Enlightenment. Documenting the history of those extraordinary years of democratic self-government set the agenda for federal history for many decades. Members of the initial Congresses authorized the printing of *The Journals of the Continental Congress*. The first national leaders established the Library of Congress, authorized the printing of the *Congressional Record,* and assembled and then contributed their papers to state historical societies or state libraries. They wanted the history of the new national government preserved, recorded, and placed in a permanent institution of learning. In 1818 Congress funded the publication of the *Journal of the Constitutional Convention*. Two years later, in 1820, it authorized the printing of *The Secret Journals of the Constitutional Congress*. Then, following a decade of inactivity, Congress funded another historical series, prepared by the State Department, entitled *Diplomatic Correspondence*.

With the administration of President Andrew Jackson (1828–1836) the preparation and funding of federal history took a turn toward contract history. In 1832 Congress authorized funds for publishing two series of documents: the noted printers Galen and Seaton collected, assembled, and printed *American State Papers* (38 vols., 1832–1861), while Peter Force and Matthew St. Clair Clarke were contracted to publish their remarkable collection of documents on the American Revolution, *Documentary History of the American Revolution* (9 vols., 1838–1853). Concern with documenting the writings of the Founding Fathers began in 1840 with the publication of the papers of James Madison, constitutional scholar, senator, and president. This volume spurred ef-

forts over the next two decades to publish the collected papers of John Adams, Thomas Jefferson, and Alexander Hamilton. This effort to record and disseminate the key documents of the federal government to the citizens continued past midcentury with the publication in 1861 of the inaugural volume of the U.S. State Department's *Foreign Relations of the United States* series. This distinguished historical series has been collected, edited, and published continuously since 1861. By 1996 it comprised 340 volumes.

During the first seventy years of the federal government, no event caused such intense historical activity as the Civil War. National politicians, military leaders, veterans' groups, and ordinary citizens demanded that this fundamental event in the life of the nation be thoroughly researched and documented, and that the findings be published and disseminated to the American public. The result, *The Official Records of the War of the Rebellion,* (131 vols., 1880–1901), was the largest and most expensive documentary collection ever published by the federal government to that time. Even today it remains perhaps the most widely read and continually studied of all the federal historical series. It set a pattern for documenting and publishing the records of the major wars in the twentieth century.

After World War I had ended, the U.S. Army's Historical Branch projected a sixty-five-volume history of the Army's participation in the war, but rapid postwar demobilization and Secretary of War Newton D. Baker's concern about controversy over economic, political, and diplomatic issues stopped the project. Instead, Baker restricted Army historians to "the collection, indexing, and preservation of the records of the war." Baker's policy limited the influence of historical work in the Army for more than twenty-five years. Military historians in the U.S. Army Air Service were similarly inhibited, as they collected but did not publish a four-volume series on the Air Service in its first war. The U.S. Army Medical Division did manage to publish a fifteen-volume history of its clinical and administrative war efforts.

As of 1920, the federal government employed a very small number of historians in only three departments: War, Navy, and Agriculture. The federal government had 655,000 employees, approximately eighty-five percent of whom worked in just two areas, the Post Office and the military services. The rest worked in accounting, budgeting, and enforcing federal regulations. The Government Accounting Office, which reviewed every voucher, check, and dollar spent by every federal employee, had fewer than one thousand employees. Not until the administration of President Franklin D. Roosevelt (1932–1945) would the transition take place from a small federal government to a large, activist government with programs in virtually every aspect of American life. By 1936 the Roosevelt administration had 250,000 projects under way—40,000 new schools, 500,000 miles of new highways, 1,000 airports, and thousands of new hospitals. More than 4.2 million people worked for the federal government. From this point, the presence of historians in the federal government grew with the expansion of the national government. In many ways this growth paralleled the government's increasing reliance on engineers, economists, physicists, librarians, statisticians, and other educated professionals as the century progressed.

The creation of this large, activist, bureaucratic state came during a time when public accountability and public dissemination of information about the working of these federal projects was encouraged and even sponsored. Public administrators and national park leaders led the way, hiring historians who set to work documenting, researching, writing, and publishing monographs and histories. This development was particularly evident in the Interior Department, where the National Park Service began to employ a corps of National Park Rangers to manage and serve the public. Parks with a historical theme, such as Independence Park in Philadelphia, and the National Mall in Washington, D.C., employed a number of federal historians. The relevance of historical study to the national parks was patent, since many parks owed their existence to one or more national historical events. But the connection was not so obvious when federal historians were employed to document, record, and interpret histories of engineering, construction, and federal dam projects. Hundreds of such historical monographs were written and published in limited numbers during the New Deal.

In 1934 Congress established the National Archives of the United States as the first modern archives for the federal government. Public availability of essential federal records had its origin in this act. The standards for becoming an archivist were rooted in the study of history, especially the history of the American government. The first archivist was a historian, and in subsequent years this link has remained strong.

Beginning during World War II and continuing for almost fifty years, historians of the military services researched, wrote, and published multivolume histories of the war, the largest and probably the most comprehensive of which is the *U.S. Army's History of World War II* (80 vols., 1946–1990). Kent Roberts Greenfield and Stetson Conn served as general editors of these well-known Army histories. The U.S. Air Force recruited a distinguished staff of military historians for *The Army Air Forces in World War II* (7 vols., 1948–1958). Samuel Eliot Morison, the nation's most distinguished maritime historian, guided the production of *The History of the United States Navy in World War II* (15 vols., 1947–1952). The U.S. Marine Corps documented its unique experiences in the war with a historical series of its own, *The United States Marines in World War II* (5 vols., 1961–1971). The importance of these multivolume series for federal history cannot be overestimated. First, they served the nation well as a record of the national military experience during World War II. Few of the fundamental interpretations in these histories have been challenged by subsequent historians. Second, they established a new pattern for published federal histories, embodying the shift from documentary series, such as that which appeared after the Civil War, to narrative history series researched and written by professional historians. Finally, they pointed the way for all modern federal history programs: research in original sources, narrative writing, focus on campaigns, process, and leadership, and publication in letterpress volumes. Each of these series was distributed widely to the public, to military academies, and to universities in the United States and abroad.

World War II contributed directly to a virtual

explosion of government records in every area. The National Archives, located in a single neo-classical building in Washington, D.C., before the war, now was faced with huge warehouses bulging with federal records from the far-flung campaigns of American military forces all over the world. In the decade following the war, the National Archives had to be redefined, expanded, and extensively reorganized. Out of this process came the creation of federal records centers and the presidential library system. The former enabled the national government to expand its records management system outside of the capital city, while the latter brought together the records of each of the modern presidents into a central library and archives. These were significant developments to federal historians because virtually all of their research was rooted in original federal records; the retention, location, and organization of these records was a major concern to all historians.

For much of the postwar era, the federal government was dominated by a concern with maintaining the national security state. The consequences of these developments for federal historians were far-reaching. Military historians became perhaps the dominant force in the field of federal history. They had achieved status and standing as a result of their published work on World War II; now following the war they became public historians working directly for the military commanders and their senior staffs. History offices were established by the Office of the Secretary of Defense, the Joint Chiefs of Staff, the Defense Intelligence Agency, and the Central Intelligence Agency. The U.S. Air Force led the way in creating a corps of professional historians who worked directly for field commanders, recording and documenting their planning, preparations, and operations. This documentary record proved useful to many senior planning and operational officers. During the Korean and Vietnam wars, all of the military services utilized field historians to collect, record, and document combat operations.

In the same decade (1945–1955), the national security state created entirely new departments of the federal government. In the 1950s, there were historians working in a cluster of federal

agencies devoted to energy, nuclear power, and nuclear weapons. Richard Hewlett and Oscar Anderson researched and wrote a series of masterful federal histories documenting the U.S. government's management of nuclear weapons in these precedent-setting years. They wrote interpretative narrative histories of the Manhattan Project, the Atomic Energy Commission and the Truman administration, the nuclear navy, and other topics. Contributing to these volumes at one time or another were a dozen professional historians who in addition developed an archival and management system for their organizations. Perhaps the most significant accomplishment of these federal historians has been to help shape national discussion over the past fifty years about the control and use of nuclear energy. Deeply researched historical volumes have provided an intellectual foundation for much of the serious debate on this topic.

If fifties witnessed the growth of federal history in the service of the national security state, the next decade saw historians responding to the public's insatiable desire to know more about American life and culture. One consequence for the federal government was that the national museum, the Smithsonian Institution, grew significantly during the sixties and seventies. The Smithsonian's Museum of History and Technology was renamed the National Museum of American History. Social historians were employed to create museum displays focusing on diverse aspects of American life and history: displays concentrating strictly on government activity fell into disfavor, while major shows focusing on civil rights, immigration, women, and technology in American life predominated. Meanwhile, the National Museum of American Art and the National Air and Space Museum, entirely new museums that were added to the Smithsonian Institution during these years, came to be regarded as premier museums in the United States and the world in their respective fields. (The twenty-five to thirty federal historians and curators employed by the National Air and Space Museum would spark a major political controversy during the mid-nineties with their handling of a commemorative exhibit featuring the Enola Gay aircraft, and ultimately would be forced to withdraw contentious references to the U.S. military's use of the atomic bomb during World War II.) Another significant development of the sixties was the rise of the environmental movement in the United States, one that did not confine itself to the natural environment but manifested a concern for the nation's historical environment as well. The National Historical Preservation Act of 1966 created the legal authority for a system of federal regulations governing a national register of historic places, houses, and cultural landmarks. Federal historians in the National Park Service, and state historical preservation officers administering the program have worked closely with architects, preservationists, public historians, and archeologists to create a substantial body of preserved sites throughout the United States. Numerous historic structures of the U.S. military services, including forts, ports, and airfields, likewise would have been lost had it not been for the work of these federal regulators, many of whom were federal historians.

One of the most interesting developments of the late seventies and eighties was the concern with documenting, recording, and disseminating the history of the Senate and the House of Representatives. As a consequence of the national interest in political history generated by the 1976 Bicentennial, the House of Representatives created the Office of the Historian. Staffed by three professional historians, its work, in addition to substantial reference work, has been to publish documentary biographical histories of House members. Established during the same years, the Senate historical office developed a multifaceted operation, assisting senators and their staffs with office record keeping and the retention of their personal papers. Working with Senate majority leader Robert Byrd (D-W.Va.), Senate historians researched and published a multivolume history of the upper house. The office has recorded an interesting series of oral histories with senior Senate staffers.

During what might be termed the post–Cold War nineties, there have been several interesting developments in federal history programs. New programs have been created in new arms control agencies, the Postal Service, and the Defense Communications Agency. The Department of Agriculture, the Internal Revenue Service, and the Federal Bureau of Investigation, meanwhile, have eliminated history offices altogether. In a fascinating development, the history offices associated with the national intelligence services—the Central Intelligence Agency, the National Security Agency, the Defense Intelligence Agency, and even the National Reconnaissance Office—have begun to publish a documentary record of their Cold War activities. The National Archives was reinvigorated with new leadership and a new "Archives II" structure. It will house many of the federal government's critical records into the twenty-first century.

Two professional organizations have been established to encourage the federal government to preserve its history and to support federal historians. The Society for History in the Federal Government was founded in 1979 as a nonprofit organization to promote the study and broad understanding of the history of the federal government. It has approximately 450 members and serves as the "voice" of federal historians. The National Council for Public History promotes the cause of public history at the local, state, and national levels. It has a broader constituency and conducts national meetings annually. Both of these organizations, as well as the American Historical Association, have championed federal history programs before Congress.

[See also Library of Congress; National Archives; and Smithsonian Institution.]

BIBLIOGRAPHY

Harahan, Joseph P., and David M. Pemberton. "United States Federal History: A Bibliography." Government Publications Review. Vol. 16, 463–488.
Holl, Jack M. "The New Washington Monument: History in the Federal Government." Public Historian (Fall 1985): 9–20.
Jessup, John E., and Robert W. Coakley. A Guide to the Study and Use of Military History. Washington, D.C., 1987.
Morton, Louis. "The Historian and the Federal Government: A Proposal for a Government-wide Historical Office." Prologue (Spring 1977): 1–14.

—JOSEPH P. HARAHAN

Hoover Commission Report.

See Appendix: Basic Documents of Public Administration.

House of Representatives

ESSAY As intended by the framers of the U.S. Constitution, the House of Representatives is the more popularly oriented of the nation's two legislative bodies. The House of Representatives is distinctive in its origins, traditions, rules, and leadership, and its procedures and style differ from those found in the Senate, its legislative counterpart. Members of the House of Representatives are elected to two-year terms every even year by a direct popular vote. They are elected from evenly populated congressional districts within each state, and more populous states send more representatives to Congress than do those with fewer people. Because of these characteristics and others, James Madison, one of the framers of the Constitution, called the House "the grand repository of the democratic principle of government."

ORIGINS

During the summer of 1789, the members of the Constitutional Convention gathered in Philadelphia to revise the Articles of Confederation. They soon decided to scrap the old decentralized system for something that would better preserve the nationalist feeling growing out of the American Revolution. Madison and the other framers had to grapple with the fresh fears of central authority while strengthening the system; moreover, any plan would certainly advantage some states at the expense of others.

Based on an understanding of the British Parliament and on experience in the Colonial assemblies, a consensus grew for a new bicameral legislature empowered to directly adopt laws. This "Virginia Plan" called for a lower house elected by the people, with representation to be determined on a proportional basis. Yet many of the Framers were also convinced that some voice in national government should be reserved to the states regardless of size. Eventually a "Great Compromise" was reached, leading to the creation of the House of Representatives and the Senate, the former chamber based on population and the latter equally represented among the states.

The House was intended to be the more responsive to the people. Each member would stand for election every two years. The Constitution (Art. I, Sec. 2) specifies that a census be taken every ten years, and the number of representatives is apportioned among the several states in accordance with this enumeration. [*See* Census, Bureau of the.] The First Congress had sixty-five members, and as the country grew, so did the House. By 1911, when the House had 435 members, the Congress stopped the expansion of seats and decided to reapportion them as necessary at this fixed number. Today, each House district contains slightly more than half a million people.

POWERS

The House is granted three special powers, the first and most fundamental of which is the power to tax. Though this responsibility is shared with the Senate, all revenue bills must originate in the House (Art. I, Sec. 7). The Framers felt that the power to initiate taxation must be placed in the body that faces the electorate directly and frequently. The House soon assumed the power to originate all spending or appropriation bills as well.

The second special power of the House is to recommend removal of federal officials through the impeachment process (Art. I, Sec. 2), a procedure that is similar to that of an indictment in a criminal trial; the trial itself takes place in the Senate. The most noteworthy example of this procedure was the impeachment of President Andrew Johnson in 1868. (Actual removal from office failed by one vote in the Senate.) The procedure has been used sixty times since 1789, with the Senate sitting as a court of impeachment fifteen times, and with seven individuals (all federal judges) being removed from office. The power remains an effective check on the executive and judicial branches. In 1974 the impeachment process commenced over the Watergate affair, but President Richard Nixon resigned before a vote of the full House was taken.

The third power of the House is to elect the president when the electors fail to do so because of a tie or lack of a majority, a circumstance that has happened twice in U.S. history. The Constitution (Art. II, Sec. 1) provides that the "House . . . shall choose one of them for President." Each state delegation has one vote, and a majority of all states is needed for a decision. In 1800, when Thomas Jefferson and Aaron Burr tied in electoral balloting, Jefferson was subsequently chosen by the House. In 1824 a four-candidate field prevented Andrew Jackson, winner of the popular vote, from gaining an electoral majority. John Quincy Adams was then chosen by the House when a third candidate, Henry Clay, threw his support to him. Clay was later named secretary of state by Adams, leading to calls of a "corrupt bargain" by the supporters of Jackson.

The House's having to decide a presidential election takes on heightened importance whenever strong third-party candidates enter the presidential race. In 1968 independent George Wallace won forty-six electoral votes, but Republican Richard Nixon won enough states to receive a majority of electoral votes over Hubert Humphrey, the Democratic nominee, and Wallace. In 1992 independent Ross Perot received nineteen percent of the popular vote but did not win a majority of votes in any single state, and hence earned no electoral votes. Democrat Bill Clinton easily won an electoral majority over Republican George Bush, 370 to 168.

LEADERSHIP

After each election, the House is reorganized when leaders and administrative officers are elected and rules are formally adopted. The votes for the Speaker of the House and the adoption of rules are usually cast along party lines since each party falls in behind its own leader and the two parties often differ on rules of procedure. The leadership and the rules then govern legislative and administrative activity in the House.

Article I, Section 2, of the Constitution specifies that the House "shall choose their Speaker and other Officers," but there is no reference to specific duties. For the first two decades, the Speaker was largely a presiding officer much like the Speaker in the British House of Commons. But beginning with Henry Clay in 1811, Speakers took a more active role in partisan policy-making and legislative strategy. Over time, the Speaker became the paramount majority party leader. Particularly influential individuals such as Thomas Brackett Reed, Joseph G. Cannon, Sam Rayburn, and Thomas P. O'Neill, Jr., have put their own imprint on the role of Speaker of the House. "Uncle Joe" Cannon, for example, consolidated formal powers of the Speaker to such an extent that the membership eventually stripped him of some of those powers. Sam Rayburn, on the other hand, employed the powers of persuasion along with his long years of experience to cultivate support and ensure discipline among the members.

The Speaker is responsible for the administration of the House. In this capacity the Speaker is assisted by other elected officers, including the clerk of the House (who keeps the House journal and records legislation), the House sergeant-at-arms (who ensures decorum in the chamber and security in the Capitol), and the chief administrative officer (who handles building supplies and payroll).

The Speaker has important legislative responsibilities. Aside from acting as presiding officer (a role that is often delegated to another member of the majority party), the Speaker refers bills and resolutions to appropriate committees, appoints members to special committees like conference committees, and acts as chief spokesman for the House. In addition, the Speaker is second in line behind the vice president to succeed to the presidency, making the position inherently one of high visibility.

A Speaker's principal deputy is the majority leader, who is primarily responsible for managing activities on the House floor such as the daily and weekly agendas. The majority leader has a counterpart in the party out of power—the minority leader. The majority and minority leaders consult with members to gauge sentiment and work to advance the goals of the party in question. When the president meets with the leadership in Congress, the House representation includes the Speaker of the House, the House majority leader, and the House minority leader.

The assistants to the party leaders are the whips. As the term implies, the majority and minority whips encourage party discipline, count votes, and generally mobilize support for their respective parties. They are assisted through a whip system that includes a variety of deputies and assistants.

RULES AND PROCEDURES

The House formally adopts or readopts its rules every Congress. The 104th Congress, elected in 1994, had fifty-two rules. All in all, about two hundred different precepts were reflected in these rules. Some thirty-five rules can be traced to the First Congress. House rules govern organizational, administrative, and legislative matters.

Organizational rules include the duties and responsibilities of House officers: the Speaker, the clerk, the sergeant-at-arms, the chief administrative officer, and others. The jurisdiction and oversight responsibilities of the standing committees are also described in the rules. Administrative rules describe such matters as accounting for expenses, the recording of proceedings, use of the chamber and galleries, and codes of conduct: rule 52, for example, prohibits members, officers, and staff from accepting gifts under most circumstances. Legislative rules proscribe the conduct of business in the committees and on the floor of the House. Such rules detail the use of motions, the amending process, and procedures for reconciling differences between House and Senate versions of bills. Rules may also be specified within a statute: the Congressional Budget Act of 1974, for example, contains specific rules governing budget preparation and consideration.

The precedents of the House, that is, the accumulated decisions of the Speakers and other presiding officers, provide a rich foundation for rule interpretation. The House follows precedent in ruling on points of order or inquiry, and its decisions are published in such works as Deschler and Brown's *Procedure in the United States House of Representatives*. To assist the Speaker or presiding officer in procedural rulings and interpretation

of rules is the job of the House parliamentarian. As noted, rules and procedures govern all components of the legislative process.

ON THE FLOOR OF THE HOUSE

Under most circumstances the House convenes at noon. The chaplain of the House or a guest delivers a prayer. The Speaker, or more likely a member of the majority party appointed by the Speaker to preside temporarily, announces the approval of the House journal, the official proceedings of the previous day. The Speaker then chooses a member to lead the Pledge of Allegiance. This is usually followed by a series of one-minute speeches on various subjects by selected members from each party. These speeches publicize concerns of the day to both colleagues and constituents since floor proceedings are televised and can be seen in most areas around the country. Routine House business then begins.

Uncontroversial bills are cleared by unanimous consent through the use of the consent calendar. Bills affecting individuals are dispensed with through the private calendar. "Suspension days" involve a suspension of the rules, requiring a two-thirds vote. This provides for the immediate consideration of a bill, limits debate, and restricts amendments. For the majority, suspensions speed up the legislative process provided they have the votes. The opposition needs only one-third of the House to defeat measures.

A common procedure for handling major legislation, usually measures that contain some controversial matters or those dealing with money, is for the House to act as a Committee of the Whole. In this case, the Speaker appoints a majority member to serve as presiding officer. This officer is now addressed "Mister" or "Madam Chairman" rather than Speaker. The full House can then employ the more expeditious rules that govern committees.

The most contentious issues are usually considered under a "special rule" provided by the House Committee on Rules that first must be adopted by the House in the Committee of the Whole. This rule governs the time allotted for debate and sets terms for amendments. Once the rule is passed (on rare occasions a rule may be defeated, in effect stopping the process cold), time for debate is divided evenly between the majority and minority. Floor managers, usually the committee chairperson and the ranking member of the committee handling the bill, direct the action.

When the debate time has expired and the amendments, if any, have been disposed of, the Committee of the Whole disbands and the chamber again becomes the House. The chairman leaves and the Speaker returns to the rostrum. The mace, the symbol of legislative authority, is returned to the high pedestal next to the Speaker's desk. The mace is moved to a lower position during the Committee of the Whole process and is taken out of the chamber by the sergeant-at-arms when the House is in recess.

The measure debated by the Committee of the Whole is now available for a vote on final passage. The opposition can now move to recommit the bill back to a committee, a tactic that, if approved, effectively kills the measure. Once the recommittal motion is disposed of, the House can vote on final passage.

By late afternoon or early evening, the majority and minority leaders usually have a short dialogue on the upcoming legislative schedule. Following this, the House goes to special orders, a series of short or long (up to one hour) speeches on any topic by members subject to prior approval to speak. Since legislative business for the day has been concluded, the members speaking during special orders often face an empty chamber. Since the advent of televised proceedings, however, members have used the special orders procedures as a vehicle to focus attention on certain matters, highlight differences with the opposing party, and to communicate directly to voters watching on television. Many observers trace the rise of Speaker Newt Gingrich to his use of special orders speaking opportunities early in his career.

The final motion of the day, to adjourn, is usually given by the member delivering the last special order speech. The Speaker, more likely the Speaker *pro tempore,* and the clerks then leave the rostrum, and a day in the House is over.

COMMITTEES

The real action in the legislative process takes place in committee. This is where bills are assem-

bled and refashioned; where they come to life. It is also where most of them die. In the House there are nineteen standing committees with eighty-six subcommittees; there are also four joint committees and one permanent select committee. Proposed legislation can be referred to committees or originate with them. Subcommittees usually consider proposed legislation first. Hearings are held and testimony taken. The subcommittee may approve, change, or kill a bill. The full committee takes it next. Additional testimony may be needed. If the full committee approves, the measure then goes to the floor, where it is managed by the subcommittee or full committee leaders.

Committees also have oversight authority over departments and agencies of government. Through hearings and sometimes investigations, committees can review performance, expenditures, and management decisions. This information is often important in determining appropriations or spending on programs. Oversight power originated with the Legislative Reorganization Act of 1946, which directed the House and Senate committees to exercise "continuous watchfulness of the execution of administrative agencies."

RELATIONS WITH THE PRESIDENT

As the House cannot act without the involvement of the Senate, the Congress cannot act without the involvement of the president, even if cooperation is not forthcoming. The president remains a key figure in the legislative process. Under Article II, the president can convene one or both houses of Congress in special session. Though the president cannot introduce legislation directly, the State of the Union message offers the opportunity to recommend "measures he shall judge necessary and expedient." The president and his staff can, of course, lobby Congress for measures being introduced or debated.

The president can veto legislation. Often, the mere threat of a veto can influence the version of legislation likely to be passed by the Congress. The House and Senate can override a veto by a two-thirds vote, but this is a difficult vote to achieve in both chambers. Though a president does not have to sign a bill for it to become law, Article I, Section 7, provides that a bill "shall not be law" if Congress adjourns before a president signs a measure. In this case a president can pocket the legislation—hence, "pocket veto." Shortly before the end of the Civil War, for example, President Lincoln, seeking to avoid strained relations with Congress over a formal veto, simply pocketed what he viewed as a particularly harsh Reconstruction measure bill and then waited for Congress to adjourn.

The relations between the president and Congress can be smooth or rocky. When one party controls the White House and the other controls Congress—"divided government" as it is called—relations can be especially contentious. Problems may arise even when a single party controls both branches and both chambers. Events, politics, and the institutional prerogatives of each branch and chamber play important roles.

Membership in the House of Representatives has been the first step in national service for many significant future leaders. Eighteen presidents first were members of the House of Representatives, including James Madison, Abraham Lincoln, John Kennedy, Richard Nixon, and George Bush. John Quincy Adams was elected to the House after serving as senator and president.

FUTURE DIRECTIONS

Until recently, the House had been slow to adopt new technology, but important strides have been taken to make the institution more effective and accountable. For example, House documents are now available through the THOMAS system via Internet access to the Library of Congress. The 104th Congress reorganized and renamed some committees, disbanded others, revamped administrative offices, reduced staff, and applied to itself the workplace laws it passed.

The House has changed in other ways too. As of May 1996, its membership included forty-eight women, thirty-nine African Americans, and eighteen Hispanic members. Though attorneys still make up the largest single block of professions represented in the House, an increasing number of new members come from careers in business and education.

Majoritarian in character, rule-laden in operation, and bound by the traditions of some two hundred years of practice, the House of Representatives remains an unwieldly and frustrating place to many. Most scholars agree, however, that the Founders devised a system of representative government and separation of powers knowing full well that a price would be paid in efficiency. As one Russian visitor once remarked when viewing the House from the gallery, "Congress is so strange. A man gets up and speaks. Nobody listens—then everybody disagrees." Behind the apparent confusion lies a strong yet malleable body. The U.S. House of Representatives has demonstrated throughout its history that it can adapt to both political and social change.

[*See also* Executive Power; Judicial Branch; President as Chief Executive; Presidential Succession and Disability; Senate; *and* Supreme Court Decisions on the Presidency.]

BIBLIOGRAPHY

Josephy, Alvin M. *The American Heritage History of the Congress of the United States.* New York, 1975.
Smith, Steven S. "The House of Representatives." In *The Encyclopedia of the United States Congress,* edited by Donald C. Baker, Roger H. Davidson, and Morton Keller. New York, 1995.
U.S. Congress. House Commission on the Bicentenary. *Origins of the House of Representatives: A Documentary Record.* 101st Cong., 1st sess., 1990. H. Doc. 101–118.
U.S. Congress, House Committee on House Administration. *History of the House of Representatives.* 87th Cong., 1st sess., 1962. H. Doc. 87–246.
U.S. Congress. House Committee on House Administration. *History of the House of Representatives, 1789–1994.* 103d Cong., 2d sess., 1994. H. Doc. 103–324.
—JOHN J. KORNACKI

Housing and Urban Development, Department of

Tenth among the fourteen cabinet departments by date of origin, the Department of Housing and Urban Development (HUD) is a comparatively recent and somewhat insecure arrival on the Washington scene. It celebrated its thirtieth anniversary in 1995 amid continuing congressional calls for its abolition. The political forces that called for its establishment have dissipated thanks to the flow of people and jobs out of large central cities. Its precise origins remain a matter of some speculation, even for the contemporary professional historian. However tenuous, HUD's institutional survival bears witness to our persistent national problems of affordable housing, especially for the poor and homeless, and the seething discontent of urban newcomers trapped in large central cities. These anxieties have been compounded by the arrival of unparalleled numbers of new immigrants since the 1980s.

HUD's affairs have been directed by ten secretaries, divided equally between Democratic and Republican administrations. Policies and programs have shifted sharply, but the persistent dilemma has been how to substantially underwrite the provision of housing for middle-income and poor families while working primarily to ensure stable and genuine community life in a "suitable metropolitan environment." In pursuing this mission, HUD has had to address the operational issue as to whether it is more effective to provide affordable housing for most income levels by subsidizing production or by relying on consumer vouchers to enhance individual choice. Hard on the heels of this question is what steps are feasible and desirable to encourage sound and manageable community building, especially communities that accommodate the increasing diversity of the American people. The sometimes contradictory thrusts of departmental missions and their political saliency must be viewed in the context of the dramatic changes in land use that have occurred as the nation transforms itself from a densely packed, largely self-contained urban country to one exhibiting a more thinly settled and expansive metropolitan pattern of settlement.

THE UNCERTAIN ORIGINS

Even though the department is only a little over a generation old, accounting accurately for HUD's elevation to departmental status is not a straightforward matter. The trail goes back at least to the 1949 Housing Act and the growing political concern about what was occurring in post–World War II cities. By the late 1950s that political concern surfaced in the Democratic Na-

tional Committee, which had brought together a coalition of academics specializing in urban affairs and big-city mayors who were faced with severe problems and were trying to put cities on the national agenda.

But the precise sequence of events remains poorly understood, marked by "obscure reference to unrecorded conversations," "occasional papers by policy instigators with disparate motives," "poorly drafted memoranda," "purportedly learned treatises," "intemperate Congressional debates," and "excessively enthusiastic presidential rhetoric" (Wood). These forces gradually built momentum that accelerated rapidly in 1965 after the first contemporary urban riot in Watts, California. Soon afterward President Johnson established the first of a series of urban task forces, and in his speech at Ann Arbor, Michigan, calling for a Great Society, he called attention to the problem of cities as being an area of national concern on a par with those of health and education.

The same forces that were pushing to put urban affairs on the national policy agenda—academics who had come to see cities as a respectable field of inquiry in the social sciences and an increasingly vigorous lobby of big-city mayors, downtown business leaders, and urban renewal directors—pushed for departmental status. The call for a cabinet seat became explicit during the 1960 Kennedy presidential campaign—the new department would supersede the Housing and Home Finance Agency (HHFA) created by President Eisenhower—and a pre-inauguration task force of housing developers, mortgage financiers, and academics joined in recommending departmental status. [See Cabinet.]

The Kennedy initiative to create HUD failed. An important factor was the assumption on the part of Congress, mostly expressed by southern members, that the president would appoint as secretary Robert Weaver, administrator of the HHFA, who would thereby become the first-ever black cabinet member. Another was opposition in the Executive Office of the President from staff members who preferred a coordinating arrangement that would combine presidential oversight. [See President, Executive Office of the.]

It remained for President Johnson to win approval for departmental status in 1965 after the Watts riot drew public attention to the problem of urban blight and racial injustice. Thanks to Johnson's delay in appointing Weaver as HUD's first secretary, however, only a Justice Department declaration that the HHFA's status had "lapsed" permitted important program commitments to continue.

Weaver's eventual appointment and confirmation signaled three years of intensive action, both legislatively and in department-building. Within days after Weaver's appointment, Johnson forwarded legislation proposing the 1966 Housing and Urban Development Act. It had been preceded by the rent-supplement program, enacted but not yet funded in 1965, which had occasioned the first presidential message explicitly concerned with cities, and one that included a rare footnote: "for cities read Metropolitan areas." It would be followed by the 1968 act, breaking more new ground in a massive commitment to build twenty million new housing units in ten years, including six million set aside for the poor.

Simultaneously, Weaver faced the administrative challenges of reorganizing the predecessor HHFA, adding two new programs (rent supplements and Model Cities) to the structure, and providing a separate office of assistant secretary for metropolitan development and planning. It was truly a time of great activity. In Weaver's words, to make HUD "an ongoing concern . . . The President counted on us to create a new department and we did."

CRITICAL OMISSIONS IN THE HUD CHARTER

Impressive as Robert Weaver's record proved to be, the new HUD operated under sizable constraints as it undertook to help care for the old core cities and help shape the emerging new metropolitan areas. The academics who dominated the Johnson urban task forces had come forward with some genuinely new policy ideas—the politics of innovation, as textbooks later defined it, in contrast to the politics of distribution and redistribution: the 1965 rent supplement and 1966 Model Cities metropolitan development programs fell into that category. But what the task forces recommended and did not secure

was the incorporation of the new poverty and environmental programs that had just preceded them as separate parts of the Great Society. The absence of these programs prevented HUD from possessing a coherent portfolio that might have counterbalanced the bricks-and-mortar tradition inherited from the HHFA. So at the outset, the department's capacity to strengthen the neighborhood and metropolitan components of its mission was weak.

Two years later the establishment of the Department of Transportation stripped HUD of a vigorous mass transportation initiative that had funded the revival of old rapid transit systems in Boston, New York, and Philadelphia and had underwritten new ones in San Francisco and Maine. As Anthony Downs has observed, "not placing highway planning and finance under HUD's jurisdiction removed from its influence the single most important determinant of the way our metropolitan areas were to grow over the next several decades." Meanwhile, HUD was unable to absorb existing housing guarantee programs in the Department of Agriculture and the Veterans Administration because a classic version of turf protection, Washington-style, prevailed. So the great expectations of a new department, led by the first African American in the cabinet and committed to urban dwellers, were dashed owing to the restricted scope of authority of the first secretary and the lack of resources available to him.

These problems were compounded by the riots of 1967 and the stark conclusion of the President's National Advisory Commission on Civil Disorders that "our nation is moving toward two societies, one black, one white—separate and unequal." Most of all, the continuation and escalation of the Vietnam War robbed all the domestic departments of projected resources. It splintered the consensus that now was the time to tackle the president's great new domestic priorities— aid to the cities, to health, and to education. For all the legislative triumphs and administrative innovation, HUD never had an unchallenged mandate and sufficient resources. Instead, racked by successive tragic events—the assassinations of Dr. Martin Luther King, Jr., and Robert Kennedy, the riots extending over three years in more than

150 cities, the 1968 election—HUD had neither a honeymoon nor a shakedown cruise.

THE ROLLER COASTER OF CHANGING ADMINISTRATIONS

Although the Nixon administration would never support HUD on the scale that Johnson had achieved in the landmark 1966 and 1968 Housing and Urban Development Acts, neither did it seriously try to shut the department down. In reality, the pipeline of urban projects was now substantial, and HUD's program was increasingly popular in Congress. To be sure, the academic experts, most prominently Edward Banfield and James Wilson, now were conservatives, and an early presidential task force recommended the elimination of Model Cities and scaling back the ambitious goals of the 1968 act (revised in 1970 to include the first serious venture into subsidizing demand instead of production: the Experimental Housing Allowance Program). But Secretary George Romney chose to ignore academic counsel. Instead the former governor of Michigan focused on the implementation of the 1968 and 1970 acts by increasing the volume of private housing production and demonstrating the feasibility of mass production and by reorganizing the department to carry out these assignments. The results were dramatic: in a year the number of subsidized housing units rose from 162,000 to 190,000, and by 1970 HUD had authorized the production of 400,000 units for the poor. Romney also initiated Operation Breakthrough, emphasizing factory-based housing construction instead of building on-site. The results of the new primarily privately subsidized programs were mixed, both in terms of appropriate location and financial viability, and subsequent secretaries viewed the loan defaults and property abandonment as excessive.

But the shift from demonstration and experimental programs was significant, and the secretary showed genuine commitment to enforcing fair housing laws in the suburbs and restoring a metropolitan perspective in his advocacy of a "real city" approach to regional issues. His strong advocacy of minority housing throughout metropolitan regions led to a conservative suburban backlash; in response to the equivocal support

shown him by the Nixon administration, Romney announced his resignation in August 1972, effective after the presidential election. Nonetheless, although HUD dropped out of the headlines, federal appropriations tied to overall federal aid to municipalities exceeded $6 billion.

Romney's successor, James Lynn, was a corporate lawyer and general consul and had been under secretary of commerce in Nixon's first term; he concentrated on "dealing as effectively as possible with a disastrous default situation" and on "test[ing] the desirability of housing allowances and vouchers." In 1974 the Housing and Community Development Act made explicit the award of block grants calculated on a formula basis and established a new subsidized housing program emphasizing the leasing and rehabilitation of existing housing stock.

With the resignation of Nixon two weeks after the 1974 act was enacted, President Ford appointed Assistant Attorney General Carla Hills as secretary. To her fell the task of implementing the new act, which promised an annual production of an additional 400,000 housing units. She also encouraged the expansion of the block grant program ("community development block grants," or CDBGs), and by her last year the production and sales of housing ranked as third-best in U.S. history. Names of the Great Society programs had been changed, and a shift from housing subsidies for producers to those for consumers by rent and voucher assistance was detectable. But overall the appropriations and level of program activity were maintained. By 1980 total federal aid exceeded $10 billion, although priorities had been shifted to include suburban constituencies, and revenue sharing to almost every locality (administered by the Treasury Department, not HUD) found substantial popularity. In fact, Nixon had declared that the urban crisis had been resolved and had turned increasing attention to environmental issues.

In comparison with its immediate predecessors, the Carter administration in terms both of philosophy and political compatibility was far more attuned to urban constituencies and needs. Seeking to formulate a comprehensive urban policy and committed to a policy process involving extensive interagency collaboration, by 1978 Carter announced a somewhat complex urban policy with seven governing principles, four goals, ten policies, and thirty-eight strategies. The major legislative breakthrough was the concept of "urban development action grants" (UDAGs), successor to the Model Cities and CDBG programs, whereby attention was retargeted toward distressed areas and the poor, especially in inner cities. The president's support in Congress was limited, however, as metropolitan spread continued now in the form of "urban villages" springing up outside traditional downtowns. The energy crisis, inflation, and unemployment also emerged to become the domestic preoccupation of national policymakers. The pipeline would still yield about $11 billion, but 1980 would be the high-water mark of federal support to the nation's cities.

The Reagan years brought a sharp reversal in two policies. Samuel Pierce, Jr., held office for eight years, the longest term of any secretary to date. His administration emphasized support for the deregulation of private thrift institutions and extra assistance for the private housing industry as the ceilings for mortgage insurance by the Federal Housing Administration and the Federal National Mortgage Association ("Fannie Mae") were doubled and tripled. The secretary also gave increasing attention to international arrangements for the expansion of housing mortgage credit and the exchange of information among nations.

In two other ways, however, the Reagan administration undid the work of years both in budget and program authorizations. It savaged the HUD programs and left it little room for a national role in urban affairs except for a small number of sharply restricted block grants and a vague new policy concept of "enterprise zones." HUD's budget fell fifty-seven percent from 1980 to 1987, the largest cut for any federal department. Authorization for federally assisted housing dropped from $27 billion to $1.5 billion. CDBGs were cut from $3.7 to $2.6 billion and UDAGs from $675 million to $20 million. Overall intergovernmental aid to cities was reduced from almost $14 billion in 1980 to about $9 billion in 1986, a drop from twenty-three percent

of federal support for local budgets to twelve percent. Hit most severely was public housing, with reservations reduced by ninety-three percent, from 205,000 to 14,000 units. As an alternative, the Reagan administration offered a housing voucher program in which sixty-two percent of the applications learned that no housing was available to them.

Besides almost shutting down the HUD programs and watching passively as changes in the tax and banking laws in 1981 and 1983, ignited a commercial building explosion, the Pierce administration savaged the department ethically and morally as well. For eight years the programs originally designed to house the poor and to encourage home ownership were manipulated to benefit the rich and the powerful, for the most part developers with strong political ties. As the subsequent report of the federal special prosecutor makes clear, an estimated $2 billion was lost owing to fraud and mismanagement. Staff members in the secretary's immediate office were convicted of wrongdoing, as was a former secretary of agriculture. The scandal matched if not surpassed any in federal administrative history.

Appointed by George Bush in 1989, Secretary Jack F. Kemp gave due priority to restoring the integrity of the department and to ensuring that appropriate arrangements for oversight and compliance were in place. The HUD Reform Act of 1989 was a first result, with appropriate emphasis on the role of the department's investigatory facilities. It was followed by the Financial Institutions Reform, Recovery, and Enforcement Act, undertaken to cope with similar scandals in the thrift industry. With these initiatives under way, Kemp turned to his own policy agenda: home ownership for the poor, the growing problem of homelessness as identified by the 1987 McKinney Act, and the enactment of a substantial funded enterprise zone program that he had long advocated. On balance, although not satisfied with the resources available to this program initiative, Kemp restored morale and a sense of purpose in a department that had been badly shaken. His efforts to respond to the 1993 Los Angeles riots were for the most part turned aside by the Bush administration.

The tenth secretary, Henry G. Cisneros, has

worked hard to restore the department's budget and readdress its priorities in an increasingly hostile political environment. In its first two years, the Clinton administration expressed appropriate concern for the urban condition, expanded funds for homeless support and the renovation of public housing, and initiated another demonstration program in empowerment zones. But its early efforts to enact a fiscal stimulus package with a strong urban focus did not pass Congress, and following the 1994 congressional elections, the very existence of HUD was once more put in jeopardy.

In September 1995 Secretary Cisneros set forth his priorities for the department. They included internal consolidation of sixty individual programs to three performance-based funds designed to give state and local authorities maximum flexibility in implementation. They also stressed a continued preference for demand-oriented subsidies in the form of vouchers, a "continuum of care" approach to the homeless, the expansion of empowerment zones, and renewed emphasis on home ownership by supporting initiatives to improve financing and access in the housing market. While opting for consumer choice in housing assistance, Cisneros stressed a need for advocates not only for neighborhoods and cities but also for entire metropolitan regions. He regarded regionalism as the "new geography of opportunity." In an atmosphere of fixation on the deficit and presidential and legislative standoff, the success of these initiatives was uncertain. According to the secretary, during the 104th Congress the department was targeted for elimination, but the "move to dismantle HUD was postponed." "The proponents of elimination will be back; we will be hunted," Cisneros went on, observing that the 1996 Congress pushed through a "massive cut in HUD's budget, more than 20% in 1 year. *No other Secretary has faced such a cut.*" Thus the outcome of the 1996 national election may have been critical to the future of the department and its programs.

TRANSFORMATION OF THE URBAN ENVIRONMENT

Throughout the department's thirty years, America's urban demographic and economic patterns have evolved along largely predictable lines. First, decisions by the private sector—the marketplace—have increasingly prevailed. In retrospect, the brief five years of the Great Society represented the last period in which a majority of Americans supported public intervention to help solve domestic problems of poverty, education, health, and community enhancement. In the wake of Vietnam and Watergate, HUD has had to make its case to a public grown cynical and skeptical about the efficacy of government. The depth of this disillusionment has allowed the private sector to win substantial subsidies and tax relief, unleashing it to make the truly significant decisions regarding land use and the location of jobs and households. It was the private sector, checked only by environmental concerns, that underwrote the boom and bust in commercial development that the banking and tax reform acts of 1981 and 1983, respectively, made possible. The tax breaks and banking deregulation of those years produced a series of off-budget tax incentives that increased eight times between 1980 and 1986, from $2 billion to $9 billion. Accelerated or depreciated allowances on nonrental housing buildings added another $13 billion. Tax exclusions on state bonds added another $6 billion. Thus almost $40 billion dollars became available for building commercial and industrial space in old downtowns and in the new urban villages. The crash came in the late 1980s when incompetence, fraud, and corruption overwhelmed the savings and loan industry and required a federal bailout during the Bush administration.

A largely unrestrained private sector has cultivated a public perception that, whatever public assistance is warranted in housing and urban development, allegiance should be paid first to consumer choice. If vouchers in housing and education do not suffice and charity is not sufficient, then any necessary intervention should come from the state and local levels. Accordingly, land use policy is the appropriate province of local government. The care of the homeless is also best carried out at the grass roots. As the twenty-first century approaches, the marketplace stands secure. An opportunity was missed with the rejection of Richard Nixon's proposal of an income maintenance floor, and there now exists no comprehensive national response to ensure, in the words of the 1949 Housing Act, "a decent home in a suitable environment."

PROSPECTS

The chronicle of HUD over thirty years ends on a somber note. The vigorous defense of the department by Secretary Cisneros is clearly to be commended. Indeed, the sincerity, competence, and commitment of all the secretaries save one have been exemplary. Yet the questions remain: Who shall provide shelter for the poor? Who profits from that provision? Who is not served? For now the market prevails, and concern for people as consumers has replaced concern for places where people can be neighbors.

[*See also* Housing Finance Board, Federal.]

BIBLIOGRAPHY

Califano, Joseph, Jr. *The Triumph and Tragedy of Lyndon Johnson.* New York, 1991.
Downs, Anthony. "HUD'S Basic Missions and Some of Their Key Implications." *Cityscape* I, no. 3 (September 1995): 125–141.
Foote, Joseph. "As They Saw It: HUD's Secretaries Reminisce About Carrying Out the Mission." *Cityscape* I, no. 3 (September 1995): 71–92.
Kaplan, Marshall. *Urban Affairs Review* 30, no. 5 (May 1995).
Wood, Robert, and Beverly Klimkowsky. "HUD in the Nineties: Doubt-Ability and Do-Ability. In *The Future of National Urban Policy,* edited by Marshall Kaplan and Franklin James. Durham, N.C., 1990.

—ROBERT WOOD

Housing Finance Board, Federal

Established as an independent agency in the executive branch by the Financial Institutions Reform, Recovery, and Enforcement Act of 1989, the Federal Housing Finance Board is the supervisory authority for the Federal Home Loan Bank System and the Office of Finance. Located in Washington, D.C., the Finance Board ensures that banks operate safely and soundly by supervising lending and related operations of member-owned banks that comprise the Federal Home Loan Bank System. Bank system members include federal and state chartered thrift institutions, commercial banks, credit unions, and insurance companies.

A financial institution can join the district bank that serves the state where the institution's home office or principal place of business is located. Member financial institutions own stock in the banks and receive competitive returns on their investment through dividends. The system serves as a lender of first resort for its members and finances its own operations by charging for credit products and services provided to member institutions. Assessments, in turn, from the twelve Federal Home Loan Banks located in twelve districts across the country support the Finance Board.

The Finance Board also administers the Affordable Housing and Community Investment Programs, which provide low-cost advances and direct subsidies to members to finance housing for low- and moderate-income households. In addition, under the Federal National Mortgage Association Charter Act, the Finance Board conducts monthly surveys of major lenders to calculate a national average for interest rates on mortgages for single-family homes on behalf of the Federal National Mortgage Association. The Federal Home Loan Mortgage Corporation conducts a similar survey.

The Office of Finance, on the other hand, operates jointly with the Federal Home Lenders Banks, but its operations and management are subject to the oversight of a board of directors consisting of two district bank presidents and an outside director, each of whom serves for a term of three years. Regulated by the Federal Housing Finance Board, its primary role is to manage the sale of Bank System consolidated obligations to investors and to service the system's debt. The Office of Finance executes the Bank System's funding programs: bond sales, the issuance of discount notes, and medium-term bonds. The Office of Finance also sells daily medium-term bonds that offer the buyer a selection of maturity, interest payment dates, and price/yield balance.

The Finance Board, governed by a five-member board of directors, sets agency policy and issues resolutions. Four directors, appointed by the president with the advice and consent of the Senate, serve seven-year terms. The secretary of housing and urban development, the fifth director, serves in an *ex officio* capacity. Not more than three directors can belong to the same political party, and by law, four appointed directors must have backgrounds in housing finance or a demonstrated commitment to providing specialized housing credit. One of the directors is a "consumer/community director" and has at least a two-year record of representing consumer or community interests on either banking or housing issues.

BIBLIOGRAPHY

"Fact Sheet." *Federal Housing Finance Board News.* Washington, D.C., 1994.
Federal Housing Finance Board News. Washington, D.C., 1995.
"Federal Home Loan Bank System." *Federal Housing Finance Board News.* Washington, D.C., 1995.
"Statistics." *Federal Housing Finance Board News.* Washington, D.C., 1995.

—VERONICA D. DICONTI

HUD.

See Housing and Urban Development, Department of.

I

Immigration and Naturalization Service

Americans encouraged relatively free and open immigration during the eighteenth and early nineteenth centuries and did not question that policy until the late 1800s.

After certain states passed immigration laws following the Civil War, the Supreme Court in 1875 declared that regulation of immigration is a federal responsibility. Thus, as the number of immigrants rose in the 1880s and economic conditions in some areas worsened, Congress began to issue immigration legislation. The Chinese Exclusion Act of 1882 and alien contract labor laws of 1885 and 1887 prohibited certain laborers from immigrating to the United States. The more general Immigration Act of 1882 levied a head tax of fifty cents on each immigrant and blocked the entry of (or *excluded*) "idiots, lunatics, convicts, and persons likely to become a public charge." These national immigration laws created the need for a federal enforcement agency.

In the 1880s state boards or commissions enforced immigration law with direction from U.S. Treasury Department officials. At the federal level U.S. customs collectors at each port of entry collected the head tax from immigrants while "Chinese inspectors" enforced the Chinese Exclusion Act. Congress soon expanded the list of excludable classes and in doing so made regulation of immigration more complex. As a result, when the Immigration Act of 1891 barred polygamists, persons convicted of crimes of moral turpitude, and those suffering loathsome or contagious diseases from immigrating, it also created the Office of the Superintendent of Immigration.

Located within the Treasury Department, the office oversaw a new corps of "U.S. immigrant inspectors" stationed at the United States' principal ports of entry.

Under the 1891 law the federal government assumed the task of inspecting, admitting, rejecting, and processing all immigrants seeking admission to the United States. The Immigration Service's first task was to collect arrival manifests (passenger lists) from each incoming ship, a responsibility of the Customs Service since 1820. Enforcing immigration law was a new federal function, and the 1890s witnessed the Immigration Service's first attempts to implement national immigration policy.

Operations began in New York Harbor at a new federal immigration station on Ellis Island, which opened 2 January 1892. The largest and busiest station for decades, Ellis Island housed inspection facilities, hearing and detention rooms, hospitals, cafeterias, administrative offices, railroad ticket offices, and representatives of many immigrant aid societies. Ellis Island station also employed 119 of the Immigration Service's entire staff of 180 in 1893. The service continued building additional immigrant stations at other principal ports of entry through the early twentieth century. At New York, Boston, Philadelphia, and other traditional ports of entry, the Immigration Service hired many immigrant inspectors who previously worked for state agencies. At other ports, both old and new, the service built an inspector corps by hiring former customs inspectors and "Chinese inspectors" and training recruits. An "immigrant fund" created from collection of immigrants' head taxes financed the Immigration Service until 1909, when Congress replaced the fund with an annual appropriation.

During its first decade at Ellis Island and other ports, the Immigration Service formalized basic immigration procedures. Inspectors questioned arrivals about their admissibility and noted their admission or rejection on manifest records. Detention guards and matrons cared for those people detained pending decisions in their cases or, if the decision was negative, awaiting deportation. Inspectors also served on Boards of Special Inquiry that closely reviewed each exclusion case. Often, aliens were excluded because they lacked funds or had no friends or relatives nearby. In these cases the Board of Special Inquiry usually admitted the person if someone could post bond or one of the immigrant aid societies would take responsibility for the alien. Those denied admission by the board were deported at the expense of the transportation company that brought the alien to the port.

Congress continued to exert federal control over immigration with an act of 2 March 1895 that upgraded the Office of Immigration to the Bureau of Immigration and changed the agency head's title from superintendent to commissioner-general of immigration. An act of 6 June 1900 further consolidated immigration enforcement by assigning both alien contract labor law and Chinese Exclusion Act responsibilities to the commissioner-general. Because most immigration laws of the time sought to protect American workers and wages, an act of 14 February 1903 transferred the Bureau of Immigration from the Treasury Department to the newly created Department of Commerce and Labor.

Attention then turned to naturalization, a duty assigned to Congress by the Constitution but carried out by "any court of record" since 1802. A commission charged with investigating naturalization practice and procedure reported in 1905 that there was little or no uniformity among the nation's more than five thousand naturalization courts. Congress responded with the Basic Naturalization Act of 1906, which framed the rules for naturalization still in effect. The 1906 law also prescribed standard naturalization forms, encouraged state and local courts to relinquish their naturalization jurisdiction to federal courts, and expanded the Bureau of Immigration into the Bureau of Immigration and Naturalization.

To standardize naturalization procedures na-

tionwide, the new Naturalization Service collected copies of every naturalization record issued by every naturalization court. To prevent fraud, bureau officials checked immigration records to verify that each applicant for citizenship had been legally admitted into the United States. When the Department of Commerce and Labor was divided into separate cabinet departments in 1913, the Bureau of Immigration and Naturalization was divided into the Bureau of Immigration and the Bureau of Naturalization. The two bureaus existed separately within the Department of Labor until 1933.

The Immigration Service took form during an unprecedented rise in immigration to the United States. While Congress continued to strengthen national immigration law with acts such as the Immigration Act of 1907, a presidential commission investigated the causes of massive emigration from southern and eastern Europe and a congressional commission studied conditions among immigrants in the United States. These commission reports influenced the writing and passage of the Immigration Act of 1917, which, among other provisions, required that immigrants be able to read and write in their native languages. The Immigration Service then began administering literacy tests.

The outbreak of World War I reduced immigration from Europe but also imposed new responsibilities on the agency. Internment of enemy aliens (primarily seamen who worked on captured enemy ships) became an Immigration Service function. Passport requirements imposed by a 1918 presidential proclamation increased agency paperwork during immigrant inspection and deportation activities. The passport requirement also disrupted routine traffic across United States land borders with Canada and Mexico, and the Immigration Service consequently began to issue border crossing cards.

Mass immigration resumed after the war, and Congress responded with a new immigration policy, the national origins quota system. Established by Immigration Acts of 1921 and 1924, the system limited immigration by assigning each nationality a quota based on its representation in past United States census figures. The State Department distributed a limited number of visas each year through United States embassies abroad, and the Immigration Service admitted only immigrants who arrived with a valid visa.

The corollary to severely restricted immigration is increased illegal immigration. In response to rising illegal entries and alien smuggling, especially along land borders, Congress in 1924 created the U.S. Border Patrol within the Immigration Service. The strict new immigration policy coupled with Border Patrol successes shifted more agency staff and resources to deportation activity. Rigorous enforcement of immigration law at the ports of entry also swelled appeals under the law and led to creation of the Immigration Board of Review within the Immigration Bureau in the mid-1920s. (The Immigration Board of Review became the Board of Immigration Appeals after moving to the Justice Department in the 1940s and since 1983 has been known as the Executive Office of Immigration Review.)

A grass roots Americanization movement popular before World War I influenced developments in the Naturalization Bureau during the 1920s. The bureau published the first *Federal Textbook on Citizenship* in 1918 to prepare naturalization applicants, and its Education for Citizenship program distributed textbooks to public schools offering citizenship education classes and notified eligible aliens of available educational opportunities. Legislation of 1926 introduced the designated examiner system that assigned a naturalization examiner to each naturalization court to monitor proceedings, interview applicants, and promote uniform implementation of federal naturalization policy.

Executive Order 6166 of 10 June 1933 reunited the two bureaus into one agency, the Immigration and Naturalization Service (INS). Consolidation resulted in significant reduction of the agency's work force, achieved through merit testing and application of civil service examination procedures. [*See* Civil Service.] During the 1930s immigration volume dropped significantly. Deportation constituted a larger share of INS operations, as did certain repatriation programs later in the decade.

With the threat of war in Europe, immigration came to be perceived as a national security rather than an economic issue. President Roosevelt's Reorganization Plan No. 5 of 1940 moved the INS from the Department of Labor to the Department of Justice, and the U.S. entry into World War II brought additional change when many agency personnel enlisted in the armed forces, leaving the INS short of experienced staff. At the same time, INS headquarters moved to Philadelphia to sit out the war.

New responsibilities led to the agency's rapid growth during World War II. The INS's war-related duties included recording and fingerprinting every alien in the United States through the Alien Registration Program, the organization and operation of internment camps and detention facilities for enemy aliens, constant guarding of the nation's borders by the Border Patrol, record checks related to security clearances for immigrant defense workers, and administration of a program to import agricultural laborers to harvest the crops left behind by Americans who went to war. The only agency responsibility to end during the war was enforcement of the Chinese Exclusion Act, which Congress repealed in 1943. Other wartime changes included a conversion to a new record-keeping system, the implementation of the Nationality Act of 1940, and the doubling of the agency work force from four thousand to eight thousand employees.

Immigration remained relatively low following World War II because the national origins system of the 1920s remained in place after Congress recodified and combined all previous immigration and naturalization law into the Immigration and Nationality Act of 1952. Seasonal farm labor continued to be imported from Mexico, as it had been during the war, under a formal agreement between the United States and Mexico in 1951 that made the Bracero Program permanent. Other INS programs of the late 1940s and 1950s addressed conditions in postwar Europe. The War Brides Act of 1945 facilitated admission of the spouses and families of returning American soldiers. The Displaced Persons Act of 1948 and Refugee Relief Act of 1953 allowed for admission of many refugees displaced by the war and unable to come to the United States under regular immigration procedures. With the onset of the Cold War, the Hungarian Refugee Act of

308 • INDIAN AFFAIRS, BUREAU OF

1956, Refugee-Escapee Act of 1957, and Cuban Adjustment Program of the 1960s served the same purpose.

By the mid-1950s INS enforcement activities focused on two areas of national concern. Public alarm over illegal aliens resident and working in the United States caused the service to strengthen border controls and launch targeted deportation programs, most notably "Operation Wetback." Additional worry over criminal aliens within the country prompted INS investigation and deportation of Communists, subversives, and organized crime figures.

In 1965 amendments to the 1952 immigration law, Congress replaced the national origins system with a preference system designed to reunite immigrant families and attract skilled immigrants to the United States. This change in national policy responded to changes in the sources of immigration since 1924. The majority of applicants for immigration visas now came from Asia and Central and South America rather than Europe. The preference system continued to limit the number of immigration visas available each year, however, and Congress still responded to refugees with special legislation, as it did for Indochinese refugees in the 1970s. Not until the Refugee Act of 1980 did the United States have a general policy governing the admission of refugees.

The INS's functional responsibilities expanded again under the Immigration Reform and Control Act of 1986. The act charged the INS with enforcing sanctions against U.S. employers who hired undocumented aliens. Carrying out employer sanction duties involved investigating, prosecuting, and levying fines against corporate and individual employers, as well as deportation of those found to be working illegally. The 1986 law also allowed certain aliens illegaly in the United States to legalize their residence here, and the INS administered that legalization program.

Changes in world migration patterns, the growing ease of international travel for business and pleasure, and an increased emphasis on controlling illegal immigration all fostered growth of the INS during the late twentieth century. The INS work force, which numbered approximately eight thousand from World War II through the

late 1970s, grew to more than twenty thousand employees in thirty-six INS districts at home and abroad. The original force of Immigrant Inspectors is now a corps of officers specializing in inspection, examination, adjudication, legalization, investigation, patrol, and refugee and asylum issues. As it enters its second century, the INS continues to enforce laws providing for selective immigration and controlled entry of tourists, business travelers, and other temporary visitors. It does so by inspecting and admitting arrivals at land, sea, and air ports of entry, administering benefits such as naturalization and permanent resident status, and apprehending and removing aliens who enter illegally or violate the requirements of their stay.

[*See also* Customs Service *and* Public Health Service.]

BIBLIOGRAPHY

Calavita, Kitty. *Inside the State: The Bracero Program, Immigration and the INS.* New York, 1992.
Congressional Research Service. *History of the Immigration and Naturalization Service.* Senate Judiciary Print. Washington, D.C., 1980.
Morris, Milton D. *Immigration: The Beleaguered Bureaucracy.* Washington, D.C., 1985.
Smith, Darrell Hevenor. *Bureau of Immigration: Its History, Activities, and Organization.* Baltimore, 1924.
Smith, Darrell Hevenor. *Bureau of Naturalization: Its History, Activities, and Organization.* Baltimore, 1926.
U.S. Department of Labor. *Historical Sketch of Naturalization in the United States.* Washington, D.C., 1926.
U.S. Immigration and Naturalization Service. *INS Monthly Review.* Periodical. 1943–1952.
U.S. Immigration and Naturalization Service. *I&N Reporter.* Periodical. 1952–1982.

—MARIAN L. SMITH

Indian Affairs, Bureau of

The Department of the Interior's Bureau of Indian Affairs (BIA) and its precursors form one of the oldest bureaucratic institutions in the United States. The BIA is the primary agent of the federal government in its relations with Indians and Indian tribes and a dominant administrative force in tribal government.

Services provided by the BIA include education, housing, law enforcement, and asset management for 319 federally recognized tribes in the continental United States and 223 village groups in Alaska. Through the BIA the United States holds 56 million acres of land in trust for Indian tribes and individuals. The fiscal year budget for 1995 was $1.8 billion.

Scholars typically divide the federal government's relations with the Native Americans into six policy eras. The first, the Treaty Era, extends from the colonial period to approximately 1830. The early relationship between Native Americans and the English Crown and, later, the United States was characterized by the conclusion of treaties that, by definition, recognized tribes as sovereign entities.

The seeds of U.S. Indian policy can be found in the British government's Proclamation of 1763, which ordered that all colonial-tribal relations be conducted centrally, through authorized Crown agents. Centralization of relations was designed to eliminate the expense of quelling disorder along the colonial frontier, where colonists—often unscrupulously and out of sight of authorities—provoked tribes by making disputable land deals and by outright encroachment.

In 1775 the Second Continental Congress established a Committee on Indian Affairs with three departments—one each for the north, south, and central colonies—to conduct relations between the colonists and the Indian tribes. Such notables as Patrick Henry and Benjamin Franklin assumed seats on the new panel, which consisted of eleven commissioners. These commissioners were to treat "with the Indians . . . to preserve peace and friendship."

When the U.S. Constitution was adopted, the practice of handling Indian affairs centrally was retained. The power to "regulate Commerce with Indian Tribes" was granted to Congress in Article I, Section 8, of the Constitution. The treaty-making power, to be shared by the president and the Congress (Art. II, Sec. 2), was understood to include Indian treaties (until 1871, when Congress unilaterally declared that it would no longer treat with Indians). The new Congress, in its 1790 Trade and Intercourse Act, also forbade individuals or states from concluding separate treaties with Indians or tribes and subjected Indian trade to federal regulation.

Indian commissioners often were accompanied by armed militia during negotiations with the tribes. Hence, when Congress established the War Department in 1789, Henry Knox, secretary of war, assumed responsibility for Indian-U.S. relations. Throughout its history, U.S. policy toward Indians has swerved back and forth between actions that articulate and encourage tribal self-determination and those that encourage assimilation. This contradiction can be seen from the nation's first days, when Knox drafted a report recommending assimilation and the civilizing of Indians as policy aims. Meanwhile, Congress soon passed the first of several trade and intercourse acts that dealt with tribes as independent sovereigns.

In 1824, without authorization from Congress, Secretary of War John C. Calhoun established what he called the Bureau of Indian Affairs. After some debate, and in recognition of the growing complexity of U.S.-Indian relations, Congress sanctioned Calhoun's action by creating the Indian Office (also called the Indian Service). To head the new office, Congress created the position of commissioner of Indian affairs, to be appointed by the president with the advice and consent of the Senate. The office would have "the direction and management of all Indian affairs, and of all matters arising out of Indian relations." The commissioner of Indian affairs had supervision over agents, whose responsibilities included negotiating treaties, trading with Indians, and attempting to resolve disputes between U.S. citizens and tribal members. The commissioner also was responsible for overseeing the removal of Indians to reservation lands farther west.

Scholars call the period from approximately 1830 to 1887 the Removal/Reservation Era. Although earlier presidents had broached plans for the removal of Indians from their homelands in the East, it was Andrew Jackson who pushed vigorously for their implementation.

Indian advocates in Congress and elsewhere bitterly decried the proposals, and Supreme

Court Chief Justice John Marshall, in his decisions at this time, speaks of the unconstitutionality of such policy. In a series of decisions often referred to as "the Marshall trilogy" (*Johnson v. McIntosh* [1823], *Cherokee Nation v. Georgia* [1831], and *Worcester v. Georgia* [1832]), the chief justice laid down judicial doctrine that still forms the bedrock of federal Indian law. Although Marshall did not go so far as to label tribes complete sovereigns, he did recognize them as "domestic dependent nations" and "distinct political communities." Taken as a whole, these cases articulated the right of tribes to maintain their own internal affairs and to hold "Indian title" to their lands, a status somewhat less than that of title in fee simple but one that nonetheless constrained appropriation by the federal and state governments.

Eventually, the proponents of removal won out. In 1830 Congress passed the Indian Removal Act, which required that Indians in certain areas submit to state law, or that they be removed—by force, if necessary—to lands west of the Mississippi River. Alexis de Tocqueville included a moving eyewitness account of the devastation of Indian removal in his study of American democracy while noting the divergence between rhetoric and reality in U.S. policy concerning Native Americans.

The movement of tribes from their homelands, coupled with their containment on lands of inadequate size for hunting, led to disease and starvation. In a majority of the treaties and agreements reached during this period, the federal government promised to assume responsibility for the health, welfare, and education of Indians in exchange for some tract of land. Such agreements naturally expanded the role of the Indian Office into social service provision and beyond its roles of treaty negotiation and Indian containment. In 1849—in recognition of the evolving nature of the Indian Office—Congress transferred responsibility for Indian affairs from military to civilian control, housing the bureau in the newly established Department of the Interior.

In the following decades the role of the BIA would again shift. Indian Agents—those employees of the BIA in the field—became increasingly involved in the inner workings of tribal societies. The BIA became involved in such specialized reservation activities as irrigation, forestry, Indian employment, and law enforcement. Thus, by the last two decades of the nineteenth century, the presence of the federal government, through the BIA, became the dominant force in reservation life.

The federal government was not the sole outside influence on tribal affairs, however. It not only sanctioned, but encouraged, various religious groups to establish educational missions on the reservations. Over time, the federal government itself would come to view the education of Indians as one of its core responsibilities. (Indeed, during most years since 1900 education has remained the largest single item in BIA budgets.) The first off-reservation boarding school was established in Carlisle, Pennsylvania, in 1879. Within the next few years, dozens more of these schools were established, and thousands of Indian children were taken from their parents to attend them.

The period from 1887 to 1934 is typically labeled the Allotment/Assimilation Era. As previously mentioned, the practice of treating with Indians formally ended in 1871. This paved the way for passage of the Land Severalty Act (Dawes Act) in 1887, which allowed reservation lands to be divided among individual Indians and their families, wresting control of the land from the tribes and effectively crippling the authority of most tribal governments. Allotment was intended to encourage farming and private property ownership. Besides parceling out tribal lands, the BIA would negotiate with tribes for the disposal of "excess lands." Consequently, Indian land holdings fell from 138 million acres in 1887 to forty-eight million acres by 1934.

By the 1920s it was painfully obvious that federal policy was failing to improve the economic well-being of indigenous Americans. Indian reservations persistently remained in a condition of abject poverty and owing to the influence of missionaries, the bureau's Indian Agents, and allotment policy, little was left of tribal governments. The harmful effects of the allotment/assimilation policy were detailed in a 1928 report conducted for the BIA by the Institute for Government Research (later the Brookings Institution). Known as the Meriam Report, the study is attributed with ushering in a decade of policy activity known as the Indian New Deal, and a new era of Indian policy more generally, the Indian Reorganization Era (1934 to 1950).

The era draws its name from the 1934 Indian Reorganization Act, which formally halted the allotment policy and instructed the secretary of the Interior to restore Indian lands where possible. The statute also encouraged the cultivation of tribal governments, creating a provision under which tribes could create and adopt written constitutions with the approval of the secretary of the Interior. Adoption of a tribal constitution (typically resembling state constitutions) was up to tribal members. The bureau continued in its role as service provider but also assumed the role of protector of Indian lands and resources.

Called the Termination/Relocation Era, the period between 1953 and 1968 witnessed the passage of legislation that severed the special relationship between several tribes and the U.S. government, subjected certain tribal members to state laws and state jurisdiction, and again transferred tribal lands to private ownership. Congress was effectively "terminating" its relationship with a number of tribes. Although the stated objective of some who supported the policy was to free Indian's from the heavy hand of the federal government (particularly the BIA), the effect has often been judged disastrous, leaving tribes as economically troubled as before.

Concomitant with congressional termination directives, the BIA worked to relocate many Indians to urban areas where they would receive job training. Although some indigenous Americans did find success through this program, many were simply left stranded in metropolitan areas, far from their families.

Scholars have dubbed the years since 1968 the Era of Self-Determination. Again, assimilationist agendas were assessed a failure. In 1968 Congress passed the Indian Civil Rights Act, part of which amended legislation dating from the Termination Era so as to require tribal consent to the extension of any state jurisdiction over them. The law also created certain protections for individual tribal members against their tribal governments. The Indian Civil Rights Act, or "Indian Bill of Rights," is in many ways similar to its namesake, with the notable exception that it does not require formal separation of church and state.

The Era of Self-Determination was announced most clearly by President Nixon, who condemned termination policies and stressed the idea that tribes were independent governments and should be allowed to act as such. He also reiterated the federal government's trust responsibility toward tribes. The trust relationship is not specifically defined in any one place but has gradually evolved in treaties, acts of Congress, executive mandates, and court decisions. Its precise implications, therefore, remain open to controversy and interpretation. The U.S. government assumed the trust relationship when it promised to safeguard Indian lands and provide social support in exchange for resettlement.

Prominent among moves toward greater tribal self-government was the Indian Self-Determination and Education Assistance Act of 1975. The law allowed tribes to assume administrative control over some social services from the BIA contractually. Although the law was considered a marked improvement over previous policy, many tribes were frustrated by the slow pace with which the BIA relinquished its former responsibilities. Tribal administration, for instance, was strictly limited to a few types of contract services, which were subject to strict budgetary scrutiny.

In 1988, at the initiative of several tribal leaders, Congress passed the Self-Governance Demonstration Project Act. The purpose of the act was to allow tribes more flexibility and authority in the contracting process. The pilot project initially involved ten tribes and offered increased sums of money for service provision. These sums resembled federal block grants to the states (though the project's language was careful to distinguish tribes' status from that of the states). The Self-Governance Project became permanent by an act of Congress in 1994 and currently involves fifty tribes.

The organizational profile of the BIA within the federal government has, at times, been viewed as a disadvantage. In 1973 Congress placed the commissioner of Indian affairs directly under the secretary of the Interior. Before this time the bureau reported to an Interior Department assistant secretary. Four years later the BIA received another organizational promotion when an assistant secretary post was devoted specifically to Indian affairs.

Since 1949 the BIA has been organized in a three-tiered structure. While its headquarters is in Washington, D.C., twelve relatively autonomous area offices have been established along with 109 field offices, most of which are on reservations. Although the 1990 census reported that about two million people identified themselves as American Indian, only about half that number live on or near Indian reservations and are thus eligible for services from the BIA.

The staffing practices of the BIA are unique among U.S. governmental institutions. With the approval of both Congress and the Supreme Court, it is not required to adhere to the equal employment opportunity guidelines in force for other agencies. Thus, nearly ninety percent of the BIA's fourteen thousand employees claim Indian ancestry. Precedent for preferential hiring was set in the Indian Reorganization Act of 1934, in which Congress directed that Indians "shall hereafter have the preference to the appointment to vacancies" in offices that administer to any tribes. In 1972, by directive of the commissioner of Indian affairs, preferential consideration was extended to job promotion as well. This internal policy survived legal challenge by several non-Indian employees when the Supreme Court, in *Morton v. Mancari* (1974), held that preferential practices furthered the congressional goal of greater Indian self-government.

A tension remains at the heart of the BIA's Indian policy. While Congress and the last few presidents have praised and encouraged the development of Indian self-determination, the bureau remains charged with trust responsibility over tribal assets. In recent years tribal leaders have been careful to ensure that Indian legislation reiterate this responsibility.

The bureau, however, has at time used the trust relationship as a reason not to relinquish control to tribes. Such actions would, argue BIA officials, abrogate the trust relationship. The tension between Indian self-determination and the federal-tribal trust relationship continues to be one of the greatest challenges to sound policy and reform at the BIA.

BIBLIOGRAPHY

Champagne, Duane. "Organizational Change and Conflict: A Case Study of the Bureau of Indian Affairs." *American Indian Culture and Research Journal* 7, no. 3 (1983): 3–28.
Institute for Government Research. *The Problem of Indian Administration.* Baltimore, 1928.
O'Brien, Sharon. *American Indian Tribal Governments.* Norman, Okla., 1993.
Schmeckebier, Laurence Frederick. *The Office of Indian Affairs: Its History, Activities, and Organization.* Baltimore, 1927.
Senate Select Committee on Indian Affairs. *Final Report and Legislative Recommendations.* Report 101–216. Washington, D.C., 1989.
Taylor, Theodore W. *The Bureau of Indian Affairs.* Boulder, Colo., 1984.

—TOM HOFFMAN and
GWEN-TORGES HOFFMAN

Indian Health Service.
See Public Health Service.

Information, Government.
See Government Information.

Information Agency, United States.
See United States Information Agency.

INS.
See Immigration and Naturalization Service.

Interior, Department of the

Charged statutorily by a gaggle of nineteenth- and twentieth-century statutes embodying competing values, missions, and constituencies, the Department of the Interior approaches the twenty-first century as the federal agency most responsible for managing the nation's resources on over 500 million acres of lands. More precisely, the Department of the Interior has to reconcile the nation's disparate desires to develop, conserve, and preserve natural resources on these economically, ecologically, and anthropologically robust properties. What is more, it must do so within the constraints afforded by the administrative, cultural, and political legacies bequeathed to it by six analytically distinct, yet overlapping, eras of natural resource management. Daunting enough in their own right, these legacies take on additional import for Interior as the department runs pell-mell into the downsizing, reinventing, and budget-trimming emphases of its turbulent present.

Created in 1849, the Interior Department today comprises three bureaus (Indian Affairs, Reclamation, and Land Management), three services (Fish and Wildlife, National Park, and Minerals Management), the U.S. Geological Survey, the National Biological Survey, the Office of Surface Mining Reclamation and Enforcement, and the office of Insular Affairs. These report variously to six assistant secretaries who, in turn, report to the secretary of the Interior: policy, management, and budget; fish and wildlife and parks; water and science; territorial and international affairs; Indian affairs; and land and minerals management.

Ranked from highest to lowest in budget size as a percentage of Interior's fiscal year 1995 funding were the Bureau of Indian Affairs (26.6%), the National Park Service (21.3%), the Bureau of Land Management (16.9%), the Fish and Wildlife Service (10.3%), the Geological Survey (8.8%), the Office of Surface Mining Reclamation (4.5%), the Minerals Management Service (3%), the National Biological Survey (2.5%), and Insular Affairs (1.9%). Illustrative of the relative power of these agencies within the department today, these figures fail to convey the enormous changes in mandates, methods, and motives that have informed Interior's responsibilities over the past century and a half.

TOWARD PRIVATIZATION

The first two eras of natural resource management—acquisition (1792–1867) and disposal (1812–1933)—fostered a crazy-quilt pattern of land ownership and competing interests that still plagues the Department of the Interior today. Propelled during the acquisition era by the rhetoric of "manifest destiny," the federal government amassed hundreds of millions of acres of land through direct purchase, peace treaties, and international agreements. Among the most significant of these were the Louisiana, Gadsden, Pacific Northwest, and Alaska purchases; the Guadalupe-Hidalgo pact with Mexico; and peace treaties with various Indian tribes.

Responsibility for managing and disposing of these lands rested initially with the General Land Office (GLO) in the Treasury Department. Fearing, however, that the GLO would become scandal-ridden, Treasury Secretary Robert Walker persuaded President Polk to move the GLO along with the Patent, Pension, and Indian Affairs offices from the State, War, and Navy Departments—into an independent Department of the Interior. In rapid order, Congress also added a miscellany of important, but tangential, duties. Most notable among these were: colonizing freed slaves in Haiti, conducting the decennial census, exploring the western wilderness, overseeing the District of Columbia jail, regulating territorial governments, managing hospitals and universities, and maintaining public parks.

Using terms presaging those used by today's Property Rights, Wise-Use, and Sagebrush Rebellion proponents, those who had unsuccessfully opposed creating the department (e.g., John C. Calhoun and James Mason) considered it a "monstrous" and "ominous" assault on states' rights. More compelling as the years passed, however, were arguments that Interior's lack of focus was hampering its operations: "A slop bucket for executive fragments," railed one editorialist; a "hydraheaded monster," wailed another; the "Department of Everything Else," ridiculed others (Utley and Mackintosh, p. 5). Thus, during the disposal era, Congress began whittling Interior's more ancillary functions from it: its agricultural division became the Department of Agriculture in 1862; its Bureau of Labor became the Department of Commerce and Labor in 1903 (later the Department of Labor); its Patent Office moved to the Department of Commerce in 1925; and its Bureau of Pensions became the Veterans Affairs Office in 1930 (later the Department of Veterans Affairs).

With these divestitures came a sharper focus on natural resource management in the West. By the 1880s the Bureau of Indian Affairs (1849)—founded originally in the War Department (1824)—employed anywhere from two thousand to three thousand personnel overseeing the tribal affairs of 260,000 Native Americans living on 138 reservations located primarily in the West. Likewise, the U.S. Geological Survey (1879) explored newly acquired lands in the West. Similarly situated were most of the national parks assigned to Interior over the last quarter of the nineteenth century—for example, Yellowstone, Sequoia, Yosemite, and Mount Rainier.

Interior is remembered most, however, for presiding over a land-rich, settlement-poor, and debt-ridden nation's "fire sale" of its western lands during the disposal era. Initially, these transfers were few, scattered, and unprofitable. Consequently, Congress passed—and Interior implemented—a series of statutes designed to promote homesteading by settlers and economic development by mining, railroad, and timber companies. Among these were the Public Land Sales Act of 1820, the Mining Control Act of 1832, the Homestead Act of 1862, the Pacific Railroad Acts of 1862 and 1864, the Mining Act of 1872, the Timber Culture Act of 1873, and the Desert Land Act of 1877. Interior eventually turned ninety-four million acres over to the railroads, and nearly 290 million acres to homesteaders, miners, and timber companies.

From the Interior Department's perspective today, the disposal era produced a crazy-quilt pattern of land ownership that sorely compromises effective, efficient, and apolitical land management. Only scattered parcels near scarce water supplies, adjacent to population centers, and flush with forage were transferred. This left western lands in noncontiguous blocks of random sizes, owned by different purchasers, and unamenable to comprehensive land management. Moreover, such a "checkerboard" pattern of ownership made federal land management decidedly ripe for conflict with private and municipal owners.

Even discounting ownership patterns, however, the lands retained by Interior suffered mis-

erably under the GLO's stewardship. At its peak in the 1880s, GLO staffing barely exceeded a thousand employees. Half of these were clerks working in Washington recording land transactions. Moreover, the GLO and local land offices often did little more than "[front] for powerful private interests adept at using existing legislation to obtain additional landholdings" (Gottlieb, p. 21).

Perhaps most illustrative of these dynamics was the Mining Law of 1872. Interior had to allow miners to buy, or "patent," mining claims on public lands for as little as $2.50 per acre. Neither was Interior to charge royalties on any hardrock minerals (e.g., gold, silver, or copper) that miners extracted. Moreover, the law did not require miners to restore damaged lands. As for corruption in the program, Interior secretaries were not in any position to deal effectively with it. Congress typically allowed Interior's agencies to retain full legal authority for programs. As such, Interior secretaries were "denied . . . the machinery for controlling [their] bureaus and shaping policy" (Utley and Mackintosh, p. 14). Thus, despite their typically good character and high integrity, they were often unsuccessful executives.

Two episodes occurring near the end of the disposal era tarnished Interior's image immeasurably. In the first, a GLO employee accused President Taft's Interior secretary, Richard Ballinger, of impeding an investigation of fraudulent coal claims in Alaska. Importuned by Forest Service chief Gifford Pinchot, who took the employee's side against Taft's wishes, Congress investigated. Ballinger was cleared of the charges, and Taft forced the legendary Pinchot to resign for insubordination. However, the taint of scandal remained, and already distrustful conservationist allies of Pinchot grew more disaffected. Even more damaging, however, was the Teapot Dome scandal. President Harding's Interior secretary, Albert Fall (1921–1923), was convicted in 1931 of accepting $400,000 in bribes for oil leases at the Teapot Dome Reserve in Wyoming and the Elk Hills Reserve in California. Still, these eras were not without "heroes," who began transitioning parts of Interior into a more progressive, conservationist, and preservationist mode. Most prominent among these were John Wesley Powell, first director of the U.S. Geological Survey (1881–1894), and Carl Schurz, progressive reformer and Interior secretary (1877–1881).

TOWARD MINIMALIST MANAGEMENT

With the progressive conservationist movement came the next two eras of natural resource management at the Interior Department: reservation (1890–1940) and custodial management (1910–1950). In these overlapping eras, Congress recognized the need for Interior to preserve natural, historic, and cultural resources of uniquely national import. Concomitantly, it recognized that the economic prosperity of future generations required Interior to become an apolitical "custodian" managing federal lands according to the multiple use–sustained yield conservation principles of Europe's scientific management movement.

What could not be "imported," however, were adequate resources and expertise to perform these tasks, broad-based political support for the agencies applying these principles, and hence, a congressional commitment to anything greater than minimal stewardship of public lands. Most illustrative of these dilemmas are the travails, cultures, and prodevelopment constituencies bequeathed to Interior today by the five agencies established during these two eras: the Bureau of Reclamation (1902), the Bureau of Mines (1910), the National Park Service (1916), the Fish and Wildlife Service (1940), and the Bureau of Land Management (1946).

The Bureau of Reclamation (BuRec)—established originally in the Geological Survey by Frederick Newell—embodied the conservationists' faith in comprehensive regional development. This faith, however, was not shared by all, as the initial opposition of powerful local interests and the Army Corps of Engineers attests. All initially saw BuRec as an interloper on their bureaucratic turf, but the bureau's implementation of the Reclamation Act of 1902 would assuage such concerns. BuRec could only develop river basins in arid western states, thus preserving the Corps' monopoly in the East. Moreover, it would build large-scale hydropower dams capable of providing low-cost irrigation and electric power for whatever agricultural, industrial, or personal needs might arise. These subsidies, a clear mission, and the creation of rural irrigation districts dominated by user interests did three things: they deflected local fears, created *esprit de corps* among BuRec engineers, and built formidable political support for BuRec's operations.

The blossoming of the West during the twentieth century testifies to the efficacy of BuRec's strategy. But in its success were sown the seeds of contemporary dilemmas for Interior. Irrigation farmers have, since 1902, repaid only 3.3 percent of BuRec's original capital costs for building these dams. Likewise, the West's water doctrine of "prior appropriation and beneficial use" meant that farmers using massive amounts of heavily subsidized irrigation water fought tenaciously any shift to urban users in the 1980s and 1990s. Moreover, BuRec's dam-building culture had a difficult and politically charged transition to make when a switch to water conservation was needed during those same decades.

Likewise, Congress instructed the Bureau of Mines (1910)—created after a series of coal mine disasters in 1907 took over three thousand lives—to both promote the industry and ensure the safety of miners. However, the bureau's focus—by nature of its early leadership, its organizational odyssey, and the signals it received from Congress during the two eras—was on developing technology rather than safety. Not only was its first director, Joseph Holmes, recruited from the Geological Survey, but the bureau was shifted in 1925 to the Department of Commerce, where it resided until returning to Interior in 1934. What is more, while mining inspection functions remained in Interior during this interregnum, the Geological Survey performed them. To be sure, Interior developed first-aid training, built rescue stations, and conducted coal dust research during this period. Nonetheless, it did not have authority to enforce health and safety standards until the late 1960s.

In contrast, preservationists like John Muir saw the National Park Service (NPS) as a cover for unbridled development in national parks after Interior let the Hetch Hetchy Valley in Yosemite Park be dammed to supply water for San Francisco. Originally responsible for the fourteen national parks and twenty-one national monuments preserved under the Antiquities Act of 1906, the NPS's responsibilities swelled by the 1990s to include 360 parks, monuments, historic battlefields, and forts. Remaining constant, however, was the managerial conundrum spawned by the "use, but don't spoil" goals of the act establishing the NPS in 1916. The NPS was to "conserve the scenery and the natural and historic objects and the wildlife therein," but also to "provide for the enjoyment of the same in such manner and by such means as will leave them unimpaired for the enjoyment of future generations" (16 U.S.C. 1).

Until Director George Hartzog divided park lands into three areas managed for different purposes in 1964 (recreational, natural, and historic), park use trumped preservation as the NPS's primary mission. The service's politically savvy first two directors—Stephen Mather and Horace Albright—believed that the agency could survive and flourish only if they aggressively encouraged public access to national parks. Better roads and accommodations, alliances with railroads transporting users to remote areas, and formidable marketing campaigns ensued. Simultaneously, the NPS nurtured sinewy political alliances with pro-use state governments reaping revenue from mining, timber, hunting, and grazing fees. Cultivated as well were alliances with local communities dependent on recreational use for economic growth; with sportsmen's associations wishing to hunt and fish in the parks; and with ranchers wishing to protect their livestock from predators wandering off park lands.

Brilliant politically, Mather's and Albright's strategy left a disturbing legacy that their successors had to grapple with as the NPS's statutory responsibilities expanded. In protecting animals popular for viewing or hunting (e.g., antelope and elk) and in allowing massive kills of predators (e.g., coyotes, wolves, and cougars), NPS policy created significant ecological imbalances at many parks. Moreover, as the number of visitors spiraled over these two eras, crowd control quickly trumped scientific research as the primary concern of park rangers. Indeed, to protect animals and visitors from each other, Mather staffed park ranger positions with soldiers recruited for their firearms skills.

Thus, as late as the 1920s, the NPS had only five naturalists on its staff. Chagrined, ecologists such as Joseph Grinnel, George Wright, and Milton Skinner eventually persuaded Albright—and, in turn, legendary Interior Secretary Harold Ickes (1933–1946)—to create a Wildlife Division within the NPS. The division published over a thousand reports during the 1930s. Developed in the process, however, was a tension that remains today between park rangers and scientists. The former worried that a "good science" rather than a "control" model of park management would prevail. Given the dominance of park rangers in the NPS, research remained a stepchild at the agency until the early 1960s. Those years brought a higher profile for research with the publication of the Leopold Report, the arrival of Stewart Udall as Interior secretary (1961—1969), and a spate of legislation emphasizing preservation. Still, less than two percent of the NPS budget today is devoted to research.

Similarly, the Fish and Wildlife Service (F&WS) faced cultural, stakeholder, and structural dilemmas that pushed it inexorably toward a minimalist custodial ethic ill-suited to today's pressing demands. "An incidental appendage buried deep in Interior" (Tobin, p. 37), the F&WS inherited in 1940 a system of wildlife refuges, fisheries, and waterfowl production areas. By the 1990s agency holdings had grown to 434 refuges and 150 waterfowl areas. The agency's responsibilities had also expanded to include protecting migratory birds, inland sport fisheries, and threatened or endangered species. What is more, it had to perform the reams of research necessary to support these activities.

Decisions made during the minimalist management era today render the capacities of the F&WS woefully inadequate to its responsibilities. The agency was created by combining the Bureau of Fisheries from the Department of Commerce and Labor with the Biological Survey from the Department of Agriculture. Given the low stature of each politically, however, this merger left the agency desperate for alternative funding sources, for politically potent constituencies, and for wildlife biologists with training and organizational experiences better-suited to ecosystem management. Nor did its reporting relationship to the assistant secretary for fish and wildlife and parks help its cause; the F&WS has had to vie for resources at a severe political disadvantage with the constituency-rich, expanding, and popular NPS. Thus, the latter garners approximately seventy percent of all expenditures allocated today by the assistant secretary, while the F&WS's Office of Endangered Species receives only one-tenth of one percent of Interior's budget.

Like the NPS, the F&WS grew increasingly more dependent during these two eras on getting revenues from, and providing services for, prodevelopment and pro-use constituents. For example, a primary revenue source for acquiring and preserving new wetlands was afforded by the Migratory Bird Hunting Stamp Act of 1934. Requiring all waterfowl hunters over fifteen years old to purchase a stamp annually, the act generated enough revenue to purchase 3.7 million acres of additional wetlands by 1987. Likewise, additional revenue—some shared with the states—accrued to the NPS by allowing farming, hunting and fishing, logging, and oil and gas extraction on or near refuges. These are permissible activities when compatible with the primary purpose of the refuge. However, a resource-strapped F&WS was under attack by the mid-1980s for tilting too far toward allowing incompatible uses. These resulted, the General Accounting Office concluded, in the pollution of over one hundred refuges by oil spills, toxic wastes, or fertilizer and pesticide runoff.

Finally, the biologists inherited by the F&WS came from cultures emphasizing resource development and from career training focused on higher-level vertebrate animals. This would become a problem in the 1970s when the Threatened and Endangered Species Act of 1973 also required the agency to consider plants and other invertebrate animals for listing. Unaccustomed to thinking in these terms, biologists typically failed to list these species for many years, much to the chagrin of environmental critics. So, too, did meager congressional appropriations for staffing during these eras cause environmentalists to bray at the agency's slow pace in listing species. Meanwhile, outraged property owners and developers alleged that the species the F&WS *did* list reduced property values without adequately compensating landowners.

Still, Congress designed no agency in Interior more explicitly for minimally managing federal lands than the Bureau of Land Management (BLM). Created in 1946 in a merger of the GLO and the Grazing Service, the bureau took as its primary responsibility the promoting of grazing, mining, and logging on public lands. Without its own multiple-use "organic" statute until the Federal Land Policy and Management Act of 1976, the BLM's behavior was guided primarily by such unabashedly prodevelopment statutes as the Taylor Grazing Act of 1934.

The act charged the Grazing Service—overwhelmingly staffed by former ranchers—with establishing district advisory boards dominated by the cattle industry. These boards resolved issues of vital interest to ranchers regarding who could graze livestock on the public lands, at what cost, at what levels, and with what range improvements. Not surprisingly, the boards kept grazing fees inordinately low and kept sheepherders away by assigning land use exclusively to ranchers with adjoining water supplies. They also severely restricted the access of miners to public lands by denying rights-of-way across their properties. Meanwhile, they promoted their own access by ignoring range studies calling for sizable grazing reductions. Finally, they shackled the Grazing Service (and, later, the BLM) by having Congress slash agency budgets—a legacy of underfunding, understaffing, and professional deskilling from which the bureau still sorely suffers.

Further complicating the BLM's situation today is a final legacy of the reservation and custodial management eras: the transfer of Interior's Division of Forestry to the Department of Agriculture in 1905. As Congress began reserving timber lands for national forests, progressive conservationists led by Gifford Pinchot persuaded President Roosevelt that forests would be decimated if managed by an Interior Department ill-suffused with a conservation ethic. The merits of this argument aside, transferring this responsibility to the new U.S. Forest Service under Pinchot's leadership did two things. First, forest management on public lands was split between two departments, a situation that subsequent Interior secretaries and presidential commissions have tried unsuccessfully to redress by proposing a Department of Natural Resources. Second, the transfer placed the BLM at a sorely disadvantageous budgetary and staffing position relative to the more professionalized, scientifically based, and, hence, congressionally favored Forest Service. Thus, although the BLM managed four times as many acres as the Forest Service by 1980, it did so with only one-third the budget and one-seventh the personnel.

FROM DOMINANT TO MULTIPLE CLIENTELISM

The final two eras of natural resource management at Interior—intensive management (1950–1960s) and consultation-confrontation (post-1960s)—are the product of the changing socioeconomic, demographic, and political situation in the West. More precisely, public land issues turned during these eras from local management affairs into national policy issues. This began as recreational lifestyles changed, as ecological awareness expanded, and as Washington began coveting "energy independence." In turn, it solidified as recreationists, aesthetes, and Frostbelt émigrés to the urban West wrought a more diverse constituency for the Interior Department. Provoked in the process was a turbulent decoupling of Interior from the dominant clientelism of traditional users that had inspired much of its past. Forged by statute in its place was a multiple clientelism, one that inexorably places Interior's agencies in the cross hairs of competing, hostile, and sometimes extremist interest groups and values.

The era of intensive management spawned infinitely more aggressive, comprehensive, and integrated attempts to regulate traditional users during the consultation-confrontation era. For example, President Kennedy's and President Johnson's Interior secretary, Stewart Udall, pressed successfully during his eight years for, among other statutes, the Clean Air Act of 1963, the Wilderness Act of 1964, the Land and Water Conservation Fund Act of 1965, and the Wild and Scenic Rivers Act of 1968. President Nixon's Interior secretaries—Walter Hickel (1969–1970) and Rogers Morton (1971–1975)—presided, respectively, over the shutdown of oil leasing on the Outer Continental Shelf and the Alaska Native Claims Settlement Act. The latter provided major additions to the national park, forest,

scenic river, and wildlife refuge systems. These trends continued apace during the tenure of President Carter's Interior secretary, Cecil Andrus (1977–1981), when Congress enacted the Alaska National Interest Lands Conservation Act (ANILCA) of 1980. The single largest expansion of federal lands in the twentieth century, the ANILCA conveyed forty-seven million acres to the national park system and added fifty-four million acres to the wildlife refuge system.

Crafted as well during these presidencies were such multiple-use statutes as the Federal Land Policy and Management Act of 1976, as well as such comprehensive planning statutes as the National Environmental Policy Act of 1970, the Endangered Species Act of 1973, the National Forest Management Act of 1976, and the Federal Coal Leasing Amendments Act of 1976. Predicated on notions of consultation with affected interests, the implementation of these statutes required an influx of professionals into Interior with less pro-development philosophies (e.g., recreation planners, biologists, and botanists). Moreover, significant strides were made toward incorporating a wider range of citizen values into public land decision-making processes. These also, however, slowed those processes, made them more litigious, and wrought a backlash from traditional users from which Interior is still reeling.

With their control over management decisions waning, traditional users began pillorying Interior's mandates, methods, and motives. Ironically, these tensions surfaced with most notoriety, first, in the East. This occurred when the F&WS tried to stop the Tennessee Valley Authority from completing the Tellico Dam because it threatened the extinction of the snail darter. [See Tennessee Valley Authority.] They then grew infinitely more virulent in the West as traditional users fell increasingly on harder economic times. Demands spiraled for the federal government to return public lands to the states. Termed the "Sagebrush Rebellion" during the Carter and Reagan years, and metastasizing into the "Property Rights" and "Wise Use" movements during the Clinton administration, an angry and sometimes violent campaign arose to "return" public lands to the states.

These attacks against Interior's land management agencies were largely muted during the Reagan and Bush years as these presidents and their Interior secretaries—James Watt (1981–1983), Donald Hodel (1983–1988), and Manuel Lujan (1989–1992)—moved aggressively to accelerate development on public lands. They did so by revamping rules and regulations, defunding and deskilling agencies, and redelegating authority to traditional users on grazing boards expanded to include environmentalists by the Carter administration. Comity ended, however, when Bruce Babbitt became Interior secretary under President Clinton.

Babbitt's agenda was as incendiary to traditional users as Watt's prodevelopment agenda had been to environmentalists. Most anathematized were his efforts to raise grazing fees over three years from $1.86 per animal-unit-month (AUM) to $4.28 per AUM, a rate still considerably lower than what private owners or the Forest Service charge. Excoriated as well were his efforts to link grazing permits to good stewardship of the land, to have the BLM retain water rights on public lands, and to overhaul the 1872 Mining Law. The latter brought exorbitant profits to mining corporations exempt from resource extraction royalties, environmental restoration requirements, and fair market prices for leases.

Babbitt's agenda stalled almost immediately, impaled by the congressional *realpolitik* that stymied earlier reform efforts in Congress. While the House of Representatives had routinely passed bills sympathetic to Babbitt's agenda since 1987, these died in the Senate with its unique filibuster and cloture rules, its more rural bias, and the prodevelopment bent of Interior's oversight committees. Moreover, even the administration's "victories"—for example, its plan for the logging of old growth forests in the Pacific Northwest—won only brickbats from its multiple clienteles. Indeed, when the administration's forest management plan for the Pacific Northwest was announced, it was roundly criticized by environmentalists for allowing too much cutting and by the timber industry for allowing too little.

Yet, even under less volatile circumstances, the Interior Department's multiple clientelism poses daunting dilemmas for its leaders. The assistant secretary for land and minerals management oversees the BLM, the Minerals Management Service (created in 1982 by Secretary Watt), and the Office of Surface Mining Reclamation and Enforcement (1977). Thus, the assistant secretary must ensure that these agencies both conserve and develop oil, gas, mineral, and water resources on public lands, Native American reservations, and the Outer Continental Shelf. Moreover, this must be done in ways that protect and reclaim the environment from the scars of development but that maximize federal and state revenues.

Meanwhile, the assistant secretary for fish, wildlife, and parks oversees the NPS, the F&WS, and the National Biological Survey (NBS). The assistant secretary must ensure that the NPS preserves national parks and historic areas while it accomodates spiraling demands for visitor access to them by car, from plane overflights, by off-road vehicles, and by backpackers seeking solitude and scenic vistas. The assistant secretary must also help find a balance between the ecosystem needs of wolves reintroduced into Yellowstone Park and the needs of nearby ranchers for livestock protection. Likewise, the assistant secretary must ensure that the F&WS enforces provisions of the Endangered Species Act against prodevelopment private landowners, against other federal agencies (including those within Interior), and even against wildlife refuge managers within the F&WS! Finally, the assistant secretary has to deal with the internal bureaucratic turf wars spawned by the NBS, as well as the opposition of the Property Rights movement to the Survey's activities. By taking scientific staff from other divisions within Interior to form the NBS in 1993, Babbitt raised the hackles of units who lost personnel and pressed Congress for redress in the 104th Congress. By inventorying lands for ecosystem management, the NBS struck traditional users as another challenge to their property rights.

No less herculean challenges confront the assistant secretaries for Indian affairs, for water and science, and for insular affairs. The assistant secretary for Indian affairs has to ensure that the Bureau of Indian Affairs acts as a trustee preserving Native American and Alaskan Native communities, traditional values, and antiquities on fifty million acres of tribal lands. At the same time, however, the assistant secretary has to guarantee a fair hearing to nontraditional Indians demanding resource development on reservations, to non-Native Americans wishing to develop these lands, and to those concerned that the social costs of these activities do not fall disproportionately on Native Americans. What is more, the assistant secretary must do so without appearing paternalistic, indifferent, or callous.

Similarly, the assistant secretary for water and science—now responsible for only BuRec and the Geological Survey after the 104th Congress eliminated the Bureau of Mines—has to reorient BuRec from a "demand supply" to a "demand control" ethic. In a post-dam-building era this involves stressing environmental protection, more market-oriented water regimes, and groundwater conservation. Moreover, with both quantity and quality of surface and groundwater supplies under stress in many parts of the United States, the assistant secretaries for water and science and for insular affairs have a difficult task. They must reconcile Interior's role as trustee of Indian and Alaskan Native water rights with non-Native demands for supplies.

Finally, all the assistant secretaries must reconcile their disparate responsibilities within budgets bequeathed to them by preceding eras. Typically, these budgets are woefully incommensurate with Interior's evolving multiple-use responsibilities. Indeed, the General Accounting Office reports that most are not large enough to meet a growing backlog of infrastructure and staffing needs in the department. For example, a $2.1 billion cumulative shortfall exists in funding for maintenance at the NPS, while a $27 billion cumulative shortfall exists at the Office of Surface Mining Control and Reclamation for refurbishing lands around abandoned coal mines. Meanwhile, the F&WS faces such severe staffing shortfalls that it cannot consider at least six hundred species for designation as threatened or endangered; the agency lacks the research and information bases necessary to make these judgments. Even the Minerals Management Service is collecting less in revenues than it should because of staffing shortages.

How likely is it that this situation will improve at Interior? Legislatively, two "reform" perspectives vied for ascendancy in the 104th Congress. Neither fared well amidst threats of presidential vetoes and the dominance of prodevelopment interests on Interior's oversight committees. The first perspective—pressed by traditional users—was to dramatically reduce or redirect Interior's responsibilities. Sought, for example, were the release of contested timber sales in the Pacific Northwest, the opening of the Arctic National Wildlife Refuge to oil drilling, and the prohibition of new Endangered Species Act listings. The second perspective—pressed by a "Baptist-Bootlegger" coalition of budget hawks, "reinventing government" devotees, and environmentalists—was to resize, reengineer, and reprioritize Interior's agenda, while cutting user subsidies.

Present stalemates notwithstanding, elements of both perspectives may eventually lead to an ecosystem management approach that can help overcome past parochialism at the department. Indeed, restricted budgets and reengineering initiatives in some cases are pushing Interior's agencies to work more cooperatively with each other, to set priorities, and to "leverage" their funding across programs. Still, if Interior's history is any guide, these efforts—as well as more durable legislative reforms—will succeed only to the extent, in the form, and at the pace that traditional users of the public lands concede. Neither, however, will litigious environmentalists flushed with success in previous court battles "go gentle into that good night." Thus, the epic battle spawned by multiple clientelism for Interior's "heart and soul" has only begun.

[See also Fish and Wildlife Service; Forest Service; Geological Survey; Indian Affairs, Bureau of; Land Management, Bureau of; Minerals Management Service; National Park Service; and Reclamation, Bureau of.]

BIBLIOGRAPHY

Chase, Alston. *Playing God in Yellowstone: The Destruction of America's First National Park.* San Diego, 1987.
Clarke, Jeanne N., and Daniel McCool. *Staking Out the Terrain: Power Differentials among Natural Resource Management Agencies.* Albany, 1985.
Clawson, Marian. *The Federal Lands Revisited.* Baltimore, 1983.
Culhane, Paul J. *Public Lands Politics.* Baltimore, 1981.
Durant, Robert F. *The Administrative Presidency Revisited:*

Public Lands, the BLM, and the Reagan Revolution. Albany, 1992.

Foss, Phillip O. *Politics and Grass.* Seattle, 1960.

Francis, John G., and Richard Ganzel, eds. *Western Public Lands: The Management of Natural Resources in a Time of Declining Federalism.* Totowa, N.J., 1984.

Freemuth, John C. *Islands under Siege: National Parks and the Politics of External Threats.* Lawrence, Kans., 1991.

Gottlieb, Robert. *Forcing the Spring: The Transformation of the American Environmental Movement.* Washington, D.C., 1993.

Henning, Daniel H., and William R. Mangun. *Managing the Environmental Crisis: Incorporating Competing Values in Natural Resource Administration.* Durham, N.C., 1989.

McCool, Daniel. *Command of the Waters: Iron Triangles, Federal Water Development, and Indian Water Rights.* Berkeley, Calif., 1988.

Paehlke, Robert, ed. *Conservation and Environmentalism: An Encyclopedia.* New York, 1995.

Portney, Paul R., ed. *Natural Resources and the Environment: The Reagan Approach.* Washington, D.C., 1984.

Reisner, Marc. *Cadillac Desert: The American West and Its Disappearing Water.* New York, 1987.

Rosenbaum, Walter A. *Environmental Politics and Policy.* 4th ed. Washington, D.C., 1996.

Smith, Zachary A., ed. *Water and the Future of the Southwest.* Albuquerque, 1990.

Tobin, Richard. *The Expendable Future: U.S. Politics and the Protection of Biological Diversity.* Durham, N.C., 1990.

Udall, Stewart L. *The Quiet Crisis and the Next Generation.* Salt Lake City, 1988.

Utley, Robert M., and Barry Mackintosh. *The Department of Everything Else: Highlights of Interior History.* Washington, D.C., 1989.

White, Leonard D. *The Republican Era, 1869–1901: A Study in Administrative History.* New York, 1963.

Wilkinson, Charles F. *Crossing the Next Meridian: Land, Water, and the Future of the West.* Washington, D.C., 1992.

—ROBERT F. DURANT

Internal Revenue Service

It is the responsibility of the Internal Revenue Service (IRS) to collect taxes enacted by Congress to pay for government operating costs and expenses. The mission statement of the IRS charges the agency with collecting the proper amount of revenue at the least cost to the American people.

Although its mission may sound straightforward, the role of taxes in American history and public attitudes toward taxation have done much to shape our tax collection agency and define its role in American life.

The history of taxation in the United States reaches back beyond the days of the American Revolution and its battle cry, "No taxation without representation." Even the colonists relied on a system of property taxes, poll taxes, and faculty taxes to support limited government functions, but certainly they were not interested in developing a centralized system of raising revenue to support even the burden of financing the Revolutionary War. In fact, the colonies relied primarily on paper money and loans to support the war effort. Each colony was asked to make voluntary "contributions" from their own revenues to finance the war.

So it was that the newly independent United States, born largely out of frustration with what were considered repressive and unfair taxes, trade restrictions, and excises imposed by the British empire, was faced with a need to develop its own system of taxation to support its governmental structure. The depth of this dilemma showed in the results of the first attempt at self-government, the Articles of Confederation, which did not grant Congress the power to levy taxes.

A national government without the ability to raise revenue was a government almost assuredly doomed to failure. The end of the Revolutionary War brought economic chaos. The newly independent states looked upon federal requests for "donations" to pay the war debt more as voluntary contributions than obligations. For the most part, the states ignored pleas from the federal government for money. By 1782 the national treasury was virtually empty.

Growing frustrations from a financially destitute country and a restless citizenry prompted the nation's new leaders to support a constitutional convention in 1787. Two years later the country had a new constitution that outlined broader and more well defined authorities. Especially important was the power to tax granted by Article I, Section 8, of the new constitution.

While not granting unlimited powers, this section gave the federal government "the power to lay and collect taxes, duties, imposts, and excises, to pay the debts and provide for the common defense and general welfare of the United States." Also important was the limitation that "duties, imposts, and excises shall be uniform throughout the United States."

The leaders of the young nation preferred to rely primarily on "external" revenue sources, such as customs duties and tariffs, to protect budding domestic enterprises and discourage imports. But it did not take long before Congress passed its first "internal" revenue measure under the encouragement of strong Federalist Alexander Hamilton, George Washington's first secretary of the Treasury.

The Revenue Act of 1791 became law on 3 March of that year and brought with it the first internal taxes—excises on distilled spirits and tobacco products. Additional excises were levied in the following years on carriages, snuff, the refining of sugar, property sold at auction, and many other items. In 1798 Congress adopted the first direct tax on property owned by individuals, including dwellings, land, and slaves, based on their value.

These early internal taxes required an administrative machinery for collection. The 1791 revenue act delegated the power to collect taxes to the Treasury Department and provided for the establishment of fourteen revenue districts, each headed by a "supervisor of revenue" appointed by the president and operating under the direction of an assistant secretary of the Treasury. By 1792 the assistant secretary responsible for internal tax collection was given the title "commissioner of the revenue."

The first individual to occupy the tax collector's position in the United States was Tench Coxe, a Pennsylvania lawyer who earned $1,900 a year for this work. During his first year Coxe collected $209,000 from internal excise taxes, one-tenth of what was collected from "external" sources, including customs duties.

These early taxes were not universally praised. The tax on distilled spirits levied by the act of 1791 became the famed "whiskey tax" and precipitated the first major challenge to the authority of the federal government—the Whisky Rebellion. As an outgrowth of the mounting frustrations among farmers in America's rural areas, many farmers in western Pennsylvania took up arms against federal tax inspector John Neville, burned his home, and looted his possessions in 1794.

Interpreting these events as a serious threat to national authority he could not afford at this early stage in the young nation's development, President Washington, at the urging of Secretary of the Treasury Hamilton, called upon the militia to suppress the rebellion. Nearly thirteen thousand troops were mustered to march across Pennsylvania to suppress the rebellion.

As Thomas Jefferson assumed the presidency at the dawning of the nineteenth century, he quickly dismantled this entire system of early internal taxation. With his strong agrarian background and belief in self-government and individual rights, Jefferson called for the immediate abolition of all internal taxes. Congress complied, and for the next decade the country's revenue needs were supported primarily by tariffs and customs duties.

The commissioner of the revenue disappeared from the Treasury Department and the four hundred employees of the tax collector were released from duty. Establishing a pattern that has persisted throughout American history, it took a war to bring the next fundamental change to the tax system. The need to finance the War of 1812 resulted in a brief revival of the position of commissioner of the revenue and numerous excise taxes.

The country narrowly escaped the burden of a permanent internal revenue system during this period when Secretary of the Treasury Alexander Dallas unsuccessfully advocated the establishment of an annual assessment of internal taxes, including an income tax, in an 1814 report to Congress. It would take a century for the country to establish a permanent income tax. After the War of 1812, the United States again reverted to a revenue system dependent upon external sources and the sale of public lands to finance its activities. Until the outbreak of the Civil War the federal government levied no internal taxes of any kind.

Upon assuming the presidency, Lincoln found a nearly empty treasury, a rapidly growing national debt, a decline in customs revenues, and a country on the verge of civil war. The financial demands required that Congress seek new ways to raise revenue. A combination of excises, internal duties, and increased tariffs was proposed, including the first income tax to be levied on the American people.

On 1 July 1862 Congress passed a bill that recreated the position of tax collector in the Treasury Department, this time to be known as the commissioner of internal revenue. This act also authorized the establishment of up to 182 collection districts around the country, with the president to appoint a collector and assessor for each district. This was the most comprehensive piece of tax legislation ever enacted and also included the first income tax ever enacted in the United States. Although this tax on personal incomes was very minor, with rates ranging from three to five percent on incomes greater than $600, it was important in that it set a precedent for future income taxes.

President Lincoln appointed former Massachusetts governor George S. Boutwell as the first commissioner of internal revenue. Within a short time Boutwell's staff grew to more than four thousand tax collectors. Tax revenues began pouring in. In Boutwell's first year, $37 million was collected. The following year internal tax revenues jumped to $109 million. The Bureau of Internal Revenue collected approximately $311 million in excise, income, and inheritance taxes during the Civil War years.

The years following the Civil War witnessed many changes in the income tax, as the new tax came under increasing scrutiny and criticism. Progressive rates were abandoned in 1870 and the inheritance tax was repealed. Two years later, an election year, Congress repealed the income tax completely. For the next forty-one years the country relied primarily on the tariff and various excise taxes for its revenue.

The Bureau of Internal Revenue kept busy during the postwar years collecting and enforcing the many excise taxes and license fees enacted by Congress. Alcohol and tobacco excises remained staples of the American revenue system. Regulatory taxes appeared during this period as Congress began using internal revenue collection as a method to regulate business, social policy, and economics. The first successful regulatory tax appeared in 1886, when Congress enacted an excise on the sale of oleomargarine and placed stiff license fees on manufacturers and dealers in this new product.

Despite efforts to restrict margarine production through the tax system, the tax reaped revenues of nearly $1 million in its first year, and margarine continued to grow in popularity. The Bureau of Internal Revenue collected the tax, inspected oleomargarine factories, and analyzed samples of both butter and margarine in new laboratories built in Washington, D.C.

The oleomargarine tax and similar duties of the late nineteenth century expanded the official duties of the bureau well beyond that of basic tax collection. Since its beginnings the bureau had employed gaugers and inspectors to work in breweries and distilleries, but the advent of excise taxes on controversial products such as margarine, opium, and marijuana further broadened the work of the bureau.

Although it disappeared from the list of annual taxes, the income tax had not disappeared from the minds of politicians in the late nineteenth century. Between 1873 and 1879, fourteen different bills proposing an income tax were introduced in Congress. In 1894, Congress passed a new income tax law.

Challenges to the new tax began almost immediately, culminating in the tax case of *Pollock v. Farmers' Loan and Trust Company*, which led the Supreme Court to declare the income tax unconstitutional on 20 May 1895 in a 5–4 decision. In rendering their decision that income was personal property and, as such, a tax on it was a direct tax, the justices cited Article I, Section 8, of the Constitution, which required that taxes be "uniform throughout the United States."

But the income tax would rise again. By 1909 Congress approved a constitutional amendment to revive this tax, and four years later, the Sixteenth Amendment became part of the Constitution, once again authorizing a tax on incomes. The rates of this new tax remained low, ranging from one to six percent on incomes greater than $3,000. The average American worker, who earned about $800 a year, remained unaffected by this new tax.

The Bureau of Internal Revenue unveiled the first 1040 form on 5 January 1914, only three months after enactment of the income tax. By the middle of 1914, the administrative force dedicated to enforcing the income tax numbered 277 in Washington, D.C., with 3,723 employees in the field forces.

Changes came rapidly to the income tax. The Emergency Revenue Act of 1916 doubled the base income tax rates and raised the highest rate to fifteen percent. The 1916 act also required the Bureau of Internal Revenue to publish an annual statistical summary of its tax collection activity, which became a standard reference used widely by policy analysts in debating changes to the American tax system.

The era of World War I taxation brought many significant changes in the tax system. The traditional reliance on tariff and excise revenues was now a vestige of a bygone era, replaced with higher income taxes and excess profits taxation. Never again would customs revenues challenge internal taxes as the staple of revenue for the United States.

For the Bureau of Internal Revenue, the administrative demands of income and estate taxation brought vastly increased demands. The staff of the bureau expanded more than fourfold in the ten years following the advent of the income tax, so that by 1920 nearly twenty thousand employees worked for the bureau. Tax collections rose from about $350 million in 1913 to $5.5 billion by 1920.

In 1919 worries about increased fraud prompted the bureau to create an Intelligence Division, with the mission of ferreting out corruption both outside and internal to the organization. This unit would gain recognition over the years for investigations of notorious criminals for tax evasion. Most notable was Al Capone, brought down by the Bureau of Internal Revenue for failure to file tax returns and underpayment of income taxes.

The bureau was also given the unenviable task of enforcing national prohibition, after ratification of the Eighteenth Amendment in 1919. The commissioner was responsible for issuing permits for the manufacture, sale, and transportation of alcoholic beverages. The bureau established a Prohibition Unit to carry out this responsibility. By 1925, more than thirty-seven hundred Internal Revenue employees worked in alcohol and narcotics enforcement, making more than seventy-seven thousand arrests that year alone.

In 1930 the bureau shifted enforcement responsibility for Prohibition to the Department of Justice. It did not take long for the bureau to regain similar responsibilities. In 1934, after the national experiment with Prohibition ended, an Alcohol Tax Unit was established to monitor the production, warehousing, and payments of taxes on alcoholic beverages. This unit grew into the Alcohol, Tobacco and Firearms Division, which ultimately gained its independence from the IRS in 1972 as the Bureau of Alcohol, Tobacco and Firearms.

The growth of the Bureau of Internal Revenue in the twentieth century was rapid, creating space and personnel problems. In the 1920s employees in Washington, D.C., worked out of ten buildings scattered in a several-mile radius of the Treasury Department. The need for a dedicated building for the IRS became part of a major architectural project in Washington, D.C., known as the Federal Triangle. The bureau's new headquarters was the first of these buildings to be constructed, with a design inspired by that of Somerset House, home of Britain's tax collection agency. Completed sixteen months ahead of schedule at a construction cost of $6.4 million, the new Internal Revenue building was designed to house up to forty-five hundred workers.

The election of Franklin D. Roosevelt in 1932 brought increased federal spending as the government expanded programs to pull people out of the lingering effects of the Great Depression. A Social Security Tax Division was created in the bureau to administer the collection of taxes under the Social Security Act of 1935.

By 1941 more than twenty-seven thousand employees worked for the bureau and tax collections reached $7.4 billion. Although this represented significant growth, these numbers would be dwarfed as the bureau struggled to meet the financial demands of World War II. The need for dramatically increased revenue to fund the war effort pushed the income tax to new levels and brought millions of new taxpayers onto the income tax rolls. By 1945 Internal Revenue brought in $45 billion in tax revenues.

The bureau tried to ease the tax burden as much as possible for the millions of new taxpayers added to the rolls during the war years as the tax base was broadened to reach most American citizens for the first time. A short form 1040 was created in 1941; withholding of taxes at the source came with the Current Tax Payment Act of 1943; the standard deduction began in 1944.

As the nation returned to normalcy following World War II, signs began to appear that the traditional method of politically appointing collectors of internal revenue in each state might be outmoded. The system was a vestige of the Civil War tax structure established by President Lincoln. By the late 1940s serious concerns over ethical violations of the tax laws by some of the highest-ranking individuals of the Bureau of Internal Revenue prompted a series of congressional investigations led by Representative Cecil R. King of California.

King's committee investigated numerous cases of alleged misconduct, bribery, and other unscrupulous behavior on the part of bureau employees. By the end of 1951, Commissioner of Internal Revenue John Dunlap announced that 113 Internal Revenue employees had been fired or forced to resign, including six collectors and a former commissioner.

In large part, these investigations provided a catalyst for a massive reorganization of the Bureau of Internal Revenue in 1952. The existing organizational structure was the result of haphazard growth and change as new taxes were implemented and existing taxes altered over the years. The Bureau of Internal Revenue had grown like patchwork, adding a new organization whenever a new tax was created. This created overlap as employees in different areas performed similar work on different types of tax returns. Employees of the Income Tax Section processed, filed, and audited income tax returns, while employees of the Alcohol and Tobacco Division performed the same duties for their tax returns.

The Bureau of Internal Revenue of the early 1950s was a political organization functioning in an increasingly specialized and professional world of tax administration. The 1952 reorganization combined all field functions of Internal Revenue into the basic organizational unit of a district office, headed by a career civil service director rather than a political appointee. [See Civil Service.]

The Bureau also created regional offices to manage the vast nationwide field organization and provide a buffer between district offices and the headquarters in Washington, D.C. Only the commissioner remained a political appointee, completing the transformation of Internal Revenue from one of the most political organizations of the federal government to one of the least. Also created with the reorganization was an internal inspection organization, with the mission of ensuring the integrity of the tax system and investigating cases of official misconduct.

In 1953 the official designation of the organization was changed to Internal Revenue Service, reflecting the overall change in philosophy and direction. For the first time, Internal Revenue was organized along functional lines, such as collection of revenue and examination of tax returns. The filing deadline for individual tax returns was shifted from 15 March to 15 April in 1955, reflecting the need for more time to process the millions of tax returns flowing into the IRS.

The dawning of the electronic age of American business coincided with the expansion and reorganization of the tax administration system, and the IRS recognized the need to automate its processing techniques. Automation promised to eliminate many labor-intensive tasks associated with processing tax returns, decreasing processing time and resulting in fewer errors.

The IRS ventured into the world of automated data processing in the 1960s as it developed a plan to build a series of "service centers" around the country. These new centers, which grew to a total of ten by 1972, centralized the tax processing operations in buildings filled with computer systems, in contrast to the manual handling of returns in every district office that dominated the tax processing system through the 1950s. The system was linked by the National Computer Center in Martinsburg, West Virginia, which opened in 1961. The center housed the heart of the automatic data processing system, known as the "master file," which consisted of data extracted from individual tax returns.

By the late 1960s the IRS realized that changes in technology were already outpacing its computer systems. A long-range study of technology requirements for the tax processing system began in 1967, leading to the first of many plans to upgrade existing computer systems. By the late 1970s budgetary constraints and increasing concerns over the security and privacy of more and more computerized information prompted Congress to withdraw support for the first of several major computer upgrades for the IRS.

Despite the setback, the IRS moved towards the twenty-first century by replacing aging computer hardware in its service centers in the early 1980s. A major step into the advanced world of electronic processing for the IRS began in 1986, as the agency accepted the first successful transmission of a tax return by electronic means. By the 1990s, electronic filing had transformed the process of filing tax returns for millions of Americans.

[See also Alcohol, Tobacco and Firearms, Bureau of and Treasury, Department of the.]

BIBLIOGRAPHY

Adams, Charles, W. For Good and Evil: The Impact of Taxes upon the Course of Civilization. New York, 1993.
Brown, Thomas H. George Sewall Boutwell: Human Rights Advocate. Groton, Mass., 1989.
Burnham, David. A Law unto Itself: Power, Politics and the IRS. New York, 1989.
Chommie, John C. The Internal Revenue Service. New York, 1970.
Commissioner of Internal Revenue. Report of the Commissioner of Internal Revenue. Washington, D.C., annually.
Dorris, Lillian, ed. The American Way in Taxation: Internal Revenue, 1862–1962. Englewood Cliffs, N.J., 1963.
Gurney, George. Sculpture and the Federal Triangle. Washington, D.C., 1985.
Irey, Elmer. The Tax Dodgers: The Inside Story of the T-Men's War with America's Political and Underworld Hoodlums. London, 1949.
IRS Historical Studies. IRS Historical Fact Book: A Chronology, 1646–1992. Washington, D.C., 1992.
Messick, Hank. Secret File. New York, 1969.
Paul, Randolph E. Taxation in the United States. Boston, 1954.
Ratner, Sidney. Taxation and Democracy in America. New York, 1967.
U.S. Department of the Treasury. Statistics of Income. Washington, D.C., annually.

—SHELLEY L. DAVIS

International Development Cooperation Agency

The functions of the United States International Development Cooperation Agency (IDCA) include policy planning, policy making, and policy coordination on international issues affecting developing countries. Established on 1 October 1979, the IDCA is composed of three separate agencies: the Agency for International Development (USAID), the Overseas Private Investment Corporation (OPIC), and the Trade and Development Agency (TDA). Prior to the founding of the IDCA, the secretary of state, acting as the agent of the president and working through the State Department and other agencies, coordinated planning and strategy for U.S. economic policies affecting developing countries. These functions were taken over by the IDCA.

The IDCA is headed by an administrator assisted by a deputy administrator. The administrator serves as the principal international development adviser to the president and the secretary of state. He works with other government agencies in formulating the policies the United States will take in negotiations with other countries and in international conferences regarding issues concerning developing countries.

Since 1981 the USAID administrator has also served concurrently as the acting administrator of the IDCA. The staff of USAID currently performs the staff functions for the IDCA.

The IDCA's administrator also serves as chairman of the OPIC. The administrator or designated assistants also serve on a number of interagency committees. The administrator is chairman of the Development Coordination Committee, an interagency body coordinating development programs and policies. As chair of this committee, the administrator submits to Congress a report on development issues. He is also a member of the National Committee on International and Monetary Affairs, the Trade Policy Committee, and the Advisory Committee on Agricultural Assistance.

USAID is the largest of the three component agencies of the IDCA. It was founded during the Kennedy administration to amalgamate existing U.S. foreign assistance programs. The purpose of USAID was to administer U.S. foreign economic and humanitarian programs worldwide in developing countries. It provides humanitarian assistance and aid to countries in transition and crisis. When major disasters occur in developing countries USAID provides disaster relief and short-term rehabilitation supplies and services during periods of national transitions.

USAID supports voluntary family planning programs in developing countries as well as health care, educational, and service programs for women and children. It provides programs to encourage and promote private-sector enterprises, including job skills and training programs. It has programs on environmental education, programs to strengthen democratic institutions, and those to promote human rights. It also administers the foreign aid programs to Israel and Egypt that were pledged under the Camp David Accords.

In 1990 the Bush administration established a commission to examine the management of USAID. In the spring of 1992, the commission issued a series of recommendations for changes to promote efficiency and obtain better results from foreign aid dollars. One of the recommendations was that USAID lose its independence as a separate agency and be folded into the State Department. In response to criticism that too much money was being spent on foreign assistance programs, in the last few years Congress began to cut the foreign aid appropriations to USAID with the result that USAID has sharply cut its staff and closed many missions abroad.

The OPIC, a component of the IDCA and a self-sustaining federal agency, was established in 1969 and began operations in 1971. Some of its programs began as early as 1948 and were administered by several foreign aid agencies including USAID.

According to its 1969 enabling legislation, the OPIC is a U.S. government agency "under the policy guidance of the Secretary of State," created to "mobilize and facilitate the participation of the United States' private capital and skills in the economic and social programs of less developed countries and areas, thereby complementing the development assistance objectives of the United States."

The OPIC's chief executive officer is its president. The IDCA's administrator is chairman of the OPIC's fifteen-member board of directors, eight of whom are from the private sector and seven from the federal government.

The OPIC assists U.S. investors with three basic programs: 1) insuring U.S. investors for up to twenty years against a broad range of political risks through political risk insurance; 2) financing investment projects through direct loans and/or guarantees; and 3) providing a variety of investor services. The OPIC insures U.S. investors against inconvertibility, expropriation, and war. Each term is specifically defined: inconvertibility, as the inability to convert to dollars local currencies received as income, repayment, or return of investment; expropriation, as including confiscation and nationalization; and war, as embracing revolution, insurrection, and civil strife.

As a self-sustaining agency, the OPIC conducts its insurance operations with due regard for the principles of risk management. Its finance program provides financing in conjunction with U.S. private investment. It provides medium- to long-term funding to small- and medium-sized firms who invest in new facilities or expand or modernize existing facilities. Since it began operations in 1971, the OPIC has supported investments in projects valued at over $60 billion. In 1994 it did business in 144 countries and made a profit of $167 million.

The TDA, with less than thirty employees, is the smallest component of the IDCA. Established in 1980, it was made an independent agency within the IDCA in 1988. It is headed by a director. The TDA's mandate is to promote economically developing countries by financing planning services for development projects leading to the export of U.S. goods and services. It assists U.S. firms in planning overseas investment projects by funding feasibility studies as well as by carrying out a program of tied aid credits for U.S. exports.

BIBLIOGRAPHY

Brennglass, Alan C. *The Overseas Private Investment Corporation: A Study in Political Risk.* New York, 1983.

Federal Staff Directory. Mount Vernon, Va., 1995.

"International Development Cooperation Agency." *Business America* 8 (1985): 11–12.

Madeo, David. "Clinton Administration Policy Ties Economic Aid to Foreign Policy Goals." *Law and Policy in International Business* 25 (1994): 1215–1223.

The United States Government Manual. Lanham, Md., 1995.

U.S. Overseas Private Investment Corporation. *Annual Report.* Washington, D.C., 1972–.

—ALAN C. BRENNGLASS

International Trade Administration

The task of the International Trade Administration (ITA) is to promote and strengthen the international trade and investment position of the United States. A cabinet-level agency in the Department of Commerce, the ITA was created because of a bureaucratic reorganization proposal that was submitted to Congress by President Carter in July 1979. After consultation and revisions, Carter's proposal was accepted and became effective on 2 January 1980.

Carter's submission of the reorganization plan was instigated because of a general feeling in Congress that trade policy had not been given very high priority or attention by most top government officials, and that major trade policy operations were spread too thinly throughout the executive branch, resulting in the "haphazard" formulation and implementation of U.S. trade policy. Although the Office of the U.S. Trade Representative (USTR) had established itself as a major player in multilateral negotiations and had taken the lead on bilateral and product-specific negotiations as well, other policy tasks were spread around the executive branch. The Department of Commerce promoted exports, the Department of the Treasury handled unfair trade practices cases, the Department of Agriculture oversaw grain sales, and many departments evi-

dently tried to influence escape clause cases in which the president has final decision-making authority over whether or not to grant protection to industries that claim to be injured by negotiated trade concessions. For a brief time the idea of creating a Trade Department was floated in Congress, but with only weak support. Under political pressure from the Senate, Carter submitted his proposal for bureaucratic reform that was later adopted.

The Carter reforms enlarged and enhanced the USTR, giving it "international trade policy development, coordination and negotiation functions" and encompassing some responsibilities previously handled by the State Department (Destler, p. 117). The Department of Commerce became the focus of nonagricultural trade operations and was to play a supporting role in the trade policy negotiation efforts of the USTR. Evidently for political reasons, the Department of Agriculture would retain its power over farm products. However, power was transferred from the Department of the Treasury to the ITA for the investigation and implementation of the anti-dumping and countervailing duty laws. Thus all future investigations of the so-called unfair trade practices of foreign firms dumping their goods on the U.S. market or of foreign governments subsidizing their industries' exports would be conducted by the ITA.

As originally conceived, the ITA provides support to the USTR for trade policy negotiation efforts but has no jurisdiction over agricultural trade programs. The agency is headed by the under secretary for international trade, who coordinates the operations of four major subdivisions of the agency: International Economic Policy, Trade Development, U.S. and Foreign Commercial Service, and Import Administration.

The International Economic Policy sector seeks to increase U.S. trade and investment by identifying foreign barriers to commerce and taking part in negotiations to remove them. It also helps to identify commercial opportunities for U.S. businesses and counsels them regarding those opportunities. As international economic policy may be bilateral, multilateral, or regional in nature, there are five deputy assistant secretaries who report to the assistant secretary of the

International Economic Policy sector, one for each of the major regions: Europe, the Western Hemisphere, Asia and the Pacific, Africa and the Near East, and Japan. Regional secretaries are responsible for trade and investment issues for the particular countries in their regions.

The Trade Development sector of the ITA is headed by an assistant secretary who provides advice on international trade and investment policies for particular industrial sectors, carries out programs to strengthen domestic exports, and promotes U.S. industries in international markets. Various sectors receive specific attention including technology and aerospace industries, textiles and apparel, environmental technology, service sectors, and basic industries such as forest products, chemicals, minerals, and metals.

The U.S. and Foreign Commercial Service division, headed by the assistant secretary and director general, provides marketing information and assistance to U.S. exporting industries and international businesses through its offices around the United States and the world. In 1995 it supported forty-seven domestic offices and 132 international posts in sixty-eight foreign countries. Among other duties, these offices offer export counseling to U.S. business owners, put U.S. companies into contact with potential foreign buyers, and conduct conferences and seminars to help companies enter new markets.

Perhaps the most controversial sector of the ITA is Import Administration. Headed by an assistant secretary, the Import Administration division has the authority to implement the antidumping and countervailing duty laws of the United States. These laws are meant to protect U.S. industries against unfair trade practices. The antidumping law is used to counter the practice of foreign firms dumping their goods on the U.S. market, where dumping is defined as selling goods at below home market price or cost of production. The countervailing duty law is implemented against foreign firms whose goods are believed to be subsidized by their governments, giving them an unfair market advantage.

Typically, firms or industries petition the ITA to investigate the existence of an unfair trade practice. The products investigated under these laws are diverse, including such goods as canned pineapple, fresh garlic, cut flowers, saccharin, pencils, leather, lumber, and steel wire, pipes, and bars. The ITA then investigates the behavior of the foreign firm(s) or government to determine whether or not an unfair practice has occurred or is occurring. If the investigation results in a positive ruling, the ITA determines the size of the duty that may be imposed on U.S. imports of the unfairly traded goods. This is typically the difference between the domestic and foreign prices or costs in the case of dumped goods, or an amount equivalent to the degree of foreign government assistance to its firms in the case of subsidized goods. However, before these duties can be officially collected by the government, the International Trade Commission (ITC), an independent regulatory agency, must rule on whether or not the dumped or subsidized imports are causing or threaten to cause injury to the domestic industry. For most cases, a positive ruling from both agencies is required before duties can be imposed. The only exception is for cases against countries that have not signed the subsidy code of the General Agreement on Tariffs and Trade (or its successor, the World Trade Organization). Under the countervailing duty law, these countries do not get an injury test from the ITC; in these cases, the ITA is the sole policymaker.

The implementation of these laws by the ITA is controversial largely because it is believed that the laws are biased in favor of domestic firms that petition the ITA for protection against alleged unfair practices. For example, in its investigations the Import Administration requests detailed price and cost information from foreign firms accused of an unfair trade practice. If that information is deemed incomplete or is not provided in the proper format and in a timely fashion, the ITA can choose to ignore the foreign producer's information and use the "best information available," which typically means information provided by the domestic firm. This biases the case in favor of the domestic petitioner.

In addition to its enforcement of these unfair practices laws, the Import Administration also implements various trade agreements, such as the U.S.-Japan Semiconductor Agreement and the President's Machine Tool Program with Taiwan and Japan, and ensures the proper creation and administration of foreign trade zones in the United States, which allow firms within those zones to operate free of customs duties in the importation of any goods that are used in the production of products for export.

[*See also* International Trade Commission *and* Trade Representative, Office of the U.S.]

BIBLIOGRAPHY

Boltuck, Richard, and Robert E. Litan, ed. *Down in the Dumps.* Washington, D.C., 1991.

Destler, I. M. *American Trade Politics.* 3d ed. Washington, D.C., 1995.

The United States Government Manual: 1995/1996. Washington, D.C., 1995.

U.S. Congress. Senate. Committee on Finance. *Trade Agreements Act of 1979.* 96th Cong., 1st sess., 1979. S. Rep. 96–249.

U.S. Department of Commerce. *Business America.* Washington D.C., 1980–.

—Wendy L. Hansen

International Trade Commission

 Although it has been known by its present name since 1974, the beginnings of the International Trade Commission (ITC), an independent, quasi-judicial federal agency, date back to 1916, when Congress established the United States Tariff Commission, as an investigative body for Congress and the executive branch. The commission was to collect information broadly related to international trade and provide this information to congressional committees and administrative officials to aid them in policy-making. Occasionally the commission would make recommendations on policy. To avoid the partisanship problems that doomed its predecessor, the short-lived Tariff Board (1909–1912), the commission was supposedly made nonpartisan by a provision that no more than three of the six presidentially appointed commissioners could be members of the same political party. Primarily a fact-finding agency, the Tariff Commission in its early years

lacked any direct policy-making powers. One of the commission's primary tasks was to conduct general fact-finding investigations involving the monitoring of imports, impact of tariff changes, and the like under Section 332 of the U.S. Tariff Act of 1930. These investigations, which are conducted on its own initiative, or upon request from the president, the Senate Finance Committee, the House Ways and Means Committee, or the office of the U.S. Trade Representative, continue to be a major task of the ITC.

With the delegation of power by Congress to the president under the 1934 Reciprocal Trade Agreements Act and with the creation of the General Agreement on Tariffs and Trade (GATT) in 1947, the importance of the commission began to grow. In 1947, first by executive order and later by act of Congress, the "escape clause," which had been incorporated into GATT, became part of U.S. law. The escape clause (also known today as Section 201 of the Trade Act of 1974) requires the commission to investigate complaints of serious injury to the domestic industry or threat thereof owing to negotiated trade concessions, and recommend a remedy to the president. The president then has the authority to accept the ITC's recommendation, modify that recommendation, or offer his or her own policy, including a denial of protection to the domestic industry. This law became an important political factor in the adoption of future multilateral trade agreements because it allows the U.S. to "escape" from concessions offered in international agreements. Since 1980 the ITC has conducted twenty-five escape clause investigations on products as diverse as mushrooms and automobiles. Protection, if granted, usually takes the form of quotas or tariffs and typically lasts for five years, after which review investigations determine whether or not the protection will be continued. The case most often cited as evidence of how successful the use of the escape clause can be is the case of Harley-Davidson's request for protection from imports of motorcycles, largely from Japan and Europe. In 1982 the motorcycle industry was granted five years of protection. After a few years Harley evidently recovered enough economically to request that the protection be removed early.

A second major addition to the tasks of the ITC in the post-GATT era is its administration of the antidumping law. In its early years enforcement of the Antidumping Act of 1921 had fallen on the Department of the Treasury alone. In 1954 the ITC was granted the power under Section 731 of the Tariff Act of 1930, as amended, to jointly enforce the antidumping law, first with the Department of the Treasury, and then, since 1980, with the International Trade Administration (ITA), a cabinet agency in the Department of Commerce. The antidumping law is used to punish foreign firms that are believed to be dumping goods on the U.S. market, where dumping is defined as selling goods in the U.S. market at a price below home market price or cost of production. Typically, a firm or industry association petitions the ITC and ITA to investigate a foreign firm or firms for engaging in the unfair practice of dumping. Once a petition is filed, two investigations are conducted virtually simultaneously—the ITA investigates the allegation of dumping and determines the margin by which goods are being dumped, while the ITC investigates the domestic industry's claim of injury owing to dumped imports. Both agencies have veto power over granting protection to the U.S. industry, and affirmative rulings are required by both agencies for protection from imports to be granted under the antidumping law. If both agencies rule in the affirmative, a duty is imposed on imports of the good, in addition to any existing tariff, equivalent to the margin of dumping as determined by the ITA. Since 1980 the largest number of investigations conducted by the ITC has been under the antidumping law; a total of 718 investigations were conducted from 1980 through 1994. The products investigated under this law are diverse, including such goods as canned pineapple, fresh garlic, cut flowers, saccharin, pencils, and steel wire, pipes, and bars.

Another major law enforced by the ITC is the countervailing duty law, also known as Section 701 of the Tariff Act of 1930. This law is designed to counter the practice of foreign governments subsidizing their industries. The United States had had a statute since 1897 that allowed it to impose countervailing duties against goods that were allegedly subsidized by foreign governments. But it was not until 1974 that the United States, under international pressure, adopted an injury test that would require it to show that the domestic industry had been "materially injured" by the subsidized imports, if those imports come from a country that has signed the GATT subsidy code. Investigations of alleged subsidization are similar to those under the antidumping law. When a firm or industry association petitions the government for protection from the unfair practice of subsidization, the ITA investigates whether or not subsidization is occurring and determines the margin of subsidization (before 1980 this task was performed by the Treasury Department). The ITC investigates the domestic industry and determines whether U.S. firms are being injured by the subsidized imports. As under the antidumping law, either agency has veto power, and affirmative decisions are required from both agencies in order for protection to be granted to the domestic industry. Since 1980, 364 countervailing duty investigations have been conducted by the ITC. While a variety of industries, from lumber to leather, have requested such investigations, steel and steel-related industries have been the predominant petitioners under this law.

Three other types of investigations conducted by the ITC are worthy of mention. In its early years, before the creation of GATT, the commission was granted power under Section 337 of the Tariff Act of 1930 to investigate alleged unfair practices, largely allegations of patent infringement or copyright violations. An administrative law judge holds hearings and makes an initial determination, which the ITC can modify or accept. The ITC's decision then becomes final sixty days after issuance, unless disapproved by the president. Since 1980 the ITC has conducted 330 such investigations. Far less frequent are the ITC's investigations under Section 22 of the Agricultural Adjustment Act. Under this law the ITC investigates agricultural imports and their impact on or interference with U.S. agricultural programs; only fourteen investigations have been conducted by the ITC under this law since 1980. Finally, under Section 406 of the Trade Act of 1974, the ITC was given the power to investigate market disruption in the United States owing to imports from a communist country and to recommend a remedy to the president. Only nine such investigations have been conducted since 1980.

The impact that the ITC has on U.S. trade policy varies by the statutes it is involved in enforcing. Although no decisions are made by the ITC in its general fact-finding investigations, policymakers may use the information gathered by the ITC to shape policy. In its enforcement of the escape clause, the Agricultural Adjustment Act, and the Trade Act of 1974 for market disruptions from communist countries, the ITC has the opportunity to make policy recommendations to the president to remedy market disruptions in the United States, though in each case the president has final decision-making authority. It is under the unfair practices law, the antidumping law, and the countervailing duty law that the ITC has the greatest policy-making authority. Though power is shared with other policy-making bodies, the ITC has the ability to directly affect international trade.

Investigations conducted under the aforementioned body of laws make up the bulk of the activities of the ITC. However, in addition to these formal investigations, the ITC also conducts numerous studies every year on the request of members of the U.S. House of Representatives and Senate to determine the potential impact of proposed trade legislation on U.S. industries or the economy. However, the effect of these studies on U.S. policy has not been systematically studied.

In addition to using the ITC as a source of information for policy-making, the U.S. Congress has taken actions to ensure that the ITC would be under its control, not that of the executive. Under the 1974 Trade Act the budget for the ITC was put outside the control of the executive branch's Office of Management and Budget; thus, the president must pass the ITC's budget request along to Congress unchanged. Permanent authorization for the ITC was canceled, requiring it to obtain annual authorization as well as annual appropriations through congressional legislation in order to continue to function. Commissioners' terms were extended from six

years to nine years, with reappointment forbidden. Finally, the 1974 Trade Act maintained the bipartisan nature of the commission as originally conceived, requiring that no more than three commissioners be members of the same political party.

As with other top presidential appointees, the six commissioners must be confirmed by the Senate. Under current rules reappointment is only allowed a commissioner who was appointed to a vacated seat but has served no more than five years. Terms are staggered so that one commissioner's term expires every eighteen months. The chair and vice chair of the commission are appointed by the president for two-year terms, but the current chair may not be of the same political party as the preceding chair, nor may the president designate a chair and vice chair from the same political party. Decision-making at the ITC is accomplished by majority rule. In the case of ties, the decision goes to the affirmative, benefiting U.S. firms that seek protection. In their decision-making, the commissioners are supported by a staff of economists, lawyers, and other personnel that assists them in their investigations. On occasion, fewer than six commissioners vote owing to vacancies or abstentions for possible conflict of interest.

Major trade statutes passed by Congress in 1979, 1984, and 1988 have further affected the implementation of trade policy under this body of U.S. trade laws. For example, in 1984 Congress mandated that the ITC use cumulation in its investigation of antidumping and countervailing duty petitions. This provision requires that the ITC pool all imports of "like products" together, from all countries that are under investigation within a "reasonably coincidental" time period, in its investigation and determination of domestic injury. Some experts believe that this provision and many other such congressional amendments to the U.S. laws have made it easier for U.S. firms to get protection from foreign imports.

Finally, as a check on the discretionary powers of the ITC, any party (foreign or domestic) to an unfair practices, antidumping, or countervailing duty case has the right to appeal the ITC's decision. Unfair practices cases are appealed to the U.S. Court of Appeals for the Federal Circuit.

Cases under the antidumping and countervailing duty laws are appealed the to U.S. Court of International Trade, or in cases involving Canada or Mexico, to a binational panel under the auspices of the North American Free Trade Agreement. Decisions at the Court of International Trade can be further appealed to the U.S. Court of Appeals for the Federal Circuit, and all the way to the U.S. Supreme Court.

[*See also* International Trade Administration *and* Trade Representative, Office of the U.S.]

BIBLIOGRAPHY

Boltuck, Richard, and Robert E. Litan, eds. *Down in the Dumps.* Washington D.C., 1991.
Dobson, John M. *Two Centuries of Tariffs.* Washington D.C., 1976.
Hansen, Wendy L., and Thomas J. Prusa. *Cumulation and ITC Decision-Making: The Sum of the Parts Is Greater than the Whole.* National Bureau of Economic Research Working Paper No. 5062. Cambridge, Mass., 1995.
Jackson, John H. *The World Trading System.* Cambridge, Mass., 1989.
U.S. International Trade Commission. *Annual Report.* Washington D.C., 1979–.
—WENDY L. HANSEN

Interstate Commerce Commission

 Congress created the Interstate Commerce Commission (ICC) to regulate railroads by passing the Interstate Commerce Act (ICA), which President Grover Cleveland signed into law on 4 February 1887. Representing a break with traditional laissez-faire notions (even though they were imperfectly held), the ICA culminated demands for regulation that became heated in the decades following the Civil War. In those years railroads crisscrossed the United States and developed old and new regions by speeding essential goods to distant markets, but these roads were unlike any business Americans had experienced. With their steel tentacles stretching across many states, railroads monopolized transportation in large areas, where they set rates not by simple weight and distance formulas, reflecting the cost of transportation, but by an estimate of what the market would bear. At points, however, where other railroads or modes of transportation existed, railroads were fiercely competitive, charged low rates, and even offered large shippers rebates on published rates. Shippers without rebates and those without alternative means of transportation were infuriated that common carriers, contrary to their charters, discriminated against them, and they clamored for government regulation.

In the years following the Civil War, states established railroad commissions. Massachusetts and several other states sought to end discrimination and abuses through publicity, while midwestern commissions, like the one in Illinois, set maximum freight rates by a weight and distance formula. Railroads challenged state regulation, but in the Granger cases (1877) the Supreme Court ruled that in the absence of federal legislation the states could regulate railroads. Reversing itself, however, in *Wabash v. Illinois* (1886), the Court refused to allow the Illinois commission to set freight rates between Illinois and New York, declaring that if interstate commerce were to be regulated it should be by "the Congress of the United States under the commerce clause of the Constitution."

By 1886 farmers, merchants, and industrialists demanded regulation and railroad managers were resigned to it. All four groups had a hand in creating the ICA—a compromise measure that passed Congress by overwhelming majorities. Opponents in the main came from California and the Northeast, where discrimination often worked to their advantage and where railroad interests were strong. Creating a five-member ICC, the ICA outlawed pools and rate discrimination and demanded that rates be published and be "reasonable and just." Its commissioners were appointed for six-year terms, and no more than three were to be from the same party. The ICC could investigate railroads, compel witnesses to testify, secure relevant materials, and require the railroads to submit annual reports and to use a uniform accounting system. If a railroad ignored an ICC ruling, it had recourse to the appropriate U.S. Circuit Court. Parts of the ICA were fuzzy.

Traffic pools were illegal, but collective rate setting was not; the prohibition against charging less for a long than for a short haul was qualified with the ambiguous phrase "under substantially similar circumstances"; and the value-of-service rate system was not replaced with a cost-of-service system, making it difficult to determine "reasonable and just" rates. Nevertheless, the ICC had potential. Able and energetic commissioners backed by the courts could eliminate abuses and shape a national transportation system, but a weak, court-harassed commission would annoy railroads without helping the public.

Cleveland appointed an outstanding jurist, Thomas M. Cooley, as chair of the ICC. Under his leadership the ICC in its early years was reasonably effective. Discrimination waned, and, since the ICC allowed only few exceptions under the long- short-haul clause, small shippers benefited as railroads reduced short-haul rates. But its case-by-case approach made it difficult for the ICC to enunciate a transportation policy. With Cooley's superior guidance, it might have shaped a grand design out of individual cases, but his health failed, and in 1891 he resigned.

The panic of 1893 led to a severe economic depression, which devastated interstate commerce, bankrupted railroads, and undermined the effectiveness of the ICC. Suffering railroads defied the commission by offering rebates to attract traffic, and preoccupied politicians neglected it. While presidents did little beyond appointing commissioners and Congress ignored the ICC's pleas for additional power, the Supreme Court all but destroyed the commission. For a decade it had decided on replacements for unfair rates, but the Supreme Court in *ICC v. Cincinnati, New Orleans and Texas Pacific Railway* (1897) declared that the ICC could not prescribe rates. After the Court, in *ICC v. Alabama Midland Railroad* (1897), made so many exceptions to the long- short-haul clause that it was rendered useless, railroads raised thousands of rates for intermediate points, which once again were at their mercy. Dissenting, Justice John Marshall Harlan declared that the ICC was left only "with power to make reports and issue protests."

With the return of prosperity, railroads consolidated or purchased stock in competing railroads to form a "community of interest" and embarked on a rebuilding program to handle greater freight volume. By 1906 railroads appeared prosperous, but inflation increased construction and operating costs, and they needed higher rates. President Theodore Roosevelt, however, opposed railroad consolidation and wished to empower the ICC to regulate maximum freight rates, claiming that regulation would give both shippers and railroads a square deal. The House of Representatives responded with the Hepburn bill, specifically giving the ICC power to set maximum rates. Several senators, however, tried to weaken the bill by including a broad judicial review of the facts of a case, which would in effect lodge the rate-setting power in the courts. These senators failed because Roosevelt orchestrated public opinion and forced them to allow the courts to decide on the extent of judicial review. Besides allowing the ICC to set maximum rates and to inspect railroad accounts, the Hepburn Act (1906) increased the commission to seven members and its jurisdiction to include express and sleeping car companies, oil pipelines, switches, spurs, yards, depots, and terminals. The act prohibited discrimination in providing shippers with freight cars and switches for their sidings, restored imprisonment as a punishment for giving or taking rebates, and forbade giving railroad passes to anyone not employed by the railroad. The Hepburn Act made the ICC a powerful regulatory agency, especially after the Supreme Court adopted a narrow-review policy. Even if it believed the ICC were mistaken, the Court refused to usurp administrative functions.

Roosevelt urged that the ICC adopt a positive administrative rather than a passive judicial approach to regulation. Increased jurisdiction, however, led to a flood of cases, and the ICC found it even more difficult to rise above the minutiae to engage in imaginative administration and develop an adequate national transportation system. Ignoring Roosevelt's injunction, the ICC only tinkered with the status quo, legitimatized value-of-service rates (which maximized the use of railroad tracks and rolling stock but built the economy on false and wasteful premises) rather than instituting cost-of-service rates (which would raise bulk commodity rates for many farmers and industrialists, but would lower consumer prices for manufactured goods). In an expanding inflationary economy, the ICC froze freight rates at their 1906 level.

Redeeming a Republican campaign promise, Congress passed the Mann-Elkins Act of 1910. Carriers could continue to set rates by concerted action, but the ICC could suspend the new rates for ten months, pending an investigation, and the railroads would have to prove the reasonableness of existing and proposed rates. The act also revived the long- short-haul clause and added to the ICC's jurisdiction telephone, telegraph, and cable lines. Congress also set up a Commerce Court to review the ICC's decisions, but killed it in October 1913, when it tended to reverse the ICC's antirailroad decisions.

In 1911 the ICC rejected railroad proposals for rate advances. Not only were value-of-service rates impossible to defend as reasonable, but the ICC (reflecting the attitudes of the Progressive Era) regarded railroad managers as inefficient and unethical and, assuming that railroad stock was watered, stressed that reasonable rates could be determined only when profits could be compared with the true value of railroads. Consequently, Congress in 1913 authorized the ICC to valuate railroad property, but after twenty years of study the ICC concluded that the roads were not overcapitalized and that excessive profits were not masked by watered stock.

With determined leadership, the ICC could be a positive force. In 1912 the archaic, disorganized practices of the nation's thirteen express companies made their service inefficient, discriminatory, and frequently dishonest. Mirroring the railroads, express companies had a complex classification and pricing system that resulted in roundabout routing and over 600 million confusing rates. Wisely rejecting a case-by-case approach, the ICC made all express companies party to one proceeding and after a thorough investigation (largely the work of Commissioner Franklin K. Lane) allowed only two classifications (general and perishables), divided the nation into 950 blocks (each bounded by a degree of latitude and longitude), and required that all rates be calculated by counting the blocks a ship-

ment traversed. Overhauling the express system was the ICC's most significant accomplishment in its 108 years. It failed to impose a comparably rational rate system on the railroads.

World War I strained the American rail system. Enormous traffic snarls occurred (with the West needing empty cars while loaded freight cars glutted eastern ports), and the railroads could not untangle them because of the antipooling provision of the ICA. When the United States entered the war in April 1917, the American Railway Association, with the blessing of the Woodrow Wilson administration as well as the ICC, formed a War Board to coordinate rail operations. To keep up with the ICC's increasing responsibilities, Congress in August enlarged it to nine members and authorized it to form three divisions with power to act independently, subject to review by the whole commission. With its reorganization complete in October, the ICC got through more work, but the shift of power from commissioners to their staff was accentuated. This shift had started when the 1906 Hepburn Act created special examiners, whose findings were usually accepted by the commissioners.

By December 1917 the rail system was in shambles. The War Board could not eliminate traffic snarls, and the ICC would not allow the railroads a fifteen percent rate increase, despite their plea that they were near bankruptcy. Recognizing the crisis, the ICC suggested that the antitrust acts and the antipooling clause of the ICA be suspended and the entire rail system be operated as one unit by either the carriers or the government. On 28 December the Wilson administration took over the rail system. Public control replaced private enterprise; compulsory unification replaced voluntary cooperation; and an aggressive Railroad Administration replaced the negative adjudication of the ICC. Federal control, while successfully consolidating rail facilities and expediting interstate commerce, ended the shipper-dominated progressive phase of railroad regulation, which had aimed to keep costs down. The Railroad Administration doubled hourly wages of railroad labor and raised freight rates twenty-eight percent and passenger fares eighteen percent.

With peace, Congress refused to extend federal control, but passed the Esch-Cummins Transportation Act (1920) to preserve the advantages of unified operation. This act enlarged the ICC to eleven members and gave it power to fashion "a more rationally conceived, stable, and profitable railroad industry." Specifically, the ICC could set minimum and exact rates as well as maximum ones that would give railroads a fair return on their value; could compel railroads to build new lines, or extend or abandon existing ones; and could permit pools and combinations if they promoted efficiency. The commission was asked to prepare a plan consolidating the nation's railroads into major competing systems. Rather than hamper the ICC as it had in the 1890s, the Supreme Court agreed that the commission was responsible for fashioning an adequate interstate commerce system.

The ICC did not rise to the occasion. Although reorganized into five divisions and supported by two thousand staff members, the ICC was swamped in the 1920s by thousands of individual rate cases; overwork, fragmentation, and specialization made it difficult to formulate broad principles. The congressional shift from just-and-reasonable rates to fair-investment-return rates changed the perspective of the ICC from shippers to railroads and led to increased rates in 1920. Following the abrupt downturn of the business cycle the next year, however, the ICC pared down the advances in 1922. Reluctant to disturb a network of discriminations balancing discriminations, the ICC after 1922 froze rates. Its greatest opportunity for constructive leadership was in planning consolidations, and its 1921 tentative plan reorganizing railroads into nineteen systems was sound. But strong railroads, unwilling to absorb weak lines and anxious to merge with profitable railroads, bitterly opposed the plan. And by vacillating for years and even approving 298 combinations at the expense of its plan, the commission hindered reorganization. While the ICC traditionally preferred inaction, its lethargy in the 1920s reflected its subservience to railroads and the drift of the federal government away from progressivism and scientific management toward laissez-faire.

The Great Depression following the stock market crash of 1929 brought disaster to American railroads. Tonnage and revenues were halved between 1929 and 1932. With enormous fixed charges (mostly interest on bonds), railroads were vulnerable and could only be saved by federal intervention, but even with generous government aid bankruptcies multiplied. In addition, railroads faced a serious challenge from the new unregulated trucking industry, in which anarchy prevailed, with cutthroat competition reducing rates and diverting traffic from the railroads. Congress in 1935 passed the Motor Carrier Act, giving the ICC control over maximum and minimum common carrier truck rates, as well as driver qualifications, the maximum hours worked, and the safety of equipment. To prevent trucks from threatening existing rail rates, the ICC tied truck rates to rail rates, but that move proved disastrous to the railroads. Parity rates assured competition on a service basis, which was advantageous for the more convenient trucks, rather than on a cost basis, which would have favored the more efficient railroads. When Congress in the Transportation Act of 1940 gave the ICC jurisdiction over water carriers, it made the ICC the regulator of all significant modes of interstate commerce except air. Congress also tried to give the ICC some guidance by calling for a national transportation policy that would impartially regulate all modes of transportation, while recognizing "the inherent advantages of each." But in World War II the Franklin Roosevelt administration, rather than turn to the ICC to coordinate transportation, established the Office of Defense Transportation, with ICC Commissioner Joseph B. Eastman at its head.

In the post–World War II years, motor and water carriers enormously expanded their share of intercity freight. Despite the challenge of the 1940 Transportation Act, the ICC failed to devise a formula that would enable carriers to flourish where they had inherent cost advantages. The ICC's power to set minimum rates determined whether trucks or trains would carry the nation's interstate commerce. If railroads could cut their rates to reflect actual costs, they would win back traffic lost to trucks. With its case-by-case approach, the ICC did not enunciate a uniform minimum rate policy. Rather, it leaned toward "umbrella" rate making (artificially high rail rates to protect motor and water carriers), which allowed trucks by 1956 to capture the profitable high tariff shipments of less than forty tons. Congress attacked umbrella rate making in its Transportation Act of 1958, but then reiterated that the objective of national transportation policy was to preserve the inherent advantages of each mode. Receiving contradictory instructions, the ICC continued to hand down contradictory decisions.

Criticism of the ICC became strong in the 1960s. In his 1961 report *National Transportation Policy,* John P. Doyle concluded that rail and motor carriers were subjected to "unequitable and destructive" ICC regulation that tried to preserve the status quo. President John F. Kennedy in 1962 presented Congress with a comprehensive transportation proposal that would have increased competition and lowered rates by permitting railroads and trucks to cut bulk commodity rates without ICC approval. Although railroads favored these deregulatory proposals, water and motor carriers and the ICC opposed them, and Congress refused to act. Economists agreed that competing transportation companies charging cost-of-service rates and utilizing trains, trucks, barges, and planes to move freight in the most rational manner would solve the transportation malaise. But railroads, aided by the ICC, turned to the merger panacea to eliminate competition and achieve savings. From 1955 to 1968 the ICC approved thirty-three out of thirty-eight merger applications, including that of the giant Pennsylvania and New York Central railroads (1966), which ended rail competition in the Northeast. Savings from mergers proved elusive, the great Penn Central went bankrupt (1970), and the ICC was castigated for passively losing the opportunity to create competing intermodal transportation companies.

The energy crisis of the late 1970s brought criticism of the ICC to a head during the Jimmy Carter administration. Since transportation consumed half the nation's fuel, the shortage of petroleum and its skyrocketing price inspired consumer demands that wasteful rules be eliminated

and competition be promoted. To the dismay of established trucking firms and the Teamsters Union, the Motor Carrier Act of 1980 deregulated the seventeen thousand companies in the $41 billion interstate trucking business. In addition, the Staggers Rail Act (1980) made railroads more competitive with trucks by allowing them to adjust their rates rapidly and by deregulating "piggyback" (trucks carried on trains) traffic. Deregulation threatened the ICC's demise. In 1982 Congress cut its membership from eleven to seven, and to five by 1986, while its staff dropped from 1,946 in 1981 to under thirteen hundred in 1983.

Deregulation in the 1980s resulted in larger trucking firms and railroads. While the number of trucking companies rose dramatically to twenty-five thousand by 1983, the share of the industry controlled by its ten largest carriers rose from 40.7 percent in 1980 to 48.5 percent in 1983. Railroad deregulation spurred a new round of mergers, designed less to eliminate competition by parallel lines serving the same markets (which had been largely accomplished) than to enable a railroad to carry freight over the longest possible distance. Apart from issuing guidelines stressing the need to improve operating efficiencies and reduce excess facilities, the ICC approved merger proposals that resulted in fifteen major rail systems by 1984.

Deregulation killed the ICC, but its death was slow. By the end of 1985, the Office of Management and Budget proposed that the ICC be abolished, but major rail and motor carriers staved off its departure for ten years. While they had complained about filing their rate changes with the ICC, this process, giving advance warning of competitors' price changes, tended to stabilize rates. The ICC could no longer set rates except in rare and unimportant instances in which one carrier had a complete monopoly over a route, but it controlled railroad mergers until its demise, when that power was shifted to the Department of Transportation. The ICC's last important act approved the creation in 1995 of the nation's largest rail network, the Burlington Northern Santa Fe Corporation. When the ICC finally died on the last day of 1995, the budget-cutting mania sweeping Washington administered its coup de grace. The savings, however, were minuscule, since the ICC's last budget of $40 million was mere pin money by Washington standards.

Everyone agrees that the ICC was a failure, but for some it regulated too much and for others it regulated too little. Everyone is right, for it chose to regulate where it should not have regulated and chose not to where it should have. For many of its 108 years, the commission had the power to shape a rational nationwide transportation system, but instead of accomplishing this needed job it used its authority to maintain the status quo. It did not replace value-of-service rates with cost-of-service rates. It did not implement its 1920s' plan to consolidate the nation's railroads into nineteen systems that would have improved service and increased efficiency. It did not allow railroads to raise rates to secure badly needed revenue, nor did it allow them to reduce rates to compete with motor carriers. Rather than promote intermodal competing transportation companies, it approved mergers that created regional rail monopolies. Rather than stimulate the New York Central and Pennsylvania railroads to move freight throughout the Northeast by the most feasible mode, whether rail, highway, water, or air, the ICC let that vision perish. With its weak, inexperienced, unimaginative commissioners led by their entrenched staff and dominated by shippers in the Progressive Era, railroads between the world wars, and truckers after World War II, the ICC squandered its opportunities.

[*See also* Appendix: Act to Regulate Commerce (1887).]

BIBLIOGRAPHY

Bernstein, Marver H. *Regulating Business by Independent Commission.* Princeton, N.J., 1955.
Cushman, Robert E. *The Independent Regulatory Commissions.* New York, 1941.
Friedlaender, Ann F. *The Dilemma of Freight Transport Regulation.* Washington, D.C., 1969.
Hoogenboom, Ari, and Olive Hoogenboom. *A History of the ICC: From Panacea to Palliative.* New York, 1976.
Kolko, Gabriel. *Railroads and Regulation, 1877–1916.* Princeton, N.J., 1965.
McCraw, Thomas K. *Prophets of Regulation: Charles Francis Adams, Louis D. Brandeis, James M. Landis, Alfred E. Kahn.* Cambridge, Mass., 1984.
Martin, Albro. *Enterprise Denied: Origins of the Decline of American Railroads, 1897–1917.* New York, 1971.
Sharfman, I. L. *The Interstate Commerce Commission: A Study in Administrative Law and Procedure.* 5 vols. New York, 1931–1937.

—Ari Hoogenboom

IRS.

See Internal Revenue Service.

J

Joint Chiefs of Staff

The body known as the Joint Chiefs of Staff (JCS), which came into being on 9 February 1942, was modeled on the British Chiefs of Staff Committee; its purposed was to enable the Americans to participate properly in the U.S.-U.K. Combined Chiefs of Staff, which had been created six weeks earlier. The members of the JCS were General George C. Marshall, Army chief of staff; General Henry H. Arnold, chief of Army Air Forces; Admiral Ernest J. King, chief of Naval Operations; and from 20 July 1942, Admiral William D. Leahy, chief of staff to the commander in chief of the Army and Navy. Although President Franklin Roosevelt never issued the JCS a formal charter, thereby leaving them free to expand their activities as necessary, the JCS assumed responsibility for planning and strategic direction of the U.S. war effort. The JCS prepared joint war plans and ordered field commanders to implement them, allocated critical resources such as munitions, petroleum, and shipping, and supervised the collection of strategic intelligence. Admiral Leahy presided over JCS meetings, but his main job was as liaison between the JCS and the president. General Marshall emerged as the dominant member, shaping the Europe-first strategy that culminated in the 1944 cross-Channel invasion. General Arnold was Marshall's subordinate and could speak authoritatively only for the Army Air Forces. The JCS were assisted by part-time joint committees drawn from the Army, Navy, and Army Air Forces (e.g., strategic plans, logistics, intelligence, transportation) that in turn drew support from full-time working groups. The shortcomings of this approach were soon obvious; Americans often felt outclassed by the quality of British staff work.

World War II highlighted the problems of divided command, which clearly contributed to the Pearl Harbor disaster. The National Security Act of 1947 represented a compromise between the Army's advocacy of a single Defense Department with a chief of staff of the armed forces and the Navy's wish for three separate departments: war, navy, and air. The act legally established the JCS as principal military advisers to the president and secretary of defense, responsible for preparing strategic plans and providing for strategic direction of the armed forces, for preparing joint logistic plans, for establishing unified commands, and for reviewing major materiel and personnel requirements. The act also created a Joint Staff headed by a director and not exceeding one hundred officers, organized by committees and prohibited from operating as an Armed Forces General Staff or exercising command authority. These prohibitions have been included in all subsequent legislation. As the Air Force was now an independent service, the Air Force chief of staff became a JCS member.

The new JCS organization became mired in fundamental disagreements about strategy and force levels that culminated in the Navy–Air Force "B-36 controversy." The remedy, 1949 amendments to the National Security Act, increased the Joint Staff to 210 and created the position of chairman of the JCS. Admiral Leahy's position was abolished. The chairman was to serve as presiding officer of the JCS, provide agendas for JCS meetings, and inform the secretary of defense when the JCS could not agree, although the chairman could cast no formal vote when positions were being recorded. The first chairman, General Omar N. Bradley, U.S. Army, behaved as an impartial mediator at JCS meetings. But his successor, Admiral Arthur W. Radford, acted within the JCS as a spokesman for the Eisenhower administration's "New Look" policy, and bypassed recalcitrant service chiefs to work out solutions directly with the secretary of defense. With Radford there began the practice of the chairman serving as the president's advocate. As an example, General Maxwell D. Taylor, U.S. Army, was instrumental in securing JCS concurrence to the 1963 Limited Test Ban Treaty.

In 1952 Congress gave the commandant of the Marine Corps coequal status when matters of direct concern to the Marines were under JCS consideration. The commandant was made a full legal member in 1978.

During World War II the JCS were part of the chain of command and sent directives to field commanders. During the Korean War the Army chief of staff acted as executive agent for the JCS in transmitting directives and overseeing field activities. President Eisenhower, in 1953, decided to strengthen civilian control by removing the JCS from the chain of command, so that the chain went from the secretary of defense through the appropriate service secretary to the military commander. The Department of Defense Reorganization Act of 1958 gave the chairman a formal vote, increased the Joint Staff to four hundred officers, and revised the chain of command to run from the secretary of defense through the JCS to the unified and specified commands. To fulfill this new responsibility of assisting the secretary in directing these commands, the Joint Staff was reorganized into six directorates (e.g., J-3, Operations; J-4, Logistics; J-5, Plans and Policy) and the joint committees were abolished. However, the new JCS system did not seem to work much better than the old. Critical issues often continued to be handled by either negotiating lowest common denominator compromises or submitting split opinions to the secretary of defense. President Eisenhower, disappointed that most service chiefs appeared unable to rise above what he saw as parochial interests, relied increasingly on the chairman.

Robert McNamara, secretary of defense from 1961 to 1968, broadened the secretary's role so much that JCS members felt their own functions were being usurped. McNamara's planning, pro-

gramming, and budgeting system extended civilian influence far into the details of military force planning. During the Vietnam War civilians' selection of targets during the air campaign against North Vietnam, and their rejection of the JCS recommendation to strike a hard blow in favor of graduated escalation of pressure, caused deep resentment. General Harold K. Johnson, Army chief of staff during 1964–1968, later described JCS influence in this period as minimal and likened his own role to that of a frustrated spectator. General Earle G. Wheeler, U.S. Army, who was chairman during 1964–1970, tried to uphold military influence by persuading the JCS to present a united front. The number of split JCS recommendations dropped from forty in 1965 to six in 1967. That approach failed, however, because even a united front usually did not persuade the secretary. The JCS permitted complex and cumbersome command arrangements to remain in place throughout the Vietnam War. But, concurrently, the chairman was steadily gaining influence at the service chiefs' expense. General Wheeler and then Admiral Thomas H. Moorer, who was chairman during 1970–1974, became far more involved with operational matters during the Vietnam War than General Bradley had been during the Korean War. Particularly with Admiral Moorer, the chairman at times acted on his own and later informed the service chiefs what he had done.

The most significant change in JCS history was initiated in 1982 by the chairman, General David C. Jones, just before he retired. Four years as Air Force chief of staff followed by four as chairman convinced Jones that the military had inadequate cross-service and joint experience "from the top down," and that the service chiefs faced built-in conflicts because they bore both service and JCS responsibilities. Jones recommended:

- Making the chairman rather than the corporate JCS the principal military adviser to the president, the secretary of defense, and the National Security Council

- Giving the chairman a deputy

- Having the Joint Staff work for the chairman alone and not for the corporate JCS

- Limiting the involvement of service staffs in the preparation of JCS positions

- Making joint assignments more career enhancing.

Among the service chiefs only General Edward C. Meyer, Army chief of staff from 1979 to 1983, supported such major reforms.

General John W. Vessey, Jr., U.S. Army, who was chairman from 1982 to 1985, believed that many of the Jones-Meyer proposals could be effected without legislation. Accordingly, he and the service chiefs implemented a number of internal reforms. In 1984 legislation did designate the chairman as spokesman for unified and specified commanders on operational requirements. Congress, however, rejected a JCS recommendation to put the chairman directly in the chain of command.

Public demands for fundamental reforms along the lines of General Jones's proposals were fueled by the failed hostage rescue attempt in Iran in 1980, problems of interoperability during the 1983 Grenada operation, and the cumbersome chain of command revealed after the 1983 bombing of Marine barracks in Beirut. A presidential commission formulated proposals that were embodied in the Goldwater-Nichols Department of Defense Reorganization Act of 1986. The chairman, rather than the corporate JCS, was designated principal military adviser to the president, the National Security Council, and the secretary of defense, with responsibilities that included:

- Assisting the president and the secretary in the strategic direction of the armed forces

- Preparing strategic and logistic plans as well as net assessments

- Providing for the preparation and review of contingency plans

- Advising the secretary of defense on requirements, programs, and budgets

- Developing doctrine for joint employment of the armed forces.

The Joint Staff, limited to a total of 1,627 military and civilian personnel, was to work for the chairman alone. Steps were taken to increase the prestige and rewards for joint duty. The chairman would consult with the service chiefs at his discretion, but service chiefs retained the right to submit dissenting views to the secretary. The act provided for a vice chairman who would assist the chairman, act for the chairman in his absence or disability, outrank all officers except the chairman, and participate in JCS meetings but vote only when acting for the chairman. The service chiefs had opposed creating a vice chairman, even though each of them had his own vice chief, because they believed it would diminish their own influence.

Admiral William J. Crowe, Jr., chairman during 1985–1989, was rather circumspect in exercising his new powers, usually seeking a JCS consensus. He added two directorates to the Joint Staff: J-7, Operational Plans and Interoperability, and J-8, Force Structure, Resources and Assessment. The Joint Staff began to emerge as the premier planning and warfighting staff.

General Colin L. Powell, U.S. Army, chairman during 1989–1993, made full use of the authority granted by the Goldwater-Nichols Act. In developing his "Base Force" concept, designed to guide the post–Cold War reduction of the armed forces, Powell took the initiative. He never asked for a vote by the service chiefs; instead, Powell focused his efforts on winning the secretary of defense's approval of his ideas. During the Persian Gulf War of 1991 and the six-month buildup of U.S. forces that preceded it, General Powell dominated the direction of strategy and operations, although he kept the service chiefs well informed of developments.

The vice chairman's position steadily gained prominence. The first incumbent, General Robert T. Herres, U.S. Air Force (1987–1990), performed formally delineated duties; his tenure emphasized ways in which to extend the chairman's influence. Admiral David E. Jeremiah (1990–1994) supported Chairman Powell across the whole range of responsibilities. In 1992 legislation supported by the service chiefs made the vice chairman a full JCS member without restrictions. Admiral William A. Owens (1994–1996) used his position as chairman of the Joint Requirements Oversight Council to press programming initiatives.

In sum, the JCS of the 1990s bears very little resemblance to the organization of the 1940s. Change occurred gradually because the need for efficient decision-making conflicted with fears that a "man on horseback" or a Prussian general staff in some guise would dominate the national security apparatus. Accumulated experience demonstrated the need for greater jointness. Even so, the military could not find common ground; the landmark changes of 1947, 1949, 1958, and 1986 were imposed by Congress and the president. Ultimately, centralization largely supplanted corporate consensus.

[*See also* Defense, Department of *and* National Security Council.]

BIBLIOGRAPHY

Betts, Richard K. *Soldiers, Statesmen, and Cold War Crises*. New York, 1991.
Cole, Ronald H., Lorna S. Jaffe, Walter S. Poole, and Willard J. Webb. *The Chairmen of the Joint Chiefs of Staff*. Washington, D.C., 1996.
Korb, Lawrence J. *The Joint Chiefs of Staff: The First Twenty-Five Years*. Bloomington, Ind., 1976.

—WALTER S. POOLE

Judicial Branch

ESSAY   The federal judiciary is an independent, coequal branch of the national government. Article III of the Constitution vests the judicial power "in one supreme Court, and in such inferior Courts as the Congress may from time to time ordain and establish." Besides guaranteeing federal judges basically lifetime tenure, subject only to impeachment, Article III extends the judicial power to all cases in law and equity arising under the Constitution and the laws of the United States. Yet, the Constitution remains silent as to the power of judicial review and the structure of the federal judiciary.

The power of judicial review is the power of the Supreme Court and the lower federal courts to overturn any congressional and state legislation or other official governmental action deemed inconsistent with the Constitution, the Bill of Rights, or federal law. The power was first asserted in *Marbury v. Madison*, 5 U.S. 137 (1803).

Since that landmark decision, the Supreme Court has overturned more than 146 congressional acts, 927 state laws, and 111 municipal ordinances.

While the president is authorized in Article II to nominate and appoint, subject to the Senate's confirmation, federal judges, Congress has the power to determine the structure, size, and appellate jurisdiction of the federal judiciary. There have been 108 justices appointed to the Supreme Court. The Senate has rejected or forced the president to withdraw twenty-eight nominations to the Supreme Court.

The First Congress established the federal judiciary with the enactment of the Judiciary Act of 1789. That act authorized five associate justices and one chief justice, and created two "inferior" courts: district courts, which serve as the trial courts in the federal judicial system, and circuit courts of appeals, which are located in various geographical regions of the country. Along with thirteen district judgeships, the Judiciary Act required the justices to "ride circuit" twice a year and sit with district judges to hear appeals in the circuit courts. There were no permanent appellate court judges until after the passage of the Circuit Court of Appeals Act in 1891.

The size of the Supreme Court and the federal judiciary is not constitutionally mandated and has often reflected Congress's attempt to either enhance or thwart a president's influence over the federal courts by giving or denying him opportunities to fill judicial vacancies. Congress, for instance, frequently declines to authorize new judgeships in order to deny lame-duck presidents additional judicial appointments.

As the country grew in population, the size of the federal bench gradually grew as well. The number of justices and circuits grew from seven in 1807, to nine in 1837, and to ten in 1863. Owing to the Reconstruction Congress's antagonism toward President Andrew Johnson, the number of justices was reduced from ten to seven in order to deny him appointments to the Court. After General Ulysses S. Grant was elected president, Congress in 1869 again authorized nine justices—the number that has prevailed.

From the original nineteen federal judges, the number grew to more than one thousand by the mid-1990s, including more than seven hundred full-time judges and more than three hundred who have senior status and continue to hear cases. There are ninety-four district courts with at least one in each state, depending on caseloads. District judges sit alone and preside over trials, with or without juries, and other criminal and civil proceedings. They also approve plea bargains, supervise settlements, monitor remedial decrees, and manage the processing of cases.

The number of federal circuit courts of appeals has grown to thirteen. Eleven geographical regions, or circuits, each have one appellate court with general appellate jurisdiction over appeals from the district courts, rulings by independent regulatory commissions, and decisions from federal agencies' enforcement actions. The Court of Appeals for the District of Columbia Circuit also has general jurisdiction over federal cases, but by statute handles mostly challenges to federal agencies' regulations. In 1982 Congress added the Court of Appeals for the Federal Circuit, which is also located in the District of Columbia but hears primarily tax, patent, and international trade cases and appeals.

Unlike district courts, federal appellate courts have twenty or more judges. They generally hear cases on the basis of rotating three-judge panels. In important and divisive cases, particularly in cases that present issues on which two or more three-judge panels have reached opposite results in other similar cases, the entire circuit court sits as a panel, or *en banc*, to reach a decision and to resolve conflicting interpretations of the law within the circuit.

Along with the increasing number of federal judges, there has been a significant growth in the number of law clerks, secretaries, support staff, magistrate and bankruptcy judges, probation and pretrial workers, and hence in the size of the entire federal judiciary. Whereas in 1900 there were 2,770 employees, by 1960 there were 4,992 employees in the federal judicial system, with only further modest increases thereafter until the late 1970s, and then the size of the federal judiciary swelled to 14,500 in 1980, and to more than 24,600 in the 1990s.

The changes in the size and the operation of the judiciary reflect the increasing flow of litigation into the federal courts. The caseloads of the federal judiciary, moreover, skyrocketed in the second half of the twentieth century owing to the expansion of federal regulations and criminal law. From 1950 to 1990, for instance, federal district courts experienced a three-hundred-percent increase in cases. Whereas in 1950 they faced a little more than ninety thousand new filings each year, by the mid-1990s they annually confronted more than 260,000 cases. Because the bulk of federal litigation takes place in district courts, they basically function as courts of first and last resort for the overwhelming majority of cases. Approximately forty-five thousand appeals are annually filed in federal appellate courts.

The increased federal litigation also affected the Supreme Court's role in the federal judicial system and has diminished its capacity for reviewing the decisions of the lower federal courts. Whereas in 1920 there were just 565 cases on the Court's docket, the number each decade since World War II has incrementally grown, from 1,300 in 1950, to more than 2,300 cases by 1960, to 4,200 by 1970, to 5,300 in 1980, and to more than 8,000 cases by the mid-1990s.

In response to these increases in the size of the high court's docket, Congress expanded the Court's discretionary jurisdiction, giving it the power to deny the vast majority of case reviews. As a result, the Supreme Court annually reviews only about 100 cases (or only about one percent of the cases arriving on its docket). The Court hears only those cases that pose major questions of national importance. The contemporary Court thus no longer serves primarily to supervise or correct the errors of lower courts. Instead, the Court functions like a "super-legislature," reviewing major issues of public law and policy of interest to the national government and the states.

The nature of the business of the judiciary has changed as well. Along with broader social and economic forces, federal legislation and administrative regulations have affected the business of the federal courts. The work of federal district courts has generally evolved toward less criminal and more civil litigation. In the late nineteenth century, sixty-one percent of the work of federal trial courts involved criminal cases. The filing of criminal cases rapidly increased during the 1920s and early 1930s, when it leveled off until another surge in the late 1960s, and then declined from 1975 to the end of the decade. In 1980 criminal cases amounted to only fifteen percent of federal district courts' caseloads; they further declined to less than one percent by 1991 owing to a dramatic increase in civil litigation. Although not keeping pace with the increasing rate of civil litigation, the number of criminal cases steadily climbed throughout the 1980s. The number of drug-related criminal cases alone more than doubled between the 1980s and the 1990s.

The changes in the business of the federal judiciary register shifts in the national government's legal policies and litigation strategies. District courts' caseloads were significantly affected by the decriminalization of internal revenue offenses and the abolition of federal Prohibition in the early twentieth century, a subsequent change in the government's prosecutorial policy on immigration and the diversion of criminal cases to state courts, and then in the 1980s by the "war" on crime and drugs. The increase in civil litigation also reflects changes in the policies and priorities of the federal government. In the 1980s, for instance, the federal government made a concerted effort to recover defaulted student loans and overpaid veterans' benefits in federal courts. As a result, the federal government was a plaintiff in almost sixty-five percent of all civil government cases, as compared with just fifty-one percent a decade earlier.

The changing nature of the business coming before the Supreme Court further underscores how the federal judiciary's role in determining national public law and policy became more significant in the twentieth century. During much of the early nineteenth century more than forty percent of the Court's business consisted in admiralty and prize cases and approximately fifty percent matters of common law. But by the 1880s, although almost forty percent continued to deal with common law disputes, more than forty-three percent of the Court's business involved questions of statutory interpretation, and only about four percent concerned matters of constitutional law. That change in the Court's business registered the national government's increased regulation of interstate commerce and enforcement of antitrust laws and other economic regulations.

In the twentieth century the trend continued toward a Court that principally decides issues of national importance for federal law and public policy. In the 1990s about forty-seven percent of the cases annually decided by the Court raised questions of constitutional law, while thirty-eight percent dealt with the interpretation of congressional statutes, and the remaining fifteen percent involved controversies over federal taxation, administrative law, and federal agencies' regulations.

The federal judiciary generally, though not invariably, supports the Congress and the executive branch. There have been decisions, to be sure, that have gone against one or both of the other two branches of the national government. In *United States v. Nixon,* 418 U.S. 683 (1974), for example, the Court rejected President Richard M. Nixon's claim of executive privilege to withhold confidential White House communications from disclosure in a criminal trial. There have also been periods of time, such as before 1937, when the Court invalidated much of the early New Deal legislation, when the Court has ruled against Congress and the president. Still, in historical perspective the Court tends to legitimate the legal policies of the national government. Between 1950 and 1990, for instance, the Court annually upheld the executive branch's position from fifty-five to more than eighty percent of the time.

The Court's rulings are self-enforcing and the judiciary depends on other political institutions to ensure compliance with its decisions. Both the Congress and the president have the means to effectively thwart or limit compliance with controversial judicial rulings. For example, Congress delayed implementation of the watershed school desegregation decision in *Brown v. Board of Education of Topeka, Kansas,* 347 U.S. 483 (1954), by not authorizing the executive branch to enforce the decision before the enactment of the Civil Rights Act of 1964. Presidents may attack the legitimacy of the Court's rulings, refuse to follow its rulings, and direct the solicitor general to appeal cases, enabling him to ask the justices to reconsider their prior rulings. The president's major influence over the federal courts, though, resides in the power of selecting federal judges. Through federal judicial appointments, presidents may in the long run influence the direction of the federal judiciary.

Congress may also reverse the judiciary's interpretation of federal statutes by simply passing new legislation. Between 1967 and 1990, Congress thus overrode 344 decisions of the Court and lower federal courts. The reversal of judicial decisions based on the Constitution, however, requires Congress to pass a constitutional amendment, which three-fourths of the states must ratify. Only six of the Court's rulings have been overturned by constitutional amendments.

The business and role of the federal judiciary has evolved with changes in American politics. The federal judiciary is no longer, as Alexander Hamilton observed in *the Federalist,* "the least dangerous branch." Instead, the federal judiciary is a coequal branch within the national government, and the Supreme Court, in particular, decides only cases and controversies of national importance.

[*See also* Executive Power; House of Representatives; Senate; *and* Supreme Court Decisions on the Presidency.]

BIBLIOGRAPHY

Abraham, Henry J. *Justices and Presidents: A Political History of Appointments to the Supreme Court.* 3d ed. New York, 1992.
Abraham, Henry J. *The Judicial Process.* 6th ed. New York, 1993.
Carp, Robert, and C. K. Rowland. *Policymaking and Politics in the Federal District Courts.* Knoxville, Tenn., 1983.
Coffin, Frank M. *On Appeal: Courts, Lawyering, and Judging.* New York, 1994.
Hall, Kermit L., ed. *The Oxford Companion to the Supreme Court of the United States.* New York, 1992.
Howard, J. Woodford, Jr. *Courts of Appeals in the Federal Judicial System.* Princeton, N.J., 1981.
Lasser, William. *The Limits of Judicial Power.* Chapel Hill, N.C., 1988.
O'Brien, David M. *Storm Center: The Supreme Court in American Politics.* 4th ed. New York, 1996.
Rosenberg, Gerald N. *The Hollow Hope: Can Courts Bring About Social Change?* Chicago, 1991.
Witt, Elder. *Guide to the U.S. Supreme Court.* 2d ed. Washington, D.C., 1990.

—DAVID M. O'BRIEN

Justice, Department of

 Established by the Judiciary Act of 1870, the U.S. Department of Justice handles most of the legal work of the federal government, including investigations and enforcement of federal law. It assists in prosecutions in lower federal courts through its role overseeing the U.S. attorneys and represents the government before the Supreme Court. In addition, the department provides legal advice and opinions to the president and heads of the executive departments.

The U.S. attorney general administers the Department of Justice and serves as a member of the cabinet and a presidential adviser. Seventy-six men have served in that capacity; in 1993, Janet Reno became the first woman attorney general. The attorney general's office, created by the Judiciary Act of 1789, predates the Justice Department by eighty years. Initially, the duties of the attorney general were almost exclusively legal, centering on Supreme Court litigation and advice to the executive branch on questions of law. But with the growth of the department and expansion of its activities, the attorney general's post has become primarily administrative. This development was noted as early as 1927, when Albert Langeluttig wrote, "His duties as administrative head of the Department of Justice require his entire attention, and since the creation of the office of Solicitor General, the Attorney General has not always been appointed primarily for his legal ability."

Reflecting the growth in the federal government as a whole, the Justice Department has expanded dramatically in the last thirty years, from a budget outlay of about $300 million in 1962 to almost $10 billion in 1992. Its expenditures have also increased as a percentage of the national budget, from about 0.3 percent to 0.7 percent in the same time period.

The department houses more than thirty divisions, bureaus, offices, and boards that cover the range of federal legal issues. The staff includes the deputy attorney general, the associate attorney general, the solicitor general, assistant attorneys general for the different litigation divisions, the Office of Legal Counsel (OLC), and the inspector general. In addition, the Federal Bureau of Investigation (FBI), the Drug Enforcement Administration (DEA), the Federal Bureau of Prisons, and the Immigration and Naturalization Service are located in the department, as are numerous other agencies. Twenty-two of the top positions in the department are presidential appointments requiring Senate confirmation.

The deputy attorney general, the second in command, is responsible for supervising the department and assisting in the implementation of programs and policies. The associate attorney general is charged with overseeing civil and immigration issues. The solicitor general, whose post was created by the Judiciary Act of 1870, handles cases before the Supreme Court, acting either as a litigant when the federal government is a party or as an *amicus curiae* ("friend of the court") when the government has an interest in the outcome of a case. The department also has an office of the inspector general to conduct internal audits.

The government's litigation is divided into six subject areas, with an assistant attorney general heading each division. The oldest is the Civil Division, which developed out of the 1868 appointment of the first assistant attorney general. It represents the government's interests in civil litigation. The Environment and Natural Resources Division (known as the Public Lands Division until 1965) was created in 1910 and reorganized twenty years later; it handles litigation arising from the government's buying, managing, and using land and natural resources, including enforcement of environmental laws. The Criminal Division, formed in 1928, enforces the growing body of federal criminal statutes. In 1933 both the Tax and Antitrust Divisions were formed to create a corps of attorneys with expertise in those particular areas of federal law. The newest component is the Civil Rights Division. Dwight Eisenhower's attorney general, Herbert Brownell, began advocating a new division in 1955 to ensure effective government enforcement of civil rights laws and judicial rulings. The Civil Rights Act of 1957 subsequently authorized the attorney general to create the division.

An assistant attorney general also heads the OLC. The OLC, established in 1933, issues official legal opinions on the request of the president and executive department heads. Prior to this statutory delegation, the advisory function rested with the attorney general. It derives from a need to assist the president in his constitutional duty to "take care that the laws be faithfully executed."

The FBI, with nine divisions, three offices, and almost twenty-four thousand personnel, is the largest unit in the Justice Department. Initially a small detective staff formed in 1908, it was reorganized along more professional lines in 1924 and renamed in 1935. The DEA, added to the department in 1973, investigates the illicit manufacturing and trafficking in controlled substances. Specialized task forces also operate in such areas as financial institution fraud and drug involvement of organized crime.

The Justice Department supports the offices of the ninety-four U.S. marshals and the U.S. attorneys and their staffs, representing each federal judicial district. Historically, the U.S. attorneys have exercised considerable autonomy in handling federal litigation at the district court level, in part because they are subject to presidential appointment and Senate confirmation. The department primarily provides assistance and nonlitigative oversight.

Several nonlawyering responsibilities also are handled by the Justice Department, such as the quasi-judicial Board of Immigration Appeals and the Foreign Claims Settlement Commission of the United States. The Bureau of Prisons, the U.S. Parole Commission, and the Office of Pardon Attorney also serve under the attorney general.

Other programs include the Office of Tribal Justice; the Office of Community Oriented Policing Services; the Office of Justice Programs, which supports criminal justice research and publishes crime statistics; the Office of Policy Development, which assesses the entire system of justice and makes recommendations for change; and the Community Relations Service, providing mediation and assistance when local problems arise under federal civil rights laws. The Executive Office for United States Trustees operates out of the department as well, a nationwide administrative network to assist in processing bankruptcies. The Office of Intelligence Policy and Review represents the government before the Foreign Intelligence Surveillance Court, and the Interpol-U.S. National Central Bureau serves as a liaison with other Interpol member nations.

Internal housekeeping duties rest primarily with the Justice Management Division, which develops budget requests, handles personnel matters, and oversees department finances. Other responsibilities are handled by the Office of Executive Secretariat, the Office of Information and Privacy, and the Office of Legislative Affairs. The Office of Professional Responsibility investigates charges of misconduct of Justice employees.

A review of the U.S. budget over the past thirty years illustrates the shifting enforcement priorities of the department, in large part reflecting the policy directions of the president. A particularly strong example is evident in civil rights. Actual gross outlays in civil rights increased from $962,000 in 1963 to $5,416,000 in 1971, an increase of 463 percent, compared with a general departmental budget increase of 291 percent over the same period. After 1971 increases in the area of civil rights were generally more modest. During the 1980s, responding to the Reagan administration's priorities, the department spent heavily on drug control operations. Both the DEA and the Interagency Law Enforcement Agency, dealing with drug trafficking, benefited. Other administrations have focused their resources on prosecuting antitrust violations or pursuing organized crime.

LAW AND POLITICS

The Department of Justice has periodically been the subject of political controversy stemming from the unique position it holds in the government. On one hand, it is a political office, headed by presidential appointees and sensitive to the larger political context of the law. On the other hand, the Justice attorneys are officers of the court and the attorney general the chief law officer of the nation. On occasion the department has been caught between serving an elected president or serving the ideal of the law. This tension is inherent in the office.

Griffin Bell, attorney general during the Carter administration, described one source of the tension. "Under our present system, the attorney general wears so many hats that his independence is difficult to establish or sustain. . . . These responsibilities require varying degrees of contact and coordination with the executive branch on the one hand and independence from the executive branch on the other." The distinction between political and legal roles can be murky. The department often participates in drafting bills and testifying before congressional committees. It also sets its budgetary priorities for law enforcement and prosecution. Both of these functions have political and legal dimensions. The same is true of the advisory role. Elliot Richardson, serving briefly in the Justice Department under Richard Nixon, noted in a 1987 interview with the author that the attorney general often is both a legal adviser and personal adviser to the president. "Advice to a president needs to have the political dimension clearly in view, without any pejorative attached to the word political. The presidency is by definition a political job."

Critics periodically charge that the Justice Department has become politicized, subverting the law to advance political ends. Some of these charges are unfounded, stemming from a failure to understand the connection between law and politics in the U.S. system. Legal choices are not neutral, nor are political choices inherently corrupt. Daniel Meader writes, "There is a tendency toward an over-simplification of a subtle and complex relationship . . . a failure to appreciate the appropriate political setting within which the laws are executed . . . an overlooking of constitutional responsibilities and accountability."

Yet the overt use of the department for political—especially partisan—purposes is unsettling. There is evidence that some incumbents have abused the office for political ends, oblivious to legal considerations.

The charge that law officers are too politicized is not new. Incumbents have periodically been accused of manipulating their legal opinions to support a president's legally questionable policy decision. One example often cited is Attorney General Robert Jackson's opinion in 1940 justifying Franklin Roosevelt's exchange of bases for destroyers with Britain early in the Second World War. This transfer appears to violate a neutrality statute of 1917 and neutrality resolutions of 1935, 1936, 1937, and 1939. Another is Attorney General Robert Kennedy's assurance that the blockade of Cuba in October 1962 was not an act of war, when international law suggests otherwise. Yet the assertion that these decisions were political contrivances bereft of legal support cannot be sustained under a historical review.

Because of its legal role, the Justice Department may be subject to heightened expectations and greater congressional scrutiny than the other executive branch departments. One indication of this higher standard may be found in confirmation battles. While other cabinet nominees have not been confirmed, the attorney generalship seems particularly vulnerable to Senate rejection. Three of the nine nominations rejected by the Senate over the past two hundred years were attorney general designates, and a fourth was an attorney general who was rejected for a different post. Allegations of wrongdoing held up the confirmation process of Edwin Meese in 1985 for fifteen months while a special prosecutor probed his activities as White House counsel. Two of Clinton's early choices for attorney general withdrew their names from consideration rather than face an anticipated fight in the Senate.

Another possible indication of the different standard applied to Justice is the number of congressional inquiries into the department's affairs. In 1884 the Springer Committee in the House of Representatives investigated Justice for its handling of two politically explosive cases: one the prosecution of extensive postal route fraud on the frontier, and the other the prosecution of some U.S. marshals who had submitted false accounts and arrested people without cause in order to receive government fees. Both cases involved prominent leaders in the president's political party; one involved the department itself. For these reasons, the House instigated an investigation, even though the attorney general appears to have pushed rigorously for convictions.

On occasion, the actions by Justice officials themselves have triggered the scrutiny. For example, the House Rules Committee conducted hearings in 1921 to review charges that Attorney General A. Mitchell Palmer had condoned illegal searches, seizures, and mass detentions during his "Red Raids" against Russian immigrants and others suspected of communism and anarchism.

Just three years later, a Senate select committee investigated the department following Attorney General Harry Daugherty's forced resignation. Daugherty was accused of selling judgeships, obstructing justice in war and land fraud cases, and failing to prosecute illegal monopolies. His two closest associates operated a criminal ring out of the department, involving shady stock deals, influence peddling, and the sale of confiscated liquor. The head of the bureau of investigation was implicated in jury packing, spying on political opponents, breaking and entering, and fomenting labor unrest. The Senate hearings ran for two months and produced almost three-thousand pages of testimony.

In 1952 the House Judiciary Committee held hearings to discuss removing Justice from improper political influence following a scandal involving tax collectors and the assistant attorney general for the Tax Division. Adding to the controversy was the fact that five years earlier, the same person had failed to act on allegations of election fraud involving a candidate favored by the president. The impact of the tax scandal worsened when Attorney General J. Howard McGrath fired the special prosecutor. Truman forced McGrath out.

The actions of John Mitchell and Richard Kleindienst, Nixon's attorneys general, also brought the department under congressional fire in 1973. Mitchell's involvement with the break-in of Democratic National Headquarters and subsequent cover-up was examined during the Watergate hearings of the Senate Select Committee on Presidential Campaign Activities. His successor, Kleindienst, pleaded guilty to a contempt of Congress charge for failing to report that the White House had pressured the department to drop an antitrust suit against a powerful corporation. The department was further undermined by allegations that an assistant attorney general had leaked to the president secret grand jury testimony.

These events culminated in another congressional inquiry in 1974 under the auspices of a subcommittee of the Senate Judiciary Committee. The hearings focused on a systemic concern: was subversion of the law inevitable as long as the Justice Department remained under presidential control? Heading those hearings, Senator Sam J. Ervin, Jr., proposed legislation to make the department independent of the president. Ervin explained that Justice was the "one agency in the federal government that has the solemn responsibility of furthering the rule of law." But his proposal to separate the department from political oversight raised some concerns. First, the underlying cause of much of the Watergate misconduct was personal and not institutional. Second, without political accountability, prosecutorial power would be unchecked and potentially dangerous. Ervin's bill was not enacted; nor was a proposal made by Senator Lloyd Bentsen in 1977 to prohibit campaign managers from heading Justice. But legislation providing for an office of special prosecutor eventually was incorporated into the 1978 Ethics in Government Act.

HISTORY

No federal law office existed under the Articles of Confederation, although in February 1781 the Continental Congress debated a proposal to create one. The states did have experience with an office of attorney general, derived from the colonial officer who served as a delegate of the attorney general of England.

The need for a law officer on the national level became apparent with the decision to eschew the state courts for adjudication of federal law. One of the first actions of the First Congress was consideration of a bill creating both a system of lower federal courts and an office of U.S. attorney general. Signed into law on 24 September 1789, the Judiciary Act reads in part:

And there shall also be appointed a meet person, learned in the law, to act as attorney general for the United States, who shall be sworn or affirmed to a faithful execution of his office; whose duty it shall

be to prosecute and conduct all suits in the Supreme Court in which the United States shall be concerned, and to give his advice and opinion upon questions of law when required by the President of the United States, or when requested by the heads of any of the departments, touching any matters that may concern their departments, and who shall receive such compensation for his services as shall by law be provided. (1 Stat. 73, Sec. 35)

The attorney general had no department, initially serving without even a desk, much less a clerk. The salary was a meager $1,500 a year, half that paid to the other department heads, because incumbents were expected to continue their private law practices. The United States was just one client among many. This situation caused the first attorney general, Edmund Randolph, to complain, "I am a sort of mongrel between the State and the U.S.; called an officer of some rank under the latter, and yet thrust out to get a livelihood in the former,—perhaps in a petty mayor's or county court."

The Judiciary Act itself was not liked by either Anti-Federalists or Federalists in Congress. In 1790 Congress directed the attorney general to recommend revisions. Randolph's response—communicated to Congress on 28 December 1791 by the president—made two basic recommendations. He asked that Congress provide funds for a clerk to transcribe the attorney general's opinions and correspondence. He also recommended that he be granted authority over the federal district attorneys and marshals; as it was, they operated largely without oversight. Congress, still torn over the issue of centralizing federal legal machinery, ignored both requests. This was the first of many efforts to consolidate the nation's legal affairs and institutionalize the administration of justice at the federal level. Yet little changed during the first thirty years of the new government, owing in part to continued suspicion of executive power. [See Executive Power.]

One obstacle to creating a law office was the fact that the attorney general was not required to reside in the District of Columbia. Since private business often drew early law officers out of the capital, they were not readily available when the president and others sought legal advice. Further, the attorney general seldom met with the cabinet, despite being considered a member since 1792. The House of Representatives in 1814 debated a residency requirement for the office, but no bill was passed. Two years later James Madison advocated making the position full-time, with rank and salary equal to the other department heads. Again, no bill was passed. James Monroe pushed for greater resources in 1817, explaining to one congressman, "The office has no apartment for business, nor clerks, nor a messenger, nor stationery, nor fuel allowed. These have been supplied by the officer himself, at his own expense." Finally, the plea met some success. Congress provided funds for a clerk in 1819 and, the next year, funds for a messenger and $500 per annum for expenses. Then the attorney general was given an office. However, his salary, while increased from Randolph's day, remained well below that of other cabinet secretaries until 1853.

Even so, by 1817 the movement toward institutionalization had begun. A major impetus was provided by William Wirt, attorney general under Monroe and John Quincy Adams. Wirt contributed substantially to the office during his twelve-year tenure. First, he moved his residence to Washington, D.C. This meant that he was able to attend cabinet meetings regularly and provide legal advice to the administration. In addition, for the first time in the history of the office, he kept records of his official opinions and compiled and indexed documents of earlier opinions that the department heads provided to him.

The position still was part-time, which kept the attorney general's attention divided between public and private obligations. This question came before Congress in 1829, when Andrew Jackson recommended an increase in the attorney general's salary and duties, including supervision of district attorneys, Treasury Department lawsuits, and all federal criminal proceedings. Congress refused, under the leadership of Senator Daniel Webster, a staunch Jackson opponent. Webster asserted that the bill would turn the attorney general into "a half accountant, a half lawyer, a half clerk, in fine, a half everything and not much of anything." His counterproposal, to create a solicitor's office in the Treasury Depart-

ment, passed instead. This measure established a precedent for other departments to demand their own legal staffs. Congress did, however, provide $500 in 1831 for law books, augmented by $1,000 in 1840, which formed the nucleus of the department's extensive law library.

The effort to consolidate the nation's legal affairs did not evaporate. In 1845 James Polk unsuccessfully lobbied Congress for a Justice Department, as did Millard Fillmore's administration in 1851. Franklin Pierce had better success in dealing with Congress, winning a salary increase for his attorney general and two more clerk positions. By this time, the attorney general's office was often referred to as the "law department."

Pierce's choice for attorney general—Caleb Cushing—also had a significant impact on the development of the Department of Justice. With the higher salary, Cushing was the first attorney general to abandon his private practice and concentrate solely on national legal affairs. Furthermore, he was an energetic, experienced, and forceful cabinet officer who managed to draw more and more responsibilities into his domain. Contemporary newspaper accounts noted his leadership role in the administration. Cushing considered his office to be the administrative head of the legal business of government. By 1856 he had joined in pressuring Congress to establish a Justice Department in his influential essay on the "Office and Duties of Attorney General." By the end of his tenure, he had four permanent clerks on staff; a small legal bureaucracy had begun to emerge.

Congress still did not create a law department. In 1858 Cushing's successor also asked Congress to establish a law department; the bill was defeated. Instead, Congress created yet another external law office, the solicitor of the court of claims.

Gradually, however, Congress moved toward consolidation. In 1859 the administration hired an assistant attorney general to handle civil claims against the government, and two years later the attorney general was given some control over the district attorneys scattered around the country.

Congressional resistance to the formation

of a Justice Department broke down in the wake of the Civil War. The war had brought a tremendous increase in federal litigation in courts throughout the country involving everything from personal rights to property titles. Without a legal department, the federal government had to contract with private counsel at prevailing market rates to argue government cases. According to the *Congressional Globe* of the Forty-first Congress, the expenditures on extra legal counsel from 1861 to 1867 amounted to nearly half a million dollars, with another quarter of a million spent from 1868 to 1869. These enormous costs fueled the drive for a Department of Justice. Not only would a law department help ensure consistency and accountability in the government's legal business, it would save tax money.

Many in Congress remained convinced that a consolidated law department would create a stronger and more dangerous presidency. This concern is evident in the debates on the Justice Department in 1866 and 1870. Some charged that the attorney general was only a tool of the White House and not independent. Despite this, the act did pass on 20 June 1870, creating a Department of Justice effective 1 July 1870. It added two more assistant attorneys general and a solicitor general for the U.S. Supreme Court to the attorney general's staff. The act also transferred some solicitors and legal business from other departments into Justice, and gave the attorney general greater authority over the U.S. attorneys and marshals.

Yet legislation alone could not consolidate the nation's dispersed legal offices. For one thing, Congress had continued to add law posts to other departments, including the Internal Revenue Service, War Department, Navy, and Post Office. Further, two seemingly minor oversights in the Judiciary Act of 1870 effectively undermined the effort to transfer legal business to Justice. First, Congress failed to provide centralized office space for the new department. Solicitors in the other departments, out of necessity, stayed where they were. In addition, Congress failed to repeal the originating legislation of these departmental solicitors. So, while nominally under the attorney general's purview, they continued to operate largely outside the control of the department.

This fragmented legal machinery was maintained despite pleas to Congress in 1903 and 1909. By 1915 solicitors operated in the Departments of State, Treasury, Interior, Commerce, Labor, Agriculture, Navy, the Post Office, and Internal Revenue. Each acted independently of Justice in conducting its department's litigation and giving legal advice. President Woodrow Wilson sought to change this during the First World War. He issued an executive order mandating that departmental solicitors operate under the attorney general's supervision, that litigation be left to the Justice Department, and that other executive officers were bound by the attorney general's legal opinions. After the war, however, the executive order lapsed and the old system of fragmentation reemerged. The department's 1928 annual report lists only about thirteen percent of the legal positions in the executive branch as under the attorney general's control. (According to Griffin Bell, the percentage had increased to twenty-four percent by 1978.) Not until 1933 did serious efforts at consolidation begin again, when President Franklin Roosevelt issued another executive order.

In practice, the legal system in the executive branch remains divided, with each department maintaining its own law staff. However, most of the government's litigation now is handled by the Justice Department. Independent agencies, such as the Tennessee Valley Authority, have kept their right to conduct their own litigation if they so choose.

In cases where executive departments take opposite sides, the attorney general and solicitor general make the determination of which side will be defended in court. On rare occasions conflict has occurred between Justice and the administration over the handling of a case at the Supreme Court stage. This can happen when a new administration repudiates the legal position taken by an earlier Justice Department. While attorneys in the Justice Department recognize that the president has the constitutional authority to act, they also on occasion have resisted switching positions on a case at the behest of the White House.

[*See also* Cabinet; Drug Enforcement Administration; Federal Bureau of Investigation; Immigration and Naturalization Service; Marshals Service; Prisons, Federal Bureau of; *and* Appendix: An Act to Establish the Judicial Courts of the United States, 24 September 1789.]

BIBLIOGRAPHY

American State Papers, 1801–1823. Vol. 2. Washington, D.C., 1834.

Baker, Nancy V. *Conflicting Loyalties: Law and Politics in the Attorney General's Office, 1789–1990*. Lawrence, Kans., 1992.

Bell, Griffin. *Taking Care of the Law*. New York, 1982.

"Budget Authority and Outlays by Agency." *Budget of the United States Government, Fiscal Years 1963, 1965, 1971, 1973, 1980, 1985, 1989, 1993*. Washington, D.C., 1964, 1972, 1979, 1984, 1988, 1992.

Clayton, Cornell. *The Politics of Justice: The Attorney General and the Making of Government Legal Policy*. Armonk, N.Y., 1992.

Clayton, Cornell, ed. *Government Lawyers: The Federal Legal Bureaucracy and Presidential Politics*. Lawrence, Kans., 1995.

Conway, Moncure Daniel. *Omitted Chapters of History Disclosed in the Life and Papers of Edmund Randolph*. New York, 1888.

Cummings, Homer, and Carl McFarland. *Federal Justice: Chapters in the History of Justice and the Federal Executive* (1937). Reprint, New York, 1970.

Cushing, Caleb. "Office and Duties of the Attorney General." *American Law Register* 5 (December 1856): 5–94.

Dunar, Andrew J. *The Truman Scandals and the Politics of Morality*. Columbia, Mo., 1984.

Fuess, Claude M. *The Life of Caleb Cushing*. Vol. 2. New York, 1923.

Giglio, James N. *H. M. Daugherty and the Politics of Expediency*. Kent, Ohio, 1978.

Harris, Richard. *Justice: The Crisis of Law, Order, and Freedom in America*. New York, 1970.

Huston, Luther. *The Department of Justice*. New York, 1967.

Langeluttig, Albert. *The Department of Justice of the United States*. Baltimore, 1927.

Learned, Henry B. "The Attorney General and the Cabinet." 24 *Political Science Quarterly* 24 (1909): 444.

Learned, Henry B. *The President's Cabinet*. New Haven, Conn., 1912.

Meador, Daniel J. *The President, the Attorney General, and the Department of Justice*. Charlottesville, Va., 1980.

U.S. Congress. House. Rules Committee. *Hearings on Attorney General A. Mitchell Palmer on Charges Made against the Department of Justice by Louis F. Post and Others*. Washington D.C., 1921.

U.S. Congress. Senate. *Register of Debates*. 1829–1830.

U.S. Congress. Senate. *Hearings before the Select Committee on Investigation of Attorney General Harry M. Daugherty*. 68th Cong., 1st sess. Washington, D.C., 1924.

U.S. Congress. Senate. Subcommittee on Separation of Powers of the Committee on the Judiciary. *Hearings on S. 2803 and S. 2978 on Removing Politics from the Administration of Justice*. 93d Cong., 2d sess. Washington, D.C., 1974.

U.S. Department of Justice. *Annual Report of the Attorney General*. Washington, D.C., 1873–.

Warren, Charles. "New Light on the History of the Federal Judiciary Act of 1789." *Harvard Law Review* 37 (November 1923): 49.

The Watergate Hearings: Break-In and Cover-up; Proceedings of the Senate Select Committee on Presidential Campaign Activities. Edited by the *New York Times* staff. New York, 1973.

—NANCY V. BAKER

L

Labor, Department of

The organic act establishing the Department of Labor was signed on 4 March 1913 by a reluctant President William Howard Taft, the defeated and departing incumbent, just hours before Woodrow Wilson took office. A federal Department of Labor was the direct product of a half-century campaign by organized labor for a "voice in the cabinet" and an indirect product of the Progressive Movement. In the words of the organic act, the department's purpose is "to foster, promote and develop the welfare of working people, to improve their working conditions, and to enhance their opportunities for profitable employment."

Initially the department consisted of the new U.S. Conciliation Service (USCS), which mediated labor disputes, plus four preexisting bureaus: the Bureau of Labor Statistics, the Bureau of Immigration, the Bureau of Naturalization, and the Children's Bureau. Woodrow Wilson's appointee as secretary of labor was Scottish-born Congressman William B. Wilson (1913–1921), a founder and former secretary-treasurer of the United Mine Workers of America.

In his first annual report Secretary Wilson enunciated a philosophy, echoed by many secretaries since, that the department was created "in the interest of the wage earners," but must be administered in fairness to labor, business, and the public at large. Under Wilson's early leadership the bureaus functioned fairly autonomously and the department focused most of its remaining resources on the USCS. He also set up a national employment service within the Bureau of Immigration.

With the entry of the United States into World War I on 5 April 1917, adequate war production became a national necessity and issues of working conditions and labor peace assumed paramount importance. The department assumed the major responsibility for implementing the nation's war labor policies, which included recognition of the right of workers to bargain collectively, establishment of machinery to adjust grievances, and an eight-hour workday. The War Labor Administration, headed by Wilson, was placed in charge of most of the government's labor programs. Its principal component was the War Labor Board, which adjudicated labor disputes not resolved by the USCS.

When the war ended, an upsurge in labor-management conflict resulted in an alarming strike wave that threatened to paralyze the rebounding postwar economy. At the same time, a nationwide "Red Scare" led to a series of government raids resulting in the arrests of thousands of "dangerous" aliens. The Justice Department demanded that the Bureau of Immigration deport them all, but the department insisted on observing strict legal standards, and it dismissed most of the charges. Only 556 proven communists were deported.

After the activism of President Wilson there was a sharp reversal in policy by the Republican administrations from 1921 to 1933, and the department reflected their desire for less government. President Warren Harding appointed James J. Davis (1921–1930), who had attained national prominence as a charitable fund raiser. Although Davis was a union member, the department now followed a neutral course toward organized labor and focused on other areas. Administration of a series of new, restrictive immigration laws and deportation of undesirable aliens became its main function. The department also expanded the activities of the Children's Bureau and led the unsuccessful fight for a constitutional amendment limiting child labor. The employment service directed seasonal farm workers to areas of labor shortage, establishing a departmental tradition of aid to migrant farm workers. The Women's Bureau, a wartime agency that had been made a permanent bureau in 1920, promoted the welfare of working women, primarily through information dissemination.

The department took few positive steps to cope with the Depression under Davis's successor, William N. Doak (1930–1933), an official with the Brotherhood of Railway Trainmen. One of the principal departmental programs for fighting the Depression was the Davis-Bacon Act of 1931, which fought wage slashing on federal construction projects by requiring that contractors match local rates.

In 1933 President Franklin D. Roosevelt appointed Frances Perkins (1933–1945), the first woman ever to serve in the cabinet. While FDR was governor of New York, Perkins had served as commissioner of labor and had developed plans to alleviate unemployment as the Depression deepened. She survived a politically motivated impeachment attempt over her refusal to deport communist labor leader Harry Bridges and served until shortly after FDR died in April 1945.

Taking office in the depths of the Depression, Perkins believed that government had a major role to play in achieving a recovery, and she had the president's ear. However, her first crisis involved the Bureau of Immigration and Naturalization, whose efforts to deport aliens had become extreme. She disbanded a special corps devoted to deportation and ceased the bureau's harassment of this group. This sometimes troublesome bureau was transferred to the Department of Justice in 1940.

Perkins next helped set up the Civilian Conservation Corps, which sent young, unemployed men from the cities to work on conservation projects in rural areas at a dollar a day. She played a major role in the design of many of the other economic assistance and social programs of the New Deal, but her main contribution was in the enactment of Social Security. She led a campaign to convince the nation that a pension system would be humanitarian and would help prevent future depressions. The Social Security Act passed in 1935.

A number of New Deal programs directly involved the Department of Labor. The Wagner-Peyser Act of 1933 revitalized the existing U.S. Employment Service (USES) and established a nationwide system of employment offices. The USES also provided placement and recruitment for the unemployed and later helped administer Unemployment Insurance (UI) under the Social Security Act. The Walsh-Healey Public Contracts Act of 1936 required that firms manufacturing goods for the government establish an eight-hour day and assure that the work would be done under safe and healthful conditions. It also authorized the secretary to set minimum wages based on locally prevailing rates.

This act prepared the way for a much broader labor standards bill, which Perkins had long supported, setting minimum wages and maximum work hours for most industrial workers. Both the American Federation of Labor and the National Association of Manufacturers opposed it, but after a prolonged legislative battle the Fair Labor Standards Act (FLSA) became law in 1938. Administered by the Department of Labor, the act set a minimum wage of 25 cents per hour and a maximum workweek of forty hours (to be phased in by 1940) for most workers in manufacturing. The forty-hour week has not changed since 1938, but the wage level has been raised numerous times and the coverage has broadened to include most salaried workers.

One of Perkins's favorite activities was helping state governments. In July 1933 she began a series of conferences on state labor legislation that continued annually for more than twenty years. She also created the Bureau of Labor Standards in 1934 as a service agency and informational clearinghouse for state governments and other agencies to improve conditions of work.

The department played only a limited role in the World War II war production effort, focusing on maintaining labor standards. The Bureau of Labor Statistics served as the research arm for the Office of Price Administration, the War Labor Board, and the armed forces. The USCS worked with the War Labor Board.

When Harry S. Truman succeeded FDR in

THE DEPARTMENT OF LABOR BUILDING IN WASHINGTON, D.C. *Completed in 1935, the Department of Labor Building houses the United States Custom Service, the Departmental Auditorium, and the Interstate Commerce Commission.*

April 1945, Perkins resigned voluntarily. Truman then appointed Lewis B. Schwellenbach (1945–1948), a federal judge and former U.S. senator, to carry the "Fair Deal" program forward at the Department of Labor. Noble goals for workers quickly foundered on high inflation and, as was the case after World War I, a massive wave of strikes. Reaction to the strikes led to the anti-union Taft-Hartley Act of 1947 (despite strong opposition by Schwellenbach). As a result, the USCS was reconstituted outside the department as the Federal Mediation and Conciliation Service (FMCS). Congress also ordered severe budget cuts in the department, which many saw as a hotbed of unionism. The hardest-hit agency was the Bureau of Labor Statistics, which suffered a draconian forty percent reduction in its staff. A reshuffling of agencies in and out of the depart-

ment added to the disruptions. Responding to Cold War needs, the department established an Office of International Labor Affairs.

When Schwellenbach died in office in June 1948, he was succeeded by Maurice J. Tobin (1948–1953), popular governor of the state of Massachusetts. With Tobin's help Truman won reelection, and the department saw a rebirth in which the cuts of 1947 and 1948 were largely restored. Tobin transferred several dispersed labor functions into the department, including the USES, which had been removed in 1939, and the UI system. Congress also gave the secretary direct authority over the traditionally independent bureau heads. During the Korean War the strengthened department played a major role in mobilizing for defense production. In the process it began to deal with the need to raise the educational levels of workers and make better use of the capacities of women, older workers, and minorities.

In 1953 President Eisenhower appointed Martin P. Durkin, a Democrat and president of the plumbers and steamfitters union. The unions took Durkin's appointment as a sign that the new administration was open to change in the hated Taft-Hartley Act. Durkin drew up amendments to the act, but when Eisenhower refused to support them Durkin resigned in protest in September 1953. The main legacy of his brief tenure was in the improvement of the department's administrative efficiency. He clarified and strengthened the role of the secretary, assigned each bureau to one assistant secretary to promote better cooperation, and established the principle that the secretary normally takes the lead in government labor policy-making.

Eisenhower replaced Durkin with James P. Mitchell (1953–1961), vice president in charge of labor relations and operations at a New York department store. Mitchell served during a period of high prosperity and low unemployment. He continued Durkin's quest for organizational improvement, establishing himself as the administration's representative for all federal agencies concerned with labor and reducing the overlapping of functions. Internally, he concentrated on coordinating the work of the bureaus, and, to promote greater continuity of policy, he appointed civil servants as deputies to top political staff.

The FLSA was amended in 1955 to broaden coverage and raise the minimum wage from 75 cents to $1 per hour. In 1958 Congress authorized the department to enforce safety and health standards to protect workers in longshoring and harbor work. The problem of assuring an adequate supply of trained workers became a major concern. A departmental policy group developed projections on skills which would be needed twenty years later. The department also examined the employment problems of women, minorities, and the handicapped. Mitchell headed a commission that investigated and publicized the problems of migrant farm workers. The department also provided better protections from unscrupulous employers under its Bracero Program,

which imported seasonal Mexican farm workers.

New laws on misconduct by unions and employers led to new responsibilities for the department. Under the Welfare and Pension Plans Disclosure Act it collected and made available information on companies' pension and benefits plans. The Landrum-Griffin Act of 1959 required filing of reports on union funds with the Department of Labor, banned Communists from holding union office, and toughened restrictions on secondary boycotts by unions.

In 1961 President Kennedy brought into government an able throng anxious to implement his "New Frontier." His first appointee as secretary of labor was Arthur J. Goldberg (1961–1962), special counsel to the American Federation of Labor and Congress of Industrial Organizations. Known as the "Davy Crockett of the New Frontier," Goldberg became involved in a wide range of social and cultural issues. He regularly acted to settle or prevent strikes, particularly in the aerospace and transportation industries. He even settled a strike against the New York Metropolitan Opera. Strongly conscious of the rights of African Americans and other minorities, he abolished segregation in the department.

The department developed a major role in dealing with the emerging problems of automation and unemployment. Under the Area Redevelopment Act of 1961 it provided training and assistance in regions of serious unemployment. In 1962 the broader Manpower Development and Training Act gave the department responsibility for identifying labor shortages, training the unemployed, and sponsoring manpower research. Amendments to the FLSA in 1961 raised the minimum wage to $1.25 an hour and further broadened the scope of the law.

When Goldberg left the department to become a Supreme Court justice, he was succeeded by Under Secretary W. Willard Wirtz (1962–1969), a former labor lawyer and law professor active in Democratic politics. Wirtz generally left labor disputes to the FMCS and focused on training and equal opportunity programs. The department soon developed a wide range of programs to meet the social and economic goals of President Lyndon Johnson's "Great Society" and "War on Poverty," and it established the Manpower

Administration to coordinate these programs. One of the most important was the Neighborhood Youth Corps, which helped 1.5 million poor, unemployed youths work and earn income while completing high school. It was administered by local sponsors and provided public service jobs. Other programs included Special Impact for people in very poor neighborhoods; New Careers, providing training in health, education, and public safety; and the Work Incentive Program, to move able-bodied persons off welfare and into jobs.

With passage of the Civil Rights Act of 1964 an Office of Federal Contract Compliance Programs (OFCCP) was established to fight discrimination by government contractors. In the hope of opening more jobs for American farmworkers, the Bracero Program was terminated. Efforts by the department to secure passage of a job safety and health law were unsuccessful, but they laid the foundations for future legislative action.

During the Nixon and Ford administrations a succession of five secretaries carried out policies of restructuring parts of the Great Society and decentralizing federal labor programs. George P. Shultz (1969–1970), an academic economist with special expertise in labor issues, was President Nixon's first appointee. Shultz set the general course that the department followed until January 1977 and also helped formulate the administration's economic policies. He went to other posts in the administration and was succeeded by his under secretary, James D. Hodgson (1970–1973), former vice president for industrial relations with Lockheed Aircraft Corporation. Hodgson departed involuntarily after Nixon's reelection and was succeeded by Peter J. Brennan (1973–1975), a unionist from the New York City building trades who had supported Nixon's Vietnam War policies. Brennan was replaced by President Ford with John T. Dunlop (1975–1976), an academic labor economist and longtime government adviser. He served less than a year, resigning when President Ford vetoed a labor bill whose passage Dunlop had supported. Ford's second appointee was Willie J. Usery (1976–1977), another unionist then serving as director of the FMCS.

The department's main goal now became to strengthen and rationalize the massive employment and training effort. In 1969 the Manpower Administration was restructured and the Comprehensive Employment and Training Act (CETA) of 1973 established a targeted form of revenue-sharing to transfer funds and decision-making for training activities closer to local officials. The Emergency Employment Act of 1971 provided 170,000 temporary public service jobs. In 1969 the Job Corps, which provided training for needy youths, was shifted from the Office of Economic Opportunity to the department.

In 1970 the movement for a job safety and health law was successful, and the next year the department established the Occupational Safety and Health Administration (OSHA) to enforce rules, or oversee state-run programs, to protect against hazards in most of the nation's workplaces. Controversy soon dogged OSHA as inspectors were criticized for being "nitpickers." The costs of compliance with rules provoked opposition from manufacturers, and attempts to accommodate them caused consternation among the unions.

Promotion of equal job opportunity became an ever more important activity of the department. In the largely white construction industry the department promoted voluntary minority-hiring agreements between unions and contractors. Later these "Philadelphia Plans" set numerical minority hiring goals for contractors in a number of cities. The OFCCP coordinated these and other equal opportunity efforts and helped to improve their management.

The Employee Retirement Income Security Act (ERISA) of 1974 gave the department a major role in protecting and improving the nation's private retirement systems. The Congress raised the minimum wage in stages to $2.30 an hour by January 1976, and coverage was initially extended to 1.5 million domestic workers. UI coverage was expanded to cover an additional five million persons, and extended benefits were authorized during periods of high unemployment.

The department continued to avoid involvement in most labor-management disputes. However, in 1970 it successfully mediated an illegal strike by postal workers after federal troops were called up. It also focused on labor-management relations in the turbulent construction industry. In 1971 a Construction Industry Stabilization Committee within the department began to oversee construction contract settlements, resulting in a moderating trend in annual wage increases.

In January 1977 Jimmy Carter succeeded Gerald Ford. His primary domestic goal was to stimulate the economy and create jobs for the unemployed. He selected Ray Marshall (1977–1981), a labor economist at the University of Texas specializing in unemployment and minority group issues. Marshall helped develop an economic stimulus program that included 725,000 public service workers under the CETA and an expanded Job Corps. The CETA was reauthorized in 1978 with sharper targeting of assistance to the most disadvantaged persons and a new Private Sector Initiatives Program to help private firms provide job training for the needy. The Youth Employment and Demonstration Projects Act of 1977 set up programs to assist young people. The Targeted Jobs Tax Credit gave employers tax credits for hiring disadvantaged people. The Humphrey-Hawkins Act of 1978 called on the federal government to simultaneously reduce unemployment and eliminate inflation.

OSHA was under intense attack by 1977, and Marshall quickly instituted a "common sense priorities" program to focus on serious dangers, simplify safety and health regulations, and help small businesses reduce occupational hazards. Enforcement became much stricter, safety standards were simplified, and tough health standards were issued for benzene, cotton dust, lead, and other hazards. In addition, OSHA issued an innovative generic cancer policy which regulated a whole class of cancer-causing substances at once. In 1978 OSHA was joined by a sister agency, the Mine Safety and Health Administration (MSHA), consisting largely of functions transferred from the Interior Department.

Amendments to the FLSA raised the minimum wage from $2.30 to $3.35 an hour by 1 January 1981, and farm workers were covered for the first time. To strengthen enforcement of equal employment programs, federal contract compliance functions were centralized under the OFCCP. After the United States withdrew from the International Labor Organization for foreign policy reasons in 1977, the department helped lay the groundwork for a return to the organization in 1980. To strengthen the department's capacity to analyze complex issues, its economic research functions were consolidated under the Office of the Assistant Secretary for Policy Evaluation and Review.

In January 1981 Ronald Reagan took office as president with a domestic agenda for economic recovery that emphasized reduced government spending and relief for business from burdensome government rules. To carry out these programs at the department Reagan appointed Raymond J. Donovan (1981–1985). Donovan was vice president of a construction company in his home state of New Jersey and had been active in Reagan's presidential campaign.

One of Donovan's primary goals was regulatory relief, and OSHA was the lead agency in this effort. It immediately froze rules proposed during the Carter administration and sought to weaken existing standards to make them less costly for business. However, because of the complexity of rule-making procedures, existing rules proved difficult to change. OSHA adopted a less punitive approach to enforcement and encouraged voluntary compliance. The MSHA, the OFCCP, and the other regulatory agencies followed similar deregulatory policies.

Discretionary spending was slashed by sixty percent and departmental employment fell by twenty-one percent. CETA programs were cut from $8 billion per year to $3.7 billion, largely through elimination of public service employment jobs. Replacing the CETA in 1983 was the Job Training and Partnership Act (JTPA), which shifted significant decision-making and oversight from the federal level to the states while continuing to allow local officials to shape their own programs, subject to approval by special private industry councils.

Donovan was replaced by William E. Brock (1985–1987), the U.S. trade representative and a former senator. Brock's initial goal was to improve the department's efficiency, and he instituted a "Secretary's Management System" to track and assure timely meeting of the department's goals. The department began to focus on both long- and short-term employment and training policies. It initiated a "Work Force in the Year 2000" project to help make plans to meet future skilled labor needs. It also cooperated with the broadcast industry in "Project Literacy U.S."

OSHA and the MSHA shifted emphasis from reducing compliance costs for business to providing more effective protection for workers. The MSHA undertook an accident reduction program in small coal mines. To accelerate the process of setting protective standards, OSHA explored mediated rule-making, under which the interested parties would seek a consensus on the best regulation. Generic standard-setting, suspended by Secretary Donovan, was resurrected.

A task force under ERISA developed proposals to assure that pension plans would have enough funds to pay promised retirement benefits. The department helped develop proposals to reform government welfare programs at the state and community levels and to help working mothers and displaced homeworkers in the work force.

After Brock departed to join Senator Robert Dole's presidential campaign, Reagan selected Ann Dore McLaughlin (1987–1989), who had served as assistant secretary of the Treasury and under secretary of the Interior. During her brief tenure, McLaughlin sought to reconcile demands of work and family life largely through nongovernmental means, establishing a Commission on Workforce Quality and Labor Market Efficiency. The department helped shape an amendment to ERISA that required employers to eliminate underfunding of pension plans, and it set up a program to help displaced workers.

Newly elected President George Bush appointed Elizabeth Hanford Dole (1989–1990). Dole had held several high government positions and was the wife of Senate Republican Leader Robert Dole. While Dole resigned in 1990, she set the main policies that guided the department until the end of the Bush administration. She was succeeded by Lynn Morley Martin (1991–1993). Martin was a former schoolteacher who had gone into electoral politics, serving ten years in the U.S. House of Representatives.

The department followed a more activist approach to workforce issues than it had during the Reagan administration. The OFCCP undertook a "Glass Ceiling" initiative to reduce barriers to advancement by women and minorities within corporations. OSHA and the MSHA issued final standards on air quality and other hazards and assessed record penalties for violations of safety and health regulations. Dole helped broker a settlement of the protracted Pittston coal mine strike in southwest Virginia. A Secretary's Commission on Achieving Necessary Skills was appointed which prepared national competency guidelines to improve the education and skills of American workers, and JTPA amendments were enacted to target training resources toward the neediest. The first raise in the minimum wage in over a decade was enacted, accompanied by a special subminimum youth training wage, long opposed by Democrats.

In January 1993 Robert B. Reich was appointed by President Bill Clinton, who was elected on a platform of "Putting People First" and reinvigorating the economy. A teacher of government at Harvard, an author, and a radio and television commentator, Reich had previously served in the Justice Department and the Federal Trade Commission.

Under his leadership the Labor Department focused on building up the skills of American workers. The School-to-Work Opportunities Act, enacted in 1994, was designed to ease the transition from secondary education to employment for the seventy-five percent who do not graduate from college. "Goals 2000" established a national system of skill standards to certify that workers had the skills that employers needed. States were given funds to establish one-stop career centers, linking unemployment insurance, job counseling, and access to job training.

As chairman of the Pension Benefit Guaranty Corporation, Reich oversaw the enactment of the Retirement Protection Act, aimed at assuring that millions of workers in underfunded pension plans would receive adequate retirement benefits. [See Pension Benefit Guaranty Corporation.] He emphasized protection of workers by waging active campaigns against sweatshops, unsafe work sites, and fraudulent purveyors of health insurance. The department collected tens of millions of dollars in back pay for victims of job discrimination. The department administered the Family and Medical Leave Act of 1993, which provided workers with up to twelve weeks of unpaid leave to care for a new child or ill family member. While these efforts went forward, the department's operations were streamlined and its staff was reduced by more than one thousand employees. From its reluctant birth in 1913 as primarily an immigration agency with limited data collection, labor relations, and social welfare duties, the department has evolved into one of the principal regulatory and human resources development departments of the federal government.

[*See also* Cabinet *and* Occupational Safety and Health Administration.]

BIBLIOGRAPHY

Goldberg, Joseph P., and William T. Moy. *The First Hundred Years of the Bureau of Labor Statistics.* Bureau of Labor Statistics Bulletin 2235. Washington, 1985.
Grossman, Jonathan. *The Department of Labor.* New York, 1973.
Grossman, Jonathan. "The Origin of the U.S. Department of Labor." *Monthly Labor Review* (March 1973): 3–7.
Lombardi, John. *Labor's Voice in the Cabinet: A History of the Department of Labor from Its Origin to 1921.* New York, 1942.
MacEachron, David Wells. "The Role of the United States Department of Labor." Ph.D. diss., Harvard University, 1953.
MacLaury, Judson. *The U.S. Department of Labor: The First Seventy-Five Years.* Washington, D.C., 1988.
Martin, George. *Madam Secretary: Frances Perkins.* Boston, 1976.
Morris, Richard B., ed. *The U.S. Department of Labor History of the American Worker.* Washington, D.C., 1976.
Shor, Edgar L. "The Role of the Secretary of Labor." Ph.D. diss., University of Chicago, 1954.
U.S. Department of Labor. *Annual Report.* Washington, D.C., 1913–.
U.S. Department of Labor. *The Anvil and the Plow: A History of the United States Department of Labor.* Washington, D.C., 1963.
U.S. Department of Labor. Correspondence Files of the Secretary of Labor. Record Group 174. National Archives and Records Administration. College Park, Md.
U.S. Department of Labor. *Growth of Labor Law in the United States.* Washington, D.C., 1967.
U.S. Department of Labor. "Histories of the Department of Labor during the Administrations of Presidents Johnson, Nixon, Ford and Carter." Unpub-
lished, in the Historical Office, U.S. Department of Labor, Washington, D.C.

—JUDSON MACLAURY

Land Management, Bureau of

 In terms of acreage, the Bureau of Land Management (BLM) is the federal government's largest natural resources agency. Its personnel manage 270 million acres of land in eleven western states of the continental United States and in Alaska. In Alaska alone, the BLM has jurisdiction over approximately ninety-two million acres. The agency manages these vast public lands with an annual budget of about $1.2–$1.3 billion and a work force of twelve thousand. It is headed by a director, who is nominated by the president and confirmed by the Senate, and by twelve state directors.

The BLM was created by an executive order issued by President Harry Truman in 1946. The reorganization order combined two Interior Department agencies into a single agency: the Grazing Service, established in 1934, and the General Land Office, created in 1812. It was not until 1976, however, that Congress sanctioned the merger by passing an organic act for the BLM. The Federal Land Policy and Management Act of 1976, and a corollary statute, the Public Rangelands Improvement Act of 1978, put the BLM on a firm statutory footing while directing its personnel to employ a multiple-use management philosophy similar to that developed earlier in the century by the U.S. Forest Service.

Notwithstanding these clear expressions of legislative intent, the BLM, like its predecessors (the General Land Office and the Grazing Service), has been at the center of a historic controversy over federal versus state ownership of these public lands. In its 1930 report the Garfield Commission, which was created by President Herbert Hoover to propose a solution to the "public domain" lands, recommended ceding those lands to the states in which they lay. The Congress did not accept the proposal. Voicing the majority sentiment, Senator Robert Borah of Idaho scoffed at the gift of federal acres "on which a jack rabbit could hardly live."

The controversy erupted again in 1980 with the election of Ronald Reagan as president. The "Sagebrush Rebellion" was composed primarily of western ranchers and owners of mining companies who felt that their interests were threatened by the BLM's 1976 multiple-use mandate. For decades ranchers had controlled the bureau, leading political scientists to point to the BLM as the epitome of the "captured agency phenomenon." When these 270 million acres became available for other uses such as outdoor recreation, wilderness preservation, and endangered species protection, the traditional users of the public domain organized the Sagebrush Rebellion to protect their interests.

Although very little acreage actually was transferred from federal to state ownership during the 1980s, the BLM lost the important function of managing a large portion of the nation's mineral resources to a new Interior Department agency, the Minerals Management Service, created in 1984. However, during the Bush administration, all Interior Department fire-fighting activities were consolidated and placed under the BLM's jurisdiction.

Recent efforts by the Clinton administration to revise the 1872 Mining Act and to increase grazing fees on BLM lands have found little support in Congress. This is testimony to the influence that ranching and mining interests still hold over the BLM and in the legislative branch. Moreover, proponents of the present-day "wise use" movement have introduced bills in Congress that once more call for state and private ownership of these public lands. In the midst of this controversy, bureau personnel continue incorporating a multiple-use management philosophy within an organization that historically has been a dominant-use agency. With such initiatives as riparian area protection, preservation of Native American cultural sites, and a wilderness inventory program, the BLM presently struggles with implementing its 1976 mandate to allow a wider range of uses on its lands.

[*See also* Forest Service; Interior, Department of the; *and* Minerals Management Service.]

BIBLIOGRAPHY

Clarke, Jeanne Nienaber, and Daniel McCool. *Staking Out the Terrain: Power and Performance in Natural Resource Agencies.* 2d ed. Albany, 1996.

Culhane, Paul J. *Public Lands Politics: Interest Group Influence on the Forest Service and the Bureau of Land Management.* Baltimore, 1981.

Durant, Robert F. *The Administrative Presidency Revisited: Public Lands, the BLM, and the Reagan Revolution.* Albany, 1992.

Robbins, Roy M. *Our Landed Heritage: The Public Domain, 1776–1936.* Lincoln, Neb., 1962.

—JEANNE NIENABER CLARKE

Legislative Branch.
See House of Representatives *and* Senate.

Library of Congress

 Occupying a unique place in U.S. government as well as in the world of libraries, the Library of Congress is at once the legislative library and research arm of the U.S. Congress, copyright agency of the U.S. government, research center for scholars in every subject and in more than 450 languages, law library for the judiciary and the legal profession, national library for the blind, publisher of bibliographic data and products, home of the nation's poet laureate, research center for the preservation and conservation of library materials, and the world's largest repository of maps, atlases, printed and recorded music, motion pictures, and television programs. The Library of Congress is housed in three massive structures on Capitol Hill: the Jefferson Building, opened in 1897, the Adams Building, opened in 1939, and the Madison Building, completed in 1980. Even though the Library of Congress functions as a *de facto* national library, it does not have that official appellation; it is still part of the legislative branch, subject to congressional oversight and budgetary appropriations and scrutiny.

The fledgling United States had no national

THE LIBRARY OF CONGRESS IN WASHINGTON, D.C. *The original building to house the Library of Congress, the Jefferson Building opened in 1897. As collections grew, the Adams building was opened in 1939, and the Madison Building in 1980.*

library for the first twenty-four years of its existence. On 24 April 1800 President Adams approved legislation appropriating $5,000 for the purchase of "such books as may be necessary for the use of Congress." The first package of books arrived from London in 1801. It consisted of 740 volumes and three maps, and they were placed in the Capitol, the library's first home. Two years later, Adams's successor, Thomas Jefferson, approved a law appointing a librarian and creating a Joint Congressional Committee on the Library with authority to set the budget. In the absence of a national library, the Library of Congress assumed that role almost by default. The right to appoint the librarian of Congress became a presi-

dential responsibility. The law also permitted the president and the vice president to borrow books, a privilege that was extended in the course of time to most government agencies and the judiciary. The major influence in transforming the scope of the Library of Congress was Thomas Jefferson, no mean bibliophile himself. He took a personal interest in the library during his eight-year term and personally recommended many of the earliest acquisitions.

Tragedy struck in 1812 when the British invaded Washington and burned the Capitol, including all three thousand volumes in the library. To restart the library, Jefferson, by now retired to his estate at Monticello, offered to sell to Congress his personal library, then the largest and finest in the country. The purchase of Jefferson's 6,487 volumes was approved in 1815. The Jefferson purchase changed the character of the library at a single stroke. Far from being a library exclusively devoted to legislative interests, it became an encyclopedic collection with works on art, architecture, science, literature, and geography. It contained books in French, Spanish, German, Latin, and Greek, and even one three-volume statistical work in Russian.

For a while, the Smithsonian Institution emerged as a rival to the Library of Congress. During the early 1850s Smithsonian librarian Charles Coffin Jewett promoted the idea of a national library based in his institution. Jewett's efforts, however, were opposed by Smithsonian Secretary Joseph Henry, who wanted the institution to focus exclusively on scientific research and publication. With the dismissal of Jewett in 1854 and the transfer of the Smithsonian library's forty thousand volumes to the Library of Congress in 1866, this chapter ended.

The 1850s proved a rough patch for the Library of Congress. The looming prospect of civil war hindered any real planning. In 1851 the most serious fire in the library's history destroyed about two-thirds of the fifty-five thousand volumes, including most of the Jefferson collection. Congress responded quickly by appropriating $168,700 to restore the library and replace the lost volumes. An even more serious setback was the loss of several of the library's functions to other agencies. In 1857 a joint resolution of Congress transferred the responsibility for distribution of public documents to the Bureau of the Interior and the responsibility for the international exchange of books and documents to the Department of State. Moreover, all copyright activities were transferred to the Patent Office, which meant that the library could no longer receive free copies of all books published in the United States. As the Civil War came to a close, the library had only eighty thousand volumes and a staff of seven.

The person who was responsible for transforming the sleepy institution was Ainsworth Rand Spofford, a former Cincinnati bookseller and journalist who served as librarian for thirty-

two years, from 1865 to 1897. The Spofford era, as these years are called in the library's annals, marked the transition to the modern period and equipped the library to meet the challenges of the twentieth century. Spofford was responsible for establishing the basis of strong bipartisan support for the library's ambitious expansion programs, and for beginning a comprehensive collection of Americana. It was also in Spofford's time that the magnificent Jefferson Building was planned; it opened the year that he retired. Spofford took full advantage of the favorable political and cultural climate to promote the library's expansion. He was instrumental in securing congressional approval of five laws defining and expanding the library's role as the national library. They were the Copyright Amendment of 1865 and the Copyright Act of 1870, which brought back all copyright registration and deposit activities to the library; the transfer of the Smithsonian Institution Library to the Library of Congress; the 1867 purchase for $100,000 of the private library of the historian and archivist Peter Force, which became the core of the library's Americana and incunabula collections; and the International Exchange Resolution of 1867, restoring to the library the development of a foreign books and documents collection. It was the expansion of the Copyright Act that served as the foundation of the Spofford plans. The library had received single copies of all works published in the United States from 1846 to 1859, and the practice was revived by Spofford from 1865. From 1870 the receipt by the library of two copies of every work was made mandatory. The international copyright law of 1891 brought deposits of foreign works into the library for the first time. More than forty percent of the library's print holdings and more than ninety percent of its nonprint holdings were acquired through copyright deposit. Among the more important items thus received were the first photographs of Matthew Brady. By 1876 the U.S. Bureau of Education ranked the Library of Congress and the Boston Public Library as the two largest libraries in the country, containing 300,000 volumes each. However, by the time Spofford left, the Library of Congress had become the largest, with over 840,000 volumes.

In 1897 the Jefferson Building opened as the new home of the Library of Congress. An imposing structure in the style of the Italian Renaissance, its Main Reading Room is a triumph of architectural decoration. Spofford is also credited with two major innovations: extending the hours of service so that the library remained open every weekday all year round and reinstating the earlier policy of lending books to the public on the strength of an advance deposit. In 1896 the congressional committee overseeing the library held hearings about the state of the library and its possible reorganization. The American Library Association sent six witnesses, including a future Librarian of Congress, Herbert Putnam. The library was reorganized on the basis of the committee's recommendations. The size of the staff was increased from 42 to 108 and new administrative divisions were established for the reading room, the art gallery, maps and charts, cataloging, copyright, manuscripts, music, and periodicals.

Following Spofford's retirement, President McKinley appointed John Russell Young as librarian. Young's brief two-year tenure was marked by unusual activity. He established a special room in the library for the Jefferson Collection, sought the help of U.S. embassies abroad in the collection of books, newspapers, magazines, pamphlets, manuscripts, broadsides, and documents "illustrative of the history of the various nationalities," and established the library service to the blind and the physically challenged.

Young's successor was Herbert Putnam of the Boston Public Library, who was appointed by President McKinley in 1899 and served for forty years under eight presidents. Putnam was the man who made the library a national institution by creating a program of wider access and opening the collections to the public in its broadest sense. He was also the first professional librarian, and he enjoyed the full confidence and support of the community of librarians. He was the first to forge strong links between the Library of Congress and the thousands of other libraries scattered throughout the nation. Just two years after he took office, the first volume of a completely new classification scheme, based on the library's own collections, was published, access to the library was extended to all "duly qualified individuals" throughout the United States, the interlibrary loan service was inaugurated, and the sale and distribution of the Library of Congress printed catalog cards was begun. His goals were to democratize knowledge, raise bibliographic standards, and encourage cooperation among libraries. In defending the interlibrary loan system, Putnam said that "a book used is better than a book that is merely preserved." In 1903 Putnam persuaded his friend Theodore Roosevelt to issue an executive order transferring the papers of many of the Founding Fathers, including George Washington, Thomas Jefferson, and James Madison, from the State Department archives to the library's Manuscript Division. In 1904 the library began publishing important historical texts from its collection, such as *Journals of the Continental Congress*. Putnam also was tireless in his efforts to secure important private collections from domestic and foreign sources. His major coups were the purchase in 1904 of a four-thousand-volume library of Indica, the eight-thousand-volume G. V. Yudin Library from Russia, the Schatz Collection of early opera librettos, and, notably, the Otto F. Vollbehr Collection, which included one of the three perfect existing vellum copies of the Gutenberg Bible. The purchase of the Vollbehr collection for $1.5 million was approved by Congress at the height of the Depression, and Putnam personally went to Europe to bring the Gutenberg Bible to the library's vaults. As the library had now outgrown its original purpose to serve as a research adjunct of Congress, Putnam established a special division known as the Legislative Reference Service (LRS). The LRS was designed as a problem solver and information provider to members of Congress. In 1925 Congress passed the Library of Congress Trust Fund Board Act enabling the institution to accept gifts and bequests from private citizens. One of the first donors under this act was Elizabeth Sprague Coolidge, whose endowment promoted the understanding and appreciation of music. She also bore the costs of the construction of a new concert hall within the library and commissioned new works of music. Other benefactors included John D. Rockefeller, Gertrude Clarke Whittall, Archer Huntington, and James

MAIN READING ROOM, LIBRARY OF CONGRESS. *Modeled on the reading room of the British Museum Library, the Main Reading Room is the principal point for gaining access to the library's vast holdings. The card catalog cases, visible at the rear of this photo, have now been moved to another location, and reader desks now completely encircle the Central Desk, where call slips are submitted.*

B. Wilbur. The trust fund also allowed the library to establish chairs and consultantships for scholars and poets, the latter evolving into today's poet laureate consultant in poetry.

The continuing expansion of library collections required more space. Additional book stacks were built in the Jefferson Building in 1910 and 1927. When this space also ran out, adjacent land was acquired in 1928 and the Annex Building (later the Adams Building) was authorized in 1930. Construction was delayed during the Depression years, and it was not until 1939 that it was opened to the public.

Putnam's successor as Librarian of Congress was a typical New Deal intellectual, the poet Ar-

chibald MacLeish, who was handpicked by FDR in 1939. As an *homme engagé,* MacLeish was the first librarian whose interests went beyond books into politics and social issues. In 1941 MacLeish dedicated the South (Jefferson) Reading Room in the Adams Building, decorated by artist Ezra Winter with four Jeffersonian murals, and also established a democracy alcove in the Main Reading Room, where readers could find the classic texts of the American tradition. In 1943 the library celebrated the bicentennial of Jefferson's birth with an exhibition, an annotated catalog of the books in Jefferson's personal library, and a project to microfilm the Jefferson papers. MacLeish also launched an administrative reorganization so thorough that it lasted until the 1970s. MacLeish's wide-ranging interests were reflected in the growing emphasis on collections from and about foreign countries.

MacLeish resigned in 1944, and President Truman appointed assistant librarian Luther H. Evans, a political scientist by background, to the post. Although hampered by a penurious Congress, Evans strengthened the bibliographic services of the library. The library also become more active in copyright and intellectual freedom issues. As part of his commitment to international library cooperation, Evans initiated automatic book purchase agreements with foreign dealers and the international exchange of official publications.

Evans's successor as librarian of Congress was L. Quincy Mumford, director of the Cleveland Public Library, who was nominated by President Eisenhower in 1954. Mumford presided over the most ambitious program of expansion in the library's history, including ground-breaking for the Madison Building in 1957. The library benefited from higher levels of federal funding for education, libraries, and research. In 1958 the library was authorized by Congress to acquire books abroad by using U.S.-owned nonconvertible foreign currency under the terms of the Agricultural Trade Development and Assistance Act of 1954 (P.L. 480). Under this act the library established centers in New Delhi and Cairo in 1961 to purchase publications and distribute them to research libraries in the United States. The Higher Education Act of 1965 authorized the Office of Education to transfer funds to the Library of Congress to enable it to acquire all current library materials of scholarly value published throughout the world and provide cataloging information for these materials after they had been received. The new effort, christened the National Program for Acquisitions and Cataloging, led to the establishment over the next two decades of six foreign offices, including one in London. Shared acquisitions and cataloging made international bibliographical standards imperative. To meet this need, the library created "Machine-Readable Cataloging" (MARC) for converting, maintaining, and distributing bibliographic in-

formation. MARC became the official national standard for this purpose in 1971 and the international standard in 1973. Another Mumford innovation was a pilot project to study techniques for the preservation of brittle books printed on acidic paper. This project has grown into the Preservation Office. Before his retirement in 1974, Mumford went on record as opposing the change of the library's name to the National Library of the United States. The Legislative Reorganization Act of 1970 in fact reaffirmed the library's primary commitment to serving the research and reference needs of the U.S. Congress. The act also changed the name of the Legislative Reference Service to the Congressional Research Service.

On Mumford's retirement in 1974, President Gerald R. Ford appointed Daniel Boorstin, director of the Smithsonian's National Museum of History and Technology (now American History), as the twelfth Librarian of Congress. Boorstin's intellectual flair added immensely to the visibility of the library as a national asset and helped to forge and strengthen links to scholars, authors, publishers, journalists, cultural leaders, and businesspeople. The annual budget had grown to $250 million. Boorstin took a keen interest in copyright, collection development, and promotion of reading. In 1976 Boorstin created a Task Force on Goals, Organization and Planning and incorporated its recommendations in a far-reaching reorganization, the first since the days of Archibald MacLeish. The move to the Madison Building was completed in 1982 and helped to relieve the pressures on space—at least for a few more years. The Boorstin years saw the establishment of two significant units: the American Folklife Center under the American Folklife Preservation Act, and the Center for the Book, with John Y. Cole as director. The next librarian of Congress was James H. Billington, a renowned scholar in Russian history, who was director of the Wilson International Center. He took the oath of office as the thirteenth librarian of Congress on 14 September 1987. Through his Management and Planning Committee, Billington set up an ongoing review of the means of bringing the Library of Congress to the American people.

The American Memory Project provides electronic copies of selected collections of American history and culture to schools and libraries. Billington's tenure coincided with vast technological leaps in communication, including the development of CD-ROM, online transmission of text and data, the Internet, video, and digitization of photographs. All these breakthroughs had serious implications for the library and provided avenues for realizing the age-old dream of a library without walls, or a new "Electronic National University." To strengthen the library's educational outreach, Billington established the Education Office. To enlist the support of the private sector, Billington established the James Madison Council, some of whose members, such as Walter Annenberg and John Kluge, have provided generously for the expansion of the electronic projects.

The Library of Congress is headed by a librarian of Congress assisted by a deputy librarian and an assistant librarian. These three officers have immediate overview of all administrative functions and of the Legislative Liaison Office, the Exhibits Office, the Information Office, and the Publications Office. The library is divided into six departments: 1) the Administrative Office, responsible for the buildings, the Photoduplication Service, information systems, security, budget, accounting, personnel, matériel, training, and preservation; 2) the Processing Department, consisting of eighteen major organizational units and fifteen overseas offices whose responsibilities cover MARC, the National Union Catalog, the Exchange and Gift Division, cataloging, decimal classification, the Card Division, and the Serial Record Division; 3) the Reference Department, comprising sixteen divisions including the Division for the Blind and Physically Handicapped, Federal Research, Reference and Bibliography, Geography and Map, Latin America, Africa, Loan, Manuscript, Music, Orientalia, Motion Pictures, Prints and Photographs, Rare Books and Special Collections, Science and Technology, Serials, and Slavic Studies; 4) the Copyright Office; 5) the Law Library; and 6) the Congressional Research Service, with eight research divisions covering law, government, economics, education and public welfare, environment and natural resources, foreign affairs and national defense, and science policy.

BIBLIOGRAPHY

Cole, John Y. *Jefferson's Legacy*. Washington, D.C., 1993.
Goodrum, Charles. *The Library of Congress*. Columbia Mo., 1987.
—GEORGE THOMAS KURIAN

Life-Saving Service

The saving of lives imperiled by shipwreck was a private endeavor in the United States until 1847, when Congress appropriated $1,000 for lifesaving equipment. This money was not spent immediately; the next year Congressman William A. Newell of New Jersey amended the lighthouse bill to include $10,000 for such equipment, to be procured under supervision of the Revenue-Cutter Service. Captain Douglas Ottinger oversaw the construction of eight lifeboat stations along the coasts in the vicinity of New York, and subsequent years brought further expansion, but the absence of personnel left the system less than fully effective. Loss of life in shipwrecks in 1854 led to the engagement of station-keepers, although these had to rely on volunteer crews and no regulations for their guidance existed.

The sectional crisis and the Civil War diverted attention thereafter; in 1869 the new Division of Revenue Marine in the Treasury Department assumed control of lifesaving stations. Two years later Sumner I. Kimball became chief of the division, and he took advantage of increased appropriations to invigorate the stations. Crews of experienced surfmen were engaged for alternate stations along the coast; when this proved inadequate, all were manned during winter months. With regular drills, conducted in accordance with detailed regulations, personnel of the lifesaving stations became more professional.

The *Huron* and *Metropolis* disasters of 1877 and 1878, respectively, with heavy loss of life, led to proposals that the lifesaving stations be transferred to the U.S. Navy; instead, the Life-Saving Service became a separate entity in 1878, with

Sumner Kimball as its superintendent, a position he held during the thirty-seven years of the service's existence. Connections with the cutter service remained close—officers of the latter served as inspectors, and others oversaw the construction of stations, lifeboats, surfboats, and related equipment, while cutters and station personnel frequently cooperated in rescue operations.

By 1881 there were 189 lifesaving stations, 139 on the Atlantic coast, 5 on the Gulf coast, 7 on the Pacific coast, 37 on the Great Lakes, and 1 at the Falls of the Ohio River. Most were manned only during the months when stormy weather was expected, although the rise of recreational boating led to the season's being extended to ten months—1 August to 1 June—in 1894. Consequently, surfmen could no longer find employment in the fishing industry during the brief period of inactivity, and their pay was generally so low that many left the Life-Saving Service. The lack of a retirement system was a further deterrent; Kimball's efforts to rectify this situation came to naught, and neither was he able to arrange adequate pensions for the families of those who died or were disabled in the line of duty.

These problems were solved when the Life-Saving Service was merged with the Revenue-Cutter Service to form the U.S. Coast Guard on 28 January 1915, for personnel of the former became members of a military service. For the next twenty years the lifesaving branch of the Coast Guard retained its separate identity; thereafter, the service was truly unified.

[See also Coast Guard and Revenue-Cutter Service.]

BIBLIOGRAPHY

Bennett, Robert F. Surfboats, Rockets, and Carronades. Washington, D.C., 1976.
Evans, Stephen H. The United States Coast Guard, 1790–1915: A Definitive History. Annapolis, 1949.
Lombard, Asa C. P., Jr. East of Cape Cod. New Bedford, Mass., 1976.
Means, Dennis R. "'A Heavy Sea Running': The Formation of the U.S. Life-Saving Service, 1846–1878." Prologue (Winter 1987): 223–243.
Noble, Dennis L. That Others Might Live: The U.S. Life-Saving Service, 1878–1915. Annapolis, 1994.

—ROBERT E. JOHNSON

Lighthouse Service

The ninth act of the U.S. Congress (I Stat.L. 53), the first to deal with a public work, made the federal government responsible for the establishment and maintenance of aids to navigation. In 1789 there were twelve lighthouses at harbor entrances, with three more under construction. These were brought under the Treasury secretary, Alexander Hamilton, who made them the charge of the commissioner of revenue in 1792. When that office was finally abolished in 1820, the fifth auditor of the Treasury assumed the responsibility for the lighthouses, which numbered fifty-five by that time.

In the absence of a field organization, it was the responsibility of customs collectors to supervise lights in the various ports, with building and maintenance done by contract. Discontent in maritime circles occasioned periodic investigations by naval officers, leading to some reorganization, and in 1851 a board composed of two senior naval officers, two army engineers, and one civilian scientist investigated the service and recommended extensive changes, including organization as a single system under a permanent board. In 1852 the board, with the addition of a second civilian scientist, was made permanent. Reorganization followed; the country's sea and lake coasts were divided into twelve districts, each of which was assigned an inspector, usually a naval officer. After a study of European systems, the Lighthouse Board adopted the illuminating lens and classification system introduced in France by Augustin Jean Fresnel.

Although the Civil War was a blow to the service—164 lights were destroyed and military and naval officers could not be spared for the Lighthouse Service—recovery was rapid after the war. Thereafter, expansion continued: the 332 lighthouses and lightships of 1850 had grown to 1,523 by 1880, while fog signals and buoys numbered 3,343. Shipwrecks in Alaskan waters led to the establishment of buoys there in 1884, and the first lighthouse was built in Alaska in 1895. Within a few years after the acquisition of noncontiguous islands in 1898, the Lighthouse Board's authority was extended to these as well.

The act creating the Department of Commerce and Labor in 1903 specified that the Lighthouse Service be transferred from the Treasury Department, with the secretary of commerce and labor assuming the authority heretofore vested in the secretary of the Treasury. There was no immediate change in the structure of the Lighthouse Board, but the first two secretaries of commerce and labor, Oscar Strauss and Charles Nagel, pointed out the inefficiency resulting from the lack of an executive head with definite authority and responsibility and from the use of military and naval officers who were assigned to the Lighthouse Service for short periods only. In 1910 Congress passed legislation eliminating the Lighthouse Board and establishing the Bureau of Lighthouses under a civilian commissioner. George R. Putnam was appointed the first commissioner; he held that post until 1935, when he was succeeded by Harold D. King. The military and naval officers who had served as lighthouse inspectors were replaced by civilians. On 1 July 1939, Congress returned the Lighthouse Service to the Treasury Department, where it became part of the U.S. Coast Guard.

[See also Coast Guard.]

BIBLIOGRAPHY

Collins, Francis A. *Sentinels along Our Coast.* New York, 1922.

Conway, John S. *The United States Lighthouse Service, 1923.* Washington, D.C., 1923.

Holland, F. Ross, Jr. *America's Lighthouses.* Brattleboro, Vt., 1972.

Johnson, Arnold B. *The Modern Light-House Service.* Washington, D.C., 1889.

Putnam, George R. *Lighthouses and Lightships of the United States.* Boston, 1917.

Strobridge, Truman R. *Chronology of Aids to Navigation and the Old Lighthouse Service, 1716–1939.* Washington, D.C., 1974.

Weiss, George. *The Lighthouse Service: Its History, Activities, and Organization.* Baltimore, 1926.

—ROBERT E. JOHNSON

M

Management and Budget, Office of

 An agency located in the Executive Office of the President, the Office of Management and Budget (OMB) has the primary responsibilities for preparing the president's budget requests to Congress. It also assists the president in preparation of the administration's legislative program, advises the president about signing or vetoing bills passed by Congress, recommends management innovations in the bureaucracy, improves interagency coordination, and determines the quarterly allocations of funds for each department.

The Budget and Accounting Act of 1921 created the predecessor of the OMB, known as the Bureau of the Budget (BOB). [*See* Appendix: Budget and Accounting Act (1921).] Although created in the Harding administration, one of the most corrupt in American history, the Bureau of the Budget was a good-government reform strongly supported by the business community of the Republican party. It was expected to function as a neutral mechanism to promote the most efficient and economical administration. The first director, Charles Dawes, told Congress in 1921, "The Budget Bureau must be impartial, impersonal, and non-political." It had the duty to assist the president to "assemble, correlate, revise, reduce, or increase the estimates of the several departments or establishments." Originally located in the Treasury Department, the BOB was moved to the newly created Executive Office of the President in 1939 as part of the administrative reform proposals developed by President Franklin Roosevelt in Reorganization Plan No. 1. [*See* Appendix: Reorganization Plan No. 1

(1939).] Since 1947 the budget director and deputy director have been Executive Level III positions, requiring Senate consent. The agency was renamed the OMB in the Reorganization Plan No. 2 proposed by President Richard Nixon and approved by Congress in 1970. The director of the OMB has had an office in the West Wing of the White House since 1971 and has had the title "assistant to the president" since 1973, serving as one of the president's key advisers. The OMB itself is located in the old State, War and Navy Building, now known as the Old Executive Office Building, right next to the White House.

The main function of the OMB is to assist with preparation of the president's budget requests to Congress, submitted annually as the "Budget of the United States." President Harding's first budget director, Charles Dawes, instructed all departments to submit their requests to the BOB rather than to Congress, for inclusion in the president's budget. The BOB, acting on behalf of the president, reserved the right to change the figures requested by the departments. Since then, as early as two years before the president's budget is sent to Congress, the OMB sends departments its budget call. Depending on its forecasts in revenues, the OMB, from Conference Room 248 in the Old Executive Office Building, instructs departments (in what are known as OMB "marks") to plan either for increases, adjustments for inflation (the current services budget), a freeze in expenditures (the zero-base option), targeted or across-the-board cutbacks, or reductions in nonessential activities. Departments submit their proposed budgets to the OMB for review. These traditionally included *language sheets*, which estimated spending authority requested from Congress, and *green sheets*, which estimated annual outlays (a combination of past and present spending authority). Today agencies transmit computerized equivalents (spreadsheets) to the OMB. Examiners from the OMB's Budget Review Division then make recommendations for every agency and program. They look for padding in requests and suggest management reforms, or even consolidation of agencies and functions. Preliminary department budgets prepared by OMB examiners are sent to the OMB program associate directors, a set of White House political appointees, for revision in accord with White House priorities.

The budget director and top White House aides then hold "review sessions" so each cabinet secretary may make final arguments to restore cuts. Sometimes secretaries are given one last chance to appeal directly to the president. Truman, Ford, Carter, and Clinton listened to these appeals carefully, acting like judges deciding cases. Other presidents, such as Nixon, Reagan, and Bush, used an intermediate "appellate division" consisting of the OMB director and the White House chief of staff to screen appeals. Presidents rarely reverse decisions of their budget directors: to do so would simply invite more appeals. The military budget is often handled differently. Since 1951 the review is held at the Pentagon (and not on the OMB's home turf) by OMB and Defense officials, and many presidents, following Kennedy's lead, have made the OMB appeal to the president against Department of Defense requests, rather than leave the burden of proof with the department. During the Nixon years, the assistant for national security Henry Kissinger controlled interdepartmental committees that helped the president resolve disputes between the OMB and Defense Department.

The final OMB product, submitted to Congress each year by the president along with a special message, is the executive budget, more formally known as the "Budget of the United States," though in fact it is nothing of the sort. It is actually the presidential request for budget authority. It comes in five volumes (8 inches by 11), totals more than two thousand pages, and provides current and projected budget figures for every agency and activity of the national government (secret intelligence and defense activities excepted). The budget covers proposed spending for a fiscal year that begins 1 October and ends 30 September. The budget is numbered for the calendar year in which it ends.

The OMB director testifies on the president's budget before the House Ways and Means and Senate Finance Committees, the House and Senate Appropriations Committees, and the House and Senate Budget Committees. The OMB reviews the testimony of department secretaries when they appear before the appropriations committees to defend the president's budget. It also advises the president whether to veto congressional spending bills. Once funds are appropriated by Congress, the OMB controls departmental spending by monitoring the levels of expenditure and making quarterly allotments (a power it has had since 1933), as well as by directing the Treasury to hold certain agency funds as "reserves." It may permit reprogramming of funds (transferring money from one activity to another) within an agency or across agency lines with the concurrence of congressional committees with jurisdiction. It conducts audits of past spending to ensure that they conform to White House priorities.

The OMB handles the staff work involved in presidential requests to defer or rescind spending authorized by Congress. Under the provisions of the Budget and Impoundment Act of 1974, the president may recommend that scheduled spending be deferred to a later fiscal year. The recommendation goes into effect unless Congress blocks it within a specified period of time. The president may also recommend that some or all budget authority be rescinded, a proposal that does not go into effect unless Congress affirmatively acts in favor. The OMB is also responsible for implementing impoundments required by law, including those involving state and local governments that have violated antidiscrimination statutes, projects that have failed environmental review procedures, and programs in which corruption in intergovernmental administration has been uncovered. It also administers any across-the-board impoundments authorized by statute, as well as rescissions or sequesters required by spending caps instituted under such procedural laws as the Budget Enforcement Act of 1990. It is in charge of seeing that agencies remain under their spending ceilings instituted under the reconciliation act passed by Congress each fiscal year.

The OMB's role in preparing the presidential budget gives it informal influence in economic policy-making, particularly in the formulation of the budget resolution proposed by the administration to Congress each spring and the recommendations for the reconciliation measure adopted by Congress just prior to the start of the fiscal year in mid-September (or later if the process is stalled). Along with the chair of the Council of Economic Advisers and the secretary of the Treasury, the OMB director is part of the president's "troika" that meets regularly to discuss macroeconomic issues and meets occasionally with the president to offer economic advice. Most of the OMB directors have been appointed from the business, financial, or legal communities, or from the ranks of professional economists. Since the Nixon administration the OMB director has become a visible media spokesperson for the administration, and presidents expect the director to support the president's program before Congress and the American people. Often the OMB director becomes embroiled in debate with the director of the Congressional Budget Office (CBO) over the probability of OMB forecasts of future government expenditures, a debate that is exacerbated any time the White House is controlled by one party and Congress by the other. (Until 1993 most independent observers believed that the CBO was more accurate in its forecasts.) Under the provisions of the Balanced Budget and Emergency Deficit Control (Gramm-Rudman-Hollings) Act of 1986, the OMB and CBO had joint responsibility for forecasting the projected deficit, and if the forecast exceeded specified deficit reduction targets, the president was to sequester funds appropriated by Congress to keep projected spending under the mandated deficit ceilings. The sequester provision was eliminated by Congress in 1990, reducing the significance of the OMB forecasts. The different forecasts of accumulated seven-year deficits forecast by President Clinton's OMB and the Republican-dominated CBO were at the heart of the confrontation between president and Congress that paralyzed the budget process and led to the temporary "shutdown" of the departments in 1995.

The OMB assists the White House in preparing a presidential program for Congress (known as legislative clearance). The practice began in 1921 during the Harding administration: the BOB occasionally helped the president decide if a departmental proposal should become part of Harding's program, and President Coolidge institutionalized the practice under the second director, Herbert Lloyd, in 1924. During the New Deal the National Economic Council performed the legislative clearance function, but after its demise Roosevelt assigned all clearance to the bureau. After 1947 the budget agency's Legislative Reference Division was assigned by President Harry Truman the responsibility of creating much of the presidential program out of agency submissions, a practice that President Dwight Eisenhower continued. By the 1960s the OMB was involved in the task forces organized by President Lyndon Johnson that developed the Great Society programs, and was at the height of its influence in the legislative clearance process. In 1970, however, President Nixon reduced the agency's rule in program formulation. Nixon established a Domestic Council to innovate programs. In a message to Congress in 1970 explaining his reorganization plan, he indicated that "the Domestic Council will be primarily concerned with *what* we do; OMB will be primarily concerned with *how* we do it, and *how well* we do it." The result, however, in the Nixon and subsequent administrations, was not a neat separation of functions, but rather a series of turf struggles between the OMB and those planners of domestic programs functioning in various White House innovating agencies. The OMB emphasized economies, efficiencies, and cutbacks in program functions, and became a prime instrument in presidential retrenchment politics, especially in reorganizing or partially dismantling the Great Society programs of the 1960s.

The OMB also performs a "veto clearance" function. Since 1960 it has had the primary responsibility for organizing the analytical studies within the bureaucracy that are used by senior

White House staff in recommending to the White House whether or not the president should sign bills passed by Congress, let them become law without signature, or return the measure with a veto message. The agency is required to do so within five days of receiving measures from Congress, in order to give the White House an additional five days to make a decision after its recommendations. When the OMB recommends that the president sign a measure, the president almost always does so. When it recommends a veto the picture is mixed: Eisenhower and Johnson tended to side with the bureau, while subsequent presidents have often gone against OMB recommendations.

The OMB does the staff work when a president prepares an executive order or proclamation. It coordinates all agency comments on the proposed orders, prepares its own analysis of the impact of the order, and makes its recommendation to the president.

The OMB recommends improvements in departmental operations. Its General Management Division, established in 1970, suggested changes in departmental operations. Between 1971 and 1973 OMB director Roy Ash was given a "second hat" as an assistant to the president in charge of management. Over the years the BOB and the OMB have promoted such concepts as "program budgeting," "cost-benefit" and "systems" analysis in the 1960s (using sophisticated quantitative tools to weigh costs against benefits in current and proposed programs), "Management by Objective" (a Ford initiative of 1975, developed by OMB director Frederick Malek, according to which agencies were encouraged to set goals), "zero-based budgeting" (a Carter innovation of 1977 according to which all activities were to be reviewed and justified annually), and Clinton's "total quality management" (an approach to improving operations taken from the corporate sector). The bureau has proposed information collection and management improvements as well as methods of assessing program performance and efficiency. Often its recommendations fell on deaf ears in the departments, though the OMB did provide some tangible budget incentives to go along with its recommendations for management improvements. In 1994, during the

Clinton administration, the management division was reintegrated into the budget division, and the two major units were then reorganized into five "resource management offices" (Natural Resources and Energy and Science, National Security and International Affairs, Health and Personnel, Human Resources, General Government) each headed by a program associate director. Each office is further subdivided into divisions headed by a deputy associate director, and each division subdivided into branches headed by an assistant director.

The OMB develops reorganization plans: President Carter created the President's Reorganization Project within the OMB, and it formulated ten plans designed to give the administration greater control over departments. President Reagan established an OMB Reform Task Force to implement "Reform '88," a special effort to establish more "businesslike" procedures in departments, to be implemented through the President's Council on Management Improvement.

The OMB's Office of Information and Regulatory Affairs reviews all regulations proposed by departments to see if they should go into effect (known as regulatory clearance). During the Bush administration the OMB was superseded by an unofficial regulatory review group headed by Vice President Dan Quayle; eventually Congress cut off funding for the officials in Quayle's group, and the OMB once again assumed primary responsibility for regulatory review.

The OMB's Division of Federal Procurement Policy recommends ways of cutting procurement costs, which are higher than in the private sector. In 1994 it participated in drafting the Federal Acquisition Streamlining Act, which made major savings in the cost of procurement in federal agencies, repealing or modifying more than 225 onerous contracting regulations that had formerly been imposed by Congress, promoting "electronic procurement" via e-mail (Federal Acquisitions Network, or Facnet), and promoting use of "off-the-shelf" commercial products rather than those made according to government specifications.

Harold Smith, an influential budget director during the New Deal, said in 1940 that "deciding basic policies is clearly outside the Bureau's role."

The "neutral competence" model of the budget agency did not survive into the 1960s, when the bureau became a policy advocate for the Great Society; since the Nixon era the OMB has functioned as a highly visible and politicized agency involved in presidential politics.

BIBLIOGRAPHY

Berman, Larry. *The Office of Management and Budget and the Presidency, 1921–1979.* Princeton, N.J., 1979.

Brundage, Percival. *The Bureau of the Budget.* New York, 1970.

Dawes, Charles. *The First Year of the Budget of the United States.* New York, 1923.

Fisher, Louis. *Presidential Spending Powers.* Princeton, N.J., 1975.

Ippolito, Daniel. *Uncertain Legacies: Federal Budget Policy from Roosevelt through Reagan.* Charlottesville, Va., 1990.

Rose, Richard. *Managing Presidential Objectives.* New York, 1976.

Schick, Allen. *The Federal Budget: Politics, Policy, Process.* Washington, D.C., 1994.

Willoughby, William F. *The Problem of a National Budget.* New York, 1918.

—RICHARD M. PIOUS

Marine Corps

The Continental Congress, following British "sea soldier" practice, authorized the raising of two battalions of marines for service with the Continental army on 10 November 1775. The date became the "Marine Corps birthday," observed worldwide by today's U.S. Marine Corps.

The two battalions were never fully raised, but marines recruited for the purpose, about three hundred in number, were deflected into service with Commodore Esek Hopkins's squadron being mounted out from Philadelphia in December 1775 for a raid into the Bahamas. These marines, under command of Captain Samuel Nicholas (regarded by the Marine Corps as its first "commandant"), landed successfully at Nassau on 3 March 1776, overrunning two small forts and capturing a significant amount of military stores.

It was taken for granted that all ships of any size in the Continental navy would have marine detachments. John Paul Jones used them especially well in the *Ranger* and *Bonhomme Richard.*

At home, a small party of marines fought at Princeton in January 1777. A larger number landed at Penobscot, Maine, in June 1779, an amphibious operation that ended disastrously because of quarreling between the land and sea commanders.

The Continental marines disappeared at the end of the Revolution, as did the Continental navy. Rebirth as the United States Marine Corps came by act of Congress on 11 July 1798. The new corps was to provide detachments for the new frigates being built and guards for naval bases ashore. This new Corps of Marines was uniformed in blue coats with red piping, colors that continue in today's dress uniforms. The fifers and drummers provided for in the act became the nucleus for what emerged in President Jefferson's administration as the Marine Band, the "President's Own."

Marines would share the glory in the romantic victories of the frigates, such as *Constitution* ("Old Ironsides"), in the Quasi-War with France (1798–1801), the Barbary Wars (1801–1815), and the more important Second War of Independence (1812–1815). The adventures of Lieutenant Presley O'Bannon in North Africa, where in 1805 he and seven marines marched with a polyglot "army" that successfully stormed the fortified Tripolitan city of Derna, became embedded in the legends of the Corps. The Marine Corps' officer's sword, adopted in 1826, is modeled after the Mameluke scimitar reputedly given O'Bannon for his exploits. In the War of 1812, marines, in addition to serving in the sea battles (including those on the Great Lakes), fought ashore, notably in the defense of Washington in August 1814 and at New Orleans in December 1814 and January 1815.

From then until the Civil War, the Marine Corps, which would seldom number as many as a thousand men, would be largely shaped by its longtime commandant, Archibald Henderson (1820–1859). Until the war with Mexico, the Marine Corps' service was chiefly seagoing, with adventures against "pirates" in the Caribbean and the Far East and operations against slave runners in the South Atlantic. The Mexican War (1846–1847) was particularly suited to the modest amphibious capabilities of the Corps, both in the

Gulf of Mexico and in the conquest of California.

Considering its successes in the Mexican War, the Marine Corps was curiously somnolent in the Civil War. Its chief service was to provide battalions for landings against the Confederacy, notably at Fort Hatteras (September 1861), New Orleans (April 1862), Charleston (1863–1864), and Fort Fisher (December 1864–January 1865).

After the Civil War, as the Navy converted from sail to steam, the Marine Corps struggled to redefine its purposes and uses. The so-called "Gilded Age" was marked by many small-scale landings by shipboard marines against smaller nations in response to real or perceived affronts to U.S. diplomatic or economic interests. This period also saw the adoption of the familiar "Eagle, Globe, and Anchor" insignia; the motto "Semper Fidelis," the tenure of John Philip Sousa as leader of the Marine Band, and the metamorphosis of the marching song "From the Halls of Montezuma" into "The Marines Hymn."

The war with Spain (1898) marked the beginning of the modern Marine Corps. Seizure of an advance naval base at Guantánamo, Cuba, by a Marine battalion captured the public's attention and became the prototype of many such amphibious assaults to come. During the period of imperialism following the war with Spain, the Marine Corps, at a strength of about five thousand, continued its expeditionary service to such places as China, Panama, Nicaragua, Cuba, Haiti, the Dominican Republic, and Vera Cruz, Mexico.

The National Defense Act of 1916 expanded the Marine Corps to an unprecedented strength of fifteen thousand. Propelled by its recruiting slogan, "First to Fight," the Marine Corps, after the declaration of war against Germany in April 1917, argued for and got a place for a regiment of marines in the first convoy to sail for France. Despite a lukewarm reception by General John J. Pershing, commanding general of the American Expeditionary Forces (AEF), the marines in France were built up to brigade strength. The big (nearly ten thousand men) Fourth Brigade of Marines, as one of two infantry brigades in the U.S. Second Division, AEF, attracted international attention with its bloody successes at Belleau Wood, Soissons, Saint-Mihiel, and the Meuse-Argonne. In its last battles of the war, the Second Division was commanded by Marine Major General John J. Lejeune.

Throughout World War I and after, the Marine Corps continued its shipboard duties, its guarding of naval bases, its brigade-size interventions in Haiti, Santo Domingo, and Nicaragua, and its largely parade-ground garrisons in Peking, Tientsin, and Shanghai, China. This was accomplished with a peacetime strength of from fifteen to twenty thousand marines.

Lejeune became commandant in 1921 and would so serve for nine years. His planners looked toward the Pacific and what was increasingly regarded as an inevitable war with Japan. The Orange Plan, the Army-Navy plan for such a war, foresaw the loss of the Philippines and little chance, in the initial stages, of holding a line west of Hawaii. The Navy saw subsequent operations as being essentially a naval campaign fought westward through the Central Pacific. Complementing this strategy, the Marine Corps saw its role as being initially *defensive,* holding what could be held, and then *offensive,* seizure of advanced naval bases to support the navy's drive across the Central Pacific.

Staff work, largely concentrated at Quantico, Virginia, then the Marine Corps' major East Coast base, developed a theoretical amphibious doctrine that was tested in a series of fleet exercises. Prototype landing craft and amphibian vehicles for the critical ship-to-shore movement were developed. In 1933 the Fleet Marine Force was formally organized with a brigade and aircraft group on the East and West Coasts. In early 1941 these were expanded into the First and Second Marine Divisions with accompanying First and Second Marine Aircraft Wings.

A provisional brigade was sent to Iceland in the summer of 1941 to relieve the British garrison. Defense battalions were formed and sent to Oahu, Palmyra, Johnson, Midway, and Wake islands in the Pacific. These defense battalions were hit heavily in the opening Japanese offensive of December 1941. In early 1942 provisional brigades were committed to the defense of Samoa. In May 1942 the First Marine Division deployed to New Zealand and on 7 August landed at Guadalcanal, marking the crossover from the strategic defensive to the offensive. Next in the Southwest Pacific came the Central Solomons, Bougainville, Cape Gloucester, and the reduction of Rabaul.

The Central Pacific offensive began in November 1943 with Tarawa in the Gilbert Islands and continued through the Marshalls, the Marianas (Saipan, Guam, and Tinian), Peleliu, Iwo Jima, and eventually, in April 1945, Okinawa. By then the Marine Corps had expanded to two amphibious corps totaling six divisions supported by five aircraft wings. Strength peaked at 485,000.

After the war the Marine Corps fought, seemingly for its life, in the unification struggle that eventuated in the National Defense Act of 1947. Budget cuts shriveled the Marine Corps by summer 1950 to 75,000 marines and two skeleton divisions and wings. A prevalent military opinion was that the atomic bomb had made future large-scale amphibious assaults impossible. The Marine Corps, in countering that opinion, sought means to achieve greater dispersion in the amphibious objective area and a swifter ship-to-shore movement. After some exploration of the possibilities of huge transport seaplanes and transport submarines, the Corps settled on a "vertical envelopment" concept centered on the use of helicopters, at that time still in their infancy.

Marine helicopters proved their practicality in the Korean War, not in a ship-to-shore movement, but in reconnaissance, medical evacuation, and limited movement of men and supplies. A provisional brigade was dispatched in July 1950 to help shore up the threatened Pusan Perimeter. On 15 September the First Marine Division, brought together on the battlefield, landed at Inchon in MacArthur's master stroke that turned the direction of the war. Marines would be embroiled in Korea for the next three years, including the epic withdrawal from Chosin Reservoir in late 1950. Marine Corps performance in the Korean War caused a friendly Congress in 1952 to establish a legislative floor of three divisions and wings for the active Marine Corps, with a fourth division and wing in the Reserve.

The late 1950s and early 1960s saw the maturing of Marine air-ground tactical concepts. Combined Marine air and ground task forces, known by their acronym, MAGTF ("Mag-taff"), were established at levels ranging from battalion/squadron to division/wing size. A Marine brigade equivalent of four battalions landed in Lebanon in 1958 in an almost blood-free shoring up of the Chamoun regime.

Marine involvement in Vietnam began in 1954 with the providing of "advisers" to the Vietnamese Marine Corps. The landing of the Ninth Marine Expeditionary Brigade at Danang in March 1965 marked the first significant introduction of U.S. ground forces.

Almost coincident with the Danang landing, in April 1965 a Marine brigade went ashore in the Dominican Republic in an intervention, initiated by the Johnson administration's fear of a Communist takeover. The intervention turned into a contest between two strategic mobility systems: Army–Air Force airlift vs. Navy–Marine Corps sealift.

The buildup in Vietnam continued. The Marine Corps would have a much larger percentage of its total strength involved than any of the other U.S. armed services. In 1968, at the peak of the war, III Marine Amphibious Force, employed in the northernmost five provinces, totaled eighty thousand marines, more than had been ashore at either Iwo Jima or Okinawa. Only a few set-piece battles, such as Khe Sanh and Hue City, were fought. In 1975, in the final days of the war, amphibious operations became critical to the evacuation of Phnom Penh and Saigon.

The Marine Corps during the Vietnam conflict, with the pressure of the draft, kept its ranks filled in numbers but not always in quality. Strength reached a peak of 350,000. During the early 1970s the Corps grappled with problems of drug abuse, drinking, racism, and unauthorized absence. In the postwar period the Marine Corps argued for an end-strength of 204,000 and settled for a manning level of about 196,000. By the beginning of the 1980s more stringent recruiting standards and more demanding training had improved quality immensely.

A North Atlantic Treaty Organization (NATO) mission was essential to get the dollars needed for force modernization. The Marine Corps concentrated on a reinforcing mission of NATO's northern flank—Norway and Denmark's Jutland peninsula. The United States and Norway agreed in 1982 to stock an "in-the-rock" mountain depot with supplies and equipment sufficient to support a Marine amphibious brigade. These would be exercised annually with a Marine brigade flown in for winter training exercises.

The introduction of "helicopter carriers," typified by the *Tarawa*-class, first commissioned in 1976 as the primary amphibious ships, revolutionized landing operations. But there could never be enough of these increasingly costly ships. By 1982 the Navy was down to sixty-seven amphibious ships.

In August of that year eight hundred marines landed in Lebanon as part of a multinational force (the other members were French, British, and Italian) to oversee the evacuation of several thousand members of the Palestine Liberation Organization who had concentrated in Beirut as a result of the Israeli invasion. This began the ill-defined "presence" of marines, chiefly at the Beirut International Airport. Several Marine amphibious units took their turn ashore. On early Sunday morning, 23 October 1983, a five-ton truck laden with explosives plunged under the building housing the headquarters of a battalion landing team. The explosion killed 241 Americans, 220 of them marines. In other incidents marines continued to die and be wounded in small numbers. In late February 1984 the marines were pulled out. The whole affair caused bitter recriminations and a reexamination of so-called "peacekeeping" missions.

Two days after the Beirut disaster, on 25 October 1983, a U.S. joint task force piled U.S. forces, including a Marine amphibious unit, onto the tiny island of Grenada to prevent a perceived Cuban-Communist takeover and to "rescue" some six hundred Americans, most of them medical students. Against minimal resistance by Grenada irregulars, a Marine battalion landing team helicopter-landed at Pearls Airport on the northeastern coast. In a five-day operation the marines proceeded south through seven-eighths of the island including the capital city of St. George's. Meanwhile, a much larger Army force—an airborne brigade and two ranger battalions—was bogged down near Point Salines, more by air traffic conditions at the uncompleted airfield than by the resistance posed by Cuban construction workers.

As a partial offset to the chronic shortage of amphibious shipping, the Marine Corps, although historically distrustful of forward-area logistical prepositioning, embraced the concept of "Maritime Prepositioned Shipping" (MPS). This would be a fleet of from thirteen to seventeen specially configured commercial ships organized into three squadrons. These squadrons had taken station in the eastern Atlantic, western Pacific, and Indian Ocean by 1986. Each was preloaded with the logistic support for a Marine amphibious brigade.

Marines would play only a minor role in Operation Just Cause, aimed at snatching Panama's dictator and drug dealer, General Manuel Antonio Noriega, after months of irritation. Triggered by the murder of a Marine lieutenant, the operation was launched during the early hours of 20 December 1989. In an operation carried out primarily by Army airborne troops and rangers, Marine Corps participation was limited to the 650 marines in the reinforced resident Marine Security Force Panama. The operation did give the Corps a chance to employ new light armored vehicles and its antiterrorist teams.

Since the end of World War II, and in some cases earlier, the Marine Corps has provided uniformed security detachments to American embassies and consulates around the world. In the 1990s there were some 140 such detachments, averaging about ten marines each, serving in some 120 countries. In the terrorist-ridden world of the late twentieth century these minuscule squads of marines were frequently the frontline protection for the American diplomatic community abroad.

The all-service Rapid Deployment Joint Task Force, originally intended for operations primarily in the Middle East ("from Marrakesh to Bangladesh"), was organized in 1980 and three years later became the U.S. Central Command. Command alternated between Army and Marine Corps generals.

On 7 August 1990, five days after Saddam Hussein's invasion of Kuwait, Colin L. Powell, chairman of the Joint Chiefs of Staff, ordered the movement of U.S. forces to the Persian Gulf. [*See* Joint Chiefs of Staff.] Three Marine expeditionary brigades, the Seventh at Twentynine Palms, California, the First in Hawaii, and the Fourth in North Carolina, were alerted for deployment. The Seventh and First moved by airlift, taking with them virtually nothing but their individual arms and equipment. MPS ships were to provide logistical wherewithal at the scene. The Fourth would move in amphibious shipping. The maritime prepositioning concept required a "benign" port for unloading. This was provided by the superbly modern port facilities bought by oil dollars in Saudi Arabia. The flow of marines to the Gulf continued, smaller units being combined with larger in a process called "compositing," until a I Marine Expeditionary Force was fully formed.

The I Marine Expeditionary Force, with two divisions, faced the supposedly formidable defensive line the Iraqis had constructed on the Kuwaiti–Saudi Arabian border. On 16 January 1991, D-day for Desert Storm, the air campaign against the Iraqis began. The Third Marine Aircraft Wing provided about one-quarter of the total fixed wing aircraft.

G-day, the day the ground campaign began, was 24 February. A month before that, on 29 January, marines had repelled three sizable Iraqi mechanized columns that had crossed the border near the coastal town of El Khafji. The first major ground move on G-day was the predawn jump-off of the First Marine Division, which went through the Iraqi fortifications with surprising ease. The Second Marine Division, on the left, in a deeper and wider move, had equal success. The marines' smashing of the Iraqi line caused General H. Norman Schwarzkopf, then commanding the U.S. Central Command, to advance the timing of his massive "Hail Mary" left hook by twenty-four hours. Meanwhile, Marine forces afloat were demonstrating against the Iraqi seaward flank. By the end of the hundred-hour war, the First Marine Division had paused at the outskirts of Kuwait City to allow Arab troops the honor of liberating the capital, and the Second Marine Division was north and west of the city, cutting off Iraqi routes of escape. Marine forces, including two divisions, two amphibious brigades, an amphibious unit, a very large aircraft

wing, and a force logistic command, totaled nearly ninety-three thousand, making it the largest Marine Corps combat operation in history.

Marines of the I Marine Expeditionary Force landed in Somalia in December 1992 as part of a U.S. Joint Task Force, seizing the Mogadishu airport and port complex. What began as a humanitarian mission turned into an antiterrorist campaign. However, by early May 1993 most marines were out of the troubled country. Two Marine expeditionary units again took station off the Somali coast in October 1993 to add protection to the U.S. forces still ashore. These marines covered the withdrawal of U.S. forces from Somalia, with all U.S. troops withdrawn by the end of March 1994.

In September 1994 a Marine special MAGTF landed and secured Cap Haitien in the north of Haiti. Meanwhile, larger U.S. Army formations executed the main effort at Port-au-Prince to dislodge dictator Raoul Cedras and reinstate President Jean-Bertrand Aristide.

Throughout the remainder of the 1990s the Corps strained to maintain an unprecedented level of peacetime readiness. The "downsizing" by the Clinton administration of the armed services reduced the Corps to about 175,000 marines. Even with these numbers the Corps could argue persuasively that it was the armed force that could best project American power onto hostile shores.

[*See also* Navy, Department of the.]

BIBLIOGRAPHY

Alexander, Joseph H. *Utmost Savagery: The Three Days of Tarawa*. Annapolis, 1995.
Asprey, Robert B. *At Belleau Wood*. New York, 1965.
Frank, Benis M. *U.S. Marines in Lebanon, 1982–1984*. Washington, D.C., 1987.
Griffith, Samuel B. *The Battle for Guadalcanal*. New York, 1963.
Hammel, Eric. *Chosin: Heroic Ordeal of the Korean War*. New York, 1981.
Hammel, Eric. *Khe Sanh*. New York, 1989.
Heinl, Robert D., Jr. *Soldiers of the Sea: The U.S. Marine Corps, 1775–1962*. Annapolis, 1962.
Heinl, Robert D. *Victory at High Tide: The Inchon-Seoul Campaign*. Philadelphia, 1968.
Isely, Jeter A., and Philip A. Crowl. *The U.S. Marines and Amphibious War: Its Theory and Practice in the Pacific*. Princeton, N.J., 1951.

Krulak, Victor H. *First to Fight: An Inside View of the U.S. Marine Corps.* Annapolis, 1984.

Leckie, Robert. *Strong Men Armed: The United States Marines against Japan.* New York, 1962.

Lejeune, John A. *The Reminiscences of a Marine.* Philadelphia, 1930.

Melson, Charles D., Evelyn A. Englander, and David A. Dawson, compilers. *U.S. Marines in the Persian Gulf, 1990–1991: Anthology and Annotated Bibliography.* Washington, D.C., 1992.

Mersky, Peter B. *U.S. Marine Corps Aviation: 1912 to the Present.* Baltimore, 1987.

Metcalf, Clyde H. *A History of the United States Marine Corps.* New York, 1939.

Millett, Allan R. *Semper Fidelis: The History of the United States Marine Corps.* New York, 1980, 1991.

Montross, Lynn. *Cavalry of the Sky: The Story of U.S. Marine Helicopters.* New York, 1954.

Moran, John B., compiler. *Creating a Legend.* Chicago, 1973.

Moskin, J. Robert. *The U.S. Marine Corps Story.* New York, 1977, 1992.

Musicant, Ivan. *The Banana Wars.* New York, 1990.

Quilter, Charles J., II. *With the I Marine Expeditionary Force in Desert Shield and Desert Storm.* Washington, D.C., 1993.

Rankin, Robert H. *Uniforms of Marines.* New York, 1970.

Ross, Bill D. *Iwo Jima: Legacy of Valor.* New York, 1985.

Sherrod, Robert. *Tarawa: The Story of a Battle.* New York, 1944.

Sherrod, Robert. *History of Marine Corps Aviation in World War II.* Washington, D.C., 1952.

Simmons, Edwin H. *The United States Marines: The First Two Hundred Years, 1775–1975.* New York, 1976.

Simmons, Edwin H., et al. *The Marines in Vietnam, 1954–1973: An Anthology and Annotated Bibliography.* Washington, D.C., 1974.

Sledge, Eugene B. *With the Old Breed at Peleliu and Okinawa.* Novato, Calif., 1981.

Smith, Charles R. *Marines in the Revolution: A History of the Continental Marines in the American Revolution.* Washington, D.C., 1975.

Spector, Ronald H. *U.S. Marines in Grenada.* Washington, D.C., 1987.

Spector, Ronald H. *After Tet: The Bloodiest Year in Vietnam.* New York, 1993.

Thomason, John W., Jr. *Fix Bayonets!* New York, 1926.

—EDWIN H. SIMMONS

Maritime Administration

An agency of the Department of Transportation since 1981, the Maritime Administration (MARAD) is responsible for overseeing and promoting the U.S. maritime industry and interests.

As the needs of the nation have changed over the years, so have the name and the responsibilities of the agency.

MARAD's origins can be traced to the United States Shipping Board, created by the Shipping Act of 1916. The board was an independent agency of the executive branch with regulatory, investigatory, and quasi-judicial functions related to maritime operations. It was also directed to promote the growth of the maritime industry. The board was composed of five commissioners appointed by the president to six-year terms, with no more than three members belonging to the same political party. The board selected its own chairman.

The board's duties were varied. It was responsible for building, buying, and leasing merchant vessels for use by the U.S. armed forces. When these vessels were not in use by the government, the board was permitted, under terms approved by the president, to charter or lease the vessels. Eventually, and under the same approved terms, the board could sell vessels in its possession when they became unfit for use. During times of war or national emergency, board approval was needed for the sale of a U.S. vessel to a foreign citizen or organization or the transfer of an American vessel to foreign registry (the registration of a U.S.-owned vessel in a foreign nation). At all times, the board was empowered to investigate the cost of building vessels in the United States and abroad, the problems related to navigational laws and marine insurance, and the legal status of mortgage loans on vessels. In addition, it held the power to request the issuing of bonds when necessary.

In terms of regulatory oversight, the shipping board had broad powers. It was charged with the responsibility of approving, disapproving, and, when it deemed necessary, modifying carrier agreements as they related to interstate and foreign maritime commerce. It could readjust carrier rates it felt were discriminatory as well as issue new or revised regulations related to waterborne traffic. It was the board that determined how and when carriers had to file their schedule of rates, fares, and charges, and it had to approve any variations of those filings before they could take effect.

Almost immediately the board's main focus became the urgent need to produce vessels supplying matériel for the war in Europe and to prepare for America's eventual entry in the conflict. One of the broad powers of the board was the authority to form a corporation for the "purchase, construction, equipment, lease, charter, maintenance and operation of merchant vessels in the commerce of the United States" (Shipping Act of 1916). On 16 April 1917 the board established the Emergency Fleet Corporation (EFC). To assist the EFC in its efforts the board requested and received a presidential embargo on the transfer of any U.S.-flagged vessel to foreign registry. At the board's urging the Senate passed a resolution authorizing the president to seize any vessel in its jurisdiction that was owned wholly or in part by a citizen or corporation of a nation at war with the United States. In June 1917 President Wilson issued an order for the board to seize and take title to eighty-eight vessels. The corporation also began an aggressive shipbuilding effort, and by the end of the war an average of forty steel and ninety wooden ships were being built in shipyards every month.

But with the end of World War I came the end to the mass production, and with the new administration came a more relaxed policy toward government action in the economic and business arenas. The size and condition of the U.S. merchant fleet began to decline. And in the early years of the Depression resources were directed elsewhere. This postwar laissez-faire attitude of the government toward the maritime industry and the problems of the Great Depression left the American maritime industry in a very poor state by the mid-1930s. President Roosevelt, an assistant secretary of the Navy during World War I, fully appreciated the need for a strong merchant fleet, and with the growing troubles in Europe he knew America would soon have need of that strength.

At his urging, Congress passed the Merchant Marine Act of 1936, creating the United States Maritime Commission as an independent agency and dissolving the United States Shipping Board. The commission was given the responsibilities and powers of the now-defunct shipping board. While its mission and composition were almost identical to the board's, there were some important differences. First, the chairman was chosen not by the commission, but by the president. (President Roosevelt designated Joseph P. Kennedy, father of the future president, as the first chairman of the commission.) The most important difference, however, was the way the government would subsidize the merchant fleet.

Recognizing that it was necessary to maintain an active fleet in peacetime so that defense needs could be met in times of war, the government had been awarding mail delivery contracts to subsidize the shipping lines. But problems had arisen over the size and scope of the contracts, creating turmoil and embitterment with the program. Under the 1936 act, the commission would award direct monetary subsidies to the shipping lines. In return the commission would have approval rights over certain business practices under the act and could call upon the vessels in times of war or national emergency.

As with the old board, the commission was soon distracted from its oversight of normal carrier operations and forced to begin preparations for America's impending entry into the war in Europe. Once again regulatory concerns were shelved and a massive shipbuilding program was begun. In this endeavor the commission made a vital contribution to the war effort. Unlike the other services, the U.S. Merchant Marine became involved in the fighting long before 7 December 1941. Through various aid and lease programs the United States began sending the French and British supplies and munitions in 1939. Although the U.S. and German governments had yet to formally declare war upon each other, the German navy—its U-boats in particular—had declared war on American vessels supplying the Allies. Even after America's formal entry into World War II, the German naval attacks took a heavy toll. By the end of hostilities, the U.S. Merchant Marine had suffered heavy casualties, with seven hundred vessels sunk and more than sixty-seven hundred lives lost at sea.

As with all aspects of the home front war effort, the shipbuilders were under pressure to replace these losses. In the end, roughly seven thousand "Victory" and "Liberty" ships had been constructed, and shortly after the war the United

States could boast of a merchant fleet thirty-three hundred ships strong.

With the end of World War II and the return to normal business operations, concerns were raised both within Congress and the Truman administration over the wide scope of the commission's jurisdiction. It was proposed that the promotional aspects and regulatory function of the commission be separated. In 1950, under Reorganization Plan No. 21, the commission, like its predecessor, was abolished and its duties transferred to the newly created MARAD and the Federal Maritime Board, both new agencies of the Department of Commerce.

The Federal Maritime Board consisted of three commissioners appointed by the president, who also designated the chairman. The Maritime Board was given most of the commission's commercial regulatory functions. It oversaw the filings of rates and routes; carrier agreements, schedules and fares; and issues pertaining to maritime insurance. It continued to run the direct subsidy programs to U.S. shipping lines and operated the shipbuilding programs. MARAD became responsible for the remainder of the commission's duties, primarily that as promoter of the U.S. maritime industry.

But from the outset there were problems. Very early on, it became readily apparent that the division between these agencies was a false one. The Federal Maritime Board chairman was also the maritime administrator, and under Section 302 of Reorganization Plan No. 21 he was directed to make "joint use of the officers and employees of the agencies" in order to save on expenditures. Soon the chairman became too engaged in the business of the Maritime Board to properly execute his duties as maritime administrator, and so he delegated much of that work to the deputy administrator. In time the commissioners began to argue with each other over the direction of the board, and regulatory activity slowed considerably.

In 1961 the Kennedy administration expressed concern with the situation. There were questions as to whether it was proper for an agency to be responsible for regulating foreign commerce at the same time that it operated a ship subsidy program. A new reorganization plan was issued to completely sever the relationship between the two functions and agencies. Reorganization Plan No. 7 of 1961 dissolved the Federal Maritime Board and divided its duties between MARAD and a newly formed independent agency, the Federal Maritime Commission (FMC). The FMC was granted regulatory duties regarding foreign and domestic waterborne commerce; carrier agreements; rate, route, and scheduling filings; tariffs; and licensing. The FMC consists of five commissioners appointed by the president, who also designates the chairman.

With the passage of the Maritime Act of 1981, MARAD was transferred to the Department of Transportation in order to facilitate management of the nation's transportation concerns. Currently MARAD is responsible for much the same issues that faced the original Shipping Board. MARAD continues to administer subsidy payments to shipping lines and provide loan guarantees for construction and repairs in U.S. shipyards. MARAD manages a cargo preference program that guarantees that a certain percentage of U.S. aid shipments will be sent on American merchant vessels, and it maintains the National Defense Reserve Fleet, vessels available for government service in times of need, as well as the Ready Reserve Fleet (RRF), vessels maintained by the government at a heightened state of readiness for periods of five, ten, or thirty days. (Components of the RRF were used in the Persian Gulf War of 1991.) MARAD also operates the U.S. Merchant Marine Academy, one of the nation's four service academies, at Kings Point, New York, and provides federal assistance to state-run maritime academies in California, Maine, Massachusetts, Michigan, New York, and Texas.

[See also Maritime Commission, Federal.]

BIBLIOGRAPHY

Kessler, Ronald. Sins of the Father: Joseph P. Kennedy and the Dynasty He Founded. New York, 1996.

Smith, Darrell Hevenor, and Paul Betters. "The United States Shipping Board." Service monograph. Washington, D.C., 1931.

Tindall, George Brown. America: A Narrative History. New York, 1984.

U.S. Congress. House. Committee on Merchant Marine and Fisheries. Jones Act Waivers and the National Defense Reserve Fleet. Serial No. 103-53. Washington D.C., 1993.

U.S. Congress. House. *The Merchant Marine Act of 1936 and Related Acts.* Serial No. 103-A. Washington D.C., 1993.

The United States Government Manual 1995/96. Washington, D.C., 1995.

Whitnah, Donald R. *Government Agencies.* London, 1983.

—DAVID HONNESS

Maritime Commission, Federal

Created by Reorganization Plan No. 7 of 1961 as an independent agency of the executive branch, the Federal Maritime Commission (FMC) is responsible for ensuring that oceangoing foreign and domestic commerce is maintained under fair and open conditions. Its primary responsibility is to regulate and oversee steamship conferences and common carriers to prevent discriminatory rates and unreasonable competition. The president appoints five commissioners for rotating six-year terms. The president designates the chairman when making the appointment, and no more than three members of the same political party may serve at one time. The FMC's role is crucial because carriers were given an exemption to antitrust laws in the formation of conferences. In exchange for the exemption, the FMC must approve much of the conferences' operations.

A "conference" is made up of two or more operators in the same trade who come together to stabilize prices and set mutually agreed-upon rates for freight and passenger fares. The conference submits documentation outlining its scope and objectives and submits it to the FMC. The FMC will assign the agreement to an administrative law judge, who will review the documentation after holding public hearings and then make a recommendation to the commissioners. The commissioners can then accept, reject, or amend the agreement as they see fit. Final action on the agreement must be taken by a vote of all five commissioners. The operators may not conduct business as a conference until the FMC has made its final decision, under penalty of heavy fines for violations.

Once a conference is approved and a chairman selected, public notification is made. Throughout the conference's continued operation, the chairman must supply the FMC with copies of minutes of all conference meetings. The conference is also responsible for supplying various business information to the FMC, referred to as "filings." The conference must file all freight and passenger tariffs and any proposed changes to previously approved tariffs, schedules of operation, and route information. It must also supply copies of any material made available to the general public. There is one exception to the conference's notification requirement: while it must submit a request and await approval for any increase in freight rates, it may reduce rates effective at the time of filing with the commission.

Conferences operate under a "dual-rate system." The conference seeks a binding agreement with shippers to patronize its members and in exchange offers the shipper a lower rate than that of a nonconference carrier. This is legal under the conference agreement as long as it is not discriminatory or used in an effort to selectively put a nonconference competitor out of business. This "exclusive patronage contract" must be approved before it is offered to the general public. Any shipper or independent carrier who has a grievance with a conference can file a protest with the FMC, which will assign the case to an administrative law judge for investigation and a recommendation. Action on such a filing can take a year or more.

A second type of multicarrier association the FMC must regulate is a "pool" agreement. Under such an agreement carriers agree to pool their earnings into a mutual account and distribute the proceeds on a percentage basis according to the percentage of tonnage transported in a given period. As with conferences, pooling agreements must be filed and approved by the commission.

In the pursuit of its responsibilities the FMC attempts to regulate foreign as well as domestic carriers engaged in commerce with the United States, making it the only agency in the world that attempts to supervise carriers of foreign nations as well as its own. This has led to protests by foreign nations on occasion. The FMC is also responsible for approving and issuing maritime licenses for ocean freight forwarding, investigating foreign government practices that hinder the operations of the U.S. shipping trade, and ensuring that owners and operators maintain proper passenger indemnity and certificates of financial responsibility to guarantee the payment of compensation to passengers in cases of injury, loss of life, or in the event of cancellations or interruptions of service.

Before 1961 the powers and responsibilities of the FMC were held by a succession of agencies that evolved into what is now the Maritime Administration. The Shipping Act of 1916 established the United States Shipping Board, an independent government agency responsible for regulating oceanborne commerce as well as promoting the U.S. maritime industry. Shortly after the board's formation it became heavily involved in the effort to procure and construct vessels to aid the nation's efforts during World War I. In the years that followed there was little regulatory oversight, and the Great Depression had a devastating effect on the American merchant fleet.

At President Roosevelt's urging, the Congress acted to rectify this situation by dissolving the board and ceding its responsibilities to a new independent agency, the U.S. Maritime Commission, first chaired by Joseph P. Kennedy, father of the president who would create the FMC. Like the Shipping Board, the new commission soon became involved in preparations for European conflict. While performing its duties admirably, the commission's primary focus was the production of merchant vessels called "Victory" and "Liberty" ships to supply the war effort.

In the early years following World War II, concerns were raised about the divided mission of the commission. In an effort to address these concerns President Truman issued Reorganization Plan No. 21 of 1950, abolishing the commission and dividing its duties between the newly created Maritime Administration, which would oversee the promotion of American maritime interests, and the Federal Maritime Board, which would continue to oversee the regulatory and operational aspects of the U.S. Merchant Marine.

This arrangement proved to be problematic. The firewall created between these two new agencies of the Department of Commerce proved to be a false one. The Maritime administrator was also the chairman of the Federal Maritime Board. In addition, several other employees acted as agents for both organizations. This created a diversion of attention and a slowdown of the regulatory and operational effectiveness of both agencies. There were also concerns about an agency's operating a subsidy program and overseeing international commerce at the same time.

To solve these problems President Kennedy broke the ties between the agencies and moved the regulatory functions for oceanborne carriers out of the Department of Commerce. Reorganization Plan No. 7 of 1961 eliminated the Federal Maritime Board and transferred its ship subsidy, shipbuilding, and other promotional and support operations to the Maritime Administration. Its other regulatory functions were given to the newly created Federal Maritime Commission. The current division of maritime oversight between the Maritime Administration and the Federal Maritime Commission has lasted for over thirty-five years, the longest period without organizational reform of the federal government's regulation of the maritime industry in the twentieth century.

[See also Maritime Administration.]

BIBLIOGRAPHY

Kessler, Ronald. Sins of the Father: Joseph P. Kennedy and the Dynasty He Founded. New York, 1996.
Smith, Darrell Hevenor, and Paul Betters. "The United States Shipping Board." Service monograph. Washington, D.C., 1931.
U.S. Congress. House. Committee on Merchant Marine and Fisheries. The Merchant Marine Act of 1936 and Related Acts. Serial No. 103-A. Washington, D.C., 1993.
The United States Government Manual 1995/96. Washington, D.C., 1995.
Whitnah, Donald R. Government Agencies. London, 1983.

—DAVID HONNESS

Marshals Service

The Judiciary Act of 1789 created the offices of United States marshal and deputy United States marshal, thus intimately tying both the function and the history of each office to the federal judicial system. From the first, the president appointed one U.S. marshal to each federal judicial district. Each marshal then hired as many deputies as the work in the district could support. Marshals served four-year terms at the pleasure of the president; deputies served at the pleasure of the marshal or (as a safeguard against miscreant marshals employing corrupt deputies) the district judge. A $20,000 bond posted by each marshal gave surety against any improprieties by either the marshal or his deputies.

The act assigned the marshals two responsibilities: "to attend the federal courts" sitting in their judicial districts and "to execute all lawful precepts [written orders] issued under the authority of the United States." In executing these duties, the marshals could "command all necessary assistance" from the community by forming citizen posses. The broad sweep of the law's language disguised the crucial role played by the marshals in the original judicial system. "Attending" the courts meant the marshals took care of all the necessary arrangements. They managed the court's money, leased the courtrooms, bought the firewood, filled the water pitchers, hired the bailiffs and court criers, hauled in the prisoners, and protected the judges, witnesses, and jurors from angry litigants and outraged defendants.

Executing precepts imbued the marshals with even more authority. Until the twentieth century, most federal law enforcement officers—customs agents, revenuers, and postal inspectors, for example—did not have the authority to arrest lawbreakers. They had to take their suspicions and accusations to the U.S. attorney, who applied to the judiciary for an arrest warrant, one of the many precepts executed by the marshals. Everyone then waited for the marshal to effect the arrest. The marshals then held the prisoner in custody, usually by leasing jail space from the local sheriffs, until the accused's acquittal or delivery to the penitentiary.

In 1792 Congress recognized that certain emergencies outpaced the slow process which it had devised. With no federal official empowered to make an arrest without a warrant, felons had plenty of opportunity to escape. To deal with problems such as these, Congress empowered each marshal with the same powers and authority enjoyed by the sheriffs in their district. The effect was to make the marshals federal peace of-

ficers, with full authority to arrest on probable cause alone.

The marshals paid a price for their broad powers. On 11 January 1794 U.S. Marshal Robert Forsyth (1789–1794) of Georgia was shot and killed while trying to execute a legal precept. Forsyth was the first marshal—and probably the first federal law enforcement officer—killed in the line of duty. Since Forsyth, as many as three hundred marshals have been killed enforcing federal law, a staggeringly high figure that further underscores their central role in the federal judicial system.

NINETEENTH-CENTURY DUTIES

The process of accusation, warrant, and then arrest remained the government's principal law enforcement system throughout the nineteenth century. As long as federal law severely restricted criminal violations to but a handful of offenses, it worked. Executing these and other court orders also involved the U.S. marshals in a fascinating array of events. U.S. Marshal David Lenox's (1793–1795) efforts to summons delinquent taxpayers into court sparked the violent consummation of the Whisky Rebellion in 1794. Under the infamous Alien and Sedition Acts of 1798, marshals arrested citizens who dared criticize federal officials or authority. During the War of 1812 (and again in World War I), marshals registered enemy aliens and imprisoned in special camps those who were suspected of espionage or sabotage. Marshals tried to block the myriad filibustering expeditions of armed mercenaries against neutral South American nations and enforced the laws banning the African slave trade. They sold at auction Africans seized from illegal slave ships.

The marshals also tracked down counterfeiters, and during the 1850s they enforced the roundly hated Fugitive Slave Act by returning escaped slaves to their southern masters. During the Civil War marshals in the North seized the property of Confederate sympathizers. After the war marshals throughout the South protected the newly freed slaves from the Ku Klux Klan and other violent groups of recalcitrant southerners. They also fought illicit distillers in the famous Moonshine Wars. Since the marshals alone enjoyed arrest authority, a deputy marshal usually accompanied the revenuers. The tax men seized the stills, the marshals the moonshiners. For their services, marshals were paid specific fees for each type of precept they served or for each day they physically attended a session of court.

Since the marshals also provided the new federal government with its only nationwide regional structure, they also ended up carrying out a curious assortment of administrative tasks. From 1790 through 1870 the marshals took the constitutionally mandated decennial census of the population. [*See* Census, Bureau of the.] On other occasions marshals distributed presidential proclamations, summoned congressmen to special sessions of Congress, maintained lists of local federal employees, registered enemy aliens during times of war, and compiled information on the type and diversity of industries within their districts. In 1841 U.S. Marshal Alexander Hunter of the District of Columbia (1834–1848) even handled the funeral arrangements for President William Henry Harrison, the first president to die in office. Similarly, in 1865 U.S. Marshal Ward Hill Lamon of the District of Columbia (1861–1863) escorted the body of his friend and former law partner, Abraham Lincoln, home to Springfield, Illinois.

MARSHALS IN THE TERRITORIES

The role of the territorial marshals constituted that of the federal courts. In the unorganized territories, the courts sat as district or circuit courts hearing all manner of cases. Marshals were the only lawmen. They essentially introduced law to the territory, chasing murderers, thieves, brigands, rapists, robbers, and embezzlers. In the Indian Territory alone, U.S. marshals hauled hundreds of outlaws before "Hanging Judge" Isaac Parker (1875–1896). The judge sentenced 160 of them to death; the marshals actually hanged 79.

Once the government organized the territory, the federal courts acted in a dual capacity. They continued to sit as federal courts hearing federal issues, but with the rap of the judge's gavel they transformed themselves into territorial courts hearing cases on appeal. The marshals supported the courts in their federal capacity and, at the behest of the territorial legislature, could also act as an officer of the territorial court. As the individual territory passed through the organized

stage toward statehood, the marshals surrendered their authority to territorial sheriffs and town marshals. As the territory verged on statehood, the marshals were usually concerned solely with the federal courts and federal laws.

Many sheriffs and town marshals also served as federal deputy marshals. The double office gave the lawmen considerable authority, as well as the opportunity to earn extra fees. In October 1882 Virgil Earp (1843–1905) was the town marshal of Tombstone, Arizona, and a deputy U.S. marshal of the Arizona Territory. When he, his brothers, and Doctor John ("Doc") Holliday gunned down the Clantons and McLaurys just down the street from the O.K. Corral, they were exercising Virgil's authority as town marshal. Their excuse was their opponents' violation of Tombstone's gun laws; their intent was murder.

Frontier lawmen frequently moved from one office to the other with disconcerting frequency. James Butler ("Wild Bill") Hickok (1837–1876) worked sometimes as town marshal, sometimes as a deputy U.S. marshal, depending on who would hire him. Pat Garrett (1850–1908) moved from deputy U.S. marshal of the New Mexico Territory to sheriff of Lincoln County and back again, forever clouding by what authority he killed William H. ("Billy the Kid") Bonney (1859–1881). Almost as frequently, frontier lawmen worked both sides of the law. The Dalton brothers worked as deputy U.S. marshals of the Indian Territory until Frank Dalton (d. 1887) was killed in the line of duty. His death apparently convinced his brothers that they could, for the same risk, reap higher profits as outlaws than as lawmen. Even Billy the Kid, notoriously disrespectful of the law, rode in a deputy marshal's posse early in the Lincoln County cattle war.

TWENTIETH-CENTURY DUTIES

Toward the end of the nineteenth century, federal power dramatically widened its embrace, ultimately encroaching almost every aspect of the lives of the citizenry, from inspecting the food and drugs people consumed to guaranteeing them a minimum wage, then taxing their personal incomes. Federal law enforcement kept pace with the expansion in federal power. The marshals could not.

Consequently, Congress began empowering

federal agents with specific arrest authority, thus sparing them from having to wait on the marshals to make arrests. Secret Service operatives and customs agents gained it early (1865 and 1866, respectively), while other officers waited longer. Postal agents got arrest powers in 1896, and agents of the Federal Bureau of Investigation were so empowered in 1934. The list kept growing until, in 1993, Vice President Al Gore counted more than 140 federal agencies assigned some responsibility for enforcing forty-one hundred federal criminal laws.

Although their monopoly on arrest authority was broken, the marshals retained the broadest law enforcement responsibilities within the federal system. Still charged with attending the federal courts, the marshals took greater and more sophisticated measures to ensure judicial security. They electronically fortified the federal courthouses with alarms, X-ray machines, and magnetometers and provided teams of deputies to personally protect threatened judicial officials.

Still charged, too, with executing precepts, the marshals kept custody of all federal prisoners, no matter who effected the arrest, until acquittal or delivery to prison. Marshals seized the ill-gotten gains of drug dealers and organized criminals and pursued fugitives from federal justice. The marshals, too, executed a startling array of federal court orders. They enforced the integration of Southern schools and colleges—perhaps most famously James Meredith's (1933–) attendance at the University of Mississippi during 1962–63–compelled mandatory busing, and in 1995 escorted Shannon Faulkner, the first female cadet, onto the campus of the Citadel in Charleston, South Carolina.

ORGANIZATIONAL AUTONOMY

Originally, the secretary of state loosely supervised the work of the disparate marshals. The attorney general was literally the government's attorney and did not have a managerial role. By the 1850s, however, presidents were relying on their lawyer not only for legal advice but for guidance on enforcing the law as well. Slowly, the attorneys general began to oversee the marshals and U.S. attorneys. In 1861 Congress confirmed this trend with special legislation as-

signing the attorney general full supervision over both offices. Nine years later it created the Department of Justice and folded the district offices into it.

The marshals retained considerable independence within their districts. Their oversight by the department was general, not detailed. In 1896 Congress finally abolished the fee system and put both the marshals and their deputies on a salary. Since the department was now paying for the deputies, it began to take an interest in who the marshal hired, initially by requiring the marshal to report on each person and ultimately by insisting on approving each candidate. In 1956 the department established an Executive Office of U.S. Marshals, staffed with a half-dozen people, to help oversee the district marshals.

Six years later, concerned about potential southern opposition to desegregation, President John F. Kennedy appointed James J. P. McShane, a former New York City homicide detective, as chief U.S. marshal and head of the executive office. McShane's principal responsibility was to put together the teams of deputies sent throughout the South to escort black students into all-white schools. In 1969 Attorney General John Mitchell approved the establishment of the U.S. Marshals Service as a departmental agency charged with superintending and coordinating the district U.S. marshals. Headed by a director, the service took control over budget and personnel (except the selection of the presidentially appointed U.S. marshals). In 1974 the service was made a full-fledged bureau within the department. Fourteen years later, in 1988, the service's bureau status and principal duties were embedded in law. After more than 150 years of nearly complete autonomy, the district marshals were integrated into a national law enforcement organization.

To this day, that organization retains striking characteristics of its past and traditions. District operations are marked by a streak of independence forever challenging national management. The diverse tasks confronting the marshals bred diverse talents, giving the organization enormous flexibility and innovation. At the same time, deep within the service lay buried the sense that somehow the marshals had peaked a century earlier when the Earps shot it out with the Clantons and McLaurys and Wild Bill Hickok held eights and aces.

BIBLIOGRAPHY

Ball, Larry D. *The United States Marshals of New Mexico and Arizona Territories, 1846–1912.* Albuquerque, 1978.

Calhoun, Frederick S. *The Lawmen: United States Marshals and Their Deputies, 1789–1989.* Washington, D.C., 1990.

Prassel, Frank Richard. *The Western Peace Officer: A Legacy of Law and Order.* Norman, Okla., 1972.

Shirley, Glenn. *Law West of Fort Smith: A History of Frontier Justice in the Indian Territory, 1834–1896.* Lincoln, Neb., 1968.

—FREDERICK S. CALHOUN

Mediation Board, National

Established in 1934 by an amendment to the Railway Labor Act, the National Mediation Board (NMB) is composed of three members appointed for three-year terms by the president and confirmed by the Senate. The board mediates disputes between rail and air carriers and their employees. The NMB may respond to a request for mediation by the employers or employees and their unions, or it may initiate proceedings on its own. If the board is unsuccessful in its efforts at mediation, it may persuade both parties to submit to arbitration. If arbitration is not acceptable to either party, the board may impose a thirty-day cooling-off period. If such a dispute seriously threatens interstate commerce, the board notifies the president who, in turn, appoints an emergency board to investigate the dispute. Strikes are banned during the investigation. Individual grievances in the railroad industry are handled by the National Railroad Adjustment Board. There is no similar provision for the airline industry.

—GEORGE THOMAS KURIAN

Minerals Management Service

Established in 1982 as an agency within the Department of the Interior, the Minerals Manage-

ment Service (MMS) is headed by a director who is appointed by the secretary of the Interior. The MMS is responsible for collecting revenues generated from mining leases offshore and on federal and Indian lands through the Royalty Management Program. Through the Offshore Minerals Management Program the service develops offshore mineral and energy resources while safeguarding the environment. The royalties collected by the MMS are distributed to Indian tribes and allotted to the states in which the minerals were found. A portion of the funds goes to the U.S. Treasury.

—GEORGE THOMAS KURIAN

Minority Business Development.

See Commerce, Department of.

Mint, U.S.

"The Congress shall have Power . . . To coin Money." The United States Mint, a unit of the Treasury Department, is the agency that fulfills this constitutional directive. The Mint has two primary missions: producing coins for the nation's money supply and safeguarding the nation's monetary stocks of gold, silver, and other monetary assets. The Mint is responsible for distributing coins to the Federal Reserve Banks and branches, which circulate coins to the public through banks. The U.S. Mint is the world's largest coin-producing enterprise and one of the few government agencies producing a profit from its operations. In addition, the Mint manufactures and sells a variety of numismatic coins, American eagle gold and silver bullion coins, and national and historic medals.

Mint headquarters are located in Washington, D.C. Mints are in Philadelphia, Denver, San Francisco, and West Point, New York. The Mint is responsible for the Bullion Depository in Fort Knox, Kentucky, where the nation's gold bullion is stored.

The only colony to establish a mint was Massachusetts. The first mint in the United States began operation in 1652 and produced pine tree shillings until 1684, when the Crown closed the mint. It took several attempts before a mint was finally established by the federal government more than one hundred years later.

Robert Morris, Thomas Jefferson, and Alexander Hamilton were responsible for the Mint and the world's first adoption of a currency based on the decimal system. In 1776 the Continental Congress received appeals to establish a mint. On 20 February 1777 the Congress recommended that "a Mint be forthwith established for coining money" (*Journals of the Continental Congress*, vol. 7, p. 138). The project was abandoned. On 3 September 1780, and again on 30 April 1781 in a letter to Robert Morris, Alexander Hamilton proposed a mint as an annex to a national bank.

Robert Morris, superintendent of finance (1781–1784) under the Articles of Confederation, recommended the adoption of an American coin, was the first to suggest a system of decimal coinage, and proposed the establishment of a mint in his report of 15 January 1782. On 21 February 1782 Congress approved the establishment of a mint and directed the superintendent to prepare a plan. Morris prepared specimen coins in April 1783 whose design included the first use of the words *Libertas* ("Liberty") and *U S* on a proposed national coin.

On 5 August 1783 a committee directed Morris "to lay before Congress an Estimate of the expence which will attend the establishment of a mint including Buildings, Tools, Salaries to officers, etc." (*Journals of the Continental Congress*, vol. 24, p. 487). Congress did not act on the committee's report, thus ending Morris's attempts to establish a mint.

Thomas Jefferson returned to Congress in November 1783. Appointed chairman of the currency committee, he learned of Morris's plan. Between March and May 1784 Jefferson prepared his own plan in *Notes on Coinage*. These notes do not outline a mint but present a clear and simple alternative of a unit of account based on the Spanish dollar to Morris's cumbersome unit of account based on the English pound.

Jefferson called for a decimal system and a unit of money that was close in value to a known coin and a convenient size when applied as a measure to the common money transactions of life; its parts and multiples were to be in easy proportion to one another, the easiest ratio being 10. The Spanish dollar, already adopted by the Americans, fulfilled all these conditions. Jefferson's ideas were adopted unanimously by the Continental Congress. A resolution of 6 July 1785 decreed that "the money unit of the United States of America be one dollar" and that the pieces be in decimal ratio (*Journals of the Continental Congress*, vol. 29, p. 500). On 8 August 1786 Congress accepted a report from the Board of Treasury establishing the decimal parts of the dollar. The names mill, cent, dime, and eagle were introduced for the first time. Congress also ordered the Board of Treasury to draft an ordinance to establish a mint. The mint law was approved on 16 October 1786. Because the Continental mint was never established, a resolution of 6 July 1787 provided for the minting of Franklin or Fugio cents by contractors. These are claimed to be the first coins issued by authority of the United States.

Indeed, it was the very machinations of Congress with contract coinage that ended Jefferson's direct effort to establish a mint. In 1787 Jefferson made an unsuccessful attempt to get Congress to hire a Swiss coiner, Jean Pierre Droz, who had invented a coin press that would strike both sides and edge at one stroke. (The U.S. Mint did not adopt this technology until 1907!)

The Articles of Confederation permitted states to strike coins (Art. IX). Three of the thirteen states, Massachusetts, Connecticut, and New Jersey, did so; but only Massachusetts operated a mint in 1787 and 1788.

The Constitution of the United States, adopted on 17 September 1787, gave Congress the sole authority over coinage, made only gold and silver coins legal tender, and expressly forbade the right of the states to coin money (Art. I, Sec. 8, 10). On 15 January 1790 the First Congress directed Secretary of State Thomas Jefferson to make a report on a uniform system of coinage, weights, and measures. Exactly three months later, on 15 April 1790, the House directed Secretary of the Treasury Alexander Hamilton to prepare a plan for a mint. Jefferson, who cleared his report with Hamilton, consequently omitted any reference to the mint in his report on coinage of 13 July 1790.

Alexander Hamilton's *Report on the Establishment of a Mint* was dated 28 January 1791. In preparing his report, Hamilton used earlier proposals but was indebted to Thomas Jefferson, with whom he cleared his report. The general outlines of Hamilton's proposals on coinage agree with Jefferson's.

Hamilton's plan set out in detail the internal organization of the mint. He provided for a director, assayer, master coiner, a cashier, an auditor, clerks, and workmen. An assay commission of high officials was to make an annual inspection of the coins. The secretary of the Treasury agreed with Jefferson and determined that the dollar be the unit of account and correspond in weight to the circulating Spanish silver dollar. On 3 March 1791 Congress passed a resolution authorizing a mint and directing the president to engage the principal artists (1 Stat. 225). The Mint was established by law on 2 April 1792 (1 Stat. 246).

The Mint Act was much as Hamilton had proposed. The U.S. Mint was to produce free (meaning any private person has the right to have bullion coined at legal rates) and unlimited coinage of both gold and silver. Coinage was to be gratuitous (meaning without seigniorage, the charge paid by persons to have their bullion coined at the Mint; 1 Stat. 249). The ratio of silver to gold was fifteen pounds of silver to one pound of gold (1 Stat. 249).

The Mint Act of 1792 provided for three gold coins—the eagle ($10), half-eagle ($5), and quarter eagle ($2.50); five silver coins—the dollar, half-dollar, quarter, dime, and half-dime; and two copper coins—the cent and half-cent (1 Stat. 248). The act decreed that all coins had to have an emblem of Liberty (the Liberty design originates with Benjamin Franklin's Libertas Americana medal of 1782), the word *Liberty*, and the year of coinage on one side of the coin; all gold and silver coins had to have an eagle and the inscription *United States of America* on the reverse side; and the copper coins had to show the de-

nomination on the reverse (1 Stat. 248). Most of these design regulations are still in effect today.

The first Mint was built in Philadelphia on Seventh Street, the first public building erected by the United States government. The first Mint director was the noted Philadelphia scientist David Rittenhouse. A sum of $3 was paid in 1793 for Nero, the watchdog. But Hamilton had not asked Congress to assign the Mint to the Treasury Department. Jefferson was not anxious to increase Hamilton's growing control over the new federal government and wanted the Mint placed under his authority.

Given the political antagonism between the two leaders, Congress refrained from assigning the Mint to either man and placed the Mint under the president of the United States. George Washington assigned the Mint to Thomas Jefferson and the State Department. ". . . I am more inclined to add it to . . . State than to multiply the duties of the [Treasury]" (*The Writings of George Washington*, vol. 32, pp. 127). The Mint director reported to Congress through the secretary of state from 1792 to 1799. In 1799 the Mint became an independent agency reporting directly to the president of the United States.

Copper coins were first produced in 1793; silver coinage began in 1794; gold coinage in 1795. But the early record of the Mint was disappointing. Attempts were made to terminate it. Although the act of 1792 required that the Mint operate at the seat of government, Congress declined to spend any money in 1800 to move it to Washington, and to this day the Mint remains in Philadelphia.

The Mint hired the first two women employed by the Treasury Department in 1795. They were adjusters who earned fifty cents a day to weigh gold coins. Men earned $1.20 for the same work. Two more women were hired in 1798.

THE MINT BECOMES A BUREAU OF TREASURY

In 1816 an attempt was made to place the Mint under the Treasury Department, but the bill failed in Congress. An act of 3 March 1835 (4 Stat. 775) made the Philadelphia Mint director's management of the three new branch mints subject to the approval of the secretary of the Treasury. This was the first statutory grant of supervisory authority given to the secretary of the Treasury over the Mint. By an act of 18 January 1837 (5 Stat. 136) the director of the Mint was required to submit certain reports on operations to the secretary. By an act of 21 February 1857 (11 Stat. 164) the director of the Mint was required by law to submit his annual report to the secretary of the Treasury.

An independent agency, the Mint was falling more and more under the management of the Treasury. Secretary of the Treasury George Boutwell wrote in his 1869 annual report that the mining and coining of precious metals was now so large a national interest that it deserved more attention, yet there was no official in the department on whom the secretary could rely for information. In addition, examinations by the secretary revealed that irregularities and discrepancies at the branch mints had resulted in large losses to the government. More stringent control was needed. The secretary recommended a bureau in Washington headed by an officer under the secretary's direction.

On 12 February 1873 the Mint was made a bureau of the Treasury Department (17 Stat. 424). The Coinage Act of 1873 was controversial from the start. The act reorganized the Mint and placed the Mint superintendents and the assay offices under the supervision of Washington. The director of the Mint is appointed by the president with the consent of the Senate for a five-year term (17 Stat. 424). The Mint was no longer an independent agency.

The Coinage Act of 1873 revised and codified all coinage laws. The law added to the 1792 coin design requirements that coins must contain the inscription *E Pluribus Unum.* The secretary of the Treasury could approve the use of the motto *In God We Trust* (17 Stat. 427). The act of 1873 dropped the two-cent and silver three-cent coins and the half-dime (made redundant by the introduction of the nickel in 1866; 17 Stat. 427, 429). But it went down in history as the "Crime of 1873" for discontinuing the standard silver dollar, which had long since ceased to circulate.

By an act of 29 January 1874 the U.S. Mint was authorized to strike coins for foreign governments (18 Stat. 6). Coin designs could not be changed for twenty-five years following passage of an act of 1890 (26 Stat. 484). In 1892 the Mint was authorized to issue commemorative coins (27 Stat. 389). The first commemorative coin was the Columbian Exposition coin; the Sesquicentennial of American Independence was celebrated in 1926; and the last commemoratives to be issued in over a quarter of a century were the coins struck in honor of African-American leaders Booker T. Washington and George Washington Carver from 1946 through 1954.

On 3 May 1933 Nellie Tayloe Ross became the first woman director of the Mint. She was appointed to four five-year terms, serving until 1953.

Gold coins were withdrawn from circulation in 1933. The public was ordered to turn in gold coins and gold bullion to the government by Executive Order 6102 of 5 April 1933. The minting of gold coins was ended by the Gold Reserve Act of 30 January 1934 (48 Stat. 340).

During World War II the composition of the penny and the nickel was changed to conserve metals needed for the war effort. By an act of 23 July 1965 (79 Stat. 254) clad coins were authorized, replacing silver in quarters and dimes with a nickel and copper alloy in order to resolve a silver crisis. The Mint began producing silverless clad dollars and fifty-cent pieces in 1971.

Today the Mint produces five coins. New designs for each denomination honoring five American presidents were introduced by the Mint in the twentieth century: the Lincoln penny (1909), the Jefferson nickel (1938), the Roosevelt dime (1946), the Washington quarter (1932), and the Kennedy half dollar (1964).

The dollar coin is currently not being produced. The Eisenhower dollar was struck from 1971 to 1978 in honor of President Dwight Eisenhower. The Susan B. Anthony dollar, honoring the nineteenth-century advocate for women's rights and the first coin to bear the likeness of an American woman, was minted between 1979 and 1981.

The Mint was authorized to produce coins with special designs for the American Bicentennial by an act of 18 October 1973 (87 Stat. 455).

The designs were chosen through national competitions and were minted for issue between 4 July 1975 and 1977.

On 31 December 1974 the ban on American citizens owning gold was ended (88 Stat. 445). The American Eagle gold bullion coins (December 1985, 99 Stat. 1177), the first U.S. noncommemorative numismatic gold coins struck by the United States Mint for U.S. consumption since 1933, were first issued in October 1986.

Commemorative coins, issued again by the Mint starting in 1982, included the Olympic coins of 1984, the Statue of Liberty/Ellis Island coin in 1986, the Bicentennial of the U.S. Constitution in 1987, and the Jackie Robinson commemorative of 1997 honoring the African American who expanded civil rights by breaking the color barrier in professional baseball.

An act of 14 March 1980 (94 Stat. 98) abolished the Assay Commission. On 9 January 1984 the secretary of the Treasury changed the official name of the bureau to the United States Mint.

THE MINTS

The Philadelphia Mint, which has remained in continuous operation, outgrew its first home, and a new Mint, begun on 4 July 1829 on Chestnut Street, operated for seventy years. (An act of 19 May 1828 [4 Stat. 277] had continued the Mint in Philadelphia.) The third Philadelphia Mint was built in 1900, and the fourth building opened on 14 August 1969.

The California Gold Rush of 1849 led to the establishment of a branch mint in San Francisco in July 1852 (10 Stat. 11). Twenty years later, in 1872–1873, Alfred B. Mullett's Mint building was constructed at Fifth and Mission streets. Occupied in 1874, it was one of the few buildings to withstand the earthquake of 1906. A modern Mint facility was opened in 1937 and produced coins until 1955; coinage was resumed in 1965. The Old Mint, restored in 1972–1976, was closed after the 1989 earthquake.

Gold was first discovered in Colorado in 1858; in January 1862 the Treasury proposed to Congress that a branch mint be built in Denver. After passage of the April 1862 law (12 Stat. 382), a private mint was purchased, but it served only as an assay office from September 1863 until 1906 and as a refuge during Indian raids in the early years. In March 1895 Congress provided for a Mint building in Denver (28 Stat. 931), and a site was purchased in April 1896. The new Mint building was occupied in September 1904, and coin production began in 1906.

The Fort Knox Gold Bullion Depository was opened in 1937. The West Point Bullion Depository was opened in 1938 to store silver bullion and since 1973 has produced coins. Mints in New Orleans, Charlotte, North Carolina, Dahlonega, Georgia, and Carson City, Nevada are now closed.

BIBLIOGRAPHY

Bowers, Q. David. *Commemorative Coins of the United States: A Complete Encyclopedia.* Wolfeboro, N.H., 1991.

Breen, Walter H. *Walter Breen's Complete Encyclopedia of United States and Colonial Coins.* Garden City, N.Y., 1988.

Coin World Almanac. 6th ed. Sidney, Ohio, 1990.

Evans, George G. *Illustrated History of the United States Mint.* Philadelphia, 1892.

Failor, Kenneth M., and Eleanora Hayden. *Medals of the United States Mint.* Washington, D.C., 1972.

Julian, R. W. *Medals of the United States Mint: The First Century, 1792–1892* (1892). Reprint, El Cajon, Calif., 1977.

Stewart, Frank H. *History of the First United States Mint* (1924). Reprint, Lawrence, Mass., 1974.

Taxay, Don. *The U.S. Mint and Coinage: An Illustrated History from 1776 to the Present.* New York, 1966.

U.S. Bureau of the Mint. *Domestic and Foreign Coins Manufactured by Mints of the United States, 1793–1980.* Washington, D.C., 1981.

U.S. Mint. *Annual Report of the Director of the Mint, 1793–.* Title varies. Publisher varies. Washington, D.C.

Watson, Jesse P. *The Bureau of the Mint: Its History, Activities, and Organization.* Institute for Government Research, Service Monographs of the United States Government, no. 37. Baltimore, 1926.

Wolman, Paul. *The U.S. Mint.* New York, 1987.

—ABBY L. GILBERT

Museums, National.

See Smithsonian Institution.

N

National Aeronautics and Space Administration

On 20 July 1969 people around the world watched in awe as Neil Armstrong became the first human to walk on the moon. The event symbolized, as Armstrong laconically radioed to earth, a "giant leap for mankind." A U.S. government agency—the National Aeronautics and Space Administration (NASA)—made that amazing feat happen.

THE CREATION OF NASA

America emerged from World War II confident in its technological leadership, especially because it led in the development of atomic weapons and the means to deliver them. That confidence was shattered on 4 October 1957, when the Soviet Union launched into orbit the earth's first man-made satellite, called *Sputnik*. Most Americans were alarmed by the event because it implied that the Soviets had acquired the missile technology to deliver nuclear warheads to American targets.

The American public demanded action. President Dwight Eisenhower saw no need to rush exploration of the universe and thought priority should be given to the military applications of space. He was reluctant to establish a separate civilian government agency to oversee the nation's space program, which he believed might emphasize satellites at the expense of missiles. Yet Congress, the public, and many scientists strongly favored such an agency, and Eisenhower acquiesced.

The president proposed the creation of NASA in April 1958, and Congress quickly passed the National Aeronautics and Space Act of 1958.

NASA came into existence on 1 October of that year, absorbing the National Advisory Committee for Aeronautics, an obscure and poorly funded agency created in 1915 to conduct research in aeronautics.

NASA enjoyed a highly favorable political environment in its early years. The Cold War was raging, and the American public's fear that the Soviets would dominate space translated into potent political support for the American space program. The public recognized the importance of space exploration and was intrigued by NASA's activities. Congress also supported NASA enthusiastically. As a result, the young agency got just about everything it wanted, with few hostile questions asked.

PROJECT MERCURY AND THE DECISION TO GO TO THE MOON

NASA's first major program was Project Mercury, designed to study humans' ability to function in space and to develop the technology and equipment needed for manned space exploration. The Mercury program and NASA's original seven astronauts fascinated the public. The media showered attention on the Mercury astronauts, and they emerged as national heroes.

One of those astronauts, Alan Shepard, became the first American in space with his suborbital flight on 5 May 1961. Although acclaimed in the United States, Shepard's voyage was overshadowed by the earlier orbital flight of Soviet Yuri Gagarin, who had become the first human in space on 12 April 1961. President John F. Kennedy, whose 1960 campaign for the White House had used the space race as an issue, commended Shepard and NASA, but said that the nation should put forth "a substantially larger effort" in space.

The Mercury program continued as Kennedy

and NASA looked to the future. Virgil ("Gus") Grissom took the second suborbital Mercury flight in July 1961. After splashdown, however, the capsule's hatch opened prematurely. Grissom survived, but the capsule filled with water and sank. On 20 February 1962, in the third Mercury mission, John Glenn became the first American to orbit the earth. Glenn and NASA were hailed by the American public even though the Soviet Gagarin had orbited the earth nearly a year earlier. Three more Mercury flights, although somewhat anticlimactic, were executed successfully.

Having promised to accelerate the nation's space program, Kennedy had to decide how to do so. The president, chagrined at the repeated space firsts achieved by the Soviets, wanted a dramatic goal that America could accomplish before the Soviet Union. In a speech to Congress on 25 May 1961, Kennedy declared his objective: "I believe that this nation should commit itself to achieving the goal, before this decade is out, of landing a man on the moon and returning him safely to the earth."

Kennedy admitted that the lunar program, called Project Apollo, would be risky and costly. As he said to Congress, "No single space project in this period will be more impressive to mankind, or more important for the long-range exploration of space; and none will be so difficult or expensive to accomplish." Yet the nation quickly supported Apollo. Congress approved the program, the largest civilian project ever undertaken by America, virtually without debate.

NASA wanted to go to the moon but had not planned to do so in the near future, and was therefore excited by the goal and its deadline. In setting that objective and securing the funding, Kennedy energized NASA and gave the agency its clearest mandate ever.

Both Mercury and the subsequent Gemini program served as preliminary steps to the Apollo program. Although already under way when Apollo was announced, the six Mercury flights between 1961 and 1963 and the ten Gemini flights during 1965 and 1966 provided the basic information about human and mechanical capabilities in space needed for more advanced space activities. The Gemini spacecraft, larger and more sophisticated than its Mercury prede-

cessor, enabled NASA to practice some of the procedures astronauts would have to perform in the Apollo program.

NASA embarked on a massive building program in the 1960s to construct the ground facilities needed to support the Apollo program. In Houston NASA built the Manned Spacecraft Center (later renamed the Johnson Space Center in honor of Lyndon Johnson), and the agency made significant improvements at the Marshall Space Flight Center in Alabama and at the Kennedy Space Center in Florida. NASA also expanded its network for tracking the progress of space flights. James Webb, later called "one of the giants of American public administration," skillfully ran NASA from 1961 to 1968.

APOLLO

Tragedy struck NASA on 27 January 1967. Three astronauts—Gus Grissom, Edward White, and Roger Chaffee—conducting tests in a sealed Apollo spacecraft died when a fire broke out inside the capsule. NASA and the nation were stunned by the fire. A review board charged that NASA had been lax about safety, and some public doubts about NASA and space exploration began to arise. NASA quickly made some management changes and established new safety guidelines, but it also reiterated that space exploration was a risky endeavor and that the lunar landing posed many obstacles.

NASA also faced the challenge, starting in the mid-1960s, of declining political support. Americans began to wonder, especially after it became clear that the U.S. space program was catching up to the Soviet program, if being the first nation on the moon really mattered. America's deepening involvement in Vietnam and the accompanying economic problems and domestic unrest also contributed to NASA's waning support.

After several unmanned Apollo test flights and one manned mission in earth orbit, NASA was ready to send a spacecraft into lunar orbit. On 21 December 1968 *Apollo 8* began its flight to the moon. Orbiting the moon on Christmas Eve, the crew beamed back to earth spectacular pictures of the moon's surface while reading from the Bible.

After two more test missions, *Apollo 9* and

Apollo 10, NASA was ready to fulfill the goal set by Kennedy in 1961. On 16 July 1969, *Apollo 11* lifted off, carrying astronauts Neil Armstrong, Edwin ("Buzz") Aldrin, and Michael Collins toward the moon. Four days later, Armstrong and Aldrin descended to the moon's surface in the lunar excursion module, called the *Eagle.* On touchdown Armstrong calmly radioed to earth: "Houston, Tranquillity base here. The *Eagle* has landed."

A few hours after landing, as much of the world watched televised coverage in awe, Neil Armstrong became the first human to set foot on the moon. Armstrong exited the *Eagle* and slowly climbed down the ladder on its side. Standing on the last step, he described what the moon's surface looked like and then announced that he was going to step down. Armstrong stepped, paused, and then spoke his immortal line: "That's one small step for a man, one giant leap for mankind." The safe return to earth of the *Apollo 11* crew on 24 July capped one of the most spectacular voyages in history. President Richard Nixon even called *Apollo 11* "the greatest week in the history of the world since the Creation."

After the smooth *Apollo 12* mission, sending men to the moon began to look easy. That changed dramatically with *Apollo 13* in April 1970. On the way to the moon, one of the spacecraft's oxygen tanks exploded, crippling the ship and leaving serious doubt as to whether the crew would make it back alive. The nation and much of the world waited and watched for several days as NASA struggled to return the crew safely. Some ingenious work by NASA engineers and managers as well as the astronauts did bring *Apollo 13* back with the crew alive. Ironically, that flight received more attention than any Apollo mission other than the first moon landing.

NASA successfully completed four more missions to the moon. The missions had scientific value, but the public showed little interest. Drastically smaller NASA budgets and increased debate over the value of the Apollo project forced the cancellation of two additional planned flights to the moon, and the lunar program ended with the return of *Apollo 17* in December 1972.

THE SPACE SHUTTLE ERA

As the Apollo program came to an end, NASA needed a new mission. The agency made some bold proposals, including a manned lunar base, a large orbiting space station, and a manned mission to Mars. However, NASA's political support had eroded so badly that most of its ideas were rejected as too costly. Only a new space transportation system called the "space shuttle" won approval, and even that was subject to strict budgetary limits. In the unfamiliar position of struggling for political support, NASA stressed that the shuttle would provide economical and routine access to space.

While it spent most of the 1970s developing the shuttle, NASA did pursue some other projects. It launched a small orbital "workshop" called Skylab in May 1973, which was visited by three crews over the following year to study humans' ability to live and work in space. Skylab did see many experiments performed but failed to generate much public interest, at least until the station's unplanned and uncontrolled reentry into the atmosphere in 1979.

The decade also featured the 1975 Apollo-Soyuz Test Project, a joint American-Soviet project that sprang from the détente of the period. The project entailed an American Apollo spacecraft docking in space with a Soviet Soyuz spacecraft, exchanging crews, and performing a number of experiments. The 1970s also saw NASA exploring the planets through a series of unmanned projects, including the series of Viking probes that sent back spectacular detailed photos of the surface of Mars.

The space shuttle began flying in 1981, two years behind schedule. NASA conducted twenty-two more shuttle flights by the end of 1985. Despite a few glitches, the shuttle performed well during these years. NASA accomplished a string of space "firsts" in this period: first American spacecraft landing on the ground, first reusable space vehicle, first American woman and first African American in space, largest number of crew members (eight) in a single spacecraft, and first members of Congress launched into space. NASA also aggressively pursued its plan to use the shuttle for deploying satellites and conducting scientific experiments. The agency was especially delighted by the 1984 *Challenger* mission that retrieved, repaired, and returned a satellite to orbit.

The second shuttle mission of 1986, to be flown by *Challenger,* generated unusually high prelaunch interest because its crew included a personable high-school teacher. Christa McAuliffe, NASA's choice as the first "Teacher in Space," planned to transmit lessons from space to thousands of schoolchildren on earth. After several embarrassing launch delays, *Challenger* finally took off on the unusually cold morning of 28 January 1986.

Seventy-three seconds after lift-off, the *Challenger* exploded. The seven crew members aboard—Francis Scobee, Michael Smith, Judith Resnik, Ronald McNair, Ellison Onizuka, Gregory Jarvis, and Christa McAuliffe—were killed. The tragedy was captured on tape, which was shown repeatedly on television.

Americans were deeply shocked and sorrowed by the accident, and NASA itself was badly shaken. The *Challenger* explosion marked the nadir of the agency's history. The dismay of the public and NASA soon intensified, however, when reports surfaced contending that the accident could and should have been prevented. President Ronald Reagan appointed a panel, the Presidential Commission on the Space Shuttle *Challenger* Accident (chaired by former secretary of state William P. Rogers, and better known as the Rogers Commission), to investigate the matter.

The Rogers Commission identified the cause of the accident: a gasket, called an O-ring, between two sections of a solid rocket booster lost its resiliency because of the cold weather and failed to maintain its seal, allowing burning propellant to spew out of the booster and cause the explosion. The Rogers report sharply criticized NASA management and safety procedures, and it made numerous suggestions for changes both in the shuttle system and in NASA itself. The commission's report received wide praise, although numerous observers doubted its conclusion that NASA was under no demonstrable outside pressure to maintain its launch rate. James Fletcher, in his second stint as NASA administrator, vowed to implement the report's recommendations.

AFTER *CHALLENGER*

The shuttle program resumed successfully in September 1988, yet a new round of problems soon beleaguered the agency. NASA's plans for its next major project, an orbiting space station, received criticism as being poorly defined, enormously expensive, and technologically unfeasible. NASA also suffered continuing problems and delays with the shuttle program. In addition, a manufacturing flaw in the highly touted Hubble Space Telescope blurred the scope's vision and embarrassed the agency.

President George Bush showed support for NASA in 1989 when he proposed that NASA build a manned base on the moon and pursue manned exploration of Mars. The plan excited NASA but elicited skepticism elsewhere, since Bush did not set a deadline or explain the financing of the plan, estimated to cost $500 billion or more. Aside from the tremendous fiscal obstacles, several observers wondered whether NASA, beset by troubles from much less ambitious programs, had the technical competence to attain such a lofty goal.

NASA rebounded somewhat in the 1990s. The agency continued the shuttle program (including a flight that repaired the Hubble telescope) and its successful unmanned exploratory missions. NASA also pursued a series of joint missions with the Russian Space Agency as a prelude to constructing a permanently manned international space station. NASA is leading the international space station project, with help from Russia, Canada, Japan, Italy, and the nine European nations supporting the European Space Agency. Assembly of the station, in orbit, is scheduled to begin in 1998.

[*See also* Global Change Research Program *and* Science and Technology Policy, Office of.]

BIBLIOGRAPHY

Bilstein, Roger E. *Orders of Magnitude: A History of the NACA and NASA, 1915–1990.* SP-4406. Washington, D.C., 1989.

Byrnes, Mark E. *Politics and Space: Image Making by NASA.* Westport, Conn., 1994.

Hirsch, Richard, and Joseph John Trento. *The National Aeronautics and Space Administration.* New York, 1973.

Lambright, W. Henry. "James Webb and the Uses of Administrative Power." In *Leadership and Innovation: A Biographical Perspective on Entrepreneurs in Government,* edited by Jameson W. Doig and Erwin C. Hargrove, pp. 174–203. Baltimore, 1987.

Levine, Arthur L. *The Future of the U.S. Space Program.* New York, 1975.

McCurdy, Howard E. *Inside NASA: High Technology and Organizational Change in the American Space Program.* Baltimore, 1993.

McDougall, Walter A. *. . . The Heavens and the Earth: A Political History of the Space Age.* New York, 1985.

Murray, Charles, and Catherine Bly Cox. *Apollo: The Race to the Moon.* New York, 1989.

Trento, Joseph J. *Prescription for Disaster.* New York, 1987.

The United States Government Manual, 1995/96. Washington, D.C., 1995.

Wolfe, Tom. *The Right Stuff.* Toronto, 1979.

—MARK BYRNES

National Archives

From its declaration as an independent nation in 1776 until 1934, when the National Archives Act was passed, the United States operated without a central archival system. The nation carried the dubious distinction of being the last major country to establish its national archives. Over this period of time vermin, floods, and fires compounded the problems of preserving the historical records of the federal government. In the nation's early history much depended upon the faithful clerks of executive departments preserving essential documents relating to the government's political, diplomatic, and military activities. To recordkeepers such as Charles Thompson, who served as secretary to both the Continental and Confederation Congresses, the nation is indebted for creating and preserving the nation's records.

One early alternative resorted to was documentary publication at public expense of important federal records such as the *American State Papers* (Washington, D.C., 1832–1861), edited and published by Lowrie and Clarke. During the mid-nineteenth century, the growth in government and the explosion in military records generated by the Civil War caused the War Department and the Department of State to initiate publications of records relating to the Civil War and the foreign relations of the United States. At the same time the emergence of academic historians and the establishment of the American Historical Association in 1884 renewed the call for the federal government to take better care of its records. Historians argued that until they had access to the records of the nation little satisfactory American history could be written.

Concern for federal records gained more support with publication of Van Tyne and Leland's *Guide to the Archives of the Government of the United States in Washington* (Washington, D.C., 1904). Five years later the American Historical Association established an annual conference of archivists where all records of local, state, and federal government were discussed. By 1910 states had pushed ahead of the federal government by forming history and archives departments to care for their historical records. Slowly a federal hall of records proposal gained acceptance whereby federal departments would simply deposit their records in a large warehouse but keep control of them. The most influential historian advocating a true archives system was J. Franklin Jameson. With energy and savvy worthy of any politician, Jameson persuaded people in Washington that the hall of records plan would not work. As editor of the *American Historical Review* and the leading spokesman for historians, Jameson could speak with authority. By the 1920s Jameson and his colleagues had convinced Presidents Coolidge and Hoover and persons in Congress that it was time to establish a National Archives.

In 1926 Congress appropriated almost $7 million for a National Archives building to be built on prime land between Pennsylvania and Constitution avenues. With this choice location it was clear that this was more than a low-cost hall of records. Hoover laid the cornerstone on a cold February day in 1933. Over the next two years

ROTUNDA ENTRANCE OF THE NATIONAL ARCHIVES IN WASHINGTON, D.C. *Displayed in the Rotunda are the foundational documents of U.S. government—the Declaration of Independence, the Constitution, and the Bill of Rights—along with numerous other historically significant documents.*

the massive two-block neoclassical structure slowly took shape. When the exterior of the National Archives building was complete, the seventy-two massive limestone columns stood like immobile Roman centurions ready to protect the nation's documentary heritage. In the midst of the Great Depression, Congress was preoccupied with Roosevelt's New Deal and had not provided an organization for the building. Questions about whether it was to be an independent agency or part of an existing department were being debated into the late spring of 1934. Finally President Roosevelt intervened in June 1934 to settle the squabbling, and a bill passed the Senate the next day. On 19 June 1934 the National Archives Act became law.

THE EARLY NATIONAL ARCHIVES

The National Archives was established as an independent agency within the executive branch. The Archivist of the United States was selected by the president and confirmed by the Senate. It specifically authorized the archivist or the staff to inspect the records maintained by all three branches of government. With the approval of a National Archives Council defined in the law, the National Archives could transfer records of enduring value from all three branches of government. The records of state and local governments, in contrast with other countries' archival systems, were not included in this legislation. The archivist had full power and responsibility over the new building and had wide latitude in hiring competent persons to assist in bringing together the nation's storehouse of historic documents.

The first Archivist of the United States was the history professor R. D. W. Connor of the University of North Carolina. In addition to his noteworthy teaching career, Connor earlier had developed a strong North Carolina Department of Archives and History as the executive secretary of the North Carolina Historical Commission, a state agency. Vital American Historical Association support and good Democratic party connections brought Connor a personal interview with FDR in October1934. Liking what he heard and saw, the president forwarded his name to the Senate, where it was confirmed on 20 March 1935. By the end of 1935 the staff of the Archives numbered 130 and was made up mostly of historians, although librarians and manuscript curators were employed.

As the staff increased it began the formidable job of locating and determining what federal records had survived. The National Archives Act of 1934 empowered the archivist to take custody of "all archives or records belonging to the Federal Government" including the executive, judicial, and legislative branches as long as the transfers were approved by the National Archives Council—an approving body composed of senior members from all three branches of government. Connor could also inspect, either personally or by deputy, all records "whatsoever and wheresoever" located. With the council's approval, he could direct the transfer of inactive records that were judged to be of permanent value or historical interest. In early years the archivist had four key assistants: a director of archival service, an executive director, a director of publications and guides to records, and a secretary to the National Historical Publications Commission. The last named was established by the 1934 act but did little for two decades. The major professional duties of the National Archives rested with the director of archival service. This division was to acquire the government's archival materials, provide repair and preservation of them, and classify

them according to a cataloging system—in a word, accession them—and make them available to the public. This was a major challenge because of the small staff and the 150-year buildup of inactive government records.

During the agency's first year of operation Congress passed the Federal Register Act and placed it under the National Archives. The Office of the Federal Register provided for notice, through publication of or access to proclamations, orders, regulations, notices, and other documents promulgated by federal agencies. The law provided that any agency document or order that prescribed a penalty or contained general applicability and legal effect had to be announced in the *Federal Register* and a reading copy made available at the Office of the Federal Register. As the size and complexity of the executive branch grew under FDR, the role of the *Federal Register* as a purveyor of governmental activity likewise grew.

During the mid-1930s archivists called deputy examiners began searching over 6,570 rooms, closets, and hallways in Washington looking for records. The examiners identified almost three million cubic feet of records and about 2.5 million photographs. This amounted to about 7.5 trillion pages of federal records in the Washington, D.C., area. Less than half were judged to be of enduring value and eligible for transfer to the new archives building. In the meantime a Works Progress Administration survey of federal records in the rest of the United States identified over four million cubic feet of records. By 1940 records storage space of the new building was over half full. In hindsight it is fair to conclude that these examiners appraised too much to be of permanent value.

Another event that had a major impact on the future structure of the National Archives was the establishment of a special library at Hyde Park, New York, on the grounds of Franklin Roosevelt's estate. Since the time of George Washington the papers of presidents were considered personal property and taken when they left office. On 4 July 1938 FDR told Archivist Connor that he wanted to build a small repository on his estate with private funds, deed his papers to the United States, and deposit them there for the use of scholars. Congress passed and FDR signed a bill on 18 July 1939 authorizing the National Archives to accept the building and operate the Franklin D. Roosevelt Library. This would serve as a model for future presidential libraries under the management of the National Archives.

During its early years the Archives was managed more as a special library, but by 1940 professional archivists realized that the cataloging and classification of individual records would not work because of the tremendous quantity of documents. Descriptions of records in the aggregate became the norm in the National Archives. As records are created or accumulated in government offices, they are kept together and make up a file—or, in archival terminology, form a records series. The records series provides the fundamental arrangement and description pattern for most records; however, special media such as photographs, motion pictures, or manuscript maps may require individual description and control. Adoption of this collective or aggregate description was necessitated by the tremendous quantity of records being accessioned by the National Archives. Also, in order to better administer the records of agencies, the Archives adopted the concept of the record group—a classification or grouping of records accessioned from major organizations of the federal government.

According to the annual report of the archivist for 1940–1941, the "National Archives must inevitably be concerned with the creation, arrangement, and administration as well as the appraisal, disposal, and preservation of Government records": the National Archives had realized, in other words, that it could no longer be a passive agency waiting to peruse records after they were no longer needed for business. The entire life-cycle of records had to be taken into account; better records management in agencies would make the subsequent archival functions much easier. Archivists from the National Archives would be sent to assist agencies in their preparations for World War II. Masses of records poured into the Archives, very little description was done, and service to the public was curtailed while that to agencies was increased. The National Archives published *The Care of Records in a National Emergency* in order to pro-

vide government guidance to agencies seeking to maintain control over their recordkeeping. The National Archives served the needs of the government during the war, and normal archival activities resumed once the fighting stopped.

In 1949 the National Archives was merged into a new agency of the executive branch, the General Services Administration (GSA), whose purpose was to streamline executive branch operations in the interest of economy and efficiency. This was a major blow to many in the National Archives, henceforth to be known as the National Archives and Records Service. Successive Archivists of the United States experienced frustration on occasion but usually maintained silence on policy matters. As part of the GSA, the National Archives was one of several organizations that provided facilitative services for executive branch agencies. Its fundamental character as a custodial institution holding the permanently valuable records of the federal government remained unchanged under the GSA, but for the next twenty years the focus was on better management of semicurrent records through a national system of federal records centers and the establishment of a cadre of professional records managers working to assist agencies.

THE NATIONAL ARCHIVES TODAY

In October 1984 the Congress passed a bill reestablishing the National Archives and Records Administration as an independent agency effective 1 April 1985. The National Archives immediately established the Office of Records Administration in order to provide guidance and assistance to the federal community. In 1992 the Office of Special and Regional Archives was established by combining the Center for Electronic Records, the Center for Legislative Archives, and the Regional Archives System. This organizational structure remained intact until 1995, when the Office of Management and Administration was divided and policy and planning was split from the administrative services function. During 1995–1996 a major strategic planning effort was undertaken with the goal of streamlining the agency in order to provide better service to federal agencies and the American people.

OFFICE OF THE ARCHIVIST

The Office of the Archivist consists of the Archivist of the United States, a deputy, and the staff of the general counsel, congressional affairs, public affairs, professional development and training, and equal employment opportunity and diversity programs. Also reporting to the archivist is an inspector general and the executive director of the National Historical Publications and Records Commission (NHPRC). By statute the archivist is vested with the authority to manage the staff, real property, and programs of the agency. There is statutory guidance relating to the roles and responsibilities of the director of the Federal Register and the NHPRC. The other major offices include the Office of Policy and Information Resources Management, Administrative Services, Office of Federal Records Centers, Office of Public Programs, Office of Special and Regional Archives, Office of the National Archives, and the Office of Presidential Libraries. The archivist delegates major program responsibilities to these offices.

OFFICE OF THE NATIONAL ARCHIVES

The Office of the National Archives has custodial responsibility for those federal records of enduring or permanent value held in the Washington, D.C., area, including a wide spectrum of archival materials dating from 1774 to the present. In brief, these records provide accountability for why and how the national government acted over the past two hundred years. Other documents provide information about people, programs, events such as wars and natural disasters, and many other activities that took place within the affairs of the nation. Important diplomatic records such as treaties, accords, and conventions can be found within the holdings of this office. This also includes treaties made with Native Americans relating to land cessions, tribal removal, and fishing and hunting rights. An abundance of subjects are documented in a wide variety of media including parchment, paper, photographs, audio and video recording, and an increasing number of electronic media. For almost fifty years this office has preserved and made available that body of records known as the National Archives of the United States. This archival mother lode of over one million cubic feet of paper records, two million maps, and six million photographs is in the custody of the Office of the National Archives. Over the years millions of reference inquiries have been answered by this unit.

OFFICE OF SPECIAL AND REGIONAL ARCHIVES

The Office of Special and Regional Archives was created in 1992 and is made up of thirteen regional archives scattered throughout the United States. These centers provide a full range of archival services and contain almost 500,000 cubic feet of archival materials that document local and regional history. Each regional center also contains almost 60,000 rolls of National Archives microfilm publications, including the federal population census schedules from 1790 to 1920, selected passenger arrival lists, and many military service and pension records used by researchers conducting family history. The regional archives participate widely in public events such as workshops, classes, symposia, and exhibits that make records more accessible.

The Center for Legislative Archives has custody of the permanent records of the United States Senate and the United States House of Representatives. In 1994 the center produced *The Presidency of Thomas Jefferson,* a packet containing colored document facsimiles that was distributed to social studies teachers in a six-state area in order to encourage them to use the documentary resources of the National Archives. Another unit of the Office of Regional and Special Archives is the Center for Electronic Records, which is responsible for appraising, accessioning, preserving, and providing access to permanently valuable records in electronic format.

The electronic revolution of the last twenty years—especially the ever increasing speed and capacity of personal computers—has led to the decrease of large central filing systems and the growing ability of individuals in agencies to create, maintain, and preserve or destroy electronic records. This democratization of record keeping has a downside because of a lack of agency control over the management of current records. As more records are created, maintained, and preserved by federal agencies in electronic media, demands for archivists knowledgeable in electronic record keeping systems are increasing rapidly.

OFFICE OF PRESIDENTIAL LIBRARIES

The Office of Presidential Libraries administers nine presidential libraries and two presidential materials projects. Following the precedent set by FDR, presidential libraries have been established for Hoover, Truman, Eisenhower, Kennedy, Johnson, Ford, Carter, and Reagan. The Presidential Libraries Act of 1955 provides the model for the creation of these facilities. The presidential materials of Richard Nixon, seized by the United States in the midst of the Watergate crisis, are being processed for release to the public by a special staff. Considerable litigation has caused delay in the release of much of the Nixon materials. The Nixon Library in Yorba Linda, California, is a privately operated library. A special staff also is preparing materials in anticipation of the formal opening of the Bush Presidential Library. All presidential libraries operate museums; however, the Ford Museum is situated in Grand Rapids, Michigan, rather than at Ann Arbor, the site of the library.

The Presidential Records Act of 1978 spelled an end to the tradition that these were personal papers and established by law a new species of records—presidential records. Starting with the administration of President Reagan, records were no longer owned by the president but by the United States government. The small number of personal papers of presidents and the personal papers of cabinet and White House officials can still be deposited in presidential libraries by the signing of a deed of gift.

Today the presidential library system contains a combination of donated historical materials, agency records, and, since 1980, presidential records. The size and variety of holdings vary considerably. The Hoover Library is the smallest, with just over eight million pages of material, while the Reagan Library is the largest, with over forty-seven million pages. Thanks to their importance and accessibility, these research materials attract scholars from all over the world. Because of gifts made over the years to the presidents and their spouses, 287,815 museum objects are held

by the presidential libraries. In addition, the libraries offer a variety of scholarly and public programs. The libraries have individual foundations that support various programs and fund research scholarships. This office adds an important historical manuscripts dimension to the National Archives and Records Administration that differentiates it from the national archives of many other countries.

OFFICE OF FEDERAL RECORDS CENTERS

The Office of Federal Records Centers plays an essential role in providing federal agencies with low-cost storage of records no longer needed for conducting current business but not yet ready for destruction. This nationwide system of fifteen large records warehouses permits agencies to transfer large blocks of inactive records from high-cost agency office space to economical storage space, thus saving American taxpayers millions of dollars each year. (It is estimated to be about twenty times more expensive to keep records in agencies than in records centers.) This nationwide system currently holds almost nineteen million cubic feet of records and in fiscal year 1994 destroyed one million cubic feet of temporary records.

Because these records are in the physical custody of records centers yet still in the legal custody of federal agencies, discovery and requests related to the Freedom of Information and Privacy Acts remain the responsibility of the federal agencies in question. [*See* Appendix: Freedom of Information Act *and* Privacy Act.] Records centers answered almost fifteen million reference requests in fiscal year 1994, almost two million of which were completed by the National Personnel Records Center located in Saint Louis. This latter category includes inquiries from former government employees, former members of the armed services, and their families. By means of the Centers Information Processing System started in 1992, reference requests totaling more than sixty thousand per month are processed electronically.

OFFICE OF RECORDS ADMINISTRATION

The Office of Records Administration focuses on the federal bureaucracy's meeting its statutory and regulatory responsibilities in managing current records. This office provides guidance to agencies in managing their recorded information by issuing records management regulations and publications, conducting various training courses in records management, and performing in-depth evaluations of records management programs in agencies. In addition, a small group of senior archivists appraises federal records for their evidential and informational content and assists the agencies in the proper disposition of records by means of an agency disposition schedule. The appraisal process is critical and is done with care because it decides what is earmarked for permanent retention as part of the National Archives of the United States and what is destroyed. Although the percentage of records appraised as permanent can vary from agency to agency, the federal government is currently destroying between ninety-five and ninety-seven percent of what it creates. Without such managed destruction, the federal government would quickly suffer from information overload.

OFFICE OF THE FEDERAL REGISTER

The Office of the Federal Register is an information link between the federal government and the American people. Although the essential mission of this small but crucial office has not changed much since 1935, when it was established, the volume of laws, regulations, and announcements has increased tremendously. Just as important, the office has utilized advances in technology to circulate government news: on 8 June 1994 it initiated the first official electronic version of the *Federal Register* on the Internet. The Office of the Federal Register is also the publisher of the *Code of Federal Regulations,* the *United States Government Manual,* the *United States Statutes at Large,* and the *Public Papers of the Presidents.* It is noteworthy that the *Federal Register* has been published every day since its first issuance on 14 March 1935.

OFFICE OF PUBLIC PROGRAMS

The Office of Public Programs brings the resources of the National Archives to the public through exhibitions, workshops, publications,

media programs, lectures and dramatic performances, and tours led by trained volunteers. During recent years about one million visitors came annually to Exhibition Hall to see the Declaration of Independence, the Constitution, and the Bill of Rights. A major exhibition highlight was the traveling exhibit of 1991–1995, "World War II: Personal Accounts—Pearl Harbor to V-J Day," on display in several cities, presidential libraries, and the National Archives Building. Public workshops in family history and archival research are popular services given several times a year, and a lecture series features authors who have used documentary resources in the writing of their books. In addition, film series are held at both the original building and the College Park, Maryland, facility. *Prologue,* the quarterly journal of the National Archives, is produced in this office.

POLICY AND PLANNING AND ADMINISTRATIVE SERVICES

In a recent development, a new Office of Policy and Information Resources Management Services was split from the Office of Management and Administration. This new office has two major divisions. One provides guidance to the entire agency on the management of information resources available to the agency and determines what resources will be needed in the future. The Policy and Planning Division determines the long-term policies of the agency and plans how best to carry them out. Both divisions work closely with the major program offices of the agency and with the archivist and deputy archivist. The Office of Administrative Services performs the facilitative services normally associated with any agency. It contains acquisitions, budget, finance, facilities, human resources, and information and personnel security staffs. The planning, financing, coordination of construction, and opening of the National Archives at College Park, Maryland, in 1994 was the responsibility of this office. When the building opened to researchers, it was the largest and most technologically advanced archives facility in the world. It has a records storage capacity of two million cubic feet.

THE NATIONAL HISTORICAL PUBLICATIONS AND RECORDS COMMISSION

Although the National Historical Publications and Records Commission was included in the provisions of the original National Archives Act of 1934, it was not until the Federal Records Act of 1950 was passed and President Truman lent his support that the commission became active. The archivist serves as the chairman, and the composition of the commission is determined by law.

Most of its funding is appropriated; however, it can accept grants from foundations. The executive director and staff report to the archivist. Most of the budget of the commission is dispersed through the awarding of grants for a wide variety of publications or records projects. In a typical year the commission will support over one hundred records or publications projects throughout the United States. Both the publications and records grants programs are dedicated to the principle that the nation's historical documents are a priceless national legacy and are essential to an understanding of the country's history and culture.

FUTURE CHALLENGES FOR THE NATIONAL ARCHIVES AND RECORDS ADMINISTRATION

The National Archives is staffed by three thousand employees scattered in thirty-three facilities nationwide. The agency budget is just over $200 million. The fixed costs of building upkeep will put a strain on future budgets. Planners will need to assess whether the Internet and other information transmission technologies can permit users to access records without going to these facilities. As time goes on, the number of presidential libraries and museums will continue to grow, thus adding more buildings and fixed costs. More challenging is the question of whether the National Archives should be the repository of textual information and data bases produced by federal agencies. The rapidly evolving technologies of creating, maintaining, transmitting, and storing recorded information in the next century will test the planners of tomorrow's National Archives.

[*See also* Federal Register *and* History and Historians in the Federal Government.]

BIBLIOGRAPHY

Annual Reports of the National Archives. Washington, D.C., 1935–.

Bradsher, James Gregory, ed. *Managing Archives and Archival Institutions.* London, 1988.

Jones, H. G. *The Records of a Nation.* New York, 1969.

McCoy, Donald L. *The National Archives: America's Ministry of Documents, 1934–1968.* Chapel Hill, N.C., 1978.

U.S. National Archives. *Guide to the National Archives of the United States.* Washington, D.C., 1974.

U.S. National Archives and Records Administration. *Guide to the Federal Records in the National Archives of the United States.* 3 vols. Washington, D.C., 1995.

Viola, Herman J. *The National Archives of the United States.* New York, 1984.

Walch, Timothy, ed. *A Modern Archives Reader: Essays on the History of the National Archives.* Washington, D.C., 1984.

Walch, Timothy, ed. *Guardian of Heritage: Essays on the History of the National Archives.* Washington, D.C., 1985.

—GEORGE C. CHALOU

National Capital Planning Commission

The central planning agency for the federal government in the national capital region is called the National Capital Planning Commission. The capital region consists of the District of Columbia, the Maryland counties of Prince George's and Montgomery, and Arlington, Fairfax, Prince William, and Loudoun counties in Virginia. The capital region also includes the city of Alexandria.

The federal agency is headed by twelve commission members, each selected by the president or by the mayor of the District of Columbia. The presidential appointees include a resident from Maryland and Virginia, as well as one from anywhere in the United States. The two mayoral appointees must be District residents. Additionally, the commission has seven *ex officio* members, representing various cabinet-level departments, two members of Congress (one from the House, the other from the Senate), the mayor of the District, and the chairman of the District's Council.

The commission meets monthly to plan projects for the capital region. The responsibilities and areas of concern of the commission have evolved through time. For example, in June 1924, when Congress first established the agency, originally named the National Capital Park Commission, the objective was to acquire lands to complete a park, a parkway, and a playground system for the capital. By 1926, however, Congress reestablished the agency as the National Capital Park and Planning Commission and added the responsibilities of including recommendations on highways, parks, bridges, waterfronts, public and private buildings, and zoning regulations. The new act further designated it as the central planning agency for natural and historical features.

A 1952 act of Congress expanded the responsibilities of the commission and charged it with the duty of preparing and adopting a comprehensive plan for the national capital. Additionally, the new legislation required the commission to review federal and District master plans. Finally, in 1973, the District of Columbia Self-Government and Governmental Reorganization Act, known as the Home Rule Act, amended the National Capital Planning Act of 1952. Although the new act made the mayor chief planner for the District, it left projects considered part of the federal master plan under the jurisdiction of the commission.

During the 1990s, with the dual, but perhaps sometimes opposing goals of preserving historic features of the national capital while permitting development, the commission continues to represent the federal interest in planning by coordinating plans with local, state, and regional plans and programs. The agency conducts reviews of proposed rezoning, site plans, and special project developments to determine if there is an adverse impact on the federal interest.

To ensure that it meets its dual goals, the commission also prepares, adopts, and submits annually to the Office of Management and Budget (OMB) a five-year federal capital improvements program for the region containing land acquisitions and development proposals from all federal agencies. Following the OMB's review of the budget, it is forwarded to Congress for funding. For the fiscal years 1995–1999, for example, the National Capital Planning Commission request amounted to over $5.41 billion in proposed projects.

BIBLIOGRAPHY

National Capital Planning Commission. *Worthy of the Nation: The History of Planning for the National Capital.* Washington, D.C., 1977.
National Capital Planning Commission Fact Sheet. Washington, D.C., 1995.
U.S. Congress. House. *Reorganization Plan Number Five of 1966: National Capital Regional Planning Council; Hearing before a Subcommittee of the Committee of Government Operations.* 89th Cong., 2d sess., 1966. Washington, D.C., 1966.

—VERONICA D. DiCONTI

National Center for Atmospheric Research.

See Atmospheric Research, National Center for.

National Credit Union Administration.

See Credit Union Administration, National.

National Endowments for the Arts and Humanities

According to their enabling legislation, the National Endowments for the Arts (NEA) and Humanities (NEH)—established as part of the National Foundation for Arts and Humanities (NFAH) Act of 1965—were to "develop and promote a broadly conceived national policy of support for the humanities and the arts in the United States and for institutions that preserve the cultural heritage of the United States" (P.L. 89-209, Sec. 953). The NEA and NEH are independent executive agencies: that is, they do not fall within the jurisdiction of any cabinet department, and each of their chairpersons reports directly to the president. In 1976 a third operating agency—the Institute for Museum Services—was established; it was incorporated as a part of the

NFAH in 1984. The NFAH Act also provided for a Federal Council on the Arts and Humanities (FCAH) that might serve as an interagency coordinating mechanism between the endowments and between these and other federal agencies and departments responsible for other cultural programs. Historically, the FCAH has been active only with regard to the administration of the Arts and Artifacts Indemnity Act of 1975 and during the presidency of Jimmy Carter; in fact, it appears to have been superseded by the President's Committee on the Arts and Humanities (PCAH), which was established by executive order of Ronald Reagan during the early 1980s and is primarily concerned with stimulating private support for national cultural needs and opportunities. The PCAH includes up to thirty-two private citizens appointed by the president as well as thirteen statutory members who serve as officials of various federal agencies that administer cultural programs.

Although the federal government had occasionally undertaken other federal programs in the arts and humanities, the creation of the NEA and NEH marked the first instance of explicit and ongoing programs of direct support for the arts and humanities on a national scale. Historically, governments have granted indirect benefits to nonprofit cultural organizations in the form of tax exemptions and of tax deductibility for donor gifts. During the 1930s the federal government had briefly experimented with employment programs for artists and intellectuals under the auspices of the Works Progress Administration. By the 1950s the federal government had developed interest in international cultural exchanges, the design and decoration of public buildings, government collections (such as the National Gallery of Art, the Smithsonian Institution, and the Library of Congress), and in the design of commemorative coins, stamps, monuments, and artworks.

Passage of the NFAH Act was facilitated by a number of political developments and responded to social and economic conditions facing cultural organizations in the 1960s. On the political side, a small but strategically positioned set of cultural policy supporters in Congress had been incubating ideas and rationales for a federal

role for over a decade. This group included Senators Claiborne Pell (D-R.I.), Jacob Javits (R-N.Y.), J. William Fulbright (D-Ark.), and Hubert Humphrey (D-Minn.) as well as Representative Frank Thompson (D-N.J.). Second, presidential interest in the arts and humanities began to develop late in the Eisenhower administration and gathered greater momentum during the Kennedy years. President Kennedy appointed a special consultant, August Heckscher, to write a report with policy recommendations on "The Arts and the National Government." In addition, after a number of futile attempts to secure congressional approval for the establishment of a Federal Advisory Council on the Arts, President Kennedy announced plans to do so by executive order. Finally, following the assassination of President Kennedy, federal sponsorship of cultural activities was promoted both as a tribute to the slain president and by the legislative skills and resources of his successor, Lyndon B. Johnson.

Coincidentally, financial problems facing many arts institutions became increasingly evident. Private national foundations prepared the ground for federal action by sponsoring research and model programs and by articulating policy arguments. A privately organized national commission on the humanities issued a report calling for policy parity with the sciences through the creation of a National Foundation for the Humanities. Following his reelection in 1964, President Johnson combined these arts and humanities developments into the NFAH Act and attached it as an education initiative of the Great Society legislative agenda.

According to the NFAH Act's declaration of purpose, the creation of the NEA and NEH rested on the following principles or assumptions: "encouragement and support of national progress and scholarship in the humanities and the arts" are primarily a matter for private and local initiative but also a matter of federal concern; in accordance with the principles of American civilization and democracy as well as the requirements of world leadership, the arts and humanities must be cultivated no less than the sciences and technology; federal programs and support can assist local, state, regional, and private activities in the arts and humanities; the federal government can help to "create and sustain not only a climate encouraging freedom of thought, imagination, and inquiry [but also] the material conditions facilitating the release of this creative talent"; and commitment must be shown to the encouragement of professional excellence and cultural diversity, access for all citizens, and freedom of expression.

These principles have underwritten the NEA and NEH throughout their history. In 1990, when the agencies were last reauthorized, additional declarations of purposes were attached. There was an acknowledgment that the agencies and the policies they administered were of a public nature—"the arts and the humanities belong to all the people of the United States"—and that "Government must be sensitive to the nature of public sponsorship. Public funding . . . is subject to the conditions that traditionally govern the use of public money. Such funding should contribute to public support and confidence in the use of taxpayer funds [and] must ultimately serve public purposes the Congress defines" (Sec. 951[5]). Other declarations underlined a concern with the nation's "multicultural artistic heritage" (Sec. 951[10]) as well as the federal government's interest in "transmit[ting] the achievement and values of civilization from the past via the present to the future" (Sec. 951[11]).

According to the NEA's enabling legislation, the arts are broadly defined as including without being limited to:

> music (instrumental and vocal), dance, drama, folk arts, creative writing, architecture and allied fields, painting, sculpture, photography, graphic and craft arts, industrial design, costume and fashion design, motion pictures, television, radio, tape and song recording, the arts related to the presentation, performance, execution, and exhibition of such major arts forms, and the study and application of the arts to human environment (Sec. 952 [3 b]).

The NEA developed a program division structure that reflected this essentially discipline-based definition of the arts; by the 1990s, categories included dance, design arts, expansion arts, folk arts, the international program, literature, media arts, museums, music, opera–musical theater, presenting and commissioning, theater, visual arts, challenge and advancement grants, arts in

education, the local arts agencies program, and the state and regional program. In the wake of sustained controversy over and criticism of its operations and in the face of a significant budget cut, the NEA announced a major reorganization effective as of January 1996. As a consequence, while the agency continues to support all the arts disciplines and fields that it has in the past, the traditional discipline-based structure was replaced with four thematic categories: heritage and preservation, creation and presentation, education and access, and planning and stabilization.

Thanks to the recent reorganization, the NEA now bears a closer resemblance structurally to the NEH, which has traditionally been organized around functional program areas such as education, fellowships and seminars, preservation and access, public programs, research programs, and state programs. Even these have been consolidated somewhat as a result of recent budget reductions into four categories: research and education, public programs and enterprises, preservation and access, and federal-state partnerships. The fields to which the NEH, according to its enabling legislation, is charged with providing support include but are not limited to:

> the study and interpretation of . . . language, both modern and classical; linguistics; literature; history; jurisprudence; philosophy; archeology; comparative religion; ethics; the history, criticism and theory of the arts; those aspects of the social sciences which have humanistic content and employ humanistic methods; and the study and application of the humanities to the human environment with particular attention to reflecting out diverse heritage, traditions, and history and to the relevance of the humanities to the current conditions of national life. (Sec. 952)

In many ways the organization and operations of the two endowments are similar. Each is headed by a presidentially appointed chairperson who is subject to Senate confirmation and who is eligible for reappointment upon completion of a four-year term. By law, the chairperson is the only person with authority to establish policy and to award grants. In addition, a number of advisory mechanisms assist the chairperson and the agency in the administration of programs. These include a National Council for the

Arts and a National Council for the Humanities as well as grant advisory panels or peer panels. Twenty-six private citizens recognized for their achievements in and knowledge of the arts are appointed by the president, with the advice and consent of the Senate, for staggered terms of six years. A similar group of citizens with broad knowledge of, commitment to, and expertise in the humanities serves on the National Council for the Humanities. These national councils each meet quarterly to review grant applications, to discuss policy, and to advise the chairperson on policies, programs, and field conditions. In addition, the members of the national councils often work on behalf of the agencies to drum up support among lawmakers, to increase public awareness of and interest in the arts and humanities, and to encourage greater support for the arts and humanities by corporations, foundations, and other public agencies.

Although grant advisory panels were not formally a part of the structure of the two endowments, they quickly became key components of the grant-making process. Panels are convened to review grant applications for all categories in each of the program divisions. Panel size varies between five and twenty members who are appointed by the chairperson to one-year terms (renewable for up to three years). Panelists may be recommended by endowment staff, cultural lobbying organizations, national council members, elected officials, and other concerned members of the cultural community. Panelists are selected for their expert knowledge, with an eye toward geographic, gender, ethnic, racial, and professional diversity. Panel members serve as individuals, not as representatives of their institutions. To assure diverse representation and fairness, there is considerable turnover each year in the membership of specific panels. Since 1990 NEA grant advisory panels have been required to have at least one member who is a knowledgeable layperson.

In the case of the NEH, *ad hoc* panels are assembled each year depending on the composition of the applicant pool. Panel deliberations are further informed by the solicitation of written assessments prepared by outside peer reviewers for each grant application. In the case of the

NEA, the panel composition and rotation have worked a bit differently. Beginning in the late 1970s, the NEA convened two types of panels: grant advisory panels and policy panels. Policy panels provided an overview of a field and advice on priorities, practices, guidelines, and the allocation of resources within individual agency programs. Typically, members of policy panels also served on a grant advisory panel within the same program. In both types of panels, efforts were made to maintain some continuity in membership from year to year. An exception was fellowship panels, where membership turned over completely each year.

In 1994 the NEH asked some twelve hundred humanities experts to serve on nearly 250 panels to review 8,319 applications that resulted in the award of 1,563 grants. Meanwhile, in 1993 the NEA called upon 1,005 experts to serve on 138 panels; 16,259 applications were reviewed, and 4,096 grants were awarded.

The recommendations of advisory panels have traditionally carried great weight in the grant-making process. Only a small percentage of the award recommendations put forward by the panels have been questioned, remanded, or rejected by either the national council or the chairperson. Differences of opinion or assessment were exceptionally rare during the first fifteen years of operation of the NEA and NEH, but since then they have become more frequent—although still unusual. Because they exercise such great influence in the allocation and award of federal moneys as well as in the direction and character of program policy, endowment panels have periodically been the subject of political scrutiny and comment. Concern has been voiced about the potential for "cronyism" and "closed-circle decision-making," about representativeness, and about possible conflicts of interest. Conversely, panels have been praised as having broadened the base of private citizen participation, as a time-tested principle, and as a valuable source of expert knowledge and judgment. Peer panels seemed to play a particularly influential role in the arts both because the NEA's panels came to constitute the broadest, most comprehensive evaluation system in the nation and because the arts, in contrast to the humanities or the sciences, had few other systems of professional validation and recognition.

Beginning in 1989, controversies over specific NEA grants brought the agency escalating congressional criticism. The photographic works of Robert Mapplethorpe and Andres Serrano were attacked as obscene and blasphemous. The works of various performance artists as well as literary works also drew public, and especially conservative, censure. Eventually the grant-making processes, the organization, and even the very idea of federal support for the arts were called into question. Meanwhile, the NEH encountered controversy over "political correctness," especially concerning its support for the development of history curriculum standards for primary and secondary education. With both the NEA and the NEH battlefields in the so-called "culture wars," Congress has not reauthorized the agencies since 1993. Congressional criticism of the agencies increased in the wake of the midterm elections of 1994 that ushered in Republican control of both houses of Congress. Following the election of many new members who opposed one or both of the endowments and the selection of House leaders who were critical of the agencies, the NEA sustained budget cuts of approximately forty percent, dropping from $162 million in fiscal year 1995 to $99.5 million for fiscal year 1996. The NEH's appropriation was also dropped to $99.5 million. Despite these sizable funding cuts, supporters did succeed in saving the two agencies from elimination; however, the future of the NEA and NEH remains precarious.

BIBLIOGRAPHY

American Council of Learned Societies, Council of Graduate Schools of the United States, and United Chapters of Phi Beta Kappa. *The Report of the Commission on the Humanities*. New York, 1964.

Berman, Ronald. *Culture and Politics*. Lanham, Md., 1984.

Biddle, Livingston. *Our Government and the Arts: A Perspective from the Inside*. New York, 1988.

Cummings, Milton C., Jr. "To Change a Nation's Cultural Policy: The Kennedy Administration and the Arts in the United States." In *America's Commitment to Culture*, edited by Kevin Mulcahy and Margaret Jane Wyszomirski, pp. 95–120. Boulder, Colo., 1995.

Hughes, Robert. *Culture of Complaint: The Fraying of America*. New York, 1993.

Independent Commission. *A Report to Congress on the National Endowment for the Arts*. Washington, D.C., 1990.

McDonald, William F. *Federal Relief Administration and the Arts*. Columbus, Ohio, 1968.

McKinzie, Richard D. *The New Deal for Artists*. Princeton, N.J., 1973.

Marquis, Alice Goldfarb. *Art Lessons: Learning from the Rise and Fall of Public Arts Funding*. New York, 1995.

Miller, Stephen. *Excellence and Equity: The National Endowment for the Humanities*. Lexington, Ky., 1984.

Mulcahy, Kevin V. and Margaret Jane Wyszomirski, eds. *America's Commitment to Culture: Public Policy and the Arts*. Boulder, Colo., 1995.

National Endowment for the Arts. *1994 Annual Report*. Washington, D.C., 1995.

National Endowment for the Arts. "Reorganization Fact Sheet." Washington, D.C., 1995.

National Endowment for the Humanities. *1994 Annual Report*. Washington, D.C., n.d.

Netzer, Dick. *The Subsidized Muse: Public Support for the Arts in the United States*. New York, 1978.

Taylor, Fannie, and Anthony L. Barresi. *The Arts at a New Frontier: The National Endowment for the Arts*. New York, 1984.

—MARGARET J. WYSZOMIRSKI

National Highway Traffic Safety Administration.

See Highway Traffic Safety Administration, National.

National Institute of Standards and Technology.

See Standards and Technology, National Institute of.

National Institutes of Health

The mission of the National Institutes of Health (NIH)—the U.S. federal government's principal agency for the support of medical research—is to uncover new knowledge that will lead to improved human health. The NIH is a part of the Public Health Service, which, in turn, is one component of the Department of Health and Human Services. Its task is implemented through its intramural and extramural programs, through support for the training of new investigators, and through the dissemination of biomedical information for the public and health care professionals. The extramural programs comprise grant and contract awards to biomedical research scientists across the United States and, on a much smaller scale, in foreign countries. The intramural programs are made up of research laboratories sponsored directly by the agency on its 320-acre campus in Bethesda, Maryland, and at field stations in Maryland, North Carolina, Montana, New Mexico, and Puerto Rico. More than sixteen thousand people work in the NIH intramural programs, of whom about six thousand are physicians and scientists directly involved in research projects. In 1997 the budget for the NIH was just over $12 billion. Of this amount, eighty percent was designated for the extramural program, about eleven percent for the intramural program, and about nine percent for other uses. The focus of NIH awards is on the extension of basic scientific knowledge rather than on applications such as the drug discovery process, which is supported primarily by industry.

This configuration for federal biomedical research emerged after World War II, but the NIH itself traces its roots to 1887, when a one-room laboratory was created within the Marine Hospital Service (MHS), predecessor agency to the U.S. Public Health Service. The MHS had been established in 1798 to provide for the medical care of merchant seamen. One clerk in the Treasury Department collected twenty cents per month from the wages of each seaman to cover costs at a series of contract hospitals. Treasury remained the administrative home of the service until 1939, when it was transferred to the newly created Federal Security Agency (FSA). In 1953 FSA agencies were transferred to the new Department of Health, Education, and Welfare, which in 1980 was renamed the Department of Health and Human Services when a separate Department of Education was created.

By the 1880s the MHS had been charged by Congress with examining passengers on arriving ships for clinical signs of infectious diseases, es-

pecially for the dreaded diseases cholera and yellow fever, in order to prevent epidemics. During the 1870s and 1880s, the French chemist Louis Pasteur, the German physician Robert Koch, and their associates had presented compelling evidence that microscopic organisms were the causes of several infectious diseases. In 1884, for example, Koch described a comma-shaped bacterium as the cause of cholera. Officials of the MHS followed these developments with great interest and, in 1887, authorized Joseph J. Kinyoun, a young physician trained in the new bacteriological methods, to set up a laboratory in the Marine Hospital at Stapleton, Staten Island, New York. Kinyoun called his facility a "laboratory of hygiene" in imitation of German facilities, which were considered the finest in the world and were so designated. Within a few months Kinyoun had identified the cholera bacillus and demonstrated it to his colleagues as confirmation of their clinical diagnoses.

In 1891 the laboratory was moved to Washington, D.C., and housed in the Butler Building, a facility near the U.S. Capitol that was demolished in 1929 when the Longworth House Office Building was constructed. For the next decade Kinyoun remained the sole full-time staff member. He inaugurated a training program in bacteriology for MHS officers and conducted numerous tests of water purity and air quality for the District of Columbia and the Congress. During this period the laboratory gradually, and without apparent design, became known as the Hygienic Laboratory.

In 1901 the Hygienic Laboratory was belatedly recognized in law when Congress authorized $35,000 for construction of a new building in which the laboratory could investigate "infectious and contagious diseases and matters pertaining to the public health." Occupied in 1904, this building was located at Twenty-fifth and E streets, N.W., in Washington, D.C. The organic legislation for the NIH, therefore, resides not in a visionary health act; it is, instead, buried in a routine supplemental appropriations act. Many other scientific agencies of the federal government were also created via "money bills." Congress was not convinced that such bureaucracies would prove demonstrably useful, so it chose to preserve the option of divesting the government of them simply by not renewing their funding.

In 1902 two acts contributed significantly to the emergence of the Hygienic Laboratory as a center for research within the federal government. The first reorganized the MHS and renamed it the Public Health and Marine Hospital Service (PH-MHS), moving it forward toward its status as the chief U.S. public health agency. More important for the Hygienic Laboratory, the act launched a formal program of research by designating the pathological and bacteriological work as the Division of Pathology and Bacteriology and by creating three new components that represented the most fruitful areas for research at that time: the Divisions of Chemistry, Pharmacology, and Zoology. The importance of these new programs was underscored by the provision that the PH-MHS could hire Ph.D. specialists to head them. Before this, the professional staff had been limited to physicians. The Division of Zoology was first headed by Charles Wardell Stiles, who came to the Hygienic Laboratory from the Department of Agriculture, having just identified *Necator americanus,* the hookworm, as the cause of anemia in the southern United States. Stiles and his staff prepared a definitive *Index Catalog of Medical and Veterinary Zoology.* Within the Division of Chemistry, Joseph Hoeing Kastle, its first director, developed a chemical method to identify and estimate the amount of hydrochloric acid in the stomach. The division also developed a hemoglobinometer for measuring the amount of hemoglobin in the blood. The Division of Pharmacology, under the direction of Reid Hunt, studied the biological action of acetylcholine on blood pressure, described the toxicity of methyl and ethyl alcohols, and developed a practical test for thyroid activity. The original Division of Pathology and Bacteriology, headed by the Hygienic Laboratory's director, conducted a major study of typhoid fever in the District of Columbia; identified a new disease, tularemia, carried by California ground squirrels; and conducted research on undulant fever that hastened the pasteurization of milk in the United States.

The Biologics Control Act was the second piece of legislation enacted in 1902 that had major consequences for the Hygienic Laboratory. It charged the laboratory with regulating the production of vaccines and antitoxins, thus making it a regulatory agency four years before passage of the better-known 1906 Pure Food and Drugs Act. The danger posed by biological products resulted from their production in animals and their administration by injection. Diphtheria antitoxin, for example, was made by inoculating horses with increasingly concentrated doses of diphtheria bacteria, then bleeding them to obtain the antibodies in their blood serum, which was injected into the bodies of patients. Possibilities for contamination lurked at every stage of the production process, and the amount of antitoxin necessary to cure was initially undefined. In 1901, thirteen children in St. Louis died after receiving diphtheria antitoxin contaminated with tetanus spores. This tragedy spurred Congress into passing the Biologics Control Act. Between 1903 and 1907 standards were established and licenses issued to pharmaceutical firms for making smallpox and rabies vaccines, diphtheria and tetanus antitoxins, various other antibacterial antisera, thyroidectomized goat serum, and horse serum. This regulatory work also protected the Hygienic Laboratory from political assault because of its practical value to the U.S. citizenry.

In 1912 another service reorganization act shortened the name of the PH-MHS to the Public Health Service (PHS). This brief act also authorized the laboratory to conduct research into noncontagious diseases and into the pollution of streams and lakes in the United States. Under this law, PHS officer Joseph Goldberger in 1914 was able to conduct an epidemiological study that identified the disease pellagra, a scourge of poor Southerners, as a dietary deficiency and to promote brewer's yeast as a cheap and widely available cure. Earl B. Phelps, then director of the Division of Chemistry, described the behavior of oxygen in water, thus fostering better understanding of the effects of pollution in lakes and rivers. During World War I, the PHS attended primarily to the sanitation of areas around military bases in the United States. The staff of the Hygienic Laboratory traced the cause of anthrax outbreaks among the troops to contaminated shaving brushes and discovered that the bunion pads widely used to cover smallpox vaccinations could harbor tetanus spores. During the 1918 influenza epidemic physicians from the laboratory were pressed into service treating patients in the District of Columbia because so many local doctors were ill.

In 1930 the Ransdell Act changed the name of the Hygienic Laboratory to the National Institute of Health (NIH) and authorized the establishment of fellowships for research into basic biological and medical problems. The roots of this act extended to 1918, when chemists hoped to attract a philanthropic patron to support basic studies in chemistry and medicine. In 1926, after no wealthy individual had come forward, the proponents joined with Senator Joseph E. Ransdell of Louisiana to seek federal sponsorship. This bill marked a key transition within the U.S. scientific community from reliance only on private support for medical research to a willingness to seek public funding. The truncated form in which the bill was finally enacted in 1930 reflected the harsh economic realities imposed by the Great Depression.

Seven years later the National Cancer Institute (NCI) was created with sponsorship from every senator in Congress. This unusual agreement among lawmakers revealed growing concern in the nation about cancer and foreshadowed the categorical-disease structure of the NIH that has characterized the agency since that time. The NCI was authorized to award grants to nonfederal scientists for research on cancer and to fund fellowships for young researchers. Under the original legislation the NCI's administrative relationship to the NIH was unspecified. A research facility was constructed, however, as "Building 6" of a new NIH campus in Bethesda, Maryland, that was occupied between 1938 and 1941. In 1944 PHS legislation, the NCI was specifically described as a component of the NIH.

During World War II the NIH focused almost entirely on war-related problems. At the outset a Division of Public Health Methods worked with the Selective Service to analyze why forty-three percent of potential inductees were unfit for general military service and twenty-eight percent unfit for any military service. The most common cause of rejection, they found, was defective teeth; many of those rejected also had syphilis.

To protect workers in war industries, the Division of Industrial Hygiene collaborated with the Divisions of Pathology and Pharmacology to conduct research on hazardous substances and conditions, examining new explosives, developing methods to determine the amount of lead or TNT in urine so that workers could be tested for undue exposure, and demonstrating the affinity of lead for bone tissue. Other investigators determined that vapors of methyl, ethyl propyl, isopropyl, and butyl ether were acutely toxic to workers. This work improved conditions of employment for more than 300,000 workers in defense industries.

Vaccines and therapies to deal with tropical diseases were also critically important to the war effort. At the NIH's Rocky Mountain Laboratory in Hamilton, Montana, yellow fever and typhus vaccines were prepared for military forces. In Bethesda—as well as through grants to investigators at universities—a synthetic substitute for quinine was sought to treat malaria. The Division of Biologics investigated the fever-producing properties of bacteria that might appear as contaminants of plasma, serum albumin, or whole blood and developed sampling techniques to avoid contamination. Research in the Division of Chemotherapy revealed that sodium deficiency was the critical element leading to death after burns or traumatic shock. This led to the widespread use of oral saline therapy as a first-aid measure on the battlefield. NIH and military physiologists collaborated on problems related to high-altitude flying. They determined the altitude at which oxygen had to be administered to prevent pilots from blacking out and designed an apparatus to supply extra oxygen efficiently. They also studied the relation of pressure changes to bubble formation in liquids to address the problem of emboli forming in the blood of pilots. Other tests were made to evaluate the efficiency of flight clothing, especially electrically heated suits, and to determine the effect of altitude on visual acuity and the use of visual devices for improvement of night vision.

As the war drew to a close, PHS leaders guided through Congress the 1944 Public Health Service Act, which defined the shape of medical research in the postwar world. Two provisions in particular proved key for NIH. First, the successful grants program of the NCI was expanded to the entire NIH. From slightly more than $4 million in 1947, the program grew to more than $100 million in 1957 and $1 billion in 1974. The entire NIH budget expanded from $8 million in 1947 to more than $1 billion in 1966. Concomitant with growth in the grants program came the proliferation of new categorical institutes. Between 1946 and 1949, voluntary health organizations spurred Congress to create institutes for research on mental health, dental diseases, and heart disease. In 1948 language in the National Heart Act also made plural the name of the umbrella organization: National Institutes of Health. By 1960 there were ten components. This number increased by 1970 to fifteen, and in 1995 there were twenty-four institutes, centers, and divisions:

- National Cancer Institute
- National Eye Institute
- National Heart, Lung, and Blood Institute
- National Institute of Allergy and Infectious Diseases
- National Institute of Arthritis and Musculoskeletal and Skin Diseases
- National Institute of Child Health and Human Development
- National Institute of Dental Research
- National Institute of Diabetes and Digestive and Kidney Diseases
- National Institute of Environmental Health Sciences
- National Institute of General Medical Sciences
- National Institute of Mental Health
- National Institute of Neurological Disorders and Stroke
- National Institute of Nursing Research
- National Institute on Aging
- National Institute on Alcoholism and Alcohol Abuse
- National Institute on Deafness and Other Communication Disorders

- National Institute on Drug Abuse
- National Library of Medicine
- John E. Fogarty International Center
- National Center for Human Genome Research
- National Center for Research Resources
- Warren Grant Magnuson Clinical Center
- Division of Computer Research and Technology
- Division of Research Grants

In addition, specialized offices such as the Office of AIDS Research, the Office of Minority Health, the Office of Research on Women's Health, and the Office of Alternative Medicine were created but subsumed administratively under existing components.

The grants program succeeded in attracting talented investigators into medical research, but it also altered teaching and research priorities within medical schools and expanded institutional reliance on the federal government for a significant portion of personnel costs and program activities. Toward the end of the 1960s, the growth of NIH budgets slowed considerably, in part because of inflation in the U.S. economy and the advent of new programs such as Medicare and Medicaid that competed for congressional "health" funding. This shift posed a problem for young scientists whose numbers did not drop as rapidly as available grant funds. Competition with each other and with experienced senior scientists for limited funding has meant that fewer applications for NIH grant support are successful. As federal grants became more competitive, the funds that they authorized became known as "soft money," meaning that its future was uncertain, in contrast to the "hard money" that represented nonfederal, institutional commitments to personnel and projects. Tighter budgets also led to debate over the relative efficacy of unfettered basic research versus goal-directed applied research, the latter most visibly embodied in the so-called war on cancer. Similarly, the AIDS crisis of the 1980s at first provided an opportunity for goal-directed research quickly to uncover an effective therapy or vaccine. When no quick solution was forthcoming, leaders of the research effort against AIDS began to emphasize study of basic immunological processes as the most effective strategy to find an effective therapy or preventative.

The second key provision of the 1944 PHS act authorized the NIH to conduct clinical research. After the war Congress provided funding to build a research hospital, now called the Warren Grant Magnuson Clinical Center, on the NIH campus in Bethesda. Opened in 1953 with 540 beds, the hospital was designed to bring research laboratories into close proximity to hospital wards in order to promote productive collaboration between laboratory scientists and practicing physicians. Special care was taken to communicate to local physicians that the clinical center dealt only with research and did not represent a move toward "socialized medicine," which was opposed by most physicians in the 1950s. Meanwhile, because the center was launched in the shadow of revelations about Nazi medical experiments during World War II, from the outset a medical board was charged with reviewing research protocols to ensure that they would not harm participants. In 1979 the oversight process was codified into written guidelines for research on human subjects and expanded to all clinical research supported by NIH.

In the 1970s other thorny social and ethical issues also became topics of public concern. The first recombinant DNA experiments, for example, revealed scientific and public concern over a new technology whose implications were unknown. To address concerns about public safety yet permit such research to continue, investigators drew up guidelines for physical and biological containment of recombinant organisms. In addition, a panel of nonfederal physicians, scientists, and laypeople was appointed to review proposed experiments and grant approval only to those that were judged safe. As research proceeded under these rules, biological containment of recombinant organisms—accomplished by utilizing altered organisms that could not survive outside the laboratory—proved to be the preferred strategy, supplanting the elaborate physical containment facilities that are used to perform research on lethal microorganisms.

The NIH investment in biomedical research—that is, in the study of fundamental life processes—can be evaluated, at least in part, by examining some of the discoveries produced and their applications to human health. More than eighty Nobel prizes have been won by investigators supported by the NIH. Five of these medals have been awarded to investigators working in the NIH intramural programs. Their discoveries have included breaking the genetic code that governs all life processes, demonstrating how chemicals act to transmit electrical signals between nerve cells, and describing the relationship between the chemical composition of proteins and how they fold into biologically active conformations. These discoveries have led to greater understanding of genetically based diseases, to better antidepressants, and to drugs specially designed to target proteins involved in particular disease processes. In the 1980s research on AIDS produced a test that permitted screening of the blood supply for antibody to the AIDS virus. Long-term research has dispelled preconceptions that morbidity and dementia are a normal part of the aging process. Some cancers have been cured and deaths from heart attack and stroke have been significantly lowered. Research has also revealed that preventive strategies such as a balanced diet, an exercise program, and not smoking can reduce the need for therapeutic interventions and thus save money otherwise expended for health care.

Physicians, scientists, and political leaders have viewed the NIH as a national treasure, a federal bureaucracy operating on the merit system with minimal political interference and maximum benefit to the taxpayer for the monies expended. Its exceptional status has been reflected in vigorous congressional resistance to members who seek to bypass the scientific peer review system and to earmark research projects solely on the basis of their location in the member's home state. Whether the agency will be able to maintain this position depends upon a number of factors. The most important is public confidence that medical research benefits the people of the United States. Another requirement is the continued perception that fraud in science is an exception to common practice that will be dealt with effectively. Current challenges to medical research come from those who discount the methods of modern science as no more valid than those of any other political interest group. In light of Congress's historical tendency to allocate funds for immediately practical undertakings, expenditures for open-ended basic research require continual justification. NIH administrators and their private-sector supporters must annually reeducate the public and members of Congress in order to make the political case for ongoing public funding of medical research.

[*See also* Public Health Service *and* Science and Technology Policy, Office of.]

BIBLIOGRAPHY

Dickson, David. *The New Politics of Science.* Reprint, Chicago, 1988.

Dyer, R. E. "Medical Research in the United States Public Health Service." *Bulletin of the Society of Medical History of Chicago* 6 (1948): 58–68.

Fox, Daniel M. "The Politics of the NIH Extramural Program, 1937–1950." *Journal of the History of Medicine and Allied Sciences* 42 (1987): 447–466.

Furman, Bess. *A Profile of the United States Public Health Service, 1798–1948.* DHEW Publication No. (NIH) 73–369. Washington, D.C., 1973.

Harden, Victoria A. *Inventing the NIH: Federal Biomedical Research Policy, 1887–1937.* Baltimore, 1986.

Mider, G. Burroughs. "The Federal Impact on Biomedical Research." In *Advances in American Medicine: Essays at the Bicentennial,* edited by John Z. Bowers and Elizabeth F. Purcell, vol. 2, pp. 806–871. New York, 1976.

National Institute of Allergy and Infectious Diseases. *Intramural Contributions, 1887–1987.* Edited by Harriet R. Greenwald and Victoria A. Harden. Bethesda, Md., 1987.

Shannon, James A. "The Advancement of Medical Research: A Twenty-Year View of the Role of the National Institutes of Health. *Journal of Medical Education* 42 (1967): 97–108.

Stetten, DeWitt, Jr., and William T. Carrigan, eds. *NIH: An Account of Research in Its Laboratories and Clinics.* Orlando, Fla., 1984.

Stimson, Arthur H. "A Brief History of Bacteriological Investigations of the U.S. Public Health Service." *Public Health Reports,* supp. no. 141, 1938.

Strickland, Stephen P. *Politics, Science, and Dread Disease: A Short History of United States Medical Research Policy.* Cambridge, Mass., 1972.

Strickland, Stephen P. *The Story of the NIH Grants Program.* Lanham, Md., 1989.

Swain, Donald C. "The Rise of a Research Empire: NIH, 1930–1950." *Science* 138 (1962): 1233–1237.

U.S. National Library of Medicine. *Notable Contributions to Medical Research by Public Health Service Scientists: A Biobibliography to 1940.* Compiled by Jeanette Barry. Public Health Service Publication No. 752. Washington, D.C., 1960.

Williams, Ralph C. *The United States Public Health Service, 1798–1950.* Washington, D.C., 1951.

—VICTORIA A. HARDEN

National Labor Relations Board

An independent agency, the National Labor Relations Board (NLRB) was established by the National Labor Relations (Wagner) Act of 1935. The protection of the rights of workers had not been a federal concern until the Wilson administration—the first Democratic administration in this century—set up the National War Labor Board during World War I. The board, which operated for little more than a year (April 1918–August 1919), worked to protect the rights of employees to bargain collectively and to bar management from interfering with this right and discriminating against employees engaging in legitimate union activity. The following years witnessed the passage of such legislation as the Railway Labor Act of 1926, which set up a board to mediate disputes between railroads and their employees (a similar board was set up for airlines and their employees); the Norris–La Guardia Act of 1932, which restricted judicial power to issue injunctions against unions engaged in peaceful strikes and prohibited federal courts from enforcing "yellow dog" contracts requiring employees not to join a union as a precondition for employment or to quit a union if employed; and the National Industry Recovery Act, an engine of the New Deal, which was passed on 16 June 1933 and which sought to preserve an employee's right to collective bargaining. When employers began ignoring the provisions of this last act, Roosevelt responded by creating a National Labor Board, under the chairmanship of Senator Robert Wagner, consisting of three members drawn from industry and three drawn from labor. Twenty regional baby boards were set up for the same purpose. The board did not last long, as the employers continued to defy it. Further, the Supreme Court declared the board unconstitutional. To remedy the situation, Congress passed in 1935 the National Labor Relations Act, known commonly as the Wagner Act, setting up the NLRB. The board was granted strong regulatory powers, including the right to issue subpoenas, cease-and-desist orders, and other remedies. The act barred employers from engaging in five kinds of illegal practices:

- interfering with the right of employees to organize

- establishing, or contributing to the support of, a pro-company or sweetheart union

- discriminating against actual or potential employees on the basis of union membership

- discriminating against employees who testified against employers or filed charges under the act

- refusing to bargain collectively with the union.

The Wagner Act survived five challenges in the Supreme Court brought by employer groups and remained substantially unchanged until 1947, when the Republican-controlled Congress passed the Taft-Hartley Act over Truman's veto. The act added to the original legislation a list of unfair labor practices that unions were barred from practicing. A free speech amendment allowed employers to campaign against unions prior to an NLRB election so long as no threats or promises were made. While still protecting the right of employees to bargain collectively, join a union, or strike, it allowed the unions to be sued for contract violations and to be held liable for damages resulting from illegal actions. Closed shops were declared illegal, but union shops were permitted. Union officials had to file financial reports and swear they were not Communists. Public servants were denied the right to strike. Federal courts could intervene in "national emergency strikes" and issue injunctions after an eighty-day cooling-off period. The NLRB itself was expanded to five members. To remove the appearance of its dual role as prosecutor and judge, the office of an independent general counsel was created. The act also created the Fed-

eral Mediation and Conciliation Service and the Joint Committee on Labor Management.

The next landmark in the evolution of the NLRB was the Landrum-Griffin Act of 1959, passed in the aftermath of reports of union corruption. Titled the Labor-Management Reporting and Disclosure Act, the act required all unions to adopt formal constitutions and bylaws and register them with the secretary of labor. In addition, the unions were required to prepare annual reports detailing assets, liabilities, receipts and their sources, payments to union members exceeding $10,000, loans to union members and businesses, and other disbursements. The Postal Service was brought within NLRB jurisdiction in 1970, and private health care institutions in 1974. Later the coverage was expanded to professional sports teams, private universities, and law firms.

The NLRB has used its rule-making powers sparingly. In 1987 the board recognized eight appropriate bargaining units in acute care hospitals, and this rule was upheld by the Supreme Court in 1991. In an effort to comply with another Supreme Court decision, the board decided that non-union workers who had to pay fees to a union were entitled to withhold that portion of the fee not related to administration or collective bargaining. On various occasions the Supreme Court has acted to curtail the scope of the NLRB's powers. It has established that the NLRB has no jurisdiction over teachers in church-affiliated schools and faculty members in private universities. It has overturned the NLRB on other occasions, based on its interpretation of statutes.

The gradual erosion of the Wagner Act continued even through the Democratic administrations of the 1960s. Carter was generally pro-labor but failed to influence Congress to pass two pieces of legislation designed to reverse the trend. One was the legalization of common-site picketing in the construction industry, and the other was a simplification of the union certification procedures. The Reagan era represented the triumph of conservative forces and the rout of the labor movement. Attrition allowed Reagan to appoint new board members, all of whom were described by organized labor as "union busters." These Reagan appointees handed down a number of decisions calculated to turn the balance in favor of management. Employers were given the right to demand loyalty from supervisors. The board refrained from interfering in "minor" workplace disputes and also relaxed rules on management neutrality when rival unions competed in the workplace. During this period the American Federation of Labor and Congress of Industrial Organizations (AFL-CIO) has estimated that the NLRB sided with employers sixty percent of the time as against thirty percent for previous boards. A huge case backlog also developed as a deliberate strategy to discourage unions from seeking government help. Workers were sometimes forced to wait for years. President Bush's appointees to the board succeeded in restoring a more impartial approach to board decisions. Although they were conservative, they were more evenhanded in their application of the law.

Even as the NLRB was losing both the image and the clout invested in it by the Wagner Act, the labor movement as a whole was in serious trouble. Unions and labor leaders suffered major political defeats, especially when the Democratic Clinton administration pushed the North American Free Trade Agreement through Congress against bitter union opposition. By 1994 labor was spending more money on political action committees but showing less for it. It was unable to prevent Congress from permitting permanent replacement of striking workers. The possibility that they might be replaced by permanent nonunion workers was a strong disincentive to many workers to strike, and a volatile and downsizing economy did not provide any motivation either. In fact, an AFL-CIO study in 1994 concluded that "confrontation and conflict are wasteful and a cooperative approach to solving shared present and future problems is desirable."

The NLRB is governed by a board of five members nominated by the president and confirmed by the Senate. Board members serve five-year terms and the general counsel a four-year term. The board conducts representational and decertification elections, certifies the results of elections, and acts to prevent employers and unions from engaging in unfair labor practices.

The NLRB does not have the power to initiate proceedings; it acts only when cases are brought before it and only in cases in which the labor dispute affects commerce. The standard procedure is for employers or employees to file a petition under oath with NLRB regional offices. Several classes of employers/employees are exempt from the NLRB's purview: racetracks, horse trainers, real estate brokers, agricultural laborers, domestic servants, independent contractors, managers or supervisors, employees subject to the Railway Labor Act, federal, state, or local government employees, employees of Federal Reserve Banks, and employees of church-affiliated schools. Many NLRB cases are decided in one of the thirty-four NLRB offices, and only five percent reach the board for review.

The most significant activity conducted by the NLRB is the holding of elections in the workplace. Such elections are held after lengthy investigations into the rival claims, credentials of the parties, and related matters. In the case of a dispute, the NLRB may order a secret ballot election in accordance with established board rules. The other major responsibility of the NLRB is monitoring of unfair labor practices and prescription of suitable remedies. The NLRB is authorized to issue cease-and-desist orders requiring offending parties to take appropriate action. In about one-third of the cases, arbitration procedures result in acceptable agreements. Unsettled charges are decided by an administrative law judge in accordance with procedures that apply to a U.S. District Court. Decisions of the administrative law judge may be appealed to the board, and then to the U.S. Court of Appeals. Board cases account for more litigation in the U.S. Courts of Appeals than do those of any other federal agency. Many of these cases go all the way to the Supreme Court.

BIBLIOGRAPHY

Gross, James A. *The Making of the National Labor Relations Board, 1933–1937.* New York, 1974.
Gross, James A. *The Reshaping of the National Labor Relations Board: National Labor Policy in Transition, 1937–1947.* New York, 1978.
Miscimarra, Philip A. *The NLRB and Managerial Discretion.* Philadelphia, 1983.

Murphy, Betty S., and Elliott S. Azaoff. *Practice and Procedure before the National Labor Relations Board.* Washington, D.C., 1989.

—GEORGE THOMAS KURIAN

National Mediation Board.

See Mediation Board, National.

National Museums.

See Smithsonian Institution.

National Oceanic and Atmospheric Administration.

See Oceanic and Atmospheric Administration, National.

National Park Service

The concept of the national park is generally credited to the artist George Catlin. On a trip to the Dakotas in 1832, he worried about the impact of America's westward expansion on Indian civilization, wildlife, and wilderness. They might be preserved, he wrote, "by some great protecting policy of government . . . in a magnificent park. . . . A *nation's park,* containing man and beast, in all the wild and freshness of their nature's beauty!"

Catlin's vision was partly realized in 1864, when Congress donated Yosemite Valley to California for preservation as a state park. Eight years later, in 1872, Congress reserved the spectacular Yellowstone country in the Wyoming and Montana territories "as a public park or pleasuring-ground for the benefit and enjoyment of the people." With no state government there yet to receive and manage it, Yellowstone remained in the custody of the U.S. Department of the Interior as a national park—the world's first area so designated.

Congress followed the Yellowstone precedent with other national parks in the 1890s and early 1900s, including Sequoia, Yosemite (to which California returned Yosemite Valley), Mount Rainier, Crater Lake, and Glacier. The idealistic impulse to preserve nature was often joined by the pragmatic desire to promote tourism: western railroads lobbied for many of the early parks and built grand rustic hotels in them to boost their passenger business.

The late nineteenth century also saw growing interest in preserving prehistoric Indian ruins and artifacts on the public lands. Congress first moved to protect such a feature, Arizona's Casa Grande Ruin, in 1889. In 1906 it created Mesa Verde National Park, containing dramatic cliff dwellings in southwestern Colorado, and passed the Antiquities Act authorizing presidents to set aside "historic and prehistoric structures, and other objects of historic or scientific interest" in federal custody as national monuments. Theodore Roosevelt used the act to proclaim eighteen national monuments before he left the presidency. They included not only cultural features like El Morro, New Mexico, site of prehistoric petroglyphs and historic inscriptions, but natural features like Arizona's Petrified Forest and Grand Canyon. Congress later converted many of these natural monuments to national parks.

By 1916 the Interior Department was responsible for fourteen national parks and twenty-one national monuments but had no organization to manage them. Interior secretaries had asked the Army to detail troops to Yellowstone and the California parks for this purpose. There military engineers and cavalrymen developed park roads and buildings, enforced regulations against hunting, grazing, timber cutting, and vandalism, and did their best to serve the visiting public. Civilian appointees superintended the other parks, while the monuments received minimal custody. In the absence of an effective central administration, those in charge operated without coordinated supervision or policy guidance.

The parks were also vulnerable to competing interests, including some within the ascendant conservation movement. Utilitarian conservationists favoring regulated use rather than strict preservation of natural resources advocated the construction of dams by public authorities for water supply, power, and irrigation purposes. When San Francisco sought to dam Yosemite's Hetch Hetchy Valley for a reservoir after the turn of the century, the utilitarian and preservationist wings of the conservation movement came to blows. Over the passionate opposition of John Muir and other park supporters, Congress in 1913 permitted the dam, which historian John Ise later called "the worst disaster ever to come to any national park."

Hetch Hetchy highlighted the institutional weakness of the park movement. While utilitarian conservation had become well represented in government by the U.S. Geological Survey and the Forest and Reclamation services, no comparable bureau spoke for park preservation in Washington. Among those recognizing the problem was Stephen T. Mather, a wealthy and well-connected Chicago businessman. When Mather complained to Secretary of the Interior Franklin K. Lane about the parks' mismanagement, Lane invited him to Washington as his assistant for park matters. Twenty-five-year-old Horace M. Albright became Mather's top aide upon Mather's arrival in 1915.

Crusading for a national parks bureau, Mather and Albright effectively blurred the distinction between utilitarian conservation and preservation by emphasizing the economic value of parks as tourist meccas. A vigorous public relations campaign led to supportive articles in *National Geographic,* the *Saturday Evening Post,* and other popular magazines. Mather hired his own publicist and obtained funds from seventeen western railroads to produce *The National Parks Portfolio,* a lavishly illustrated publication sent to congressmen and other influential citizens.

Congress responded as desired, and on 25 August 1916 President Woodrow Wilson approved legislation creating the National Park Service within the Interior Department. The act made the bureau responsible for Interior's national parks and monuments, Hot Springs Reservation in Arkansas (made a national park in 1921), and "such other national parks and reservations of like character as may be hereafter created by Congress." In managing these areas, the Park Ser-

vice was directed "to conserve the scenery and the natural and historic objects and the wild life therein and to provide for the enjoyment of the same in such manner and by such means as will leave them unimpaired for the enjoyment of future generations."

Secretary Lane named Mather the Park Service's first director and Albright assistant director. A policy letter Lane approved in 1918 elaborated on the bureau's dual mission of conserving park resources and providing for their enjoyment. While reemphasizing the primacy of preservation, it reflected Mather's and Albright's conviction that more visitors must be attracted and accommodated if the parks were to flourish. Automobiles, not permitted in Yellowstone until 1915, would be allowed throughout the system. Hotels would be provided by concessionaires. Museums, publications, and other educational activities were encouraged as well.

The policy letter also sought to guide the system's expansion. "In studying new park projects, you should seek to find scenery of supreme and distinctive quality or some natural feature so extraordinary or unique as to be of national interest and importance," it directed. "The national park system as now constituted should not be lowered in standard, dignity, and prestige by the inclusion of areas which express in less than the highest terms the particular class or kind of exhibit which they represent."

Through the 1920s the national park system was really a western park system. Only Acadia National Park in Maine lay east of the Mississippi. The West was home to America's most spectacular natural scenery, and most land there was federally owned and thus subject to park or monument reservation without purchase. If the system were to benefit more people and maximize its support in Congress, however, it would have to expand eastward. In 1926 Congress authorized Shenandoah, Great Smoky Mountains, and Mammoth Cave national parks in the Appalachian region but required that their lands be donated. With the aid of John D. Rockefeller, Jr., and other philanthropists, the states involved gradually acquired and turned over most of the land needed for these parks in the next decade.

But the Park Service's greatest opportunity in

the East lay in another realm—that of history and historic sites. Congress had directed the War Department to preserve a number of historic battlefields, forts, and memorials there as national military parks and monuments, beginning in 1890 with Chickamauga and Chattanooga National Military Park in Georgia and Tennessee. After succeeding Mather as director in 1929, Albright was instrumental in getting Congress to establish three new historical parks in the East under Park Service administration. Colonial National Monument, Virginia, which included Yorktown Battlefield, and Morristown National Historical Park, New Jersey, the site of Revolutionary War encampments, edged the Park Service into the War Department's domain.

Soon after Franklin D. Roosevelt took office in 1933, Albright accompanied the new president on a trip to Shenandoah National Park and mentioned his desire to acquire all the military parks. Roosevelt agreed and directed Albright to initiate an executive transfer order. Under the order, effective 10 August 1933, the Park Service received not only the War Department's parks and monuments but the fifteen national monuments then held by the Forest Service as well as the national capital parks, including the Washington Monument, Lincoln Memorial, and White House. The addition of nearly fifty historical areas in the East made the park system and Park Service truly national and deeply involved with historic as well as natural preservation.

As Roosevelt launched his New Deal, the Park Service received another mission: depression relief. Under its supervision the Civilian Conservation Corps (CCC) employed thousands of young men in numerous conservation, rehabilitation, and construction projects in both the national and state parks. The program had a lasting impact on the Park Service. Many professionals hired under its auspices remained on the bureau's rolls as career employees, and regional offices established to coordinate CCC work in the state parks evolved into a permanent regional system for park administration.

During the 1930s the Park Service also became involved with areas intended primarily for mass recreation. Begun as depression relief projects, the Blue Ridge Parkway between Shenandoah and Great Smoky Mountains national parks and the Natchez Trace Parkway between Nashville, Tennessee, and Natchez, Mississippi, were designed for scenic recreational motoring. In 1936, under an agreement with the Bureau of Reclamation, the Park Service assumed responsibility for recreational development and activities at the vast reservoir created by Hoover Dam. Lake Mead National Recreation Area, as it was later titled, was the first of several reservoir areas in the park system. In 1937 Congress authorized Cape Hatteras National Seashore, the first of several seashore and lakeshore areas.

Albright left the Park Service for private business in 1933 and was succeeded by his able associate director, Arno B. Cammerer. Newton B. Drury, who had directed the Save-the-Redwoods League in California, followed Cammerer in 1940. America's entry into World War II a year later forced Drury to preside over a drastic retrenchment in Park Service activity and defend the parks against pressures for consumptive uses in the name of national defense. Timber interests sought Sitka spruce in Olympic National Park for airplane manufacture. Ranchers and mining companies pressed to open other parks to grazing and prospecting. Scrap drive leaders eyed historic cannon at the Park Service's battlefields and forts. Drury successfully resisted most such demands, which eased as needed resources were found elsewhere.

The postwar era brought new pressures on the parks as the nation's energies were redirected to domestic pursuits. Bureau of Reclamation plans to dam wilderness canyons in Dinosaur National Monument in Colorado and Utah touched off a conservation battle recalling Hetch Hetchy. Interior Secretary Oscar L. Chapman's decision to support the project contributed to Drury's resignation in March 1951. But this time the park preservationists won: Congress finally declined to approve the Dinosaur dams.

Conrad L. Wirth, a landscape architect and planner who had led the Park Service's CCC program, became director in December 1951. Facing a park system with a deteriorating infrastructure overwhelmed by the postwar travel boom, he responded with Mission 66, a ten-year, billion-dollar program to upgrade facilities, staffing, and resource management by the bureau's fiftieth anniversary in 1966. A hallmark of Mission 66 was the park visitor center, a multiple-use facility with interpretive exhibits, audiovisual programs, and other public services. By 1960, fifty-six visitor centers were open or under construction in parks from Antietam National Battlefield Site, Maryland, to Zion National Park, Utah.

Mission 66 development, criticized by some as overdevelopment, nevertheless fell short of Wirth's goals—in large part because the Park Service's domain kept expanding, diverting funds and staff to new areas. Congress added more than fifty parks to the system during the ten-year period, from Virgin Islands National Park to Point Reyes National Seashore in California. Expansion continued apace under George B. Hartzog, Jr., who had superintended the Jefferson National Expansion Memorial in St. Louis before succeeding Wirth in 1964. Under his leadership through 1972, the Park Service and system branched out in several new directions.

Natural resource management was restructured along ecological lines following a 1963 report by a committee of scientists chaired by A. Starker Leopold. "As a primary goal, we would recommend that the biotic associations within each park be maintained, or where necessary recreated, as nearly as possible in the condition that prevailed when the area was first visited by the white man," the Leopold Report declared. "A national park should represent a vignette of primitive America." Environmental interpretation, emphasizing ecological relationships, and special environmental education programs for school classes reflected and promoted the nation's growing environmental awareness.

"Living history" programs became popular attractions at many historical parks, ranging from frontier military demonstrations at Fort Davis National Historic Site, Texas, to period farming at Lincoln Boyhood National Memorial, Indiana. The Park Service's historical activities expanded beyond the parks as well. Responding to the destructive effects of urban renewal, highway construction, and other federal projects during the postwar era, the National Historic Preservation Act of 1966 authorized the bureau to maintain a comprehensive National Register of Historic Places. Listed properties—publicly and privately owned, locally as well as nationally significant— would receive special consideration in federal project planning and federal grants and technical assistance to encourage their preservation.

Several new types of parks joined the system during the Hartzog years. Ozark National Scenic Riverways in Missouri, authorized by Congress in 1964, foreshadowed the comprehensive Wild and Scenic Rivers Act of 1968, which led to the acquisition of other free-flowing rivers. On the Great Lakes, Pictured Rocks and Indiana Dunes became the first national lakeshores in 1966. The National Trails System Act of 1968 made the Park Service responsible for the Appalachian National Scenic Trail, running some two thousand miles from Maine to Georgia. Gateway National Recreation Area in New York City and Golden Gate National Recreation Area in San Francisco, both established in 1972, were precedents for other national recreation areas serving metropolitan Cleveland, Atlanta, and Los Angeles.

During the bicentennial of the American Revolution in the mid-1970s, the two dozen historical parks commemorating the Revolution benefited from another big development program. At Independence National Historical Park in Philadelphia the Park Service reconstructed the house where Thomas Jefferson drafted the Declaration of Independence, installed elaborate exhibits at the site of Benjamin Franklin's house, and moved the Liberty Bell to a new pavilion outside Independence Hall. On 4 July 1976 President Gerald R. Ford, once a seasonal ranger at Yellowstone, spoke at Independence Hall and signed legislation making Valley Forge a national historical park.

Four years later, the Alaska National Interest Lands Conservation Act of 1980 more than doubled the size of the national park system by adding over forty-seven million wilderness acres. The largest of the new areas in Alaska, Wrangell–Saint Elias National Park, comprises more than 8.3 million acres, while the adjoining Wrangell–Saint Elias National Preserve comprises nearly 4.9 million. Together they cover an area larger than New Hampshire and Vermont combined and contain the continent's greatest array of glaciers and peaks above sixteen thousand feet. The national preserve designation was applied to ten of the new Alaska areas because they allowed certain activities, like sport hunting and trapping, not permitted in national parks.

Russell E. Dickenson, a former park ranger and manager, took the helm in 1980. Because the Park Service's funding and staffing had not kept pace with its growing responsibilities, Dickenson sought to slow the park system's expansion. The Reagan administration and the Congress that took office with it in 1981 were of like mind. Rather than creating more parks they backed Dickenson's Park Restoration and Improvement Program, which allocated more than a billion dollars over five years to resources and facilities in existing parks.

William Penn Mott, Jr., a landscape architect who had directed California's state parks when Ronald Reagan was governor, followed Dickenson in 1985. Deeply interested in interpretation, Mott sought a greater Park Service role in educating the public about American history and environmental values. He also returned the bureau to a more expansionist posture, supporting such additions as Great Basin National Park, Nevada, and Steamtown National Historic Site, a railroad collection in Scranton, Pennsylvania. Steamtown, championed by Scranton's congressman for its local economic benefits, was a costly venture much criticized as an example of "park barrel" politics, but Mott was convinced of its educational potential.

James M. Ridenour, formerly head of Indiana's Department of Natural Resources, served as director during the Bush administration (1989–1993). Doubting the national significance of Steamtown and other proposed parks driven by economic development interests, he spoke out against the "thinning of the blood" of the national park system and sought to regain the initiative from Congress in charting its expansion. He also worked to achieve a greater financial return to the Park Service from park concessions. In 1990 the Richard King Mellon Foundation made the largest single park donation yet: $10.5 million for additional lands at the Antietam, Gettysburg, Fredericksburg, and Petersburg Civil War battlefields and at Shenandoah National Park.

Roger G. Kennedy, who had directed the Smithsonian Institution's Museum of American History, was the Clinton administration's choice to head the Park Service in 1993. Like Mott, he took particular interest in the bureau's educational role and sought to enlarge its presence beyond the parks via electronic media. His tenure coincided with a government-wide effort to restructure and downsize the federal bureaucracy, which accelerated after the Republicans took control of Congress in 1995 promising to balance the federal budget by 2002. The Park Service restructured its field operations and embarked on a course of reducing its Washington and regional office staffs by forty percent.

By this time the national park system comprised some 370 areas in nearly every state and U.S. possession. In addition to managing these parks—as diverse and far-flung as Hawaii Volcanoes National Park and the Statue of Liberty National Monument—the Park Service was supporting the preservation of natural and historic places and promoting outdoor recreation outside the system through a range of grant and technical assistance programs. Amid growing pressures to curtail federal funding and staffing, increased emphasis was placed on cooperation and partnerships with other government bodies, foundations, corporations, and other private parties to protect the parks and other significant properties and advance Park Service programs.

Public opinion surveys consistently rated the National Park Service among the most popular federal agencies. The high regard in which the national parks and their custodians were held augured well for philanthropic, corporate, and volunteer support, present from the beginnings of the national park movement but never more vital to its prosperity.

[See also Forest Service; Geological Survey; Interior, Department of the; and Reclamation, Bureau of.]

BIBLIOGRAPHY

Albright, Horace M., and Robert Cahn. The Birth of the National Park Service: The Founding Years, 1913–33. Salt Lake City, 1985.
Dilsaver, Lary M., ed. America's National Park System: The Critical Documents. Lanham, Md., 1994.

Everhart, William C. *The National Park Service.* Boulder, Colo., 1983.

Foresta, Ronald A. *America's National Parks and Their Keepers.* Washington, D.C., 1985.

Hartzog, George B., Jr. *Battling for the National Parks.* Mount Kisco, N.Y., 1988.

Hosmer, Charles B., Jr. *Preservation Comes of Age: From Williamsburg to the National Trust, 1926–1949.* 2 vols. Charlottesville, Va., 1981.

Ise, John. *Our National Park Policy: A Critical History.* Baltimore, 1961.

Mackintosh, Barry. *The National Parks: Shaping the System.* Washington, D.C., 1991.

Rettie, Dwight F. *Our National Park System: Caring for America's Greatest Natural and Historic Treasures.* Urbana, Ill., 1995.

Ridenour, James M. *The National Parks Compromised: Pork Barrel Politics and America's Treasures.* Merrillville, Ind., 1994.

Rothman, Hal K. *Preserving Different Pasts: The American National Monuments.* Urbana, Ill., 1989.

Runte, Alfred. *National Parks: The American Experience.* 2d ed. Lincoln, Neb., 1987.

Shankland, Robert. *Steve Mather of the National Parks.* 3d ed. New York, 1976.

Swain, Donald C. *Wilderness Defender: Horace M. Albright and Conservation.* Chicago, 1970.

Wirth, Conrad L. *Parks, Politics, and the People.* Norman, Okla., 1980.

—BARRY MACKINTOSH

National Performance Review

In March 1993 President Bill Clinton announced the creation of an interagency working group that he dubbed the National Performance Review (NPR) and asked Vice President Al Gore to lead it. He asked Gore to report back to him in six months with a blueprint for reforming the government to make it work better and cost less. Gore did, and Clinton endorsed the recommendations. Clinton then asked Gore to make sure the recommendations were implemented and ultimately asked him to undertake additional reform efforts.

The NPR took place in a broader context of governmental changes around the world, and in the midst of a period of significant social changes brought about by rapid technological advances. The NPR learned from, and built upon, the reform efforts that began in the early 1980s in other countries, states and localities across the nation, and private industry.

The NPR's approach was inspired by David Osborne and Ted Gaebler's book *Reinventing Government,* which studied successful innovators in the public sector. It also drew upon the quality management movement that swept private sector organizations in the 1980s, as well as the reengineering efforts of the early 1990s. The NPR was premised on the belief that there was a different understanding of human capacity that diverged from the traditional "command and control" approach in use in most large organizations. Individuals in organizations were capable of more than previously thought, and traditional hierarchies impeded their full potential. A second development brought about revolutionary changes in management. Information technology has allowed the creation of flatter organizations and much faster information sharing. This technology allows decentralized operations while still assuring accountability for results.

The NPR began with a simple vision, that is, to make government work better and cost less. It proposed doing this by acting on the four common characteristics it identified in successful organizations:

- put customers first
- empower employees to put their customers first
- cut the red tape that prevents employees from being empowered
- cut back to basics

To guide managers on how to put these characteristics into action in their own organizations, the NPR described eight steps leaders should take. These steps are based in part on some of the observations made popular in Osborne and Gaebler's *Reinventing Government:*

- create a clear sense of mission
- steer more, row less
- delegate authority and responsibility
- replace regulations with incentives
- develop budgets based on outcomes
- inject competitive spirit into everything we do

- search for market, not administrative, solutions
- measure our success by customer satisfaction

Taken together, these twelve items served as the basic operating instructions for the NPR's teams, the agency teams, and the reinvention labs. The NPR's project director, Bob Stone, announced these as the "operating manual" for the review and had them printed on wallet-size cards for each of the NPR's team members. He felt strongly that relatively simple principles had a greater chance of being actually applied than any set of elaborate theories.

The NPR also relied on several other premises during the course of its review:

- focus on "how" government works, not on "what" it does
- focus on incentives, not changes to organizational structures
- recognize that the problem is systems, not people
- target overhead, not frontline, positions for reduction
- focus on solutions, not studies
- focus on administrative, not legislative, solutions

Taken together, these three sets of characteristics, steps, and premises served as the NPR management team's criteria to assess the thousands of recommendations proposed by its teams.

MAJOR RECOMMENDATIONS IN PHASE I

Gore's September 1993 report to President Clinton offered a wide-ranging vision of how government could be transformed to work better and cost less. It was targeted to two audiences—the general public and the career civil service. For the public, it promised $108 billion in savings, a smaller government by cutting twelve percent of the federal work force, and better services. For the civil service, it promised greater flexibility in getting their jobs done and more authority on the front line to do their jobs. The report contained over one hundred key recommendations organized by the four characteristics of successful public organizations that guided the review. [See

Civil Service.] After concluding that the quality of most government services is below what its customers routinely get from the private sector, the NPR proposed a series of incentives to change the behavior of federal agencies.

Set Challenging Customer Service Standards

The NPR challenged agencies to provide customers services equal to the best in business and to measure customer satisfaction. To help agencies meet this goal, the NPR proposed loosening a number of constraints on agencies by allowing them to conduct surveys of their customers without review by the Office of Management and Budget, encouraging the creation of cross-agency "one-stop" centers, and eliminating statutory restrictions on cross-cutting agency activities that are in the public interest.

Reduce Internal Monopolies

The NPR found the federal government, in the name of economies of scale, had created a series of monopolies that provided agencies poorer services at higher prices. It proposed eliminating the existing printing, supplies, real estate, and furniture monopolies across government. In addition, it proposed taking away the power of monopolies within agencies by allowing managers to obtain services from other parts of their organization or from other agencies via "franchises" in areas such as legal services, audit services, personnel services, and contract services.

Create Market Dynamics

Another approach to improving services is to subject agencies to customer demands by making them market driven. The NPR proposed restructuring the nation's air traffic control system into a corporation to improve its performance. Likewise, it proposed turning over management of HUD's "market-rate" properties and mortgage loans to the private sector. It also proposed encouraging market-based approaches to reducing pollution and housing vouchers for tenants of public housing.

Decentralize Decision-Making and Hold Employees Accountable

To encourage decentralization, Gore recommended that the executive branch decentralize decision-making and increase the average span of control of managers from 1:7 to 1:15. He also recommended holding agencies accountable for developing and using measurable objectives and reporting results. He proposed that this would begin by having the president develop written performance agreements with his key department and agency heads. More broadly, he recommended that the president issue an annual "accountability report to the citizens," starting with the financial condition of the government. To support this, he recommended the creation of accounting standards for the federal government—first proposed by the Hoover Commission in 1949.

Give Federal Workers the Tools They Need To Do Their Jobs

Transforming the work force to being more customer oriented and results focused means recasting how people see and do their jobs. The vice president recommended giving agencies more flexibility to finance their training needs, in part by reinvesting a portion of the savings they realized from streamlining their staffs. The government also would commit to upgrading information technology and the accompanying training.

Enhance the Quality of Work Life

Only half of the work force believes their agencies support family issues, such as dependent-care, flexible work schedules, and telecommuting policies. The vice president recommended expanding "family-friendly" workplace options and abolishing employee time sheets and time cards for the standard workweek.

Form Labor-Management Partnerships

Corporate executives told Gore that no move to reorganize for quality can succeed without the full and equal participation of workers and their unions. As a result, Gore proposed the creation of labor-management partnership councils throughout the government, with representatives of unions, senior career managers, and top political leaders. The council was charged with creating a high-performance, high-quality government.

Exert Leadership

Vice President Gore was counseled by an experienced reinventor from New Zealand "that government won't change unless the chief executive is absolutely 100 percent committed to making it change" (Gore, 1993, p. 89). With this advice, he asked every department and agency to designate a chief operating officer and formed the President's Management Council to lead the quality revolution and ensure the implementation of the NPR's recommendations.

Cut Overhead Staff in Half

The NPR found nearly one-third of the federal work force could be classified as "overhead," responsible for "systems of over-control and micro-management"—headquarters staffs, supervisors, regional offices, and specialists in personnel, procurement, and budget. It proposed cutting these staff in half, eliminating about 252,000 positions over a five-year period. This roughly matched the projected attrition rate for the federal work force during that period. For the staff affected by the reductions, layoffs would be avoided by providing incentives for affected employees to resign or retire. Of the estimated $40 billion in savings expected to accrue, a portion would be reinvested to expand performance measuring, benchmarking best practices, and training the remaining work force.

Streamline the Budget Process

The NPR proposed three sets of changes in the budget area. First, it recommended increasing accountability for results by shifting the emphasis of the budget process from a focus on "inputs" (such as personnel and equipment) to "results" (such as improved child immunization rates). It proposed adopting pending legislation—the Government Performance and Results Act—that would require agencies to develop performance measures and justify their future budgets based on performance. It also advocated that the president and his cabinet members prepare written performance agreements on what he expected of them in key areas. In addition, it recommended better accountability by allowing the president line item veto authority.

Second, it recommended changes in the existing budget development and execution processes, which consumed an enormous amount of energy, resources, and time but did not contribute to good decision-making by policymakers. For example, policy decisions and broad spending allocations were made nine months after agencies began developing their budgets. The NPR proposed that the president start with an executive budget resolution to set priorities and to propose a budget only every other year. This would create greater stability in a budget process whereby, despite the fact that all but about fifteen percent of the budget was fairly stable and contained predictable spending patterns, the entire amount was annually subjected to the uncertainties of the general process.

And third, it proposed minimizing restrictions on the budget implementation processes imposed by both the administration and Congress. It advocated the elimination of personnel ceilings in favor of budget controls and letting agencies keep a portion of their savings from one year to the next to discourage wasteful year-end spending sprees.

Decentralize Personnel Policy

Believing the government could no longer afford a personnel system premised on a policy of "one size fits all," the NPR recommended devolving significant personnel authority to the agencies away from the Office of Personnel Management. [See Personnel Management, Office of.]

Streamline Procurement

This was an area that required substantial legislative changes. Part of the changes were to allow frontline managers more authority for small item purchases by allowing them the use of VISA cards to replace authorization forms and raising the definition of a "small purchase" from $25,000 to $100,000. Larger purchases still required substantial written justifications and the use of specialized procurement staffs, but now nearly ninety percent of the federal government's purchase actions could be conducted using the new, simplified process.

The NPR also recommended a number of administrative actions that could be undertaken immediately to begin changing the culture of procurement officers to make them more results and customer oriented. For example, it proposed the rewrite of the federal acquisition regulation and all its supplements to shift from thousands of pages of rigid rules to guiding principles. It also encouraged the General Services Administration (GSA) to delegate more authority to agencies to allow them to buy information technology directly instead of through the GSA. It also proposed that the GSA eliminate its "mandatory supply schedules" whereby agencies were required to buy only from these schedules instead of local stores, even when costs were lower at the latter. [See General Services Administration.]

Reorient the Inspectors General

Many employees Vice President Gore met with were concerned about the atmosphere of fear created by inspectors general in the agencies. The NPR recommended that the inspectors general maintain their traditional audit and investigative functions, but broaden their focus from strict compliance auditing to evaluating management controls systems. They were to hold managers accountable for managing, but not second-guess managerial decisions.

Eliminate Regulatory Overkill

The NPR found thousands of outdated, overlapping regulations affecting people inside as well as outside government. It recommended that all federal agencies reduce their internal regulations—those affecting government workers—in half. It also recommended the elimination of half of the five thousand congressionally mandated reports and the coordination of the reporting schedules of similar congressional reports. It also advocated streamlining the regulatory review process for rules affecting businesses and the public so that review by the Office of Management and Budget would be more selective and less of a bottleneck.

Empower State and Local Governments

Washington allocates federal money to states and localities through an array of more than six hundred different grant programs, three-quarters of which distribute less than $50 million a year nationwide. People who run programs struggle to knit together funding from different grants, and yet they have to separately report on the uses of funds from each of these grants. The NPR proposed the creation of a cabinet-level Community Enterprise Board to improve the way the federal government works with states and localities. The board would look for ways to empower innovative communities by letting federal agencies waive rules that conflict with agreed-upon results, and increasing state and local flexibility in combining federal aid if the states and localities agree to achieve agreed-upon levels of performance. The NPR also recommended limiting the use of "unfunded mandates" whereby states and localities are required to act on a federal priority but there is no accompanying financial support to meet the requirement.

[*See also* Management and Budget, Office of.]

BIBLIOGRAPHY

Barrett, Katherine, and Richard Greene. "An Open Letter to the President." *Financial World,* 25 October 1994.

Church, George. "Gorezilla Zaps the System." *Time,* 13 September 1993, 24.

Cooper, Matthew, and Paul Glastris. "Al Gore's Biggest Fix." *U.S. News and World Report,* 13 September 1993, 40.

Gleckman, Howard. "Where to Prune and Where to Hack Away." *Business Week,* 13 September 1993, 98.

Gore, Al. *From Red Tape to Results: Creating a Government That Works Better and Costs Less; A Report of the National Performance Review.* Washington, D.C., 1993.

Gore, Al. *Creating a Government That Works Better and Costs Less: September 1994 Status Report; A Report of the National Performance Review.* Washington, D.C., 1994.

Gore, Al. "The New Role of the Federal Executive." *Public Administration Review* 54 (July–August 1994): 317–321.

Gore, Al. *Common Sense Government: Works Better and Costs Less.* Washington, D.C., 1995.

Gore, Al. *Reinvention's Next Steps: Governing in a Balanced Budget World.* Washington, D.C., 1996.

Kettl, Donald F., and John J. DiIulio, Jr., eds. *Inside the Reinvention Machine: Appraising Governmental Reform.* Washington, D.C., 1995.

Moe, Ronald C. "The 'Reinventing Government' Exercise: Misinterpreting the Problem, Misjudging the Consequences." *Public Administration Review* (March–April 1994): 111–122.

Office of Management and Budget. "Making Government Work." In *Budget of the United States: Fiscal Year 1997,* supp., pp. 117–137. Washington, D.C., 1997.

Osborne, David, and Ted Gaebler. *Reinventing Government: How the Entrepreneurial Spirit Is Transforming the Public Sector from Schoolhouse to State House, City Hall to Pentagon.* Reading, Mass., 1992.

"Poll: People Want Government to Work, Period." *USA Today,* 13 September 1993, 1.

U.S. General Accounting Office. *Quality Management: Survey of Federal Organizations.* GAO/GGD-92-9BR. Washington, D.C., 1992.

U.S. General Accounting Office. *Management Reform: GAO's Comments on the National Performance Review's Recommendations.* GAO/OCG-94-1. Washington, D.C., 1993.

U.S. General Accounting Office. *Management Reform: Implementation of the National Performance Review's Recommendations.* GAO/OCG-95-1. Washington, D.C., 1994.

—JOHN KAMENSKY

National Science Foundation

Congress established the National Science Foundation (NSF) as an independent federal agency in 1950. In 1945 Vannevar Bush, director of the wartime Office of Scientific Research and Development, had recommended the creation of a federal agency to develop national policy for science and to support basic scientific research and education. Bush's seminal 1945 report, *Science: The Endless Frontier,* became the basis for the legislation that created the agency.

The subsequent five-year debate over federal support of research and education revolved around several issues: ownership of patents; geographic and institutional distribution of funds; eligibility of the social sciences; basic research versus applied; and control of the agency. The 1950 act sidestepped or compromised most of these issues. It directed the NSF to avoid "undue concentration" of its funds. The social sciences were not mentioned, but the act's term "other sciences" allowed their inclusion in the NSF's portfolio.

The most important compromise concerned control and direction of the foundation. Backers of the Bush proposal wanted to place control in an independent board that would appoint a director responsible to it. In 1947 President Harry

NATIONAL SCIENCE FOUNDATION · 427

S. Truman vetoed a bill providing such an arrangement. The 1950 law instead created a policy-making Science Board and a full-time director, all appointed by the president and confirmed by the Senate.

The five-year debate left a science vacuum to be filled by other agencies. The explosion of atomic bombs over Japan in August 1945 ushered in public awareness of nuclear energy. For national security reasons, American policymakers quickly decided that this powerful energy source would continue to be guarded closely by the government. The ensuing Atomic Energy Act of 1946 restricted the use of nuclear data and effectively carved off the field of nuclear energy as an independent area of research. The Atomic Energy Commission, which assumed control of the wartime Manhattan Project facilities in January 1947, soon became a leading scientific government agency. It concentrated its support of basic research and fellowships primarily in physics.

The Bush report called for support of biomedical research in the new research foundation. During the war Bush's Office of Scientific Research and Development had great success coordinating the government's sponsorship of medical research. But when the creation of the NSF ran afoul of politics in the postwar period, the Public Health Service assumed these responsibilities within what was then called the National Institute of Health (NIH). Much NIH research was conducted in its own laboratories, but after 1945 the agency added a popular extramural grant program that increasingly gained from Congress sizable appropriations and an enduring political constituency. [See National Institutes of Health.]

Bush's report also called for a continuation of military research in peacetime by the civilian-controlled organization, with close liaison with the Army and Navy. That recommendation was based on Bush's wartime experience. When the Office of Scientific Research and Development went out of existence in December 1947, the secretaries of war and the Navy created a new board to fill the void. In the meantime, the Navy quickly moved to establish close ties with the nation's research universities. It gained statutory approval in 1946 for an Office of Naval Research. Although headed by a naval officer, the office had as its deputy administrator a civilian chief

scientist to direct the scientific program. While the primary purpose of the office was to perform research of direct use to the Navy, the office also supported wide-ranging unclassified fundamental research that had little bearing on naval issues. Developing a good working relationship with the civilian science community, the office allowed results of research to be published in the open literature and pioneered in using eminent scientists to evaluate the research projects it sponsored. It consequently became a model for government grant-making agencies, and the NSF later adopted many of its techniques. So by 1950, when the NSF came into existence, there was already an extensive though disjointed government sponsored research system for the sciences.

The first NSF director, Alan T. Waterman (1951–1963), took care to keep the agency out of politics as well as to avoid the enmity of other federal science agencies in the science policy area. Waterman and the science board defined the agency's policy role as one of compiling reliable information on scientific research and manpower, advocating support for fundamental research, and improving government-university relations. In 1962 President John F. Kennedy issued an executive reorganization plan that transferred the national science policy-making functions from the NSF to a permanent Office of Science and Technology located in the Executive Office of the President. [See President, Executive Office of the.]

The NSF's original charter restricted its support to fundamental research—research performed without thought of practical ends. The agency planned a program to support individual research projects in the mathematical, physical, nonclinical medical, biological, and engineering sciences. It concluded that the project grant system would work best. In adopting this procedure, the agency followed the pattern of most of the private foundations and the Public Health Service. Agency officials thought the project grant, with its nonrestrictive features, was the best method to achieve two agency objectives: encourage the finest fundamental research and ensure a comprehensive research program.

Early guidance to prospective researchers suggested what should be included in the proposal in order for the staff to make an evaluation. It should contain a description of the intended research, procedures to be followed, facilities and equipment available, biographical information on the principal investigator and others participating in the research, and a budget. The proposal had to have the approval of the originating institution and be signed by an official authorized by the institution. Although an individual researcher submitted a proposal, for administrative purposes, a successful grant would be awarded to the institution to support the research of the individual. Grants covered direct costs plus up to fifteen percent for indirect costs.

Proposals went to the appropriate division and subsequently to the program officer responsible for either the discipline or function. The programs were generally organized by discipline in the mathematical, physical, and engineering sciences, and by function in the biological and medical sciences (regulatory, systematic, molecular, etc.). Program officers were the agency's frontline people. They had to work within budgets and always had more good proposals than they had money to support. Program officers read each proposal and arranged for external review. Generally, program officers solicited mail reviews in the mathematical, physical, and engineering sciences, and used a combination of mail and assembled panel reviews in the life sciences and later in the social sciences. From the beginning, keen competition meant that only the best proposals were funded.

Program officers were also frontline decisionmakers in that they often had to select among seemingly equal proposals. Scientific merit was the main criterion, but it was combined with others: capability of the investigator, relevance of the research, and the effect of the research on the science and engineering infrastructure. The budget alone prevented all meritorious projects from being funded; in some instances, proposals were awarded but the funding had to be carried over to the next fiscal year. This created backlogs and merely increased the pressure on program officers to limit selections even more. This procedure, although modified somewhat over time, remains to the present time as the principal NSF proposal process.

Emphasis on quality also characterized the

NSF's first educational program—fellowships for graduate students and postdoctoral scientists. NSF graduate fellows tended to concentrate in a rather small number of graduate schools, causing criticism from "have-not" universities. Later programs of "cooperative" fellowships and traineeships offset most of the criticism by spreading NSF support of graduate education among a larger number of institutions during the 1960s.

Support for precollege science education expanded greatly following the launching of Sputnik by the Soviet Union in October 1957. Newly developed curricula in physics, biology, chemistry, and mathematics were widely adopted. Some of the new courses came under attack in the 1970s as too difficult for most students. An elementary school social science course—"Man: A Course of Study"—met especially harsh criticism from conservatives.

Since the late 1950s, the NSF increasingly sponsored "big science" enterprises. National centers for radio and optical astronomy and for atmospheric research required facilities and instruments so costly that only the federal government could build and equip them and pay for their continuing operation. The agency, by law, could not directly operate research laboratories, so universities managed the facilities under contract to the NSF.

NSF sponsorship of other large-scale activities also began in the 1950s and expanded across the disciplines over the next four decades. During the 1958–1959 International Geophysical Year, the NSF's interests focused on Antarctica. In 1959 the United States and the eleven other nations engaged in Antarctic operations signed a treaty reserving the continent for peaceful and scientific purposes. The NSF continues as the lead federal agency for Antarctic activities. In the 1960s the NSF supported an ambitious attempt to gain knowledge of Earth by drilling through its mantle from an ocean platform (the Mohole project). Escalating costs ended the effort, but a continuing deep-sea drilling program yielded knowledge of such geologic phenomena as plate tectonics, including what is popularly called continental drift. In the 1980s the agency funded other new research centers in engineering, science and technology, and supercomputing. These centers featured cooperative matching funding from industry.

A controversial program blossomed and faded between 1971 and 1978. Research Applied to National Needs (RANN) stemmed from a major 1968 amendment to the NSF's charter that expanded the agency's authority to include support of applied research. Organized around designated problems rather than science disciplines, the program used criteria and management practices heretofore foreign to the foundation. RANN addressed many of the domestic problems of that time: pollution, energy, transportation, and urban difficulties. It attempted to link industrial enterprises and academic research with the hope that industry eventually would support parts of the program. Criticism came from segments of Congress, other agencies, and particularly from the science community, which feared that RANN would drain funding from the NSF's traditional support of basic research. The program began to be phased out in 1975 and 1976.

The NSF constantly sought out and supported research based on the best ideas from the most qualified people. The Internet, one of the phenomenal technologies of the late twentieth century, grew from experimental networks funded by the NSF and other federal agencies. Work supported by NSF grants also led to analysis of microbursts and development of Doppler radar systems to detect and warn of treacherous wind shears at airports. NSF grantees have accumulated twelve Nobel Prizes, thirty MacArthur Awards, and numerous other awards. More than thirty thousand fellowships and traineeships have been awarded to the most promising graduate students in science, mathematics, and engineering. Several hundred former NSF fellows have been inducted into the National Academy of Sciences.

The agency's expanding programs increased its budget. The first large boost—to $40 million—came in 1957. Sputnik sparked a series of increases—to $134 million in 1959 and to nearly $500 million by 1968. The budget passed the half-billion mark in 1971 and generally continued to rise thereafter. By the opening of the next decade, the budget reached the billion-dollar level and by the mid-1990s, it stood at over $3 billion. A cost-effective agency, its internal operations consume about four percent of its total budget, leaving the remainder for investment in scientific research and education.

Over the years NSF reorganizations reflected the changing nature of the research disciplines it supported. Engineering, science and engineering education, computer science, and the social sciences, long supported by the agency but at lesser organizational and budgetary levels, were given equal organizational stature with the traditional disciplines in mathematics, the physical sciences, and the biological sciences. The changes mirror the fact that over its forty-five-year history, the NSF has established itself as the only general-purpose science agency and the United States government's flagship for fundamental research.

[*See also* Atmospheric Research, National Center for; Global Change Research Program; *and* Science and Technology Policy, Office of.]

BIBLIOGRAPHY

England, J. Merton. "Dr. Bush Writes a Report: 'Science—The Endless Frontier.'" *Science* 191 (1976): 41–47.

England, J. Merton. *Patron for Pure Science*. Washington, D.C., 1982.

England, J. Merton. "The National Science Foundation and Curriculum Reform: A Problem of Stewardship." *The Public Historian* 11 (1989): 23–36.

England, J. Merton. "Investing in Universities: Genesis of the National Science Foundation's Institutional Programs, 1958–63." *Journal of Policy History* 2 (1990): 131–156.

Kevles, Daniel J. "Scientists, the Military, and the Control of Postwar Defense Research: The Case of the Research Board for National Security, 1944–1946." *Technology and Culture* 16 (1975): 20–47.

Kevles, Daniel J. "The National Science Foundation and the Debate over Postwar Research Policy, 1944–1946." *Isis* 68 (1977): 5–26.

Kevles, Daniel J. "Principles and Politics in Federal R&D Policy, 1945–1990: An Appreciation of the Bush Report." In *Vannevar Bush: Science—The Endless Frontier*. Washington, D.C., Reprint, 1990: ix–xxx.

Kleinman, Daniel Lee, and Mark Solovey. "Hot Science/Cold War: The National Science Foundation After World War II." *Radical History Review* 63 (1995): 110–139.

Lomask, Milton. *A Minor Miracle: An Informal History of the National Science Foundation*. Washington, D.C., 1976.

Maddox, Robert F. "The Politics of World War II Science: Senator Harley M. Kilgore and the Legislative Origins of the National Science Foundation." *West Virginia History* 41 (1979): 20–39.

Mazuzan, George T. *NSF: A Brief History.* Washington, D.C., 1988.

Mazuzan, George T. "Up, Up, and Away: The Reinvigoration of Meteorology in the United States, 1958–1962." *Bulletin of the American Meteorological Society* 69 (1988): 1152–1163.

Mazuzan, George T. "'Good Science Gets Funded . . .': The Historical Evolution of Grant Making at the National Science . Foundation." *Knowledge: Creation, Diffusion, Utilization* 14 (1992): 63–90.

Schaffter, Dorothy. *The National Science Foundation.* New York, 1976.

Stine, Jeffrey K. "Scientific Instrumentation as an Element of U.S. Science Policy: National Science Foundation Support of Chemistry Instrumentation." In *Invisible Connections: Instruments, Institutions, and Science,* edited by Robert Bud and Susan E. Cozzens, pp. 238–263. Bellingham, Wash., 1992.

—GEORGE T. MAZUZAN

National Security Council

Established in 1947, the National Security Council (NSC) coordinates policy among the various agencies involved in the formation and implementation of foreign and defense policy. The president has the authority to alter the size and functions of the NSC, so while the overall size of the NSC has varied as different administrations have added or removed members, the council itself has generally been made up of the president, vice president, the secretaries of state and defense, the chairman of the Joint Chiefs of Staff, the director of the Central Intelligence Agency (CIA), and the president's national security adviser. Besides resources and information provided by its members, the NSC also has the National Security Agency (NSA) to provide it with intelligence. The influence and role of the NSC have varied greatly from president to president, but it has become increasingly central as the president's main source of advice and information in security matters.

Under the National Security Act of 1947, the Department of War and the Department of the Navy were combined into the Department of Defense, while a separate intelligence agency, the CIA, was created to gather and analyze information and conduct covert actions abroad. The act also created the NSC as a means to give the military a voice in foreign policy at the same time that it coordinated intelligence information and surrounded the president with a team of foreign and security policy professionals to advise him. Over the years, the NSC has provided a means to ensure continuity in American foreign policy despite the elections of different presidents from different political parties.

During the first few years of its existence, President Harry S. Truman convened the NSC sparingly, preferring to keep policy formulation squarely in his own hands. The NSC itself consisted of a senior staff, made up of assistant secretaries and senior officials, and an administrative staff appointed by the various departments represented on the council. Truman initially used the NSC mainly as a body to conduct long-term strategic studies and forecasts and left policy development and recommendations to the major departments such as State and Defense.

Events of the Cold War soon greatly enhanced the significance of the NSC. With the fall of China, the Soviet explosion of an atomic bomb, and increased domestic pressure to take a hard line against communism, Truman ordered a reappraisal of American security policy to be written in 1950. The resulting document, written by Paul Nitze and dubbed NSC-68, called for a militarization of American foreign policy in order to counter a perceived growth in Soviet influence and power. NSC-68 stated that unless the United States greatly expanded its military capabilities, the Soviet Union would be able to overwhelm American conventional and nuclear forces as early as 1954.

The document asserted the need to triple the American defense budget and proposed an increased American presence in the Third World in order to fill the vacuum created by the retreating colonial powers and thereby forestall Soviet expansionism. NSC-68 would serve as the centerpiece of American security policy in regard to the Soviet Union for the next twenty years.

With the North Korean invasion, the NSC became increasingly involved in policy decisions of the Truman administration. The NSC advocated a "rollback" strategy that called for an end to containment of communism through an aggressive offensive strategy to reclaim communist-dominated lands. For instance, the NSC recommended crossing the 38th parallel and uniting Korea under control of the South Koreans after the Inchon landings. The entrance of China into the Korean War signaled the failure of the rollback strategy under the Truman administration.

With the election of Dwight D. Eisenhower as president in 1952, the NSC increased in size and importance. The NSC quickly became the center of policy coordination during the Eisenhower administration. Unlike the Truman administration, under Eisenhower the NSC met frequently and for lengthy sessions. Eisenhower also reduced the importance of the State Department within the NSC by having the vice president chair the council in his absence, instead of the secretary of state as had been the practice under Truman. New subgroups and committees such as the Policy Planning Board and the Operations Coordination Board were created as Eisenhower entrusted his friend General Robert Cutler with establishing a staff and support system for the NSC that would mirror the military system with which the president was familiar. The expanded staff created a system that allowed Eisenhower to reach and implement policy decisions without significant interaction with Congress and, thus, without significant public debate. This provided the secrecy and security necessary for operations such as the CIA-backed coup against the Mossadegh regime in Iran in 1953.

Under Eisenhower the NSC initially advocated the policy of rollback and military buildup espoused by the NSC under Truman. Secretary of State John Foster Dulles called for a "policy of boldness" that would "liberate" communist areas. However, the bloody Soviet suppression of the Berlin uprising in June of 1953 and the Soviet detonation of a hydrogen bomb in August of the same year caused the NSC to propose that direct confrontation against communist aggression be confined to the Third World.

In 1953 President Eisenhower implemented the policy of "massive retaliation" toward the Soviet Union as part of a "new look" for American security policy called for by NSC-162/2. Under this "new look," American nuclear capabilities, rather than ground forces, would become the major deterrent against Soviet expansion since henceforth American military planners were instructed to plan for the use of nuclear weapons at both the tactical and strategic level so that a major act of aggression by the Soviet Union would be met by an overwhelming American nuclear response. This virtually ensured that superpower conflict would be confined to the Third World, where it would be less likely to escalate. At the same time, NSC-162/2 also advocated a new policy of negotiation with the Soviet Union if American interests could be furthered through cooperation.

The result of NSC-162/2 was that conflict between the Soviets and the Americans came to be increasingly fought by proxy and marked by covert operations. American covert successes such as the aforementioned Iranian coup or the CIA-sponsored toppling of Jacobo Arbenz Guzmán in Guatemala in 1954 seemed to vindicate hawks on the NSC, such as Dulles, who promoted active American involvement in the Third World in order to secure American economic and security interests. Unfortunately, these early American successes created an aura of overconfidence within the NSC that would lead to later failures, most notably in the case of Cuba.

In fact, the failure of the Bay of Pigs invasion, which was planned by the CIA and approved by the NSC under Eisenhower, caused the newly elected John F. Kennedy to take a dim view of the NSC. Kennedy implemented two major changes in the NSC. He changed the role of the assistant for national security affairs so that the adviser henceforth served the president directly, instead of the NSC itself. He also ended the practice of having the various departments and agencies represented on the NSC appoint the NSC staff and instead appointed the staff directly. As a result of these two changes, Kennedy ensured that the NSC staff came to serve the president directly and not represent the interests of the various agencies involved with the NSC.

Under McGeorge Bundy, Kennedy's special assistant for national security affairs, many of the bureaucracy and staff structures that Eisenhower had established were dismantled. The Operations Coordination Board and the Policy Planning Board were abolished along with some thirty subcommittees and working groups. While the NSC continued to exist, Kennedy stopped the regular meetings of the council and instead turned its coordinating role over to Bundy and his staff. Like Truman, Kennedy preferred to concentrate the formulation of policy in the hands of a select few advisers, rather than delegating tasks to a large staff system. Nonetheless, Kennedy continued to follow the same basic policy line as his predecessors—the main architects of NSC-68 including Paul Nitze, Dean Acheson, and Dean Rusk were all influential members of the Kennedy administration.

Despite his preferences, Kennedy soon found himself turning to the NSC in response to the Cuban missile crisis. The revelation that the Soviets were building medium range missile silos in Cuba caused Kennedy to form a special eleven-member executive committee of the NSC to deal with the crisis in October of 1962. The executive committee was unanimous in its rejection of negotiations, insisting that some show of force was necessary in order to restore American credibility in the wake of the Bay of Pigs fiasco. The thirteen-day crisis was resolved when the Soviets agreed to withdraw their missiles in exchange for an American pledge not to invade Cuba.

While Lyndon B. Johnson followed the same overall security policy objectives as Kennedy, and even retained basically the same NSC staff members, he made the NSC even more informal than it had been under his predecessor. He replaced regular NSC meetings with *ad hoc* meetings of his principal advisers. He even established a rival to the main NSC—the Senior Interdepartmental Group (SIG). The SIG, which technically was part of the NSC system and was made up of many of the same officials as the NSC, took over the main policy formulation functions of the NSC. Under the chairmanship of the secretary of state, the SIG also marked the reemergence of the State Department as the main voice in American foreign policy.

As time went on and the conflict in Vietnam escalated, Johnson increasingly concentrated the policy coordination functions of the NSC into informal working groups while both the formal

NSC and the SIG meetings effectively stopped. The special assistant for national security emerged as the key foreign policy adviser to the president. This trend continued in the administration of President Richard M. Nixon. Nixon's special assistant for national security affairs, Dr. Henry Kissinger, was clearly the main architect of foreign policy in the administration. At the same time, however, the Nixon-Kissinger foreign policy team did develop an interlocking system of committees and working groups that very much resembled those of the Eisenhower administration. All of these advisory groups reported to the Senior Review Group (SRG) of the NSC, which was made up of the principal NSC members and chaired by Kissinger. The SRG would then publish policy goals and statements in a series of documents entitled "national security study memoranda" (NSSMs).

The NSC became not only a coordinating body for the development of American foreign policy, but the origin of a major amount of that strategy as Nixon concentrated the formulation of foreign policy around the White House staff. The State Department was again relegated to a secondary position in the formulation of security policy. Given considerable latitude by Nixon, the NSC developed a number of policies that reflected a recalculation of American priorities during the Cold War. A series of NSC memoranda (NSSM-14, -35, and -68) called for a reassessment of American foreign policy priorities that resulted in the development of "triangular diplomacy" through which the United States sought to exploit hostilities between China and the Soviet Union. The fruition of this policy ultimately came with Nixon's historic restoration of ties with China in 1972.

Kissinger's brand of diplomacy required a degree of secrecy and concentration of power that was perfectly matched by the Nixon NSC. The first set of Strategic Arms Limitation Talks (SALT I), the shuttle diplomacy in the Middle East following the Yom Kippur War, and the American intervention in the Cyprus crisis were all conducted mainly through the use of the CIA and with little or no involvement by the State Department.

Kissinger continued to dominate the NSC

after his appointment as secretary of state and after the resignation of Nixon in 1974. During the presidency of Gerald Ford, the NSC continued to be the main instrument in determining American foreign policy and continued to implement the basic policies initiated during the Nixon administration. However, with the election of Jimmy Carter in 1976 and the appointment of Zbigniew Brzezinski as national security adviser, subtle changes emerged in both the structure and direction of the NSC. While decision-making remained concentrated in the NSC, there was a significant diffusion of power as agencies such as the State Department and the CIA regained a significant voice in policy formation.

Carter laid out the formal structure of his NSC in Presidential Directive/NSC-2 (PD-2) in January of 1977. PD-2 created two subgroups within the NSC framework. The first was the Policy Review Committee (PRC), which was given the task of formulating policy, while the second, the Special Coordinating Committee (SCC), dealt with issues requiring collaboration among agencies. The SCC was significant in that it was the first cabinet-level group to be formally chaired by the president's national security adviser. Carter also replaced the NSSMs of the Nixon-Ford years with a new series of memoranda entitled "presidential review memoranda" (PRMs) and "presidential directives" (PDs). PRMs and PDs were issued during the Carter presidency as a means of establishing or stating broad policy goals.

Although the Carter NSC did initially continue the major components of the Nixon-Ford-Kissinger foreign policy such as détente (through the SALT II negotiations), it also advocated an emphasis on human rights rather than stressing stability as the previous six administrations had done. In the summer of 1978, in response to increased Soviet activism in the Third World, a three-month NSC review recommended deployment of Pershing II missiles in Europe and an increase in American military capabilities. This deployment and the normalization of relations between China and the United States effectively marked the end of détente and signaled a dramatic increase in tensions between the United States and the Soviet Union. In July of 1980, at the urging of the NSC, Carter secretly signed PD-59, which called for expanded military construction and a renewal of American military commitments abroad. Carter was plagued by a series of foreign policy crises during his last year in office, and the failure of the Carter NSC to deal decisively with events such as the Soviet invasion of Afghanistan and the Iran hostage crisis set the stage for a reappraisal of American foreign policy undertaken early in the first term of President Ronald W. Reagan.

Like Eisenhower, Reagan came to rely heavily on the NSC for policy advice and formulation. Upon entering office Reagan surrounded himself with professional military officers such as Secretary of State Alexander Haig and men who had significant ties with the defense industry such as Secretary of Defense Caspar Weinberger and Secretary of State George Shultz. The NSC staff also reflected this trend as the main NSC advisers such as Robert McFarlane, John Poindexter, and Colin Powell were all career military officers. This propensity for the military reflected an overall remilitarization of American foreign policy, initiated at the end of the Carter administration, but carried to its conclusion under Reagan. Reagan also took a much more active role in NSC meetings, usually chairing NSC meetings himself.

Reagan replaced the PRMs and PDs of the Carter administration with "national security decision directives" (NSDDs). NSDD-2 defined the NSC structure of the Reagan presidency and formalized the NSC by reducing the ability of the president to use ad hoc or informal working groups for consultation and concentrating duties and capabilities in the official bodies that made up the NSC staff.

In 1982, after formulation by the NSC, national security adviser William Clark enunciated the implementation of what became known as the "Reagan Doctrine," which stressed the importance of America's leadership of the free world against communist aggression anywhere on the globe and the importance of supporting anti-communist nations and groups while at the same time working to undermine communist governments and groups.

The NSC became the main focal point of an

aggressive covert policy to undermine existing communist regimes and fight against the emergence of new ones. Like the earlier Eisenhower administration, the Reagan administration attempted to keep these covert actions out of the public eye by having the NSC develop the policies and the CIA carry them out. This practice caused considerable problems for the Reagan administration when it became public that NSC and CIA officials had broken both domestic and international law in some of their operations, such as the mining of Nicaraguan waters and the Iran-*contra* scandal (a complex scheme to use money generated by the sale of missiles to Iran to fund the Nicaraguan *contras*).

The NSC reacted slowly to the changes brought about by Mikhail Gorbachev's reform efforts in the Soviet Union, adopting a wait-and-see approach. This caution carried over into the administration of President George Bush, who was often criticized for reacting too slowly to the events surrounding the Cold War and thus being reactive instead of proactive. The Bush NSC also miscalculated in its policy of building up Iraq in order to prevent Iran from becoming a hegemon in the Persian Gulf region. Nonetheless, the Bush foreign policy team also accomplished a major success by building the coalition that eventually won the Gulf War.

During the Bush administration, the role of the president's national security adviser and his staff continued to increase in importance. Bush appointed his adviser, Brent Scowcroft, to chair the main committee of the NSC and the deputy national security adviser to chair the deputies committee. In doing so, Bush reaffirmed the importance of the national security adviser as the principal figure in security policy formulation.

By the 1990s the NSC system had clearly emerged as the main forum for the discussion of and formulation of American foreign policy. Throughout the post–World War II era, the NSC did succeed in providing a continuum in American foreign policy despite changes in both administrations and personnel. It established a framework through which incoming presidents, often unfamiliar with the complexities of diplomacy and policy formulation, could surround themselves with a circle of foreign policy experts.

Finally, the NSC has provided a coordinating body for the various agencies involved in American foreign policy.

[*See also* Advising the President; Central Intelligence Agency; Defense, Department of; Joint Chiefs of Staff; *and* State, Department of.]

BIBLIOGRAPHY

Andrianopoulos, Gerry. *Kissinger and Brzezinski: The NSC and the Struggle for Control of U.S. National Security Policy.* New York, 1991.
Brown, Seyom. *The Faces of Power: United States Foreign Policy From Truman to Clinton.* 2d ed. New York, 1994.
Carnes, Lord. *The Presidency and the Management of National Security.* New York, 1988.
Gaddis, John Lewis. *Strategies of Containment: A Critical Appraisal of Postwar American National Security Policy.* London, 1982.
Menges, Constantine C. *Inside the National Security Council.* New York, 1988.
Miscamble, Wilson D. *George F. Kennan and the Making of American Foreign Policy, 1947–1950.* Princeton, N.J., 1992.
Prados, John. *Keepers of the Keys: A History of the National Security Council From Truman to Bush.* New York, 1991.
Shoemaker, Christopher C. *The NSC Staff: Counseling the Council.* Boulder, Colo., 1991.
Shoemaker, Christopher C. *Structure, Function and the NSC: An Officer's Guide to the National Security Council.* Washington, D.C., 1989.
—TOM LANSFORD

National Technical Information Service.
See Technical Information Service, National.

National Transportation Safety Board.
See Transportation Safety Board, National.

Naturalization Service.
See Immigration and Naturalization Service.

Natural Resources Conservation Service

The Soil Conservation Service (SCS), predecessor to the Natural Resources Conservation Service

(NRCS), was created on 27 April 1935 by Public Law 46 (Seventy-fourth Congress), which declared that soil erosion was a menace to the national welfare and authorized broad powers to the new agency to attack the problem. (As part of the Department of Agriculture Reorganization Act of 1994, the name was changed to the Natural Resources Conservation Service on 20 October 1994.) The enactment testified to a continuing federal commitment to soil conservation and was the culmination of the efforts of the agency's first chief, Hugh Hammond Bennett. A North Carolina native, Bennett joined the Bureau of Soils in the U.S. Department of Agriculture (USDA) in 1903, shortly after graduating from the University of North Carolina. About four years earlier, the bureau had begun making soil surveys to assist agricultural development. Usually mapped on a county basis, these descriptions of the physical and chemical properties of the soil would help make farmers aware of the potentials and limitations of particular soils.

BENNETT'S CRUSADE

During the years of making surveys, Bennett came to believe that soil erosion was taking such a toll on farmland that, if left unchecked, it would impair the nation's ability to produce food. He launched a crusade of speaking and article-writing to draw attention to the problem. Through professional contacts and writings such as the influential USDA bulletin *Soil Erosion: A National Menace*, Bennett became the department's acknowledged soil erosion expert. Largely owing to Bennett's efforts, Congress approved a group of soil erosion experiment stations in 1929.

Recognition of these contributions proved crucial when the emergency employment programs of the Great Depression offered an opportunity to work on erosion. A clause in the National Industrial Recovery Act of 16 June 1933 permitted erosion control work. Several plans were offered for carrying out this provision. In reacting to plans to simply build terraces, Bennett argued persuasively that soil conservation, in addition to terracing, was based on a variety of management and vegetative measures such as contouring, strip cropping, crop rotations, pas-

ture improvement and management, reforesting of land not suited to cropland, wildlife enhancement, and use of land according to its potential. Thus, according to Bennett soil conservation was multidisciplinary and depended on numerous specialists—agronomists, soil scientists, engineers, foresters, wildlife biologists, and social scientists—to develop mutually supporting soil and water conservation measures.

THE SOIL EROSION SERVICE

Bennett's arguments proved persuasive, and on 19 September 1933 he became the first director of the Soil Erosion Service, which was funded with $5 million in emergency employment funds and operated out of the Department of the Interior. Bennett planned demonstrations of soil and water conservation on farms in selected watersheds. He located the earliest of the demonstration projects near the erosion experiment stations so that the head of the experiment station could also supervise the project and use the experiment station's findings. Working along with Raymond H. Davis, director of the Upper Mississippi Soil Erosion Experiment Station at La Crosse, Wisconsin, and officials of the University of Wisconsin, Bennett selected the Coon Creek watershed as the first demonstration project. Farmers in demonstration projects could sign five-year cooperative agreements to install conservation measures. The Soil Erosion Service furnished equipment, seed, seedlings, and assistance in planning the measures. Boys from nearby Civilian Conservation Corps (CCC) camps or workers hired by the Soil Erosion Service would do much of the work. A project staff might consist of an engineer, soil scientist, forester, economist, and biologist to work with farmers on rearranging the farm for conservation practices. Eventually the service developed the conservation farm plan, written cooperatively by the farmer and the service, to detail the needed work. The personal connection between the trained conservationist and the land user became the hallmark of agency activities.

THE SOIL CONSERVATION SERVICE

As the work found favor with farmers and more requests were made for demonstration projects, friends of the soil conservation movement intro-duced bills into Congress to give the work a more assured legislative footing. This too was one of Bennett's objectives. The congressional hearing provided one of the most memorable events in conservation history. In the mid-1930s it was not uncommon during the early spring for one of the dust storms from the Dust Bowl region to be swept up into the atmosphere and to be carried out to the Atlantic seaboard. Bennett recounted the events five years after his testimony before the Senate Public Lands Committee on Public Law 46:

> The hearing was dragging a little. I think some of the Senators were sprinkling a few grains of salt on the tail of some of my astronomical figures relating to soil losses by erosion. At any rate, I recall wishing rather intensely, at the time, that the dust storm then reported on its way eastward would arrive. I had followed the progress of the big duster from its point of origin in northeastern New Mexico, on into the Ohio Valley, and had every reason to be-lieve it would eventually reach Washington.
> It did—in sun-darkening proportions—and at about the right time—for the benefit of Public Forty-six.
> When it arrived, while the hearing was still on, we took a little time off the record, moved from the great mahogany table to the windows of the Senate Office Building for a look. Everything went nicely thereafter.

Shortly before the bill passed Congress, Presi-dent Franklin Roosevelt resolved a struggle be-tween the secretaries of the Departments of the Interior and Agriculture by transferring the ser-vice, now called the SCS, to the USDA. With pas-sage of legislation giving the SCS a promising fu-ture, the work expanded rapidly. By mid-1936 there were 147 demonstration projects, 48 nurs-eries, 23 experiment stations, 454 CCC camps, and over 23,000 Works Progress Administration workers on the rolls.

The demonstration projects were important to the history of the conservation movement. During the depths of the depression, many farm-ers were receptive to the help. Owing to the availability of labor and equipment, the young service was able to transform farms into models of conservation. Moreover, by concentrating work on the selected watersheds, the service

could demonstrate the cumulative effects of work on individual farms and its value to the whole watershed.

CONSERVATION DISTRICTS

Still, some people questioned whether demon-stration projects were the best method for spreading conservation from this promising be-ginning. One criticism was that farmers should take a more active part in planning and install-ing the work. M. L. Wilson, under secretary of agriculture, devoted considerable thought to spreading conservation from the scattered dem-onstration projects to the rest of the country. In order to develop the legal framework for the new mechanisms, he enlisted the aid of Philip Glick, a young lawyer in the USDA. Together they drew on the strengths and flexibility of federalism to develop a new unit of government, the conserva-tion district. The district would be organized un-der state, not federal, law. Most of each district's directors, or supervisors, would be elected by the people living within the district's boundaries.

Thus the district concept fulfilled many of Wilson's objectives. Local groups would be more involved in planning and in control of setting priorities in their districts. The district likewise provided a means of spreading the conservation activities nationwide. The federal government could contribute to the conservation effort with financial aid as well as provide trained personnel. The arrangement allowed federal assistance to conservation without complete federal control.

President Franklin D. Roosevelt transmitted the law regarding standard state soil conserva-tion districts to the governors of the states on 27 February 1937 along with the suggestion that each state pass the law. Arkansas passed the first such state law on 3 March 1937. The Brown Creek Soil Conservation District in North Caro-lina, in whose boundaries lay the home farm of Hugh Bennett, signed the first memorandum of understanding with the USDA on 4 August 1937. Not surprisingly, many of the demonstration project areas and CCC work areas quickly orga-nized conservation districts. In some areas SCS personnel and farmers friendly to the district movement had to overcome opposition. At the end of 1939 there were eighty-eight million acres in districts. The acreage in districts topped the one-billion mark in 1947 and the two-billion mark in 1973.

The nearly three thousand districts, their state associations, and the National Association of Conservation Districts became the grass-roots support for federal conservation programs and helped sustain SCS and conservation funding through difficult times. In states and counties where districts had funds, they added personnel to work alongside SCS employees and thus speeded the conservation work. The SCS field office in many states might have a mixture of federal and district employees working alongside one another.

The districts could further conservation by purchasing equipment and supplies needed for conservation work. For instance, they promoted the adoption of conservation tillage by purchasing no-till drills which they lent or leased to farmers. As private citizens, district officials could influence state laws and regulations in areas where it would be inappropriate for federal employees to do so. As units of state government, the districts could play a role in planning and zoning, areas of the law reserved to state government.

WATER RESOURCES

The agency's title highlighted soil, but the scope of the agency's work encompassed the interaction of soil and water. A hallmark of the SCS has been its emphasis on treating the whole watershed—not just in-stream and floodplain conditions, but also the upland areas of the watershed. Before, or in conjunction with, installing flood control, streambank erosion control, or other structures, the SCS worked with landowners to use conservation measures that would increase infiltration, reduce runoff, and prevent sediments from moving to the stream. Some of the early demonstration projects combined flood control structures and water supply structures with conservation measures on the watershed lands. The Flood Control Act of 1936 authorized the SCS to study measures regarding soil erosion control, runoff, and water flow retardation in se-

lected watersheds. The Flood Control Act of 1944 approved eleven of these plans for operation. The Watershed Protection and Flood Prevention Act of 1954 established a different, more streamlined procedure for the SCS to carry out what came to be called the small watershed program on upstream watersheds of less than 250,000 acres: federal assistance would be provided for the building of structural works that could not possibly be realized by individual parties; local communities were expected to provide land rights and become legally responsible for the operation and maintenance of these structures, and landowners above them were expected to apply conservation measures that would reduce erosion and slow runoff.

Some of these projects, usually those involving drainage and channel modifications, became the objects of the severest criticism the SCS had yet received, as part of the environmental movement's critique of federal assistance in matters of flood control and drainage. But it bears remembering that the projects were to treat the whole watershed: work for which individuals bore primary responsibility was matched by community responsibility, and federal assistance was provided to the latter.

Most projects have involved more than flood prevention and watershed protection: drainage has been involved in nineteen percent of the projects, recreation in seventeen percent, municipal and industrial water supply in eleven percent, fish and wildlife habitat enhancement in six percent, irrigation in six, and water quality protection in seven. Since the Flood Control Act of 1944, the service has contributed to 1,596 projects covering more than 106 million acres.

EXPANDING RESPONSIBILITIES AND ACTIVITIES

The primary method of operation of the renamed NRCS continues to be working directly with farmers in cooperation with conservation districts. In its ongoing mission to conserve, maintain, and enhance the quality of resources, it has had to adapt and tailor its services to changing agricultural conditions, congressional mandates, and public concerns. In addition to working with individuals, the NRCS and the districts may work with groups and units of government at all levels.

During the mid-1960s there was great emphasis on using soil survey data and other information to help communities and local governments in their planning and development efforts. Over the next twenty years the Service undertook river basin surveying and planning activities at scales large and small in order to identify needed conservation work. Public concerns about water pollution have been addressed in a series of amendments to the Clean Water Act. While the original focus was on municipal and industrial sources of pollution, agricultural sources, sometimes referred to as nonpoint sources, became an area of concern in the 1970s. The NRCS works with farmers to reduce these sources of sediments and other pollutants from cropland and pasture. The NRCS works with livestock and poultry farmers on waste management systems as well as composting, manure storage facilities, and other practices that lessen and control water runoff. The NRCS assists farmers in the arid and semiarid West on water conservation, irrigation scheduling, and measures to combat saline concentrations in soil, surface water, and groundwater. Range and pasture management techniques developed by the SCS aid ranchers in maintaining soil- and moisture-retaining ground cover and reducing erosion. The service worked with private landowners on timber management. Farm conservation plans can include information to help owners increase wildlife habitat.

The Food Security Act of 1985, more commonly called the 1985 farm bill, linked farmers' eligibility for USDA programs to conservation performance. The highly erodible lands provision, sometimes known as conservation compliance, required farmers to use conservation measures on erodible land in order to remain eligible for USDA programs such as price support payments and crop insurance. The agency also became responsible for identifying wetlands that farmers could not alter without also losing benefits. These requirements placed a considerable work load on SCS field staff and altered the relationship of the SCS to its clientele. While participation in programs was still voluntary, the SCS had assumed a role different from its tradition of using persuasion with farmers.

HERITAGE AND PHILOSOPHY

Work on farmlands growing commodities is only one part of the agency's work. Through sixty years of experience the agency has developed numerous scientifically based tools and standards in agronomy, forestry, engineering, economics, wildlife biology, and other disciplines that local NRCS field office conservationists use in helping landowners plan and install conservation practices. Also, historical experience has created a philosophy that the service still follows: Assess the resources on the land, the conservation problems and opportunities. Draw on various sciences and disciplines and integrate all their contributions into a plan for the whole property. Work closely with land users so that the plans for conservation mesh with their objectives. Through implementing conservation on individual projects, contribute to the overall quality of life in the watershed or region.

BIBLIOGRAPHY

Archer, Sellers G. *Soil Conservation*. Norman, Okla., 1956.

Bennett, Hugh Hammond. *Soil Conservation*. New York, 1939.

Bennett, Hugh Hammond. *Elements of Soil Conservation*. New York, 1947.

Brink, Wellington. *Big Hugh: The Father of Soil Conservation*. New York, 1951.

Buie, Eugene C. *A History of the United States Department of Agriculture Water Resources Activities*. Washington, D.C., 1979.

Hardin, Charles M. *The Politics of Agriculture: Soil Conservation and the Struggle for Power in Rural America*. Glencoe, Ill., 1952.

Held, R. Burnell, and Marion Clawson. *Soil Conservation in Perspective*. Baltimore, 1967.

Helms, J. Douglas. *Readings in the History of the Soil Conservation Service*. Washington, D.C., 1992.

Morgan, Robert J. *Governing Soil Conservation: Thirty Years of the New Decentralization*. Baltimore, 1965.

Parks, W. Robert. *Soil Conservation Districts in Action*. Ames, Iowa, 1952.

Sampson, R. Neil. *For Love of the Land: A History of the National Association of Conservation Districts*. League City, Tex., 1985.

Simms, D. Harper. *The Soil Conservation Service*. New York, 1907.

U.S. Soil Conservation Service. *The Preparation of the Standard State Soil Conservation Districts Law: An Interview with Philip M. Glick.* Washington, D.C., 1980.
—J. DOUGLAS HELMS

Navy, Department of the

 On 13 October 1775 the Marine Committee was authorized by the Continental Congress, with John Adams of Massachusetts as chairman and Silas Deane of Connecticut and John Langdon of New Hampshire as members. On 11 December 1775, Congress expanded the committee to thirteen members to oversee the administration of the navy and direct the deployment of its warships. This body administered the navy until December 1779, when it was replaced by a Board of Admiralty. During the Revolutionary War years (1775–1781), the Continental navy struggled to obtain eighty vessels of all types, including packets, while the number of privateers operating under letters of marque totaled 1,697. Despite the energetic efforts of the committee and later the admiralty, the results of the fledgling Continental navy during the Revolutionary War were on first impression less than satisfactory. With the notable exception of Captain John Paul Jones, the victories of its captains were far outweighed by their defeats. In thirteen ship-to-ship engagements the Continental navy won on four occasions, lost eight, and fought to a draw once. In seven squadron engagements, Great Britain captured a total of forty-three vessels and forced the Continental navy to scuttle eighteen others. These losses seemed to compare poorly with the successes of the privateers, which had captured 450 British merchantmen between 1775 and 1781. It should be noted, however, that the original strategy set forth by the Marine Committee was not that of fleet or squadron engagements with the Royal Navy, but rather the harrying and destruction of British commerce. In this regard, despite its losses, the Continental navy succeeded. The navy captured about two hundred merchantmen in all, resulting in an average 0.4 merchantmen per navy vessel, compared to 0.2 merchantmen per privateer.

Despite its valiant efforts, many members of Congress called for the navy's disestablishment after the conclusion of hostilities in 1781. The navy survived this, the first of many future postwar reductions in force, owing largely to the efforts of Superintendent of Finance Robert Morris, who took control of the navy as agent of marine on 8 September 1781. The depredations of the Mediterranean corsairs on American merchantmen in the Mediterranean in 1785, and their effect on the pocketbooks of the merchants filling the seats of Congress, also helped justify the survival of the navy. To further strengthen the organization, naval affairs were placed under the War Department in 1788, when the Constitution of the United States was adopted. The requirement for a national "blue water" navy was further reinforced during the Quasi-War with France (1797–1801).

The official birth of the Navy Department occurred by act of Congress on 30 April 1798. It was followed shortly thereafter by the establishment of the United States Marine Corps as a separate service within the department on 11 July 1798. In the years after the Revolution naval strength was reduced to six active cruisers. By 1800 the Navy had an onboard total strength of fifty-four hundred personnel. The organizational structure of the early department was simple, with the secretary of the Navy having direct control over six navy yards and their corresponding naval hospitals. Control over the operating forces at sea was difficult at best, given the communications of that period.

BOARD OF NAVY COMMISSIONERS, 1815

During the War of 1812, the civilian secretary had frequently needed professional assistance in the conduct of naval affairs, especially when faced with problems in the international arena. Even ex-president Thomas Jefferson, formerly an ardent isolationist, conceded that it was no longer possible, and he recommended a stronger Navy to protect the nation's interests abroad. By an act of Congress on February 7, 1815, a board of three senior naval officers was established to serve as an organizational entity over the Navy and the Shore Establishment. The board also served as an advisory body to the secretary of the Navy.

From 1815 to 1842, the commissioners did their work well. There were no major conflicts to tax the slender resources of the Navy, other than the elimination of pirate strongholds in the Caribbean (1817–1824). Efforts were made to upgrade the quality and efficiency of the service with the establishment of the Naval Academy and scientific establishments such as the Naval Observatory, Hydrographic Office, and Naval Gun Factory.

BUREAU SYSTEM, 1842

The need for improved administration of the increasingly complex Navy Department of the 1840s led Congress to abolish the Board of Navy Commissioners on 31 August 1842 and replace it with the bureau system. Five bureaus were created: Yards and Docks; Provisions and Clothing; Ordnance and Hydrography; Medicine and Surgery; and Construction, Equipment and Repair.

The operating forces were also reorganized in 1842 by Secretary of the Navy Abel P. Upshur. The fleet was divided into six squadrons: Pacific (California to Hawaii), Mediterranean, East India (Hawaii to China), Brazil (Rio de Janeiro to Cape Horn), African (Atlantic), and Home (Gulf of Mexico). A senior captain was designated commodore in charge of each squadron during its deployment.

Concerns over inhumane conditions aboard U.S. naval vessels led Congress to pass a bill revoking flogging that President Fillmore signed into law on 28 September 1850. Many leading officers of the day objected to the dropping of flogging ". . . without being offered a reasonable alternative."

An Efficiency Board, also known as the "Star Chamber," was established by Congress in 1855 to weed out the officer corps. As there was no mandatory retirement age, superannuated officers were kept on the advancement list, blocking the progress of younger officers. The files of 712 officers were reviewed; forty-nine were dismissed from the service, seventy-one were put on leave

of absence with pay on the retired list, and eighty-one were placed in the retired reserve with furlough pay.

CIVIL WAR, 1861–1865

The expansion of naval operations at the start of the Civil War persuaded the Congress to authorize an assistant to the secretary of the Navy in July 1861. Gustavus Vasa Fox, the newly appointed assistant secretary, was a former naval officer with eighteen years' experience at sea. Working closely with Secretary Gideon Welles and the Congress, Fox reorganized the Navy Department bureaus in 1862. The new bureaus were Yards and Docks, Equipment and Recruiting, Navigation, Ordnance, Construction and Repair, Steam Engineering, Provisions and Clothing, and Medicine and Surgery. Welles and Fox realized early in the war that the winning strategy would be concentration of naval assets along the American inland rivers and coastlines, and not fleet engagements at sea with ships of the line. Accordingly, the fleet was expanded and reorganized into blockade squadrons: the North Atlantic Squadron, South Atlantic Squadron, East Gulf Squadron, West Gulf Squadron, and the Mississippi Flotilla.

Fox was also responsible for the abolishment of the grog ration in the Naval Appropriation Bill of 1862. This action was taken after more than three hundred officers had been relieved since the start of the war owing to drunkenness. A corresponding increase in the pay of both officers and enlisted personnel helped to mitigate its loss.

POST–CIVIL WAR, 1865–1891

Civil War admirals influenced the Navy of the postwar period until the last retired in the 1880s. After the war, cutbacks in appropriations reduced the Navy from a first-rate, modern seapower to the level of a twelfth-rank seapower behind China and Denmark. Limitations were placed on the power of the bureaus, and the supremacy of line officers over civilian officials became widely accepted. The fusty old-timers of flag rank acting as advisers to the secretary of the Navy even required full sets of sails on all Navy vessels and limited the use of coal for economy reasons.

Ironclad warships, breech-loading rifled guns, and triple expansion steam engines were put on the shelf while other navies forged ahead in their development.

The decade between 1881 and 1891 was one of renewal for the Navy. The Naval War College was established by Admiral Stephen B. Luce; Alfred Thayer Mahan wrote his seminal works on naval strategy; and three modern, armored battleships were authorized. Kenneth J. Hagan has characterized the decade as one in which the United States Navy, by adopting the Mahanian precepts of capital ships, fleet engagements, and command of the seas, was joining a naval league long dominated by Great Britain.

THE MODERN NAVY, 1892–1915

The war with Spain began on 25 April 1898 and established the United States as a naval power in two fleet actions—one under Admiral William T. Sampson at Santiago Harbor, Cuba; the other under Admiral George Dewey at Manila Bay, Philippines. The U.S. Navy rose to a position of preeminence it had not enjoyed since the Civil War, owing largely to the strength of the reformed Navy Department and the commitment of its backers in Congress. The status of the Navy was further enhanced in 1908, when President Theodore Roosevelt's "Great White Fleet" toured ports around the globe in a move calculated to impress potential international adversaries.

The bureau system had survived the doldrums of the postwar period to emerge as an effective support structure for the operating forces. The only change to the system during these years was the disestablishment of the Bureau of Equipment (formerly Equipment and Recruiting) in 1910, with its functions being transferred to the Bureau of Steam Engineering and the Bureau of Construction and Repair.

Scientific advances did not pass unnoticed by the Navy Department. In the naval appropriation of 1901, six Holland-class submarines were added to the fleet. On 14 November 1910 the navy began its first experiments with aviation aboard naval vessels when George Ely flew a Curtiss A-1 Triad aeroplane from a platform aboard the battleship *Birmingham* in Hampton Roads, Virginia.

The resolve of the United States to use its Navy as an instrument of international persuasion was demonstrated in 1914, when President Woodrow Wilson sent the fleet to Vera Cruz, Mexico, to help quell an insurrection. It was also the first test under combat conditions for naval aviation, when scouting aircraft came under fire while flying over rebel positions.

WORLD WAR I AND THE INTERWAR PERIOD

In 1915 the office of chief of naval operations (CNO) was established. The position met the long-standing need for a legally responsible professional naval adviser to the secretary of the Navy. The CNO was placed in direct line of authority over the operating forces, with responsibility for the operation of the fleet and preparation of naval war plans, while reporting directly to the secretary of the Navy.

The entry of the United States into the First World War in 1917 caused little in the way of organizational change for the Navy Department, other than scaling up the size of its operations. The overall design of the organization withstood the test of war and remained largely unaltered during the curtailment of its activities in the interwar period of 1919–1939. With the CNO assuming responsibility for the operational concerns of the Navy, the five bureaus and the assistant secretary concentrated on the business and administrative affairs of the Navy Department.

As the naval establishment grew, it became increasingly ungainly. In 1920 the CNO split the Battle Fleet into the Atlantic Fleet, Pacific Fleet, and Asiatic Fleet to enable quicker responses to global requirements. The commandants of the nine naval districts established during the period 1915–1919 began to assist the CNO in the administration of the now burgeoning Shore Establishment.

The importance of aviation in the fleet was acknowledged with the establishment of a new Bureau of Aeronautics in 1921 and an assistant secretary of the Navy (Air) in 1926. Aviation had proved itself during World War I, and confrontations with the Army and Brigadier General Billy Mitchell over unification of aviation assets forced the Navy hierarchy to take a stand for keeping aviation in the fleet. The controversy ended with the court martial of General Mitchell in 1925 and the recommendations of the Morrow Board in November of that same year that the services should retain control over their own air services.

WORLD WAR II, 1939–1945

The Second World War did not result in any major change in the basic organizational structure of the Navy Department, but the scope of its responsibility was vastly expanded with the requirements of a two-ocean war. The bureaus assisted the CNO and naval district commandants by assuming a greater role in the administration of the Shore Establishment so that they might devote their energies to the conduct of the war. In 1940 the Bureau of Construction and Repair was merged with the Bureau of Engineering to form the Bureau of Ships. In 1942 the Bureau of Navigation was redesignated the Bureau of Personnel.

Since 1798 only two military departmental secretaries had advised the president—the War Department and the Department of the Navy. In the spring of 1942, the Joint Board of the Army and Navy was redesignated the Joint Chiefs of Staff (JCS). Almost immediately the JCS became embroiled in a controversy over control of forces in the Pacific theater of operations. General Douglas MacArthur, planning his return to the Philippines, wanted control over all forces in that zone, including naval forces. That the issue was resolved through diplomacy and interservice cooperation proved the soundness of the JCS concept.

At the beginning of the war, the Navy was still reliant on the battleship as its linchpin to naval strategy. Two new elements soon changed this view of warfare. By 1939 long-range submarines were being built in American yards, and in July 1940 six aircraft carriers were authorized for construction. Both represented a turning point for the Navy Department and its conduct of the naval war. In the finest tradition of American privateers in the Revolutionary War, and Captain Raphael Semmes of the CSS *Alabama* in the Civil War, American submarines joined with naval aviation to sweep the Pacific of enemy merchant shipping. It has been estimated that even with-

out the use of the atomic bomb, Japan would have eventually been forced to capitulate owing to the destruction of the merchant fleet on which it was so totally dependent.

REVOLT OF THE ADMIRALS, 1947

By the end of World War II, the U.S. fleet was built around battle groups of Essex-class carriers. There was little debate with the Army Air Force over the issue of strategic weapons, as the atomic bombs of the day were far too heavy to be carried in carrier-based aircraft. By 1947 the situation had changed. Nuclear weapons were small enough to be carried by carrier aircraft, and many high-ranking naval officers felt that the Navy should have a stake in the emerging nuclear strategy of the Cold War. This concept was directly opposed by the recently established United States Air Force. The newest member of the armed forces was rapidly defining its responsibilities in the nation's defense structure, laying claim to the area of strategic weapons delivery. Within the Navy Department there was strong feeling that the responsibility of the Air Force should be confined to the continental defense of the U.S. against enemy air attack. In response, the Air Force pointed to the Joint Strategic Survey Committee (JSSC) report of 1946, which recommended that the Air Force assume responsibility for all land-based aviation, air transport, Marine Corps aviation, and naval air antisubmarine warfare and reconnaissance functions.

By 1948 the controversy had escalated, with both services requesting new strategic delivery platforms—the Navy, with its super-carrier, the United States; and the Air Force, with its long-range strategic bomber, the Convair B-36. The Berlin crisis of 1948, with its emphasis on long-range airlift capability, settled the debate in favor of the Air Force. Contracts for the B-36 were authorized, and plans for the super-carrier United States were scuttled.

The efforts of the Air Force to get Congress to approve the 1946 JSSC report seemed to the Navy Department like a revisitation of the controversy begun by Billy Mitchell twenty years earlier. But on 1 March 1950 the Armed Services Committee investigation on unification, like the Morrow Board of 1925, rejected the Air Force position that it be responsible for all air-power strategy. The Armed Services Committee stated that the Air Force, Navy, and Marine Corps aviation all had their separate roles to fulfill.

THE COLD WAR, 1946–1989

The postwar debates on unification and intense interservice rivalries led to the passage by Congress of the National Security Act of 1947, which, with a 1949 amendment, created a centralized Department of Defense. Much of the power of the service secretaries of the Navy, Army, and Air Force in the operational employment of their forces ended with the passage of this act. The United States Marine Corps was the only service to improve its position, moving out from under the Navy undersecretaries with the commandant reporting directly to the secretary of the Navy.

With the dust from debates over service roles settled, the Congress and the president were more inclined to consider the Navy Department's role in the emerging Cold War period. The resurrection of the super-carrier came in the spring of 1950, when the National Security Council issued its memorandum NSC-68. It allowed the Navy to acquire carriers large enough to fulfill the classical Mahanian concepts of control of the seas while carrying aircraft capable of delivering nuclear weaponry.

Shortly after the super-carrier was restored to the Navy, a new strategic arm was added to the inventory. In 1952 the keel of the first nuclear submarine, the *Nautilus* (SSN-571), was laid. This vessel and its ballistic missile–carrying offspring would become an essential part of the U.S. nuclear deterrence triad destined to exist well into the next century.

By the mid-1970s the bureau system adopted in 1842 was gradually put aside, with functions being assumed by a myriad of new systems commands. The Bureau of Aeronautics became the Naval Air Systems Command in 1966, Yards and Docks became the Naval Facilities Engineering Command in 1966, Supplies and Accounts became Naval Supply Systems Command in 1966, Ordnance and Ships merged to become the Naval Sea Systems Command in 1974, and Personnel became the Naval Military Personnel Command in 1978.

The irony of the Cold War period was that the operational experience of the Navy leaned more toward "gunboat diplomacy" than it did the employment of large fleets of nuclear-equipped carrier battle groups. Carriers used in Korea and Vietnam served as floating airfields and used little of their inherent mobility for combat operations. This was largely due to the fact that the only potential superpower adversaries, Russia and China, were land powers. The more recent experience in the Gulf War of 1990–1991 was a repeat of these earlier conflicts, with carriers reluctantly exposed to a combat air support role in the shallow, confined waters of the Gulf.

THE CLOSING DECADE, 1990–2000

The Department of Defense Reorganization Act of 1986 (the Goldwater-Nichols Act), continued the policy of weakening the power of the separate service chiefs begun with the National Security Act of 1947. The JCS (Army, Air Force, Navy, and Marines) lost power, with the chairman of the JCS given full authority over the conduct of operations, reporting directly to the president. Debate in the last half of this decade may well be focused on whether there is any longer a need for the administrative layer of separate service secretaries and their staffs. The sizes of the service secretaries' departments have not been reduced in the past fifty years, despite the changes taking place in the overall defense structure. The role of the Navy Department in the next century may depend on the perceived need for submarine nuclear deterrence, mobility of carrier tactical air support in littoral warfare, and the proven expertise of the Marine Corps in rapid-strike, amphibious warfare. Whatever streamlining takes place in the management of the department, it is evident, in the words of Kenneth J. Hagan, that the navy of the twenty-first century "will be smaller in every respect than the capital ship fleet of Alfred T. Mahan, the two Roosevelts and John F. Lehman."

[*See also* Defense, Department of; Joint Chiefs of Staff; Marine Corps; *and* National Security Council.]

BIBLIOGRAPHY

Barlow, Jeffrey G. *Revolt of the Admirals: The Fight for Naval Aviation, 1945–1950.* Washington, D.C., 1994.
Dudley, William S., and Michael A. Palmer. "No Mis-

take About It: A Response to Jonathan R. Dull." *The American Neptune* (Fall 1985).

Dull, Jonathan R. "Was the Continental Navy a Mistake?" *The American Neptune* (Summer 1984).

Hagan, Kenneth J. *This People's Navy: The Making of American Seapower.* New York, 1991.

Hurley, Alfred F. *Billy Mitchell: Crusader for Air Power.* Bloomington, Ind., 1975.

Knox, Dudley W. *The History of the United States Navy.* Washington, D.C., 1948.

Merrill, James M. *DuPont: The Making of an Admiral.* New York, 1986.

Palmer, Michael A. "The Navy." In *The Encyclopedia of the American Military,* edited by John E. Jessup. New York, 1994.

Roscoe, Theodore. *Pig Boats: United States Submarine Operations in World War II.* New York, 1982.

Smith, David A. "Who Needs the Secretariats." *Naval Institute Proceedings* (December 1995).

Sullivan, William J. *Gustavus Vasa Fox and Naval Administration, 1861–1866.* Washington, D.C., 1977.

Swansborough, Gordon, and Peter M. Bowers. *United States Navy Aircraft since 1911.* London, 1990.

U.S. Department of the Navy. *Report of the Secretary of the Navy, 1861–65.* Washington, D.C., 1866.

U.S. Department of the Navy. *Department of the Navy Organization.* NAVEXOS P-861. Washington, D.C., 1960.

—MIKE ROBERTS

NIH.

See National Institutes of Health.

NSC.

See National Security Council.

Nuclear Regulatory Commission

Regulating the safety of commercial nuclear power and other civilian applications of nuclear energy is the responsibility of the Nuclear Regulatory Commission (NRC). Its predecessor agency, the Atomic Energy Commission (AEC), was established in the aftermath of World War II by the Atomic Energy Act of 1946. The legislation that created the AEC emphasized military considerations in the context of growing tensions with the Soviet Union and pervasive fear of a future nuclear confrontation. Within a few years, however, the AEC, the Joint Committee on Atomic Energy (the AEC's powerful oversight committee), and some industry leaders began to look for ways to encourage the development of peaceful uses of nuclear energy, particularly nuclear power plants for generating electricity. Their efforts culminated in a new law, the Atomic Energy Act of 1954, that for the first time made possible the growth of the commercial nuclear industry.

The 1954 act eased the stringent restrictions on dissemination of technical information in the 1946 law and directed the AEC to promote the peaceful uses of nuclear technology actively. At the same time it assigned the agency the responsibility for regulating the safety of civilian applications of nuclear energy. The 1954 act was not the result of an immediate need for electrical power or a pending energy crisis. It reflected instead a bipartisan commitment to exploiting the nonmilitary potential of the atom, and above all, to maintaining American scientific leadership in the field of nuclear energy in the face of challenges from Great Britain and especially the Soviet Union.

The AEC carried out its new mandate by offering modest incentives to utilities to explore the potential of nuclear power by building pilot plants. In response to the 1954 act and the AEC's programs, several utilities, either individually or as members of consortiums, made plans to construct "demonstration" nuclear plants. The AEC sought a partnership between government and industry in which private enterprise would take the primary responsibility for building and running power reactors. But at a time when conventional fuels were cheap and plentiful, industry was reluctant to make a major commitment to an unproven technology with high capital costs and potentially severe safety hazards. By 1962 six nuclear power reactors were operating and several more were under construction.

The growth of the nuclear power industry dramatically expanded in the late 1960s and early 1970s. The boom in orders for and construction of nuclear power plants, labeled by one observer as the "great bandwagon market," exceeded even the most optimistic expectations of nuclear proponents. Nuclear power gained sudden acceptance because of cost-cutting offers by nuclear plant vendors, signs that the technology was becoming economically competitive with coal, increasing demand for large units that took advantage of "economies of scale," and widening concerns about the effects of air pollution from plants that burned coal and other fossil fuels. The reactors that utilities ordered not only increased sharply in numbers but also in the size of individual units. The demonstration plants licensed in the late 1950s ranged in size from less than 20 to 265 electrical megawatts; most of the facilities ordered less than a decade later ranged from 800 to 1100 electrical megawatts.

The boom market for power reactors, although gratifying for nuclear proponents, placed severe pressure on the regulatory staff of the AEC. The license applications that poured into the AEC had to be carefully reviewed. The greater size of the plants that utilities were ordering made licensing a much more complicated and time-consuming task. The applications for larger plants raised new safety questions for which answers were not always readily available. The AEC and the industry relied heavily on the concept of "defense-in-depth," which used a series of redundant safety features and systems to assure the safety of plant operation. The primary danger of an accident was that it would release large amounts of radiation to the environment and cause a major public health hazard. Reactor experts, both inside and outside the AEC, were concerned that an unlikely but plausible series of events could overwhelm the safety systems of larger plants and allow a massive escape of radiation.

While the AEC and the industry were trying to deal with new safety issues, opposition to nuclear power was increasing. At the same time that the nuclear industry experienced a boom, the environmental movement was emerging and winning broad public support. One of the main issues on which it focused was nuclear power. Critics of the technology raised questions about the chances and the consequences of a nuclear accident, the environmental impact of the nuclear plants, the disposition of nuclear waste, the likelihood that nuclear power could lead to the proliferation of nuclear weapons, and the health effects of radiation. All of those issues generated widely reported and at times acrimonious debate after the late 1960s. Furthermore, cultural trends in the United States produced growing support for the idea that "small is beautiful." Nuclear power, which to its opponents represented regrettable bigness in business, government, technology, environmental effects, and risk, was an obvious target. Nuclear power's defenders denied that the risks were nearly as threatening as the critics claimed and cited the advantages of nuclear power in providing power with less damage to the environment than fossil-fuel plants.

By the mid-1970s the AEC was the subject of intense attack; one of the most damaging charges was that it was incapable of ensuring safety when it was also responsible for promoting the nuclear power industry. This was, said one critic, "like letting the fox guard the henhouse." In 1974, in the wake of an energy crisis, Congress passed and President Gerald R. Ford signed the Energy Reorganization Act, which abolished the AEC and created the NRC to perform its regulatory functions. The purpose of the new law was not only to separate regulatory and promotional duties but also to establish an agency that could focus on, and presumably speed up, the licensing of plants.

The NRC was committed to demonstrating that it would be an effective regulator. Nuclear critics were not convinced, however, and the controversy over nuclear safety continued unabated after the NRC began operations in January 1975. Meanwhile, utilities sharply curbed orders for new plants, partly because of antinuclear opposition but mostly because of inflation, rising costs, and diminishing demand for power. By the late 1970s the nuclear industry was in a slump, though dozens of plants were still under construction.

In an atmosphere of political controversy and economic uncertainty, the most serious crisis in the history of commercial nuclear power in the United States took place. On 28 March 1979 an accident at Unit 2 of the Three Mile Island nuclear station near Harrisburg, Pennsylvania, uncovered the reactor's core and melted about half of it. A "loss-of-coolant accident" of this magnitude had been the focus of concern of reactor experts since the middle 1960s. The safety systems in the plant worked according to design, and the accident could have been little more than a minor incident. But the plant's operators failed to recognize the nature of the problem and reduced the flow of emergency cooling water to a trickle. The lack of coolant in the core caused irreparable damage to the reactor.

From all indications, the Three Mile Island accident did not release enough radiation to threaten public health; only tiny amounts escaped from the plant. Nevertheless, the accident undermined the credibility of both the industry and the NRC, which experienced difficulty figuring out what had happened and deciding what to do about it. The events at Three Mile Island demonstrated that a severe reactor accident could occur in ways that experts had not fully appreciated. This enhanced the credibility of nuclear critics and eroded public support for nuclear power.

In the aftermath of Three Mile Island, the NRC took many steps to correct weaknesses that the accident revealed. It imposed new requirements for plant equipment intended to reduce the likelihood of the problems that had contributed to the severity of the accident. It placed much greater emphasis than previously on operator training and other "human factors" that affected reactor safety. It devoted more attention to small failures that could lead to major consequences, as had happened at Three Mile Island. The agency established a new office to evaluate information from and the performance of operating reactors. It expanded research programs on a number of key issues that the accident had highlighted, and it took action to upgrade emergency preparedness and planning.

After a moratorium that lasted over a year, the NRC began to issue operating licenses for completed plants in August 1980. In the following nine years it granted full-power licenses to more than forty other reactors, most of which had received construction permits in the mid-1970s. There were no new orders for plants after 1978. The NRC devoted an increasing amount of its resources to regulating the safety of operating plants rather than reviewing applications for new ones.

BIBLIOGRAPHY

Balogh, Brian. *Chain Reaction: Expert Debate and Public Participation in American Commercial Nuclear Power, 1945–1975.* New York, 1991.

Bedford, Henry F. *Seabrook Station: Citizen Politics and Nuclear Power.* Amherst, 1990.

Joppke, Christian. *Mobilizing against Nuclear Energy: A Comparison of Germany and the United States.* Berkeley, 1993.

Mazuzan, George T., and J. Samuel Walker. *Controlling the Atom: The Beginnings of Nuclear Regulation, 1946–1962.* Berkeley, Calif., 1984.

Miner, Craig. *Wolf Creek Station: Kansas Gas and Electric Company in the Nuclear Era.* Columbus, Ohio, 1993.

Morone, Joseph G., and Edward J. Woodhouse. *The Demise of Nuclear Energy? Lessons for Democratic Control of Technology.* New Haven, Conn., 1989.

Okrent, David. *Nuclear Reactor Safety: On the History of the Regulatory Process.* Madison, Wis., 1981.

Rees, Joseph V. *Hostages of Each Other: The Transformation of Nuclear Safety since Three Mile Island.* Chicago, 1994.

Walker, J. Samuel. *Containing the Atom: Nuclear Regulation in a Changing Environment, 1963–1971.* Berkeley, Calif., 1992.

Weart, Spencer R. *Nuclear Fear: A History of Images.* Cambridge, Mass., 1988.

Wellock, Thomas R. *Critical Masses: Opposition to Nuclear Power in California, 1958–78.* Ph.D. diss., University of California, Berkeley, 1995.

Winkler, Allan M. *Life under a Cloud: American Anxiety about the Atom.* New York, 1993.

—J. Samuel Walker

O

Occupational Safety and Health Administration

Established pursuant to the Occupational Safety and Health Act of 1970 (P.L. 91-596; also known as the Williams-Steiger Act), the Occupational Safety and Health Administration (OSHA) is responsible for workplace safety and health based on vague and far-reaching statutory authority, and is perhaps the best-known and most controversial of all federal regulatory agencies. Records of workplace injuries, illnesses, and deaths were documented long before the creation of OSHA. The hazards of the Industrial Revolution and concern about work-related accidents and injuries prompted state governments to respond as early as 1867. States generally focused on the safety aspect rather than health, and their response took one of two basic forms: 1) a legal approach which classified occupational injuries as torts for which an employer could be sued, or 2) a workers' compensation system that provided compensatory benefits for workers who were harmed during the course of their job. Both alternatives provided only minimal protection for the average worker and were reactive rather than proactive in nature.

The primary contributing factors to the initial proposal of a federal bill to address the issues of workplace safety and health were rather idiosyncratic. In the mid-1960s one of President Lyndon Johnson's speech writers, Robert Hardesty, repeatedly inserted references to worker safety and health in presidential speeches. This was done at the request of Hardesty's brother who worked at the Bureau of Occupational Safety and Health, a small research organization with no regulatory authority. Simultaneously, Assistant Secretary of Labor Esther Peterson encouraged Secretary Willard Wirtz to make the issue of occupational

health problems a priority for the Department of Labor. Wirtz responded largely because he viewed the issue as a program that would have presidential support.

A national workplace safety bill was first introduced in Congress in 1968, prompting an immediate battle between organized labor and business groups. Despite the attention it received, the bill never made it out of committee. It lost priority in the face of several significant political events including Johnson's withdrawal from the presidential race, the assassinations of Martin Luther King, Jr., and Robert Kennedy, and the Democratic National Convention in Chicago.

A serious West Virginia mining accident in late 1968 and increased activities by organized labor combined to increase momentum and support for a federal government response to workplace hazards. In 1969 the bill was reintroduced by Democrats in Congress. President Richard Nixon, recognizing the potential to increase labor support for his party, developed and introduced a Republican alternative.

The Democratic proposal called for a new regulatory agency to be located within the Department of Labor, whereas Republicans advocated the creation of an independent commission owing to President Nixon's concerns about the influence of organized labor in the Department of Labor. The Democratic version delegated substantial rule-making authority to the agency along with the power to impose fines on violators. The Nixon version of the bill called for extensive reliance on voluntary compliance, favored case-by-case adjudication over rule-making authority, and would allow fines only in rare cases of willful violations. Labor unions expressed support for the original Democratic version of the bill, while business groups rallied to support the administration's alternative. The final bill passed in both chambers with overwhelming support. While technically representing a compromise, the final bill more closely approximated the Democratic version. President Nixon signed the Occupational Safety and Health Act of 1970 into law on 29 December 1970.

The act nationalized regulatory policy of occupational safety and health and demanded a new emphasis on prevention of injury and illness to replace or augment the compensatory system previously in place. The act also represented a shift from reliance on criminal charges to an emphasis on civil procedures, and the movement from a process that excluded employees from participation to one that guaranteed them rights to participate. The act did not entirely remove the regulation of workplace safety and health from the control of state governments. States can maintain responsibility for health and safety enforcement if their programs are "at least as effective as" the federal program.

The act itself is a surprisingly brief document, only thirty pages in length. Its stated goal is "to assure so far as possible every working man and woman in the Nation safe and healthy work conditions." OSHA is part of a three-agency contingency assigned with the task of protecting the safety and health of the American worker. The National Institute for Occupational Safety and Health in the Department of Health and Human Services conducts research and prepares reports on proposed occupational safety and health standards; OSHA serves as the principal regulator; and the Occupational Safety and Health Review Commission decides appeals of OSHA citations.

OSHA is located within the Department of Labor and is headed by an assistant secretary appointed by the president with the advice and consent of the Senate. The agency is empowered to accomplish its mission by developing health and safety standards, promulgating regulations, conducting inspections and investigations to insure compliance, and issuing citations and proposing penalties for noncompliance. The agency also serves as a source of information and training for employers and employees. Regulations issued by OSHA are found under Title 29 of the Code of Federal Regulations, Parts 1900 through 1990.

OSHA is widely criticized for being both overbearing and ineffective. Labor groups have argued that the agency has not gone far enough to provide a safe and healthy workplace while management organizations complain of the insensitivity of agency officials to the costs of compliance. The criticisms, however, do not focus on the fundamental objective of the agency. There appears to be widespread acceptance of the legitimacy and desirability of the goal; the controversy surrounds the means of accomplishing that goal.

In determining where to focus their limited energies and resources, OSHA officials have applied the general philosophy that the worst situations need attention first. The top priority is the investigation of situations in which there is reasonable certainty that the hazard will cause death or serious physical harm. The second priority is investigations of catastrophes and fatal accidents, followed by the inspection of workplaces based on employee complaints. Next in priority are inspections aimed at "target industries" with notoriously high accident and illness rates (e.g., lumbering, meat packing, longshoring, and roofing). Remaining resources, if there are any, are used to conduct follow-up inspections of workplaces that were found previously to be in violation, and random inspections of all other workplaces.

OSHA has undergone significant changes since its creation but not owing to any modifications or amendments to the Occupational Safety and Health Act itself. This is despite the fact that revision of the act has been a topic of discussion during almost every legislative session since the original bill became law. The changes experienced by OSHA have instead occurred in response to changing leadership within the agency and a changing political, economic, and social environment.

For much of the 1970s, the primary focus of OSHA regulations was on workplace and worker safety. It was recognized that more deaths occurred as a result of occupational disease than industrial accidents—indeed, labor and management leaders agreed that occupational diseases were the most pressing concern—yet health issues received little attention from OSHA for several years. One explanation for the emphasis on safety is the relative ease of identification and correction of safety problems as opposed to occupational health hazards. The latter may take years to manifest, and at that stage attributing illnesses to specific occupational conditions is extremely difficult.

Eula Bingham was appointed to the position of administrator of OSHA on 19 May 1977. She immediately announced a change in the agency's focus to emphasize health issues. The redirection was reflected in both rule-making and enforcement activities. Bingham also eliminated or modified close to one thousand regulations and made efforts to increase the use of market regulation techniques.

Legal challenges of OSHA regulations, particularly health regulations, are so routine they can be considered part of the regulatory process. In 1980 the Supreme Court imposed a benefit level threshold on OSHA standards in response to OSHA's benzene standard; in effect, the Court declared that the reduction of risks gained by an OSHA regulation must be significant. The Court later explicitly ruled out strict benefit-cost tests for OSHA regulations, arguing that the legislative intent was not to have worker health or safety sacrificed for the sake of money.

OSHA was a prime target of President Ronald Reagan's "regulatory relief" plan. The appointment of Thorne Auchter as administrator of OSHA in 1981 signaled a change in both the rule-making and enforcement approach of the agency. The number and scope of rule-makings were reduced dramatically, as were levels of enforcement, and numerous exemptions were developed for inspections.

President Bill Clinton's "National Performance Review" identified frequent conflicts between OSHA standards and those of other agencies as an example of the need for greater coordination among regulatory agencies. OSHA's primary challenge in the 1990s is to develop a less adversarial approach to working with employers while still protecting the health and safety of workers.

BIBLIOGRAPHY

Eisner, Marc Allen. *Regulatory Politics in Transition*. Baltimore, 1993.
Harter, Philip J. "In Search of OSHA." *Regulation* 1 (1977): 33–39.
Kelman, Steven. "Occupational Safety and Health Administration." In *The Politics of Regulation*, edited by James Q. Wilson. New York, 1980.
Lave, Lester B. *The Strategy of Social Regulation: Decision Frameworks for Policy*. Washington, D.C., 1981.
MacAvoy, Paul W. *Industry Regulation and the Performance of the American Economy*. New York, 1992.
McCaffrey, David P. *OSHA and the Politics of Health Regulation*. New York, 1982.
Meier, Kenneth J. *Regulation: Politics, Bureaucracy, and Economics*. New York, 1985.
Reagan, Michael D. *Regulation: The Politics of Policy*. Boston, 1987.
Smith, Robert S. *The Occupational Safety and Health Act*. Washington, D.C., 1976.
Smith, Robert S. "The Impact of OSHA Inspections on Manufacturing Injury Rates." *Journal of Human Resources* 4 (1979): 145–170.
U.S. Department of Labor, Occupational Safety and Health Administration. *All about OSHA*. Washington, D.C., 1985.
U.S. Department of Labor, Occupational Safety and Health Administration. *OSHA Reference Book*. Washington, D.C., 1985.
Viscusi, W. Kip. "Reforming OSHA Regulation of Workplace Risks." In *Regulatory Reform: What Actually Happened*, edited by Leonard W. Weiss and Michael W. Klass. Boston, 1985.
—NADIA RUBAII-BARRETT

Oceanic and Atmospheric Administration, National

The principal functions of the National Oceanic and Atmospheric Administration, an agency within the Commerce Department under Reorganization Plan No. 4 of 1970, are to explore, map, and chart the oceans and to manage, use, and conserve their living resources. Specifically, the NOAA monitors and predicts atmospheric conditions; reports the weather; issues warnings and alerts regarding impending natural disasters; collects environmental data; manages a network of meteorological, oceanographic, geophysical, and solar-terrestrial data centers; manages and conserves living marine habitats, including those of certain endangered marine species; produces charts for safe navigation of the nation's waterways, territorial seas, and airspace; draws up policies on ocean and coastline management; and provides grants for marine research. The NOAA is the lead agency involved in the study of global climatic change. The most famous division of the NOAA is the National Weather Service, which provides the data on which the media base their weather forecasts. The National Weather Service has six regional offices, in Alaska, Hawaii, Missouri, New York, Texas, and Utah. Another NOAA unit, the National Marine Fisheries Service, develops and manages the nation's marine fishery resources for both commercial and recreational use, assists the fishing industry in production and marketing, issues fishing permits, regulates the protection of marine animals and their habitats, and coordinates the activities of the eight Regional Fisheries Management Councils. A third unit, the National Environmental Satellite Data and Information Service, operates the Satellite Operational Control Center and Command and Data Acquisition. The NOAA conducts extensive oceanic and atmospheric research in collaboration with other federal science agencies. The NOAA Corps, the nation's seventh uniformed service, operates a twenty-three-ship research fleet and research and hurricane warning aircraft.

—GEORGE THOMAS KURIAN

Office of _____.
See under latter part of name.

On-Site Inspection Agency

When President Reagan and Soviet leader Mikhail Gorbachev signed the Intermediate-Range Nuclear Forces (INF) Treaty in December 1987, it opened a new age for arms control treaties and agreements. Within six years the Conventional Armed Forces in Europe (CFE) Treaty, Strategic Arms Reduction Treaty (START), Threshold Test Ban Treaty (TTBT), Vienna Documents of 1990, 1992, and 1994, Chemical Weapons Convention (CWC), and Open Skies Treaty had been negotiated, signed, and were either being implemented

or were being considered for ratification. The United States was a signatory to each of these post–Cold War arms control treaties.

These treaties were bilateral (signed by two nations) and multilateral (signed by up to 160 nations). A key element in treaty verification was on-site inspections. Small teams of inspectors had the treaty right to travel to a site and confirm the number and location of weapons at operational bases, storage depots, and weapon production factories. The inspectors would confirm and report, under strict provisions of the treaty's protocols, on the destruction, modification, or removal of the nuclear, conventional, and chemical weapons.

As a direct consequence of these new arms control treaties, President Reagan issued a national security directive that instructed the secretary of defense to set up a new organization, the On-Site Inspection Agency (OSIA). Under the INF Treaty, the OSIA was responsible for conducting inspections in the Soviet Union and for escorting Soviet inspectors carrying out inspections in the United States and Western Europe. Established in January 1988, the new agency began INF Treaty inspections following U.S. Senate ratification and the exchange of treaty instruments at the Moscow Summit of 1 June 1988. Within the treaty's first sixty days, the United States and the Soviet Union conducted more than two hundred on-site inspections of the sites in question. The OSIA led and conducted all U.S. inspections and escorts.

Brigadier General Roland Lajoie of the U.S. Army served as the first director of the OSIA. The agency's initial cadre of forty people was later doubled, then more than doubled again, reaching 240 within three years. Thanks to the signing and ratification of new treaties, each with the verification right of on-site inspections, this number had grown to 830 by December 1995. General Lajoie decided that for the INF Treaty inspections, teams would be manned by military personnel. Team chiefs were U.S. Army, U.S. Marine Corps, or U.S. Air Force officers with 15–17 years of experience, Russian language skills, and advanced study in international relations. Team members were drawn from a mixture of officers and noncommissioned officers who had either language skills (Russian) or weapon system skills (nuclear weapons specialists). Such skills and experience proved to be important in conducting the INF Treaty inspections, especially during the first phases, which set precedents in the United States and the Soviet Union for carrying out more recent, and much larger, arms control treaties and agreements.

In May 1990 President George Bush directed the expansion of the agency's mission beyond implementation of the INF Treaty. The president directed the OSIA to prepare to conduct on-site inspections under several pending arms control treaties: the CFE Treaty, START, two nuclear testing treaties—the TTBT and the Peaceful Nuclear Explosions Treaty (PNET)—and several agreements for reducing chemical weapons, including the CWC. As of May 1990, none of these agreements had been signed or had entered into force; within six years, all but the CWC would be in force, with verification monitored by on-site inspectors.

On 1 June 1990 President Bush and President Gorbachev signed new protocols to two treaties permitting the monitoring of underground nuclear tests. That same month, OSIA inspectors went to the Soviet Union and conducted the first on-site visits to implement a new bilateral agreement: the Destruction and Non-Production Agreement for Chemical Weapons. This accord was an attempt to establish a schedule for the destruction of each nation's chemical stockpiles. In the summer and fall of 1990, another major treaty reached completion: the CFE Treaty. It was, by any measure, the largest multinational arms reduction treaty in modern European history. On 19 November 1990 the leaders of twenty-two nations—sixteen of which were members of the North Atlantic Treaty Organization, the rest of which were Warsaw Pact signatories—met in Paris, France, and signed the CFE Treaty. It mandated the reduction within forty months of entry into force of more than 38,500 modern offensive weapons—tanks, artillery, armored personnel carriers, fighters, and helicopters. Inspections covered the territory of all 22 nations, stretching across 2.4 million square miles from the Atlantic Ocean to the Ural Mountains. More than 200,000 pieces of military equipment and forty-five hundred military sites were subject to inspection.

All these treaties were submitted to the U.S. Senate for ratification. The TTBT and protocols were ratified by both U.S. Senate and the Supreme Soviet in early November 1990. The treaty entered into force on 11 December 1990. The Soviet Union conducted the first inspection of a U.S. underground nuclear test in July 1991. The OSIA led the official escort team, serving on-site as the U.S. government representative. Escorting consisted of hosting a series of preliminary meetings to coordinate the inspection schedule with the planned nuclear test at the Department of Energy's Nevada test site, transporting the Soviet test equipment to the site (from San Francisco), transporting the Soviet inspection team, hosting it on-site, and then, after the test, completing the final binational inspection report. Under the TTBT, the Soviet Union monitored on-site two nuclear tests, and the United States underwent preparations for monitoring two scheduled Soviet nuclear tests. A moratorium by both nations in the fall of 1991 stopped all testing.

In June 1991 the OSIA gained another mission as the National Security Council directed it to assume the United States' inspection and escort responsibilities under the Vienna Document agreements of 1990. Conducted in Europe under the auspices of the Conference on Security and Cooperation in Europe, these inspections by small teams of national military officers encouraged the open exchange of information across the old East-West boundaries of the Cold War. The fifty-four-nation agreement was expanded in the Vienna Document of 1992, and yet again in a broader, more comprehensive agreement, the Vienna Document of 1994.

Another inspection mission came in July 1991 when the under secretary of defense for acquisition assigned the OSIA responsibility for coordinating all Department of Defense support for the on-site inspections conducted by the United Nations Special Commission on Iraq. Established following the Gulf War of 1991, the special commission was to monitor Iraq's commitment to United Nations Resolution 687, which stipulated the elimination of its weapons of mass destruction. OSIA inspectors have served as U.S. government representatives on UN inspection teams in Iraq.

On 31 July 1991 President Bush and President

Gorbachev signed START in Moscow. Three weeks later, the Soviet leader was nearly overthrown in a coup d'état. Despite this foreboding event, START went forth. OSIA inspection teams conducted a series of START exhibition inspections in the fall and winter of 1991–92. These were the months when the Soviet Union collapsed as an empire and a nation. Throughout these months inspections continued under the INF Treaty, the chemical weapons destruction agreement, the TTBT, and the aforementioned START. The carrying out of these arms control treaties, especially the escorting and hosting of on-site inspection teams, was one of the few signs of continuity in the international system during these chaotic times.

In the winter of 1991–92 there were fears that the peoples of the former Soviet Union would face a harsh winter without adequate food, heat, or critical medical supplies. In Washington, Secretary of State James Baker initiated a large multinational humanitarian aid project, "Provide Hope." Baker requested that the OSIA send small, experienced teams on three weeks' notice to cities and towns throughout Russia and the new nations of the former Soviet Union. Their mission was to receive air-transported humanitarian aid and to insure its delivery to schools, orphanages, and hospitals. In the first phase the OSIA sent thirty-eight people to twenty-five cities, where they distributed over twenty-two hundred tons of food and medical supplies. The second phase involved 120 people from the OSIA; they assisted in the delivery of twenty-five thousand tons of aid to twenty-eight cities between April and August 1992. A third phase saw the deployment of sixty-eight OSIA people in twenty-five teams. They delivered forty-three thousand tons of food, heating fuel, medical supplies, and even medical field hospitals to cities and towns across Eurasia from October 1992 to September 1993.

The United States entered into another treaty, the Open Skies Treaty, on 24 March 1992. Signed by twenty-four nations in Helsinki, Finland, this treaty gave the signatory nations the right, under a quota system based on size of national territory, of flying unarmed aircraft, equipped with cameras and infrared devices, over other nations' territories. On 24 November 1992 the OSIA, along with the U.S. Air Force, received from the National Security Council responsibility for conducting and hosting treaty overflights.

Two months later, in January 1993, the United States and 120 other nations signed the CWC in Paris, France. The OSIA was assigned responsibility by the U.S. government for escorting all international inspection teams while on U.S. territory. Because of the large number of signatory states—currently 160—this treaty (which was sponsored by the United Nations) had not entered into force as of December 1995.

In summary, the OSIA's existence was tied directly to the verification of major post–Cold War arms control treaties. It began by organizing and conducting precedent-setting inspections in the Soviet Union under a single treaty agency, the INF Treaty; it grew substantially as newer, larger arms control treaties—the CFE Treaty, START, TTBT, Vienna Documents, United Nations Special Commission on Iraq, and the bilateral chemical weapons destruction agreement—entered into force. Since 1988, when the first treaty entered into force, agency inspection teams have conducted more than fifteen hundred inspections in foreign nations. Meanwhile, they have escorted more than one thousand foreign inspection teams monitoring U.S. facilities and weapons sites. The work is far from finished, for larger and more recent arms control treaties—the CWC, Open Skies Treaty, and START II—await ratification and entry into force.

[*See also* National Security Council.]

BIBLIOGRAPHY

Harahan, Joseph P. *On-Site Inspections under the INF Treaty.* Washington, D.C., 1993.
Harahan, Joseph P., and John S. Kuhn III. *On-Site Inspections under the CFE Treaty.* Washington, D.C., 1996.
SIPRI Yearbook: Armaments and Disarmament. New York, 1988–.
Willford, David M. *Brief History of the On-Site Inspection Agency.* Washington, D.C., 1995.

—JOSEPH P. HARAHAN

OSHA.

See Occupational Safety and Health Administration.

P

Packers and Stockyards Administration

The responsibilities of the Packers and Stockyards Administration include regulation of the practices of livestock and live poultry marketers as well as those of meat and poultry packers engaged in interstate commerce. These regulations cover unfair, deceptive, discriminatory, fraudulent, and anticompetitive marketing practices such as false weighing, price manipulation, livestock switches, and misrepresentation of the source, origin, and health of livestock. The Packers and Stockyards Administration is an agency within the Department of Agriculture set up under the 1921 Packers and Stockyards Act. It is headed by an administrator who is appointed by the secretary of agriculture.

—GEORGE THOMAS KURIAN

Paperwork Reduction Act.
See Appendix: Basic Documents of Public Administration.

Park Service, National.
See National Park Service.

Parole Commission

Established within the Justice Department in 1930 as the U.S. Board of Parole, the Parole Commission administers the parole system for federal prisoners and develops federal policy on parole. The commission consists of nine commissioners appointed by the president and confirmed by the Senate for six-year terms. Five of the commis-

sioners head regional offices; the chairperson and three other commissioners make up the National Appeals Board in Washington, D.C. The commissioners meet every three months to determine parole eligibility, impose conditions on the release of any prisoner from custody, revoke parole, or terminate prison sentences before the expiration of the supervision period.

—GEORGE THOMAS KURIAN

Patent and Trademark Office

The basic function of the Patent and Trademark Office is to examine and issue patents and trademarks. It also sells printed copies of issued documents, hears and decides appeals, and represents the United States in international bodies involved in patents. Patents have been issued by the federal government since 10 April 1790, making it one of the oldest federal agencies. The fees charged and the term of the patent have changed over the years, but not substantially. The first superintendent of patents was appointed in 1802 by Thomas Jefferson. At first part of the State Department, it was moved to the Interior Department in 1949, and then to the Commerce Department in 1925. The name of the agency was expanded from the Patent Office to Patent and Trademark Office in 1975.

BIBLIOGRAPHY

U.S. Patent and Trademark Office. *The Story of U.S. Patent and Trademark Office.* Washington, D.C., 1988.
Weber, Gustavus A. *The Patent Office: Its History, Activities and Organization.* Washington, D.C., 1924.

—GEORGE THOMAS KURIAN

Peace Corps

The mission of the Peace Corps calls for volunteers to live and work with people in developing countries at the grass-roots level. The Peace Corps Act, signed into law on 22 September 1961, declares three goals: To promote world peace and friendship by helping people of interested countries to meet their needs for trained manpower; helping to promote a better understanding of the American people on the part of the people served; and helping to promote a better understanding of other people on the part of the American people.

Peace Corps volunteers have been fighting hunger, disease, illiteracy, poverty, and lack of opportunity around the world since 1961. The efforts of more than 140,000 volunteers in ninety-four countries over the course of thirty-five years have encouraged better productivity on millions of acres of cropland; sanitization of water and other health programs; English instruction; and the launching of thousands of new small businesses.

Peace Corps programs have evolved as the world has changed. While the need continues for volunteers to work in agriculture, education, forestry, health, engineering, and skilled trades, more countries are beginning to request help in business, the environment, urban planning, youth development, and the teaching of English for commerce and technology.

Until the establishment of the Peace Corps in 1961 by President John F. Kennedy, the federal government had not, by and large, considered voluntary assistance programs to be part of its responsibility. Kennedy's New Frontierism, however, aimed to improve the quality of the nation and the world and was expressed in the Peace Corps. In the late 1950s Senator Hubert H. Humphrey (D-Minn.) and Representative Henry S. Reuss (D-Wis.) developed the general idea of sending volunteers overseas for personal aid in the form of training and education. Reuss wrote the first Peace Corps–type legislation, HR 9638, in January 1960 to study the practicality of the establishment of a Peace Corps. Humphrey used

the phrase "Youth Peace Corps" in Senate bill S 3675 in June 1960. The House Foreign Affairs Committee responded favorably in August 1960, when it added a rider to the Mutual Security Act that authorized $10,000 for a study of a "Point Four Youth Corps," as Reuss called it after President Harry S. Truman's Point Four technical assistance agency of 1949.

Kennedy advanced the idea of a people-to-people foreign assistance initiative during his campaign for the presidency in October 1960. Kennedy addressed an audience of approximately ten thousand students at the University of Michigan in the early hours of the morning. The students' warm reception of Kennedy inspired him to challenge them and to declare that their willingness to contribute a part of their lives to their country would determine the ability of a free society to compete. Following the speech, two University of Michigan graduate students launched an initiative to recruit volunteers and compel Kennedy to enact the youth service idea he advocated.

The concept of the Peace Corps resembled the Civilian Conservation Corps (CCC) of 1933, one of the first New Deal programs enacted by President Franklin D. Roosevelt, in both its mission and in the way it created political disputes. The CCC was a public works project intended to promote environmental conservation and build good citizens through vigorous, disciplined outdoor work. The way that the Republican party reacted to the Peace Corps in 1960 mirrored its response to the CCC nearly thirty years earlier. In 1933 the CCC was viewed as entirely visionary, and, in 1960, the Peace Corps was labeled a juvenile experiment. Kennedy's Republican opponent, Richard M. Nixon, believed that volunteers would really be attempting to escape the draft. Even some Democrats felt the Peace Corps was being used primarily for campaign purposes. Other critics felt that the program should not be a part of the federal government and that Third World countries might view the program as imperialistic. However, the enthusiasm of the younger generation had motivated Kennedy to give the Peace Corps its initial national publicity. He believed there to be a wealth of idealism among the youth of America, and the Peace

Corps was a method of revealing it to the world.

Following his famous inaugural address asking Americans to "ask not what your country can do for you—ask what you can do for your country," Kennedy appointed his brother-in-law, R. Sargent Shriver, to head a task force to develop Peace Corps ideology and design a program. On 1 March Kennedy established a pilot Peace Corps, one of his most positive and enduring legacies, by signing Executive Order 10924 and sent a message to Congress requesting legislation. He appointed Shriver as the Peace Corps' first director.

The Peace Corps was originally slated for placement in the Agency for International Development, which incorporated all government economic and social development initiatives. However, Peace Corps advisers wanted to preserve the uniqueness and autonomy of the newly established program. They felt that the Peace Corps had a spirit and appeal to young people that would be stifled if entangled in red tape and contained within the government's traditional foreign aid establishment. Therefore, the Peace Corps was organized as a semi-autonomous unit within the State Department. Although subject to continuous supervision and general direction to insure that the foreign policy of the United States was best served, the Peace Corps was essentially independent and apolitical.

To Congress, however, the concept of a humanitarian foreign assistance program established in the context of the Cold War was generally unpopular, and Kennedy's use of the executive order was seen as an offensive display of his executive powers. Many members were hesitant to approve Peace Corps legislation. They voiced concerns about the value of the program, the amount of tax dollars spent on a foreign aid scheme, and the security of volunteers sent overseas amidst America's concern over communist expansion in the Third World.

In response, Shriver and his team of lobbyists saturated Capitol Hill with Peace Corps information to urge members to pass legislation and further the program beyond the pilot stage. Humphrey announced Senate bill S 2000 on 1 June 1961. It passed in the Senate on 25 August 1961 and in the House on 14 September 1961. It became law on 22 September 1961, and fifty-two trainees departed for Ghana.

The early years of the Peace Corps were inspired by the same values traditionally associated with the Kennedy administration: youth, idealism, and vigor. Peace Corps volunteers were known as "Kennedy's children." By December 1963 there were 6,988 volunteers and trainees assigned to forty-four countries. Volunteers had already assisted countries in developing mass education, administering vaccinations, establishing recreational programs, and launching cooperatives. Early training of volunteers consisted of eight to twelve weeks of rigorous academic training, physical exercise, psychological tests, and the fundamentals of a foreign language. Once overseas, volunteers lived on wages equal to those of their host counterparts and were assigned as co-workers instead of supervisors. They strived to share the lives of the people of a village, work side-by-side with them, speak their language, and adopt their customs.

Despite its accomplishments, the Peace Corps battled both internal and external problems. Many volunteers and host countries felt the Peace Corps had not provided sufficient training to enable volunteers to meet the needs of the countries they served. They felt that the early effort to launch the Peace Corps as quickly as possible placed many volunteers in unessential jobs that did not seem to produce tangible results. Some of the first volunteers lowered their expectations and realized they would not be working miracles, contrary to what the American press publicized.

The Peace Corps responded to these problems by rethinking its volunteer development and expectations. Some volunteers were trained in the country in which they would be living, instead of on America's college campuses. Language instruction improved, and cultural sensitivity was stressed more than physical exercise. Former Peace Corps volunteers were used to train future volunteers. Recruiters emphasized that the Peace Corps was a challenging and rewarding experience, and an opportunity to learn about another culture while helping people to learn to help themselves. This new approach superseded the spirited rhetoric of the early years of the Peace

Corps, such as volunteers revolutionizing the social and economic patterns of the countries. In addition, applicants were cautioned that the experience could include periods of frustration and, on occasion, no visible signs of progress.

The Vietnam crisis made America and Third World countries alike reconsider the virtue of the Peace Corps. The antiwar sentiment and activity expressed in the United States was also practiced by volunteers stationed overseas, despite the Peace Corps' attempt to remain politically detached in its mission. During that period the Nixon administration reduced the Peace Corps' budget and, in July 1971, incorporated the agency with all other federal volunteer programs in a new and large bureaucratic agency called ACTION. Peace Corps advocates viewed Nixon's move as an attempt to phase out the agency. The Peace Corps did, in fact, lose some prominence and institutional independence as part of ACTION, and recruitment and training functions slowed as operations were centralized in the larger agency.

The effects of linking the Peace Corps to ACTION extended to the Carter administration, when the number of volunteers overseas sank to a record low, and the agency's continued vitality was uncertain. On 16 May 1979 President Jimmy Carter signed Executive Order 12137 to make the Peace Corps autonomous within ACTION. The move was designed to renew the agency's original spirit of independence. It was also an opportunity to emphasize one of the government's purely humanitarian functions. Similarly, the Peace Corps was seen during the Reagan administration as an alternative to the stereotypical selfishness of the 1980s. In 1983 the Peace Corps once again achieved its status as an independent agency.

Peace Corps operations are, at times, the subject of bipartisan dispute, and many of the same problems and issues continue to exist. Countries' needs for technical skills and "specialists" instead of "generalists" sometimes inhibit the Peace Corps' goal of cultural reciprocity. In addition, political crises have forced volunteers to leave countries hostile to the United States. Nonetheless, Shriver's 1981 speech to commemorate the twentieth anniversary of the founding of the Peace Corps called the program the most memorable and continuing way an American had to serve his or her country and fellow human beings worldwide. Shriver viewed the Peace Corps as service in the purest form, and a vehicle to exhibit America's talents. Despite the problems inherent in fulfilling its mission, the Peace Corps has served its volunteers, the United States, and developing nations alike.

BIBLIOGRAPHY

Peace Corps Handbook. Washington, D.C., 1974, 1978, 1990.

Rice, Gerard T. *Twenty Years of the Peace Corps.* Washington, D.C., 1981.

Rice, Gerard T. *The Bold Experiment.* Notre Dame, Ind., 1985.

Schlesinger, Arthur M., Jr. *A Thousand Days: John F. Kennedy in the White House.* Boston, 1965.

Schwarz, Karen. *What You Can Do for Your Country: Inside the Peace Corps.* New York, 1991.

To Touch the World: The Peace Corps Experience. Washington, D.C., 1995.

Viorst, Milton, ed. *Making a Difference: The Peace Corps at Twenty-Five.* New York, 1986.

—KATHERINE A. COLLADO

Pendleton Act.

See Appendix: Basic Documents of Public Administration.

Pension Benefit Guaranty Corporation

The Employment Retirement Income Security Act (ERISA) of 1974 extended federal regulatory control over private pension plans. The Pension Benefit Guaranty Corporation (PBGC), created under Title IV of the act, is one of the three government agencies administering ERISA, the others being the Pensions and Welfare Benefits Administration (PWBA) and the Internal Revenue Service. The PBGC is a nonprofit corporation wholly owned by the federal government and financed by premiums levied on covered pension plans. The corporation is administered by a board of directors composed of the secretaries of labor, commerce, and the treasury, with the labor secretary serving as chairman. It has a seven-member advisory committee appointed by the president.

The PWBA administers and enforces ERISA's fiduciary standards on reporting and disclosure and employee protection. These standards mandate that:

- employees cannot be forced to work for an unreasonable amount of time before becoming eligible to participate in a pension plan

- the plans must meet certain minimum funding standards

- a copy of the plan must be filed with the PWBA along with annual or triennial financial reports, and these plans and reports must be open to public inspection

- participants must be informed of any changes regarding benefits

- the directors of the plan must avoid conflict of interest and have a track record of integrity

Pension plans not covered by ERISA include government plans, pension plans of churches, plans related to workers' compensation, unemployment compensation and disability insurance, and excess benefit plans where the level of benefits or contributions are higher than those required by law. In 1990 the Supreme Court upheld the PBGC's power to require the reinstatement of terminated plans. The PBGC's termination insurance program covers single-employer and multiemployer pension plans. Under legislation enacted in 1980, if a multiemployer plan becomes insolvent the PBGC will provide financial assistance for the period of insolvency but does not take over the administration of the plan. Employers who withdraw from a multiemployer plan are held liable for a portion of the plan's unfunded vested benefits. The PBGC also may force a plan to be terminated if the plan is unable to pay benefits or if the long-term losses would be a burden on the PBGC. In such cases the PBGC takes over the plan to assure continued payments of benefits.

—GEORGE THOMAS KURIAN

Personnel Management, Office of

Created by executive order in 1978 after the passage of the Civil Service Reform Act, the Office of Personnel Management (OPM) replaced the Civil Service Commission, which had been responsible for administering the civil service system since its creation by the Pendleton Act of 1883. The OPM was intended to remedy some of the problems that reformers felt had developed over the previous century's experience with the merit system.

THE LEGACY OF THE PENDLETON ACT

As the spoils system developed over the nineteenth century, reformers argued that it led to corruption through the selling of public offices. Spoils also led to incompetence because of the lack of qualifications of many of those who received government jobs purely through their political affiliation. The intent of the Pendleton Act was to change this by establishing the merit system and the Civil Service Commission to administer it. The original principles of merit included hiring people based on open and competitive examinations (not political affiliation), promotion (and demotion) based on job performance, and protection of government workers from partisan political pressure.

The merit system was to be administered by an agency under the direction of the three-person, bipartisan Civil Service Commission. As the percentage of federal government workers covered by the merit system grew over the decades, the merit regulations came to include other personnel regulations that were added to the system. These new requirements included a complex classification system, extensive examination and recruitment systems, veterans' preferences, equal opportunity, and affirmative action rules.

As the system developed and rules were created to prevent partisan abuse or discrimination, it became more cumbersome to use. The system was seen as unresponsive, too slow to hire, and too protective of employee rights at the expense of managerial flexibility. Agencies wishing to hire personnel were forced to recruit through the Civil Service Commission, which administered examinations and provided lists of those qualified to agencies, often with significant delays. Line managers felt that their managerial authority was undermined by personnel specialists who controlled much of the hiring process. In addition, the complex set of rules and regulations had not succeeded in entirely eliminating partisan tampering with the Civil Service.

THE CIVIL SERVICE REFORM ACT OF 1978 CREATES THE OFFICE OF PERSONNEL MANAGEMENT

The reorganization that created the OPM transferred to it most of the functions of the expiring Civil Service Commission. The oversight of the merit system and enforcement of its rules were given to a much smaller bipartisan Merit Services Protection Board and an Office of Special Counsel, with independent authority to prosecute abuses in the system.

The bipartisan structure of the commission was replaced by an OPM director appointed (subject to removal) by the president for a four-year term. In keeping with the rest of the Civil Service Reform Act, the intent was to make the civil service system more responsive to presidential direction; the OPM director reported to the president, and agency personnel offices reported to agency directors, who were presidentially appointed. Emphasis was to shift from merely administering merit system rules in a passive way to an active approach to personnel management. The goal would now be on work force planning and human resource management rather than merely the administration of the civil service rules and regulations. The new OPM would be the president's management agent in personnel management as well as the federal government's central personnel management agency.

The primary mission of the newly created agency was to carry out the provisions of the Civil Service Reform Act, including the implementation of the Senior Executive Service provisions, merit pay for mid-level managers, the designing of performance appraisal systems, and, importantly, the delegation of personnel func-

tions to departments and agencies. The remedy for past centralization and lack of responsiveness was to be the delegation, and thus decentralization, of personnel functions to agencies themselves and the responsiveness of agency personnel offices to the line managers. The OPM was to act as a consultant to agencies in designing their own personnel systems in conformance with merit principles and federal laws. The OPM would also conduct research on recruiting systems, examinations, and performance appraisal systems, and it would supervise experimental demonstration projects that could waive personnel regulations to see if better ways of personnel management could be developed. The OPM would be a general overseer of the system and expert consultant rather than the administrator of the system and enforcer of compliance with civil service rules.

President Carter appointed Alan K. ("Scotty") Campbell to be the first director of the OPM and Jule M. Sugarman to be his deputy (and later acting director). Their first challenge was to assist executive branch agencies in implementing the Civil Service Reform Act, and the agency invested significant resources in research on performance appraisal systems, merit pay practices, managing the newly created Senior Executive Service, and work force management. Demonstration projects were begun.

Most important, the new leadership began to delegate personnel authorities to agencies in order to loosen the rigid central controls under which line managers had chafed. The most important delegations involved the authority to examine job candidates and select persons for employment. By the end of 1981, these new delegations of examining authority were used to hire more than twenty-five percent of new employees.

THE REAGAN AND BUSH YEARS

With the election of 1980, major changes came to the leadership of the OPM when President Reagan appointed one of his campaign supporters, Donald Devine, to be director. Devine wanted the OPM to return to the "basics" of traditional personnel administration. The most important policy change that was instituted was the reversal of the delegation of hiring authority to departments and agencies. By 1987 almost half of the specific delegations had been withdrawn. This approach was in accord with the general Reagan administration policy of cutting the federal work force in the domestic area.

One of the intentions of the Civil Service Reform Act was to increase the responsiveness to presidential direction, and the new OPM was more responsive than the old Civil Service Commission in several ways. First, it was responsive to the Carter administration priorities of implementing the act and delegating personnel authority to agencies. During the Reagan administration it reversed the delegation of authority and assisted in the downsizing of the domestic work force and the narrowing of the OPM's mission. The number of political appointees in the OPM increased from fifteen in 1980 to thirty-six in 1983, assuring responsiveness of the OPM to its political leadership. The OPM also was in charge of overseeing the Senior Executive Service of about seven thousand executives, ten percent of whom could be political appointees. The creation of Schedule C positions, political appointments below the GS-15 level, was controlled by the OPM, and their number increased significantly (from about nine hundred to about seventeen hundred) during the Carter and Reagan years.

During the 1980s the OPM as an agency was subject to considerable turbulence that decreased its capacity to carry out its functions. Under Devine the OPM was reorganized three different times during the period that the agency mission was being revised. At the same time its staffing resources were significantly reduced. Between 1979 and 1989 the staffing that was devoted to direct personnel management functions (not including administering the retirement system or providing investigative services to other agencies) was cut by more than fifty percent, and the funding level was cut forty-five percent (in constant dollars).

When Constance Horner succeeded Donald Devine as director in 1985, she began cutting red tape for federal managers and began to return to some of the decentralizing concerns of the first several years of the OPM. In 1989 President Bush appointed Constance B. Newman to direct the OPM; her priorities included capacity building for the OPM and reinvigorating the recruitment of high-quality applicants for the federal work force. Newman moved to implement some of the recommendations of the bipartisan National Commission on the Public Service (the Volcker Commission) to improve recruitment, increase pay, and enhance training in the civil service. But the efforts of each of these OPM directors were constrained by the steady decline in resources that the OPM was able to bring to bear on their rebuilding priorities.

PRESIDENT CLINTON AND THE NATIONAL PERFORMANCE REVIEW

When Bill Clinton was elected, his administration decided that one of its priorities would be to "reinvent" the way the government did business. He put Vice President Al Gore in charge of the National Performance Review (NPR) in an effort to create "a government that works better and costs less." Many of the NPR initiatives had profound personnel implications, not the least of which was cutting the federal work force by 272,900 over several years. Another priority was getting rid of red tape and many of the rules and regulations that continued to clog the personnel process. It was argued that decision making, including personnel actions, was best made closest to the actual place where the work was being done. This implied the active delegation of personnel authority to the agencies again.

Because of the predominance of the NPR initiatives, President Clinton's OPM director, James B. King, was not the initiator of the most important personnel policies of the administration, but he was an enthusiastic implementer of them. King's actions included cutting OPM merit system regulations, reducing OPM personnel, privatizing functions, delegating to agencies, and abandoning the Bush administration efforts on training.

One of the most highly visible of King's actions was to abolish the *Federal Personnel Manual,* a compilation of hundreds of pages of interpretation of Title V of the U.S. Code, which deals with federal government personnel. Many managers were glad to see the end of the detailed and sometimes frustrating rules covering all aspects of personnel actions. On the other hand, since Title V had not been repealed, agencies had to interpret the law themselves and make up new personnel rules, and many continued to use the processes mandated by the newly obsolete manual. Another action that King took was to abolish the standard employment history form (SF171) that had been used throughout the federal government. This was also a relief for many who had struggled with the cumbersome standardized form. Agencies could now create their own forms for application for government employment or depend on whatever type of résumé that applicants submitted.

As the reductions in personnel began to take their effect throughout the federal government, the OPM contributed more than its share of cuts. By the end of 1996 the federal government had 250,000 fewer employees than it had had when the Clinton administration took office in 1993. This brought federal employment down to fewer than two million, the smallest it had been since the early 1960s. The OPM lost more than thirty-eight percent of the employees it had had in 1993, further reducing its capacity to act as the central personnel agency of the federal government. Thus the OPM would be delegating personnel functions to agencies as much by abdication as by policy. By the middle of the 1990s the OPM no longer had the capacity to act as the personnel manager for the government even if it had wanted to.

AN UNCERTAIN FUTURE

The Civil Service Reform Act of 1978 was intended to relieve the rigidities in the system and create an OPM that would be both the president's personnel management agent and the promoter of personnel professionalism throughout the government. But the OPM and the Merit Services Protection Board never fulfilled the high hopes of the framers of the act. The failure can be attributed to several factors, including drastic cutbacks in resources and a turbulent political environment.

The OPM began the 1980s with the full-strength capacity and resources to accomplish its new policy initiatives and with the motivation and professionalism necessary to carry out its mission. But it was soon hit with a series of challenges that undermined its capacity and spirit. With the transition to the new Reagan administration in 1981, several key changes were made. Along with other domestic agencies, and in accord with President Reagan's priorities, OPM budgets and personnel were cut. At the same time, the number of political appointees doubled, the agency underwent three reorganizations, and the mission of delegation of personnel authority to agencies was reversed.

With the coming of directors Horner and Newman the worst aspects of the early 1980s were ameliorated, but the overall level of resources in both personnel and budget continued to decrease. These internal challenges were exacerbated by a turbulent environment. Encouraged by bipartisan criticism of the federal government, public trust in the government continued to decline throughout the 1980s, and many of the perceived failings of the federal government were blamed on those who carried out its policies. In addition, work force planners had to plan for a future of rapid change in the demographics of the American work force at the same time that technological innovations were transforming the nature of work.

Under the Clinton administration and the priorities of the NPR, the OPM's mission was further undermined and its work force drastically cut. Thus, in the late 1990s the OPM was merely a shadow of its former self, either at its birth or in its previous incarnation as the Civil Service Commission; and the Merit Services Protection Board never developed the enforcement clout that the framers of the reform act had intended. Whether the system of merit, developed over a century of U.S. history, would suffer irreparably from the reduced oversight and developmental capacity was not yet clear at the end of the century.

[See also Civil Service; National Performance Review; and Appendix: Civil Service (Pendleton) Act (1883).]

BIBLIOGRAPHY

Campbell, Alan K. "Civil Service Reform: A New Commitment." *Public Administration Review* (March–April 1978): 99–103.

General Accounting Office. *Managing Human Resources: Greater OPM Leadership Needed to Address Critical Challenges*. GGD-89-19. Washington, D.C., 1989.

Ingraham, Patricia W., and David H. Rosenbloom, eds. *The Promise and Paradox of Civil Service Reform*. Pittsburgh, 1992.

Ingraham, Patricia Wallace. *The Foundation of Merit*. Baltimore, 1995.

Ingraham, Patricia Wallace, and Carolyn Ban, eds. *Legislating Bureaucratic Change*. Albany, 1984.

Levine, Charles H., and Rosslyn S. Kleeman. *The Quiet Crisis of the Civil Service: The Federal Personnel System at the Crossroads*. Washington, D.C., 1986.

Merit Services Protection Board. *U.S. Office of Personnel Management and the Merit System*. Washington, D.C., 1989.

National Academy of Public Administration. *Civil Service Reform, 1978–1981: A Progress Report*. Washington, D.C., 1981.

Newland, Chester A. "Crucial Issues for Public Personnel Professionals." *Public Personnel Management* (Spring 1984): 15–46.

Rosenbloom, David H. "Civil Service Reform, 1978: Some Issues." *Midwest Review of Public Administration* (September 1979): 171–175. —JAMES P. PFIFFNER

Political Parties and the Federal Government

ESSAY From its beginnings, government has had a paradoxical place in the American polity. In its essence, the state is a system of authority: to distribute, to withhold, to regulate. Yet the United States, in its underlying revolutionary beliefs and its chartering Constitution, was shaped by the belief that government's was a power as much to be checked and constrained as to be enhanced and asserted.

The Constitution is most of all a document of checks and balances: among the three branches—legislative, executive, judicial—of the federal government; and between the levels of government, national and state. The functions assigned to the federal government were, from a modern point of view, limited indeed: defense and diplomacy, taxation and finance, tariff-making. Social and economic regulation—"all the objects, which, in the ordinary course of affairs, concern the lives, liberties, and properties of the people; and the internal order, improve-ment, and prosperity of the state"—were, James Madison declared in his *Federalist,* no. 45, the province of the states.

But then into this classic eighteenth-century construct of order and balance was suddenly injected a quite unexpected form of the interest-group factionalism that Madison and the other Founders so feared. This was the national political party system: a product in part of the size and diversity of the American Republic, but more so of the ground rules of winner-take-all national elections set down in the Constitution. During the 1790s two major political parties, the Federalists and the Jeffersonian Republicans, became the dominant reality in American public life.

The first stage of the interplay between government and party lasted from 1790 to 1825. Foreign policy, from the fight over the Jay Treaty with England in 1794 to the War of 1812, played a major role in party politics: a new development for a realm of public policy that was traditionally regarded as the special province of elites. The Monroe Doctrine of 1823 was not an elite declaration of foreign policy in the spirit of the Congress of Vienna that had ended the Napoleonic period a decade before, but rather a product of the intense domestic politics of the 1824 presidential election.

The classic Republican ideal of high-minded, well-educated civil servants—something to which both Thomas Jefferson and Alexander Hamilton, political adversaries though they were, subscribed—quickly gave way before the dictates of patronage: not the aristocratic patronage of the Old Regime, distributed by grandees to their associates and relatives, but the broad distribution of government jobs—what by the 1830s was called the spoils system—required by an increasingly democratic politics.

The full emergence, between 1825 and 1845, of (white, male) mass parties in the era of the Jacksonian Democrats and the Whigs had an even more profound impact on the shape and substance of American government. Before 1825 politicians as varied as Washington's Secretary of the Treasury Alexander Hamilton, Jefferson's Secretary of the Treasury Albert Gallatin, John Quincy Adams of Massachusetts, Kentucky Whig leader Henry Clay, and the (later) Southern states' rights spokesman John C. Calhoun called for large-scale government programs of internal improvements and protective tariffs. As Calhoun grandly put it in 1816: "Let us bind the Republic together with a perfect system of roads and canals. Let us conquer space." But tariffs and transportation, and indeed government policy in general, turned out to be the work not of national planners but of party and local politics.

Canals and railroads were planned, financed, and constructed by state and, increasingly, private enterprises, closely linked to the political parties. They served local, not national, purposes. The same was true of banking and finance. The Bank of the United States turned out not to be the beginning of a national bank, but an experiment in central banking soon overridden by conflicting state and local political and economic interests.

A dramatic demonstration of the weakened state of the federal government in the early nineteenth century was the fate of the national capital. Washington was planned on a grand scale in the 1790s, as befitted the capital of an ambitious republic. The reality a half century later was very different: no thriving metropolis, no national center of culture, commerce, and industry, but rather a tawdry, fever-ridden, half-built town, with a small contingent of federal employees clustered around the White House and boarding house–dwelling congressmen clustered around the Capitol. So far removed was L'Enfant's plan of an imperial capital from the reality of early-nineteenth-century American government that when the Treasury building was constructed in the early 1830s, it was placed square on the axis of Pennsylvania Avenue, the grand boulevard that was supposed to link the Capitol and the White House (with the Supreme Court placed halfway between) in a physical expression of the balance-of-power concept of the Constitution.

The most consequential result of government's subordination to the dictates of party politics was the crisis of the late 1840s and the 1850s that resulted in Southern secession and Civil War. The weakness and incapacity of government seemed to be steadily growing. This was a time of one-term presidents with little administrative capacity; Congress did not provide funding for administrative assistants or even a private secretary for the chief executive until 1857. The federal bureaucracy was small and ineffective: in 1851, of the 26,274 civilian employees of the government, 21,391 worked for the patronage-ridden Post Office. Major national issues—the construction of a transcontinental railroad, tariff policy, most of all the question of the place of slavery in the lands secured by the Louisiana Purchase of 1803 and the Mexican War of 1846–1848—were less and less subject to resolution as intersectional animosity and intense partisanship grew in intensity and stymied the workings of government.

The Civil War seemed for a time to have fundamentally reversed the decay of government and its subordination to party politics. The mobilization of men, money, matériel, and public opinion by which Lincoln and his administration won the war led to the emergence of a powerful American state.

References to the "Nation" and to the "great Republic" were common during the wartime and postwar years. Large-scale federal taxation (including an income tax) and borrowing financed the war. An outburst of legislation by the Republican-controlled Congress—a higher tariff, a national paper currency (greenbacks), nationally chartered banks, a Pacific Railroad Act, the Land Grant College and Homestead Acts—constituted the first large-scale national program since the 1790s. And Reconstruction—the Thirteenth, Fourteenth, and Fifteenth Amendments, the Republican Reconstruction policy toward the defeated South—seemed to presage a federal commitment to race-blind national citizenship.

But as the passions of the war faded, what emerged—or, better, reemerged—was something more familiar: a limited American state dominated by the party system. The Republicans and Democrats of the late nineteenth century ever more skillfully merged intense organization, large-scale money-raising (through officeholder kickbacks, contractor payoffs, and the like), and powerful regional and ethnocultural appeals to voter loyalties.

More than ever, government was the handmaiden of party politics. True, the federal work force increased almost fivefold, from 51,020 in

1871 to 239,476 in 1901. And a national civil service system was finally instituted in 1884. But the bulk of federal employees worked in intensely party-oriented departments: the Post Office, the Agriculture Department, the Pension Bureau, and the customs houses. They served the interests of party more than the dictates of the American state. And while forty-four percent of federal employees were under the civil service by 1900, the great majority of these were party appointees protected in office by outgoing administrations (the Republicans in 1885 and 1893, the Democrats in 1889 and 1895).

The closest approach to an autonomous, relatively nonpartisan governmental presence in this period was to be found not in the bureaucracy, but in the courts. Federal judges were more and more ready to decide whether taxation and regulation were proper applications of the states' police power or were unconstitutional violations of the Fourteenth Amendment's due process clause. While this new judicial activism came under popular and political challenge, more striking was the degree to which it was accepted—presumably as a necessity in a system where rule by bureaucrats was so out of favor. The late-nineteenth-century American state was one of courts as well as parties.

The prevailing view today is that an American government with national administrative capacities emerged in the late nineteenth and early twentieth centuries. Certainly there are grounds for so believing. The years from 1887 to 1932 might properly be called the Age of Regulation, as government, both federal and state, entered into a dramatic expansion of its authority over wide areas of American economic, social, and political life.

Independent regulatory agencies began with the Interstate Commerce Commission of 1887. The Sherman Antitrust Act of 1890 and the Federal Trade Commission of 1914 were among a number of new laws and agencies designed to deal with the rise of big business. The Federal Reserve Act of 1914 gave the federal government an authority over the nation's banking system denied it since the end of the Second Bank of the United States in 1836; the income tax amendment of 1913 gave it the potential of broad new revenue-collecting powers. Immigration restriction, World War I restraints on freedom of speech and the press, and Prohibition were among the more significant social constraints imposed by federal authority; national woman suffrage was the broadest expansion of the right to vote in the nation's history.

As important as these developments was the rise of a new view of government as a public function best performed free from the constraints of party politics. This was a central theme in the Progressive movement of the early twentieth century. It led to a substantial assault on the dominance of party machines and bosses through such devices as the Australian ballot (secret voting on uniform ballots printed at public expense), new registration laws, and primaries. And it fostered a new belief in expertise and nonpartisanship in the conduct of government affairs. Mass-circulation newspapers and magazines, independent of party affiliation, became a powerful new force in the shaping of public opinion, more powerful, it seemed, than that of the major political parties.

Still, it cannot be said that when the Great Depression of the early 1930s struck, the late nineteenth century state of courts and parties had been fundamentally altered. In the wake of the Progressive movement and the First World War, the major parties reasserted their control over the public agenda. The appeal of the Republican party to white, Protestant America, and its representation of the interests of big business, gave it both great popular support and control over government policy during the 1920s. The Democrats similarly reasserted their dominance over the agendas of those unlikely bedfellows the white Protestant rural South and the urban, Catholic–new immigrant North. This meant that the initial response to the Depression, the most profound challenge to American government since the Civil War, was solidly within the framework of the prevailing values of the party system: suspicion of active government, wariness of the welfare state.

The reluctance of the Hoover administration to deal directly with the human costs of the Depression is a familiar story. But comparable ideological constraints were evident among the Democrats as well. True to his party's tradition of hostility to a strong federal government, Franklin D. Roosevelt in his 1932 campaign castigated the Hoover administration for spending and agency-making: "I accuse the present administration of being the greatest spending administration in peace times in all our history. It is an administration that has piled bureau on bureau, commission on commission. . . . I regard the reduction in Federal spending as one of the most important issues in this campaign."

But in fact FDR's presidency led to the New Deal and the mobilization of World War II, developments commonly regarded as the watershed events of modern American government. It was during this period that the legislative and administrative infrastructure of the modern welfare state (if not its levels of expenditure from the 1960s on) took shape. And it was during the war that levels of government spending (and taxation) and economic planning and control previously undreamed of came into being. Just as important, it appeared to most Americans, and to most American politicians, that New Deal spending and economic planning and control had done the jobs that they were designed to do. Not only did the United States win the war, but massive unemployment, the grimmest specter of the Depression, finally was laid to rest.

The political and economic exigencies of the Depression wrought one of the most dramatic transformations in the history of American government. During the most intense years of the New Deal, from 1933 to 1937, about a hundred new government agencies were created, and the American state took on a range of regulatory, welfare, recovery, and relief activities far beyond anything in its past.

The contribution of the New Dealers—the academics, social workers, reformers, economists, and lawyers who gave this outburst its statutory shape—has been widely recognized. Less familiar is the intensely political—indeed, partisan—context of the New Deal. There was a powerful reciprocal relationship between politics and policy. Much of the agricultural activity of the New Deal was closely attuned to the interests and influence of southern Democratic leaders. And

while ultimately the welfare state may have eroded the power of city and state party organizations, the initial effect of the New Deal was quite the reverse. The burgeoning New Deal vote in the industrial cities and towns both sustained and shaped the relief, welfare, and labor legislation of the Roosevelt administration. In return, these programs gave sustenance to the urban Democrats' core voters, and to party workers as well (it was estimated that over ninety percent of the ward committeemen of the newly victorious Pittsburgh Democratic machine were employed as foremen in the Works Progress Administration).

If the New Deal was as much the product of the Democratic party as of FDR's Brains Trusters, so too was the Republican response as much political as ideological. The unpopularity of a wholesale rejection of the New Deal was evident, and GOP presidential candidates from Alfred M. Landon in 1936 to Wendell Willkie in 1940 and New York governor Thomas E. Dewey in 1944 and 1948 promised to run a more efficient and economical, not a dismantled, modern American government. While to some degree opposing the New Deal on class terms, Republican (and southern Democratic) anti–New Deal conservatism rested as much on the ethnocultural opposition of white, Anglo-Saxon, native-born Protestant Americans to the new immigrants, their children, and blacks, who were the most enthusiastic beneficiaries of the New Deal. And beyond that, conservative critics of the New Deal tapped an American suspicion of government and bureaucracy that would not be easily laid to rest, even in so traumatic a time as that of the Great Depression and the Second World War.

The relationship of party politics to American government during the half century since the end of the Second World War has been more tenuous and indirect than in the past. For most of this period both the foreign and domestic policies of the government have been far less subject to partisan definition and resolution than was the case before.

The American positions during the Cold War toward the Soviet Union, Communist China, Israel and the Arab states—the flashpoint issues of the period—reflected, if anything, declining party divisions. Thus there was more of a partisan response to the triumph of the Chinese Communists in the late 1940s and to the Korean War of the 1950s than there was to the Vietnam War of the 1960s or to Richard Nixon's resumption of relations with the Chinese Communists in the 1970s. For the most part the foreign policy of the American government over the past half century has been bipartisan. And the opposition—often the fierce opposition—to that policy has come primarily from groups (the New Right, the New Left) defined by social-cultural ideology rather than by party affiliation.

Much the same can be said of domestic policy. Since the 1940s the scale of American government activism has greatly expanded, through both Democratic and Republican administrations. Government expenditure measured as a percentage of the gross national product has gone from twenty percent in 1940 to thirty-one percent in 1962, thirty-six percent in 1980, and forty percent in 1990. Major regulation and expenditure affecting new areas of concern—health, poverty, the environment, civil rights, equal access for disadvantaged groups—were created by Lyndon Johnson's Great Society program and Richard Nixon's presidency during the 1960s and the early 1970s.

At least until recently, it has been difficult to see clear-cut party positions on issues such as civil rights, Medicare and Medicaid, Aid to Families with Dependent Children, food stamps, or environmental regulation, any more than it was possible to speak of Republican and Democratic positions on social security, defense spending, or highways in earlier decades. The issues that have most deeply divided the parties in recent times have been social and cultural, and to some extent class. It is true that many Republicans since at least the time of the New Deal have defined themselves as the party of limited government and many Democrats as the party of expansive government. But more often than not this distinction has broken down in the practice of legislative enactment and statutory enforcement: most recently in the Reagan years, when the rhetoric of government downsizing was overshadowed by the sheer, persistent reality of a government immune to reduction.

Is this still the case? Are we now in the throes of a redefinition of the parties' relationship to government more sharply partisan than at any time since the New Deal? Does the Gingrich/congressional Republican Contract with America mark the demarcation of a new era in the relationship of political parties to American government?

Prediction is foolhardy. But surely the long postwar history of the growth of government, and the ambiguous love-hate relationship that most Americans bear to it, argue against a major and lasting ideological polarization. If government shrinks, or changes in any substantial way, it is much more likely to do so through a complex interparty process of policy and practice rather than through sharply divided partisan positions. Our pluralistic society, and our diffuse and amorphous parties, all but assure that this will be the case.

BIBLIOGRAPHY

Bensel, Richard F. *Sectionalism and American Political Development, 1880–1980*. Madison, Wis., 1984.

Bensel, Richard F. *Yankee Leviathan: The Origins of Central State Authority in America, 1859–1877*. Cambridge, U.K., 1990.

Campbell, Ballard C. *The Growth of American Government: Governance from the Cleveland Era to the Present*. Bloomington, Ind., 1995.

Farnham, Wallace D. "'The Weakened Spring of Government': A Study in 19th-Century American History." *American Historical Review* 68 (1963): 62–80.

Keller, Morton. *Affairs of State: Public Life in Late Nineteenth Century America*. Cambridge, Mass., 1977.

Keller, Morton. *Regulating a New Economy: Public Policy and Economic Change in America, 1900–1933*. Cambridge, Mass., 1990.

Keller, Morton. *Regulating a New Society: Public Policy and Social Change in America, 1900–1933*. Cambridge, Mass., 1994.

McCormick, Richard L. "The Party Period and Public Policy: An Exploratory Hypothesis." *Journal of American History* 66 (1979): 279–298.

May, Ernest R. *The Making of the Monroe Doctrine*. Cambridge, Mass., 1975.

Skocpol, Theda. *Protecting Soldiers and Mothers: The Political Origins of Social Policy in the United States*. Cambridge, Mass., 1992.

Skowronek, Stephen. *Building a New American State: The*

Expansion of National Administrative Capacities, 1877–1920. Cambridge, U.K., 1982.
Sundquist, James L. *Politics and Policy: The Eisenhower, Kennedy, and Johnson Years.* Washington, D.C., 1968.
Young, James S. *The Washington Community, 1800–1828.* New York, 1966.

—MORTON KELLER

Postal Rate Commission

An independent agency that was created by the Postal Reorganization Act of 1970 as amended by the Postal Reorganization Act Amendments of 1976, the Postal Rate Commission (PRC) considers proposed changes in postal rates, fees, and mail classifications and submits recommendations to the governors of the United States Postal Service. Specifically, the commission schedules public hearings on rate changes, solicits comments, and publishes proposals in the *Federal Register.* [*See* Federal Register.] The PRC may also issue advisory opinions on changes in postal services. It also has appellate jurisdiction to review decisions to close or consolidate small post offices. The PRC has five members nominated by the president and confirmed by the Senate for six-year terms. No more than three commissioners can be members of the same political party.

—GEORGE THOMAS KURIAN

Postal Service

The mission of the United States Postal Service, an independent establishment of the executive branch of the federal government, is to provide prompt, reliable, and efficient mail service to all residents of the United States. In fiscal year 1995 the Postal Service delivered 180.7 billion pieces of mail to nearly 128 million addresses, working within a $50.7 billion budget funded through the sale of stamps and services. No tax dollars support this organization. The Postal Service is the country's largest civilian employer, with some 750,000 employees, and compensation and benefits account for 79.5 percent of the costs incurred. Although part of the federal government, the Postal Service is expected to operate in a businesslike manner and has a structure comparable to that of a publicly owned corporation. It also is required to provide service to all communities, even those where post offices are not self-sustaining, and to "break even" financially over time.

ORIGINS

The first official notice of a postal service in the American colonies appeared in 1639, when the General Court of Massachusetts designated Richard Fairbanks's tavern in Boston as the official repository of mail brought from or sent overseas. A monthly post was established between New York and Boston in 1673, although most mail traveled between the colonies and England. A central postal organization within the colonies began after 1691, when Thomas Neale received a grant from the Crown, a franchise that left him heavily in debt. By 1775 and as a rival to the Crown's post, William Goddard had set up a Constitutional Post for intercolonial mail service. It operated by subscription, and net revenues were reinvested in postal improvements rather than paid back to subscribers.

Today's Postal Service dates its origin to 26 July 1775, when the Second Continental Congress agreed "that a Postmaster General be appointed for the United States" and named Benjamin Franklin to the position. The Articles of Confederation gave Congress "the sole and exclusive right and power . . . [of] establishing and regulating post offices from one State to another," with postal laws and regulations revised and codified in the Ordinance of 18 October 1782.

Following adoption of the Constitution, the Act of September 22, 1789, temporarily established a post office and created the Office of the Postmaster General. The Act of February 20, 1792, made detailed provisions for the Post Office, and subsequent legislation enlarged the duties of the Post Office, developed its organization, and issued rules and regulations regarding postal operations. In 1829, upon the invitation of President Andrew Jackson, the postmaster general became a member of the president's cabinet.

In its earliest days, the Postal Service was referred to as the Post Office, then, nationally, as the General Post Office. In the 1820s Postmaster General John McLean began referring to the organization as the Post Office Department, but it was not specifically established as an executive department by Congress until 8 June 1872. On 1 July 1971 it became known as the United States Postal Service, when major organizational changes were made.

Early postmasters general usually were public figures who would, for example, go on to serve as secretary of war, Supreme Court justice, or U.S. senator. Today, the postmaster general is usually selected from the ranks of top corporate executives.

THE POSTAL REORGANIZATION ACT

Despite its best efforts, by the mid-1960s the Post Office Department was in deep trouble. Years of financial neglect and fragmented control had left it with inadequate facilities, outdated equipment, low wages, and inefficient management, along with highly subsidized rates that bore little relation to the costs of processing the mail.

In 1966 the Chicago Post Office virtually shut down owing to a logjam of mail. At a congressional hearing on the problem in 1967, the chairman of the House Appropriations Subcommittee on Treasury–Post Office, Congressman Tom Steed of Oklahoma, stated the case for postal reform while questioning Postmaster Lawrence O'Brien. Congressman Steed asked:

> Would this be a fair summary—that at the present time, as manager of the Post Office Department, you have no control over your workload; over the rates or revenue; over the pay rates of the employees that you employ; you have very little control over the conditions of the service of these employees; you have virtually no control, by the nature of it, of your physical facilities; and you have only limited control, at best, over the transportation facilities that you are compelled to use—all of which adds up to a staggering amount of "no control" in terms of the duties you have to perform?

The bipartisan move toward postal reform began under President Lyndon Johnson and Postmaster General O'Brien and became effective under President Richard Nixon and Postmaster General Winton M. Blount. In May 1969 Postmaster General Blount proposed a basic reorganization of the Post Office Department. The president asked Congress to pass the Postal Service Act of 1969, calling for removal of the postmaster general from the cabinet and the creation of a self-supporting postal corporation wholly owned by the federal government. In March 1970 a compromise measure was passed, but postal employees called it "too little, too late," and a work stoppage began that involved approximately 152,000 postal employees. Following negotiations that included a pay increase, management and the unions agreed to jointly develop a reorganization plan, which was embodied in a legislative proposal sent to Congress by the president. With some modifications, the proposal was passed, and on 12 August 1970 President Nixon signed into law the most comprehensive postal legislation since the founding of the American Republic, Public Law 91-375, the Postal Reorganization Act.

The Post Office Department, symbolized by the post rider for a century and a half, was transformed into the United States Postal Service, symbolized by a blue eagle, effective 1 July 1971. On that date, the postmaster general left the cabinet; the Postal Service received: operational authority vested in a board of governors and Postal Service management rather than in Congress; authority to issue public bonds to finance postal buildings and capital equipment; direct collective bargaining between representatives of management and unions; and a new rate-setting procedure, built around an independent Postal Rate Commission.

Title 39, the Postal Reorganization Act, also vested direction of the powers of the Postal Service in an eleven-member board of governors. Nine governors are appointed by the president, by and with the advice and consent of the Senate, and serve staggered nine-year terms. No more than five governors may belong to the same political party, and each governor represents the public interest generally. The nine governors appoint the postmaster general, who is the chief executive officer of the Postal Service and serves at their discretion. These ten people select the deputy postmaster general. All eleven members of the board direct the Postal Service, review its practices and policies, and control its expenditures, but only the nine governors approve rates and classification changes following a recommendation by the Postal Rate Commission.

TRANSPORTATION

Because the Postal Service primarily delivers hard-copy, material messages, transportation has been the single most important element in mail delivery. The Postal Service has helped develop and subsidize many modes of transportation in the United States, including the stagecoach, steamboat, railroad, automobile, and airplane and still uses mules to reach an Indian reservation in the Grand Canyon. It operates water routes, used dogsleds to deliver mail in Alaska until the mid-1960s, and has experimented with camels, balloons, helicopters, and pneumatic tubes as means of carrying the mail. Federal support for the development of post roads—a post road being defined as any road on which mail travels—encouraged the improvement of roads for commercial travel as well. In fact, an eighteenth-century disagreement between the third postmaster general, who wanted to hire less costly post riders to carry the mail, and President George Washington, who wanted more costly coaches used in order to encourage commercial travel, soon led to the appointment of the fourth postmaster general.

Waterways were declared post roads in 1823, two years after the Post Office began using steamboats to carry mail between towns where no roads existed, and in 1836, shortly after the development of steam-driven engines traveling on tracks, Congress designated railroads as post roads. As early as 1896, the Post Office Department experimented with the "horseless wagon," the automobile, to carry mail, although it was not until 1914 that it began operating the first government-owned motor vehicle service at the Washington, D.C., Post Office under the direction of the man who would later oversee the start of airmail service, Otto Praeger.

The Post Office first experimented with airmail during an exhibition in 1911, and on 15 May 1918 it began scheduled airmail service between New York City and Washington, D.C. Congress authorized airmail postage of twenty-four cents, although the public was reluctant to use this more expensive service. However, when a transcontinental route between New York and San Francisco was completed in 1920, airmail—despite the fact that it was then flown only by daylight—beat the best railroad time of twenty-two hours, thus stimulating its use by financial companies. On 22 February 1921 it was flown across the country through the night, impressing Congress, which then appropriated money for the expansion of airmail service equipment and fields.

The Post Office Department received several awards for its contributions to the development of aeronautics and for demonstrating the feasibility of night flight. In 1926 the Post Office awarded its first contract for commercial carriage of airmail, and by 1 September 1927 all airmail was carried under contract. The Post Office transferred its lights, airways and radio service, stations, emergency landing fields, and beacons to the Department of Commerce, and most airports were transferred to the municipalities in which they were located. According to Charles Stanton, an early airmail pilot who later headed the Civil Aeronautics Administration, "the cornerstones on which our present world-wide transport structure is built . . . came, one by one, out of our experience in daily, uninterrupted flying of the mail."

SERVICE

Annual reports of the Post Office Department over nearly two centuries show the struggle to balance public service against operational costs. One of the most obscure and criticized postal developments at its onset, yet most valued once established, was rural free delivery. Postmaster General John Wanamaker advocated rural free delivery in the early 1890s, but it did not begin until 1896 under Postmaster General William L. Wilson.

In the days before telephones, radios, or television, the farmer's main links to the outside world were the mail and newspapers that came to the nearest post office. However, since this meant a special trip to the post office, the farmer might delay picking up mail for days or even weeks. To serve rural families better, the Post Office Department began three experimental rural delivery routes in West Virginia in 1896. Critics claimed it was impractical and too expensive to have a carrier trudge over rutted roads and through forests trying to deliver mail in all kinds of weather. Without exception, however, farmers were delighted with the new service and, where necessary, paid to grade roads to qualify for it. Stimulated by petitions for rural delivery, between 1897 and 1908 local governments spent an estimated $72 million on bridges and other improvements to qualify for the service, which had a cultural and social impact on millions of Americans, linking industrial and rural parts of the country.

The establishment of rural delivery also increased demand for small packages and other commodities not easily available to farmers. Although private express companies and country retail merchants fought against parcel post, the more than half of the U.S. population that lived in rural areas pressed for a reasonably priced parcel service. The Post Office Department began parcel post service on 1 January 1913, giving rise to great mail order houses such as Montgomery Ward and Sears, Roebuck and Company.

Response to customer needs, operational requirements, and new technology had stimulated other services as well. The department began issuing postage stamps in 1847, with Benjamin Franklin and George Washington appearing, respectively, on five- and ten-cent stamps. Registered mail was offered in 1855 to allow secure transmittal of money and valuables, and letter collection boxes were placed on city streets in 1858 for customers' convenience. Despite the disruptions of the Civil War, in 1863 the department began offering free delivery to residences and businesses in most cities and divided mail into classes requiring different rates. A year later, stimulated by the need of soldiers to safely send money home to their families, the Post Office began selling money orders.

Postal cards were introduced in 1873, and special delivery in 1885. Certified mail, which offered proof of a mailing where necessary, began

in 1955. In 1971 the Postal Service experimented with overnight delivery of mail, called Express Mail, and made the service permanent in 1977. Service standards for the delivery of first-class mail were established in 1971, and beginning in 1972 customers could buy stamps by mail without having to go to their post offices.

TECHNOLOGY

At the turn of the twentieth century, despite growing volumes and limited work space, the Post Office Department still sorted mail manually into pigeonholes, much as was done during Benjamin Franklin's time. Crude sorting machines were proposed in the 1920s, but the Depression and World War II postponed development of postal mechanization until the mid-1950s. At that time the Post Office Department began awarding contracts for the development of machines to sort letters, cancel them, read addresses automatically, sort parcels, use conveyors to transport mail within a facility, and tag letters and stamps to help in sorting mail. In 1957 the first letter-sorting machine, the Transorma, was tested in an American post office. By 1959 a modified version was installed in the Detroit Post Office; this model became the backbone of letter-sorting operations during the 1960s and 1970s, allowing a clerk to process approximately 1,750 pieces of mail per work hour.

Early in the 1980s the Postal Service entered the age of automation when it began using computer-driven optical character readers to read the city and state line of an address, then print a bar code on an envelope. Later, other automated equipment would scan the bar code and sort the mail to the delivery post office or letter carrier. Modern automated sorting equipment reads the entire address, including the street name and number, sprays a bar code, and sorts mail to a small geographic area, such as the floor of an apartment building, one side of a street between intersecting streets, or a group of post office boxes. Automated equipment sorts mail at an average rate of sixty-two hundred pieces per work hour.

ZIP CODES

In 1943 postal customers were encouraged to place one- and two-digit numerical codes between the city and state. These zone codes allowed postal clerks to more quickly sort mail to the post office, postal station, or branch that served the addressee. By 1963 the character, volume, and transportation of mail had changed, with eighty percent of all mail being business mail and computers affecting mass mailings. In 1962 a presidentially appointed advisory board on the Post Office Department recommended that a coding system be developed. The result was the five-digit ZIP (Zone Improvement Plan) code system that began on 1 July 1963. Compliance was voluntary, but within two years and following an extensive public relations campaign featuring a cartoon figure called Mr. ZIP, most mail included the ZIP code in its address. The ZIP code allowed faster sorting of mail to the delivering post office, station, or branch.

Twenty years later, in 1983, the ZIP + 4 code, featuring the ZIP code and a hyphen followed by four more digits, would be used to sort mail more specifically, not only to the post office or postal station serving the addressee, and not only to the letter carrier delivering the mail, but to a segment of the carrier's route. Translated into a bar code by automated equipment, today's mail can be sorted into the order a carrier delivers it for the most efficient service.

RATES

Domestic postal rates were charged on a per sheet–per distance basis until a three thousand-mile cutoff was set in 1855, essentially giving universal service, that is, service at the same rate to any destination in the United States and its territories. During the same year the Post Office Department began requiring prepayment of postage, since the earlier common practice of the recipient's paying the postage had invited abuse of the mail by persons making solicitations.

In 1863 rates were charged solely on the basis of weight, with distance and the per sheet considerations discontinued. On occasion, rates were increased as a means of raising general revenues in times of war. Such increases were put into effect in 1815 and 1816 as a result of the War of 1812 and from 1917 to 1919 because of World War I. Rates were set by Congress until the

Postal Reorganization Act of 1970 became effective on 1 July 1971. Since that time, rates have been set by the nine governors of the Postal Service. The governors propose rates to the Postal Rate Commission, which has ten months to conduct open hearings in which customers, competitors, and consumer advocates testify on the proposed rates. The commission then gives a recommended decision to the Postal Service's governors, who can accept it, reject it and request reconsideration by the commission, or modify it by a unanimous vote.

[*See also* Postal Rate Commission.]

BIBLIOGRAPHY

Fuller, Wayne E. *The American Mail: Enlarger of the Common Life.* Chicago, Ill., 1972.
Rich, Wesley. *The History of the United States Post Office to the Year 1829.* Cambridge, Mass., 1924.
Scheele, Carl H. *A Short History of the Mail Service.* Washington, D.C., 1970.
Tierney, John T. *The U.S. Postal Service: Status and Prospects of Public Enterprise.* Dover, Mass., 1992.
U.S. Postal Service. *History of the United States Postal Service, 1775–1993.* Washington, D.C., 1993.

—MAGAERA AUSMAN HARRIS

President, Executive Office of the

As Hugh Heclo has pointed out, the Executive Office of the President (EOP) is neither executive in the sense of conducting major government operations nor an office in the sense of being a single control structure. It is, rather, a holding company of many offices, some of them bureaucracies of several hundred people, that serve the president in a variety of ways. All of the units are ultimately responsible to the president, though some report to him through different White House staffers.

Franklin Roosevelt created the EOP in 1939 through Reorganization Plan No. 1 and Executive Order 8248. The original function of the EOP was to provide coordination for executive branch departments and agencies from a presidential perspective and to manage the development of policies that cut across departmental

THE WHITE HOUSE IN WASHINGTON, D.C. *Completed in 1803, the White House has been home to every U.S. president except George Washington. The south portico is shown here.*

boundaries. The White House Office was an original unit in the EOP whose purpose was to house the personal and political advisers to the president. The rest of the EOP, in contrast, was to include offices whose mission would be to serve the presidency rather than the individual occupant of the office. Professional staffers in these units were to remain in their jobs across administrations and provide institutional memory and a continuing capacity for each new president to use.

Over the years the mission of the EOP and its subunits has shifted from merely coordinating executive branch departments and agencies to helping the president control the executive branch. The growth in size and numbers of the offices in the EOP has enabled presidents to formulate and develop policy, in addition to the EOP's traditional role of fine-tuning and final deliberation before presidential decision. Presidents now also fill all of the leadership positions in EOP units with political appointees, though the larger units, such as the Office of Management and Budget and the Office of the U.S. Trade Representative, are staffed primarily with career civil servants.

Since 1939 more than forty separate units have been added to the EOP by different presidents, though many have been dropped by subsequent chief executives. Historically, most of the units that have had relatively brief stays in the EOP as offices were added to symbolize presidential concerns (e.g. inflation, drug abuse, consumer protection, space exploration, etc.) or to incubate them before transferring them to larger, more established executive branch bureaucracies or independent status (e.g. the Office of Economic Opportunity, the National Aeronautics and Space Administration).

The core functions of the EOP have survived in units that perform functions that presidents consider central to the presidency. These units advise the president and engage in coordination, control, policy development, and enforcement of presidential priorities.

The most important office in the EOP is the White House Office, which contains about 430 staffers (1994) and more than a dozen subunits that make up the top levels of the White House staff. The White House Office contains what is often referred to as the White House staff. In addition to the White House Office, the five major units in the EOP that provide coordination and enforcement as well as advisory functions are the Office of Management and Budget (572 personnel), the National Security Council staff (147), the Office of Policy Development (50), the National Economic Council, and the Office of the U.S. Trade Representative (191). Each of these units coordinates presidential policy in the executive branch and ensures that narrow departmental perspectives do not prevail in the making of administration policy.

The units in the EOP primarily concerned with advising the president but that do not have the clout or the staff to give direction to the line departments or agencies include the Council of Economic Advisers (35), the Office of Science and Technology Policy (46), the Council on Environmental Quality, and the Office of National Drug Control Policy. The Office of Administration deals with records, personnel, and physical space of the Executive Office units. Regardless of the personal preferences or campaign promises of future presidents, a large and complex collection of bureaucracies is likely to constitute the EOP of the future.

[See also Advising the President; Economic Advisers, Council of; Environmental Quality, Council on; Management and Budget, Office of; National Security Council; Science and Technology

Policy, Office of; Trade Representative, Office of the U.S.; White House Office; and Appendix: Reorganization Act (1939), Reorganization Plan No. 1 (1939), and Executive Order No. 8248 (1939).]

BIBLIOGRAPHY

Burke, John P. *The Institutional Presidency.* Baltimore, 1992.
Hart, John. *The Presidential Branch.* 2d ed. Chatham, N.J., 1995.
Heclo, Hugh. "The Changing Presidential Office." In *Politics and the Oval Office,* edited by Arnold J. Meltsner. San Francisco, 1981.
Heclo, Hugh. "The Executive Office of the President." In *Modern Presidents and the Presidency,* edited by Mark Landy. Lexington, Mass., 1985.
Pfiffner, James P. *The Modern Presidency.* New York, 1994.
—JAMES P. PFIFFNER

President as Chief Executive

ESSAY There are several thousand national government programs. No president has the time, energy, or motivation to run all of them. Presidents are not "hands-on" administrators except when implementing new initiatives or modifying existing departmental programs is an important White House priority. The White House interest in the bureaucracy is more political than administrative, more concerned with "macro" characteristics than with "micro" management. Presidents want the bureaucracy to be managerially and technologically up to date; they want to avoid scandals (or at least avoid the blame for scandals when they occur); they want to use the resources of the departments as patronage to reward their electoral coalitions; they want officials to be responsive to their party platform and priorities; and in an era of deficit reduction efforts, they want the bureaucracy to downsize and provide savings through management reforms.

Since Thomas Jefferson's era, presidents have been in the forefront of those calling for managerial reforms. It is no accident that all three of the presidents who won two terms in the forty years after World War II (Dwight Eisenhower, Richard

Nixon, and Ronald Reagan) were very adept at aligning themselves against the Washington bureaucrats. Presidents often create national commissions and task forces to recommend changes in the way the bureaucracy works. Most commissions have not had a major impact until a decade or so after their reports have been submitted.

President William Howard Taft's Commission on Economy and Efficiency proposed in 1912 that the president be given vast budgetary powers and recommended reorganizing agencies by function—but its recommendations were ignored by Congress at the time, though an executive budget was implemented in 1921. President Franklin Roosevelt appointed the Brownlow Committee, a group of three academic experts on public administration, who made recommendations to strengthen the president's grip on government agencies: it recommended that independent regulatory and New Deal agencies be brought into the departments to establish a unified chain of command, a recommendation that Congress disregarded. In 1939 Congress did act on its recommendations that a White House Office (for political aides) and an Executive Office of the President (for managerial agencies involving personnel and budgeting) be created. Presidents Harry Truman and Dwight Eisenhower appointed the first and second Hoover Commissions, (chaired by former president Herbert Hoover), which in 1949 and 1955 called for sweeping changes in the departments to reduce costs and increase efficiency. President Richard Nixon appointed the Ash Council in 1970, which concentrated on improving the federal system by promoting revenue sharing and block grants to state and local governments to replace grants earmarked for particular programs (which were adopted in part by Congress), and which recommended the consolidation of several cabinet departments along functional lines—recommendations that Congress ignored. The President's Private Sector Survey on Cost Control made close to twenty-five hundred recommendations to President Ronald Reagan about putting government on a more "businesslike" basis by emulating the practices of large corporations, and promised hundreds of billions of dollars in savings. But most of its recommendations about

cutbacks were not implemented. In 1988 a Commission on Privatization issued eighteen recommendations to turn over mail delivery, air traffic control, and other functions to private companies, to sell off Amtrak, and to provide educational vouchers to help pay private school tuitions—recommendations that went nowhere. The Volcker Commission proposed that the merit system be extended upward and the number of political appointees in the departments be reduced, but President George Bush made no recommendations to Congress. President Bill Clinton's National Performance Review, sent to Congress in the fall of 1993, specified agency-by-agency reductions to save $11 billion by closing field offices and research facilities, authorizing the sale of assets to private industry, opening up government jobs to private bidders, combating fraud, merging duplicative programs, increasing fees for government services, freezing many programs, reforming federal procurement, and providing incentives for the early retirement of careerists. Two years later, Republicans in control of Congress made even more drastic cutbacks, an unusual outcome in Washington, where recommendations for deep cuts have almost always been ignored.

The main influence the president has on the bureaucracy is through the powers of appointment and removal. The president nominates and, by and with the advice and consent of the Senate, appoints fourteen cabinet secretaries, fifty or so directors of other nondepartmental agencies, and ninety or so commissioners of independent regulatory agencies, as well as six hundred to seven hundred subordinate political executives in the departments (with titles such as deputy secretary, under secretary, assistant secretary, and deputy assistant secretary). The president also appoints the two hundred or so U.S. attorneys and marshals, more than two hundred ambassadors, and approximately two hundred members of the boards of directors of government quasi-independent corporations. Without the advice or consent of the Senate, the president appoints about four hundred aides in the White House Office and officials in the Executive Office of the President, about seven hundred senior managers, and about seventeen hundred lower-

THE OVAL OFFICE IN THE WHITE HOUSE. *The Oval Office is where the president carries out his official duties as chief executive: signing bills and executive orders and meeting with staff and visitors.*

level managers in the bureaucracy. These White House, departmental, and agency appointees are the officials who constitute "the administration."

Although it may seem that the Constitution assigns the president the dominant role in making departmental appointments, both constitutional law and political tradition often suggest otherwise. Senate committee leaders often propose nominees to the president. Senators routinely "nominate" officials for positions affecting their states: regional and district personnel, U.S. attorneys, and federal marshals. Often they are given a "veto" by the administration over appointments. Senatorial courtesy allows a senator from a state affected by a presidential nomina-tion subject to Senate confirmation to declare that the prospective appointee is "personally obnoxious," in which case the Senate committee considering the nomination will put it on hold until the president or the nominee provides assurances that get the senator to withdraw his or her objection. Members of the House from committees with jurisdiction over agencies are often influential in "sponsoring" officials for promotion, especially into the Senior Executive Service (SES). High-level appointments to many departments, especially those that serve "clienteles," such as Agriculture, Labor, Commerce, and Interior, are often proposed by interest groups that benefit from existing distributions of contracts, goods, and services. Congress itself often specifies particular qualifications for appointees to administrative positions, to guarantee that positions will be filled by professionals attuned to the interests of particular constituencies.

By the mid-1990s appointment politics as it was played out in the capital at times made the presidential appointment power more of a liability than an asset: when a president made a nomination of a person affiliated with one of the liberal or conservative "issue networks," the nominee might be subject to "attack politics" from the other ideological side. This sometimes involved attempts to marginalize and demonize the nominee and the issue position he or she was identified with, thereby damaging the president as well. A president who stood by a controversial nominee took a political risk and might come under pressure from the senatorial party to back off, but to cut and run from a nasty ideological fight would weaken the president's reputation in the Washington community, embolden the opposition, and make it difficult for the White House to attract the best people into the administration.

The Senate consents to presidential nominees by majority vote of those present. It blocks few presidential appointments. Before the 1960s only eight cabinet nominations had been turned down by Senate vote; since then George Bush's nomination of John Tower for secretary of defense in 1989 was also defeated. Other cabinet-level nominees have withdrawn before a Senate vote if the president senses they will be defeated: President Carter withdrew the nomination of Theodore Sorensen for the position of director of central intelligence in 1977, and two nominees for Clinton's attorney general withdrew in 1993.

Most appointees are not personally acquainted with the president, and therefore the incumbent in the Oval Office presides over a "government of strangers." Not only does the president not know them; they do not know him. His personnel operation can provide him with people who are nominally members of his party, and who come from constituencies that he favors. But what the appointees need, and often cannot get from him without personal contact, is a sense of the "big picture." They do not know the president's priorities, they do not know the

White House's political strategy, and they do not know whether the White House will back them up when they start to make policy. Presidents often find out too late that they disagree with their appointees about the specifics of program administration.

As soon as most administration officials have accepted their jobs, they are cut adrift by the White House and its personnel office. No one is in charge of seeing to it that new officials are properly oriented and that their transition to life in Washington is smooth. They and their families have a rough time getting settled, and they complain of overwork, stress in their personal life, salaries that are inadequate, and isolation from the president. Turnover is high: about one-third at the subcabinet level leave within eighteen months, another third last it out for three years, and less than one-third remain beyond that. The consequence is that most political appointees supervise career officials who have far more expertise and experience than they do. The more savvy of these political executives will build their own power bases and constituencies. They abandon presidential priorities and develop their own support by currying favor with career officials, lobbyists, reporters, and congressional committees, becoming part of what political scientists refer to as a "policy subgovernment" that functions without White House supervision.

Presidents since Jimmy Carter have been given new management tools to better influence the direction of senior civil servants. The top-level career officials consist of approximately seven thousand members of the SES and most of the fifteen hundred high-level officials of the Foreign Service. The SES was created by President Carter after Congress passed the Civil Service Reform Act of 1978. The purpose of the law was to make top-level civil servants more responsive to the White House. Members are given greater responsibility and can get pay increases and bonuses on the basis of superior performance. But they give up some of the protections of the civil service system: it is easier for their political superiors to transfer them, demote them back to the civil service, or even remove them (after a 120-day waiting period at the start of a new administration). The president also may appoint people to the SES from outside the career service, not exceeding ten percent of the total SES.

Presidents, using their discretionary appointment power within the SES, can select program managers who share their party or ideological orientation, or who are independent and "neutral," and therefore willing to do their bidding and work harmoniously with the noncareer officials of their administrations. President Reagan filled about 850 SES positions with his own political appointees and promoted to the SES careerists who were ideologically in sympathy with his administration. Officials who have been promoted into the SES or appointed to it from the outside operate within the bureaucracy at low levels, and presidents can cluster them in key agencies that deal with their priorities. Presidents can also remove or transfer officials whose attitudes make them liabilities. Personnel decisions can be made by the White House to maximize administrative control. This may mean transferring recalcitrant officials, giving them low-priority assignments, and encouraging them to retire. It may also mean not filling career slots when vacancies arise or leaving noncareerist SES appointees in full control of a particular program targeted for White House influence. Political scientists have found some evidence that SES officials who share the president's party and ideology receive preferential treatment, and that other officials are more likely to be subject to transfers or reductions in rank. This may not involve favoritism, but it does reflect the fact that a Republican administration is likely to cut back on bureaucracies that harbor liberal Democratic careerists—especially domestic social welfare agencies. Top-level careerists at the SES level (which runs from GS 16 through Executive Level IV) and at the managerial ranks slightly below the SES (the fifteen hundred or so positions, ranked at GS 15 and below, that require political discretion and confidentiality) usually begin and end their careers in government working for only one or two agencies. They average about twenty years of service by the time they attain SES rank and are put in charge of programs or bureaus. They identify strongly with the goals and missions of their units. They may fight to maintain programs that the president wants to modify or eliminate. Because the political executives above them in the administration hardly have time to learn their jobs before they move on, careerists often discount their nominal superiors in the administration. They do not take kindly to directives from these "revolving-door" assistant secretaries instructing them that, for the good of a president who may serve for only four years, they should sacrifice programs on which they have worked all their professional lives.

In dealing with political executives attempting to carry out White House directives, senior civil servants try to engage in "education from below." Instead of refusing to carry out orders, they present their superiors with unpleasant alternatives: they may claim that proposed budget cuts would mean the elimination of popular programs. They may inform their superiors that proposed policies cannot be implemented without first obtaining new statutory authorization from Congress. They often delay or block presidential priorities. Officials may refuse to carry out orders from political appointees they believe violate laws or ethical guidelines.

Although the Constitution does not specifically mention a removal power, since the Supreme Court ruled on the issue in *Myers v. U.S.* in 1926 presidents can remove political appointees who serve at their pleasure in the departments. But in *Humphrey's Executor v. U.S.* (1935) and *Wiener v. U.S.* (1953), the Supreme Court ruled that officials with legislative or judicial functions (such as commissioners of independent regulatory agencies) are insulated from presidential removal. The Ethics in Government Act of 1978 prohibits the removal of an independent counsel except for extraordinary impropriety, physical disability, mental incapacity, or "any other condition that substantially impairs the performance of such special prosecutors' duties." In *Nader v. Bork* (1973) a federal district court ruled that a special prosecutor may be protected from removal by departmental regulations as well as by congressional statute. Below the level of political appointees and SES officials, most administrators are protected by civil service regulations from presidential dismissal, further limiting the president's administrative control.

What gets an administration into more trouble than almost anything is corruption or criminal behavior by high-level appointees and subsequent attempts by the president to cover it up. Had President Nixon come clean at the beginning about the Watergate affair and admitted low-level White House involvement, the issue probably would not have taken on great significance. It was his role in the conspiracy to conceal White House involvement in the burglary that formed the basis of the impeachment charges against him. The Clinton administration fell into the same trap. High-level White House aides and subcabinet officials misled Congress (either deliberately or inadvertently) about briefings that had occurred between officials of the Resolution Trust Corporation (RTC), the Treasury, and the White House. These meetings dealt with the question of whether a recommendation for a criminal referral (indictment) against business associates of the Clintons would be referred to the Department of Justice. (The indictment involved a failed savings and loan in Arkansas that might have benefited from decisions taken by Clinton while he was governor.) Republicans pressed for congressional hearings, then exploited the inconsistencies in testimony of top Clinton officials, charging a cover-up. Eventually Clinton was forced to assert attorney-client privilege in order to keep notes of a meeting between Clinton's government and private attorneys out of the hands of a Senate committee investigating the matter.

Under certain circumstances the prosecutions for wrongdoing by top-level officials pass from the Justice Department to an independent counsel. Title VI of the Ethics in Government Act of 1978 provides for the appointment of an independent counsel to investigate and prosecute the president, vice president, members of the cabinet, or other political executives appointed by the president if the attorney general receives "specific information" about their possible violation of federal criminal law. The attorney general conducts a preliminary investigation and then may request appointment of independent counsel by the Special Division of the Court of Appeals for the District of Columbia circuit. The panel is appointed by the chief justice of the

United States. The Judiciary Committee may also request that the attorney general conduct a "threshold inquiry": if the attorney general fails to apply for an independent counsel, he or she must explain the decision to Congress within thirty days, and a majority of either party on either the House or Senate judiciary committees may request the Special Division to appoint an independent counsel. The law provides that he or she may not be dismissed by the president, or by the attorney general except on the grounds of "extraordinary impropriety," thus ensuring the independence of the counsel and the integrity of the investigation and prosecution.

The Reagan administration, through its Department of Justice, argued that the statute was unconstitutional since it infringed upon the presidential removal power (although Reagan himself had not vetoed its extension in 1987). The law was upheld by the Supreme Court in *Morrison v. Olson* in 1988 by a 7–1 vote. The act, according to Chief Justice William Rehnquist, did not violate the appointments clause; it did not expand the role of federal courts beyond that contemplated by the Constitution; and it did not infringe on the presidential power to remove executive officials.

Since the New Deal the institutionalized presidency has been created to allow the president to function as a "chief executive." The presidential staff in the White House Office in theory provides capabilities for managerial control, particularly when staffers wear "two-hats" as both assistant to the president and head of a department or staff agency. Often, however, the presidential aides are not interested in or capable of managing complicated policy areas, but instead function more as troubleshooters to resolve particular political problems. When exposed by the media through the well-timed leaks of their bureaucratic adversaries, the activities of these aides result in charges of favoritism, cronyism, conflict of interest, or illegal *ex parte* interference in matters concerning regulatory agencies.

Several agencies in the Executive Office of the President are involved in administrative oversight, including the Office of Management and Budget and the Office of Personnel Management. These agencies struggle with appointees in the departments for operational control over personnel, budgeting, data reporting and analysis, and other administrative functions, and their struggles lead to charges of incompetence among competing officials, jockeying for position with the president, and leaks to the media that reporters translate into stories about overbearing White House interference. The public receives the impression of an administration in disarray, and that image keeps the president on the political defensive. Although these presidential staff agencies provide the president with an opportunity to craft a legislative program and influence how departments will handle their personnel decisions, budget matters, and management of programs, there is a limit to what presidential staffing can accomplish in "running the government"—especially when there is open resistance to White House interference by officials from the cabinet secretaries all the way down the line, as well as by their allied interest group constituencies and congressional and judicial allies, all of whom constitute a permanent government in Washington devoted to limiting the president's power as chief executive of the administrative establishment.

[See also Brownlow Committee; Cabinet; Civil Service; Executive Power; Management and Budget, Office of; National Performance Review; Personnel Management, Office of; President, Executive Office of the; Senate Confirmation of Presidential Appointees; Supreme Court Decisions on the Presidency; Twenty-Second Amendment; Vice Presidency; White House Office; and Women and the Executive Branch.]

BIBLIOGRAPHY

Arnold, Peri. *Making the Managerial Presidency.* Princeton, N.J., 1986.
Burke, John P. *The Institutional Presidency.* Baltimore, 1992.
Heclo, Hugh. *A Government of Strangers.* Washington, D.C., 1977.
Hess, Stephen. *Organizing the Presidency.* 2d ed. Washington, D.C., 1988.
Kettl, Donald F., and John J. DiIulio, eds. *Inside the Reinvention Machine.* Washington, D.C., 1994.
Lessig, Lawrence, and Cass Sunstein. "The President and Administration." *Columbia University Law Review* 94, no. 1 (January 1994): 1–123.
Light, Paul. *Thickening Government.* Washington, D.C., 1995.
MacKenzie, G. Calvin. *The Politics of Presidential Appointments.* New York, 1981.
MacKenzie, G. Calvin, ed., *The In-and-Outers.* Baltimore, 1987.
Maranto, Robert. *Politics and Bureaucracy in the Modern Presidency.* Westport, Conn., 1993.
Moe, Ronald C. "Traditional Organizational Principles and the Managerial Presidency: From Phoenix to Ashes." *Public Administration Review* 50 (1990): 129–140.
Nathan, Richard. *The Administrative Presidency.* New York, 1983.
Pfiffner, James. *The Strategic Presidency.* Chicago: 1988.
Seidman, Harold, and Robert Gilmour. *Politics, Position and Power.* New York, 1986.
Waterman, Richard. *Presidential Influence and the Administrative State.* Knoxville, Tenn., 1989.

—RICHARD M. PIOUS

Presidential Personnel, Office of

Each president has the opportunity to make thousands of appointments at the beginning of a new administration. While most of these are part-time, honorary, or *pro forma* appointments of military officers, the most important are appointments to leadership positions in the executive branch. These include, at the highest level, presidential appointees who require Senate confirmation and who help lead the executive branch, from cabinet secretaries to assistant secretaries (Executive Levels I–V). In the 1990s these positions numbered close to one thousand.

A full-scale Office of Presidential Personnel (in different administrations called the White House Personnel Office or the Presidential Personnel Office) has developed only in recent decades. Presidents have always made appointments, but before the 1960s these appointments were dominated by the president's political party and heavily influenced by members of the president's party in Congress. Political patronage was a mainstay of the party system, and presidents relied on the party to provide candidates for presidential appointment.

But as the power of political parties declined and presidential nominations came to be dominated by primary elections, the parties began to lose influence in presidential appointments, and presidents began to want more personal control over the recruitment of their appointees. The need for policy expertise and the desire for appointees who were personally loyal to the president led to the creation of a political recruitment capacity in the White House.

Jimmy Carter was the first presidential candidate to begin organizing a personnel search operation (the "Talent Inventory Program") before he was elected. But the largest and most sophisticated personnel recruitment effort of the modern presidency was organized by Pendleton James for Ronald Reagan. James was given the title of assistant to the president (the highest level on the White House staff), a signal of the importance that Reagan attached to the personnel recruitment task. In the first year of the Reagan administration James had one hundred people working for him, though some were detailees and volunteers rather than officially on the White House staff.

The large number of people working on political recruitment reflected the intensive effort at political recruitment of the Reagan White House. The Reagan operation was marked by two factors: the close scrutiny of candidates' political values to ensure that they adhered to the Reagan philosophy, and the decision to scrutinize *all* political appointments, not only *presidential* appointments.

This unprecedented step of systematically screening lower-level political appointees included those to the noncareer Senior Executive Service (about seven hundred) and to Schedule C positions (about seventeen hundred), which technically are made by agency heads. This comprehensive approach added to the time and complexity of filling administration jobs, but it ensured heavier White House influence on the total political appointments for an administration than had ever existed.

The modern presidency has seen the personnel recruitment function develop from a one-person job to a highly sophisticated and systematic operation supported by the latest computer capabilities and scores of professionals. While the size of the White House personnel operation will depend on presidential preferences, a professional personnel office is now a permanent fixture in the White House.

BIBLIOGRAPHY

Mackenzie, G. Calvin. *The Politics of Presidential Appointments.* New York, 1981.

Mackenzie, G. Calvin. *The In-and-Outers: Presidential Appointees and Transient Government in Washington.* Baltimore, 1987.

Mackenzie, G. Calvin. "Partisan Leadership Through Presidential Appointments." In *The Parties Respond,* edited by L. Sandy Maisel. Boulder, Colo., 1994.

Macy, John, Bruce Adams, and J. Jackson Walter. *America's Unelected Government: Appointing the President's Team.* Cambridge, Mass., 1983.

Pfiffner, James P. *The Strategic Presidency: Hitting the Ground Running.* 2d ed. Lawrence, Kans., 1996.

Weko, Thomas J. *The Politicizing Presidency.* Lawrence, Kans., 1995.

—JAMES P. PFIFFNER

Presidential Succession and Disability

ESSAY   When a healthy president occupies the White House, the topic of presidential succession and disability (or inability) attracts little attention. When the president dies or becomes ill, however, the provisions for filling presidential vacancy become paramount. Indeed, nine of the forty-two presidents left office prematurely; numerous others suffered illnesses that impaired their ability to lead.

Presidential succession and, particularly, disability present difficult problems that have created some trying situations. The original Constitution addressed the issue in Article II, Section 1. Two constitutional amendments and three statutes have since focused on some part of the issue.

Presidential succession and inability was first addressed relatively late at the Constitutional Convention. The proposal from a representative committee suggested that the vice president would exercise the powers and duties of the president in case of the death, resignation, removal, absence, or disability of the president "until another president be chosen, or until the inability of the president be removed." The delegates seemed to contemplate that the vice president would act as, but not become, president and that his tenure (except in case of presidential inability) could be limited by a special election. Yet in refining this provision, a Committee on Style—which was to make stylistic, rather than substantive, changes—obscured this intent. The language included in the Constitution reads:

> In Case of the Removal of the President from Office, or of his Death, Resignation, or Inability to discharge the Powers and Duties of the said Office, the same shall devolve on the Vice President, and the Congress may by Law, provide for the Case of Removal, Death, Resignation or Inability, both of the President and Vice President, declaring what Officer shall then act as President, and such Officer shall act accordingly, until the Disability be removed, or a President shall be elected.

The text alone did not make clear whether the office or merely its powers and duties devolved in case of vacancy or inability. Although the text clearly gave Congress the option to provide for a special election if both the president and vice president left office prematurely, it did not seem to do so if the term of only the president was abbreviated.

These questions raised only hypothetical concerns during the first fifty-two years of the Republic, during which time all elected presidents completed their terms. On 4 April 1841, however, President William Henry Harrison died of pneumonia contracted during his inauguration one month earlier. His vice president, John Tyler, insisted that he succeeded to the presidency, not simply its powers and duties. Tyler's claim was controversial but soon won acceptance. The Tyler precedent was followed when other presidents died during the nineteenth century. When President Zachary Taylor died on 9 July 1850, his vice president, Millard Fillmore, succeeded to the presidency. Similarly, upon the death of Abraham Lincoln on 15 April 1865, his vice president, Andrew Johnson, became president. And when James Garfield died on 19 September 1881 from gunshot wounds inflicted more than eleven weeks earlier, Vice President Chester A. Arthur succeeded to the presidency.

These four episodes of presidential succession in the nineteenth century shared some common features. In each case the vice president who succeeded to the presidency came from a different wing of the president's party (or in Johnson's case, from a different party) than the president. The political differences often contributed to instability in government. Tyler, Fillmore, and Arthur replaced in relatively short order virtually the entire cabinet they inherited; Johnson, more than half of Lincoln's cabinet appointees. None of these nineteenth-century presidents won election to their own term.

During the twentieth century, five vice presidents have succeeded to the presidency following the death or resignation of their predecessors. Upon the death of William McKinley on 14 September 1901 (following an assassination attempt eight days earlier), Theodore Roosevelt became president. The deaths of Warren G. Harding on 2 August 1923 and Franklin D. Roosevelt on 12 April 1945 resulted in the elevation of their vice presidents, Calvin Coolidge and Harry S. Truman, respectively. The assassination of John F. Kennedy on 22 November 1963 brought Vice President Lyndon B. Johnson to the presidency.

On 9 August 1974 Richard M. Nixon became the first president to leave office prematurely owing to a cause other than death. Nixon resigned after being advised by Republican congressional leaders that his removal was inevitable. Vice President Gerald R. Ford was sworn in as president that day. Ford's succession was unique in a second respect. Whereas other vice presidents laid claim to the presidency based upon language quoted above from Article II of the Constitution as embellished by the Tyler precedent, Ford became president under section one of the Twenty-fifth Amendment to the Constitution. It confirmed Tyler's insistence that a vice president who succeeds following his predecessor's removal, death, or resignation becomes president.

Presidential succession this century has been handled more smoothly. Except for Truman, presidential successors have retained their inherited cabinet largely in place for at least a year. Most followed the programmatic outlines of their predecessors. All except Ford were elected to a term of their own; Ford narrowly lost in

1976, hampered by his status as Nixon's heir and by his pardon of his predecessor.

The more difficult problems relate to presidential disability. Other causes of presidential vacancy—death, resignation, or removal—share at least three attributes: they all are relatively easy to identify, established procedures exist for recognizing them, and they create a permanent vacuum. Presidential disability differs. The original Constitution provided no guidance regarding the definition of presidential disability nor the manner in which it was to be established. John Dickinson's question at the Constitutional Convention—"What is the extent of the term 'disability' and who is to be the judge of it?"—remained unanswered. Moreover, disability may be temporary rather than permanent. Since the original Constitution used the same language to define the status of the vice president in case of presidential disability as for the three causes of permanent vacancy, the Tyler precedent created a significant problem. If the vice president became president upon the death of his predecessor, arguably he also became president upon his disability. But if the vice president was elevated when the president was disabled, presumably the chief executive lost office since the Constitution does not provide for two presidents. The prospect that vice presidential action would displace the president from office was a deterrent to action.

During most of American history the system did not respond well when situations arose involving instances of presidential disability. The lack of constitutional procedures to define or determine disability and the ambiguity regarding the status of the president once his disability ended accounted for the poor performance as did the distant relations between presidents and vice presidents. When Garfield lay unconscious for more than eighty days his cabinet failed to summon Arthur to act—it was uncertain regarding the consequence of such a step and perhaps was affected by the political antipathy between Arthur and the administration. After suffering a stroke in September 1919, Woodrow Wilson was confined to his quarters for months, unable to perform much government business. Although his disability was clear, no action was taken to transfer power to Vice President Thomas R. Marshall. Wilson and his aides viewed as disloyal suggestions of Secretary of State Robert Lansing that Wilson be declared disabled and accused Lansing of trying to "oust" Wilson.

President Dwight D. Eisenhower suffered three serious illnesses during his two terms—a heart attack in 1955, an ileitis attack in 1956 that required surgery, and a stroke the following year. Vice President Richard M. Nixon presided over government meetings and informally assumed some of Eisenhower's engagements. Presidential power was never transferred to Nixon.

Eisenhower and Nixon subsequently agreed to procedures to govern any future disability. Eisenhower would advise Nixon of his disability if possible, in which case Nixon would act as president. If Eisenhower could not communicate, Nixon would decide the issue after consultation he deemed appropriate. In any case, Eisenhower would decide when to resume presidential powers. President John F. Kennedy and Lyndon B. Johnson entered into similar agreements with their designated successors.

Efforts to craft a legislative solution began following the Eisenhower illnesses. Not until Kennedy was assassinated did they gather momentum, when Senator Birch Bayh, the newly appointed chair of the Senate Subcommittee on Constitutional Amendments, embraced the issue. On 6 July 1965 Congress proposed the Twenty-fifth Amendment to the Constitution, which was ratified by the required number of states within two years. The amendment made clear that in cases of presidential disability the vice president merely acts as president; the chief executive retains office. It provided, in section three, that the president could declare his own disability (in letters to the Speaker of the House of Representatives and president *pro tempore* of the Senate), thereby transferring power to the vice president. The president would also determine when his disability ended. Alternatively, if the president was unable or unwilling to proclaim his own disability, the vice president and a majority of the cabinet could declare the president disabled, in which event the vice president would act as president during the incapacity. The president could reclaim powers when his disability ended subject to the right of the vice president and cabinet to contest that determination; in that case, Congress was to decide the issue.

Presidential disability became an issue on several occasions during the tenure of Ronald Reagan. On 30 March 1981 Reagan was shot in an assassination attempt. Although Reagan's condition was precarious for several days, the new administration elected not to invoke the disability provisions. When Reagan underwent surgery under anesthesia in July 1985 he did transfer powers to Vice President George Bush for nearly eight hours. Although Reagan insisted at the time that he was not invoking the Twenty-fifth Amendment, he followed its procedures to the letter.

In addition to the constitutional provisions, Congress has enacted three different lines of successors to act as president in case both the president and vice president are unavailable. In 1792 Congress placed the Senate's president *pro tempore* and the Speaker of the House next in line. In 1886 Congress replaced the legislative successors with a line that ran through the cabinet members. Congress reverted to a legislative line in 1947, placing the Speaker and president *pro tempore* before the various cabinet secretaries. Although these statutory successors have never been called upon to act as president, they have stood first in line on eighteen different occasions when the vice presidency was vacant.

Section two of the Twenty-fifth Amendment reduced the likelihood that succession would go beyond the vice presidency. It provided that in the event of a vice presidential vacancy, the president could nominate a vice president subject to confirmation of both houses of Congress. By that procedure, Nixon appointed Ford to replace Spiro T. Agnew as vice president. When Ford succeeded to the presidency, he named Nelson A. Rockefeller to succeed him.

The Twentieth Amendment to the Constitution provides that the vice president–elect become president if the president-elect dies before inauguration and act as president if the president-elect has failed to qualify. It empowers Congress to specify who acts as chief executive if neither president-elect nor vice president–elect qualifies.

The Twenty-fifth Amendment clarified America's laws regarding succession, vice presidential vacancy, and disability. Some question whether the cabinet would declare a president disabled; the amendment would allow Congress to replace the cabinet with "such other body as Congress" provides. Others believe the cabinet would so act in an appropriate situation and believe that it should be involved both to insulate the vice president from being attacked as opportunistic and to ensure that disability questions are not lightly raised. Some question whether legislative officers should follow the vice president, contending either that legislative succession is unconstitutional or could work a change in party control of the White House. Others believe such succession is valid and preferable since it results in an elected, not appointed, successor. Many who favor cabinet succession also endorse some special election scheme if both president and vice president leave office; others doubt an election could or should be called in such circumstances. Congress has not addressed all contingencies that could result.

BIBLIOGRAPHY

Abrams, Herbert L. *"The President Has Been Shot."* New York, 1992.

Amar, Akhil R., and Vikram D. Amar. "Is the Presidential Succession Law Constitutional." *Stanford Law Review* 48 (1995): 113–139.

Bayh, Birch. *One Heartbeat Away: Presidential Disability and Succession.* Indianapolis, 1968.

Crispell, Kenneth R., and Carlos F. Gomez. *Hidden Illness in the White House.* Durham, N.C., 1988.

Feerick, John D. *From Failing Hands.* New York, 1965.

Feerick, John D. *The Twenty-Fifth Amendment: Its Complete History and Applications.* 2d ed. New York, 1992.

Ferrell, Robert H. *Ill-Advised: Presidential Health and Public Trust.* Columbia, Mo., 1992.

Gilbert, Robert. *The Mortal Presidency: Illness and Anguish in the White House.* New York, 1992.

Goldstein, Joel K. *The Modern American Vice Presidency: The Transformation of a Political Institution.* Princeton, N.J., 1982.

Goldstein, Joel K. "The New Constitutional Vice Presidency." *Wake Forest Law Review* 30 (1995): 505–561.

Hansen, Richard. *The Year We Had No President.* Lincoln, Neb., 1962.

Schlesinger, Arthur M., Jr. "On the Presidential Succession." *Political Science Quarterly* 89 (1974): 475–505.

Silva, Ruth C. *Presidential Succession.* Ann Arbor, Mich., 1951.

"The Twenty-Fifth Amendment: Preparing for Presidential Disability." Symposium. *Wake Forest Law Review* 30 (1995): 427–648.

Thompson, Kenneth W., ed. *Papers on Presidential Disability and the Twenty-Fifth Amendment.* 2 vols. Lanham, Md., 1988, 1991.

—JOEL K. GOLDSTEIN

Printing Office.

See Government Printing Office.

Prisons, Federal Bureau of

Before 1930 the U.S. federal prison system operated in a decentralized manner, with each of the seven prisons separately funded and operating under local policies and procedures established by each warden. A 1930 act by Congress, however, created the Federal Bureau of Prisons (BOP), which would direct the development of an integrated system of prisons to provide custody and programs based on the individual needs of offenders. The mission of the BOP is "to protect society by confining offenders in the controlled environments of prison and community based facilities that are safe, humane, and secure, and [provide] . . . opportunities to assist offenders in becoming law-abiding citizens."

Today, the BOP is responsible for the confinement of almost 100,000 offenders committed to the custody of the attorney general. The bureau director oversees the operations of eighty-one federal institutions, six geographical regional offices, and a staff of more than twenty-seven thousand. The bureau's central office, located in Washington, D.C., controls and coordinates all agency activities. Major functions include planning, developing policy, staffing, budgeting, and monitoring the quality of programs and services. In addition to these management activities, the central office is responsible for public information activities, legal and legislative affairs, and relations with Congress. The central staff also carries out such functions as adjudicating appeals by inmates and employees, directing research and evaluation projects, and negotiating with the sole bargaining agent for bureau employees, the American Federation of Government Employees Council of Prison Locals.

In conjunction with the central office, six regional offices provide technical support and on-site assistance to field locations. Regional offices located in Philadelphia, Pennsylvania; Annapolis Junction, Maryland; Atlanta, Georgia; Dallas, Texas; Kansas City, Kansas; and Dublin, California, are each operated by a regional director and deputy regional director. Additionally, administrators in such areas as human resource management, education, health services, financial and case management, correctional services, psychology services, chaplaincy services, facilities operations, food service, and community corrections operate in each regional office.

Because the services for prisons greatly vary, the BOP negotiates a number of contractual agreements with various vendors. For example, under the direction of the bureau's Community Corrections and Detention Division, the agency hires private vendors for prison services such as halfway houses. Most inmates serve the last few months of their sentence in a halfway house, or a "community corrections center," and often hold jobs in the community while preparing for their release. The bureau contracts with these facilities to house federal offenders on a per capita basis. Almost six hundred halfway houses nationwide operate privately.

Additionally, through federal, state, county, and city government agencies, a number of facilities and services also operate on a contractual basis. For example, services provided by these agencies include prerelease programs; short-term and long-term detention; juvenile and adult boarding; and electronic monitoring for home confinement programs. As approximately twenty-five percent of the bureau's population consists of foreign nationals, the Detention Branch has been active in obtaining additional contract bed space for this group. Nonbureau staff operate all contract facilities.

The BOP also operates facilities that include penitentiaries, federal correctional institutions, federal prison camps, metropolitan correctional centers, and other more "traditional" prisons. The bureau operates institutions of several different security levels to house a broad spectrum of offenders. Security levels are based on such features as the presence of external patrols, gun towers, security barriers, and detection devices; the type of housing within the institution; internal security features; and staff-to-inmate ratio. Each facility is placed in one of five groups—minimum, low, medium, high, and administrative.

Minimum-security institutions, also known as federal prison camps, have dormitory housing, a low staff-to-inmate ratio, and no fences. Many times, they are located adjacent to larger institutions or on military bases, where inmates help serve the labor needs of the institution or the base. Federal inmates who are able must work and receive a small wage, a portion of which some inmates use to make restitution to victims through the Inmate Financial Responsibility Program. Federal Prison Industries, Inc., a government corporation that produces a range of goods and services from office furniture to electronic cable assemblies for sale to federal government clients, employs about one-fourth of the inmates.

Low-security federal correctional institutions, on the other hand, have double-fenced perimeters, mostly dormitory housing, and strong work and program components. Medium-security federal correctional institutions provide greater internal controls than their low-security counterparts, with strengthened perimeters, cell-type housing, and a higher staff-to-inmate ratio.

High-security institutions, also known as U.S. penitentiaries, have highly secure perimeters (either walled or double-fenced), multiple and single-occupant cell housing, and close staff supervision and movement controls.

Finally, administrative facilities are institutions that perform various duties, such as the detention of noncitizen or pretrial offenders, the treatment of inmates with serious or chronic medical problems, and the containment of dangerous, violent, or escape-prone inmates. Administrative facilities are capable of holding inmates of all security categories.

Two separate organizations currently accredit all bureau facilities: the American Correctional Association (ACA) and the Joint Commission on Accreditation of Healthcare Organizations (JCAHO). Both the ACA and the JCAHO accredit many of the same institutions but evaluate different aspects of the institutional programs. The ACA accreditation provides certification that the federal prisons offer decent living conditions and provide adequate programs and services, and safeguards inmate rights by ensuring compliance with more than 450 adult correctional living standards developed by the ACA. At the end of 1994, fifty-five bureau facilities received accreditation and eleven actively pursued accreditation from the ACA. JCAHO accreditation, on the other hand, provides certification that the health care provided in BOP facilities is consistent with community standards for health care in such areas as ambulatory, hospital, mental health, and long-term care.

Recent projects by the bureau include an effort to reduce overcrowding. To accomplish this mission, the bureau has undertaken new construction projects to accommodate the growing federal inmate population. In 1996 at least ten new institutions were completed.

BIBLIOGRAPHY

Federal Bureau of Prisons. Federal Bureau of Prisons Documents. Washington, D.C., 1996.

—VERONICA D. DICONTI

Privacy Act.

See Appendix: Basic Documents of Public Administration

Public Debt, Bureau of the

The establishment of the Bureau of the Public Debt took place on 30 June 1940 under Reorganization Plan No. 3 of 1939. The bureau was created when several functions carried out by the Department of the Treasury (1789) and the Public Debt Service (1919–1940) were combined into a single bureau, which became part of the Fiscal Service of the Treasury.

The bureau's mission is to administer the public debt. This means that it has to do three tasks. First, it has to borrow the money needed to operate the federal government. The federal government has had a deficit for most of this century—that is, its spending has been greater than what it receives from taxes. Thus, the bureau has to raise the money needed to finance the deficit. Second, the bureau conducts the sale of Treasury securities in the market so that the public finances the debt. If the bureau is to sell securities it has to attract buyers. This implies that it has to create confidence in the federal government's ability to manage the debt. Alexander Hamilton (1755–1804) first articulated this policy, which still decides the bureau's mission. Also, the bureau has to:

- offer a competitive rate of return, given different buyers' needs and resources

- offer a rate that will not undermine the aim of reducing the cost of the debt

- sell securities to refund the maturing debt and issue new securities to those who expect a payment

- supervise and set the regulations on all debt-servicing activities in the country

- keep track of what happens with the securities—who owns them and when and how they can be replaced

Third, the bureau has to report and account for the resulting public debt and the interest costs generated by the debt.

From an organizational perspective, the bureau establishes its policies according to the guidelines set by the secretary of the Treasury, the under secretary for domestic finance, and the Office of the Fiscal Assistant Secretary. This office, which also oversees the activities of the Financial Management Service, is in charge of the administration of fiscal affairs—financing operations and management of cash balances. The secretary and the under secretary communicate with the commissioner, who is the bureau's head, through this office.

Internally, the bureau is organized into seven offices: 1) Commissioner; 2) Financing; 3) Securities and Accounting Services; 4) Administration; 5) Automated Information Systems; 6) Savings Bond Operations; and 7) Public Debt Accounting. An assistant commissioner heads each office, except the Office of the Commissioner. The Office of Savings Bond Operations is located in Parkersburg, West Virginia; all other bureau activities are conducted in Washington, D.C. The number, name, and responsibilities of the offices have changed over time, but not the bureau's tasks, which are as old as the Department of the Treasury. Still, the activities and responsibilities that the bureau performs are twentieth-century developments fueled by two world wars and by the increased size of the public debt during the 1960s and the 1980s.

The offices, as they exist today, are in charge of the following activities:

- The Office of the Commissioner sets the policy for the bureau, coordinates the bureau's activities with the Federal Reserve Banks—the federal government's fiscal agents—and carries out the regulations for the government securities market. The bureau has had six commissioners in its fifty-six year history: William S. Broughton (1940–1945; he was also the commissioner of the public debt from 1919 to 1940), Edwin L. Kilby (1946–1960), Donald M. Merritt (1960–1971), H. J. Hintgen (1971–1981), William M. Gregg (1983–1987; acting commissioner, 1981–1983), and Richard L. Gregg (1987–).

- The Office of Financing manages and directs the offer and auction of marketable securities—Treasury bills, notes, and bonds—provides technical advice and assistance to management officials on security offerings, and assesses how these auctions may affect book-entry systems.

- The Office of Securities and Accounting Services establishes and maintains investor accounts, authorizes the payment of interest and redemption proceeds to the owners of securities, and keeps control records on all public debt securities.

- The Office of Administration meets the administrative requirements of the bureau.

- The Office of Automated Information Systems provides data processing support. It also maintains electronic communications between the bureau and the Federal Reserve Banks.

- The Office of Savings Bond Operations supervises the issue, service, and retirement of U.S. savings bonds and notes, and settles claims for lost, stolen, destroyed, or mutilated bonds.

- The Office of Public Debt Accounting reports the composition and size of the outstanding public debt and the annual interest costs generated by the debt.

The bureau decides its policies not only according to the needs and preferences of the actors within the Treasury or the public that buys the securities, it also has to consider the needs and preferences of other actors. First, it has to deal with the president and Congress, which set policies according to national, state, and local needs, and according to their electoral concerns. Then it has to consider the needs and preferences of the Federal Reserve, with whom it shares the realm of monetary policy. These "external actors" may help or hinder the bureau's ability to achieve its mission.

The needs and concerns of other actors are important because the tasks done by the bureau create two different, yet related, problems. On the one hand, the bureau needs to create confidence in the securities that it sells, but this depends on what others do. Congress, for example, has the authority to raise the public debt ceiling. Failure to raise it disrupts the auction of Treasury securities and may undermine the bureau's aim of maintaining confidence in the government's ability to honor its debts. On the other hand, the bureau has to consider the effect that these securities may have on the economic performance of the nation. Here, the bureau's policy of reducing the cost of financing the debt may create inflationary pressures.

To understand how and why maintaining confidence and assessing the economic impact of the securities creates problems, it is necessary to consider that the debt can be financed in three different ways. The first solution is via inflation—the creation of new money. This solution is neither good public policy nor feasible because the Federal Reserve controls the monetary supply. A second way is to raise taxes. The problem here is that it is not possible to raise taxes beyond a certain limit. Also, tax increases create political risks for elected officials. A third alternative is to borrow money from the public—that is, issue securities. The Treasury depends on the Federal Reserve Banks, especially the trading desk at the Federal Reserve Bank of New York, to do this. This dependence does not imply, however, that the Federal Reserve buys the securities that the public does not want to buy.

A second problem is that securities vary according to different elements. First, securities can be either marketable or nonmarketable. Marketable securities are those in which secondary market trading is allowed. This includes Treasury bills, bonds, and notes. Owners can sell these bills, bonds, and notes to other actors besides the Treasury. Nonmarketable securities are those in which secondary market trading is not possible. U.S. saving bonds are an example, for they can only be sold to the Treasury. Second, securities have different maturity dates, interest rates, and conditions under which they can be redeemed. The problem is to assess the impact of these elements on the economy.

The major administrative problem for the bureau is that it has to—in the words of Jeffrey A. Cantor and Donald R. Stabile—"plan how, to whom, and in what form [the government] sells its debt." This goes beyond the issue of public confidence because it implies that the bureau needs to sell securities without creating inflationary pressures. Still, the bureau has no control over this. The problem is that if the bureau wants to reduce the cost of the debt, then—all other things being equal—it will favor a policy of low interest rates. High interest rates imply that the bureau will not contain the cost of the debt. Low interest rates may also attract more people to borrow money, and thus ease the task of financing the debt. However, low interest rates create the risk of inflation, which will disrupt economic activity and will eventually make it difficult for the bureau to manage the debt. The main problem for the bureau is that it has no control over interest rates, which are set by the Federal Open Market Committee.

[*See also* Federal Reserve System *and* Financial Management Service.]

BIBLIOGRAPHY

Bach, George L. *Federal Reserve Policy-Making.* New York, 1950.
Cantor, Jeffrey A., and Donald R. Stabile. *A History of the Bureau of the Public Debt.* Washington, D.C., 1989.
Hamilton, Alexander. *The Federalist Papers.* Nos. 7, 15, and 34. New York, 1987.
Havrilesky, Thomas. *The Pressures on American Monetary Policy.* Boston, 1993.
Keech, William R. *Economic Politics.* New York, 1995.
Kettl, Donald F. *Leadership at the Fed.* New Haven, Conn., 1986.
Kettl, Donald F. *Deficit Politics.* New York, 1992.
Mayer, Thomas, ed. *The Political Economy of American Monetary Policy.* New York, 1993.
Ritter, Lawrence S., and William L. Silber. *Principles of Money, Banking, and Financial Markets.* New York, 1993.
Stein, Herbert. *Presidential Economics.* New York, 1984.
Taus, Esther R. *Central Banking Functions of the United States Treasury, 1789–1941.* New York, 1943.
Taus, Esther R. *The Role of the U.S. Treasury in Stabilizing the Economy, 1941–1946.* Washington, D.C., 1981.
Timberlake, Richard H. *Monetary Policy in the United States.* Chicago, 1993.
U.S. Department of the Treasury, Bureau of the Public Debt. *An Introduction to the Bureau of the Public Debt.* Washington, D.C., 1988.
The United States Government Manual, 1995/96. Washington, D.C., 1995.
Woolley, John T. *Monetary Politics.* New York, 1985.

—ARMANDO PALACIOS-SOMMER

Public Health Service

 The origins of the United States Public Health Service may be traced to the passage of an act in 1798 that provided for the care and relief of sick and injured merchant seamen. The leaders of the young American nation recognized that a healthy merchant marine was necessary to protect the economic prosperity and national de-

fense of the country. The 1798 law created a fund to be used by the federal government to provide medical services to merchant seamen in American ports. The marine hospital fund was administered by the Treasury Department and financed through a monthly deduction from the wages of the seamen. Medical care was provided through contracts with existing hospitals and, increasingly as time went on, through the construction of new hospitals for this purpose. The earliest marine hospitals were located along the Atlantic coast, with Boston being the site of the first such facility, but later they were also established along inland waterways, the Great Lakes, and the Gulf and Pacific coasts.

The marine hospitals hardly constituted a system in the antebellum period. Funds for the hospitals were inadequate, political rather than medical reasons often influenced the choice of sites for hospitals and the selection of physicians, and the Treasury Department had little supervisory authority over the hospitals. During the Civil War, the Union and Confederate forces occupied the hospitals for their own use, and in 1864 only eight of the twenty-seven hospitals listed before the war were operational. In 1869 the secretary of the Treasury commissioned an extensive study of the marine hospitals, and the resulting critical report led to the passage of reform legislation in the following year.

The 1870 reorganization converted the loose network of locally controlled hospitals into a centrally controlled Marine Hospital Service, with its headquarters in Washington, D.C. The position of supervising surgeon (later surgeon general) was created to administer the service. John Maynard Woodworth was appointed as the first supervising surgeon in 1871, and he moved quickly to reform the system. In 1872 he began publishing annual reports of the service. He also adopted a military model for his medical staff, instituting examinations for applicants and putting his physicians in uniforms. Woodworth created a cadre of mobile, career service physicians who could be assigned and moved as needed to the various marine hospitals. The uniformed services component of the Marine Hospital Service was formalized as the Commissioned Corps by legislation enacted in 1889. At first open only to physicians, over the course of the twentieth century the corps expanded to eventually include dentists, sanitary engineers, pharmacists, nurses, and other health professionals.

The scope of activities of the Marine Hospital Service also began to expand well beyond the care of merchant seamen in the closing decades of the nineteenth century, beginning with the control of infectious disease. Responsibility for quarantine was originally a function of the states rather than the federal government, but an 1877 yellow fever epidemic that spread quickly from New Orleans up the Mississippi River served as a reminder that infectious diseases do not respect state borders. The epidemic resulted in the passage of the National Quarantine Act of 1878, which conferred quarantine authority on the Marine Hospital Service. Since the service already had hospitals and physicians located in many port cities, it was a logical choice to administer quarantine at the federal level. Over the course of the next half century, the Marine Hospital Service increasingly took over quarantine functions from state authorities.

As immigration increased dramatically in the late nineteenth century, the federal government also took over the processing of immigrants from the states, beginning in 1891. The Marine Hospital Service was assigned the responsibility for the medical inspection of arriving immigrants. Immigration legislation prohibited the admission of persons suffering from "loathsome" or dangerous contagious diseases, those who were insane or had serious mental deficiencies, and anyone who was likely to become a public charge (e.g., owing to a medical disability). Officers of the Marine Hospital Service were assigned to immigration depots to examine immigrants for medical fitness. The largest center of immigration was Ellis Island in New York, opened in 1892, and service physicians could examine as many as five thousand immigrants on a busy day. Under such conditions the medical examination was necessarily brief and superficial, and the experienced eye of the physician was the best diagnostic instrument at hand. When an immigrant's condition aroused concern, he or she was detained for further examination.

The newly emerging science of bacteriology was just beginning to make its impact felt on medicine in the late nineteenth century (e.g., by aiding in the diagnosis of infectious diseases). In 1887 the service established a bacteriological laboratory at the marine hospital at Staten Island. Originally concerned mainly with practical problems related to the diagnosis of disease, the Hygienic Laboratory, as it was called, was later moved to Washington, D.C., and became a center for biomedical research, eventually known as the National Institutes of Health.

Because of the broadening responsibilities of the service, its name was changed in 1902 to the Public Health and Marine Hospital Service. The service continued to expand its public health activities as the nation entered the twentieth century. The 1902 law that changed the name of the service also led to increased cooperation between federal and state public health authorities. The surgeon general was charged with convening a conference of state health authorities at least on an annual basis and was also directed to prepare and distribute to state health officers forms for the uniform compilation of vital statistics. This statistical information was published in the service's journal, *Public Health Reports*. Service physicians also cooperated with local health departments in campaigns against plague and yellow fever in cities such as San Francisco and New Orleans in the early part of the century.

Another law passed in 1902, the Biologics Control Act, gave the service regulatory authority over the production and sale of vaccines, serums, and other biological products. Rural sanitation also became central to the work of the service beginning in 1911, when Dr. Leslie Lumsden was sent to the state of Washington at the request of Yakima County officials to investigate the source of typhoid fever there. Lumsden identified the cause of the spread of the disease as feces and initiated a campaign for sanitary privies. The rural sanitation efforts of Lumsden and his colleagues spread to other areas of the country and helped to encourage the establishment of county health departments.

The increasing involvement of the service in public health activities led to its name being changed again in 1912 to the Public Health Service (PHS). At the same time, the PHS was given clear legislative authority to "investigate the diseases of man and conditions influencing the propagation and spread thereof, including sanitation and sewage and the pollution either directly or indirectly of the navigable streams and lakes of the United States" (*Annual Report of the Surgeon General of the Public Health Service*, 1912, p. 9). All types of illness, whatever their cause (including environmental pollution), now came within the purview of the PHS.

In the period following the passage of the 1912 law, the PHS devoted significant attention to trachoma and pellagra, carrying out surveys, laboratory and field research, and efforts to control these diseases. PHS physician Joseph McMullen worked with state and local health officials to wage a campaign against trachoma, a contagious eye disease that could lead to blindness. He organized a string of temporary trachoma hospitals and clinics, staffed by nurses employed by the PHS, for the treatment of the disease. Another PHS physician, Joseph Goldberger, demonstrated that pellagra, a disease that was especially common in the South, was caused by a dietary deficiency and that it could be eliminated by the addition of milk, meat, or eggs to the diet.

The entry of the United States into World War I had a significant impact on the PHS. Some PHS commissioned officers were detailed to the Army and the Navy, but most PHS staff were involved in war-related efforts on the home front. The service was given the responsibility of working with local health departments to keep the areas around military training camps free from disease. Venereal disease was a particular concern to the military, and a PHS Division of Venereal Disease was established in 1918 to control the spread of "social disease." In that same year the "Spanish influenza" pandemic reached the United States, and the PHS was given increased funding and staff specifically to battle this disease.

Following the war the PHS was given the responsibility for the care of all returning veterans, leading to a threefold increase in the number of hospitals operated by the service and an eightfold increase in patients. This situation was short-lived, however, because Congress established an independent Veterans' Bureau in 1921, and the following year the responsibility and facilities for the medical treatment of veterans were transferred from the PHS to the new bureau.

The wartime concern with potential industrial hazards for workers served to stimulate PHS activities in the field of industrial hygiene, an area with which the service had been concerned since about 1910. In the postwar period staff and activities in industrial hygiene were increased, and important investigations were undertaken on the hazards of radiation and toxic chemicals in various industrial settings and lung disease in miners and granite cutters. The PHS also became more actively involved in studies of water pollution in this period.

In the two decades between the two world wars, the PHS expanded the population to which it provided health care beyond the traditional categories of merchant seamen and the Coast Guard. In 1921 the PHS assumed responsibility for individuals suffering from leprosy when it converted the state leprosy facility in Carville, Louisiana, to a national leprosy hospital. Under the PHS the hospital at Carville carried out pioneering research on the nature and treatment of leprosy. In 1928 the service detailed a commissioned officer to serve as director of health of the Bureau of Indian Affairs of the Department of Interior, as well as assigning a number of other officers to the bureau to provide medical assistance in the field. This cooperative arrangement continued until the PHS eventually took over full responsibility for the health of American Indians from the Department of the Interior almost forty years later. The law creating the Federal Bureau of Prisons in 1930 included provisions for the assignment of PHS officers to supervise and provide medical and psychiatric services in federal prisons, thus adding another category of beneficiaries to the roster of those served by the PHS.

Although the PHS had become significantly involved with the issue of mental health in connection with the screening of arriving immigrants, it did not establish a formal organizational unit in this area until 1929. Initially, the Division of Mental Hygiene focused largely on questions of substance abuse, as is suggested by the fact that it was called the Narcotics Division for the first year of its existence. The 1929 law that established the division also authorized the creation of two hospitals for the treatment of narcotics addicts, and these facilities were opened in Lexington, Kentucky, and Fort Worth, Texas, in the 1930s.

Under the New Deal the PHS became more involved in the broader health concerns of the nation. The Social Security Act of 1935 provided the PHS with the funds and the authority to build a system of state and local health departments, an activity that it had already been doing to some extent on an informal basis. Under this legislation the service provided grants to states to stimulate the development of health services, train public health workers, and undertake research on health problems. These programs were to be aided by the federal government but run at the state and local level, joining the various government units in a public health partnership.

These new authorities were embraced by Thomas Parran, who was appointed as PHS surgeon general in 1936 and was of a more activist bent than his predecessor. Venereal disease was an area of particular concern to Parran, who sought to focus the battle against syphilis and gonorrhea on scientific and medical grounds, rather than emphasizing moral or ethical views concerning sex. His articles in widely read magazines and his 1937 book, *Shadow on the Land,* were a major factor in breaking down the taboo against the discussion of the subject in the popular press. His efforts were instrumental in leading to the passage of the National Venereal Disease Control Act in 1938. This legislation provided federal funds to the states through the PHS for venereal disease control programs, as well as supporting research into the treatment and prevention of these diseases.

After being housed in the Treasury Department ever since its establishment, the PHS suddenly found itself in a new administrative home as the result of a government reorganization in 1939. President Franklin D. Roosevelt aligned the PHS along with a number of social service agencies, such as the Social Security Board, in a newly created Federal Security Agency. The reorganiza-

tion had little effect, however, on the functions and operation of the service.

As it became obvious that the United States might become involved in World War II, the PHS, along with many other American institutions, began to emphasize preparation for war. With the entry of this country into the war, some PHS officers were detailed to the military services. The PHS also provided personnel to the United Nations Relief and Rehabilitation Administration to staff medical care and disease prevention programs in refugee camps in Europe and the Middle East. The Coast Guard was militarized in November 1941, and 663 PHS officers served with the Guard during the war.

A concern about a wartime shortage of nurses led to the passage of the Nurse Training Act of 1943, creating a program known as the Cadet Nurse Corps, administered by the PHS. The program provided participants with a tuition scholarship and a small monthly stipend while attending a qualified nursing school. In return for this support, the cadets agreed to work after graduation in essential nursing services for the duration of the war, whether in the military or in civilian life. To symbolize their commitment to the war effort, the cadets wore uniforms. Between 1943 and the termination of the corps in 1948, over 124,000 nurses (including some three thousand African Americans) were graduated, making the Cadet Nurse Corps one of the most fruitful federal nursing programs in history. The program also marked the beginning of PHS involvement on a large scale in funding the training of health professionals.

The war contributed to expansion in the service's programs and personnel, the latter doubling in size to sixteen thousand employees between 1940 and 1945. It also increased the involvement of the service in international health activities, leading to the creation of an Office of International Health Relations. Two legislative acts during this period also had a significant impact on the PHS. A 1943 law reorganized the service, consolidating its programs into four subdivisions: the Office of the Surgeon General, the National Institute (later Institutes) of Health, and two new entities, the Bureau of Medical Services and the Bureau of State Services. The 1944

Public Health Service Act codified on an integrated basis all of the authorities of the service and strengthened the administrative authority of the surgeon general. This act also allowed the PHS to develop a major postwar program of grants for medical research through the National Institutes of Health, building upon the earlier example of the extramural grants for cancer research given by the service's National Cancer Institute since its creation in 1937.

Another legacy of World War II grew out of a wartime program of the PHS to control malaria in areas around military camps and maneuver areas in the United States, most of which were established in the South. Over the course of the war, the Malaria Control in War Areas program, based in Atlanta, expanded its responsibilities to include the control of other communicable diseases such as yellow fever, dengue, and typhus. By the end of the war, the program had demonstrated its value in the control of infectious disease so successfully that it was converted in 1946 to the Communicable Disease Center (CDC). The mission of the CDC continued to expand over the next half century, going beyond the bounds of infectious disease to include areas such as nutrition, chronic disease, and occupational and environmental health. To reflect this broader scope of the institution, its name was changed to the Center for Disease Control in 1970. It received its current designation, Centers for Disease Control and Prevention (but retaining the acronym CDC), in 1992.

In 1946 two major legislative acts had a significant impact on the PHS. The National Mental Health Act was to greatly increase the involvement of the PHS, which administered the programs established by the law, in the area of mental health. The act supported research on mental illness, provided fellowships and grants for the training of mental health personnel, and made available to states grants to assist in the establishment of clinics and treatment centers and to fund demonstration projects. It also called for the establishment within the PHS of a National Institute for Mental Health, which was created in 1949. The Hospital Survey and Construction Act, more commonly referred to as the Hill-Burton Act, authorized the PHS to make grants to the states for surveying their hospitals and public health centers and for planning construction of additional facilities, and to assist in this construction. Over the next twenty-five years, the program disbursed almost $4 billion.

The Federal Security Agency was elevated to cabinet status as the Department of Health, Education, and Welfare (DHEW) in 1953, but this change in status of the service's parent organization had little direct impact on the PHS at the time. The service did assume several new tasks, however, in the 1950s. For example, it became fully responsible for the health of American Indians in 1955, when all Indian health programs of the Bureau of Indian Affairs were transferred to the PHS. A new Division of Indian Health was established to administer these programs. In 1956 the Armed Forces Medical Library became the National Library of Medicine and was made a part of the PHS.

The 1960s witnessed continued expansion of the PHS. Two agencies that were also housed in the DHEW were incorporated into the PHS in this decade. St. Elizabeths Hospital, which had begun as the Government Hospital for the Insane in 1855, was brought into the PHS in 1967 (although much of the hospital's physical plant and programs were transferred to the District of Columbia in 1987). The Food and Drug Administration was made a part of the PHS in 1968, thus involving the PHS much more heavily and visibly in the area of regulation.

Undoubtedly many Americans became much more aware of the PHS and the surgeon general with the publication of the famous surgeon general's report on *Smoking and Health* in 1964. Although not the first statement from a PHS surgeon general concerning the dangers of smoking, the publicity surrounding this report brought Surgeon General Luther Terry into the limelight. It led eventually to the now-familiar surgeon general's warnings on cigarette packages.

The major health event of the 1960s, the passage of Medicare and Medicaid legislation, actually had little impact on the PHS. When these programs became law in 1965, they were placed elsewhere within the DHEW. Thomas Parran's successors as surgeon general had been much less involved in matters of medical care policy, and many within the PHS saw Medicare and Medicaid as essentially insurance programs in which the service need not involve itself.

While expanding its responsibilities in a number of areas, the PHS also saw its activities circumscribed in one field in this period, namely environmental health. In the 1960s water pollution control was moved from the PHS to the department level, and eventually transferred to the Department of the Interior. The creation of the Environmental Protection Agency (EPA) in 1970 led to the loss of PHS programs in areas such as air pollution and solid waste to the new agency. Although some PHS commissioned officers were detailed to the EPA to assist it in its work, the service had lost its role as the leader of the federal environmental movement.

A major reorganization in 1968, prompted by the concerns of some that the PHS needed to be more responsive to the policies of elected public officials and more of a modern political bureaucracy, dramatically changed the leadership structure of the service. From the reorganization of 1870 through the middle of the 1960s, the PHS was led entirely by career commissioned officers (who represented less than twenty percent of PHS employees by the 1960s), with no member of the civil service having ever run a bureau. The surgeon general, although appointed by the president, had always been a career member of the Commissioned Corps. The 1968 reorganization transferred the responsibility for directing the PHS from the surgeon general to the assistant secretary for health and scientific affairs (a political appointee position that had been created originally as an adviser to the department secretary). For the first time, a noncareer official became the top official in the PHS. Although the assistant secretary for health (as the position was later renamed) could come from the ranks of the PHS Commissioned Corps, this has not typically been the case. In general, beginning in this period the heads of PHS bureaus were increasingly not members of the corps, and were frequently brought in from outside the federal government. The surgeon general was no longer responsible for the management of the PHS but became largely an adviser and spokesperson on public health matters. Candidates for the position of surgeon general no longer necessarily came from the ranks of the corps but were often appointed from outside the PHS and commissioned upon their appointment.

A series of further reorganizations over the next three decades continued to reshape the structure, but not the major functions, of the PHS. The PHS did assume responsibility for the first time for the health of certain members of the general public (as opposed to specific groups such as seamen or prisoners or Indians) with the creation of the National Health Services Corps (NHSC) in 1970. Under this program the PHS sent physicians, nurse practitioners, and other health professionals into clinical practice in areas where there were critical health manpower shortages. Beginning in 1972 the PHS could offer health profession students scholarships in exchange for a commitment to serve in the NHSC. A decade later, however, the PHS lost another group of patients when the health care entitlement for merchant seamen was terminated. By that time the provision of health care to merchant seamen played only a small part in the work of the PHS, but nevertheless the closing of the remaining eight marine hospitals and twenty-seven clinics in 1981 represented the end of the activity for which the service was originally created.

There has been no lack of challenges for the PHS since that time, with the AIDS epidemic just one example of health care issues confronting the service in the 1980s and 1990s. The service remains a component of the Department of Health and Human Services (DHHS), as the DHEW was renamed upon the creation of a separate Department of Education in 1980. A major reorganization in 1995 once again changed the leadership structure of the PHS. The PHS agencies, by this time numbering eight, no longer reported to the assistant secretary for health, but directly to the secretary of the DHHS. The agencies, now considered operating divisions of the department, are as follows: the Agency for Health Care Policy and Research, the Agency for Toxic Substances and Disease Registry, the Centers for Disease Control and Prevention, the Food and Drug Administration, the Health Resources and Services Administration, the Indian Health

Service, the National Institutes of Health, and the Substance Abuse and Mental Health Services Administration. Together with the Office of Public Health and Science (headed by the assistant secretary for health and including the surgeon general) and the department's regional health offices, these eight divisions comprise today's Public Health Service, an organization of some fifty thousand employees.

[*See also* Food and Drug Administration *and* National Institutes of Health.]

BIBLIOGRAPHY

Etheridge, Elizabeth. *Sentinel for Health: A History of the Centers for Disease Control.* Berkeley, Calif., 1992.

Furman, Bess. *A Profile of the United States Public Health Service, 1798–1948.* Bethesda, Md., 1973.

Greenberg, George D. "Reorganization Reconsidered: The U.S. Public Health Service, 1960–1973." *Public Policy* 23 (1975): 483–522.

Harden, Victoria. *Inventing the NIH: Federal Biomedical Research Policy, 1887–1937.* Baltimore, 1986.

Kaiser, Margaret. *The United States Public Health Service: An Historical Bibliography of Selected Sources.* Bethesda, Md., 1989.

Kondratas, Ramunas. *Images from the History of the Public Health Service: A Photographic Exhibit.* Washington, D.C., 1994.

Lee, Philip R., and A. E. Benjamin. "Governmental and Legislative Control and Direction of Health Services in the United States." In *Oxford Textbook of Public Health,* edited by Walter W. Holland, Roger Detels, and George Knox, vol. 1, pp. 217–230. Oxford, U.K., 1991.

Miles, Rufus E., Jr. *The Department of Health, Education, and Welfare.* Washington, D.C., 1974.

Mullan, Fitzhugh. *Plagues and Politics: The Story of the United States Public Health Service.* New York, 1989.

Schmeckebier, Laurence F. *The Public Health Service: Its History, Activities, and Organization.* Baltimore, 1923.

Snyder, Lynne Page. "Passage and Significance of the 1944 Public Health Service Act." *Public Health Reports* 109 (1994): 721–724.

Williams, Ralph Chester. *The United States Public Health Service, 1798–1950.* Washington, D.C., 1951.

—JOHN PARASCANDOLA

R

Railroad Administration, Federal

The authority to regulate safety on U.S. railroads belongs to the Federal Railroad Administration (FRA), an agency within the Department of Transportation. The FRA is headed by an administrator appointed by the president and confirmed by the Senate. The regulatory authority of the FRA extends to safety of locomotives, signals, hours of service, and transportation of hazardous materials. The FRA employs 361 inspectors in eight regional offices to monitor safety equipment and procedures. Rail accidents are reported to and investigated by the Office of Safety within the FRA. The FRA also extends financial assistance through loans and grants to Amtrak and other railroads and subsidies to small freight lines so that they will be able to continue service.

[*See also* Amtrak.]   —GEORGE THOMAS KURIAN

Reclamation, Bureau of

Many Americans associate the Bureau of Reclamation with recreation. Indeed, more than 87 million visitors enjoy more than three hundred Reclamation recreation sites each year, where fishing, boating, water skiing, sailing, kayaking, swimming, and hiking are available. But this is only a small part of the role that Reclamation plays in the contemporary American West.

Inadequate precipitation in the American West required settlers to use irrigation for agriculture. At first settlers simply diverted water from streams, but in many areas demand outstripped supply. As demand for water increased, settlers wanted to store "wasted" runoff from rains and snow for later use, thus maximizing use by mak-

ing more water available in drier seasons. At that time private and state-sponsored storage and irrigation ventures were pursued but often failed because of lack of money and/or lack of engineering skill.

Pressure mounted for the federal government to undertake storage and irrigation projects. Congress had already invested in America's infrastructure through subsidies to roads, river navigation, harbors, canals, and railroads. Westerners wanted the federal government also to invest in irrigation projects in the West. The irrigation movement demonstrated its strength when pro-irrigation planks found their way into both Democratic and Republican platforms in 1900. Eastern and midwestern opposition in the Congress quieted when Westerners filibustered and killed a bill containing rivers and harbors projects favored by opponents of western irrigation. Congress passed the Reclamation Act on 17 June 1902. The act required that water users repay construction costs from which they received benefits.

In the jargon of that day, irrigation projects were known as "reclamation" projects. The concept was that irrigation would "reclaim" arid lands for human use. In addition, "homemaking" was a key argument for supporters of reclamation. Irrigation's supporters believed reclamation programs would encourage western settlement, making homes for Americans on family farms. President Theodore Roosevelt supported the reclamation movement because of his personal experience in the West, and because he believed in homemaking.

In July of 1902, in accordance with the Reclamation Act, Secretary of the Interior Ethan Allen Hitchcock established the United States Reclamation Service within the U.S. Geological Survey

(USGS). The new Reclamation Service studied potential water development projects in each western state with federal lands—revenue from sale of federal lands was the initial source of the program's funding. Because Texas had no federal lands, it did not become a reclamation state until 1906, when Congress passed a special act including it in the provisions of the Reclamation Act.

From 1902 to 1907, the Reclamation Service began about thirty projects in western states. Then, in 1907, the secretary of the Interior separated the Reclamation Service from the USGS and created an independent bureau within the Department of the Interior. In the early years many projects encountered problems: lands/soils included in projects were unsuitable for irrigation; land speculation sometimes resulted in poor settlement patterns; proposed repayment schedules could not be met by irrigators who had high land preparation and facilities construction costs; settlers were inexperienced in irrigation farming; waterlogging of irrigable lands required expensive drainage projects; and projects were built in areas that could grow only low-value crops. In 1923 the agency was renamed the Bureau of Reclamation. Then, in the face of increasing settler unrest and financial problems for the reclamation program, in 1924 the "Fact Finders' Report" spotlighted the issues. The Fact Finders' Act in late 1924 sought to resolve some of the financial and other problems.

In 1928 Congress authorized the Boulder Canyon (Hoover Dam) Project, and large appropriations began, for the first time, to flow to Reclamation from the general funds of the United States. The authorization came only after a hard-fought debate about the pros and cons of public power versus private power.

The heyday of Reclamation construction of water facilities occurred during the Depression and the thirty-five years after World War II. The last major authorization for construction projects occurred in the late 1960s while a parallel evolution and development of the American environmental movement began to result in strong opposition to water development projects. Even the 1976 failure of Teton Dam as it filled for the first time did not diminish Reclamation's strong

international reputation in water development circles. However, this first and only failure of a major Reclamation dam did shake the bureau, which subsequently developed a very strong dam safety program designed to avoid similar problems in the future. However, the failure of Teton Dam, the influence of the environmental movement, and the announcement of President Jimmy Carter's "hit list" on water projects profoundly affected the direction of Reclamation's programs and activities in the United States.

Reclamation operates about 180 projects in the seventeen western states. The total Reclamation investment for completed project facilities in September of 1992 was about $11 billion. Reclamation projects provide agricultural, household, and industrial water to about one-third of the population of the American West. About five percent of the land area of the West is irrigated, and Reclamation provides water to about one-fifth of that acreage (in 1992, some 9.1 million acres). Reclamation is a major American generator of electricity. In 1993 Reclamation had fifty-six powerplants on-line and generated 34.7 billion kilowatt-hours of electricity.

Between 1988 and 1994 Reclamation underwent major reorganization as construction on projects authorized in the 1960s and earlier drew to an end. A Reclamation report stated, "The arid West essentially has been reclaimed. The major rivers have been harnessed and facilities are in place or are being completed to meet the most pressing current water demands and those of the immediate future." Emphasis in Reclamation programs shifted from construction to operation and maintenance of existing facilities. Reclamation's redefined official mission is to "manage, develop, and protect water and related resources in an environmentally and economically sound manner in the interest of the American public." In redirecting its programs and responsibilities, Reclamation substantially reduced its staff levels and budgets but remains a significant federal agency in the West.

BIBLIOGRAPHY

"Irrigation." In *History of Public Works in the United States, 1776–1976,* edited by Ellis L. Armstrong, pp. 303–340. Chicago, 1976.

Kollgaard, Eric B., and Wallace L. Chadwick, eds. *Development of Dam Engineering in the United States*. New York, 1988.

Lowitt, Richard. *The New Deal and the West*. Bloomington, Ind., 1984.

Robinson, Michael C. *Water for the West: The Bureau of Reclamation, 1902–1977*. Chicago, 1979.

Smith, Karen L. *The Magnificent Experiment: Building the Salt River Reclamation Project, 1890–1917*. Tucson, 1986.

Warne, William E. *The Bureau of Reclamation*. Boulder, Colo., 1985.

—Brit Allen Storey

Reform of the Federal Government

ESSAY Especially since the late nineteenth century, reform has proven a constant companion to federal management. Major reform movements have been episodic, rooted in both improvement efforts and occasional crises. More than anything else, the great constant of federal management has been change.

Reformers over the years have struggled to balance often-conflicting goals. They have sought to make government more professional and free from excessive political influence, but at the same time they have struggled to make it more responsive and accountable. Reformers have frequently also promised to make government more efficient and effective, both cheaper and smaller. Finally, they have struggled with the classic distinction between ends and means: *what* government ought to do versus *how* government ought to do it.

On one level, of course, these goals represent the very core of public debate about government. Reformers have always believed that they could craft a government both professional and accountable, more efficient and cheaper, more effective and smaller. In practice, however, the steps taken to secure some of these goals have often made it far harder to achieve others. Strengthening the professionalism of government has typically meant building protections against political favoritism and interference. That, in turn, has made it harder to secure responsiveness. Reforms to shrink government have sometimes made government work less well.

In the end, it has proven impossible truly to separate ends from means. The "what" has meaning only in the "how": ambitious goals come to life only as administrators implement them. The "how" requires the "what" to guide administrators' actions: government managers need a value-based compass, since management is never a purely technical matter of mechanically translating goals into reality.

The interconnections among these themes are inescapable, but that has never prevented reformers from trying to construct a neater world that favors one side or another of these tradeoffs. Administrative reform in the United States has long revolved around these issues—and around enduring efforts to find some simpler or more productive balance among fundamentally conflicting core principles. The reforms have progressed through four identifiable periods: the Progressive era (1875 through 1929); the institutionalization of expertise (1929 through 1955); consolidation (1955 through 1975); and privatization and reinvention (1975 through 1995).

THE PROGRESSIVE ERA

With the Progressives in the last fifteen years of the nineteenth century, American public administrators self-consciously began crafting the idea of a modern administrative state. Woodrow Wilson's famous essay "The Study of Administration" (1887) is celebrated for its argument about the separation of politics and administration. But it is perhaps most important for the sense of *purpose* with which Wilson, and the other Progressives, imbued administration. In their view government had a job to do, and the job could not execute itself. Moreover, although amateur government might produce some progress toward the goal, it could never perform the job as effectively or efficiently as a strong and professional bureaucracy. Theirs was not a case for big government or an all-powerful bureaucracy. It was, rather, a case for a government that worked. They believed that an effective government demanded bureaucratic reform.

Americans, of course, had been tinkering with the government's administrative system since the very beginning. In the nation's early days, Frederick C. Mosher points out, administration was dominated by a "government by gentlemen." "Fitness of character" dominated the criteria for selecting government officials, and that inevitably brought society's elite into government. That, of course, made government service a preserve dominated by Eastern well-educated males.

Andrew Jackson's election as president in 1828 brought a revolution, a "government by the common man," as Mosher put it, in which the spoils system came to dominate government service. The spoils system had existed before Jackson's administration, and Jackson himself was equivocal on the role of public service. He did, however, believe that government's work was simple enough that ordinary people could perform it. That, in turn, laid the foundation for hiring based on political support. Ordinary people could do ordinary work; loyalty, on the other hand, enhanced responsiveness.

These two approaches set the foundation for generations of reform that followed. Should government bureaucracy be dominated by the highly skilled, at the risk of having government populated mostly by an elite? Or should it be opened more broadly to political influence? That would improve responsiveness, but it would also risk making government less effective and efficient. These themes, established in the nation's first generation, provided the foundation for much of what followed in the next two centuries.

In 1883 the nation started on a profoundly different direction. Congress passed the Pendleton Act, which created a nonpartisan civil service system to reduce the role of patronage in government positions. The Pendleton Act was, in many ways, the cornerstone of the Progressive reform movement.

From the British the new system borrowed the ideas of competitive examinations for entrance to the service and political neutrality. Examinations would secure the best people for the positions, while political neutrality would insulate the system from political pressure. Other aspects of the new civil service, however, were very different from the British system. The British had established a relatively closed system built on scholarly exams and generalist knowledge. The

American system, by contrast, grew on practical exams. If there were to be practical exams, the exams would have to be tailored to the needs of individual positions. This set the stage for detailed classification of government jobs, of the exams to assess job qualifications, and therefore of the people who filled the jobs. Moreover, the American system allowed "open" entry, unlike the British system, which staffed the civil service from graduates of the nation's leading universities and then promoted officials from within. The American system had no such provision for generalists or for limiting lateral entry to higher-level positions. Finally, the British system created an administrative class to manage the top levels of the agency. The American system, in its eagerness to insulate the civil service from political pressures, maintained political control at top levels.

American pragmatism and egalitarianism—based on allowing entry to the service to anyone who could do the job, but defining the job according to the qualifications required—produced extensive rules and procedures to guarantee equality and access. It also, however, built rigidity into the system, which would in later years prove the source of extensive complaints and fuel continuous reform. The argument to protect civil servants from political pressure, moreover, limited just how far in the bureaucracy career administrators could rise. It created the need for extensive political appointments at the top levels and introduced substantial conflicts between the permanent career and temporary political officials. These problems, in turn, have also led over time to substantial reform proposals: to make the civil service more responsive, to improve careers for government employees, and in the end to make government more effective.

Most important, the creation of the civil service built on the assertion of a separation of policy-making and policy administration. Thinkers like Woodrow Wilson and Frank Goodnow argued vigorously for political neutrality. The civil service was to be an impartial instrument used to support the government's policies. But it also separated people from management: those carrying out government's work from the work to be done. That, in turn, built the foundation for substantial reforms in the latter half of the twentieth century.

The Progressive reforms stretched far past the creation of the civil service, however, into new structures and processes. Congress established important independent regulatory agencies, including the Interstate Commerce Commission (1887), to prevent monopolies from controlling the nation's rail and water transportation. The movement to bring scientific management to government helped support the creation of a new cabinet department for Commerce and Labor (1903), later split into separate departments for Commerce and Labor (1913). (There were political pressures as well—each of these constituencies wanted its own department to represent its interests.) The passage of the federal income tax in 1913 led to the expansion of tax collection in the Treasury Department. Meanwhile, the need to stabilize the currency led reformers to create the Federal Reserve System (1913). The 1910s, in fact, marked a period of surprisingly frenzied creation of new agencies.

Meanwhile, the Taft Commission on Economy and Efficiency (1912–1913) made a strong case for the creation of an executive budget and a central budget staff agency. Budgeting to this point had largely been *ad hoc,* with the president's budget little more than the accumulation of individual agencies' spending requests. Scientific management, reformers argued, demanded that the president carefully review all spending proposals, combine them into a single presidential recommendation, and submit them to Congress in a government-wide budget. These tasks, in turn, required a substantial staff agency to help the president with the job. With the passage of the Budget and Accounting Act of 1921, Congress in one stroke created the foundation of the nation's modern fiscal management: a presidential budget, to be submitted annually to Congress; a new Bureau of the Budget, housed in the Treasury Department, to assist the president in preparing the budget; and the General Accounting Office (GAO), a congressional agency, to audit federal spending on behalf of Congress. The act simultaneously increased the president's power by creating an executive budget, yet balanced congressional leverage by establishing the GAO. [*See* General Accounting Office.]

Thus, by the mid-1920s, reformers had dramatically transformed the American administrative state. They had created a new civil service system to shift political influence from routine administrative tasks. They had established new agencies to do the government's work. They had formulated new processes to manage the nation's money. More than anything else, these reforms combined to enhance executive power and capacity. Reform had firmly established a muscular administrative state.

THE INSTITUTIONALIZATION OF EXPERTISE

During the 1930s economic crisis proved to be the engine of management reform. The Depression fueled public demands that the federal government help pull the economy out of its slump, and President Franklin D. Roosevelt responded with his New Deal. The New Deal was far more a tactic of responding pragmatically to pressing problems than a coherent strategy of increasing the size and power of the federal government. People were hungry and out of work; Roosevelt and his advisers struggled to create jobs and lessen the misery. The product of the New Deal, however, was a remarkable collection of new government agencies, from short-term organizations like the Works Progress Administration to monumental creations like the Social Security Administration.

Perhaps even more important, the New Deal redefined the federal government's role: it could help steer the economy, lessen citizens' problems, and strengthen the public infrastructure. More subtly, these reforms also strengthened the executive branch. The creation of new programs demanded new agencies to run them. New agencies coupled with more money increased the president's importance in framing policy. They also dramatically increased the president's problems in managing the executive branch, however, and that prompted Roosevelt in 1935 to appoint a three-member Committee on Administrative Management, composed of Louis Brownlow as chair, Luther Gulick, and Charles Merriam. The committee's members were among the best-known and most respected public management experts of their day. Moreover, the committee was especially successful in recruiting young staffers who went on to become the leaders of the next generation of American public management.

The committee's report (1937) proved the most searching reexamination of the role of management in the federal government since the ratification of the Constitution. The committee concluded that the president, as head of the executive branch, had the central role as chief administrator. To serve effectively as chief administrator, however, "the president needs help," as the committee wrote in its most famous conclusion. Moreover, the committee argued for clear authority and accountability connecting the president at the top with administrators at the bottom of the bureaucracy.

These principles supported sweeping recommendations: that the lines of control ought to be streamlined and clarified; that the president's span of control ought to be reduced by consolidating administrative agencies into a small number of cabinet departments; that the president be supported in this job by creating a small but effective White House staff with "a passion for anonymity"; and that the president's power over personnel, planning, and budget policy be strengthened. The committee was especially strong in its attack on independent regulatory agencies, which it said constituted a "headless fourth branch of government." These agencies, it concluded, ought to be incorporated into cabinet departments.

Roosevelt submitted most of the committee's recommendations to Congress in 1938. Many members of Congress, however, were still angry at the administration for its earlier "court-packing" plan, and they saw the reorganization proposals as part of a broader Roosevelt strategy to establish a virtual dictatorship. Some scholars, moreover, fiercely contested these recommendations, in particular the committee's assertion that the president's executive power included all administrative power. Congress eventually approved a far more modest plan in 1939, which most notably created the Executive Office of the President. The plan moved the Bureau of the Budget to the president's own executive office and created the foundation for the modern presidential establishment. Perhaps most important, however, the Brownlow Committee made explicit the basic ideas that defined the keystone of administrative orthodoxy for the remainder of the century: the president's job was to act as chief executive officer for the government of the United States.

World War II soon erupted, and the nation mounted an enormous effort—with a substantially bigger executive branch—to win it. In the war's aftermath, some reduction in the size and scope of government was inevitable. Moreover, Republicans, who had captured both houses of Congress, questioned the continuing need for the New Deal agencies and programs. To examine these problems, Democratic president Harry S. Truman and the Republican Congress jointly created a new twelve-member Commission on the Organization of the Executive Branch of Government. Former president Herbert Hoover was chosen as the commission's chair, and it came to bear his name.

The Hoover Commission was a far larger effort than the Brownlow Committee. It created task forces to study problems ranging from the management of the executive branch to budgeting. Each task force wrote a report and made recommendations to the commission. The commission never wrote a final report but, rather, debated the task force recommendations and submitted nineteen separate reports to Congress in 1949.

The most notable report was on the *General Management of the Executive Branch* (1949), which Harold Seidman and Robert Gilmour have called "the hard core of fundamentalist dogma" on American public management. The Hoover Commission amplified the themes of the Brownlow Committee: there ought to be clear lines of control from the president to operating departments and their heads; related agencies ought to be consolidated in larger departments, according to their major purpose, to reduce the president's span of control; independent regulatory agencies, in particular, ought to be eliminated to prevent the diffusion of responsibility throughout the executive branch; the president, not agency officials, ought to control policy; agency officials, not the president, ought to be responsible for administrative details. The commission also recommended that the president be given substantial authority to reorganize the executive branch to improve its effectiveness.

Congress approved many of the recommendations, including the reorganization authority, the creation of a new General Services Administration, and many agency reorganization proposals. [See General Services Administration.] Most important, the commission confirmed the core values first defined in the Brownlow Committee's report: that the president served as the government's manager-in-chief, and that he ought to be given the authority needed to do the job.

The Hoover Commission's success led to the creation of a second Hoover Commission in 1953. Some government critics, especially congressional Republicans, were concerned that, although the first Hoover Commission had improved the "how" of government, it did little to focus on the "what." They were eager in particular to attack "big government" and pressed the new commission, with many of the same members and staff, to take on directly the question of what functions government ought to perform. President Dwight Eisenhower, just elected, had little enthusiasm for commissions in general and for commissions outside his control in particular. The second commission, however, proved much less successful in delivering a sharp message. Like its predecessor, it relied on task forces, but, once again, it made no effort to meld their recommendations into a single set of conclusions. Cutting government functions, moreover, proved not nearly as popular as its creators had hoped. The second Hoover Commission therefore had far less influence than the first.

Nevertheless, the Hoover Commissions, coupled with the work of the Brownlow Committee, defined an administrative orthodoxy that shaped both thought and practice about public management until the mid-1970s. They envisioned a strong president whose job was managing and controlling the government. Such a president

would require help, which grew up around him in a powerful executive office. The commissions focused squarely on improving the president's administrative leverage: on getting the organizational structure right, and on creating central management processes, like personnel, budgetary, and property management, to help him do his job.

The commissions, moreover, had two far more subtle features. First, they quietly and gradually moved more responsibility from Congress to the executive branch and, within the executive branch, from the agencies to the White House. Second, even if they worked on the "how" of government, they showed how hard it was to tackle the "what." Reformers had little success in directly defining what government ought to do. They also discovered, however, that the "how" very often shaped the "what." That set the stage, in the years that followed, for using management reform in pursuit of a far larger policy agenda.

RATIONALIZING THE EXECUTIVE BRANCH

During the 1960s reform of the federal government took a very different tack. The orthodoxy of the Brownlow Committee and the Hoover Commissions had become well established, and the Executive Office of the President had matured into a muscular arm of the presidency. That orthodoxy found its high water mark with President Lyndon B. Johnson's War on Poverty, an aggressive expansion of federal programs that simultaneously confirmed the Progressives' confidence in government's ability to solve public problems; the earlier reformers' strategy of presidential management of public programs; and the New Deal's commitment to social policy.

The very success of the Johnson administration programs, in fact, gave root to new strategies to reform the federal government. President Richard M. Nixon and his advisers were concerned that the programs were too expansive, that the federal government was becoming too big to be manageable, and that the president lacked adequate leverage to steer it. In 1969 Nixon appointed a six-member task force, the President's Advisory Council on Executive Organization, to examine the problem. The council, chaired by Litton Industries president Roy L. Ash, spent just over a year preparing more than a dozen reports to the president. The Ash Council concluded that government had become too fragmented to be managed well. It relied on the ruling orthodoxy to argue that federal agencies ought to be consolidated and that the president's ability to control the executive branch ought to be enhanced. In particular, the Ash Council concluded that the executive branch ought to move from constituency-based departments, like Agriculture, Labor, and Commerce, to broader departments organized by function. Ronald C. Moe, in fact, ironically notes that the business executives called in to shape up the government relied far more on the traditional theory of public administration than private sector models of management.

In early 1971 Nixon took up the Ash Council's recommendations to urge the transformation of the Bureau of the Budget into a new Office of Management and Budget (OMB). The change was to be more than cosmetic. Nixon clearly wanted stronger management support close to the president, in part to improve his ability to control the executive branch, in part to balance what administration officials believed was a domination of Great Society programs by liberal Democrats who would fight him on his policies. This logic led as well to Nixon's proposal to consolidate seven existing departments into four "super-departments": human resources, community development, natural resources, and economic affairs.

The Democratic Congress, however, rejected virtually all of the proposals as part of the broader Watergate-era battles over control of government policy and process. Congress did approve the reorganization of the Bureau of the Budget into the OMB and, in the process, put management in an unprecedented position at the center of government. At the same time, however, Congress enhanced its own power by establishing a new congressional budget process and a Congressional Budget Office to counter the OMB. These changes enhanced the congressional role in budgeting, which gradually had

been eroding since the passage of the Budget and Accounting Act of 1921.

President Jimmy Carter likewise promised to streamline the federal bureaucracy, but his model was his experience as governor of Georgia. He created a reorganization project within the OMB and pledged to trim the number of federal agencies by nearly ninety percent, to just two hundred; no one, though, could document the numbers. Carter promised, moreover, to introduce a new budget process, zero-base budgeting, to the federal government and to use it to bring federal spending under control. In the end, however, zero-base budgeting proved to give the president little leverage over federal spending. The principal effect of Carter's reorganization effort was the creation of two new federal departments, Energy and Education, to fulfill campaign promises.

The battles of the Nixon and Carter administrations to rationalize the executive branch underlined several important themes. First, the orthodoxy of public administration, first established by the Progressives and later embroidered by the reform commissions of the middle third of the century, had reached full maturity. This ideology defined the ultimate goals and fundamental options that the presidents considered. Second, successful as the orthodoxy was in framing the debate, it had also contributed to an executive branch that critics increasingly argued was unmanageable. The stage was being set for fundamental reforms in the years that followed.

Third, even though restructuring, by consolidating related functions in the same department, dominated the reform movement, other pressures to make the bureaucracy more politically responsive often crowded out rationalist goals. The creation of the Department of Education, widely viewed as the Carter administration's effort to repay teachers' unions for their support in the 1976 presidential campaign, only reinforced the sense left over from the Nixon administration that effective management was but one goal driving federal reform. Finally, many of the reforms sought to strengthen the president's control of the executive branch through strategies ranging from new support agencies to fresh budgetary tactics. But even though reform for a century had rested on the belief that the president had to be made powerful enough to act as a real chief administrator, members of Congress and administration critics alike grew increasingly nervous about such strategies. They were not at all sure that real reform would come from stronger presidential control of the executive branch.

PRIVATIZATION, DEVOLUTION, AND REINVENTION

By the late 1970s public administration orthodoxy had badly frayed. Taxpayer revolts spread from California to other parts of the country and, eventually, to Washington. Citizens and elected officials alike increasingly complained that government in general, and bureaucracy in particular, was inefficient and unresponsive. Instead of looking to the long history of bureaucratic reform for fixes, reformers increasingly argued that government ought to be run more like a private business. Indeed, the most conservative reformers argued that government was inherently inefficient. Wherever possible, they argued, government functions ought simply to be turned over to the private sector; where that was not possible, government needed to be subject to the competitive pressures of the marketplace. In a remarkably short time, "privatization," as this strategy came to be known, replaced a century-old tradition of reform through strengthening and rationalizing the executive.

These reform ideas took strong root during the presidency of Ronald Reagan. Reagan appointed corporate leader J. Peter Grace to head a special commission of private sector executives, the President's Private Sector Survey on Cost Control (popularly known as the Grace Commission). The commission, filled with more than 160 business leaders, never actually met. Instead, armies of private sector analysts, lent by their companies, swarmed through the federal government and produced nearly 2,478 recommendations. These recommendations varied widely, from very narrow suggestions dealing with individual agencies to sweeping proposals covering the entire federal government. The commission concluded that these recommendations would produce $424.4 billion in savings over just three years. The federal government, the commission argued, was "suffering from a critical case of inefficient and ineffective management." Only more businesslike practices and huge cuts in government programs could solve the problems.

The Grace Commission differed substantially from virtually all earlier government reform studies. It did not focus on administrative reorganization. Most proposals, instead, argued for cutting programs outright, for imposing more private sector–style management, and for increasing top-level policy control through a new Office of Federal Management. Most important, it shifted the target from improving the executive branch's performance to shrinking its size. Deficit politics had begun to crowd out the Progressives' confidence that government could be structured to produce public good.

Although Grace and his supporters afterwards claimed a broad victory for their effort, few of the commission's proposals were enacted. The commissioners had launched their effort with little sense of what government did or how it differed from the private sector. Their proposals, moreover, quickly ran into powerful opposition from the Democrats who controlled Congress. They saw it as a central part of the Reagan policy revolution, and they were committed to blocking that revolution on every front.

If the Grace Commission had little direct impact, it did fundamentally transform the debate. It marked a fundamental retreat from presidential concern with management. It stimulated a subtle but clear shift in the policy debate from bureaucratic effectiveness to deficit cutting. And it changed the view of public management from an instrument wielded for the public good, as the Progressives envisioned, to the embodiment of some of the government's worst problems.

President Bill Clinton promised a very different approach with his program to "reinvent government." The administration borrowed heavily from the best-selling book of the same name by David Osborne and Ted Gaebler, who had investigated reform at the state and local levels of government. Unlike Hoover-style commissions, in which outside public management experts studied government, and the Grace Commission, which sought to impose private-sector reforms on public agencies, the Clinton reinventing government campaign recruited government bureaucrats to conduct the study. Their job was to recommend changes that could reduce the cost and improve the performance of the federal government.

In just six months the effort, christened the National Performance Review (NPR) and led by Vice President Al Gore, produced a report on "creating a government that works better and costs less." The report identified 130 major recommendations that, the NPR claimed, would save $108 billion over five years. About sixty percent of its savings came from reducing the number of federal employees by 272,900, to less than two million (smaller than at any time since the Kennedy administration). The remaining savings were to come from management improvements that were hard to implement and even harder to quantify.

Gore's effort courted attack from two fronts. Congressional Republicans argued that the effort was far too modest, and that the government needed a more fundamental, Grace Commission–style housecleaning. Especially after the 1994 midterm congressional elections, when Republicans took control of both the House and Senate, the NPR found itself struggling to offer budget cuts large enough to be taken seriously amidst the far more aggressive Republican "Contract with America." On the other hand, many federal administrators felt that the NPR betrayed them. They had at first been reassured because the Clinton administration sought their input, but then they became annoyed because the NPR seemed to them to be focused simply on reducing the number of bureaucrats. In fact, the NPR aimed to reduce the federal work force by at least one-eighth.

The NPR promised a middle ground between improving performance and reducing costs, between traditional reformers and government's more modern critics. It produced genuine improvements in customer service and procurement. It also provided high-level support for many reform ideas that had long been floundering. These savings were real and progress within the executive branch genuine, if overpowered by the downsizing battles. But the NPR struggled to satisfy agency bureaucrats, who desperately wanted affirmation of their work and new processes to help make it more effective, and budget cutters, in Congress and outside, who wanted even deeper cuts. If the NPR produced far more results than the Grace Commission, it nevertheless grappled with the same fundamental dilemma: deciding what government ought to do, and how best it could be done. After a century of reform, the difficult questions about the "what" and "how" of government once again became intertwined, this time in disputes far more difficult to disentangle.

FUZZY RESULTS

Reform has in fact been the great constant of the federal government since the late nineteenth century. Elected officials, especially presidents, have worked to make the bureaucracy more effective, efficient, responsive, and compact. They have differed on whether bureaucracy was a neutral instrument that ought to be honed to do the public's work well, or whether it had itself become part of the problem that needed to be trimmed.

These ongoing struggles have been magnified, in turn, by fundamental fuzziness over the purpose of administrative reform. Some reformers have sought to reinforce or even magnify existing policy by making the bureaucracy stronger. Other reformers have fundamentally disagreed with existing policy and have done battle against it by trying to cut the bureaucracy responsible for implementing it. Reformers have in many cases made substantial progress in managing public programs, but reform has also focused on devising boundaries between the making and administration of public policy. The century of the American reform tradition shows just how fuzzy those boundaries are at best. More important, the reform tradition demonstrates that shaping of the "how" of policy powerfully affects the "what." Elected officials therefore have not only pursued reform for its own sake but also to pursue policy changes through indirect means.

[*See also* Brownlow Committee; Cabinet; Civil Service; Executive Power; Management and Budget, Office of; National Performance Review; *and* President, Executive Office of the.]

BIBLIOGRAPHY

Chandler, Ralph Clark. *A Centennial History of the American Administrative State*. New York, 1987.

Goodnow, Frank. *Politics and Administration*. New York, 1900.

Gore, Al. *From Red Tape to Results: Creating a Government That Works Better and Costs Less*. Washington, D.C., 1993.

Moe, Ronald C. "Traditional Organizational Principles and the Managerial Presidency: From Phoenix to Ashes." *Public Administration Review* 50 (1990): 129–140.

Moe, Ronald C. *Reorganizing the Executive Branch in the Twentieth Century: Landmark Commissions*. Washington, D.C., 1992.

Mosher, Frederick C. *Democracy and the Public Service*. 2d ed. New York, 1982.

Nathan, Richard P. *The Plot That Failed: Nixon and the Administrative Presidency*. New York, 1975.

Osborne, David, and Ted Gaebler. *Reinventing Government: How the Entrepreneurial Spirit Is Transforming the Public Sector*. Reading, Mass., 1992.

President's Committee on Administrative Management [Brownlow Committee]. *Report of the Committee with Special Studies*. Washington, D.C., 1937.

President's Private Sector Survey on Cost Control. *A Report to the President*. Washington, D.C., 1984.

Savas, E. S. *Privatizing the Public Sector: How to Shrink Government*. Chatham, N.J., 1982.

Seidman, Harold, and Robert Gilmour. *Politics, Position, and Power: From the Positive to the Regulatory State*. 4th ed. New York, 1986.

Short, Lloyd M. *The Development of National Administrative Organization in the United States*. Washington, D.C., 1923.

Skowronek, Stephen. *Building a New American State: The Expansion of National Administrative Capacities, 1877–1920*. Cambridge, U.K., 1982.

U.S. Commission on Organization of the Executive Branch of the Government. *General Management of the Executive Branch*. Washington, D.C., 1949.

Wilson, Woodrow. "The Study of Administration." *Political Science Quarterly* 2 (1887): 197–222.

—DONALD F. KETTL

Regulation and Regulatory Agencies

ESSAY   Regulatory agencies are bureaucratic institutions entrusted with the implementation, management, and administration of public policy. They are generally considered inferior to the three constitutional branches of government because their power is derived from and subject to the oversight of the Congress, the presidency, and the judiciary. However, their rules are law and carry the same weight as congressional legislation, presidential executive orders, and judicial decisions. Through the device of delegation of authority, bureaucratic regulatory agencies are vested with the powers pertaining to all three branches of government.

Regulation is defined by Kenneth Meier as "an attempt by the government to control the behavior of citizens, corporations or subgovernments." They are federal requirements, standards, and procedures, backed by the use of penalties or other sanctions, that are intended specifically to govern, modify, and direct the behavior of public and private entities.

When people think of regulation, they usually think of only one type: the command and control regulations whereby the government decides precisely and within quite narrow bounds the actions the regulated entities must take. A requirement that coal-fired power plants must install a scrubber is an example of command and control regulation. However, there are other regulatory forms that give the regulated entities more discretion and take advantage of market forces to achieve the desired results. For example, performance standards require power plants to emit not more than a given number of pounds of sulfur dioxide per million BTU produced. Individual plants are then free to decide the best means of achieving this standard. In addition to issuing binding regulations, agencies also rely on other methods to establish policy, such as policy statements, guidance documents, enforcement manuals, and memos to agency personnel.

Once largely economic in scope—such as the nature of products and prices charged—regulation has seeped over the years into other areas and concerns such as health, safety, protection of the environment, and aesthetics. In each of these areas regulation has a different set of rationales and historical precedents. In the economic domain, regulations attempt to control monopolistic tendencies inherent in the marketplace. Regulations also introduce considerations of equity and fairness that are extraneous to the workings of unchecked capitalism and curtail predatory activities of industries in the pursuit of profit. In this sense, regulations are designed to protect the powerless against the powerful. Historically, this aspect provides the high moral ground that forms the ideological bedrock of regulation. The call for regulation was first raised in the nineteenth century by union leaders, muckrakers, and writers with a strong social conscience who sought the intervention of government as the only defense against the exploitative greed of the robber barons and industrial cartels. In laying down minimum wages for sweatshop workers or monitoring the sanitary conditions in the meatpacking industry, regulators were concerned not merely with expanding the powers of the bureaucracy but in ensuring a decent quality of life for all Americans. But the regulators were fighting not only monopolies but also destructive forms of competition. The railroad price wars of the 1880s and 1890s created anarchic conditions that threatened the creation of a stable transportation system. It was to meet this threat that the Interstate Commerce Commission (ICC), the first regulatory agency, was created in 1887. Technology is another regulatory domain where the rationale is different. Technology has externalities or spillovers, unintended consequences that can cause havoc if not properly controlled. Regulatory agencies establish standards and norms and set the conditions for orderly growth and development. Neither the legislature nor the judiciary is equipped to deal with the velocity of change in a technology-driven world. Environment is another fertile domain for regulations. Such regulations are the corollary of the concept of nature as the global commons to be preserved for future generations and protected against excessive depradations. The most controversial regulations are those that apply to society and morals. Although the state is historically neutral on religious issues, norms of public morality need to be upheld to preserve the integrity of interpersonal relationships and family values. Under this rubric, the state may try to regulate and censor forms of speech and conduct, and also the content of print media, films, and television programs. The common thread running through economic, environmental, technological, and social regulations is the elusive concept of public good. A government's ultimate authority in issuing regulations is as the guardian of this public good.

HISTORY AND GROWTH OF REGULATIONS

The constitutional bedrock of regulations is the commerce clause (Art. 1, Sec. 8), which grants government the legal authority to regulate commerce with foreign nations and among the several states. In the early years of the republic certain regulatory powers, such as the imposition of tariffs, were assigned to the president directly. In 1816 Congress granted sweeping powers to the secretary of the Treasury to regulate the importation of goods into the United States. Subsequently regulatory agencies were established as part of the executive departments. These included the Patent and Trademark Office in 1836, the Comptroller of the Currency in 1863, the Copyright Office in the Library of Congress in 1870, and the Bureau of Fisheries in 1871. As the railroad monopolies began to unravel in the 1880s, the Congress created the ICC as the first true regulatory agency in 1887. As the first effort to shift regulatory powers to the federal government the ICC became the organizational model for later agencies and for serial interventions by the federal government in other sectors of the economy. The Wilson era saw the creation of the Coast Guard and the Tariff Commission in 1915 and 1916 respectively, while the three Republican administrations that followed established the Commodities Exchange Authority in 1922, the Customs Service in 1927, the Federal Radio Commission in 1927, the Federal Power Commission in 1930, and the Food and Drug Administration in 1931. In each case the executive was responding to rather than anticipating industrial and economic changes. It is interesting to note that by the end of the Hoover administration regulation had become a bipartisan activity.

The New Deal was the most fertile spawning ground for regulation, and the period witnessed the creation of numerous regulatory agencies and their expansion into social and administrative areas. In sheer volume of legislation, the

New Deal had no equal. In the economic domain, the New Deal led to the establishment of 1) the Federal Home Loan Bank Board in 1932, 2) the Federal Deposit Insurance Corporation in 1933, 3) the Securities and Exchange Commission in 1934, 4) the National Labor Relations Board in 1935, 5) the Motor Carrier Act of 1935, 6) the U.S. Maritime Administration in 1936, and 7) the Civil Aeronautics Authority in 1938 (renamed the Civil Aeronautics Board in 1940). New legislation conserved wildlife, protected livestock and agricultural production from contamination, ensured the quality of food and grain, the efficacy of drugs, and the purity of milk, and regulated the operation of stockyards and packing houses. The federal government ventured into the energy arena by passing the Federal Water Power Act and increased the powers of the ICC with the Hepburn Act. The centerpiece of the New Deal was the National Industrial Recovery Act, enacted in 1933. It authorized the president to create bodies of rules called codes. In the social domain, New Deal birthed Social Security and a host of social programs channeling benefits to certain groups of people. Agriculture, labor relations, employment conditions, assistance for the aged and disadvantaged, housing and home ownership, and consumer protection were all profoundly affected. Third, the Administrative Procedures Act of 1946 established administrative procedures for the operation of regulatory programs. In 1934, with the creation of the *Federal Register* and the *Code of Federal Regulations* (CFR), this period of extraordinary regulatory growth changed the nature and scope of American government permanently. In 1938 the CFR was made up of 121 chapters. It rose to 138 in 1949, 221 in 1969, 284 in 1979, and 313 in 1989. Agriculture filled eight chapters and twelve hundred pages whereas labor made up just thirty-nine pages. One regulation on which two hundred lawyers worked had seven hundred supporting documents.

The next wave of regulatory expansion was the Great Society era of the 1960s. More than one hundred regulatory statutes were enacted in the 1960s alone, including the crucial Civil Rights Act of 1964 and the National Environmental Policy Act of 1969. The consumer movement that peaked in the 1970s also spawned a number of regulatory agencies. The first auto safety legislation, passed in 1966, was inspired by Ralph Nader, the nemesis of the old laissez-faire auto industry. It was the first of many pieces of regulatory legislation affecting automobiles. Safety was the catchword in three other agencies set up during this period: the National Highway Traffic Safety Administration in 1970, the Federal Highway Administration in 1966, and the Federal Railroad Administration in 1966. The financial and banking sectors were the next to come under the regulatory umbrella. Between 1968 and 1977 Congress enacted the Truth in Lending Act, the Fair Credit Billing Act, the Equal Credit Opportunity Act, the Home Mortgage Disclosure Act, the Consumer Leasing Act, and the Fair Debt Collection Practices Act. The passage of the Consumer Product Safety Act in 1972 led to the establishment of the Consumer Products Safety Commission.

The next wave was the environmental decade that began with the setting up of the Environmental Protection Agency (EPA) in 1970. Environmental legislation, as a whole, required the regulators to identify, locate, prevent, control, or mitigate virtually every form of harmful pollutant or dangerous substance in the air, water, and ground. The EPA sponsored a panoply of acts and statutes including the Clean Air Act of 1970, the Clean Water Act of 1972, the Safe Drinking Water Act of 1974, the Toxic Substances Control Act of 1976, and the Resource Conservation and Recovery Act of 1976. In the wake of these new efforts the words *hazards* and *toxic materials* entered regulatory language. The Materials Transportation Board began in 1975 to regulate the transport of toxic materials and the Office of Surface Mining Reclamation and Enforcement began in 1977 to regulate the strip-mining industry. Workplace safety became another regulatory concern. The Occupational Safety and Health Administration (OSHA) was created in 1970. Within the first month, OSHA adopted some forty-four hundred standards. In 1973 the Mining Enforcement and Safety Administration was established within the Interior Department, and in 1977 it was reorganized as the Mine Safety and Health Administration. Another area of aggressive regulation was energy. On a broad front, the energy problem was attacked by the Federal Energy Administration (FEA) of 1973, the Energy Research and Development Administration (ERDA) of 1974, and the Nuclear Regulatory Commission. In 1977 Carter abolished the FEA and the ERDA and created a cabinet-level Department of Energy in their place. Authority to set energy prices was given to the Federal Energy Regulatory Commission. Finally in the 1980s regulation entered the political arena with the Federal Election Commission.

By the end of the 1980s regulation had become so pervasive that it affected many aspects of American society. At the same time, negative fallout from the web of regulations began to cause concern to legislators and policymakers. For one thing, the cost of compliance with the regulations of these various agencies was estimated in the 1980s at several hundred billion dollars. The law of unintended consequences made some of the most humane regulations the source of new and intractable problems. Aid to Families with Dependent Children was said to be the main culprit in encouraging out-of-wedlock births. Medicare and Medicaid not only altered the physician-patient relationships for the worse but also discouraged children from looking after their parents. There was also the potential for increasing conflicts through lack of coordination among regulatory agencies and among state governments on the one hand and the federal government on the other. Many regulations created uneasy partnerships between federal and state governments in which standards and policies were set in Washington but enforced by the states.

THE TIDE TURNS

The end of the 1970s was a time of disenchantment with government and its social engineering programs. This widespread antiregulatory sentiment crystallized in the election of Ronald Reagan, who had campaigned on the theme that big government is inefficient and wasteful. Following the policy models of British prime minister Margaret Thatcher, a fellow conservative, Reagan set in motion an avalanche of deregulation that eventually extended to air-

lines, telecommunications, securities, trucking, railroads, buses, cable television, oil, natural gas, financial institutions, and public utilities. In each of these areas, deregulation was implemented differently. Only in a few cases were these institutions totally deregulated, but, nevertheless, their cumulative effect was far-reaching. The most severely affected were those in the economic sector, where deregulation represented an effort to reinstate the free market to its dominant role in the American economy. Social regulation was also under attack, but not frontally. The focus of criticism was on the goals of social regulation and on escalating costs. Republican strategy was flexible. In some cases a moratorium was imposed; in others, new rules were enforced, existing procedures were altered, and budgets were cut. In 1981 the Office of Management and Budget was given extensive powers over the regulatory apparatus—the most important reform of the rule-making process since the Administrative Procedures Act of 1946. Executive Order 12291 required the use of cost-benefit analysis and established a net benefit criterion for rule-making. These changes fostered the use of nonregulatory options imposing the least burden on affected parties. Under George Bush, regulatory reform became muted, except for sporadic attempts, such as the creation of the Competitive Council chaired by Vice President Dan Quayle, an aggressive advocate of deregulation. Under Bill Clinton, the first Democratic president in twelve years, the regulatory impulse received an impetus, but he did not want to go against public opinion, which held that regulation was at best a necessary evil to be constantly kept in check and periodically defanged. The major initiative under Clinton was Executive Order 12866, "Regulatory Planning and Review," establishing eleven guidelines for the development of regulations: 1) identification of problems and assessment of their magnitude; 2) review of existing regulations for possible elimination or modification; 3) exploration of nonregulatory alternatives; 4) use of risk assessment to establish regulatory priorities; 5) use of cost-benefit studies to justify regulations; 6) utilization of all available information in reaching regulatory decisions; 7) use of performance objectives; 8) consultation with below-federal-level governments; 9) resolution of conflicts among regulations and deletion of duplication; 10) adoption of the principle of the least burden on society in tailoring regulations; and 11) use of simple language in writing regulations. The National Performance Review was another initiative in the same vein directed by Vice President Al Gore. Described as an effort to "reinvent government," it planned to reduce existing rules by fifty percent within three years and to set up better interagency coordination and reduce red tape.

Despite these efforts, new regulatory statutes continued to proliferate. The new statutes included the Government Securities Act of 1986, the Hazardous and Solid Waste Amendments of 1984, the Safe Drinking Water Act Amendments of 1986, the Electric Consumers Protection Act of 1986, and the Superfund of 1980.

REGULATORY TOOLS

All regulations are born not in the dark recesses of Washington bureaucracy, but in acts of Congress. Statutes define the goals and assign an oversight agency. They also may contain substantive details and procedural guidance. Some statutes are broad and give agencies considerable freedom in devising mechanisms and guidelines. In other cases, Congress microlegislates the details. For example, the Clean Air Act of 1990 and the Delaney amendment to the Pure Food, Drug and Cosmetic Act gave strict guidelines and spelled out the various pollutants to be regulated. The agency has little discretion in these cases. Statutory provisions calling on the agencies to mediate conflicting interests, increase public participation, and conduct specified analyses also limit regulatory discretionary powers and blunt their thrust.

Rule-making is the single most important function of a regulatory agency. Rules are laws in working clothes. The Administrative Procedures Act defines rules as "the whole or part of an agency statement of general or particular applicability and future effect designed to implement, interpret or prescribe law or policy." The keywords are 1) interpret or adapt laws to meet new and changing conditions or technologies; 2) prescribe the details on how the law is to be implemented or put into operation or how specific

goals are to be achieved and quantitatively measured; and 3) consider future effect, or go beyond the merely legal implications of a statute by structuring the future—that is, create new conditions, eliminate existing ones, and prevent others from coming into being. Congress first established uniform methods for rule-making in the Administrative Procedures Act. These principles guide rule-making even today: information, participation, and accountability. Rule-making is also governed by a number of other acts like the Regulatory Flexibility Act, the Paperwork Reduction Act, and the National Environmental Policy Act. Additional constraints are imposed by executive orders, agency- and program-specific authorizations, and appropriations bills. Judicial decisions may mandate some form of public participation, special studies, and feedback from interest groups.

Another effective regulatory tool is the granting of licenses and permits for various activities. Licenses and permits serve a number of interrelated purposes. They are used to impose conditions on the activity for which the permit is being issued. Most environmental, health, safety, and natural resource regulations involve licenses and permits. They also require the applicants to submit extensive background information and consult in advance with other agencies and groups with a stake in the activity. Sometimes, licenses may contain dozens of conditions or articles committing the licensee to regard the public interest and also reserve the right to revoke the license if these conditions are not met. These licenses invariably carry substantial fees that form a source of income for the regulatory agencies.

IMPLEMENTATION

The enforcement of regulations begins with their publication in the *Federal Register*. Sometimes regulatory agencies may communicate directly with the regulated parties. Agencies provide technical supplements to rules. OSHA goes further and provides free regulatory audits, that is, no-fault surveys of a corporation's compliance records. In this manner, a company can obtain authoritative information on its compliance status without threats of enforcement. Monitoring is another regulatory activity. Some regulations require regulated parties to monitor their own activities, submit periodic reports, and make these available to inspectors. Inspection is the most common form of monitoring. In some cases inspection can be constant, like supervision; in others, it may be random, depending on the number of establishments on the books and the number and budget of the agency staff. Enforcement of the last resort is intervention after a violation has occurred. Inspectors may issue citations or negotiate with the violators for a settlement on terms that may not be burdensome to the affected parties. As a last resort, an agency may impose a range of sanctions based on the nature and intensity of the noncompliance. Sanctions come in the form of warnings, fines, product recalls, suspension or termination of licenses and permits, and criminal penalties. Some statutes grant authority to the agency to impose sanctions while others require the agency to seek court orders. When criminal penalties are involved, the matter is usually referred to the Department of Justice for prosecution. Sanctions are also public relations debacles for the corporations involved and often lead to serious losses.

Conflict is common between enforcing agencies and the regulated parties. Congress has provided for dispute resolution. The most common form of dispute resolution is adjudication, a time-consuming and cumbersome court trial with hearings, evidence, oral arguments, and formal judicial decisions. Many disputes are resolved through a consent order, which is a regulatory plea bargain. Thus the regulatory process moves from the legislative to the executive and from the executive to the judicial domain in order to achieve its goals.

ANALYSES

The regulatory process involves at least five types of analyses. An analysis is made at every stage before a significant decision is made. 1) Legal analysis assesses the mandate given by the relevant statute to the agency and relevant judicial and other administrative decisions affecting the regulation. 2) Policy analysis takes place as well. Regulators must hew to the priorities and preferences of the political leadership of the agency. These policy preferences need to be incorporated into the rules. 3) Scientific and technical analysis

must ask whether the proposed regulation conforms to the state of the art in technology, is compatible with environmental and other requirements, and is technically feasible. The accuracy of the technical analysis determines the success of the regulation. 4) Risk analysis is perhaps the most controversial. It seeks to establish the nature and degree of risk of a regulation to the health and safety of humans, animals, and plants, and whether this risk is more than that posed by the activity the regulation is designed to control. Risk analyses may vary widely in their conclusions; even within a single agency the criteria used to establish risk may vary. The EPA administers several statutes each seeking different levels of risk reduction. 5) Cost-benefit analysis emerged during the Reagan era as a major tool to slow the regulatory process. Such analyses began in 1976 under President Ford as economic impact analysis. The program was continued under Carter, who required agencies to prepare statements on the economic impact of major government regulations. Executive Order 12044 set the criteria to govern the analyses: "a succint statement of the problem, a description of alternatives, and an explanation for choosing one option over the others." Carter also created the Regulatory Analysis Review Group chaired by a member of the Council of Economic Advisers. Reagan's Executive Order 12291 of 1981 required a cost-benefit analysis from agencies and gave the Office of Management and Budget broad authority to review compliance. The administration called for a review of major regulations having a measurable impact on the economy of $100 million or more, and likely to have an adverse effect on competition, employment, investment, productivity, innovation, and the ability of the United States to compete in foreign markets or with foreign-based enterprises in domestic markets. Cost-benefit analyses may sound scientific, but present a number of problems. They introduce political ideology into the regulatory process and also suffer from the difficulty of measuring intangible benefits that may take a long time to materialize while costs are immediate and painful. Other analytic tools include the Regulatory Flexibility Act, which considers the effects of rules on small business; environmental impact statements; and the Paperwork Reduction

Act, which requires agencies to think carefully about their information needs.

OVERSIGHT

Regulatory agencies remain subject to a number of oversight mechanisms. The most important are the controls exercised by the White House. Presidents exert their control through two principal means: appointive power over the personnel of regulatory agencies and budgetary control under the Budget and Accounting Act of 1921 and its extension in 1939. Presidents may use their powers to increase or slash budgets of the regulatory agencies. Presidents also issue executive orders centralizing review of regulations within the Office of Management and Budget. Congressional oversight is based on six principles: 1) ensuring compliance with legislative intent, 2) determining the effectiveness of regulatory policies, 3) preventing waste and dishonesty, 4) preventing abuse in the administrative process, 5) representing the public interest, and 6) preventing agency usurpation of legislative authority. Congress uses several tools in ensuring the political accountability of regulatory agencies. The first is the annual review of budgetary appropriations, when Congress may specify purposes for which funds may be used. The second is the authorization process, when Congress determines whether the agency should be continued. Congress may also decide to narrow the agency's mandate periodically. In addition to formal oversight powers, there are nonstatutory controls, such as hearings, directives in committee reports, sunset provisions, and individual case work. Congress may launch investigations into specific abuses and into disregard of the public interest. Statutes require regulatory agencies to submit detailed reports to committees. Nevertheless, Congress is hampered in the exercise of its oversight functions by the committee structure, information lag, and inadequate staff. Often oversight is undertaken only in response to crises or complaints. Routine surveillance is replaced by episodic fire alarms. Judicial control over regulatory agencies consists in the right of the judiciary to intervene and review the actions of the regulators.

Regulatory agencies are in a state of transition. An improved regulatory system needs to produce regulations that achieve their goals more efficiently, with less delay, and more economically. To do this regulatory agencies must have the flexibility to strike the proper balance and focus clearly on the public good.

[*See also* Federal Register *and* Appendix: Paperwork Reduction Act, Executive Order 12044, Executive Order 12291, Executive Order 12498, *and* Executive Order 12866.]

BIBLIOGRAPHY

Bryner, Gary. *Bureaucratic Discretion: Laws and Policy in Federal Regulatory Agencies.* Elmsford, N.Y., 1987.

Eads, George C., and Michael Fix. *Relief or Reform? Reagan's Regulatory Dilemma.* Washington, D.C., 1984.

Kerwin, Cornelius. *Rulemaking: How Government Agencies Write Law and Make Policy.* Washington, D.C., 1994.

Meier, Kenneth. *Regulation: Politics, Bureaucracy and Economics.* New York, 1985.

—GEORGE THOMAS KURIAN

Reorganization Act.

See Appendix: Basic Documents of Public Administration.

Republican Party.

See Political Parties and the Federal Government.

Resolution Trust Corporation

In August 1989 Congress passed the Financial Institution Reform, Recovery, and Enforcement Act, which in turn created the Resolution Trust Corporation (RTC). The RTC's mission was to resolve one of the worst financial disasters in United States history. Financial problems began when savings and loan institutions, which served mainly to finance home purchases, could not compete with banks because interest rate fluctuations left thrifts paying more to depositors than they were earning on loans. In order to solve the problems, in the 1980s Congress deregulated the thrift industry. Deregulation in turn created a wave of real estate speculation that resulted in massive losses in the thrift industry. Once created, the RTC shut down faltering institutions. Headquartered in Washington, D.C., and with the help of field offices and sales centers in Atlanta, Georgia, Newport Beach, California, Dallas, Texas, Denver, Colorado, Kansas City, Missouri, and Valley Forge, Pennsylvania, the agency held auctions to sell mortgages and real estate to the highest bidders. Additionally, a low-income housing program made homes available to the poor.

Additionally, the RTC brought violators to justice and recovered money. The Justice Department reported that more than thirty-seven hundred senior executives and owners of failed thrifts served time in prison for crime, including loan fraud and insider dealing that was rampant in many institutions.

On 21 December 1991 Congress expanded the powers and scope of the RTC when it passed the Resolution Trust Corporation Refinancing, Restructuring, and Improvement Act. The new law provided the RTC with $25 billion in funding through 1 April 1992, extended the RTC's ability to accept appointment as conservator, and redesignated the RTC Oversight Board as the Thrift Depositor Protection Oversight Board. The board's members included the secretary of the Treasury, who also chaired the board, and the chairperson of the Board of Directors of the Federal Deposit Insurance Corporation (FDIC). The Improvement Act also abolished the RTC Board of Directors and removed the FDIC as exclusive manager of the RTC.

To replace the FDIC role, it created the Office of the Chief Executive Officer of the RTC, requiring appointment to that office by the president with the advice and consent of the Senate. The chairperson of the Board of Governors of the Federal Reserve System serves on the board along with two independent members appointed by the president, with the advice and consent of the Senate.

The RTC closed its doors and ceased to exist on 31 December 1995, nearly six and a half years after its creation and one year ahead of the closure date originally mandated by Congress. By that time the agency closed or merged 747 thrifts, protected twenty-five million depositor accounts, and sold more than $465 billion in assets, including 120,000 real estate properties at a cost to taxpayers of $145 billion. Estimates of the final cost, however, are near $400 billion after counting the years of interest on the money borrowed to finance the federal cleanup. The FDIC handled the unfinished business of the RTC.

[See also Thrift Supervision, Office of.]

BIBLIOGRAPHY

Grimsley, Kirstin Downey. "After Closing Many Doors, RTC Shuts Its Own." Washington Post, 29 December 1995, D1.
Resolution Trust Corporation. 1989 Annual Report: Resolution Trust Corporation. Washington, D.C., 1989.
Resolution Trust Corporation. 1994 Annual Report: Resolution Trust Corporation: Resolving the Crisis, Restoring the Confidence. Washington, D.C., 1994.
Resolution Trust Corporation. "RTC to Offer $700 Million in Loans in Final National Loan Auction in Kansas City." News Release. Washington, D.C., 24 October 1995.
—VERONICA D. DICONTI

Revenue-Cutter Service

On 4 August 1790 Congress authorized Treasury Secretary Alexander Hamilton to "establish and support" ten cutters to enforce the nation's maritime revenue laws. Stationed in the principal seaports, these small vessels were commanded by customs officers and controlled by local collectors of customs. Until 1797 they composed the nation's only maritime armed force.

A year later several were ordered to duty with the Navy in the Quasi-War with France, and with the exception of the war against Tripoli (1803–1806), revenue cutters served in all of the United States' nineteenth-century wars. Other duties followed, some temporary—enforcement of President Thomas Jefferson's unpopular embargo (1807–1809) and suppression of piracy on the Gulf coast (1819–1820)—while others were longer-lived: support of health and quarantine laws passed by some states to curb infectious diseases that might be transmitted by vessels trading to tropical regions beginning in 1799; prohibition of the foreign slave trade after 1807; and in 1832, prevention of illegal logging in live oak forests and cruising off the coast during winter months to assist vessels in distress. When the U.S. government appropriated public funds for lifesaving equipment on the shores adjacent to the approaches to New York in 1848, the act specified that cutter service officers supervise the expenditures, and from that point forward, what eventually grew into the U.S. Life-Saving Service was fostered by the Revenue-Cutter Service, albeit not under that name.

The "Revenue Service" or the "Revenue-Marine," as the service was usually called, did not have a formal appellation during its first century; only during the 1890s was it named the Revenue-Cutter Service. Similarly, it had no true central organization, although in 1843 a captain was ordered to head the Revenue-Marine Bureau in the Treasury Department to oversee all matters pertaining to the service. That experiment ended in 1849; twenty years later, Secretary George S. Boutwell established boards to consider the condition of the service, leading to a recommendation for a central organization. In 1871 Sumner I. Kimball became chief of the Revenue-Marine Division in the Treasury Department, holding that position until 1878, when he assumed control of the new Life-Saving Service. The service continued to be headed by a civilian until 1889, when Captain Leonard G. Shepard became commandant. He was followed by Captains Charles F. Shoemaker (1895–1905), Worth G. Ross (1905–1911), and Ellsworth P. Bertholf (1911–1915).

Meanwhile, the service's duties continued to expand. Cutters reconnoitered Alaskan waters immediately following the territory's acquisition in 1867, supported governmental authorities, protected the fur seal herd from poachers, and patrolled the Bering Sea and Arctic Ocean off Alaska. Harbor cutters enforced anchorage regulations in the larger seaports, beginning with New York in 1888, and patrolled regattas, while larger cutters were active in derelict destruction during the 1880s and thereafter. Its facilities grew

as well: the School of Instruction for officers began in 1877, and in 1899 a ship-repair and boat-building yard took shape at Curtis Bay, Maryland. On 28 January 1915 the Revenue-Cutter Service was merged with the Life-Saving Service to form the U.S. Coast Guard.

[See also Coast Guard and Life-Saving Service.]

BIBLIOGRAPHY

Canney, Donald L. U.S. Coast Guard and Revenue Cutters, 1790–1935. Annapolis, 1995.
Evans, Stephen H. The United States Coast Guard, 1790–1915: A Definitive History. Annapolis, 1949.
Kern, Florence. The United States Revenue Cutters in the Civil War. Washington, D.C., 1988.
King, Irving H. George Washington's Coast Guard. Annapolis, 1978.
King, Irving H. The Coast Guard under Sail. Annapolis, 1989.
Smith, Darrell H., and Fred W. Powell. The Coast Guard: Its History, Activities, and Organization. Washington, D.C., 1929.
—ROBERT E. JOHNSON

Rural Development Administration

Created in 1990, the Rural Development Administration (RDA) was the successor to the Farmers Home Administration and was assigned additional programs to promote economic development, health care, and water supply in rural areas. The RDA is headed by an administrator who is appointed by the president and confirmed by the Senate. The RDA provides technical assistance and administers credit programs of the Rural Development Insurance Fund. It has seven regional offices and approximately 125 area offices. Financial assistance is provided through three programs: Water and Waste Disposal, Business and Industry, and Community Facilities. The RDA also provides administrative assistance to public and private agencies through its Rural Development Strategy Assistance Program. The Water and Waste Disposal Program extends assistance to towns with fewer than ten thousand people (five thousand for emergency grants), the Business and Industry Program provides loans to towns with fewer than fifty thousand people, and the Community Facilities Program provides loans to towns with fewer than twenty thousand people.

—George Thomas Kurian

Rural Utility Service

A lending agency within the Department of Agriculture, the Rural Utility Service (RUS) was set up under the Rural Electrification Act of 1936 as the Rural Electrification Administration. It adopted the new name in 1994. It is headed by an administrator who is appointed by the president and confirmed by the Senate. The RUS makes insured loans and loan guarantees to more than nineteen hundred rural electric and telephone cooperatives and companies at variable and fixed rates established by Congress. The RUS also guarantees through the Federal Financing Bank loans from non-RUS sources and operates the Rural Telephone Bank (of which the RUS administrator is the governor), which makes loans to telephone systems. In addition the RUS makes ten-year interest-free loans under the Rural Economic Development Loan and Grant Program and also grants to water and sewage services.

—George Thomas Kurian

S

Science and Technology Policy, Office of

 The primary functions of the Office of Science and Technology Policy (OSTP), a federal agency located within the Executive Office of the President, are to provide the president with expert advice on all matters relating to science and technology and to coordinate the federal government's research and development (R&D) activities. [*See* President, Executive Office of the.] It is also responsible for communicating the president's science and technology policies and programs to Congress and the public. The OSTP is led by a director and four associate directors, all of whom are appointed by the president and confirmed by the Senate. The director also carries the title of assistant to the president for science and technology (or, more popularly, the president's science adviser).

The OSTP advises the president on the scientific and technical aspects of major issues such as health care, environmental regulation, and national security, as well as on matters of direct concern to the R&D community. In order to address these issues effectively, the OSTP is organized into four divisions, each headed by an associate director. The Environment Division seeks to ensure that federal policies relating to air and water quality, toxic substances, hazardous wastes, and other related issues are based upon sound scientific and technical principles. The National Security and International Affairs Division is concerned with defense technologies, the technical aspects of arms control and nonproliferation policies, and export controls. The Science Division and Technology Division cover federal policies on fundamental scientific research and technological development, including education in science and engineering.

The science and technology programs sponsored by the federal government are spread across a large number of agencies and departments. The National Science and Technology Council (NSTC, known prior to 1993 as the Federal Coordinating Council on Science, Engineering and Technology) is charged with coordinating all this activity and ensuring that it is consistent with other federal goals. The NSTC is a cabinet-level organization within the OSTP, chaired by the president, consisting of the vice president, the science adviser, the national security adviser, the director of the Office of Management and Budget, the chair of the Council of Economic Advisers, and the heads of all cabinet departments (Energy, Defense, Health and Human Services, Commerce, Interior, Education, Transportation, Agriculture, and State) and independent agencies (National Science Foundation, National Aeronautics and Space Administration, National Institutes of Health, and the Environmental Protection Agency) concerned with R&D policy.

Since most research and development in the United States is done in the private sector, it is extremely important that the views of scientists and engineers from corporations and universities be represented in federal R&D policy. Accordingly, President Clinton created the President's Committee of Advisers on Science and Technology (PCAST) in 1993. The PCAST is made up of eighteen prominent individuals from business and academe, appointed by the president, plus the science adviser.

Although the OSTP is a relatively young organization—it was officially established in 1976—its origins go back more than fifty years. During World War II the federal government began investing heavily in science and technology and sought to organize the work of large numbers of the nation's scientists and engineers in support of the war effort. The primary vehicle for this was the Office of Scientific Research and Development (OSRD). Little attempt was made, however, to bring science directly into the White House, or to provide the president with full-time expertise on scientific or technical matters. For the most part, President Roosevelt felt more comfortable with generalists rather than specialists for his closest advisers, although he did make use of experts from the OSRD on an *ad hoc* basis. In fact, it was in response to a presidential request that the head of the OSRD, Dr. Vannevar Bush, produced the report that ultimately led to the creation of the National Science Foundation. President Truman followed a similar approach. He established a science committee within the Office of Defense Mobilization that could provide expert advice "from time to time," but it does not appear that he consulted it very often.

It was the launch of *Sputnik,* the world's first artificial satellite, by the Soviet Union in October 1957 that finally brought science advising into the Oval Office. With the opening of the "space race," President Eisenhower saw the need for continuing high-level advice on scientific and technical issues. A few weeks after *Sputnik,* Eisenhower announced the creation of the President's Science Advisory Committee (PSAC), in many ways a forerunner of the OSTP. James R. Killian, Jr., then president of the Massachusetts Institute of Technology, became the first presidential science adviser.

The PSAC was abolished by President Nixon in 1973. As would later happen with the OSTP, historians of science policy still debate the committee's overall effectiveness during its sixteen-year existence. In some areas, such as the space program of the 1960s, the PSAC's influence was negligible. In a few other cases, however, like the development of the U.S. national air traffic control system and the early laws governing communication satellites, it did play a significant role.

From 1973 to 1976 presidential science advising briefly returned to the early postwar model, although it should be noted that the level of sci-

entific expertise available in most federal agencies and cabinet departments had risen significantly. Still, given that throughout the late 1960s and 1970s public officials were becoming increasingly involved with highly specialized issues like environmental quality, energy supplies, toxic wastes, and nuclear power, many in government felt that there was a need for "in-house" scientific and technical advice. By 1972 Congress had established its own advisory body, the Office of Technology Assessment (which was abolished in 1995). Four years later, in passing the National Science and Technology Policy, Organization, and Priorities Act, it did the same for the president, creating the OSTP and reestablishing the post of (official) science adviser.

While it has outlasted the PSAC and is generally well regarded in both scientific and political circles, the OSTP has had to deal with its own share of controversy. Much of this has stemmed from the inherent ambiguity of its role. As a purely advisory body, it has no power to set policy on its own. Its actual level of influence, even over its primary areas of concern, is really a function of how the president chooses to use it, which, of course, varies from one administration to the next. Thus, it is not unusual for a science adviser to feel caught between the demands and views of the scientific community and the pronouncements of the chief executive.

In the Reagan administration, for example, science advisor George Keyworth was a strong supporter of the president's proposed Strategic Defense Initiative (a plan to create a defensive system against nuclear missiles), despite strong reservations on the part of the science and engineering community. Similarly, during the mid-1990s a top priority of the Clinton administration and Congress was balancing the federal budget. This required large cuts in discretionary spending, including funding for scientific research programs. Not surprisingly, such moves faced strong opposition from scientists and engineers. The OSTP (and particularly Clinton science adviser John Gibbons) had to play a difficult role in balancing out administration policies with the growing hostility of its primary constituency.

A more recent controversy involved priorities

within R&D spending itself. As the cost of carrying out research programs rises (and the budget for supporting them shrinks), there has been an increasing level of competition among various disciplines, and different ideas on how such money should be spent. During the 1970s, for example, a large number of scientists expressed concern over the resources being devoted to the development of the space shuttle, fearing that it would mean less money not only for other space-based projects, but for most other areas of R&D as well. More recently, many physicists (as well as scientists from other fields) complained about the proposed $8 billion price tag of the Superconducting Super Collider, which probably played some role in the project's 1993 cancellation. As the most highly placed, centralized, and visible agency concerned with federal science policy, the OSTP often finds itself at the center of such disputes.

Finally, there has been increasing controversy about the role of government in science and technology. Most elected officials, and much of the public at large, support the idea of investing in basic scientific research, particularly in fields that—for reasons of cost, risk, or time—private industry will not fund. Not everyone agrees, however, on how the federal government should deal with applied science, that is, R&D intended for direct use in the private sector. Some think that federal support is necessary to ensure U.S. competitiveness in world markets. Others feel that such investments are the responsibility of private business. However this debate is resolved (and, given its importance, it will likely continue for some time), the OSTP will certainly play a central role, both in the discussion and the implementation of whatever policy changes result.

BIBLIOGRAPHY

Bromley, D. Allan. "Science and Technology: From Eisenhower to Bush." *Presidential Studies Quarterly* 21 (1991): 243–250.

Brooks, Harvey. "Issues in High-Level Science Advising." In *Science and Technology Advice to the President, Congress, and the Judiciary*, 2d ed., edited by William T. Golden. New Brunswick, N.J., 1995.

Dickson, David. *The New Politics of Science.* New York, 1984.

Katz, James Everett. *Presidential Politics and Science Policy.* New York, 1978.

Killian, James R., Jr. *Sputniks, Scientists, and Eisenhower: A Memoir of the First Special Assistant to the President for Science and Technology.* Cambridge, Mass., 1982.

Lambright, W. Henry. *Presidential Management of Science and Technology: The Johnson Presidency.* Austin, 1985.

Morin, Alexander J. *Science Policy and Politics.* Englewood Cliffs, N.J., 1993.

Smith, Bruce L. R. *American Science Policy since World War II.* Washington, D.C., 1990.

Smith, Bruce L. R. *The Advisors: Scientists in the Policy Process.* Washington, D.C., 1992.

Teich, Albert H., and Jill H. Pace. *Science and Technology in the USA.* Harlow, U.K., 1986.

Wiesner, Jerome B. "The Rise and Fall of the President's Science Advisory Committee." In *Science and Technology Advice to the President, Congress, and the Judiciary*, 2d ed., edited by William T. Golden. New Brunswick, N.J., 1995.

—W. D. KAY

Secret Service

The United States Secret Service has two distinct and unique missions, those of protection and of investigation. The Secret Service was originally organized on 5 July 1865 as an investigative division of the Department of the Treasury to suppress widespread counterfeiting of United States currency. At the close of the Civil War, between one-third and one-half of all United States paper currency in circulation was counterfeit. Within less than a decade, efforts by the Secret Service sharply reduced this crisis. In 1883 the Secret Service was officially acknowledged as a distinct organization within the Treasury Department. However, it was still dependent on the annual appropriations and the availability of funds since enabling legislation was nonexistent. (This was rectified with the passage of Public Law 82-79 on 16 July 1951, which provided permanent authority for the Secret Service to perform certain functions and activities that had been carried out through authority contained in the Department of the Treasury's annual appropriations acts.)

INVESTIGATIVE MISSION

During its early years the Secret Service investigated many cases unrelated to counterfeiting.

These included the Ku Klux Klan, the "Whisky Ring," naturalization document fraud, the "Louisiana Lottery," government land fraud, the "Beef Trust" monopoly, and the Teapot Dome oil scandals. The service also conducted counterespionage activity during the Spanish-American War and World War I. During World War II the Secret Service assisted the Office of Price Administration in detecting and arresting persons who manufactured, used, or distributed counterfeit ration stamps.

The Secret Service continues to suppress the counterfeiting of currency and securities of the United States and of foreign governments. The service is also responsible for investigating the fraud and forgery of United States checks, bonds, and other obligations. In 1984 Congress passed legislation expanding Secret Service investigative jurisdiction further to include fraud related to false identification documents and devices; fraud and related activities involving credit and debit cards; investigative authority relating to computer fraud; and, at the direction of the secretary of the Treasury, authorization to investigate fraud associated with the electronic funds transfer system of the United States Treasury. In 1990 Congress further expanded the service's jurisdiction regarding criminal violations against federally insured financial institutions to include savings and loan investigations.

PROTECTIVE MISSION

In addition to its investigative mission, the Secret Service is also responsible for protecting the president. The service had provided informal security beginning in 1894 to President Grover Cleveland and later to William McKinley. However, after the assassination of President McKinley in 1901, over seventeen bills concerning the protection of the president were introduced yet unsuccessfully acted on by Congress. As a result, the secretary of the Treasury assigned the Secret Service to protect President Theodore Roosevelt on a full-time basis. In 1906 Congress enacted legislation that provided funds for presidential protection by the Secret Service and finally authorized permanent protection of the president in 1913. In 1917 the protection of the president's immediate family was authorized by statute. In

that same year Congress enacted legislation making it a crime to threaten the president of the United States by mail or any other manner. Since that time the service's protection responsibilities expanded to include a number of temporary assignments. Among these were the protection of foreign leaders during World War II; the protection of valuable documents such as the Declaration of Independence, the United States Constitution, and the Gutenberg Bible; and providing security for Leonardo da Vinci's *Mona Lisa* during its exhibition in the United States (1962–1963).

Following the assassination of President John Kennedy in 1963, President Lyndon Johnson established the President's Commission on the Assassination of President Kennedy (The Warren Commission). Based on the commission's recommendations in its extensive report, the Secret Service increased its number of agents assigned to presidential protection, worked to expand its special agent training, further developed the protective intelligence function, and increased its liaison with law enforcement and other federal agencies. The service added new technical security apparatus, automated data processing, and improved communications equipment. Also, the organization's internal structure was reorganized to include: director; assistant to the director—Inspection and Audit; assistant to the director—Information and Liaison Counsel; assistant director—Investigations; assistant director—Protective Intelligence; assistant director—Protective Forces; and assistant director—Administration.

As a result of the assassination of presidential candidate Robert Kennedy in 1968, Congress authorized that the Secret Service protect major presidential and vice presidential candidates and nominees, unless protection is declined. In 1971 the service was sanctioned to protect visiting heads of a foreign state or government. Today, the Secret Service is charged with protecting the president, vice president, the president-elect, vice president–elect and their immediate families, former presidents and their spouses, widows of former presidents until death or remarriage, children of a former president until age sixteen, visiting heads of foreign states or governments, major presidential and vice presidential candidates and their spouses, and other individuals at the direction of the president.

THE SECRET SERVICE UNIFORMED DIVISION

The first formal attempt to provide security at the White House occurred during the Civil War. The "Bucktail Brigade," composed of the 150th Regiment of the Pennsylvania Volunteers, and four officers from the Metropolitan Washington Police Force were assigned to protect White House property. On 14 September 1922 President Warren G. Harding created the White House Police under the supervision of the White House military aide's office.

After an incident in which an unexpected and unknown visitor entered the White House dining room in 1930, President Herbert Hoover recommended that the White House Police and the Secret Service could better coordinate their efforts if they were under centralized control. Since the Secret Service protected presidents, it should handle all aspects of presidential protection. On 14 May 1930 Congress instructed that the chief of the Secret Service supervise the White House Police Force.

White House Police responsibilities increased sharply in 1970 to include security for foreign diplomatic missions in the Washington, D.C., area. In addition, the force was renamed the Executive Protective Service in March 1970. In 1974, when Congress authorized the protection of the vice president's immediate family, the Executive Protective Service gained further duties. On 15 November 1977 the name of the force officially became the United States Secret Service Uniformed Division.

The Secret Service Uniformed Division provides security at the White House, the vice president's residence, buildings in which presidential offices are located, the United States Treasury Building and the Treasury Annex, foreign diplomatic missions in the Washington, D.C., metropolitan area, and foreign diplomatic establishments in other parts of the United States as the president may direct. Uniformed Division officers carry out their protective responsibilities through a network of foot and vehicular patrols and fixed posts. They also provide additional assistance to the overall Secret Service protective

mission through special support programs such as the canine, magnetometer, and counter sniper units.

ORGANIZATION

The Secret Service has approximately forty-six hundred employees, with field offices located throughout the continental United States and in Alaska, Hawaii, and Puerto Rico, as well as liaison offices in Paris, France; London, England; Bonn, Germany; Rome, Italy; and Bangkok, Thailand.

The Secret Service is under the direction of its eighteenth director, Eljay B. Bowron. Deputy Director Richard J. Griffin assists the director in planning and directing activities of the Secret Service and in formulating general policies for the enforcement of the laws over which the service has jurisdiction. To accomplish its various missions, the Secret Service is organized into seven major offices, each headed by an assistant director. These offices are Inspection, Protective Operations, Protective Research, Investigations, Administration, Government Liaison and Public Affairs, and Training. In addition, the Office of the Chief Counsel provides specialized support to the organization as a staff function to the director.

Throughout their careers special agents serve on both investigative and protective assignments. Agents while assigned to investigative duties in the service's field offices also serve as a source of additional manpower for temporary protective details, such as those for candidates or visiting foreign dignitaries.

During the first year on the job, a special agent receives five months of formal classroom and simulation training. The remaining seven months are spent in an on-the-job training program. Special agents begin general investigative training at the Federal Law Enforcement Training Center in Glynco, Georgia. They continue to receive comprehensive and specialized protective and investigative training at Secret Service facilities in the Washington, D.C., area. The training curriculum consists of protective techniques, investigative procedures, criminal law, rules of evidence, surveillance techniques, undercover operations, interviewing techniques, defensive measures, and emergency medicine. Special emphasis is placed on the jurisdiction areas of counterfeiting, forgery, financial crimes, and physical protection.

Numerous specialists in a wide variety of occupations also contribute their expertise to the Secret Service's investigative and protective missions. They include security specialists, electronics engineers, communications technicians, research psychologists, computer experts, armorers, intelligence analysts, polygraph examiners, forensic experts, and professionals in many other fields.

BIBLIOGRAPHY

Bowen, Walter S., and Harry Edward Neal. *The United States Secret Service.* Philadelphia, 1960.
Report of the President's Commission on the Assassination of President John F. Kennedy. Washington, D.C., 1964.
U.S. Department of the Treasury. *Excerpts From the History of the United States Secret Service, 1865–1975.* Washington, D.C., 1975.
U.S. Department of the Treasury. *United States Secret Service Moments in History, 1865–1990.* Washington, D.C., 1990.

—MIKE SAMPSON

Securities and Exchange Commission

An independent agency of the federal government, the Securities and Exchange Commission (SEC) is charged with regulating the distribution, sale, and trading of stocks, bonds, and other securities in order to protect the investing public. Its authority is vast, extending to the major markets for trading securities, corporations that sell securities to the public, investment companies such as mutual funds, and the accounting profession through oversight of the Financial Accounting Standards Board. The agency makes rules and regulations for market operations and for participation in the markets by the companies that issue securities, professionals who facilitate the trading of securities, and investors who buy and sell them. The SEC also brings enforcement actions when regulations are violated.

When a company needs to raise capital it works with an investment banking firm to finance and sell an initial distribution of securities in the primary market. Investors who buy the securities own shares of the company. Following the initial sale, these securities are bought and sold (or traded) by investors in one of two types of secondary markets. A centralized trading market, or floor, is called an exchange, such as the New York or American Stock Exchange. Here, a secondary market for securities is made by brokers and specialists who are members of that exchange. Brokers take orders to buy and sell securities from investors and pass them on to the exchange specialist who maintains a book of orders for buying and selling securities. Trades are made when the specialist matches book orders with the orders brought to the floor by brokers, or when the specialist acts as an auctioneer taking bids for the sale and purchase of broker orders. In exchange for their privileged position on the exchange floor, specialists have an obligation to buy securities through their own account when the market is falling, and to sell securities when the market is rising. This offers investors and companies that issue and trade securities some assurance of market continuity and liquidity.

A secondary market is also made over the counter. Unlike an exchange, trading does not take place on a central floor but through dealers who trade over the phone and with computers— and before the days of computer, by telegraph. These dealers compete to make a market in particular securities by charging a competitive markup to other dealers and investors: investors who want to purchase securities are charged an increment above the current market value (what the dealer views as the value of the securities) and those who want to sell are given an increment below that value. As long as dealers are willing to buy and sell, or as long as the markup is attractive to buyers and sellers, trading continues. Unlike the specialists in an exchange market, over-the-counter dealers are not obligated to buy and sell securities from their accounts during falling and rising markets, respectively. Without such safeguards, this market is a low-cost alternative for companies unable to meet the capital requirements necessary to have their securities listed and traded on an exchange, or unwilling to pay the listing fee, and to investors and other dealers wanting to avoid brokerage fees—which is typically more expensive than a dealer's markup.

Before 1933 a combination of state laws and industry self-governance provided scant regulatory protection for the investing public in both the primary and secondary markets. A collection of "blue sky" laws, intended to protect investors from securities dealers selling shares of anything (even the sky), provided some protection on a state-by-state basis, in part by regulating the information contained in a prospectus—a statement about the company issuing the securities intended to promote the sale of an issue. But the rigor of enforcement varied between states, and the regulations did not extend to securities traded interstate. Meanwhile, in the two largest secondary markets, the New York Stock Exchange and the American Stock Exchange (before 1930, the New York Curb Exchange), a system of internal regulation covered trading practices, qualifications for membership (an exchange seat), and the requirements for corporations listing their securities with the exchange.

The stock market crash in October 1929 and a series of Wall Street scandals, however, exposed the limitations of both state regulation and internal exchange regulation for protecting investors. In the early 1920s a growing economy and buoyant stock market drew investors of all kinds to the securities markets. Before the market fell in October 1929, 1.125 billion shares of stock were traded on the New York Stock Exchange for the year. Approximately $10.2 billion in new securities flooded the primary markets in the same year, and speculative interest in many unknown companies pushed the price of securities higher than warranted. In the rush to invest, many investors lost a great deal of money as the price of new securities fell in secondary market trading. On the exchanges, market professionals often manipulated the price of securities through collusive buying and selling and the "leaking" of untrue information about any given issue of securities. In the wake of the crash, the vulnerability of the small investor to the sale of "hot" issues (new issues often from unknown companies) and the manipulation of securities prices in the secondary market was evident.

With strong public sentiment for the federal regulation of Wall Street, President Franklin Roosevelt took office in 1933 with an agenda to prevent fraudulent issues of securities, to restrict the trading practices of insiders on the stock exchanges, and to make the markets more accountable to the public. The Securities Act of 1933 and the Securities Exchange Act of 1934 met both objectives.

The Securities Act requires companies selling new securities to the public to disclose financial information that is material for making an investment decision. Before the creation of the SEC in 1934, this legislation required companies to register a new issue of securities with the Federal Trade Commission (FTC). The agency would review the disclosure documents for irregularities in the content or reporting of the information, register the issue, and allow the sale of the issue on the twentieth day after the company filed. If the filing were incomplete or incorrect, the FTC could place a stop order on the issue. In the event of a delay, the company would be unable to raise necessary capital, brokers and dealers would have to wait to trade and sell the issue, and the investment banking firm would have to wait for the underwriting fees. Further, a stop order might diminish public interest in the securities when the issue did go to market. Hence, there was a built-in incentive to disclose the relevant information correctly, the first time.

Under the Securities and Exchange Act of 1934, this authority over company disclosure was transferred to the SEC. The creation of the SEC was a compromise between Wall Street and supporters of the new legislation. Wall Street was very much opposed to additional regulation of its activities, and the fear among members of the Roosevelt administration and in Congress that harsh regulation might provoke a cessation of trading in securities and hence harm the economic recovery effort of the country made it necessary to compromise. Most important, the industry wanted authority over the markets transferred from the FTC to a new agency responsible only for securities regulation. The FTC had a reputation for being quite vigorous in its enforcement of the Securities Act, and two of its commissioners, James Landis and George Mathews, were strong supporters of the New Deal. A new agency, focused on the securities markets, might be more attentive to the concerns of Wall Street than was the FTC, which had many other responsibilities.

The 1934 act did, however, place significant regulatory restrictions on Wall Street by requiring stock exchanges to register with the new SEC. The agency could then "alter or supplant" exchange rules to protect investors and "maintain fair and orderly markets." The legislation also prohibited particular trading practices that allowed exchange members to manipulate the price of securities, and it required all companies that listed their stock with an exchange to meet the disclosure requirements of the 1933 act and to provide regular disclosure filings with the SEC throughout the year.

Three key participants in developing the 1933 and 1934 acts were James Landis, Benjamin Cohen, and Thomas Corcoran. When an initial draft of the 1933 legislation by Houston Thompson—formerly the chairman of the FTC and responsible for the Democratic party platform on securities regulation in 1932—drew controversy in Congress, FDR contacted longtime friend and Harvard law professor Felix Frankfurter for assistance. Frankfurter came to Washington with Landis, Cohen, and Corcoran, three former law students, to take on the task of legislative drafting. Each played a role in developing the 1934 legislation as well.

President Roosevelt chose Joseph Kennedy, father of John F. Kennedy, to be the first chairman of the SEC in 1934. For many strong New Deal supporters, the choice was an odd one. Kennedy made a fortune on Wall Street engaging in many of the manipulative practices the SEC was created to prevent. But for FDR, the choice was pragmatic. Kennedy could send the signal to his associates on Wall Street that the administration wanted the markets to continue to grow and flourish to support economic recovery. At the same time, the appointment of James Landis, George Mathews, and Robert Healy to the commission (all formerly with the FTC) along with Ferdinand Pecora (the chief counsel to the Senate Banking and Currency Committee during its investigation of the 1929 market crash) provided some reassurance to supporters of the New Deal that the agency would be vigorous in its enforcement of the disclosure statute and the regulation of trading practices on the exchanges. Kennedy stayed with the commission for only one year, and Roosevelt named Landis as chairman in 1935.

As an independent regulatory commission, the SEC is not part of an executive branch department. Five commissioners are appointed by the president and approved by the Senate and serve for five-year terms. One of the five members is selected by the president as chair of the commission. Members cannot be removed by the president before their term is over. No more than three members of the commission can be from the same political party. The backgrounds of commissioners since 1934 have varied from an expertise in law to economics and investment banking.

Once the SEC was created, Congress gradually extended its responsibilities. In 1935 the Public Utility Holding Company Act required public utility holding companies to disclose their financial activities and information relevant to their securities issues to the SEC. The production and interstate transmission of electricity, as well as the control over natural gas pipelines, was in the hands of several large public utility holding companies. This concentration resulted from the often-fraudulent sale of new securities to the public in a utility subsidiary that existed on paper alone. The result was oligopolistic companies and high energy rates for the consumer. Disclosure and registration with the SEC was argued to provide better information to investors.

In 1938 Senator Francis Maloney of Connecticut sponsored legislation that gave the SEC oversight of the over-the-counter market. Similar to the agency's authority in the exchange markets, the SEC was authorized to regulate the trading practices and professional qualifications of over-the-counter dealers. The Investment Company Act of 1940 and the Investment Company Advisers' Act of 1940 further expanded SEC jurisdiction by requiring investment companies and investment advisers to register with the SEC and to disclose any conflict of interest that might exist between an adviser and the investing public. A series of amendments in 1964, 1970, and 1975 expanded and sharpened the agency's authority. Perhaps most significantly, the 1975 Securities Exchange Act Amendments required the SEC to oversee the development of a national market system that eventually breaks down the barriers between markets in the trading of securities. In this move to "deregulate" Wall Street from the inside out, the Office of the National Market System was established within the SEC to facilitate the transformation, which is still very much in progress.

Throughout its history the SEC's regulatory efforts have received a great deal of public attention. During the 1970s the SEC began to expand the information deemed material to the investor in order to reveal management fraud and to make publicly traded corporations more accountable to the investing public. For corporate America and many critics of the SEC, this was an expansion of the agency's jurisdiction in an attempt to regulate corporate behavior rather than provide investors with relevant information. For example, the agency wanted companies with publicly traded securities to voluntarily disclose "questionable payments," or bribes, made to secure shares of foreign markets often through favorable legislation or regulation in the targeted country. This, the SEC argued, was a misuse of funds by publicly owned companies. The voluntary disclosure of such information would prevent prosecution by the SEC. The agency also required the disclosure of executive perquisites, such as salaries, fees, and bonuses.

The 1980s were marked by an increased interest in prosecuting insider trading and by the stock market crash of 1987. The prosecution of arbitrageur Ivan Boesky, investment banker Dennis Levine, and the investment house of Drexel Burnham Lambert and its executive Michael Milken brought the practice of insider trading (trading in securities based upon nonpublic information) to the front pages and the headlines of the evening news. Following the stock market crash in October of 1987, in which the Dow Jones Industrial Average fell by 508 points in one day, members of Congress and the public alike turned to the SEC for solutions to prevent such a free-fall in the future. Today, with the definition of a "security" blurred by the trading of stock index futures and other hybrid products—products whose value depends on the value of a security or a "basket" of securities, but which are pack-aged and trade in different markets, such as the futures market—the SEC is faced with the challenge it confronted when it was created: how to provide regulation in a manner that protects investors without dampening the vigor of the capital markets.

BIBLIOGRAPHY

Bernheim, Alfred, and Margaret Grant Schneider, eds. *The Securities Markets: Findings and Recommendations of a Special Staff of the Twentieth Century Fund.* New York, 1935.

Chatov, Robert. *Corporate Financial Reporting: Public or Private Control?* New York, 1975.

de Bedts, Ralph F. *The New Deal's SEC: The Formative Years.* New York, 1964.

Karmel, Roberta S. *Regulation by Prosecution.* New York, 1981.

Khademian, Anne M. *The SEC and Capital Market Regulation: The Politics of Expertise.* Pittsburgh, 1992.

Kripke, Homer. *The SEC and Corporate Disclosure: Regulation in Search of a Purpose.* New York, 1979.

Landis, James. *The Administrative Process.* New Haven, Conn., 1938.

Macey, Jonathan R., and David D. Haddock. "Shirking at the SEC: The Failure of the National Market System." *University of Illinois Law Review* 2 (1985): 315–362.

McCraw, Thomas K. *Prophets of Regulation.* Cambridge, Mass., 1984.

Parrish, Michael E. *Securities Regulation and the New Deal.* New Haven, Conn., 1970.

Phillips, Susan M., and J. Richard Zecher. *The SEC and the Public Interest.* Cambridge, Mass., 1981.

Poser, Norman. "Restructuring the Stock Markets: A Critical Look at the SEC's National Market System." *New York University Law Review* 56 (1981): 883–898.

Ritchie, Donald A. *James M. Landis: Dean of the Regulators.* Cambridge, Mass., 1980.

Seligman, Joel. *The Transformation of Wall Street: A History of the Securities and Exchange Commission and Modern Corporate Finance.* Boston, 1982.

Seligman, Joel. *The SEC and the Future of Finance.* New York, 1985.

Sobel, Robert. *N.Y.S.E.: A History of the New York Stock Exchange, 1935–1975.* New York, 1975.

—ANNE M. KHADEMIAN

Senate

ESSAY The Senate of the United States relates to the executive branch through its joint power with the House of Representatives to appropriate the funds for running the government, to conduct oversight investigations, to override presidential vetoes, and to pass or block legislation sought by an administration. Equally important, however, are the three constitutional powers that the Senate alone possesses: the power to approve treaties, the right to confirm the president's nominations to high executive branch posts and federal judgeships, and its role as judge in the impeachment process.

BACKGROUND

The Constitutional Convention created the U.S. Senate as part of the "Great Compromise" between the large and small states. In contrast to the House of Representatives in which membership was based on population, the Senate would have two senators from each state—large or small—as protection for the interests of small states. The Framers also intended the Senate to be a more stable body than the House and less subject to transient political pressures. Thus, senators were to be elected by the legislatures of their respective states rather than by direct popular vote, a practice ended only with ratification of the Seventeenth Amendment in 1913. In addition, while all House members stand for election every two years, senators serve six-year terms, with one-third of the members to be chosen in each election year. As a result, the Senate is a continuing body in which two-thirds of the membership carries over from the previous Congress. Also, by setting a minimum age of thirty—rather than the twenty-five required for House members—the Framers hoped to ensure that senators would be more mature individuals who could serve as thoughtful statesmen.

In its early days the Senate met in secret—as had the Continental Congress and the Congress under the Articles of Confederation—while the House of Representatives held its deliberations in public. Not until 1795 did the Senate change its rules and begin meeting in open session.

Under the Constitution (Art. I, Sec. 3), the vice president of the United States is the president of the Senate and its official presiding officer, who is empowered to vote only if necessary to break a tie. Since its earliest days, the Senate has also chosen a president *pro tempore* to preside in the absence of the vice president. This individ-

ual is third in the line of succession for the presidency, after the vice president and the Speaker of the House. During the nineteenth century vice presidents regularly presided over the Senate, but the practice diminished in the twentieth century. Since the 1950s the vice president has generally presided only on occasions when the administration expects a close vote on important legislation that may require him to break a tie. As of March 1996, vice presidents had cast tie-breaking votes on at least 235 occasions.

The Senate handles legislation through a committee system. After electing committee members in an *ad hoc* fashion for each piece of legislation during its early years, the Senate in 1816 created its first standing committees as a more efficient way of conducting business. Since that time periodic reorganizations have revised the numbers and jurisdictions of Senate committees in order to make the system more effective and reduce the number of each senator's committee assignments. Through its committees, the Senate, like the House, appropriates money for executive branch programs. It also exercises oversight of such programs, both through its standing committees and with in-depth investigations by panels specially created for the purpose. The latter practice has increased in the twentieth century, with high profile probes ranging from the Teapot Dome investigation of the 1920s to the Truman Committee investigation of defense contracts during World War II, the Army-McCarthy hearings of the 1950s, and the Watergate hearings in 1973 and 1974.

By the 1920s both political parties had established the position of floor leader to be responsible for managing the movement of legislation, assisted by party whips and party conference chairmen. The system has since been expanded by the addition of party conference secretaries and staff members who serve as majority and minority party secretaries, as well as the Democratic and Republican policy committees. From its earliest years the Senate has entrusted administrative duties to an elected secretary of the Senate and a sergeant at arms. It also elects a chaplain, who offers a prayer at the opening of each daily session.

Because the Constitution's framers viewed the

Senate as the guardian of minority views, its rules historically have permitted nearly unlimited debate, unlike the strict controls in the House of Representatives. Even the present cloture rule requires the votes of sixty senators (three-fifths of the members) to cut off debate, thus permitting a minority of forty-one senators to block passage of controversial legislation.

The lack of restrictions on the length of speeches—combined with a carefully maintained numerical balance in the body between the slave and free states—contributed to the so-called Golden Age of the Senate from the 1830s to the 1850s, with its intense and extensive deliberations over slavery by such noted orators as Henry Clay of Kentucky, Daniel Webster of Massachusetts, and John C. Calhoun of South Carolina. During the later nineteenth century, however, opponents of legislation increasingly used the lack of constraints on debate to delay or block measures, especially in the closing days of a Congress—an approach that became known as a filibuster. The situation worsened in the early twentieth century, as small numbers of senators managed to obstruct legislation sought by the executive branch. In 1915, for example, a six-week filibuster against a bill to purchase merchant ships eventually killed the measure, and in 1917 legislation supported by President Woodrow Wilson to arm merchant vessels in World War I was defeated by another lengthy filibuster. This action caused public outrage and a bitter attack by President Wilson against "a little group of willful men" who had blocked the bill he considered to be in the national interest. Shortly thereafter, on 8 March 1917, the Senate finally adopted a cloture rule to make it possible to shut off debate. The first successful use of the rule came on 15 November 1919, allowing a vote on the Treaty of Versailles—although the Senate then failed to produce the necessary two-thirds majority to approve the pact.

The original cloture rule required a vote by two-thirds of all those present and voting to end debate. In 1975 the Senate changed the rule to the present three-fifths of *all* senators, except on rules changes, which still need two-thirds of those present and voting. As cloture has become more attainable, those opposing legislation have developed new obstructive techniques, such as the "post-cloture" filibuster, which has in turn been limited by controls on the number of hours of debate permitted after cloture has been invoked. In spite of the changes, a filibuster or the threat of one is still frequently used to frustrate an administration's initiatives, as well as occasionally to block confirmation of a controversial presidential appointment. The president possesses the veto power as a weapon against legislation he opposes, which can only be overridden by a two-thirds vote in both the Senate and the House. Overrides are generally difficult to achieve; Congress has only been able to override some four percent of the more than twenty-five hundred vetoes to date.

SPECIAL SENATE POWERS

As part of the nation's system of checks and balances, the Constitution in Article II, Section 2, establishes the Senate's authority to "advise and consent" by a two-thirds vote in the adoption of treaties, giving the body a strong voice in the nation's foreign policy, which is generally conducted by the executive branch. During the First Congress (1789–1791), President George Washington and the Senate faced the need to determine how this role would be carried out. Initially, Washington believed he could simply visit the Senate in person, have a treaty read aloud to the members, and receive their advice or vote of approval. A small group of resistant senators, however, urged referral to a committee for more careful consideration. Although Washington took offense at the time, he found that, after the committee review, the Senate approved the treaties. As a result of this experience, the first president resolved to submit future treaties in writing rather than by appearing in person, and all subsequent presidents have followed this procedure.

In the nineteenth and early twentieth centuries the Senate debated treaties in closed executive session, but descriptions of the debate and even the provisions of the treaties themselves were frequently leaked to the press. Finally, in 1929 the Senate began considering treaties in open session. Today, the body meets in secret only to debate matters dealing with national security.

As early as 1794, the Senate established the precedent that it had the right to refuse its consent when it rejected a treaty negotiated by the executive branch with several Indian tribes. In 1825 the body for the first time rejected an international treaty when it turned down a pact with Colombia aimed at ending the slave trade. In practice, if a treaty is to receive the necessary two-thirds vote for approval, it needs bipartisan Senate support. Some presidents have sought to build such support by seeking advice from senators during treaty negotiations, and scholars have sometimes criticized Woodrow Wilson for failing to consult senators during negotiations over the Treaty of Versailles, the best-known treaty rejected by the Senate. Perhaps learning from this incident, both Presidents Franklin D. Roosevelt and Harry S. Truman involved senators in the planning for the United Nations.

An 1868 Senate rule change permits the body to amend a treaty by a simple majority vote. Such amendments may have the effect of alienating some of the original supporters—or the foreign government involved—but they may also be instrumental in building the necessary bipartisan coalition. The Senate may also add reservations, which the president and the country involved must then accept or reject. In addition, the Senate has the option of simply taking no action at all, leaving the treaty hanging. Since 1789 the full Senate has rejected twenty treaties by failing to achieve the necessary two-thirds majority, while approving some ninety percent of those it considered. It has killed a number of other treaties by simply failing to act when there did not appear to be sufficient votes for approval. For less important matters the executive branch may use the alternative approach of an executive agreement with another country, which has the force of law but does not require Senate approval. The United States has entered into many more of these agreements than formal treaties, especially since World War II.

The Constitution also gives the Senate the power of advice and consent regarding presidential nominations (Art. II, Sec. 2) by a simple majority vote. In practice, the Senate usually allows a president wide latitude to select his executive branch appointees, who will be carrying out the policies of the administration. Judicial appointments that are for life and thus carry on far beyond the end of a particular administration receive closer Senate scrutiny, especially Supreme Court nominations that can influence national policy for decades. Thus, the Senate has formally voted to reject twenty-seven Supreme Court appointees and only nine cabinet nominees (another six were withdrawn or abandoned when the Senate took no action). The first Senate rejection of a Supreme Court nomination occurred in 1795 (in 1793 George Washington had withdrawn a nomination), but not until 1834 did the Senate first reject a nominee to a cabinet post.

After voting on George Washington's early appointments by secret ballot, the Senate changed to its present procedure of handling such matters by voice vote. Originally, the Senate considered nominations, like treaties, in closed executive session. As with treaties, however, much of the information leaked to the press, and nominations have been considered in open session since 1929. Opposition by a Georgia senator to one of George Washington's appointments led to the practice known as senatorial courtesy, in which the Senate will not confirm a nominee for federal office in a state if one of the senators from that state objects.

In Article I, Section 3, the Constitution gives the Senate "the sole power to try all Impeachments," which are initiated by the House. Such cases require a two-thirds vote for conviction and removal from office. Over the years the Senate has sat as a court of impeachment in sixteen cases; in seven of these it has voted to convict and removed the official from office. Congress has rarely used impeachment against executive branch officials. The sixteen cases handled by the Senate included one senator, one president, and one cabinet member. The remainder were federal judges. In the only case dealing with a cabinet officer, former secretary of war William Belknap was impeached by the House in 1876 for accepting bribes and was tried after he had already resigned the post. The Senate acquitted him, apparently on the grounds that he had already left office.

Impeachments of presidents are generally viewed as political rather than legal remedies.

The only such case that went to trial was that of President Andrew Johnson in 1868. Johnson had repeatedly clashed with the Congress controlled by Radical Republicans over the mildness of his approach to Reconstruction. When he fired Secretary of War Edwin Stanton, ignoring the recently passed Tenure of Office Act that required Senate approval to remove an official appointed with the consent of the Senate, the House voted to impeach him. After the two-month-long trial, the Senate vote was thirty-five for conviction and nineteen against, one vote short of the two-thirds needed to convict. When it became clear that the additional "guilty" vote could not be obtained, the Radicals adjourned the Senate and ended the trial.

The only other attempt to impeach a president occurred in 1974, when the House Judiciary Committee voted a resolution of impeachment against Richard M. Nixon for his role in the Watergate cover-up. When he realized that the full House was also prepared to vote to impeach him, the president resigned.

[See also Executive Power; House of Representatives; Judicial Branch; President as Chief Executive; Presidential Succession and Disability; Senate Confirmation of Presidential Appointees; and Supreme Court Decisions on the Presidency.]

BIBLIOGRAPHY

Bacon, Donald, Roger Davidson, and Morton Keller, eds. *The Encyclopedia of the United States Congress.* 4 vols. New York, 1995.

Baker, Richard A. *The Senate of the United States: A Bicentennial History.* Melbourne, Fla., 1988.

Byrd, Robert C. *The Senate, 1789–1989: Addresses on the History of the United States Senate.* Senate Document 100-20. Washington, D.C., 1989–1994.

Dole, Bob. *Historical Almanac of the United States Senate.* Senate Document 100-35. Washington, D.C., 1989.

Frumin, Alan S. *Riddick's Senate Procedure: Precedents and Practices.* Senate Document 101-28. Washington, D.C., 1992.

Schulz, George J., ed. *Creation of the Senate: From the Proceedings of the Federal Convention* (1937). Senate Document 100-7. Reprint, Washington, D.C., 1987.

Silbey, Joel H. *Encyclopedia of the American Legislative System.* 3 vols. New York, 1994.

Swanstrom, Roy. *The United States Senate, 1787–1801* (1962). Senate Document 100-31. Reprint, Washington, D.C., 1988.

U.S. Congress. Senate. *Biographical Directory of the United States Congress, 1774–1989.* Senate Document 100-34. Washington, D.C., 1988.

U.S. Congress. Senate. *Guide to the Records of the United States Senate at the National Archives, 1789–1989: Bicentennial Edition.* Prepared by the National Archives' Center for Legislative Archives. Senate Document 97-41. Washington, D.C., 1989.

U.S. Congress. Senate. *Senate Election, Expulsion and Censure Cases from 1793 to 1990.* Senate Document 103-33. Washington, D.C., 1995.

U.S. Congress. Senate. *Guide to Research Collections of Former United States Senators, 1789–1995.* Senate Document 103-35. Washington, D.C., 1995.

U.S. Congress. Senate. *Senators of the United States: A Historical Bibliography.* Senate Document 103-34. Washington, D.C., 1995.

—WENDY WOLFF

Senate Confirmation of Presidential Appointees

ESSAY One measure of presidential leadership is the president's ability to select individuals for executive and judicial positions that collectively determine the manner in which national legislation, and ultimately the Constitution itself, will be executed and interpreted. The Constitution (Art. II, Sec. 2) gives the president authority to nominate "ambassadors, other public ministers and consuls, judges of the Supreme Court, and all other officers of the United States, whose appointments are not herein otherwise provided for, and which shall be established by law. . . ."

Most nominations require approval by a majority vote of the Senate. However, the Twenty-fifth Amendment authorizes the president to select nominees when the office of vice president is vacant, with the consent of a majority of both houses of Congress. This amendment has been invoked twice, in 1973 to confirm Gerald Ford, and in 1974 to endorse Nelson Rockefeller.

Constitutionally, Congress can authorize the president, the courts, or department heads to appoint some individuals without requiring Senate confirmation. Presidents can make temporary recess appointments when the Senate is not in session, but if unconfirmed, these expire at the end of the congressional session.

Senate confirmation of presidential nominations is essentially an American practice, an important power of the Senate, and a basic part of the division of powers between the president and Congress. It stems from historical precedent established in colonial times, when appointments of some governors required approval by their councils. Under the Articles of Confederation, several state constitutions provided for legislative endorsement of gubernatorial appointees.

The adoption of Senate confirmation was the result of a compromise in the Constitutional Convention. Some favored appointment by the president alone, others by the Senate alone, and still others by a president acting with an executive council chosen by the legislature. Supporting the constitutional compromise in *The Federalist,* no. 76, Alexander Hamilton predicted the role of the Senate would be largely reactive and passive, and that there would be "no difference between nominating and appointing." Hamilton's prediction was largely accurate. More than ninety-nine percent of the forty to seventy thousand nominations made annually by the president are quickly approved by voice vote without debate. Most are to minor positions, including military, foreign service, and Public Health Service officers.

There are more than two thousand major civilian positions the president directly fills on federal courts, in executive departments, and on regulatory bodies. Major nominations receive more individual attention during each stage of the confirmation process than minor ones, but only a small number each year are challenged. However, those few are highly publicized in the media because of the underlying policy and political significance of opposition and possible rejection.

Developments since the enactment of the Constitution have influenced an evolving confirmation process. For example, while the president may select all civilian employees, much of this task has been delegated to a civil service system. This allows for sharper focus on the remaining positions. Also, the confirmation process has been systematized to diminish expenditure of time and resources while permitting careful consideration of key appointees. Political parties play a central role in the process, as do

Senate committees and their staffs. Since 1868 each nomination has been sent to a standing committee that holds hearings (public since 1929), opening the process to interested groups and the media, which intensifies the impact of the proceedings on senators' electoral considerations. Following a committee vote the nomination goes to the full Senate. At any step along the way it may be challenged, blocked, withdrawn, or defeated.

Presidents who are in poor standing with what Richard Neustadt called their "publics," as reflected in low ratings in opinion polls or a negative press, are more likely to have nominations challenged, as are lame-duck presidents and presidents not of the same party as the Senate majority. Challenge may arise because of questions about a nominee's qualifications, competence, or ethical record, or it may be a surrogate for opposition to the president, whether personal, political, or policy-related. For, as G. Calvin Mackenzie reminds us, the confirmation process involves more than an individual nomination. It also provides another arena for the continuing struggle between the executive and legislative branches over public policy.

Only a few major nominations each year come to a roll call vote. Most roll call votes result in approval, but every few years a nomination has been rejected by the Senate. When a nomination faces powerful challenge and possible rejection, even the strongest president must decide if a battle is politically worthwhile, and strategic considerations become critical in determining if it is possible to win the marginal votes of uncommitted senators or if the nomination should be withdrawn.

Conflict has been a recurrent part of the process almost from the outset. During the eighteenth and nineteenth centuries, partisanship, patronage, and personality clashes played a central role in conflict over nominations, while ideology became a major factor in the twentieth century. In 1789 the Senate rejected George Washington's nominee to a minor post in Georgia because senators from that state, desiring patronage, backed a different candidate. They insisted on senatorial courtesy, or rejection by the Senate of any candidate for an office in a state who was not acceptable to senators from that state. Only with the passage of the Pendleton Act of 1883, which inaugurated the civil service system, did the role of patronage begin to decline. More recently this decline has even affected the selection of district court judges.

In 1795 the Senate rejected George Washington's nomination of John Rutledge as chief justice of the United States because he criticized the Jay Treaty. This was the first instance of opposition to the appointment of a Supreme Court nominee. In the process the Senate began to define what it considered legitimate cause for rejection of high court candidates.

Contention over nominations escalated in the nineteenth century. After Andrew Jackson's attorney general, Roger Taney, was rejected as secretary of the Treasury in 1834, Jackson nominated him to a seat on the Supreme Court. This nomination was also defeated, but Taney finally secured confirmation as chief justice in 1836. John Tyler, the first person to become president without being elected to that office, had four nominees to cabinet posts and four Supreme Court appointees rejected during his brief single term.

Faced with the overwhelming task of conducting a Civil War, Abraham Lincoln tried to avoid conflict over nominations by asking members of the Senate to name people whom he would then nominate. Post–Civil War presidents were less pliant than Lincoln, and the Senate responded by rejecting nominees who were not supported by powerful senators. The first president to face such difficulty was Andrew Johnson, who was unsuccessful in getting his impeachment trial counsel, Henry Stanbery, reappointed as attorney general or seated on the Supreme Court. Least successful during this period was Rutherford B. Hayes, who had a total of fifty-one nominations rejected during his single term.

A number of twentieth-century nominees to the Supreme Court were not approved, and ideology played a central part in their rejection. Herbert Hoover's nomination of John Parker (1930) was the first such rejection since 1894. Lyndon Johnson had little difficulty with appointments until the last year of his presidency (1968), when his nomination of Supreme Court associate justice Abe Fortas to become chief justice was withdrawn under the threat of likely defeat. Richard Nixon had two Supreme Court nominations rejected, and George Bush also lost two. Overall, of 133 individuals nominated to the Court since 1789, twenty-seven were not confirmed by the Senate, and twenty-two of these rejections occurred before 1968. Historically, the Senate has given closest attention to Supreme Court nominees, and they now rank first in the rate of rejection, which befits the long-term impact these justices have on public policy.

Increasing involvement in the nominations process by interest groups and a consequent interjection of ideology also played a role in the Senate's failure to confirm Dwight Eisenhower's nomination of Lewis Strauss as secretary of commerce in 1959. This was a rare case of rejection of a department head, and one not repeated until the defeat of George Bush nominee John Tower as secretary of defense in 1989. The Senate has historically granted the president the widest latitude when he selects members of his cabinet, and since 1789 only nine cabinet-level nominations have been rejected, six before 1900.

A spate of recent highly politicized controversies has led one critic of the confirmation process, Stephen L. Carter, to label it the "confirmation mess." Placed in perspective, however, contemporary battles result from a number of historical developments, including the direct election of senators, the growth of interest groups, the institutionalization of the White House's approach to appointments, and the increasing openness of, and media attention to, the confirmation process in the Senate. These have been accompanied in recent years by circumstances that have historically intensified controversy, such as divided government, and such polarizing issues as crime, race, and abortion, as well as the vulnerability of presidents vis-à-vis their publics. Together these developments help explain the highly publicized "selling and shelling" of nominees, particularly those to the Supreme Court.

[*See also* Civil Service *and* Senate.]

BIBLIOGRAPHY

Abraham, Henry J. *Justices and Presidents: A Political History of Appointments to the Supreme Court.* New York, 1974.

Cameron, Charles M., Albert D. Coover, and Jeffrey A. Segal. "Senate Voting on Supreme Court Nominees: A Neoinstitutional Model." *American Political Science Review* 84 (1990): 525–534.

Carter, Stephen L. *The Confirmation Mess: Cleaning Up the Federal Appointments Process.* New York, 1994.

Chase, Harold W. *Federal Judges: The Appointing Process.* Minneapolis, 1972.

Fenno, Richard F., Jr. *The President's Cabinet.* Cambridge, Mass., 1959.

Harris, Joseph P. *The Advice and Consent of the Senate.* Berkeley, Calif., 1953.

Mackenzie, G. Calvin. *The Politics of Presidential Appointments.* New York, 1981.

Maltese, John Anthony. *The Selling of Supreme Court Nominees.* Baltimore, 1995.

Neustadt, Richard E. *Presidential Power: The Politics of Leadership.* New York, 1960.

Scigliano, Robert. *The Supreme Court and the Presidency.* New York, 1971.

Silverstein, Mark. *Judicious Choices: The New Politics of Supreme Court Nominations.* New York, 1994.

Tannenbaum, Donald G. "Explaining Controversial Nominations: The Fortas Case Revisited." *Presidential Studies Quarterly* 17 (1987): 573–586.

Welco, Thomas J. *The Politicizing Presidency: The White House Personnel Office, 1948–1994.* Lawrence, Kans., 1995.

—DONALD G. TANNENBAUM

Small Business Administration

Congress created the U.S. Small Business Administration (SBA) in 1953 as an independent agency of the federal government to help America's entrepreneurs form successful small enterprises. At that time, members of Congress argued that small business would be an essential ingredient to economic recovery, building America's future and helping the United States compete in the global marketplace. Their argument proved sound. As of the 1990s, more than twenty million small companies provide opportunities for working Americans by creating two of every three new jobs, producing thirty-nine percent of the gross national product, and inventing more than half the nation's technological innovation.

In an effort to foster small enterprise, the SBA operates programs with offices in every state as well as the District of Columbia, the Virgin Islands, and Puerto Rico. Through the local offices, the SBA works with thousands of lending, educational, and training institutions nationwide providing workshops, individual counseling, publications, and videotapes. These programs help new proprietors understand and meet the challenges of starting a business in areas such as financing, marketing, and management, for example.

Additionally, three partner organizations that are sponsored by the SBA offer training and counseling. The first organization, Service Corps of Retired Executives, more popularly referred to as SCORE, has more than thirteen thousand volunteers who provide training and one-on-one counseling. Retirees constitute most of the SCORE volunteers; however, full-time employed executives are also eligible for membership. In addition to their volunteer work, about twenty percent of SCORE's membership are gainfully employed.

The SCORE program began in 1964 with the express goal of helping American small businesses prosper. SCORE volunteers are members of 390 locally organized, self-administered chapters offering services in more than eight hundred locations throughout the nation. SCORE volunteers work in or near their home communities to provide management counseling and training to small businesses and to those considering going into business. Through counseling and training SCORE volunteers help business owners and managers identify basic management problems, determine the causes, and become better managers. The program makes appropriate matches between volunteers with expertise in a certain area of business and small businesses that need that particular expert advice. Counselors analyze each business and its problems. The collective experience of these men and women spans the full range of American enterprise. They offer suggestions, such as the ways and means whereby a client can successfully correct problems or institute changes to the business.

Although SCORE volunteers share their expertise at no charge, there is a nominal fee for training programs. SCORE also offers business workshops as well as a variety of other workshops nationwide for prospective small business entrepreneurs. These workshops take place in local communities and provide a general overview of what it takes to start a business.

The second program offered by the SBA is the Small Business Development Center (SBDC) program. Like the SCORE program, the SBDC program provides training, counseling, research, and other specialized assistance at more than six hundred locations nationwide. The program is a cooperative effort of the private sector, the educational community, and federal, state, and local governments. Its purpose is to enhance economic development by providing management and technical assistance to small businesses. By 1995, there were fifty-seven SBDCs, one or more in fifty states, the District of Columbia, Puerto Rico, and the Virgin Islands, with a network of more than seven hundred service locations. In each state there is a lead organization that sponsors the SBDC and manages the program. The lead organization coordinates program services offered to small businesses through a network of subcenters and satellite locations in each state. Subcenters, located at colleges, universities, community colleges, vocational schools, and area chambers of commerce and economic development corporations tailor assistance to the local community and individual client needs. Each center develops services in cooperation with local SBA district offices to ensure statewide coordination with other available resources. Each center has a director, staff members, volunteers, and part-time personnel. Qualified individuals recruited from professional and trade associations, the legal and banking communities, academia, chambers of commerce, and SCORE are among those who donate their services. Paid consultants, consulting engineers, and testing laboratories from the private sector are used to help clients who need specialized expertise. Assistance from an SBDC is available to anyone who is interested in beginning a small business for the first time, or in improving or expanding an existing small business, and who cannot afford the services of a private consultant.

Two sources provide funding for the SBDC program. The first source is the SBA, which provides fifty percent or less of the operating funds for each state SBDC. One or more sponsors provide the rest. These matching fund contributions are provided by state legislatures, private sector foundations and grants, state and local chambers of commerce, state-chartered economic development corporations, public and private universities, vocational and technical schools, community colleges, and so on.

The third and final program that works in partnership with the SBA is the Small Business Institute (SBI) program. The SBI program gives small business owners an opportunity to receive intensive management counseling from qualified graduate and undergraduate business students working under faculty guidance. The program began in 1972 when the SBA created SBIs in cooperation with thirty-six colleges and universities across the country. SBIs at more than five hundred universities provide free management studies, performed by advanced business students. Any accredited four-year college or university is eligible to apply to become an SBI school.

The students participating in the program provide counseling to small businesses. The SBI students meet frequently over the course of an academic term with a small business owner to solve specific management problems. Business clients receive a detailed report and an oral presentation on the actions they need to take to improve their business operations. The SBI team also occasionally works with other SBA business development resources, such as SBDCs and SCORE volunteers. All small business owners and managers are eligible to participate. In order to participate, however, the business must meet several requirements. For example, it must be independently owned and operated, not dominant in its field, and must conform to SBA business size and standards.

In addition to the training and counseling provided by the three partnership organizations, the SBA also provides financing to new businesses. Business clients, however, do not need to have an SBA loan to participate in any SBA partnership program.

Since its creation by Congress in 1953, the SBA has been guaranteeing bank loans to small businesses. About eight thousand lenders made at least one SBA loan in the period from 1990 to 1995. Most lenders utilize regular processing on loan guarantees. This processing requires a thorough analysis of the application and a decision by the SBA. There are, however, two types of programs for lenders. The first is the Certified Lenders Program, which includes 1) lenders who have been more heavily involved in regular SBA guaranty loan processing and 2) lenders who meet certain criteria. This loan process accounts for thirty percent of all business loan guarantees. These lenders may use regular processing when necessary. There are 660 certified lenders participating in this particular program across the nation.

The second type of program, the Preferred Lenders Program, permits the lender to unilaterally decide on SBA participation in eligible business loans. The purpose is to more fully utilize the resources of the SBA's best lenders and to reduce processing time on strong credits. Preferred loans have a maximum SBA guaranty of eighty percent with preferred authority renewed every two years. Preferred loans are about fourteen percent of all business loan guarantees. Preferred lenders may use certified or regular processing when necessary. There are 156 preferred lenders across the nation. The SBA backs eligible small businesses that are having trouble securing conventional financing by offering loan guarantees on loans made by private lenders.

Additionally, the SBA offers a range of specialized financing such as International Trade Loan Guarantees, which help finance U.S.-based facilities or equipment for producing goods or services for export, and the Small Loan Program, which helps businesses needing capital of $50,000 or less. Other types of loans include the Seasonal Line of Credit Program for firms facing seasonal business increases and Pollution Control Loans for firms involved in pollution control and reduction. The SBA also fosters rural and urban economic development and Development Company Loans, geared to creating and retaining jobs

in those areas. Finally, the SBA expands access to surety bonds through guarantees on bonding for small and emerging contractors, including minorities, who otherwise cannot secure bid, payment, or performance bonds.

BIBLIOGRAPHY

Field, Thomas G. *Trademarks and Business Goodwill.* Washington, D.C., 1990.
Pelissier, Raymond Francis. *Planning and Goal Setting for Small Business.* Washington, D.C., 1991.
Rhyne, Elizabeth Holmes. *Small Business, Banks, and SBA Loan Guarantees: Subsidizing the Weak or Bridging a Credit Gap?* New York, 1988.
Small Business Administration. *SBA Legislative Handbook.* Washington, D.C., 1992.
Small Business Administration. *Profile: Who We Are and What We Do.* Washington, D.C., 1995.
Small Business Administration. *Small Business Answer Card.* Washington, D.C., 1995.
Small Business Administration. *SBA Resources.* Washington, D.C., 1996.
                                          —VERONICA D. DiCONTI

Smithsonian Institution

On 10 August 1846 President James K. Polk signed the legislation founding the Smithsonian Institution as an establishment dedicated to the "increase and diffusion of knowledge." This legislation was the culmination of more than a decade of debate among the general public and the Congress over a peculiar bequest. In 1829 an English chemist and mineralogist, James Smithson, died, leaving a will that stated if his heir died without heirs, his estate should go to the United States to found in Washington, under the name of the Smithsonian Institution, an establishment for the increase and diffusion of knowledge among men. After his sole heir died in 1835, the United States was notified of this bequest. President Andrew Jackson asked the United States Congress for authorization to pursue the bequest, sparking a heated debate between states' rights advocates and federalists. Senators John C. Calhoun and William Campbell Preston argued that there was no constitutional

provision for the creation of a national institution. However, the federalists prevailed, and in 1836 Richard Rush was dispatched to London to file a claim for the Smithson estate in the British Court of Chancery, then eight hundred cases in arrears. In just two years, Rush won a judgment for the United States, sold Smithson's properties, and converted them to gold sovereigns. When the proceeds of the estate were delivered to the U.S. Mint in Philadelphia on 1 September 1838, they totaled $508,318.46.

Another decade passed, however, before the Smithsonian was actually created. Congressmen, educators, scientists, social reformers, and the general public all voiced opinions as to what they believed Smithson had meant by "the increase and diffusion of knowledge." Initially most Americans assumed that Smithson intended to found a university; thus debate centered on what type of school. Gradually other ideas were introduced—an observatory, a scientific research institute, a national library, a publishing house, or a museum. The final legislation represented a compromise among these ideas, leaving out only the university. The Smithsonian Institution was created as a federal establishment, not part of the three branches of government, managed by a self-perpetuating board of regents.

The Smithsonian regents were left to decide how to carry out Smithson's vague mandate and the broad legislation. Their first act was to build a home for the Institution, a Norman "castle" designed by architect James Renwick, Jr., located on the National Mall in Washington, D.C. The regents selected as the first chief operating officer, or secretary, Joseph Henry, a distinguished physicist from the College of New Jersey (now Princeton University), who was an expert on electromagnetic induction. During his years as secretary (1846–1878), Henry focused on increasing knowledge through scientific research and diffusing knowledge through publication of *Smithsonian Contribution to Knowledge* and through international exchange of publications. He established a national network of weather observers, which led to the founding of the National Weather Service. The first objects donated to the institution were scientific apparatus, the

gift of Robert Hare of the University of Pennsylvania in 1848. The following year the Institution purchased its first collection, art books and works collected by regent George Perkins Marsh. During the Civil War years programs were curtailed, but the Institution was not affected substantially by the nearby fighting. A fire in the Castle in 1865, caused by a careless workman, destroyed the central portion of the building and many of the early collections. Henry was reluctant to use the Smithson fund for a national library or museum. Thus, in 1865 he transferred the art collection to the Library of Congress and Corcoran Gallery of Art. In 1866 he transferred the Smithsonian library to the Library of Congress and had the provision for copyright deposit at the Smithsonian repealed from the legislation.

Henry accepted natural history collections, as necessary for research, but worried about the costs of maintaining a museum collection and exhibits. Starting in 1858, the Congress provided an annual appropriation to the Smithsonian for the care of the national collections. The second secretary, Spencer Fullerton Baird, turned his energies enthusiastically to creating a great national museum during his tenure (1878–1887). As Henry's assistant since 1850, he had established a natural history collecting network across the country, relying on citizens from all walks of life, including soldiers, trappers, farmers, teachers, and doctors. Baird's goal was a comprehensive collection of all the natural resources of the continent in the United States National Museum. Based on his knowledge of the natural resources of Russian America, in 1867 Baird presented persuasive testimony to the Congress in favor of the purchase of Alaska. The government's collection of artworks, historical memorabilia, and scientific specimens, housed at the National Institute gallery in the Patent Office Building, was transferred to the Smithsonian as well. Baird prepared all of the government exhibits for the Centennial Exposition in Philadelphia in 1876. The Smithsonian exhibits gave the Institution national visibility. At the close of the exposition, Baird convinced most exhibitors to donate their displays to the Smithsonian and persuaded the Congress to build a new National Museum Building. Now known as the Arts and

Industries Building, its first event was to host President James A. Garfield's inaugural ball on 4 March 1881. When the building opened to the public in October of that year, it housed exhibits on natural history and history. During Baird's tenure the Bureau of American Ethnology was added to the Smithsonian's programs in 1879. Under the direction of John Wesley Powell, Smithsonian anthropologists documented Native American cultures rapidly vanishing from the West. Baird also served simultaneously as U.S. commissioner of fish and fisheries (1871–1887), overseeing research on the fishing industry that later led to the creation of the National Marine Fisheries Service.

During the tenure of the third secretary, Samuel Pierpont Langley (1889–1906), programs were added and expanded. Langley created the Smithsonian Astrophysical Observatory in 1890 to facilitate his research on solar phenomena, founded the National Zoological Park in 1891, opened a "Children's Room" in 1901 designed to awaken the curiosity of the young, and secured funding for a new National Museum Building. Langley also attempted to design the first flying machine, but his "aerodrome" lacked the aerodynamic features of the Wright Brothers' airplane that flew successfully at Kitty Hawk, North Carolina, in 1903.

Charles Doolittle Walcott, paleontologist and director of the United States Geological Survey, succeeded Langley as the fourth secretary, from 1907 to 1927. Under Walcott, the new museum building, now known as the National Museum of Natural History, opened in 1911 to house natural history and art collections. The building was closed during World War I to house the Bureau of War Risk Insurance. A National Gallery of Art, now the National Museum of American Art, was formally created in 1920. In 1923 the Freer Gallery of Art also opened, housing industrialist Charles Lang Freer's collection of Oriental art and the works of James McNeill Whistler.

The fifth secretary, Charles Greeley Abbot, served from 1928 to 1944, through the Great Depression and World War II. At the National Zoological Park, director William M. Mann secured assistance from the Works Progress Administration and Public Works of Art program for con-struction of new zoo buildings and the creation of murals and backgrounds for animal displays. During World War II the National Museum collections were moved to a warehouse in Shenandoah National Park, near Luray, Virginia, for safekeeping. The Smithsonian housed the Ethnogeographic Board, whose mission was to provide the military with ethnographic and geographic information about little-known areas of the world, especially the Pacific.

From 1945 to 1952, Alexander Wetmore, the sixth secretary, oversaw a program of exhibits modernization at the National Museum. In 1946 the Canal Zone Biological Area was placed under Smithsonian aegis. Now known as the Smithsonian Tropical Research Institute, this research station in the Panama Canal was founded in 1923 to facilitate research on the tropics. The National Museum's growing aeronautical collection, which included Charles Lindbergh's *Spirit of St. Louis,* was formally designated the National Air Museum in 1946. The Smithsonian Traveling Exhibition Service was inaugurated in 1952 to facilitate exhibits at venues outside the institution.

During the 1950s groundwork was laid for substantial growth in Smithsonian programs under the seventh secretary, Leonard Carmichael (1953–1964). Carmichael secured the appropriation for a new museum building for the history collections, which opened in 1964 and is now the National Museum of American History. New wings were added to the Natural History Building in the 1960s to house additional collections. The Patent Office Building was transferred to the Smithsonian in 1958 to house the national art collections. A major capital improvement program was initiated at the National Zoological Park in the 1960s, and the Smithsonian Astrophysical Observatory was revitalized and transferred to Cambridge, Massachusetts, in 1955. After the launching of *Sputnik* in 1957, the observatory played a major role in the tracking of artificial satellites.

S. Dillon Ripley, eighth secretary from 1964–1984, oversaw a major expansion in Smithsonian programs. New museums included the Anacostia Museum (1967), the Cooper-Hewitt, the National Design Museum, located in New York (1968), the National Museum of American Art and the National Portrait Gallery (1968), the Renwick Gallery (1972), the Hirshhorn Museum and Sculpture Garden (1974), the National Museum of African Art (1979), the Sackler Gallery (1983), and the International Center (1987). A new building for the National Air and Space Museum opened on 4 July 1976 in celebration of the Bicentennial of the American Revolution, and the Arts and Industries Building was renovated to re-create the Centennial Exposition in Philadelphia in 1876.

New programs included the Office of Fellowships and Grants in 1964, the Smithsonian Associates and Smithsonian Environmental Research Center in 1965, the Office of Museum Programs in 1966, the first Festival of American Folklife in 1967, the Conservation Analytical Laboratory in 1969, *Smithsonian* magazine, the Smithsonian Institution Archives, and the Archives of American Art in 1970, the Smithsonian Marine Station at Link Port in 1971, the Office of Elementary and Secondary Education in 1974, the Office of Telecommunications in 1975, and the Office of Horticulture in 1976. Expansions of existing programs included the Fred L. Whipple Observatory in Arizona, housing the Multiple Mirror Telescope, in 1968, the Conservation and Research Center of the National Zoological Park, located in Front Royal, Virginia, in 1975, and the Museum Support Center in 1983 to house collections storage and handling.

From 1984 to 1993, Robert McCormick Adams served as ninth secretary, presiding over a period of consolidation and renewed emphasis on research. Museums founded during his tenure were the National Museum of the American Indian in 1989, located in both New York and Washington, D.C., and the National Postal Museum in 1990. New research programs focused on the role of humans in the environment, including the Biodiversity Program established in 1986 in conjunction with the United Nations Educational, Scientific and Cultural Organization's Man and the Biosphere Program and the Mpala Research Station established in Kenya in 1992. The National Science Resource Center was established in 1985 in cooperation with the National Academy of Sciences to develop pre-college curriculum resources in mathematics and science. Expansions of existing programs included the

Arctic Studies Center established in the National Museum of Natural History in 1988 and a new observatory in Hawaii in 1991. In 1994 the Commission on the Future of the Smithsonian Institution issued its report, *E Pluribus Unum: This Divine Paradox,* setting forth its vision for the Smithsonian of the twenty-first century. As the national museum seen by some twenty-nine million visitors per year, in the 1980s and 1990s Smithsonian exhibits such as "The West as America," "Science in American Life," and "Enola Gay" became the focus for public debates over issues of cultural and historical identity.

When the tenth secretary, I. Michael Heyman, took office in 1993, he turned his attention to disseminating information electronically and celebrating the 150th anniversary of the Institution in 1996. A planned museum of African American culture was converted to the Center for the Study of African American History and Culture in 1995. Sesquicentennial programs included the largest traveling exhibit ever mounted, "America's Smithsonian," which traveled to twelve cities over a two-year period, a major development campaign, and a celebration on the National Mall on 10 August 1996. By its sesquicentennial the Institution housed over 140 million artifacts and specimens in its sixteen museums. The Smithsonian endowment had grown to some $378 million, part of a net operating budget in 1994 of $421.4 million. A staff of over sixty-seven hundred and some fifty-two hundred volunteers carried out its programs in museums and research institutes in Washington, D.C., across the continent, and around the world. In 1995 inauguration of the Smithsonian Institution's Home Page on the World Wide Web made the Institution's resources and exhibits available worldwide.

BIBLIOGRAPHY

Field, Cynthia R., Richard E. Stamm, and Heather P. Ewing. *The Castle: An Illustrated History of the Smithsonian Building.* Washington, D.C., 1993.
Hagen, Joel B. "Problems in the Institutionalization of Tropical Biology: The Case of Barro Colorado Island Biological Laboratory." *History and Philosophy of the Life Sciences* 12 (1990): 225–247.
Hellman, Geoffrey T. *The Smithsonian: Octopus on the Mall.* Philadelphia, 1967.
Hinsley, Curtis M., Jr. *Savages and Scientists: The Smith-*

sonian Institution and the Development of American Anthropology, 1846–1910. Washington, D.C., 1981.

Jones, Bessie Zaban. Lighthouse of the Skies: The Smithsonian Astrophysical Observatory; Background and History, 1846–1955. Washington, D.C., 1965.

Mergen, Alexa. From Bison to Biopark: 100 Years of the National Zoo. Washington, D.C., 1989.

Meyer, Agnes E. Charles Lang Freer and His Gallery. Washington, D.C., 1970.

Oehser, Paul H. Sons of Science: The Story of the Smithsonian Institution and Its Leaders. New York, 1949.

Oehser, Paul H. The Smithsonian Institution. Boulder, Colo., 1983.

Park, Edwards. "Secretary S. Dillon Ripley Retires after Twenty Years of Innovation." Smithsonian (September 1984): 77–85.

Rathbun, Richard. The National Gallery of Art, Department of Fine Arts of the National Museum. Bulletin of the United States National Museum, no. 70. Washington, D.C., 1906.

Reingold, Nathan, ed. The Papers of Joseph Henry, vol. 1–5. Washington, D.C., 1972, 1975, 1979, 1981, 1985.

Rivinus, Edward F., and Elizabeth M. Youssef. Spencer Baird of the Smithsonian. Washington, D.C., 1992.

Rothenberg, Marc, ed. The Papers of Joseph Henry, vols. 6–7. Washington, D.C., 1992, 1996.

"Smithsonian Institution Centennial Issue." Science 104: 2693 (August 1946).

Washburn, Wilcomb E. "Joseph Henry's Conception of the Purpose of the Smithsonian Institution." In A Cabinet of Curiosities: Five Episodes in the Evolution of American Museums, pp. 106–166. Charlottesville, Va., 1967.

Yochelson, Ellis L. National Museum of Natural History: 75 Years in the Natural History Building. Washington, D.C., 1985.

—PAMELA HENSON

Social Security Administration

Headquartered in Baltimore, the Social Security Administration (SSA) employs sixty-five thousand people, who work across the nation in thirteen hundred district and branch offices, ten regional offices, eight processing centers, three data operations centers, thirty-seven teleservice centers, and 132 hearings offices. The agency maintains an annual budget of $384 billion, most of which goes toward the monthly checks mailed to 37.8 million old-age and survivors' insurance (OASI) beneficiaries. In addition to administering this core program, the agency runs the Social Security Disability Insurance and Supplemental Security Income programs. These programs reach approximately 6.1 and 6.5 million people, respectively (all figures from 1995).

THE SOCIAL SECURITY ACT

The legislative antecedent of the SSA was the Social Security Act, signed into law by President Franklin Roosevelt on 14 August 1935. The act stemmed from the president's desires to prepare a comprehensive economic security program, including unemployment compensation and old-age insurance components, in time for congressional consideration in January 1935. In the summer of 1934, he put Department of Labor Secretary Frances Perkins in charge of a cabinet-level committee to write the necessary legislation.

Although the members of this committee agreed on the basic outlines of the program, they disagreed over administrative details. After a great deal of internal discussion, the committee recommended the creation of state-run unemployment compensation programs, a federally administered old-age insurance program, and state-run but federally assisted welfare or public assistance programs. To run these and other federal social welfare programs, some technical advisers to the committee hoped to start a new Department of Public Welfare. Allies of Frances Perkins preferred to retain the United States Employment Service, the Children's Bureau, and the Women's Bureau in the Department of Labor. Perkins and Harry Hopkins, head of the Federal Emergency Relief Administration, settled the matter through personal negotiations. A social insurance board within the Department of Labor would run unemployment compensation and old-age insurance. Old-age assistance and aid to dependent children, the two major welfare programs, would be run by Hopkins's Federal Emergency Relief Administration.

Congress upset these arrangements and established the Social Security Board (SSB) as an independent agency, in charge of both the social insurance and welfare programs created by the Social Security Act. Late in August 1935, the Senate confirmed the first three members of the SSB and, even though the agency lacked permanent appropriations, it began operations. Named as original members of the SSB were Democrats Arthur Altmeyer, a former secretary of the Wisconsin Industrial Commission, and Vincent Miles, a lawyer from Arkansas, and Republican John Winant, a former governor of New Hampshire. Winant chaired the board.

THE SOCIAL SECURITY BOARD

The SSB met nearly every day through the fall of 1935 and most of 1936 to decide on matters of policy. The earliest priorities consisted of staffing the board's three operating bureaus, five service bureaus, and twelve regional offices. The three operating bureaus were the most important. The Bureau of Public Assistance, run between 1936 and 1953 by Jane Hoey, oversaw the distribution of funds to the states to pay for aid to the elderly, aid to dependent children, and aid to the blind. The Bureau of Unemployment Compensation certified state unemployment compensation laws and made grants to the states for the administration of unemployment compensation programs. The Bureau of Federal Old-Age Benefits devised systems to maintain wage records and to pay old-age benefits.

During 1938 the SSB established the Office of the Actuary, which became an integral part of the agency's operations. After 1939 the chief actuary received responsibility for preparing a report on the financial status of the trust fund supporting OASI. This report carried great weight with policymakers in Congress. In addition, the chief actuary, advising Congress on proposed amendments to the program, held an informal veto over which amendments Congress would accept. Illustrating the tight relationship between the actuary and Congress, Robert J. Myers, who served as chief actuary between 1947 and 1970, periodically spent time as, in effect, a staff member of the Finance and Ways and Means Committees as they considered social security legislation.

The board faced its first crisis during the presidential campaign of 1936. In a speech delivered in September, Governor Alfred Landon, the Republican candidate, denounced the old-age insurance program as a fraud and a hoax. Winant immediately resigned as chairman of the SSB to defend the program. The issue was in part that the program was scheduled to begin taking deductions from the paychecks of industrial and commercial workers (one percent of the first $3,000 in wages to be matched by an equal amount from the employer), although the first benefits were not scheduled to be paid until 1942. Landon questioned the fiscal solvency of the program and the administrative ability of the SSB to maintain accurate records.

Immediately preceding the election, an intensive effort began to educate the public on the details of the old-age insurance program. Soon after the election, the SSB issued the first social security card to John Sweeney of New Rochelle, New York. A young Princeton graduate working for his father's company, Sweeney had voted for Landon. Issuing the first card coincided with a national campaign to register workers for the social security system.

In February 1937 President Roosevelt named Altmeyer the new chairman of the SSB. From then until 1953, Altmeyer served as the head of the agency. Other members of the board included George E. Bigge, a Republican and a professor at Brown University, who served until 1946, Molly Dewson, an influential member of the Democratic Women's Committee, who replaced Miles in 1937, and Ellen Woodward of Mississippi, who succeeded Dewson at the end of 1938.

In 1939 the SSB took two important steps, one that increased and one that decreased the agency's power. In 1937 Arthur Altmeyer and other SSB personnel, including I. S. Falk, who served between 1937 and 1953 as head of the Bureau of Research and Statistics, wrote the legislation that resulted in the 1939 Social Security Act Amendments. At the end of June 1939, the SSB lost its independent status and became a charter member of the Federal Security Agency, a subcabinet agency that was the predecessor to the Department of Health, Education, and Welfare. As a result, the chair of the SSB reported to the federal security administrator, rather than directly to the president of the United States.

The 1939 amendments broadened the program to include survivor benefits and special benefits for the spouses of retired workers. In addition, the amendments changed the starting date for the receipt of regular benefits from 1942 to 1940. On 31 January 1940 the SSB issued the first monthly retirement check. It went to Ida

May Fuller of Ludlow, Vermont, who received more than $20,000 from the Social Security program before she died at the age of 100.

When Miss Fuller received her first check, the SSB employed about twelve thousand people, most of whom worked in the Bureau of Old-Age and Survivors' Insurance (BOASI). During the war the board faced an increased work load with a decreased staff. The expansion of the labor force meant, for example, that the SSB received many more wage reports from employers. In fiscal 1941 the board collected 135 million wage items; in fiscal 1944, this number increased to 196 million.

THE SOCIAL SECURITY ADMINISTRATION

In 1946 the SSB faced a major reorganization. President Truman's second reorganization plan of that year abolished the SSB and replaced it with the SSA. Instead of being governed by a three-person board, the social security program would be headed by a commissioner. Arthur Altmeyer, the former chairman of the SSB, became the first commissioner of social security. As part of the same reorganization, the Children's Bureau moved from the Department of Labor to the SSA.

Despite the loss of the Bureau of Unemployment Compensation to the Department of Labor in 1949, the passage of major new amendments in 1950 provided a substantial boost to the program. As the agency recorded in its annual report, regular work in the BOASI was deferred during much of the year to cope with requests for information from Congress. On 28 August 1950 the process paid off in the form of a law that raised the average level of OASI benefits and that extended social security coverage to many urban self-employed, to many agricultural and domestic workers, and to other groups. As Arthur Altmeyer later remarked, the 1950 legislation proved crucial to the program's survival; without it, old-age insurance might well have been superseded by some form of welfare.

The arrival of the Eisenhower administration in 1953 interrupted the internal continuity that had governed the social security program since 1935. First, the Eisenhower administration succeeded in convincing Congress to elevate the Federal Security Administration to a cabinet-level agency. The new Department of Health, Education and Welfare included the SSA as one of its component parts. Then, in the same legislation, the administration earned the right to name the commissioner and deputy commissioner of social security, as well as to replace the agency's bureau chiefs. That meant the departure, among others, of Arthur Altmeyer, I. S. Falk, and Jane Hoey. In the fall of 1953, the administration announced the appointment of John Tramburg, director of Wisconsin's Department of Public Welfare, as commissioner of social security. Jay Roney succeeded Hoey as head of the Bureau of Public Assistance, and Victor Christgau took over as head of the BOASI.

Despite these changes, continuity prevailed both in the program and its operations. No wholesale cutbacks occurred among social security personnel. At the end of June 1953, SSA staff totaled 14,623. Wilbur Cohen, Falk's successor as head of the Bureau of Research and Statistics, and Robert Ball, the deputy chief of the BOASI, both of whom had played important roles in the Altmeyer regime, remained key advisers to Tramburg and Charles Schottland, SSA commissioner between 1954 and 1959. As a result of Ball's and Cohen's advice, Eisenhower decided to recommend a major expansion of the OASI program in 1954. Indeed, incremental expansions in benefit levels and coverage occurred throughout the decade, as amendments in 1956, 1958, and 1960 indicated.

To be sure, the Democratic holdovers did not agree completely with the legislative desires of the Eisenhower administration. In the 1950s employees of the BOASI and the Bureau of Research and Statistics continued to press for the passage of disability insurance, even in the face of administrative opposition. In 1954 the Republican Congress acquiesced in the administration's desire for a modest program that protected the retirement benefits of a person disabled before retirement age. In 1956 SSA employees worked closely with Democratic congressmen in the passage of Social Security Disability Insurance. This program operated under a complex administrative apparatus in which states, acting under contract to the SSA, made disability determinations. SSA employees received applications for disability benefits in district offices and sent them to state disability determination offices for adjudication. Only people judged "unable to engage in substantial gainful activity" because of a demonstrable medical impairment that was expected to last for a year or end in death received benefits. Passage of Social Security Disability Insurance caused the SSA to grow. On 30 June 1957, 22,472 people worked for the agency.

In 1962 Robert Ball became the commissioner of social security, a position he held for the next eleven years. After entering the agency as a field representative in northern New Jersey in 1939, he had worked his way to the very top. And he was just one of the SSA's celebrated employees in the 1960s and early 1970s: as Martha Derthick has pointed out, the six highest ranking executives as of 1970 had 191 years of service at the agency among them. Rufus Miles, a student of public administration, aptly described the SSA as a "career-oriented organization." It was an organization with a well-developed sense of mission and a reputation for administrative competence.

The sheer magnitude of the SSA's operations was impressive. In fiscal year 1963, for example, the SSA processed about five million claims for OASI benefits and 700,000 claims for Social Security Disability Insurance benefits. The agency established new social security account numbers for six million people. It issued 3.5 million duplicate account cards and posted more than 270 million earnings items from employers and the self-employed. In the district offices, SSA employees handled sixteen million inquiries for information about the program.

In the same year, the SSA underwent a significant reorganization. Robert Ball decided to remove the welfare programs from the agency's control and to consolidate many of the functions of the BOASI within the Office of the Commissioner. The bureau itself was abolished. No longer did the SSA run the aid to dependent children or other public assistance programs. What had been the Bureau of Public Assistance moved to the newly created Welfare Administration, as did the Children's Bureau.

MEDICARE

Between 1963 and 1965 the SSA prepared for its next major challenge, the administration of a

health insurance program for its beneficiaries known as Medicare. Robert Ball and others at the SSA played an active role in the politics of Medicare's enactment, providing advice to key congressmen such as Wilbur Mills (D-Ark.) and Clinton Anderson (D-N.Mex.). In lobbying actively for Medicare, the SSA worked closely with Nelson Cruikshank and other representatives of organized labor.

Although it took more than four years from President Kennedy's introduction of Medicare to its passage, Medicare became part of a large package of social security amendments in 1965. In addition to starting Medicare (hospital insurance), Medicaid (health insurance for welfare beneficiaries), and Supplemental Medical Insurance (for doctors' bills), the legislation also raised the earnings base on which social security taxes were paid, contained a substantial seven-percent increase in social security benefits, made it easier for social security beneficiaries to work without losing their benefits, liberalized the definition of disability, began a program of rehabilitation services for people on disability insurance, extended the scope of childhood disability benefits, and lowered the age at which widows could receive benefits. On 28 July 1965 the measure, the most far-reaching amendment to the Social Security Act since the act's passage in 1935, received final approval from Congress and reached the president's desk.

The SSA geared up for a major task as daunting as anything that the government had ever attempted in a time of peace. People needed to be contacted about the voluntary supplementary health insurance program and offered every chance to participate. Fiscal intermediaries and carriers who would help to administer the program had to be selected. Hospitals would have to be inspected to see if they met the criteria for participation, and all of these things would happen simultaneously with preparations for putting many changes in the basic rules of social security into effect. Robert Ball later noted that his agency opened a hundred district offices, hired thousands of people, and issued nineteen million Medicare cards. "As I look back on it . . . I don't how in the hell we did it, to tell you the truth," Ball said.

The implementation of Medicare proved to be a high-water mark for the SSA's self-confidence. The agency continued to grow as it became responsible for more complex tasks. Medicare required the addition of a Bureau of Health Insurance. In 1973, as part of President Nixon's welfare reform effort, the SSA agreed to administer the adult welfare categories, those that covered the blind, the disabled, and the elderly, in a program known as Supplemental Security Income. That required the establishment of a Bureau of Supplemental Security Income. As a result of these new assignments and the growth of the basic programs, the SSA reached a high of 80,054 employees in 1977.

DECLINE AND REBIRTH

In 1977 the SSA became part of a major departmental reorganization initiated by Joseph Califano, President Carter's secretary of health, education, and welfare. Califano decided to create the Health Care Financing Administration, and as a result the SSA lost the Bureau of Health Insurance, which ran the Medicare program. [See Health Care Financing Administration.] In the same reorganization, the SSA gained responsibility for administering the Aid to Families with Dependent Children and child support enforcement programs. This arrangement lasted until 1986.

Between 1935 and 1973, Arthur Altmeyer and Robert Ball dominated the administration of the SSA. After 1973 the organization entered a period of substantial instability. Between 1973 and 1996, no fewer than thirteen individuals served as SSA commissioner. Martha McSteen, a Reagan appointee, held the job between 1983 and 1986 without ever being confirmed by Congress.

Changes in the top personnel were mirrored by frequent internal bureaucratic reorganizations. In January 1975 the SSA established an Office of Program Operations to run the cash benefit programs under its charge. The move effectively undid Ball's 1963 changes. In 1979 Stanford Ross, President Carter's choice as SSA commissioner, moved to abolish the program bureaus and to substitute functional offices. In 1983 the Reagan administration decided to return to program bureaus.

These changes and the rise of political criticism of the social security programs had an unsettling effect on SSA personnel. Legislation in 1977 and 1983 attempted to address a growing deficit in the OASI trust funds. People debated whether the social security program would be able to meet the financial challenge of the retirement of the baby boom generation. The Social Security Disability Insurance and Supplemental Security Income programs also engendered their share of controversy, as legislation in 1980 and 1984 demonstrated.

In response to the changes at the SSA, program defenders proposed that the SSA be removed from the Department of Health and Human Services and reestablished as an independent agency. Congress commissioned a report that appeared in 1984 on the possibility of making the SSA independent. The report led to hearings in both houses of Congress. In 1986 the Committee on Ways and Means noted that the SSA had been viewed as a flagship federal agency, providing efficient and courteous service. In recent years, however, it had begun to decline. As an "important step toward restoring integrity and competence within SSA," the committee recommended that the agency become independent.

For the next eight years, the independence of the SSA became a matter of intense political debate. The Bush administration opposed the move. Daniel Patrick Moynihan (D-N.Y.) of the Senate Finance Committee and Daniel Rostenkowski (D-Ill.) of the House Ways and Means Committee eventually prevailed, however, and on 15 August 1994 President Clinton signed the Social Security Independence and Program Improvements Act of 1994 into law.

On 31 March 1995, nearly sixty years after the passage of the Social Security Act, the SSA once again became an independent agency. The modest old-age insurance program established in the 1935 act had grown into the nation's largest social program. The small SSB with less than ten thousand employees had grown into a major bureaucratic entity employing sixty-five thousand people. It seems certain that further reforms of the program will be necessary to ensure solvency into the twenty-first century.

BIBLIOGRAPHY

Achenbaum, W. Andrew. *Social Security: Visions and Revisions*. New York, 1986.

Altmeyer, Arthur. *The Formative Years of Social Security*. Madison, Wis., 1966.

Berkowitz, Edward. *Mr. Social Security: The Life of Wilbur J. Cohen*. Lawrence, Kans., 1995.

David, Sherri I. *With Dignity*. Westport, Conn., 1965.

Derthick, Martha. *Policymaking for Social Security*. Washington, D.C., 1979.

Derthick, Martha. *Agency under Stress*. Washington, D.C., 1991.

Falk, I. S. *Security Against Sickness: A Study of Health Insurance*. Garden City, N.Y., 1936.

Kingson, Eric, and Edward Berkowitz. *Social Security and Medicare: A Policy Primer*. Westport, Conn., 1993.

McKinley, Charles, and Robert W. Frase. *Launching Social Security: A Capture and Record Account, 1935–1937*. Madison, Wis., 1970.

Miles, Rufus. *The Department of Health, Education, and Welfare*. New York, 1974.

Witte, Edwin. *The Development of the Social Security Act*. Madison, Wis., 1963.

—EDWARD BERKOWITZ

Special Counsel, Office of

 The Office of Special Counsel for Immigration-Related Unfair Employment Practices (OSC) enforces the antidiscrimination provision of the Immigration and Nationality Act (INA), formerly the Immigration Reform and Control Act of 1986. The 1986 act was the first federal law making it illegal for employers to knowingly hire, recruit, or refer for a fee any persons not authorized to work in the United States. The act also made it unlawful to employ an undocumented worker or a worker who loses authorization to work. (Those hired before 6 November 1986 do not fall within this category.)

The 1986 law was an attempt to reduce the stream of undocumented workers entering the United States for employment. But the act, some argued, was a double-edged sword. On the one side, hiring undocumented workers would result in a penalty, and on the other, these employer sanctions might discourage employers from hiring certain eligible workers if they looked or sounded foreign. To combat this problem, members of Congress made the law also prohibit discrimination in hiring and firing on the basis of citizenship status or national origin. Penalties for employers who discriminate include fines, the hiring or rehiring of the employee, and payment of back wages.

The antidiscrimination provision of the INA protects workers from several types of discrimination including, for example, national origin discrimination, which takes place when an employer treats a job applicant or employee differently because of the individual's (or his or her ancestors') birthplace or the physical, cultural, or linguistic characteristics of a particular nationality. Another form of discrimination, citizenship status discrimination, occurs when an employer rejects a job applicant, fires an employee, or retaliates against an employee because of the individual's citizenship or immigration status.

Document abuse is another type of discrimination and occurs when an employer refuses to accept documents that appear to be genuine and prove identity, work authorization, or both. Requiring more or specific documents to prove an employee's identity and/or work authorization also constitutes document abuse. Finally, an employer may not retaliate against any individual for filing a complaint, cooperating in an investigation, or testifying at a hearing.

OSC research has consistently shown that many incidents of immigration-related employment discrimination stem from the employer's confusion about acceptable work-authorization documents, and not discrimination. Therefore, with a focus on the antidiscrimination provision of the INA, the OSC educates workers about their rights and how to defend them and informs employers about their rights and responsibilities under the provision. For example, in 1994 the OSC awarded nearly $1 million in grants to nine community-based organizations and employer groups to help combat job discrimination against work-authorized immigrants.

Finally, the OSC, a component of the Department of Justice's Civil Rights Division, covers all cases of discrimination based on citizenship status by employers of four to fourteen employees. The Equal Employment Opportunity Commission has jurisdiction over employers of fifteen or more.

[*See also* Equal Employment Opportunity Commission.]

BIBLIOGRAPHY

U.S. Department of Justice. Office of Special Counsel. *Look at the Facts, Not at the Faces.* Washington, D.C., 1993.

U.S. Department of Justice. Office of Special Counsel. *OSC Update.* Washington, D.C., 1993.

U.S. Department of Justice. Office of Special Counsel. *OSC Update.* Washington, D.C., 1994.

U.S. Department of Justice. Office of Special Counsel. *OSC Update.* Washington, D.C., winter, 1995.

U.S. Department of Justice. Office of Special Counsel. *OSC Update.* Washington, D.C., summer, 1995.

U.S. Department of Justice. Office of Special Counsel. *You Have the Right to Work: Don't Let Anyone Take it Away.* Washington, D.C., 1996.

—VERONICA D. DICONTI

Standards and Technology, National Institute of

In 1957 the National Institute of Standards and Technology completed its first cesium atomic beam clock. In 1967 the cesium atom's natural frequency was formally recognized as the new international unit of time: the second was defined as exactly 9,192,631,770 oscillations of the cesium atom's resonant frequency.

What is now known as the National Institute of Standards and Technology (NIST) was created by an act of Congress in 1901 and was first called the National Bureau of Standards. At first a part of the Department of the Treasury, its name was changed in 1988, and it was moved to the Department of Commerce in 1989. After the passage of the enabling legislation, Samuel Wesley Stratton was appointed as the first director. The bureau's mission included:

- Custody of the national standards

- Comparison of the standards used in science, engineering, manufacturing, and commerce with the national standards

- Construction of standards when necessary

- Testing and calibration of standards-measuring apparatus

- Determination of physical constraints and the properties of materials when such data are of great importance to science and manufacturing and are not available in sufficient accuracy elsewhere.

The bureau was given no policing or regulatory authority. Since it was staffed by eminent scientists, it became gradually involved in broader technology development beyond measurements, standards, and data. In 1951 Edward Condon resigned in the midst of a McCarthy probe. He was followed by Allen V. Astin, who led the bureau for the next seventeen years. In 1953 the Kelly Committee was formed "to evaluate the present functions and operations of the National Bureau of Standards." Its report is one of the most important documents in the bureau's history, and it set the goals that have guided the bureau since.

The NIST administers an array of technology-based programs. The Advanced Technology Program provides cost-shared awards to industry to develop high-risk technologies with commercial potential and build bridges between basic research and product development. The Manufacturing Extension Partnership helps small and medium-sized companies adopt new technologies. The Malcolm Baldrige National Quality Award administered by the NIST has become the most prestigious award in American industry. NIST research is done in eight laboratories: Building and Fire Research, Chemical Science and Technology, Computing and Applied Mathematics, Computer Systems, Electronics and Electrical Engineering, Manufacturing Engineering, Materials Science and Engineering, and Physics. Technology Services is a division that fosters technology transfer.

BIBLIOGRAPHY

Cochrane, Rexmond C. *Measures for Progress: A History of the National Bureau of Standards.* Philadelphia, 1976.

Weber, Gustavus A. *The Bureau of Standards: Its History, Activities and Organization.* New York, 1925.

—GEORGE THOMAS KURIAN

State, Department of

Now in its third century as the flagship foreign affairs agency of the U.S. federal government, the Department of State has provided support and expertise to presidents and secretaries of state, worked with Congress, and served and protected the citizens of the United States as the nation grew to become a great power. For more than two hundred years, the Department of State has conducted American diplomacy through war and peace, amidst the competing currents of isolationism and internationalism that have shaped American foreign policy and its commitment to liberty and democracy.

THE EMERGING STATE DEPARTMENT, 1789–1860

The Constitution of the United States, drafted in Philadelphia in the summer of 1787 and ratified by the states the following year, gave the president responsibility for the conduct of the nation's foreign relations. It soon became clear, however, that an executive branch was necessary to support President Washington in the conduct of the affairs of the new federal government. The House and Senate approved legislation to establish a Department of Foreign Affairs on 21 July 1789, and President Washington signed it into law on 27 July, making the Department of Foreign Affairs the first federal agency to be created under the new Constitution. This legislation remains the basic law of the Department of State. In September 1789 additional legislation changed the name of the agency to the Department of State and assigned to it a variety of domestic duties.

These responsibilities grew to include management of the Mint, keeper of the Great Seal of the United States, and the taking of the census. President Washington signed the new legislation on 15 September. Most of these domestic duties of the Department of State were eventually turned over to various new federal departments and agencies that were established during the nineteenth century.

President Washington appointed Thomas Jefferson in September 1789 to be the first secretary of state. In February 1790 Jefferson reluctantly returned from Paris, where he was serving as the American minister to France. The new Department of State under Secretary Jefferson was set up briefly in New York until the capital was moved to Philadelphia. Under Jefferson and his immediate successors, the department consisted of several clerks and a part-time translator. The Department of State and the rest of the new government finally moved to its permanent home in Washington, D.C., in early 1800.

During the first thirty-five years under the Constitution of 1789, the Department of State was led by the greatest leaders of the new republic. For Thomas Jefferson, James Madison, James Monroe, and John Quincy Adams, service as secretary of state proved to be the stepping-stone to election as president. At no time in the history of the United States would foreign relations be so critical to the very existence of the nation and the well-being of its citizens. During these years of the Napoleonic Wars and their aftermath, the new republic had to complete its revolutionary struggles, free itself from entangling alliances with the Old World, and complete the largest part of the expansion of the country to the Caribbean, across the Mississippi, and, with the Louisiana Purchase, to the Pacific Ocean. The Department of State, which grew to more than twenty employees by 1825, also continued to carry out a wide variety of domestic duties assigned to it by Congress in 1789.

From 1825, when John Quincy Adams left the department to become president, until the Civil War, America experienced the great initial expansion of its industry and commerce and the surge of the population westward across the Great Plains and the western mountains and deserts. Foreign affairs, while important, mostly lost the urgency of the founding years. The Department of State focused on managing the gradual broadening of U.S. diplomatic relations and the spread of American ships and commerce to all corners of the world. There were few major foreign policy problems: negotiating with the British the northern border with Canada and resolving, through diplomacy and sometimes war, the conflicts with Mexico over the southwestern frontier. Congress gradually removed from the Department of State its domestic duties and transferred them to new departments and agencies like the Department of the Interior. The secretaries of state continued to be the preeminent members of the president's cabinet, but only twice more would former secretaries of state (Martin Van Buren and James Buchanan) become president. Presidents from Andrew Jackson to James Buchanan made the nation's few really important foreign affairs decisions.

The Department of State changed little during these years. John Quincy Adams was the first secretary of state to introduce some basic organizational and management practices so that the small agency could handle its slowly expanding responsibilities. In 1833 Secretary of State Louis McLane carried out the first overall reorganization of the department, the most important aspect of which was the establishment of bureaus, including the Diplomatic, Consular, and Home Bureaus. The number of employees grew from eight in 1790 to twenty-three in 1830 and to forty-two in 1860.

The American diplomatic service expanded slowly in the late eighteenth and early nineteenth century, when the nation was adamantly opposed to extensive diplomatic contacts with European nations. In 1790 the United States sent ministers plenipotentiary to only two countries—France and Great Britain. By 1830 the number grew to fifteen; by 1860, to thirty-three. The consular service, on the other hand, grew steadily during this time. Consuls, commercial agents, and consular agents protected American ships and crews abroad and promoted the expansion of American commerce. American consular posts grew in number from ten in 1790 to 141 in 1831 and 253 in 1860.

THE DEPARTMENT COMES OF AGE, 1861–1895

Under William Henry Seward the Office of the Secretary of State became a position of unprecedented power and importance during the Civil War. Secretary Seward was President Abraham Lincoln's principal counselor on a broad range of urgent wartime domestic matters as well as on the vital diplomatic effort to prevent European powers from recognizing or assisting the Confed-

eracy. The success of the State Department and American diplomatic representatives abroad in the early years of the Civil War was critical to isolating the South until the Union armies and navy could be mobilized to win the struggle. The State Department's authority grew in size and activity even as the whole federal government was centralized, expanded, and strengthened during the Civil War.

After the Civil War the State Department gained a more appropriate bureaucratic structure to deal with its increasing responsibility of serving the interests of a rapidly industrializing America, whose economic growth was beginning to outdistance most European powers. In 1870 Secretary Hamilton Fish redefined the department's bureau structure and issued a series of rules and regulations updating its administrative practices. Fish also secured from Congress the addition of a third assistant secretary of state. (Secretary Seward had a second assistant secretary added to the department in 1866.)

Continuity and experience in the conduct of the responsibilities of the State Department and of its management before, during, and after the Civil War were assured by the long-term presence of William Hunter. Hunter, who served in the department for more than forty years, was chief clerk from 1852 until 1866, when he was promoted to the newly established position of second assistant secretary of state. He had served as acting secretary during the convalescence of Secretary Seward and his son, Assistant Secretary Frederick Seward, after the April 1865 assassination attempt. Hunter occupied the position of second secretary under seven secretaries of state until his death in 1886. In so doing he confirmed the establishment of a leadership role for the most senior member of the department's permanent bureaucracy. Hunter was succeeded as second assistant secretary by Alvey A. Adee, who filled that post until his death in 1924. Thanks to their long service as the top career officers of the Department of State from 1841 to 1924, William Derrick, William Hunter, and Alvey Adee had a profound impact on American foreign affairs by serving in their time as guarantors of institutional memory, by coordinating the work of the department, and by developing and main-

THE DEPARTMENT OF STATE HEADQUARTERS IN WASHINGTON, D.C. *Originally intended to house the Department of Defense, the structure was turned over to the Department of State on the eve of World War II, when the Department of Defense decided instead to construct the massive Pentagon across the Potomac River in Arlington, Virginia.*

taining a distinctive style of American diplomacy.

During the three decades after the Civil War, the United States reverted to a basically isolationist foreign policy and confronted no real overseas crises. Beneath the orderly management of minor diplomatic issues of America's Gilded Age, the rapidly expanding American economy was pushing the nation and its State Department toward important changes in the conduct of foreign affairs. The American presence and commerce abroad increased at an astounding rate. Between the end of the Civil War and the outbreak of the Spanish-American War thirty-four years later, American exports tripled, and the United States was second only to Great Britain in export trade. The consular service became the

lead instrument in the search for American markets abroad. In 1860 there were 480 consulates, commercial agencies, and consular agencies abroad, and by 1890 this number had risen to 760. Congress began to adopt measures to place American diplomatic representatives in the front rank of international diplomacy and to ensure that both the consular and the diplomatic services were more efficiently and tightly managed to represent American interests abroad. In 1893 Congress finally acknowledged that the United States had come of age diplomatically when it authorized the appointment of ambassadorial-rank representatives to Great Britain and other major powers. In 1895 President Grover Cleveland issued regulations requiring the filling of vacancies on the basis of written examinations, including language tests. Other measures were adopted to deal with the salaries and inspection of consular posts.

A corps of professional American diplomats was emerging to meet the new challenges of foreign policy. Although the system of patronage continued to dominate the presidential appointment process, able and experienced men (but not yet women) were retained in service despite changes of administration and party. In the years preceding World War I, such distinguished diplomats as George Seward, Robert McLane, Charles Denby, and William Rockhill provided outstanding American representation in the Far East; Henry White had a long and important career caring for American interests in Great Britain; Henry Vignaud spent nearly thirty-five years in the embassy in Paris; and George Schuyler served in a variety of posts in eastern Europe.

MANAGING THE FOREIGN AFFAIRS OF A GREAT POWER, 1900–1940

From the Spanish-American War at the turn of the century until the first years of the presidency of Franklin D. Roosevelt, the United States, the reluctance of many Americans notwithstanding, joined the ranks of the great world powers. The nation's overseas involvements and responsibilities expanded dramatically. Theodore Roosevelt ushered in the imperial phase of U.S. diplomacy with the building of the Panama Canal, the dispatch of the U.S. fleet around the world, the Russo-Japanese peace settlement at Portsmouth, New Hampshire, and the brokering of great power arrangements to ward off war over European colonialism in Africa. Secretary of State John Hay heralded the emergence of the United States as a Pacific power with his policies in China. The Department of State and the diplomatic and consular services expanded and modernized in response to the expanding interests abroad of twentieth-century American commercial and cultural interests. Caution and a traditional conservatism, reflecting the ambivalences of the general citizenry, however, continued to dominate the Department of State.

During this time the Department of State grew from ninety-one employees in Washington, D.C., and a budget of $141,000 in 1900, to 708 employees and a budget of $1.4 million in 1920, to 1,128 employees and a budget of $2.8 million in 1940. Secretary of State Philander Knox in 1909 introduced new political-geographic divisions to handle the main substantive work of the department, greatly expanded the role of the department's solicitor, and assigned the growing administrative tasks to the third assistant secretary of state. Divisions for Information and for Trade Relations also were created.

World War I imposed global responsibilities on the United States government. In 1914 the United States had active and purposeful diplomatic relations with few of the nations of the world, recognized national interests in few of them, and held coherent policies toward hardly any of them. The war changed this completely. During the war and the peace negotiations that followed, President Woodrow Wilson, with the help of the Department of State, developed a comprehensive American foreign policy with respect to all the major issues and problems arising from the war and the peace settlement. High-level diplomatic negotiations involved American diplomats and the Department of State. To assist the secretary of state in managing the growing overseas responsibilities, Congress created the position of under secretary of state in 1919.

Modernized communications were developed to carry out the department's global business. The number of telegrams increased tenfold between 1900 and 1914 and continued to rise steadily thereafter. The use of telegraphic codes and ciphers, little needed before World War I, also expanded during and after World War I. The department introduced security measures for the protection of information and began the process of labeling and controlling "secret" and "confidential" documents. Effective American diplomatic codes were introduced after the war, and an "American Black Chamber" operation was experimented with in an effort to decipher the coded diplomatic messages of other nations. Cordell Hull was the first secretary of state to make use of the telephone to instruct overseas missions and delegations.

Professionalization of the Foreign Service and the Department of State in the first decades of the twentieth century did little initially to undo the elitist character of U.S. diplomacy. Appointment to the Foreign Service continued to be essentially confined to members of the prosperous white Anglo-Saxon Protestant community. Foreign policy was made at the Department of State with little reference to broad democratic community of people and interests. President Wilson's progressivist policies began to change the style of American diplomacy.

World War I set in motion some changes that could not be held back. One of the most important consequences of the war was the increased employment of women and their rise to places of greater leadership in the Department of State. Margaret M. Hanna had served as a clerk in the department for twenty-three years when she was made chief of the Correspondence Bureau. She was succeeded by Blanche Halla in the late 1930s. Ruth Shipley, who for a time was Hanna's assistant, later served for twenty-five years as head of the Passport Bureau. Women were admitted into the new Foreign Service beginning in 1925. President Franklin D. Roosevelt appointed the first two women chiefs of mission: Ruth Bryan Owen served as minister to Denmark from 1933 to 1936, and Florence Jaffrey Harriman served as minister to Norway from 1937 until 1940. The advancement of women in the department remained, however, slow.

In the period between World Wars I and II, women made up more than half of the departmental work force, although most of these positions were lower-ranking clerical jobs. African-Americans were also well represented in the lowest-paying department positions. The separation of the races in the government workplace that set in during the Wilson presidency was felt in the Department of State and confined African Americans to the bottom of career ladders. Exceptions occurred. Clifton Wharton passed his oral and written examinations and became the first black Foreign Service officer in August 1925. Jews also felt the exclusionary practices that were prevalent elsewhere in the government establishment and the wider business and professional world.

After several decades of effort by the Department of State, led by the long-serving career officer and assistant secretary of state Wilbur J. Carr, Congress adopted on 24 May 1924 the Rogers Act, creating a unified (combining the diplomatic and consular services) and professional Foreign Service of the United States. The act made merit rather than politics the basis for appointment and promotion, and it fostered a permanent career service to represent the nation abroad. Diplomatic and consular officers were amalgamated into a single service and could and did serve in either function. Improved salaries and benefits opened the service to those with limited means. Subsequent reforms and modifications emphasized language training and expertise. The Foreign Services Buildings Act of 1926 provided for the first time for the construction of embassy and consular buildings overseas.

The professionalization of the diplomatic service was reflected in the changing composition of the heads of American diplomatic missions. The percentage of career officers serving as chief of mission rose from zero before 1920 to thirty percent in 1924 following the Rogers Act, to nearly fifty-five percent during World War II. The rotation of diplomatic officers from overseas posts into positions of leadership in the department was begun during World War I and was greatly enhanced by the Rogers Act. By 1939 the Foreign Service had become the single personnel service for all overseas service except for military and naval attachés. By the time the United States entered World War II, President Roosevelt and Secretary of State Cordell Hull were being served by a Foreign Service of about 830 trained officers.

THE DEPARTMENT OF STATE AND THE UNITED STATES AS A SUPERPOWER, 1945–1960

The United States emerged from World War II as the most powerful nation in the world. During the next fifteen years American foreign policy was dominated by the series of crises, great and small, that marked the struggle to contain the aggressive communism of the Soviet Union. The basic American government analysis of its postwar task was set forth in 1950 in National Security Council (NSC) document no. 68, which postulated a protracted period of world crisis resulting from communist aggression and urged a major military buildup of nuclear and conventional arms supported by large U.S. budgets and increased taxes. Against the backdrop of the Cold War, the United States led the search for a lasting peace settlement in Europe and Asia, took the lead with the Marshall Plan and other forms of economic and technical assistance to rebuild the shattered world economy, and pushed forward, even to the dismay of its great power allies, the decolonization of the Third World. Secretaries of State James F. Byrnes, George C. Marshall, Dean Acheson, John Foster Dulles, and Christian A. Herter worked closely with Presidents Truman and Eisenhower to fashion U.S. foreign policy. Byrnes and his successors traveled frequently to conferences and negotiations around the world. In his five years in office, John Foster Dulles traveled 480,000 miles. The United States and its diplomats gave the postwar peace settlement its direction and stood as a guarantor of its durability. In the United Nations, the vehicle for the building of a new standard and style of international relations, the United States provided much of the resources and initiative and the Department of State was at the forefront of the extensive multilateral diplomacy that arose to harness the experience of the older nations and the expectations of the newly emergent states.

To administer the new and complex responsibilities of the Department of State during and after World War II, the number of domestic employees grew from 1,128 in 1940 to more than 3,700 in 1945 and nearly 9,000 by 1950. The postwar Department of State was completely overhauled and restructured. New bureaus and offices were created and staffed. Bureaus for Administration and Economic Affairs were established in 1944. When the war ended, a large new Bureau of Public Affairs was created by sweeping together the remnants of a variety of wartime information and propaganda agencies. Secretary Marshall, who sorely missed the tightly coordinated conduct of affairs that characterized his military command experiences, set up an Executive Secretariat and a Policy Planning Staff in 1947 to organize and manage the department's decision-making and undertake long-range policy planning. Marshall's secretariat proved so

successful that it has continued, without significant change, to the present day. The Policy Planning Staff, initially manned by such luminaries as George Kennan and Paul Nitze, lost its original luster under later secretaries, and instead of tending to long-range planning became a troubleshooting staff for the department leadership.

In the years after the end of the war, it became apparent that the Department of State, swollen by the personnel and tasks of countless wartime agencies and saddled with the broad new global tasks of a world superpower, was unable to perform as decisively or quickly as the world situation usually demanded. Worse still, the conflict between the growing and powerful Foreign Service and the civil service, including many workers from disparate wartime agencies, was thwarting efficient government. In 1949 a comprehensive department restructuring was carried out in response to the commission on governmental organization headed by former president Herbert Hoover. The work of the department was reorganized to center on major policy-making bureaus for Inter-American Affairs, Far Eastern Affairs, European Affairs, Near Eastern and African Affairs, International Organization Affairs, and Congressional Relations. Personnel systems for the Foreign Service and the civil service were placed under central leadership with the aim of ameliorating the tensions between the two.

The geographic bureau structure was rounded out in 1958, in advance of the rapid decolonization of Africa in the 1960s, with the establishment of a Bureau of African Affairs. Meanwhile, in response to the increasing diversification of foreign policy issues, the department created a Bureau for Consular Affairs in 1952, a Bureau of Intelligence in 1957, and a Bureau of Cultural Affairs in 1960. The expanding department gradually gained a new level of policymakers and coordinators, including the creation of the position of under secretary for economic affairs in 1946. A deputy under secretary for management was first appointed in 1949, and by 1953 the position had been raised to under secretary for management. The proliferating political bureaus were first overseen in 1949 by a deputy under secretary for political affairs; this position was raised to under secretary of state for political affairs in 1959.

Although the Department of State expanded substantially to meet its growing responsibilities around the world and to respond to communist threats as the Cold War deepened, it lost its role as the sole federal agency involved in the preparation and execution of foreign policy. Military units were stationed at bases around the world, and American air and naval power might be called upon by the president at any moment to deal with a crisis abroad. Department of State leaders were uncomfortable with the penchant for aggressive intelligence gathering and covert political action that emerged from World War II. As a result, a separate Central Intelligence Agency was created in 1947 to coordinate intelligence activities outside the United States, and it soon developed a worldwide operational apparatus that offered presidents secret operations to further foreign policy goals. The Departments of Treasury, Commerce, and Agriculture were also involved in major international programs. Separate agencies managed expanding overseas information programs and economic assistance efforts in war-ravaged Europe and in the developing nations of Asia and Africa. Above all, the NSC was created in 1947 as part of the White House apparatus to coordinate for the president the principal international issues confronting the government and the several agencies concerned with foreign affairs. While Secretaries of State Acheson and Dulles held the lead role in the NSC for its first few years, the balance of control had flowed to the White House staff. The Department of State sought to work out effective relationships with these agencies in Washington and at posts abroad. The successes in State Department coordination of the foreign policy establishment were often overlooked by critics who focused on the increasingly complicated decision-making process and the different voices defining the scope of American interests and commitments abroad.

A major development in the conduct of foreign affairs was the significant involvement of the public in the formulation of policies. From the last days of World War II, the Department of State has worked to inform and educate the American public about the problems and possibilities posed by the world political scene. The press conference grew to be the principal means by which the secretary of state and the Department of State provided the nearly insatiable demand for foreign policy information and insight from the news media. News conferences by the secretary of state, begun on an informal basis by Secretary Hull in the 1930s, expanded as the news corps accredited to the department grew. In the 1950s press conferences by Secretaries Dean Acheson and John Foster Dulles grew increasingly infrequent. Instead, Department of State spokesmen, such as the veteran Lincoln White, became the intermediaries for correspondents assigned to "Foggy Bottom." The State Department also reached beyond the news media to explain America's deepening involvement in international affairs and to listen to the views of the public. Quality publications ranging from authoritative statements on current policy to historical background documentaries were developed, and a broad program of conferences, briefings, and speeches sought to illuminate complex policies and negotiations for interested citizens and for the growing number of nongovernmental organizations concerned with America's role and involvement abroad.

In 1940 the United States was represented abroad by nineteen embassies, thirty-nine legations, and one other mission. Twenty years later, there were seventy-eight embassies, three legations, and two other missions. The Foreign Service Reform Act of 1946 established the structure for a modern, efficient service with a consolidated classification system, promotion and retirement programs, and improved allowances and assignment policies. The Foreign Service Institute provided special language and area training. In the 1950s the department and the Foreign Service made the first serious efforts to recruit women, blacks, and other minorities at the officer level. The number of Americans employed overseas grew from about two thousand in 1939 to thirty-five hundred in 1946 to more than six thousand by 1960. In addition the department employed more than nine thousand foreign personnel overseas by 1960. An independent U.S. Information Agency was established in 1951 to coordinate the public affairs and cultural efforts abroad and to manage the expanding Voice of America. Other agencies coordinated expanding economic and military assistance.

The emerging modern and comparatively large Department of State and Foreign Service, with their greatly broadened scope of activities, found themselves threatened by dangers at home and abroad. Threats by agents of the wartime Fascist enemies were followed by the even more insidious menace of a world communism aiming at not only espionage but the subversion of the governments of America's allies and the expansion of the Soviet Union by whatever means available. Security measures for the protection of both information and personnel, both at the department in Washington and at the individual missions abroad, began on a limited scale in the years leading to the outbreak of World War II, but really became extensive and even intrusive in the decade after the end of the war. These security practices culminated in the accusations of treasonous activity eventually aimed at several hundred department and Foreign Service officers by Senator Joseph McCarthy and other members of Congress in the 1950s. Some dismissals did occur, and in other cases careers were needlessly destroyed. The security "scare" injured the morale of department personnel just as the department shouldered its most difficult new tasks around the world. Some of the most bitter consequences of the McCarthyite purges became evident years later during American involvement in the Vietnam War when American leaders found themselves blundering ever deeper into the quagmire in significant part because they lacked vital expertise in Asia.

The first postwar decades witnessed accelerated changes in the role of minorities in the Department of State. The mobilization of men for the war effort made the recruitment of even more women into the department an urgent necessity. Racial barriers were gradually undone pursuant to President Roosevelt's orders to introduce fair employment practices in the federal government. The desegregation of African Americans in the Department of State cafeteria occurred quietly during World War II, and other

restrictive hiring and promotion practices began to be reversed. It was not until 1958, however, that Clifton Wharton became the first black chief of mission in the Foreign Service. Segregation in the District of Columbia, the home of many of those who worked in the State Department, gave way slowly through these years.

This expansion of American diplomatic activities and responsibilities abroad gave rise to a program to build American embassies either to replace smaller buildings or to establish the U.S. presence in areas where there had been none. The first American-designed and -owned embassies abroad had been those in Paris and Tokyo built between the two world wars. The availability of nearly $175 million in "counterpart" funds resulting from the repayment in local currencies for lend-lease provided the basis for an ambitious program in the 1950s for building embassies and consulates in Europe, Africa, and Asia. These buildings, designed in the modern international style by leading American architects, projected a powerful image abroad of America as superpower. The need for increased security for the larger American diplomatic establishments abroad, many in countries where political instability was chronic, led to the deployment of Marine guard detachments at many of the embassy buildings.

THE DEPARTMENT OF STATE'S ROLE IN THE U.S. FOREIGN AFFAIRS COMMUNITY, 1961–1996

The last thirty-five years have seen the cresting of American power and responsibility in world affairs, the climax and end of the Cold War, and the slow emergence of a new and different world order. Presidents from John F. Kennedy and Lyndon Johnson to George Bush and Bill Clinton have personally directed the response to challenges to American interests, threats to national security, and disturbances to international peace and stability. These foreign affairs crises ranged from the imminent danger of war with the Soviet Union during the Cuban missile crisis in 1962 and the confrontation in a divided Berlin in 1963, the involvement in the Vietnam War in the 1960s and early 1970s, and the resort to massive military force against Iraqi aggression during Operation Desert Storm in 1991. Crises erupted recurrently during this period in the Caribbean, Africa, the Mediterranean, the Middle East, and Southeast Asia. The emergence of the nations of the Third World brought with it unavoidable and ever-widening American responsibilities and involvements in the economic well-being of developing peoples and their essential human rights.

In attempting to manage or at least respond to the often-complex foreign affairs crises of these recent decades, presidents have not only turned to the secretaries of state and their department but have also drawn into the management and decision-making process a growing number of other agencies that acquired major foreign affairs responsibilities. The form and nature of this involvement varied from president to president. John Kennedy concentrated more on crisis management and major policy coordination in the White House and in an NSC system pared down from the elaborate staffing of the Eisenhower administration. Lyndon Johnson experimented with a "senior interdepartmental group" that gave the secretary of state primary responsibility for policy coordination. Presidents Nixon and Ford favored a decision-making style that concentrated authority as much as possible in the White House and the NSC. Presidents Carter, Reagan, and Bush depended on the development of an NSC system featuring a powerful national security adviser and steadily expanding staff that mediated, with greater or lesser success, among the increasing number of departments and agencies with foreign affairs responsibilities.

Within these changing systems for high-level policy formulation, the Department of State worked alongside various other agencies of government with major national security responsibilities. A conglomerate "foreign affairs community" emerged reflecting the burgeoning bureaucracy involved in the formulation and execution of foreign policy. The overall impact and effectiveness of the Department of State within this community varied from presidency to presidency. Most observers agreed, however, that the erosion of the traditional preeminence in foreign affairs of the Department of State and the Foreign Service would only be reversed for brief periods during the incumbency of a secretary of state

who enjoyed the close confidence of the president and the support of advisers and lieutenants who could wrest leadership of diplomatic crises from the hands of competing agencies and officials.

Below the "principals" level, the department policy-making leadership was further redefined and expanded to deal with the new issues of foreign policy. The Department of State and the Congress responded to the modern problems of crisis management, terrorism, science and the environment, human rights, narcotics, and refugee affairs by creating new organizations at the bureau level. The proliferation of bureaus (there were thirty by 1990) allowed the department to bring expertise to bear on the new problems of foreign policy, but it also threatened policy-making with recurrent bottlenecks as overlapping responsibilities too often deprived the secretary of state of timely recommendations and decisive policy recommendations. In the Nixon, Ford, and Carter administrations, determined national security advisers were tempted to ignore or evade department policymakers. In the Reagan and Bush administrations, Secretaries Alexander Haig and George Schultz drew the department more closely into the inner decision-making circles, but some observers feared that Secretary James Baker's close group of advisers seemed too often to conduct the main lines of foreign policy without input from the department as a whole. Secretary of State Warren Christopher revived the essential role of State Department policy recommendations across the spectrum of foreign policy concerns and sought to streamline the policy-making pyramid.

Terrorist activity in recent years aimed at overseas American personnel has brought about intensified concern about the protection of embassies and missions abroad and at home. Congress in 1985 authorized the Department of State's Bureau of Diplomatic Security to undertake a prodigious program to defend U.S. diplomatic and consular establishments from the threats of terrorists and espionage. The open outreach of the modernist architecture of American embassies and consulates of the 1950s was abandoned in place of secure perimeters and bombproof walls.

The Department of State, working with other agencies of the U.S. government, has in recent years spearheaded the international struggle to combat terrorism on a global basis.

The secretaries of state and their close advisers sought to make use of the most modern technology, communications, and management in order to be better able to meet the recurrent crises and threats to American interests around the world. An Operations Center was established in April 1961 to provide the Department of State with instant worldwide crisis communications. The first computer was installed in the department in 1962, and by 1972 computers managed the bulk of department communications with posts abroad. Secretaries of state often had to take the department "on the road" in order to deal in person with critical negotiations, such as Secretary Kissinger's "shuttle diplomacy" in 1974 to stabilize the tensions in the Middle East and begin the long peace process in the region.

The expanded Department of State had moved in 1947 from the elegant State, War, and Navy Building on Seventeenth Street to a new home on Twenty-first Street in Foggy Bottom, but these quarters were almost immediately too small, and additional temporary buildings multiplied. In the 1960s a new State Department building attached to the old one brought together most, although not all, of about seven thousand department employees in Washington, D.C. State Department principals and most of the assistant secretaries occupied suites on the seventh floor while the staffs were arranged vertically below them, to the extent possible. The Agency for International Development, which coordinated U.S. foreign assistance programs, and the Arms Control and Disarmament Agency also shared space with the State Department, and by the 1980s State Department personnel and activities had spread into more than twenty buildings around the District of Columbia.

The Department of State and the American people enjoyed a long period of consensus regarding the goals and direction of foreign policy in the first twenty years following World War II. Public support was consistently forthcoming for presidentially mandated overseas initiatives in Europe, the Middle East, East Asia, and even in the Caribbean against the perceived threat of international communism. An essentially unanimous nation followed the president in frequent diplomatic interventions and generous efforts of aid and assistance, and even in the case of limited wars and secret political actions. The involvement of the United States in the Vietnam War, however, proved to be rancorously divisive to American public opinion. The longstanding national consensus on the use of power became frayed if not completely torn. Suspicion of American leadership and government grew, and the Department of State received its share of condemnation at the hands of critics. Beginning with the demonstrations and disasters of Vietnam, the conduct of foreign policy became snarled in contentious public debate as it had never been before. As the danger from world communism and nuclear war declined, external threats to the nation in the form of terrorist attacks, uncontrolled immigration, and relentless economic competition gnawed at many Americans and made foreign policy more of an everyday concern.

The principal vehicle for informing the public regarding foreign policy issues, apart from the speeches and press conferences of the president and the secretary of state, were the briefings provided to the diplomatic press corps at the Department of State. The informal give-and-take between briefers and correspondents at the department of the immediate postwar years was soon overwhelmed by the wide scope and complexity of recurrent foreign policy crises and high-level negotiations. U.S.-Soviet summit meetings and shuttle diplomacy in the Middle East were examples of foreign affairs events that gained the interest and attention of the nation. In the early 1960s in the wake of the widening Vietnam War, daily noon briefings by the State Department spokesman became a principal vehicle for disseminating the administration's views on current crises and its responses to public anguish and concern over threats to Americans and their interests. Occasionally these briefings, brought live on evening television to millions of Americans, became a focus of intense national attention, as during the 444 days when American diplomatic personnel were held hostage by Iranian authorities in 1979 and spokesman Hodding Carter kept a fascinated and horrified nation up to date.

MODERNIZING THE DEPARTMENT OF STATE AND THE FOREIGN SERVICE

Since the inauguration of President Kennedy, two new generations of Foreign Service officers and Department of State personnel have served in Washington and around the world. These officers have been different from their predecessors. They were recruited broadly from around the nation, and many have advanced education, including a significant number of doctorates of philosophy. The newer generation of Foreign Service officers also reflected more closely the general makeup of the population in terms of the numbers of women and minorities. Beginning with President Jimmy Carter and Secretary of State Cyrus Vance, affirmative action programs were introduced in the Department of State to better guarantee fairness in the hiring of new personnel. Efforts at broadening and balancing the makeup of the department and the Foreign Service moved too slowly to make up fully for decades of denial and exclusionary recruitment and promotion practices. The Foreign Service Reform Act of 1980 provided for more rigorous standards for recruitment and promotion, improved the rewards of service, and sought to deal with the problems of promotion and tenure that were sapping the once very high morale of the service.

New Foreign Service officers and department personnel recruited after 1960 were part of the generation that questioned and challenged traditional social and political values. As American involvement in the Vietnam War deepened, many among the younger Foreign Service officers joined in the public opposition to the war and actively protested American actions and policies. Doubts about leadership decisions spread from Vietnam issues to other American involvements abroad. In 1968 Secretary of State Dean Rusk authorized the establishment of a "dissent channel" through which officers could offer critiques of official policies and alternative approaches. An "Open Forum" was begun in 1970 to allow Foreign Service and Department of State personnel to hear a wide spectrum of opinion and expertise on foreign policy issues.

The Foreign Service Institute made ever-greater efforts to give officers throughout their careers a variety of specialized training. In addition to area and language training, the Institute's Center for the Study of Foreign Affairs provides symposia and publications on important foreign affairs issues. The capstone of the department's educational program was the "Senior Seminar," begun in 1958. In this program, small groups of the most promising midlevel Foreign Service officers, together with some military officers and officials of other agencies, undergo a year of special experience in what has come to be considered the most advanced professional development program available to senior career officials in the U.S. government.

The culmination of the challenges and improvements of the Foreign Service through the 1960s and 1970s was the Foreign Service Reform Act of 1980, which provided far more rigorous standards for recruitment and performance, improved the rewards of service, and sought to deal with the problems of promotion and tenure. The act created a new Senior Foreign Service for top grades and established the sharp distinction between Foreign Service and civil service employment by abolishing the Foreign Service Reserve.

Attempts at reform and reorganization in the department during the last fifteen years have often been obscured and even vitiated by the impact on department personnel and functions caused by recurrent budget cuts and resource reductions that were part of the overall governmental budget deficits and spending constraints. State Department resources were reduced by fifty percent between 1986 and 1996. Despite expanding responsibilities, the department and the Foreign Service grew little between 1960 (when there were about seven thousand domestic and six thousand overseas American personnel) and 1988 (when there were eight thousand domestic and six thousand overseas personnel). The department has remained one of the smallest of major government agencies yet has an ever-increasing daily impact upon the lives of Americans—not only those who travel or conduct business abroad but those who are concerned about the role of the United States in the world.

The collapse of international communism culminating in the 1991 breakup of the Soviet Union eliminated for the foreseeable future the danger of nuclear warfare and Soviet-style sponsorship of massive insurgencies around the world. It did not make the world easier for diplomacy. Even as its resources are being reduced, the Department of State's tasks have become far more complicated and the expectations of the American public for effective actions far greater. In the wake of the Cold War, terrorism, nuclear proliferation, international crime, and economic issues that were always present, if on the margins, have become the central focus of foreign affairs. Resurgent nationalism in Europe and the former Soviet Union has sparked civil wars and rebellions that the United Nations, the United States and its allies, or any other combination of states have been unable to quell or even restrain. Respect by nations great and small for the human rights of their citizens has become the measure by which many Americans gauge the worthiness of foreign policy goals and the effectiveness of the Department of State's performance.

[See also Arms Control and Disarmament Agency; Central Intelligence Agency; International Development Cooperation Agency; National Security Council; United States Information Agency; White House Office; and Appendix: Basic Documents of Public Administration.]

BIBLIOGRAPHY

Barnes, William, and John Heath Morgan. The Foreign Service of the United States. Washington, D.C., 1961.
Calkin, Homer. Women in the Department of State: Their Role in American Foreign Affairs Washington, D.C., 1978.
Craig, Gordon A., and Francis L. Lowenheim. The Diplomats, 1939–1979. Princeton, N.J., 1994.
DeConde, Alexander. The American Secretary of State: An Interpretation. New York, 1962.
Mayer, Martin. The Diplomats. Garden City, N.Y., 1983.
Plischke, Elmer. Conduct of American Diplomacy. 3d ed. Princeton, N.J., 1967.
Rubin, Barry. Secrets of State: The State Department and the Struggle over U.S. Foreign Policy. New York, 1985.
Schulzinger, Robert. The Making of the Diplomatic Mind: The Training, Outlook, and Style of United States Foreign Service Officers, 1908–1931. Middletown, Conn., 1975.
Steigman, Andrew L. The Foreign Service of the United States: First Line of Defense. Boulder, Colo., 1985.
Stuart, Graham H. The Department of State: A History of Its Organization, Procedure, and Personnel. New York, 1949.
—WILLIAM Z. SLANY

States and the Federal Government

ESSAY The government of the United States is federal in form. It consists of one national government and fifty state governments, each with its own territory, ranging in size from Rhode Island (1,545 sq. mi.) to Alaska (656,424 sq. mi.). At the time of its formation in 1787–1789, the union consisted of thirteen states. Between 1791 and 1959 Congress admitted thirty-seven others.

Although in practice these numerous governments are highly interdependent, in form they exist independently of one another. Each has its own written constitution, which in American political theory comes from the people, who are sovereign. The United States government cannot abolish the state governments, nor they it. States do not have a right to secede from the union. In the succinct, benign, balanced phrase of the Supreme Court, speaking shortly after the close of the Civil War in Texas v. White (1869), the United States is "an indestructable Union, composed of indestructible States."

The conception of this union was pragmatic and ingenious. No such form of government had existed before. Previous federations had consisted of states that had entered into alliances for limited purposes—ordinarily, defense and foreign affairs—without surrendering their autonomy. The Articles of Confederation, predecessor of the union of 1787–1789, was classical in form. Each state retained its "sovereignty, freedom, and independence, and every power, jurisdiction, and right" that was not "expressly delegated" to the federation. The federation depended for revenue and armed force, and thus for its very existence, on the member states. They selected delegates to the legislative assembly annually and could recall them at will. Within the assembly their delegations, though permitted to range from two to seven members, were obliged to vote as units. Each state had one vote.

The leaders of the movement for union judged this form to be deeply defective—indeed, "imbecilic," in Alexander Hamilton's phrase—and succeeded in substituting for it a much stronger union that was not, however, completely unitary. Rather than one government, it was an intricate, subtle combination of one and many. The crucial difference from the Articles of Confederation was that the new national government derived powers directly from the people rather than the member states. It could raise its own revenue and army and navy. It had its own executive and judiciary, and thus the capacity to enforce as well as enact laws. One house of its legislature was elected by the people and, within state delegations, was proportioned to their numbers.

Yet this government incorporated certain federal features. In the second house of its legislature, each state was represented equally, with two members, who were chosen by state legislatures. No state could be deprived of equal representation without its consent. Likewise, the boundaries of a state could not be altered without the consent of its legislature. The chief executive of the new government was to be elected by an electoral college whose members would be chosen as state legislatures decided. To amend the Constitution required the assent of three-fourths of the state legislatures. And, to undergird the whole structure and affirm a guiding principle, the Tenth Amendment declared that "[t]he powers not delegated to the United States by the Constitution, nor prohibited by it to the States, are reserved to the States respectively, or to the People."

The outcome of 1787–1789 was thus a compromise between a purely national form and a classical federal form. It was arrived at with utmost difficulty, only after the Constitutional Convention very nearly broke up over the question of how far to carry union. James Madison, the most influential framer of the Constitution and the most profound student of federations,

called the result a "compound" republic in which "[t]he different governments will control each other, at the same time that each will be controlled by itself."

On balance, though, the compound was weighted in favor of the national side. This bias is made explicit in the supremacy clause, which stipulates that the Constitution and laws made in pursuance of it "shall be the Supreme Law of the Land; and the Judges in every State shall be bound thereby. . . ." It may also be seen in the very broad and elastic grants of power given to Congress under Article I, in particular the "necessary and proper" clause ("The Congress shall have Power . . . To make all Laws which shall be necessary and proper for carrying into Execution the foregoing [enumerated] powers, and all other Powers vested by this Constitution in the Government of the United States. . . ."

The bias is manifest, too, in a series of prohibitions imposed on the states in section 10 of Article I: "No State shall enter into any Treaty, Alliance, or Confederation; . . . coin money . . . ; make any Thing but gold and silver Coin a Tender in Payment of Debts . . . or [pass any] Law impairing the Obligation of Contracts. . . ." And perhaps above all is the fact, not fully explicit in the Constitution yet well understood, that the Supreme Court of the United States, an institution of the national government, would interpret the meaning of the Constitution and thus settle disputes between the national government and the state governments.

Each side in the founding struggle feared that in the long run the other would prevail. Anti-Federalists, who were partisans of the states, anticipated that a consolidated form would emerge. "Brutus," perhaps the most trenchant critic of the proposed constitution, wrote in The *New York Journal* in October 1787 that "although the government reported by the convention does not go to a perfect and entire consolidation, yet it approaches so near to it, that it must, if executed, certainly and infallibly terminate in it." Simultaneously, Madison in a letter to Jefferson was lamenting the failure of the convention to lodge in Congress the power to veto acts of state legislatures. "Without such a check in the whole over the parts, our system involves the evil of imperia in imperio." He thought the danger of encroachments much greater from the state than from the national side.

One can argue over whether Brutus or Madison was the more prescient. There has not occurred, as Brutus feared, a "perfect and entire consolidation." State governments continue to exist, to raise a great deal of revenue ($516.4 billion from their own sources in 1991, or forty-three percent of that raised by the federal government), and to perform many functions. On the other hand, it was not long before Madison was himself devising responses to national "encroachments"—as in the Kentucky and Virginia Resolutions of 1798, which he and Jefferson prepared to counter the Federalist party's Alien and Sedition Acts. In the twentieth century, certainly, the national side has generally been the more encroaching of the two.

A compound republic, composed of features from two contrasting forms of government, was certain to be unstable, and the relation between the federal government and the states has changed steadily and profoundly over time. The original constitutional contest, involving a conflict between states' sovereignty and popular sovereignty, persisted in the nineteenth century until the Civil War decisively ended it in favor of popular sovereignty and union. Of three constitutional amendments adopted in the aftermath of the war, the Fourteenth in particular sharply increased the nationalizing bias of the fundamental law. It added new prohibitions on the states: "No State shall . . . deprive any person of life, liberty, or property, without due process of law; nor deny to any person within its jurisdiction the equal protection of the laws." In effect, this was an immense grant of power to the federal judiciary to invalidate state laws.

If prohibitions on the states mounted over time, restraints on the federal government tended to fall. Madison had written in *The Federalist*, no. 39, as reassurance to partisans of the states, that the jurisdiction of the new government "extends to certain enumerated objects only, and leaves to the several States a residuary and inviolable sovereignty over all other objects." Before the Civil War this constitutional principle gave rise to impassioned debates over

the power of the national government to create a bank and an equally impassioned and more prolonged debate over whether it had power to build roads and canals and otherwise make "internal improvements." Even when a constitutional power was not conceded, Congress found ways to act. Before the Civil War it used military appropriations, land grants, and corporate stock subscriptions to aid public works. After the Civil War it freely authorized public works. The constitutional principle of limitation had proved ineffective; the Tenth Amendment, a mere parchment barrier.

Nevertheless, as custom and belief, the doctrine of enumerated powers continued to exert some effect even as the United States turned into a great industrial nation and international power. As the twentieth century advanced, bringing industrial conflict, ever-increasing economic and social interdependence, catastrophic depression, and world wars, pressures mounted for action by the national government. For a long time advocates of national legislation bore a heavy burden of proof because of the constitutional tradition that the national government was a government of limited powers. A strong presumption existed against national action, so that advocates of major new measures of economic regulation or social provision had to be prepared to meet, both generally and before the Supreme Court, constitutionally grounded opposition.

Centralization prevailed. By 1950 the constitutional scholar Edward S. Corwin declared that the doctrine of "dual federalism," as he called it, was dead. This had consisted, he said, of four postulates of constitutional interpretation:

- The national government is one of enumerated powers only

- The purposes which it may constitutionally promote are few

- Within their respective spheres the two centers of government are "sovereign" and hence "equal"

- The relation of the two centers with each other is one of tension rather than collaboration.

Corwin wrote after the Great Depression, the New Deal, and World War II had wrought their nationalizing effects but before the further impact of the civil rights revolution and Lyndon Johnson's Great Society. Greater nationalizing change was to come. Programs of grants-in-aid to state and local governments, which had begun in 1862 with land grants for colleges and grown selectively during the early twentieth century, multiplied many times during the Johnson administration, covering every conceivable domestic activity and paying no heed whatever to a constitutional custom of residual sovereignty. It is fair to say that by the end of the Johnson administration, the burden of proof had shifted. The presumption now was that every domestic problem or public activity was national in scope. Whoever wanted to argue that schooling, or police conduct, or enforcement of housing codes or gun control should be left to state and local governments bore a heavy burden of proof.

As the responsibility of the national government increased in scope, touching every type of domestic function, there also occurred a change in the distribution of authority between the federal government and the states. The states became less the equals of the national government, which in constitutional doctrine, at least, they had previously been, and became instead its subordinates, subject to commands.

The commands took various forms. Increasingly, Congress subjected state and local governments to direct regulation, just as private organizations were subject to regulation—in regard to employment practices, for example. Whereas states would once have been granted immunity on the ground that they were independent, sovereign governments, this ceased to be the case.

Sometimes the commands developed as a byproduct of Congress's using the states as instruments of national purpose. Federal grants-in-aid to the states had traditionally come with conditions attached. Historically, these had addressed mainly administrative and financial practices that were closely related to effectuating the purposes of the grant. Over time the conditions expanded in scope and substance. In particular, through the Civil Rights Act of 1964 they became an instrument for prohibiting racial discrimination, and thus for ending segregation in schools throughout the South.

In programs that depended on regulation rather than expenditure, Congress developed a different technique for employing the states. It would enact standards—say, for purity of the air or water, or for occupational health and safety—and give states the option of adopting such standards as their own and enforcing them as such. This technique, commonly practiced beginning in the 1970s, became known to scholars as "partial preemption." States routinely accepted this offer rather than resort to its alternative, which would have been to surrender the function to the federal government.

Another form that federal commands took was decrees issuing from the judiciary. The courts after the 1960s did not merely confine themselves to telling states what they could not do under the Constitution and laws of the United States. Increasingly, they issued affirmative decrees telling states and their local subdivisions what they must do. As with grant-in-aid conditions, school desegregation was the paradigmatic, precedent-setting case, but the practice extended over the whole range of state government activity, including in particular the administration of prisons.

Despite these many measures of formal subordination, the states as the twentieth century drew to a close were typically judged by students of American government to be gaining in importance. Whereas earlier in the century they were derided as backward and obsolete, with irrational boundaries, lethargic legislatures, and patronage-ridden agencies, by the 1980s they were beginning to be perceived as competent and respectable, even energetic and innovative.

In the sweep of time, they had gained in relation to their own subdivisions if not the federal government. In 1940, on the eve of World War II, state governments accounted for 22.3 percent of public spending, while local governments accounted for 28.5 percent and the federal government for 49.3 percent. Half a century later, at 22.4 percent, the states' share was essentially unchanged, but localities had fallen to 18.7 percent while the federal government had risen to 59 percent, taking up all of the difference.

BIBLIOGRAPHY

Beer, Samuel H. *To Make a Nation: The Rediscovery of American Federalism.* Cambridge, Mass., 1993.

Berns, Walter. "The Meaning of the Tenth Amendment." In *A Nation of States,* edited by Robert A. Goldwin. Chicago, 1963.

Corwin, Edward S. "The Passing of Dual Federalism." *Virginia Law Review* 36 (1950).

Diamond, Martin. *As Far as Republican Principles Will Admit: Essays by Martin Diamond.* Edited by William A. Schambra. Washington, D.C., 1992.

Hart, Henry M., Jr. "The Relations between State and Federal Law." In *Federalism Mature and Emergent,* edited by Arthur W. Macmahon. Garden City, N.Y., 1955.

Riker, William H. "The Senate and American Federalism." *American Political Science Review* 49 (1955): 452–469.

Texas v. White, 74 U.S. 700 (1869).

U.S. Advisory Commission on Intergovernmental Relations. *Regulatory Federalism: Policy, Process, Impact and Reform.* ACIR A-95. Washington, D.C., 1984.

U.S. Advisory Commission on Intergovernmental Relations. *Federal Regulation of State and Local Governments: The Mixed Record of the 1980s.* ACIR A-126. Washington, D.C., 1993.
                                        —MARTHA DERTHICK

Statistical Information

ESSAY Over one hundred agencies are authorized to collect and disseminate statistics, the three largest of which are the Bureau of the Census, the Bureau of Economic Analysis, and the Bureau of Labor Statistics. The eight largest agencies account for one-third of the total output. Federal statistical activity is coordinated by the Office of Management and Budget. Agencies collect statistics to support their missions and to meet legislative mandates. Up to three-quarters of the federal budget is allocated on the basis of the data collected in this manner. Federal agencies also receive statistical data from state and local governments and private agencies. Because statistics are so well suited to electronic storage and manipulation, some of them are available from the government in electronic form only. Fees are sometimes charged for ac-

cessing data electronically. The most popular statistical publication in the country is *The Statistical Abstract of the United States,* which has been described as "the best book published by the government." *The Statistical Abstract* also updates *Historical Statistics of the United States, Colonial Times to 1970.*

Next to the Bureau of the Census, the seven largest statistical agencies in the federal government are the Bureau of Economic Analysis, the Bureau of Justice Statistics, the Bureau of Labor Statistics, the Energy Information Administration, the National Agricultural Statistical Service, the National Center for Education Statistics, and the National Center for Health Statistics. The Commerce Department's Bureau of Economic Analysis prepares basic economic indicators, analyzes business trends, and constructs national income and product accounts. The data are made available through the Commerce Department's Economic Bulletin Board. It publishes the monthly *Economic Indicators.*

The Bureau of Justice Statistics is an arm of the National Institute of Justice. It gathers statistics on crime, courts, and corrections. Its largest statistical series is the National Crime Survey. Its annual *Sourcebook of Criminal Justice Statistics* is a one-volume compendium of data from more than one hundred sources. The Federal Bureau of Investigation publishes the annual *Uniform Crime Reports.*

The Bureau of Labor Statistics (BLS) gathers data on labor-oriented topics, such as employment and unemployment, hours and earnings, and productivity, and produces key economic indicators, such as the Consumer Price Index, the Producer Index, the Employment Cost Index, and the Employment Situation. The irregularly published *Handbook of Labor Statistics* incorporates many of these data. These indicators are available electronically through the BLS Electronic News Release Service. The National Trade Data Bank is a Commerce Department Database and CD-ROM containing international trade and economic information. The National Economic, Social and Environmental Data Bank is a similar data warehouse, containing not only statistics but also full text of related government publications.

The Energy Information Administration is the Department of Energy's statistical and analytical arm, gathering and publishing data on energy reserves production, demand, consumption, distribution, and technology. It publishes the *International Energy Annual* and the *Annual Energy Review.*

The National Agricultural Statistical Service collects data on the production, supply, and price of agricultural products and related data on the farm sector. A related agency, the Economic Research Service, analyzes the outlook for domestic and foreign farm products. These data are published in the annual *Agricultural Statistics.*

Collection of educational statistics began in 1867 and is now handled by the National Center for Education Statistics (NCES), a subunit of the Office of Educational Research and Improvement. The NCES produces two invaluable annual statistical abstracts: *The Condition of Education* and the *Digest of Education Statistics.*

The National Center for Health Statistics collects and disseminates statistics about public health and provides data on health and nutrition, illness and disability, health resources, health expenditures, and vital statistics. Its flagship publication is *Vital Statistics of the United States,* supplemented by *Health United States,* both annuals, and the biennial *Mental Health United States.* Other important statistical publications of the federal government include *Statistics of Communications Common Carriers, HUD Statistical Yearbook, Highway Statistics, FAA Statistical Handbook of Aviation, National Transportation Statistics,* and *Public Land Statistics.*

[*See also* Census, Bureau of the.]

BIBLIOGRAPHY

Bureau of the Census. *Reflections of America: Commemorating the Statistical Abstract Centennial.* Washington, D.C., 1980.
Fishbein, Meyer H. *The National Archives and Statistical Research.* Athens, Ohio, 1974.
Office of Technology Assessment. *Statistical Needs for a Changing U.S. Economy.* Washington, D.C., 1989.
Scott, Ann Herbert. *Census U.S.A.: Fact Finding for the American People.* New York, 1968.
Wallman, Katherine K. *Losing Count: The Federal Statistical System.* Washington, D.C., 1988.

—GEORGE THOMAS KURIAN

Supreme Court Decisions on the Presidency

ESSAY — Although the case of *Marbury v. Madison* (1803) is best known for its holding that the federal judiciary may declare acts of Congress unconstitutional, it also articulated the proposition that the courts have power to review the legality of acts of the executive branch when presented in a case. *Marbury* involved the claim of William Marbury and others that Secretary of State James Madison (at President Thomas Jefferson's direction) had wrongfully withheld their commissions to serve as justices of the peace of the District of Columbia. The Court concluded that even high officers of the executive branch are answerable in court for violations of legal duties (although not with respect to actions where they have constitutional or political discretion); it did not order Madison to deliver the commissions because the Court concluded it lacked jurisdiction of the case (and thereby avoided a confrontation with Jefferson).

In many respects, *Marbury* foreshadowed the approach subsequent cases would take to the presidency. Following *Marbury,* the Court has established the right of the judiciary to define in important respects the powers and limits of the presidency. At the same time the Court has acknowledged that the executive branch has a separate constitutional responsibility which may at times be immune from judicial scrutiny. Since *Marbury* the judiciary has generally proceeded cautiously in cases regarding the presidency, being most deferential in those involving foreign and defense policy.

Marbury, of course, involved an action against Secretary of State James Madison, not the president. It made clear that in an appropriate case a court could assert jurisdiction over a cabinet member, a scenario that has frequently occurred. Could, however, the judiciary require the president to defend a case and impose its will upon him? In *Mississippi v. Johnson* (1867) the Court stated that it lacked jurisdiction to enjoin President Andrew Johnson "in the performance of his official duties" at least with respect to discretionary acts and implied that judicial process could not usually reach the president.

The issue arose again more than one hundred years later in *United States v. Nixon* (1974) when Watergate special prosecutor Archibald Cox issued a subpoena *duces tecum* for tape recordings and related documents of conversations between President Richard M. Nixon and aides. Nixon asserted that the president was immune from judicial process; alternatively, he claimed that executive privilege protected his conversations. The Court rejected Nixon's claim that the judiciary could not subject the president to its process, since "it is the province and duty" of the judiciary to articulate the law regarding a president's claim of executive privilege. The Court did recognize a presumptive privilege for the president's confidential communications with close associates in the executive branch. That privilege was outweighed, however, in *United States v. Nixon,* by the need for evidence in a criminal trial. The result might have been different, the Court suggested, had the president sought to protect state or military secrets rather than asserting a "generalized" claim of privilege, or had the presidential papers been sought by a congressional committee or for a civil trial.

United States v. Nixon, was, of course, a rare case in which the president himself became the defendant because he claimed that he, not a subordinate, controlled the tapes at issue. More often, however, the president acts through associates, as in *Marbury,* and accordingly the president's appointees are generally named as defendants. *Youngstown Sheet & Tube Co. v. Sawyer* (1952) is instructive in this regard; although President Harry S. Truman issued the order directing his secretary of commerce to possess and operate the nation's steel mills in the face of a threatened strike, it was Secretary Charles Sawyer who took action and emerged as the defendant in the "steel seizure" case.

The president enjoys greater insulation from lawsuits seeking damages from him for official duty. In *Nixon v. Fitzgerald* (1982) a former government employee who traced his termination to President Nixon's official acts sued the former president for damages arising from those acts. The Court held (5–4) that as a former president Nixon enjoyed absolute immunity from damage actions based upon his official acts.

This protection does not extend to the president's unofficial conduct. In *Clinton v. Jones* (1997) the Supreme Court unanimously refused to delay a civil lawsuit in federal court against President Clinton until his term ended. Unlike other claims at issue in *Fitzgerald,* the lawsuit alleged wrongdoing by President Clinton *before* he became president. Moreover, the president did not assert absolute or qualified immunity. Rather, he argued that since the presidency is a unique and unusually demanding position, judicial proceedings should be postponed to avoid diverting his time and attention from the nation's business. The Supreme Court did not view these arguments as raising separation of power concerns that justified a stay of the lawsuit. It recognized that the federal trial court could, and indeed should, accommodate the president's schedule through appropriate case-management techniques; granting a stay of the trial under present circumstances abused the court's discretion.

Just as *United States v. Nixon* demonstrated that the president's right to protect the privacy of his communications is diminished when not cloaked in the protective garb of military or state secrets, *Youngstown* suggested that judicial deference to the president declines when he acts in a domestic context without constitutional or congressional support. The Court rejected President Truman's claim that he had inherent power to seize the steel mills as implied from the aggregate of specific constitutional provisions—the vesting in him of the "executive power," his duty to execute faithfully the laws, and his power as commander in chief.

To be sure, the six justices in the majority produced six opinions, obscuring somewhat the case's meaning. *Youngstown's* most important legacy is probably Justice Jackson's concurrence, which delineated three categories of presidential power. Justice Jackson stated that when the president acts pursuant to "an express or implied authorization of Congress" his power is at its maximum because it rests not only on his constitutional authority but that that Congress has given. Where the president acts without either congressional approval or dissent, his power depends on constitutional grants of power or the contention that he is acting in a "twilight zone" where he shares power with Congress. The president is most vulnerable when acting contrary to "the expressed or implied will of Congress."

Most in the majority (and all three dissenters) agreed that the president possessed some inherent powers beyond those the Constitution specified. As Justice Jackson put it, in the "zone of twilight" in which the president and Congress have concurrent authority, if Congress is quiescent, the president may act to fill the void. And a pattern of congressional acquiescence to presidential action could shift constitutional power to the executive branch, thought most justices. As Justice Felix Frankfurter put it, "a systematic, unbroken, executive practice, long pursued to the knowledge of the Congress and never before questioned . . . making as it were such exercise of power part of the structure of our government, may be treated as a gloss on 'executive power' vested in the President."

Yet many in the majority were influenced by the fact that Congress had considered, and rejected, a proposal that it give the president power to seize property. As such, Justice Frankfurter concluded, Congress had "expressed its will to withhold this power from the President as though it had said so in so many words." Since President Truman's actions were "incompatible with the expressed or implied will of Congress," Justice Jackson explained, his constitutional power was at its weakest.

The Court has not, however, been oblivious to claims that the constitutional provisions referred to above—the duty to take care that the laws be faithfully executed and the vesting of the executive power in the president—have implications for presidential power. In *In re Neagle* (1890), for instance, the Court held that the president had inherent power to assign a bodyguard to protect a Supreme Court justice (who had been threatened by a disgruntled litigant) even absent statutory authorization. The president's duty to "take Care that the Laws be faithfully executed" made him responsible not only for enforcing statutes but also other rights and duties fairly derived from the Constitution. And in *In re Debs* (1895) the Court upheld the president's power to employ governmental power to preserve domestic peace.

The Constitution's more general grants to the president are especially important when joined with other, specific provisions. The Court has held, for instance, that Congress's power to create offices does not allow it to reserve for itself the power to appoint officers. Thus, in *Springer v. Government of the Philippine Islands* (1928) the Court held that Congress cannot control the execution of the laws by arrogating to itself the power to appoint the enforcing officer; such a power, the Court explained in *Buckley v. Valeo* (1976), was reserved to the chief executive, at least with respect to "officers of the United States" like commissioners of the Federal Election Commission.

Whereas *Springer* and *Buckley* could rely upon explicit language in the Constitution that the president "shall nominate, and by and with the Advice and Consent of the Senate, shall appoint" officers, the Constitution does not expressly give the president power to remove subordinates. Yet the Court, in a series of decisions, has accorded the president the exclusive right to remove many executive officials and has circumscribed the ability of Congress to reserve removal power for itself.

In *Myers v. United States* (1926) the Court declared unconstitutional a statute that prevented the president from removing certain postmasters without Senate consent. Speaking for the Court, Chief Justice (and former president) William Howard Taft associated the power to remove with the power to appoint and concluded that "the President has the exclusive power of removing executive officers of the United States whom he has appointed by and with the advice and consent of the Senate."

Yet the Court soon made clear that *Myers* did not establish that the president possessed unlimited power to remove all executive officials. In *Humphrey's Executor v. United States* (1935) the Court held that the "necessary and proper" clause of the Constitution authorized Congress to create certain quasi-legislative or quasi-judicial agencies, such as the Federal Trade Commission, independent of the president; as such, the president could not remove a commissioner before his term expired, thereby compromising the independence Congress sought to achieve.

THE SUPREME COURT BUILDING IN WASHINGTON, D.C. *Designed by Cass Gilbert and opened in 1935, this building was the first in the Court's then 145-year history that it did not share with other government institutions.*

The Court subsequently refined the distinction that separated *Myers* and *Humphrey's Executor* in *Wiener v. United States* (1958); there, it held that the president could remove those who are part of the executive establishment but not those "whose tasks require absolute freedom from Executive interference."

More recently, the Court has made clear that *Myers* rests on the premise that Congress cannot itself reserve power to remove executive officials rather than on the idea that the president's removal power is unlimited. In *Bowsher v. Synar* (1986) the Court struck down part of the Balanced Budget and Emergency Deficit Control Act of 1985, which conferred on the comptroller general certain executive functions. Since the comptroller general was an agent of Congress removable (for cause, upon joint resolution) by it, the Court held the act unconstitutionally gave Congress control over the execution of the laws.

In *Morrison v. Olson* (1988) the Court confirmed that the president's power to appoint and remove certain officers charged with executive functions could be limited in appropriate circumstances. The Court there upheld the constitutionality of the Ethics in Government Act of 1978, although it provided that independent counsel (who would investigate and prosecute acts of wrongdoing by executive branch officials) would be appointed by a panel of three judges and be removable by the attorney general only upon "good cause." The Court relied on constitutional language that allowed Congress to place in the courts the power to appoint certain inferior officers. The Court was influenced by the perceived need to insulate an independent counsel from executive control. The Court rejected any formalistic test to define when the president's power to remove could be restricted, concluding that the "real question" is whether the restrictions "impede the President's ability to perform his constitutional duty." The "good cause" limitation on removal of an inferior officer like the independent counsel did not "unduly trammel . . . on executive authority."

The Constitution also limited Congress's ability to control the executive by a legislative veto in *Immigration and Naturalization Service v. Chadha* (1983). Congress had delegated certain power to the executive, subject to the right of either house of Congress to "veto" that action. The Court held the "legislative veto" unconstitutional since it represented lawmaking without approval of both houses of Congress (bicameralism) and without reserving to the president the right to veto any measure subject only to a two-thirds override in both houses (presentment).

The Court has often been more deferential to the president in international and military matters. The seminal case of *United States v. Curtiss-Wright Export Corp.* (1936) raised the question of whether Congress could delegate to the president power to prohibit certain sales of military equipment. The Court used the case to articulate an expansive theory of unenumerated presidential power to conduct foreign policy. It argued that the president's foreign affairs powers were not confined, as were his domestic powers, to the provisions the Constitution enumerated. Moreover, the other branches of government were "significantly limited" in their ability to participate in decision-making regarding foreign affairs. "In this vast external realm, with its important, complicated, delicate and manifold problems, the President alone has the power to speak or listen as a representative of the nation," said the Court. To avoid national embarrassment and to exploit the president's access to confidential information, the president, the Court thought,

must enjoy greater autonomy in conducting international than domestic affairs. Although the opinion contains words of limitations and has been attacked by leading academic critics, presidents have frequently invoked it to justify actions over the past sixty years.

Consistent with this vision of broad executive powers in the international arena, the Court has recognized the constitutionality of executive agreements whereby various presidents have committed the United States without obtaining the Senate's advice and consent. For instance, in *United States v. Belmont* (1937) and *United States v. Pink* (1942) the Court upheld the Litvinov Assignment, an executive agreement whereby President Franklin D. Roosevelt recognized the Soviet Union and, in doing so, affected certain property rights. The Court found that the president could proceed by executive agreement although it had the effect of law and overrode contrary state law. Significantly, these cases involved actions related to the recognition of a nation, an inherent power of the presidency implied from the ability to receive and dispatch ambassadors; they do not support the proposition that the president can conduct all foreign policy by executive agreement, nor do they establish that an executive agreement would prevail over inconsistent federal (rather than state) law.

More recently, in *Dames & Moore v. Regan* (1981), the Court upheld the authority of Presidents Jimmy Carter and Ronald Reagan, by executive agreements, to take various actions affecting private property rights as part of the agreement that secured Iran's release of American hostages. The Court held the president had authority to cancel judicial attachments of Iranian assets, to order the transfer of frozen Iranian assets, and to suspend claims against Iran pending in American courts that would be adjudicated instead in a special Iranian–United States Claims Tribunal. Significantly, the Court found that the president's actions had either been authorized in advance by Congress (and accordingly fell within category one of Justice Jackson's analysis in *Youngstown*) or were consistent with similar presidential conduct that had won congressional acquiescence.

The Court's references in *Dames & Moore* to

Justice Jackson's *Youngstown* formulation suggest that the Court has not embraced the *Curtiss-Wright* approach totally without considering other theories regarding constitutional constraints on the president in international affairs. As Professor Harold Koh has pointed out, *Youngstown* provides a competing vision of foreign affairs power being shared by the three branches of government, and one which finds some support in the Constitution, American history, and judicial precedents.

Presidents have claimed broad powers regarding defense matters, too, resting their claims largely on the fact that the Constitution designates the president commander in chief of the Army and Navy. By the same token, the same document vests in Congress the power to declare war. The extent of the president's power to commit troops absent a congressional declaration is not entirely clear, in part because few cases address the subject. In *The Prize Cases* (1863), the Court narrowly affirmed the president's power unilaterally to direct the military to respond to foreign invasion or domestic insurrection. The case did not, however, decide whether without congressional approval, presidents could, for instance, deploy troops to defend Americans abroad or to repel an attack against allies or send forces pursuant to a treaty.

Although the president's domestic powers may also increase during wartime, they are not without limit. Thus, in *Youngstown*, military needs for steel during the Korean War were insufficient to allow President Truman to seize the steel mills. And the Court held in *Ex Parte Milligan* (1866) that President Abraham Lincoln could not impose martial law in states where the authority of civil government was recognized and the courts were functioning.

At times the Court has simply refused to review certain presidential actions regarding international affairs on the grounds that they were political questions—either issues committed by the Constitution to the president or beyond the competence of the judiciary. For instance, in *Chicago and Southern Air Lines, Inc. v. Waterman Steamship Corp.* (1948) the Court justified its refusal to review a presidential order granting an overseas air route because "the very nature of executive decisions as to foreign policy is political, not judicial." More recently, in *Goldwater v. Carter* (1979), petitioners sought to enjoin President Carter from unilaterally terminating a defense treaty with Taiwan, an action taken in connection with this country's recognition of the People's Republic of China. They contended that the president could not terminate a treaty without the Senate's advice and consent. The Court, without opinion, ordered the complaint dismissed. Justice William Rehnquist and three colleagues, in a separate statement, argued that the issue was a political question since it involved the ability of the president to conduct foreign policy and accordingly was not justiciable. Although Justice William Brennan believed this to be an erroneous application of the political question doctrine, he would not question the president's action because it related to the recognition of a nation.

Similarly, the Court has refused to hear challenges to military actions. In *Mora v. McNamara* (1967) the Court refused to hear a case challenging the legality of the war in Vietnam. In criticizing the Court's decision not to accept the case, Justice Potter Stewart urged that it raised "questions of great magnitude" including whether American military activity constituted a "war" as meant by the Constitution and whether the president could send citizens to fight in Vietnam absent a declaration of war by Congress.

BIBLIOGRAPHY

Corwin, Edward S. *The President: Office and Powers.* 4th rev. ed. New York, 1957.

Ely, John Hart. *War and Responsibility.* Princeton, N.J., 1993.

Fisher, Louis. *The Politics of Shared Power: Congress and the Executive.* 3d ed. Washington, D.C., 1993.

Freund, Paul A. "On Presidential Privilege." *Harvard Law Review* 88 (1974): 13–39.

Koh, Harold H. *The National Security Constitution.* New Haven, Conn., 1990.

Nowak, John E., and Ronald D. Rotunda. *Constitutional Law.* 5th ed. Saint Paul, 1995.

Pyle, Christopher H., and Richard M. Pious. *The President, Congress and the Constitution.* New York, 1984.

Shane, Peter M., and Harold H. Bruff. *The Law of Presidential Power: Cases and Materials.* Durham, N.C., 1988.

Tribe, Lawrence H. *American Constitutional Law.* 2d ed. New York, 1988.

—Joel K. Goldstein

T

Taft Commission Report.

See Appendix: Basic Documents of Public Administration.

Technical Information Service, National

Access to U.S. and foreign government–sponsored research and development in engineering and business is provided by the National Technical Information Service (NTIS), the primary mission of which is to foster the transfer of technology from the government to the private sector and to improve the competitiveness of U.S. business and industry in a global economy. In 1945 President Truman established the Publications Board to review all scientific and technical research produced during World War II and to determine how it could be made available to the American public. In 1950 Public Law 81-776 directed the Department of Commerce to operate a national clearinghouse to collect and distribute scientific and technical information. In 1970 this clearinghouse became the NTIS.

In 1992 the American Technology Preeminence Act mandated government agencies to submit all federally produced or financed scientific, technical, and engineering information to the NTIS in a timely manner. Until then such information was delivered to the NTIS on a voluntary basis. The NTIS data base covers 1964 to the present and includes more than 2.5 million titles. Each year 70,000 to 80,000 titles are added to the data base. Approximately twenty-five percent of all new titles come from foreign sources

through various international exchange agreements. The NTIS also maintains an electronic bulletin board gateway, "Fedworld," as a clearinghouse for technical reports and literature emanating from federal agencies. In addition, Fedworld maintains large files of military and technical standards, weather satellite images, and White House press statements. However, unlike the Government Printing Office, which receives appropriated funds, the NTIS is a self-sustaining agency that must recover its costs and charge for its services.

BIBLIOGRAPHY

McClure, Charles R., and Peter Hernon. *U.S. Scientific and Technical Information Policies: Views and Perspectives.* Norwood, N.J., 1989.
McClure, Charles R. M., Peter Hernon, and Gary R. Purcell. *Linking the U.S. National Technical Information Service with Academic and Public Libraries.* Norwood, N.J., 1986.
Office of Technology Assessment. *Helping America Compete: The Role of Federal Scientific and Technical Information.* Washington, D.C., 1990.

—GEORGE THOMAS KURIAN

Technology Assessment, Office of

The first organizational casualty of the Republicans' 1994 takeover of Congress was the Office of Technology Assessment (OTA), which had been created in 1972 to provide the Congress with in-house analytic support on issues with major science and technology (S&T) content. Although its initial seven years had been fraught with controversy, most observers believed the OTA had become one of the nation's most competent, unbiased, and valuable sources of information on the increasing number of issues that had S&T embedded in them.

Key factors in the termination were the desire by the new majority to demonstrate its commitment to reducing government and the fact that the OTA's specialized focus meant it had a limited constituency among the members of Congress. The late 1994 decision by the Senate Republican leadership to make the OTA's elimination one of its five "major" congressional reform proposals was also surprising in that it violated traditional Senate protocol. The three Republican members of the OTA's governing board, Orrin Hatch of Utah, Charles Grassley of Iowa, and David Durenberger of Minnesota, were not consulted by the leadership.

The origins of this unique congressional support agency can be traced to the explosion of technological innovation that followed World War II. In the late 1960s and early 1970s Congress found itself dealing with three particularly difficult sets of technology-related issues. The first was the growing recognition that new technologies often had unanticipated negative consequences. Rachel Carson's 1962 book, *Silent Spring*, is commonly identified as the turning point in a set of developments that generated public concern about unanticipated consequences. The second was a rapid growth in federal expenditures for technological research and development; by the mid-1960s such expenditures represented nearly fifteen percent of the federal budget (entitlements were not included at that time). The third was a growing perception in Congress of a need for its own S&T expertise—highlighted by its struggle with President Nixon over the supersonic jet transport.

Congressman Emilio Q. Daddario (D-Conn.), chairman of the House Subcommittee on Science, Research and Development, was the key figure in creating and shaping the OTA. From 1963 until he resigned to run for governor of Connecticut in 1970, Daddario used congressional hearings, seminars, and studies by the National Academies of Science and Engineering to push for a technology assessment agency. The OTA's organic statute, the Technology Assessment Act of 1972 (P.L. 92-484), however, included significant changes from Daddario's conception. Specifically, the early warning role for the OTA was deemphasized and the proposal for

a governing board composed of a mix of public and congressional members was modified to one composed only of members of the Congress.

These compromises represented the first efforts to deal with two of the controversies that were to plague the OTA intermittently throughout its existence—how responsive the OTA should be to Congress and to its individual members, and whether technology assessment acted as a barrier to technology development. Although these concerns were sometimes muted for long periods by the OTA's effective performance, they never completely disappeared. And ironically, the compromised structure became both the source of the OTA's technical strength and its political vulnerability.

In significant ways the OTA's structure was different from that of its sister agencies—the General Accounting Office, the Congressional Research Service, and the Congressional Budget Office. First, it was governed by a Technology Assessment Board (TAB), composed of members of Congress. To ensure politically balanced assessments, the TAB was a bipartisan, bicameral mix of six Republicans and six Democrats, divided evenly between the two houses. The chair rotated annually between the House and Senate. To assure technical quality control and public input, the organic act required a Technology Assessment Advisory Committee composed of eminent people appointed by the TAB. To provide stability the OTA director was appointed by the TAB for a relatively long term (six years), like other support agencies.

The OTA study requests could only be made by the chairs and ranking minority members of full committees, by the TAB itself, or the OTA director, and to be accepted all studies had to be approved by the TAB. The TAB also reviewed and approved all studies when they reached final draft form. These arrangements spared the OTA the task of rejecting purely partisan or narrow requests from individual members and helped assure balance in its studies. But the arrangements also limited the number of members of the House and Senate who were knowledgeable about its work—a serious disadvantage when it came under attack.

The structure also allowed the OTA to be selective, that is, to undertake only a relatively small number of carefully done studies at any point in time. The eighteen to twenty-four months typically required for the data collection and broad review by external experts and interested parties that made the studies so trusted, however, also exposed the agency to criticism that the studies were not conducted and delivered in a manner consistent with the needs of the legislative cycle.

The OTA was also unique in its broad use of contractors and advisory panels. Though small in size, the agency used contracting authority to tap the best scientific and technical talent in the country. The OTA quickly learned that its status as a congressional agency made access to information from expert organizations and individuals easily available at low cost. Similarly, throughout its tenure, the OTA's study teams relied on advisory panels composed of a balance of recognized technical experts and representatives of groups and individuals with a stake in the issues being investigated. This process magnified the OTA's technical capacity well beyond its relatively small staff.

The OTA's organizational history can be quite clearly divided into the periods associated with its four directors: Emilio Daddario (1973–1977), Russell Peterson (1978–1979), John Gibbons (1979–1993), and Roger Herdman (1993–1995). Shortly after his defeat in Connecticut's 1970 gubernatorial race, Daddario was chosen as the OTA's first director. Initially, Daddario had the OTA staff serve primarily as managers, contracting for technology assessments with universities and research firms. This approach failed in part because the contractors lacked a close connection to Congress, impairing their capacity to complete relevant, balanced studies. In rescuing these initial studies, the OTA learned an enduring lesson about how to structure successful technology assessments—to use experts and stakeholders for data and review, but retain responsibility in-house for scoping, synthesizing, and writing the reports.

Daddario's tenure was marked by controversy as he sought to walk a line between the demands of Congress and the scientific community. Crit-

ics accused the OTA of undertaking studies of marginal importance to satisfy congressional demands. Concerns about senatorial patronage generated friction because each Senate TAB member had authority to appoint a member of the OTA research staff. Finally, major controversy revolved around the allegation that Senator Edward M. Kennedy (D-Mass.), the first chairman of the TAB, was using the OTA as staff for his expected presidential campaign.

Russell Peterson, the former Republican governor of Delaware, was chosen as the second director. Mindful of the controversy over patronage appointments within the OTA, Peterson gained assurance prior to accepting his position that he would have sole control over hiring staff members. Upon taking office he tackled the issue of how to select studies based on both the judgments of experts and congressional interest. He favored the longer-term studies envisioned during the debates preceding the OTA's founding. Some in Congress decided that he was not sufficiently responsive to their concerns, and Peterson resigned after two years to assume leadership of the National Audubon Society.

The OTA's third director, John Gibbons, was warned that his term was the OTA's last chance—either it performed satisfactorily or Congress would kill it. With a staff that by now had learned how to carry out technology assessments and with control of staff hiring, Gibbons presided over a fourteen-year period during which the OTA earned a reputation for high-quality studies. OTA assessments became a model for technical accuracy and sociopolitical balance on a wide range of topics: for example, the Strategic Defense Initiative (Star Wars); the use of taggents for explosives; lie detector technologies; and information technologies in rural communities. During this period the OTA's work also became widely used by policy researchers in both private and public sector organizations, including state and local legislative bodies in framing and making policy choices. The press reported on and cited OTA studies often, finding them useful as policy stories in their own right and as credible, clearly written sources for understanding the technical information underlying many policy issues. And finally, other countries began to emulate the OTA model for dealing with public issues involving S&T content. By the time the OTA was eliminated, several countries had established their own versions of the OTA.

When Gibbons left in 1993 to become the science adviser to the newly elected president, Bill Clinton, Roger Herdman was appointed director. Herdman, who had been an assistant director at the OTA, inherited what was generally believed to be an exceptionally successful organization requiring only relatively minor organizational and managerial changes. Before the 1994 congressional election, Herdman initiated a number of organizational and personnel changes, resulting in a voluntary twenty-five percent reduction in the OTA's fiscal year 1996 budget request. Before these changes were implemented, however, and even before the opening of the 104th Congress, the new Republican leadership in the Senate initiated the process that led to the OTA's end. The technique used was to eliminate funding, leaving the OTA's enabling legislation intact. The key tactical event occurred when the leadership, in a surprise move early on a Saturday morning, called for a unanimous voice vote in support of the five major reform proposals.

—Don E. Kash and
Elizabeth M. Gunn

Tennessee Valley Authority

Congress created the Tennessee Valley Authority (TVA) in May 1933 as a response to questions over what to do with the government-owned properties at Muscle Shoals, Alabama. During World War I the government built two nitrate plants and a dam, which later came to be known as Wilson Dam. For the fifteen years that followed the war, two presidential commissions, President Calvin Coolidge's Muscle Shoals Inquiry of 1925 and President Herbert Hoover's Muscle Shoals Commission of 1931, tried to address the issue of

whether the government ought to be producing and distributing fertilizer and electricity or whether the operation should be sold to private industry. The commissions sought bids from private industry for the facilities. Bids were submitted by the Ford Motor Company and the American Cyanamide Company. These bids were rejected, however, because commissioners believed that the companies were primarily interested in the energy production capabilities and not the fertilizer research and production that both commissions considered critical.

In 1933 the Franklin D. Roosevelt administration decided to use this small government installation as a way to achieve wider goals. Roosevelt regarded the creation of the TVA as the first step in a series of regional authorities that would have included the Columbia and Missouri Valleys. This system of national planning would be managed through the National Resources Planning Board (NRPB). However, when Congress dismantled the NRPB in 1943, the ideal of centralized planning came to an end.

The May 1933 legislation that produced the TVA authorized the creation of an independent corporate agency charged with the responsibility to develop the resources of the Tennessee Valley. As an "authority" the TVA was not attached to any existing federal government department. This independence gave the TVA greater flexibility because it had to report only to the Executive Office of the President. In fact, its decisions were not subject to ordinary approval by the Treasury, General Accounting Office, or the Civil Service Commission. Many agencies with overlapping functions and interests like the Department of Commerce, the Army Corps of Engineers, and the Agriculture Adjustment Agency had mixed feelings about the creation of an autonomous body. Additionally, private power companies even challenged the constitutionality of the government's competing in the provision of electricity.

The primary functions of the TVA were, and continue to be, to provide the region with flood control, electricity, agricultural and industrial development, and improved navigation of the river. The TVA has grown dramatically since its inception in 1933 to serve over ninety-one thousand square miles in seven states—Alabama, Georgia, Kentucky, Mississippi, North Carolina, Tennessee, and Virginia. The agency has nearly fifty thousand full-time employees. This vast $5.5 billion corporate entity is headed by a three-member board of directors appointed for nine-year terms by the president with the advice and consent of the Senate. However, the day-to-day operations are run by the general manager, who reports directly to the board of directors.

The TVA has three main administrative centers, Muscle Shoals, Alabama, and Knoxville and Chattanooga, Tennessee. In addition, the agency maintains a liaison office in Washington, D.C., and nine district offices throughout the region. The agency is divided into three primary divisions: Power and Engineering, Natural Resources and Economic Development, and Agricultural and Chemical Development.

The Office of Power and Engineering is responsible for the supply of electricity to over seven million customers—many of whom had no electricity before the construction of the authority—through 160 municipal and cooperative power distributors. The system contains more than seventeen thousand miles of transmission lines, twenty-nine hydroelectric dams on the Tennessee River and its tributaries, three nuclear-generated units, and eleven coal-fired plants. The office oversees the daily operations and maintenance of the nation's largest power system. Unlike the other activities of the agency, which are funded by congressional appropriations, the power system is funded by the revenues generated from the sale of electricity to its customers.

In 1994 the coal plants produced seventy percent of the TVA's electricity, the hydroelectric dams generated sixteen percent, and the nuclear plants accounted for fourteen percent. In 1995 the TVA sold more than 130 billion kilowatt-hours of electricity—enough energy to power more than three cities the size of New York. The agency is committed to keeping electricity inexpensive in order to aid in the economic development of the area. In fact, the TVA has not had a general electric rate increase since 1987, even though the cost of living has risen thirty percent

in that same time. In addition to providing electricity, the dams were estimated to have saved more than $1 billion in flood damage during the severe rains of 1994 that devastated other parts of the country.

The Office of Natural Resources and Economic Development is charged with designing programs to use and to protect the natural resources of the Tennessee Valley region. The office runs programs that include land use, water conservation, development, and management. Additionally, the TVA uses government appropriations to fund programs that improve water quality and conditions for aquatic life on the Tennessee River. The TVA also offers work force training, business information, industrial site studies, and related technical assistance to help businesses better compete in the local and global markets. The agency's efforts are centered on the nine regional offices and cover a broad range of activities that included a $4 million investment in the development of the Ocoee River Olympic venue for the 1996 Atlanta Summer Olympic Games and a $20 million loan fund established to promote industrial development.

Development of the region is not a new activity for the agency. In fact, one of the most dramatic events for the area's economic development was the improved navigability of the Tennessee River. When the TVA was formed, there were lengthy periods of time when water levels were too low to support large ships. Today, however, as a result of damming the river and various tributaries, the Tennessee River is navigable from Knoxville, Tennessee, to Paducah, Kentucky, 652 miles downstream. This has enabled the connection of eastern Tennessee and northern Alabama to the Ohio and Mississippi Rivers. In addition to the improved shipping conditions, the agency manages 164 public recreation areas including Land Between the Lakes—the agency's national recreation and environmental education center.

A more recent economic development initiative has been the TVA's telecommunications network. The authority owns and maintains an extensive telecommunications network to enable automated process control of its transmission and generating facilities and to provide intra-agency voice and data communications. In addition to these internal functions, the network is also being set up to accommodate rural communities, schools, and business partners, giving them access to the information superhighway.

The Office of Agricultural and Chemical Development conducts research into new fertilizers and fertilizer manufacturing. Additionally, the office helps develop the agricultural resources of the area through activities like soil conservation, strategic planning, and total quality management so that the rural communities can be more competitive.

In 1995 the TVA developed a twenty-five-year strategic plan. Energy Vision 2020, as it is called, is an integrated plan that provides information on long-range energy strategies that the agency can employ as it enters into a new era of deregulation and increased competition from the utility industry. The comprehensive study identified major objectives for the authority, including keeping electric rates low to stimulate growth, lessening the potential impact on the environment by the agency's operations, controlling its bond-funded debt, continuing to encourage economic development in the region, and ensuring a reliable source of power throughout the Tennessee Valley through the year 2020.

The agency helped to secure its future when it was able to convince enough members of the House of Representatives not to eliminate funding for its appropriated programs. The Republican-held Congress considered an amendment to HR1905, Fiscal 1996 Energy and Water Appropriations, that would have cut off all federal funding to the TVA. However, through a bipartisan vote, the amendment was defeated by a margin of 2 to 1.

While the TVA has been successful in accomplishing its major goals of regional economic development, rural electrification, and management of natural resources, the future of the agency as an independent government corporation will continue to come under heightened scrutiny. Many critics argue that the agency has outlived its original purposes and that the authority ought to be sold to private industry in much the same way as Conrail, the government-created freight train corporation, was. As budget cutting continues in Washington, D.C., the TVA will likely fall victim even though it has been given a reprieve.

BIBLIOGRAPHY

Hargrove, Erwin C., and Paul K. Conkin, eds. *TVA: Fifty Years of Grass Roots Bureaucracy*. Urbana, Ill., 1983.

Lilienthal, David E. *TVA: Democracy on the March*. New York, 1953.

Owen, Marguerite. *The Tennessee Valley Authority*. New York, 1973.

—JEFFREY D. SCHULTZ

Thrift Supervision, Office of

 Created as a bureau of the Treasury Department by authority of the Financial Institutions Reform, Recovery, and Enforcement Act (FIRREA) of 9 August 1989, the Office of Thrift Supervision (OTS) replaced the Federal Home Loan Bank Board (FHLBB) as the primary regulator of federal- and state-chartered savings and loan (S&L) institutions belonging to the Savings Association Insurance Fund (SAIF). The agency is headed by a director who is appointed by the president and confirmed by the Senate to serve a five-year term.

The OTS was a product of the S&L crisis of the 1980s. Between 1980 and 1989 hundreds of S&Ls failed in the biggest collapse of financial institutions since the Great Depression. Scholars agree that the crisis originated in the mismatch of low-yield mortgage assets held by the S&Ls and the rising cost of funds beginning in the late 1960s. The government responded with legislation enabling S&Ls to offer new products and services in hopes of obtaining higher returns. However, poor (sometimes corrupt) S&L management, inadequate supervision by thrift regulators, a declining market for energy and real estate (into which S&Ls had gone on to pour millions of dollars), changes in the tax code, and outright fraud doomed rescue efforts. By 1988, despite infusions of federal financial assistance, the Federal Savings and Loan Insurance Corporation was essentially out of money with which to pay off S&L

depositors, and the FHLBB was being held responsible for the worsening crisis. Thus, when Congress addressed the problem comprehensively in 1989, it abolished both entities in favor of the OTS, the regulator, and the SAIF, the insurer.

Under Timothy Ryan, a Washington, D.C., attorney who became the agency's first director, the OTS sought to stabilize a shaken industry and return it to profitability. Over the next two and a half years, more than seven hundred insolvent S&Ls were closed. Usually, their assets were turned over for sale by the Resolution Trust Corporation, another FIRREA creation. In other cases, sick thrifts were acquired by healthy thrifts or commercial banks. By 1995 there were fewer than half as many thrifts (1,522) as there were in 1989 (3,547).

A significant share of OTS resources went into the identification and prosecution of individuals charged with perpetrating and abetting S&L fraud. In a landmark 1992 action, the OTS filed a $275 million enforcement action against Kaye Scholer, the law firm that had represented Charles Keating, one of the most notorious of the S&L manipulators of the 1980s. This action, which led to a $41 million settlement agreement, raised important ethical questions about the dual responsibility of attorneys, accountants, and other professionals to their clients and to the public interest.

OTS supervision and an improving economy helped the much-reduced thrift industry to begin posting profits again in the early nineties. Questions continued, however, about the future of the thrift charter and the OTS itself. With bank and thrift powers essentially equalized, many S&Ls switched to a bank charter, which offered a big reduction in deposit insurance premiums. With a declining base of institutions to supervise, the OTS steadily shrank (from 3,442 employees in 1990 to 1,477 in 1995), and OTS executives publicly advocated folding their agency into one of the existing bank regulatory agencies. The Clinton administration's decision to leave in place an acting director (Jonathan Fiechter, who had taken over when Ryan resigned in December 1993) instead of making an official appointment seemed to support assump-

tions that the OTS would soon disappear from the scene.

[*See also* Resolution Trust Corporation.]

BIBLIOGRAPHY

Lowy, Martin. *High Rollers: Inside the Savings and Loan Debacle*. New York, 1991.
Savings and Community Banker. 1990–1995.
White, Lawrence J. *The S&L Debacle: Public Policy Lessons for Bank and Thrift Regulators*. New York, 1991.

—JESSE STILLER

Trade Representative, Office of the U.S.

 The United States trade representative (USTR) is a cabinet-level official who serves as the principal negotiator and government-wide leader on U.S. trade policy. The office which s/he heads, located within the Executive Office of the President, includes three deputy U.S. trade representatives with ambassadorial rank and a staff of about 160 in Washington, D.C., and Geneva, Switzerland. The Washington staff is housed in the Winder Building, one short block from the White House.

For most of American history, primary responsibility for trade rested with the Department of State. It was Secretary of State Cordell Hull (1933–1944) who led the historic shift, during the Roosevelt administration, from a policy of high trade barriers (protectionism) to one stressing reciprocal, negotiated reductions of tariffs and other trade barriers by the United States and its trading partners. By the 1950s, however, members of the U.S. Congress had become very critical of the State Department for its insensitivity to the interests of American industry and its alleged tendency to bargain away commercial interests in pursuit of good political relations or other diplomatic goals.

Thus in 1962, when President John F. Kennedy sought congressional authorization for a major new round of multilateral trade bargaining, particularly with the new European Economic Community, legislators pressed for an organizational change. Representative Wilbur Mills (D-Ark.), chairman of the House Ways and Means Committee and the most important member of Congress on trade matters, believed that no existing U.S. department was appropriate for directing these negotiations. So he inserted in the authorizing legislation a provision that the U.S. delegation in the new talks be led by a special trade representative (STR) reporting directly to the president. Kennedy accepted this condition, the law was enacted, and the first STR, Christian A. Herter, was sworn in before the end of the year.

Herter and his successor, William Roth, negotiated far-reaching tariff-reduction agreements, concluded in 1967, in what had become known as the "Kennedy Round." It brought average U.S. tariff rates down to below ten percent, compared to about sixty percent under the Smoot-Hawley Act of 1930. So the next global trade negotiating round centered on nontariff barriers to trade. When the Nixon administration sought authorization to launch such a round, STR William Eberle (1971–1974) and his deputies played a major role in winning legislative approval. The Trade Act of 1974 also strengthened the trade office by giving it permanent statutory existence within the Executive Office of the President (the 1962 law had only established the *position* of STR) and by awarding its leader cabinet rank. President Carter's STR, Robert Strauss (1977–1979), took advantage of this enhanced position and succeeded in completing the global negotiation, labeled the Tokyo Round, that Congress had authorized. He worked closely with Congress throughout the process, and his assiduousness was rewarded with overwhelming approval of the results—only seven representatives and four senators voted against the Tokyo Round implementing legislation when it came to a vote in the summer of 1979.

But before the final vote, Congress insisted that the administration act to strengthen its trade policy institutions. The Office of the STR had grown in staff and role since its creation: its officials were now leading not just in global trade rounds—the original purpose—but in many bilateral negotiations as well. Senators and representatives saw U.S. trade competitiveness as

eroding in key sectors—initially textiles and apparel, then steel, then consumer electronics, then automobiles. They felt that trade policy was not receiving very high priority from the U.S. government and that power over trade issues was dispersed too broadly among executive branch agencies. So they delayed final action on the Tokyo Round until President Carter presented a reorganization proposal to Congress.

The plan that Carter submitted (Reorganization Plan No. 3 of 1979) enlarged and strengthened the trade representative's office. Its permanent staff was increased from 59 to 131 officials. Its mandate was broadened to include a range of "international trade, policy development, coordination and negotiation functions," including some previously assigned to the State Department. The Reorganization Plan made the trade representative the president's principal adviser and chief spokesman on trade issues. Finally, the name of the institution was changed to the Office of the *United States* Trade Representative, or USTR.

The Carter reorganization went into effect in 1980, and the Office of the USTR has been the lead trade agency ever since. Its position has not gone unchallenged: In the first Reagan administration the office experienced spirited competition from the Department of Commerce, which had also been given new trade authorities in the Tokyo Round legislation and the Carter reorganization. Moreover, there have been periodic proposals that it be replaced by a full-fledged Department of Trade which would bring a much broader range of trade functions under one bureaucratic roof. But the current office has retained strong support from Congress and in particular from the House Ways and Means and Senate Finance Committees, the panels with primary trade policy jurisdiction. It fended off reorganizers during the tenure of USTR William Brock (1981–1985) and was given added authority by Congress in the Omnibus Trade and Competitiveness Act of 1988. It launched the Uruguay Round of multilateral trade negotiations under USTR Clayton Yeutter (1985–1989) and brought it near completion under President Bush's trade representative, Carla Hills (1989–1993).

The USTR office also took the lead in negotiating a free-trade agreement with Canada (approved by Congress in 1988) and the North American Free Trade Agreement (NAFTA) signed by President Bush in 1992 and approved by Congress in 1993 after a tough legislative battle. President Clinton's USTR, Mickey Kantor (1993–1996), played a key role in the NAFTA fight; he also led the negotiations that completed the Uruguay Round in December 1993 and won congressional approval a year later. And all USTRs since Robert Strauss of the Carter administration have devoted major energy to bilateral market-opening negotiations with key U.S. trading partners such as Japan.

As this brief history illustrates, trade negotiations are the primary function of the Office of the USTR. The object of these negotiations is usually *trade liberalization,* achieved through agreements with other countries to remove or reduce barriers to their imports of foreign (particularly U.S.) goods. The global, regional, and bilateral talks described above all had this as their primary purpose. However, the office has also negotiated agreements with other countries to restrict their sales of certain products to the United States. Most prominent and elaborate have been long-standing arrangements to limit imports of textile and apparel by category of product. (The Uruguay Round agreements provide for elimination of this restrictive Multi-Fiber Arrangement by the year 2005.) The Office of the USTR has operated within a set of general international trade rules set forth initially by the General Agreement on Tariffs and Trade in the late 1940s and carried over, sometimes in strengthened form, to the World Trade Organization, launched in 1995 under the Uruguay Round agreements.

The Office of the USTR carries out trade negotiations as the lead agency on trade working with other executive agencies, particularly the Departments of Commerce, State, the Treasury, and Agriculture. To both underscore and facilitate this leadership, trade legislation provides for an interagency trade process chaired by the USTR. At the working level, the Trade Policy Staff Committee (TPSC) coordinates routine issues. The Trade Policy Review Committee, chaired by a deputy USTR, handles broader issues as well as appeals from the TPSC. Standing formally above them is the cabinet-level Trade Policy Committee, which seldom meets. Trade policy, in turn, must be coordinated with overall economic policy and overall foreign policy. The long-standing National Security Council and the National Economic Council (a creation of the Clinton administration) are presidential staffs that help to bring this about.

As these interagency relationships suggest, the role of the Office of the USTR in negotiating with other nations inevitably involves it in negotiations *within* the United States. These not only involve reconciling competing perspectives within the executive branch but also maintaining broad support in the Congress and working closely with U.S. industries that produce goods that are traded internationally. To facilitate the latter, Congress has established a three-tiered system of private sector advisory committees through which the office is expected to solicit and respond to the views of American business. And to please domestic constituencies, the Office of the USTR talks tough with foreign governments in order to extract maximum concessions—or at least to leave an impression of having done so—regarding the opening of their markets to U.S. products.

One important means of USTR leadership has been the "fast-track procedures" for congressional action on trade agreements. Originally established by the Trade Act of 1974, these provide for expeditious, up-or-down House and Senate votes on legislation submitted by the president for the purpose of implementing trade agreements that Congress has authorized. This process enhances the credibility of U.S. trade negotiators. In practice, USTR officials work closely with the key congressional trade committees—Senate Finance, House Ways and Means—to draft such presidential legislation in order to assure the broadest possible support.

BIBLIOGRAPHY

Destler, I. M. *American Trade Politics.* 3d ed. Washington, D.C., 1995.
Dryden, Steve. *Trade Warriors: USTR and the American Crusade for Free Trade.* New York, 1995.

—I. M. DESTLER

Transit Administration, Federal

One of the nine operating divisions of the Department of Transportation, the Federal Transit Administration (FTA) was authorized under the Housing and Urban Development Act of 1961 and expanded by the Federal Transit Act of 1964. It became an operating entity in 1968 and was called the Urban Mass Transportation Administration until 1991, when the present name was adopted. The FTA is headed by an administrator appointed by the secretary of transportation. The FTA's powers are defined under the Federal Transit Act of 1964, the Federal Transit Assistance Act of 1970, and the Surface Transportation Assistance Act of 1982. The last named act imposed a penny a gallon tax on gasoline for financing a fund devoted to mass transit. The FTA undertakes major research and development projects on its own as well as for other private and public organizations.

—GEORGE THOMAS KURIAN

Transportation, Department of

 The mission of the Department of Transportation (DOT), a cabinet-level executive department of the United States government, is to develop and coordinate policies that will provide an efficient and economical national transportation system, with due regard for need, the environment, and the national defense. It is the primary agency in the federal government with the responsibility for shaping and administering policies and programs to protect and enhance the safety, adequacy, and efficiency of the transportation system and services.

The DOT was established by an act of Congress, signed by President Lyndon B. Johnson on 15 October 1966. Its first secretary, Alan S. Boyd, took office on 16 January 1967. The department's first official day of operation was 1 April 1967.

The Department of Transportation contains the Office of the Secretary and ten individual operating administrations, each headed by a presidential appointee. They are the United States Coast Guard, the Federal Aviation Administration, the Federal Highway Administration, the Federal Railroad Administration, the National Highway Traffic Safety Administration, the Federal Transit Administration, the Maritime Administration, the Saint Lawrence Seaway Development Corporation, the Research and Special Programs Administration, and the Bureau of Transportation Statistics.

From its inception the United States government has wrestled with its role in developing transportation infrastructure and transportation policy. Often, the result has been confusion and needless complexity, leading to an overabundance of aid for some means of transportation and inadequate support for others. The law that established a cabinet-level DOT did not pass Congress until ninety-two years after one was first introduced. Lyndon Johnson called that bill "the most important transportation legislation of our lifetime . . . one of the essential building blocks in our preparation for the future. . . ."

Passage of the Department of Transportation enabling act in 1966 fulfilled a dream at least as old as that of Thomas Jefferson's Treasury secretary, Albert Gallatin. Even before that, the Coast Guard and the Army Corps of Engineers had helped to foster trade and transportation. [See Army Corps of Engineers.] To enhance the prosperity of struggling new states and to fulfill the need for rapid, simple, and accessible transportation, Gallatin recommended in 1808 that the federal government subsidize such internal improvements as the National Road.

Just before he left office in June 1965, Najeeb Halaby, administrator of the independent Federal Aviation Agency (as it was then called), proposed the idea of a cabinet-level DOT to Johnson administration planners. He argued that the department should assume the functions then under the authority of the under secretary of commerce for transportation. Moreover, he recommended that the Federal Aviation Agency become part of that department. As he later wrote, "I guess I was a rarity—an independent agency head proposing to become less independent."

Frustrated because he thought the Defense Department had locked the Federal Aviation Agency out of the administration's supersonic transport decision-making, Halaby decided that a DOT was essential to secure decisive transportation policy development. After four and a half years as administrator, he concluded that the agency could do a better job as part of an executive department that incorporated other government transportation programs. "One looks in vain," he wrote Johnson, "for a point of responsibility below the President capable of taking an evenhanded, comprehensive, authoritarian approach to the development of transportation policies or even able to assure reasonable coordination and balance among the various transportation programs of the government."

Charles Schultze, director of the Bureau of the Budget, and Joseph A. Califano, special assistant to the president, pushed for the new department. They urged Boyd, then under secretary of commerce for transportation, to explore the prospects of having a transportation department initiative prepared as part of Johnson's 1966 legislative program. On 22 October the Boyd Task Force submitted recommendations that advocated establishing a DOT that would include the Federal Aviation Agency, the Bureau of Public Roads, the Coast Guard, the Saint Lawrence Seaway Development Corporation, the Great Lakes Pilotage Association, the Car Service Division of the Interstate Commerce Commission, the subsidy function of the Civil Aeronautics Board, and the Panama Canal.

With modifications, Johnson agreed, and on 6 March 1966 he sent Congress a bill to establish a DOT. The new agency would coordinate and effectively manage transportation programs, provide leadership in the resolution of transportation problems, and develop national transportation policies and programs. The department would accomplish this mission under the leadership of a secretary, an under secretary, and four staff assistant secretaries whose functions, though unspecified, expedited the line authority between the secretary and under secretary and the heads of the operating administrations.

With the proposed legislation Johnson sent Congress a carefully worded message recom-

mending that it enact the bill as part of his attempt to improve public safety and accessibility. Johnson recognized the dilemma the American transportation system faced. While it was the best-developed system in the world, it wasted lives and resources and had proved incapable of meeting the needs of the time. "America today lacks a coordinated transportation system that permits travelers and goods to move conveniently and efficiently from one means of transportation to another, using the best characteristics of each." Johnson maintained that an up-to-date transportation system was essential to the national economic health and well-being, including employment, standard of living, accessibility, and the national defense.

After much compromise with a Congress that was jealous of its constitutional power of the purse, Johnson signed the Department of Transportation enabling act on 15 October 1966. Compromise made the final version of the bill less than what the White House wanted. Nevertheless, it was a significant move forward, producing the most sweeping reorganization of the federal government since the National Security Act of 1947.

On 1 April 1967 the DOT opened for business, celebrating the "Pageant of Transportation" five and a half months after Johnson had signed the enabling legislation. Dignitaries from the department, the Smithsonian Institution, the transportation industry, and the public gathered for ceremonies on the Mall celebrating the start of the new department. Alan S. Boyd, named by Johnson as its first secretary, guaranteed that the new department would "make transportation more efficient, more economical, more expeditious and more socially responsible."

By 1 April this newest cabinet-level department was suddenly the fourth largest, with a blueprint of organization, an order providing for essential authorizations, and several leading officials on the job. It brought under one roof more than thirty transportation agencies and functions scattered throughout the government and about ninety-five thousand employees, most of whom had been with the Federal Aviation Agency, the Coast Guard, and the Bureau of Public Roads.

To Alan S. Boyd, the former Civil Aeronautics Board chairman and under secretary of commerce for transportation, fell the challenge of setting up the new department: structuring it around Congress's recommendations in the enabling act, organizing it, and setting it in motion. The new secretary faced a host of problems: creating his own immediate office, providing appropriate missions for his assistant secretaries, building the new Federal Highway Administration and the Federal Railroad Administration, helping to start the National Transportation Safety Board, and setting up an organization and management plan for the entire department.

Acknowledging the connection between transportation systems and the needs of urban areas, the White House drafted a plan to transfer urban mass transit functions to the DOT that formerly resided in the Department of Housing and Urban Development (HUD). As mandated by the Department of Transportation Act, Johnson directed the secretaries of housing and urban development and transportation to inform Congress where the most "logical and efficient organization and location of urban mass transportation functions within the Executive Branch" would be. When this failed to resolve the issue, Johnson transferred most of HUD's mass transit capacity to the DOT, effective 1 July 1968. Responsibility for these programs resided in the newly established Urban Mass Transportation Administration (now the Federal Transit Administration).

By the conclusion of Boyd's administration, the department embraced the Coast Guard, the renamed Federal Aviation Administration, the Federal Highway Administration, the Federal Railroad Administration, the Saint Lawrence Seaway Development Corporation, the Urban Mass Transportation Administration, and, tangentially, the National Transportation Safety Board. Boyd's most significant achievement was to organize the department and to get it operating as a constructive governmental entity.

During his first administration, Richard Nixon presided over several transportation-related matters, including the bailout of the Penn Central Railroad, the launching of Amtrak, and the attempted extension of federal support for supersonic transport. He nominated as his secretary of transportation the moderate, thrice-elected governor of Massachusetts, John A. Volpe. A modern Horatio Alger, Volpe headed a construction firm that built hospitals, schools, shopping centers, public buildings, and military installations along the Eastern Seaboard and in other parts of the country. In 1968 the former federal highway administrator was a rumored vice presidential nominee until Maryland governor Spiro Agnew received the nod.

In 1970 the Highway Safety Act authorized the establishment of the National Highway Traffic Safety Administration. Although the law added somewhat to the department's safety mission, the Federal Highway Administration originally had handled most of the functions that the new agency assumed.

Besides establishing another operating administration and adding to the secretary's span of control and coordination workload, the Highway Safety Act separated highway administration into two parts: design, construction, and maintenance on the one hand, highway and automobile safety on the other. Such organization ran counter to the original DOT organizing concept for the various modes of transportation: unlike the Coast Guard and the Federal Aviation Administration, for example, the Federal Highway Administration no longer bore responsibility both for facilities and infrastructure and for safety programs.

Volpe gave highest priority to coordinating the missions of the diverse agencies placed under the department's umbrella and developing a national transportation policy. Symbolic of this effort was the establishment of the Transportation Systems Center in Cambridge, Massachusetts. He thought that he had effectively begun to coordinate separate agencies, each of which had its own constituencies on Capitol Hill, in industry, and among the public. For years, these agencies had acted autonomously and with little thought for the nation's transportation needs and for teamwork among themselves. Volpe believed he had begun to forge them into a united transportation agency.

During Volpe's tenure the DOT assumed a higher profile in resolving national transportation problems. These included airline hijackings, the sick-out of the fledgling Professional Air Traffic Controllers Organization, the decision to end federal support for production of the supersonic transport and to handle applications for Concorde landing slots, the financial insolvency of the Penn Central Railroad and the creation of Amtrak, and the Coast Guard's mishandling of the case of the defection of the Lithuanian seaman Simas Kudirka.

On 1 December 1972 Nixon named Claude Brinegar to succeed Volpe. Brinegar, a senior vice president of the Los Angeles–based Union Oil Company, had a doctorate in econometrics and was a self-styled professional manager. Reserved in management style and conservative in political philosophy, Brinegar successfully steered the department through Watergate and the energy crisis of 1973–1974.

Watergate finished the Nixon presidency. Gerald Ford, Nixon's successor, decided that he wanted to run for president in his own right, a campaign that Brinegar had no wish to join. He returned to California, and Ford named William T. Coleman to succeed him. Coleman's background in transportation had been limited to serving on several airline and transit boards, including the Southeastern Pennsylvania Transportation Authority, Philadelphia's transit system. Coleman was a distinguished lawyer who, with Thurgood Marshall, had played a major role in landmark civil rights cases, including *Brown v. the Board of Education of Topeka,* which ended *de jure* school segregation in 1954. Later, Coleman met and impressed Ford, when the then–House Minority Leader served on the Warren Commission investigating the assassination of John F. Kennedy; Coleman was senior consultant and assistant counsel to the commission. During Coleman's tenure, on 1 April 1975 Congress granted the National Transportation Safety Board, which had been established within the DOT, its independence from the department.

Ford lost the election of 1976 to Jimmy Carter, the former governor of Georgia. For secretary of transportation, Carter chose Brock Adams, a six-term member of the House of Representatives from Washington. Adams, a leading authority on transportation matters in the House, had been

Brinegar's nemesis and the primary author of the legislation that reorganized the bankrupt northeastern rail lines into the government-backed Conrail system.

Adams's establishment of the Research and Special Programs Administration (RSPA) on 23 September 1977 was a significant institutional development. When Adams created the RSPA, he combined the Transportation Systems Center, the hazardous materials transportation and pipeline safety programs, and diverse program activities from the Office of the Secretary that did not readily fit in any of the existing operating administrations. The establishment of the RSPA set a precedent in that it was a creation of the secretary, not Congress. (Passage of the Pipeline Safety Act of 1992 gave the RSPA equal statutory standing with the other operating administrations.) The RSPA simultaneously moved crosscutting research and development pursuits from the Office of the Secretary to an autonomous operating administration.

During Adams's administration, the Inspectors General Act of 1978 imposed on the department, and most other executive agencies as well, an inspector general, appointed by the president and confirmed by the Senate. The mission of the inspector general was to help the secretary cope with waste, fraud, and abuse. Although housed in the department and given the rank of assistant secretary, the inspector general was generally autonomous.

Before leaving office, Adams recommended that the Federal Highway Administration and the Urban Mass Transportation Administration be reorganized into a Surface Transportation Administration, an idea to which James Burnley and Federico Peña would later return. Adams was succeeded by Neil Goldschmidt, mayor of Portland, Oregon, since 1972, and later president of the United States Conference of Mayors. Meanwhile, legislative triumphs in transportation deregulation included the Railroad Regulatory Act (better known as the Staggers Rail Act), the Truck Regulatory Reform Act, the International Airlines Reform Act, and the Household Goods Regulatory Reform Act.

Goldschmidt expressed an interest in government industrial policy, an early example of which was the Chrysler Corporation Assistance Program, worked out largely by the Treasury Department. When Congress drafted the Chrysler Loan Guarantee Act of 1979, he began a review of the automobile industry's problems. Goldschmidt also established the Office of Small and Disadvantaged Business Utilization in the Office of the Secretary. It was responsible for carrying out policies and procedures consistent with federal statutes to provide policy guidance for minority, women-owned, and disadvantaged businesses taking part in the department's procurement and federal financial assistance activities.

Ronald Reagan's first secretary of transportation, Andrew ("Drew") Lewis, a management consultant and political leader from Pennsylvania, successfully negotiated the transfer of the Maritime Administration from the Commerce Department to the DOT and provided the department with the maritime connection it needed to formulate national transportation policy. The department assumed greater visibility during the air traffic controllers' strike in August 1981, during which Lewis spoke for the administration. After personally negotiating with the Professional Air Traffic Controllers Organization in the days leading up to the strike, Lewis forcefully explained the government's response to the strike—firings and no amnesty for strikers.

Lewis's successor, Elizabeth Dole, had been Reagan's assistant for public liaison. A consumer adviser in two administrations and a member of the Federal Trade Commission during the Nixon and Ford administrations, Dole brought to her new position experience in consumer and trade matters. While Dole was secretary, the Commercial Space Launch Act of 1984 gave the department a multifaceted new mission to promote and to regulate commercial space launch vehicles. Because no operating administration had a comparable mission and because of its modest funding, Dole located the Office of Commercial Space Transportation in the Office of the Secretary. (It was transferred to the Federal Aviation Administration in a 1995 restructuring.)

The Airline Deregulation Act of 1978 and the Civil Aeronautics Board Sunset Act of 1984 had abolished the board and transferred to the department many of its functions relating to the economic regulation of the airline industry. Specifically, these included the aviation economic fitness program, functions related to consumer protection, antitrust oversight, airline data collection, and the review of international route negotiations and route awards to carriers. On 1 January 1985 the Office of the Secretary took over most of these functions, under the jurisdiction of the Office of the Assistant Secretary for Policy and International Affairs.

Continuing a trend begun when the department transferred the Alaska Railroad to the state of Alaska, the DOT divested itself of entities that it thought should be in the private sector. Dole moved to end Federal Railroad Administration ownership of Conrail, finally realized in April 1987. She also encouraged the establishment of the Metropolitan Washington Airports Authority in June 1987, transferring administration of Washington National Airport and Dulles International Airport from the Federal Aviation Administration to that authority.

To succeed Dole, Reagan chose her deputy, former general counsel James Burnley. While deputy secretary, Burnley had helped to negotiate the sale of Conrail, directed the privatization of Amtrak, enabled the transfer of the Washington airports to the regional authority, and helped to assemble an air traffic control work force in the wake of the 1981 strike. He also helped to produce the department's policies on aviation safety and security.

Disappointed with the Federal Aviation Administration's apparent foot-dragging on safety regulations, and seeking to increase the secretary's management oversight capacity within the department, Burnley proposed to curtail the autonomy of the operating administrations. A working paper recommended integration of the functions of the Maritime Administration, the Federal Aviation Administration, and the surface transportation administrations under three under secretaries, for water, air, and surface transportation, respectively, the very antithesis of the rationale for the department as conceived by its organizers.

Burnley's reorganization proposal was made at the conclusion of Ronald Reagan's second term in the hope that it would provide Congress, his successor, and the public with an alternative to proposals according to which one agency or another would leave the department. His successor, Samuel Skinner, a George Bush appointee, chose to emphasize national transportation policy instead. Skinner also welcomed expansion of the department's role in crisis management response. His handling of a succession of disasters, both natural and manufactured, earned Skinner the Washington moniker "the Master of Disaster." For Skinner, it began with additional evidence that a terrorist bomb had destroyed Pan American Airways flight 103. (The explosion over Lockerbie, Scotland, on 21 December 1988 had killed 270, including eleven on the ground.) In rapid sequence followed the machinists' strike at Eastern Airlines (March 1989) and the company's subsequent bankruptcy, the *Exxon Valdez* oil spill (March 1989), the Loma Prieta earthquake (October 1989), and Hurricane Hugo (September 1990), all high-profile incidents that took place during Skinner's first twenty-one months in office.

Skinner identified the development of a national transportation policy as the department's highest priority. In *Moving America,* national transportation policymakers outlined six objectives: to maintain and expand America's national transportation system; to nurture a sturdy financial footing for transportation; to keep the nation's transportation industry vigorous and competitive; to guarantee that the transportation system enhances public safety and the national security; to maintain the environment and the quality of life; and to ready American transportation technology and expertise for the next century. By March 1990 conditions had persuaded Skinner that to realize the national transportation policy goals, diverse departmental offices would have to work together. As a result, the secretary launched NTP—Phase 2 under the leadership of Thomas Larson, administrator of the Federal Highway Administration. NTP—Phase 2 activities combined to help the department inventory its strengths and weaknesses and identify room for improvement.

On 18 December 1991 Bush signed the Intermodal Surface Transportation Efficiency Act (IS-TEA), developed in part from the NTP, which provided a six-year reauthorization to restructure the department's highway, highway safety, and transit programs. One effect of this legislation was that the Urban Mass Transportation Administration became the Federal Transit Administration. The ISTEA legislation also required the department to establish two new organizational entities: the Bureau of Transportation Statistics, which was to provide timely transportation-related information through the compilation, analysis, and publishing of comprehensive transportation statistics, and the Office of Intermodalism, in the Office of the Assistant Deputy Secretary, which was charged with coordinating and initiating federal policy on intermodal transportation.

Skinner, meanwhile, became White House chief of staff. A month and a half later, Bush named Andrew Card, his deputy White House chief of staff, to be secretary of transportation. Disaster response to Hurricane Andrew, which hit southern Florida in August 1992, highlighted Card's term at the department.

Bush lost the election of 1992 to Arkansas governor Bill Clinton. In a move to enhance diversity in his cabinet, Clinton selected Federico Peña, an Hispanic American and the former mayor of Denver, Colorado, initially to head the "cluster group" that dealt with transportation issues during the transition, and ultimately to manage the Department of Transportation.

In March 1993 Clinton announced an initiative that the Democratic Leadership Council embraced, a plan for a six-month National Performance Review (NPR) of the federal government. Following a highly successful program analysis by Texas governor Ann Richards, Clinton asked Vice President Al Gore to head his administration's effort to improve the quality of the government and to reduce the cost of delivering services to the American taxpayer. The NPR challenged federal agencies to identify what worked and what did not, to propose new ways of doing the job that would eliminate red tape and improve both operations and customer service, and to think about doing their work in smarter, more cost-effective ways.

While the NPR laid the groundwork for "reinventing government," the department had been responding to several congressional initiatives, including the Chief Financial Officers Act of 1990, the Federal Managers' Financial Integrity Act, and the Government Performance and Results Act of 1993. The outcome was the *DOT Strategic Plan*, which Peña announced in January 1994. The plan delineated the department's mission and enumerated seven broad strategic goals to carry it out:

- "tying America together" through an effective intermodal transportation system

- investing strategically in transportation infrastructure

- creating a new alliance between the nation's transportation and technology industries in order to make them more efficient and economically competitive

- promoting safe and secure transportation

- actively enhancing the environment

- "putting people first" in the transportation system

- transforming the DOT.

The NPR had promised a government that not only did its job better but cost less as well. Consequently, the Clinton administration was able, by 19 December 1994, to propose a "middle-class" tax cut, one that would be funded, in part, by restructuring several federal departments and agencies, including the DOT. That same day, Peña outlined a plan to restructure the department by the end of the decade. After a month and a half of workshops and discussions with Congress, the public, and department employees throughout the country, Peña announced a restructuring plan for the department. Pending congressional approval, three operating administrations, a Federal Aviation Administration, a new Intermodal Transportation Administration, and the Coast Guard, would replace the current ten. Meanwhile, the department continued to be at the center of the federal government's crisis management response team, as exemplified by its response to flooding in the Mississippi River Basin in the summer of 1993 and the Northridge earthquake of January 1994.

[*See also* Amtrak; Coast Guard; Federal Aviation Administration; Highway Administration, Federal; Highway Traffic Safety Administration, National; Maritime Administration; Railroad Administration, Federal; Transit Administration, Federal; *and* Transportation Safety Board, National.]

BIBLIOGRAPHY

Burby, John. *The Great American Motion Sickness; or, Why You Can't Get from There to Here.* Boston, 1971.
Davis, Grant Miller. *The Department of Transportation.* Lexington, Mass., 1970.
Dean, Alan L. *The Organization and Management of the Department of Transportation.* [National Academy of Public Administration], March 1991.
Halaby, Najeeb E. *Crosswinds: An Airman's Memoir.* Garden City, N.Y., 1978.
Harr, John E., comp. *Administrative History of the United States Railway Association.* National Academy of Public Administration, n.d.
Hazard, John L. "The Institutionalization of Transportation Policy: Two Decades of DOT." *Transportation Journal* (Fall 1986).
Hazard, John L. *Managing National Transportation Policy* Westport, Conn., 1988.
                                                        —R. DALE GRINDER

Transportation Barriers Compliance Board.

See Architectural and Transportation Barriers Compliance Board.

Transportation Safety Board, National

 Established by the Department of Transportation Act of 1966, the National Transportation Safety Board (NTSB) was an autonomous agency within the Department of Transportation until it was granted independent status in 1975. The board consists of five members appointed by the president and confirmed by the Senate for five-year terms. No more than three members of the board may be members of the same party. A majority of the members are required to be technically

competent in transport regulation, safety engineering, and accident reconstruction. There are ten regional offices.

The NTSB's special responsibility is to investigate all civil aviation, railroad, pipeline, highway, and marine accidents. It also investigates and reports on the transportation of hazardous materials, assesses and recommends procedures for accident regulations, and reviews on appeal the suspension and revocation of certificates or licenses issued to any airline, railroad, motor vehicle, carrier, or ship. The NTSB can only make recommendations, and it has no authority to impose them or to enforce remedial action. However, some eighty percent of the NTSB's recommendations are generally accepted.

—GEORGE THOMAS KURIAN

Travel and Tourism Administration

Until it was dismantled in 1996 as part of the budget deal between the Republican Congress and Democratic president Bill Clinton, the United States Travel and Tourism Administration (USTTA) worked to develop tourism policy, to promote inbound tourism from abroad, and to stimulate travel within the United States. The USTTA, an agency of the Department of Commerce, was originally established by the International Travel Act of 1961 as the United States Travel Service. Congress created the agency in order to address a $1.2 billion balance-of-payments deficit in tourism. The agency changed its name as part of the National Tourism Policy Act of 1981.

Based in Washington, D.C., the agency also maintained ten international field offices in the countries that account for eighty-five percent of international tourists to the United States. The agency was guided by a fifteen-member industry-based Travel and Tourism Advisory Board.

The USTTA coordinated and negotiated international tourism policy, conducted statistical and market research, and directed programs of tourism trade development. While the USTTA's programs were to benefit states, cities, and private businesses, there was a special emphasis on small businesses, cultural and ethnic communities, and rural areas.

Headed by the under secretary of commerce for travel and tourism, who reported directly to the secretary of commerce, the agency was divided into four offices: Tourism Marketing, Policy and Planning, Research, and Strategic Planning and Administration.

The Office of Tourism Marketing was responsible for the agency's tourism trade development programs. The office helped American regions and companies sell their products and services abroad. Additionally, the office administered among its various programs the International Tourism Development Financial Assistance Program, which supported regional marketing initiatives, and the Disaster Relief Financial Assistance Program, which provided funds to encourage international tourism promotion after a natural disaster. The ten international field offices were administered by Tourism Marketing. The field offices conducted market analysis, participated in cooperative advertising, and provided consumer/trade information.

While the Office of Policy and Planning developed broad policy initiatives to encourage travel to and within the United States, it had no jurisdiction over state, local, or private-sector policies. The office identified and addressed bilateral and multilateral tourism issues that might create travel barriers. The Office of Policy and Planning represented the United States tourism interests in several international organizations including the World Tourism Organization, the Organization for Economic Cooperation and Development, the Organization of American States, and the Asian-Pacific Economic Cooperation Group.

The Office of Research provided tourism data for both the USTTA and for industry. The office conducted the In-Flight Survey of International Air Travelers, which profiled demographic and travel characteristics of international travelers. Additionally, the office collected travel information that was generated by other departments, including the Immigration and Naturalization Service and the Department of Transportation. Using econometric models, the office forecast international visitor arrivals from twenty-one countries and several world regions. The Office of Strategic Planning and Administration advised the USTTA on all administrative matters including budget planning and preparation, personnel training, and resource management.

BIBLIOGRAPHY

Department of Commerce. *USTTA: United States Travel and Tourism Administration.* Washington, D.C., 1993.
—JEFFREY D. SCHULTZ

Treasury, Department of the

 Established on 2 September 1789 (1 Stat. 65), the Department of the Treasury is the second oldest department in the federal government. Its central position within the federal government is due to Treasury's functions, size, leadership, and important role in the economic development of the United States.

Treasury has three missions: the development of tax, debt, financial, and economic policies; the management of the government's finances; and law enforcement. Money is the one element that ties together the varied activities of the department. Treasury helps to develop domestic and international economic policy, collects taxes, coins money, prints paper currency, manufactures stamps, regulates national banks and thrift institutions, and manages the government's fiscal accounts, cash, and the public debt. As the second largest law enforcement agency in the federal government, Treasury protects the country's borders, combats drug and other smuggling, enforces federal regulation of commerce in firearms, investigates bombings, apprehends counterfeiters, guards the president, trains law enforcement officers, and enforces tariff, trade, patent, and copyright laws. Support for the policy functions is provided by the departmental offices of the Treasury Department; the operations missions are carried out by operating bureaus under the oversight of the secretary of the Treasury, deputy secretary, heads of bureaus, and other officials.

Many of the main functions of the Treasury remain essentially the same today as in 1789, although the department has expanded and its functions have grown more sophisticated. The Treasury Department consists of eighteen departmental offices and eleven operating bureaus:

Customs Service (established in 1789)

U.S. Mint (1792)

Internal Revenue Service (1862)

Bureau of Engraving and Printing (1862)

Office of the Comptroller of the Currency (1863)

Secret Service (1865)

Bureau of the Public Debt (1919)

Financial Management Service (1920)

Federal Law Enforcement Training Center (1970)

Bureau of Alcohol, Tobacco and Firearms (1972)

Office of Thrift Supervision (1989).

TREASURY ADMINISTRATION DURING THE AMERICAN REVOLUTION

Treasury's history goes back to the American Revolution. On 22 June 1775 the Second Continental Congress approved the printing of $2 million in bills of credit to finance the war. Between 1775 and 1779 more than $241 million Continentals were issued. The value of this first national paper money fell so low it gave rise to the expression "not worth a Continental."

On 29 July 1775 Congress appointed joint treasurers; on 1 April 1776 a Treasury Office of Accounts with an auditor general was established; and on 6 September 1777 Michael Hillegas was named treasurer of the United States. Treasury's organization over the next three years proved so cumbersome that a congressional committee reported in November 1780 that "the Demon of Discord pervaded the whole Department" and determined that Treasury should be under a single officer.

Robert Morris, who served as superintendent of finance (20 February 1781 through 30 September 1784) under the Articles of Confederation, brought some stability to the nation's finances, secured foreign loans, financed the surrender of the British at Yorktown, wrangled with Congress over the budget, and reorganized Treasury operations. His staff included a comptroller, a register, the treasurer, and auditors. A private citizen, the broker Haym Salomon, raised most of the money needed to finance the American Revolution. Although a three-man Treasury Board ran Treasury operations from 1785 until 1789, the efficiency of a single administrator was not lost on the framers of the new government under the Constitution.

ESTABLISHMENT OF THE TREASURY DEPARTMENT

The Department of the Treasury was created by the First Congress on 2 September 1789 (1 Stat. 65). The law created six officers: "a Secretary of the Treasury, to be deemed head of the department; a Comptroller, an Auditor, a Treasurer, a Register, and an Assistant to the Secretary of the Treasury, which assistant shall be appointed by the said Secretary." The major financial officers were modeled on earlier experience.

The act establishing the Treasury Department followed a unique pattern and showed that Congress wanted to keep in close touch with the administration of finance. The laws creating the State, War, and Navy Departments were brief and general. Only in the Treasury Department did Congress fix in detail the internal organization and specify the duties of the six officers. Congress required the secretary to report in person or in writing on "all matters referred to him . . . or which shall appertain to his office." These requests for financial information did not refer to the chief executive. The president's control was mentioned only as to his removal power; nowhere, as in the statutes establishing the other departments, did the law specifically give the president power to assign additional duties to the secretary or to direct him in the performance of his duties. Reports went directly to Congress from the secretary of the Treasury and the treasurer.

Congress determined Treasury should be administered by a single executive with checks provided by the comptroller to supervise expenditures; the auditor to examine and verify accounts and certify balances; the treasurer to receive, store, and disburse public money; and the register to keep records of all receipts and expenditures and all debts due to or owed by the United States. The system has ever since provided protection against payments from the Treasury not authorized by law.

The formulation of financial policy and general direction of the Treasury Department were assigned to the secretary. Some of these functions strengthened the secretary's ties to Congress:

1. to prepare plans for improving and managing the revenue and for support of the public credit;

2. to prepare and report estimates of the public revenue and public expenditures;

3. to superintend the collection of the revenue;

4. to decide on forms for keeping and stating accounts;

5. to grant all warrants for money issued from the Treasury; and

6. to execute services relating to the sale of public lands.

ALEXANDER HAMILTON AND THE FEDERALISTS, 1789–1800

The first secretary of the Treasury, Alexander Hamilton, worked in the nation's first two capitals, New York City and Philadelphia. Renowned for his bold plans to restore America's credit, it is little known that he was the administrative architect of the new federal government. His policies strengthened the central government, established a strong financial basis for the nation, and provided the stability needed for economic development.

The secretary of the Treasury, in response to requests from Congress, wrote five reports that organized the fiscal service of the federal government. The policies contained in Hamilton's reports on the public debt and national bank were controversial. They created divisions in Congress and the cabinet and helped to define the difference between the nascent political parties by aligning those who wanted to make the central authority preeminent against those who sought a limited government.

Hamilton made three recommendations in his report on the public credit of 9 January 1790. The American Revolutionary War debt would be paid in full: "The debt of the United States . . . was the price of Liberty."

1. The debt of the United States to foreign creditors ($11.8 million, including interest) would be paid in full.

2. The debt of the United States to its people ($42.4 million, including interest) would be paid at face value rather than the greatly depreciated market value. The debt would be paid by replacing it with new bonds issued by the federal government, thus binding public creditors to the national interest rather than to the states.

3. The federal government would assume the Revolutionary War debts of the states. The third suggestion led to a stalemate in Congress. Alexander Hamilton, Thomas Jefferson, and James Madison worked out a compromise whereby Virginia and other southern states would vote for assumption of the debt of northern states in return for northern votes placing the nation's capital on the Potomac.

Secretary Hamilton's second report on the public debt of 16 January 1795 emphasized plans for paying off the public debt from existing revenues, in order, as Hamilton quoted from President George Washington's sixth annual message to Congress of 19 November 1794, "to prevent that progressive accumulation of debt which must ultimately endanger all governments."

Hamilton's report of 13 December 1790 on a national bank urged the establishment of a bank as a way to assist the Treasury. Congress chartered the Bank of the United States in February 1791 for twenty years as a private corporation. The government purchased one-fifth of the bank's $10 million capital stock, and the secretary of the Treasury could examine its general accounts. The first Bank of the United States acted in several ways like a modern central bank: it was the government's fiscal agent, held most of the Treasury's funds, helped sell government bonds, and made loans to the government. The bank issued its own paper currency that was soon accepted as a national uniform currency.

The principal source of revenue in the eighteenth century was customs duties. The need to increase revenues resulted in internal excise taxes, and a tax on whiskey was adopted by Congress in March 1791. The tax led to the Whisky Rebellion of August 1794, the first challenge to the authority of the federal government. Hamilton led the militia that caused the opposition to flee. Treasury's firm response gave the government new strength.

The Treasury Department, not the president, was at the center of the budget process for 130 years. The department secretaries and other branches of the government submitted estimates to the register of the Treasury, who brought them together and published annually *An Account of the Receipts and Expenditures of the United States.*

The act of 2 September 1789 did not specifically authorize the Treasury to revise figures supplied by the departments. Secretaries did so infrequently. Hamilton began the custom of sending the estimates directly to Congress; thus the Treasury became the agency for transmitting the budget. Appropriation acts followed closely the amounts requested by the departments. The Jeffersonian Republicans in Congress pushed unsuccessfully for specifically itemized appropriations that more closely controlled expenditures. The Federalists held that appropriations should be large lump sums of money allowing wide executive discretion.

The Constitution (Art. I, Sec. 9) directed that "No Money shall be drawn from the Treasury, but in Consequence of Appropriations made by Law." Administrative control over expenditures was detailed in the organic act creating the Treasury Department. The secretary was directed to grant all warrants for money issued from the Treasury. The Treasury's responsibility was to keep sums in excess of appropriations from being paid out. The auditing system also provided control. The act of 2 September 1789 made the Treasury primarily and finally responsible for all public accounts. Treasury auditors verified all balances and sent them to the comptroller for review and final settlement. The comptroller, not the secretary, had the responsibility of settling accounts. The comptroller was also empowered to direct prosecutions for all debts due to the United States and to institute suit against revenue officers for failing to remit money to the government. The prosecutorial functions of the government were placed in the Treasury Department and not given to the attorney general.

The Treasury Department quickly became the largest and most comprehensive agency in the government. The greatest expansion and development of government responsibilities occurred in it. Treasury's importance in the cabinet derived from its functions, size, and constituency.

Before America had a navy, Alexander Hamilton saw to the establishment of the Revenue-Cutter Service. By the act of 4 August 1790 (1 Stat. 175), Treasury would operate a fleet of armed sailing ships to patrol American waters and enforce the revenue laws. Customs collectors were designated to pay military pensions in 1790, and the purveyor of public supplies was created in 1795 to purchase military supplies (1 Stat. 419). The Marine Hospital Service, established in 1798 to provide medical care to seamen (1 Stat. 605), was financed from the seamen's wages by one of the federal government's earliest systems of payroll deduction. [See Public Health Service and Revenue-Cutter Service.]

Treasury was the only department with an extensive field service located in every section of the country. The Customs Service, created before the Treasury Department on 31 July 1789, was placed within Treasury (1 Stat. 38); internal revenue collectors and land agents enlarged the field force.

Through the Customs Service and revenue cutters, Treasury dealt with merchants, fishermen, and shipowners; through its fiscal agent, the Bank of the United States, it dealt with bankers, businessmen, and professionals; through the purveyor of public supplies, large contractors; through the Post Office, annexed loosely to the Treasury from 1789 until 1829, the newspapers; and through the revenue officers and land agents, the average citizen.

In 1789 the headquarters office in New York employed thirty-nine people; in 1790 the staff in Philadelphia numbered seventy. When Treasury opened for business on 15 June 1800 in Washington, D.C., there were seventy-eight officers and employees and a field force of 1,615, more than half the total civil service. Treasury occupied a brick Georgian-style building designed by the English architect George Hadfield and built (1798–1800) next to the White House on a site chosen by George Washington.

ALBERT GALLATIN AND THE JEFFERSONIAN REPUBLICANS, 1800–1829

Thomas Jefferson's secretary of the Treasury was Albert Gallatin. He remains the longest-termed secretary, serving from 14 May 1801 until 20 April 1813, when he left to negotiate the end of the War of 1812. Like Hamilton, Albert Gallatin was an eminent financier and one of America's great administrators.

Gallatin's job was to put into practice the economic views of the Jeffersonian Republicans—reduction of the public debt, the abolition of internal excise taxes, and making public land affordable. The reduction of the public debt was Gallatin's first priority. From 1801 through 1811, Secretary Gallatin succeeded in cutting the public debt in half. In May 1801 the public debt, both foreign and domestic, was $82 million. Eight years later it had been reduced $25 million, to $57 million; on 31 December 1811, the public debt had been reduced a total of $37 million, to $45.2 million.

Gallatin was the first secretary of the Treasury to realize that the control of budget expenditures meant control of the administration's public policy and the whole machinery of government. Secretary Gallatin relentlessly strove to cut expenditures in the Army, Navy, and U.S. legations abroad; made savings in the Customs Service; and specifically applied the annual budget surplus from increased revenues to the public debt.

The Louisiana Purchase (1803), stretching from the Mississippi to the Rockies, doubled the size of the United States. Secretary Gallatin financed the $15.2 million purchase price by issuing $11.2 million of stock to the French government and assuming $3.7 million of American claims on France.

Secretary Gallatin was one of America's strongest supporters of internal improvements that opened up eastern and southern markets to western produce and that were instrumental in knitting America's regions into a single national economy. In his 1808 report on *Roads and Canals,* based on an extensive national survey, Gallatin wrote: "Good roads and canals will . . . unite . . . the United States. No other single operation, within the power of Government can more effectually tend to strengthen and perpetuate that Union."

Albert Gallatin's land policies directly aided the group that formed the backbone of Jeffersonian democracy—the independent farmers. Gallatin supported sales of 160-acre tracts—plots that were workable and affordable. To administer his policy Gallatin established the General Land Office in 1812.

In financing the War of 1812, Gallatin faced the same problems that confronted every other wartime secretary of the Treasury: he had to choose between taxes or borrowing. Gallatin chose borrowing, in part because Congress was reluctant to pass adequate taxes. The $87 million cost of the war left a huge public debt.

In April 1816 Congress called for the first administrative reorganization of the government and asked the four cabinet secretaries to report on "a more certain accountability of the public expenditure." Their report of December 1816 supported the primary and final settlement of all accounts in the Treasury and a complete separation between civil and military accounts. Five (later six) auditors and two comptrollers were appointed to carry out the law. This system lasted until the end of the nineteenth century.

Treasury's responsibilities expanded under the Jeffersonians as they had under the Federalists. The Revenue-Cutter Service became active after 1807 in suppressing the slave trade. The register of the Treasury began the annual publication of U.S. trade statistics in 1821. *Commerce and Navigation of the United States* was produced by Treasury until 1903, when the function was transferred to the new Department of Commerce and Labor.

The department held one of the oldest governmental libraries, established about 1817. Treasury clerks totaled 181 in 1826 and were becoming an increasingly aged work force. In 1827 Secretary Richard Rush called the Treasury "the octogenarian department."

On the night of 24 August and the early morning of 25 August 1814, the Treasury Building was burned to the ground by Admiral George Cockburn and General Robert Ross in the British attack on Washington during the War of 1812. The Treasury was reconstructed on George Hadfield's design by architect James Hoban. The staff moved back into the building by March 1816.

THE JACKSONIANS AND THE WHIGS, 1830–1860

The outstanding financial issue of Andrew Jackson's term was the recharter of the Second Bank of the United States. Established in 1816, it had effectively become a central bank by 1830, controlling the quantity of money in the economy and providing a depository for government funds. At times it took countercyclical action to offset swings in economic activity. Its bank notes were the national currency.

In the summer of 1832 Henry Clay made President Jackson's veto of the bill to recharter the bank a political issue. Jackson saw his reelection as a victory for his policy. The president removed two secretaries of the Treasury for refusing to withdraw government funds. The next Treasury secretary, Roger Taney, agreed and in 1833 began to place government deposits in state-chartered banks called "pet banks." The register of the Treasury assumed the sale of government bonds from the bank, a function carried out in part until the register was abolished in 1956.

The president's removal of two secretaries of the Treasury was significant because the president was asserting his power to remove a cabinet member for failure to follow the president's wishes in a matter specifically granted by law only to the secretary of the Treasury. Administrative historians have concluded that removal of the two secretaries ended the ambiguous position the secretary of the Treasury had under the act of 1789. Whatever his responsibility to Congress, it was now clear the secretary had a more direct responsibility to the president, and his duties had to be exercised within the framework of the president's policy.

The second important economic issue was the tariff. The protective tariff was increasingly dividing the country along sectional lines. When South Carolina declared the tariff void, President Jackson issued the Nullification Proclamation and sent seven Treasury revenue cutters and a Navy warship to Charleston harbor. A compromise tariff lowering rates over ten years ended the confrontation.

In 1846 the Jacksonian Democrats established the Independent Treasury System by the act of 6 August 1846 (9 Stat. 59; briefly created in 1840 [5 Stat. 385]). All government funds would be kept in the vaults of the Treasury or in the subtreasuries in major cities. The government would be its own banker. The subtreasuries were not abolished until 1920.

Secretary of the Treasury Robert J. Walker was a strong proponent of a tariff for revenue only. His 1845 annual report presented his views on free trade and the results of an extensive survey the secretary made of manufacturers and farmers, obtaining statistics and seeking their views on the tariff. In 1848 the secretary recommended reciprocal free trade between the United States and Canada and Mexico.

In 1835 Albert Gallatin's dream was realized when the public debt was paid off for the only time in American history. "An unprecedented spectacle is thus presented to the world, of a Government . . . virtually without any debts," boasted Secretary Levi Woodbury in his annual report. In 1837 Congress authorized the Treasury to distribute about $28 million of surplus revenue to the states in four installments. The distribution was legally a loan, but in practice was like modern grants. The fourth installment was never paid out because the Panic of 1837 ushered in the second longest depression, seven years, in U.S. history.

The Mexican War, which cost $82 million, was popular and readily financed. But the ensuing debt called President James Polk's attention to the budget process. Polk held that the proce-

dure by which bureau heads asked for more money than was necessary because they counted on congressional reductions of their appropriation requests was wrong.

Treasury's nonfiscal responsibilities continued to grow until midcentury. In 1838 Treasury was assigned supervision of the Steamboat Inspection Service. Treasury thus administered the first regulation of transportation by the federal government.

Treasury was affected by the turnover from one administration to another that was initiated by Andrew Jackson's "spoils system." The secretary spent much of his time dealing with office seekers. Nonetheless, a nucleus of experienced clerks remained. Their tenures ranged from twelve to twenty years. The chief clerks, many of whom had been promoted from the permanent employees, managed the daily business of their Treasury offices. In 1860 a chief clerk of a division earned $2,000 a year; a Class 4 clerk earned $1,800; a Class 3 clerk $1,600; Class 2, $1,400; and Class 1, $1,200. Watchmen and laborers earned $600. The treasurer earned $3,000. The secretary's salary was $8,000. Among the employees was a handful of women, including a female nurse in the Revenue-Cutter Service in 1827.

THE TREASURY BUILDING, 1833–1860

On 31 March 1833 the Treasury Building was again burned to the ground. On 4 July 1836 Congress authorized construction of a "fire-proof building of such dimensions as may be required for the present and future accommodations of the Treasury Department" (5 Stat. 115). Robert Mills, later architect of the Washington Monument, was chosen to design the Treasury Building. Mills designed a granite Greek-revival building whose commanding feature is the 336-foot-long colonnade along the entire east front. Robert Mills's Treasury Building changed the character of the capital's architecture. The stately government buildings, envisioned by Pierre L'Enfant in his design of the federal city, began to be constructed. The two Mills wings were constructed between 1836 and 1842; occupancy dates from 1839. The south wing was completed in 1860; the west wing in 1864. Thomas Ustick Walter,

THE DEPARTMENT OF THE TREASURY BUILDING IN WASHINGTON, D.C. *This is the third structure to house the Department of the Treasury, the first two having been destroyed by fire. Robert Mills, the architect of the Washington Monument, designed the Greek Revival building in 1836.*

Ammi B. Young, and Isaiah Rogers were the architects.

THE CIVIL WAR, 1861–1865

The Civil War wrought enormous changes in the Treasury. Under the leadership of Secretary Salmon P. Chase, the U.S. government issued the first paper money, established an entirely new banking system, initiated an unprecedented program of emergency taxation, introduced the income tax, and created four new bureaus in the Treasury Department.

The Civil War was the first modern war demanding enormous capital. The cost of the four-year war was $2.3 billion to the U.S. government and $1 billion to the Confederacy. Less than one-fifth of the North's cost was paid for in taxes; four-fifths was financed by borrowing and the issue of unredeemable paper currency.

The Legal Tender Act of 25 February 1862 (12 Stat. 345) authorized the U.S. government to issue $150 million of non-interest-bearing notes not redeemable in specie but legal tender for all debts except customs duties and interest on the public debt. These notes were the first issue of paper money by the U.S. government. Their issue ended seventy-five years of debate as to the constitutionality of the issue of paper money by the federal government. The currency was printed by the newly established Bureau of Engraving and Printing (12 Stat. 346), first in the attic and later in the basement of the Treasury Building.

The notes were nicknamed greenbacks from the color on the back side. A total of $450 million were issued during the war. In 1865 the Secret Service was established in the Treasury Department by the secretary to stop counterfeiting. (There was no organic law creating the Secret Service until 1951; its legislative authority derived from annual appropriation acts providing money to punish counterfeiting starting with coins, 23 June 1860 [12 Stat. 102], and notes, 23 December 1860 [12 Stat. 123].)

Secretary Chase followed Secretary Gallatin's example and financed the war primarily through borrowing. But the market for Treasury securities was weak. Secretary Chase developed three proposals to create a new national banking system whose currency issues had to be secured by government bonds. Purchase of the bonds would help finance the war. National banks would supply a uniform national currency. On 25 February 1863 President Abraham Lincoln signed the National Currency Act (12 Stat. 665), which reestablished the government's relations with banks and created a new Treasury bureau, the Office of the Comptroller of the Currency, to regulate the new federally chartered banks.

The Republicans enacted a vast array of taxes that the Treasury implemented through another new bureau established on 1 July 1862 (12 Stat. 432), the Bureau of Internal Revenue. Treasury collected the nation's first income tax, enacted on 5 August 1861 (12 Stat. 309), with a tax of three percent on incomes over $800 that rose, by 1865, to five percent on incomes between $600 and $5,000 and ten percent on incomes over $5,000 (13 Stat. 479). The tax remained in effect until 1872, but at reduced rates. Excise taxes were placed on many consumer goods, and Treasury collected the first federal inheritance tax, special taxes on corporations, and a very high tariff with duties equal to almost half the total value of all imports.

Treasury clerks numbered 380 when the Civil War began in 1861; by 1865 more than 2,000 were employed. To make up for the shortage of men, the Treasury hired the first large numbers of women in the federal government. Treasurer Francis E. Spinner hired women as note cutters because it was thought that women could use scissors better than men and would do it cheaper. By 1862 seventy women had been hired in the Treasury, including the first black woman hired by the U.S. government.

Able-bodied clerks between eighteen and forty-five were required to join the Treasury Guards called up in July 1864 when the threat of an attack on Washington led to a call for volunteer troops. The Treasury Guards drilled each day after work. The women clerks purchased a navy blue silk flag for the guards. It was the Treasury Guards Flag, loaned to Ford's Theater, on which John Wilkes Booth tripped as he jumped to the stage from the president's box after assassinating Abraham Lincoln on 14 April 1865.

The Treasury Building became a temporary White House. President Andrew Johnson wished to give Mary Lincoln time to move out of the Executive Mansion. The president worked in the large reception room of Secretary Hugh McCulloch's suite on the third floor of the west wing for six weeks from 15 April to 24 May 1865.

THE REPUBLICAN ERA, 1865–1899

The major issues during the next thirty-five years were resumption of specie payments, management of the huge war debt (paid off by the 1880s), and three controversial questions that divided Americans by class and section—the silver question (the on-again, off-again policy of basing the nation's currency on gold and silver), the gold standard (basing the value of all U.S. money on gold), and the high level of tariffs.

Resumption of specie payments, a deflationary policy, was the most controversial economic issue after the Civil War. The goal was to return to the exchange rate of $1 in gold for $1 in greenbacks, rather than the immediate postwar rate of $100 in gold for $140 in paper currency. Treasury Secretary Hugh McCulloch's policy of contraction was so severe that it was ended by Congress in February 1868. The Gold Resumption Act of 1875 (18 Stat. 296) maintained a strict convertibility between greenbacks and gold. This law effectively put the United States on a gold standard. The Gold Standard Act of 1900 (31 Stat. 45) legalized the gold standard.

The high tariffs administered by Treasury made protection, incentives, and subsidies important elements in America's and Treasury's political economy. High protective tariffs were supported by both the new giant American corporations and workers, and their revenues funded America's first major system of social insurance—pensions for Union veterans.

The depression and budget deficits of the 1890s turned Treasury's attention to additional revenue. Congress returned to an income tax (two percent on all incomes above $4,000) in 1894 (28 Stat. 553). The Supreme Court declared the income tax unconstitutional in 1895. The Spanish-American War, which cost $270 million, was financed by borrowing. The Dockery Act of 31 July 1894 (28 Stat. 205), the most influential law on government accounting between 1789 and 1921, changed Alexander Hamilton's historic system of a double audit to a single audit with final settlement in the auditor's office.

Work on the Treasury Building was completed between 1867 and 1869. The last wing was designed by Treasury's supervising architect, Alfred B. Mullett. The Office of the Supervising Architect also left its stamp on American architecture through its designs of post offices and courthouses for the expanding eastern cities and western states.

The secretary of the Treasury's influence was greatly enlarged during these years through the power of his patronage, which was far greater than that of any other cabinet officer. Congress kept close watch on the department through the very subordinate level of officers requiring Senate confirmation. Inadequate pay for officials and clerks made it difficult to hold on to expert staff.

The Civil Service Act of 1883 (the Pendleton Act, 22 Stat. 403) enabled Treasury to extend the merit system and strengthen its control over its field staff. Women competed under the new merit system; a woman made the highest score on the first examination in 1883 and was hired as a clerk in Treasury. Blanche Kelso Bruce, a former slave and senator from Mississippi, was the first African American to be appointed to a high position in Treasury. He served as register from 1881 to 1885 and again from 1897 to 1898. His name appears on the U.S. currency of the period.

THE NEW CENTURY, 1900–1914

The creation of the Federal Reserve System on 23 December 1913 (38 Stat. 251) ended Treasury's control over note issue. America's new central bank would issue a new paper currency, Federal Reserve notes; U.S. notes and silver certificates would soon become a negligible part of the money supply; and national bank notes issued by Treasury-chartered banks would be retired. The secretary of the Treasury and the comptroller of the currency sat on the Federal Reserve Board until February 1936, and the seven-member board was housed in the Treasury Building until 1937. The Federal Farm Loan Bureau was established in Treasury in July 1916 to regulate the agricultural credit system. The ratification of the Sixteenth Amendment in 1913 making the income tax constitutional gave Treasury permanent contact with most Americans.

Treasury grew more vocal about the need for a budget. In his 1909 annual report Secretary Franklin MacVeagh wrote: "The absence of anything like a budget in our Government has undoubtedly led to a great deal of extravagant appropriation. Originally . . . it was contemplated that a budget should be presented by the Secretary of the Treasury. . . . But the complete plan of a budget was never fully realized. . . . [T]he Government arrived at the farthest extreme from a responsible budget."

WORLD WAR I, 1914–1918

World War I cost $32.7 billion. The need to finance this enormous cost led President Woodrow Wilson and Secretary William G. McAdoo to transform the income tax into the foremost instrument of federal taxation. They used the income tax not only to raise revenue but also as a means to achieve social justice: to attack concentrations of wealth, special privilege, and public corruption; and to promote a more competitive economy. The Revenue Acts of 1916 and 1917 (39 Stat. 756, 1000) imposed the first significant taxes on corporate profits and personal incomes and introduced a graduated federal estate tax, but rejected a mass-based income tax. An excess profits tax became the centerpiece of wartime finance.

In its borrowing campaign Treasury appealed for the first time to the average citizen in four Liberty Loan drives and a Victory Loan. Treasury raised $21.5 billion. Thrift Stamps, War Savings Stamps, and War Savings Certificates raised an additional $1.6 billion and provided a way for the low-income citizen to participate. The bond drives were advertised through one of America's finest collections of poster art. The huge borrowing left a debt of $25 billion at the end of 1919.

ANDREW MELLON AND THE ROARING TWENTIES

Andrew W. Mellon was the first secretary of the Treasury since Hamilton, Gallatin, and Chase to dominate the era he served. His leadership made Treasury the focal point for the central financial issue of the 1920s—tax reduction. The Bureau of Internal Revenue placed Treasury foursquare in the decade's other issue—Prohibition.

Secretary of the Treasury Mellon personally outlined the tax reductions of the 1920s. His program was based on two convictions:

1. Business counted above all other activities and would prosper in proportion to the lightening of its tax burdens.

2. Taxation was to raise revenue for the government and not to redistribute wealth: "I have never viewed taxation as a means of rewarding one class of taxpayers or punishing another."

Mellon, like his predecessor, Democrat David Houston, believed that high marginal tax rates were counterproductive. They encouraged investment in tax shelters and tax-exempt activities, distorted resource allocation, biased the flow of capital away from savings and productive investment, and lessened tax receipts. Mellon presented the case for tax reduction in the upper-income brackets and predicted his program would get the economy out of the postwar recession and increase Treasury revenues from the very wealthy.

Mellon's program was embodied in the Revenue Acts of 1921, 1924, and 1926 (42 Stat. 227, 43 Stat. 253, 44 Stat. 9). The Revenue Act of 1921 abolished the wartime excess profits tax, made the individual income tax much less progressive, favored capital gains, and increased the corporate income tax to 12.5 percent. The three laws reduced the top marginal tax rate from seventy-three percent in 1919 to twenty-five percent in 1926. The tax reductions encouraged economic growth, drew capital away from tax shelters and into investments that increased employment, and increased substantially, rather than decreased, the percentage of total income tax paid by the very wealthy over the decade.

Mellon's critics also proved to be correct. While the secretary stood firm against a national sales tax that would affect lower-income Americans, Mellon drastically reduced taxes for the very wealthy while the average middle-income taxpayer received little relief. It was the Progressives in Congress who reduced taxes for those earning $6,000 or less.

Like Albert Gallatin, Mellon made reduction of the public debt central to his policies. When Mellon came into office the public debt was $24 billion. By 1929 he had lowered the debt to about $17 billion. Mellon's insistence on keeping spending under income was universally approved by a country eager to return to "normalcy." Treasury enjoyed an era of budget surpluses.

The Budget and Accounting Act of 10 June 1921 (42 Stat. 20) forever changed two of Treasury's basic missions. The act created the General Accounting Office as an independent agency responsible to Congress and transferred the auditors, comptroller, and function of settling the government's accounts, established in 1789, to the legislative branch.

The creation of the Bureau of the Budget in the Treasury Department (1921, 42 Stat. 22) meant that Treasury would continue to prepare the revenue estimates, but Alexander Hamilton's precedent of sending the estimates directly to Congress was ended after 130 years. The bureau would act under the president's direction, and the president was responsible for submitting the budget to Congress.

The Treasury Department became actively involved in foreign economic affairs in the 1920s. The secretary of the Treasury was the chairman of the World War Foreign Debt Commission, established in February 1922 (42 Stat. 363). The commission was authorized to extend the time of repayment of the debts of foreign governments held by the U.S. government as a result of the Great War.

Andrew Mellon established a bureaucratic base for his technical staff. The secretary changed the name of the Section of Statistics (established in December 1921) to the Section of Financial and Economic Research in June 1927 to more clearly reflect its functions. The section maintained statistical series on taxes, the public debt, and monthly changes in general economic and financial conditions and conducted confidential economic studies for Treasury officials.

HENRY MORGENTHAU, THE GREAT DEPRESSION, AND THE NEW DEAL

Henry Morgenthau, Jr., was the second longest-termed secretary of the Treasury. His eleven and a half years spanned the Great Depression and World War II.

On 5 April 1933 President Franklin D. Roosevelt took U.S. currency off the gold standard (Executive Order No. 6102). On 31 January 1934 President Roosevelt stabilized the price of gold at $35 an ounce and issued a proclamation (48 Stat. 1730) devaluing the dollar by lowering the official gold content to 15 and 5/21 grains of gold nine-tenths fine. Since gold had been nationalized in April, the profit from devaluation went to the federal government. By the Gold Reserve Act of 30 January 1934 (48 Stat. 344), Congress placed $2 billion of the profit into an Exchange Stabilization Fund under the control of the president but operated by the secretary of the Treasury with the president's approval. Treasury uses the fund to manage the international exchange value of the dollar by buying gold and foreign exchange. The Gold Reserve Act of 1934 also required the Federal Reserve Banks to transfer all their gold to the Treasury. Henceforth, the monetary gold stock was legally owned by the Treasury. To store the gold reserves Treasury built the bullion depository at Fort Knox.

Secretary Morgenthau wrote: "The important repercussions of taxes . . . make it vital that . . . our tax system be responsive to social and economic change" and be "based upon the democratic principle of ability to pay." The Revenue Acts of 1934 (48 Stat. 680), 1935 (49 Stat. 1014), and 1936 (49 Stat. 1648) lowered taxes on small individual and corporate incomes, increased estate and gift taxes, taxed undistributed profits in order to curb the avoidance of income taxes, and closed many loopholes. "Tax loopholes do more than confer unfair tax benefits on some at the expense of others. They distort normal business relationships and act as a drag on the economy."

Secretary Morgenthau said the Treasury's New Deal borrowing operations had three major objectives:

1. to restore the money supply wiped out in the deflation of the Great Depression

2. to reduce interest rates on U.S. securities (the average interest rate on outstanding U.S. debt fell from 3.3 percent to 2.5 percent between June 1933 and June 1940)

3. to increase the number of Americans holding the public debt. (For this purpose, small denomination savings bonds, called "baby bonds," were introduced in March 1935. Like Alexander Hamilton, Morgenthau wished to increase the number of citizens having a direct financial interest in the affairs of government.)

On 12 November 1934 Secretary Morgenthau issued regulations that established a reporting system for specified international capital movements. Banks, brokers, and dealers were required to submit weekly reports to their respective Federal Reserve Banks on security and foreign exchange transactions and changes in bank balances between the United States and foreign countries. Commercial and industrial firms reported their foreign assets and liabilities. The present Treasury International Capital reporting system, an ongoing statistical program, evolved from the 1934 data collection efforts.

On 25 March 1938 the secretary separated the technical staff into three separate divisions: Research and Statistics, Tax Research, and Monetary

Research. In 1935 the first woman assistant secretary was appointed by President Roosevelt.

The Treasury was a leader in New Deal relief programs. The Public Works of Art Project (December 1933–April 1934) assisted thirty-five hundred artists who produced over fifteen thousand paintings and other artwork for federal buildings, and the Treasury Relief Art Project (July 1935–December 1938) paid artists on relief a monthly fee. In October 1934 Henry Morgenthau established the Section of Painting and Sculpture (renamed Section of Fine Arts in October 1938) in Treasury's Office of the Supervising Architect, which designed public buildings. The artists, chosen in local competitions, painted murals in post offices and courthouses. Some of America's greatest New Deal artists, including Reginald Marsh and Rockwell Kent, painted the murals in the Justice and Interior Departments. The program ended on 30 June 1943.

WORLD WAR II, 1940–1945

World War II drastically changed the American tax system. It changed who paid, how many paid, and how they paid. The tax system shifted from a narrow base to a broad base—the basis of our current tax system.

President Roosevelt and Secretary Morgenthau preferred to finance the war with taxes that bore heavily on business and upper income groups. Morgenthau wanted taxes to help reduce inflation, preserve the social progress of the New Deal, distribute the tax burden by ability to pay, and prevent war profiteering. But a diverse group of leaders vigorously promoted mass-based income taxation as a way to reduce inflation.

Congress instituted mass-based taxation in 1940 (54 Stat. 519). Millions of Americans were added to the tax rolls for the first time. The number of income tax payers grew from 3.9 million in 1939 to 42.6 million in 1945. Income tax collections rose from $2.2 billion in 1939 to $35.1 billion in 1945. Tax revenues came predominantly from wages and salaries rather than from profits, dividends, and interest. The Office of Tax Research helped to design the pay-as-you-go payroll withholding system by which most Americans pay taxes. It was enacted in June 1943 (Current Tax Payment Act, 57 Stat. 126).

Wartime revenue acts increased income tax rates to a top rate of ninety-four percent on $200,000 (from seventy-nine percent on $5 million); raised the lowest rates from eight percent to twenty-three percent; raised corporate taxes from nineteen percent to forty percent; and reinstituted the excess profits tax, which reached ninety-five percent in 1945. Exemptions were repeatedly cut. Excise taxes rose steeply. And in 1941 Secretary Morgenthau succeeded in getting Congress to eliminate the tax exemption on federal securities (only state and municipal bonds would be tax exempt), meaning that an income stream would be realized from Treasury borrowing.

Total revenues during the war rose from $5.3 billion in 1940 to $43.8 billion in 1945. Nearly one-half of America's national product went to war. Taxes financed forty-one percent of the war in 1940 and reached a peak of forty-six percent in 1945. By contrast, taxes financed less than one-third of the cost of World War I. World War II was the most costly war in the country's history—$360 billion. Total wartime borrowing by the U.S. government reached $185.7 billion. The war increased the public debt by February 1946 to a total of $279.2 billion.

Secretary Morgenthau personally helped to design the Savings Bond campaign, expanding the low-denomination "baby bond" program so that Series E bonds could be available to all Americans. The sales campaigns were managed by a special staff in the Secretary's Office. Bond drives, appeals by movie stars, and the "Treasury Radio Hour" raised almost $20 billion in E Bonds between May 1941 and December 1945.

Treasury engaged in economic warfare. Morgenthau and the Treasury were instrumental in organizing lend-lease (act of 11 March 1941, 55 Stat. 31), by which war materials were manufactured in the United States and loaned or leased to the allies. Treasury's Procurement Division purchased the nonmilitary industrial commodities and automotive equipment turned over to the allies.

Treasury designed and implemented Foreign Funds Control in 1940 to protect in the United States the assets of invaded countries and to keep them from the enemy. Foreign Funds Control froze Axis assets in 1941, regulated international financial transactions, administered wartime trade restrictions under the Trading with the Enemy Act (6 October 1917, 40 Stat. 411) as amended, and by 1945 froze $8.5 billion of assets belonging to thirty-five countries. Treasury also conducted a comprehensive survey of foreign-owned property in the United States in 1941 and of American property abroad in 1943.

The production of military invasion currency was among the Treasury's most highly secret work, since any knowledge of production would reveal Allied invasion plans. Treasury loaned fourteen thousand tons of silver to help produce uranium for the atom bomb and financed the top-secret Manhattan Project, though Treasury did not know at the time what the metals and funds were being used for. And Secretary Morgenthau and three Treasury attorneys persuaded President Roosevelt to reverse U.S. policy and establish the War Refugee Board in January 1944, the only government effort to save European Jews.

International monetary cooperation, freer trade, the IMF, and the International Bank for Reconstruction and Development are the legacies of World War II international economic policies. On 14 December 1941 Secretary Morgenthau asked Harry Dexter White, chief of the Division of Monetary Research, to prepare a memorandum on a postwar inter-Allied stabilization fund. Dr. White's plans for a fund and a bank and John Maynard Keynes's proposal for an international clearing union became the basis of three years of international discussion. The Bretton Woods Conference (1–22 July 1944), attended by forty-four nations and chaired by Secretary Morgenthau, established the IMF and the World Bank. The United States officially became a member by the Bretton Woods Agreements Act of 31 July 1945 (59 Stat. 512). Treasury was directed to use $1.8 billion of the Exchange Stabilization Fund to pay part of the U.S. subscription to the IMF (59 Stat. 514); $300 million of capital and earnings from operations were left in the fund.

THE POSTWAR YEARS, 1945–1965

During the war Treasury and the Federal Reserve Board cooperated to reduce the average interest

rate on government securities from 2.53 percent on 30 June 1939 to 1.94 percent on 30 June 1945. The need to stabilize government security prices led to Treasury control of interest rates, which were pegged at .375 percent for short-term Treasury bills and 2.5 percent for long-term Treasury bonds. As a result, the debt was monetized and the Federal Reserve System abandoned control over the volume of bank reserves because when the central bank had to buy government securities at fixed prices, it enlarged bank reserves, enabling banks to expand credit. By 1950 the conflict between the Federal Reserve's need to restrain private credit expansion and Treasury debt management had to be resolved. Consequently, under the Treasury–Federal Reserve accord of 3 March 1951 the Federal Reserve discontinued fixed-price support for government securities, enabling the central bank to regain control over the money supply.

Treasury developed international monetary policy in a world that was rapidly changing. By the end of the Korean War (which cost $50 billion) American world dominance was ending. The free nations America had helped to regain financial soundness were becoming vigorous economic competitors. By 1958 the United States began running large balance of payments deficits. The trade surpluses on current account were unable to pay for the deficits caused by the U.S. government's huge overseas aid and military programs and U.S. industry's foreign investments. As the United States settled these accounts its monetary gold stock fell alarmingly.

Secretary of the Treasury C. Douglas Dillon persuaded President John F. Kennedy that the nation's most pressing economic problem in the early 1960s was the balance of payments deficit and gave priority to its reduction. One reason was that by 1960 domestic stabilization policies had international repercussions. Lower interest rates at home sent American capital abroad; the dollars then were returned for gold. Programs such as the Interest Equalization Tax (1963–1974) and voluntary reduction of capital exports were not enough to stem the outflow of gold. To increase the gold available for international settlement, the gold reserve required against Federal Reserve member-bank deposits and notes was removed by the acts of 3 March 1965 (79 Stat. 5), and 18 March 1968 (82 Stat. 50), ending the gold standard. U.S. money was fiat money.

Treasury's increased international responsibilities brought administrative changes. Secretary of the Treasury John Snyder established the Office of International Finance in July 1947 (renamed the Office of International Affairs in October 1962) to assist the secretary in international monetary matters arising out of the Bretton Woods Agreements Act. The duties of the Monetary Research Division were absorbed, Treasury attachés (assigned to foreign posts sporadically since the mid-1930s) were sent to U.S. embassies on a regular basis, and Foreign Funds Control was liquidated by June 1948. Secretary Snyder reestablished foreign funds control in December 1950 under the name Foreign Assets Control.

A fairer tax system that would "get the country moving again" was the goal of President Kennedy and Treasury Secretary Dillon, who was a proponent of tax reform. Congress, however, rejected the reforms but did pass tax reductions that stimulated the economy. Kennedy and Dillon presented their program in language reminiscent of Secretary Mellon: lower taxes would bring economic growth.

Secretary Dillon persuaded President Kennedy to follow Treasury's cautious approach to fiscal stimulus and phase in the $11.5 billion tax cut over three years in order to forestall inflation and an unmanageable budget deficit that would impact the balance of payments deficit. The Revenue Act of 1964 reduced maximum personal income tax rates from ninety-one percent to seventy percent, the lowest rates went down from twenty percent to fourteen percent, and corporate tax rates dropped from fifty-two percent to forty-eight percent (78 Stat. 20, 25). To assist in tax and economic analysis and bureau data collection efforts, Treasury purchased its first computer in 1955.

TREASURY IN AN INTEGRATED WORLD, 1966–1996

The "guns and butter" policy of Lyndon B. Johnson's administration led Secretary Henry Fowler to propose a tax increase and a surtax to help pay for both the Vietnam War (total cost $140.6 billion) and the social programs of the Great Society. A temporary tax surcharge of ten percent was enacted on 28 June 1968 that lasted fifteen months. The Revenue and Expenditure Control Act of 1968 (82 Stat. 251) was the first general income tax law to raise taxes since 1951.

In January 1969 in testimony before Congress, Secretary Joseph Barr warned Congress of a "taxpayers' revolt" over inequities in the tax laws. Treasury played a key role in significant peacetime tax reforms and the legal and economic staffs of the Office of the Assistant Secretary for Tax Policy helped to draft three important tax laws. The Tax Reduction and Simplification Act of 1977 (91 Stat. 126) eliminated several million low-income families from the tax rolls, reduced taxes on low- and middle-income taxpayers, and provided for an innovative jobs tax-credit. The Economic Recovery Tax Act of 1981 (95 Stat. 172) and the Tax Reform Act of 1986 (100 Stat. 2085) together lowered tax rates substantially. The top rate fell from seventy percent to twenty-eight percent (thirty-three percent in some income ranges) and corporate tax rates were reduced to thirty-four percent. The 1981 law indexed individual income tax rates and the 1986 act eliminated many tax shelters. The technical staffs helped to formulate the Revenue Reconciliation Act of 1990, which increased the top tax rate from twenty-eight percent to thirty-one percent (104 Stat. 1388-403).

The Treasury Department administered the Revenue Sharing program (1972–1986), an initiative of the Nixon administration. The program distributed $82.6 billion among 39,000 states, cities, and other general-purpose local governments. And the department developed the Financial Institutions Reform, Recovery, and Enforcement Act of 1989, which addressed the savings and loan crisis.

The Office of the Assistant Secretary for Economic Policy participated in the formulation of the four phases of wage and price controls (15 August 1971–30 April 1974), conducted statistical surveys of foreign portfolio investment (reinstituted in 1974), led the effort to develop the Reagan administration's policy on the transfer of technology developed in federal laboratories to the commercial sector and the Bush administration's policy regarding the encouragement of private sector activity in space, analyzed the deficit reduction packages enacted in the early 1990s, and helped to formulate the Clinton administration's health care reform proposals of 1993–1994.

Treasury cooperated with other government departments and nations in expanding the Bretton Woods system, the world payments system of fixed exchange rates for major currencies centered on the dollar and in its convertibility into gold. Treasury helped to develop Special Drawing Rights for the IMF first introduced in 1969. The Treasury, in support of other U.S. agencies, developed comprehensive proposals for the reform of the international monetary system after announcing in 1971 that the dollar would no longer be redeemed in gold and the collapse of the Bretton Woods system in the early 1970s; took the lead in the Smithsonian Agreement of December 1971, which was a last attempt to realign fixed exchange rates; helped to revise the articles of the IMF, the basis for a new system of management of floating rates; and designed the Plaza Accord of 1985, which was the first substantive effort of the United States, Britain, France, Germany, and Japan to coordinate their economic and exchange rate policies. Treasury developed policies to resolve the international debt crises of the 1980s and early 1990s. Since 1989, Treasury has led U.S. participation in the Financial Services negotiations of the Uruguay Round of multilateral trade talks under the General Agreement on Trade in Services and the new World Trade Organization. Treasury financed the Gulf War of 1991, which cost $7.4 billion.

At the time of Treasury's bicentennial in 1989, the department had 164,000 employees worldwide. In June 1996 there were 155,840 employees worldwide, reflecting policies of streamlining in the 1990s.

[See also Alcohol, Tobacco and Firearms, Bureau of; Comptroller of the Currency, Office of the; Customs Service; Engraving and Printing, Bureau of; Federal Reserve System; Financial Management Service; Internal Revenue Service; Mint, U.S.; Public Debt, Bureau of the; Secret Service; Thrift Supervision, Office of; and Appendix: An Act to Establish the Treasury Department, September 2, 1789.]

BIBLIOGRAPHY

Contreras, Belisario R. *Tradition and Innovation in New Deal Art.* Lewisburg, Pa., 1983.
Morris, Robert. *The Papers of Robert Morris, 1781–1784.* Edited by E. James Ferguson et al. 9 vols. Pittsburgh, 1973–1997.
Sanders, Jennings B. *Evolution of Executive Departments of the Continental Congress, 1774–1789.* Chapel Hill, N.C., 1935.
Studenski, Paul, and Herman E. Krooss. *Financial History of the United States.* New York, 1963.
Taus, Esther R. *Central Banking Functions of the United States Treasury, 1789–1941.* New York, 1943.
Taus, Esther R. *The Role of the U.S. Treasury in Stabilizing the Economy, 1941–1946.* Washington, D.C., 1981.
U.S. Department of the Treasury. *Department of the Treasury.* Washington, D.C., 1995.
U.S. Department of the Treasury. *Annual Report of the Secretary of the Treasury on the State of the Finances, 1789–.* Washington, D.C.
Walston, Mark. *The Department of the Treasury.* New York, 1989.
White, Leonard D. *The Federalists: A Study in Administrative History.* New York, 1948.
White, Leonard D. *The Jeffersonians: A Study in Administrative History, 1801–1829.* New York, 1951.
White, Leonard D. *The Jacksonians: A Study in Administrative History, 1829–1861.* New York, 1954.
White, Leonard D. *The Republican Era, 1869–1901: A Study in Administrative History.* New York, 1958.

—ABBY L. GILBERT

TVA.
See Tennessee Valley Authority.

Twenty-second Amendment

ESSAY According to the Twenty-second Amendment to the United States Constitution, the service of anyone as president of the United States is limited to two elected terms or ten years. The amendment provides, in pertinent part:

No person shall be elected to the office of the President more than twice, and no person who has held the office of President, or acted as President, for more than two years of a term to which some other person was elected President shall be elected to the office of the President more than once. . . .

Although the Founders provided that presidents would be perpetually eligible for reelection, a two-term tradition developed when first George Washington, then Thomas Jefferson refused to consider a third term. Those of their immediate successors who won a second term—James Madison, James Monroe, and Andrew Jackson—followed their example. Although Ulysses S. Grant sought nomination for a third (though nonconsecutive) term in 1880 and Theodore Roosevelt tried to supplant William Howard Taft in 1912 after completing most of President McKinley's second term and one of his own, neither succeeded. As such, the two-term tradition survived until Franklin D. Roosevelt was elected to a third term in 1940 and a fourth four years later.

Although more than two hundred attempts were made before 1945 to amend the Constitution to limit presidential tenure, the effort gained impetus following President Roosevelt's death that year and the election of Republican majorities in Congress in 1946. Approximately one month after the new Congress convened, the House of Representatives proposed by the required two-thirds majority H.J. Res. 27, which imposed a two-term limit, 285 to 121. The supermajority included all 238 Republicans who voted (including Representative Richard M. Nixon) and forty-seven Democrats (including Representative John F. Kennedy and thirty-seven southerners). The following month the Senate passed a similar proposal, 59 to 23; all forty-six Republicans who voted supported the limit, as did thirteen Democrats, mostly from the South. On 21 March 1947 the House agreed to the Senate version, 81 to 29, thereby sending the proposed amendment to the state legislatures. By 27 February 1951 thirty-six

of the forty-eight states had ratified the amendment, providing the required three-fourths margin; five other states soon added their approval.

Those who favored the amendment argued that the tenure limitation was needed to prevent the presidency from becoming too powerful. They claimed that a president could use executive powers virtually to assure retention in office. They contended that lengthy tenure would render the public apathetic and posed risks to presidential health. They insisted that no leader was indispensable.

Opponents dismissed the amendment as a politically motivated repudiation of Franklin Roosevelt. They condemned as undemocratic removal from the people of the ability to reelect a popular president who had served the requisite time. They foresaw emergency situations in which the electorate would be precluded from continuing an able leader. They feared the amendment would weaken the presidency, especially during a second term. They also worried that second-term presidents would be less responsive to public opinion.

By its terms, the amendment did not apply to President Harry S. Truman, the incumbent at the time of its ratification. It did preclude Dwight D. Eisenhower and Ronald Reagan from seeking third terms.

BIBLIOGRAPHY

Cronin, Thomas E. "Presidential Term, Tenure and Reeligibility." In *Inventing the American Presidency,* edited by Thomas E. Cronin. Lawrence, Kans., 1989.

Koenig, Louis W. *The Chief Executive.* Rev. ed. New York, 1968.

Rossiter, Clinton. *The American Presidency.* Rev. ed. New York, 1960.

Stathis, Stephen W. "The Twenty-Second Amendment: A Practical Remedy or Partisan Maneuver?" *Constitutional Commentary* 7 (Winter 1990): 61–88.

—JOEL K. GOLDSTEIN

U

United States Information Agency

The mission of the United States Information Agency (USIA) is to understand, to inform, and to influence foreign publics as a means of promoting U.S. national interests and dialogue between Americans and their institutions and their counterparts abroad. Two of the USIA's primary activities include conducting U.S. government (nonmilitary) international broadcasting and administering foreign exchange programs. Overseas, the USIA is the United States Information Service (USIS).

Historically, the U.S. information program began on 4 July 1776 with a "decent respect for the opinions of mankind" in the Declaration of Independence. That December, Benjamin Franklin arrived in France as the first *de facto* public affairs officer with a mandate "to sell America abroad." He was a successful conveyor of this mission, as were the American diplomats that followed him in other European countries. Throughout the nineteenth century, the United States maintained unofficial information programs in countries where it was important to win friends for the American cause. This was facilitated by an emerging communication revolution. The first telegraph message was sent from Washington, D.C., to Baltimore in 1844; the first Atlantic cable was completed in 1866; Bell patented his telephone in 1876; Marconi patented his wireless telegraph in 1896; and Lindbergh completed the first solo flight from New York to Paris in 1927, opening up a new way of travel that revolutionized cultural relations. In 1910 the Carnegie Endowment for International Peace established a philanthropic initiative to foster cultural relations as a vehicle for transnational contacts.

The first official U.S. information program began during World War I, when President Wilson established the Committee on Public Information to handle wartime information activities: distribute publications, supply articles to the foreign-language press, open offices in major capitals, give rapid distribution to presidential speeches, establish reading rooms (all in Mexico City), and bring foreign journalists to the United States, all activities later carried out by the USIA.

After World War I U.S. government–sponsored information activities dwindled considerably, although there was an unofficial exchange program with Latin America after 1927, when the first binational center (BNC) was established in Buenos Aires. In 1938 the Interdepartmental Committee for Scientific Cooperation and Division of Cultural Cooperation were formed in the State Department to counterattack German and Italian propaganda in Latin America. Two years later, Nelson Rockefeller was appointed coordinator of commercial and cultural affairs between the United States and the other American republics. Some of the programs Rockefeller initiated included exchanges of persons and the establishment of libraries and of BNCs.

In World War II President Roosevelt combined several government agencies into the Office of War Information in June 1942, with responsibility for all U.S. government information activities, domestic and foreign, including the Voice of America (VOA), which went on the air in February of that year. With the war's end all information activities were absorbed into the State Department, which was uncomfortable with these functions, under a variety of names, and the need arose for more systematic control of U.S. information and cultural activities. Two basic pieces of legislation were passed to fulfill this need. An amendment to the the Surplus Property

Act of 1946 (Fulbright Act; P.L. 79-584) mandated a peacetime international exchange program; it was superseded by the Mutual Educational and Cultural Exchange Act of 1961 (Fulbright-Hays Act; P.L. 87-256), which consolidated previous educational and cultural exchange laws. In 1948 Congress approved the United States Information and Educational Exchange Act (Smith-Mundt Act; P.L. 80-402), which chartered the peacetime overseas information program and which remains one of the USIA's governing statutes. The next year the Hoover Commission on Organization of the Executive Branch recommended creation of an independent U.S. government information corporation separate from State. From 1949 to 1952, State conducted a massive reorientation and reeducation program in Germany and in Japan, the first such foreign cultural, information, and education endeavor by the U.S. government, while the Marshall Plan agencies (Economic Cooperation Administration and Mutual Security Agency) conducted multimedia information programs to promote the European Recovery Program. In 1951 Senate Resolution 74 (Bentley-Wiley resolution) authorized the Senate Committee on Foreign Relations to conduct "an investigation with respect to the effectiveness of existing foreign information programs."

At the beginning of his administration, President Eisenhower established committees to further study an independent information agency separate from the State Department, in which Secretary of State Dulles did not want "propagandists." Recommendations were almost unanimous that a separate agency, independent of State but responsible to it for policy direction, was necessary. On 1 August 1953 President Eisenhower created the USIA under Reorganization Plan No. 8 as an independent foreign affairs agency within the executive branch of the U.S. government, responsible for the conduct of all information programs abroad ("telling America's story to the world"). The new agency consolidated the information activities formerly carried on by the International Information Administration of the State Department, the Technical Cooperation Administration, the Mutual Security Agency, and programs financed in connection

with the U.S. government in occupied areas. The educational exchange programs were retained in State. The USIA director was to report to the president through the National Security Agency and receive complete, daily guidance on U.S. foreign policy from the secretary of state. The agency was patterned on lines recommended by the President's Commission on International Information Activities (Jackson Committee) and by the Senate's Special Subcommittee on Overseas Information Programs (Hickenlooper Committee). On 22 October the president issued a directive defining its mission: promote "mutual understanding between the United States and other nations by conducting educational and cultural activities." Unfortunately, the new agency began in the turmoil of Senator Joseph McCarthy's (R-Wis.) persecution of individual USIA officers and his claims of communist infiltration of USIA programs and libraries, all unfounded and unproven, that seriously undercut employees' morale.

On 15 October 1954 twenty-eight members in the fields of communication, public opinion, and international affairs formed a voluntary, nonpartisan group, the National Committee for an Adequate U.S. Overseas Information Program, headed by Edward L. Bernays. The committee found a good information program a "powerful offensive and defensive weapon for our nation and vital to our national strength," but the USIA would be "unable to do the important job before it until, and unless, the American people and the Congress recognize its vital importance." Six years later, USIA overseas polls indicated a drop in the level of U.S. prestige throughout the world; these were leaked by someone in the State Department to a Kennedy aide during the presidential campaign and turned over to the *New York Times,* which printed the findings.

Reorganization Plan No. 2 of 1977 merged the USIA and the State Department's Bureau of Educational and Cultural Affairs as the U.S. International Communication Agency (USICA). Under this reorganization the USICA received responsibility for nearly all official exchange programs along with a second mandate from President Carter "to reduce the degree to which misperceptions and misunderstandings complicate relations between the United States and other nations." In 1982 the agency and its functions were left intact but the name was restored to the more familiar USIA under Public Law 97-241, the agency's authorization bill for fiscal year 1982–1983. The next year, the Fulbright-Hays Act was amended to give the USIA authority to conduct educational and cultural affairs in nonpolitical fashion and according to the highest academic and artistic standards.

DOMESTIC DISSEMINATION

There were also changes in the ban on domestic dissemination (Section 501 of the Smith-Mundt Act). This is a congressionally imposed restriction on dissemination within the United States of the USIA's output that makes the agency's work virtually unknown in this country. Congressional intent was to avoid creating a propaganda agency that mirrored the powerful state information ministries of Nazi Germany and of the Soviet Union; to ensure that no administration or political party would have potential to use the means available to the VOA to influence the American people; and to prohibit the VOA from competing with domestic media organizations. There are certain authorized exceptions: to *English Teaching Forum* (the other journal exempted was *Problems of Communism,* which was abolished in 1994); to USIA-commissioned research reports that are sent to selected repositories around the United States; and to certain films distributed by the National Audiovisual Center. Congress attempted a more flexible policy in 1990, when it passed an amendment (P.L. 101-507) to the Smith-Mundt Act that authorized the USIA director to make certain program materials available to the archivist of the United States for domestic distribution twelve years after their distribution abroad or, if not disseminated, twelve years after the material was prepared. The new policy focused primarily on motion pictures, films, and videotapes.

A challenge to the domestic dissemination ban came in 1989 in *Gartner v. United States Information Agency* (726 F. Supp. 1183) in the U.S. District Court for the Southern District of Iowa. Michael Gartner, then editor of Iowa's *Ames Register and Tribune* and former head of NBC News, filed

a lawsuit against the USIA after a *Register* reporter was unable to obtain copies of VOA editorials. The two central issues for the court were whether the First Amendment included a right to make copies of USIA documents and whether the domestic dissemination ban prevented the plaintiffs from disseminating any USIA materials they obtained. The court ruled in favor of the USIA, but it narrowed the application of the ban to the agency and its employees only, not to private individuals or entities. The court ruled that there exists no constitutional "right to access to all sources of information within government control."

MAJOR PROGRAMS

The USIA's information and cultural work abroad is mainly performed by its Foreign Service officers assigned to American missions. With guidance, support, and material from Washington headquarters, they manage cultural and information programs in support of American foreign policy objectives and of greater mutual understanding between the United States and foreign societies.

Exchange Activities

Perhaps the agency's best-known exchange activity is the Fulbright scholarship program, however, it is not the only exchange program that the USIA administers. The legislation was signed by President Truman on 1 August 1946. Since then, the Fulbright program has expanded several times. The Smith-Mundt Act of 1948 served as a charter for a peacetime overseas information program and authorized the State Department to seek appropriations to pay some dollar expenses of foreign grantees, as well as to carry out academic exchanges in countries with minimal surplus property sales. This responsibility was transferred to the USIA in 1953. Also in 1953 and in 1954, the House and the Senate gave permission to use other foreign currencies owed the United States, most notably from surplus agricultural commodity sales abroad, to finance educational exchange. This was an important step because in some countries surplus property proceeds were already exhausted. In the mid-1950s Congress also authorized the extension of exchanges to additional countries, including eight in Latin America, where previously there had been none. Finally, the Fulbright-Hays Act (1961) consolidated various U.S. international educational and cultural exchange activities and codified the existing program. At the end of that year, the Bureau of Educational and Cultural Affairs (CU) was established in the State Department to administer the educational exchange programs, which it did until April 1978, when CU was abolished and its programs were transferred to the USIA as part of President Carter's reorganization. In November 1983 Congress amended the Fulbright-Hays Act to include a "Bureau of Educational and Cultural Affairs (E Bureau) Charter," outlining the programs to be administered by the agency's E Bureau for the conduct of exchange programs. By 1993 there were 130 Fulbright Commissions around the world; of these, more than half share in the costs of the program. The presidentially appointed J. William Fulbright Foreign Scholarship Board (formerly the Board of Foreign Scholarships) sets policies and has final responsibility for awarding grants.

The term "Fulbright Program" encompasses a variety of exchange programs, including several types of individual and institutional grants: the U.S. Scholar Program, which sends scholars and professionals to lecture and/or conduct research; the Fulbright Student Program for U.S. and foreign graduate students to study and do research abroad; the Visiting Scholar Program and the Scholar-in-Residence Program; the Fulbright Teacher Exchange Program; the Hubert H. Humphrey Fellowship Program for midcareer professionals; and the College and University Affiliations Program.

During the Reagan administration the exchange program expanded with an International Youth Exchange Initiative (1982), which called for a greatly expanded exchange of youths (aged fifteen to nineteen), and a new scholarship program in the mid-1980s designed to offer educational opportunities at U.S. universities for disadvantaged Central Americans, the Central American Program of Undergraduate Scholarships. The first group of students to complete the program returned home in August 1987.

Another exchange program, older than the Fulbright, is the International Visitors (IV) Program. It began in 1940 with tightly funded programs, mostly in Latin America; it now brings approximately five thousand visitors from abroad to the United States to meet professional counterparts and to experience the United States firsthand. The agency also assists an additional twenty-five hundred individuals who visit the United States at their own or their home institution's expense. IVs come for either individual or group programs keyed to their professional interests and travel to different parts of the United States where they are hosted by volunteer community organizations, many belonging to the National Council for International Visitors, a nonprofit service organization. IV alumni now include more than 150 current and former chiefs of state and heads of government, more than six hundred cabinet-level ministers around the world, and thousands of prominent figures worldwide.

Under the Arts America program, the USIA administers the overseas performing and fine arts programs of the U.S. government. The Office of Arts America has principal responsibility for the agency's arts programs. It presents American culture abroad through performances, exhibitions, and consultancies; sponsors Artistic Ambassador musicians' tours; and supports inter-institutional relationships by providing to private sector organizations for joint exchange projects. There is also a presidentially appointed Cultural Property Advisory Committee, which reviews requests from other countries seeking U.S. assistance in reducing pillage of cultural objects and makes its recommendations to the USIA director. The Office of Academic Programs, the Office of International Visitors, and the Office of Citizen Exchanges support international arts exchanges through Fulbright and other academic programs, international visitor grants, and citizens and youth exchanges.

With the fall of communism signifying the end of the Cold War, the USIA has obtained funding from Congress to initiate new exchange programs. Major ones are with the Newly Independent States (NIS; formerly the Soviet Union) and eastern European initiatives. Programs focus on academic, cultural, and information exchanges that encourage democracy and free market economy building. In addition, the USIA provides technical assistance to NIS countries, as part of a government-wide initiative, through programs in public policy and public administration. The Edmund Muskie Fellowship Program is bringing qualified college graduates from the new states of the former Soviet Union for one- or two-year graduate study programs in law, business, economics, and public administration. With funds from the Freedom Support Act, the USIA launched the Secondary School Initiative, which began in fiscal year 1993. The program's goal is to provide opportunities to secondary students from NIS countries to visit and study in the United States, and to enable American youth to visit and study in NIS countries. The initiative will enable up to eighty-four hundred students from the United States and twelve NIS countries to participate in the exchange. There is also the NIS-U.S. Teacher Exchange Program, a two-year program also funded under the Freedom Support Act and designed to support democratic and educational reform in the NIS by advancing the development of civics education.

The latest NIS program is "Corridors of Culture," created in 1993 to support and encourage writers in emerging democracies in their efforts to live and work in free societies. The program sends delegations of American writers, editors, and literary agents to meet their counterparts and share insights and practical information about the writer's craft in a free society.

Eastern European initiatives are designed to help central and eastern European countries develop democratic and free market institutions. For this purpose, the agency participates in the Support for Eastern European Democracies (SEED) program. Since fiscal year 1990, the agency has used over $72 million in SEED monies to fund training programs in a broad range of fields that include English teaching, management principles, media, education reform, book donations and library training, and the rule of law. SEED funding also supports an in-country grant program at each American embassy, coordinated by the ambassador, to respond to immediate opportunities to enhance and support democratic initiatives by local universities, human rights organizations, media organizations, and others.

The U.S. Speakers Program sends American experts abroad to consult and speak on economics, international affairs, democracy and rule of law, journalism, U.S. politics, sports, science and technology, environment, and narcotics abuse prevention. Under USIA sponsorship participants meet with foreign government officials, journalists, labor leaders, students, entrepreneurs, and parliamentarians. There are also the Professionals-in-Residence, who serve for tours of up to six months as consultants to government and private institutions on promoting democratic development. Teleconference programs enable foreign audiences to communicate by telephone with American counterparts, often on short notice.

Broadcasting

The oldest and best-known element is the VOA global radio network. It currently broadcasts in forty-seven languages more than eleven hundred programming hours weekly, which always changes as new countries are targeted; it is considered one of the U.S. government's most effective communication tools. Broadcast mostly by shortwave, the VOA reaches some 127 million listeners worldwide who tune in regularly to the VOA for news and information. During times of crisis, such as the tragic events in Tiananmen Square, the Gulf War, and the 1991 failed Soviet coup, listenership increases dramatically.

The first international broadcasts of the U.S. government were those of the Coordinator for Inter-American Affairs, led by Nelson A. Rockefeller, which began transmitting programs in English, Portuguese, and Spanish to the American republics in 1941. The Office of the Coordinator of Information (COI), a predecessor to the Central Intelligence Agency, was responsible for U.S. government information activities for all areas of the world. COI's Foreign Information Service (FIS) was assigned the task of communicating by radio. By November 1941 the FIS produced reports and features in Cantonese, Czech, Danish, Finnish, French, German, Italian, Mandarin, Norwegian, Polish, Portuguese, Spanish, Swedish, and Turkish for the shortwave broadcast of private American stations. Direct broadcasts to Asia were begun by the FIS's San Francisco division in December 1941, but the New York division transmitted the first direct broadcast to Europe in February 1942. William Harlan Hale, the announcer of that first broadcast in German ("The news may be good. The news may be bad. We shall tell you the truth."), identified the new program as a "voice from America," which was adopted for all FIS broadcasts a few months later as the VOA. On 31 December 1945 the two radio activities were transferred to the State Department, where their operations were merged. When the USIA came into existence, the VOA was its single largest element.

To protect the integrity of VOA programming and to define the organization's mission, a VOA mission statement was created in 1960 by USIA Director George Allen, then congressionally mandated as the VOA's charter in 1976 under Public Law 94-350 (fiscal year 1977 Foreign Relations Authorization Act). The charter charged the VOA with serving "reliable and authoritative" news, representing "a balanced and comprehensive projection" of America, and presenting U.S. policies "clearly and effectively."

Presently, the VOA is part of the new Bureau of Broadcasting established by the 1994/1995 Foreign Relations Authorization Act (P.L. 103-236), which officially combined, for the first time, all U.S. government international broadcast services under a Board of Broadcasting Governors. The board oversees the VOA, Radio Free Europe/Radio Liberty (RFE/RL), the newly created Radio Free Asia, and Radio and TV Martí. The act provides independent grantee status for RFE/RL and Radio Free Asia and is expected to save approximately $400 million over four years while enhancing the program quality and effectiveness of U.S.-funded broadcast services.

Radio Martí broadcasts news, features, and other information about events in Cuba and elsewhere to promote the cause of freedom in Cuba. Named for Cuban patriot José Martí, the radio service was established by the Radio Broadcasting to Cuba Act (P.L. 98-111) and began broadcasting in May 1985. The law stipulated that Radio Martí should parallel all VOA standards to ensure the broadcasting of objective, accurate, balanced, and varied programs.

The Television Broadcasting to Cuba Act (P.L. 101-246) established TV Martí to provide the Cuban people with entertainment programming, uncensored news, and information. TV Martí programming consists of originally produced news and programs in addition to material acquired from commercial sources. Programs are produced in Washington and Miami, then sent by satellite to Cudjoe Key, Florida. From there, a balloon (aerostat) housing a broadcast transmitter and antenna tethered ten thousand feet in the air forwards the signal to Cuba. Presently, Cuban dictator Fidel Castro is jamming TV Martí programs, and the service has not been cost effective.

The USIA's WORLDNET Television and Film Service acquires, produces, and distributes television programs to enhance U.S. public diplomacy efforts. The first original agency television programs were shown overseas in 1955. Almost thirty years later, the Television and Film Service initiated a weekly half-hour Satellite File for the European Broadcast Union in 1983, the agency's first regular satellite program service to Europe. That same year, WORLDNET, a global satellite television network, was inaugurated by USIA Director Charles Z. Wick, then agency director. Today, it reaches almost 130 countries with live and taped television programming daily to more than 225 television receive-only antennas at U.S. embassies and USIS posts worldwide. In addition, various broadcast and cable systems receive WORLDNET public affairs programs direct via satellite. In 1987 Congress included the Television and Film Service within the VOA charter to "foster democracy and free market economies in a new information age." Three years later, the agency acquired commercial programming for rebroadcast, such as "NewsHour with Jim Lehrer," "Economics USA," "Firing Line," "George Michael's Sports Machine," and C-Span selections, while in 1993 WORLDNET launched a Ukrainian-language TV series, "Windows on America."

Other Information Tools

The USIA uses printed materials and other tools to project an accurate image abroad of the United States and its policies, including the Wireless File, whose two major products are the daily "Washington File" and the projected electronic journals in five languages, linked by a computerized communication system to all overseas posts. The Wireless File, which was started in 1935 in the State Department, provides time-sensitive information, including full transcripts of speeches, press conferences, congressional testimony, and texts of published articles and interviews. In 1985 the file began its first-ever computer-to-computer Arabic language transmission when the Arabic Wireless File switched from telex to personal computer. Seven years later, the first edition of the Russian Wireless File was distributed in Russia and several states of the former Soviet Union. It now has five regional files.

The agency also produces a number of publications, in both print and electronic form, dealing with issues of democratic development, market economies, trade, security, and other transnational issues. Until 1994 the USIA had an active publications program. Besides its special pamphlets, the agency published selected magazines. These included *Al Majal* (Arabic); *America Illustrated* (Polish and Russian); the oldest of the magazines, *Dialogue* (with its various language editions); *Economic Impact; Free World* (and its successor, *Horizons*); *Problems of Communism; Span;* and *Topic*. With the end of the Cold War, the expanding democratization of formerly Iron Curtain countries, increasing production costs, and the funding cuts in the early 1990s, the agency decided to cease publication of its in-house produced journals. Today, only *Span* is still published (at one of the agency's regional printing centers).

Another service that was abolished completely was Exhibits. This office produced paper shows along with major exhibitions. Some highlights were the American National Exhibition in Moscow (1959), the scene of the famous Nixon-Khrushchev "kitchen debate"; "The Family of Man," with the photos of Edward Steichen that toured in the 1950s; "Design USA" (1990), the last major cultural exchange exhibit in the Soviet Union; "Information—USA: Linking People With Knowledge," the most complex show ever launched by the USIA; and "Seeds of Change," a paper show based on a major Smithsonian exhibition and presented for the Columbus Quincen-

tenary. A 1993 exhibit, "Good Design Is Good Business," opened in Tallinn, Estonia, as the first American exhibition seen in the Baltic region and in one of the NIS countries.

The Exhibits Service also produced, through its expo staff, the American pavilions at the international expositions (or world's fairs). Under the Fulbright-Hays Act, the agency still has responsibility for U.S. participation at those fairs held overseas. Unlike the exhibitions, which could last for years as they toured from post to post, expos were no more than six months in duration and were regulated by the Bureau of International Expositions in Paris. The USIA was a presence at the expos beginning in Brussels (1958) up to Seville and Genoa (both 1992). After that, the expo staff was abolished and the private sector was responsible for U.S. participation, a most likely precondition at any future fairs. This happened at Taejon (1993), when the American presence was made possible entirely by private sector support and the states, with no federal funds expended. The USIA provided advice and liaison with other U.S. government agencies. This is expected to continue with the planned expo in Lisbon (1998).

The foreign press centers in Atlanta (opened 7 February 1996), Los Angeles, New York, and Washington are the U.S. government's principal points of contact for foreign journalists resident in the United States or visiting on assignment. The centers arrange briefings by U.S. officials and private experts and provide a wide variety of special activities for visiting journalists aimed at explaining U.S. policies and programs and increasing their understanding of the United States and its people. They also coordinate programs between the international media and the White House, State Department, and other U.S. agencies.

The USIA now supports nearly 160 reference libraries in developing countries and reading rooms in 130 countries, and provides substantial support for library programs in binational centers (BNCs) in more than 20 countries. USIS libraries contain over 900,000 books and 17,000 periodical subscriptions that are used by some 3.8 million users annually. The focus is on materials that will help people in foreign countries learn about the United States, its people, history, culture, and political and social processes. USIS library programs provide special library and information services to foreign publics, primarily under the direction and funding of a USIS post or on the USIS's behalf. They are distinguished from other agency program activities by their focus on acquiring existing materials in response to specific requests from posts. USIS-supported libraries, distinct from USIS libraries, operate primarily under the direction of an indigenous organization rather than a USIS post. Agency support usually consists of donations of materials and services or a grant of funds for rent, materials, and staff. Supported libraries are often located in BNCs, a research center, or other local institution. The ongoing nature of USIS support distinguishes such libraries from other indigenous libraries to which the USIS may donate collections of materials on an occasional one-time basis.

Binational centers are autonomous, foreign institutions dedicated to the promotion of mutual understanding between the host country and the United States. The BNCs work closely with USIS posts overseas but are independent in their financial and administrative management. At the invitation of their governing boards, four BNCs (Brasília, San José, Montevideo, Bangkok) have USIS officers as executive directors. English teaching is usually a major component of a BNC's cultural, educational, and information activities; it started in 1941 in the State Department. It is coordinated by the USIS post, although some posts conduct their own English teaching program. A local-hire course director administers these programs. Affiliated English teaching programs overseas, which are supported by USIA/USIS resources, include activities conducted by universities, ministries of education, and private institutes.

Books continue to have impact and enduring value in an age of instant communication, particularly in countries developing new political and economic institutions. The USIA promotes the distribution of selected American books abroad through English reprints and translations into some fifteen languages. The agency also engages in book donations and a variety of book promotion activities, including sponsoring displays at foreign and international book fairs each year and organizing thematic book exhibits in multiple sets for worldwide circulation in a joint public/private sector initiative.

Cultural centers have played an important role in U.S. cultural programming for over fifty years. They are different from BNCs in their programs' focus, such as lectures, film presentations, art exhibits, and musical performances, although many also host English teaching programs. In June 1993 the first American Cultural Center opened in Moscow to provide students, scholars, professionals, and other citizens of the country greater access to information about America. Centers were also opened in Prague, Tallinn, Riga, and Sofia at the same time, joining a string of new centers in Kiev, Tirana, Warsaw, and Budapest. America House resource centers in these countries demonstrate U.S. commitment to democratic and economic reform. They have an important practical value as "home base" for government information programs and for the activities of American grass-roots volunteers engaged in nongovernment assistance.

The Office of Research staff surveys foreign public opinion and provides daily reports on foreign media commentary to assess reaction to issues, policies, and events. These products are used by the White House, Department of State, and other government agencies as well as the USIA. Most popular is the daily digest of foreign media reaction prepared by the Media Reaction Branch in Washington. Each report provides a global roundup of editorial and op-ed reaction to a major foreign policy issue or event. The reports include the most recent commentary taken from major newspapers, magazines, and broadcast media around the world. The agency also supports academic programs relating to the study of American history and civilization (American studies); provides liaison between American and foreign universities, academic associations, and scholars; and gives annual grants to the National Endowment for Democracy, a private, nonprofit corporation that encourages and strengthens the international development of democratic institutions.

THE POST–COLD WAR AGENCY

The fall of the Berlin Wall, followed by the collapse of communism in Eastern Europe and in the Soviet Union, ushered the USIA into a post–Cold War era. The agency was forced to redefine its mission. The situation today as a post–Cold War agency is one of constant change as the USIA redefines its mission amidst smaller budgets and staff. An early step was the elimination of most of the agency's magazines by 1994 and a serious reevaluation of many of its programs. On 1 October, 1994 a new Information Bureau was created to take the USIA onto the information superhighway and to fulfill many of the goals of Vice President Gore's "Reinventing Government" program. It was designated a reinvention laboratory with a flexible, team-based approach that incorporated functions from two bureaus within the agency and established self-directed teams that set goals and produced materials and programs around selected global issues for the USIA's overseas posts; democracy building was one of its primary mandates. With the Republican takeover of Congress in 1995, there was a further attempt to rethink U.S. government foreign policy by refocusing the role of the four foreign affairs agencies: the USIA, the Agency for International Development (AID), the Arms Control and Disarmament Agency (ACDA), and the State Department. The debate was prompted by a perceived necessity to tighten the foreign policy budget and the changing common foreign policy goals of a post–Cold War world. Critics held that these agencies sometimes maintained conflicting agendas, housed duplicative functions and bureaus, and deemphasized current issues, such as U.S. economic opportunities abroad.

In March 1995 Senator Jesse Helms (R-N.C.), chairman of the Senate Foreign Relations Committee, proposed a plan to reorganize the foreign policy structure by eliminating the three independent agencies (USIA, AID, ACDA) no later than 1 March 1997 and merging their functions into a "new," more effective State Department (to be called the U.S. Department of International Relations); by creating an under secretary of public diplomacy within the State Department; and by requiring the USIA director to reduce the number of employees by twenty-five percent before 28 February 1997. The committee marked up and ordered reported its version (S. 908) of the consolidation bill, but it was

stalled in July. John Kerry's (D-Mass.) amendment temporarily blocked debate on the bill, but it is expected to come up again in future Congresses, probably as early as the 105th Congress, which began in 1997. There was also a House bill to abolish the USIA. President Clinton has threatened to veto this legislation. According to Helms, putting these functions into the State Department would "make certain that the exchange and broadcasting functions paid for by the American taxpayers reflect American policy."

Critics question whether international broadcasting can maintain its present level of credibility with foreign publics in promoting democracy and the U.S. perspective if it is administered by the State Department. They also question whether international exchange programs should continue to emphasize cross-cultural understanding or should only promote political-military goals of U.S. foreign policy. Supporters argue that it is an inexpensive and safe way to promote democracy and that it strengthens the link between broadcasting and U.S. foreign policy objectives. To counter the charge that consolidation proposals would reduce expensive duplication, increase program effectiveness, and transfer coordination authority to the State Department, the USIA contends that they would be detrimental to the effectiveness of the program. The idea to consolidate foreign policy agencies was considered by the Clinton administration, but it was rejected by Vice President Gore and his National Performance Review.

Appropriations enacted for fiscal year 1995 totaled $1.4 billion, but the agency requested a 1.6 percent decrease in its fiscal year 1996 budget. The House approved even more reductions, decreasing the USIA's funding level from the fiscal year 1995 level of $1.4 billion. Cuts included decreases to the educational and cultural exchange programs and to international broadcasting expenditures. However, no agency funding bill was signed six months into fiscal year 1996 as the agency continued operations under a continual resolution.

Today, the USIA has a new post–Cold War mission. To support it, the agency now practices public diplomacy, loosely defined as an activity that complements traditional diplomacy between governments through open communication of U.S. policies and information about the United States to people and governments in other countries, and by fostering people-to-people contacts and mutual understanding through educational and cultural programs; its chief instruments are publications, motion pictures, cultural exchanges, radio, and television.

DIRECTION

To date, the USIA has had thirteen directors. The first, Theodore C. Streibert (1953–1956), a former New York radio executive, pulled the new agency together and increased the number of the VOA's transmitters to compete with the British Broadcasting Corporation. Arthur Larson (1956–1957), a former speech writer for President Eisenhower, was included in regular meetings of the National Security Council but resigned under congressional pressure. His successor, George V. Allen (1957–1960), a career diplomat, headed the U.S. overseas information program in 1948–1949; he fought strongly for increases in teaching English abroad, translating American books, broadcasting in English by the VOA, participating in foreign trade fairs, and encouraging American experts to lecture and to visit their overseas counterparts. Edward R. Murrow (1961–1964), probably the USIA's best-known director thanks to a solid reputation as a broadcaster and a journalist, gained regular contacts between the White House and the USIA and encouraged a better relationship between agency media programs and foreign policy; his administration is still remembered fondly by many USIA alumni. Carl T. Rowan (1964–1965), the first, and to date only, African American director, a newspaper reporter and former ambassador to Finland, continued the cordial agency relations with the president but soon resigned. Lyndon Johnson's lawyer, Leonard H. Marks (1965–1968), carried through the Great Society programs, effectively instigated better control of media programming, and tailored the cultural agenda to individual posts abroad. Frank J. Shakespeare (1969–1973), a former CBS executive, was attacked by the press for the strong anticommunist programs he promoted, including his stand on the agency's role in Vietnam, and for not coordinating policy with the State Department. James Keogh (1973–1976),

former *Time* executive editor, directed the withdrawal of the agency staff and their information programs (Joint U.S. Public Affairs Office, field research surveys) from Vietnam, and focused on USIA efforts to increase trade and tourism in the United States. John E. Reinhardt (1977–1981), the first USIA career Foreign Service officer to become the agency's director, started his tenure with the USIA but ended as director of its temporary successor, the USICA. Charles Z. Wick (1981–1989) was the longest-serving director and also one of its most effective, with a direct line to the White House; he was instrumental in the name change back to the USIA. Bruce S. Gelb (1989–1991) left to become U.S. ambassador to Belgium while Henry E. Catto (1991–1993) came to the USIA from an ambassadorship in Great Britain. The present director, Joseph Duffey (1993–), was formerly assistant secretary of state for educational and cultural affairs in the State Department at the time of the 1978 reorganization, a duty he may perform again if the proposed Helms reorganization succeeds.

OVERSIGHT

The bipartisan United States Advisory Commission on Public Diplomacy is an independent, presidentially appointed citizens' panel created by Congress to advise the president, the secretary of state, and the USIA's director. It has broad oversight authority of U.S. government activities intended to understand, to inform, and to influence foreign public opinion. The commission assesses the policies and the programs of the agency; it reports its findings and recommendations to the president, to Congress, to the secretary of state, to the USIA director, and to the American people. The Office of the Inspector General has oversight authority of all USIA programs but in fiscal year 1996 is expected to be merged into its counterpart program in the State Department.

BIBLIOGRAPHY

Barrett, Edward W. *Truth Is Our Weapon*. New York, 1953.
Bernays, Edward L., and Burnet Hershey, eds. *The Case for Reappraisal of U.S. Overseas Information Policies and Programs*. New York, 1970.

Bogart, Leo. *Cool Words, Cold War: A New Look at USIA's Premises for Propaganda.* 2d ed. Washington, D.C., 1995.

Doggett, Clinton L., and Lois T. Doggett. *The United States Information Agency.* New York, 1989.

Elder, Robert E. *The Information Machine: The United States Information Agency and American Foreign Policy.* Syracuse, 1968.

Gordon, George N., and Irving A. Falk. *The War of Ideas: America's International Identity Crisis.* New York, 1973.

Gormly, Charles F. "The United States Information Agency Domestic Dissemination Ban: Arguments for Repeal." *Administrative Law Journal* 9 (Spring 1995), 191–220.

Green, Fitzhugh. *American Propaganda Abroad.* New York, 1988.

Hansen, Allen C. *USIA: Public Diplomacy in the Computer Age.* 2d ed. New York, 1989.

Henderson, John W. *The United States Information Agency.* New York, 1969.

Hitchcock, David I. *U.S. Public Diplomacy.* Washington, D.C., 1988.

Malone, Gifford D. *Political Advocacy and Cultural Communication: Organizing the Nation's Public Diplomacy.* Lanham, Md., 1988.

Ninkovich, Frank. *The Diplomacy of Ideas: U.S. Foreign Policy and Cultural Relations, 1938–1950.* New York, 1981.

Pirsein, Robert. *The Voice of America.* New York, 1979.

Roth, Lois. "Public Diplomacy and the Past: The Search for an American Style of Propaganda, 1952–1977." *Fletcher Forum* 8 (Summer 1984): 353–396.

Snyder, Alvin. *Warriors of Disinformation.* New York, 1995.

Sorenson, Thomas C. *The World War: The Story of American Propaganda.* New York, 1968.

Thompson, Kenneth W., ed. *Rhetoric and Public Diplomacy: The Stanton Panel Revisited.* Lanham, Md., 1987.

Tuch, Hans. *Communicating with the World: The U.S. Practice of Public Diplomacy.* New York, 1990.

U.S. Congress. House. Committee on International Relations. Subcommittee on International Relations. *Public Diplomacy and the Future.* Hearings, 95th Cong., 1st sess. Washington, D.C., 1977.

U.S. Congress. Senate. Committee on Foreign Relations. Subcommittee on International Operations. *Reorganization and Revitalization of America's Foreign Affairs Institutions.* Hearings, 95th Cong., 1st sess. Washington, D.C., 1977.

—MARTIN J. MANNING

V

Veterans Affairs, Department of

 At the end of the Civil War, which had killed nearly 500,000 uniformed men and boys and scarred the bodies and lives of millions of other Americans in both the North and South, President Abraham Lincoln made a moving appeal to the nation. His words created what gradually became a massive government bureaucracy that, perversely enough, has not been noted for its compassion.

The language of empathy used by Lincoln in his call to the nation during his second inaugural address in 1865— "... *to care for him who shall have borne the battle, and for his widow and his orphan* ..." —is displayed today on metal plaques at both sides of the entrance of the eleven-story, city-block-square Washington headquarters of the Department of Veterans Affairs (DVA). The building and its huge bureaucracy, whose $36 billion annual budget is exceeded only by that of the Defense Department, are the unintended consequence of Lincoln's appeal.

Lincoln's words never applied to Confederate veterans, and by 1958, when Congress finally pardoned the Confederate army, only one of them survived to receive veterans' benefits for his last year of life. It is also ironic that the words of Lincoln's century-old appeal were not put on display at the agency's entrance until 1959. By then the demands of successive wars, the influences of partisan and pandering congressional politics, and decades of unredeemed departmental mismanagement had turned Lincoln's vision of care for veterans and their kin into a mammoth ministry with a Kafkaesque reputation.

The cabinet-rank coronation of the Veterans Administration (VA) in 1988, an elevation from its status as a mere "independent agency" to the fourteenth federal department and an honorific new name, encapsulated to "the DVA," has done little to alter its image. The agency is perceived as so basically unchanged that it is still almost universally referred to as "the VA."

The VA's bureaucratic growth came by eras, marked by wars. In the five years following the Civil War, for example, the government spent more money caring for its veterans than in the preceding seventy-five years of supporting veterans of the Revolutionary War, the War of 1812, and the Mexican War. Corruption came with the money. As even self-congratulatory official agency publications concede, during the late nineteenth and early twentieth centuries the department's predecessor, then called the Bureau of Pensions, was "the most uncompromisingly political agency of the federal government."

In 1921 a commission formed to investigate the chaos found that "an imperfect organization" was responsible for "a deplorable failure on the part of government to properly care for disabled veterans." A Senate investigation in 1923 found "waste, extravagance, irregularities and mismanagement." But the Bureau of Pensions survived until it was merged in 1930 with other veterans' offices to become the VA.

In its geometrical growth since then, the veterans' agency has been marred repeatedly by political scandals, and congressional investigations have revealed continuing incompetence and abuse. But even when it has been put on the defensive, attempts to diminish it by ideological critics of "the federal leviathan" have largely failed. The grass-roots political power of the multimillion-member national veterans' organizations, known collectively on Capitol Hill as "the hat people" for their attachment to wearing military-style overseas caps, gives the agency strong legislative armor.

The VA as we know it now was created midway through the administration of President Herbert Hoover by the consolidation of various small veterans' bureaus that had been established separately, war by war. The VA remained one of the hundreds of Washington's low-visibility bureaucracies that rarely attract the attention of the press. In the aftermath of World Wars I and II and the Korean and Vietnam Wars, however, the low-profile agency grew to such massive proportions that its $36 billion annual budget now exceeds all but that of the Defense Department. The VA staff of about a quarter-million employees includes one of every eight federal government workers.

The world's history of government compensation for active combat, much less for support of the wounded and survivors of the dead, spans only a few centuries. In primitive tribal clans, able-bodied males served as warriors with no thought of compensation. Military forces were maintained by plunder and tributes exacted from fallen foes. Soldiers of the Greek city-states received no pay, but children of the war dead were meagerly supported. As the Romans and their successors in the medieval feudal states of Europe recruited mercenaries from across the known world, troops began to be paid wages. But not until four years after the legendary British naval mobilization that smashed the invading Spanish Armada in 1588, with heavy casualties among British seamen, did Parliament feel sufficiently threatened by begging, robbing, and rioting armada veterans to enact the world's first pension law. The cost, which was to rise astronomically over following centuries of ceaseless warfare, was conveniently fastened on the veterans' home counties—if they could collect it there.

In Colonial America, where the Pilgrims are sometimes said to have "fallen upon their knees, and then upon the aborigines," the Plymouth Colony's fierce combat with American Indians cost many a colonist an arm and a leg. To encourage enlistments in spite of such hazards, the colony adopted a military pension plan in 1636, the first ever paid out of a general government treasury. The Plymouth Colony Records contain this language: *"If any man shalbee sent forth as a souldier and shall returne maimed, hee shallbee majntainted competently by the Collonie during his life."*

This system was incorporated into state law when Plymouth merged with the Massachusetts Bay Colony in Boston in 1691. Other Colonial governments gradually did the same, but with class-conscious distinctions. In Maryland and Virginia disabled veterans and the widows and families of the war dead were deemed "objects of charity" who were due a stipend according to rank and "quality," a distinction that favored officers over enlisted men. The first federal act granting pensions to officers and enlisted men of the United States "disabled in the line of duty" was passed by the Continental Congress in 1789.

The steady growth of the government's largess for veterans has had only occasional setbacks. One of them came in what seemed a harshly heretical speech by President Franklin D. Roosevelt, delivered to an American Legion convention in the Depression year of 1933. "No person, because he wore a uniform, must thereafter be placed in a special class of beneficiaries over and above all citizens," Roosevelt declared. He expressed a "duty to country" sentiment shared by the majority of physically fit American veterans who are not members of veterans' organizations and have had little or no contact with, or dependence on, the VA. Roosevelt's 1933 Economy Act severely cut the Depression-strained veterans' benefit budget, a politically popular move at the time.

But then came World War II. In 1944 the Roosevelt administration enormously broadened veterans' benefits by creating what is widely believed to have been the most enlightened and successful veterans' compensation program ever enacted by any country, the Servicemen's Readjustment Act of 1944, known as the GI Bill of Rights. Enrolled in a program that elevated a whole generation of blue-collar Americans to the middle class, nearly two million veterans of World War II were given personal and family financial support and tuition payments while they enrolled in colleges and universities. Gauged by its impact on the nation, the GI Bill is widely judged to have had more powerful and lasting effects than the Homestead Act of 1862, which gave Civil War veterans land in the West. Other millions of World War II veterans advanced their talents and their employability in government-paid vocational training.

Veterans of the war in Korea, from 1950 to 1955, were offered reduced GI Bill benefits. The Vietnam veterans' ratio of participation in GI education and training programs was higher than among veterans returning from either World War II or Korea. But many thousands of Vietnam veterans, disillusioned by the war and feeling rejected by civilian society in the 1960s and 1970s, were estranged and alienated as they returned home. This forced the VA to a belated response with alcohol, drug, and psychiatric treatment programs. In the post-Vietnam years the agency's performance was in decline, but, because the VA receives little press attention, both its mismanaged benefits-granting process and its invigorated response to the special problems of Vietnam veterans were not widely reported.

Today there are five basic veterans' compensation and pension programs:

- Monthly compensation for disability incurred or aggravated on active duty, with the dollar amount based on a VA determination of the scope of disability, from ten to one hundred percent

- Indemnity compensation for surviving dependents of veterans who die of a service-connected injury or illness

- Pension benefits for veterans of wartime duty who are sixty-five or older, are disabled for non-service-connected causes, and who meet low income limits

- Death benefits for surviving dependents

- Burial allowances.

By now, with more than seventy thousand interments each year, some 2.4 million veterans and members of their families have been buried in the VA's 130 national cemeteries—fifty-seven of them filled and closed—in thirty-nine states, the District of Columbia, and Puerto Rico.

The agency has also guaranteed millions of GI home loans since World War II. By the 1990s the DVA home loan program, part of the original GI Bill, had helped 14.6 million veterans with $493 billion in mortgage guarantees. About 6.9 million active service members and veterans also have some form of low-cost VA life insurance.

Twenty-one children of deceased Civil War veterans were still receiving benefits from the VA in 1996. They were among more than three million disabled and unemployably aged veterans and veterans' dependents supported by monthly checks that totaled about $19 billion a year in tax-free monthly benefit checks. The VA spends another $16.5 billion a year to operate the world's largest hospital and medical care network—172 hospitals with 75,000 beds, 365 outpatient clinics, 128 nursing homes, and 37 domiciliaries, or old folks' homes.

Although it is rarely mentioned, apparently to avoid impacts on the morale of active duty forces and their families, one quiet rationalization for the huge and underutilized VA hospital network is that it is on standby to treat the war wounded in the event of sudden combat. But the agency seems not content to be merely mammoth. To justify its size the VA uses census data to support exaggerated estimates of its constituency. In its published reports it asserts that some seventy-six million Americans, or nearly a third of the nation, are its *potential* beneficiaries." This inflated estimate includes the 26.5 million living veterans; 21.6 million of their wives or husbands; 15.4 million of their children under eighteen who might be eligible for benefits as dependents, and just under two million veterans' widows and their children.

In 1996 only about ten percent of all living veterans and their widows, children, and dependents were receiving veterans' benefits. The beneficiaries are only one or two percent of the total population of 264.8 million.

A new demographic characteristic that began to appear in Vietnam and became increasingly visible in the media coverage of the armed forces' missions in Somalia, Kuwait, and Bosnia was the servicewoman. Women are equally eligible with men for veterans' benefits. Female veterans of World War II, limited to clerical and support duties, numbered only 319,000, but by 1990 women veterans totaled more than one million.

Two-thirds of the U.S. presidents—twenty-five of the thirty-nine through George Bush—

had some prior military service, ranging from high command (George Washington, Ulysses S. Grant, Dwight D. Eisenhower), to wounded or decorated heroism in combat (James Monroe, Rutherford B. Hayes, John F. Kennedy, George Bush), to three months of volunteer service in 1832 in the Indian Wars (Abraham Lincoln). Aside from the rhetoric of Memorial Day and Veterans Day speeches, their views of the veteran population have seemed to be that of President Roosevelt in 1933—that veterans are not a special class "over and above all citizens."

Accordingly, for decades, the veterans agency's presidentially appointed leaders were for the most part unmemorable. One early choice, Charles R. Forbes, appointed by President Warren G. Harding in 1921 to head what was then called the Veterans Bureau, was sentenced to prison for fraud. His successor, retired Brigadier General Frank T. Hines, served in obscurity at the bureau and the VA for the next two decades. In the crush of returning World War II veterans in 1945, Hines's lengthy tenure was ended by President Harry S. Truman a month after President Roosevelt's death. President Truman then appointed General Omar Bradley, a hero of World War II, but Bradley could bear command of this chaotically intransigent bureaucracy for little more than two years. He returned to the Army, restoring the top control of the agency to patronage.

Over the years, those given presidential appointments to head the veterans' agency have often been men championed by the leadership of the national veterans' service organizations. In the rapid turnover of top VA administrators after the Korean War, four of the fourteen men appointed were former national or state commanders of the American Legion or the Veterans of Foreign Wars (VFW), the two largest of the politically active veterans' organizations. President Clinton's choice as secretary of veterans affairs in 1993 was Jesse Brown, the former executive director of the Disabled American Veterans (DAV). Mr. Brown, an African-American former Marine whose right arm was partially paralyzed in combat in Vietnam in 1965, was also a veteran of twenty-six years in the DAV.

It was President Ronald Reagan, whose World War II service involved making movies, who un-expectedly proposed elevating the VA to cabinet rank. Reagan had come to Washington in 1981 pledged to abolish at least two existing government departments, the Department of Energy and the Department of Education. Instead, he created a new one by enlisting Congress to make the VA the fourteenth cabinet department.

Since 1965 the number of cabinet departments had already been increased from nine to thirteen, and the VA proposal came at a time when the veteran population was declining. Aging ex-service men and women were expiring at nearly twice the rate of discharge from the armed forces. Reagan nonetheless reversed the firm judgment of his White House predecessors and of his own advisers and, in an unexpected speech on Veterans Day 1987, proposed the VA cabinet elevation, effective in 1988. The House of Representatives approved it in a week.

Reagan partisans felt betrayed. The conservative journal *Human Events* accused the president of "bureaucratic pork-barreling." In William F. Buckley, Jr.'s monthly *National Review,* the cabinet elevation was called "a joke" and "the worst new idea of the new year." Despite a strongly negative report prepared for the Senate by a panel of management experts at the National Academy of Public Administration, the Senate also finally complied.

Bills to create a cabinet department for veterans had been introduced first in 1929 and had reappeared with regularity—in every Congress after 1963. In part because President Jimmy Carter in 1977 had already designated the VA administrator a *de facto* cabinet member, with a chair at the cabinet table, few took the idea seriously until Reagan's surprise announcement.

The critical study before the Senate warned that the grant of cabinet status imposed no requirement for reform of the VA's "internal weaknesses," its seemingly unremediable administrative mismanagement and its programmatic failures. The study concluded that departmental rank for the VA not only was unnecessary, but also that the departmental escalation raised "the possible danger" of "a perception that this elevation, in and of itself, has done something to address veterans' needs."

It did not. Problems and political repercussions at the VA worsened and became more visible. In 1989, given the choice of naming the first secretary of veterans affairs, President Bush seemed to break the political patronage mold by nominating Edward J. Derwinski, until 1982 a twelve-term Republican member of the House from Chicago. At the end of his twenty-four years in Congress, Mr. Derwinski had been appointed during the Reagan administration first as the State Department's top lawyer and then as under secretary of state for security assistance. He was regarded as a capable and credible public servant. But as an apolitical reformist, he proved to be a disposable misfit. When the new secretary discovered how many VA hospitals had empty beds, he proposed opening them to limited care of the nonveteran poor in Appalachia and elsewhere. The Lincolnesque extension of care so offended the VFW that President Bush, correctly fearing a reelection defeat in 1992, sought to keep the VFW's campaign support by summarily dismissing Mr. Derwinski. After a year's vacancy, he was succeeded as secretary in 1993 by Jesse Brown.

The broad array of VA abuses disclosed in the 1980s by congressional investigators was added proof of the journalists' abdications that helped conceal them. Evidence of bizarrely systematic bureaucratic abuse of due process in the VA was laid before a subcommittee of the House Government Operations Committee chaired by Representative Ted Weiss, a Democrat from New York City. Its investigators obtained copies of unpublished VA staff critiques that showed that the agency knew that it was violating the concept of "non-adversarial" treatment of veterans' claims for benefits, which is supposed to give them "the benefit of the doubt."

The VA was found to have been aware that some of its claims examiners were denying veterans' claims with little or no attention in order to enhance their own careers. The Weiss subcommittee showed that some VA regional office managers had encouraged staff employees to gain the "work credits" needed for promotion by padding their logs with quick claims denials. Some veterans were not notified of the denials, as required, and accordingly their claims denials were never appealed. Unaware of their rights, veterans' hopes vanished in the wastebaskets of a bureau-

cratic maze. VA studies obtained by the subcommittee also showed that the agency was reporting to Congress artificially low claims error rates—as many as three times lower than the rate generated in the haste of management-fostered slipshod paperwork.

Congressional scrutiny also forced the VA to abandon years of quota-controlled speed in ruling on veterans' appeals of quixotic claim denials. Appeals adjudicators at VA headquarters who ground out the highest number of rulings were offered cash bonuses of up to $3,000 for exceeding the goal of forty cases a week. It was a production quota that one retired adjudicator told House investigators could be met only by giving each complex medical claim no more than a twenty-minute review.

Congressional interrogation revealed that appeals decision makers held back some of these quickly scanned cases for strategic release at the start of new bonus-counting periods. The House investigators learned that one bonus winner had received a cash award for withholding decisions and then bundling them together in a way that appeared to show that he had processed 102 cases in one week, a pace that could have been accomplished only by giving each case 7.8 minutes. The VA manager of this pressurized pace of appeals decisions defended it by telling the House committee that "if you emphasize quality too much, you are not going to get production and you are going to get way behind."

When consistency was tested in the hasty VA process of rating disability benefits—awarding the degree of medical disability, from ten to one hundred percent, on which the amount of compensation checks is now pegged at from $91 to $1,870 a month—the system was found to be subject to other vagaries. Based on a survey run by VA program analysts in Washington, the agency was forced to acknowledge that it had sent hypothetical veterans' medical case folders to disability raters in VA regional offices in different states as a test. Reviewing identical case files that appeared to describe an actual case of PTSD, or posttraumatic stress disorder—the controversial Vietnam-era diagnosis of what had been called "shellshock" or "battle fatigue" in other wars—two regional offices rated the test case disability at zero, sixteen of them at ten percent, nineteen of them at thirty percent, thirteen of them at fifty percent, and one at seventy percent. Support for some of the 470,000 troubled Vietnam veterans then estimated by the VA to be "current cases of PTSD" seemed to depend on where they lived.

Some of the worst VA abuses are gradually ending thanks to the creation of a new seven-judge U.S. Court of Veterans Appeals, the first veterans' panel before which claimants can be represented by lawyers. The absolute preclusion of lawyers in all veterans' appearances before VA hearing officers and boards began in post–Civil War days. Before the practice of law was licensed or regulated, Congress suspected that carpet bagging lawyers would bilk veterans and their widows of their benefits. Congress acted more directly in 1887 to deny veterans any access to the courts. Again in 1924, to block a surge of new attempts at court challenges by veterans of World War I, Congress specified by law that all findings of the veterans' agency's "nonadversarial" claims adjudicators were final and were not subject to appeal.

The VA, its allies on the powerful House Veterans Affairs Committee, and, astonishingly, until 1988, the major national veterans' organizations, supported the preclusion of lawyers. They argued that allowing any intrusions by the courts would force the abandonment of an assertedly benevolent VA process, described for decades as more favorable to veterans than any court could be.

To fill the advocacy void in entry-level contacts by veterans with the VA bureaucracy, the major national veterans' organizations had gradually installed cadres of salaried nonlawyer "service representatives," who act as the claimants' *pro bono* advocates. However, because an impenetrable maze of more than four hundred fine-print pages of federal statutes on veterans' benefits now fill Title 38 of the United States Code, and because VA rules and regulations are also gargantuan, the new veterans' appeals court has held that the nonlawyer representation of veterans sometimes yields ineffective advocacy. Lawyers are now permitted to represent veterans before the Court of Veterans Appeals itself, an inroad

that VA authorities do not appear to relish. In 1994 the chief judge of the special Court of Veterans Appeals, Frank Nebeker, accused the VA's claims-judging and medical bureaucracies of simply ignoring orders of the court.

Held at somewhat shorter arm's length, the special appeals court and the gradual advance of lawyer advocacy at some levels of veterans' appeals have improved the outlook for claimants. More servicemen exposed to radiation during World War II nuclear bomb tests, more Vietnam veterans claiming injury by the chemical defoliant Agent Orange, and more veterans of Desert Storm claiming symptoms from still-disputed exposures to chemical warfare weapons or air pollution in Kuwait, are gradually being allowed to make their case.

BIBLIOGRAPHY

Knight, Amy W. and Robert L. Worden. *The Veterans Benefits Administration: An Organizational History.* Washington, D.C., 1995.
National Academy of Public Administration. *Evaluation of Proposals to Establish a Department of Veterans Affairs.* Washington, D.C., 1988.
Severo, Richard, and Lewis Milford. *The Wages of War: When America's Soldiers Came Home; From Valley Forge to Vietnam.* New York, 1989.
Stewart, Anne C. *Proposals in the 100th Congress to Make the Veterans Administration a Cabinet-Level Department: Background Information and Analysis of Issues.* Washington, D.C., 1987.
U.S. Congress. House. Committee on Government Operations. *Investigation of Disability Compensation Programs of the Veterans' Administration.* House Report 100–886. Washington, D.C., 1988.

—BEN A. FRANKLIN

Vice Presidency

 A classic American political fable tells of two brothers: one went to sea, the other became vice president; neither was ever heard from again. That tale well describes the anonymity and futility of the vice presidency during much of U.S. history. During the nineteenth and early twentieth century, the

office was a sinecure, often occupied by someone whose sparse credentials hardly qualified him as a presidential successor. The vice presidency was generally ignored, except by political satirists, for whom it was an easy mark.

The vice presidency has grown in stature this century, particularly since World War II. Its development has occurred primarily owing to changes in American politics and government—the increased American international role, the growth of national government, the enhanced role of the presidency—which have transformed the vice president from a legislative officer, whose only duty was to preside over the Senate, to an integral part of the executive branch. That change received constitutional confirmation in 1967 when the Twenty-fifth Amendment to the Constitution was ratified; it rested on the premise that the vice presidency was an indispensable part of the executive branch, a radical departure from the Founders' view.

The office has advanced most over the last twenty years. During that time vice presidents have assumed a prominent role as presidential advisers. Those vice presidents who have established easy rapport with the chief executive have gained most access to the decision-making process. The changes have made the vice presidency not simply a station to house, and hopefully prepare, a presidential successor but an institution that contributes to American government on an ongoing basis.

THE FOUNDERS' VICE PRESIDENCY

The vice presidency was an afterthought at the Constitutional Convention, where it received little comment. The Constitution specified only that the vice president 1) would be president of the Senate empowered to break tie votes, 2) would be the runner-up in a presidential election in which electors would have two votes, 3) would be elected for the same term as the president, 4) would succeed to the presidency upon vacancy in that office, and 5) along with the president and civil officers of government, could be removed upon impeachment and conviction.

Why the Founders created the office remains a mystery. Some have suggested the office was to provide the Senate a neutral chair or the nation

a presidential successor. Neither rationale alone is convincing. Other evidence suggests the Framers made the vice president the Senate's presiding officer to occupy his time; otherwise he would have nothing to do. Nor was presidential succession the problem the office was to remedy. The Framers said little about it. Moreover, if they created the vice presidency to solve either problem they probably would have provided some means to fill a vice presidential vacancy. They did not. Apparently, they thought the nation could occasionally function without a vice president.

Most likely, the office was created to facilitate the election of a national president. The Framers feared parochial tendencies would inhibit the election of a national president as each state supported its own favorite son. Accordingly, they provided that each elector would have two votes, only one of which could be cast for a citizen from the elector's state. To give electors incentive to vote seriously, the Framers created a second office for the presidential runner-up and assigned him his two constitutional functions—presiding over the Senate and acting as first successor. By fashioning the vice presidency as a consolation prize for the second-place finisher, the system afforded some assurance that the second spot would be filled with people fit to be president.

Initially, the system worked. The first vice presidents, John Adams and Thomas Jefferson, were towering figures later elected president in their own right. But the Framers had apparently not anticipated two developments that undermined their design. First, before 1800 national political parties fielded candidates. Thus in 1796 the electoral system awarded Federalist Adams the presidency and Republican Jefferson the vice presidency. Partisan differences complicated a difficult relationship.

A second development proved more problematic. Although electors cast two presidential ballots, in fact the parties designated one person for the presidency, the other for the second spot. The system worked as intended only if a few electors withheld votes from the vice presidential candidate so the standard-bearer received more votes. In 1800, however, Jefferson, the intended presidential candidate, and Aaron Burr, the true vice presidential candidate, received an equal vote. Some thirty-six ballots of the House of Representatives were required to elect Jefferson.

The experience exposed a defect in the electoral design. In 1804 the Twelfth Amendment remedied that problem by providing for separate election of the president and vice president. Some legislators preferred abolishing the vice presidency. They reasoned that the new electoral system eliminated the rationale for the office; they predicted that the vice presidency would be depreciated and would no longer attract people of substance.

Their concerns were prophetic. With few exceptions (John Calhoun [1825–1832] and Martin Van Buren [1833–1837], for instance), the office was inhabited by undistinguished figures during the remainder of the nineteenth century. Chester A. Arthur (1881), for instance, had never held a position higher than collector of customs for the port of New York before serving as James Garfield's vice president. Garret A. Hobart's (1897–1899) long tenure in the New Jersey state legislature represented the pinnacle of his accomplishment before party leaders placed him on a ticket with William McKinley in 1896. Some vice presidents with respectable résumés—George Clinton (1805–1812), Elbridge Gerry (1813–1814), William R. King (1853), and Thomas A. Hendricks (1885)—were ill during much of their tenures and died in office.

Although a few nineteenth-century vice presidents established rapport with the chief executive, more often the relationship was distant or even acrimonious. George Clinton refused to attend James Madison's inauguration. Calhoun openly opposed some of Andrew Jackson's important initiatives. Arthur publicly condemned President Garfield for not being truthful, or "square."

Troubled relationships were predictable. The presidential candidate typically had little, if any, say in choosing the running mate. Party leaders made that decision to balance the ticket ideologically or geographically. Accordingly, vice presidents had little loyalty to their presidents and were unlikely to become their confidants.

Nineteenth-century vice presidents had few duties. In the Senate, they could not debate or

vote (except when ties occurred); often the Senate was not in session. Some found other outlets: Richard M. Johnson (1837–1841) operated a tavern; Henry Wilson (1873–1875) wrote history books. Many did little to distinguish themselves. Andrew Johnson (1865) came to his inauguration drunk. Daniel D. Tompkins (1817–1825) and Schuyler Colfax (1869–1873) were occupied answering allegations of financial improprieties.

Developments in the nineteenth century did, however, strengthen the status of vice presidents who filled presidential vacancies. The Founders expected the vice president simply to "act" as, not to become, president upon death, resignation, removal, or disability of the chief executive. Yet when William Henry Harrison died in 1841, John Tyler insisted that he was president. Although Tyler's claim was controversial, both houses of Congress ultimately accepted it; Millard Fillmore (1849–1850), Johnson, and Arthur were all treated as "president" upon their predecessors' death.

The four vice presidents who succeeded to the presidency were anomalies; the office was the last stop in a mediocre career for most of its nineteenth-century occupants. Daniel Webster turned down the chance to be vice president, saying "I do not propose to be buried until I am dead." Only one of the twenty-two men who served as vice president from 1804 to 1899 was later elected president (Van Buren); the four nineteenth-century vice presidents who succeeded to the office following the death of their predecessors failed to win their own term. Six were not renominated for the vice presidency. Six died in office. Most, like the brother who went to sea, were not heard from again.

THE EARLY TWENTIETH-CENTURY VICE PRESIDENCY

The vice presidency began a slow metamorphosis near the turn of the twentieth century. Although party leaders continued to select the vice presidential candidates at the beginning of the century, the new era occasioned a rise in the caliber of those chosen. Theodore Roosevelt (1901), Charles W. Fairbanks (1905–1909), Charles Curtis (1929–1933), John Nance Garner (1933–1941), and Alben Barkley (1949–1953) were prominent leaders of their parties when chosen to run. Others, like Calvin Coolidge (1921–1923), Charles Dawes (1925–1929), Henry Wallace (1941–1945), and Harry S. Truman (1945), were respected public servants.

Presidents began to make some assignments to vice presidents. Woodrow Wilson, for instance, invited Thomas R. Marshall (1913–1921) to preside over the cabinet during Wilson's absence from the country; since Franklin Roosevelt's first administration, vice presidents have received a regular invitation to cabinet meetings. Roosevelt used Garner as a legislative liaison during his first term and included him at meetings with legislative leaders, a practice most subsequent presidents have followed. And Garner became the first vice president to take a goodwill trip abroad at the president's request, another role his successors copied. Roosevelt appointed Henry Wallace to head the Economic Defense Board, which helped coordinate wartime preparations; it became the Board of Economic Warfare once the United States entered World War II.

The vice presidency began to experience enhanced status as a political springboard. The three vice presidents who became president following the death of their predecessors—Roosevelt, Coolidge, and Truman—all won a term of their own, unlike their nineteenth-century predecessors. Others made credible runs for the presidential nomination or were viewed as serious presidential contenders.

Yet advances in the office during the first half century were more subtle than substantial. Relations remained cool between most presidents and vice presidents, a circumstance that impeded vice presidential activity in the executive branch. When Wilson was sick for the last eighteen months of his tenure, Marshall was kept at bay, ignorant of the true state of the president's health. Theodore Roosevelt and Hoover had little use for their vice presidents. Franklin Roosevelt and Garner, after working together for one term, broke during their second term. Roosevelt allowed Wallace to be dropped from his ticket; he kept Truman in the dark regarding America's progress toward perfecting an atomic bomb. Vice presidents testified to the poverty of the office. Marshall likened the vice president to "a man in a cataleptic fit; he cannot speak; he cannot move; he suffers no pain; he is perfectly conscious of all that goes on, but has no part of it." Garner was more blunt; he was quoted as disparaging his job as "not worth a pitcher of warm spit."

THE VICE PRESIDENCY TRANSFORMED

The conspicuous growth in the vice presidency occurred during the last half century. The office has been transformed from the hollow shell that so attracted satirists' scorn to a significant institution. The increased international and domestic role of the United States since the New Deal and World War II increased the prominence of the president, a change that showered benefits on the vice presidency.

First, the vice presidency became firmly lodged in the executive branch of government during the last fifty years. Developments during the first half century had eroded the traditional view of the vice presidency as strictly a legislative office. Following World War II that view lost all credibility. In 1949 Congress made the vice president a statutory member of the National Security Council. [See National Security Council.] Barkley, diffident at embracing an executive role, continued to preside over the Senate regularly. His successor, Richard M. Nixon (1953–1961), betrayed no such inhibitions. He spent little time presiding over the Senate and eagerly gravitated to the executive branch.

Beginning with Nixon, vice presidents routinely fielded assignments from presidents. As the presidency assumed responsibility for a greater range of issues, presidents often appointed vice presidents to chair commissions dealing with a myriad of problems, large and small. Nixon and his two immediate successors, Lyndon B. Johnson (1961–1963) and Hubert H. Humphrey (1965–1969), chaired executive branch committees that addressed discrimination in government contracts. Beginning with Johnson, vice presidents chaired the space council. Nelson A. Rockefeller (1974–1977) headed the Domestic Council and an investigation of the Central Intelligence Agency. Others received additional assignments.

Although these presidential grants identified

the vice president more closely with the executive branch, they also carried risks. Some assigned tasks were not commensurate with the status of the vice president. Conversely, entrusting the vice president with significant ongoing responsibilities risked offending officials whose turf was invaded.

Vice presidents also served as an emissary abroad. Many trips were ceremonial—to attend inaugurations and funerals. Yet vice presidents drew foreign assignments of substance, too. Nixon's seven trips abroad included travels to the Soviet Union (where he engaged in a well-publicized "kitchen debate" with Premier Nikita Khrushchev). Johnson led an American delegation to West Germany following erection of the Berlin Wall in an important show of Western solidarity. Humphrey traveled to Vietnam on "fact-finding" trips on several occasions. The White House choreographed the trips to extract from them the maximum political advantage upon Humphrey's return.

Recent vice presidents have also assumed political roles in at least three respects. They have emerged as administration spokespersons on important issues. Nixon, for instance, frequently articulated the administration's policy with respect to communism and defended its record addressing internal subversion. Humphrey was used as a frequent champion of Johnson's Great Society programs and of his Vietnam policy. Agnew devoted much of his time to attacking administration critics. Albert Gore (1993–) articulated administration policy on a range of issues; most prominent, perhaps, was his debate with Ross Perot on the North American Free Trade Agreement.

Vice presidents have also worked as legislative liaison for the administration. The role of occasional lobbyist has suited well those vice presidents who previously served in Congress and could exploit knowledge of the institution and friendships with its members. Humphrey spent much of his first year advancing legislation. Mondale and Gore frequently contacted legislators on pending measures.

Finally, vice presidents have emerged as energetic party workers. By attending party functions they fulfill multiple objectives. They raise funds and generate enthusiasm for local candidates. By sparing the chief executive some of that burden, they allow him to husband his time and to appear "presidential" rather than partisan. Party work enables the vice president to build a following. Nixon, for instance, embraced this role; his skill at it enabled him to secure the Republican nomination in 1960 without opposition. Increasingly, vice presidents devote much of their time in the last year of their first term campaigning for the renomination and reelection of the president.

Most significantly, vice presidents have emerged as presidential advisers on a range of topics. Although Nixon, Johnson, and Humphrey played this role to some extent, the advisory vice presidency has developed primarily since Walter Mondale's tenure (1977–1981). His predecessor, Rockefeller, had won a weekly meeting with President Gerald R. Ford. An expanded staff provided Rockefeller with necessary support. Carter and Mondale continued the weekly private meetings as have all pairs since then. Carter gave Mondale an office only paces from his own; physical proximity gave Mondale opportunities to influence. Carter also gave Mondale the right to attend all meetings on his schedule and access to all paper that came to the Oval Office. Subsequent vice presidents—George Bush (1981–1989), J. Danforth Quayle (1989–1993), and Gore—have all enjoyed these advantages, all of which have enhanced their roles. Information, staff support, and access to the president have enabled these vice presidents to participate in meaningful ways. Mondale's role was aided by the rapport he established with President Carter and his ranking aides. His successors have been sensitive to the need to foster similar relationships and have largely been successful.

Since Nixon's tenure, the vice presidency has also become the best springboard to the presidency. Johnson and Ford succeeded to the office upon death or resignation of their predecessors. Of the three sitting vice presidents who have been nominated to run for the presidency, Bush was elected in 1988, and Nixon (1960) and Humphrey (1968) fell just short. Of former vice presidents, Nixon (1968) won while Mondale (1984) did not. Agnew seemed a likely contender in

1972 before being forced to resign; Gore and Quayle may be future candidates. Still, incumbent vice presidents may have difficulty distancing themselves from controversial policies of the administration.

Changes in the method of selecting vice presidential candidates have contributed to reshaping the vice presidency. Since 1940, most presidential candidates have played the leading role in selecting their running mates, a change that has encouraged compatibility between the two in at least three ways: 1) allowing the presidential candidate to select someone with whom he can work, 2) giving the vice president reason for loyalty to his superior, and 3) giving the chief executive reason to want his subordinate to succeed. Although candidates often seek some form of ticket-balancing, the rise of electronic media has made more costly the extreme ideological balancing that once occurred. Indeed, the Clinton-Gore ticket reflected a relatively new phenomenon—a ticket with candidates from the same region, generation, and wing of a party (although with different government experience).

Although some have called for the abolition of the office, the vice presidency seems destined to remain part of America's constitutional apparatus. The development of the office has not removed all flaws. Vice presidents rely on the chief executive for meaningful assignments, a reality that leaves the vice president weak and dependent. Moreover, vice presidents are not always presidential caliber. Over the years, reform proposals have accumulated, the most prominent of which would provide for separate election of the vice president or would allow him to hold an additional appointed or elective position. These suggestions have attracted little support. Separate elections might install presidents and vice presidents from different parties. Allowing the vice president to hold a second office would create some problems. Presidents would be reluctant to appoint their vice presidents to major cabinet positions; even if removed from that position they would remain as vice president, leaving an embarrassed president with a disgruntled second.

It seems more likely that the further development of the office will depend on informal changes designed to promote vice presidential involvement in decision-making. The precedents in that regard from the Rockefeller and Mondale terms have been followed, and they will no doubt create expectations for future vice presidents. Although the office remains vulnerable, the more recent experience suggests the office can offer its occupant opportunity to contribute to policy-making while gaining insight into problems facing the presidency.

[See also Advising the President; Cabinet; Presidential Succession and Disability; and Senate.]

BIBLIOGRAPHY

David, Paul. "The Vice-Presidency: Its Institutional Evolution and Contemporary States." Journal of Politics 29 (1967): 721–748.
Davis, James W. The American Presidency. 2d ed. Westport, Conn., 1995.
Feerick, John D. From Failing Hands. New York, 1965.
Goldstein, Joel K. The Modern American Vice Presidency: The Transformation of a Political Institution. Princeton, N.J., 1982.
Goldstein, Joel K. "The New Constitutional Vice Presidency." Wake Forest Law Review 30 (1995) 505–561.
A Heartbeat Away. Report of the Twentieth Century Fund Task Force on the Vice Presidency. New York, 1988.
Light, Paul C. Vice-Presidential Power: Advice and Influence in the White House. Baltimore, 1984.
Milkis, Sidney M., and Michael Nelson. The American Presidency: Origins and Development, 1776–1993. 2d. ed. Washington, D.C., 1994.
Natoli, Marie D. American Prince, American Pauper: The Contemporary Vice Presidency in Perspective. Westport, Conn., 1985.
Pika, Joseph A. "The Vice Presidency: New Opportunities, Old Constraints." In The Presidency and the Political System, 4th ed., edited by Michael Nelson. Washington, D.C., 1995.
Schlesinger, Arthur M., Jr. "On the Presidential Succession." Political Science Quarterly 89 (1974): 475–505.
"Symposium on the Vice-Presidency." Fordham Law Review 45 (1977): 707–799.
Williams, Irving G. The Rise of the Vice Presidency. Washington, D.C., 1956.
Witcover, Jules. Crapshoot: Rolling the Dice on the Vice Presidency. New York, 1992.
Young, Donald. American Roulette: The History and Dilemma of the Vice Presidency. Rev. ed. New York, 1972.
—JOEL K. GOLDSTEIN

W

White House Office

In 1939, using his recently granted reorganization authority, Franklin Roosevelt established the Executive Office of the President (EOP); among the several offices included therein, the White House Office (WHO) would be most important and would be the home of those advisers closest to the president. In the latter part of the twentieth century the WHO has grown to be an institutionalized bureaucracy containing more than fifteen offices that conduct the core activities of the modern presidency. The offices include about 450 staffers and can be grouped by the functions they perform:

- Policy Coordination: National Security Affairs, Domestic Policy, Legislative Affairs, Presidential Personnel, and Counsel's Office
- Outreach and Communications. Press Secretary, Strategic Planning Communications (including speech writing and research), Speech Writing, Public Liaison, Intergovernmental Affairs, and Political Affairs
- Internal Coordination: Chief of Staff, Staff Secretary, Cabinet Affairs, Management and Administration (including the Military Office), and Scheduling and Advance.

In addition, the Office of the First Lady is located within the WHO. It has grown over the years to include a sizable staff. [See Women and the Executive Branch.]

Senior advisers to the president, sometimes given the title of counselor, may also be included in the WHO, depending on presidential preference. The staffs of the assistant to the president for national security affairs and the domestic policy adviser are located organizationally in the EOP, but in fact they work for their superiors in the WHO.

POLICY COORDINATION

The policy coordination offices ensure that narrower departmental perspectives and turf do not prevail over the president's priorities.

Assistant to the President for National Security Affairs

The National Security Act of 1947 created the National Security Council (NSC) and established the position of executive secretary to head it; the position was elevated to that of assistant to the president by President Eisenhower. This adviser to the president wields considerable authority throughout the executive branch in military and international affairs. The power of the national security adviser reached its apogee during the Nixon administration when Henry Kissinger's control of foreign policy making overshadowed the advisory roles of the secretaries of state and defense.

The NSC staff grew from a few administrative aides in the early 1950s to fifty foreign policy professionals in the 1980s, with a total staff of 150–200. The NSC staff, housed in the Old Executive Office Building, has been accused of dominating foreign policy advice to the president to the exclusion of the secretaries of state and defense. The rivalry between the NSC staff and the departments was considerably lessened during the Bush and Clinton administrations. The NSC staff functions as an umbrella for the president's closest foreign policy advisers, providing a forum for policy advice and a center for policy formulation. Most of the NSC staff are considered to be part of the EOP, with only the top few aides belonging to the WHO.

Domestic Policy Advisor

Presidents Kennedy and Johnson had some of their White House aides specialize in domestic policy development to coordinate their activist domestic agendas. This White House capacity was formalized and expanded considerably by Richard Nixon when he created the Domestic Policy Council in 1970. John Ehrlichman put together a staff of sixty–seventy domestic policy professionals to enable the White House to develop policy independent of the domestic departments and agencies. Even though the name has changed in different administrations, a domestic policy staff capacity has existed in the White House since the 1960s. The staff aides are in the WHO and supporting staff are officially in the EOP.

Office of Legislative Affairs

President Eisenhower formalized White House relations with Congress by creating the Office of Congressional Relations (now Legislative Affairs). This office is charged with staying in touch with the president's partisans on Capitol Hill and being on top of all issues involving the president's legislative agenda. Members of this office count votes for the president. While they occasionally trade favors for votes, their main duties are to keep open lines of communications between the White House and the Hill, particularly with members of the president's party.

Office of Presidential Personnel

Before the 1960s recruitment of political appointees was done primarily by the political parties. While the top cabinet positions were, of course, handled by the president and his top aides, most lower-level political appointees were recruited by cabinet secretaries in conjunction with the president's political party. But with the decline of political parties and the increasing need for policy expertise in the government, presidents began to do more political recruiting with their top aides. The few White House aides were replaced by the White House Personnel Office in the 1970s and by the Office of Presidential Personnel, headed by an assistant to the president, in the 1980s. The Office of Presidential Personnel now is an entrenched and important part of the WHO and is responsible for more than five thousand presidential appointments.

Counsel's Office

The president used to receive most legal advice from the attorney general, but as the legal implications of the president's duties have expanded, the legal advice function has gravitated to the White House. The title of counsel to the president in the Roosevelt and Truman administrations meant trusted top-level advisers but nowadays includes a legal staff that coordinates all presidential legal issues, advises on ethical and conflict-of-interest issues, and advises on judicial selection. The counsel is the president's lawyer for official purposes.

COMMUNICATIONS AND OUTREACH

The offices charged with outreach and communications primarily provide advice to the president and mostly do not have the independent power or staff to prevail over departments and agencies.

Press Secretary

Ever since President Hoover designated one staffer to be his spokesman, the job of the presidential press secretary has been to deal with the host of questions from journalists who want to know about the president's personal life as well as public policy issues. In addition to dealing with the press, the press secretary's office helps prepare the president for news conferences and puts the president's "spin" on news events.

Office of Communications

The task of the Office of Communications is to coordinate the administration's overall political message. It is particularly concerned with actively projecting the administration's perspective to the media, circumventing the national media (which tend to be critical) and reaching out instead to regional and local news media outlets.

Speech Writing

Because they must give many more speeches than they can possibly compose themselves, modern presidents have come to rely on the work of the speech writing office. Major policy statements and speeches are also drafted by speech writers and are cleared with all of the appropriate policy officials in the White House and departments.

Office of Public Liaison

Presidents from Franklin Roosevelt to Lyndon Johnson had White House staffers charged with providing liaison with different groups from the president's electoral coalition. These *ad hoc* approaches to building presidential coalitions were formalized in the White House when President Ford created the Office of Public Liaison. The purpose of the office is to help organize the political activities of groups (whether religious, business, labor, ethnic, or other social or interest groups) which might support presidential initiatives. It is the focus of contacts of most interest groups with the White House.

Intergovernmental Affairs

The function of the Office of Intergovernmental Affairs, established by Dwight Eisenhower, is to provide access to the president for governors, mayors, and other state and local officials. It reflects an increasing attention to concerns of state and local governments as well as the large role that the federal government plays in funding and regulating the activities of other units in the federal system.

Office of Political Affairs

The creation of the Office of Political Affairs by President Reagan underscored the fact that presidents want partisan political advisers close to them in the White House. With the decline of political parties, presidential candidates have had to put together a personal organization to capture the nomination. Once elected, presidents tend to keep together the team that ran the campaign and to use them if they choose to run for reelection. The Bush and Clinton administrations followed Reagan's precedent in regard to this office.

INTERNAL COORDINATION

The offices charged with internal coordination ensure that all of the units of the bureaucracy work together as smoothly as possible. Two offices originally created by President Eisenhower provide some of that necessary coordination. The staff secretary controls the paper flow to the president and ensures that all presidential paperwork is in order. The assistant to the president for cabinet affairs provides liaison and coordination for cabinet secretaries and the White House staff and does the preparation and follow-through for all cabinet meetings. The Office of Management and Administration deals with personnel administration, office space, and the other routine administrative chores necessary for running the White House offices. The Advance and Scheduling Office provides for the preparation for all presidential travel and cooperates with the Secret Service to ensure that presidential trips run smoothly. The Executive Residence staff cares for routine functioning of the White House. The task of ensuring that all of the separate units of the WHO function smoothly in the service of the president falls to the chief of staff, the one person short of the president who is in charge of White House operations and administration policy.

[*See also* Advising the President; National Security Council; President, Executive Office of the; Presidential Personnel, Office of; *and* Appendix: Executive Order No. 8248.]

BIBLIOGRAPHY

Burke, John P. *The Institutional Presidency.* Baltimore, Md., 1992.

Hart, John. *The Presidential Branch.* 2d ed. Chatham, NJ: 1995.

Heclo, Hugh. "The Changing Presidential Office." In *Politics and the Oval Office,* edited by Arnold J. Meltsner. San Francisco, 1981.

Hess, Stephen. *Organizing the Presidency.* 2d ed. Washington, D.C., 1988.

Kernell, Samuel. "The Evolution of the White House Staff." In *Can the Government Govern?,* edited by John E. Chubb and Paul E. Peterson. Washington, D.C., 1989.

Moe, Terry. "The Politicized Presidency." In *The New Direction in American Politics,* edited by John E. Chubb and Paul E. Peterson. Washington, D.C., 1985.

Patterson, Bradley. *Ring of Power.* New York, 1988.

Pfiffner, James P. *The Modern Presidency.* New York, 1994.

Walcott, Charles E., and Karen M. Hult. *Governing the White House.* Lawrence, Kans., 1995.

—JAMES P. PFIFFNER

Women and the Executive Branch

ESSAY It is only in the twentieth century that women have begun to play a prominent role in the executive branch. While women had filled clerical posts in the federal government, not until 1912 was the first woman appointed to a top-level executive branch post: Julia Lathrop, appointed by President William Howard Taft to head the Children's Bureau. With women's suffrage in 1920, presidents began to take note of this new constituency and a few more women began to be appointed to posts in executive branch departments and agencies. Additionally, women's suffrage also helped prod Congress into establishing a permanent Women's Bureau in the Department of Labor. The Women's Bureau, established in 1920 to investigate working conditions for women, was a successor to "Women in Industry Service," which had come into being in 1918 in response to the mobilization of women into the work force during World War I to meet defense and production needs.

The social welfare legislation of Franklin D. Roosevelt's New Deal both resulted from women serving in influential posts in the administration, including the first woman appointed to head a cabinet department, Frances Perkins as secretary of labor, and attracted women to the Democratic party who worked to get Roosevelt elected in 1932, and subsequently helped get Roosevelt's legislative program passed. This important constituency of the Democratic party was rewarded with a number of political appointments, including "26% of all postmasterships by 1938" (Deckard, p. 291), and posts in several departments and new agencies. While Frances Perkins did help bring women into the Department of Labor, she did not name any women to head major divisions in the department, since it was thought that with a woman heading the department, it would be better not to appoint any more women to major policy posts in the department.

THE CAREER FEDERAL SERVICE

Women faced legal barriers against working in the career federal service from 1870 until 1962, with some jobs classified on the basis of sex. President John F. Kennedy's Presidential Commission on the Status of Women, chaired by Eleanor Roosevelt, convinced Kennedy to work toward ending sex discrimination in the civil service, and an executive order was issued in 1962 "to all federal agencies requiring them to make selections for appointments, advancement, and training without regard to sex, except in a few unusual circumstances justified by the Civil Service Commission (which ruled that women could be excluded from jobs requiring the use of firearms)" (Peterson, p. 29).

Women's advancement through the ranks of the federal civil service, while slow, has seen some progress. Throughout the 1970s and 1980s, more than seventy percent of those working in the lowest civil service pay grades (mostly clerical and secretarial jobs) were women, and, as of 1970, only 1.4 percent of the highest grade posts (GS 16–18) were held by women. But by 1991 the percentage of women in the highest grades had increased to 9.1 percent.

The specialized ranks of the Foreign Service and career military service have placed additional hurdles in the advancement of women. In fact, efforts had begun under President Harry S. Truman to make the Foreign Service more representative of the American people by including women. While there was a gradual increase in the percentage of women in the Foreign Service, obstacles remained to women's entrance as well as progression through the ranks, as reflected in the 1976 class action lawsuit filed by Allison Palmer and the Women's Action Organization against the State Department for "discriminatory practices including administration of the Foreign Service Exam, assignments, evaluations, and awards" (McGlen and Sarkees, 1993, p. 199). In the past twenty years there have been a number of court decisions in Palmer's favor, with resulting changes in the evaluation process of Foreign Service officers.

In the military service, under President Clinton there has been some easing of combat restriction rules for women, both in allowing women to fly combat planes and serve on combat ships, which will enable women to gain the military experience needed to progress up the career ladder in both the military as well as the civilian policy-making posts in the Defense Department. Clinton's appointment of Sheila Widnall as secretary of the Air Force in 1993 marked the first time a woman was named to head a branch of the armed forces.

APPOINTIVE POSITIONS

Only in the last twenty years have women made appreciable gains in receiving appointments to high-level, Senate-confirmed positions in the executive departments, agencies, and on regulatory commissions. For instance, during the period from 1933 until 1965, only 12 of 1,041 appointments made by presidents to such posts went to women. After Frances Perkins was named secretary of labor in 1933, it took twenty years before a second woman was appointed to the cabinet, Oveta Culp Hobby, secretary of the Department of Health, Education, and Welfare under President Eisenhower, and another twenty-two years until a third woman was appointed, Carla Anderson Hills, named by President Ford to serve as secretary of the Department of Housing and Urban Development in 1975. Of more than six hundred appointments to posts as cabinet secretaries or attorneys general in the last two hundred years, only sixteen appointments had gone to women as of the beginning of 1996.

Since the 1960s there has been a gradual increase in the numbers of women serving in the highest-level appointive posts. For example, in the Kennedy administration, women held but 2.1 percent of all appointments to high-level, full-time, Senate-confirmed positions in the cabinet departments, independent agencies, and on regulatory commissions and boards. By comparison, in the first two years of the Clinton administration women had received 30.5 percent of such appointments.

In recent years women's advancement to high-level posts has benefited from intense activity on the part of the Coalition for Women's Appointments of the National Women's Political Caucus in suggesting candidates and lobbying each new administration for the inclusion of women. This activity parallels earlier efforts on the part of a "network" of women who during the 1930s "recruited women for prominent positions, demanded increased political patronage, and generally fostered an awareness of women as a special interest group with a substantial role to play in the New Deal" (Ware, p. 7). The women's network included Eleanor Roosevelt, who did much to advance the appointment of women and issues of concern to women on the president's agenda, Molly Dewson, the head of the Women's Division of the Democratic party, who played a major role in getting women constituents into political appointments, and Frances Perkins. The creation of new social welfare agencies during the New Deal, such as the Works Progress Administration, the Social Security Administration, and the National Recovery Administration, gave opportunities for women to move into positions not viewed as being held only by men. The Truman administration's use of the Democratic party's Women's Division in providing names of women for consideration also helped further the advancement of women.

THE WHITE HOUSE OFFICE

The modern presidency has seen a tremendous growth in the institutionalization of the presidency, with a growing Executive Office of the President (EOP) and White House Office in the EOP. However, not until 1967 was a woman included in the White House Office in a policy role: Betty Furness, special assistant to the president for consumer affairs under President Lyndon B. Johnson. While the number of women holding posts in the White House Office has increased, especially during the Carter and Clinton administrations, and women have served as "assistant to the president," the highest title, women have tended to serve in the offices of Personnel/Administration, Congressional Liaison, and Political Affairs/Public Liaison, rather than in the major foreign, domestic, and economic policy posts. No woman has served as national security adviser as of 1996, but Karna Small was deputy assistant to the president for national security affairs and senior director for public affairs on the National Security Council under President Ronald Reagan, the first woman to serve in a foreign policy position in the White House. In 1993, under President Clinton, Laura D'Andrea Tyson became the first woman to chair the Council of Economic Advisers, and subsequently was named chair of the National Economic Council in the White House.

THE OFFICE OF THE FIRST LADY

In looking at women and the executive branch, one post is unlike any other—that of the First Lady. While the First Lady is viewed as a public official, she is not elected, has no constitutional or statutory responsibilities, and receives no salary. Since the administration of President Theodore Roosevelt, First Ladies have had a clerk or social secretary for official correspondence, but the position was not viewed as part of the institutionalized presidency. However, beginning in the 1950s during the Eisenhower administration, the Office of the First Lady began to be recognized, with the inclusion of Mary McCaffree as "Acting Secretary to the President's Wife," in the *Congressional Directory*'s listing of top White House personnel. Twenty years later, in 1978, Congress for the first time authorized personnel assistance to be provided to the spouse of the president and spouse of the vice president "when such spouses are assisting the President or Vice President, respectively, in carrying out their duties" (P.L. 95-570).

In recent administrations First Ladies have taken on substantive policy roles. Pat Nixon served as the official representative of the president on a trip to Africa in 1972, in which she met and conferred with several heads of state. Eleanor Roosevelt, Rosalynn Carter, and Hillary Clinton all testified before congressional committees on public policy issues. Rosalynn Carter, with her service as chair of a commission on mental health and attendance at cabinet meetings, advanced the role of First Spouse as a policy activist. Hillary Clinton's work as chair of a health care task force, a major legislative agenda item of the Clinton presidency, has caused debate as to the institutionalization of a policy advisory role for the First Spouse that has yet to be resolved.

Throughout the twentieth century the role of women in the executive branch has been expanded from the inclusion of a few women as "tokens" in high-level posts to women fulfilling greater symbolic and substantive roles as their numbers and positions of power increase. The impact of the greater inclusion of women in the executive branch, a late twentieth-century phenomenon, in a substantive policy sense and in terms of understanding gender and political leadership is only now being studied.

BIBLIOGRAPHY

Borrelli, MaryAnne, and Janet M. Martin, eds. *The Other Elites: Women, Politics, and Power in the Executive Branch.* Boulder, Colo., 1997.

Burrell, Barbara. "The Office of the First Lady and Public Policy Making." In *The Other Elites: Women, Politics, and Power in the Executive Branch,* edited by MaryAnne Borrelli and Janet M. Martin. Boulder, Colo., 1997.

Deckard, Barbara Sinclar. *The Women's Movement.* 3d ed. New York, 1983.

Duerst-Lahti, Georgia, and Rita Mae Kelly, eds. *Gender Power, Leadership, and Governance.* Ann Arbor, Mich., 1995.

Harrison, Cynthia. *On Account of Sex: The Politics of Women's Issues, 1945–1968.* Berkeley, Calif., 1988.

Martin, Janet M. "Women Who Govern: The President's Appointments." In *The Other Elites: Women, Politics, and Power in the Executive Branch,* edited by MaryAnne Borrelli and Janet M. Martin. Boulder, Colo., 1997.

Matthews, Glenna. *The Rise of Public Woman: Woman's Power and Woman's Place in the United States, 1630–1970.* New York, 1992.

McGlen, Nancy E., and Meredith Reid Sarkees. *Women in Foreign Policy: The Insiders.* New York, 1993.

McGlen, Nancy, and Meredith Sarkees. "Style Does Matter: The Impact of Presidential Leadership on Women in Foreign Policy." In *The Other Elites: Women, Politics, and Power in the Executive Branch,* edited by MaryAnne Borrelli and Janet M. Martin. Boulder, Colo., 1997.

Peterson, Esther. "The Kennedy Commission." In *Women in Washington,* edited by Irene Tinker. Beverly Hills, Calif., 1983.

Skocpol, Theda. *Protecting Soldiers and Mothers: The Political Origins of Social Policy in the United States.* Cambridge, Mass., 1992.

Stanley, David T., Dean E. Mann, and Jameson W. Doig. *Men Who Govern.* Washington, D.C., 1967.

Tenpas, Kathryn Dunn. "Women on the White House Staff: A Longitudinal Analysis, 1939–1994." In *The Other Elites: Women, Politics, and Power in the Executive Branch,* edited by MaryAnne Borrelli and Janet M. Martin. Boulder, Colo., 1997.

Ware, Susan. *Beyond Suffrage: Women in the New Deal.* Cambridge, Mass., 1981.

—JANET M. MARTIN

Appendix

Basic Documents of
Public Administration

U.S. political history began with a document—the Constitution—and American administrative history has been propelled and guided by the creation of ever more documents. Such documents serve two purposes: First, they have a descriptive function, dealing with government as it is. They survey the administrative terrain, clarify the organizational levels and structures of government, and identify the channels of communication and the flow of authority. Second, they have a prescriptive function, dealing with government as it ought to be. They identify problem areas, suggest reforms, and, to use a recent term, reinvent or reengineer government. The evolution of government is thus best illustrated by these documents, which number several hundred over the course of the last 220 years. Extracts from the more important of these documents are reproduced in the appendix. Many of them, such as the Pendleton Act, have had enduring influence on the very concepts, values, doctrines, techniques, and philosophies undergirding government. Those documents that are covered by an article in the body of *A Historical Guide to the U.S. Government,* such as the Brownlow Committee Report and the National Performance Review, are not reproduced here.

■ An Act for Establishing an Executive Department, To Be Denominated the Department of Foreign Affairs, July 27, 1789

SECTION 1. *Be it enacted by the Senate and House of Representatives of the United States of America in Congress assembled,* That there shall be an Executive department, to be denominated the Department of Foreign Affairs, and that there shall be a principal officer therein, to be called the Secretary for the Department of Foreign Affairs, who shall perform and execute such duties as shall from time to time be enjoined on or instructed to him by the President of the United States, agreeable to the Constitution, relative to correspondences, commissions or instructions to or with public ministers or consuls, from the United States, or to negotiations with public ministers from foreign states or princes, or to memorials or other applications from foreign public ministers or other foreigners, or to such other matters respecting foreign affairs, as the President of the United States shall assign to the said department; and furthermore, that the said principal officer shall conduct the business of the said department in such manner as the President of the United States shall from time to time order or instruct.

SEC. 2. *And be it further enacted,* That there shall be in the said department, an inferior officer, to be appointed by the said principal officer, and to be employed therein as he shall deem proper, and to be called the chief Clerk in the Department of Foreign Affairs, and who, whenever the said principal officer shall be removed from office by the President of the United States, or in any other case of vacancy, shall during such vacancy have the charge and custody of all records, books, and papers appertaining to the said department.

SEC. 3. *And be it further enacted,* That the said principal officer, and every other person to be appointed or employed in the said department, shall, before he enters on the execution of his office or employment, take an oath or affirmation, well and faithfully to execute the trust committed to him.

SEC. 4. *And be it further enacted,* That the Secretary for the Department of Foreign Affairs, to be appointed in consequence of this act, shall forthwith after his appointment, be entitled to have the custody and charge of all records, books, and papers in the office of Secretary for the Department of Foreign Affairs, heretofore established by the United States in Congress assembled.

■ An Act To Establish an Executive Department, To Be Denominated the Department of War, August 7, 1789

SECTION 1. *Be it enacted by the Senate and House of Representatives of the United States of America in Congress assembled,* That there shall be an executive department to be denominated the Department of War, and that there shall be a principal officer therein, to be called the Secretary for the Department of War, who shall perform and execute such duties as shall from time to time be enjoined on, or entrusted to him by the President of the United States, agreeably to the Constitution, relative to military commissions, or to the land or naval forces, ships, or warlike stores of the United States, or to such other matters respecting military or naval affairs, as the President of the United States shall assign to the said department, or relative to the granting of lands to persons entitled thereto, for military services rendered to the United States, or relative to Indian affairs; and furthermore, that the said principal officer shall conduct the business of the said department in such manner, as the President of the United States shall from time to time order or instruct.

SEC. 2. *And be it further enacted,* That there shall be in the said department an inferior officer, to be appointed by the said principal officer, to be employed therein as he shall deem proper, and to be called the chief clerk in the department of war, and who, whenever the said principal officer shall be removed from office by the President of the United States, or in any other case of vacancy, shall, during such vacancy, have the charge and custody of all records, books, and papers, appertaining to the said department.

SEC. 3. *And be it further enacted,* That the said principal officer, and every other person to be appointed or employed in the said department, shall, before he enters on the execution of his office or employment, take an oath or affirmation well and faithfully to execute the trust committed to him.

SEC. 4. *And be it further enacted,* That the Secretary for the department of war, to be appointed in consequence of this act, shall forthwith after his appointment, be entitled to have the custody and charge of all records, books, and papers in the office of Secretary for the department of war, heretofore established by the United States in Congress assembled.

■ An Act To Establish the Treasury Department, September 2, 1789

SECTION 1. *Be it enacted by the Senate and House of Representatives of the United States of America in Congress assembled,* That there shall be a Department of Treasury, in which shall be the following officers, namely: A Secretary of the Treasury, to be deemed head of the department; a Comptroller, an Auditor, a Treasurer, a Register, and an Assistant to the Secretary of the Treasury, which assistant shall be appointed by the said Secretary.

SEC. 2. *And be it further enacted,* That it shall be the duty of the Secretary of the Treasury to digest and prepare plans for the improvement and management of the revenue, and for the support of public credit; to prepare and report estimates of the public revenue, and the public expenditures; to superintend the collection of the revenue; to decide on the forms of keeping and stating accounts and making returns, and to grant under the limitations herein established, or to be hereafter provided, all warrants for monies to be issued from the Treasury, in pursuance of appropriations by law; to execute such services relative to the sale of the lands belonging to the United States, as may be by law required of him; to make report, and give information to either branch of the legislature, in person or in writing (as he may be required), respecting all matters referred to him by the Senate or House of Representatives, or which shall appertain to his office; and generally to perform all such services relative to the finances, as he shall be directed to perform.

SEC. 3. *And be it further enacted,* That it shall be the duty of the Comptroller to superintend the adjustment and preservation of the public accounts; to examine all accounts settled by the Auditor, and certify the balances arising thereon to the Register; to countersign all warrants drawn by the Secretary of the Treasury, which shall be warranted by law; to report to the Secretary the official forms of all papers to be issued in the different offices for collecting the public revenue, and the manner and form of keeping and stating the accounts of the several persons employed therein. He shall moreover provide for the regular and punctual payment of all monies which may be collected, and shall direct prosecutions for all delinquencies of officers of the revenue, and for debts that are, or shall be due to the United States.

SEC. 4. *And be it further enacted,* That it shall be the duty of the Treasurer to receive and keep the monies of the United States, and to disburse the same upon warrants drawn by the Secretary of the Treasury, countersigned by the Comptroller, recorded by the Register, and not otherwise; he shall take receipts for all monies paid by him, and all receipts for monies received by him shall be endorsed upon warrants signed by the Secretary of the Treasury, without which warrant, so signed, no acknowledgment for money received into the public Treasury shall be valid. And the said Treasurer shall render his accounts to the Comptroller quarterly, (or oftener if required), and shall transmit a copy thereof, when settled, to the Secretary of the Trea-

sury. He shall moreover, on the third day of every session of Congress, lay before the Senate and House of Representatives, fair and accurate copies of all accounts by him from time (to time) rendered to, and settled with the Comptroller as aforesaid, as also, a true and perfect account of the state of the Treasury. He shall, at all times, submit to the Secretary of the Treasury, and the Comptroller, or either of them, the inspections of the monies in his hands; and shall, prior to the entering upon the duties of his office, give bond, with sufficient sureties, to be approved by the Secretary of the Treasury and Comptroller, in the sum of one hundred and fifty thousand dollars, payable to the United States, with condition for the faithful performance of the duties of his office, and for the fidelity of the persons to be by him employed, which bond shall be lodged in the office of the Comptroller of the Treasury of the United States.

SEC. 5. *And be it further enacted,* That it shall be the duty of the Auditor to receive all public accounts, and after examination to certify the balance, and transmit the accounts with the vouchers and certificates to the Comptroller for his decision thereon: *Provided,* That if any person whose account shall be so audited, be dissatisfied therewith, he may within six months appeal to the Comptroller against such settlement.

SEC. 6. *And be it further enacted,* That it shall be the duty of the Register to keep all accounts of the receipts and expenditures of the public money, and of all debts due to or from the United States; to receive from the Comptroller the accounts which shall have been finally adjusted, and to preserve such accounts with their vouchers and certificates; to record all warrants for the receipt or payment of monies at the Treasury, certify the same thereon, and to transmit to the Secretary of the Treasury, copies of the certificates of balances of accounts adjusted as is herein directed.

SEC. 7. *And be it further enacted,* That whenever the Secretary shall be removed from office by the President of the United States, or in any other case of vacancy in the office of Secretary, the Assistant shall, during the vacancy, have the charge and custody of the records, books, and papers appertaining to the said office.

SEC. 8. *And be it further enacted,* That no person appointed to any office instituted by this act, shall directly or indirectly be concerned or interested in carrying on the business of trade or commerce, or be owner in whole or in part of any sea-vessel, or purchase by himself, or another in trust for him, any public lands or other public property, or be concerned in the purchase or disposal of any public securities of any state or of the United States, or take or apply to his own use, any emolument or gain for negotiating or transacting any business in the said department, other than what shall be allowed by law; and if any person shall offend against any of the prohibitions of this act, he shall be deemed guilty of a high misdemeanor, and forfeit to the United States the penalty of three thousand dollars, and shall upon conviction be removed from office, and forever thereafter incapable of holding any office under the United States: *Provided*, That if any other person than a public prosecutor shall give information of any such offense, upon which a prosecution and conviction shall be had, one half the aforesaid penalty of three thousand dollars, when recovered, shall be for the use of the person giving such information.

■ An Act To Provide for the Safe-keeping of the Acts, Records and Seal of the United States, and for Other Purposes, September 15, 1789

SECTION 1. *Be it enacted by the Senate and House of Representatives of the United States of America in Congress assembled,* That the Executive department, denominated the Department of Foreign Affairs, shall hereafter be denominated the Department of State, and the principal officer therein shall hereafter be called the Secretary of State.

SEC. 2. *And be it further enacted,* That whenever a bill, order, resolution, or vote of the Senate and House of Representatives, having been approved and signed by the President of the United States, or not having been returned by him with his objections, shall become a law, or take effect, it shall forthwith thereafter be received by the said Secretary from the President; and whenever a bill, order, resolution, or vote, shall be returned by the President with his objections, and shall, on being reconsidered be agreed to be passed, and be approved by two-thirds of both Houses of Congress, and thereby become a law or take effect, it shall, in such case, be received by the said Secretary from the President of the Senate, or the speaker of the House of Representatives, in whichsoever House it shall last have been so approved; and the said Secretary shall, as soon as conveniently may be, after he shall receive the same, cause every such law, order, resolution, and vote, to be published in at least three of the public newspapers printed within the United States, and shall also cause one printed copy to be delivered to each Senator and Representative of the United States, and two printed copies duly authenticated to be sent to the Executive authority of each State; and he shall carefully preserve the Originals, and shall cause the same to be recorded in books to be provided for the purpose.

SEC. 3. *And be it further enacted,* That the seal heretofore used by the United States in Congress assembled, shall be, and hereby is declared to be, the seal of the United States.

SEC. 4. *And be it further enacted,* That the said Secretary shall keep the said seal, and shall make out and record, and shall affix the said seat to all civil commissions, to officers of the United States, to be appointed by the President by and with the advice and consent of the Senate, or by the President alone. *Provided,* That the said seal shall not be affixed to any commission, before the same shall have been signed by the President of the United States, nor to any other instrument or act, without the special warrant of the President therefor.

■ An Act To Establish the Judicial Courts of the United States, September 24, 1789

. . .

SEC. 35. *And be it further enacted,* That in all courts of the United States, the parties may plead and manage their own causes personally or by the assistance of such counsel or attorneys at law as by the rules of the said courts respectively shall be permitted to manage and conduct causes therein. And there shall be appointed in each district a meet person learned in the law to act as attorney for the United States in such district, who shall be sworn or affirmed to the faithful executions of his office, whose duty it shall be to prosecute in such district all delinquents for crimes and offenses, cognizable under the authority of the United States, and all civil actions in which the United States shall be concerned, except before the Supreme Court in the district in which that court shall be holden. And he shall receive as a compensation for his services such fees as shall be taxed therefor in the respective courts before which the suits or prosecutions shall be. And there shall also be appointed a meet person, learned in the law, to act as attorney-general for the United States, who shall be sworn or affirmed to a faithful execution of his office; whose duty it shall be to prosecute and conduct all suits in the Supreme Court in which the United States shall be concerned, and to give his advice and opinion upon questions of law when required by the President of the United States, or when requested by the heads of any of the departments, touching any matters that may concern their departments, and shall receive such compensation for his services as shall by law be provided.

■ Civil Service (Pendleton) Act (1883)
An Act To Regulate and Improve the Civil Service of the United States

Be it enacted by the Senate and House of Representatives of the United States of America in Congress assembled, That the President is authorized to appoint, by and with the advice and consent of the Senate, three persons, not more than two of whom shall be adherents of the same party, as Civil Service Commissioners, and said three commissioners shall constitute the United States Civil Service Commission. Said commissioners shall hold no other official place under the United States.

The President may remove any commissioner; and any vacancy in the position of commissioner shall be so filled by the President, by and with the advice and consent of the Senate, as to conform to said conditions for the first selection of commissioners.

The commissioners shall each receive a salary of three thousand five hundred dollars a year. And each of said commissioners shall be paid his necessary traveling expenses incurred in the discharge of his duty as a commissioner.

SEC. 2. That it shall be the duty of said commissioners:

First. To aid the President, as he may request, in preparing suitable rules for carrying this act into effect, and when said rules shall have been promulgated it shall be the duty of all officers of the United States in the departments and offices to which any such rules may relate to aid, in all proper ways, in carrying said rules, and any modifications thereof, into effect.

Second. And, among other things, said rules shall provide and declare, as nearly as the conditions of good administration will warrant, as follows:

First, for open, competitive examinations for testing the fitness of applicants for the public service now classified or to be classified hereunder. Such examinations shall be practical in their character, and so far as may be shall relate to those matters which will fairly test the relative capacity and fitness of the persons examined to discharge the duties of the service into which they seek to be appointed.

Second, that all the offices, places, and employments so arranged or to be arranged in classes shall be filled by selections according to grade from among those graded highest as the results of such competitive examinations.

Third, appointments to the public service aforesaid in the departments at Washington shall be apportioned among the several States and Territories and the District of Columbia upon the basis of population as ascertained at the last preceding census. Every application for an examination shall contain, among other things, a statement, under oath, setting forth his or her actual bona fide residence at the time of making the application, as well as how long he or she has been a resident of such place.

Fourth, that there shall be a period of probation before any absolute appointment or employment aforesaid.

Fifth, that no person in the public service is for that reason under any obligations to contribute to any political fund, or to render any political service, and that he will not be removed or otherwise prejudiced for refusing to do so.

Sixth, that no person in said service has any right to use his official authority or influence to coerce the political action of any person or body.

Seventh, there shall be non-competitive examinations in all proper cases before the commission, when competent persons do not compete, after notice has been given of the existence of the vacancy, under such rules as may be prescribed by the commissioners as to the manner of giving notice.

Eighth, that notice shall be given in writing by the appointing power to said commission of the persons selected for appointment or employment from among those who have been examined, of the place of residence of such persons, of the rejection of any such persons after probation, of transfers, resignations, and removals, and of the date thereof, and a record of the same shall be kept by said commission. And any necessary exceptions from said eight fundamental provisions of the rules shall be set forth in connection with such rules, and the reasons therefor shall be stated in the annual reports of the commission.

Third. Said commission shall, subject to the rules that may be made by the President, make regulations for, and have control of, such examinations, and, through its members or the examiners, it shall supervise and preserve the records of the same; and said commission shall keep minutes of its own proceedings.

Fourth. Said commission may make investigations concerning the facts, and may report upon all matters touching the enforcement and effects of said rules and regulations, and concerning the action of any examiner or board of examiners hereinafter provided for, and its own subordinates, and those in the public service, in respect to the execution of this act.

Fifth. Said commission shall make an annual report to the President for transmission to Congress, showing its own action, the rules and regulations and the exceptions thereto in force, the practical effects thereof, and any suggestions it may approve for the more effectual accomplishment of the purposes of this act.

SEC. 3. That said commission is authorized to employ a chief examiner, a part of whose duty it shall be, under its direction, to act with the examining boards, so far as practicable, whether at Washington or elsewhere, and to secure accuracy, uniformity, and justice in all their proceedings, which shall be at all times open to him. The chief examiner shall be entitled to receive a salary at the rate of three thousand dollars a year, and he shall be paid his necessary traveling expenses incurred in the discharge of his duty. The commission shall have a secretary, to be appointed by the President, who shall receive a salary of one thousand six hundred dollars per annum. It may, when necessary, employ a stenographer, and a messenger, who shall be paid, when employed, the former at the rate of one thousand six hundred dollars a year, and the latter at the rate of six hundred dollars a year. The commission shall, at Washington, and in one or more places in each State and Territory where examinations are to take place, designate and select a suitable number of persons, not less than three, in the official service of the United States, residing in said State or Territory, after consulting the head of the department or office in which such persons serve, to be members of boards of examiners, and may at any time substitute any other person in said service living in such State or Territory in the place of any one so selected. Such boards of examiners shall be so located as to make it reasonably convenient and inexpensive for applicants to attend before them; and where there are persons to be examined in any State or Territory, examinations shall be held therein at least twice in each year. It shall be the duty of the collector, postmaster, and other officers of the United States, at any place outside of the District of Columbia where examinations are directed by the President or by said board to be held, to allow the reasonable use of the public buildings for holding such examinations, and in all proper ways to facilitate the same.

. . .

SEC. 5. That any said commissioner, examiner, copyist, or messenger, or any person in the public service who shall willfully and corruptly, by himself or in co-operation with one or more other persons, defeat, deceive, or obstruct any person in respect of his or her right of examination according to any such rules or regulations, or who shall willfully, corruptly, and falsely mark, grade, estimate, or report upon the examination or proper standing of any person examined hereunder, or aid in so doing, or who shall willfully and corruptly make any false representations concerning the same or concerning the person examined, or who shall willfully and corruptly furnish to any person any special or secret information for the purpose of either improving or injuring the prospects or chances of any person so examined, or to be examined, being appointed, employed, or promoted, shall for each such offense be deemed guilty of a misdemeanor, and upon conviction thereof, shall be punished by a fine of not less than one hundred dollars, nor more than one thousand dollars, or by imprisonment not less than ten days, nor more than one year, or by both such fine and imprisonment.

SEC. 6. That within sixty days after the passage of this act it shall be the duty of the Secretary of the Treasury, in as near conformity as may be to the classification of certain clerks now existing under the one hundred and sixty-third section of the Revised Statutes, to arrange in classes the several clerks and persons employed by the collector, naval officer, surveyor, and appraisers, or either of them, or being in the public service, at their respective offices in each customs district where the whole number of said clerks and persons shall be all together as many as fifty. And thereafter, from time to time, on the direction of the President, said Secretary shall make the like classification or arrange-

ment of clerks and persons so employed, in connection with any said office or offices, in any other customs district. And, upon like request, and for the purposes of this act, said Secretary shall arrange in one or more of said classes, or of existing classes, any other clerks, agents, or persons employed under his department in any said district not now classified; and every such arrangement and classification upon being made shall be reported to the President.

Second. Within said sixty days it shall be the duty of the Postmaster-General, in general conformity to said one hundred and sixty-third section, to separately arrange in classes the several clerks and persons employed, or in the public service, at each post-office, or under any postmaster of the United States, where the whole number of said clerks and persons shall together amount to as many as fifty. And thereafter, from time to time, on the direction of the President, it shall be the duty of the Postmaster-General to arrange in like classes the clerks and persons so employed in the postal service in connection with any other post-office; and every such arrangement and classification upon being made shall be reported to the President.

Third. That from time to time said Secretary, the Postmaster-General, and each of the heads of departments mentioned in the one hundred and fifty-eighth section of the Revised Statutes, and each head of an office, shall, on the direction of the President, and for facilitating the execution of this act, respectively revise any then existing classification or arrangement of those in their respective departments and offices, and shall, for the purposes of the examination herein provided for, include in one or more of such classes, so far as practicable, subordinate places, clerks, and officers in the public service pertaining to their respective departments not before classified for examination.

SEC. 7. That after the expiration of six months from the passage of this act no officer or clerk shall be appointed, and no person shall be employed to enter or be promoted in either of the said classes now existing, or that may be arranged hereunder pursuant to said rules, until he has passed an examination, or is shown to be specially exempted from such examination in conformity herewith. But nothing herein contained shall be construed to take from those honorably discharged from the military or naval service any preference conferred by the seventeen hundred and fifty-fourth section of the Revised Statutes, nor to take from the President any authority not inconsistent with this act conferred by the seventeen hundred and fifty-third section of said statutes; nor shall any officer not in the executive branch of the government, or any person merely employed as a laborer or workman, be required to be classified hereunder; nor, unless by direction of the Senate, shall any person who has been nominated for confirmation by the Senate be required to be classified or to pass an examination.

SEC. 8. That no person habitually using intoxicating beverages to excess shall be appointed to, or retained in, any office, appointment, or employment to which the provisions of this act are applicable.

SEC. 9. That whenever there are already two or more members of a family in the public service in the grades covered by this act, no other member of such family shall be eligible to appointment to any of said grades.

SEC. 10. That no recommendation of any person who shall apply for office or place under the provisions of this act which may be given by any Senator or member of the House of Representatives, except as to the character or residence of the applicant, shall be received or considered by any person concerned in making any examination or appointment under this act.

SEC. 11. That no Senator, or Representative, or Territorial Delegate of the Congress, or Senator, Representative, or Delegate elect, or any officer or employee of either of said houses, and no executive, judicial, military, or naval officer of the United States, and no clerk or employee of any department, branch or bureau of the executive, judicial, or military or naval service of the United States, shall, directly or indirectly, solicit or receive, or be in any manner concerned in soliciting or receiving, any assessment, subscription, or contribution for any political purpose whatever, from any officer, clerk, or employee of the United States, or any department, branch, or bureau thereof, or from any person receiving any salary or compensation from moneys derived from the Treasury of the United States.

SEC. 12. That no person shall, in any room or building occupied in the discharge of official duties by any officer or employee of the United States mentioned in this act, or in any navy-yard, fort, or arsenal, solicit in any manner whatever, or receive any contribution of money or any other thing of value for any political purpose whatever.

SEC. 13. No officer or employee of the United States mentioned in this act shall discharge, or promote, or degrade, or in manner change the official rank of compensation of any other officer or employee, or promise or threaten so to do, for giving or withholding or neglecting to make any contribution of money or other valuable thing for any political purpose.

SEC. 14. That no officer, clerk, or other person in the service of the United States shall, directly or indirectly, give or hand over to any other officer, clerk, or person in the service of the United States, or to any Senator or Member of the House of Representatives, or Territorial Delegate, any money or other valuable thing on account of or to be applied to the promotion of any political object whatever.

SEC. 15. That any person who shall be guilty of violating any provision of the four foregoing sections shall be deemed guilty of a misdemeanor, and shall, on conviction thereof, be punished by a fine not exceeding five thousand dollars, or by imprisonment for a term not exceeding three years, or by such fine and imprisonment both, in the discretion of the court.

■ Act To Regulate Commerce (1887)

. . .

SEC. 11. That a Commission is hereby created and established to be known as the Inter-State Commerce Commission, which shall be composed of five Commissioners, who shall be appointed by the President, by and with the advice and consent of the Senate. The Commissioners first appointed under this act shall continue in office for the term of two, three, four, five, and six years, respectively, from the first day of January, anno Domini eighteen hundred and eighty-seven, the term of each to be designated by the President; but their successors shall be appointed for terms of six years, except that any person chosen to fill a vacancy shall be appointed only for the unexpired term of the Commissioner whom he shall succeed. Any Commissioner may be removed by the President for inefficiency, neglect of duty, or malfeasance in office. Not more than three of the Commissioners shall be appointed from the same political party. No person in the employ of or holding any official relation to any common carrier subject to the provisions of this act, or owning stock or bonds thereof, or who is in any manner pecuniarily interested therein, shall enter upon the duties of or hold such office. Said Commissioners shall not engage in any other business, vocation, or employment. No vacancy in the commission shall impair the right of the remaining Commissioners to exercise all the powers of the Commission.

SEC. 12. That the Commission hereby created shall have authority to inquire into the management of the business of all common carriers subject to the provisions of this act, and shall keep itself informed as to the manner and method in which the same is conducted, and shall have the right to obtain from such common carriers full and complete information necessary to enable the Commission to perform the duties and carry out the objects for which it was created; and for the purposes of this act the Commission shall have power to require the attendance and testimony of witnesses and the production of all books, papers, tariffs, contracts, agreements, and documents relating to any matter under investigation, and to that end may invoke the aid of any court of the United States in requiring the attendance and testimony of witnesses and the production of all books, papers, and documents under the provisions of this section.

And any of the circuit courts of the United States within the jurisdiction of which such inquiry is carried on may, in case of contumacy or refusal to obey a subpoena issued to any common carrier subject to the provisions of this act, or other person, issue an order requiring such common carrier or other person to appear before said Commission (and produce books and papers if so ordered) and give evidence touching the matter in question, and any failure to obey such order of the court may be punished by such court as a contempt thereof. The claim that any such testimony or evidence may tend to criminate the person giving such evidence shall not excuse such witness from testifying; but such evidence or testimony shall not be used against such person in the trial of any criminal proceeding.

SEC. 13. That any person, firm, corporation, or association, or any mercantile, agricultural, or manufacturing society, or any body politic or municipal organization complaining of anything done or omitted to be done by any common carrier subject to the provisions of this act in contravention of the provisions thereof, may apply to said Commission by petition, which shall briefly state the facts; whereupon a statement of the charges thus made shall be forwarded by the Commission to such common carrier, who shall be called upon to satisfy the complaint or to answer the same in writing within a reasonable time, to be specified by the Commission. If such common carrier, within the time specified, shall make reparation for the injury alleged to have been done, said carrier shall be relieved of liability to the complainant only for the particular violation of law thus complained of. If such carrier shall not satisfy the complaint within the time specified, or there shall appear to be any reasonable ground for investigating said complaint, it shall be the duty of the Commission to investigate the matters complained of in such manner and by such means as it shall deem proper.

Said Commission shall in like manner investigate any complaint forwarded by the railroad commissioner or railroad commission of any State or Territory, at the request of such commissioner or commission, and may institute any inquiry on its own motion in the same manner and to the same effect as though complaint had been made.

No complaint shall at any time be dismissed because of the absence of direct damage to the complainant.

SEC. 14. That whenever an investigation shall be made by said Commission, it shall be its duty to make a report in writing in respect thereto, which shall include the findings of fact upon which the conclusions of the Commission are based, together with its recommendation as to what reparation, if any, should be made by the common carrier to any party or parties who may be found to have been injured; and such findings so made shall thereafter, in all judicial proceedings, be deemed prima facie evidence as to each and every fact found.

All reports of investigations made by the Commission shall be entered of record, and a copy thereof shall be furnished to the party who may have complained, and to any common carrier that may have been complained of.

SEC. 15. That if in any case in which an investigation shall be made by said Commission it shall be made to appear to the satisfaction of the Commission, either by the testimony of witnesses or other evidence, that anything has been done or omitted to be done in violation of the provisions of this act, or of any law cognizable by said Commission, by any common carrier, or that any injury or damage has been sustained by the party of parties complaining, or by other parties aggrieved in consequence of any such violation, it shall be the duty of the Commission to forthwith cause a copy of its report in respect thereto to be delivered to such common carrier, together with a notice to said common carrier to cease and desist from such violation, or to make reparation for the injury so found to have been done, or both, within a reasonable time, to be specified by the Commission; and if, within the time specified, it shall be made to appear to the Commission that such common carrier has ceased from such violation of law, and has made reparation for the injury found to have been done, in compliance with the report and notice of the Commission, or to the satisfaction of the party complaining, a statement to that effect shall be entered of record by the Commission, and the said common carrier shall thereupon be relieved from further liability or penalty for such particular violation of law.

SEC. 16. That whenever any common carrier, as defined in and subject to the provisions of this act, shall violate or refuse or neglect to obey any lawful order or requirement of the Commission in this act named, it shall be the duty of the Commission, and lawful for any company or person interested in such order or requirement, to apply, in a summary way, by petition, to the circuit court of the United States sitting in equity in the judicial district in which the common carrier complained of has its principal office, or in which the violation or disobedience of such order or requirement shall happen, alleging such violation or disobedience, as the case may be; and the said court shall have power to hear and determine the matter, on such short notice to the common carrier complained of as the court shall deem reasonable; and such notice may be served on such common carrier, his or its officers, agents, or servants, in such manner as the court shall direct; and said court shall proceed to hear and determine the matter speedily as a court of equity, and without the formal pleadings and proceedings applicable to ordinary suits in equity, but in such manner as to do justice in the premises; and to this end such court shall have power, if it think fit, to direct and prosecute, in such mode and by such persons as it may appoint, all such inquiries as the court may think needful to enable it to form a just judgment in the matter of such petition; and on such hearings the report of said Commission shall be prima facie evidence of the matters therein stated; and if it be made to appear to such court, on such hearing or on report of any such person or persons, that the lawful order or requirement of said Commission drawn in question has been violated or disobeyed, it shall be lawful for such court to issue a writ of injunction or other proper process, mandatory or otherwise, to restrain such common carrier from further continuing such violation or disobedience of such order or requirement of said Commission, and enjoining obedience to the same; and in case of any disobedience of any such writ of injunction or other proper process, mandatory or otherwise, it shall be lawful for such court to issue writs of attachment, or any other process of said court incident or applicable to writs of injunction or other proper process, mandatory or otherwise, against such common carrier, and if it be a corporation, against one or more of the directors, officers, or agents of the same, or against any owner, lessee, trustee, receiver, or other person failing to obey such writ of injunction or other proper process, mandatory or otherwise; and said court may, if it shall think fit, make all order directing such common carrier or other person so disobeying such writ of injunction or other proper process, mandatory or otherwise, to pay such sum of money not exceeding for each carrier or person in default the sum of five hundred dollars for every day after a day to be named in the order that such carrier or other person shall fail to obey such injunction or other proper process, mandatory or otherwise; and such moneys shall be payable as the court shall direct, either to the party complaining, or into court to abide the ultimate decision of the court, or into the treasury; and payment thereof may, without prejudice to any other mode of recovering the same, be enforced by attachment or order in the nature of a writ of execution, in like manner as if the same had been recovered by a final decree in personam in such court. When the subject in dispute shall be of the value of two thousand dollars or more, either party to such proceeding before said court may appeal to the Supreme Court of the United States, under the same regulations now provided by law in respect of security for such appeal; but such appeal shall not operate to stay or supersede the order of the court or the execution of any writ or process thereon; and such court may, in every such matter, order the payment of such costs and counsel fees as shall be deemed reasonable. Whenever any such petitions shall be filed or presented by the Commission it shall be the duty of the district attorney, under the direction of the Attorney-General of the United States, to prosecute the same; and the costs and expenses of such prosecution shall be paid out of the appropriation for the expenses of the courts of the United States. For the purposes of this act, excepting its penal provisions, the circuit courts of the United States shall be deemed to be always in session.

SEC. 17. That the Commission may conduct its proceedings in such manner as will best conduce to the proper dispatch of business and to the ends of justice. A majority of the Commission shall constitute a quorum for the transaction of business, but no Commissioner shall participate in any hearing or proceeding in which he has any pecuniary interest. Said Commission may, from time to time, make or amend such general rules or orders as may be requisite for the order and regulation of proceedings before it, including forms of notices and the service thereof, which shall conform, as nearly as may be, to those in use in the courts of the United States. Any party may appear before said Commission and be heard, in person or by attorney. Every vote and official act of the Commission shall be entered of record, and its proceedings shall be public upon the request of either party interested. Said Commission shall have an official seal, which shall be judicially noticed. Either of the members of the Commission may administer oaths and affirmations.

. . .

SEC. 20. That the Commission is hereby authorized to require annual reports from all common carriers subject to the provisions of this act, to fix the time and prescribe the manner in which such reports shall be made, and to require from such carriers specific answers to all questions upon which the Commission may need information. Such annual reports shall show in detail the amount of capital stock issued, the amounts paid therefor, and the manner of payment for the same; the dividends paid, the surplus fund, if any, and the number of stock-holders; the funded and floating debts and the interest paid thereon; the cost and value of the carrier's property, franchises, and equipment; the number of employees and the salaries paid each class; the amounts expended for improvements each year, how expended, and the character of such improvements; the earnings and receipts from each branch of business and from all sources; the operating and other expenses; the balances of profit and loss; and a complete exhibit of the financial operations of the carrier each year, including an annual balance-sheet. Such reports shall also contain such information in relation to rates or regulations concerning fares or freights, or agreements, arrangements, or contracts with other common carriers, as the Commission may require; and the said Commission may, within its discretion, for the purpose of enabling it the better to carry out the purposes of this act; prescribe (if in the opinion of the Commission it is practicable to prescribe such uniformity and methods of keeping accounts) a period of time within which all common carriers subject to the provisions of this act shall have, as near as may be, a uniform system of accounts, and the manner in which such accounts shall be kept.

SEC. 21. That the Commission shall, on or before the first day of December in each year, make a report to the Secretary of the Interior, which shall be by him transmitted to Congress, and copies of which shall be distributed as are the other reports issued from the Interior Department. This report shall contain such information and data collected by the Commission as may be considered of value in the determination of questions connected with the regulation of commerce, together with such recommendations as to additional legislation relating thereto as this Commission may deem necessary.

SEC. 22. That nothing in this act shall apply to the carriage, storage, or handling of property free or at reduced rates for the United States, State, or municipal governments, or for charitable purposes, or to or from fairs and expositions for exhibition thereat, or the issuance of mileage, excursion, or commutation passenger tickets; nothing in this act shall be construed to prohibit any common carrier from giving reduced rates to ministers of religion;

nothing in this act shall be construed to prevent railroads from giving free carriage to their own officers and employees, or to prevent the principal officers of any railroad company or companies from exchanging passes or tickets with other railroad companies for their officers and employees;

and nothing in this act contained shall in any way abridge or alter the remedies now existing at common law or by statute, but the provisions of this act are in addition to such remedies; *Provided*, That no pending litigation shall in any way be affected by this act.

■ Report of the (Taft) Commission on Economy and Efficiency (1912)

THE NEED FOR A NATIONAL BUDGET

June 19, 1912

The President:

The Commission on Economy and Efficiency has the honor to submit the following report on "The Need for a National Budget," and makes the following recommendations, each of which is fully discussed in Part 11 of this report.

RECOMMENDATIONS

The commission recommends:

1. That the President, as the constitutional head of the executive branch of the Government, shall each year submit to the Congress, not later than the first Monday after the beginning of the regular session, a budget.

2. That the budget so submitted shall contain:

(a) *A budgetary message*, setting forth in brief the significance of the proposals to which attention is invited.

(b) *A summary financial statement*, setting forth in very summary form: (1) the financial condition; (2) a statement of the condition of appropriations and other data pertaining to the "general fund" as well as to the other funds of the Government; (3) an account of revenues and expenditures for the last completed fiscal year; and (4) a statement showing the effect of past financial policy as well as of budget proposals on the general-fund surplus.

(c) *A summary of expenditures*, classified by objects, setting forth the contracting and purchasing relations of the Government.

(d) *Summaries of estimates*, setting forth: (1) the estimated revenues compared with actual revenues for a period of years; (2) estimated expenditures compared with actual expenditures for a period of years.

(e) *A summary of changes in law*, setting forth what legislation it is thought should be enacted in order to enable the administration to transact public business with greater economy and efficiency, i.e., changes in organic law which, if enacted, would affect appropriations as well as the character of work to be done.

3. That the Secretary of the Treasury be required to submit to the Congress the following detailed reports supporting the general summaries and Executive conclusions or recommendations contained in the budget, as follows:

(a) *A book of estimates*, containing the supporting details to the summaries of estimates of expenditure contained in the budget.

(b) *A consolidated financial report*, containing a detailed statement of revenues and a consolidated statement of expenditures by departments and establishments for the last five fiscal years, with such explanatory matter as is necessary to give information with respect to increases or decreases in revenue or expenditure or other relations to which it is thought that the attention of the executive and legislative branches is to be given.

4. That the head of each department and independent establishment should be required to submit to the Secretary of the Treasury and to the Congress annual reports which, among other things, would contain detailed accounts of expenditures so classified as to show amounts expended by appropriations, as well as by classes of work, together with the amounts of increases or decreases in stores, equipment, property, etc., including lands, buildings, and other improvements, as well as such other data or operative statistics and comment in relation thereto as may be necessary to show results obtained and the economy and efficiency of doing Government work, as well as of contracting and of purchasing.

5. That the President and heads of departments issue orders which will require that such accounts be kept, such reports be made, and such estimates be prepared as will enable them to obtain the information needed to consider the different conditions, relations, and results above enumerated before the estimates are submitted; that the President recommend to the Congress the enactment of such laws as will enable the administration to comply with the requirements of the Congress.

6. That the President recommend for the consideration of the Congress such changes in the form of appropriation bills as will enable the Government to avail itself of the benefits of the exercise of discretion on the part of the Executive in the transaction of current business in order that the Government may do work and accomplish results with economy and efficiency and as will definitely fix responsibility for failure so to exercise such discretion.

INTRODUCTION

If we follow the accepted usage of most civilized nations, we must conclude that a budget is a collection of documents assembled by an officer who is at the head of or is responsible for the administration and submitted to the legislative branch of the Government. Whatever else such a budget contains, in every case it carries with it an estimate of expenditures to be made by the Government during the coming financial period. While each nation has a revenue policy, the lack of emphasis which has been laid by nations in their budget upon the revenues and the relation of expenditures thereto has probably been due to the fact that by far the larger part of the revenues have come into the Public Treasury as the result of the operation of permanent law. No regular periodical action upon the part of the legislative authority has been necessary in order that revenues might be collected. As a consequence, the budget has been regarded primarily as an estimate of expenditures. Inasmuch, however, as no nation can safely adopt for a long period of policy of expenditures which has no regard to the amount of its revenues, it has been usual in most national governments to fix the amount of the expenditures in view of the expected revenue. Where, as is the case in this country, the estimates have been a matter of legislative rather than executive responsibility, the legislature has imposed upon the Treasury the duty of acquainting it with the estimated revenue for the coming budgetary period. It thus is the case that even in political systems in which revenues are based on permanent law rather than on periodical legislative action the demands of a conservative financial policy require that expenditures shall be estimated in view of revenue possibilities. We may say, therefore, that a budget should consist of estimates of revenue as well as of expenditures.

It has been said that a budget is primarily an estimate of the expenditures made necessary by the operations of the Government. That is, it is assumed that a government already exists which operates in a given way. A budget is based upon the theory that the Government for whose operations expenditures must be made is already organized and discharges certain activities whose number and extent have already been determined. The purpose of a budget is thus to finance an existing organization in order that it may successfully prosecute defined lines of work. In case it is thought desirable to have changes made in organization and in number and extent of activities, as compared with the organization and activities financed in the preceding budgetary period, these changes should be indicated at the time the budget is drawn up, and in any case, the changes must be determined before or at the time that appropriations are granted, since the appropriation is primarily a method of financing the existing organization and predefined activities.

Nevertheless since changes in organization and in number and extent of activities can hardly fail to affect expenditures, a budget, while primarily having to do with the expenditures made necessary by the defined operations of an existing governmental organization, must in the nature of things be concerned secondarily at any rate with questions of governmental organization and activities. It is, of course, to be borne in mind that other than financial considerations primarily control the decision of these questions, but it can not be forgotten that no State can enter upon an administrative program, however desirable, the expense of which its financial resources do not admit it to assume. Thus, a comprehensive naval program is entered upon for military and not for financial reasons. But if the resources of the country are insufficient the nation will have to forego the advantages of such a program, however marked they may be.

In this sense it may be said that a budget is in the nature of a prospectus and that its purporse is to present in summary form the facts necessary to the shaping of the policies of the Government so far as they affect its finances.

Budgetary practice has been influenced by the constitutional relations existing between the executive and legislative branches of government. Generally speaking, the executive authority (apart from the United States) has been conceived of as possessing powers of initiation and leadership while the legislative authority is regarded as possessing merely powers of final determination and control. In the United States, however, the legislature is usually regarded as the authority which initiates and determines a policy which it is the duty of the Executive to carry out. The effect of this conception of the relations of the Legislature to the Executive has been that the budget has been primarily an affair of the Congress rather than of the President. The Congress makes use of administrative officers in order to obtain the information which it must have to determine the important questions of policy devolved upon it by the American system. These administrative officers are acting as the ministerial agents of the Congress rather than as representatives of the President. The result is that while in most other countries the budget is in the nature of a proposal or program submitted on its responsibility by the executive to the legislature, in the United States the Book of Estimates, our nearest approach to a budget, is rather a more or less well-digested mass of information submitted by agents of the Legislature to the Legislature for the consideration of legislative committees to enable the Legislature both to originate and to determine the policy which is to be carried out by the Executive during the coming budgetary period.

DEFINITION AND PURPOSE OF THE BUDGET

As used in this report the budget is considered as a proposal to be prepared by the administration and submitted to the legislature. The use of a budget would require that there be a complete reversal of procedure by the Government—that the executive branch submit a statement to the Legislature which would be its account of stewardship as well as its proposals for the future. A national budget thus prepared and presented would serve the purposes of a prospectus. Its aim would be to present in summary form the facts necessary to shape the policy of the Government as well as to provide financial support. The summaries of fact included in the budget would also serve as a key or index to the details of transactions and of estimates which would be submitted with the budget or which would be contained in accounting records and reports.

An act of appropriation which follows a budget is a grant of money by the legislative branch to the executive branch of the Government. In the United States Government, in which the Congress habitually exercises the right to add to the estimates proposed by the Executive, and in which the President has no right to veto specific items in appropriation bills, items are usually found in appropriation acts which can hardly be said to have received Executive approval even where the appropriation acts containing them have been signed by the President. For, in many cases, formal Executive approval has been accorded to an appropriation act as a whole which contains items for which the Executive is not in any way responsible or to which he is positively opposed. In case the President has thus approved an appropriation act as a whole, he may, however, by instruction to his subordinates in the administration, prevent the expenditure of public money for many items of which he disapproves, since an appropriation act frequently is an authorization rather than a command.

The constitutional inhibition that "no money shall be drawn from the Treasury but in consequence of appropriations made by law" makes the budget an instrument of *legislative control* over the administration. The act of appropriation as the legal means of making funds available to the executive branch, also enables the Executive, or some officer directly responsible to the Executive, to exercise *administrative control* over liabilities incurred and over expenditures made by the many officers and agents employed by the Government in the conduct of its business.

Every branch of the business of the Government is necessarily highly complex and technical. One of the most important offices of a budget is to supply the need for an effective means whereby those who are responsible for direction and control over technical processes and who understand the technical needs of the service may formally present to the Legislature and through the Legislature to the people a well-defined plan or prospectus of work to be financed in order that the Government may make provision for the needs of the country as seen by those whose duty it is to serve these needs.

The Congress, as a deliberative body, while not in a position to know what are the technical service requirements, is by reason of its representative character best able to determine questions of policy involving the expenditure of money, i.e., decide what shall and what shall not be undertaken. An act of appropriation of public money should therefore be the result of the most careful consideration of both branches of the Government.

The financing of the Government calls into action both the "money raising" and the "appropriating" powers of the Congress—the one to provide funds, the other to authorize expenditures. The exercise of both of these powers affects immediately the welfare of the people. For the purpose of considering the relations of "revenue" and "borrowing" to welfare, a budget should present for the consideration of the Congress a definite financial program.

For the purpose of considering the relation of expenditure authorizations to welfare, a budget should present a definite statement of the business to be done, or a work program.

The immediate relations of revenue raising to welfare have been a subject of constant national concern since the first year the Federal Government was organized. In fact, it reaches back through the Revolutionary period; it was one of the chief subjects of popular interest and agitation which culminated in the Declaration of Independence. During the entire national period a more or less definite revenue policy has been recognized. Though not presented in budgetary form, definite policies pertaining to the welfare relation of revenue raising have furnished a definite basis for appeal to the electorate for support. With respect to revenue, there has been a well-defined policy of government which may be traced from the beginning.

With respect to the relation of Government expenditure to welfare, there has been no conscious policy, nor has the subject of Government financing (the relation of revenues and borrowings to expenditures) been a matter of great public concern except in times of war, when the problem of defending our national integrity has depended on ability to finance the Government's needs. The result has been that the United States has had no definite financial program; appropriations have been regarded as special or local in their significance. It has only been within the last few years that what the Government does with its vast organization and resources has received the attention which it deserves. As was said by the President in a recent message:

> In political controversy it has been assumed generally that the individual citizen has little interest in what the Government spends. Now that population has become more dense, that large cities have developed, that people are required to live in congested centers, that the national resources frequently are the subject of private ownership and private control, and that transportation and other public-service facilities are held and operated by large corporations, what the Government does with nearly a thousand million dollars each year is of as much concern to the average citizen as is the manner of obtaining this amount of money for public use.

It is to the expenditure side of a budget that special attention is given in this report.

Budget and Accounting Act (1921)

TITLE I—DEFINITIONS

SECTION 1. This Act may be cited as the "Budget and Accounting Act, 1921."

SEC. 2. When used in this Act—

The terms "department and establishment" and "department or establishment" mean any executive department, independent commission, board, bureau, office, agency, or other establishment of the Government, including the municipal government of the District of Columbia, but do not include the Legislative Branch of the Government or the Supreme Court of the United States;

The term "the Budget" means the Budget required by Section 201 to be transmitted to Congress;

The term "Bureau" means the Bureau of the Budget;

The term "Director" means the Director of the Bureau of the Budget; and

The term "Assistant Director" means the Assistant Director of the Bureau of the Budget.

TITLE II—THE BUDGET

SEC. 201. The President shall transmit to Congress on the first day of each regular session, the Budget, which shall set forth in summary and in detail:

(a) Estimates of the expenditures and appropriations necessary in his judgment for the support of the Government for the ensuing fiscal year; except that the estimates for such year for the Legislative Branch of the Government and the Supreme Court of the United States shall be transmitted to the President on or before October 15th of each year, and shall be included by him in the Budget without revision;

(b) His estimates of the receipts of the Government during the ensuing fiscal year, under (1) laws existing at the time the Budget is transmitted and also (2) under the revenue proposals, if any, contained in the Budget;

(c) The expenditures and receipts of the Government during the last completed fiscal year;

(d) Estimates of the expenditures and receipts of the Government during the fiscal year in progress;

(e) The amount of annual, permanent, or other appropriations, including balances of appropriations for prior fiscal years, available for expenditure during the fiscal year in progress, as of November 1 of such year;

(f) Balanced statements of (1) the condition of the Treasury at the end of the last completed fiscal year, (2) the estimated condition of the Treasury at the end of the fiscal year in progress, and (3) the estimated condition of the Treasury at the end of the ensuing fiscal year if the financial proposals contained in the Budget are adopted;

(g) All essential facts regarding the bonded and other indebtedness of the Government; and

(h) Such other financial statements and data as in his opinion are necessary or desirable in order to make known in all practicable detail the financial conditions of the Government.

SEC. 202. (a) If the estimated receipts for the ensuing fiscal year contained in the Budget, on the basis of laws existing at the time the Budget is transmitted, plus the estimated amounts in the Treasury at the close of the fiscal year in progress, available for expenditure in the ensuing fiscal year, are less than the estimated expenditures for the ensuing fiscal year contained in the Budget, the President in the Budget shall make recommendations to Congress for new taxes, loans, or other appropriate action to meet the estimated deficiency.

(b) If the aggregate of such estimated receipts and such estimated amounts in the Treasury is greater than such estimated expenditures for the ensuing fiscal year, he shall make such recommendations as in his opinion the public interests require.

SEC. 203. (a) The President from time to time may transmit to Congress supplemental or deficiency estimates for such appropriations or expenditures as in his judgment (1) are necessary on account of laws enacted after the transmission of the Budget, or (2) are otherwise in the public interest. He shall accompany such estimates with a statement of the reasons therefor, including the reasons for their omission from the Budget.

(b) Whenever such supplemental or deficiency estimates reach an aggregate which, if they had been contained in the Budget, would have required the President to make a recommendation under subdivision (a) of section 202, he shall thereupon make such recommendation.

SEC. 204. (a) Except as otherwise provided in this Act, the contents, order, and arrangement of the estimates of appropriations and the statements of expenditures and estimated expenditures contained in the Budget or transmitted under section 203, and the notes and other data therein, submitted therewith, shall conform to the requirements of existing law. (b) Estimates for lump-sum appropriations contained in the Budget or transmitted under section 203 shall be accompanied by statements showing, in such detail and form as may be necessary to inform Congress, the manner of expenditure of such appropriations and of the corresponding appropriations for the fiscal year in progress and the last completed fiscal year. Such statements shall be in lieu of statements of like character now required by law.

SEC. 205. The President, in addition to the Budget, shall transmit to Congress on the first Monday in December, 1921, for the service of the fiscal year ending June 30, 1923, only, an alternative budget, which shall be prepared in such form and amounts and according to such system of classification and itemization as is, in his opinion, most appropriate, with such explanatory notes and tables as may be necessary to show where the various items embraced in the Budget are contained in such alternative budget.

SEC. 206. No estimate or request for an appropriation and no request for an increase in an item of any such estimate or request, and no recommendation as to how the revenue needs of the Government should be met, shall be submitted to Congress or any committee thereof by any officer or employee of any department or establishment, unless at the request of either House of Congress.

SEC. 207. There is hereby created in the Treasury Department a Bureau to be known as the Bureau of the Budget. There shall be in the Bureau a Director and an Assistant Director, who shall be appointed by the President and receive salaries of $10,000 and $7,500 a year, respectively. The Assistant Director shall perform such duties as the Director may designate, and during the absence or incapacity of the Director or during a vacancy in the office of Director he shall act as Director. The Bureau, under such rules and regulations as the President may prescribe, shall prepare for him the Budget, the alternative Budget, and any supplemental or deficiency estimates, and to this end shall have authority to assemble, correlate, revise, reduce, or increase the estimates of the several departments or establishments.

. . .

SEC. 209. The Bureau, when directed by the President, shall make a detailed study of the departments and establishments for the purpose of enabling the President to determine what changes (with a view of securing greater economy and efficiency in the conduct of the public service) should be made in (1) the existing organization, activities, and methods of business of such departments or establishments, (2) the appropriations therefor, (3) the assignment of particular activities to particular services, or (4) the regrouping of services. The results of such study shall be embodied in a report or reports to the President, who may transmit to Congress such report or reports or any part thereof with his recommendations on the matters covered thereby.

SEC. 210. The Bureau shall prepare for the President a codification of all laws or parts of laws relating to the preparation and transmission to Congress of statements of receipts and expenditures of the Government and of estimates of appropriations. The President shall transmit the same to Congress on or before the first Monday in December, 1921, with a recommendation as to the changes which, in his opinion, should be made in such laws or parts of laws.

SEC. 211. The powers and duties relating to the compiling of estimates now conferred and imposed upon the Division of Bookkeeping and Warrants of the office of the Secretary of the Treasury are transferred to the Bureau.

SEC. 212. The Bureau shall have at the request of any committee of either House of Congress having jurisdiction over revenue or appropriations, to furnish the committee such aid and information as it may request.

SEC. 213. Under such regulations as the President may prescribe, (1) every department and establishment shall furnish to the Bureau such information as the Bureau may from time to time require, and (2) the Director and the Assistant Director, or any employee of the Bureau, when duly authorized, shall, for the purpose of securing such information, have access to, and the right to examine, any books, documents, papers, or records of any such department or establishment.

SEC. 214. (a) The head of each department and establishment shall designate an official thereof as budget officer therefor, who, in each year under his direction and on or before a date fixed by him, shall prepare the departmental estimates.

(b) Such budget officer shall also prepare, under the direction of the head of the department or establishment, such supplemental and deficiency estimates as may be required for its work.

SEC. 215. The head of each department and establishment shall revise the departmental estimates and submit them to the Bureau on or before September 15 of each year. In case of his failure so to do, the President shall cause to be prepared such estimates and data as are necessary to enable him to include in the Budget estimates and statements in respect to the work of such department or establishment.

SEC. 216. The departmental estimates and any supplemental or deficiency estimates submitted to the Bureau by the head of any department or establishment shall be prepared and submitted in such form, manner, and detail as the President may prescribe.

TITLE III—GENERAL ACCOUNTING OFFICE

SEC. 301. There is created an establishment of the Government to be known as the General Accounting Office, which shall be independent of the executive departments and under the control and direction of the Comptroller General of the United States. The offices of Comptroller of the Treasury and Assistant Comptroller of the Treasury are abolished, to take effect July 1, 1921. All other officers and employees of the office of the Comptroller of the Treasury shall become officers and employees in the General Accounting Office at their grades and salaries on July 1, 1921, and all books, records, documents, papers, furniture, office equipment and other property of the office of the Comptroller of the Treasury shall become the property of the General Accounting Office. The Comptroller General is authorized to adopt a seal for the General Accounting Office.

SEC. 302. There shall be in the General Accounting Office a Comptroller General of the United States and an Assistant Comptroller General of the United States, who shall be appointed by the President with the advice and consent of the Senate, and shall receive salaries of $10,000 and $7,500 a year, respectively. The Assistant Comptroller General shall perform such duties as may be assigned to him by the Comptroller General, and during the absence or incapacity of the Comptroller General, or during a vacancy in that office, shall act as Comptroller General.

SEC. 303. Except as hereinafter provided in this section, the Comptroller General and the Assistant Comptroller General shall hold office for fifteen years. The Comptroller General shall not be eligible for reappointment. The Comptroller General or the Assistant Comptroller General may be removed at any time by joint resolution of Congress after notice and hearing, when, in the judgment of Congress, the Comptroller General or Assistant Comptroller General has become permanently incapacitated or has been inefficient, or guilty of neglect of duty, or of malfeasance in office, or of any felony or conduct involving moral turpitude, and for no other cause and in no other manner except by impeachment. Any Comptroller General or Assistant Comptroller General removed in the manner herein provided shall be ineligible for reappointment to that office. When a Comptroller General or Assistant Comptroller General attains the age of seventy years, he shall be retired from his office.

SEC. 304. All powers and duties now conferred or imposed by law upon the Comptroller of the Treasury or the six auditors of the Treasury Department, and the duties of the Division of Bookkeeping and Warrants of the Office of the Secretary of the Treasury relating to keeping the personal ledger accounts of disbursing and collecting officers, shall, so far as not inconsistent with this Act, be vested in and imposed upon the General Accounting Office and be exercised without direction from any other officer. The balances certified by the Comptroller General shall be final and conclusive upon the executive branch of the Government. The revision by the Comptroller General of settlements made by the six auditors shall be discontinued, except as to settlements made before July 1, 1921.

SEC. 305. Section 236 of the Revised Statutes is amended to read as follows:

Sec. 236. All claims and demands whatever by the Government of the United States or against it, and all accounts whatever in which the Government of the United States is concerned, either as debtor or creditor, shall be settled and adjusted in the General Accounting Office.

SEC. 306. All laws relating generally to the administration of the departments and establishments, shall, so far as applicable, govern the General Accounting Office. Copies of any books, records, papers, or documents, and transcripts from the books and proceedings of the General Accounting Office, when certified by the Comptroller General or the Assistant Comptroller General under its seal, shall be admitted as evidence with the same effect as the copies and transcripts referred to in sections 882 and 886 of the Revised Statutes.

SEC. 307. The Comptroller General may provide for the payment of accounts or claims adjusted and settled in the General Accounting Office, through disbursing officers of the several departments and establishments, instead of by warrant.

SEC. 308. The duties now appertaining to the Division of Public Moneys of the Office of the Secretary of the Treasury, so far as they relate to the covering of revenues and repayments into the Treasury, the issue of duplicate checks and warrants, and the certification of outstanding liabilities for payment, shall be performed by the Division of Bookkeeping A1 and Warrants of the Office of the Secretary of the Treasury.

SEC. 309. The Comptroller General shall prescribe the forms, systems, and procedure for administrative appropriation and fund accounting in the several departments and establishments, and for the administrative examination of fiscal officers' accounts and claims against the United States.

SEC. 310. The offices of the six auditors shall be abolished, to take effect July 1, 1921. All other officers and employees of these offices except as otherwise provided herein shall become officers and employees of the General Ac-counting Office at their grades and salaries on July 1, 1921. All books, records, documents, papers, furniture, office equipment, and other property of these offices, and of the Division of Bookkeeping and Warrants, so far as they relate to the work of such division transferred by section 304, shall become the property of the General Accounting Office. The General Accounting Office shall occupy temporarily the rooms now occupied by the office of the Comptroller of the Treasury and the six auditors.

. . .

SEC. 312. (a) The Comptroller General shall investigate, at the seat of government or elsewhere, all matters relating to the receipt, disbursed, and application of public funds, and shall make to the President when requested by him, and to Congress at the beginning of each regular session, a report in writing of the work of the General Accounting Office, containing recommendations concerning the legislation he may deem necessary to facilitate the prompt and accurate rendition and settlement of accounts and concerning such other matters relating to the receipt, disbursement, and application of public funds as he may think advisable. In such regular report, or in special reports at any time when Congress is in session, he shall make recommendations looking to greater economy or efficiency in public expenditures.

(b) He shall make such investigations and reports as shall be ordered by either House of Congress or by any committee of either House having jurisdiction over revenue, appropriations, or expenditures. The Comptroller General shall also, at the request of any such committee, direct assistants from his office to furnish the committee such aid and information as it may request.

(c) The Comptroller General shall specially report to Congress every expenditure or contract made by any department or establishment in any year in violation of law.

(d) He shall submit to Congress reports upon the adequacy and effectiveness of the administrative examination of accounts and claims in the respective departments and establishments and upon the adequacy and effectiveness of departmental inspection of the offices and accounts of fiscal officers.

(e) He shall furnish such information relating to expenditures and accounting to the Bureau of the Budget as it may request from time to time.

SEC. 313. All departments and establishments shall furnish to the Comptroller General such information regarding the powers, duties, activities, organization, financial transactions, and methods of business of their respective offices as he may from time to time require of them; and the Comptroller General, or any of his assistants or employees, when duly authorized by him, shall, for the purpose of securing such information, have access to and the right to examine any books, documents, papers, or records of any such department or establishment. The authority contained in this section shall not be applicable to expenditures made under the provisions of section 291 of the Revised Statutes.

■ Classification Act (1923)

Be it enacted by the Senate and the House of Representatives of the United States of America in Congress assembled, That this Act may be cited as "The Classification Act of 1923."

SEC. 2. That the term "compensation schedules" means the schedules of positions, grades, and salaries, as contained in section 13 of this Act.

The term "department" means an executive department of the United States Government, a governmental establishment in the executive branch of the United States Government which is not a part of an executive department, the municipal government of the District of Columbia, the Botanic Garden, Library of Congress, Library Building and Grounds, Government Printing Office, and the Smithsonian Institution.

The term "the head of the department" means the officer or group of officers in the department who are not subordinate or responsible to any other officer of the department.

The term "board" means the Personnel Classification Board established by section 3 hereof.

The term "position" means a specific civilian office or employment, whether occupied or vacant, in a department other than the following: offices or employments in the Postal Service; teachers, librarians, school attendance officers, and employees of the community center department under the Board of Education of the District of Columbia; officers and members of the Metropolitan police, the fire department of the District of Columbia, and the United States park police; and the commissioned personnel of the Coast Guard, the Public Health Service, and the Coast and Geodetic Survey.

The term "employee" means any person temporarily or permanently in a position.

The term "service" means the broadest division of related offices and employments.

The term "grade" means a subdivision of a service, including one or more positions for which approximately the same basic qualifications and compensation are prescribed, the distinction between grades being based upon differences in the importance, difficulty, responsibility, and value of the work.

The term "class" means a group of positions to be established under this Act sufficiently similar in respect to the duties and responsibilities thereof that the same requirements as to education, experience, knowledge, and ability are demanded of incumbents, the same tests of fitness are used to choose qualified appointees, and the same schedule of compensation is made to apply with equity.

The term "compensation" means any salary, wage, fee, allowance, or other emolument paid to an employee for service in a position.

SEC. 3. That there is hereby established an ex officio board, to be known as the Personnel Classification Board, to consist of the Director of the Bureau of the Budget or an alternate from that Bureau, designated by the Director, a member of the Civil Service Commission or an alternate from that commission designated by the commission, and the Chief of the United States Bureau of Efficiency or an alternate from that bureau designated by the chief of the bureau. The Director of the Bureau of the Budget or his alternate shall be chairman of the board.

Subject to the approval of the President, the heads of the departments shall detail to the board, at its request, for temporary service under its direction, officers or employees possessed of special knowledge, ability, or experience required in the classification and allocation of positions. The Civil Service Commission, the Bureau of the Budget, and the Bureau of Efficiency shall render the board such cooperation and assistance as the board may require for the performance of its duties under this Act.

The board shall make all necessary rules and regulations not inconsistent with the provisions of this Act and provide such subdivisions of the grades contained in section 13 hereof and such titles and definitions as it may deem necessary according to the kind and difficulty of the work. Its regulations shall provide for ascertaining and recording the duties of positions and the qualifications required of incumbents, and it shall prepare and publish an adequate statement giving (1) the duties and responsibilities involved in the classes to be established within the several grades, illustrated where necessary by examples of typical tasks, (2) the minimum qualifications required for the satisfactory performance of such duties and tasks, and (3) the titles given to said classes. In performing the foregoing duties, the board shall follow as nearly as practicable the classification made pursuant to the Executive order of October 24, 1921. The board may from time to time designate additional classes within the several grades and may combine, divide, alter, or abolish existing classes. Department heads shall promptly report the duties and responsibilities of new positions to the board. The board shall make necessary adjustments in compensation for positions carrying maintenance and for positions requiring only part-time service.

SEC. 4. That after consultation with the board, and in accordance with a uniform procedure prescribed by it, the head of each department shall allocate all positions in his department in the District of Columbia to their appropriate grades in the compensation schedules and shall fix the rate of compensation of each employee thereunder, in accordance with the rules prescribed in section 6 herein. Such allocations shall be reviewed and may be revised by the board and shall become final upon their approval by said board. Whenever an existing position or a position hereafter created by law shall not fairly and reasonably be allocable to one of the grades of the several services described in the compensation schedules, the board shall adopt for such position the range of compensation prescribed for a grade or a class thereof, comparable therewith as to qualifications and duties.

In determining the rate of compensation which an employee shall receive, the principle of equal compensation for equal work irrespective of sex shall be followed.

SEC. 5. That the compensation schedule shall apply only to civilian employees in the departments within the District of Columbia and shall not apply to employees in positions the duties of which are to perform or assist in apprentice, helper, or journey man work in a recognized trade or craft and skilled and semiskilled laborers, except such as are under the direction and control of the custodian of a public building or perform work which is subordinate, incidental, or preparatory to work of a professional, scientific, or technical character. The board shall make a survey of the field services and shall report to Congress at its first regular session following the passage of this Act schedules of positions, grades, and salaries for such services, which shall follow the principles and rules of the compensation schedules herein contained in so far as these are applicable to the field services. This report shall include a list prepared by the head of each department, after consultation with the board and in accordance with a uniform procedure prescribed by it, allocating all field positions in this department to their approximate grades in said schedules and fixing the proposed rate of compensation of each employee thereunder in accordance with the rules prescribed in section 6 herein.

SEC. 6. That in determining the compensation to be established initially for the several employees the following rules shall govern:

1. In computing the existing compensation of an employee, any bonus which the employee receives shall be included.

2. If the employee is receiving compensation less than the minimum rate of the grade or class thereof in which his duties fall, the compensation shall be increased to that minimum rate.

3. If the employee is receiving compensation within the range of salary prescribed for the appropriate grade at one of the rates fixed therein, no change shall be made in the existing compensation.

4. If the employee is receiving compensation within the range of salary prescribed for the appropriate grade, but not at one of the rates fixed therein, the compensation shall be increased to the next higher rate.

5. If the employee is not a veteran of the Civil War, or a widow of such veteran, and is receiving compensation in excess of the range of salary prescribed for the appropriate grade, the compensation shall be reduced to the rate within the grade nearest the present compensation.

6. All new appointments shall be made at the minimum rate of the appropriate grade or class thereof.

SEC. 7. Increases in compensation shall be allowed upon the attainment and maintenance of the appropriate efficiency ratings, to the next higher rate within the salary range of the grade: *Provided, however,* That in no case shall the compensation of any employee be increased unless Congress has appropriated money from which the increase may lawfully be paid, nor shall the rate for any employee be increased beyond the maximum rate for the grade to which his position is allocated. Nothing herein contained shall be construed to prevent the promotion of an employee from one class to a vacant position in a higher class at any time in accordance with civil service rules, and when so promoted the employee shall receive compensation according to the schedule established for the class to which he is promoted.

SEC. 8. That nothing in this Act shall modify or repeal any existing preference in appointment or reduction in the service of honorably discharged soldiers, sailors, or marines under any existing law or any Executive order now in force.

SEC. 9. That the board shall review and may revise uniform systems of efficiency rating established or to be established for the various grades or classes thereof, which shall set forth the degree of efficiency which shall constitute ground for (a) increase in the rate of compensation for employees who have not attained the maximum rate of the class to which their positions are allocated, (b) continuance at the existing rate of compensation without increase or decrease, (c) decrease in the rate of compensation for employees who at the time are above the minimum rate for the class to which their positions are allocated, and (d) dismissal.

The head of each department shall rate in accordance with such systems the efficiency of each employee under his control or direction. The current ratings for each grade or class thereof shall be open to inspection by the representatives of the board and by the employees of the department under conditions to be determined by the board after consultation with the department heads.

Reductions in compensation and dismissals for inefficiency shall be made by heads of departments in all cases whenever the efficiency ratings warrant, as provided herein, subject to the approval of the board.

The board may require that one copy of such current ratings shall be transmitted to and kept on file with the board.

SEC. 10. That, subject to such rules and regulations as the President may from time to time prescribe, and regardless of the department or independent establishment in which the position is located, an employee may be transferred from a position in one grade to a vacant position within the same grade at the same rate of compensation, or promoted to a vacant position in a higher grade at a higher rate of compensation, in accordance with civil service rules, any provision of existing statutes to the contrary notwithstanding: *Provided,* That nothing herein shall be construed to authorize or permit the transfer of any employee of the United States to a position under the municipal government of the District of Columbia, or any employee of the municipal government of the District of Columbia to a position under the United States.

SEC. 11. That nothing contained in this Act shall be construed to make permanent any temporary appointments under existing law.

SEC. 12. That it shall be the duty of the board to make a study of the rates of compensation provided in this Act for the various services and grades with a view to any readjustment deemed by said board to be just and reasonable. Said board shall, after such study and at such subsequent times as it may deem necessary, report its conclusions to Congress with any recommendations it may deem advisable.

SEC. 13. That the compensation schedules be as follows:

PROFESSIONAL AND SCIENTIFIC SERVICE

The professional and scientific service shall include all classes of positions the duties of which are to perform routine, advisory, administrative, or research work which is based upon the established principles of a profession or science, and which requires professional, scientific, or technical training equivalent to that represented by graduation from a college or university of recognized standing. . . .

SUBPROFESSIONAL SERVICE

The subprofessional service shall include all classes of positions the duties of which are to perform work which is incident, subordinate, or preparatory to the work required of employees holding positions in the professional and scientific service, and which requires or involves professional, scientific, or technical training of any degree inferior to that represented by graduation from a college or university of recognized standing. . . .

CLERICAL, ADMINISTRATIVE, AND FISCAL SERVICE

The clerical, administrative, and fiscal service shall include all classes of positions the duties of which are to perform clerical, administrative, or accounting work, or any other work commonly associated with office, business, or fiscal administration. . . .

CUSTODIAL SERVICE

The custodial service shall include all classes of positions the duties of which are to supervise or to perform manual work involved in the custody, maintenance, and protection of public buildings, premises, and equipment, the transportation of public officers, employees or property, and the transmission of official papers. . . .

CLERICAL-MECHANICAL SERVICE

The clerical-mechanical service shall include all classes of positions which are not in a recognized trade or craft and which are located in the Government Printing Office, the Bureau of Engraving and Printing, the Mail Equipment Shop, the duties of which are to perform or to direct manual or machine operations requiring special skill or experience, or to perform or direct the counting, examining, sorting, or other verification of the product of manual or machine operations. . . .

Reorganization Act of 1939

TITLE I—REORGANIZATION

PART I

SECTION 1. (a) The Congress hereby declares that by reason of continued national deficits beginning in 1931 it is desirable to reduce substantially Government expenditures and that such reduction may be accomplished in some measure by proceeding immediately under the provisions of this Act. The President shall investigate the organization of all agencies of the Government and shall determine what changes therein are necessary to accomplish the following purposes:

(1) To reduce expenditures to the fullest extent consistent with the efficient operation of the Government;

(2) To increase the efficiency of the operations of the Government to the fullest extent practicable within the revenues;

(3) To group, coordinate, and consolidate agencies of the Government, as nearly as may be, according to major purposes;

(4) To reduce the number of agencies by consolidating those having similar functions under a single head, and to abolish such agencies as may not be necessary for the efficient conduct of the Government; and

(5) To eliminate overlapping and duplication of effort.

(b) The Congress declares that the public interest demands the carrying out of the purposes specified in subsection (a) and that such purposes may be accomplished in great measure by proceeding immediately under the provisions of this title, and can be accomplished more speedily thereby than by the enactment of specific legislation.

SEC. 2. When used in this title, the term "agency" means any executive department, commission, independent establishment, corporation owned or controlled by the United States, board, bureau, division, service, office, authority, or administration, in the executive branch of the Government.

SEC. 3. No reorganization plan under section 4 shall provide—

(a) For the abolition or transfer of an executive department or all the functions thereof or for the establishment of any new executive department;

(b) In the case of the following agencies, for the transfer, consolidation, or abolition of the whole or any part of such agency or of its head, or of all or any of the functions of such agency or of its head: Civil Service Commission, Coast Guard, Engineer Corps for the United States Army, Mississippi River Commission, Federal Communications

Commission, Federal Power Commission, Federal Trade Commission, General Accounting Office, Interstate Commerce Commission, National Labor Relations Board, Securities and Exchange Commission, Board of Tax Appeals, United States Employees' Compensation Commission, United States Maritime Commission, United States Tariff Commission, Veterans Administration, National Mediation Board, National Railroad Adjustment Board, Railroad Retirement Board, the Federal Deposit Insurance Corporation, or the Board of Governors of the Federal Reserve System; or

(c) For changing the name of any executive department or the title of its head, or for designating any agency as "Department" or its head as "Secretary"; or

(d) For the continuation of any agency beyond the period authorized by law for the existence of such agency; or

(e) For the continuation of any function of any agency beyond the period authorized by law for the exercise of such function; or

(f) For authorizing any agency to exercise any function which is not expressly authorized by law.

SEC. 4. Whenever the President, after investigation, finds that—

(a) the transfer of the whole or any part of any agency or the functions thereof to the jurisdiction and control of any other agency; or

(b) the consolidation of the functions vested in any agency; or

(c) the abolition of the whole or any part of any agency which agency or part (by reason of transfers under this Act or otherwise, or by reason of termination of its functions in any manner) does not have, or upon the taking effect of the reorganizations specified in the reorganization plan will not have, any functions, is necessary to accomplish one or more of the purposes of section 1 (a), he shall—

(d) prepare a reorganization plan for the making of the transfers, consolidations, and abolitions, as to which he has made findings and which he includes in the plan. Such plan shall also—

(1) designate, in such cases as he deems necessary, the name of any agency affected by a reorganization and the title of its head;

(2) make provision for the transfer or other disposition of the records, property (including office equipment), and personnal affected by such transfer, consolidation, or abolition;

(3) make provision for the transfer of such unexpended balances of appropriations available for use in connection with the function or agency transferred or consolidated, as he deems necessary by reason of the transfer or consolidation for use in connection with the transferred or consolidated functions, or for the use of the agency to which the transfer is made, but such unexpended balances so transferred shall be used only for the purposes for which such appropriation is originally made;

(4) make provision for winding up the affairs of the agency abolished; and

(e) transmit such plan (bearing an identifying number) to the Congress, together with a declaration that, with respect to each transfer, consolidation, or abolition referred to in paragraph (a), (b), or (c) of this section and specified in the plan, he has found that such transfer, consolidation, or abolition is necessary to accomplish one or more of the purposes of section 1 (a). The delivery to both Houses shall be on the same day and shall be made to each House while it is in session.

The President, in his message transmitting a reorganization plan, shall state the reduction of expenditures which it is probable will be brought about by the taking effect of the reorganizations specified in the plan.

SEC. 5. The reorganizations specified in the plan shall take effect in accordance with the plan:

(a) Upon the expiration of sixty calendar days after the date on which the plan is transmitted to the Congress, but only if during such sixty-day period there has not been passed by the two Houses a concurrent resolution stating in substance that the Congress does not favor the reorganization plan.

(b) If the Congress adjourns sine die before the expiration of the sixty-day period, a new sixty-day period shall begin on the opening day of the next succeeding regular or special session. A similar rule shall be applicable in the case of subsequent adjournments sine die before the expiration of sixty days.

SEC. 6. No reorganization under this title shall have the effect—

(a) of continuing any agency or function beyond the time when it would have terminated if the reorganization had not been made; or

(b) of continuing any function beyond the time when the agency in which it was vested before the reorganization would have terminated if the reorganization had not been made; or

(c) of authorizing any agency to exercise any function which is not expressly authorized by law.

SEC. 7. For the purposes of this title any transfer, consolidation, abolition, designation, disposition, or winding up of affairs, referred to in section 4 (d), shall be deemed a "reorganization."

SEC. 8. (a) All orders, rules, regulations, permits, or other privileges made, issued, or granted by or in respect of any agency or function transferred to, or consolidated with, any other agency or function under the provisions of this title, and in effect at the time of the transfer or consolidation, shall continue in effect to the same extent as if such transfer or consolidation had not occurred, until modified, superseded, or repealed.

(b) No suit, action, or other proceeding lawfully commenced by or against the head of any agency or other officer of the United States, in his official capacity or in relation to the discharge of his official duties, shall abate by reason of any transfer of authority, power, and duties from one officer or agency of the Government to another under the provisions of this title, but the court, on motion or supplemental petition filed at any time within twelve months after such transfer takes effect, showing a necessity for a survival of such suit, action, or other proceeding to obtain a settlement of the questions involved, may allow the same to be maintained by or against the head of the agency or other officer of the United States to whom the authority, powers, and duties are transferred.

(c) All laws relating to any agency or function transferred to, or consolidated with, any other agency or function under the provisions of this title, shall, insofar as such laws are not inapplicable, remain in full force and effect.

SEC. 9. The appropriations or portions of appropriations unexpended by reason of the operation of this title shall not be used for any purpose, but shall be impounded and returned to the Treasury.

SEC. 10. (a) Whenever the employment of any person is terminated by a reduction of personnel as a result of a reorganization effected under this title, such person shall therafter be given preference, when qualified, whenever an appointment is made in the executive branch of the Government, but such preference shall not be effective for a period longer than twelve months from the date the employment of such person is so terminated.

(b) Any transfer of personnel under this title shall be without change in classification or compensation, except that this requirement shall not operate after the end of the fiscal year during which the transfer is made to prevent the adjustment of classification or compensation to conform to the duties to which such transferred personnel may be assigned.

SEC. 11. If the reorganizations specified in a reorganization plan take effect, the reorganization plan shall be printed in the Statutes at Large in the same volume as the public laws, and shall be printed in the Federal Register.

SEC. 12. No reorganization specified in a reorganization plan shall take effect unless the plan is transmitted to the Congress before January 21, 1941.

TITLE III—ADMINISTRATIVE ASSISTANTS

SEC 301. The President is authorized to appoint not to exceed six administrative assistants and to fix the compensation of each at the rate of not more than $10,000 per annum. Each such administrative assistant shall perform such duties as the President may prescribe.

◼ Reorganization Plan No. 1 (1939)

PART I.—EXECUTIVE OFFICE OF THE PRESIDENT

SECTION 1. *Bureau of the Budget.*—The Bureau of the Budget and all of its functions and personnel (including the Director and Assistant Director) are hereby transferred from the Treasury Department to the Executive Office of the President; and the functions of the Bureau of the Budget shall be administered by the Director thereof under the direction and supervision of the President.

SEC. 2. *Central Statistical Board.*—The Central Statistical Board and all of its functions and personnel (including the Chairman and the members of the Board) are hereby transferred to the Bureau of the Budget in the Executive Office of the President. The Chairman of the Board shall perform such administrative duties as the Director of the Bureau of the Budget shall direct.

SEC. 3. *Central Statistical Committee Abolished and Functions Transferred.*—The Central Statistical Committee is hereby abolished, and its functions are transferred to the Director of the Bureau of the Budget to be administered by him under the direction and supervision of the President. The Director of the Bureau of the Budget shall promptly wind up any outstanding affairs of the Central Statistical Committee.

SEC. 4. *National Resources Planning Board.*—(a) The functions of the National Resources Committee, established by Executive Order No. 7065 of June 7, 1935, and its personnel (except the members of the Committee) and all of the functions of the Federal Employment Stabilization Office in the Department of Commerce and its personnel are hereby transferred to the Executive Office of the President. The functions transferred by this section are hereby consolidated, and they shall be administered under the direction and supervision of the President by the National Resources Planning Board (hereafter referred to as the Board), which shall be composed of five members to be appointed by the President. The President shall designate one of the members of the Board as Chairman and another as Vice Chairman. The Vice Chairman shall act as Chairman in the absence of the Chairman or in the event of a vacancy in that office. The members of the Board shall be compensated at the rate of $50.00 per day for time spent in attending and traveling to and from meetings, or in otherwise exercising the functions and duties of the Board, plus the actual cost of transportation: *Provided,* That in no case shall a member be entitled to receive compensation for more than thirty days' service in two consecutive months.

(b) The Board shall determine the rules of its own proceedings, and a majority of its members in office shall constitute a quorum for the transaction of business, but the Board may function notwithstanding vacancies.

(c) The Board may appoint necessary officers and employees and may delegate to such officers authority to perform such duties and make such expenditures as may be necessary.

SEC. 5. *National Resources Committee Abolished.*—The National Resources Committee is hereby abolished, and its outstanding affairs shall be wound up by the National Resources Planning Board.

SEC. 6. *Federal Employment Stabilization Office Abolished.*—The Federal Employment Stabilization Office is hereby abolished, and the Secretary of Commerce shall promptly wind up its affairs.

■ **EXECUTIVE ORDER NO. 8248: Establishing the Divisions of the Executive Office of the President and Defining Their Functions and Duties (1939)**

By virtue of the authority vested in me by the Constitution and Statutes, and in order to effectuate the purposes of the Reorganization Act of 1939, Public Resolution No. 19, Seventy-sixth Congress, approved April 3, 1939, and of Reorganization Plans Nos. 1 and 11 [4 F.R. 2727, 2733 DI] submitted to the Congress by the President and made effective as of July 1, 1939 by Public Resolution No. 2, Seventy-sixth Congress, approved June 7, 1939, by organizing the Executive Office of the President with functions and duties so prescribed and responsibilities so fixed that the President will have adequate machinery for the administrative management of the Executive branch of the Government, it is hereby ordered as follows:

I

There shall be within the Executive Office of the President the following principal divisions, namely: (1) The White House Office, (2) the Bureau of the Budget, (3) the National Resources Planning Board, (4) the Liaison Office for Personnel Management, (5) the Office of Government Reports, and (6) in the event of a national emergency, or threat of a national emergency, such office for emergency management as the President shall determine.

II

The functions and duties of the divisions of the Executive Office of the President are hereby defined as follows:

1. *The White House Office.* In general, to serve the President in an intimate capacity in the performance of the many detailed activities incident to his immediate office. To that end, The White House Office shall be composed of the following principal subdivisions, with particular functions and duties as indicated:

(a) *The Secretaries to the President.* To facilitate and maintain quick and easy communication with the Congress, the individual members of the Congress, the heads of executive departments and agencies, the press, the radio, and the general public.

(b) *The Executive Clerk.* To provide for the orderly handling of documents and correspondence within The White House Office, and to organize and supervise all clerical services and procedure relating thereto.

(c) *The Administrative Assistants to the President.* To assist the President in such matters as he may direct, and at the specific request of the President, to get information and to condense and summarize it for his use. These Administrative Assistants shall be personal aides to the President and shall have no authority over anyone in any department or agency, including the Executive Office of the President, other than the personnel assigned to their immediate offices. In no event shall the Administrative Assistants be interposed between the President and the head of any department or agency, or between the President and

any one of the divisions in the Executive Office of the President.

2. *The Bureau of the Budget.* (a) To assist the President in the preparation of the Budget and the formulation of the fiscal program of the Government.

(b) To supervise and control the administration of the Budget.

(c) To conduct research in the development of improved plans of administrative management, and to advise the executive departments and agencies of the Government with respect to improved administrative organization and practice.

(d) To aid the President to bring about more efficient and economical conduct of Government service.

(e) To assist the President by clearing and coordinating departmental advice on proposed legislation and by making recommendations as to Presidential action on legislative enactments, in accordance with past practice.

(f) To assist in the consideration and clearance and, where necessary, in the preparation of proposed Executive orders and proclamations, in accordance with the provisions of Executive Order No. 7298 of Feburary 18, 1936.

(g) To plan and promote the improvement, development, and coordination of Federal and other statistical services.

(h) To keep the President informed of the progress of activities by agencies of the Government with respect to work proposed, work actually initiated, and work completed, together with the relative timing of work between the several agencies of the Government; all to the end that the work programs of the several agencies of the Executive branch of the Government may be coordinated and that the monies appropriated by the Congress may be expended in the most economical manner possible with the least possible overlapping and duplication of effort.

3. *The National Resources Planning Board.* (a) To survey, collect data on, and analyze problems pertaining to national resources, both natural and human, and to recommend to the President and the Congress long-time plans and programs for the wise use and fullest development of such resources.

(b) To consult with Federal, regional, state, local, and private agencies in developing orderly programs of public works and to list for the President and the Congress all proposed public works in the order of their relative importance with respect to (1) the greatest good to the greatest number of people, (2) the emergency necessities of the Nation, and (3) the social, economic, and cultural advancement of the people of the United States.

(c) To inform the President of the general trend of economic conditions and to recommend measures leading to their improvement or stabilization.

(d) To act as a clearing house and means of coordination for planning activities, linking together various levels and fields of planning.

4. *The Liaison Office for Personnel Management.* In accordance with the statement of purpose made in the Message to Congress of April 25, 1939, accompanying Reorganization Plan No. 1, one of the Administrative Assistants to the President, authorized in the Reorganization Act of 1939, shall be designated by the President as Liaison Officer for Personnel Management and shall be in charge of the Liaison Office for Personnel Management. The functions of this office shall be:

(a) To assist the President in the better execution of the duties imposed upon him by the Provisions of the Constitution and the laws with respect to personnel management, especially the Civil Service Act of 1883, as amended, and the rules promulgated by the President under authority of that Act.

(b) To assist the President in maintaining closer contact with all agencies dealing with personnel matters insofar as they affect or tend to determine the personnel management policies of the Executive branch of the Government.

5. *The Office of Government Reports.* (a) To provide a central clearing house through which individual citizens, organizations of citizens, state or local governmental bodies, and, where appropriate, agencies of the Federal Government, may transmit inquiries and complaints and receive advice and information.

(b) To assist the President in dealing with special problems requiring the clearance of information between the Federal Government and state and local governments and private institutions.

(c) To collect and distribute information concerning the purposes and activities of executive departments and agencies for the use of the Congress, administrative officials, and the public.

(d) To keep the President currently informed of the opinions, desires, and complaints of citizens and groups of citizens and of state and local governments with respect to the work of Federal agencies.

(e) To report to the President on the basis of the information it has obtained possible ways and means for reducing the cost of the operation of the Government.

III

The Bureau of the Budget, the National Resources Planning Board, and the Liaison Office for Personnel Management shall constitute the three principal management arms of the Government for the (1) preparation and administration of the Budget and improvement of administrative management and organization, (2) planning for conservation and utilization of the resources of the Nation, and (3) coordination of the administration of personnel, none of which belong in any department but which are necessary for the over-all management of the Executive branch of the Government, so that the President will be enabled the better to carry out his Constitutional duties of informing the Congress with respect to the state of the Union, of recommending appropriate and expedient measures, and of seeing that the laws are faithfully executed.

IV

To facilitate the orderly transaction of business within each of the five divisions herein defined and to clarify the relations of these divisions with each other and with the President, I direct that the Bureau of the Budget, the National Resources Planning Board, the Liaison Office for Personnel Management, and the Office of Government Reports shall respectively prepare regulations for the governance of their internal organizations and procedures. Such regulations shall be in effect when approved by the President and shall remain in force until changed by new regulations approved by him. The President will prescribe regulations governing the conduct of the business of the division of The White House Office.

V

The Director of the Bureau of the Budget shall prepare a consolidated budget for the Executive Office of the President for submission by the President to the Congress. Annually, pursuant to the regular request issued by the Bureau of the Budget, each division of the Executive Office of the President shall prepare and submit to the Bureau estimates of proposed appropriations for the succeeding fiscal year. The form of the estimates and the manner of their consideration for incorporation in the Budget shall be the same as prescribed for other Executive departments and agencies.

The Bureau of the Budget shall likewise perform with respect to the several divisions of the Executive Office of the President such functions and duties relating to supplemental estimates, apportionments, and budget administration as are exercised by it for other agencies of the Federal Government.

VI

Space already has been assigned in the State, War and Navy Building, adjacent to The White House, sufficient to accommodate the Bureau of the Budget with its various divisions (including the Central Statistical Board), the central office of the National Resources Planning Board, the Liaison Office for Personnel Management, and the Administrative Assistants to the President, and although for the time being, a considerable portion of the work of the National Resources Planning Board and all of that of the Office of Government Reports will have to be conducted in other quarters, if and when the Congress makes provision for the housing and of the Department of State in a building appropriate to its function dignity and provision is made for the other agencies now accommodated in the State, War and Navy Building, it then will be possible to bring into this building, close to The White House, all of the personnel of the Executive Office of the President except The White House Office.

This Order shall take effect on September 11th 1939.

■ Hatch Act
Act To Prevent Pernicious Political Activities (1939), as Amended (1940)

Be it enacted by the Senate and House of Representatives of the United States of America in Congress assembled, That it shall be unlawful for any person to intimidate, threaten, or coerce, or to attempt to intimidate, threaten, or coerce any other person for the purpose of interfering with the right of any such other person to vote or to vote as he may choose, or of causing such other person to vote for, or not to vote for, any candidate for the office of President, Vice President, Presidential elector, Member of the Senate, or Member of the House of Representatives at any election held solely or in part for the purpose of selecting a President, a Vice President, a Presidential elector, or any Member of the Senate or any Member of the House of Representatives, Delegates or Commissioners from the Territories and insular possessions.

SEC. 2. It shall be unlawful for (1) any person employed in any administrative position by the United States, or by any department, independent agency, or other agency of the United States (including any corporation controlled by the United States or any agency thereof, and any corporation all of the capital stock of which is owned by the United States or any agency thereof), or (2) any person employed in any administrative position by any State, by any political subdivision or municipality of any State, or by any agency of any State or any of its political subdivisions or municipalities (including any corporation controlled by any State or by any such political subdivision, municipality, or agency, and any corporation all of the capital stock of which is owned by any State or by any such political subdivision, municipality, or agency), in connection with any activity which is financed in whole or in part by loans or grants made by the United States, or by any such department, independent agency, or other agency of the United States, to use his official authority for the purpose of interfering with, or affecting, the election or the nomination of any candidate for the office of President, Vice President, Presidential elector, Member of the Senate, Member of the House of Representatives, or Delegate or Resident Commissioner from any Territory or insular possession.

SEC. 3. It shall be unlawful for any person, directly or indirectly, to promise any employment, position, work, compensation, or other benefit, provided for or made possible in whole or in part by any Act of Congress, to any person as consideration, favor, or reward for any political activity or for the support of or opposition to any candidate or any political party in any election.

SEC. 4. Except as may be required by the provisions of subsection (b), section 9 of this Act, it shall be unlawful for any person to deprive, attempt to deprive, or threaten to deprive, by any means, any person of any employment, position, work, compensation, or other benefit provided for or made possible by any Act of Congress appropriating funds for work relief or relief purposes, on account of race, creed, color, or any political activity, support of, or opposition to any candidate or any political party in any election.

SEC. 5. It shall be unlawful for any person to solicit or receive or be in any manner concerned in soliciting or receiving any assessment, subscription, or contribution for any political purpose whatever from any person known by him to be entitled to or receiving compensation, employment, or other benefit provided for or made possible by any Act of Congress appropriating funds for work relief or relief purposes.

SEC. 6. It shall be unlawful for any person for political purposes to aid or assist in furnishing or disclosing, any list of names of persons receiving compensation, employment, or benefits provided for or made possible by any Act of Congress appropriating, or authorizing the appropriation of, funds for work relief or relief purposes, to a political candidate, committee, campaign manager, or to any person for delivery to a political candidate, committee, or campaign manager, and it shall be unlawful for any person to receive any such list of names for all purposes.

SEC. 7. No part of any appropriation made by any Act, heretofore or hereafter enacted, making appropriations for work relief, or otherwise to increase employment by providing loans and grants for public-works projects, shall be used for the purpose of, and no authority conferred by any such Act upon any person shall be exercised or administered for the purpose of, interfering with, restraining, or coercing any individual in the exercise of his right to vote at any election.

SEC. 8. Any person who violates any of the foregoing provisions of this Act upon conviction thereof shall be fined not more than $1,000 or imprisoned for not more than one year, or both.

SEC. 9. (a) It shall be unlawful for any person employed in the executive branch of the Federal Government, or any agency or department thereof, to use his official authority or influence for the purpose of interfering with an election or affecting the result thereof. No officer or employee in the executive branch of the Federal Government, or any agency or department thereof, shall take any active part in political management or in political campaigns. All such persons shall retain the right to vote as they may choose and to express their opinions on all political subjects and candidates. For the purposes of this section the term "officer" or "employee" shall not be construed to include (1) the President and Vice President of the United States; (2) persons whose compensation is paid from the appropriation for the office of the President; (3) heads and assistant heads of executive departments; (4) officers who are appointed by the President, by and with the advice and consent of the Senate, and who determine policies to be pursued by the United States in its relations with foreign powers or in the Nation-wide administration of Federal laws.

(1) It shall be unlawful for any person employed in any capacity by any agency of the Federal Government, whose compensation, or any part thereof, is paid from funds authorized or appropriated by any Act of Congress, to have membership in any political party or organization which advocates the overthrow of our constitutional form of government in the United States.

(2) Any person violating the provisions of this section shall be immediately removed from the position or office held by him, and thereafter no part of the funds appropriated by any Act of Congress for such position or office shall be used to pay the compensation of such person.

SEC. 10. The provisions of this Act shall be in addition to and not in substitution for any other provision of law.

SEC. 11. If any provision of this Act, or the application of such provision to any person or circumstance, is held invalid, the remainder of the Act, and the application of such provision to other persons or circumstances, shall not be affected thereby.

SEC. 12. (a) No officer or employee of any State or local agency whose principal employment is in connection with any activity which is financed in whole or in part by loans or grants made by the United States or by any Federal agency shall (1) use his official authority or influence for the purpose of interfering with an election or a nomination for office, or affecting the result thereof, or (2) directly or indirectly coerce, attempt to coerce, command, or advise any other such officer or employee to pay, lend, or contribute any part of his salary or compensation or anything else of value to any party, committee, organization, agency, or person for political purposes. No such officer or employee shall take any active part in political management or in political campaigns. All such persons shall retain the right to vote as they may choose and to express their opinion on all political subjects and candidates. (b) For the purposes of the second sentence of this subsection, the term "officer" or "employee" shall not be construed to include (1) the Governor or the Lieutenant Governor of any State or any person who is authorized by law to act as Governor, or the mayor of any city; (2) duly elected heads of executive departments of any State or municipality who are not classified under a State or municipal merit or civil-service system; (3) officers holding elective offices.

. . .

SEC. 14. For the purposes of this Act, persons employed in the government of the District of Columbia shall be deemed to be employed in the executive branch of the Government of the United States, except that for the purposes of the second sentence of section 9 (a) the Commissioners and the Recorder of Deeds of the District of Columbia shall not be deemed to be officers or employees.

SEC. 15. The provisions of this Act which prohibit persons to whom such provisions apply from taking any active part in political management or in political campaigns shall be deemed to prohibit the same activities on the part of such persons as the United States Civil Service Commission has heretofore determined are at the time this section takes effect prohibited on the part of employees in the classified civil service of the United States by the provisions of the civil-service rules prohibiting such employees from taking any active part in political management or in political campaigns.

SEC. 16. Whenever the United States Civil Service Commission determines that, by reason of special or unusual circumstances which exist in any municipality or other political subdivision, in the immediate vicinity of the National Capital in the States of Maryland and Virginia or in municipalities the majority of whose voters are employed by the Government of the United States, it is in the domestic interest of persons to whom the provisions of this Act are applicable, and who reside in such municipality or political subdivision, to permit such persons to take an active part in political management or in political campaigns involving such municipality or political subdivision, the Commission is authorized to promulgate regulations permitting such persons to take an active part in such political management and political campaigns to the extent the Commission deems to be in the domestic interest of such persons.

SEC. 17. Nothing in the second sentence of section 12 (a) of this Act shall be construed to prevent or prohibit any officer or employee of a State or local agency (as defined in section 12 (b), from continuing, until the election in connection with which he was nominated, to be a bona fide candidate for election to any public office and from engaging in any political activity in furtherance of his candidacy for such public office, if (1) he was nominated before the date of the enactment of this Act, and (2) upon his election to such public office he resigns from the office or employment in which he was employed prior to his election, in a State or local agency (as defined in section 12).

SEC. 18. Nothing in the second sentence of section 9 (a) or in the second sentence of section 12 (a) of this Act shall be construed to prevent or prohibit any person subject to the provisions of this Act from engaging in any political activity (1) in connection with any election and the preceding campaign if none of the candidates is to be nominated or elected at such election as representing a party any of whose candidates for presidential elector received votes in the last preceding election at which presidential electors were selected, or (2) in connection with any question which is not specifically identified with any National or State political party. For the purposes of this section, questions relating to constitutional amendments, referendums, approval of municipal ordinances, and others of a similar character, shall not be deemed to be specifically identified with any National or State political party.

SEC. 19. As used in this Act, the term "State" means any State, Territory, or possession of the United States.

■ Government Corporation Control Act (1945)

Be it enacted by the Senate and House of Representatives of the United States of America in Congress assembled. That this Act may be cited as the "Government Corporation Control Act."

DECLARATION OF POLICY

SEC. 2. It is hereby declared to be the policy of the Congress to bring Government corporations and their transactions and operations under annual scrutiny by the Congress and provide current financial control thereof.

TITLE I—WHOLLY OWNED GOVERNMENT CORPORATIONS

SEC. 101. As used in this Act the term "wholly owned Government corporation" means the Commodity Credit Corporation; Federal Intermediate Credit Banks; Production Credit Corporations; Regional Agricultural Credit Corporations; Farmers Home Corporation; Federal Crop Insurance Corporation; Federal Farm Mortgage Corporation; Federal Surplus Commodities Corporation; Reconstruction Finance Corporation; Defense Plant Corporation; Defense Supplies Corporation; Metals Reserve Company; Rubber Reserve Company; War Damage Corporation; Federal National Mortgage Association; the RFC Mortgage Company; Disaster Loan Corporation; Inland Waterways Corporation; Warrior River Terminal Company; The Virgin Islands Company; Federal Prison Industries, Incorporated; United States Spruce Production Corporation; Institute of Inter-American Affairs; Institute of Inter-American Transportation; Inter-American Educational Foundation, Incorporated; Inter-American Navigation Corporation; Prencinradio, Incorporated; Cargoes, Incorporated; Export-Import Bank of Washington; Petroleum Reserves Corporation; Rubber Development Corporation; U.S. Commercial Company; Smaller War Plants Corporation; Federal Public Housing Authority (or United States Housing Authority) and including public housing projects financed from appropriated funds and operations thereof; Defense Homes Corporation; Federal Savings and Loan Insurance Corporation; Home Owners' Loan Corporation; United States Housing Corporation; Panama Railroad Company; Tennessee Valley Authority; and Tennessee Valley Associated Cooperatives, Incorporated.

SEC. 102. Each wholly owned Government corporation shall cause to be prepared annually a budget program, which shall be submitted to the President through the Bureau of the Budget on or before September 15 of each year. The Bureau of the Budget, under such rules and regulations as the President may establish, is authorized and directed to prescribe the form and content of, and the manner in which such budget program shall be prepared and presented. The budget program shall be a business-type budget, or plan of operations, with due allowance given to the need for flexibility, including provision for emergencies and contingencies, in order that the corporation may properly carry out its activities as authorized by law. The budget program shall contain estimates of the financial condition and operations of the corporation for the current and ensuing fiscal years and the actual condition and results of operation for the last completed fiscal year. Such budget program shall include a statement of financial condition, a statement of income and expense, an analysis of surplus or deficit, a statement of sources and application of funds, and such other supplementary statements and information as are necessary or desirable to make known the financial condition and operations of the corporation. Such statements shall include estimates of operations by major types of activities, together with estimates of administrative expenses, estimates of borrowings, and estimates of the amount of Government capital funds which shall be returned to the Treasury during the fiscal year or the appropriations required to provide for the restoration of capital impairments.

SEC. 103. The budget programs of the corporations as modified, amended, or revised by the President shall be transmitted to the Congress as a part of the annual Budget required by the Budget and Accounting Act, 1921. Amendments to the annual budget programs may be submitted from time to time.

Budget programs shall be submitted for all wholly owned Government corporations covering operations for the fiscal year commencing July 1, 1946, and each fiscal year thereafter.

SEC. 104. The budget programs transmitted by the President to the Congress shall be considered and, if necessary, legislation shall be enacted making available such funds or other financial resources as the Congress may determine. The provisions of this section shall not be construed as preventing wholly owned Government corporations from carrying out and financing their activities as authorized by existing law, nor shall any provisions of this section be construed as affecting in any way the provisions of section 26 of the Tennessee Valley Authority Act, as amended. The provisions of this section shall not be construed as affecting the existing authority of any wholly owned Government corporation to make contracts or other commitments without reference to fiscal-year limitations.

SEC. 105. The financial transactions of wholly owned Government corporations shall be audited by the General Accounting Office in accordance with the principles and procedures applicable to commercial corporate transactions and under such rules and regulations as may be prescribed by the Comptroller General of the United States: *Provided,* That such rules and regulations may provide for the retention at the offices of such corporations, in whole or in part, of any accounts of accountable officers, covering corporate financial transactions, which are required by existing law to be settled and adjusted in the General Accounting Office, and for the settlement and adjustment of such accounts in whole or in part upon the basis of examinations in the course of the audit herein provided, but nothing in this proviso shall be construed as affecting the powers reserved to the Tennessee Valley Authority in the Act of November 21, 1941 (55 Stat. 775). The audit shall be conducted at the place or places where the accounts of the respective corporations are normally kept. The representatives of the General Accounting Office shall have access to all books, accounts, financial records, reports, files, and all other papers, things, or property belonging to or in use by the respective corporations and necessary to facilitate the audit, and they shall be afforded full facilities for verifying transactions with the balances or securities held by depositories, fiscal agents, and custodians. The audit shall begin with the first fiscal year commencing after the enactment of this Act.

SEC. 106. A report of each such audit for each fiscal year ending on June 30 shall be made by the Comptroller General to the Congress not later than January 15 following the close of the fiscal year for which such audit is made. The report shall set forth the scope of the audit and shall include a statement (showing intercorporate relations) of assets and liabilities, capital and surplus or deficit; a statement of surplus or deficit analysis; a statement of income and expense; a statement of sources and application of funds; and such comments and information as may be deemed necessary to keep Congress informed of the operations and financial condition of the several corporations, together with such recommendations with respect thereto as the Comptroller General may deem advisable, including a report of any impairment of capital noted in the audit and recommendations for the return of such Government capital or the payment of such dividends as, in his judgment, should be accomplished. The report shall also show specifically any program, expenditure, or other financial transaction or undertaking observed in the course of the audit, which, in the opinion of the Comptroller General, has been carried on or made without authority of law. A copy of each report shall be furnished to the President, to the Secretary of the Treasury, and to the corporation concerned at the time submitted to the Congress.

SEC. 107. Whenever it is deemed by the Director of the Bureau of the Budget, with the approval of the President, to be practicable and in the public interest that any wholly owned Government corporation be treated with respect to its appropriations, expenditures, receipts, accounting, and other fiscal matters as if it were a Government agency other than a corporation, the Director shall include in connection with the budget program of such corporation in the Budget a recommendation to that effect. If the Congress approves such recommendation in connection with the budget program for any fiscal year, such corporation, with respect to subsequent fiscal years, shall be regarded as an establishment other than a corporation for the purposes of the Budget and Accounting Act, 1921, and other provisions of law relating to appropriations, expenditures, receipts, accounts, and other fiscal matters, and shall not be subject to the provisions of this Act other than this section. The corporate entity shall not be affected by this section.

TITLE II—MIXED-OWNERSHIP GOVERNMENT CORPORATIONS

SEC. 201. As used in this Act the term "mixed-ownership Government corporations" means (1) the Central Bank for Cooperatives and the Regional Banks for Cooperatives, (2) Federal Land Banks, (3) Federal Home Loan Banks, and (4) Federal Deposit Insurance Corporation.

SEC. 202. The financial transactions of mixed-ownership Government corporations for any period during which Government capital has been invested therein shall be audited by the General Accounting Office in accordance with the principles and procedures applicable to commercial corporate transactions and under such rules and regulations as may be prescribed by the Comptroller General of the United States. The audit shall be conducted at the place or places where the accounts of the respective corporations are normally kept. The representatives of the General Accounting Office shall have access to all books, accounts, financial records, reports, files, and all other papers, things, or property belonging to or in use by the respective corporations and necessary to facilitate the audit, and they shall be afforded full facilities for verifying transactions with the balances or securities held by depositories, fiscal agents, and custodians. The audit shall begin with the first fiscal year commencing after the enactment of this Act.

SEC. 203. A report of each such audit for each fiscal year ending on June 30 shall be made by the Comptroller General to the Congress not later than January 15, following the close of the fiscal year for which such audit is made. The report shall set forth the scope of the audit and shall include a statement (showing intercorporate relations) of assets and liabilities, capital and surplus or deficit; a statement of surplus or deficit analysis; a statement of income and expense; a statement of sources and application of funds; and such comments and information as may be deemed necessary to keep Congress informed of the operations and financial condition of, and the use of Government capital by, each such corporation, together with such recommendations with respect thereto as the Comptroller General may deem advisable, including a report of any impairment of capital or lack of sufficient capital noted in the audit and recommendations for the return of such Government capital or the payment of such dividends as, in his judgment, should be accomplished. The report shall also show specifically any program, expenditure, or other financial transaction or undertaking observed in the course of the audit, which, in the opinion of the Comptroller General, has been carried on or made without authority of law. A copy of each report shall be furnished to the President, to the Secretary of the Treasury, and to the corporation concerned at the time submitted to the Congress.

SEC. 204. The President shall include in the annual Budget any recommendations he may wish to make as to the return of Government capital to the Treasury by any mixed-ownership corporation.

■ Employment Act of 1946

SECTION 1. This Act may be cited as the "Employment Act of 1946."

DECLARATION OF POLICY

SEC 2. The Congress hereby declares that it is the continuing policy and responsibility of the Federal Government to use all practicable means consistent with its needs and obligations and other essential considerations of national policy, with the assistance and cooperation of industry, agriculture, labor, and State and local governments, to coordinate and utilize all its plans, functions, and resources for the purpose of creating and maintaining, in a manner calculated to foster and promote free competitive enterprise and the general welfare, conditions under which there will be afforded useful employment opportunities, including self-employment, for those able, willing, and seeking to work, and to promote maximum employment, production, and purchasing power.

SEC. 3. (a) The President shall transmit to the Congress within sixty days after the beginning of each regular session (commencing with the year 1947) an economic report (hereinafter called the "Economic Report") setting forth (1) the levels of employment, production, and purchasing power obtaining in the United States and such levels needed to carry out the policy declared in section 2; (2) current and foreseeable trends in the levels of employment, production, and purchasing power; (3) a review of the economic program of the Federal Government and a review of economic conditions affecting employment in the United States or any considerable portion thereof during the preceding year and of their effect upon employment, production, and purchasing power; and (4) a program for carrying out the policy declared in section 2, together with such recommendations for legislation as he may deem necessary or desirable.

(b) The President may transmit from time to time to the Congress reports supplementary to the Economic Report, each of which shall include such supplementary or revised recommendations as he may deem necessary or desirable to achieve the policy declared in section 2.

(c) The Economic Report, and all supplementary reports transmitted under subsection (b), shall, when transmitted to Congress, be referred to the joint committee created by section 5.

COUNCIL OF ECONOMIC ADVISERS TO THE PRESIDENT

SEC. 4. (a) There is hereby created in the Executive Office of the President a Council of Economic Advisers (hereinafter called the "Council"). The Council shall be composed of three members who shall be appointed by the President, and by and with the advice and consent of the Senate, and each of whom shall be a person who, as a result of his training, experience, and attainments, is exceptionally qualified to analyze and interpret economic developments, to appraise programs and activities of the Government in the light of the policy declared in section 2, and to formulate and recommend national economic policy to promote employment, production, and purchasing power under free competitive enterprise. Each member of the Council shall receive compensation at the rate of $15,000 per annum. The President shall designate one of the members of the Council as chairman and one as vice chairman, who shall act as chairman in the absence of the chairman.

(b) The Council is authorized to employ, and fix the compensation of, such specialists and other experts as may be necessary for the carrying out of its functions under this Act, without regard to the civil-service laws and the Classification Act of 1923, as amended, and is authorized, subject to the civil-service laws, to employ such other officers and employees as may be necessary for carrying out its functions under this Act, and fix their compensation in accordance with the Classification Act of 1923, as amended.

(c) It shall be the duty and function of the Council—

(1) to assist and advise the President in the preparation of the Economic Report;

(2) to gather timely and authoritative information concerning economic developments and economic trends, both current and prospective, to analyze and interpret such information in the light of the policy declared in section 2 for the purpose of determining whether such developments and trends are interfering, or are likely to interfere, with the achievement of such policy, and to compile and submit to the President studies relating to such developments and trends;

(3) to appraise the various programs and activities of the Federal Government in the light of the policy declared in section 2 for the purpose of determining the extent to which such programs and activities are contributing, and the extent to which they are not contributing, to the achievement of such policy, and to make recommendations to the President with respect thereto;

(4) to develop and recommend to the President national economic policies to foster and promote free competitive enterprise, to avoid economic fluctuations or to diminish the effects thereof, and to maintain employment, production, and purchasing power;

(5) to make and furnish such studies, reports thereon, and recommendations with respect to matters of Federal economic policy and legislation as the President may request.

(d) The Council shall make an annual report to the President in December of each year.

(e) In exercising its powers, functions and duties under this Act—

(1) the Council may constitute such advisory committees and may consult with such representatives of industry, agriculture, labor, consumers, State and local governments, and other groups, as it deems advisable;

(2) the Council shall, to the fullest extent possible, utilize the services, facilities, and information (including

statistical information) of other Government agencies as well as of private research agencies, in order that duplication of effort and expense may be avoided.

(f) To enable the Council to exercise its powers, functions, and duties under this Act, there are authorized to be appropriated (except for the salaries of the members and the salaries of officers and employees of the Council) such sums as may be necessary. For the salaries of the members and the salaries of officers and employees of the Council, there is authorized to be appropriated not exceeding $345,000 in the aggregate for each fiscal year.

JOINT COMMITTEE ON THE ECONOMIC REPORT

SEC. 5. (a) There is hereby established a joint Committee on the Economic Report, to be composed of seven Members of the Senate, to be appointed by the President of the Senate, and seven Members of the House of Representatives, to be appointed by the Speaker of the House of Representatives. The party representation on the joint committee shall as nearly as may be feasible reflect the relative membership of the majority and minority parties in the Senate and House of Representatives.

(b) It shall be the function of the joint committee—

(1) to make a continuing study of matters relating to the Economic Report;

(2) to study means of coordinating programs in order to further the policy of this Act; and

(3) as a guide to the several committees of the Congress dealing with legislation relating to the Economic Report, not later than May 1 of each year (beginning with the year 1947) to file a report with the Senate and House

of Representatives containing its findings and recommendations with respect to each of the main recommendations made by the President in the Economic Report, and from time to time to make such other reports and recommendations to the Senate and House of Representatives as it deems advisable.

(c) Vacancies in the membership of the joint committee shall not affect the power of the remaining members to execute the functions of the joint committee, and shall be filled in the same manner as in the case of the original selection. The joint committee shall select a chairman and a vice chariman from among its members.

(d) The joint committee, or any duly authorized subcommittee thereof, is authorized to hold such hearings as it deems advisable, and, within the limitations of its appropriations, the joint committee is empowered to appoint and fix the compensation of such experts, consultants, techniclerical and stenographic assistants, to procure such printing and binding, and to make such expenditures, as it deems necessary and advisable. The cost of stenographic services to report hearings of the joint committee, or any subcommittee thereof, shall not exceed 25 cents per hundred words. The joint committee is authorized to utilize the services, information, and facilities of the departments and establishments of the Government, and also of private research agencies.

(e) There is hereby authorized to be appropriated for each fiscal year, the sum of $50,000, or so much thereof as may be necessary, to carry out the provisions of this section, to be disbursed by the Secretary of the Senate on vouchers signed by the chairman or vice chairman.

■ Administrative Procedure Act (1946)

SECTION 1. This Act may be cited as the "Administrative Procedure Act."

DEFINITIONS

SEC. 2. As used in this Act—

(a) *Agency.*—"Agency" means each authority (whether or not within or subject to review by another agency) of the Government of the United States other than Congress, the courts, or the governments of the possessions, Territories, or the District of Columbia. Nothing in this Act shall be construed to repeal delegations of authority as provided by law. Except as to the requirements of section 3, there shall be excluded from the operation of the Act (1) agencies composed of representatives of the parties or of representatives of organizations of the parties to the disputes determined by them, (2) courts marital and military commissions, (3) military or naval authority exercised in the field in time of war or in occupied territory, or (4) functions which by law expire on the termination of present hostilities, within any fixed period thereafter, or before July 1, 1947, and the functions conferred by the following statutes: Selective Training and Service Act of 1940; Contract Settlement Act of 1944; Surplus Property Act of 1944.

(b) *Person and Party.*—"Person" includes individuals, partnerships, corporations, associations, or public or private organizations of any character other than agencies. "Party" includes any person or agency named or admitted as a party, or properly seeking and entitled as of right to be admitted as a party, in any agency proceeding; but nothing herein shall be construed to prevent an agency from admitting any person or agency as a party for limited purposes.

(c) *Rule and Rule Making.*—"Rule" means the whole or any part of any agency statement of general or particular applicability and future effect designed to implement, interpret, or prescribe law or policy or to describe the organization, procedure, or practice requirements of any agency and includes the approval or prescription for the future of rates, wages, corporate or financial structures or reorganizations thereof, prices, facilities, appliances, services or allowances therefor or of valuations, costs, or accounting, or practices bearing upon any of the foregoing. "Rule making" means agency process for the formulation, amendment, or repeal of a rule.

(d) *Order and Adjudication.*—"Order" means the whole or any part of the final disposition (whether affirmative, negative, injunctive, or declaratory in form) of any agency in any matter other than rule making but including licensing. "Adjudication" means agency process for the formulation of an order.

(e) *License and Licensing.*—"License" includes the whole or part of any agency permit, certificate, approval, registration, charter, membership, statutory exemption, or other form of permission. "Licensing" includes agency process respecting the grant, renewal, denial, revocation, suspension, annulment, withdrawal, limitation amendment, modification, or conditioning of a license.

(f) *Sanction and Relief.*—"Sanction" includes the whole or part of any agency (1) prohibition, requirement, limitation, or other condition affecting the freedom of any person; (2) withholding of relief; (3) imposition of any form of penalty or fine; (4) destruction, taking, seizure, or withholding of property; (5) assessment of damages, reimbursement, restitution, compensation, costs, charges or fees; (6) requirement, revocation, or suspension of a license; or (7) taking of other compulsory or restrictive action. "Relief" includes the whole or part of any agency (1) grant of money, assistance, license, authority, exemption, exception, privilege, or remedy; (2) recognition of any claim, right, immunity, privilege, exemption, or exception; or (3) taking of any other action upon the application or petition of, and beneficial to, any person.

(g) *Agency Proceeding and Action.*—"Agency proceeding" means any agency process as defined in subsections (c), (d), and (e) of this section. "Agency action" includes the whole or part of every agency rule, order, license, sanction, relief, or the equivalent or denial thereof, or failure to act.

PUBLIC INFORMATION

SEC. 3. Except to the extent that there is involved (1) any function of the United States requiring secrecy in the public interest or (2) any matter relating solely to the internal management of an agency—

(a) *Rules.*—Every agency shall separately state and currently publish in the Federal Register (1) descriptions of its central and field organization including delegations by the agency of final authority and the established places at which, and methods whereby the public may secure information or make submittals or requests; (2) statements of the general course and method by which its functions are channeled and determined, including the nature and requirements of all formal or informal procedures available as well as forms and instructions as to the scope and contents of all papers, reports, or examinations; and (3) substantive rules adopted as authorized by law and statements of general policy or interpretations formulated and adopted by the agency for the guidance of the public, but not rules addressed to and served upon named persons in accordance with law. No person shall in any manner be required to resort to organization or procedure not so published.

(b) *Opinions and Orders.*—Every agency shall publish or, in accordance with published rule, make available to public inspection all final opinions or orders in the adjudication of cases (except those required for good cause to be held confidential and not cited as precedents) and all rules.

(c) *Public Records.*—Save as otherwise required by statute, matters of official record shall in accordance with published rule be made available to persons properly and directly concerned except information held confidential for good cause found.

RULE MAKING

SEC. 4. Except to the extent that there is involved (1) any military, naval, or foreign affairs function of the United States or (2) any matter relating to agency management or personnel or to public property, loans, grants, benefits, or contracts—

(a) *Notice.*—General notice of proposed rule making shall be published in the Federal Register (unless all persons subject thereto are named and either personally served or otherwise have actual notice thereof in accordance with law) and shall include (1) a statement of the time, place, and nature of public rule making proceedings; (2) reference to the authority under which the rule is proposed; and (3) either the terms or substance of the proposed rule or a description of the subjects and issues involved. Except where notice or hearing is required by statute, this subsection shall not apply to interpretive rules, general statements of policy, rules of agency organization, procedure, or practice, or in any situation in which the agency for good cause finds (and incorporates the finding and a brief statement of the reasons therefor in the rules issued) that notice and public procedure thereon are impracticable, unnecessary, or contrary to the public interest.

(b) *Procedures.*—After notice required by this section, the agency shall afford interested persons an opportunity to participate in the rule making through submission of written data, views, or arguments with or without opportunity to present the same orally in any manner; and, after consideration of all relevant matter presented, the agency shall incorporate in any rules adopted a concise general statement of their basis and purpose. Where rules are required by statute to be made on the record after opportunity for an agency hearing, the requirements of sections 7 and 8 shall apply in place of the provisions of this subsection.

(c) *Effective Dates.*—The required publication or service of any substantive rule (other than one granting or recognizing exemption or relieving restriction or interpretative rules and statements of policy) shall be made not less than thirty days prior to the effective date thereof except as otherwise provided by the agency upon good cause found and published with the rule.

(d) *Petitions.*—Every agency shall accord any interested person the right to petition for the issuance, amendment, or repeal of a rule.

ADJUDICATION

SEC. 5. In every case of adjudication required by statute to be determined on the record after opportunity for an agency hearing, except to the extent that there is involved (1) any matter subject to a subsequent trial of the law and the facts de novo in any court; (2) the selection or tenure of an officer or employee of the United States other than examiners appointed pursuant to section 11; (3) proceedings in which decisions rest solely on inspections, tests, or elections; (4) the conduct of military, naval, or foreign affairs functions; (5) cases in which an agency is acting as an agent for a court; and (6) the certification of employee representatives—

(a) *Notice.*—Persons entitled to notice of an agency hearing shall be timely informed of (1) the time, place and nature thereof; (2) the legal authority and jurisdiction under which the hearing is to be held; and (3) the matters of fact and law asserted. In instances in which private persons are the moving parties, other parties to the proceeding shall give prompt notice of issues controverted in fact or law; and in other instances agencies may by rule require responsive pleading. In fixing the times and places for hearings, due regard shall be had for the convenience and necessity of the parties or their representatives.

(b) *Procedure.*—The agency shall afford all interested parties opportunity for (1) the submission and consideration of facts, arguments, offers of settlement, or proposals of adjustment where time, the nature of the proceeding, and the public interest permit, and (2) to the extent that the parties are unable so to determine any controversy by consent, hearing, and decision upon notice and in conformity with sections 7 and 8.

(c) *Separation of Functions.*—The same officers who preside at the reception of evidence pursuant to section 7 shall make the recommended decision or initial decision required by section 8 except where such officers become unavailable to the agency. Save to the extent required for the disposition of ex parte matters as authorized by law, no such officer shall consult any person or party on any fact in issue unless upon notice and opportunity for all parties to participate; nor shall such officer be responsible to or subject to the supervision or direction of any officer, employee, or agent engaged in the performance of investigative or prosecuting functions for any agency. No officer, employee, or agent engaged in the performance of investigative or prosecuting functions for any agency in any case, participate or advise in any case shall, in that or a factually related case, participate or advise in the decision, recommended decision, or agency review pursuant to section 8 except as witness or counsel in public proceedings. This subsection shall not apply in determining applications for initial licenses or to proceedings involving the validity or application of rates, facilities, or practices of public utilities or carriers; nor shall it be applicable in any manner to the agency or any member or members of the body comprising the agency.

(d) *Declaratory Orders.*—The agency is authorized in its sound discretion, with like effect as in the case of other orders, to issue a declaratory order to terminate a controversy or remove uncertainty.

Ancillary Matters

SEC. 6. Except as otherwise provided in this Act—

(a) *Appearance.*—Any person compelled to appear in person before any agency or representative thereof shall be accorded the right to be accompanied, represented, and advised by counsel or, if permitted by the agency, by other qualified representative. Every party shall be accorded the right to appear in person or by or with counsel or other duly qualified representative in any agency proceeding. So far as the orderly conduct of public business permits, any interested person may appear before any agency or its responsible officers or employees for the presentation, adjustment, or determination of any issue, request, or controversy in any proceeding (interlocutory, summary, or otherwise) or in connection with any agency function. Every agency shall proceed with reasonable dispatch to conclude any matter presented to it except that due regard shall be had for the convenience and necessity of the parties or their representatives. Nothing herein shall be construed either to grant or to deny to any person who is not a lawyer the right to appear for or represent others before any agency or in any agency proceeding.

(b) *Investigations.*—No process, requirement of a report, inspection, or other investigative act or demand shall be issued, made, or enforced in any manner or for any purpose except as authorized by law. Every person compelled to submit data or evidence shall be entitled to retain or, on payment of lawfully prescribed costs, procure a copy or transcript thereof, except that in a nonpublic investigatory proceeding the witness may for good cause be limited to inspection of the official transcript of his testimony.

(c) *Subpoenas.*—Agency subpoenas authorized by law shall be issued to any party upon request and, as may be required by rules of procedure, upon a statement or showing of general relevance and reasonable scope of the evidence sought. Upon contest the court shall sustain any such subpoena or similar process or demand to the extent that it is found to be in accordance with law and, in any proceeding for enforcement, shall issue an order requiring the appearance of the witness or the production of the evidence or data within a reasonable time under penalty of punishment for contempt in case of contumacious failure to comply.

(d) *Denials.*—Prompt notice shall be given of the denial in whole or in part of any written application, petition, or other request of any intersted person made in connection with any agency proceeding. Except in affirming a prior denial or where the denial is self-explanatory, such notice shall be accompanied by a simple statement of procedural or other grounds.

HEARINGS

SEC. 7. In hearings which section 4 or 5 requires to be conducted pursuant to this section—

(a) *Presiding Officers.*—There shall preside at the taking of evidence (1) the agency, (2) one or more members of the body which comprises the agency, or (3) one or more examiners appointed as provided in this Act; but nothing in this Act shall be deemed to supersede the conduct of specified classes of proceedings in whole or part by or before boards or other officers specially provided for by or designated pursuant to statute. The functions of all presiding officers and of officers participating in decisions in conformity with section 8 shall be conducted in an impartial manner. Any such officer may at any time withdraw if he deems himself disqualified; and upon the filing in good faith of a timely and sufficient affidavit of personal bias or disqualification of any such officer, the agency shall determine the matter as a part of the record and decision in the case.

(b) *Hearing Powers.*—Officers presiding at hearings shall have authority, subject to the published rules of the agency and within its powers, to (1) administer oaths and affirmations, (2) issue subpoenas authorized by law, (3) rule upon offers of proof and receive relevant evidence, (4) take or cause depositions to be taken whenever the ends of justice would be served thereby, (5) regulate the course of the hearing, (6) hold conferences for the settlement or simplification of the issues by consent of the parties, (7) dispose of procedural requests or similar matters, (8) make decisions or recommend decisions in conformity with section 8, and (9) take any other action authorized by agency rule consistent with this Act.

(c) *Evidence.*—Except as statutes otherwise provide, the proponent of a rule or order shall have the burden of proof. Any oral or documentary evidence may be received, but every agency shall as a matter of policy provide for the exclusion of irrelevant, immaterial, or unduly repetitious evidence and no sanction shall be imposed or rule or order be issued except upon consideration of the whole record or such portions thereof as may be cited by any party and as supported by and in accordance with the reliable, probative, and substantial evidence. Every party shall have the right to present his case or defense by oral or documentary evidence, to submit rebuttal evidence, and to conduct such cross-examination as may be required for a full and true disclosure of the facts. In rule making or determining claims for money or benefits or applications for initial licenses, any agency may, where the interest of any party will not be prejudiced thereby, adopt procedures for the submission of all or part of the evidence in written form.

(d) *Record.*—The transcript of testimony and exhibits, together with all papers and requests filed in the proceeding, shall constitute the exclusive record for decision in accordance with section 8 and, upon payment of lawfully prescribed costs, shall be made available to the parties. Where any agency decision rests on official notice of a material fact not appearing in the evidence in the record, any party shall on timely request be afforded an opportunity to show the contrary.

DECISIONS

SEC. 8. In cases in which a hearing is required to be conducted in conformity with section 7—

(a) *Action by Subordinates.*—In cases in which the agency has not presided at the reception of the evidence,

the officer who presided (or, in cases not subject to subsection (c) of section 5, any other officer or officers qualified to preside at hearings pursuant to section 7) shall initially decide the case or the agency shall require (in specific cases or by general rule) the entire record to be certified to it for initial decision. Whenver such officers make the initial decision and in absence of either an appeal to the agency or review upon motion of the agency within time provided by rule, such decision shall without further proceedings then become the decision of the agency. On appeal from or review of the initial decisions of such officers the agency shall, except as it may limit the issues upon notice or by rule, have all the powers which it would have in making the initial decision. Whenever the agency makes the initial decision without having presided at the reception of the evidence, such officers shall first recommend a decision, except that in rule making or determining applications for initial licenses (1) in lieu thereof the agency may issue a tentative decision or any of its responsible officers may recommend a decision or (2) any such procedure may be omitted in any case in which the agency finds upon the record that due and timely execution of its functions imperatively and unavoidably so requires.

(b) *Submittals and Decisions.*—Prior to each recommended, initial, or tentative decision, or decision upon agency review of the decision of subordinate officers, the parties shall be afforded a reasonable opportunity to submit for the consideration of the officers participating in such decisions (1) proposed findings and conclusions, or (2) exceptions to the decisions or recommended decisions of subordinate officers or to tentative agency decisions, and (3) supporting reasons for such exceptions or proposed findings or conclusions. The record shall show the ruling upon each such finding, conclusion, or exception presented. All decisions (including initial, recommended, or tentative decisions) shall become a part of the record and include a statement of (1) findings and conclusions, as well as the reasons or basis therefor, upon all the material issues of fact, law, or discretion presented on the record; and (2) the appropriate rule, order, sanction, relief, or denial thereof.

SANCTIONS AND POWERS

SEC. 9. In the exercise of any power or authority—

(a) *In General.*—No sanction shall be imposed or substantive rule or order be issued except within jurisdiction delegated to the agency and as authorized by law.

(b) *Licenses.*—In any case in which application is made for a license required by law the agency, with due regard to the rights or privileges of all the interested parties or adversely affected persons and with reasonable dispatch, shall set and complete any proceedings required to be conducted pursuant to sections 7 and 8 of this Act or other proceedings required by law and shall make its decision. Except in cases of willfulness or those in which public health, interest, or safety requires otherwise, no withdrawal, suspension, revocation, or annulment of any license shall be lawful unless, prior to the institution of agency proceedings therefor, facts or conduct which may warrant such action shall have been called to the attention of the licensee by the agency in writing and the licensee shall have been accorded opportunity to demonstrate or achieve compliance with all lawful requirements. In any case in which the licensee has, in accordance with agency rules, made timely and sufficient application for a renewal or a new license, no license with reference to any activity of a continuing nature shall expire until such application shall have been finally determined by the agency.

JUDICIAL REVIEW

SEC. 10. Except so far as (1) statutes preclude judicial review or (2) agency action is by law committed to agency discretion—

(a) *Right of Review.*—Any person suffering legal wrong because of any agency action, or adversely affected or aggrieved by such action within the meaning of any relevant statute, shall be entitled to judicial review thereof.

(b) *Form and Venue of Action.*—The form of proceeding for judicial review shall be any special statutory review proceeding relevant to the subject matter in any court specified by statute or, in the absence or inadequacy thereof, any applicable form of legal action (including actions for declaratory judgments or writs of prohibitory or mandatory injunction or habeas corpus) in any court of competent jurisdiction. Agency action shall be subject to judicial review in civil or criminal proceedings for judicial enforcement except to the extent that prior, adequate, and exclusive opportunity for such review is provided by law.

(c) *Reviewable Acts.*—Every agency action made reviewable by statute and every final agency action for which there is no other adequate remedy in any court shall be subject to judicial review. Any preliminary, procedural, or intermediate agency action or ruling not directly reviewable shall be subject to review upon the review of the final agency action. Except as otherwise expressly required by statute, agency action otherwise final shall be final for the purposes of this subsection whether or not there has been presented or determined any application for a declaratory order, for any form of reconsideration, or (unless the agency otherwise requires by rule and provides that the action meanwhile shall be inoperative) for an appeal to superior agency authority.

(d) *Interim Relief.*—Pending judicial review any agency is authorized, where it finds that justice so requires, to postpone the effective date of any action taken by it. Upon such conditions as may be required and to the extent necessary to prevent irreparable injury, every reviewing court (including every court to which a case may be taken on appeal from or upon application for certiorari or other writ to a reviewing court) is authorized to issue all necessary and appropriate process to postpone the effective date of any agency action or to preserve status or rights pending conclusion of the review proceedings.

(e) *Scope of Review.*—So far as necessary to decision and where presented the reviewing court shall decide all relevant questions of law, interpret constitutional and statutory provisions, and determine the meaning or applicability of the terms of any agency action. It shall (A) compel agency action unlawfully withheld or unreasonably delayed; and (B) hold unlawful and set aside agency action, findings, and conclusions found to be (1) arbitrary, capricious, an abuse of discretion, or otherwise not in accordance with law; (2) contrary to constitutional right, power, privilege, or immunity; (3) in excess of statutory jurisdiction, authority, or limitations, or short of statutory right; (4) without observance of procedure required by law; (5) unsupported by substantial evidence in any case subject to the requirements of sections 7 and 8 or otherwise reviewed on the record of an agency hearing provided by statute; or (6) unwarranted by the facts to the extent that the facts are subject to trial de novo by the reviewing court. In making the foregoing determinations the court shall review the whole record or such portions thereof as may be cited by any party, and due account shall be taken of the rule of prejudicial error.

EXAMINERS

SEC 11. Subject to the civil-service and other laws to the extent not inconsistent with this Act, there shall be appointed by and for each agency as many qualified and competent examiners as may be necessary for proceedings pursuant to sections 7 and 8, who shall be assigned to cases in rotation so far as practicable and shall perform no duties inconsistent with their duties and responsibilities as examiners. Examiners shall be removable by the agency in which they are employed only for good cause established and determined by the Civil Service Commission (hereinafter called the Commission) after opportunity for hearing and upon the record thereof. Examiners shall receive compensation prescribed by the Commission independently of agency recommendations or ratings and in accordance with the Classification Act of 1923, as amended, except that the provisions of paragraphs (2) and (3) of subsection (b) of section 7 of said Act, as amended, and the provisions of section 9 of said Act, as amended, shall not be applicable. Agencies occasionally or temporarily insufficiently staffed may utilize examiners selected by the Commission from and with the consent of other agencies. For the purposes of this section, the Commission is authorized to make investigations, require reports by agencies, issue reports, including an annual report to the congress, promulgate rules, appoint such advisory committees as may be deemed necessary, recommend legislation, subpoena witnesses or records, and pay witness fees as established for the United States courts.

CONSTRUCTION AND EFFECT

SEC. 12. Nothing in this Act shall be held to diminish the constitutional rights of any person or to limit or repeal additional requirements imposed by statute or otherwise recognized by law. Except as otherwise required by law, all requirements or privileges relating to evidence or procedure shall apply equally to agencies and persons. If any provision of this Act or the application thereof is held invalid, the remainder of this Act or other applications of such provision shall not be affected. Every agency is granted all authority necessary to comply with the requirements of this Act through the issuance of rules or otherwise. No subsequent legislation shall be held to supersede or modify the provisions of this Act except to the extent that such legislation shall do so expressly. This Act shall take effect three months after its approval except that sections 7 and 8 shall take effect six months after such approval, and no procedural requirement shall be mandatory as to any agency proceeding initiated prior to the effective date of such requirement.

■ First Hoover Commission (1949)
Concluding Report of the Commission on Organization of the Executive Branch of the Government

EXECUTIVE AUTHORITY AND ACCOUNTABILITY

It was a frequent finding of our various task forces that the President and his department heads do not have authority commensurate with the responsibility they must assume. In many instances authority is either lacking or is so diffused that it is almost impossible to hold anyone completely accountable for a particular program or operation. This tendency is dangerous and can, if extended far enough, lead to irresponsible government.

At the present time the President lacks authority to organize the agencies of the executive branch for the most effective discharge of his executive duties. While powers to reorganize have been granted to Presidents in the past, they have been intermittent and subject to many limitations and exclusions, thus seriously diminishing their effectiveness.

Likewise, the recent tendency to create by statute interdepartmental committees with specific duties and memberships has limited the President's authority to choose his advisors. Examples of such agencies are the National Security Council and the National Security Resources Board.

Similarly, statutory powers have often been granted directly to subordinate officers in such a way as to deny authority in certain areas to the President or to a department head. A case in point is the statutory authority of the Army Corps of Engineers to prepare river development plans—authority completely outside of the control of either the Secretary of the Army or the President.

In the critical area of national security, the Secretary of Defense has only a coordinating relation to the Army, Navy, and Air Force. He cannot hire and fire subordinates except on his immediate staff. Almost all appointive power not in the President's hands is vested in the subordinate service secretaries. The Defense Secretary has inadequate powers over the budget and expenditures and he possesses no authority to reorganize the Military Establishment, whose machinery is rigidly prescribed by statute.

Furthermore, when executive duties are assigned to the independent regulatory commissions the President's authority is also weakened. An example of this is the power of the Maritime Commission to operate and charter ships without regard to the views of the President.

Similarly, in the field of administrative management services, executive authority and discretion have been so weakened by rigid and detailed statutes and regulations that the effectiveness of these services has been impaired.

Likewise, requirements affecting recruitment, selection, pay increases, and dismissal of employees, intended to insure fairness and merit in personnel administration, have actually become so detailed and precise as to deprive department heads and their supervisors of important management prerogatives necessary to perform an effective and efficient job.

In another area—fiscal management—no one in the executive branch has authority to set up a central accounting system. Such an instrument is absolutely essential to management and fiscal control. The influence of the Comptroller General—an agent of the Congress—in the determination of executive expenditures also seriously impairs the authority and discretion of the President and his department heads.

Still another basic weakness is to be found in the outmoded appropriation system which concentrates on detailed listings of positions and materials rather than on well-defined functional programs. This prevents the wisest expenditure of public monies, and often diffuses the spending power among so many organization units that it becomes impossible to hold any one person or unit accountable for accomplishing program objectives.

Finally, the enormous amount of detailed substantive legislation is still another feature of present practices which is not conducive to the most effective administration of the public business. There are, for example, 199 statutes affecting personnel management alone in the Department of Agriculture. Disposition of surplus property is governed by over 369 separate laws. The Bureau of Indian Affairs is required to administer over 5,000 statutes and 370 treaties; and the laws which govern the operations of the Reclamation Bureau run to no less than 803 pages.

It is not any one of these factors alone but, like the Lilliputian threads that bound Gulliver, it is the total complex of these restrictions—lack of organization authority; grants of independent executive powers to subordinate officials; restrictive controls over personnel; divided controls over accounting and preaudit of expenditures; diffusion of the spending power of appropriations; overly detailed Legislation—that weakens the powers of management in the executive branch and makes it difficult if not impossible to fix responsibility.

Solution The solution to this problem will require some fundamental and far-reaching changes in present legislative and administrative practices. The Commission's recommendations to the Congress are covered in detail in a number of its previous reports and need not be repeated at length here. However, the reforms required must provide that sufficient authority be delegated to the President and to his department heads to permit them to carry out responsibilities that have been assigned to them by the Constitution and the Congress.

The President should be granted continuing authority to submit reorganization plans covering all agencies of the executive branch, without exception; such plans to be presented to Congress, and to become effective unless disapproved within 60 days by concurrent resolution of both houses. This authority is necessary if the machinery of government is to be made adaptable to the ever changing requirements of administration and if efficiency is to become a continuing rather than a sporadic concern of the Federal Government.

The department heads must be free, with presidential approval, to reorganize their departments in the ways that, in their judgment, best suit the requirements of efficiency and economy. This means that the internal organization structure of executive agencies should not be prescribed by legislation.

The related practice of determining the precise functions and membership of coordinating and advisory bodies by statute should be discontinued in favor of more general enabling legislation which would provide a flexible framework within which the President can act.

Detailed legislation, including rigid itemized apropriation language which unnecessarily limits executive discretion and initiative, should also be avoided.

In the further interest of responsible management, independent grants of executive authority not subject to the control of the Chief Executive should not be made to department heads and subordinate officials.

The purely executive functions of quasi-legislative and quasi-judicial agencies, too, should be brought within the regular executive departments, thus placing these responsibilities within the ambit of executive control.

Likewise, departmental authority over personnel management must be strengthened by permitting those charged with management responsibilities to exercise more discretion in such phases of personnel administration as recruiting, selection, promotions, pay administration, and dismissals.

Finally, the President must have more authority to determine the kind of fiscal reporting he needs to obtain reliable information and to maintain sound fiscal controls.

These changes are the first steps necessary to achieve not only increased efficiency and economy in the Government, but also a greater measure of accountability of the executive branch to Congress.

SHARPENING THE TOOLS OF MANAGEMENT

Beyond the need for greater executive authority and discretion, the President and top officials in the executive branch require more adequate tools in the areas of fiscal management, personnel, supply, and housekeeping services, if the public business is to be conducted efficiently and economically.

FISCAL

In the first of these areas—fiscal management—there are glaring weaknesses to be found in the budget process, in accounting controls, and in the appropriation structure.

The budget process is weakest at the departmental level where it should be strongest. The budget document itself, because of its size and complexity and its concentration on services and materials to be bought rather than programs to be undertaken, is a relatively ineffective tool of management. Perhaps the underlying reason for this is the outmoded appropriation structure, which is exceedingly complex, overly detailed in certain areas and much too broad in others, and is based upon the requirements of organizational units rather than work programs.

The apportionment system is ineffective in controlling overspending. Insufficient attention is given to the revenue side of the budget; and constant difficulty of interpretation is caused by the intermingling of current operating expenditures and capital outlays, and, in certain instances, by failure to disclose subsidies.

There is no formal accounting plan for the Government as a whole. As a consequence there is no place where the complete financial picture of our Government can be seen. Complete and current financial information cannot be obtained since Federal accounting is a mixture of the cash basis of accounting and the accrual basis; and it does not include supply accounting.

Responsibility for fiscal accounts—those relating to revenues, custody of funds, disbursements, public debt, and the currency—rests with the Treasury. Yet the Comptroller General, an agent of Congress, prescribes the form and procedure for administrative appropriation and fund accounting in the executive branch.

As a result we have not had, to this day, a system of accounting that shows the Government's true revenues and expenses for any year, that provides for property or cost accounting, or for a positive control of assets, liabilities, and appropriations.

Solution In our report on budgeting and accounting we propose far reaching changes in these areas. In order to produce a budget plan which will be a more understandable and useful instrument, both to the President and to Congress, we recommend that the budget document be completely recast along the lines of work programs and functions. Such a document, which we designate as a "performance budget," would analyze the work of Government departments and agencies according to their major functions, activities, or projects. It would thus concentrate attention on the work to be done or service to be rendered rather than on things to be acquired such as personal services, contractual services, supplies, materials, and equipment. A performance budget, moreover, would facilitate congressional and executive control by clearly showing the scope and magnitude of each Federal activity. It could also show the relationships between the volume of work to be done and the cost of the work, a measurement which cannot be made under the present system.

However, in order to obtain the full benefit of the performance budget, the appropriation structure would have to be simplified and adjusted to mesh with the budget plan.

The initial stages of budget preparation at the operational level also need to be strengthened. This will both insure better planning and relieve the Office of the Budget of the burden of detailed revisions at that level.

To further assist the President in tightening controls over spending, an Office of the Accountant General should be established under the Secretary of the Treasury with authority to prescribe general accounting methods and to enforce accounting procedures in the executive branch. These methods and procedures should be subject to the approval of the Comptroller General within the powers presently conferred upon him by the Congress.

The Accountant General should have the responsibility, on a report basis, of combining agency accounts into summary accounts of the Government and of producing complete financial reports for the information of the President, the Congress, and the public. The accounts should be kept on an accrual basis and should cover all revenues, receipts, funds, appropriations, expenditures, supplies, properties, and securities of the Federal Government.

When this new system is installed, it will make possible the development of an apportionment system that can provide what is now seriously lacking—proper executive control over the spending of appropriations.

Finally, the Commission recommends that the General Accounting Office's costly practice of minutely examining millions of expenditure vouchers be discontinued so far as possible and be replaced by spot sampling audits at the various Government agencies. In addition to reducing costs without impairing control, it would free the legislature's auditor for more comprehensive and effective post-auditing duties.

These changes in budgeting, accounting, and auditing methods must be made if sound practices in fiscal management and clearer fiscal accountability of the executive branch to the Congress are to be assured.

PERSONNEL

Probably no problem in the management of the Government is more important than that of obtaining and retaining a capable and conscientious body of public servants. Unfortunately, personnel practices in the Federal Government give little room for optimism that these needs are being met.

The Civil Service Commission has not been organized to develop as a really effective staff arm of the President. Planning and administration of the personnel program have not kept pace with the tremendous expansion of employment in the Government.

The centralization of personnel transactions in the Civil Service Commission and in the departmental personnel offices has resulted in unjustifiable delays in handling personnel problems.

Recruitment machinery has been slow, impersonal, and cumbersome. Many personnel procedures are unnecessarily complicated; and the rigidity of certain of them does not permit the necessary latitude of judgment and discretion that operating officials need to do the most effective management job.

Insufficient attention has been given to such positive aspects of sound personnel management as developing better supervisor-employee relations, training, promotion, and incentives for superior performance. In short, the system is not constituted so as to attract and retain sufficient qualified people for the Government's tasks.

These criticisms should not be construed, however, as a reflection on the vast majority of our Federal employees, who are conscientious, hardworking, and devoted, but rather upon a system which has not fully kept pace with the needs of the Federal Government.

Solution In our report on personnel management we make several recommendations to improve the quality of personnel administration in the Government. We recommend that the personnel system be decentralized so that the operating agencies of the Government will perform the day-to-day tasks of recruitment, selection, position classification, and other aspects of personnel management, under standards to be aproved and enforced by the Civil Service Commission.

This will free the Commission from the details of centralized control of personnel operations and transactions, and permit its chairman to concentrate on planning and personnel standards, and on assisting the President and his department heads in developing sound and active personnel management programs.

The chairman of the Civil Service Commission not only should serve as the President's principal staff advisor on civil service problems, but also should direct the Commission's operations.

On the agency level the personnel function should be represented in top management. The departments themselves, in recruiting employees, should use more active and attractive methods; and apply selection methods which will both give their supervisors wider latitude of judgment and insure that appointments are being made on a merit, and not on a political, basis.

To improve employee performance, line supervisors should play a greater role in the selection, advancement, and removal of employees. Forms and procedures in personnel processes should be simplified. Increased emphasis should be given to such matters as employee participation in management problems, in-service training, promotions, and the human relations aspect of management.

Salaries, pitifully low in the higher levels . . . must be substantially increased to attract and retain employees with first-rate abilities. This need was emphasized again and again by almost all of our task forces: by our task forces on personnel, on supply, on medical services, on budgeting and accounting, by our management engineering consultants, and by many other experts working in the various fields of our work.

Finally, all positions in the service with the exception of top level policy jobs should be filled by merit system methods.

All these improvements are necessary if we are to achieve a higher degree of competency, efficiency, and accountability in the Federal service.

GENERAL SERVICES

In several of the chief housekeeping services of the Government—supply, records management, and building maintenance—there are shocking instances of wasteful practices and poor business management.

SUPPLY

In the field of supply our task force reported that no large private corporation could long survive if it practiced the waste and extravagance in supply operations which is condoned in the Federal Government.

There is no adequate central organization to coordinate Government purchasing. Purchasing operations are unplanned and have degenerated largely into the routine practice of soliciting bids and awarding contracts to the lowest bidder. Purchasing officers, moreover, lack information and funds necessary to schedule purchases so as to take maximum advantage of favorable market conditions. They have failed to develop cost records and other management tools essential to performing an effective job of purchasing.

There are too many storage warehouses, many improperly located and carrying duplicating inventories. Because most agencies lack stock control systems which indicate agency needs, and because of the general practice of investing appropriation balances at the end of the fiscal year in supplies, practically all agencies have excessive stocks on hand.

The attention of most traffic personnel is directed to auditing transportation bills. Very few employees are engaged in activities connected with improving traffic management and reducing costs.

There is considerable evidence that many commodities requiring specifications do not have them; and many existing specifications are out of date. Standards are generally described in terms of physical characteristics or composition of product rather than in terms of performance required.

There is no uniformity in the quality of inspection or standard practice as to what types of commodities should be inspected. The Federal Government has no uniform system of cataloging which permits identification or classification of materials used by Federal agencies. There have been as many as 17 unrelated systems of property identification in use at one time. Some agencies maintain no property controls whatever; and numerous others have not inventoried their property in years. This situation has re-

sulted in the piling up of costly duplicating inventories throughout the Government and waste of the taxpayers' money.

Solution Putting the Government supply operations on a businesslike basis can result in enormous savings. The Government is now spending more than $6 billion a year for material, supplies, and equipment. While no one knows exactly what the Government owns, total military and civilian warehouse inventories have been estimated at $27 billion.

In order to place the supply operation on an efficient basis a number of things must be done.

First, the jungle of unduly restrictive statutes, conflicting decisions, and regulations must be swept away and supplanted by a code which will establish basic principles for an effective supply system.

A central supply agency should be created within an Office of General Services to develop, on behalf of the President, policies and regulations designed to assist the civilian operating departments in establishing efficient supply practices—practices which would give proper attention to all phases of supply such as specifications, purchasing, traffic management, inspection, property identification, storage and issue, and property utilization. The agency would also serve as the central purchasing and storage center for common use items.

RECORDS AND BUILDING MANAGEMENT

The problem of records management likewise provides fertile ground for substantial economies. Government records have accumulated at a tremendous rate during the past 20 years. They now occupy about 18 million square feet of space, equivalent to 6 buildings each the size of the Pentagon. At least 50 percent of these records are not currently used, yet many are housed in expensive office space and equipment.

Building management practices, also, are loose. No one knows exactly what property the Government owns and leases; and policies and practices on leasing and other aspects of property management differ widely.

Solution Here again we need an Office of General Services attached to the Executive Office. Through a Bureau of Records Management, it would supervise the destruction of useless records, and should transfer records not required for current operation to strategically located record centers throughout the country where they could be stored at a fraction of present costs. This organization should also assist the departments in developing more efficient and economical records management practices.

Similar economies can be obtained in the operation and maintenance of public buildings. Authority now vested in the Public Buildings Administration should be expanded and assigned to an Office of General Services which, in addition to regular duties of operation and maintenance, would prepare and issue standards of efficiency in building management, supervise space allotments, prepare standard leases and deeds, and maintain a record of buildings leased and owned by the Government.

The strengthening of each of these tools of management—fiscal, personnel, general services—now woefully inadequate, is essential for improved operation of the executive branch.

THE WASTES OF OVERLAPPING AND DUPLICATION

There is probably no place in the Government where waste is more conspicuous than in the overlapping services of the Government. Many of the duplicating and competing services have stubbornly survived through repeated exposures and attempts at reorganization. Our reports and those of the task forces give numerous examples of overlapping and duplication throughout the Government. Here, for the purpose of highlighting the problem and pointing the way toward its solution, we shall briefly cite only three. [The three, dealing with water resource development, land and forestry management, and hospital construction, and omitted herein.]

Solution In several of our reports we recommend putting an end to such wasteful competition by consolidating these overlapping services. We also propose bringing the major construction activities together in one agency.

In addition to this, a Board of Impartial Review of all major public works is required in the President's Office to insure that projects planned are feasible, are supported by adequate basic data, are not in conflict with other works projects, and are being completed with utmost efficiency.

Moreover, to avoid other overlapping and duplication, as for example in the field of statistics, we recommend that the President's authority and staff of the Office of the Budget be strengthened. Likewise, to coordinate the various scientific research programs we recommend the creation of a National Science Foundation.

Finally, in order to provide the President with the necessary information and control of all executive programs we recommend that a position of Staff Secretary be created to keep him informed on current programs. The President will thus be able to achieve better coordination of executive activities.

The basic changes in organization supplemented by additional coordinating and planning devices are vital to the elimination and prevention of tremendous wastes in money and manpower in the Government.

DECENTRALIZATION UNDER CENTRALIZED CONTROL

As a general rule, economy can be achieved in administration by centralizing services common to all agencies. There is a limit, however, in the size and complexity of Government beyond which it is no longer feasible to furnish services centrally without creating serious bottlenecks, delays, and confusion. As a result, the services become more costly and less efficient than if performed by the agencies themselves.

This point has long been reached in the operations of the Federal Government. It is no longer conceivable that personnel transactions for 2 million employees could be processed centrally, or that 3 million purchase orders for $6 billion worth of goods could be handled on a central basis. Yet in the fields of personnel, budgeting, and supply

our task forces have found over-centralized operations which are resulting in inefficient and expensive management.

Our task forces also found many instances where headquarters officials in Washington still cling to the power to make decisions even in matters of minor importance. This, too, has resulted in interminable delays in getting things done, has stultified initiative in the field services, and has resulted in decisions being made which have not taken due account of variations in local conditions.

Solution While a considerable amount of decentralization has already taken place, the necessity for further decentralization of operations under proper central controls is badly needed and has been a recurring theme in our various reports.

In our report on personnel management we recommend that recruitment, selection, and other processes of personnel administration be decentralized to the agencies under standards to be approved and enforced by the Civil Service Commission. Within the agencies themselves we recommend that a similar decentralization of personnel management be made to their field units and operating supervisors.

In our report on budgeting and accounting we recommend that the bulk of the work in the preparation of budget estimates be performed in the operating departments; that accounting reports be kept by the operating departments under a central accounting system.

With the exception of common-use items, we have recommended purchasing by departments under uniform standards prescribed by a central supply agency.

In substantive matters, too, we have recommended that a greater measure of authority be delegated to the field services of the operating departments. This will require that the headquarters agencies concentrate their attention more and more on developing policies which are unmistakably clear. They must also give more attention to establishing standards of performance and to improving their systems of reporting and inspection to insure that policies are carried out.

REORGANIZATION BY MAJOR PURPOSE

Improvements in such areas as authority, management tools, coordination, planning, procedures, and decentralization are not sufficient in themselves to bring about the maximum degree of efficiency in the operations of the Government. The organization structure of the executive branch must also undergo radical revision. Similarly, the departments and agencies themselves must be reorganized.

There are at present too many separate agencies to permit adequate attention and direction from the President. Many closely related functions also are so scattered that in certain fields such as labor, transportation, or medical services no one is charged with considering the problem as a whole.

Furthermore, many agencies contain functions which are totally unrelated to each other, if not inconsistent, creating a lack of central purpose and greatly increasing the problems of internal coordination.

Several areas of conflict, duplication and overlapping,

at least partially due to faulty organization, have been cited.

In our previous reports we have made numerous recommendations designed to improve the organization structure of the executive branch, as well as the internal structure of the various departments and agencies. . . . Our studies have shown conclusively that the areas presenting the greatest problems of duplication and coordination are those in which services of a similar nature are located in different agencies in the executive branch. This dispersion of related functions has led to interagency rivalries and conflicts which have been extremely wasteful and costly.

Solution In recommending organization changes it has been our constant objective to achieve the greatest possible degree of unity in the departmental structure. We have been mindful, too, of the excessive burden on the President of having so many agencies report to him. In our first report we recommended, as a desirable goal, the reduction of the total number of agencies reporting to the President to about one-third of their present number. While it has not been entirely possible to reach this objective, we have, nevertheless, made recommendations which will reduce the total number of agencies so reporting, to what, in our judgment, is the smallest number feasible if a maximum unity of purpose in each department is also to be achieved.

To strengthen the organization of the principal central staff services we have recommended a consolidation of the functions of supply, records management, and buildings management in an Office of General Services.

To restore the Treasury Department to its historic role in fiscal matters and to remove from it operations which are unrelated to its major purpose, we have recommended that the Bureau of Narcotics, the Coast Guard, and the Bureau of Federal Supply be transferred to other departments and that the Treasury become the focal point for the proposed central accounting system.

To integrate the scattered transportation functions of the executive branch, we have recommended combining within a single transportation service in the Department of Commerce such related functions as those of the Maritime Commission relating to the construction, operation, charter and sale of ships, the Coast Guard, the National Advisory Committee for Aeronautics, the Public Roads Administration, the Office of Defense Transportation, and certain transportation safety functions of the Civil Aeronautics Board and Interstate Commerce Commission.

To remove the major areas of overlapping and duplication, we have recommended that the functions of flood control and river and harbor improvement work of the Army Corps of Engineers be consolidated with the Reclamation Service within the Department of the Interior. Similarly, we have recommended that the Bureau of Land Management in Interior be consolidated with the Forest Service in Agriculture.

Finally, in the field of labor we have recommended that several important labor and manpower functions such as the Bureau of Employment Security, Bureau of Employees Compensation, and Selective Service System be transferred to the Department of Labor.

These are typical examples of reorganization proposals that we have made to achieve greater over-all efficiency and improved coordination in the executive branch by grouping services and activities according to major purpose.

■ Freedom of Information Act (1966)

PUBLIC INFORMATION; AGENCY RULES, OPINIONS, ORDERS, RECORDS, AND PROCEEDINGS

(a) Each agency shall make available to the public information as follows:

(1) Each agency shall separately state and currently publish in the Federal Register for the guidance of the public—

(A) descriptions of its central and field organization and the established places at which, the employees (and in the case of a uniformed service, the members) from whom, and the methods whereby, the public may obtain information, make submittals or requests, or obtain decisions;

(B) statements of the general course and method by which its functions are channeled and determined, including the nature and requirements of all formal and informal procedures available;

(C) rules of procedure, descriptions of forms available or the places at which forms may be obtained, and instructions as to the scope and contents of all papers, reports, or examinations;

(D) substantive rules of general applicability adopted as authorized by law, and statements of general policy or interpretations of general applicability formulated and adopted by the agency; and

(E) each amendment, revision, or repeal of the foregoing.

Except to the extent that a person has actual and timely notice of the terms thereof, a person may not in any manner be required to, or be adversely affected by, a matter required to be published in the Federal Register and so published. For the purpose of this paragraph, matter reasonably available to the class of persons affected thereby is deemed published in the Federal Register when incorporated by reference therein with the approval of the Director of the Federal Register.

(2) Each agency, in accordance with published rules, shall make available for public inspection and copying—

(A) final opinions, including concurring and dissenting opinions, as well as orders, made in the adjudication of cases;

(B) those statements of policy and interpretations which have been adopted by the agency and are not published in the Federal Register; and

(C) administrative staff manuals and instructions to staff that affect a member of the public;

unless the materials are promptly published and copies offered for sale. To the extent required to prevent a clearly unwarranted invasion of personal privacy, an agency may delete identifying details when it makes available or publishes an opinion, statement of policy, interpretation, or staff manual or instruction. However, in each case the justification for the deletion shall be explained fully in writing. Each agency shall also maintain and make available for public inspection and copying current indexes providing identifying information for the public as to any matter issued, adopted, or promulgated after July 4, 1967, and required by this paragraph to be made available or published. Each agency shall promptly publish, quarterly or more frequently, and distribute (by sale or otherwise) copies of each index or supplements thereto unless it determines by order published in the Federal Register that the publication would be unnecessary and impracticable, in which case the agency shall nonetheless provide copies of such index on request at a cost not to exceed the direct cost of duplication. A final order, opinion, statement of policy, interpretation, or staff manual or instruction that affects a member of the public may be relied on, used, or cited as precedent by an agency against a party other than an agency only if—

(i) it has been indexed and either made available or published as provided by this paragraph; or

(ii) the party has actual and timely notice of the terms thereof.

(3) Except with respect to the records made available under paragraphs (1) and (2) of this subsection, each agency, upon any request for records which (A) reasonably describes such records and (B) is made in accordance with published rules stating the time, place, fees (if any), and procedures to be followed, shall make the records promptly available to any person.

(4)(A) In order to carry out the provisions of this section, each agency shall promulgate regulations, pursuant to notice and receipt of public comment, specifying a uniform schedule of fees applicable to all constituent units of such agency. Such fees shall be limited to reasonable standard charges for document search and duplication and provide for recovery of only the direct costs of such search and duplication. Documents shall be furnished without charge or at a reduced charge where the agency determines that waiver or reduction of the fee is in the public interest because furnishing the information can be considered as primarily benefiting the general public.

(B) On complaint, the district court of the United States in the district in which the complainant resides, or has his principal place of business, or in which the agency records are situated, or in the District of Columbia, has jurisdiction to enjoin the agency from withholding agency records and to order the production of any agency records improperly withheld from the complainant. In such a case the court shall determine the matter de novo, and may examine the contents of such agency records in camera to determine whether such records or any part thereof shall be withheld under any of the exemptions set forth in subsection (b) of this section, and the burden is on the agency to sustain its action.

(C) Notwithstanding any other provision of law, the defendant shall serve an answer or otherwise plead to any complaint made under this subsection within thirty days after service upon the defendant of the pleading in which such complaint is made, unless the court otherwise directs for good cause shown.

(D) Except as to cases the court considers of greater importance, proceedings before the district court, as authorized by this subsection, and appeals therefrom, take precedence on the docket over all cases and shall be assigned for hearing and trial or for argument at the earliest practicable date and expedited in every way.

(E) The court may assess against the United States reasonable attorney fees and other litigation costs reasonably incurred in any case under this section in which the complainant has substantially prevailed.

(F) Whenever the court orders the production of any agency records improperly withheld from the complainant and assesses against the United States reasonable attorney fees and other litigation costs, and the court additionally issues a written finding that the circumstances surrounding the withholding raise questions whether agency personnel acted arbitrarily or capriciously with respect to the withholding, the Civil Service Commission shall promptly initiate a proceeding to determine whether disciplinary action is warranted against the officer or employee who was primarily responsible for the withholding. The Commission, after investigation and consideration of the evidence submitted, shall submit its findings and recommendations to the administrative authority of the agency concerned and shall send copies of the findings and recommendations to the officer or employee or his representative. The administrative authority shall take the corrective action that the Commission recommends.

(G) In the event of noncompliance with the order of the court, the district court may punish for contempt the responsible employee, and in the case of a uniformed service, the responsible member.

(5) Each agency having more than one member shall maintain and make available for public inspection a record of the final votes of each member in every agency proceeding.

(6)(A) Each agency, upon any request for records made under paragraph (1), (2), or (3) of this subsection, shall—

(i) determine within ten days (excepting Saturdays, Sundays, and legal public holidays) after the receipt of any such request whether to comply with such request and shall immediately notify the person making such request of such determination and the reasons therefor, and the right of such person to appeal to the head of the agency any adverse determination; and

(ii) make a determination with respect to any appeal within twenty days (excepting Saturdays, Sundays, and legal public holidays) after the receipt of such appeal. If on appeal the denial of the request for records is in whole or in part upheld, the agency shall notify the person making such request of the provisions for judicial review of that determination under paragraph (4) of this subsection.

(B) In unusual circumstances as specified in this subparagraph, the time limits prescribed in either clause (i) or clause (ii) of subparagraph (A) may be extended by written notice to the person making such request setting forth the reasons for such extension and the date on which a determination is expected to be dispatched. No such notice shall specify a date that would result in an extension for more than ten working days. As used in this subparagraph, "unusual circumstances" means, but only to the extent reasonably necessary to the proper processing of the particular request—

(i) the need to search for and collect the requested records from field facilities or other establishments that are separate from the office processing the request;

(ii) the need to search for, collect, and appropriately examine a voluminous amount of separate and distinct records which are demanded in a single request; or

(iii) the need for consultation, which shall be conducted with all practicable speed, with another agency having a substantial interest in the determination of the request or among two or more components of the agency having substantial subject-matter interest therein.

(C) Any person making a request to any agency for records under paragraph (1), (2), or (3) of this subsection shall be deemed to have exhausted his administrative remedies with respect to such request if the agency fails to comply with the applicable time limit provisions of this paragraph. If the Government can show exceptional circumstances exist and that the agency is exercising due diligence in responding to the request, the court may retain jurisdiction and allow the agency additional time to complete its review of the records. Upon any determination by an agency to comply with a request for records, the records shall be made promptly available to such person making such request. Any notification of denial of any request for records under this subsection shall set forth the names and titles or positions of each person responsible for the denial of such request.

(b) This section does not apply to matters that are—

(1)(A) specifically authorized under criteria established by an Executive order to be kept secret in the interest of national defense or foreign policy and (B) are in fact properly classified pursuant to such Executive order;

(2) related solely to the internal personnel rules and practices of an agency;

(3) specifically exempted from disclosure by statute (other than section 552b of this title), provided that such statute (A) require that the matters be withheld from the public in such a manner as to leave no discretion on the issue, or (B) establishes particular criteria for withholding or refers to particular types of matter to be withheld;

(4) trade secrets and commercial or financial information obtained from a person and privileged or confidential;

(5) inter-agency or intra-agency memorandums or letters which would not be available by law to a party other than an agency in litigation with the agency;

(6) personnel and medical files and similar files the disclosure of which would constitute a clearly unwarranted invasion of personal privacy;

(7) investigatory records compiled for law enforcement purposes, but only to the extent that the production of such records would (A) interfere with enforcement proceedings, (B) deprive a person of a right to a fair trial or an impartial adjudication, (C) constitute an unwarranted invasion of personal privacy, (D) disclose the identity of a confidential source and, in the case of a record compiled by a criminal law enforcement authority in the course of a criminal investigation, or by an agency conducting a lawful national security intelligence investigation, confidential information furnished only by the confidential source, (E) disclose investigative techniques and procedures, or (F) endanger the life or physical safety of law enforcement personnel;

(8) contained in or related to examination, operating, or condition reports prepared by, on behalf of, or for the use of an agency responsible for the regulation or supervision of financial institutions; or

(9) geological and geophysical information and data, including maps, concerning wells.

Any reasonably segregable portion of a record shall be provided to any person requesting such record after deletion of the portions which are exempt under this subsection.

(c) This section does not authorize withholding of information or limit the availability of records to the public, except as specifically stated in this section. This section is not authority to withhold information from Congress.

(d) On or before March 1 of each calendar year, each agency shall submit a report covering the preceding calendar year to the Speaker of the House of Representatives and President of the Senate for referral to the appropriate committees of the Congress. The report shall include—

(1) the number of determinations made by such agency not to comply with the requests for records made to such agency under subsection (a) and the reasons for each such determination;

(2) the number of appeals made by persons under subsection (a)(6), the result of such appeals, and the reason for the action upon each appeal that results in a denial of information;

(3) the names and titles or positions of each person responsible for the denial of records requested under this section, and the number of instances of participation for each;

(4) the results of each proceeding conducted pursuant to subsection (a)(4)(F), including a report of the disciplinary action taken against the officer or employee who was primarily responsible for improperly withholding records or an explanation of why disciplinary action was not taken.

(5) a copy of every rule made by such agency regarding this section;

(6) a copy of the fee schedule and the total amount of fees collected by the agency for making records available under this section; and

(7) such other information as indicates efforts to administer fully this section.

The Attorney General shall submit an annual report on or before March 1 of each calendar year which shall include for the prior calendar year a listing of the number of cases arising under this section, the exemption involved in each case, the disposition of such case, and the cost, fees, and penalties assessed under subsections (a)(4)(E), (F), and (G). Such report shall also include a description of the efforts undertaken by the Department of Justice to encourage agency compliance with this section.

(e) For purposes of this section, the term "agency" as defined in section 551(1) of this title includes any executive department, military department, Government corporation, Government controlled corporation, or other establishment in the executive branch of the Government (including the Executive Office of the President), or any independent regulatory agency.

■ Privacy Act (1974)

RECORDS MAINTAINED ON INDIVIDUALS

(a) DEFINITIONS

For purposes of this section—

(1) the term "agency" means agency as defined in section 552(e) of this title;

(2) the term "individual" means a citizen of the United States or an alien lawfully admitted for permanent residence;

(3) the term "maintain" includes maintain, collect, use, or disseminate;

(4) the term "record" means any item, collection, or grouping of informatin about an individual that is maintained by an agency, including, but not limited to, his education, financial transactions, medical history, and criminal or employment history and that contains his name, or the identifying number, symbol, or other identifying particular assigned to the individual, such as a finger or voice print or photograph;

(5) the term "system of records" means a group of any records under the control of any agency from which information is retrieved by the name of the individual or by some identifying number, symbol, or other identifying particular assigned to the individual;

(6) the term "statistical record" means a record in a system of records maintained for statistical research or reporting purposes only and not used in whole or in part in making any determination about an identifiable individual, except as provided by section 8 of title 13; and

(7) the term "routine use" means, with respect to the disclosure of a record, the use of such record for a purpose which is compatible with the purpose for which it was collected.

(b) CONDITIONS OF DISCLOSURE

No agency shall disclose any record which is contained in a system of records by any means of communication to any person, or to another agency, except pursuant to a written request by, or with the prior written consent of, the individual to whom the record pertains, unless disclosure of the record would be—

(1) to those officers and employees of the agency which maintains the record who have a need for the record in the performance of their duties;

(2) required under section 552 of this title;

(3) for a routine use as defined in subsection (a)(7) of this section and described under subsection (e)(4)(D) of this section;

(4) to the Bureau of the Census for purposes of planning or carrying out a census or survey or related activity pursuant to the provisions of title 13;

(5) to a recipient who has provided the agency with advance adequate written assurance that the record will be used solely as a statistical research or reporting record, and the record is to be transferred in a form that is not individually identifiable;

(6) to the National Archives of the United States as a record which has sufficient historical or other value to warrant its continued preservation by the United States Government, or for evaluation by the Administrator of General Services or his designee to determine whether the record has such value;

(7) to another agency or to an instrumentality of any governmental jurisdiction within or under the control of the United States for a civil or criminal law enforcement activity if the activity is authorized by law, and if the head of the agency or instrumentality has made a written request to the agency which maintains the record specifying the particular portion desired and the law enforcement activity for which the record is sought;

(8) to a person pursuant to a showing of compelling circumstances affecting the health or safety of an individual if upon such disclosure notification is transmitted to the last known address of such individual;

(9) to either House of Congress, or, to the extent of matter within its jurisdiction, any committee or subcommittee thereof, any joint committee of Congress or subcommittee of any such joint committee;

(10) to the Comptroller General, or any of his authorized representatives, in the course of the performance of the duties of the General Accounting Office; or

(11) pursuant to the order of a court of competent jurisdiction.

(c) ACCOUNTING OF CERTAIN DISCLOSURES

Each agency, with respect to each system of records under its control, shall—

(1) except for disclosures made under subsections (b)(1) or (b)(2) of this section, keep an accurate accounting of—

(A) the date, nature, and purpose of each disclosure of a record to any person or to another agency made under subsection (b) of this section; and

(B) the name and address of the person or agency to whom the disclosure is made;

(2) retain the accounting made under paragraph (1) of this subsection for at least five years or the life of the record, whichever is longer, after the disclosure for which the accounting is made;

(3) except for disclosures made under subsection (b)(7) of this section, make the accounting made under paragraph (1) of this subsection available to the individual named in the record at his request; and

(4) Inform any person or other agency about any correction or notation of dispute made by the agency in accordance with subsection (d) of this section of any record that has been disclosed to the person or agency if an accounting of the disclosure was made.

(d) ACCESS TO RECORDS

Each agency that maintains a system of records shall—

(1) upon request by an individual to gain access to his record or to any information pertaining to him which is contained in the system, permit him and upon his request, a person of his own choosing to accompany him, to review the record and have a copy made of all or any portion thereof in a form comprehensible to him, except that the agency may require the individual to furnish a written statement authorizing discussion of that individual's record in the accompanying person's presence;

(2) permit the individual to request amendment of a record pertaining to him and—

(A) not later than 10 days (excluding Saturdays, Sundays, and legal public holidays) after the date of receipt of such request, acknowledge in writing such receipt; and

(B) promptly, either—

(i) make any correction of any portion thereof which the individual believes is not accurate, relevant, timely, or complete; or

(ii) inform the individual of its refusal to amend the record in accordance with his request, the reason for the refusal, the procedures established by the agency for the individual to request a review of that refusal by the head of the agency or an officer designated by the head of the agency, and the name and business address of that official;

(3) permit the individual who disagrees with the refusal of the agency to amend his record to request a review of such refusal, and not later than 30 days (excluding Saturdays, Sundays, and legal public holidays) from the date on which the individual requests such review, complete such review and make a final determination unless, for good cause shown, the head of the agency extends such 30-day period; and if, after his review, the reviewing official also refuses to amend the record in accordance with the request, permit the individual to file with the agency a concise statement setting forth the reasons for his disagreement with the refusal of the agency, and notify the individual of the provisions for judicial review of the reviewing official's determination under subsection (g)(1)(A) of this section:

(4) in any disclosure, containing information about which the individual has filed a statement of disagreement, occurring after the filing of the statement under paragraph (3) of this subsection, clearly note any portion of the record which is disputed and provide copies of the statement and, if the agency deems it appropriate, copies of a concise statement of the reasons of the agency for not making the amendments requested, to persons or other agencies to whom the disputed record has been disclosed; and

(5) nothing in this section shall allow an individual access to any information compiled in reasonable anticipation of a civil action or proceeding.

(e) AGENCY REQUIREMENTS

Each agency that maintains a system of records shall—

(1) maintain in its records only such information about an individual as is relevant and necessary to accomplish a purpose of the agency required to be accomplished by statute or by executive order of the President;

(2) collect information to the greatest extent practicable directly from the subject individual when the information may result in adverse determination about an individual's rights, benefits, and privileges under Federal programs;

(3) inform each individual whom it asks to supply information, on the form which it uses to collect the information or on a separate form that can be retained by the individual—

(A) the authority (whether granted by statute, or by executive order of the President) which authorizes the solicitation of the information and whether disclosure of such information is mandatory or voluntary;

(B) the principal purpose or purposes for which the information is intended to be used;

(C) the routine uses which may be made of the information, as published pursuant to paragraph (4)(D) of this subsection; and

(D) the effects on him, if any, of not providing all or any part of the requested information;

(4) subject to the provisions of paragraph (11) of this subsection, publish in the Federal Register at least annually a notice of the existence and character of the system of records, which notice shall include—

(A) the name and location of the system;

(B) the categories of individuals on whom records are maintained in the system;

(C) the categories of records maintained in the system;

(D) each routine use of the records contained in the system, including the categories of users and the purpose of such use;

(E) the policies and practices of the agency regarding storage, retrievability, access controls, retention, and disposal of the records;

(F) the title and business address of the agency official who is responsible for the system of records;

(G) the agency procedures whereby an individual can be notified at his request if the system of records contains a record pertaining to him;

(H) the agency procedures whereby an individual can be notified at his request how he can gain access to any record pertaining to him contained in the system of records, and how he can contest its content; and

(I) the categories of sources of records in the system;

(5) maintain all records which are used by the agency in making any determination about any individual with

such accuracy, relevance, timeliness, and completeness as is reasonably necessary to assure fairness to the individual in the determination;

(6) prior to disseminating any record about an individual to any person other than an agency, unless the dissemination is made pursuant to subsection (b)(2) of this section, make reasonable efforts to assure that such records are accurate, complete, timely, and relevant for agency purposes;

(7) maintain no record describing how any individual exercises rights guaranteed by the First Amendment unless expressly authorized by statute or by the individual about whom the record is maintained or unless pertinent to and within the scope of an authorized law enforcement activity;

(8) make reasonable efforts to serve notice on an individual when any record on such individual is made available to any person under compulsory legal process when such process becomes a matter of public record;

(9) establish rules of conduct for persons involved in the design, development, operation, or maintenance of any system of records, or in maintaining any record, and instruct each such person with respect to such rules and the requirements of this section, including any other rules and procedures adopted pursuant to this section and the penalties for noncompliance;

(10) establish appropriate administrative, technical, and physical safeguards to insure the security and confidentiality of records and to protect against any anticipated threats or hazards to their security or integrity which could result in substantial harm, embarrassment, inconvenience, or unfairness to any individual on whom information is maintained; and

(11) at least 30 days prior to publication of information under paragraph (4)(D) of this subsection, publish in the Federal Register notice of any new use or intended use of the information in the system, and provide an opportunity for interested persons to submit written data, views, or arguments to the agency.

(f) AGENCY RULES

In order to carry out the provisions of this section, each agency that maintains a system of records shall promulgate rules, in accordance with the requirements (including general notice) of section 553 of this title, which shall—

(1) establish procedures whereby an individual can be notified in response to his request if any system of records named by the individual contains a record pertaining to him;

(2) define reasonable times, places, and requirements for identifying an individual who requests his record or information pertaining to him before the agency shall make the record or information available to the individual;

(3) establish procedures for the disclosure to an individual upon his request of his record or information pertaining to him, including special procedure, if deemed necessary, for the disclosure to an individual of medical records, including psychological records pertaining to him;

(4) establish procedures for reviewing a request from an individual concerning the amendment of any record or information pertaining to the individual, for making a determination on the request, for an appeal within the agency of an initial adverse agency determination, and for whatever additional means may be necessary for each individual to be able to exercise fully his rights under this section; and

(5) establish fees to be charged, if any, to any individual for making copies of his record, excluding the cost of any search for and review of the record.

The Office of the Federal Register shall annually compile and publish the rules promulgated under this subsection and agency notices published under subsection (e)(4) of this section in a form available to the public at low cost.

(g) CIVIL REMEDIES

(1) Whenever any agency

(A) makes a determination under subsection (d)(3) of this section not to amend an individual's record in accordance with his request, or fails to make such review in conformity with that subsection;

(B) refuses to comply with an individual request under subsection (d)(1) of this section;

(C) fails to maintain any record concerning any individual with such accuracy, relevance, timeliness, and completeness as is necessary to assure fairness in any determination relating to the qualifications, character, rights, or opportunities of, or benefits to the individual that may be made on the basis of such record, and consequently a determination is made which is adverse to the individual; or

(D) fails to comply with any other provision of this section, or any rule promulgated thereunder, in such a way as to have an adverse effect on an individual,
the individual may bring a civil action against the agency, and the district courts of the United States shall have jurisdiction in the matters under the provisions of this subsection.

(2)(A) In any suit brought under the provisions of subsection (g)(1)(A) of this section, the court may order the agency to amend the individual's record in accordance with his request or in such other way as the court may direct. In such a case the court shall determine the matter de novo.

(B) The court may assess against the United States reasonable attorney fees and other litigation costs reasonably incurred in any case under this paragraph in which the complainant has substantially prevailed.

(3)(A) In any suit brought under the provisions of subsection (g)(1)(B) of this section, the court may enjoin the agency from withholding the records and order the production to the complainant of any agency records improperly withheld from him. In such a case the court shall determine the matter de novo, and may examine the contents of any agency records in camera to determine whether the records or any portion thereof may be withheld under any of the exemptions set forth in subsection (k) of this section, and the burden is on the agency to sustain its action.

(B) The court may assess against the United States

reasonable attorney fees and other litigation costs reasonably incurred in any case under this paragraph in which the complainant has substantially prevailed.

(4) In any suit brought under the provisions of subsection (g)(1)(C) or (D) of this section in which the court determines that the agency acted in a manner which was intentional or willful, the United States shall be liable to the individual in an amount equal to the sum of—

(A) actual damages sustained by the individual as a result of the refusal or failure, but in no case shall a person entitled to recovery receive less than the sum of $1,000; and

(B) the costs of the action together with reasonable attorney fees as determined by the court.

(5) An action to enforce any liability created under this section may be brought in the district court of the United States in the district in which the complainant resides, or has his principal place of business, or in which the agency records are situated, or in the District of Columbia, without regard to the amount in controversy, within two years from the date on which the cause of action arises, except that where an agency has materially and willfully misrepresented any information required under this section to be disclosed to an individual and the information so misrepresented is material to establishment of the liability of the agency to the individual under this section, the action may be brought at any time within two years after discovery by the individual of the misrepresentation. Nothing in this section shall be construed to authorize any civil action by reason of any injury sustained as the result of a disclosure of a record prior to September 27, 1975.

(h) RIGHTS OF LEGAL GUARDIANS

For the purposes of this section, the parent of any minor, or the legal guardian of any individual who has been declared to be incompetent due to physical or mental incapacity or age by a court of competent jurisdiction, may act on behalf of the individual.

(i) CRIMINAL PENALTIES

(1) Any officer or employee of an agency, who by virtue of his employment or official position, his possession of, or access to, agency records which contain individually identifiable information the disclosure of which is prohibited by this section or by rules or regulations established thereunder, and who knowing that disclosure of the specific material is so prohibited, willfully discloses the material in any manner to any person or agency not entitled to receive it, shall be guilty of a misdemeanor and fined not more than $5,000.

(2) Any officer or employee of any agency who willfully maintains a system of records without meeting the notice requirements of subsection (e)(4) of this section shall be guilty of a misdemeanor and fined not more than $5,000.

(3) Any person who knowingly and willfully requests or obtains any record concerning an individual from an agency under false pretenses shall be guilty of a misdemeanor and fined not more than $5,000.

(j) GENERAL EXEMPTIONS

The head of any agency may promulgate rules, in accordance with the requirements (including general notice) of sections 553(b)(1), (2), and (3), (c), and (e) of this title, to exempt any system of records within the agency from any part of this section except subsections (b), (c)(1) and (2), (e)(4)(A) through (F), (e)(6), (7), (9), (10), and (11), and (i) if the system of records is—

(1) maintained by the Central Intelligence Agency; or

(2) maintained by an agency or component thereof which performs as its principal function any activity pertaining to the enforcement of criminal laws, including police efforts to prevent, control, or reduce crime or to apprehend criminals, and the activities of prosecutors, courts, correctional, probation, pardon, or parole authorities, and which consists of (A) information compiled for the purpose of identifying data and notations of arrests, the nature and disposition of criminal charges, sentencing, confinement, release, and parole and probation status; (B) information compiled for the purpose of a criminal investigation, including reports of informants and investigators, and associated with an identifiable individual; or (C) reports identifiable to an individual compiled at any stage of the process of enforcement of the criminal laws from arrest or indictment through release from supervision. At the time rules are adopted under this subsection, the agency shall include in the statement required under section 553(c) of this title, the reasons why the system of records is to be exempted from a provision of this section.

(k) SPECIFIC EXEMPTIONS

The head of any agency may promulgate rules, in accordance with the requirement (including general notice) of sections 553(b)(1), (2), and (3), (c) and (e) of this title, to exempt any system of records within the agency from subsections (c)(3), (d), (e)(1), (e)(4)(G), (H), and (I) and (f) of this section if the system of records is—

(1) subject to the provisions of section 552(b)(1) of this title;

(2) investigatory material compiled for law enforcement purposes, other than material within the scope of subsection (j)(2) of this section: *Provided, however,* That if any individual is denied any right, privilege, or benefit that he would otherwise be entitled by Federal law, or for which he would otherwise be eligible, as a result of the maintenance of such material, such material shall be provided to such individual, except to the extent that the disclosure of such material would reveal the identity of a source who furnished information to the Government under an express promise that the identity of the source would be held in confidence, or, prior to the effective date of this section, under an implied promise that the identity of the source would be held in confidence;

(3) maintained in connection with providing protective services to the President of the United States or other individuals pursuant to section 3056 of title 18;

(4) required by statute to be maintained and used solely as statistical records;

(5) investigatory material compiled solely for the purpose of determining suitability, eligibility, or qualifications for Federal civilian employment, military service, Federal contracts, or access to classified information, but only to the extent that the disclosure of such material would reveal the identity of a source who furnished information to the Government under an express promise that the identity of the source would be held in confidence, or, prior to the effective date of this section, under an implied promise that the identity of the source would be held in confidence;

(6) testing or examination material used solely to determine individual qualifications for appointment or promotion in the Federal service the disclosure of which would compromise the objectivity or fairness of the testing or examination process; or

(7) evaluation material used to determine potential for promotion in the armed services, but only to the extent that the disclosure of such material would reveal the identity of a source who furnished information to the Government under an express promise that the identity of the source would be held in confidence, or, prior to the effective date of this section, under an implied promise that the identity of the source would be held in confidence.

At the time rules are adopted under this subsection, the agency shall include in the statement required under section 553(c) of this title, the reasons why the system of records is to be exempted from a provision of this section.

(l) ARCHIVAL RECORDS

(1) Each agency record which is accepted by the Administrator of General Services for storage, processing, and servicing in accordance with section 3103 of title 44 shall, for the purposes of this section, be considered to be maintained by the agency which deposited the record and shall be subject to the provisions of this section. The Administrator of General Services shall not disclose the record except to the agency which maintains the record, or under rules established by that agency which are not inconsistent with the provisions of this section.

(2) Each agency record pertaining to an identifiable individual which was transferred to the National Archives of the United States as a record which has sufficient historical or other value to warrant its continued preservation by the United States Government, prior to the effective date of this section, shall, for the purposes of this section, be considered to be maintained by the National Archives and shall not be subject to the provisions of this section, except that a statement generally describing such records (modeled after the requirements relating to records subject to subsections (e)(4)(A) through (G) of this section) shall be published in the Federal Register.

(3) Each agency record pertaining to an identifiable individual which is transferred to the National Archives of the United States as a record which has sufficient historical or other value to warrant its continued preservation by the United States Government, on or after the effective date of this section, shall be considered to be maintained by the National Archives and shall be exempt from the requirements of this section except subsections (e)(4)(A) through (G) and (e)(9) of this section.

(m) GOVERNMENT CONTRACTORS

When an agency provides by a contract for the operation by or on behalf of the agency of a system of records to accomplish an agency function, the agency shall, consistent with its authority, cause the requirements of this section to be applied to such system. For purposes of subsection (i) of this section any such contractor and any employee of such contractor, if such contract is agreed to on or after the effective date of this section, shall be considered to be an employee of an agency.

(n) MAILING LISTS

An individual's name and address may not be sold or rented by an agency unless such action is specifically authorized by law. This provision shall not be construed to require the withholding of names and addresses otherwise permitted to be made public.

(o) REPORT ON NEW SYSTEMS

Each ageny shall provide adequate advance notice to Congress and the Office of Management and Budget of any proposal to establish or alter any system of records in order to permit an evaluation of the probable or potential effect of such proposal on the privacy and other personal or property rights of individuals or the disclosure of information relating to such individuals, and its effects on the preservation of the constitutional principles of federalism and separation of powers.

(p) ANNUAL REPORT

The President shall submit to the Speaker of the House and the President of the Senate, by June 30 of each calendar year, a consolidated report, separately listing for each Federal agency the number of records contained in any system of records which were exempted from the application of this section under the provisions of subsections (j) and (k) of this section during the preceding calendar year, and the reasons for the exemptions, and such other information as indicates efforts to administer fully this section.

(q) EFFECT OF OTHER LAWS

No agency shall rely on any exemption contained in section 552 of this title to withhold from an individual any record which is otherwise accessible to such individual under the provisions of this section.

■ Government in the Sunshine Act (1977)

OPEN MEETINGS

(a) For purposes of this section—

(1) the term "agency" means any agency, as defined in section 552(e) of this title, headed by a collegial body composed of two or more individual members, a majority of whom are appointed to such position by the President with the advice and consent of the Senate, and any subdivision thereof authorized to act on behalf of the agency;

(2) the term "meeting" means the deliberations of at least the number of individual agency members required to take action on behalf of the agency where such deliberations determine or result in the joint conduct or disposition of official agency business, but does not include deliberations required or permitted by subsection (d) or (e); and

(3) the term "member" means an individual who belongs to a collegial body heading an agency.

(b) Members shall not jointly conduct or dispose of agency business other than in accordance with this section. Except as provided in subsection (c), every portion of every meeting of an agency shall be open to public observation.

(c) Except in a case where the agency finds that the public interest requires otherwise, the second sentence of subsection (b) shall not apply to any portion of an agency meeting, and the requirements of subsections (d) and (e) shall not apply to any information pertaining to such meeting otherwise required by this section to be disclosed to the public, where the agency properly determines that such portion or portions of its meeting or the disclosure of such information is likely to—

(1) disclose matters that are (A) specifically authorized under criteria established by an Executive order to be kept secret in the interests of national defense or foreign policy and (B) in fact properly classified pursuant to such Executive order;

(2) relate solely to the internal personnel rules and practices of an agency;

(3) disclose matters specifically exempted from disclosure by statute (other than section 552 of this title), provided that such statute (A) requires that the matters be withheld from the public in such a manner as to leave no discretion on the issue, or (B) establishes particular criteria for withholding or refers to particular types of matters to be withheld;

(4) disclose trade secrets and commercial or financial information obtained from a person and privileged or confidential;

(5) involve accusing any person of a crime, or formally censuring any person;

(6) disclose information of a personal nature where disclosure would constitute a clearly unwarranted invasion of personal privacy;

(7) disclose investigatory records compiled for law enforcement purposes, or information which if written would be contained in such records, but only to the extent that the prdouction of such records or information would (A) interfere with enforcement proceedings, (B) deprive a person of a right to a fair trial or an impartial adjudication, (C) constitute an unwarranted invasion of personal privacy, (D) disclose the identity of a confidential source and, in the case of a record compiled by a criminal law enforcement authority in the course of a criminal investigation, or by an agency conducting a lawful national security intelligence investigation, confidential information furnished only by the confidential source, (E) disclose investigative techniques and procedures, or (F) endanger the life or physical safety of law enforcement personnel;

(8) disclose information contained in or related to examination, operating, or condition reports prepared by, on behalf of, or for the use of an agency responsible for the regulation or supervision of financial institutions;

(9) disclose information the premature disclosure of which would—

(A) in the case of an agency which regulates currencies, securities, commodities, or financial institutions, be likely to (i) lead to significant financial speculation in currencies, securities, or commodities, or (ii) significantly endanger the stability of any financial institution; or

(B) in the case of any agency, be likely to significantly frustrate implementation of a proposed agency action.

except that subparagraph (B) shall not apply in any instance where the agency has already disclosed to the public the content or nature of its proposed action, or where the agency is required by law to make such disclosure on its own initiative prior to taking final agency action on such proposal; or

(10) specifically concern the agency's issuance of a subpoena, or the agency's participation in a civil action or proceeding, an action in a foreign court or international tribunal, or an arbitration, or the initiation, conduct, or disposition by the agency of a particular case of formal agency adjudication pursuant to the procedures in section 554 of this title or otherwise involving a determination on the record after opportunity for a hearing.

(d)(1) Action under subsection (c) shall be taken only when a majority of the entire membership of the agency (as defined in subsection (a)(1)) votes to take such action. A separate vote of the agency members shall be taken with respect to each agency meeting a portion or portions of which are proposed to be closed to the public pursuant to subsection (c), or with respect to any information which is proposed to be withheld under subsection (c). A single vote may be taken with respect to a series of meetings, a portion or portions of which are proposed to be closed to the public, or with respect to any information concerning such series involves the same particular matters and is scheduled to be held no more than thirty days after the initial meeting in such series. The vote of each agency member participating in such vote shall be recorded and no proxies shall be allowed.

(2) Whenever any person whose interests may be directly affected by a portion of a meeting requests that the agency close such portion to the public for any of the reasons referred to in paragraph (5), (6), or (7) of subsection (c), the agency, upon request of any one of its members, shall vote by recorded vote whether to close such meeting.

(3) Within one day of any vote taken pursuant to paragraph (1) or (2), the agency shall make publicly available a written copy of such vote reflecting the vote of each member on the question. If a portion of a meeting is to be closed to the public, the agency shall, within one day of the vote taken pursuant to paragraph (1) or (2) of this subsection, make publicly available a full written explanation of its action closing the portion together with a list of all persons expected to attend the meeting and their affiliation.

(4) Any agency, a majority of whose meetings may properly be closed to the public pursuant to paragraph (4), (8), (9)(A), or (10) of subsection (c), or any combination thereof, may provide by regulation for the closing of such meetings or portions thereof in the event that a majority of the members of the agency votes by recorded vote at the beginning of such meeting, or portion thereof, to close the exempt portion or portions of the meeting, and a copy of such vote, reflecting the vote of each member on the question, is made available to the public. The provisions of paragraphs (1), (2), and (3) of this subsection and subsection (e) shall not apply to any portion of a meeting to which such regulations apply: *Provided,* That the agency shall, except to the extent that such information is exempt from disclosure under the provisions of subsection (c), provide the public with public announcement of the time, place, and subject matter of the meeting and of each portion thereof at the earliest practicable time.

(e)(1) In the case of each meeting, the agency shall make public announcement, at least one week before the meeting, of the time, place, and subject matter of the meeting, whether it is to be open or closed to the public, and the name and phone number of the official designated by the agency to respond to requests for information about the meeting. Such announcement shall be made unless a majority of the members of the agency determines by a recorded vote that agency business requires that such meeting be called at an earlier date, in which case the agency shall make public announcement of the time, place, and subject matter of such meeting, and whether open or closed to the public, at the earliest practicable time.

(2) The time or place of a meeting may be changed following the public announcement required by paragraph (1) only if the agency publicly announces such change at the earliest practicable time. The subject matter of a meeting, or the determination of the agency to open or close a meeting, or portion of a meeting, to the public, may be changed following the public announcement required by this subsection only if (A) a majority of the entire membership of the agency determines by a recorded vote that

agency business so requires and that no earlier announcement of the change was possible, and (B) the agency publicly announces such change and the vote of each member upon such change at the earliest practicable time.

(3) Immediately following each public announcement required by this subsection, notice of the time, place, and subject matter of a meeting, whether the meeting is open or closed, any change in one of the preceding, and the name and phone number of the official designated by the agency to respond to requests for information about the meeting, shall also be submitted for publication in the Federal Register.

(f)(1) For every meeting closed pursuant to paragraphs (1) through (10) of subsection (c), the General Counsel or chief legal officer of the agency shall publicly certify that, in his or her opinion, the meeting may be closed to the public and shall state each relevant exemptive provision. A copy of such certification, together with a statement from the presiding officer of the meeting setting forth the time and place of the meeting, and the persons present, shall be retained by the agency. The agency shall maintain a complete transcript or electronic recording adequate to record fully the proceedings of each meeting, or portion of a meeting, closed to the public, except that in the case of a meeting, or portion of a meeting, closed to the public pursuant to paragraph (8), (9)(A), or (10) of subsection (c), the agency shall maintain either such a transcript or recording, or a set of minutes. Such minutes shall fully and clearly describe all matters discussed and shall provide a full and accurate summary of any action taken, and the reasons therefor, including a description of each of the views expressed on any item and the record of any rollcall vote (reflecting the vote of each member on the question). All documents considered in connection with any action shall be identified in such minutes.

(2) The agency shall make promptly available to the public, in a place easily accessible to the public, the transcript, electronic recording, or minutes (as required by paragraph (1)) of the discussion of any item on the agenda, or of any item of the testimony of any witness received at the meeting, except for such item or items of such discussion or testimony as the agency determines to contain information which may be withheld under subsection (c). Copies of such transcript, or minutes, or a transcription of such recording disclosing the identity of each speaker, shall be furnished to any person at the actual cost of duplication or transcription. The agency shall maintain a complete verbatim copy of the transcript, a complete copy of the minutes, or a complete electronic recording of each meeting, or portion of a meeting, closed to the public, for a period of at least two years after such meeting, or until one year after the conclusion of any agency proceeding with respect to which the meeting or portion was held, whichever occurs later.

(g) Each agency subject to the requirements of this section shall, within 180 days after the date of enactment of this section, following consultation with the Office of the Chairman of the Administrative Conference of the United States and published notice in the Federal Register of at least thirty days and opportunity for written comment by any person, promulgate regulations to implement the requirements of subsections (b) through (f) of this section. Any person may bring a proceeding in the United States District Court for the District of Columbia to require an agency to promulgate such regulations if such agency has not promulgated such regulations within the time period specified herein. Subject to any limitations of time provided by law, any person may bring a proceeding in the United States Court of Appeals for the District of Columbia to set aside agency regulations issued pursuant to this subsection that are not in accord with the requirements of subsections (b) through (f) of this section and to require the promulgation of regulations that are in accord with such subsections.

(h)(1) The district courts of the United States shall have jurisdiction to enforce the requirements of subsections (b) through (f) of this section by declaratory judgment, injunctive relief, or other relief as may be appropriate. Such actions may be brought by any person against an agency prior to, or within sixty days after, the meeting out of which the violation of this section arises, except that if public announcement of such meeting is not initially provided by the agency in accordance with the requirements of this section, such action may be instituted pursuant to this section at any time prior to sixty days after any public announcement of such meeting. Such actions may be brought in the district court of the United States for the district in which the agency meeting is held or in which the agency in question has its headquarters, or in the District Court for the District of Columbia. In such actions a defendant shall serve his answer within thirty days after the service of the complaint. The burden is on the defendant to sustain his action. In deciding such cases the court may examine in camera any portion of the transcript, electronic recording, or minutes of a meeting closed to the public, and may take such additional evidence as it deems necessary. The court, having due regard for orderly administration and the public interest, as well as the interests of the parties, may grant such equitable relief as it deems appropriate, including granting an injunction against future violations of this section or ordering the agency to make available to the public such portion of the transcript, recording, or minutes of a meeting as is not authorized to be withheld under subsection (c) of this section.

(2) Any Federal court otherwise authorized by law to review agency action may, at the application of any person properly participating in the proceeding pursuant to other applicable law, inquire into violations by the agency of the requirements of this section and afford such relief as it deems appropriate. Nothing in this section authorizes any Federal court having jurisdiction solely on the basis of paragraph (1) to set aside, enjoin, or invalidate any agency action (other than an action to close a meeting or to withhold information under this section) taken or discussed at any agency meeting out of which the violation of this section arose.

(i) The court may assess against any party reasonable attorney fees and other litigation costs reasonably incurred by any other party who substantially prevails in any action brought in accordance with the provisions of subsection (g) or (h) of this section, except that costs may be assessed against the plaintiff only where the court finds that the suit was initiated by the plaintiff primarily for frivolous or dilatory purposes. In the case of assessment of costs against an agency, the costs may be assessed by the court against the United States.

(j) Each agency subject to the requirements of this section shall annually report to Congress regarding its compliance with such requirements, including a tabulation of the total number of agency meetings open to the public, the total number of meetings closed to the public, the reasons for closing such meetings, and a description of any litigation brought against the agency under this section, including any costs assessed against the agency in such litigation (whether or not paid by the agency).

(k) Nothing herein expands or limits the present rights of any person under section 552 of this title, except that the exemptions set forth in subsection (c) of this section shall govern in the case of any request made pursuant to section 552 to copy or inspect the transcripts, recordings, or minutes described in subsection (f) of this section. The requirements of chapter 33 of title 44, United States Code, shall not apply to the transcripts, recordings, and minutes described in subsection (f) of this section.

(l) This section does not constitute authority to withhold any information from Congress, and does not authorize the closing of any agency meeting or portion thereof required by any other provision of law to be open.

(m) Nothing in this section authorizes any agency to withhold from any individual any record, including transcripts, recordings, or minutes required by this section, which is otherwise accessible to such individual under section 552a of this title.

■ Paperwork Reduction Act (1980)

PURPOSE

The purpose of this chapter is—

(1) to minimize the Federal paperwork burden for individuals, small businesses, State and local governments, and other persons;

(2) to minimize the cost to the Federal Government of collecting, maintaining, using, and disseminating information;

(3) to maximize the usefulness of information collected by the Federal Government;

(4) to coordinate, integrate and, to the extent practicable and appropriate, make uniform Federal information policies and practices;

(5) to ensure that automatic data processing and tele-communications technologies are acquired and used by the Federal Government in a manner which improves service delivery and program management, increases productivity, reduces waste and fraud, and, wherever practicable and appropriate, reduces the information processing burden for the Federal Government and for persons who provide information to the Federal Government; and

(6) to ensure that the collection, maintenance, use and dissemination of information by the Federal Government is consistent with applicable laws relating to confidentiality, including section 552a of title 5, United States Code, known as the Privacy Act. . . .

OFFICE OF INFORMATION AND REGULATORY AFFAIRS

(a) There is established in the Office of Management and Budget an office to be known as the Office of Information and Regulatory Affairs.

(b) There shall be at the head of the Office an Administrator who shall be appointed by, and who shall report directly to, the Director. The Director shall delegate to the Administrator the authority to administer all functions under this chapter, except that any such delegation shall not relieve the Director of responsibility for the administration of such functions. The Administrator shall serve as principal adviser to the Director on Federal information policy.

AUTHORITY AND FUNCTIONS OF DIRECTOR

(a) The Director shall develop and implement Federal information policies, principles, standards, and guidelines and shall provide direction and oversee the review and approval of information collection requests, the reduction of the paperwork burden, Federal statistical activities, records management activities, privacy of records, interagency sharing of information, and acquisition and use of automatic data processing, telecommunications, and other technology for managing information resources. The authority under this section shall be exercised consistent with applicable law.

(b) The general information policy functions of the Director shall include—

(1) developing and implementing uniform and consistent information resources management policies and overseeing the development of information management principles, standards, and guidelines and promoting their use;

(2) initiating and reviewing proposals for changes in legislation, regulations, and agency procedures to improve information practices, and informing the President and the Congress on the progress made therein;

(3) coordinating, through the review of budget proposals and as otherwise provided in this section, agency information practices;

(4) promoting, through the use of the Federal Information Locator System, the review of budget proposals and other methods, greater sharing of information by agencies;

(5) evaluating agency information management practices to determine their adequacy and efficiency, and

to determine compliance of such practices with the policies, principles, standards, and guidelines promulgated by the Director, and

(6) overseeing planning for, and conduct of research with respect to, Federal collection, processing, storage, transmission, and use of information.

(c) The information collection request clearance and other paperwork control functions of the Director shall include—

(1) reviewing and approving information collection requests proposed by agencies;

(2) determining whether the collection of information by an agency is necessary for the proper performance of the functions of the agency, including whether the information will have practical utility for the agency;

(3) ensuring that all information collection requests—

(A) are inventoried, display a control number and, when appropriate, an expiration date;

(B) indicate the request is in accordance with the clearance requirements of section 3507; and

(C) contain a statement to inform the person receiving the request why the information is being collected, how it is to be used, and whether responses to the request are voluntary, required to obtain a benefit, or mandatory;

(4) designating as appropriate, in accordance with section 3509, a collection agency to obtain information for two or more agencies;

(5) setting goals for reduction of the burdens of Federal information collection requests;

(6) overseeing action on the recommendations of the Commission on Federal Paperwork; and

(7) designing and operating, in accordance with section 3511, the Federal Information Locator System.

(d) The statistical policy and coordination functions of the Director shall include—

(1) developing long range plans for the improved performance of Federal statistical activities and programs;

(2) coordinating, through the review of budget proposals and as otherwise provided in this section, the functions of the Federal Government with respect to gathering, interpreting, and disseminating statistics and statistical information;

(3) developing and implementing Government-wide policies, principles, standards, and guidelines concerning statistical collection procedures and methods, statistical data classifications, and statistical information presentation and dissemination; and

(4) evaluating statistical program performance and agency compliance with Government-wide policies, principles, standards, and guidelines.

(e) The records management functions of the Director shall include—

(1) providing advice and assistance to the Administrator of General Services in order to promote coordination in the administration of chapter 29, 31, and 33 of this title with the information policies, principles, standards, and guidelines established under this chapter.

(2) reviewing compliance by agencies with the re-

quirements of chapters 29, 31, and 33 of this title and with regulations promulgated by the Administrator of General Services thereunder; and

(3) coordinating records management policies and programs with related information programs such as information collection, statistics, automatic data processing and telecommunications, and similar activities.

(f) The privacy functions of the Director shall include—

(1) developing and implementing policies, principles, standards, and guidelines on information disclosure and confidentiality, and on safeguarding the security of information collected or maintained by or on behalf of agencies;

(2) providing agencies with advice and guidance about information security, restriction, exchange, and disclosure; and

(3) monitoring compliance with section 552a of title 5, United States Code, and related information management laws.

(g) The Federal automatic data processing and telecommunications functions of the Director shall include—

(1) developing and implementing policies, principles, standards, and guidelines for automatic data processing and telecommunications functions and activities of the Federal Government, and overseeing the establishment of standards under section 111(f) of the Federal Property and Administrative Services Act of 1949;

(2) monitoring the effectiveness of, and compliance with, directives issued pursuant to sections 110 and 111 of such Act of 1949 and reviewing proposed determinations under section 111(g) of such Act.

(3) providing advice and guidance on the acquisition and use of automatic data processing and telecommunications equipment, and coordinating, through the review of budget proposals and other methods, agency proposals for acquisition and use of such equipment;

(4) promoting the use of automatic data processing and telecommunications equipment by the Federal Government to improve the effectiveness of the use and dissemination of data in the operation of Federal programs; and

(5) initiating and reviewing proposals for changes in legislation, regulations, and agency procedures to improve automatic data processing and telecommunications practices, and informing the President and the Congress of the progress made therein.

(h)(1) As soon as practicable, but no later than publication of a notice of proposed rulemaking in the Federal Register, each agency shall forward to the Director a copy of any proposed rule which contains a collection of information requirement and upon request, information necessary to make the determination required pursuant to this section.

(2) Within sixty days after the notice of proposed rulemaking is published in the Federal Register, the Director may file public comments pursuant to the standards set forth in section 3508 on the collection of information requirement contained in the proposed rule.

(3) When a final rule is published in the Federal Register, the agency shall explain how any collection of information requirement contained in the final rule responds to the comments, if any, filed by the Director or the public, or explain why it rejected those comments.

(4) The Director has no authority to disapprove any collection of information requirement specifically contained in an agency rule, if he has received notice and failed to comment on the rule within sixty days of the notice of proposed rulemaking.

(5) Nothing in this section prevents the Director, in his discretion—

(A) from disapproving any information collection request which was not specifically required by an agency rule;

(B) from disapproving any collection of information requirement contained in an agency rule, if the agency failed to comply with the requirements of paragraph (1) of this subsection; or

(C) from disapproving any collection of information requirement contained in a final agency rule, if the Director finds within sixty days of the publication of the final rule that the agency's response to his comments filed pursuant to paragraph (2) of this subsection was unreasonable.

(D) from disapproving any collection of information requirement where the Director determines that the agency has substantially modified in the final rule the collection of information requirement contained in the proposed rule where the agency has not given the Director the information required in paragraph (1), with respect to the modified collection of information requirement, at least sixty days before the issuance of the final rule.

(6) The Director shall make publicly available any decision to disapprove a collection of information requirement contained in an agency rule, together with the reasons for such decision.

(7) The authority of the Director under this subsection is subject to the provisions of section 3507(c).

(8) This subsection shall apply only when an agency publishes a notice of proposed rulemaking and requests public comments.

(9) There shall be no judicial review of any kind of the Director's decision to approve or not to act upon a collection of information requirement contained in an agency rule.

ASSIGNMENT OF TASKS AND DEADLINES

In carrying out the functions under this chapter, the director shall—

(1) upon enactment of this Act—

(A) set a goal to reduce the then existing burden of Federal collections of information by 15 per centum by October 1, 1982; and

(B) for the year following, set a goal to reduce the burden which existed upon enactment by an additional 10 per centum;

(2) within one year after the effective date of this Act—

(A) establish standards and requirements for agency

audits of all major information systems and assign responsibility for conducting Government-wide or multiagency audits, except the Director shall not assign such responsibility for the audit of major information systems used for the conduct of criminal investigation or intelligence activities as defined in section 4-206 of Executive Order 12036, issued January 24, 1978, or successor orders, or for cryptologic activities that are communications security activities.

(B) establish the Federal Information Locator System;

(C) identify areas of duplication in information collection requests and develop a schedule and methods for eliminating duplication;

(D) develop a proposal to augment the Federal Information Locator System to include data profiles of major information holdings of agencies (used in the conduct of their operations) which are not otherwise required by this chapter to be included in the System; and

(E) identify initiatives which may achieve a 10 per centum reduction in the burden of Federal collections of information associated with the administration of Federal grant programs; and

(3) within two years after the effective date of this Act—

(A) establish a schedule and a management control system to ensure that practices and programs of information handling disciplines, including records management, are appropriately integrated with the information policies mandated by this chapter;

(B) identify initiatives to improve productivity in Federal operations using information processing technology;

(C) develop a program to (i) enforce Federal information processing standards, particularly software language standards, at all Federal installations; and (ii) revitalize the standards development program established pursuant to section 759(f)(2) of title 40, United States Code, separating it from peripheral technical assistance functions and directing it to the most productive areas;

(D) complete action on recommendations of the Commission on Federal Paperwork by implementing, implementing with modification or rejecting such recommendations including, where necessary, development of legislation to implement such recommendations;

(E) develop, in consultation with the Administrator of General Services, a five-year plan for meeting the automatic data processing and telecommunications needs of the Federal Government in accordance with the requirements of section 111 of the Federal Property and Administrative Services Act of 1949 (40 U.S.C. 759) and the purposes of this chapter; and

(F) submit to the President and the Congress legislative proposals to remove inconsistencies in laws and practices involving privacy, confidentiality, and disclosure of information.

FEDERAL AGENCY RESPONSIBILITIES

(a) Each agency shall be responsible for carrying out its information management activities in an efficient, effective, and economical manner, and for complying with the information policies, principles, standards, and guidelines prescribed by the Director.

(b) The head of each agency shall designate, within three months after the effective date of this Act, a senior official or, in the case of military departments, and the Office of the Secretary of Defense, officials who report directly to such agency head to carry out the responsibilities of the agency under this chapter. If more than one official is appointed for the military departments the respective duties of the officials shall be clearly delineated.

(c) Each agency shall—

(1) systematically inventory its major information systems and periodically review its information management activities, including planning, budgeting, organizing, directing, training, promoting, controlling, and other managerial activities involving the collection, use, and dissemination of information;

(2) ensure its information systems do not overlap each other or duplicate the systems of other agencies;

(3) develop procedures for assessing the paperwork and reporting burden of proposed legislation affecting such agency;

(4) assign to the official designated under subsection (b) the responsibility for the conduct of and accountability for any acquisitions made pursuant to a delegation of authority under section 111 of the Federal Property and Administrative Services Act of 1949 (40 U.S.C. 759); and

(5) ensure that information collection requests required by law or to obtain a benefit, and submitted to nine or fewer persons, contain a statement to inform the person receiving the request that the request is not subject to the requirements of section 3507 of this chapter.

(d) The head of each agency shall establish such procedures as necessary to ensure the compliance of the agency with the requirements of the Federal Information Locator System, including necessary screening and compliance activities.

PUBLIC INFORMATION COLLECTION ACTIVITIES— SUBMISSION TO DIRECTOR; APPROVAL AND DELEGATION

(a) An agency shall not conduct or sponsor the collection of information unless, in advance of the adoption or revision of the request for collection of such information—

(1) the agency has taken actions, including consultation with the Director, to—

(A) eliminate, through the use of the Federal Information Locator System and other means, information collections which seek to obtain information available from another source within the Federal Government;

(B) reduce to the extent practicable and appropriate the burden on persons who will provide information to the agency; and

(C) formulate plans for tabulating the information in a manner which will enhance its usefulness to other agencies and to the public.

(2) the agency (A) has submitted to the Director the proposed information collection request, copies of perti-

nent regulations and other related materials as the Director may specify, and an explanation of actions taken to carry out paragraph (1) of this subsection, and (B) has prepared a notice to be published in the Federal Register stating that the agency has made such submission; and

(3) the Director has approved the proposed information collection request, or the period for review of information collection requests by the Director provided under subsection (b) has elapsed.

(b) The Director shall, within sixty days of a proposed information collection request, notify the agency involved of the decision to approve or disapprove the request and shall make such decisions publicly available. If the Director determines that a request submitted for review cannot be reviewed within sixty days, the Director may, after notice to the agency involved, extend the review period for an additional thirty days. If the Director does not notify the agency of an extension, denial, or approval within sixty days (or, if the Director has extended the review period for an additional thirty days and does not notify the agency of a denial or approval within the time of the extension), a control number shall be assigned without further delay, the approval may be inferred, and the agency may collect the information for not more than one year.

(c) Any disapproval by the Director, in whole or in part, of a proposed information collection request of an independent regulatory agency, or an exercise of authority under section 3504(h) or 3509 concerning such an agency, may be voided, if the agency by a majority vote of its members overrides the Director's disapproval or exercise of authority. The agency shall certify each override to the Director, shall explain the reasons for exercising the override authority. Where the override concerns an information collection request, the Director shall without further delay assign a control number to such request, and such override shall be valid for a period of three years.

(d) The Director may not approve an information collection request for a period in excess of three years.

(e) If the Director finds that a senior official of an agency designated pursuant to section 3506(b) is sufficiently independent of program responsibility to evaluate fairly whether proposed information collection requests should be approved and has sufficient resources to carry out this responsibility effectively, the Director may, by rule in accordance with the notice and comment provisions of chapter 5 of title 5, United States Code, delegate to such official the authority to approve proposed requests in specific program areas, for specific purposes, or for all agency purposes. A delegation by the Director under this section shall not preclude the Director from reviewing individual information collection requests if the Director determines that circumstances warrant such a review. The Director shall retain authority to revoke such delegations, both in general and with regard to any specific matter. In acting for the Director, any official to whom approval authority has been delegated under this section shall comply fully with the rules and regulations promulgated by the Director.

(f) An agency shall not engage in a collection of information without obtaining from the Director a control number to be displayed upon the information collection request.

(g) If an agency head determines a collection of information (1) is needed prior to the expiration of the sixty-day period for the review of information collection requests established pursuant to subsection (b), (2) is essential to the mission of the agency, and (3) the agency cannot reasonably comply with the provisions of this chapter within such sixty-day period because (A) public harm will result if normal clearance procedures are followed, or (B) an unanticipated event has occurred and the use of normal clearance procedures will prevent or disrupt the collection of information related to the event or will cause a statutory deadline to be missed, the agency head may request the Director to authorize such collection of information prior to expiration of such sixty-day period. The Director shall approve or disapprove any such authorization request within the time requested by the agency head and, if approved, shall assign the information collection request a control number. Any collection of information conducted pursuant to this subsection may be conducted without compliance with the provisions of this chapter for a maximum of ninety days after the date on which the Director received the request to authorize such collection.

DETERMINATION OF NECESSITY FOR INFORMATION; HEARING

Before approving a proposed information collection request, the Director shall determine whether the collection of information by an agency is necessary for the proper performance of the functions of the agency, including whether the information will have practical utility. Before making a determination the Director may give the agency and other interested persons an opportunity to be heard or to submit statements in writing. To the extent, if any, that the Director determines that the collection of information by an agency is unnecessary, for any reason, the agency may not engage in the collection of the information.

DESIGNATION OF CENTRAL COLLECTION AGENCY

The Director may designate a central collection agency to obtain information for two or more agencies if the Director determines that the needs of such agencies for information will be adequately served by a single collection agency, and such sharing of data is not inconsistent with any applicable law. In such cases the Director shall prescribe (with reference to the collection of information) the duties and functions of the collection agency so designated and of the agencies for which it is to act as agent (including reimbursement for costs). While the designation is in effect, an agency covered by it may not obtain for itself information which it is the duty of the collection agency to obtain. The Director may modify the designation from time to time as circumstances require. The authority herein is subject to the provisions of section 3507(c) of this chapter.

COOPERATION OF AGENCIES IN MAKING INFORMATION AVAILABLE

(a) The Director may direct an agency to make available to another agency, or an agency may make available to another agency, information obtained pursuant to an information collection request if the disclosure is not inconsistent with any applicable law.

(b) If information obtained by an agency is released by that agency to another agency, all the provisions of law (including penalties which relate to the unlawful disclosure of information) apply to the officers and employees of the agency to which information is released to the same extent and in the same manner as the provisions apply to the officers and employees of the agency which originally obtained the information. The officers and employees of the agency to which the information is released, in addition, shall be subject to the same provisions of law, including penalties, relating to the unlawful disclosure of information as if the information had been collected directly by that agency.

ESTABLISHMENT AND OPERATION OF FEDERAL INFORMATION LOCATOR SYSTEM

(a) There is established in the Office of Information and Regulatory Affairs a Federal Information Locator System (Hereafter in this section referred to as the "System") which shall be composed of a directory of information resources, a data element dictionary, and an information referral service. The System shall serve as the authoritative register of all information collection requests.

(b) In designing and operating the System, the Director shall—

(1) design and operate an indexing system for the System;

(2) require the head of each agency to prepare in a form specified by the Director, and to submit to the Director for inclusion in the System, a data profile for each information collection request of such agency;

(3) compare data profiles for proposed information collection requests against existing profiles in the System, and make available the results of such comparison to—

(A) agency officials who are planning new information collection activities; and

(B) on request, members of the general public; and

(4) ensure that no actual data, except descriptive data profiles necessary to identify duplicative data or to locate information, are contained within the System.

PUBLIC PROTECTION

Notwithstanding any other provision of law, no person shall be subject to any penalty for failing to maintain or provide information to any agency if the information collection request involved was made after December 31, 1981, and does not display a current control number assigned by the Director, or fails to state that such request is not subject to this chapter.

DIRECTOR REVIEW OF AGENCY ACTIVITIES; REPORTING; AGENCY RESPONSE

(a) The Director shall, with the advice and assistance of the Administrator of General Services, selectively review, at least once every three years, the information management activities of each agency to ascertain their adequacy and efficiency. In evaluating the adequacy and efficiency of such activities, the Director shall pay particular attention to whether the agency has complied with section 3506.

(b) The Director shall report the results of the reviews to the appropriate agency head, the House Committee on Government Operations, the Senate Committee on Governmental Affairs, the House and Senate Committees on Appropriations, and the committees of the Congress having jurisdiction over legislation relating to the operations of the agency involved.

(c) Each agency which receives a report pursuant to subsection (b) shall, within sixty days after receipt of such report, prepare and transmit to the Director, the House Committee on Government Operations, the Senate Committee on Governmental Affairs, the House and Senate Committees on Appropriations, and the committees of the Congress having jurisdiction over legislation relating to the operations of the agency, a written statement responding to the Director's report, including a description of any measures taken to alleviate or remove any problems or deficiencies identified in such report.

RESPONSIVENESS TO CONGRESS

(a) The Director shall keep the Congress and its committees fully and currently informed of the major activities under this chapter, and shall submit a report thereon to the President of the Senate and the Speaker of the House of Representatives annually and at such other times as the Director determines necessary. The Director shall include in any such report—

(1) proposals for legislative action needed to improve Federal information management, including, with respect to information collection, recommendations to reduce the burden on individuals, small businesses, State and local governments, and other persons;

(2) a compilation of legislative impediments to the collection of information which the Director concludes that an agency needs but does not have authority to collect;

(3) an analysis by agency, and by categories the Director finds useful and practicable, describing the estimated reporting hours required of persons by information collection requests, including to the extent practicable the direct budgetary costs of the agencies and identification of statutes and regulations which impose the greatest number of reporting hours;

(4) a summary of accomplishments and planned initiatives to reduce burdens of Federal information collection requests;

(5) a tabulation of areas of duplication in agency information collection requests identified during the pre-

ceding year and efforts made to preclude the collection of duplicate information, including designations of central collection agencies;

(6) a list of each instance in which an agency engaged in the collection of information under the authority of section 3507(g) and an identification of each agency involved;

(7) a list of all violations of provisions of this chapter and rules, regulations, guidelines, policies, and procedures issued pursuant to this chapter; and

(8) with respect to recommendations of the Commission on Federal Paperwork—

(A) a description of the specific actions taken on or planned for each recommendation;

(B) a target date for implementing each recommendation accepted but not implemented; and

(C) an explanation of the reasons for any delay in completing action on such recommendations.

(b) The preparation of any report required by this section shall not increase the collection of information burden on persons outside the Federal Government.

ADMINISTRATIVE POWERS

Upon the request of the Director, each agency (other than an independent regulatory agency) shall, to the extent practicable, make its services, personnel, and facilities available to the Director for the performance of functions under this chapter.

RULES AND REGULATIONS

The Director shall promulgate rules, regulations, or procedures necessary to exercise the authority provided by this chapter.

CONSULTATION WITH OTHER AGENCIES AND THE PUBLIC

In development of information policies, plans, rules, regulations, procedures, and guidelines and in reviewing information collection requests, the Director shall provide interested agencies and persons early and meaningful opportunity to comment.

EFFECT ON EXISTING LAWS AND REGULATIONS

(a) Except as otherwise provided in this chapter, the authority of an agency under any other law to prescribe policies, rules, regulations, and procedures for Federal information activities is subject to the authority conferred on the Director by this chapter.

(b) Nothing in this chapter shall be deemed to affect or reduce the authority of the Secretary of Commerce or the Director of the Office of Management and Budget pursuant to Reorganization Plan No. 1 of 1977 (as amended) and Executive order, relating to telecommunications and information policy, procurement and management of telecommunications and information systems, spectrum use, and related matters.

(c)(1) Except as provided in paragraph (2), this chapter does not apply to the collection of information—

(A) during the conduct of a Federal criminal investigation or prosecution, or during the disposition of a particular criminal matter.

(B) during the conduct of (i) a civil action to which the United States or any official or agency thereof is a party or (ii) an administrative action or investigation involving an agency against specific individuals or entities;

(C) by compulsory process pursuant to the Antitrust Civil Process Act and section 13 of the Federal Trade Commission Improvements Act of 1980; or

(D) during the conduct of intelligence activities as defined in section 4-206 of Executive Order 12036, issued January 24, 1978, or successor orders, or during the conduct of cryptologic activities that are communications security activities.

(2) This chapter applies to the collection of information during the conduct of general investigations (other than information collected in an antitrust investigation to the extent provided in subparagraph (C) of paragraph (1)) undertaken with reference to a category of individuals or entities such as a class of licenses or an entire industry.

(d) Nothing in this chapter shall be interpreted as increasing or decreasing the authority conferred by Public Law 89-306 on the Administrator of the General Services Administration, the Secretary of Commerce, or the Director of the Office of Management and Budget.

(e) Nothing in this chapter shall be interpreted as increasing or decreasing the authority of the President, the Office of Management and Budget or the Director thereof, under the laws of the United States, with respect to the substantive policies and programs of departments, agencies and offices, including the substantive authority of any Federal agency to enforce the civil rights laws.

ACCESS TO INFORMATION

Under the conditions and procedures prescribed in section 313 of the Budget and Accounting Act of 1921, as amended, the Director and personnel in the Office of Information and Regulatory Affairs shall furnish such information as the Comptroller General may require for the discharge of his responsibilities. For this purpose, the Comptroller General or representatives thereof shall have access to all books, documents, papers and records of the Office.

AUTHORIZATION OF APPROPRIATIONS

There are hereby authorized to be appropriated to carry out the provisions of this chapter, and for no other purpose, sums—

(1) not to exceed $8,000,000 for the fiscal year ending September 30, 1981;

(2) not to exceed $8,500,000 for the fiscal year ending September 30, 1982; and

(3) not to exceed $9,000,000 for the fiscal year ending September 30, 1983.

(b) The item relating to chapter 35 in the table of chapters for such title is amended to read as follows:

"35. Coordination of Federal Information Policy."

(c)(1) Section 2904(10) of such title is amended to read as follows:

"(10) report to the appropriate oversight and appropriations committees of the Congress and to the Director of the Office of Management and Budget annually and at such other times as the Administrator deems desirable (A) on the results of activities conducted pursuant to paragraphs (1) through (9) of this section, (B) on evaluations of responses by Federal agencies to any recommendations resulting from inspections or studies conducted under paragraphs (8) and (9) of this section, and (C) to the extent practicable, estimates of costs to the Federal Government resulting from the failure of agencies to implement such recommendations."

(2) Section 2905 of such title is amended by redesignating the text thereof as subsection (a) and by adding at the end of such section the following new subsection:

"(b) The Administrator of General Services shall assist the Administrator for the Office of Information and Regulatory Affairs in conducting studies and developing standards relating to record retention requirements imposed on the public and on State and local governments by Federal agencies."

SEC. 3 (a) The President and the Director of the Office of Management and Budget shall delegate to the Administrator for the Office of Information and Regulatory Affairs all functions, authority, and responsibility under section 103 of the Budget and Accounting Procedures Act of 1950 (31 U.S.C. 18b).

(b) The Director of the Office of Management and Budget shall delegate to the Administrator for the Office of Information and Regulatory Affairs all functions, authority, and responsibility of the Director under section 552a of title 5, United States Code, under Executive Order 12046 and Reorganization Plan No. 1 for telecommunications, and under section 111 of the Federal Property and Administrative Services Act of 1949 (40 U.S.C. 759).

SEC. 4. (a) Section 400A of the General Education Provisions Act is amended by (1) striking out "and" after "institutions" in subsection (a)(1)(A) and inserting in lieu thereof "or," and (2) by amending subsection (a)(3)(B) to read as follows:

"(B) No collection of information or data acquisition activity subject to such procedures shall be subject to any other review, coordination, or approval procedure outside of the relevant Federal agency, except as required by this subsection and by the Director of the Office of Management and Budget under the rules and regulations established pursuant to chapter 35 of title 44, United States Code. If a requirement for information is submitted pursuant to this Act for review, the timetable for the Director's approval established in section 3507 of the Paperwork Reduction Act of 1980 shall commence on the date the request is submitted, and no independent submission to the Director shall be required under such Act."

(b) Section 201(e) of the Surface Mining Control and Reclamation Act of 1977 (30 U.S.C. 1211) is repealed.

(c) Section 708(f) of the Public Health Service Act (42 U.S.C. 292h(f)) is repealed.

(d) Section 5315 of title 5, United States Code, is amended by adding at the end thereof the following:

"Administrator, Office of Information and Regulatory Affairs, Office of Management and Budget."

SEC. 5. This Act shall take effect on April 1, 1981.
Approved December 11, 1980.

■ EXECUTIVE ORDER 12044: Improving Government Regulations (Revoked 17 February 1981)

As President of the United States of America, I direct each Executive Agency to adopt procedures to improve existing and future regulations.

SECTION 1. *Policy.* Regulation shall be as simple and clear as possible. They shall achieve legislative goals effectively and efficiently. They shall not impose unnecessary burdens on the economy, on individuals, on public or private organizations, or on State and local governments.

To achieve these objectives, regulations shall be developed through a process which ensures that:

(a) the need for and purposes of the regulation are clearly established;

(b) heads of agencies and policy officials exercise effective oversight;

(c) opportunity exists for early participation and comment by other Federal agencies, State and local governments, businesses, organizations and individual members of the public;

(d) meaningful alternatives are considered and analyzed before the regulation is issued; and

(e) compliance costs, paperwork and other burdens on the public are minimized.

SEC. 2. *Reform of the Process for Developing Significant Regulations.* Agencies shall review and revise their procedures for developing regulations to be consistent with the policies of this Order and in a manner that minimizes paperwork.

Agencies' procedures should fit their own needs but, at a minimum, these procedures shall include the following:

(a) *Semiannual Agenda of Regulations.* To give the public adequate notice, agencies shall publish at least semiannually an agenda of significant regulations under development or review. On the first Monday in October, each agency shall publish in the *Federal Register* a schedule showing the times during the coming fiscal year when the agency's semiannual agenda will be published. Supplements to the agenda may be published at other times during the year if necessary, but the semiannual agendas shall be as complete as possible. The head of each agency shall approve the agenda before it is published. At a minimum, each published agenda shall describe the regulations being considered by the agency, the need for and the legal basis for the action being taken, and the status of regulations previously listed on the agenda.

Each item on the agenda shall also include the name and telephone number of a knowledgeable agency official and, if possible, state whether or not a regulatory analysis will be required. The agenda shall also include existing regulations scheduled to be reviewed in accordance with Section 4 of this Order.

(b) *Agency Head Oversight.* Before an agency proceeds to develop significant new regulations, the agency head shall have reviewed the issues to be considered, the alternative approaches to be explored, a tentative plan for obtaining public comment, and target dates for completion of steps in the development of the regulation.

(c) *Opportunity for Public Participation.* Agencies shall give the public an early and meaningful opportunity to participate in the development of agency regulations. They shall consider a variety of ways to provide this opportunity, including (1) publishing an advance notice of proposed rulemaking; (2) holding open conferences or public hearings; (3) sending notices of proposed regulations to publications likely to be read by those affected; and (4) notifying interested parties directly.

Agencies shall give the public at least 60 days to comment on proposed significant regulations. In the few instances where agencies determine this is not possible, the regulation shall be accompanied by a brief statement of the reasons for a shorter time period.

(d) *Approval of Significant Regulations.* The head of each agency, or the designated official with statutory responsibility, shall approve significant regulations before they are published for public comment in the *Federal Register*. At a minimum, this official should determine that:

(1) the proposed regulation is needed;

(2) the direct and indirect effects of the regulation have been adequately considered;

(3) alternative approaches have been considered and the least burdensome of the acceptable alternatives has been chosen;

(4) public comments have been considered and an adequate response has been prepared;

(5) the regulation is written in plain English and is understandable to those who must comply with it;

(6) an estimate has been made of the new reporting burdens or recordkeeping requirements necessary for compliance with the regulation;

(7) the name, address and telephone number of a knowledgeable agency official is included in the publication; and

(8) a plan for evaluating the regulation after its issuance has been developed.

(e) *Criteria for Determining Significant Regulations.* Agencies shall establish criteria for identifying which regulations are significant. Agencies shall consider among other things: (1) the type and number of individuals, businesses, organizations, State and local governments affected; (2) the compliance and reporting requirements likely to be involved; (3) direct and indirect effects of the regulation including the effect on competition; and (4) the relationship of the regulations to those of other programs and agencies. Regulations that do not meet an agency's criteria for determining significance shall be accompanied by a statement to that effect at the time the regulation is proposed.

SEC. 3. *Regulatory Analysis.* Some of the regulations identified as significant may have major economic consequences for the general economy, for individual industries, geographical regions or levels of government. For these regulations, agencies shall prepare a regulatory analysis. Such an analysis shall involve a careful examination of alternative approaches early in the decision-making process.

The following requirements shall govern the preparation of regulatory analyses:

(a) *Criteria.* Agency heads shall establish criteria for determining which regulations require regulatory analyses. The criteria established shall:

(1) ensure that regulatory analyses are performed for all regulations which will result in (a) an annual effect on the economy of $100 million or more; or (b) a major increase in costs or prices for individual industries, levels of government or geographic regions; and

(2) provide that in the agency head's discretion, regulatory analysis may be completed on any proposed regulation.

(b) *Procedures.* Agency heads shall establish procedures for developing the regulatory analysis and obtaining public comment.

(1) Each regulatory analysis shall contain a succinct statement of the problem; a description of the major alternative ways of dealing with the problems that were considered by the agency; an analysis of the economic consequences of each of these alternatives and a detailed explanation of the reasons for choosing one alternative over the others.

(2) Agencies shall include in their public notice of proposed rules an explanation of the regulatory approach that has been selected or is favored and a short description of the other alternatives considered. A statement of how the public may obtain a copy of the draft regulatory analysis shall also be included.

(3) Agencies shall prepare a final regulatory analysis to be made available when the final regulations are published.

Regulatory analyses shall not be required in rulemaking proceedings pending at the time this Order is issued if an

Economic Impact Statement has already been prepared in accordance with Executive Orders 11821 and 11949.

SEC. 4. *Review of Existing Regulations.* Agencies shall periodically review their existing regulations to determine whether they are achieving the policy goals of this Order. This review will follow the same procedural steps outlined for the development of new regulations.

In selecting regulations to be reviewed, agencies shall consider such criteria as:

(a) the continued need for the regulation;

(b) the type and number of complaints or suggestions received;

(c) the burdens imposed on those directly or indirectly affected by the regulations;

(d) the need to simplify or clarify language;

(e) the need to eliminate overlapping and duplicative regulations; and

(f) the length of time since the regulation has been evaluated or the degree to which technology, economic conditions or other factors have changed in the area affected by the regulation.

Agencies shall develop their selection criteria and a listing of possible regulations for initial review. The criteria and listing shall be published for comment as required in Section 5. Subsequently, regulations selected for review shall be included in the semiannual agency agendas.

SEC. 5. *Implementation.* (a) Each agency shall review its existing process for developing regulations and revise it as needed to comply with this Order. Within 60 days after the issuance of the Order, each agency shall prepare a draft report outlining (1) a brief description of its process for developing regulations and the changes that have been made to comply with this Order; (2) its proposed criteria for defining significant agency regulations; (3) its proposed criteria for identifying which regulations require regulatory analysis; and (4) its proposed criteria for selecting existing regulations to be reviewed and a list of regulations that the agency will consider for its initial review. This report shall be published in the *Federal Register* for public comment. A copy of this report shall be sent to the Office of Management and Budget.

(b) After receiving public comment, agencies shall submit their revised report to the Office of Management and Budget for approval before final publication in the *Federal Register.*

(c) The Office of Management and Budget shall assure the effective implementation of this Order. OMB shall report at least semiannually to the President on the effectiveness of the Order and agency compliance with its provisions. By May 1, 1980, OMB shall recommend to the President whether or not there is a continued need for the Order and any further steps or actions necessary to achieve its purpose.

SEC. 6. *Coverage.* (a) As used in this Order, the term regulation means both rules and regulations issued by agencies including those which establish conditions for financial assistance. Closely related sets of regulations shall be considered together.

(b) This Order does not apply to:

(1) regulations issued in accordance with the formal rulemaking provisions of the Administrative Procedure Act (5 U.S.C. 556, 557);

(2) regulations issued with respect to a military or foreign affairs function of the United States;

(3) matters related to agency management or personnel;

(4) regulations related to Federal Government procurement;

(5) regulations issued by the independent agencies; or

(6) regulations that are issued in response to an emergency or which are governed by short-term statutory or judicial deadlines. In these cases, the agency shall publish in the *Federal Register* a statement of the reasons why it is impracticable or contrary to the public interest for the agency to follow the procedures of this Order. Such a statement shall include the name of the policy official responsible for this determination.

SEC. 7. This Order is intended to improve the quality of Executive Agency regulatory practices. It is not intended to create delay in the process or provide new grounds for judicial review. Nothing in this order shall be considered to supersede existing statutory obligations governing rulemaking.

SEC. 8. Unless extended, this Executive Order expires on June 30, 1980.

JIMMY CARTER
The White House,
March 23, 1978

■ EXECUTIVE ORDER 12291: **Federal Regulation (Revoked 30 September 1993)**

By the authority vested in me as President by the Constitution and laws of the United States of America, and in order to reduce the burdens of existing and future regulations, increase agency accountability for regulatory actions, provide for presidential oversight of the regulatory process, minimize duplication and conflict of regulations, and insure well-reasoned regulations, it is hereby ordered as follows:

SECTION 1. *Definitions.* For the purposes of this Order:

(a) "Regulation" or "rule" means an agency statement of general applicability and future effect designed to implement, interpret, or prescribe law or policy or describing the procedure or practice requirements of an agency, but does not include:

(1) Administrative actions governed by the provisions of Sections 556 and 557 of Title 5 of the United States Code;

(2) Regulations issued with respect to a military or foreign affairs function of the United States; or

(3) Regulations related to agency organization, management, or personnel.

(b) "Major rule" means any regulation that is likely to result in:

(1) An annual effect on the economy of $100 million or more;

(2) A major increase in costs or prices for consumers, individual industries, Federal, State, or local government agencies, or geographic regions; or

(3) Significant adverse effects on competition, employment, investment, productivity, innovation, or on the ability of United States–based enterprises to compete with foreign-based enterprises in domestic or export markets.

(c) "Director" means the Director of the Office of Management and Budget.

(d) "Agency" means any authority of the United States that is an "agency" under 44 U.S.C. 3502(1), excluding those agencies specified in 44 U.S.C. 3502 (10).

(e) "Task Force" means the Presidential Task Force on Regulatory Relief.

SEC. 2. *General Requirements.* In promulgating new regulations, reviewing existing regulations, and developing legislative proposals concerning regulation, all agencies, to the extent permitted by law, shall adhere to the following requirements:

(a) Administrative decisions shall be based on adequate information concerning the need for and consequences of proposed government action;

(b) Regulatory action shall not be undertaken unless the potential benefits to society from the regulation outweigh the potential costs to society;

(c) Regulatory objectives shall be chosen to maximize the net benefits to society;

(d) Among alternative approaches to any given regulatory objective, the alternative involving the least net cost to society shall be chosen; and

(e) Agencies shall set regulatory priorities with the aim of maximizing the aggregate net benefits to society, taking into account the condition of the particular industries affected by regulations, the condition of the national economy, and other regulatory actions contemplated for the future.

SEC. 3. *Regulatory Impact Analysis and Review.*

(a) In order to implement Section 2 of this Order, each agency shall, in connection with every major rule, prepare, and to the extent permitted by law consider, a Regulatory Impact Analysis. Such Analyses may be combined with any Regulatory Flexibility Analyses performed under 5 U.S.C. 603 and 604.

(b) Each agency shall initially determine whether a rule

it intends to propose or to issue is a major rule, *provided that,* the Director, subject to the direction of the Task Force, shall have authority, in accordance with Sections 1(b) and 2 of the Order, to prescribe criteria for making such determinations, to order a rule to be treated as a major rule, and to require any set of related rules to be considered together as a major rule.

(c) Except as provided in Section 8 of this Order, agencies shall prepare Regulatory Impact Analyses of major rules and transmit them, along with all notices of proposed rulemaking and all final rules, to the Director as follows:

(1) If no notice of proposed rulemaking is to be published for a proposed major rule that is not an emergency rule, the agency shall prepare only a final Regulatory Impact Analysis, which shall be transmitted, along with the proposed rule, to the Director at least 60 days prior to the publication of the major rule as a final rule;

(2) With respect to all other major rules, the agency shall prepare a preliminary Regulatory Impact Analysis, which shall be transmitted, along with a notice of proposed rulemaking, to the Director at least 60 days prior to the publication of a notice of proposed rulemaking, and a final Regulatory Impact Analysis, which shall be transmitted along with the final rule at least 30 days prior to the publication of the major rule as a final rule;

(3) For all rules other than major rules, agencies shall submit to the Director, at least 10 days prior to publication, every notice of proposed rulemaking and final rule.

(d) To permit each proposed major rule to be analyzed in light of the requirements stated in Section 2 of this Order, each preliminary and final Regulatory Impact Analysis shall contain the following information:

(1) A description of the potential benefits of the rule, including any beneficial effects that cannot be quantified in monetary terms, and the identification of those likely to receive the benefits;

(2) A description of the potential costs of the rule, including any adverse effects that cannot be quantified in monetary terms, and the identification of those likely to bear the costs;

(3) A determination of the potential net benefits of the rule, including an evaluation of effects that cannot be quantified in monetary terms;

(4) A description of alternative approaches that could substantially achieve the same regulatory goal at lower cost, together with an analysis of this potential benefit and costs and a brief explanation of the legal reasons why such alternatives, if proposed, could not be adopted; and

(5) Unless covered by the description required under paragraph (4) of this subjection, an explanation of any legal reasons why the rule cannot be based on the requirements set forth in Section 2 of this Order.

(e)(1) The Director, subject to the direction of the Task Force, which shall resolve any issues raised under this Order or ensure that they are presented to the President, is authorized to review any preliminary or final Regulatory Impact Analysis, notice of proposed rulemaking, or final rule based on the requirements of this Order.

(2) The Director shall be deemed to have concluded review unless the Director advises an agency to the contrary under subsection (f) of this Section:

(A) Within 60 days of a submission under subsection (c)(1) or a submission of a preliminary Regulatory Impact Analysis or notice of proposed rulemaking under subsection (c)(2);

(B) Within 30 days of the submission of a final Regulatory Impact Analysis and a final rule under subsection (c)(2); and

(C) Within 10 days of the submission of a notice of proposed rulemaking or final rule under subsection (c)(3).

(f)(1) Upon the request of the Director, an agency shall consult with the Director concerning the review of a preliminary Regulatory Impact Analysis or notice of proposed rulemaking under this Order, and shall, subject to Section 8(a)(2) of this Order, refrain from publishing its preliminary Regulatory Impact Analysis or notice of proposed rulemaking until such review is concluded.

(2) Upon receiving notice that the Director intends to submit views with respect to any final Regulatory Impact Analysis or final rule, the agency shall, subject to Section 8(a)(2) of this Order, refrain from publishing its final Regulatory Impact Analysis or final rule until the agency has responded to the Director's views, and incorporated those views and the agency's response in the rulemaking file.

(3) Nothing in this subsection shall be construed as displacing the agencies' responsibilities delegated by law.

(g) For every rule for which an agency publishes a notice of proposed rulemaking, the agency shall include in its notice:

(1) A brief statement setting forth the agency's initial determination whether the proposed rule is a major rule, together with the reasons underlying that determination; and

(2) For each proposed major rule, a brief summary of the agency's preliminary Regulatory Impact Analysis.

(h) Agencies shall make their preliminary and final Regulatory Impact Analyses available to the public.

(i) Agencies shall initiate reviews of currently effective rules in accordance with the purposes of this Order, and perform Regulatory Impact Analyses of currently effective major rules. The Director, subject to the direction of the Task Force, may designate currently effective rules for review in accordance with this Order, and establish schedules for reviews and Analyses under this Order.

SEC. 4. *Regulatory Review.* Before approving any final major rule, each agency shall:

(a) Make a determination that the regulation is clearly within the authority delegated by law and consistent with congressional intent, and include in the *Federal Register* at the time of promulgation a memorandum of law supporting that determination.

(b) Make a determination that the factual conclusions upon which the rule is based have substantial support in the agency record, viewed as a whole, with full attention to public comments in general and the comments of persons directly affected by the rule in particular.

SEC. 5. *Regulatory Agendas.*

(a) Each agency shall publish, in October and April of each year, an agenda of proposed regulations that the agency has issued or expects to issue, and currently effective rules that are under agency review pursuant to this Order. These agendas may be incorporated with the agendas published under 5 U.S.C. 602, and must contain at the minimum:

(1) A Summary of the nature of each major rule being considered, the objectives and legal basis for the issuance of the rule, and an approximate schedule for completing action on any major rule for which the agency has issued a notice of proposed rulemaking;

(2) The name and telephone number of a knowledgeable agency official for each item on the agenda; and

(3) A list of existing regulations to be reviewed under the terms of this Order, and a brief discussion of each such regulation.

(b) The Director, subject to the direction of the Task Force, may, to the extent permitted by law:

(1) Require agencies to provide additional information in an agenda; and

(2) Require publication of the agenda in any form.

SEC. 6. *The Task Force and Office of Management and Budget.*

(a) To the extent permitted by law, the Director shall have authority, subject to the direction of the Task Force, to:

(1) Designate any proposed or existing rule as a major rule in accordance with Section 1(b) of this Order;

(2) Prepare and promulgate uniform standards for the identification of major rules and the development of Regulatory Impact Analyses;

(3) Require an agency to obtain and evaluate, in connection with a regulation, any additional relevant data from any appropriate source;

(4) Waive the requirements of Sections 3, 4, or 7 of this Order with respect to any proposed or existing major rule;

(5) Identify duplicative, overlapping and conflicting rules, existing or proposed, and existing or proposed rules that are inconsistent with the policies underlying statutes governing agencies other than the issuing agency or with the purposes of this Order, and, in each such case, require appropriate interagency consultation to minimize or eliminate such duplication, overlap, or conflict;

(6) Develop procedures for estimating the annual benefits and costs of agency regulations, on both an aggregate and economic or industrial sector basis, for purposes of compiling a regulatory budget;

(7) In consultation with interested agencies, prepare for consideration by the President recommendations for changes in the agencies' statutes; and

(8) Monitor agency compliance with the requirements of this Order and advise the President with respect to such compliance.

(b) The Director, subject to the direction of the Task Force, is authorized to establish procedures for the performance of all functions vested in the Director by this Order.

The Director shall take appropriate steps to coordinate the implementation of the analysis, transmittal, review, and clearance provisions of this Order with the authorities and requirements provided for or imposed upon the Director and agencies under the Regulatory Flexibility Act, 5 U.S.C. 601 *et seq.*, and the Paperwork Reduction Plan Act of 1980, 44 U.S.C. 3501 *et seq.*

SEC. 7. *Pending Regulations.*

(a) To the extent necessary to permit reconsideration in accordance with this Order, agencies shall, except as provided in Section 8 of this Order, suspend or postpone the effective dates of all major rules that they have promulgated in final form as of the date of this Order, but that have not yet become effective, excluding:

(1) Major rules that cannot legally be postponed or suspended;

(2) Major rules that, for good cause, ought to become effective as final rules without reconsideration. Agencies shall prepare, in accordance with Section 3 of this Order, a final Regulatory Impact Analysis for each major rule that they suspend or postpone.

(b) Agencies shall report to the Director no later than 15 days prior to the effective date of any rule that the agency has promulgated in final form as of the date of this Order, and that has not yet become effective, and that will not be reconsidered under subsection (a) of this Section:

(1) That the rule is excepted from reconsideration under subsection (a), including a brief statement of the legal or other reasons for that determination; or

(2) That the rule is not a major rule.

(c) The Director, subject to the direction of the Task Force, is authorized, to the extent permitted by law, to:

(1) Require reconsideration, in accordance with this Order, of any major rule that an agency has issued in final form as of the date of this Order and that has not become effective; and

(2) Designate a rule that an agency has issued in final form as of the date of this Order and that has not yet become effective as a major rule in accordance with Section 1(b) of this Order.

(d) Agencies may, in accordance with the Administrative Procedure Act and other applicable statutes, permit major rules that they have issued in final form as of the date of this Order, and that have not yet become effective, to take effect as interim rules while they are being reconsidered in accordance with this Order, *provided that,* agencies shall report to the Director, no later than 15 days before any such rule is proposed to take effect as an interim rule, that the rule should appropriately take effect as an interim rule while the rule is under reconsideration.

(e) Except as provided in Section 8 of this Order, agencies shall, to the extent permitted by law, refrain from promulgating as a final rule any proposed major rule that has been published or issued as of the date of this Order until a final Regulatory Impact Analysis, in accordance with Section 3 of this Order, has been prepared for the proposed major rule.

(f) Agencies shall report to the Director, no later than 30 days prior to promulgating as a final rule any proposed rule that the agency has published or issued as of the date of this Order and that has not been considered under the terms of this Order:

(1) That the rule cannot legally be considered in accordance with this Order, together with a brief explanation of the legal reasons barring such consideration; or

(2) That the rule is not a major rule, in which case the agency shall submit to the Director a copy of the proposed rule.

(g) The Director, subject to the direction of the Task Force, is authorized, to the extent permitted by law, to:

(1) Require consideration, in accordance with this Order, of any proposed major rule that the agency has published or issued as of the date of this Order; and

(2) Designate a proposed rule that an agency has published or issued as of the date of this Order, as a major rule in accordance with Section 1(b) of this Order.

(h) The Director shall be deemed to have determined that an agency's report to the Director under subsections (b), (d), or (f) of this Section is consistent with the purposes of this Order, unless the Director advises the agency to the contrary:

(1) Within 15 days of its report in the case of any report under subsections (b) or (d); or

(2) Within 30 days of its report, in the case of any report under subsection (f).

(i) This Section does not supersede the President's Memorandum of January 29, 1981, entitled "Postponement of Pending Regulations", which shall remain in effect until March 30, 1981.

(j) In complying with this Section, agencies shall comply with all applicable provisions of the Administrative Procedure Act, and with any other procedural requirements made applicable to the agencies by other statutes.

SEC. 8. *Exemptions.*

(a) The procedures prescribed by this Order shall not apply to:

(1) Any regulation that responds to an emergency situation, *provided that,* any such regulation shall be reported to the Director as soon as is practicable, the agency shall publish in the *Federal Register* a statement of the reasons why it is impracticable for the agency to follow the procedures of this Order with respect to such a rule, and the agency shall prepare and transmit as soon as is practicable a Regulatory Impact Analysis of any such major rule; and

(2) Any regulation for which consideration or reconsideration under the terms of this Order would conflict with deadlines imposed by statute or by judicial order, *provided that,* any such regulation shall be reported to the Director together with a brief explanation of the conflict, the agency shall publish in the *Federal Register* a statement of the reasons why it is impracticable for the agency to follow the procedures of this Order with respect to such a rule, and the agency, in consultation with the Director, shall adhere to the requirements of this Order to the extent permitted by statutory or judicial deadlines.

(b) The Director, subject to the direction of the Task Force, may, in accordance with the purposes of this Order, exempt any class or category of regulations from any or all requirements of this Order.

SEC. 9. *Judicial Review.* This Order is intended only to improve the internal management of the Federal government, and is not intended to create any right or benefit, substantive or procedural, enforceable at law by a party against the United States, its agencies, its officers or any person. The determinations made by agencies under Section 4 of this Order, and any Regulatory Impact Analyses for any rule, shall be made part of the whole record of agency action in connection with the rule.

SEC. 10. *Revocations.* Executive Orders No. 12044, as amended, and No. 12174 are revoked.

RONALD REAGAN
The White House,
February 17, 1981

■ EXECUTIVE ORDER 12498: **Regulatory Planning Process** (Revoked 30 September 1993)

By the authority vested in me as President by the Constitution and laws of the United States of America, and in order to create a coordinated process for developing on an annual basis the Administration's Regulatory Program, establish Administration regulatory priorities, increase the accountability of agency heads for the regulatory actions of their agencies, provide for Presidential oversight of the regulatory process, reduce the burdens of existing and future regulations, minimize duplication and conflict of regulations, and enhance public and Congressional understanding of the Administration's regulatory objectives, it is hereby ordered as follows:

SECTION 1. *General Requirements.*

(a) There is hereby established a regulatory planning process by which the Administration will develop and publish a Regulatory Program for each year. To implement this process, each Executive agency subject to Executive Order No. 12291 shall submit to the Director of the Office of Management and Budget (OMB) each year, starting in 1985, a statement of its regulatory policies, goals, and objectives for the coming year and information concerning all significant regulatory actions underway or planned; however, the Director may exempt from this Order such agencies or activities as the Director may deem appropriate in order to achieve the effective implementation of this Order.

(b) The head of each Executive agency subject to this Order shall ensure that all regulatory actions are consistent with the goals of the agency and of the Administration, and will be appropriately implemented.

(c) This program is intended to complement the existing regulatory planning and review procedures of agencies and the Executive branch, including the procedures established by Executive Order No. 12291.

(d) To assure consistency with the goals of the Administration, the head of each agency subject to this Order shall adhere to the regulatory principles stated in Section 2 of Executive Order No. 12291, including those elaborated by the regulatory policy guidelines set forth in the August 11, 1983, Report of the Presidential Task Force on Regulatory Relief, "Reagan Administration Regulatory Achievements."

SEC. 2. *Agency Submission of Draft Regulatory Program.*

(a) The head of each agency shall submit to the Director an overview of the agency's regulatory policies, goals, and objectives for the program year and such information concerning all significant regulatory actions of the agency, planned or underway, including actions taken to consider whether to initiate rulemaking; requests for public comment; and the development of documents that may influence, anticipate, or could lead to the commencement of rulemaking proceedings at a later date, as the Director deems necessary to develop the Administration's Regulatory Program. This submission shall constitute the agency's draft regulatory program. The draft regulatory program shall be submitted to the Director each year, on a date to be specified by the Director, and shall cover the period from April 1 through March 31 of the following year.

(b) The overview portion of the agency's submission should discuss the agency's broad regulatory purposes, explain how they are consistent with the Administration's regulatory principles, and include a discussion of the significant regulatory actions, as defined by the Director, that it will take. The overview should specifically discuss the significant regulatory actions of the agency to revise or rescind existing rules.

(c) Each agency head shall categorize and describe the regulatory actions described in subsection (a) in such format as the Director shall specify and provide such additional information as the Director may request; however, the Director shall, by Bulletin or Circular, exempt from the requirements of this Order any class or category of regulatory action that the Director determines is not necessary to review in order to achieve the effective implementation of the program.

SEC. 3. *Review, Compilation, and Publication of the Administration's Regulatory Program.*

(a) In reviewing each agency's draft regulatory program, the Director shall (i) consider the consistency of the draft regulatory program with the Administration's policies and priorities and the draft regulatory programs submitted by other agencies; and (ii) identify such further regulatory or deregulatory actions as may, in his view, be necessary in order to achieve such consistency. In the event of disagreement over the content of the agency's draft regulatory program, the agency head or the Director may raise issues for further review by the President or by such appropriate Cabinet Council or other forum as the President may designate.

(b) Following the conclusion of the review process established by subsection (a), each agency head shall submit to the Director, by a date to be specified by the Director, the agency's final regulatory plan for compilation and publication as the Administration's Regulatory Program for that year. The Director shall circulate a draft of the Administration's Regulatory Program for agency comment, review, and interagency consideration, if necessary, before publication.

(c) After development of the Administration's Regulatory Program for the year, if the agency head proposes to take a regulatory action subject to the provisions of Section 2 and not previously submitted for review under this process, or if the agency head proposes to take a regulatory action that is materially different from the action described in the agency's final Regulatory Program, the agency head shall immediately advise the Director and submit the action to the Director for review in such format as the Director may specify. Except in the case of emergency situations, as defined by the Director, or statutory or judicial deadlines, the agency head shall refrain from taking the proposed regulatory action until the review of this submission by the Director is completed. As to those regulatory actions not also subject to Executive Order No. 12291, the Director

shall be deemed to have concluded that the proposal is consistent with the purposes of this Order, unless he notifies the agency head to the contrary within 10 days of its submission. As to those regulatory actions subject to Executive Order No. 12291, the Director's review shall be governed by the provisions of Section 3(e) of that Order.

(d) Absent unusual circumstances, such as new statutory or judicial requirements or unanticipated emergency situations, the Director may, to the extent permitted by law, return for reconsideration any rule submitted for review under Executive Order No. 12291 that would be subject to Section 2 but was not included in the agency's final Regulatory Program for that year; or any other significant regulatory action that is materially different from those described in the Administration's Regulatory Program for that year.

SEC. 4. *Office of Management and Budget.* The Director of the Office of Management and Budget is authorized, to the extent permitted by law, to take such actions as may be necessary to carry out the provisions of this order.

SEC. 5. *Judicial Review.* This Order is intended only to improve the internal management of the Federal government, and is not intended to create any right or benefit, substantive or procedural, enforceable at law by a party against the United States, its agencies, its officers or any person.

RONALD REAGAN
The White House,
January 4, 1985

■ EXECUTIVE ORDER 12866: Regulatory Planning and Review (1993)

The American people deserve a regulatory system that works for them, not against them: a regulatory system that protects and improves their health, safety, environment, and well-being and improves the performance of the economy without imposing unacceptable or unreasonable costs on society; regulatory policies that recognize that the private sector and private markets are the best engine for economic growth; regulatory approaches that respect the role of State, local, and tribal governments; and regulations that are effective, consistent, sensible, and understandable. We do not have such a regulatory system today.

With this Executive order, the Federal Government begins a program to reform and make more efficient the regulatory process. The objectives of this Executive order are to enhance planning and coordination with respect to both new and existing regulations; to reaffirm the primacy of Federal agencies in the regulatory decision-making process; to restore the integrity and legitimacy of regulatory review and oversight; and to make the process more accessible and open to the public. In pursuing these objectives, the regulatory process shall be conducted so as to meet applicable statutory requirements and with due regard to the discretion that has been entrusted to the Federal agencies.

Accordingly, by the authority vested in me as President

by the Constitution and the laws of the United States of America, it is hereby ordered as follows:

SECTION 1. *Statement of Regulatory Philosophy and Principles.* (a) *The Regulatory Philosophy.* Federal agencies should promulgate only such regulations as are required by law, are necessary to interpret the law, or are made necessary by compelling public need, such as material failures of private markets to protect or improve the health and safety of the public, the environment, or the well-being of the American people. In deciding whether and how to regulate, agencies should assess all costs and benefits of available regulatory alternatives, including the alternative of not regulating. Costs and benefits shall be understood to include both quantifiable measures (to the fullest extent that these can be usefully estimated) and qualitative measures of costs and benefits that are difficult to quantify, but nevertheless essential to consider. Further, in choosing among alternative regulatory approaches, agencies should select those approaches that maximize net benefits (including potential economic, environmental, public health and safety, and other advantages; distributive impacts; and equity), unless a statute requires another regulatory approach.

(b) *The Principles of Regulation.* To ensure that the agencies' regulatory programs are consistent with the philosophy set forth above, agencies should adhere to the following principles, to the extent permitted by law and where applicable:

(1) Each agency shall identify the problem that it intends to address (including, where applicable, the failure of private markets or public institutions that warrant new agency action) as well as assess the significance of that problem.

(2) Each agency shall examine whether existing regulations (or other law) have created, or contributed to, the problem that a new regulation is intended to correct and whether those regulations (or other law) should be modified to achieve the intended goal of regulation more effectively.

(3) Each agency shall identify and assess available alternatives to direct regulation, including providing economic incentives to encourage the desired behavior, such as user fees or marketable permits, or providing information upon which choices can be made by the public.

(4) In setting regulatory priorities, each agency shall consider, to the extent reasonable, the degree and nature of the risks posed by various substances or activities within its jurisdiction.

(5) When an agency determines that a regulation is the best available method of achieving the regulatory objective, it shall design its regulations in the most cost-effective manner to achieve the regulatory objective. In doing so, each agency shall consider incentives for innovation, consistency, predictability, the costs of enforcement and compliance (to the government, regulated entities, and the public), flexibility, distributive impacts, and equity.

(6) Each agency shall assess both the costs and the benefits of the intended regulation and, recognizing that some costs and benefits are difficult to quantify, propose or adopt a regulation only upon a reasoned determination that the benefits of the intended regulation justify its costs.

(7) Each agency shall base its decisions on the best reasonably obtainable scientific, technical, economic, and other information concerning the need for, and consequences of, the intended regulation.

(8) Each agency shall identify and assess alternative forms of regulation and shall, to the extent feasible, specify performance objectives, rather than specifying the behavior or manner of compliance that regulated entities must adopt.

(9) Wherever feasible, agencies shall seek views of appropriate State, local, and tribal officials before imposing regulatory requirements that might significantly or uniquely affect those governmental entities. Each agency shall assess the effects of Federal regulations of State, local, and tribal governments, including specifically the availability of resources to carry out those mandates, and seek to minimize those burdens that uniquely or significantly affect such governmental entities, consistent with achieving regulatory objectives. In addition, as appropriate, agencies shall seek to harmonize Federal regulatory actions with related State, local, and tribal regulatory and other governmental functions.

(10) Each agency shall avoid regulations that are inconsistent, incompatible, or duplicative with its other regulations or those other Federal agencies.

(11) Each agency shall tailor its regulations to impose the least burden on society, including individuals, businesses of differing sizes, and other entities (including small communities and governmental entities), consistent with obtaining the regulatory objectives, taking into account, among other things, and to the extent practicable, the costs of cumulative regulations.

(12) Each agency shall draft its regulations to be simple and easy to understand, with the goal of minimizing the potential for uncertainty and litigation arising from such uncertainty.

SEC. 2. *Organization.* An efficient regulatory planning and review process is vital to ensure that the Federal Government's regulatory system best serves the American people.

(a) *The Agencies.* Because Federal agencies are the repositories of significant substantive expertise and experience, they are responsible for developing regulations and assuring that the regulations are consistent with applicable law, the President's priorities, and the principles set forth in this Executive order.

(b) *The Office of Management and Budget.* Coordinated review of agency rulemaking is necessary to ensure that regulations are consistent with applicable law, the President's priorities, and the principles set forth in this Executive order, and that decisions made by one agency do not conflict with the policies or actions taken or planned by another agency. The Office of Management and Budget (OMB) shall carry out that review function. Within OMB, the Office of Information and Regulatory Affairs (OIRA) is the repository of expertise concerning regulatory issues, including methodologies and procedures that affect more than one agency, this Executive order, and the President's regulatory policies. To the extent permitted by law, OMB shall provide guidance to agencies and assist the President, the Vice President, and other regulatory policy advisors to the President in regulatory planning and shall be the entity that reviews individual regulations, as provided by this Executive order.

(c) *The Vice President.* The Vice President is the principal advisor to the President on, and shall coordinate the development and presentation of recommendations concerning, regulatory policy, planning, and review, as set forth in this Executive order. In fulfilling their responsibilities under this Executive order, the President and the Vice President shall be assisted by the regulatory policy advisors within the Executive Office of the President and by such agency officials and personnel as the President and the Vice President may, from time to time, consult.

SEC. 3. *Definitions.* For purposes of this Executive order:
(a) "Advisors" refers to such regulatory policy advisors to the President as the President and Vice President may from

time to time consult, including, among others: (1) the Director of OMB; (2) the Chair (or another member) of the Council of Economic Advisers; (3) the Assistant to the President for Economic Policy; (4) the Assistant to the President for Domestic Policy; (5) the Assistant to the President for National Security Affairs; (6) the Assistant to the President for Science and Technology; (7) the Assistant to the President for Intergovernmental Affairs; (8) the Assistant to the President and Staff Secretary; (9) the Assistant to the President and Chief of Staff to the Vice President; (10) the Assistant to the President and Counsel to the President; (11) the Deputy Assistant to the President and Director of the White House Office on Environmental Policy; and (12) the Administrator of OIRA, who also shall coordinate communications relating to this Executive order among the agencies, OMB, the other Advisors, and the Office of the Vice President.

(b) "Agency," unless otherwise indicated, means any authority of the United States that is an "agency" under 44 U.S.C. 3502(i), other than those considered to be independent regulatory agencies, as defined in 44 U.S.C. 3502(10).

(c) "Director" means the Director of OMB.

(d) "Regulation" or "rule" means an agency statement of general applicability and future effect, which the agency intends to have the force and effect of law, that is designed to implement, interpret, or prescribe law or policy or to describe the procedure or practice requirements of an agency. It does not, however, include:

(1) Regulations or rules issued in accordance with the formal rulemaking provisions of 5 U.S.C. 556, 557;

(2) Regulations or rules that pertain to a military or foreign affairs function of the United States, other than procurement regulations and regulations involving the import or export of non defense articles and services;

(3) Regulatons or rules that are limited to agency organization, management, or personnel matters; or

(4) Any other category of regulations exempted by the Administrator of OIRA.

(e) "Regulatory action" means any substantive action by an agency (normally published in the *Federal Register*) that promulgates or is expected to lead to the promulgation of a final rule or regulation, including notices of inquiry, advance notices of proposed rulemaking, and notices of proposed rulemaking.

(f) "Significant regulatory action" means any regulatory action that is likely to result in a rule that may:

(1) Have an annual effect on the economy of $100 million or more or adversely affect in a material way the economy, a sector of the economy, productivity, competition, jobs, the environment, public health or safety, or State, local, or tribal governments or communities;

(2) Create a serious inconsistency or otherwise interfere with an action taken or planned by another agency;

(3) Materially alter the budgetary impact of entitlements, grants, user fees, or loan programs or the rights and obligations of recipients thereof; or

(4) Raise novel legal or policy issues arising out of legal mandates, the President's priorities, or the principles set forth in this Executive order.

SEC. 4. *Planning Mechanism.* In order to have an effective regulatory program, to provide for coordination of regulations, to maximize consultation and the resolution of potential conflicts at an early stage, to involve the public and its State, local, and tribal officials in regulatory planning, and to ensure that new or revised regulations promote the President's priorities and the principles set forth in this Executive order, these procedures shall be followed, to the extent permitted by law: (a) *Agencies' Policy Meeting.* Early in each year's planning cycle, the Vice President shall convene a meeting of the Advisors and the heads of agencies to seek a common understanding of priorities and to coordinate regulatory efforts to be accomplished in the upcoming year.

(b) *Unified Regulatory Agenda.* For purposes of this subsection, the term "agency" or "agencies" shall also include those considered to be independent regulatory agencies, as decided in 44 U.S.C. 3502(10). Each agency shall prepare an agenda of all regulations under development or review, at a time and in a manner specified by the Administrator of OIRA. The description of each regulatory action shall contain, at a minimum, a regulation identifier number, a brief summary of the action, the legal authority for the action, any legal deadline for the action, and the name and telephone number of a knowledgeable agency official. Agencies may incorporate the information required under 5 U.S.C. 602 and 41 U.S.C. 402 into these agendas.

(c) *The Regulatory Plan.* For purposes of this subsection, the term "agency" or "agencies" shall also include those considered to be independent regulatory agencies, as defined in 44 U.S.C. 3502(10).

(1) As part of the Unified Regulatory Agenda, beginning in 1994, each agency shall prepare a Regulatory Plan (Plan) of the most important significant regulatory actions that the agency reasonably expects to issue in proposed or final form in that fiscal year, or thereafter. The Plan shall be approved personally by the agency head and shall contain at a minimum:

(A) A statement of the agency's regulatory objectives and priorities and how they relate to the President's priorities;

(B) A summary of each planned significant regulatory action including, to the extent possible, alternatives to be considered and preliminary estimates of the anticipated costs and benefits;

(C) A summary of the legal basis for each such action, including whether any aspect of the action is required by statute or court order;

(D) A statement of the need for each such action and, if applicable, how the action will reduce risks to public health, safety, or the environment, as well as how the magnitude of the risk addressed by the action relates to other risks within the jurisdiction of the agency;

(E) The agency's schedule for action, including a statement of any applicable statutory or judicial deadlines; and

(F) The name, address, and telephone number of a person the public may contact for additional information about the planned regulatory action.

(2) Each agency shall forward its Plan to OIRA by June 1st of each year.

(3) Within 10 calendar days after OIRA has received an agency's Plan, OIRA shall circulate it to other affected agencies, the Advisors, and the Vice President.

(4) An agency head who believes that a planned regulatory action of another agency may conflict with its own policy or action taken or planned shall promptly notify, in writing, the Administrator of OIRA, who shall forward that communication to the issuing agency, the Advisors, and the Vice President.

(5) If the Administrator of OIRA believes that a planned regulatory action of an agency may be inconsistent with the President's priorities or the principles set forth in this Executive order or may be in conflict with any policy or action taken or planned by another agency, the Administrator of OIRA shall promptly notify, in writing, the affected agencies, the Advisors, and the Vice President.

(6) The Vice President, with the Advisors' assistance, may consult with the heads of agencies with respect to their Plans and, in appropriate instances, request further consideration or inter-agency coordination.

(7) The Plans developed by the issuing agency shall be published annually in the October publication of the Unified Regulatory Agenda. This publication shall be made available to the Congress; State, local, and tribal governments; and the public. Any views on any aspect of any agency Plan, including whether any planned regulatory action might conflict with any other planned or existing regulation, impose any unintended consequences on the public, or confer any unclaimed benefits on the public, should be directed to the issuing agency, with a copy to OIRA.

(d) *Regulatory Working Group.* Within 30 days of the date of this Executive order, the Administrator of OIRA shall convene a Regulatory Working Group ("Working Group"), which shall consist of representatives of the heads of each agency that the Administrator determines to have significant domestic regulatory responsibility, the Advisors, and the Vice President. The Administrator of OIRA shall chair the Working Group and shall periodically advise the Vice President on the activities of the Working Group. The Working Group shall serve as a forum to assist agencies in identifying and analyzing important regulatory issues (including, among others (1) the development of innovative regulatory techniques, (2) the methods, efficacy, and utility of comparative risk assessment in regulatory decision-making, and (3) the development of short forms and other streamlined regulatory approaches for small businesses and other entities). The Working Group shall meet at least quarterly and may meet as a whole or in subgroups of agencies with an interest in particular issues or subject areas. To inform its discussions, the Working Group may commission analytical studies and reports by OIRA, the Administrative Conference of the United States, or any other agency.

(e) *Conferences.* The Administrator of OIRA shall meet quarterly with representatives of State, local, and tribal governments to identify both existing and proposed regulations that may uniquely or significantly affect those governmental entities. The Administrator of OIRA shall also convene, from time to time, conferences with representatives of businesses, nongovernmental organizations, and the public to discuss regulatory issues of common concern.

SEC. 5. *Existing Regulations.* In order to reduce the regulatory burden on the American people, their families, their communities, their State, local, and tribal governments, and their industries; to determine whether regulations promulgated by the Executive branch of the Federal Government have become unjustified or unnecessary, as a result of changed circumstances; to confirm that regulations are both compatible with each other and not duplicative or inappropriately burdensome in the aggregate; to ensure that all regulations are consistent with the President's priorities and the principles set forth in this Executive order, within applicable law; and to otherwise improve the effectiveness of existing regulations:

(a) Within 90 days of the date of this Executive order, each agency shall submit to OIRA a program, consistent with its resources and regulatory priorities, under which the agency will periodically review its existing significant regulations to determine whether any such regulations should be modified or eliminated so as to make the agency's regulatory program more effective in achieving the regulatory objectives, less burdensome, or in greater alignment with the President's priorities and the principles set forth in this Executive order. Any significant regulations selected for review shall be included in the agency's annual Plan. The agency shall also identify any legislative mandates that require the agency to promulgate or continue to impose regulations that the agency believes are unnecessary or outdated by reason of changed circumstances.

(b) The Administrator of OIRA shall work with the Regulatory Working Group and other interested entities to pursue the objectives of this section. State, local, and tribal governments are specifically encouraged to assist in the identification of regulations that impose significant or unique burdens on those governmental entities and that appear to have outlived their justification or be otherwise inconsistent with the public interest.

(c) The Vice President, in consultation with the Advisors, may identify for review by the appropriate agency or agencies other existing regulations of an agency or groups of regulations of more than one agency that affect a particular group, industry, or sector of the economy, or may identify legislative mandates that may be appropriate for reconsideration by the Congress.

SEC. 6. *Centralized Review of Regulations.* The guidelines set forth below shall apply to all regulatory actions, for both new and existing regulations, by agencies other than those agencies specifically exempted by the Administrator of OIRA:

(a) *Agency Responsibilities.*

(1) Each agency shall (consistent with its own rules,

regulations, or procedures) provide the public with meaningful participation in the regulatory process. In particular, before issuing a notice of proposed rulemaking, each agency should, where appropriate, seek the involvement of those who are intended to benefit from and those expected to be burdened by any regulation (including, specifically, State, local, and tribal officials). In addition, each agency should afford the public a meaningful opportunity to comment on any proposed regulation, which in most cases should include a comment period of not less than 60 days. Each agency also is directed to explore and, where appropriate, use consensual mechanisms for developing regulations, including negotiated rulemaking.

(2) Within 60 days of the date of this Executive order, each agency head shall designate a Regulatory Policy Officer who shall report to the agency head. The Regulatory Policy Officer shall be involved at each stage of the regulatory process to foster the development of effective, innovative, and least burdensome regulations and to further the principles set forth in this Executive order.

(3) In addition to adhering to its own rules and procedures and to the requirements of the Administrative Procedure Act, the Regulatory Flexibility Act, the Paperwork Reduction Act, and other applicable law, each agency shall develop its regulatory actions in a timely fashion and adhere to the following procedures with respect to a regulatory action:

(A) Each agency shall provide OIRA, at such times and in the manner specified by the Administrator of OIRA, with a list of its planned regulatory actions, indicating those which the agency believes are significant regulatory actions within the meaning of this Executive order. Absent a material change in the development of the planned regulatory action, those not designated as significant will not be subject to review under this section unless, within 10 working days of receipt of the list, the Administrator of OIRA notifies the agency that OIRA has determined that a planned regulation is a significant regulatory action within the meaning of this Executive order. The Administrator of OIRA may waive review of any planned regulatory action designated by the agency as significant, in which case the agency need not further comply with subsection (a)(3)(B) or subsection (a)(3)(C) of this section.

(B) For each matter identified as, or determined by the Administrator of OIRA to be, a significant regulatory action, the issuing agency shall provide to OIRA:

(i) The text of the draft regulatory action, together with a reasonably detailed description of the need for the regulatory action and an explanation of how the regulatory action will meet that need; and

(ii) An assessment of the potential costs and benefits of the regulatory action, including an explanation of the manner in which the regulatory action is consistent with a statutory mandate and, to the extent permitted by law, promotes the President's priorities and avoids undue interference with State, local, and tribal governments in the exercise of their governmental functions.

(C) For those matters identified as, or determined by the Administrator of OIRA to be, a significant regulatory action within the scope of section 3(f)(1), the agency shall also provide to OIRA the following additional information developed as part of the agency's decision-making process (unless prohibited by law):

(i) An assessment, including the underlying analysis, of benefits anticipated from the regulatory action (such as, but not limited to, the promotion of the efficient functioning of the economy and private markets, the enhancement of health and safety, the protection of the natural environment, and the elimination or reduction of discrimination or bias) together with, to the extent feasible, a quantification of those benefits;

(ii) An assessment, including the underlying analysis, of costs anticipated from the regulatory action (such as, but not limited to, the direct cost both to the government in administering the regulation and to businesses and others in complying with the regulation, and any adverse effects on the efficient functioning of the economy, private markets (including productivity, employment, and competitiveness), health, safety, and the natural environment), together with, to the extent feasible, a quantification of those costs; and

(iii) An assessment, including the underlying analysis, of costs and benefits of potentially effective and reasonably feasible alternatives to the planned regulation, identified by the agencies or the public (including improving the current regulation and reasonably viable nonregulatory actions), and an explanation why the planned regulatory action is preferable to the identified potential alternatives.

(D) In emergency situations or when an agency is obligated by law to act more quickly than normal review procedures, the agency shall notify OIRA as soon as possible and, to the extent practicable, comply with subsections (a)(3)(B) and (C) of this section. For those regulatory actions that are governed by a statutory or court-imposed deadline, the agency shall, to the extent practicable, schedule rulemaking proceedings so as to permit sufficient time for OIRA to conduct its review, as set forth below in subsection (b)(2) through (4) of this section.

(E) After the regulatory action has been published in the *Federal Register* or otherwise issued to the public, the agency shall:

(i) Make available to the public the information set forth in subsections (a)(3)(B) and (C);

(ii) Identify for the public, in a complete, clear, and simple manner, the substantive changes between the draft submitted to OIRA for review and the action subsequently announced; and

(iii) Identify for the public those changes in the regulatory action that were made at the suggestion or recommendation of OIRA.

(F) All information provided to the public by the agency shall be in plain, understandable language.

(b) *OIRA Responsibilities.* The Administrator of OIRA shall provide meaningful guidance and oversight so that each agency's regulatory actions are consistent with applicable law, the President's priorities, and the principles set forth in this Executive order and do not conflict with the policies or actions of another agency. OIRA shall, to the extent permitted by law, adhere to the following guidelines:

(1) OIRA may review only actions identified by the agency or by OIRA as significant regulatory actions under subsection (a)(3)(A) of this section.

(2) OIRA shall waive review or notify the agency in writing of the results of its review within the following time periods:

(A) For any notices of inquiry, advance notices of proposed rulemaking, or other preliminary regulatory actions prior to a Notice of Proposed Rulemaking, within 10 working days after the date of submission of the draft action to OIRA;

(B) For all other regulatory actions, within 90 calendar days after the date of submission of the information set forth in subsections (a)(3)(B) and (C) of this section, unless OIRA has previously reviewed this information and, since that review, there has been no material change in the facts and circumstances upon which the regulatory action is based, in which case, OIRA shall complete its review within 45 days; and

(C) The review process may be extended (1) once by no more than 30 calendar days upon the written approval of the Director and (2) at the request of the agency head.

(3) For each regulatory action that the Administrator of OIRA renames to an agency for further consideration of some or all of its provisions, the Administrator of OIRA shall provide the issuing agency a written explanation for such return, setting forth the pertinent provision of this Executive order on which OIRA is relying. If the agency head disagrees with some or all of the bases for the return, the agency head shall so inform the Administrator of OIRA in writing.

(4) Except as otherwise provided by law or required by a Court, in order to ensure greater openness, accessibility, and accountability in the regulatory review process, OIRA shall be governed by the following disclosure requirements:

(A) Only the Administrator of OIRA (or a particular designee) shall receive oral communications initiated by persons not employed by the Executive branch of the Federal Government regarding the substance of a regulatory action under OIRA review;

(B) All substantive communications between OIRA personnel and persons not employed by the Executive branch of the Federal Government regarding a regulatory action under review shall be governed by the following guidelines:

(i) A representative from the issuing agency shall be invited to any meeting between OIRA personnel and such person(s);

(ii) OIRA shall forward to the issuing agency, within 10 working days of receipt of the communications, all written communications, regardless of format, between OIRA personnel and any person who is not employed by the Executive branch of the Federal Government, and the dates and names of individuals involved in all substantive oral communications (including meetings to which an agency representative was invited, but did not attend, and telephone conversations between OIRA personnel and any such persons); and

(iii) OIRA shall publicly disclose relevant information about such communication(s), as set forth below in subsection (b)(4)(C) of this section.

(C) OIRA shall maintain a publicly available log that shall contain, at a minimum, the following information pertinent to regulatory actions under review:

(i) The status of all regulatory actions, including if (and if so, when and by whom) Vice Presidential and Presidential consideration was requested;

(ii) A notation of all written communications forwarded to an issuing agency under subsection (b)(4)(B)(ii) of this section; and

(iii) The dates and names of individuals involved in all substantive oral communications, including meetings and telephone conversations, between OIRA personnel and any person not employed by the Executive branch of the Federal Government, and the subject matter discussed during such communications.

(D) After the regulatory action has been published in the *Federal Register* or otherwise issued to the public, or after the agency has announced its decision not to publish or issue the regulatory action, OIRA shall make available to the public all documents exchanged between OIRA and the agency during the review by OIRA under this section.

(5) All information provided to the agency by OIRA shall be in plain, understandable language.

SEC. 7. *Resolution of Conflicts.* To the extent permitted by law, disagreements or conflicts between or among agency heads or between OMB and any agency that cannot be resolved by the Administrator of OIRA shall be resolved by the President, or by the Vice President acting at the request of the President, with the relevant agency head (and, as appropriate, other interested government officials). Vice Presidential and Presidential consideration of such disagreements may be initiated only by the Director, by the head of the issuing agency, or by the head of an agency that has a significant interest in the regulatory action at issue. Such review will not be undertaken at the request of other persons, entities, or their agents.

Resolution of such conflicts shall be informed by recommendations developed by the Vice President, after consultation with the Advisors (and other Executive branch officials or personnel whose responsibilities to the President include the subject matter at issue). The development of these recommendations shall be concluded within 60 days after review has been requested.

During the Vice Presidential and Presidential review period, communications with any person not employed by the Federal Government relating to the substance of the regulatory action under review and directed to the Advisors or their staffs or to the staff of the Vice President shall be in writing and shall be forwarded by the recipient to the affected agency(ies) for inclusion in the public docket(s). When the communication is not in writing, such Advisors or staff members shall inform the outside party that the matter is under review and that any comments should be submitted in writing.

At the end of this review process, the President, or the Vice President acting at the request of the President, shall notify the affected agency and the Administrator of OIRA of the President's decision with respect to the matter.

SEC. 8. *Publication.* Except to the extent required by law, an agency shall not publish in the *Federal Register* or otherwise issue to the public any regulatory action that is subject to review under section 6 of this Executive order until (1) the Administrator of OIRA notifies the agency that OIRA has waived its review of the action or has completed its review without any requests for further consideration, or (2) the applicable time period in section 6(b)(2) expires without OIRA having notified the agency that it is returning the regulatory action for further consideration under section 6(b)(3), whichever occurs first. If the terms of the preceding sentence have not been satisfied and an agency wants to publish or otherwise issue a regulatory action, the head of that agency may request Presidential consideration through the Vice President, as provided under

section 7 of this order. Upon receipt of this request, the Vice President shall notify OIRA and the Advisors. The guidelines and time period set forth in section 7 shall apply to the publication of regulatory actions for which Presidential consideration has been sought.

SEC. 9. *Agency Authority.* Nothing in this order shall be construed as displacing the agencies' authority or responsibilities, as authorized by law.

SEC. 10. *Judicial Review.* Nothing in this Executive order shall affect any otherwise available judicial review of agency action. This Executive order is intended only to improve the internal management of the Federal Government and does not create any right or benefit, substantive or procedural, enforceable at law or equity by a party against the United States, its agencies or instrumentalities, its officers or employees, or any other person.

SEC. 11. *Revocations.* Executive Orders Nos. 12291 and 12498; all amendments to those Executive orders; all guidelines issued under those orders; and any exemptions from those orders heretofore granted for any category of rule are revoked.

WILLIAM J. CLINTON
The White House,
September 30, 1993

Index

N.B.: Page numbers printed in boldface indicate a major discussion.
Page numbers printed in italics indicate a photograph.